# RACE TENSIONS AND THE POLICE

*A Monograph in*

THE POLICE SCIENCE SERIES

*Edited by*

V. A. LEONARD

*Professor of Police Science and Administration*
*Washington State University*
*Pullman, Washington*

# RACE TENSIONS
# and the POLICE

By **J. E. CURRY**
*Chief of Police*
*Dallas Police Department*

*and* **GLEN D. KING**
*Captain of Police*
*Dallas Police Department*

*With a Foreword by*
**GEORGE EASTMAN**
*Director, Police-Community*
*Relations Institute*
*Michigan State University*

*Police Science Series*

**CHARLES C THOMAS • PUBLISHER**
*Springfield • Illinois • U.S.A.*

CHARLES C THOMAS • PUBLISHER

BANNERSTONE HOUSE

301-327 East Lawrence Avenue, Springfield, Illinois, U.S.A.

*With THOMAS BOOKS careful attention is given to all details of
manufacturing and design. It is the Publisher's desire to present books
that are satisfactory as to their physical qualities and artistic possibilities
and appropriate for their particular use. THOMAS BOOKS will be true
to those laws of quality that assure a good name and good will.*

*Printed in the United States of America*

# FOREWORD

During the past many years, but particularly in the period following World War II, our country has been undergoing a critical reappraisal of the relations between the racial strains that characterize America and its communities. It was precipitated by an unequal application of the law by legislative bodies, enforcement agencies and the courts. Crisis after crisis has been ineffectually handled by governmental agencies and communities and each one has seldom provided a basis for avoiding or resolving the next. Thoughtful people everywhere are seeking solutions to these problems. Effective police handling of singular crisis incidents are numerous but isolated and unrecorded and there has been little pooling of experiences, good or bad, which would allow the development of sound police practices.

Perhaps no American police department has given more conscious effort to fully understand and effectively handle problems arising from racial tensions than Dallas, Texas. Most fortunately, two very able Dallas career police officers, Chief Jesse Curry and Captain Glen King, have translated the department's experience, research and study into a readable, timely and valuable contribution to the police literature.

The Dallas department has enjoyed for many years a nationwide reputation for outstanding efficiency resulting in an enviable traffic record, an unusual crime clearance rate and excellent public relations. Much of this reputation is the result of the long and successful professional stewardship of Chief Carl Hansson, Chief Curry's predecessor. However, while Chief Curry and Captain King are products of this fine department it, in part, is their product, too.

A conscience has been defined, somewhat facetiously, as a device which cannot prevent our doing those things we know we should not but which, for many of us, can prevent or hinder our enjoyment when we do them. The race relations problems of today and generations past have become an identifiable conscience. Morally, we know that we have been expedient, inept, unethical and insincere in handling the fundamental problems inherent in race relations. Morally we know also that many of our past and present courses of action often have been illegal.

We know in our hearts that the cornerstone of our great nation's foundation is the equality of men before God and the law. Although we have accepted this principle as an American creed, we have done so as a people and, all too often, not as individuals and not as communities. Communities, in the sense implied here may be neighborhoods, cities or states—or ethnic, social or other groupings.

The Dallas Police Department has embraced, not just accepted, the American creed as its vital and efficacious conscience. The result has been an objective and resolute attempt to seek an impartial and intelligent handling of major problems of all kinds and resolving them on the basis of facts, the governing law, and the compelling conscience of our American democracy.

*Race Tensions and the Police*, written for policemen by policemen, minces no words in clarifying misconceptions, discussing problems and suggesting solutions. It draws lightly but effectively, and in sufficient detail to "set the record straight," on the disciplines of sociology, anthropology and psychology.

It is adequately illustrated with examples from police files of both inept and effective handling of incidents and problems. Clearly, simply and logically it defines the police role in race relations. It frankly and sincerely lays out guide lines for the police of all jurisdictions in matters of race relations.

Patrolmen, supervisory and command officers, and police executives everywhere could read, be stimulated by, and adopt the philosophy and the proposed practices of this text to their personal gain, and to the gain of their career service and its ultimate professionalization.

The successful resolution of these problems is not only of special importance to the police service and to our communities but may also have a significant bearing on the international role of the United States in these times of stress. Even isolated instances of the improper handling of minority group problems have propaganda value to the communist nations and other unfriendly critics.

In this area, more than almost any other, is a real opportunity for the police departments of the country to be of outstanding and significant service to our communities and our nation!

GEORGE D. EASTMAN

*Director, Police-Community Relations Institute*
*Michigan State University*
*East Lansing, Michigan*

# PREFACE

THIS TEXT has been prepared to assist the law enforcement officer to better understand and mediate the differences arising between the various groups of society.

His oath of office places upon the officer the responsibility for the preservation of the peace and the protection of life and property. In his relationships with minority groups the policeman must fill his role in such a manner that his activity does not serve as an aggravating influence in an already tense situation.

In the preparation of this book the material included seemed to fall naturally into one of three classifications. Much of the text is sociological in nature, and deals perhaps no more directly with the police than with any other segment of society. It is believed, however, that the police officer who has an accurate understanding of the nature of racial differences, and the nature and effect of prejudices, will be in a better position to bring his own prejudices under control. If the officer knows the source of his prejudices, he can more ably cope with them and prevent them from influencing his official action.

The second section deals with measures which can be employed by the police, the minority groups and society as a whole to prevent racial friction from erupting into violence. It is axiomatic that the police should be extremely active in this field, for it is far better to resolve tension peacefully than to attempt to regain control of a situation which has deteriorated into lawlessness.

The inclusion of the third section—police tactics in bringing under control an unruly crowd—is not to suggest that the primary role of the police in race relations is one of riot control. Such certainly is not true. However, in view of past experience and accumulated wisdom it would be nothing short of criminal negligence for a police department to fail to develop such a plan.

It is not incumbent upon the police officer to argue the merits of segregation or desegregation. It is probable that many policemen have absorbed from the culture surrounding them attitudes which will make difficult their impartial enforcement of the law. It is mandatory that all departments achieve a unity of purpose that transcends all personal considerations, opinions, ideas, beliefs and prejudices. Only so long as the law is enforced equally and impartially will police organizations have the support of the public. That support they must have if they are to succeed in their high calling.

J. E. C.

G. D. K.

# ACKNOWLEDGMENTS

THE AUTHORS wish to express their very deep appreciation to Mr. Carl F. Hansson, retired Chief of Police of Dallas, who, while heading the Department, foresaw a possible future need and moved in his usual decisive way to meet it.

When the Supreme Court returned its now famous ruling, which declared in effect that equal but separate facilities were not in keeping with Constitutional requirements, Chief Hansson foresaw the possible effect this would have on police departments throughout the segregated areas of the country. Wishing to prepare the Dallas Police Department for an end to segregation he directed that a training manual on community tensions be prepared. This book is an outgrowth of that manual.

The authors also desire to acknowledge the invaluable assistance given by Mrs. Pearl Ayers, who not only prepared the manuscript, but who also made many constructive suggestions in its actual compilation.

J. E. C.

G. D. K.

# CONTENTS

Page

*Foreword* ........................................... v

*Preface* ...........................................

*Acknowledgments* ..................................

*Chapter*

1. INTRODUCTION ...................................... 3
2. THE LAW AND MINORITY GROUPS ...................... 5
3. CONTROL OF TENSIONS .............................. 12
4. THE HISTORY OF RACIAL TENSION..................... 17
5. THE NATURE OF RACIAL DIFFERENCES ................. 20
6. THE NATURE OF PREJUDICES ........................ 27
7. THE SOURCE OF PREJUDICE ......................... 34
8. THE EFFECT OF PREJUDICE ON MINORITIES ............ 39
9. AREAS OF CONFLICT ............................... 44
10. RUMOR ......................................... 52
11. TYPES OF CROWDS ................................ 61
12. FACTORS UNDERLYING CROWD BEHAVIOR .............. 65
13. FORMATION OF A MOB ............................. 70
14. POLICE PREVENTIVE MEASURES ..................... 74
15. MINORITY GROUP PREVENTIVE MEASURES ............. 83
16. MOBILIZATION OF COMMUNITY RESOURCES ............ 87
17. POLICE TACTICS ................................. 97
    *Index* ....................................... 137

RACE TENSIONS AND THE POLICE

*All royalties from the sale of this book will be deposited to the Dallas Police Department's Recreational Fund.*

# 1

## INTRODUCTION

THE SUPREME COURT, in a series of rulings, has declared in effect that segregation has no constitutional basis, and has ordered that integration be effected in public schools, public interstate transportation facilities, and other areas of public life "with all deliberate speed."

This produces a problem for police officers that is at the same time both simple and complex. It is simple in that there is but one course of action a department can follow: Enforce the law as it is handed down. It is complex because of the emotional factors involved. It is much like a bomb exploding, uprooting traditions and cultures centuries old.

There are widespread throughout the country deeply rooted opinions that some persons are by nature inferior, that others are by nature superior, and that some should be relegated to the status of second class citizen. Most minority groups are so looked upon. Law enforcement agencies are increasingly called upon to cope with incidents involving these opinions.

Throughout the nation efforts directed toward integration have been met with stubborn opposition. Some persons, doubting either the legality or moral rightness of Supreme Court decisions, have instituted legal proceedings, on both the federal and state levels, to halt the integrative process. One after another—without exception—these efforts have been stricken down. Still the fight goes on.

Rather than surmise on the probability of the rulings being placed into effect, law enforcement officers must accept them. There is no governmental body to whom the findings and rulings of the Supreme Court can be appealed.

The fact that officers must enforce the law as it is handed down should be obvious to every law enforcement official. While it is true that police departments are composed of individuals, any good department assumes a unity of purpose that transcends all personal considerations, opinions, ideas, beliefs and prejudices.

Sometimes an officer may be called on to enforce the law when such enforcement is directly contrary to his personal beliefs. Each person is entitled to his opinions, but when law enforcement is concerned, the officer must sublimate his personal opinions to his official duties.

It is mandatory that the officer recognize his opinions for what they are, exercise caution when and where he expresses them. He must be sure that they do not interfere with the proper performance of his job. Training, discipline and a strong sense of duty are essential to this phase of law enforcement.

Sir Robert Peel, in reorganizing the London Police Department, wrote that it is the responsibility of a police organization to enforce all the law, without regard for the political, social, economic, racial or religious condition of the persons involved.

This remains the underlying principle of modern law enforcement.

Only so long as we enforce the law equally and equitably will we have the respect and support of the people.

It is our duty to enforce all the law, and not just that part that meets with our personal approval.

# 2
## THE LAW AND MINORITY GROUPS

A POLICE OFFICER has not only the responsibility for enforcing the law, but also a corollary responsibility for acquainting himself with the law as it applies to minority groups and racial relations. He must see how this law dictates his actions.

The officer should have a very real interest in the law governing civil liberties, for it is in its enforcement that the police enter the race relations picture. The duties and responsibilities of the officer stem from the law, and from the law he derives his authority. He is then accountable to the law for a fair and impartial exercise of that authority.

The law as it applies specifically to racial minorities may be properly examined at only one level, that of the federal, since most state and local laws requiring segregation, for example, have been nullified by the Supreme Court.

For the most part, our concern is with the actual legal details, since the law is explicit in its implications for police officials. It is of prime importance, however, that we see how improper action and enforcement by individual officers may result in legal action being taken against those officers. The law not only provides what shall be done, but it also points out how it shall be done, and provides penalties for failure to comply. In the past several years the FBI has been called upon to investigate hundreds of cases involving alleged civil rights violations. Many of the complaints were proven to be unfounded but in several of the cases law enforcement officers were indicted and a few have actually been convicted and sentenced to the penitentiary.

The Constitution of the United States, as interpreted by the Supreme Court, is the basis for all our law. So we must turn to the Constitution for the amendments which bring race and minority group problems within the sphere of government.

5

The framers of the Constitution expressed no concern for the civil rights activities of state and local officers. The guarantees contained in the Bill of Rights originally applied to national officers only, and imposed no restrictions on the activities of other law enforcement officials. The so-called Civil War Amendments extended the prohibitions against the national government contained in the Bill of Rights to state governments. They allowed the federal government to take action on violations of its provisions by state and local authorities. Thus, the invasion of civil rights by the federal authorities is prohibited by the Bill of Rights, and a similar prohibition is placed on state officers by the Civil War Amendments.

The Fourteenth Amendment to the United States Constitution extended most of the guarantees of the Bill of Rights. This Amendment reads in part:

"All persons born or naturalized in the United States, and subject to the jurisdiction thereof, are citizens of the United States and of the State wherein they reside. No State shall make or enforce any law which shall abridge the privileges or immunities of citizens of the United States, nor shall any State deprive any person of life, liberty, or property, without due process of law, nor deny to any person within its jurisdiction the equal protection of the laws."

This section, as it applies to minority groups, may be broken down into three parts:

(1) privileges or immunities of citizens, (2) due process of law, and (3) the equal protection of the law.

The "privileges and immunities of citizens" in this section have been construed by the Supreme Court to include not only those rights guaranteed to all citizens under the Bill of Rights, but also others not specifically guaranteed.

The Supreme Court has held that an early California Statute denying employment to persons of Mongolian or Chinese descent invalid because it abridged both the rights of persons to hire whom they chose and the rights of the Chinese to earn a living. In effect, the Supreme Court stated that legislation enacted for the control of, or special application to, any particular group, was unconstitutional.

In another case, the Court held that a state statute denying Negroes the right to vote in primary elections in Texas was a violation of this section of the Constitution. The Court declared that while the elections in question were the Democratic primaries, these primaries in Texas are practically tantamount in election, since whoever gets the Democratic primary nomination is almost always elected.

This is an example of the inclusion of privileges not guaranteed in the Constitution. While there is no Constitutional guarantee of rights in primary elections, the Court held that the rights of the Negroes were abridged by denial of the right to vote in the decisive primary election.

The "due process of law" clause is well illustrated by the Scottsboro cases. Here nine Negro boys were indicted by a grand jury and tried by the State of Alabama on a capital charge. The boys were represented by counsel, and the trial proceedings, on the surface, conformed to established trial practice. Upon conviction, however, the sentences were appealed on the grounds that the defense was haphazard and perfunctory, and that no real attempt was made to secure the rights of the accused.

In reversing the conviction, the Supreme Court said that an appearance of conformity with established procedure was not enough, and that the defendants had been denied due process of the law. The Court cited as substantiation of this ruling the fact that the defense counsel had not been given sufficient time to prepare an adequate defense, and that both the defendants and the jury hearing the case had been threatened with mob violence in the event of a verdict of "Not guilty."

The section on "equal protection of the law" is a two-edged sword. First, it provides that no special legislation by governmental bodies shall be enacted to restrict any person because of his race, color or nationality. A statute which prohibited Negroes from serving on juries was declared in violation of this section of the Constitution. Cases in which Negroes have been convicted have been reversed by the Supreme Court when it has been shown that Negroes have been systematically excluded from service on petit and grand juries. This section thus provides that not only shall no person be prohibited from service on juries unless he is disqualified by personal considerations, but it also provides that a conviction of a Negro shall not be upheld if it appears that Negroes have been systematically excluded from service on juries because of their color.

The Fourteenth Amendment is buttressed by several provisions within the United States Civil Rights Code. When the states ratified the Civil War Amendments they gave enforcement power to Congress, which subsequently passed many civil rights statutes. Most of these were eventually declared unconstitutional. However, two statutes which originated in the Civil Rights Acts of 1866 and 1870 have stood the test of constitutionality. These two statutes are now known as Section 241 of Title 18 of the U. S. Code and Section 242 of Title 18 of the U. S. Code.

Section 242, U. S. Code reads in part: "Whoever, under color of any law, statute, ordinance, regulation, or custom, willfully subjects any inhabitant of any State, Territory, or District to the deprivation of any rights, privileges, or immunities secured or protected by the Constitution or laws of the United States, or to different punishments, pains, or penalties, on account of such inhabitant being an alien, or by reason of his color, or race, than are prescribed for the punishment of citizens, shall be fined not more than $1,000 or imprisoned not more than one year, or both."

This Section is directed against any duly constituted law enforcement officer, that is, a person who is acting under color of law. The gist of the offense is the intentional misuse of the powers of public office, and it is intended to provide a means of punishment for wrongful official action. It secures the rights of all persons which are found in the Bill of Rights and the Fourteenth Amendment.

This portion of the Civil Rights Code has frequently been invoked in cases where it was shown that public officials have discriminated against minority groups. In the case of U. S. vs. Blackburn, the defendants were indicted for conspiring to deprive certain colored citizens of equal protection of the laws. The charge to the jury in that case reads:

"Hence, if the outrages and crimes shown to have been committed in the case were well known to the community at large, and that community, and the officers of the law, willfully failed to employ the means provided by the law to ferret out and bring to trial the offenders, because of the victims being colored, it is depriving them of the equal protection of the law."

This indicates that in the mind of the Court failure of a police department to make a reasonable attempt to enforce the law as it applies to the minority groups constitutes a conspiracy, and is punishable under federal law.

Section 241 provides: "If two or more persons conspire to injure, oppress, threaten, or intimidate any citizen in the free exercise or enjoyment of any right or privilege secured to him by the Constitution or laws of the United States, or because of his having so exercised the same; or if two or more persons go in disguise on the highway, or on the premises of another, with intent to prevent or hinder his free exercise or enjoyment of any right or privilege so secured—they shall be fined not more than $5,000 or imprisoned not more than two years, or both."

So we see that failure by a police department to ferret out offenders in cases well-known to the community because the victim is a Negro constitutes a conspiracy, and we see how a conspiracy to oppress or threaten or intimidate any citizen constitutes a violation and provides a penalty.

The section on "property rights of citizens" is equally specific in extending the rights possessed by white citizens to members of other races.

The U. S. Code Annotated, Title 8, Section 42, reads in part:

"All citizens of the United States shall have the same right, in every State and Territory, as is enjoyed by white citizens thereof to inherit, purchase, lease, sell, hold and convey real and personal property."

Provision is also made for recovery of damages by injured persons. This is indicated in the section on civil action for deprivation of rights, which reads:

"Every person who, under color of any status, ordinance, regulation, custom, or usage of any Territory or State, or causes to be subjected, any citizen of the United States or other person within the jurisdiction thereof to the deprivation of any rights, privileges, or immunities secured by the Constitution and laws, shall be liable to the party injured in an action at law, and in equity, or other proper proceeding for redress."

A number of cases have appeared in the Federal Courts where it has been charged that discrimination has been practiced in the enforcement of an otherwise valid statute. In these instances, states or municipalities have adopted laws which appeared to apply to all persons alike, but which the injured persons claimed were systematically enforced against only a particular race or class of people.

In such cases, when the proof was shown that such systematic discrimination existed, the courts granted relief by prohibiting the unconstitutional enforcement.

Not only does this section provide for relief of unconstitutional enforcement of valid laws, but it also provides that the injured person may recover in a civil action against the person responsible for the unconstitutional enforcement.

So we see that the officer who allows his personal opinions to interfere with his enforcement of the law can be held liable not only in a civil action, but can be made defendant in a criminal action as well.

The Supreme Court, in recent years, has struck down, one after another, state and local laws requiring the segregation of Negroes and whites. These decisions have resulted in some of the racial conflicts that now confront us.

In 1893 the Court held that "separate but equal" facilities in the public schools were in accordance with the spirit of the Civil War Amendments to the Constitution. This doctrine was to hold for 60 years.

But in 1953, in an historic ruling, the Court stated that "separate" facilities were inherently unequal. It ordered desegregation of schools "with all deliberate speed," permitting federal district courts to determine in large measure just how rapidly integration must be carried out.

Desegregation of schools is now being accomplished in many sections of the nation. In places it has been accompanied by violence. And there is continuing controversy over the justice of the Supreme Court's decrees.

This is a matter that is outside the concern of law enforcement bodies. It is not the responsibility of law enforcement groups to interpret the law; that is a responsibility of the courts. It is the responsibility of the police to maintain the peace and enforce the law as decreed by the courts.

There is no higher legal authority than the Supreme Court, and it has spoken on segregation. The Constitution and Federal Courts have clearly outlined a peace officer's responsibilities and officers should make every effort to carry out their duties with an open mind and with impartiality.

# 3

## CONTROL OF TENSIONS

IN OUR ENFORCEMENT of the law as it applies to segregation it is obvious that we may be called upon to handle tensions initiating in or developing from racial incidents. Experience has shown that severe tensions may arise in communities where integration is being carried out.

The absolute necessity that interracial tensions not be allowed to erupt into violence is immediately apparent. Severe riots are damaging to national morale and unity. The national prestige suffers as much as it does in the loss of a major battle during a war. In the struggle between the free world and communist nations for the uncommitted peoples of the world, race relations are a most important issue. A racial incident in a United States city is flashed around the world as soon as it occurs. It is difficult for the United States to win the non-white people over to our side when they read of racial discrimination and race riots in our country.

Such disorders undermine our influence with millions of our non-white allies and neutrals, and give our enemies material for effective propaganda against us among many nations.

Racial conflicts can be extremely violent. Loss of life and extensive destruction of property are among the immediate effects. Thirty-five persons were killed in Detroit and in Harlem five million dollars worth of property was destroyed during the riots of 1943.

Furthermore, riots never clear up the bad situations that cause them. They aggravate the antagonisms between groups and frequently undermine the faith of a large number of citizens in the forces of law and order. Unless they are quickly and impartially brought under control the minority groups involved are convinced that they cannot depend upon police departments for protection.

The primary responsibility of police departments is to maintain the peace and protect life and property. Consequently, they cannot avoid censure when large scale disorders occur.

The police duty is not discharged merely by meeting violence with violence during a riot. The best opportunity for the police to escape serious criticism lies in the field of preventive work in race relations.

Due to their constant contact with all neighborhoods of a city the police are in an ideal position to maintain constant vigilance over the trouble areas, and to assume the responsibility for making known basic causes of unrest to agencies or groups that can eliminate them.

The police themselves are a tremendous force for molding public opinion. The activities and attitudes of individual policemen can influence citizens to respect the rights of others, or can give the impression that they can attack some group without fear of punishment.

The latter attitude is obviously a serious menace to the public peace, and to the prestige and effectiveness of the police force itself. If all police officers understand these basic facts, as well as the causes of friction between groups, and if they are taught how to respond in various situations involving members of such groups, every man in the department can become a positive force in developing a public attitude favorable to the efficient police handling of any disturbance between groups.

It is obviously to the advantage of the police agency for racial groups to get along with each other peacefully. The complex world in which we live depends upon the cooperation of the many groups that make it up. Each of these groups has its contribution to make in the total functioning of our society.

All of us have our jobs to do, and unless we do them with a minimum of friction and conflict the very fabric of our society will be torn beyond repair. It has been questioned whether democracy can continue to exist unless it develops a means of peacefully settling these differences. The basic idea of democracy, that private and group differences can be tolerated and utilized for the general welfare, is thoroughly in accord with our complex economic interdependence.

However, we must face the fact that ours is a competitive society. Not only individuals, but also national and racial groups are in competition with each other, as they strive individually and collectively to improve their economic and social status.

It is almost inevitable that competition for jobs, a place to live, access to higher social position—the struggle for a generally higher plane of living—will bring about some conflict. Each group, in its separate way, will seek to retain whatever superior advantages it may already possess and reach for more. It is out of this competition that conflict may arise, and the outsider, the newcomer, the stranger, is often branded and stigmatized as inferior.

Some contend that those designated as inferior racial and national groups are entitled to a lesser share of the rewards of our society regardless of individual abilities. However, these groups constantly struggle to improve themselves, and secure preferred positions.

Within this struggle the possibility of overt clashes and riotous outbreak—the resort to open warfare between racial and nationality groups—is ever-present. This creates a tense uneasy situation as competition grows keener and conditions change.

This situation is of unquestioned seriousness to every member of American Society. However, it is of even greater significance for those with whom the whole community has lodged the responsibility for maintaining civil order and protecting individual rights and liberties—the law enforcement officers of the nation.

Not only are the police charged with securing the community against riotous outbreak, but they are also the ultimate guarantors of individual liberty. This thrusts upon the police the need for an extraordinary exercise of caution and judgment, in order that their actions will not prove to be a source of further aggravation and hostility.

Unfortunately, the conduct of police officials in some localities has not always been above reproach. Unwarranted police conduct which aggravates tension will be minimized only if each police officer has the professional sense of personal and social responsibility. This must then be associated with an understanding of the possible consequence of employing varied and alternative measures.

The role of the police in these explosive situations is admittedly a difficult one. On one hand, as a person, he is a product of the same social experience to which all of us are exposed. It is likely that he has absorbed some of the prejudices and hatreds toward minority groups that are so tragically widespread in our society. It would be absurd to presume that the mere act of donning a uniform and badge would remove ideas, opinions and prejudices instilled in him from his childhood.

However, it must be stressed that as an officer of the law and as a member of the police profession he stands as a symbol of the impartial authority of society. There rests with him the task of peacefully mediating the antagonisms and conflicts between the various segments of the community.

The police officer is confronted with a most difficult task in the fulfillment of his high purpose. He must bring under control his personal sentiments and prejudices and subordinate them in a truly professional spirit. In this manner, and only in this manner, will he be able to treat fairly and impartially with the contenders in any dispute.

The private views of the individual policeman may be of such a nature as to make questionable his capacity for fairness and impartiality unless they are changed. As an officer of the law, his private views regarding the Negro, the Oriental, the Mexican, the Jew, the Catholic or the Protestant must not compromise the performance of his public duty. *He must refrain from expressing private ideas in discharging the duties of his office, and usually his private views must be kept to himself as he is looked upon as a police officer whether on or off duty.*

This entails a capacity to distinguish between his own rights as a private citizen and his responsibility as a police officer. In order that the police officer can function in a role that lies outside the area of his personal prejudices, it is necessary for him to develop an extraordinary sense of professionalism.

Just as in medicine, the law, the ministry and the teaching profession, his is a "high calling." It is not merely another occupation, distinguished only by a uniform and the size of the wage or salary.

Policing is increasingly recognized as requiring a high degree of technical skill and knowledge. This, however, is only one mark of a profession. There is the distinguishing emphasis on public duty and service to the community. The time has long passed in enlightened police circles when a man becomes an officer by merely being accepted for employment.

Training, dedication and understanding are the cornerstones of modern police science. The police officer must become increasingly aware of the role he plays as society's authority, aware that only by examining the relations of his personal sentiments to his public duties can he achieve true impartiality and neutrality. This is an educational problem. It is equal in importance to the acquisition of new information of the techniques of crime detection.

The average citizen's respect for authority is dependent upon the degree to which the authority is impartially exercised. Minority groups may have little reason to respect the law if it is apparent that they do not receive equal protection from the authorities who are administering it.

Impartial enforcement builds necessary respect for the authority of society. Only by commanding such respect can the police officer begin to cope with the various conflicts that may arise between social groups.

The modern officer in dealing with racial tensions is much like the "man on a tight rope," one false step may lead to disaster. The law enforcement officer's critical position cannot be overemphasized.

# 4

## THE HISTORY OF RACIAL TENSION

To STUDY the problem as it exists today we need to review briefly the history of the United States so far as racial tensions are concerned.

When this nation was first founded it could have truthfully been said that the racial and political frontiers were the same. The various nationality groups and races who were the first settlers largely remained separated from each other. Certain areas of the New World were settled by the English, and to these areas naturally gravitated the English part of the incoming human tide. The same is true of the German, Dutch, and French. The great area available for settlement, and the small population, made it unlikely that tension and conflict would develop between groups with widely differing ideas. The conflict as it first developed was political by nature.

It has been proven that when racial frontiers correspond with political frontiers, interracial problems are simplest. There is little exchange between groups, and when difficulties arise, diplomatic representatives can act for each, communications can be controlled and adjustment made without friction.

Rapid settlement of the western hemisphere caused the political frontiers to disappear and changed the nature of the racial frontier. Immigration continued rapidly, and to the heterogeneous population the slave trader added the Negro.

Although it is now of little importance, the Negro is not an American by choice. They were brought to the new world against their wills. If their presence creates a problem it is not one of their own devising.

The first Negroes were brought into the English colonies in 1619, when a Dutch man-of-war sold twenty Negroes to the colonists at Jamestown. This was only twelve years after the first permanent English settlement in the Western Hemisphere, and almost a year before the Pilgrims landed at Plymouth. From that beginning the importation of Negroes as slaves continued for almost two centuries, until the traffic in slaves was outlawed by Great Britian in 1807 and by the United States a year later.

Many persons in the American colonies were opposed to slavery before the United States emerged as a nation. In various ways the colonies of Virginia, Massachusetts and Pennsylvania attempted to halt the import of slaves. Their efforts were unsuccessful primarily because the mother country was getting rich from the slave trade. For many years England was placed in the paradoxical position of prohibiting slavery on her home soil, but encouraging and enforcing it in her colonies.

Because of the prohibition of slavery on English soil there was no precedent in the colonies for slavery, and they were absorbed into an existing system of apprenticeship and vagrancy laws. Their color was a basis for differential treatment, and later made easier their enslavement in the generally accepted sense of the word.

Throughout the years during which slavery existed there were many voices raised against it, both in the north and in the south. Many persons deplored the owning of human beings by others, and condemned the conditions under which the slaves had to live and work. Many persons believe that slavery would have ceased to exist without the Civil War if the problem had not become involved in the struggle for political and economical power between the slave and free states.

The war that was fought between 1861 and 1865 resulted in the emancipation of the slaves and the continuation of the federal union. In the North, which had tried slavery and abandoned it because it was not profitable there, more and more people had joined John Wesley in believing that the ownership of one human by another was the "sum of villanies."

Opposition to slavery on moral grounds had found it harder to live in the uncongenial soil of the South, and had been stifled under the weight of economic and political pressure. Prior to the Civil War most northern preachers challenged chattel slavery as contrary to the Bible and Christian teaching, while in the South equally sincere ministers were proving, at least to their own satisfaction, that slavery was conformable to Christianity.

The southern minister admitted the existence of evils in the system, but contended that they were abuses and that slavery was best for the slave and the master alike.

By comparison, in our modern times, we find ministers who disagree on whether there should be integration of the Negroes into schools and recreational and transportational facilities.

The Emancipation Proclamation, issued by President Lincoln in 1863, marked the turning point for Negroes in the United States. It marked the beginning of a new era.

It is difficult for us, almost a century after the event, to realize the conditions confronting the slaves when they were freed. They had enjoyed no rights, they had been bought and sold and they had been entirely dependent on their white masters for their existence. Naturally, a slave psychology had developed. They had come to believe that since they owned nothing, they had no responsibility. They had no ambition and no incentive to work, because their past labors had not produced for them a higher standard of living. With such a background the Negroes faced a new life at the end of the Civil War.

There were some Negroes who were better prepared to take advantage of their new-found opportunities. Manumission had not been uncommon, and when freedom came to all the Negroes in the country, almost a half million were already free. Thus there was a nucleus which had risen above the level of most of their people and had some preparation for a life of freedom and responsibility.

The sudden freedom of the slave did not accomplish what many idealists had believed would be almost immediate and automatic. The freedmen had many weary, discouraging years through which they had to travel before they attained a new and satisfying life.

# 5

## THE NATURE OF RACIAL DIFFERENCES

So THAT WE as police officers may know and understand our responsibilities and the role we must of necessity play in mediating the differences which arise between conflicting groups of society, it is necessary that we know not only the law as it specifically applies to minority group relations, but that we also have the most accurate and authentic information available on the nature and extent of racial differences.

We must arrive at an understanding of the basic principles underlying discriminatory practices. We must in addition acquire accurate knowledge on what we, as police officers, must do to function properly in situations fraught with great tension.

Our own conflicting ideas can best be brought under control if we acquire an understanding of the exact nature and extent of the differences that exist between groups.

We are much like the average citizen in our attitudes toward racial and nationality groups. The opinions we hold, and are willing to defend, rarely arise from an objective examination of the facts about racial differences. Few of our attitudes are based upon a true knowledge and analytical study of whatever differences exist in the various groups.

None of us were born with prejudices. Most of us have our beliefs because we have unconsciously gained them from the culture surrounding us. That culture has lead us to believe those ideas which we embrace, when actually the opinions we hold are likely to have very little to do with the actual facts.

We are all likely to try to explain differences in the behavior of various groups by reliance on false and unsupported assumptions. The police officer, to approach the problem in a truly professional manner, must free himself from the influences of false racial doctrines. He has the added responsibility of providing himself with realistic data about nationalities and racial differences. He must then combine this knowledge with an open mind and common sense.

A police officer cannot afford to rely on hearsay or accept without question the opinions of others. Just as we take nothing for granted in a criminal investigation and in our presentations in court—we deal only in facts we are able to substantiate and which we know to be true—so do we need to verify our thinking on problems in the field of human relations by technically accurate knowledge. It would be folly of the grossest order for us to act on the basis of laymen's hunches and speculation.

In our activities we must continually substitute thinking for prejudice. This is not easy. It is only human for us to tend to reverse the process, for it is infinitely easier for us to accept without question some other person's evaluation than to think for ourselves. Thinking remains one of man's most difficult tasks. However, only by serious thought can we arrive at the truth, and when we arrive at the truth, can we recognize it as such.

Sociologists tell us that the average human being frequently attempts to justify his racial prejudices by both physiological and psychological factors. In other words, we often contend that one race is inferior to another both because of its physical characteristics and its mental prowess.

Physiologists have come to believe, however, that there is only one basic human type. They claim that differences which are observable in the physical characteristics are differences in the individual rather than in the race. It is without question that every ethnic group contains a wide range in muscular development, weight, and height. There are Mongoloids who are short and fat and others who are tall and slender. There are similar variations among Caucasoid and Negroid representatives.

Some persons claim to be able to determine the racial grouping of an individual by an examination of the shape of the head. As a matter of fact, all shapes of heads may be found in all color groups. To a certain extent the shape of the head indicates the size of the brain, but this is by no means an accurate index of the intelligence of its possessor. Post mortem examinations have shown that extremely intelligent men sometimes have relatively small brains, whereas the largest brain yet discovered by medical science was that of an idiot.

A further contention frequently made is that the race from which it was taken can be determined by the analysis of a blood sample. Any serologist can testify to the inaccuracy of this assumption. Scientific research has proven that every racial group has all types of blood, in only slightly different percentages. No group is distinguished by possession of one particular type.

Probably because it is the most easily observed, the color of skin is frequently cited as proof of racial differences. Indeed, the average person usually makes his identification of race primarily on this basis. However, if we attempt to adopt this standard of differentiation, we again find ourselves in error, for each year approximately 20,000 persons who have lived among Negroes and who have a predominately Negro ancestry move to white areas and pass as white without question.

The classification of persons into racial categories by the shading of their skins would cause us to classify many persons with purely white ancestry as Negroes and many persons of predominately Negro ancestry as whites. In other words, there are many persons of the Negro race who have skins lighter than some persons who are classified as members of the white race. A person with a totally white skin would be odd indeed in appearance. All persons lie somewhere between absolute white and absolute black, and we cannot with accuracy classify by color alone.

However, if we choose to accept skin color as an accurate index of race, we are affording ourselves a very limited standard—one that is in actuality only skin deep. It is not possible from a laboratory examination of the vital parts of the human body—for example, the brain, heart, and lungs—to determine whether the specimen came from a Negro, a white or an Oriental.

We must then, if we attempt an analytical study of existing facts, reach the conclusion that racial differences are mostly in the outermost layers of the body. There are few if any differences deep within. It is the factors of high visibility—the color of skin, the form and appearance of the hair, and the shape of the nose, lips and eye lids—that enter into our consciousnesses and influence our judgments and attitudes.

We will usually reject any actual differences that exist as being unimportant and seize upon believed-in differences to justify our prejudices against a particular group of people. For an example, anthropologists study the relative flatness of a shin bone for classification by race, but we have no prejudice against a flat-shinned person. It is only those characteristics which are highly visible which we seize upon as a mark or a label.

A second major point frequently used in an attempt to justify a belief in racial differences is the contention that the average mentality of one group is inferior to the average mentality of another. If this difference actually existed there would be justification according to students of human behavior, for relegating certain groups to positions for which their limited mentalities would equip them.

Study has shown, however, that intelligence is in direct relation to a person's social and cultural environment, and is not dependent on racial differences.

Intelligence tests given by the Armed Forces during World War II are frequently quoted to show that the average intelligence of the Negro is appreciably lower than that of the white. Tests conducted more recently, and more recent interpretations of the World War II tests, have shown that the grades made were more influenced by geographical conditions and social background than by race membership. The studies showed that grades made by Negroes were generally lower than those made by whites, but this fails to take into consideration the geographical background of persons taking the tests and resultant differences in social environment. A great percentage of the Negroes taking the examinations were from the south and the average grade made by persons from the south, both black and white, was appreciably lower than the average grade by persons from the north. The differences actually resulted not from racial factors but from differences in the amount and quality of education and general social opportunities.

It is interesting to note that the northern Negro made a higher grade on these examinations than did the southern white. This does not necessarily prove that the northern Negro is more intelligent than is the southern white. It merely shows that the quality and quantity of education available to persons from the north, regardless of race, exceeds that available to persons from the south.

The cultural environment is the most important factor found in determining or predicating the result of so-called intelligence tests. In none of these tests have we been successful in eliminating the influence of our cultural background. Urban life, rural life, the north, the south, the east, the west, the high income group, the low income group—all have different types of cultural backgrounds to which adaptation is unconsciously made. Our total beliefs are determined by the adaptations we make, which are often so obscure that they can be detected only by a most intimate knowledge of the conditions of life.

The wide range of activities, capabilities, attitudes, and talents of members of the same race with different cultural backgrounds indicates the minimal importance of biological differences and the maximal importance of environmental factors.

Our total ethnic knowledge justifies the conclusion that while individual differences are in many cases great, biological differences in races are small. There is no apparent justification for the contention that one group is by nature so much more intelligent, endowed with greater will power or emotionally more stable than another, that its culture would be materially affected.

Social scientists then conclude that racial differences are by nature more sociological than physical. They claim that the factors which are highly visible assume a greater importance than those which are structural and conclude that we are more influenced by minor differences which are easily apparent than we are by any major differences contained deep within.

If this appraisal by qualified persons is to be accepted, then we must conclude that racial differences are actually important only so far as they affect our judgments of race. For an example, if we took special notice of green refrigerators, and believed seriously that refrigerators were less efficient and of inferior quality because they were green and believed that greenness was connected inseparably with their cooling ability, then green refrigerators would pose for us a real and important problem. It is quite obvious that our opinion of green refrigerators would not in the least affect their essential quality. They would cool just as efficiently regardless of our opinion. But if we were convinced that they were inferior, then so far as we personally were concerned they would be inferior.

A logical conclusion would then seem to be that the actual differences between races are not nearly as great as our opinions make them and that if we placed the proper evaluation on these differences there would be few attendant racial problems. While the real differences have little or no importance, the believed-in differences exert a tremendous influence. The fact that believed-in differences do not actually exist does not reduce the harmful effects of the beliefs. For "as a man thinketh so is he."

It is obviously not easy for us to change ideas, prejudices, biases and beliefs engendered in us throughout our life time. But we as police officers face the necessity for examining our ideas so that we may recognize them for what they really are.

By way of comparison, it is of great importance in police operational procedures whether we act on the assumption that criminals are born or if we believe persons become criminals because of the social environment to which they are subjected. Modern ideas of crime prevention are based on an assumption that persons become criminals because of the influences to which they are exposed and a rejection of the belief that they become criminals because of hereditary factors.

A reasonable man prefers truth to fallacy and fact to fiction. We can assume that because of his psychological make up and training the police officer is a reasonable man.

The law enforcement officer is constantly placed in contact with these believed-in differences. If he can, by analytical study of facts available, arrive at an understanding of the basis of some of the prevalent beliefs, he can then begin to subdue his prejudices and more properly perform his function.

Officers are frequently called upon to deal with other people who have strong beliefs on the racial issue. It is difficult to reason with a man on a subject that has an emotional basis. We are usually more definite in our beliefs on subjects which involve our emotions—our loves, hates, fears, and anxieties. It is more difficult to change these opinions than it is for us to change our opinions on things that do not affect us as personally. We must constantly keep in mind that while we cannot hope to change the opinions of many of the people with whom we are placed in contact, we must enforce the law even when it does not meet with the approval of one segment of society.

# 6

## THE NATURE OF PREJUDICES

To PROGRESS in the suppression of our prejudices, and it is obvious that our jobs will be made easier if our own prejudices can be controlled, we must arrive at an accurate understanding of what prejudice is sociologically and determine whether it can stand the cold light of clear logical reasoning.

Prejudice has been described as prejudgment, for it is a judgment of events or persons not based on actual personal experience. These prejudgments are frequently conditioned by experiences but are acquired vicariously. They are attitudes taken over from the culture of the group of which we are a member.

Most students of human behavior agree that racial prejudice is not usually manifested against a specific individual with observable characteristics, but against the individual as a member of the category "race." Persons identified or associated with a racial group frequently fail to emerge as an individual to a person who has a prejudice against that particular group. We have frequently heard the remark made that members of certain racial groups all look alike. Sociologists claim that the person who makes this statement is actually being truthful because he has a tendency to look on others as members of a group rather than as individuals.

Prejudices against other groups usually result in damage only to the person holding them. However, when our prejudiced ideas cause us to try to make scapegoats out of minority group members, tension inevitably arises and sometimes violence occurs.

Gordon W. Allport, an eminent psychologist, writes that 85% of the American population is ready to scapegoat one group or another. To see how violence can easily result, we should first look into the definition of scapegoating and see how it takes place. We should study its underlying factors.

When some of the aggressive energies of a person or group are
focused upon another person or group, the amount of aggression
or blame being either wholly or partly unwarranted, scapegoating
occurs. It grows out of normal predilections, normal biases, normal preferences and ordinary prejudices. It is only under the
stress of unusual frustration or hardship, misinterpreted because of
inaccurate reasoning, that the excesses which constitute scapegoating occur.

The opposite end of the scale from scapegoating is friendly,
cooperative behavior between groups. Since our concern is with
the origin and conditions of hostile relationships, we should define
the degrees or stages which are readily distinguishable. We may
start with predilection, which is the mildest and most socially
acceptable form of group exclusion.

Predilection is simply the preference of an individual for one
language, one culture or one skin color as opposed to another. If
one person likes Mexican food and another does not, they accomplish nothing by arguing about their respective tastes. Persons who
have only predilections may agree or disagree, and remain completely amicable. Every person feels that it is his privilege to disagree with all others in such matters, and almost without exception we are willing to respect the other person's choices and his
right to make them. So long as human beings must make choices,
predilections are natural and inevitable. They become socially
harmful only when they serve as a stepping stone to further discriminatory practices, which in turn lead to prejudices.

We call a rigid, inflexible and exaggerated predilection a prejudice. When we are prejudiced, we tend to have a closed mind,
and are unswayed by either logic or evidence. For example, it
would be impossible to convince some Englishmen that all Americans are not loudmouthed, boisterous spendthrifts. Some Americans think that all Englishmen are humorless bores, all Italians
are born criminals, all Germans seek war, all Frenchmen think
constantly of sex, and all Spanish people are highly emotional and
unstable. These are stereotyped judgments, which are fixed and
extremely hard to change.

Similarly, people who are prejudiced against Negroes think
that they are all stupid, that all of them will steal if given the

opportunity, that all of them prefer to resolve personal differences with a knife rather than by discussion, and that they all place a very low value on human life. Those who are prejudiced against Scotsmen think they are all penny-pinching misers. We even encountered persons who are prejudiced against women, and think that all females are incapable of succeeding in the rugged competition of business life.

Unless prejudice results in some overt action it usually harms only the person who holds it. It stagnates the mind it occupies. The great danger of prejudice lies in the probability that it will lead to discrimination, which differs from scapegoating only in the amount of violence used or aggression expressed. Discrimination is an act of total exclusion prompted by prejudice. Generally, this exclusion is not based on the individual's personal worth, but on a label branding him as a member of a discredited group.

The most aggravated form of social exclusion is scapegoating, which is the full-fledged persecution of those against whom we are prejudiced and against whom we discriminate. The scapegoat may be either physically or verbally abused. We are usually safe from retaliation, for we generally scapegoat only those persons who are weaker than we, and who cannot fight back. The basic nature of scapegoating was revealed in the persecution of the Salem witches, who were a small handful of women who could not offer effective resistance against the frustrated persons who attacked them.

The motives behind scapegoating are many, and may be unknown even to the person who seeks a scapegoat. One of the most common is thwarting and deprivation.

Because of our complex society many people are not able to attain what they want and what they think they should have. Such deprivation frequently leads to aggression, which is only rarely directed toward the cause of frustration. It can much more easily be directed toward an object, person or group which is incapable of fighting back. In many cases the anger directed against Negroes coming onto a job formerly held by whites is not because of a strong dislike of working with the Negro, but because of the basic insecurity the white feels in his job. He does not know how to direct his anger toward the reason for it, so he seeks a convenient scapegoat which can serve instead. Because employment is on a highly competitive basis, the white may feel that each added competitor increases by that much the likelihood that he may lose his job. The economic factors leading to this condition may not be clear in his mind, but the person who threatens his position is clearly visible.

Under such conditions, the scapegoat is made to pay not only for current conditions, in which he may play a part, but also for frustrations of long standing, most of which have nothing to do with the current situation.

Another basic reason for scapegoating is guilt. Most of us constantly seek to rationalize our undesirable behavior, and find some object or person on whom we can blame our shortcomings. Most of us are unwilling to admit that we might be something less than perfect, and are all too willing to project our guilt onto another. In this way we escape the pangs of conscience which assail us.

A third reason is fear and anxiety. Fear has been described as an actual feeling of danger and dread, which can be reduced or dispelled by an attack on that which we consider to be a threat. Frequently we do not properly distinguish between real and false threats, and strike out against things which actually pose no threat to us.

Anxiety is the anticipation of danger. Like fear, it is caused by a feeling of basic insecurity. It can sometimes be alleviated by rationalization which may take the form of scapegoating.

We sometimes seek a scapegoat to enhance our feelings of self-importance. A person who feels insecure can sometimes convince himself of his basic worth by increasing his feelings of strength. The bully who seeks to prove his strength by mistreatment of a physically weaker child is an example of this tendency. Conversely, a physically weak child may attempt to affirm his strength by verbally scapegoating his stronger companions. He may then physically bully a still weaker child to compensate for his own feelings of inferiority.

A feeling of basic insecurity can sometimes be overcome by membership in a group which the insecure person is eligible to join. For example, the immigrant Irishman may join a society which asserts that the Irish Catholic is the best person. Under the right conditions these societies may violently oppose other groups to highlight their own superiority.

Conformity is another reason for scapegoating, and is perhaps one of the most important. In some sections it is not socially popular to plead the cause of the minority groups. Conformity makes for security, and if a large segment of society proclaims one group inferior to another, we are inclined to accept this evaluation to maintain our popularity. Conformity does not have to be as deliberate as this. Many people conform to current patterns of persecution because they habitually imitate prevailing customs.

Children are especially inclined to take over their parent's prejudices uncritically. They may accept without question the claims of a parent that one group is inferior and unsuitable for social contact.

Another reason is "tabloid thinking" or oversimplification of a situation. Strife brings out the helplessness with which the individual faces world-wide forces. He needs to simplify issues in order to make possible some understanding of social chaos. It is less trouble to think of munition makers as being responsible for war than to figure it out in complex economic and cultural causes. Oversimplification of issues saves energy. If a person feels hostile and aggressive, it is easier for him to attack one single obstacle in his path than to spread his aggressive impulses.

Living conditions in the present world are extremely complex. The individual does not normally know enough about economics and political science to understand the reasons behind various economic and political maneuvers. Because he feels the necessity for establishing in his own mind the reasons why things are being done he is inclined to oversimplify what he thinks. Instead of figuring things out, he secures a scapegoat for his misunderstanding.

Sometimes the issue may be simplified by blaming a group or class of people rather than a specified individual. For example, in Boston's Coconut Grove fire, the public blamed "the officials" rather than concentrating its wrath on any one person, against whom a more detailed, and therefore more difficult, bill of charges would have to be drawn.

All these motives may create a pattern of aggression against someone who is partially guilty, but who in most cases is innocent.

Many factors keep us from directing our aggression against the true cause of our deprivation, fear and guilt.

1. Anxiety due to the expectation of punishment. The person who is actually responsible may be in a position to retaliate. For example, you may be really angry at your boss, but you take it out on your secretary because she is powerless to retaliate against you. The person who has had a hard day at the office, and goes home to take it out on his wife and children, is reacting in this manner.

2. Attacking the guilty person may lead to punishment by a third person. For example, a man may violate your honor in some way, but you hesitate to take action against him for fear of punishment for taking the law into your own hands.

3. There may be strong personal inhibitions against attacking the true cause of the provocation. For example, in our society a man does not strike a women, even if he has good reason. It is often more respectable to vent rage against a scapegoat.

4. Another reason for displacement of aggression is that we are unable to understand the roots of our discomfort and a prejudice we already have is made to supply the cause and receive the wrath. The economic frustration among marginal workers is no easier to bear simply because the workers do not know its cause. Having a pre-existing prejudice, it can be allowed to grow into violence because it seems to be somehow related to the complex issues which are not understood.

Displacement thus results from the remote and illogical association of ideas. Living as we do in large and impersonal cities, great numbers of individuals have been separated from the secure surroundings of family. We are dependent upon a job and an employer whom we do not even know as a means of earning a living. It is from relative strangers that we must secure personal recognition and affection. We get little genuine appreciation of ourselves from strangers, and many feel constantly disappointed and frustrated.

We may not all want to be big shots, but neither do we want to be ignored and regarded as of little or no importance. Disappointments, failures and the sense of being ignored may release aggressive tendencies. Thus we may compensate in some way for our feelings of frustration and denial.

We may build up the low esteem we have in the eyes of others by satisfying ourselves that we have a right to look down upon certain individuals and groups. No one likes to admit his shortcomings. We prefer to find scapegoats, or good explanations for our difficulties. The inability of many people to realize their social and economic goals creates pent up emotions and feelings which may be released in the form of hate, contempt or even acts of violence against scapegoat minority groups.

This is the way some men establish themselves as persons of substance and importance. Minority groups, with strange manners or appearances, become natural scapegoats. As long as large sections of a city remain economically and socially insecure, the minority groups are potential scapegoats. Unemployment, low wages and social disappointments all combine to make many men unreasonable and somewhat desperate.

We are making slow but steady progress in the satisfaction of these more basic human needs, but in the meantime we cannot permit our uncontrolled passions to destroy our society.

# 7

## THE SOURCE OF PREJUDICE

We have discussed briefly the nature of prejudice. It will possibly be of benefit to us to learn the source of prejudice, and to determine how a person becomes prejudiced.

It has been proven to the satisfaction of psychologists that racial prejudices are not instinctive reactions. For the small child there is characteristically no significance in race. This may be illustrated by the child who moved from an area where schools were segregated into a location where they were integrated. At the end of his first day in school he was asked by his parents if there were any colored children in his class. He said, "No," then asked, "What color would they be?" There is in the young no awareness of racial differences, and the children of all races can associate with each other without the question of race arising.

Children who are reared in environments where there are racial prejudices ordinarily begin to share them—or perhaps to rebel against them—at an age when self-consciousness begins.

While we are not born with hate, we do possess the ability to develop hate. What and whom we learn to hate will depend largely on our experiences at home, in our neighborhood, and in our schools, and the impressions these experiences make on us.

Even during the period of slavery, when perhaps racial prejudice was at its highest in the United States, there was no awareness on the part of the very young of race. In most slave-holding households a Negro mammy took care of the white children. She frequently served as a wet nurse, and relieved the actual mother of many of the responsibilities of caring for the child. This relationship continued, with the Negro as necessary to the comfort of the child as was the mother, until the child was old enough to be taught the socially acceptable relationship between the Negro and the white.

Frequently a Negro child, of the age of the white child, was assigned as a playmate. The two usually played together with no consciousness of their racial differences until they were both old enough to learn social custom.

If we accept the fact that we are not born with prejudice, how then do we acquire it? Social scientists claim that our views on race are not usually obtained by contact with that race, but by contact with prevailing attitudes toward that race. We then absorb our attitudes and prejudices from the culture surrounding us.

A parallel between the language we speak and the prejudices we have could be drawn. If we are born in France, and hear French spoken, then we learn to speak French. The same is true of German, Spanish or English. A Chinese boy, reared in an English home where only English is spoken, will learn not Chinese, but English. Chinese will be as unfamiliar to him as to any English boy. If then we learn our language from our society, do we not also learn our social evaluations?

The home is the most important source of our opinions and beliefs. To a very young child his parents are persons to be imitated and followed. This is not difficult to understand, when we take into consideration how dependent the child is on his parents for food, security, comfort, love and protection from danger. The attitudes of the parents become in the mind of the child associated with the food, love and protection, and he accepts them just as he accepts without question the creature comforts.

Parents also provide the child's main source of knowledge. He in a sense becomes a book, edited by his parents. If he is reared where racial prejudices are not present and where tolerance is the general attitude, then he does not develop racial prejudice at this point. But if the home has an attitude of intolerance and prejudice, then the probability is that the child will also be intolerant and prejudiced.

Let us assume, for the sake of a hypothesis, that a child's first conscious knowledge of Negroes occurs when his father comes home and tells his mother, in his presence, about a disagreeable

contact he had with a "dirty nigger." He already knows what
dirty means, and in his mind it is associated with "nigger." When
he learns that this is a term of derogation sometimes applied to
Negroes, then is born in his mind an idea that the terms dirty
and nigger are both associated with Negroes.

A short time thereafter he sees working side by side on a construction job Negroes and whites. The type of work being done
has soiled the clothing of the white and the Negro alike, but he
has heard the term "dirty nigger" and here he sees a Negro who
is dirty. Since he has never heard associated the words dirty and
white, he fails to notice that the white man working beside the
Negro is just as dirty as the Negro. He has found substantiation
for his newborn belief that Negroes are dirty.

The modern advertising man has learned to capitalize on this
association of words and attitudes. Most people, because of television commercials, associate a tattooed hand and an outdoor
type with a certain brand of cigarette. Others, who would think
for themselves, smoke still another brand. Something that is just
a little bit better is probably a cereal.

In homes where the child does not hear terms of derogation
associated with a minority group, and is not permitted to use
them, a different attitude is fostered. Not only majority groups
need to avoid the use of such terms. To many persons of Latin
American extraction an "angle" is not created by two lines coming
together, but is rather an undesirable resident of the United States.
Emotional terms, regardless of where they are used, promote
friction, but when they are used in the presence of young children,
they may establish the foundation of future prejudices.

A child imitates not only activities, but also feelings, attitudes
and opinions. In a society where he sees the Negro segregated on
public transportation facilities, where he sees the Negro attending
segregated schools, and where he sees the Negro relegated to
inferior employment then he logically supposes that the Negro
occupies this position because of his basic inferiority. He becomes
a creature of stereotyped ideas. He is molded not only by what
he sees, but also by his interpretation, in the light of current social
custom, of what he sees.

Education is not always a formal process of which we are aware. It begins with our birth, and ends with our death. All the ideas to which we are exposed play their part in the determination of our opinions. Our parents, friends, books, magazines, movies, television all play important roles in deciding what we shall believe.

We are told that our prejudices, once started, continue to grow because of several things. One is deprivation. We feel that every concession gained by the object of our prejudice results in a comparable loss to ourselves. When we compete with a member of a minority group for the job we want, he has an equal chance of getting it. If he does, we are deprived of it. Racial violence is usually initiated by the lower income group. Its members are the ones whose security is threatened or status challenged.

A second reason listed by sociologists is guilt. We are guilty of blaming our own shortcomings on others. We project our guilt to ease our own feelings of inadequacy and shortcoming. We blame others so we may excuse ourselves.

A third reason is fear and anxiety. Because we do not understand the Negro, the Latin American, the Italian or the Oriental, we ascribe to them certain attributes that do not exist except in our minds.

Another is self-enhancement. A feeling of superiority is pleasant, and feeds the ego. It makes us feel noticed and important. This self-enhancement can be acquired in either one of two ways. We can either accomplish something worthwhile which brings attention to ourselves, or we can minimize the importance of other members of society. The first is difficult. The second is all too easy.

Another is conformity to established thought. This indicates a lack of independent reasoning. We know through experience what the general public thinks about an issue, and we do not want to risk censure with an opinion to the contrary. We know that if we embrace ideas not wholly acceptable to society in general, we may become unpopular, lose our friends and become an object of ridicule. We should remember, however, that some of the greatest men of history were looked upon as crusading radicals by their contemporaries.

Prejudices frequently arise from situations for which there is justification for opposition. There was great bitterness following the Civil War between northerners and southerners. The entire social and economic structure of the South was destroyed by the war. The emancipation of the slaves removed from the southern white the source of his income and demolished his social standing.

The carpetbaggers took over the South and assumed the powers previously enjoyed by the ruling whites. The veteran of the Confederate Army was not even given the right to vote unless he repudiated the stand he took during the war. As a consequence, many veterans had no voice whatever in the government of their own affairs. The southerner who had enjoyed complete supremacy was delegated to a secondary position. It would be ridiculous to state that many cases of injustice did not occur. It would be equally absurd to presume that the southern white was not influenced by these injustices.

But we find in the South today many persons with a distinct antipathy to northerners because of events that occurred immediately following the Civil War. The initial cause of the opposition ended almost a century ago, but to a certain extent the result—prejudice of the southerner for the northerner—still exists.

# 8

## THE EFFECT OF PREJUDICE ON MINORITIES

POLICE OFFICERS have frequently commented on certain distinctive behavior traits of the Negroes as a group. Other minority groups also seem to have fallen into behavior patterns which are dissimilar from the culture of society as a whole. It is important that the real reasons for such behavior be understood.

Most minority groups live in an atmosphere where prejudice, discrimination and scapegoating are prevalent. This affects their behavior in significant ways. Because of the prejudice and discrimination so frequently directed against them, members of minority groups are more than usually sensitive and defensive. This is not too difficult to understand, for when people are made to feel from childhood that they are different from other people, they are bound to be affected in some way.

Because minority group individuals sometimes feel that other persons are prejudiced against them, they are continually fearful of assault, insult or discrimination. They live in an atmosphere of constant apprehensiveness. Because of the conditions under which they are forced to live they frequently develop strong self-protective reactions. When a person is constantly treated as if he were inferior, he must eventually begin to feel that this inferiority actually exists. He may then develop aggressiveness as a compensation for his feelings of inferiority or he may develop an overpowering shyness which causes him to retreat from the cause of his condition.

While this occurs frequently in minority groups, it is by no means restricted to them, but is a universal human reaction. Anyone who feels insecure or inferior must eventually develop some defense mechanism. Psychologists realize that arrogance is very frequently only a cover for inferiority complexes.

Many privileges which members of the majority group generally take for granted are denied to members of minority groups. In many areas the privilege of unlimited use of hotels, restaurants, theaters, free choice of residence, and free competition for jobs are included in this classification. Because of the frustration which must invariably accompany such denial many persons within minority groups react either by aggression or by withdrawal and an attempt to avoid further frustration.

This might be a partial explanation of the fact that some members of minority groups seem to be more inclined to commit crimes of violence. Others are generally withdrawn from contacts with whites which would expose them to discrimination. Still others respond by aggression of a competitive nature. They compete vigorously and try hard to excel in finance or the arts.

It should not be difficult for the police officer to understand what minority group members have to contend with and why they react defensively as they do. In many ways the police are themselves a minority group. An exaggerated illustration used in training programs for new officers is, "You may have been beating your wife for years before you joined the police department but then you were just a man up the street who beat his wife. Now you are that policeman who beats his wife." or "You were that idiotic driver who drove like wild on a quiet residential street but now you are that policeman who drives recklessly." It is almost impossible for a police officer to become involved in any activity either on or off duty in which his occupation does not enter. This is proven time and time again in social functions when members of the public feel constrained to tell the police officer about a traffic citation they received. Almost invariably the explanation will begin with, "I know that your men are normally right but on this occasion . . ."

Minority groups face much the same problem. We are inclined to think of their transgressions in terms of their race rather than in terms of the individuals involved. Many newspaper accounts relate the race of offenders when such information is not actually relevant to the story.

Carrying a bit further the parallel between police officers and other minority groups let us look at some of the generalizations made about a policeman. We all resent the portrayal of policemen so frequently found in motion pictures and in the press. Cartoons frequently show the officer as having a small head, huge stomach, and big feet. If the cartoonist really wants to show the police officer at his best, he usually shows him reaching back to get an apple or a banana off a fruit stand. Law enforcement officers who are consciously striving to improve the level of service provided and professionalize the vocation find that this constant stereotyping crucifies them. Because of the public attitude such caricatures foster, police officers find it extremely difficult to develop a code of ethics which will demand for them recognition as professionals.

Discrimination bred by such generalizations has a direct bearing on the number of offenses committed by the groups against whom the discrimination is directed. If for no other reason, the police officer should seek to avoid discriminatory practices because of this. The realization that a lessening of discrimination tends to result in a lowering of the crime rate should be incentive enough for the police officer to avoid discriminatory practices.

It is frequently pointed out that members of minority groups are responsible for a percentage of crime far out of proportion with the percentage they constitute of the total population. This is pointed to as an indication that by nature the members of the group are more than usually lawless. It must however be realized that because of discrimination a great majority of the minority groups are forced to live under conditions conducive to crime. Regardless of the race of the person involved slum conditions and a vicious environment breed criminal offenses. Practically always the highest crime rate occurs in the poorest districts.

Because of discrimination the economic status of many minority groups is very low. Due partly to poverty and partly to the fact they are not permitted residence in other sections they live mainly in the slum areas of the city. Their housing is generally poor and overcrowded. The neighborhoods in which they live usually have few recreational facilities and what do exist are normally of inferior quality. The areas in which they live are frequently centers of prostitution, gambling and other vicious activities.

The environment to which they are exposed means that the people living in these areas are more exposed to conditions conducive to crime than are other members of the public. This has been frequently cited as a part of the reason for the high delinquency and crime rates in these groups.

Restriction of the normal activities of a minority group often brings about exaggerated behavior in other directions. Minority groups suffer from restrictions in many types of activities that other people take for granted, such as the enjoyment of restaurants, hotels, bowling alleys, swimming pools and others. Discrimination results in the narrowing of the minority group member's field of opportunities and activities. It should not be surprising that many people so restricted intensify their activities in fields where they are not the subjects of discrimination.

One aspect of the sensitiveness and defensiveness of minority groups which should be of special concern to all police officers is the distrust and fear of the police which these groups frequently have. This attitude obviously makes more difficult the officer's role in dealing with racial prejudices and tensions. In many parts of the country the members of minority groups believe that, if they are arrested, they will be physically abused and that they will not be given the same sort of treatment normally afforded persons in a like condition. There is too great a resentment on the part of many members of minority groups toward the police in general. This resentment is not always justified but unfortunately in many instances there is ample justification.

There have been many instances when the police authorities were law enforcement officials, in the usually accepted meaning of the term, only so far as the majority group was concerned. Occasionally the police have made no pretense of impartiality so far as the minority groups were concerned. They seemed to feel that it was their job not only to enforce the law but also to enforce white supremacy and to keep other groups in their places.

A serious problem in public relations exists when the police are feared and distrusted by the minority group. In order to do a good job of law enforcement, officers must have the confidence and support of the public. In the field of race relations police can accomplish little unless they have the confidence of both the majority and minority groups.

If minority groups are uncooperative and antagonistic toward the police, it is only human for police officers to respond in the same manner, especially if they have had bad experiences with that group in the past. The situation then becomes a vicious circle with neither the police nor the minority group taking the first steps which could lead to a better understanding. When a condition of mutual antagonism exists, it is almost impossible for the police to do a fair and effective job of law enforcement. A situation is created which is very damaging to the public peace. For this reason it is extremely important that every police officer makes sure that in his contacts with members of a minority group his conduct is above reproach.

# 9
## AREAS OF CONFLICT

Because we will be called upon to deal with them, it is important that we understand the principal areas of conflict in American inter-cultural life. Three main areas of discrimination and conflict that demand our attention are: 1. Social; 2. Political; and 3. Economic.

Social discrimination is the widespread tendency to shut out certain groups from full participation in the shared affairs of social life. While, for example, public roads are open without discrimination to all, in the matter of hotels, schools, places of residence and jobs, segregation is more likely to develop.

The extreme of exclusion is perhaps found in formal marriage and accordingly in those social gatherings that are likely to result in marriage. The average white, indeed, we might say the normal white, does not want to see interracial marriage.

However, sociological studies on this issue reveal that the Negro is of a like mind. The thinking Negro does not want to see interracial marriage take place, but he does want to see the Negro given equal opportunities in educational, recreational and economic situations.

There is no real evidence that intermarriage has increased as a result of better human relations. This idea is sometimes used as a red herring to draw attention away from the real problem. A more pertinent question would be, "Do all groups have adequate incomes, decent housing, equal educational opportunities, and just and equal treatment under the law?"

These are real issues and have possible solutions, and are in no way affected by the problem of intermarriage. Marriage is a distinctly private and personal affair between the persons concerned and should remain so.

Minority groups have been willing to accept the separation of the social activities more often than they have been willing to accept school separation and housing segregation.

We should arrive at an understanding of the areas of agreement and disagreement between the Negroes and whites as to the meaning of social equality. By the area of agreement we mean that area where no pressure comes from the Negro race as a whole against the color line. In this area is intermarriage, cliques, churches and social clubs, and visiting and entertaining across the color line. The Negro, at this time, apparently has no desire to force the issue on intermarriage and visiting and entertaining in the homes of whites.

For example, Texas laws against intermarriage have never been challenged by Negroes in the courts.

The middle ground is the area of uncertainty. In this area some Negroes exert pressure against the color line, some whites resist, and other Negroes and whites accept the situation as semi-social. First of these is Negro residence throughout the city. Second is the use of commercial recreational facilities outside the primarily black areas. Third is use of sanitary facilities, elevators, etc., in hotels and apartment houses outside the Negro area. The fourth is attendance at social affairs of unions, professional and technical societies, and at places of employment.

On the areas of disagreement—these may be described as areas where there is increasing pressure from the Negro who does not interpret these situations as social, although white people have a tendency to do so—are (1) white-collar employment outside the Negro area, (2) membership in business and professional associations, (3) use of hospital facilities outside the Negro area, (4) unrestricted use of parks throughout the city and (5), of the most immediate concern, the integration of the public school systems.

The Negro exerts little pressure against the color line prohibiting intermarriage and visiting and entertaining across the color line, but he is increasingly protesting his denial of membership in business and professional associations, his denial of the use of hospital facilities outside his own area, his denial of unrestricted use of parks throughout cities, and his denial of opportunity to qualify for white-collar employment outside the Negro areas.

Of general concern to Negroes is their limited access to public facilities. Areas of private social relationships are not usually the main points of tension. This reveals that both Negroes and whites agree that certain matters are of a distinctly private and personal nature. As such, they should be matters of concern only to the affected individuals so long as the activities of those persons are lawful. The behavior of such individuals in this private and personal realm, as long as it falls within the boundaries of the law, is not a matter of which police consideration is necessary or relevant.

It is not difficult to understand why police interference in the field of social relationships is so strongly resented. A police officer who interferes in the lawful social relations of persons of different racial groups because he personally feels that conditions are improved, if the different races are kept apart, is a source of much difficulty.

Persons do not associate on a social plane interracially unless their views are in harmony. It is probable that in reporting their experience to their friends and neighbors, who are of a similar belief and practice, a strong resentment of the police as unfair and lacking in impartiality develops. An aftermath of such incidents is almost invariably a belief that the police officer was passing judgment on Negroes, was enforcing white supremacy, and was injecting police authority into spheres not coming under the jurisdiction of the department.

Thus, one police officer, by acting outside his proper sphere of law enforcement, can breed hatred and suspicion of police in general. This goes back to the previous statement that the police officer must exercise great caution to see that his personal beliefs and opinions do not interfere with the proper performance of his duty.

There is generally less discrimination in the use of public recreational facilities than in the use of private facilities. It should be remembered, however, that while the private business is privately financed, the public services are financed by the tax dollar. They must then be legally accessible to all members of the community.

The areas of public recreation command our attention in a very real and special sense. An examination of the history of riots reveals that many of them began on Sundays and holidays at recreational facilities.

Sundays and holidays are traditionally periods of relaxation and leisure. A majority of the population is free from work, so there is time and opportunity to gather and gossip. Rumor mongering is prevalent on those days, when all segments of community life flock to recreational areas for what may be the sole relief from the normal working week.

In our places of residence and in our work relationships the minority and majority groups are usually separated from each other. In the parks there is less isolation, with the groups mingling more freely. People meet who have only remote contact with each other in most phases of public life. The groups are also brought together on routes leading to and from the various sections of the city.

Summer months are particular periods of tension, for the tempers of people in hot weather are on edge. Under these conditions the general inclination to scapegoat others, which is always widespread, may be easily triggered.

Public parks and shopping centers frequented by both races are therefore points requiring the close attention of the police. There are sometimes certain tacitly understood divisions of the recreational facilities. They are constantly shifting, and wherever their margins meet they create points at which the races come in direct contact with each other.

When such separation exists, it is informal and unsupported by law. However, it is at these points that a constant state of tension exists, and where incidents are most likely to occur.

It was at such a place that the 1943 Detroit riot began, on a bridge crossing over onto Belle Isle. It has been estimated that approximately 100,000 persons were seeking to escape the heat and congestion of the city on the Isle that Sunday. With a background of already established tension this recreational area became a tinderbox so that an argument between a Negro and a white man became next a fist fight, then a riot of city-wide proportions.

Other locations of possible conflict are commercial recreational facilities, such as skating rinks, public dance halls, bowling alleys, taverns and amusement parks. All of these emphasize active participation. The police officer should realize the critical nature of these areas, and what could easily develop. He should perform his duties so that he is in accordance with the law. He should also take decisive action in the event of conflict so a minor incident has no chance to grow to serious proportions.

The parks, along with the schools, are locations where the young of the various nationalities and races intermingle most. This indicates the crucial role played by the administrators of the parks, and the local park policemen, in checking and minimizing minority group tensions while it is still in the formative stage.

Perhaps nowhere is the effect of discrimination bred by prejudice seen more vividly than in residential segregation. In this area the visible physical differences become all important in determining acceptability.

Although the visible differences may not be important in themselves, they serve as a brand or label, and make possible the identification of members of the minority groups.

This setting apart as unfit for residence members of the minority groups is done without consideration of the personal and social traits of the persons involved. Great singers like Mahalia Jackson and Marian Anderson, scientists like George Washington Carver, outstanding doctors, lawyers, statesmen and educators are stigmatized because of the color of their skins. They are not considered on the basis of their personal worth or individual behavior. The consideration of race outweighs all personal considerations, and they become the object of discrimination and segregation merely because of their racial membership. So long as society uses the label of race as a basis for subordinating one group to another then persons can and will be segregated racially in the community.

This systematic segregation of housing facilities causes an aggravation of housing problems in the Negro areas. A lack of access to housing in most areas forces members of the minority group to live in overcrowded and substandard areas, which are usually the most deteriorated and undesirable in the city.

The natural increase in population throughout the country, coupled with a migration from the rural to the urban areas, causes these sections to become more and more overcrowded. It is only natural that the residents of such areas seek to improve their standard of living by finding suitable quarters outside the Negro zones. It is in this attempt that they encounter the rigid wall of white opposition and strong racial tensions develop. The expansion into former white areas has been frequently marked by bitter conflict between Negroes and whites. Organizations have been set up which have attempted through restrictive covenants to prevent the sale of property in white areas to Negroes. These covenants have one after another been struck down by court action, and it is doubtful any can withstand the scrutiny of a court. Negroes who have succeeded in overcoming the restrictive covenants have frequently been terrorized and physically mistreated.

A part of the bitterness, fear and hatred which has marked the Negro's expansion has been attributable to a general belief of the whites that the Negroes are dangerous not only to their persons, but that the values of real estate are materially lowered by the Negro's presence.

It can logically be expected that any time the Negro, or any other minor racial group, makes rapid advances those advances will be met with stiff opposition from certain members of the white race. Obviously, the marginal areas of the segregated belt will be the points of greatest tension and conflict. These are the areas where the pressure of the Negro community to expand first encounters the rigid walls of white opposition.

Because of this shortage of adequate housing in the Negro areas the situation becomes a contest between the Negro, who is attempting to escape an undesirable condition, and the white residents making desperate attempts to resist the entry of the Negro families.

These are the obvious points of tension. During the period when the first Negroes are attempting to expand community feelings run high, and there is a danger of an actual resort to violence.

It is not the responsibility of police officers to enter into such disputes, or to argue the merits of either faction. Injudicious action on the part of the police can result in racial outbreaks of an extremely serious nature.

A third situation in which tension may arise is in the competition for jobs. Most minority groups are at a disadvantage in their search for employment, for in many areas they are systematically relegated to positions which are lower paying and less desirable.

This is reflected in the great differences between the Negro and the white income. A national income survey has shown that in the larger cities 21.6% of the white families were in the lower income bracket, while 77.7% of the Negro families received a comparable wage. Of the whites, 36.8% were in the middle income group, while only 19% of the Negroes were in this class, and 41.6% of the whites were in an upper income bracket while only 3.1% of the Negroes were in this bracket. It was estimated that the average income for Negroes was approximately 40% lower than that of the white families.

Job discrimination usually results from one or more of the following: (1) Prejudice of employers against hiring Negroes, (2) Fear by the employer that he will have trouble at his plant or within the structure of his social activity if he hires Negroes, and (3) The practice of some labor unions from formally excluding Negroes from membership.

Employers are also products of the society which produces them and many have accepted the prejudices prevalent in that society. Many feel that the Negro is actually inferior, and incapable of a level of work produced by the white.

Others would be willing to employ Negroes were it not for the discrimination so frequently directed against them as the consequences of such an act. A society which is prejudiced against a group is all too willing to take action against the employer who flaunts public opinion. Boycotts, social ostracization, and economic warfare has been employed against the employer who failed to honor the color line.

Labor unions in many parts of the country are willing to accept for membership Negroes who fulfill the requirements of membership, but in some areas they are still systematically excluded.

When the Negro attempts to improve his job status, he frequently becomes the object of considerable discrimination, particularly if the other workers feel somewhat insecure in their employment. Such individuals often seek to insure the security of their jobs by ruling out members of minority groups as possible competitors.

Thus within the area of employment are initiated some of the tensions which spread to all phases of human existence.

The most important area of conflict, particularly in the southern states, is the public schools. Events in Little Rock, New Orleans, Mansfield, Texas, and other cities have shown how intense feelings may become as integration is accomplished. In Little Rock the ultimate weapon of authority—force—had to be employed. The highly colorful circumstance of one level of government pitted against another was added.

There have been disorders in other southern cities, many of them caused by outside agitators in situations where a majority of local residents were reconciled to integration.

Racial conflict in schools may stem from any or all of the other areas of conflict—housing, recreational facilities and job competition—but they are also the result of years of segregation, a way of life that is being altered by court action.

Law enforcement authorities face a challenge of great magnitude as these changes are accomplished, and a task requiring diplomacy, firmness and confidence to enforce the law and maintain the peace.

# 10

## RUMOR

IT IS UNFORTUNATE but true that the normal human being has a tendency to both originate and pass on rumor. Indeed, in most social situations rumors are prevalent.

Many persons start rumors because of a lack of information on a subject under discussion. When the subject is of interest to both the teller and the listener, and when there is a lack of information on the part of either, rumors are likely to occur. Most persons do not consider the possible consequences of their acts, and most rumors are not started by persons motivated by maliciousness.

In most social situations the constant ebb and flow of rumor does not pose a particular problem because the rumors are not usually concerned with subjects about which the teller and the listener have a deep personal interest. While it is undesirable, rumor in such situations seldom poses a great danger. However, wild and unsupported rumors about minority groups are not only symptoms of tension but are one of its chief aggravating influences. Because of this they pose a very real danger and are a matter of concern for police authorities.

In dealing with rumor the police officer must be informed on its nature and the manner in which distortions develop.

Recently in a major southern city a training session was held for top city and police department administrators. At this session five participants were asked to leave the room while the remainder of the group decided on a set of facts. When an account containing thirty-two facts had been accepted by the group, one of the participants was brought into the room and the facts were related to him. Then a second was brought in and the first was asked to relate to him the facts he had heard. The second was requested to pass what he had been told on to the third and this continued down the line until the chain had been completed through five persons. The fifth person was then asked to give the facts as he understood them.

Even among these administrators who were especially trained to be observant the difference between the account given by the first person and the account of the fifth was great. The fifth person was able to relate only eight of the original thirty-two facts.

In the passage of the story there was a general simplification or loss of detail as the story traveled from person to person. It became shorter and more and more details were dropped out. The story in its original form was quite lengthy but the end product consisted of a very few sentences.

If this can occur when the participants are administrators trained in observation, think how much more distortion can occur among citizens who have no such training.

The experiment indicated that each person interpreted what he saw and heard in the light of his own experiences and in the light of what he was expecting to hear. Also the emotional value of a fact contributed greatly to its chance of being remembered.

One of the most widely circulated and false rumors of recent years was the reported existence of a shove and push day. This was reported to be a day of each week on which Negroes were organized to shove whites around in stores, on public sidewalks, and in public transportation facilities and to make themselves generally obnoxious to the whites. This shove and push day existed only in the minds of the persons who believed it, but the fact that it did not actually exist did not detract from its harmful effects. White persons, believing in its existence, were alert for any sign that such an attempt was being made by members of the Negro community. Casual brushes in stores and on street corners which normally would have gone unnoticed assumed menacing proportions and caused a build up of tension.

Every race riot we have experienced has been preceded and accompanied by wild and unsupported rumor. Without the inflammatory quality of rumor the public seldom becomes aroused to the point where race riots can occur. Areas of social activity in which emotion plays a large part are fertile grounds for rumor.

Assaults by groups upon one individual, rapes, attacks upon children and systematic discrimination have lead to many actual riots.

One such situation occurred in Detroit, Michigan, in 1943 when the rumor was widely circulated among the white populace that a Negro had raped a white woman on a bridge leading to a recreational area on Belle Isle. Simultaneously, among the Negroes it was rumored that the whites had killed a colored woman and her baby on the Isle. While these stories had absolutely no basis in fact, their effect in mobilizing the passions of the people was tremendous. The fact that they were untrue did not make them any less provocative.

Under the influence of the inflammatory rumor the trouble spread quickly. According to one of the veteran police officers who was at the scene, at least 200 sailors were fighting with Negroes before the first police arrived. The rioting was not contained at its point of origin but gradually spread into adjacent Gabriel Richard Park on the mainland side of the bridge and then to several other sections of the city. As time passed, and as more and more people were infected with the contagion, it became increasingly impossible for the authorities to contain the rioters.

One of the worst riots in our history occurred in Chicago, Illinois, in 1919. For several months prior to the actual riot, Negroes had been coming into this mid-western metropolis in large numbers. They had overcrowded the areas formerly occupied by Negroes. As the minority group sought relief from the congested conditions, they met with opposition from whites who attempted to keep them within the area. Under such conditions tension mounted rapidly.

The incident which touched off the explosion occurred on a beach used by both Negroes and whites. A fight developed between the adults of the groups. A seventeen-year-old Negro boy was swimming in the lake and remained in the water during the fight. Someone on the beach threw a stone at the boy and he sank below the water and drowned. Later, investigation showed that he had been holding onto a railroad tie for support. It was never definitely established that the stone hit the boy and caused him to drown. However, several Negroes alleged that a white man had thrown the stone and demanded that a nearby police officer place the man under arrest. The officer refused to take any action at all and the Negroes raised a cry that the boy had been stoned to death and that a white "cop" had refused to arrest the white man who had thrown the stone.

Shortly thereafter the officer, who had refused to arrest the white man on the complaint of the Negroes, arrested a Negro on the complaint of a white that he had been assaulted by the Negro. The Negroes attempted to prevent the arrest and the riot was on.

Rumor spread rapidly. Soon it was not a single stone that might have struck a boy. It was a number of stones thrown at a defenseless young Negro. Instead of one police officer being involved it was reported that a great many police officers had refused to take any action against the guilty persons. Then later, the rumor stated that the entire police department was involved in the incident. One rumor led to another. Soon there was another fatality when a Negro fired into a group of policemen and was in turn shot and killed by a Negro police officer.

This riot spread throughout the city and continued for thirteen days. At the end the tragic toll was 38 dead and 520 injured.

Another example of how rumor can provide the proper atmosphere for a riot occurred during August 1943, when a white police officer and a Negro soldier became involved in a fight in New York City. During the altercation the policeman was injured and the soldier shot in the shoulder. A rumor quickly spread throughout the neighborhood that the Negro had been shot in the back and killed. It was alleged that the killing had occurred without provocation. Here, as in many other cases, the rumor placed the incident on a highly emotional plane. The soldier was reported to have been shot in the back. The shooting was reported to be without provocation.

Soon large crowds began to gather before a nearby police station, in front of the hotel where the incident had occurred, and at the hospital to which the wounded soldier had been taken.

All attempts by city officials, who had rushed to the scene, to immediately disperse the crowd, all appeals to the reason of its individual members, were unsuccessful. The riot was brought under control only after hundreds of policemen were ordered into the area.

The result of this one incident, supplemented by exaggerated rumor, was five dead, at least 307 (including 53 policemen) wounded and approximately five million dollars worth of property destroyed.

Police experience indicates that efforts to track down the source of inflammatory rumor is seldom productive. However, officers can and should be on the lookout for rumors and the facts to counteract them.

The police are in a strategic position to stop rumor. Whenever a police officer hears a rumor, he can break the chain by himself refraining from passing the story along. If he does pass it on the hearer will probably add to the story and say, "I have it on the highest authority," since he secured his information from a policeman.

As we have noted, a police officer should never repeat a rumor, even to deny it. Rumor is usually so much more sensational than fact that the latter is likely to be overshadowed. However, the only antidote for poisonous rumor is fact and the officer should be on the look out for rumor and facts to counteract it. He should get the facts promptly and publish them as widely as possible. Cooperative relationships previously established with the press would be helpful here, but extensive use should also be made of civic organizations, minority group organizations, and other channels of information.

The police department should investigate inflammatory publications or agitating groups which promote prejudice between the Negroes and the whites. These organizations are frequently the starting place of rumor about minority groups.

We see then that the role of the police officer in dealing with rumors has a double aspect.

First, police officials must regard them as symptomatic. If rumors are plentiful, they should be reported. If they are then cleared through central police offices they can become an effective barometer of the state of mind of the community and can indicate the likelihood of trouble in any particular area.

Second, the individual officer can help minimize the effects of rumors by refraining from repeating them outside of official police circles. He can check their spread by questioning the person attempting to pass them on and insist upon verification and proof. Also it is often possible to check rumors by making plain to the carrier of the tale the implications of his acts. A rumor stopped at any point can be of great significance in cutting short its network like spread.

The relationship that exists between rumors and crowd and mob action is self-evident. Rumors may be likened to an electric charge spreading throughout the community and touching the emotional life of the people. They can serve as a stimulant which prepares many innocent people for mob action.

In times of critical tension they may serve an even more direct function. They can bring people to the scene of a minor incident where they often proceed to act on rumor rather than in the light of the facts of the situation.

It would be folly itself for a policeman to believe in or act on the basis of a rumor. Critical regard for the problem requires the utmost care on the part of the individual officer and a considered plan by which supervisory officials may evaluate the importance of the situations in which rumors are prevalent.

As was pointed out earlier, the only antidote for poisonous rumor is fact. It is axiomatic that the wider the true facts of a situation are circulated, the greater difficulty rumor will have in finding a following. Because of this necessary communication of facts, the press—by which we mean newspaper, television, and radio news gatherers—are of great importance in controlling the spread of rumor.

Depending upon the editorial policy of the news media and the relationship that exists between it and the police department, the press can play a wholesome role in the suppression of rumor, or it can cause untold difficulty for the authorities. Much of the responsibility for the type of role played by the press rests with the police.

In periods of tension it is important that the press be actively solicited to assist in campaigns calculated to dispell rumor and establish fact. A frank approach is in most cases the best policy, for if the press begins to doubt police versions of the circumstances of a particular situation, it may not act readily enough in killing rumors.

There are instances, of course, where publication of all the facts of a situation may be damaging to efforts directed toward a peaceful solution. In such cases it may be necessary to ask the press to keep these facts in confidence. This request should be honored by the press. A word of caution at this point. The police agency or individual officer who makes too great a use of facts told in confidence to the press media will alienate the members of the press. Most newspaper men feel it their duty to honor a confidence once it is given to them. They frequently feel, however, that the police officer who too often comes to them with circumstances or information on a confidential basis is restricting their right to the publication of the news. In extreme cases the press sometimes refuses to accept information received in confidence realizing that if it is so accepted, the confidence must be kept, and if it is rejected, they then have the right to find out for themselves the circumstances and print them.

It is unfortunate that at times the press can unwittingly act in an inflammatory manner. The search for a Negro rapist of a white woman, for example, can be played up by the press to such an extent that a city may be virtually terrorized. Some years ago such a situation developed in a leading midwestern city. A white woman had been criminally assaulted then murdered by a Negro. The circumstances of the offense were by their nature sensational. Accurate and truthful reporting by the press aroused the public to such an extent that it became exceedingly hazardous for newsboys and milkmen making early morning deliveries. The general public was in such a state of emotional tension that any unusual occurrence was looked on with great alarm. Incidents were reported to police in which citizens had fired shots at persons walking their dogs, at milkmen making deliveries and at police officers in the normal course of their duties.

This, of course, impeded the work of the police in solving the case and could have easily led to interracial violence. An appeal to the press when these circumstances exist may bring an end to inflammatory coverage.

Generally, it is safe to assume that a cooperative and helpful attitude toward the press will be met by considerate and fair treatment.

It has been observed in recent months that when integration is begun in southern schools and there is any hint of trouble, the press turns out in large numbers. School difficulties at such places as Little Rock, Nashville and New Orleans have attracted correspondents from all over the United States. This has created police problems that cannot be solved simply .

The function of the press is to observe and report what happens in situations of racial tension and violence. It is not the function of the press to participate in or to influence the events. In Little Rock some northern correspondents disputed with the crowd over the merits of integration. Occasionally, press representatives hired members of each race to stage demonstrations so that pictures might be taken. This tended to inflame passions that were already aroused and fostered the kind of atmosphere necessary for the spread of rumors.

If the police are to maintain the peace, they cannot allow such practices to be committed. It is not difficult to imagine the cries of righteous indignation which could arise from an arrest of a news correspondent covering a racial incident. Charges of interference with freedom of the press, control of public information and muzzling of the news gathering agencies are likely to arise from such a practice. However, a prompt statement by police officials concerning the circumstances of the arrest can do much to alleviate the fears of other press media that their rights are being subverted by the police.

Inevitably, racial disorders attract large numbers of photographers. In some instances their presence serves to stimulate individuals in the crowd who have exhibitionist tendencies. It is dependent on the police at the scene to determine how close photographers should be allowed to the areas of trouble. This is not intended to restrict the press in its covering of the events, but it is a part of the major business at hand.

In determining how close to the actual scene of violence photographers should be permitted, the nature of the press media
present must be taken into consideration. A vast majority of the
news gathering agencies which are represented at these scenes
are going to be sincerely interested in the public welfare. It is unfortunate that some press agencies place circulation above civic
and moral responsibility. In the event that a photographer or
reporter proves that his primary interest is in sensationalism and
he makes attempts to foment actual physical violence so that
he may report it, the police should take decisive action. Such
action will always be condoned and even applauded by the responsible news gathering agencies.

Frequently, news agencies with a desirable editorial policy employ photographers and reporters who are interested only in
gathering news and who will intentionally interfere with proper
police handling of incidents. These cases should be promptly reported to the management of the media concerned. Those persons
who have the responsibility for establishing the policy of a press
media are normally far removed from the field. They are sometimes not in a position to know of the activities of their individual
representatives. Frequently, the only way they have of knowing
that their representatives are furnishing misleading but highly
newsworthy material is from a contact by police officials. Again,
the foregoing comments are not made to indicate a lack on the
part of most representatives of news media to cooperate with the
police in the suppression of violence. These remarks are made
only because a very small number have not the proper attitude
toward their civic responsibility.

# 11

## TYPES OF CROWDS

Tensions usually develop into overt clashes when crowds gather under circumstances conducive to violence. It will be valuable therefore to see how crowds develop.

The demagogue has found that it is possible to control the emotions of the public and influence the course of human history by causing crowds favoring one particular ideology to develop. We have recently seen examples of this when Soviet leadership has caused to assemble throughout the world crowds advocating the communist line. These are examples of a calculated organization of crowds for a specific purpose, but the manner in which the crowds assembled are much the same as we see constantly closer to home.

Crowds of both peaceful and aggressive kinds develop in much the same way. However, it is useful to draw a distinction between the various types of crowds, since they do not all require the active intervention of the police. It is just as important to know when not to intervene as it is to know when to exercise police authority.

For purposes of classification, crowds may be divided into four types: casual, conventional, expressive, and aggressive. It must be emphasized that there is no logical sequence of development of a crowd from one stage to another. A crowd may be aggressive when it is initially formed or it may be casual and become aggressive without passing through the conventional and expressive stages.

An example of the casual crowd might be a group which has gathered in front of a store window to look at a display. It has no leadership, little organization, no unified purpose and its members come and go. Such a crowd responds easily to an order to disperse. It has no psychological unity and, so long as it remains a casual crowd, does not concern us in the present discussion.

However, it is all too easy for a casual crowd to become aggressive. The persons who are riding on a bus would under normal circumstances fall into the casual classification. One person might be thinking about the job to which he was going, another might be reading a newspaper and still another looking at the advertising cards scattered throughout the bus. These people have no community of interest and are not likely to develop one unless some incident occurs which focuses their attention on a common object. Even so small a thing as a police officer stopping the driver of the bus for a traffic violation can focus the attention of all of the passengers and command their interest. In such a situation—when two protagonists contend—people are likely to take sides. The nature of the crowd can change from one of casual interest to one of animosity toward the police officer who stopped the bus.

A conventional crowd is one that has assembled for a specific purpose, such as witnessing a ball game. While there is a community of interest, the members have no dependence on each other. Each can satisfy his individual needs without the active participation of the other persons present. The person sitting beside you at a football game is incidental to your enjoyment of the game, and he comes to your specific attention only if he conducts himself in such a manner as to draw your attention.

In such a crowd the behavior of an individual is controlled by established and understood rules and regulations which have been laid down for such occasions.

It is possible however, for such a crowd to become unruly and aggressive. The familiar throwing of pop bottles at the umpire or the quarrels that break out in the stands are an evidence of the tendency of the individual to throw off restraints and develop aggressive characteristics. These tendencies can be curbed by a rigid and scrupulous enforcement of the rules and regulations governing the occasion.

In the conventional crowd, as in the casual, aggressive tendencies can be brought on by a seemingly insignificant incident. During a professional football game at the Cotton Bowl, a well-known television and screen personality and his wife appeared for the half-time activities. As a prelude to their appearance in the center of the field, they rode around the perimeter of the field under the stands.

Just as they entered the stadium some person threw a cup containing ice into the automobile in which they were riding. This triggered a barrage of throwing and throughout the circuit of the field the performers and their automobile were pelted by cups, soft drinks, pillows, scrap paper, and any other material handy. The individual members of the crowd probably did not intend to harm the stars. Nevertheless from a conventional crowd behavior embarrassing to police authorities, the performers, and the civic leaders present developed.

In some sections of the country sporting events in which members of a minority group participate are often accompanied by a feeling of apprehension. Under such circumstances a conventional crowd can easily lose its respect for the forces of law and order. It is axiomatic that such events should be closely policed. The restraining influence of the police uniform in sufficient numbers has proven its worth on many such occasions. The presence of an adequate number of uniform officers is usually sufficient to prevent a conventional crowd from deteriorating into an active and aggressive mob.

A New Year's Day football game between the University of Syracuse and the University of Texas may be cited as an example. On the Syracuse squad were several Negro players. During the game an argument developed on the field between a University of Texas player and one of the Negroes on the Syracuse team. Arguments between opposing teams on a football field are seldom cause for alarm because they occur with almost monotonous frequency. However, to this particular incident was added the fact that not only were the two teams in contention, but also were two racial groups. The incident assumed importance all out of proportion to its actual worth, and was nationally cited as having been triggered by the fact that the Syracuse player was a Negro.

The third type of crowd, the expressive, is often mistakenly confused with the aggressive crowd and is treated as though it were dangerous. It is important for police officers to avoid this mistake, for, as was pointed out earlier, it is as important to know when to refrain from taking police action as it is to know when to exercise it.

An expressive crowd is composed of persons who are engaged in some kind of expressive behavior, such as worshipping, singing, or dancing. Because such groups are operating on an emotional level, they are giving vent to their feelings and sentiments and releasing their energies through action or movement.

The police, observing the activities of such a crowd, must decide whether such activity is harmful to others, and if it is not, refrain from intervening. If, for example, youngsters are dancing in the street or before a theater, it is not necessarily a cause for alarm, for their energies is not directed toward undesirable ends. It is frequently much better to allow such activity to continue and to permit the individual members of the group to express their emotions if there is no actual breach of the peace. Interrupting the expression of energies in an expressive manner may turn the crowd into aggressive and destructive channels.

The manner in which an expressive crowd easily deteriorates into the aggressive type may be shown by an incident that occurred at a rock and roll show in a southern city in 1957. Approximately 5,000 whites, Negroes, and Mexicans had attended and had become excited, stimulated and aroused during the show. Several minor clashes between the racial groups had occurred during the program and were resumed when the crowd broke and started to go home. Stabbings, beatings and shootings all occurred when the expressive tendencies of the crowd were diverted into aggressive channels. What started out to be an evening of entertainment became a nightmare for the police, with dozens of officers needed to quell the disturbance and restore order.

While it is mandatory that the police not intervene in the proper release of energies of an expressive crowd, it is equally necessary that its members be kept under very close surveillance. Again, the presence of an adequate number of uniform officers can frequently prevent the deterioration of expressive tendencies into aggressive channels.

# 12

## FACTORS UNDERLYING CROWD BEHAVIOR

Since we as police officers are called upon to prevent, if possible, or, if not possible, to control mobs, we should understand the factors underlying mob and crowd behavior. Many of the factors mentioned earlier, which lead to scapegoating, are also factors underlying mob violence, for the difference between scapegoating and an actual resort to violence is a difference in degree only. We shall then see how these factors gain impetus by some incident which, in a different setting, might be insignificant and how they can result in acts of overt violence.

A knowledge of the basic facts in crowd formation and mob psychology is necessary to the control of minority group tensions, for it is under the influence of the crowd or mob that feelings of tension are frequently expressed.

We have noted that many persons living in a great impersonal city have difficulty in satisfying their basic fundamental human needs. Man requires for his comfortable existence food, clothing, and shelter in adequate amounts and of adequate quality. A failure to satisfy these basic needs must result in frustration, which inevitably leads to tension. Many persons fail to receive the remuneration, the prestige, or the sense of power to which they think they are entitled and this further aggravates their frustration. The man who has a normal amount of initiative is constantly striving after greater material benefits, a higher standing in the community and increased power over his fellow man. If we are to understand the reason for crowd and mob violence, we must arrive at an understanding of how disappointment or inadequacy in each of these areas may find release in a mob situation.

Our economic welfare is of primary importance. Although earnings today are generally higher than they have been in the past, the increase in salary has been negated by a corresponding increase in the cost of living. Any wage earner knows that a dollar has considerably less purchasing power today than it did ten years ago. In the final analysis it is not the amount of money that we make, but the amount of goods we can buy with our salary that is important to us. Men and women can live happily and in normal adjustment to their fellow man only so long as they are able to provide for themselves and their families the fundamental necessities of life and such luxuries as are consistent with their normal level of existence.

It is not only in the realm of those things which were formerly considered necessities that we find a cause for frustration in men's lives, for many things which were considered luxuries a short time ago are now considered absolute necessities. All of us have a standard of living to which we have become accustomed. Any change that deprives us of things to which we have become accustomed is likely to lead to frustration.

Extremely low incomes are reflected in inadequate diet, substandard shelter and insufficient clothing. The problem, however, is not restricted just to the jobless and extremely low income groups. Most of us, regardless of our income, are chronically concerned with making our income provide us with our usual standard of living in the face of rising prices. The result of an inadequate income then is not only poverty in the narrower sense, but also a condition of denial and suffering as we attempt to live within limited means. The constant worry which accompanies trying to make ends meet is what is meant by insecurity and frustration. These worries may be expressed by hate and hostile acts if an opportunity arises for releasing our tensions upon a minority group.

Perhaps more important, or at least equally as important as our basic needs, are our derived or learned needs. Men truly do not live by bread alone. To be happy a man needs to feel that what he is doing is important, he needs to find satisfaction in his employment and in his social relationships, he needs to enjoy the respect of his friends and neighbors and he needs a sense of importance that tells him that he individually accounts for something and is not a mere nobody. While it is possible for these derived needs to assume a position of too great an importance in our lives, they are essential in varying degrees to the development of any well-adjusted person. Under modern conditions our society has many persons who have been denied these derived or learned needs and are unconsciously driven to make up for these deficiencies in other ways.

We are greatly concerned with our status, which is merely a name for the concern we have as to what others think about us, and how we are regarded as persons. At an earlier stage of our economic development man was able to derive great job satisfaction from the work he performed. Usually a man was responsible for an entire operation in the manufacture of whatever product he made. For example, if he manufactured chairs, he manufactured the entire chair and not just a part of it. He was identified by the end product of his labor and his worth to society could be measured by the quality of the material he produced.

Then businessmen found that they could produce goods in greater quantity at a lower cost by the assembly line method. While this innovation added materially to our ability to produce manufactured products, it removed from the individual laborer much of his job satisfaction. It is not as easy to take pride in a job well-done when one manufactures legs for chairs as it is when one manufactures the entire chair. In a modern factory each man has to a certain extent become a cog in a huge machine. He has become a part of a great impersonal organization that is not usually capable of attending to the achievements of the individual workman.

Many progressive businessmen have recognized this problem and are searching for means of solving it. Business has to a certain extent, through permitting the laboring force to become involved in the decision making procedures, found a partial answer. But the unfortunate fact remains that a great number of workers do not receive adequate job satisfaction.

Since they do not find the prestige and self-esteem they demand, especially in low income goups, they find it necessary to improve their status off the job. Because of this the immediate circle of their families and friends, their civic organizations, churches and labor unions have assumed greater importance.

The problem attendant to inadequate status on the job might be solved if we were able to secure a sufficient degree of prestige within the small circle of our kinsfolk. Here again we fall short, for in a typical family in a metropolitan area a man does not receive the kind and amount of recognition that he received when he was the center of a large collection of kinsfolk living in a rural community. In such a family grandparents and grandchildren lived under the same roof. In a city family the man is of importance only to his wife and children and sometimes he is not sufficiently important to them. Compounding this problem is the fact that the increasing number of distaff workers has robbed man of the prestige he formerly had of being the sole support of the family.

Today's modern city dweller possibly lives in a small apartment and usually is separated from many of the persons whom he holds dear. Quite frequently he does not even know his next-door neighbor. Thus he is forced to depend on contacts made at clubs, lodges, churches, labor unions, taverns and other areas outside the home for his wider recognition.

In extreme cases he may join organizations which foster prejudice and hate by appealing to the needs of the individual who is psychologically starved because of a lack of status. These organizations deliberately foment racial tensions by exploiting the natural human hunger for a feel of importance. The demagogue knows that it is frequently possible to change a crowd into an organized mob by playing up or taking advantage of these basic insecurities. Such well-known tactics as name calling, dealing in glittering generalities, the plain folks approach, and the band wagon approach are used to develop the unity of purpose required of a mob.

The demagogue is able to succeed because the law of the community rigidly limits the power that man is permitted to exercise over his fellow man. Nevertheless man desires power and it is no where more obvious than in the unbridled actions of a mob.

Individuals may derive a false sense of power while they are under the spell of a mob. It is incredible but true that the members of a mob can gain this kind of satisfaction from beating up members of a minority group, razing their homes and looting their places of business. This is a regression to the basic animal instinct, where the pack turns upon its weakest members.

The members of a mob receive from acts committed while a part of the mob a sense of personal satisfaction. This may be related to their ordinary helplessness and feelings of unimportance in their every day life.

For the one fleeting moment of a mob's existence its members gain a degree of personal power. They have an opportunity to exercise control and take things into their own hands. Anyone who has ever seen a mob in action is well aware that its surging power overrides reason. Its sense of power is like a gigantic tidal wave that sweeps over all in its path. Frustrated and insecure individuals, and there are many, are willing and ready to search for others who can be blamed for their own shortcomings and failures. We must not close our minds to the tragic and inescapable fact that under present conditions the population of a large city can in a twinkling be transformed into a mob that will keep the community in a state of terror and disorder for days.

The greater the tension in all phases of public life the greater is the danger of that tension erupting into an overt clash between groups with dissimilar appearances, ideologies, or attitudes. The total functioning of society must be taken into consideration when any one phase of its existence is given detailed attention.

# 13

## FORMATION OF A MOB

IN OUR DISCUSSION of the formation of a mob it will be helpful if we draw a distinction between a crowd and an unruly mob. A crowd is a collection of people without leadership and without a unity of purpose except when its members are gathered for the specific purpose of discussing or taking action on a controversial subject.

So long as it remains a crowd it will not take action even if some agitators try to foment trouble. However, even under crowd conditions the presence of a large number of people gives courage to a small group who are invariably present and willing to serve as agitators.

Although the legal definition of a mob will vary according to the location, it is generally described as an unlawful assembly of persons who are gathered together to commit, or attempt to commit, an unlawful act. A mob usually has one or more leaders, many participants and some persons who originally are observers only, but who may become infected by the mob spirit and become participants.

The steps in the development of an aggressive and destructive mob can be identified. The first stage in the transformation of a group of individuals into a mob is the occurrence of some incident which by its nature tends to attract individual attention. It may be a relatively simple thing such as an automobile accident complicated by the fact that one of the persons involved is Negro and the other white, or it may be an organized expression of resentment by a group of whites toward the presence of Negroes in the parks or schools.

Regardless of the nature of the original incident, if it is unusually exciting and commanding of attention, it will attract a group of onlookers who will mill about the scene. They may have

70

an opportunity to take sides. In an incident involving representatives of different racial groups whites are usually inclined to line up with whites, Negroes with Negroes, Latins with Latins, etc., regardless of the merits of the conflict.

The very presence of onlookers will cause an additional number of individuals to accumulate. As they are pressed together, they begin to establish oral communication with each other and initiate conversation even with strangers. They move about in a relatively aimless fashion, all the while communicating with each other the collective excitement of the situation. Rumors are numerous and spread like wildfire.

More specifically, the building of the mob spirit through a milling process takes place in the following way: The excitement of one individual stimulates excitement in another. He in turn excites a third, who may in turn restimulate the first to an even higher pitch of excitement. Through circulation, infection, stimulation, and restimulation of each other a high state of collective excitement and tension may be built up. As the tension mounts, the individuals who composed the crowd become less and less responsive to stimulations arising outside the group and respond almost completely to influence arising from within the crowd itself.

This creates among the members a kind of mass hypnosis in which the individual loses much of his ability for thoughtful, logical reasoning and responds to the dictates of the crowd as a whole. This fundamental fact every police officer who has ever dealt with a crowd has had occasion to experience. Under the influence of the mob an individual loses his ability to act in terms of cool and rational considerations. The moods and sentiments of the mob dictate his actions. Certainly under such an influence he cannot be expected to act in the same manner as if he were alone or away from the influence of the mob. Because of this, unruly crowds often exhibit an immense potential for evil behavior.

This is the type of situation in which a group of boys found themselves during the 1943 Detroit riot. After having been stimulated by a mob, they were looking for a "nigger to kill." They shot in cold blood a Negro who happened to be waiting for a streetcar. Later when they were questioned by the police, they were unable to explain why they had taken such drastic action. They were essentially truthful in their statements that they did not know why they had acted as they had, for when a person frees himself from the influence of a mob it is impossible for him to give any reasonable explanation for his actions.

The mass hypnosis which seizes the members of a mob may be compared to individual hypnosis. During the process of individual hypnosis the person being hypnotized gradually loses all awareness of any force other than the hypnotist. This is a gradual process during which the hypnotist assumes a greater and greater power and outside stimuli become less and less important. Finally, when the hypnotic trance has been completed, the subject is aware only of the commands of the hypnotist and is completely insensitive to the activities and actions of other persons. He will obey only the commands of the hypnotist and will perform any task suggested to him which is not directly contrary to his basic nature.

If persons under the influence of mob hypnosis also refused to commit an act in violation of their basic nature, the influence of the mob would be somewhat relieved, but unfortunately here the comparison ends. While the hypnotist cannot force his subjects to perform an act against which they have a deep-seated resistance, the mob in its hypnotic force can sway its subjects to perform acts of the most reprehensible nature.

The final stage of the development of a mob has been called the phase of social contagion. Here the original small crowd has been swelled by a great number of bystanders, which are almost always present at every event. These persons usually have little if any direct knowledge of the incident which gave rise to the mob. They are more often impelled by idle curiosity and are attracted by the sight of the crowd.

As ignorant as they are of the original incident, they are nevertheless captured by the mob's spirit and begin to share its collective excitement. Large segments of the population may be quickly affected in this way.

It is obvious that, as a crowd develops from one stage to another, the police will find it increasingly difficult to break up the crowd's hold upon its members. However, regardless of the stage of collective excitement which the police find when they arrive at an incident, they are faced with the responsibility for restoring law and order. A crowd is, after all, only a severe test of a police department's efficiency and proper handling of the incident by the police at any stage of a mob's development will have beneficial results.

# 14

## POLICE PREVENTIVE MEASURES

POLICE EXPERIENCE has indicated the following as essential preventive measures in subduing antagonism between the police and racial minority groups.

The police must first maintain a professional attitude toward existing minority groups. We have earlier pointed out that regardless of his personal opinions it is the responsibility of a truly professional police officer to enforce the law as it is handed down. This is absolutely essential in our normal routine work day, but it assumes even greater importance when minority groups are involved. The activities of the police are subject to constant and close scrutiny, and any activity on the part of any police officer which could be interpreted as showing racial intolerance or bigotry is likely to be seized upon and used as a reason for condemnation of the entire department.

It is entirely possible that a department may have on its roster certain officers who are by their natures unable to subordinate their personal opinions to their official responsibilities. These officers should under no conditions be assigned to an area which will place them in close proximity to a minority group. In times of racial tension, or when incidents arise showing an individual officer's lack of fitness to work with a minority group, a thorough background check should be made of the officer with a view to assigning him to an area where his prejudices and opinions will not reflect discreditably on the department.

An intolerant attitude on the part of an officer is usually revealed by complaints of slight mistreatment of members of the minority group and a general air of arrogance. One officer improperly assigned can tear down the effort toward harmonious relationships of the entire department.

Proper selection processes, training, and supervision can do much to develop the proper attitude toward minority groups within the department. The stated policy of the organization should be explicit in what is expected of each officer and no division should be tolerated.

Coupled with a professional attitude toward the minority groups there must exist a professional knowledge of conditions existing in such groups. Members of a police department are in an unusual position for developing good information. The routine activities of a squad in the field places its officers in constant contact with all elements of society. Many of these people are more than willing to talk to the police officer about anything occurring on his district. Others who have been cultivated by the police officer as informants can add the field of race relations to their scope of reporting.

In times of tension all officers should be required to report in writing any information they may receive regarding a build up of tension or an overt clash between members of different racial groups. This information properly recorded at police headquarters can quickly build a stockpile of information concerning race relationships.

Many departments have already in existence an intelligence section whose responsibility it is to collect information on criminal activity throughout the city. This can be a readymade vehicle for the collection and dissemination of information concerning racial groups. Members of the section should attend all meetings likely to result in racial tension. For example, organizations which advocate white supremacy, and organizations of minority groups which meet to discuss policy and procedures should be adequately covered by the intelligence section. In many cases it is not possible for a member of the department to attend such meetings, but constant effort will usually develop informants who are able to attend and who can then report to the police the actions taken by the groups in question.

To avoid the shoals of racial misunderstanding the police department must at all times maintain absolute impartiality. Such impartiality is essential to a professional approach but it is sometimes not an easy thing to obtain.

There must be enforcement of the law against all violators without regard for the race, color, or religious preferences of the persons involved.

An incident which occurred in California is a good example of this practice. A white man had for two or three years visited a Negro woman on weekend trips to Los Angeles. She was married, but her husband worked for a railroad and was frequently out of town. On one occasion the man went to Los Angeles and called on the woman, who told him that she could not see him that weekend. Because of their past relationship and because he had been drinking he determined that this weekend would be a repeat of several others in the past. He broke the door down, entered the woman's home and criminally assaulted her.

A crowd of people gathered. The police were called and the man was placed under arrest. A captain of detectives who had responded to the call gave instructions that the man be booked for rape. It was pointed out to him that the man was a white, the woman was a Negro, and that every white person in the district would be disturbed if the man were placed in jail and were charged with the offense. The captain pointed out that the only relevant question was whether the man was guilty and insisted that he be booked properly.

The men respected their supervisor for his cool judgment and for his insistence on equal justice so far as the racial groups were concerned. It made it a lot easier for the patrolman who worked with the Negroes, who constituted a majority of the population of that district, for the incident indicated to the Negroes that they were going to be treated fairly.

Another example of the necessary attitude of the police toward incidents involving whites and Negroes occurred in Dallas when a white postman, who was assigned to mail deliveries in a Negro area, criminally assaulted a young Negro girl. The incident was later reported by the girl to her parents, who called the police. After the necessary investigation had been made, the postman was placed under arrest and was charged with the offense. What could have resulted in racial friction, had the postmen not been booked for the violation he had committed, resulted in a greater understanding between the police department and the Negro community. The actions of the department in this instance showed the members of the minority group that their rights could not be subverted by errant members of the white race.

An example of a failure by a police officer to properly enforce the law occurred in Harlem. At about three o'clock in the morning a patrolman was working his beat when a white Navy petty officer lurched out of a subway entrance and headed for a nearby tavern. He had obviously already imbibed too freely.

The officer engaged him in conversation and pointed out to him that he was in a Negro area and that his presence and condition could possibly lead to trouble.

At that point a young Negro woman walked by and the drunk leered at her and called out, "Hey nigger, want to join me?" The woman ignored him and entered the bar. Shortly thereafter the same young woman came out of the bar accompanied by a Negro soldier, who reported to the officer that the drunk had insulted his wife. The officer admitted that the insult had taken place and offered to make an arrest if the Negro soldier wanted to prefer charges. This the Negro declined to do, but instead asked the officer a question which we must constantly keep in mind in our dealings with members of a minority group. "Tell me, officer," he asked quietly, "what would have been the outcome if I were white and he were Negro?"

Superficially, the action of the officer in this incident might have seemed to be proper, but it is doubtful that the action he took materially improved his relationship with the members of the group with which he worked daily.

Impartiality is not always easy, nor is it always popular or expedient, but it is the only course of action a department can follow and properly fulfill its responsibility to all segments of society. An attitude of impartiality will cause some members of the majority group to feel that the police officers are unduly protective of the minority groups. Such an attitude may even at times cause members of the minority group to feel that they are not being properly treated. But the officer has the responsibility for making sure that in each incident involving members of both groups, which come to his attention, his actions are beyond reproach.

A human approach is mandatory with every individual regarded as different from every other and every person treated as an individual. The contrary is a stereotyped approach which views the members of any group as all alike and regards the various groups as superior or inferior to each other. An adequate understanding of the actual differences which exist between racial groups, which we have discussed earlier, will greatly assist the individual officer in treating people as individuals rather than as members of a group.

If the individual merits of all persons handled by the police, or with whom the police come in contact, are weighed by the officer and any action taken suited to the circumstances of the incident, the stereotyped approach can be avoided.

Police officers must strenuously avoid the use of insulting terms and names. Some expressions which may be used casually without thought of offending are nevertheless offensive to members of minority groups. Expressions such as: "He looks like an Okie to me." "Black as a Nigger." "Knife wielding Wop." "Kike." "Chilipicker." "Cholo," and others of a similar brand invariably antagonize the person and group to whom they are addressed.

It is much worse to use a term that insults the group than to use one which insults the individual. It is, of course, desirable that no insulting terms of any kind be used, but terms which refer to a racial classification or a racial group should be most strenuously avoided.

It should not be too difficult for the police officer to realize that terms of derogation are usually met with resistance from the group to which they are directed. While we sometimes do not mind calling each other cops or flatfeet—we realize we have common problems and any terms we use apply equally to ourselves—we strongly resent the use of such terms by members of the public.

Because of the sensitiveness and defensiveness of minority groups and their ingrained fear of the police, every act of an officer, even to the tone of his voice, is examined for evidence of prejudice. It is necessary that we treat members of such groups with the same professional courtesy we use in our contact with the general public.

Allied to, but somewhat different from, a point previously mentioned—impartiality—is the fact that there must be the same kind of law enforcement in minority group districts as elsewhere in the city. A paternalistic attitude toward offenses committed by members of a minority group is a subtle kind of discrimination which is most difficult to avoid.

The attitude that certain types of offenses should be condoned because we can't expect too much from a minority group should be shunned. We frequently hear the expression that Negroes are inveterate gamblers and that it is impossible to control gambling in a Negro area. This is the sort of thinking into which no police officer should fall. A strong program of preventive work should be undertaken in minority group areas, the same as in any other area of the city.

There is a related attitude that the crimes of minority groups are of a relative insignificance so long as they affect only members of the same group. Too often conditions are allowed to exist in a Negro community that would never be tolerated in a white district. Negroes who are thinking about the future of their race feel that every Negro should be made to toe the mark just the same as every other individual.

It is realized that the police agency is only one member of the law enforcement team, and it is probable that this attitude is encountered in other agencies more frequently than it is among the police. An example of this might be in the penalties assessed by juries in offenses involving criminal acts committed by one Negro against another. While sentences awarded whites who have committed the offense of murder of another white is usually very severe, the penalties assessed against Negroes for the same act committed against another Negro is too often ludicrously light. It is not unusual for a jury to assess a five-year penalty against a Negro who has murdered another Negro, and frequently this light sentence is either suspended or probated.

This shortsighted attitude by juries ignores the fact that minority groups deserve the same protection by grand juries and petit juries that the whites do and that the deterrent value of the law is subverted by assessment of penalties not in keeping with the seriousness of the offense committed. The result of such jury action is too often a contempt for the total functioning of all law enforcement agencies.

It is mandatory that officers recognize the necessity of staying within the proper field of law enforcement. Police officers sometimes try to tell a white person that he can't go to this dance or into that neighborhood because it is predominately black. Usually the intent of such police action is not to subordinate any group but to preserve the peace.

There is serious question, however, whether such actions really serve the purpose for which they are intended. Without question they expose the police to criticism on the ground that they have exceeded their lawful authority and have made color rather than conduct the test of permissible activity. The only sound and impartial rule is that police activity must be directed only toward conduct.

Examples of the way in which police sometimes abandon the proper realm of enforcement are numerous. In many cities a white man and a Negro girl or a Negro man and a white girl found in company with each other are subject to immediate arrest. While such activity, because of cultural backgrounds, may properly be investigated by police agencies, the officer should never use this as a basis for an arrest. Suits against police officers for false arrest have arisen from the attempt by the officer to enforce social custom as if it were a law. It is in keeping to investigate such circumstances to determine whether an actual violation of the law exists, but the police officer who makes arrests merely because he does not like to see members of different racial groups intermingle is asking for serious trouble.

There should be frequent contact with minority group leaders and organizations. Such activity, if properly conducted, can be extremely helpful in gaining the confidence and cooperation of members of minority groups and overcoming their unfavorable attitude toward the police. On a friendly basis the police can under such circumstances make suggestions to minority groups and can receive suggestions from them for the improvement of law enforcement work among such groups.

Liaison with these groups will be extremely valuable in dealing with any troublesome situations.

Children of both minority and majority groups are usually attracted to the police uniform. If the line officer is friendly and helpful to them, if he occasionally stops to visit and exchange pleasantries with them, he can establish a grass roots relationship which can be of great benefit. The use of officers who are members of the minority groups should not be overlooked, for they are perhaps in the best position to help develop proper liaison between the police and the group of which they are a member. For an example, Negro police officers assigned to a Negro district can help immeasurably in influencing the attitudes of the members of the Negro race favorably toward law enforcement. In the first place, the assignment of members of their own race to minority group districts shows on the part of a police department confidence that Negro officers are capable of properly representing the department. An interesting side light is that Negro officers assigned to Negro districts are usually much stricter than white officers assigned to the same districts. Also, where such strictness on the part of a white officer might be misunderstood, it is accepted by the minority groups when it is applied by a member of their own group. Since the officer who is enforcing the law is also colored, there can be no possible belief on the part of the minority group that the severity is due to racial intolerance.

Neighborhoods which are in transition are traditionally powder kegs and require the assignment of men who have established liaison with the minority groups. Not too long ago in Dallas an area which had formerly been white entered a period of transition. Schools were segregated at that time and Negro youths who had entered the former white area still attended school in an all Negro zone. It was necessary for them to pass by a school that had remained white en route to the school they were permitted to attend. There developed between the Negroes and the whites a habit of pushing each other as they met on the sidewalk.

Because conflict between youths almost invariably involves the parents and hence the whole community, tension mounted rapidly. Additional police squads were assigned to the area with instructions to investigate fully all reports of such activity. Whenever it came to police attention that the groups had contended for the use of the sidewalk, a call was made to the homes of all the children involved, both Negro and white. If the same children were involved in several clashes, they were referred to the county juvenile officers.

It became apparent to members of the Negro community that the police were not enforcing the law merely against the Negroes. It also became apparent to the members of the white community that their acts of violence directed toward the minority group would not be tolerated. Thus a condition which might easily have resulted in widespread racial tension was mediated peacefully.

The police department can do a great deal to assist the local press to be a force of greater community solidarity rather than a disruptive influence in matters of group relations. The Negro press, for example, depends largely on the fact that it reports on matters concerning Negroes: matters which are treated only briefly or are omitted in other metropolitan newspapers. The police officer should have the same helpful attitude toward representatives of the colored press as he has toward members of the white press. Any information which would be released to the white press should be equally available to the colored.

Some newspapers depend on protest stories and sensationalism for circulation. A favorable target of such papers is invariably the police department.

By establishing a solid liaison with the press—both white and Negro—the police can do much to establish a better relationship through publication of facts favorable to the department. Such publicity based on facts well known to the police department would be valuable in producing harmony and helping to prevent serious clashes between members of the different groups.

# 15

## MINORITY GROUP PREVENTIVE MEASURES

THE CONTRIBUTION that can be made by the minority groups themselves toward avoiding tensions must not be overlooked.

Experience has shown that, as more and more areas of public life are integrated, certain elements of the white community will place every obstacle possible in the path of peaceful mediation.

This opposition should be expected by minority groups and should never be the cause of retaliatory measures on their part. It should be obvious to members of minority groups that a vast majority of the white population is willing to abide by court decisions and civil rights legislation. The minority group should not condemn the majority group as a whole because of the irresponsible acts of a few radicals.

It would be idealistic to presume that the majority of whites in many areas of the country eagerly anticipate an end to segregation. Many prefer to maintain the status quo, but most would not feel justified in resorting to illegal activities to defend it.

In all areas where integration has been undertaken and violence has resulted this violence has been the result of the activities of a very small segment of the population. This small segment is usually so outspoken, and even rabid, that there is a danger that the uninitiated may consider that they speak for the majority. Such a belief is the grossest error and could serve as a further aggravation of an already tense situation.

The more enlightened members of both groups realize this. They should further realize that it is their responsibility to inform other members of their own group that peaceful integration is not only possible but can be reasonably expected.

The manner in which both groups proceed can determine whether integration is effected peacefully or whether the very foundation of our government and economic life is threatened. In short, the members of neither group should place too much importance on the activities of a very few, realizing that times of transition are inherently critical times of tension in community life.

The leaders of the Negro groups know that there is danger that members of their groups, who feel that they are not making sufficiently rapid progress, may, by seizing their rights too rapidly for the majority group to adjust, serve as an aggravating influence. There must be a realization that centuries old customs cannot be destroyed over night by court decision or legislation.

As one leader expressed it, there is a danger that a man who has long been deprived of water will drink too much too fast when it is made available to him. It is the desire of most Negro leaders that an end to segregation and deprivation will not lead to excesses in the Negro groups.

An excellent example of the manner in which Negroes can curb tension is the way most Negroes conducted themselves following an end to segregation on public transportation facilities in Dallas. While there were isolated instances in which individual Negroes immediately availed themselves of the opportunity of unlimited seating these incidents were few. A vast majority of the Negro population, not wishing to immediately seize their rights at the chance of aggravating tension, continued to seat themselves in the rear of the buses. This continued until the white community had time to consider the change and arrive at an attitude of acceptance.

This did not happen without plan. Negro leaders had for some time been preparing their groups for an eventual end of segregation on the transportation facilities. The churches, which exert perhaps an even greater influence among Negroes than among whites, had conducted active campaigns exhorting their members not to act in a manner calculated to aggravate tension.

A similar campaign is being conducted by many Negro churches throughout segregated areas at the present time, in anticipation of an end to segregation in public schools.

The Negro Ministerial alliances are extremely active in preparing their congregations. Periodically and on a city wide basis

Negro ministers discuss the matter with their congregations, warning that the manner in which the Negroes conduct themselves when an end to segregation comes will determine largely their acceptance by the white community. They are urged to avoid the excesses which could so easily follow.

The leaders of the minority groups should accept as theirs the responsibility for keeping those in positions of authority informed on activities planned by the groups which might meet with resistance from other sections of community life. Included in these are any plans which would be a departure from the customary activities of their groups. Sit ins, stand ins, mass public meetings outside the Negro community are all worthy of police attention.

When police authorities know what is planned, they are in better position to squelch rumors. There should be a person known to the leaders of minority groups charged with the responsibility of receiving such information and making it known throughout the police department.

An incident which occurred in Dallas points up the necessity for the police being informed on activities planned by Negro groups. The police department received information from informants that Negroes were contemplating a mass prayer meeting to be held on the steps of the city hall. Although no comment had been made to the department by members of the Negro committee, the department sent a representative to the groups to discuss the matter with them. He informed the Negro groups that what they contemplated was a violation of a city ordinance but that the department was willing to cooperate with them in finding a suitable place for the prayer meeting. He did in fact assist them in finding a public park where the meeting was held in conformance with the requirements of the law.

The leaders with whom he talked were favorably impressed by the fact that the police department had interested itself in their affairs. They were more than willing to accept the suggestions made by the representative of the department. They had no desire to violate the law with their meeting. The free exchange of ideas and information resulted in a legal meeting being held and a possible cause of racial tension avoided.

In conclusion the leaders of both the white and Negro groups should share a belief in the basic desire of a majority of both races to do the right thing. While they should not anticipate trouble, they should urge members of their race to exercise restraint and to be sure that all of their activities are in accordance with the law.

Most Negro leaders feel that the general desires and beliefs of the Negro population can assist integration with a minimum of trouble. It is not believed that in most areas an end of segregation in the public schools will be met with a mass migration of Negroes to schools which were formerly white. Most Negroes appear to prefer to be with members of their own race and prefer to attend Negro schools if this can be accomplished without undue hardship. It has been estimated that within two years after the end of segregation in school facilities a large percentage of Negro students will still be in schools that are at the present time Negro. This is attributed to a general lack of desire on the part of the Negro to associate with whites beyond that necessary for his convenience.

It is believed that this lack of desire on the part of the Negro to force his presence on the white except in cases demanded by the welfare of the Negro will be one of the greatest factors in the avoidance of violence.

# 16

## MOBILIZATION OF COMMUNITY RESOURCES

To DEAL PROPERLY with tensions arising from racial difficulties there should be a mobilization of all of the community resources. The police are only one resource among several that must be utilized if we would master the problem of human relations and minimize the consequence of minority group tensions.

If the community is willing to wait until minority group problems become police problems, it will find that it is probably too late to effect any constructive program. The activities of the other agencies of the community, just as the activities of the police department, are much more effective if they precede any actual trouble which might arise.

Many cities have organized bi-racial committees which attempt to solve racial problems and prevent them from becoming police problems. These committees usually follow one of two lines. Some municipal administrations appoint an official bi-racial commission, of which representatives of the police department, housing agencies, fire department, public health agencies, employment services, recreational agencies, and educational departments are members. Normally under this type of organization the bi-racial commission is an official body of the municipal government and has appointed as its head an executive whose responsibility is to coordinate the efforts of all of the agencies involved.

Another form frequently followed is the establishment of a civic bi-racial committee with representatives of civic groups, churches, unions, business groups, lodges, women's clubs and parent teachers' associations actively participating. Under this form of organization there is also usually appointed an executive to fill the role occupied by his counterpart on the official commission.

The total functioning of the city must be taken into consideration in determining what type of commission or committee will

work best. Every city has established, either formally or informally, a leadership. Any bi-racial commission, if it is to have any
great chance of success, must arise from this leadership. In some
areas the city administration is recognized as the leadership of the
city. In cities with a strong governmental organization a bi-racial
committee established as an official organization of the city government will perhaps work best. In other cities where the leadership is vested in business leaders, the civic committee is perhaps
more desirable.

Several cities throughout the country have unofficial citizens'
councils composed of outstanding business and civic leaders.
These organizations are nonpolitical and wholly unofficial. However, if they are properly established and adequately controlled
from within, they can act to a certain extent as the conscience of
a community. Those cities with such an organization have a ready
made vehicle for the establishment of a civic bi-racial committee.
This committee can be appointed by the leadership of the citizens' council and should consist of men whose views and opinions
are sufficiently respected that they are likely to be followed.

Any bi-racial committee must, of course, have as members representatives of all races. Those organizations from which such
committees have sprung have expressed the opinion that it is not
desirable for the citizens' council to attempt to influence the ap-
pointment of Negroes to the committee. It is believed to be more
efficient and more acceptable to the Negro community if the Negroes themselves are permitted to appoint those who will represent them on the committee. Both as a practical operating procedure and a sound psychological principle there should be equal
representation from both races.

It has in many areas proven expedient to include high officials
of the news gathering media in the committee. Thus the cooperation of the newspapers, television and radio stations is assured.

One such organization in a southern city has proven of great
value in the peaceful implementation of court orders to integrate.
Sit ins, which have become prevalent throughout segregated areas,
have been very peaceful in this city because of a lack of newspaper publicity. The committee has further encouraged the busi-

ness leaders to serve Negroes at lunch counters and restaurants formerly restricted to whites. The newspapers have been persuaded that peaceful sit ins, stand ins and picketing are not news and have agreed not to publish anything unless actual violence results.

This organization has also been extremely helpful in curbing threatened violence. As an example, students of a university picketed a drugstore near the university campus in protest of the drugstore management's policy of refusing to serve Negroes at its lunch counter. Approximately 200 students converged on the drugstore and completely disrupted its operation. The management then decided the drugstore would be closed and enlisted the aid of the police in removing the picketing students from the premises.

The students indicated an intention of returning to the drugstore the following day and continuing the sit in. Prior to the time the drugstore was to open the following day representatives of the civic bi-racial committee called on the students on the university campus. The students were persuaded that their aims could be more easily realized if they refrained from alienating public opinion through their activities and were convinced that their proper course of action lay in legal methods rather than illegal methods.

The committee then called on business establishments throughout the area and in many cases were able to convince management that it was in the best interest of the business to serve Negroes.

The committee was equally helpful in persuading the Negroes to exercise restraint in their attempts to gain their goals. The Negro members of the committee were able to persuade a great percentage of the Negro population that it was not to the Negroes advantage to try to go too far or too fast. They were convinced that programs which sounded too radical or which brought forward too many new features at once without adequate preparation would do the Negroes more harm than good.

One such committee, composed of business leaders, realized that the amount of work to be done and the time required for this work was more than it could itself perform. To assist in the implementation of the policy and plans produced by the committee a public relations expert was employed, a staff was provided, and funds furnished so a well-trained unit could implement the plans of the committee.

This public relations expert called on business leaders throughout the city and persuaded them to review job opportunities for Negroes within their companies. He realized that if new positions were created and staffed by Negroes there would be great resistance from the white workers. Instead the companies were persuaded to re-evaluate the positions already held by Negroes within their organization and to upgrade these positions when the actual work performed warranted it. It was found that although most Negroes were classified as porters or laborers, they were already performing many functions not falling within this classification. There were found Negroes performing clerical duties, bookkeeping and a wide range of services not normally associated with Negro employees in that area. The companies who upgraded the classification of the Negroes providing these services met with little employee resistance because the white employees were already accustomed to Negroes filling this role.

It is certainly to the advantage of any police department to be informed on the activities of such bi-racial commissions, because the members of such committees can frequently make suggestions for improved police service and are usually receptive to police suggestions of needed programs.

While a police department is only one resource among several, its central role in the protection and securing of civil liberties makes it a rallying point in the mobilization of all forces in the community.

Police officials can and should do much toward indicating the responsibility of related community elements and at the same time bring about a more adequate public support in times of crises.

The police role in the mobilization of constructive community elements to deal with tension is first an informational task. There must be immediately at hand an adequate knowledge about tension, its relative state and where it is likely to occur. The police department is in an excellent position to spot locations of rising tension and to make known the fact in responsible circles. The network of police squads spread throughout the city can be invaluable in the collection of needed intelligence. We must have such knowledge if we are to encourage other resources to act and direct their influence to situations which we consider cause for alarm.

In times of rising tension each police officer should be required to report on all incidents coming to his attention which involve minority group relations. There should be made on each incident a written report which should be forwarded to the central offices of the department. Such a record should include what took place, what appeared to have caused the incident, where it occurred, who the parties were to the dispute and whether others became involved and any other details of pertinent interest.

This information should then be carefully examined by a person delegated by departmental administration. A map of the city upon which the incident is spotted is an excellent tool in determining areas of rising tension. Any information received by the delegated person within the department which could conceivably be of interest or value to other agencies should be forwarded to them. The police department would then be in a position to encourage other agencies to forward to the police reports on incidents coming to their attention.

Such strategically located persons as school teachers, community workers, ministers, transportation employees, housing directors and social workers can usually be persuaded to work in conjunction with officials from the police department to gather comprehensive and important information as to tensions and possible developments.

These public service employees can make other important contributions in the field of race relations. School teachers, for example, can teach the children in their classes racial tolerance and common courtesy. They can learn from the children the general attitudes of the homes the children represent, for the attitudes of the children will generally reflect the feelings of the parents. They can make a further important contribution to harmonious racial relationships by explaining to their students proper methods of handling incidents involving members of different races.

The community worker can develop more harmonious relationships in his sphere of activity by refusal to tolerate racial incidents and by taking appropriate action when they arise. He can insure that persons under his jurisdiction have the proper attitude and possess accurate knowledge concerning racial groups. If he is sensitive to the need for it, the community worker can also obtain much valuable information which can be forwarded to the police department for further dissemination.

The minister exerts perhaps the widest influence in our community life. If intolerance is preached in the pulpit then the congregation is likely to look upon intolerance as an acceptable attitude even for Christian people. One could logically expect a minister to believe in the equality of man. This unfortunately does not always hold true. However, if a minister does not believe that all men are created equal, he should at least believe in settling in a peaceful manner differences which might arise between groups. Since the basis of a minister's faith is established on law and order, he should be one of its most devout supporters and he should preach conformity with established law.

Most areas of the country have ministerial alliances. The minister could perhaps be persuaded to discuss racial differences at the meetings of these alliances so the group could as a body endorse a code of conduct recommended to their congregations.

Informed contacts from a wide phase of public life make possible a complete and rounded picture of the community's condition. It should not be difficult for some person in the public service to learn of incidents of a racial nature since most such incidents occur in public and quasi-public places. However, such information is ultimately valuable only in so far as it comes to the attention of the right person. Everyone concerned with service to the public should accept as his the responsibility for making known to the proper authorities all information which comes to his attention. Adequate reporting, important as it is, is of little value unless there is adequate follow up.

A spot map previously mentioned can be of great value in indicating the locations and kinds of incidents that occur and whether they are verbal, involved blows, or involve the use of lethal weapons. They can also indicate to the police administrator the necessity for the assignment of additional manpower to areas where tension is great. If the police are aware of this mounting tension, much by way of constructive educational action may be undertaken at points tending to be critical before it becomes impossible to employ such measures.

There are many ways the police can cooperate with other agencies, both public and private to improve the relationships between various groups of citizens. The basic causes of antagonisms between groups are not matters which the police alone can control, but the police usually are blamed if serious trouble develops. It is therefore very much in the interest of the police department to seek ways of supplying information and cooperation to other agencies that are able and willing to work constructively on basic problems to prevent them from becoming police problems.

It is axiomatic that the general welfare of any segment of the public contributes to or detracts from its voluntary compliance of the forces of law and order. The needs of specific members of society which come to police attention and which can be corrected by other agencies should be reported as a matter of routine procedure. The police can aid the individual further by pointing out to him the facilities and services which are available and arranging for the person in need to secure these services.

Cooperation with other city departments and public agencies can perhaps be most easily and advantageously initiated. The police in many areas are already actively cooperating with school authorities in handling problems created by interracial strife among school children.

Any preventive program must be actively directed toward the adolescent group, for youngsters are numerous and active in every race riot. The impressionability of youth makes them a danger point in any tension situation because they lack experience which causes them to reject anything other than peaceful mediation of differences. It is highly desirable therefore that the police develop close liaison with school and playground authorities in setting up programs calculated to prevent or minimize friction between children of different racial groups.

Many schools and playgrounds could do more than they now do to combat the antagonisms which arise among children. Many would undertake educational and preventive programs if the police constantly pointed out needs and dangers in concrete terms. On the other side of the coin educators would be in a better position to offer valuable suggestions concerning preventive police work if a relaxed, casual atmosphere fostered by mutual participation existed. Through the parent teachers' associations affiliated with public schools, the police could expand their realm of influence and enter every home represented.

Frequently, the facilities of a school could be made available for police operated youth programs. Many schools have as a part of their extracurricular activities boy scout, girl scout, and camp fire groups. Almost without an exception there is a need for more adult workers in such groups. Police officers on an off duty basis could volunteer as leaders or assistant leaders for these groups. They would thus be in an excellent position to indoctrinate the children in the police philosophy and explain the official attitude of the department in interracial strife.

Several departments throughout the country have active police athletic leagues which work closely with playground authorities. Here the police can perhaps become most active in an educational program. The casual atmosphere fostered by mutual cooperation in recreational activities removes from the child's mind the punitive atmosphere too often associated with the police uniform and makes the child responsive to suggestions from the police. Under such a desirable atmosphere the undesirable attitudes of many children can be changed and a more tolerant attitude toward minority groups instilled.

Another way in which police officers can actively work with school authorities is employed in many cities at the present time. Most major departments have as a part of their traffic safety education programs a unit, by whatever name it may be called, set up to work with school authorities on programs calculated to increase traffic safety in the vicinity of the schools. These officers frequently appear before school assemblies to address the student bodies. Here again the officers can explain the philosophy of the department and point out that the police will tolerate no deviation from absolute conformance with the law.

In areas with segregated schools, the police should devote as much time and effort in the schools composed of minority groups as they do in others. The attitudes and actions of minority group children are also extremely important in the prevention of racial strife.

Other local public agencies which could and should actively cooperate with the police in preventive programs are housing, welfare, health, fire and building departments. In many instances an alert police department can point out to these agencies needs which they can solve which come outside the realm of police authority. The police could in return be helped in formulation of an adequate preventive program by the information contained in the records of such agencies. Moreover, the inspectors and other employees of these agencies often discover facts concerning possible tension areas and danger points which could be used as a valuable supplement to police intelligence.

Advantageous liaisons with already existing and active private and quasi-public organizations should not be overlooked. Settlement houses, private welfare agencies, organizations like the YMCA and YWCA work constantly with youth and in many cases have established programs calculated to diminish racial strife. Many civic organizations are always looking for constructive programs in which they may engage. Frequently great benefit can be derived from pointing out to these agencies the need for constructive action in the racial field. The police could take the lead in mobilizing the interest of the members of these civic groups and give it direction by pointing out specific programs calculated to promote more harmonious relationships.

The police could make particularly valuable liaison for these purposes with some of the local minority group associations. Such organizations as the Urban League, the NAACP and the Negro Chamber of Commerce usually welcome the opportunity to cooperate with the police on constructive programs.

We may expect from such liaison not only cooperation in the implementation of nonpolice programs, devised by the police department, but also valuable information and suggestions to help the police develop more effective programs which fall within the realm of police responsibility.

In communities where another agency is set up to mobilize and coordinate community resources the police department simply cooperates. The police department should take the lead in mobilizing all available community resources when this responsibility is not delegated to some other official agency.

# 17

## POLICE TACTICS

Emphasis upon preventive and corrective procedures does not eliminate the need for a positive police plan of action in the event of physical outbreaks. While it is devoutly hoped that community programs can forestall any threatened violence a police department would be shortsighted indeed if it failed to realize that one possible result of racial tension is actual violence. There should be a formal plan of action calculated to suppress violence if it arises.

This chapter is not intended to imply that the primary role of the police in racial tensions is the suppression of disorderly crowds. Certainly such is not true. Adequate preventive measures, adequate mobilization of community resources and an adequate and accurate knowledge of the background factors in racial tension will normally head off trouble before it develops. However, in the face of past experience it would be criminally negligent for any police department not to have an established plan of action in the event actual physical overt clashes occur.

The state of mob formation present when the police arrive at the scene of an unlawful assembly should dictate the action taken by the police. In an earlier chapter we pointed out the steps in the development of an aggressive and destructive crowd. Let us now see whether certain police actions can be suited to these individual stages.

There are two possible extremes into which police authorities can easily fall. The first is a do-nothing attitude which tacitly propounds the theory that if you ignore something with sufficient studiousness, it will eventually go away. The opposite extreme, to be avoided with equal fervency, is the belief that extremely stringent police measures are required regardless of the stage of development of the crowd, and that if the police are sufficiently brutal, sufficiently forceful and make enough arrests, the aggressive tendencies of the crowd will be subdued. Proper action on the part of the police authorities obviously rests somewhere between these two extremes.

It is obvious that the individual nature of any civil disturbance must be taken into consideration in the determination of proper police measures. However, certain principles can serve as guides to our activities.

In the beginning almost every mob has been a small crowd of people who gathered together because of some exciting or stimulating incident. In this early stage of the gathering of a crowd it is often possible for a police officer to isolate the incident by making a quick yet adequate determination of the facts. Then by taking immediate action, such as arresting and removing the persons who are in violation of the law, he may avoid the involvement of many onlookers and cause them to disperse.

The speed with which the officer operates determines, to a certain extent, the ability of onlookers to accumulate. By cutting short such an accumulation, he can usually prevent an incident from becoming an affair requiring the active intervention of a large number of officers. Police throughout the country as a part of their routine duties handle such incidents every day. A measure of police efficiency is the fact that a vast majority of such incidents are controlled and are prevented from assuming major proportions.

Many times an officer is not summoned to the scene of an incident until after a large crowd has assembled and has, through the milling process, achieved a relatively high degree of aggressive unity. On such an occasion the simple and direct expedient of isolating and removing the cause of the dissension may not be possible.

Many times upon the arrival of the police at the scene the milling process is already well underway. Notwithstanding the greatly increased difficulties which confront a police officer in this stage of crowd development there are control measures which may be successfully employed. While the individual nature of the incident will indicate what steps must be taken to gain control of the crowd, it is mandatory that the milling process be stopped and the crowd broken up before it becomes hysterical and aggressive.

If it is possible, the police officer should introduce a regular formation into the crowd in order to isolate wrought up individuals from one another. By doing so the officer can transform a crowd from a potential mob into an orderly assembly.

In many cases the crowd has, on the officer's arrival, already achieved a unity of purpose that makes it unresponsive to this kind of suggestion. When this situation exists, the police officer is faced with the necessity of removing the most excited individuals from the crowd. These excited persons are always a focus of attention in the progress of an aggressive mob. Their prompt removal will frequently make it possible for the officer to disperse the remaining less excited individuals.

In the removal of these agitators the police should make an adequate show of force. It is strongly stressed that a show of force does not mean that actual force should be used. The difference is a vital one and failure to distinguish between the two can result in unnecessary bloodshed.

The presence of an adequate number of men is what is meant by a show of force. The sight of a large number of police officers in uniform frequently awes the crowd so that it is unnecessary to use force in the removal of the agitating influences. The policeman must avoid the idea of individual heroic action. It is not only unnecessary but may be damaging to the situation, and dangerous to the officer involved. The policeman who attempts to single-handedly subdue a mob or wrestle with its individual members places his own safety in jeopardy and greatly increases the likelihood of the mob's growth. In the violence that results from an individual officer attempting to subdue disruptive influences, the ugly tendencies of the crowd are likely to be stimulated. The officer who singlehandedly attempts to subdue several persons is likely to be defeated and any victory by the mob makes doubly difficult a later attempt to bring it under control. Police authority must allow the mob no victory or police authority will be undermined and the leadership of the mob reinforced. By the same token any victory by police authority diminishes the influence of the mob's leadership. Once that leadership is lost the leaders are usually unsuccessful in regaining it.

It is then of prime importance that the police emerge victorious in every dealing with an unruly crowd. This high lights the necessity for an adequate show of force and a further necessity that reinforcements be quickly available so they can be mobilized and rushed to any point in the nearest possible time and in numbers appropriate to the situation.

There will be generally scattered throughout the crowd agitators who have taken upon themselves the responsibility for building the degree of tension within the mob. Tension is usually highest at a point front and center and here usually may be found the excited individuals who are capable of exercising such unusual influences on others. Each agitator makes himself the center of the group around him. These are the points upon which police attention must be centered.

The agitators will frequently try to force police officers into retaliatory measures not warranted by the situation by heaping upon them verbal abuse and insults. The police officer should expect such abuse and should ignore it. For if he responds by an unwarranted use of force, the agitator becomes to the crowd a martyr and the ugly mood of the crowd is reinforced. In the San Francisco student riots trained agitators used this device with great success.

A tactic used by the New York Police Department in the Harlem riot and also by the Milwaukee Police Department in the dispersal of dangerous crowds has met with considerable success. Loud speaker systems were set up on the outskirts of the crowd which was directed from its outermost edges to break up and go home. The blare of the loud speaker and the authoritative tones of command attracted the attention of the members of the mob, turned their attention away from the agitating influence and broke up the influence of the mob's leaders.

This tactic has proven to be unquestionably helpful in breaking up crowds in an early stage and has been used to penetrate the consciousness of groups that were already well organized. The police should use any device by which they can attract the attention of the individual members of a mob and turn that attention away from the original incident. When the crowd's attention has been focused upon the police and the commands they give, much progress has been made toward the breaking up of a riot.

Another effective measure in the early development of a mob is the use of a police cordon. Police lines to prevent entry of spectators into the scene of an occurrence are used by most departments. Little modification is required to adapt these cordons to the control of a crowd. They are effective in reducing the influence of the crowd and lead to its more rapid dissolution. When a police cordon is properly used, persons are permitted to escape from the crowd but not to enter it. When used in a mob situation, the police cordon can be of great value in preventing the riotous infection of great masses of individuals by preventing social contagion.

By throwing police cordons around an area of danger, curiosity seekers are prevented from being exposed to the mob situation and consequently being infected with it themselves. When a person is permitted to escape the scene of a riot, he frees himself from the excitement of the mob. Such tactics can be effective in confining mob activity to a limited area.

It should be stressed, however, that when persons are permitted to leave the scene of a mob action, they should be required to do so as individuals and not as groups. If large groups are permitted to leave the scene together, the nucleus of disorder in other areas is provided.

Proper timing is as important in the control of threatened violence as is the proper police procedures. Let us review some incidents of racial violence which have occurred in the past and see how a combination of timing and procedure either did or could have brought the situation under control.

Chattanooga, Tennessee, was in February of 1960 a prosperous southern city of more than 100,000 population. Although it had, as had most other southern cities, been concerned for sometime with the tensions which almost invariably accompany desegregation, it had no indication that a possible riot was imminent. On the afternoon of Friday, February 19, a group of students from a col-

ored high school entered a variety store and staged a sit down.
School authorities claimed that this first incident was entirely
spontaneous and that the demonstrators, most of whom were
honor high school students, participated in the first sit in without
even the teachers in their school knowing it was going to happen.

Very little happened the first day. After the students had entered the store, the management closed the counter at which
they were seated and the students left. The police had been summoned to the scene and were watchfully observant. On Saturday and Sunday nothing happened. After school on Monday, however, approximately 200 Negro students appeared at dime stores
in the downtown area. Scattered throughout the crowd was a
sprinkling of Negro adults. They sat down at lunch counters.
Some quietly read school books or at least made a pretense of concentration.

At one store, however, the first physical clash with whites occurred. White students who had heard of the Friday afternoon
sit in had converged on the downtown area ahead of the Negroes
and joined them in a rush for the lunch counter seats. In the jam
which occurred in the aisles there was brief physical contact. The
police were again on the scene and ordered both groups to clear
the aisle, which they did. The police took no further action.

On Tuesday afternoon it became apparent to all city officials
that the situation was beginning to get out of hand. By 3:30 p.m.
approximately 300 whites were already downtown. Not all of
them were high school students. One newspaper account reported
that a goodly percentage was over high school age and many had
the appearance of young toughs. Shortly before four o'clock Negro students approached a variety store and the whites who had
been congregated across the street rushed into the street and ran
toward the store where the Negroes were going. The two groups
reached the store at about the same time. There was a contest for
seats at the lunch counter. The store manager rang the closing
bell, then cut off the lights.

The police, who were again on the job, ordered everyone to
leave the store. Most of the Negroes present hastened to leave
but some fought back and joined in throwing things. The Negroes

were forced into a nearby area which was occupied totally by Negroes and the white youths followed them with taunts and threats. The police attempted to be completely impartial and to arrest everyone who was fighting—Negro and white alike. However, after the Negroes had been forced into the Negro area, the whites were permitted to return to the scene of the original disturbance to jeer at Negro customers remaining in the stores. There was no apparent attempt by the police department to enforce white supremacy but the fact that the Negroes were forced to retreat to Negro areas and the whites were permitted to roam through the streets at large constituted a moral victory for the whites.

By Wednesday the right of the Negro to sit with whites at lunch counters was lost in direct conflict between the two groups. The police had made an earnest effort to be impartial and to keep the two races apart but they had not completely succeeded in establishing a clear understanding that the forces of law and order would prevail.

On Wednesday the nature of the crowd had changed. The honor students from the Negro high school who had staged the first sit in stayed at home. Older and more determined Negroes showed up. The crowd contained many adults. Many whites and Negroes were armed.

School buses entered the downtown area as usual and students from the Negro high school disembarked. They found white youths and adults already present and ready for action. In a very short time the mob had taken over. Crowds estimated at 3,000 thronged the sidewalks of a downtown street and the decision was made that the crowd could be controlled only by the use of fire hoses. The water was trained on sidewalks where the crowds were thickest and the guilty and innocent alike were drenched. Fortunately no one was hurt.

In the mean time the police had set up a cordon at the edge of the Negro area. This accomplished a dual purpose. It prevented Negroes from coming out of the Negro area into the downtown shopping section a few blocks away. It also served to contain the Negroes who were pushed out of the downtown area into the

Negro belt. When a crowd of Negroes threatened to erupt from a Negro belt, fire hoses were again brought into play and Wednesday's riot ended there.

Realizing the gravity of the situation the police doubled its strength and 150 regular and auxiliary officers patrolled the downtown area on Thursday. The Chamber of Commerce joined other civic groups in an appeal for restoration of law and order.

In a meeting with school principals the superintendent of schools pointed out that courts have clearly established the right of school authorities to direct pupils' activities from the time they leave home in the morning until they return in the afternoon. He requested all principals take whatever measures were required to see that students went home immediately following dismissal from school.

At the Negro high school the honor students who had lead the first sit in demonstration appealed to their fellow students not to go into the downtown area on Thursday afternoon. Furthermore the principal of the Negro school sent teachers into the downtown area before school was out to identify any Negro students who entered that area. He promised stern discipline to any student who went downtown.

He also directed that the school bus on which the Negro students rode be rerouted and arranged for the students to be taken on through the downtown area. School buses carrying white students were similarly rerouted.

These measures were almost totally effective, for very few entered the downtown area Thursday. When a few hoodlums did arrive, the police quickly searched and arrested them. The total arrested on Thursday was six Negroes and three whites.

The tactics employed by the Chattanooga Police Department were generally good. Officers made obvious attempts to be fair and impartial and to arrest trouble makers from both sides. They kept the crowd moving and prevented agitators from gathering about themselves groups of spectators whom they might infect. They made adequate use of the police cordon and prevented spectators from entering the scene.

They attempted to remove excited individuals who were the focus of attention and made an adequate show of force by strengthening the assignment of manpower to the downtown area.

However, as has been pointed out, timing is of as great importance as procedure. It is probable that had the police exercised firmness in advising both factions that no breach of the peace would be tolerated when the disturbance first began, it might have been more easily contained.

Another incident occurred in Montgomery, Alabama, during the same month. An essential difference existed between the citizens of Chattanooga and those of Montgomery. In Chattanooga no one, except a few extremists, wanted violence. In Montgomery many persons seemed to expect it and to take it for granted as a part of the process of mediating racial differences.

On February 25, 1960, a group of students from a Negro college in Montgomery took seats in the lunchroom of the Montgomery County Court House. The shop was immediately closed and shortly thereafter the sheriff arrived and ordered the demonstrators to line up in single file. The sheriff's force was augmented by state highway patrolmen who lined the Negroes up against the wall and took pictures of them. The governor requested an investigation and insisted that the demonstrating students be expelled from school. On Friday the governor ordered the president of the Negro university to expel any student who was involved in the sit in.

On Saturday several white men moved as a group through downtown Montgomery swinging toy baseball bats. A middle-aged Negro woman who had not taken part in the original disturbance was attacked. There were no arrests made although a photograph of the episode and the assailant was taken. In a statement the governor charged the Negroes with responsibility for the disturbance and stated that there were not enough police officers in the United States to prevent riots and protect everyone if the Negroes continued to provoke the whites. On the evening the statement was made by the governor a group of 800 Negroes held a rally to plan demonstrations for the following day.

On Tuesday when between 1,000 and 1,200 Negroes marched from the campus of the Negro college to the state capitol. Several high state officials watched the ceremony. After the Negroes had said the Lord's Prayer together and sung the Star Spangled Banner, they marched quietly back to the campus.

A plan for a prayer meeting on the capitol steps was announced for Sunday, March 6. It was scheduled to be held at 2:00 p.m. At noon a crowd began to gather. Many spectators who were idly curious converged on the scene. Some onlookers were accompanied by their wives and children.

An hour before the scheduled prayer meeting, city, county and state officials began arriving. Fifty highway patrolmen were dispersed around the capitol and city police officers lined the sidewalks. As the crowd on the capitol lawn grew, the Negroes began to gather at a Negro church across the street. When the time for the scheduled meeting arrived, a police officer was reported to have shouted to the Negroes, "Can't you tell the time, it's two o'clock. Somebody loan them a watch." When the Negroes did attempt to leave the church, the police held them at the curb. A group of whites rushed at the Negroes who were routed. The police encircled some ministers who were a part of the Negro group and led them back to the church. The police then dispersed the whites.

The attitude of the forces of law and order in Montgomery was radically different from that of Chattanooga. While the police and other city officials in Chattanooga seemed interested in enforcing the law, the officials in Montgomery gave many persons the impression of being more interested in enforcing white supremacy. Little by way of criticism could be said against the police tactics and timing in Montgomery. The authorities were—for the time at least—eminently successful in maintaining the status quo.

Experience in Little Rock, Arkansas, which has unwillingly served as a sounding board for the procedures of desegregation in the south, has proven that city officials and police administrators can profit from past mistakes. During 1957 Little Rock became a national byword as a city which had failed to meet its responsibilities in the peaceful implementation of court orders. In all fairness not all of the blame for Little Rock's dilemma could be placed on city officials. The governor of the state had become the focal point of a movement designed to maintain white supremacy and had conducted the affairs of his office in such a manner that federal troops had been sent to Little Rock to enforce the law. The 1957 attempt at desegregation had ended in disaster and such was expected for a subsequent attempt planned in 1959.

During this two-year period the city government in Little Rock had changed drastically. The aldermanic type of city administration had been abandoned and a city manager had been employed. The top administration of the police department had been changed and the activities of the new chief had earned for him the animosity of the governor who charged that the chief had been bought and paid for to enforce integration.

The chief himself had been extremely busy prior to the time set for the integrative procedure. He had implemented within his department training programs calculated to prepare his officers for any occasion. During a twenty-four month period every man on the police force had been given at least 300 hours of training. Seven attended the FBI National Academy in Washington, D. C., three went to a police-community relations school conducted by Texas A&M College, four attended the Traffic Institute at Northwestern University in Evanston, Illinois, and many others had received specialized training in their particular assignment. In addition the police department had set up a school of its own where it conducted cadet schools of 384 hours of classroom instruction.

The personal attitudes of the members of the department toward segregation were of less importance than the pride in their department they acquired. As a matter of fact, the majority of the police department believed in segregation but to a man the department was willing to subordinate personal opinions to official responsibilities.

Working with traffic supervisors the chief had made a study of forty critical street intersections at which he anticipated trouble. He had aerial photographs taken of locations where he thought the crowds might gather. In short he was to the best of his ability prepared.

On the eve of integration, as the state governor appeared on a Little Rock television station insisting that integration was being forced on the people of Little Rock, but that nothing was to be gained by disorder and violence, the chief conducted a press conference with more than 100 newspapermen from all parts of the world.

The chief declared that anyone who wanted to cover the events of the following day would need a press card. To receive a card newsmen were required to sign an agreement that they would not go onto school property, that they would not pose incidents so that photographs might be taken, that they would not interview students within two blocks of school property, that sound broadcasting and telecasting trucks would not be brought within two blocks of school property, and that they would surrender their special press cards upon demand if they violated these provisions.

The chief requested the newsmen to be on the scene at least an hour before school was scheduled to open so they could be shown where they could stand.

The commander of the police uniform division called all of his men to duty on the day integration was to be effected.

The segregationist groups were encouraged by attorneys who announced that they would defend anyone arrested during the expected demonstration.

Thus was set the stage for what could have been the worst race riot in American history.

On the day integration was effected segregationists came from miles around to hold a rally on the steps of the state capital. Following an address by the governor they started from the capitol toward the schools which were being integrated.

They never arrived.

The chief and his men blocked the path of the demonstrators and in tones of firm command ordered them to disperse. A few defied the forces of law and order and twenty-four arrests resulted. The disorderly crowd was then routed with streams of water from fire hoses.

Because of the decisive action of the police department, the crowds were kept away from the schools where integration was effected peacefully.

The events which occurred in Little Rock proved that mobs cannot operate in the face of firm police action.

The times of the race riots in Detroit and Harlem in 1943 were times of general unrest and racial tension throughout the country. It it almost certain that prompt and efficient action by the metropolitan department of Washington, D. C., prevented a race riot there during that year. Racial tensions are seldom far below the surface in Washington where a very high percentage of the population is Negro.

The Capital Transit Week occasioned the 1943 crisis. A series of demonstrations sponsored by the Washington Committee on Jobs for Negroes in Public Utilities was scheduled. The committee set May 2 for demonstrations calculated to mobilize public support for Negro operators on Washington bus and streetcar lines.

Plans were made to climax a week's demonstration with a parade and open air mass meeting on May 8. The committee arranged for adequate publicity in the Washington Negro press outlining the picketing and mass meeting so it was consequently known by a large portion of the Negro residents of the city. The white metropolitan newspapers gave no coverage to the activities of the committee and as a consequence the general public knew little about the plans and proposed activities of the pressure group.

Great numbers of white citizens read the placards carried by picketers during the week, but knew nothing of the aims and objectives of the organization responsible for the pickets and were totally unaware of the plans for the mass meeting.

Because of a lack of accurate public information properly disseminated about the Friday night mass meeting, garbled reports and frightening rumors began to circulate during the week among the white residents of Washington. The workers in various governmental offices were particularly affected. The rumors were variations on the theme that the Negro populace was planning a race riot and that it was scheduled to occur on Friday night. Some of the stories went so far as to state that large numbers of Negroes were planning an organized revolt against the whites and against the social customs which forbade them employment in the public transportation facilities.

By noon Friday the trickle of rumors had become a flood. Taxi drivers and guards in public buildings were among the most active rumor mongers. Many office workers, including supervisory personnel, were active in spreading the baseless stories.

Many well informed people who watched the situation develop were aware of its great potential for evil and feared that the situation would erupt in violence. Some of them approached the police superintendent and attempted to persuade him to revoke the permit which had already been given the Negro group for a parade and mass meeting.

The superintendent realized that the intentions of the Negro group were peaceful and insisted that they had a right to hold their parade and meeting. He told reporters on Friday afternoon that it would be cowardly to cancel the meeting and that while such action might temporarily forestall trouble, it would lead to greater difficulty in the long run.

Throughout the week extra uniformed policemen were stationed in the locations where the picketers were marching. These officers were instructed not to interfere with the picketing or with any passer by and to take enforcement action only in the event of violence.

On Friday the superintendent finalized plans for policing the evening's activities. He talked to members of the department who were scheduled to be on duty that night and told them that the policy of the department was one of complete neutrality in its effort to preserve law and order or restore it in the event of riotous outbreak.

Prior to the time of the meeting uniformed and plain-clothes officers were stationed at all intersections and scattered along the proposed line of march. An adequate number was stationed at the site where the meeting was to be held.

The police superintendent joined the demonstrators at the starting point of the parade and marched at the head of the group to the meeting place. The parade, which numbered approximately 220 at the beginning, was swelled to approximately 850 by the time it reached the meeting place. An estimated crowd of 1,000 persons, mostly Negroes but with a generous sprinkling of whites, was gathered to hear speeches by white congressmen, a local Negro clergyman and others.

No violence occurred either at the meeting place or elsewhere in the city. In addition to the civilian police the meeting was patrolled by representatives of the military service. One boisterous sailor was escorted from the park by Navy personnel and the meeting site was immediately declared out of bounds for all military personnel.

Although the parade and mass meeting was accomplished without incident, the commissioner felt the need for continuing precautions against violence and disorder after the meeting had been held. On Saturday night Negro police officers were assigned to ride on streetcars operating in the Negro districts.

Within a very short time after this decisive action taken by the police superintendent the talk of a mass riot almost entirely died out in Washington. The manner in which the incident was handled made it a good practical lesson in intercommunity relations for both the white and Negro citizens of Washington.

The whites learned that they could not rely on rumors, for the tales they had listened to were without foundation. They learned that the Negroes had no intention of committing violence.

The Negroes learned that their rights to hold peaceful meetings and to demonstrate in a legal manner would be defended by officials of the local government and that they could rely on adequate police protection when they needed it. The forthright and intelligent manner in which the police superintendent handled the entire incident appreciably decreased racial tension in Washington.

Here also we see employed some of the principles we have earlier discussed. The superintendent had provided within his department an atmosphere conducive to law and order. He made an adequate show of force by stationing police officers in uniform and in sufficient numbers to handle any violence which might have occurred. He proved to the Negroes and whites alike that the police department was determined to maintain law and order and that no illegal activity would be tolerated.

Another good example of preventive work occurred in June, 1943, in Houston, Texas. Negroes in that city traditionally celebrated "Juneteenth Day" by a parade and street carnival.

Because of the general unrest throughout the nation at that time rumors began racing through the white population that Negroes were planning to start a riot. Plans were made by some of the white citizens to attack and disperse the Negro parade.

When the police chief learned of the proposed attack, he met with the mayor, a bi-racial commission which was already in existence, and a number of influential citizens, both white and Negro. A proclamation was drawn up stating that the celebration would be held according to plan, that there would be no trouble and that any person, whether white or colored, who attempted to interfere with the parade and street carnival would be considered an unlawful citizen and would be arrested.

The proclamation was signed by the persons who drew it up and published as a full page notice in all of the daily newspapers.

The celebration was a great success. There were no disturbances. It has been said in fact that it was the most peaceful in Houston's history.

While it is, of course, highly desirable that police activity prevent a riot from beginning, this is not always possible. An example of how police authority can be properly used in quelling a riot once it has begun was given us in the Harlem incident in New York City in August 1943.

This riot was probably one of the few in American history in which police strategy and tactics was generally approved by all factions. Study of the strategy and tactics developed by the New York Police Department on that occasion will therefore be profitable to any police organization.

On the evening of August 1, 1943, a fight occurred in a south Harlem hotel between a white police officer and a Negro soldier. Both the policeman and the soldier were wounded. A rumor spread throughout the neighborhood that a soldier had been shot in the back and killed. As a result of this rumor large crowds of Negroes began to gather in front of the hotel where the incident had occurred, the 123rd Street Police Station and the hospital to which the wounded soldier had been taken.

Alert police personnel immediately reported the incident to police headquarters. Within an hour both the police commissioner

and the mayor appeared at the 123rd Street Station, set up headquarters there and assumed personal charge of the situation. Immediately upon arriving Mayor LaGuardia attempted to talk to
the crowd and urged them to break up and go home. They refused to listen to him and shouted him down. As quickly as possible approximately a third of the entire city police force was
mobilized and assigned for duty in the Harlem area.

All police vacations and days off were cancelled and forces including foot and mounted patrolmen, motorcycles, squad cars, and
detectives converged on Harlem from all five boroughs of New
York. Other city departments alerted employees who were also
called in to aid the police.

A police cordon was thrown around the area to prevent onlookers from other parts of the city from entering. All bus service in
the neighborhood was suspended, police guards were placed in
the subway stations and all trolley lines were discontinued except
one on which police guards were placed. The operation of private
automobiles in the area was similarly prohibited. This included
trucks delivering material to the district except for a few carrying
crucial material needed by the police units and these were given a
police guard.

All liquor stores were closed.

Both Negro and white military police were sent to the area to
prevent servicemen from taking part in the disturbance. All service personnel found in the area were ordered to return to their
posts.

The efficiency of such tactics was very important in containing
the riot in the neighborhood in which it originated. However, the
tactics which earned for the police the most widespread praise
were psychological.

All persons who had any responsibility for helping bring the riot
under control were instructed by the mayor and the police commissioner to use no more force than was absolutely necessary, to
be completely impartial and impersonal and to use courtesy, diplomacy and tact in their efforts to break up the street mobs. As a
result of this instruction, the police did not attempt to use overpowering force in making frontal attacks on the mob, although

by this time the rioters were breaking store windows and beginning to remove merchandise. Neither riot guns nor teargas guns were used. Police tactics were such that no possible basis for accusations of police brutality existed. Instead police sought to prevent newcomers from joining the mob and at the same time attempted to divide mobs already active and disperse the small segments that split off.

A number of the mob's ring leaders were arrested and placed in jail. They were booked in accordance with regular police procedures. Except for those individuals who were obviously agitating and controlling the activities of others, the rioters were released and ordered to go home when they were separated from the mob.

The mayor and commissioner used their knowledge of practical psychology in many other ways during the riot, all of which contributed to their success in bringing the disorderly crowds under control. Very early all the leaders of public opinion who could be reached were called together. These Negro leaders, many of whom were nationally known, made up with the mayor and police commissioner an impromptu board of strategy. They worked with the city officials all during the night of the riot. Because they were more intimately acquainted with the elements engaged in the disturbance, they were able to make many tactical suggestions which were extremely helpful to the authorities in restoring order more quickly. With the mayor they toured Harlem throughout the night in loud speaker trucks requesting people to stop rioting and go home.

Radio broadcasting equipment was set up at the 123rd Street Police Station and both the mayor and his impromptu board of strategy made many radio addresses which were broadcast by most of the area commercial radio stations. They explained in detail the true facts of the incident that started the disturbance and continued their exhortation that people get off the streets and go home. The attitude of the mayor and the line he took in his addresses made a favorable impression on the citizens of Harlem.

By morning the crowd had been dispersed and order restored.

The following steps were taken after the initial riot had been brought under control. As a precaution against further outbreaks a curfew was ordered for the entire affected area from 10:30 p.m. until complete order was restored. All theaters were closed at that hour.

The restrictions on transportation entering the area was continued and only vehicles delivering food were allowed in the area.

A ban on the sale of alcoholic beverages was established.

The police remained on twenty-four duty and in addition enlisted several hundred civilian volunteers including a large number of Negroes. The volunteers were provided with arm bands and police batons and were assigned to patrol duty.

Eight thousand members of the New York State Guard were placed on a stand-by basis in the event they were needed. One segment of the guard was all Negro. Lessons to be learned from the handling of the Harlem riot are many.

The police officers who handled the original incident realized the potential for violence and made a quick report to headquarters. Adequate numbers of police officers were speedily mobilized.

A police cordon was quickly thrown about the riot scene to prevent curiosity seekers or potential rioters from entering the trouble area.

Both the mayor and the police commissioner realized the situation demanded their immediate attention and rushed to the scene to remain there until the riot was subdued. They took special precautions to prevent an excessive use of force and insisted on impartiality and impersonal action on the part of all police officers. They further made adequate use of Negro police officers and Negro volunteers.

A large number of reinforcements were alerted and held in reserve so they would be quickly available if they were needed.

Community leaders were encouraged to join the mayor and the police commissioner in planning strategy and appealing directly to the rioters. These personal appeals continued throughout the riot.

It has been repeatedly pointed out that an adequate show of force at the proper time is of great value in bringing an unruly crowd under control. Here again timing can be as important as tactics. A police department would do well to establish as a part of its routine procedures an emergency call list whereby off duty policemen could be returned to duty as rapidly as possible. Many departments have such an emergency call list planned on a divisional basis. Under such a plan the divisional chief has the responsibility for notifying his immediate subordinates. They in turn notify a limited number of supervisors under them, who in turn are assigned to call a certain part of the operational personnel. The hierarchical structure of the organization assists in the implementation of this plan, for if there is the proper span of control, no member of the department operating in a supervisory capacity will have more persons working directly under him than he can summon in a very short period of time. The emergency call list should, of course, be written and should be maintained in a current status. Most departments using such a call list make revisions in it at least monthly.

A police department to properly handle incidents such as a riot should have an adaptable disaster control plan. One such plan is currently being used by the Dallas Police Department. Although this plan is designed to take care of all types of incidents, it is so adaptable to race riots that it is quoted in its entirety.

## POLICE DISASTER CONTROL PLAN

### *General Order No. 32*

In preparing a plan of police operation in the event of a disaster, the Department has been directly cognizant that conditions at a particular event may necessitate modification or elaboration upon this plan as it is approved. It is believed, however, after a study of conditions at several types of disaster, that the plan is sufficiently flexible to be adapted to any prevailing condition.

It is expedient to classify incidents and disasters according to severity. Incidents and disasters have been graded from the first magnitude through the seventh magnitude. All problems handled by the Police Department will fall within one of these categories.

The first through the fourth magnitudes have been classified as incidents. The fifth magnitude is classified as either an incident or a disaster, depending on circumstances, and the sixth and seventh magnitudes are definitely disasters.

A police incident, no matter how minor, is usually a disaster to somebody. When a person is injured in a disturbance of the peace, it is a disaster to the victim, his family, and friends. However, since the word "disaster" normally indicates something of a larger nature, we have not classified police incidents that are more or less routine as disasters. They have been given this classification only when they reach such proportions as to be considered out of the ordinary.

Incidents of the first four magnitudes are classified according to the amount of supervision needed, while incidents and disasters of the fifth, sixth, and seventh magnitudes are classified according to the amount of additional manpower needed to effectively control the situation.

More complete definitions of the magnitude of an incident or disaster are given later.

Basic police operating procedures will be applied to all of the named incidents and disasters. As the magnitude of the incident or disaster increases, the functions and responsibilities increase in proportion and, therefore, higher ranking supervisors are designated to command, and the delegation of authority is more diversified.

The normal organization will handle incidents up to and including the fourth magnitude, but when the incident or disaster increases to a fifth magnitude or above, it will probably be necessary to set up a separate unit to handle the problems involved, and thereby permit the Department to carry on its normal functions without too much disruption.

An incident or disaster of the fifth magnitude, or higher, requiring field command by an Inspector, or higher-ranking officer, shall require a separate command reporting directly to a Headquarters Commander designated by the Chief of Police.

The following are basic points of police responsibility and should be given consideration by the officer in charge of any police incident or disaster:

1. Preserve the peace—control of the scene.
2. Protection of life and property.
3. Aid and assistance to the citizens and strangers.
4. Prevention and detection of crime.

5. The arrest of violators.

The first thing any officer should do when arriving at the scene of a police incident is to gain control of the scene, because until this is done, he can not effectively perform the second function—protection of life and property.

After the second step has been effectively carried out, attention can be given to steps three, four, and five.

It is in accordance with accepted supervisory procedures that the senior officer present at any police incident is in charge of handling that incident. Therefore, the senior officer should immediately delegate responsibility for handling the various functions. The larger the incident or disaster, the more problems involved, and the more delegation necessary.

This responsibility should be delegated, even in the smallest incident—one of the first magnitude. As an example, when a squad of two patrolmen arrives at the scene of a disturbance, the senior patrolman should delegate to his partner a portion of the responsibility and assume the balance himself. These functions would include such things as traffic control, first aid, communication with headquarters, investigation, and the making of required reports.

Similarly, at a second, third, or fourth magnitude incident, the Sergeant, Lieutenant, or Captain in charge would delegate the authority to perform the various functions to the supervisors and officers at the scene.

Before discussing incidents and disasters of the fifth magnitude and higher it is felt that certain definitions should be given, and that a more complete breakdown of responsibility should be set out. These definitions and responsibilities follow:

First Magnitude Incident

An incident which requires only the attention of a patrolman or a squad will be considered to be of the First Magnitude.

EXAMPLES: Disturbances, minor accidents, theft investigations and other routine calls.

A First Magnitude incident becomes a Second Magnitude incident when the patrolman handling it deems it necessary to call either a Sergeant or a Detective to take charge.

## Second Magnitude Incident

An incident which requires field direction by a Sergeant or Detective shall be considered of the Second Magnitude. He shall notify Headquarters of conditions and restore to a First Magnitude as soon as possible.

EXAMPLES: Two alarm fire, major accident, homicide, or investigation requiring a crime scene search, or an incident where more than two squads are utilized.

A Second Magnitude incident increases to a Third Magnitude incident when the Sergeant or Detective handling it deems it necessary to call a Lieutenant to take charge.

## Third Magnitude Incident

An incident which requires field direction by a Lieutenant shall be considered of the Third Magnitude. The Lieutenant shall keep Headquarters informed of conditions and restore to a lower magnitude as soon as possible.

EXAMPLES: Three alarm fire, injury necessitating hospitalization of police personnel, or any incident requiring two or more first-line supervisors.

A Third Magnitude incident increases to a Fourth Magnitude incident when the Lieutenant handling it deems it necessary to call a Captain to take charge.

## Fourth Magnitude Incident

An incident which requires field direction by a Captain shall be considered of the Fourth Magnitude. The Captain shall keep Headquarters notified of the conditions and restore to a lower magnitude as soon as possible.

EXAMPLES: Explosion, plane crash, four alarm fire, minor racial disturbances and all other incidents which can be handled by personnel on duty assigned to the incident with a minimum of overtime.

A Fourth Magnitude incident becomes a Fifth Magnitude incident or disaster when a Chief Officer shall determine that circumstances warrant such a rating.

### Fifth Magnitude (Incident) Disaster

A Chief Officer shall authorize a rating of this magnitude when, in his opinion, the incident or disaster is of such proportions that it meets one of the following requirements.

1. Will require a majority of on-duty personnel to work overtime to handle the situation, but does not require the mustering of off-duty personnel.
2. Where field supervision and coordination of functions of more than one Division is necessary for an extended period of time.

The Chief Officer authorizing this magnitude shall:

1. Designate a Field Commander to take charge at the scene.
2. Establish a Disaster Headquarters Command.
3. Notify the Assistant Chief of Police of his action.
4. Notify the Administrative Assistant to the Chief of Police of the magnitude.

Inspectors of Police shall be available for assignment by the Chief Officer designating this magnitude.

The Administrative Assistant shall activate an Information Center at Headquarters, and all information shall be routed through this Center for correlation and dissemination to interested agencies. Personnel shall be drawn from all Divisions as necessary by the Headquarters Commander and assigned to the supervision of the Field Commander. Personnel so assigned shall be restored to normal duty through the Headquarters Command.

> EXAMPLES: *Incidents* include State Fair and other special events of sufficient size to warrant the rating. *Disasters* include five alarm fires, or higher, plane crashes, explosions, riots and other disasters that can be handled with on-duty personnel as set out above.

A Fifth Magnitude disaster becomes a Sixth Magnitude disaster when the Headquarters Commander shall determine that circumstances warrant such a rating.

## Sixth Magnitude Disaster

The ranking Chief Officer on duty shall authorize a disaster rating of this magnitude when, in his opinion, the disaster is of such proportions that it will require partial mobilization of off-duty personnel. The Chief Officer making this designation shall request personnel of Division Commanders and Special Unit Commanders as needed. These Commanding Officers shall mobilize such personnel as needed to comply with the request. The same plan will be followed as set out in the Fifth Magnitude incident or disaster.

> EXAMPLE: Major explosion, commercial plane crash, large strikes causing riots, and other incidents requiring more personnel to handle than is on duty.

A Sixth Magnitude disaster becomes a Seventh Magnitude disaster when the Chief of Police, or his Assistant, shall determine that circumstances warrant such a rating.

## Seventh Magnitude Disaster

The Chief of Police, or the Acting Chief of Police, shall authorize this rating when, in his opinion, the disaster is of such proportions that it will require a total mobilization of police personnel.

The Chief Officer making this designation shall cause all other Chief Officers and Special Unit Commanders to be notified, who will in turn cause their commands to be mobilized.

Each off-duty member of the Department will report to his normal duty station immediately upon learning of a disaster of this magnitude. Each Commanding Officer will keep the Headquarters Commander advised of the degree of mobilization of his unit.

> EXAMPLES: Tornado, flood, racial riots, major explosion, or any incident requiring complete mobilization of the Police Department.

## INNER BLOCKADE

This may be defined as being the blockade encircling the immediate scene and through which no one passes except those recognized by the police as being essential in the emergency control of the incident. This function will be set up and supervised by the supervisor designated by the Field Commander to handle patrol functions.

## OUTER BLOCKADE

The outer blockade may be defined as being that blockade which encircles the inner blockade at a safe distance from the disaster. It may be only the establishment of a blockade on the entrance and exit routes to and from the inner blockade for the purpose of insuring free movement of essential services. This blockade will usually stop at the first lateral roads from the outer perimeter of the inner blockade.

Entry into this area will be determined by policy of the Disaster Field Commander or by passes issued by the Disaster Headquarters Commander. Persons identifying themselves by address or drivers license and other means as residing or employed in the area between the inner and outer blockade may be permitted to enter on authority of the Field Commander. Emergency service recognized by the police as needed in the area will be permitted to pass.

The outer blockade will be set up and supervised by the traffic supervisor designated by the Field Commander.

## DISASTER HEADQUARTERS COMMAND

This command will be set up at Headquarters immediately by the Chief Officer who authorizes the rating of a fifth magnitude or greater. All information, reports, requests for manpower, equipment and supplies will be channeled through this command. In disasters of the sixth and seventh and in some of the fifth magnitude, the Assistant Chief of Police will probably assume this command, leaving the Chief of Police free to direct the overall operation of the Police Department without being tied down to a specific function. The Chief Officer who declares a disaster of the fifth magnitude, or greater, will assume this command until a designation has been made.

## DISASTER HEADQUARTERS COMMANDER

He shall designate a Disaster Field Commander. He shall notify the following:

1. Chief of Police
2. Assistant Chief of Police
3. Divisional Deputy Chiefs
4. Commanding Officers of Special Units
5. Administrative Assistant to the Chief of Police

He shall establish communications with the Disaster Field Headquarters and with Division and Special Unit Commanders.

He shall compile reports of injuries, extent of disaster, and other necessary information.

He shall obtain from the Division Chiefs and Special Unit Commanders the necessary manpower, equipment, and supplies to be assigned to the Disaster Field Commander.

He shall notify Division Chiefs and Special Unit Commanders of conditions requiring their attention.

He shall alert and maintain liaison with other agencies and city departments whose services may be needed to handle and control the disaster.

He shall be the officer who authorizes the reduction of the magnitude.

### DIVISION CHIEFS AND SPECIAL UNIT COMMANDERS

They shall mobilize their commands as requested by the Disaster Headquarters Commander.

They shall keep the Disaster Headquarters Commander fully informed of the extent of mobilization at all times.

They shall furnish manpower, supplies and equipment as requested by the Disaster Headquarters Command.

They shall provide for police services relating to the disaster that are outside the outer blockade, such as hospital details, escort duties, etc.

They shall keep a record of the services furnished and submit reports on these services to the Disaster Headquarters Command.

They shall maintain and supervise the normal police functions under their jurisdiction.

## DISASTER FIELD HEADQUARTERS

This headquarters should be set up at a point that is easily accessible somewhere outside the inner blockade. Consideration should be given to the availability of telephone communications, office space, shelter for victims and disaster workers, storage space for equipment, supplies, and property, and parking of vehicles.

All information, reports, communications, requests for manpower, equipment and supplies for the disaster area will be channeled through this command.

## DISASTER FIELD COMMANDER

He shall be the senior officer at the disaster scene until the supervisor appointed by the Headquarters Disaster Commander arrives to take charge.

He shall determine the site of the Disaster Field Headquarters and then divide functions under the following as needed:

1. Patrol Supervisor
2. Traffic Supervisor
3. Criminal Investigation Supervisor
4. Service Supervisor
5. Executive Officer

He shall make all requests for services, materials or equipment furnished by other departments of the City Government. This procedure will be followed in incidents of the first, second, third and fourth magnitudes, as well as in disasters of the fifth, sixth or seventh magnitudes.

During an incident of the first, second, third and fourth magnitudes, the senior officer acting as Field Commander will make the request through the Dispatcher.

During a disaster, the Field Commander will make his request through the Disaster Headquarters Commander.

It will be the duty of the senior officer, who has exercised command and requested the services, materials or equipment from other departments, to notify these departments when the material or equipment is no longer needed.

He shall keep Disaster Headquarters Command fully informed of events and circumstances at all times.

He shall combine supervisory functions and relieve officers for return to regular assignment as soon as possible.

## EXECUTIVE OFFICER — DISASTER FIELD HEADQUARTERS

He shall be second in command of the disaster area.

He shall be responsible that all incoming officers are mustered and a record kept of their names and date and time of reporting. Also a record of what supervisors they are assigned to in the disaster area and the time of assignment.

## SERVICE SUPERVISOR–DISASTER FIELD HEADQUARTERS

He shall be responsible to the Disaster Field Commander and set up the following functions at Disaster Field Headquarters and subdivide supervision as necessary:

*Communications:* Between Disaster Field Headquarters and Headquarters Disaster Command and Command posts within the disaster area.

*Supply Depot:* Procure and issue needed supplies and keep a current inventory of them.

*Property:* Receive, record and store all recovered property until disposition can be made.

*Transportation:* Secure vehicles for necessary transportation and keep a record of assignments and availability.

*Detention of Prisoners:* Arrange for the detention of prisoners until they can be transferred to the City Jail.

*Housing and Food:* Arrange for shelter and food for police personnel assigned to the disaster area.

*Records:* Keep and maintain records for all units in the disaster area. This would include assignments of officers, offense reports, arrest sheets, etc.

He shall see that these reports and assignment records are routed to Disaster Headquarters Command as soon as possible.

## PATROL SUPERVISOR – DISASTER AREA

He shall be responsible to the Disaster Field Commander.

He shall set up and be in charge of the inner blockade and all police functions within the inner blockade, except those that are handled by special assignment, such as investigation of a criminal matter, etc.

He shall give immediate attention to the care and evacuation of injured and dead persons and make such preliminary investigations as is normal for the Patrol Division.

He shall set up a Command Post at some convenient entrance point to the inner blockade and maintain communications with the Disaster Field Headquarters keeping the Disaster Field Headquarters fully informed of conditions and requirements.

He shall make necessary security assignments within the inner blockade.

He shall make a record of personnel assignments showing names, dates and times of assignments and inform Disaster Field Headquarters of these assignments in order that permanent records may be made.

He shall arrange relief periods for personnel under his command, particularly those on post assignment.

## TRAFFIC SUPERVISOR — DISASTER AREA

He shall be stationed at Disaster Field Command Headquarters and responsible to the Disaster Field Commander.

He shall set up and be in charge of the outer blockade and all police functions between the inner and outer blockades and set up necessary security measures.

He shall immediately survey the area and determine the best routes into and out of the disaster area for emergency services and proceed immediately to ensure the free and orderly movement of these services.

He shall set up control points of entry and exit.

He shall keep Disaster Field Headquarters fully informed of conditions and requirements.

He shall arrange relief periods for personnel under his command, particularly those on post assignment.

He shall make all assignments for escorts into and out of the disaster area. Personnel performing escort duties shall be under his supervision.

## CRIMINAL INVESTIGATION SUPERVISOR — DISASTER AREA

He shall be responsible to the Disaster Field Commander.

He shall be stationed at Disaster Field Command Headquarters and shall direct the handling of investigations, surveillances, missing persons, juveniles, and other operations normally handled by the Criminal Investigation Division.

He shall keep the Disaster Field Headquarters fully informed of conditions and requirements.

He shall check and approve all investigative reports before they are forwarded to Disaster Headquarters Command to see that proper action has been taken.

\* \* \*

It is not contemplated that it will be necessary in every disaster to expand operations to the full extent outlined above, but the full organization is listed in the event it might be needed.

\* \* \*

The use of police cordons in isolating an unruly crowd has been described. While this device is extremely efficient in preventing additional rioters from entering the scene of unrest, it is not, when used alone, adequate for it fails to disperse the crowds already gathered.

It is necessary therefore that a police agency have a tactical plan for actually breaking up mobs.

Several formations have proven effective in breaking off segments from a mob and dispersing the persons so separated. One simple expedient is the use of a diagonal line. Here the officers are in a diagonal row with each officer one pace to the side and one pace to the rear of the officer in front of him. The first officer entering the crowd forces some of the members over into the path of the second officer. The second in turn forces the rioters into the path of the third and as the police formation passes through the crowd, an entire segment is separated. There should be in reserve, following the diagonal line, a sufficient number of reserves to plug any gap that might occur. These reserves can also be used to subdue and remove any person who attempts to grapple with an officer in the line. After the segment has been separated from the main body of the mob, the line can then turn and force the section farther and farther away from the scene of the riot. Other units can then enter the crowd as a line or can take over the dispersal of the already separated segment.

Equally effective is the use of a police wedge. Here a diagonal line spreads out on each side of the leader, forming an arrowhead shaped unit. The wedge then enters the crowd and separates a segment just as in the diagonal line.

It is perhaps wise in both the wedge and the line for the supervisor to remain close to and behind the officers performing the tactic. From this position he can more easily spot the need for additional manpower and can more easily communicate with the officers of the unit. Repeated use of the line or the wedge, with a small segment of the mob broken off each time, can soon reduce the size of a disorganized crowd to manageable proportions.

Many of the weapons normally used in police work can be used to great advantage in subduing an unruly crowd. It should again be stressed that legally a police officer has the right to use only such force as is necessary to gain and maintain control of a situation. We are as accountable for our use of force in a riot situation as we are under more routine phases of police work. We have, however, the responsibility for maintenance of the peace and protection of life and property. We then have not only the authority but the responsibility for bringing a riot under control in the shortest possible length of time. The supervisor in charge of a detail on riot duty will have to decide what force is needed and then have the courage to apply that force.

No weapons should be used until the police unit has first attempted to disperse the crowd through regular police procedures. However, should the crowd refuse to abandon its disorderly tactics, the police have no alternative but to bring greater force to bear.

There are many effective weapons which may be used. The riot gun, which is standard equipment in most departments, has proven its value on many occasions. It has a great psychological effect. The riot gun should not be brought into play, however, unless the police unit intends to use it as the need arises.

The 12-gauge shotgun shell loaded with number 00 buckshot is a very lethal and effective weapon up to ranges of approximately sixty yards. By use of the riot shotgun instead of a rifle, the danger of ricochetting bullets killing persons half a mile from the riot scene is eliminated.

Not normally used in police service but available is a bayonet which may be attached to the riot gun. Such a weapon affixed to the riot gun carried by members of a diagonal line or wedge materially aids the unit's progress through the crowd. Many people who would tend to ignore a police officer carrying a riot gun give way readily when approached by a bayonet held at chest height. The sight of a steadily advancing bayonet causes the most obdurate rioter to yield.

Police dogs have proven their value on many occasions. A dog in crouched position with fangs bared is not an easy obstacle to surmount and most persons, even those infected by the spirit of a mob, will think twice and three and four times before attempting to walk past the dog. There must be in the back of the rioter's mind a realization that while a police officer is human and has a human reluctance to inflict violence on his fellow man, a well trained police dog has no such reluctance. Police dogs have been used with great success in Galveston, Texas; Jackson, Mississippi; and Baltimore, Maryland.

During the past years many civil disorders have been controlled and difficult arrests made by the use of chemicals with no appreciable loss of life or property. Any police department would do well to consider the use of tear gas and train its members in its proper use. As the San Francisco Chronicle reported some time ago, we use tear gas in riots because it stops the riot better than shooting does and leaves everybody alive.

To obtain maximum results from the use of gas, the rioters must be subjected to a prolonged and heavy concentration. It is not sufficient merely to secure a supply of gas grenades and throw them at the mob. The gas contained within the grenade can be compared to a bullet in that to be effective, it must hit the target. The effects of tear gas are only temporary and the person on whom it is used seldom receives any permanent damage.

There are several types of commercial grenades available. One type is provided with an instantaneous firing action which begins to discharge gas the instant it leaves the thrower's hand. The area around the grenade quickly becomes covered with a heavy visible gas concentration. The entire chemical contents are discharged within about twenty seconds. An added benefit is that the grenade becomes extremely hot while the gas is being discharged, thereby discouraging rioters from throwing it back at police units.

A newer type works on the same principles but separates into three parts approximately two seconds after it is thrown. Each part then travels in a different direction and functions as an individual grenade. The same effect is derived as if three separate grenades were thrown. A two-second fuse permits the thrower to toss the grenade far enough away so that when the units separate he is not himself gassed. The three sections emit a sizzling, hissing sound which, coupled with the heat, eliminates the hazards of throwbacks.

Of perhaps greatest psychological value is a jumper-repeater type recently developed. This grenade is thrown just as the others but it emits three extremely severe blasts of gas in rapid succession. At each blast the grenade jumps ten to twelve feet in the air and travels in an unpredictable direction. The rioters cannot know in which direction to move to avoid its course. The first discharge occurs two seconds after it is thrown and the two succeeding blasts occur at one second intervals. The contents are completely discharged within four seconds. The rioters have no opportunity to pick up and throw back one of these grenades. Indeed the action of the missile creates an effect of pursuit.

There are several long-range gas projectiles commercially available. These have been designed for projecting gas over a long distance into barricades or buildings. They are fired from a specially designed gas gun and most are equipped with tail fins which automatically spring into position when the shell leaves the gun barrel. In the hands of a trained operator these projectiles have a high degree of accuracy and a standard window is easily hit at ranges of 50 to 100 yards. Most such shells are equipped with an instantaneous fuse mechanism which bursts the shell on impact and allows the gas to be instantly discharged.

Some gas cartridges designed for firing in the gas gun are not contained within a projectile but leave the muzzle of the gun only as a blast of gas. While they can under certain circumstances be safely used, they pose greater danger to the user than many other types.

Wind direction and velocity must be taken into consideration before any tear gas is used. Whenever possible gas squads should maneuver so as to approach their objectives from the windward side. The most favorable wind speed for an effective gas cloud is from four to six miles per hour. Winds above twelve miles per hour rapidly dissipate the gas. If police units fail to take into consideration the direction of the wind, they may find that they are not reaching their objective but are only enveloping themselves in the gas. Although all members of a gas unit should have gas masks, proper planning will eliminate the need for such equipment.

The police baton has proven its effectiveness against an unruly crowd on many occasions. The thrust is considered the most effective movement of the baton. Good results can also be obtained by using it as a club. It should be made of very hard wood, preferably about eighteen inches long and at least one inch in diameter. The handle should be shaped so as to aid in thrusting.

A rawhide leather thong about sixteen inches long should be attached to the baton near the handle. This thong should be looped over the extended thumb as over a hook. Any surplus should be wrapped around the grip of the club. The thong should be long enough so the thumb is not restrained while the club is gripped.

In the event a rioter grapples with a police officer and seizes the club the officer should release his hold on it and attempt to bring the disorderly person under control by other measures.

It must be reassuring to any police agency that it does not stand alone. Any police department in the country stands ready to rush to the assistance of any other should the need arise. We constantly see examples of this desire to be of mutual assistance. Any department stands ready to lend whatever assistance is needed and requested by another department beset by a problem too great for it to handle alone. Other city police departments can serve as a valuable source of additional manpower. State and county units can also render valuable assistance.

A police reserve unit can prove its worth in a riot situation by relieving regular officers from routine duties for riot control work. It is questionable that reserves should be placed on the firing line but they certainly can fill office jobs and patrol quieter districts, while regular officers normally assigned to these functions are assigned to riot control.

Fire departments can frequently be of assistance in the control of unruly crowds. Water under high pressure sprayed over a crowd usually encourages it to disperse. Some cities have experimented with the use of a harmless vegetable dye used in a fire department pump truck. When the water is sprayed over the crowd, the dye settles on clothing and skin. It must be disconcerting to a rioter to see the persons standing beside him suddenly turn purple, pink, or bright green. Although current space exploration prompts considerable discussion of little green men it is difficult for a person with such color to exercise great influence on people standing near him.

It is entirely possible that a riot can assume such proportions that civil police authorities are not capable of controlling the actions of its members and breaking it up. Under such circumstances the assistance of military organizations should be enlisted. A call to the governor of any state outlining the need for national guard troops will usually result in their mobilization in short order. Most military organizations have adequate training in riot control and can bring to bear weapons effective in the dispersal of crowds not normally available to civil police agencies.

In summary, proper police tactics will include the following points:

1. Ascertaining the facts is a first necessity. Police officers must refrain from impulsive action which often leads to disaster.

2. Once the true facts have been determined the police officer should act quickly. Early decisive action by police authority can anticipate and cut short a gathering crowd. An early disposition of the incident neutralizes the possibility of widespread social disorder occurring.

3. The police officer should strive constantly to give evidence of fair and impersonal attitudes and conduct. This commands the confidence and cooperation of the best elements in any gathering of people.

4. If the persons involved in an incident are excited and emotionally agitated, they should be separated and kept apart. This allows the passions of the antagonists to cool and prevents their excitement from being communicated to the spectators.

5. Indiscriminate and mass arrests are usually not desirable. Invariably a greater number of innocent people than serious offenders are involved. This aggravates the difficulty since the arrests of innocent bystanders creates an impression of incompetency and excessive and unbridled exercise of power.

6. There should be an early awareness of a dangerous situation and adequate manpower should be summoned at once. It should be possible, through an organized plan, to mobilize adequate numbers of police quickly. It should be remembered that an incident which has passed beyond the control of the police can again be brought under control only with the greatest difficulty. As a cardinal principle, a situation should never be permitted to develop in which control has passed out of the hands of the police authority. Hence, an established plan for reinforcing the officer on the beat, the squad car in its rounds or a whole platoon of police at the scene of a conflict should be an integral feature of departmental tactics.

7. A disaster plan should be formulated to make proper use of police manpower as it reports for duty.

8. Police loud speakers should be set up on the outskirts of the crowd and its members should be directed from the outermost edges to break up and go home.

9. The use of a police cordon should be practiced by a department until this tactic can be employed easily and quickly.

10. The amount of force used should be suited to the conditions existing and only that force which is necessary to subduing riots should be employed.

11. A plan of riot control should provide for the enlistment of the cooperation of minority group leaders. They should be included at the planning level as well as in direct appeals during critical times.

12. The public relations aspect is of such an involved nature that police authorities should establish liaison with the press media to avoid work at cross purposes. Such a group should include the Negro as well as the white press.

13. A cooperative plan with other municipal police agencies, county law enforcement groups and state agencies should be developed so that such aid as may be needed can be invoked and delivered at the earliest possible moment.

14. The use of specialized weapons such as riot guns, bayonets, dogs, chemicals and police batons should be considered. The necessity for the use should be indicated without question before they are brought into play.

# BIBLIOGRAPHY

Allport, Gordon W.: *The Psychology of Rumor.* New York, H. Holt & Company, 1947, 247 pp.

Allport, Gordon W.: *The Nature of Prejudice.* Garden City, New York, Doubleday, 1958, 496 pp.

American Friends Service Committee, Southeastern Office; Department of Racial and Cultural Relations of The National Council of Churches of Christ in the United States of America; Southern Regional Council: *Intimidation Reprisal & Violence in the South's Racial Crisis,* 30 pp.

Barnes, Harry Elmer: *Society in Transition.* New York, Prentice Hall, Inc., 1946, 999 pp.

B'Nai B'Rith, Anti-Defamation League: *With Justice For All.* New York, 1959, 36 pp.

Clinchy, Everett Ross: *A Handbook on Human Relations.* New York, Farrar, Straus, 1949, 146 pp.

Kluchecky, Joseph T.: *Police Action in Minority Problems,* New York, Freedom House, 1946, 15 pp.

Lee, Alfred M.: *Race Riots Aren't Necessary.* Chicago, American Council of Race Relations, 1945, 29 pp.

Lee, Alfred McClung and Humphrey, Norman Daymond: *Race Riot.* New York, Dryden Press, 1943, 143 pp.

Lohman, Joseph D.: *The Police and Minority Groups.* Chicago, Chicago Park District, 1947, 133 pp.

McEntire, Davis and Powers, Robert B.: *A Guide to Race Relations for Police Officers.* Sacramento, California, Department of Justice, State of California, 1946, 38 pp.

McMillan, George: *Racial Violence and Law Enforcement.* Atlanta, Southern Regional Council, 1960, 32 pp.

Rosenquist, Carl M.: *Social Problems.* New York, Prentice-Hall, Inc., 1940, 519 pp.

Simpson, George Eaton and Yinger, J. Milton: *Racial and Cultural Minorities,* New York, Harpers, 1958, 881 pp.

Weckler, J. E., and Hall, Theo. E.: *The Police and Minority Groups.* Chicago, International City Managers Association, 1944, 20 pp.

Wood, Sterling A.: *Riot Control.* Harrisburg, The Military Service Publishing Company, 1952, 172 pp.

# INDEX

By-racial Committee, 87

Casual crowd, 61
Civil Rights Code, 8, 9, 10
Civil War Amendments, 6, 7, 8
Conventional crowd, 62

Disaster Control Plan, 116
Disaster Field Commander, 124
Disaster Field Headquarters, 124
Disaster Headquarters Command, 122
Disaster Headquarters Commander, 123
Due process of law, 7

Economic conflict, 50
Equal protection of the law, 7
Expressive crowd, 63

Fourteenth Amendment, 6

Housing segregation, 48

Impartiality, 78
Individuality, 78
Inner blockade, 121
Intelligence comparison, 23

Mental differences, 23

Outer blockade, 122

Physiological differences, 21
Predilection, 28
Prejudgment, 27
Prejudices, 27
Privileges and immunities of citizens, 6
Psychological differences, 21

Reactions to prejudice, 39
Reasons for scapegoating, 29
Riot control procedures, 127
Riot control weapons, 128

Scapegoating, 29
Skin color, 22
Social conflict, 44
Sociological differences, 24

Tabloid thinking, 31
Tension, information on, 75

| CENTRAL PROCESS | PRIME ADAPTIVE EGO QUALITY | CORE PATHOLOGY | APPLIED TOPIC |
|---|---|---|---|
| | | | Abortion |
| Mutuality with caregiver | Hope | Withdrawal | The role of the parents |
| Imitation | Will | Compulsion | Childcare |
| Identification | Purpose | Inhibition | School readiness |
| Education | Competence | Inertia | Violence in the lives of children |
| Peer pressure | Fidelity to others | Dissociation | Adolescent alcohol and drug use |
| Role experimentation | Fidelity to values | Repudiation | Challenges of social life |
| Mutuality among peers | Love | Exclusivity | Divorce |
| Person-environment interaction and creativity | Care | Rejectivity | Discrimination in the workplace |
| Introspection | Wisdom | Disdain | Retirement |
| Social support | Confidence | Diffidence | Meeting the needs of the frail elderly |

# Development Through Life

## A PSYCHOSOCIAL APPROACH

### NINTH EDITION

**BARBARA M. NEWMAN**
**PHILIP R. NEWMAN**
UNIVERSITY OF RHODE ISLAND

THOMSON
WADSWORTH
Australia • Canada • Mexico • Singapore • Spain
United Kingdom • United States

# THOMSON
## WADSWORTH

**Development Through Life: A Psychosocial Approach, Ninth Edition**
*Barbara M. Newman and Philip R. Newman*

Executive Editor: Michele Sordi
Assistant Editor: Jennifer Keever
Editorial Assistant: Jessica Kim
Technology Project Manager: Erik Fortier
Marketing Manager: Dory Schaeffer
Marketing Assistant: Nicole Morinon
Marketing Communications Manager: Tami Strang
Project Manager, Editorial Production: Emily Smith
Art Director: Vernon Boes
Print Buyer: Doreen Suruki

Permissions Editor: Kiely Sisk
Production Service: G&S Book Services, Jamie Armstrong
Photo Researcher: Roman A. Barnes
Copy Editor: Jan Six
Illustrator: G&S Book Services
Compositor: G&S Book Services
Cover Designer: Cheryl Carrington
Cover Image: © 2004 Estate of Pablo Picasso/Artists Rights Society (ARS), New York
Text and Cover Printer: Quebecor World/Taunton

Printed in the United States of America
1 2 3 4 5 6 7 09 08 07 06 05

For more information about our products, contact us at:
**Thomson Learning Academic Resource Center**
**1-800-423-0563**
For permission to use material from this text or product, submit a request online at **http://www.thomsonrights.com**.
Any additional questions about permissions can be submitted by email to **thomsonrights@thomson.com**.

Library of Congress Control Number: 2005922291

Student Edition: ISBN 0-534-60725-X

Instructor's Edition: ISBN 0-495-06287-1

International Student Edition: ISBN 0-495-00733-1
(Not for sale in the United States)

**Thomson Higher Education**
**10 Davis Drive**
**Belmont, CA 94002-3098**
**USA**

**Asia (including India)**
Thomson Learning
5 Shenton Way
#01-01 UIC Building
Singapore 068808

**Australia/New Zealand**
Thomson Learning Australia
102 Dodds Street
Southbank, Victoria 3006
Australia

**Canada**
Thomson Nelson
1120 Birchmount Road
Toronto, Ontario M1K 5G4
Canada

**UK/Europe/Middle East/Africa**
Thomson Learning
High Holborn House
50–51 Bedford Row
London WC1R 4LR
United Kingdom

**Latin America**
Thomson Learning
Seneca, 53
Colonia Polanco
11560 Mexico
D.F. Mexico

**Spain (including Portugal)**
Thomson Paraninfo
Calle Magallanes, 25
28015 Madrid, Spain

# Brief Contents

**1**   The Development Through Life Perspective   2

**2**   The Research Process   16

**3**   Psychosocial Theory   36

**4**   Major Theories for Understanding Human Development   60

**5**   The Period of Pregnancy and Prenatal Development   90

**6**   lnfancy (First 24 Months)   134

**7**   Toddlerhood (Ages 2 and 3)   180

**8**   Early School Age (4–6 Years)   220

**9**   Middle Childhood (6–12 Years)   262

**10**   Early Adolescence (12–18 Years)   300

**11**   Later Adolescence (18–24 Years)   346

**12**   Early Adulthood (24–34 Years)   384

**13**   Middle Adulthood (34–60 Years)   430

**14**   Later Adulthood (60–75 Years)   468

**15**   Very Old Age (75 Until Death)   502

**16**   Understanding Death, Dying, and Bereavement   536

# Contents

## ■ 1 THE DEVELOPMENT THROUGH LIFE PERSPECTIVE 2

ASSUMPTIONS OF THE TEXT 5

A PSYCHOSOCIAL APPROACH:
THE INTERACTION OF THE BIOLOGICAL,
PSYCHOLOGICAL, AND SOCIETAL SYSTEMS 6
The Biological System 6
The Psychological System 6
The Societal System 7
The Psychosocial Impact of Poverty 8
APPLYING THEORY AND RESEARCH TO LIFE:
POVERTY 8
Overview of the Psychosocial Approach 9
CASE STUDY: ROSE 11

THE LIFE SPAN 11
Projections of Life Expectancy 12
Factors That Contribute to Longevity 13
TECHNOLOGY AND HUMAN DEVELOPMENT:
THE ROLE OF TECHNOLOGY IN THE STUDY
OF HUMAN DEVELOPMENT 14

CHAPTER SUMMARY 15

## ■ 2 THE RESEARCH PROCESS 16

THE SCIENTIFIC PROCESS 18
The Positivist Approach to Research 18
Scientific Observation 18
The Qualitative Inquiry Approach to Research 20

RESEARCH DESIGN 20
Sampling 20
Random Samples 21
Stratified Samples 21
Matched Groups 21
Volunteer Samples 21
The Qualitative Approach to Sampling 22
Strengths and Weaknesses of Approaches to
Sampling 22
Research Methods 23
Observation 23
TECHNOLOGY AND HUMAN DEVELOPMENT:
OBSERVATION USING VIDEO RECORDING 23
Case Study 25
Interviews 26
APPLYING THEORY AND RESEARCH TO LIFE:
PIAGET'S INTERVIEW METHOD 27
Surveys and Tests 28
HUMAN DEVELOPMENT AND DIVERSITY: THE USE
OF THE SAT IN COLLEGE ADMISSIONS 29
Experimentation 30

DESIGNS FOR STUDYING DEVELOPMENT 31
Retrospective Studies 31
Cross-Sectional Studies 32
Longitudinal Studies 33
Cohort Sequential Studies 33

EVALUATING EXISTING RESEARCH 33

ETHICS 34

CHAPTER SUMMARY 35

## ■ 3 PSYCHOSOCIAL THEORY 36

WHAT IS A THEORY? 38

THE RATIONALE FOR EMPHASIZING
PSYCHOSOCIAL THEORY 39

BASIC CONCEPTS OF PSYCHOSOCIAL THEORY 39
Stages of Development 40
Developmental Tasks 43
Psychosocial Crisis 44
Psychosocial Crises of the Life Stages 44
The Central Process for Resolving the
Psychosocial Crisis 47
Radius of Significant Relationships 48
Contexts of Development 49
Coping Behavior 50
Prime Adaptive Ego Qualities 52
Core Pathologies 53
CASE STUDY: ERIK H. ERIKSON:
A BIOGRAPHICAL CASE STUDY
OF PSYCHOSOCIAL DEVELOPMENT 53

EVALUATION OF PSYCHOSOCIAL THEORY 54
Strengths 54
Weaknesses 55
APPLYING THEORY AND RESEARCH TO LIFE:
STUDYING PSYCHOSOCIAL DEVELOPMENT
IN ADULTHOOD 56
A Recap of Psychosocial Theory 58

CHAPTER SUMMARY 59

## ■ 4 MAJOR THEORIES FOR UNDERSTANDING HUMAN DEVELOPMENT 60

THE THEORY OF EVOLUTION 62
Implications for Human Development 63
Links to Psychosocial Theory 64

PSYCHOSEXUAL THEORY   65
APPLYING THEORY AND RESEARCH TO LIFE:
  THE COGNITIVE UNCONSCIOUS   66
  Implications for Human Development   67
  Links to Psychosocial Theory   67

COGNITIVE DEVELOPMENTAL THEORY   68
  Basic Concepts in Piaget's Theory   68
  Implications for Human Development   70
  Vygotsky's Concepts of Cognitive Development   70
    Culture as a Mediator of Cognitive Structuring   70
    Movement from Intermental to Intramental   71
    The Zone of Proximal Development   71
  Implications for Human Development   72
  Links to Psychosocial Theory   72

THEORIES OF LEARNING   73
  Classical Conditioning   73
    Implications for Human Development   74
  Operant Conditioning   74
    Implications for Human Development   75
  Social Learning Theory   75
    Implications for Human Development   76
  Cognitive Behaviorism   76
    Implications for Human Development   77
  Summary of the Learning Theories   77
  Links to Psychosocial Theory   78

CULTURAL THEORY   78
  Implications for Human Development   79
HUMAN DEVELOPMENT AND DIVERSITY:
  IMPLICATIONS OF INDIVIDUALISM
  AND COLLECTIVISM FOR PARENTING
  PRACTICES   80
  Links to Psychosocial Theory   81

SOCIAL ROLE THEORY   81
  Implications for Human Development   82
  Links to Psychosocial Theory   82

SYSTEMS THEORY   82
APPLYING THEORY AND RESEARCH TO LIFE:
  ROLE STRAIN AND PARENTHOOD   83
  Implications for Human Development   85
  Links to Psychosocial Theory   86
CASE STUDY: JACK MANASKY AND
  HIS DAUGHTER MARILYN   86

CHAPTER SUMMARY   88

■5  THE PERIOD OF PREGNANCY
      AND PRENATAL
      DEVELOPMENT   90

GENETICS AND DEVELOPMENT   92
  Genes and Chromosomes as Sources of Genetic
    Information   92
  The Laws of Heredity   93
    Alleles   93

    Genotype and Phenotype   94
    Sex-Linked Characteristics   95
  Genetic Sources of Individual Differences   96
    Genetic Determinants of Rate of Development   96
    Genetic Determinants of Individual Traits   96
    Genetic Determinants of Abnormal Development   97
  Genetic Technology and Psychosocial Evolution   98
    Ethical Considerations   98
  Evaluating the Contribution of Genetic Factors
    to Behavior   99
    Genetics and Intelligence   99
    The Reaction Range   100

NORMAL FETAL DEVELOPMENT   101
  Fertilization   101
    Twins   101
    Infertility and Alternative Means of Reproduction   102
  Development in the First Trimester   103
TECHNOLOGY AND HUMAN DEVELOPMENT:
  REPRODUCTIVE TECHNOLOGIES   104
    The Germinal Period   104
    The Embryonic Period   104
    The Fetal Period   106
  Development in the Second Trimester   108
  Development in the Third Trimester   110
TECHNOLOGY AND HUMAN DEVELOPMENT:
  LOOKING IN ON THE FETUS   110

THE BIRTH PROCESS   111
  Stages of Labor   111
  Cesarean Delivery   111
  Infant Mortality   112
APPLYING THEORY AND RESEARCH TO LIFE:
  THE IMPACT OF CESAREAN DELIVERY   113

THE MOTHER, THE FETUS, AND THE
PSYCHOSOCIAL ENVIRONMENT   113
  The Impact of the Fetus on the Pregnant Woman   114
    Changes in Roles and Social Status   114
    Changes in the Mother's Emotional State   115
APPLYING THEORY AND RESEARCH TO LIFE:
  THE DOULA OR BIRTH COMPANION   115
    Fathers' Involvement During Pregnancy
      and Childbirth   116
CASE STUDY: A FATHER'S RECOLLECTIONS
  ABOUT HIS DAUGHTER'S BIRTH   117
  The Impact of the Pregnant Woman on the Fetus   118
    The Impact of Poverty   118
    Mother's Age   118
HUMAN DEVELOPMENT AND DIVERSITY:
  PSYCHOSOCIAL FACTORS LINKED TO PRETERM
  BIRTHS FOR AFRICAN AMERICAN AND EUROPEAN
  AMERICAN WOMEN   119
    Maternal Drug Use   120
HUMAN DEVELOPMENT AND DIVERSITY: AIDS AND
  MOTHER-TO-CHILD TRANSMISSION   122
    Environmental Toxins   123
    Mother's Diet   123

THE CULTURAL CONTEXT   124
  Reactions to Pregnancy   124
    Solicitude Versus Shame   124

HUMAN DEVELOPMENT AND DIVERSITY:
    COUVADE  125
        Adequacy Versus Vulnerability  125
HUMAN DEVELOPMENT AND DIVERSITY:
    TAEGYO (FETAL EDUCATION)  126
    Reactions to Childbirth  126

APPLIED TOPIC: ABORTION  128
    The Legal Context of Abortion in the United States  129
    The Incidence of Legal Abortions  129
    The Psychosocial Impact of Abortion  129
CASE STUDY: KAREN AND DON  130
    Men's Reactions to Abortion  131

CHAPTER SUMMARY  132


■ **6  INFANCY
    (FIRST 24 MONTHS)  134**

NEWBORNS  137

DEVELOPMENTAL TASKS  137
    The Development of Sensory/Perceptual and
        Motor Functions  137
TECHNOLOGY AND HUMAN DEVELOPMENT:
    VERY SMALL BABIES  138
        Sensory/Perceptual Development  139
        Motor Development  143
HUMAN DEVELOPMENT AND DIVERSITY:
    ZINACANTECO CHILDREARING  146
        Temperament  146
CASE STUDY: THE COTTON FAMILY  148
    Attachment  148
        The Development of Attachment  149
        Formation of Attachments with Mother, Father,
            and Others  152
        Patterns of Attachment  152
        Parental Sensitivity and the Quality of Attachment  154
        The Relevance of Attachment to Later
            Development  155
    Sensorimotor Intelligence and Early Causal Schemes  157
        How Infants Organize Their Experiences  157
        The Development of Causal Schemes  157
    Understanding the Nature of Objects and
        Creating Categories  159
        The Nature of Objects  159
        The Categorization of Objects  160
    Emotional Development  161
        Emotional Differentiation  161
        Emotions as a Key to Understanding Meaning  164
        The Ability to Regulate Emotions  164
APPLYING THEORY AND RESEARCH TO LIFE:
    THE MEANING OF AN INFANT'S SMILE  165
        Emotions as a Channel for Adult–Infant
            Communication  166

THE PSYCHOSOCIAL CRISIS:
TRUST VERSUS MISTRUST  167
    Trust  167
    Mistrust  167

THE CENTRAL PROCESS FOR RESOLVING THE
CRISIS: MUTUALITY WITH THE CAREGIVER  168
    Coordination, Mismatch, and Repair of Interactions  169
    Establishing a Functional Rhythm in the Family  169
APPLYING THEORY AND RESEARCH TO LIFE:
    IS THERE A CRITICAL PERIOD FOR
    ATTACHMENT?  170
    Parents With Psychological Problems  170

THE PRIME ADAPTIVE EGO QUALITY
AND THE CORE PATHOLOGY  171
    Hope  171
APPLYING THEORY AND RESEARCH TO LIFE:
    FOSTERING MUTUALITY AMONG DISTRESSED
    MOTHERS AND THEIR INFANTS  172
    Withdrawal  173

APPLIED TOPIC: THE ROLE OF PARENTS  174
    Safety in the Physical Environment  174
TECHNOLOGY AND HUMAN DEVELOPMENT:
    INFANT SAFETY  175
    Fostering Emotional and Cognitive Development  176
    Fathers' and Mothers' Parental Behavior  176
    Parents as Advocates  177
    The Importance of Social Support  177

CHAPTER SUMMARY  178


■ **7  TODDLERHOOD
    (AGES 2 AND 3)  180**
CASE STUDY: ALICE WALKER GOES TO
    THE FAIR  183

DEVELOPMENTAL TASKS  183
    Elaboration of Locomotion  183
    Language Development  185
        Semiotic Thinking  185
        Communicative Competence  185
TECHNOLOGY AND HUMAN DEVELOPMENT:
    HOW THE BRAIN PROCESSES LANGUAGE  186
        Communication Accomplishments in Infancy  187
        Communicative Competence in Toddlerhood  189
        Language Development Beyond Toddlerhood  191
        The Language Environment  192
HUMAN DEVELOPMENT AND DIVERSITY:
    BILINGUALISM  194
    Fantasy Play  197
        The Nature of Pretend Play  197
        The Capacity for Pretense  198
        Changes in Fantasy Play During Toddlerhood  198
TECHNOLOGY AND HUMAN DEVELOPMENT:
    CHILDREN'S TOYS  199
        The Contributions of Fantasy Play to
            Development  200
        The Role of Play Companions  201
APPLYING THEORY AND RESEARCH TO LIFE:
    IMAGINARY COMPANIONS  201
    Self-Control  202
        Language and Fantasy as Strategies for Controlling
            Impulses  202

APPLYING THEORY AND RESEARCH TO LIFE:
THE CONTROL OF ANGRY FEELINGS    203
    Control of Impulses    203
    Self-Regulated Goal Attainment    206

THE PSYCHOSOCIAL CRISIS: AUTONOMY
VERSUS SHAME AND DOUBT    207
  Autonomy    208
  Shame and Doubt    208
HUMAN DEVELOPMENT AND DIVERSITY:
TOILET TRAINING    209

THE CENTRAL PROCESS: IMITATION    210

THE PRIME ADAPTIVE EGO QUALITY AND
THE CORE PATHOLOGY    211
  Will    211
  Compulsion    211

THE IMPACT OF POVERTY ON PSYCHOSOCIAL
DEVELOPMENT IN TODDLERHOOD    212

APPLIED TOPIC: CHILD CARE    214
  The Impact of Child Care on Intelligence and Academic
    Achievement    215
  The Impact of Child Care on Social Competence    216
  The Impact of Child Care on Peer Relations    217
  Directions for the Future of Child Care in the
    United States    217

CHAPTER SUMMARY    218

## ■8 EARLY SCHOOL AGE (4–6 YEARS)    220

DEVELOPMENTAL TASKS    222
  Gender Identification    223
CASE STUDY: GENDER IDENTIFICATION IN
EARLY CHILDHOOD    223
    Individual Differences Versus Constructivism    224
    Understanding Gender    225
    Gender Role Standards    226
    Identification with Parents    227
    Gender Preference    228
APPLYING THEORY AND RESEARCH TO LIFE:
CHILDREN RAISED BY GAY OR LESBIAN
PARENTS    229
  Early Moral Development    230
    Learning Theory    231
    Cognitive Developmental Theory    232
APPLYING THEORY AND RESEARCH TO LIFE:
MORAL TRANSGRESSIONS, SOCIAL CONVENTION,
AND PERSONAL CHOICE    234
    Psychoanalytic Theory    235
CASE STUDY: EARLY LEARNING ABOUT
OBEDIENCE    236
    Empathy and Perspective Taking    236
    Parental Discipline    238
    The Impact of Television on Moral Development    239
    Review of Influences on Moral Development    241

TECHNOLOGY AND HUMAN DEVELOPMENT: MEDIA USE
BY INFANTS, TODDLERS, AND PRESCHOOLERS    242
  Self-Theory    243
    The Me and the I    243
    Developmental Changes in the Self-Theory    245
    Theory of Mind    246
    Self-Esteem    247
  Peer Play    248
    Group Games    249
HUMAN DEVELOPMENT AND DIVERSITY:
HOPSCOTCH    249
    Friendship Groups    250

THE PSYCHOSOCIAL CRISIS:
INITIATIVE VERSUS GUILT    251
  Initiative    251
  Guilt    252

THE CENTRAL PROCESS: IDENTIFICATION    254

THE PRIME ADAPTIVE EGO QUALITY
AND THE CORE PATHOLOGY    256
  Purpose    256
  Inhibition    256

APPLIED TOPIC: SCHOOL READINESS    257
  Defining Readiness    257
  Measuring Kindergarten Readiness    257
  Obstacles to School Readiness    259
  Who Is Responsible for Meeting the Goal for School
    Readiness?    259
HUMAN DEVELOPMENT AND DIVERSITY:
SUPPORTING SCHOOL READINESS FOR YOUNG
CHILDREN WITH DISABILITIES    260

CHAPTER SUMMARY    260

## ■9 MIDDLE CHILDHOOD (6–12 YEARS)    262

DEVELOPMENTAL TASKS    265
  Friendship    265
    Family Influences on Social Competence    265
    Three Contributions of Friendship to Social
      Development    266
    Loneliness    268
APPLYING THEORY AND RESEARCH TO LIFE:
BULLYING    269
  Concrete Operations    270
    Conservation    271
    Classification Skills    273
    Combinatorial Skills    274
    Metacognition    275
  Skill Learning    275
HUMAN DEVELOPMENT AND DIVERSITY:
WHAT IS INTELLIGENCE?    276
    Features of Skilled Learning    277
    Reading    277
HUMAN DEVELOPMENT AND DIVERSITY:
CROSS-NATIONAL COMPARISONS OF
MATHEMATICS ABILITY    279
  Self-Evaluation    280
    Self-Efficacy    280

CASE STUDY: BECCA   281
   Social Expectations   281
   Team Play   285
      Interdependence   285
      Division of Labor   285
      Competition   286
      Ingroup and Outgroup Attitudes   287

THE PSYCHOSOCIAL CRISIS: INDUSTRY
VERSUS INFERIORITY   288
   Industry   288
   Inferiority   289
HUMAN DEVELOPMENT AND DIVERSITY:
   DISORDERS OF CHILDHOOD THAT INTERFERE
   WITH SCHOOL SUCCESS   290

THE CENTRAL PROCESS: EDUCATION   291

THE PRIME ADAPTIVE EGO QUALITY AND
THE CORE PATHOLOGY   293
   Competence   293
   Inertia   294
TECHNOLOGY AND HUMAN DEVELOPMENT:
   TECHNOLOGY AND SCHOOLING   295

APPLIED TOPIC: VIOLENCE IN THE LIVES
OF CHILDREN   296
   Consequences of Exposure to Violence   296
   Prevention Strategies   297

CHAPTER SUMMARY   298

## ■ 10 EARLY ADOLESCENCE (12–18 YEARS)   300

DEVELOPMENTAL TASKS   303
   Physical Maturation   303
CASE STUDY: CARLY PATTERSON,
   OLYMPIC GYMNAST   303
      Physical Changes in Girls   304
      Physical Changes in Boys   307
      Cultural Contexts of Puberty   308
      The Secular Growth Trend   308
      Individual Differences in Maturation Rate   308
   Formal Operations   309
APPLYING THEORY AND RESEARCH TO LIFE:
   SLEEP LOSS IN ADOLESCENCE   310
      Piaget's Theory of Formal Operational Thought   310
      Six Characteristics of Formal Operational
         Thought   312
      Egocentrism and Decentering   312
      Factors That Promote Formal Operational
         Thought   313
      Criticisms of the Concept of Formal Operational
         Thought   315
   Emotional Development   315
      Eating Disorders   316
      Delinquency   317
      Depression   318

APPLYING THEORY AND RESEARCH TO LIFE:
   ADOLESCENT SUICIDE   319
   Membership in the Peer Group   321
      Cliques and Crowds   321
      Boundaries and Norms   322
      Parents and Peers   323
   Romantic and Sexual Relationships   324
      The Transition into Sexualized Relationships   324
      Sexual Orientation   327
      Problems and Conflicts Associated with
         Sexuality   328
      Parenthood in Early Adolescence   330
HUMAN DEVELOPMENT AND DIVERSITY:
   TEEN FATHERS   332

THE PSYCHOSOCIAL CRISIS: GROUP IDENTITY
VERSUS ALIENATION   333
   Group Identity   333
      Cognitive Processes That Support Formation
         of Group Identity   333
      Four Dimensions of Group Identity   334
   Alienation   335
      The Contribution of Alienation to Group Identity
         and Individual Identity   336

THE CENTRAL PROCESS: PEER PRESSURE   336
   Affiliating with a Peer Group   337
   Peer Influence in Specific Areas   337
   Conflicts Between Belonging and Personal Autonomy   337
APPLYING THEORY AND RESEARCH TO LIFE:
   GANGS   338
   Ethnic Group Identity   339

THE PRIME ADAPTIVE EGO QUALITY
AND THE CORE PATHOLOGY   340
   Fidelity to Others   340
   Dissociation   341

APPLIED TOPIC: ADOLESCENT ALCOHOL
AND DRUG USE   341
   Factors Associated with Alcohol Use   341
      Physical Effects of Alcohol   341
      Assessment of Risk   342
      Reference Groups   342
   Early Entry Into Alcohol and Drug Use   343

CHAPTER SUMMARY   344

## ■ 11 LATER ADOLESCENCE (18–24 YEARS)   346

DEVELOPMENTAL TASKS   349
   Autonomy From Parents   349
      Autonomy and Leaving Home   350
      Autonomy and the College Experience   350
      Autonomy and Self-Sufficiency   351
APPLYING THEORY AND RESEARCH TO LIFE:
   ATTACHMENT AND IDENTITY FORMATION   352
   Gender Identity   353
      The Role of Culture   353

HUMAN DEVELOPMENT AND DIVERSITY: GENDER
   ROLES IN THE HINDU JOINT FAMILY   354
      Reevaluating Gender Constancy   354
      Reevaluating Earlier Gender Role Standards and
         Learning New Ones   355
      Revising One's Childhood Identification   355
      Adding a Sexual Dimension to Gender Identity   356
      Sexual Orientation   356
      Integrating One's Gender Identity   358
   Internalized Morality   358
      New Cognitive Capacities   359
      Stages of Moral Reasoning   359
      Experiences That Promote Moral Reasoning   359
      Expansions of Kohlberg's View of Moral
         Development   360
   Career Choice   361
      Work Experiences in Early Adolescence   362
      Factors Influencing Career Choice   362
      Career Decision Making   365
TECHNOLOGY AND HUMAN DEVELOPMENT:
   CAREER EXPLORATION ON THE WEB   368

THE PSYCHOSOCIAL CRISIS: INDIVIDUAL
IDENTITY VERSUS IDENTITY CONFUSION   369
   Individual Identity   369
      The Private and the Public Faces of Identity   370
      The Content and Evaluation Components of
         Identity   370
   CASE STUDY: HOUSTON A. BAKER, JR.   371
      Identity Status   371
   Identity Confusion   373
   Identity Formation for Men and Women   374

THE CENTRAL PROCESS:
ROLE EXPERIMENTATION   375
   Psychosocial Moratorium   375
   CASE STUDY: TURNING POINTS IN THE
      IDENTITY PROCESS   377
   Role Experimentation and Ethnic Identity   377
   HUMAN DEVELOPMENT AND DIVERSITY:
      ETHNIC IDENTITY AND ADJUSTMENT   379

THE PRIME ADAPTIVE EGO QUALITY
AND THE CORE PATHOLOGY   379
   Fidelity to Values and Ideologies   379
   Repudiation   379

APPLIED TOPIC: THE CHALLENGES
OF SOCIAL LIFE   380
   Unwanted Sexual Attention   380
   Binge Drinking   381
   Sexually Transmitted Diseases   381

CHAPTER SUMMARY   382

## ■ 12 EARLY ADULTHOOD (24–34 YEARS)   384

MAJOR CONCEPTS IN THE STUDY OF
ADULTHOOD   386
   Social Roles   387
   Life Course   388
   Fulfillment Theories   389
      Competence   390
      Self-Acceptance   390
      Self-Actualization   390

DEVELOPMENTAL TASKS   392
   Exploring Intimate Relationships   392
      Readiness to Marry   393
      Selection of a Partner   393
   TECHNOLOGY AND HUMAN DEVELOPMENT:
      COMPUTER-MEDIATED RELATIONSHIPS
      (ONLINE DATING)   396
   CASE STUDY: HOW LOVE MAKES ITS WAY INTO
      A RELATIONSHIP   398
      Cohabitation   399
      Partners of the Same Sex   400
      Adjustment During the Early Years of Marriage   402
      Adjustment in Dual-Earner Marriages   404
   Childbearing   405
      Fertility Rate   405
      Decisions About Childbearing   405
   HUMAN DEVELOPMENT AND DIVERSITY:
      THE REPRODUCTIVE CAREER OF THE GUSII   406
      The Dual Roles of Intimate Partner and Parent   407
      The Decision Not to Have Children   408
   Work   409
      The World of Work   409
   CASE STUDY: JAY CROWE   410
      Poverty and Career Opportunities   413
      Career Phases and Individual Development   413
   Lifestyle   415
      Pace of Life   415
      Social Network   415
      Competing Role Demands   415
      Health and Fitness   417

THE PSYCHOSOCIAL CRISIS:
INTIMACY VERSUS ISOLATION   417
   Intimacy   417
   APPLYING THEORY AND RESEARCH TO LIFE:
      ATTACHMENT STYLES AND RELATIONSHIP
      FORMATION   418
      Interaction Styles of Men and Women   419
      Intimacy in the Work Setting   419
   Isolation   419
      Loneliness   420
      Depression   420
      Fragile Identity   421
      Sexual Disorders   421
      Situational Factors   421
      Divergent Spheres of Interest   421
      Enmeshment   421

THE CENTRAL PROCESS: MUTUALITY
AMONG PEERS   422

THE PRIME ADAPTIVE EGO QUALITY
AND THE CORE PATHOLOGY   422
   Love   422
   Exclusivity   423

APPLIED TOPIC: DIVORCE   423
   Factors Contributing to Divorce   424
      Age at Marriage   425
      Socioeconomic Level   425
      Socioemotional Development of the Partners   426
      Family History of Divorce   426
   Coping with Divorce   426
      Attachment to a Former Spouse   427
      Coping Strategies   427

CHAPTER SUMMARY   428

## ■ 13 MIDDLE ADULTHOOD (34–60 YEARS)   430

DEVELOPMENTAL TASKS   432
   Managing a Career   432
      Achieving New Levels of Competence in the World of Work   433
      Midlife Career Changes   436
      Balancing Work and Family Life   437
      The Impact of Joblessness   440
TECHNOLOGY AND HUMAN DEVELOPMENT: WORKPLACE AGGRESSION   441
   Nurturing an Intimate Relationship   442
      Characteristics of the Partners   442
      Partners' Interpersonal Interactions   442
      Partners' Commitment to Nurturing the Future of the Relationship   443
CASE STUDY: THE STRUGGLE FOR COMMITMENT TO GROWTH IN A VITAL MARRIAGE   443
      Preserving Passion in a Long-Term Relationship   444
HUMAN DEVELOPMENT AND DIVERSITY: MENOPAUSE   445
   Expanding Caring Relationships   446
      Parenting   446
      Developmental Stages of the Family   446
      Caring for One's Aging Parents   449
CASE STUDY: A DAUGHTER CARES FOR HER AILING MOTHER   451
   Managing the Household   452
      Managing Resources and Meeting Needs   452
      Building Networks and Coalitions   453
      Remarriage and Blended Families   454
      One-Parent Families   454
APPLYING THEORY AND RESEARCH TO LIFE: HOMELESSNESS   456
      People Who Live Alone   456

THE PSYCHOSOCIAL CRISIS: GENERATIVITY VERSUS STAGNATION   457
   Generativity   457
      Measuring Generativity   458
CASE STUDY: MY LEADERSHIP JOURNEY   459
   Stagnation   460

THE CENTRAL PROCESS: PERSON–ENVIRONMENT INTERACTION AND CREATIVITY   460
   Person–Environment Interaction   460
   Creativity   461

THE PRIME ADAPTIVE EGO QUALITY AND THE CORE PATHOLOGY   463
   Care   463
   Rejectivity   463

APPLIED TOPIC: DISCRIMINATION IN THE WORKPLACE   463
   Disparities in Income and the Occupational Structure   464
   How Discrimination Perpetuates Itself   464
   Psychosocial Analysis: Discrimination and Coping   465

CHAPTER SUMMARY   466

## ■ 14 LATER ADULTHOOD (60–75 YEARS)   468

DEVELOPMENTAL TASKS   471
   Accepting One's Life   471
      Life Goals and Satisfaction   471
CASE STUDY: GOAL ADJUSTMENT IN LATER ADULTHOOD   472
      Personality and Well-Being   473
      Illness and Health   474
      The SOC Model   474
      Erikson on Accepting One's Life   475
   Promoting Intellectual Vigor   475
      Problems in Defining and Studying Intelligence in Later Adulthood   475
      Memory   476
      Postformal Operational Thinking   477
      Patterns of Change in Different Mental Abilities   478
      The Interaction of Heredity and Environment on Mental Functioning   479
APPLYING THEORY AND RESEARCH TO LIFE: AGE AND WORKPLACE PRODUCTIVITY   480
   Redirecting Energy to New Roles and Activities   481
      Grandparenthood   481
HUMAN DEVELOPMENT AND DIVERSITY: INTERGENERATIONAL RELATIONSHIPS IN VARIOUS ETHNIC GROUPS   482
      Widowhood   485
      Leisure Activities   487
TECHNOLOGY AND HUMAN DEVELOPMENT: THE USE OF THE INTERNET AMONG OLDER ADULTS   488
   Developing a Point of View About Death   490
      Changing Perspectives About Death   490
CASE STUDY: MORRIE SCHWARTZ REFLECTS ON HIS VIEWS ABOUT DEATH   491
      Death Anxiety   492

THE PSYCHOSOCIAL CRISIS: INTEGRITY VERSUS DESPAIR   493
   Integrity   493
   Despair   493
      Depression   494

THE CENTRAL PROCESS: INTROSPECTION   494

THE PRIME ADAPTIVE EGO QUALITY AND
THE CORE PATHOLOGY  495
    Wisdom  495
    Disdain  496

APPLIED TOPIC: RETIREMENT  496
    Adjustment to Retirement  497
    Difficulties with Retirement  498
    CASE STUDY: RETIREMENT AS A RELEASE FROM
    TEDIOUS WORK  498
        Income Loss  499
    The Future of Retirement  499

CHAPTER SUMMARY  500

## ■ 15 VERY OLD AGE (75 UNTIL DEATH)  502

THE LONGEVITY REVOLUTION  504
    A New Psychosocial Stage: Very Old Age  505
    The Gender Gap Among the Very Old  506

DEVELOPMENTAL TASKS  507
    Coping with the Physical Changes of Aging  507
        Fitness  507
        Behavioral Slowing  508
        Sensory Changes  510
        Health, Illness, and Functional Independence  512
    APPLYING THEORY AND RESEARCH TO LIFE:
    ORGANIC BRAIN SYNDROMES: DEMENTIA  512
        Developing a Psychohistorical Perspective  514
        Traveling Uncharted Territory: Life Structures of the
        Very Old  516
        Living Arrangements  517
    APPLYING THEORY AND RESEARCH TO LIFE:
    THE IMPACT OF GENTRIFICATION ON THE
    VERY OLD  519
    CASE STUDY: MR. Z  521
        Gender Role Definitions  522

THE PSYCHOSOCIAL CRISIS: IMMORTALITY
VERSUS EXTINCTION  525
    Immortality  525
    HUMAN DEVELOPMENT AND DIVERSITY:
    THE RESPONSIBILITY OF NATIVE HAWAIIANS
    FOR THEIR ANCESTORS' REMAINS  526
    Extinction  526
    APPLYING THEORY AND RESEARCH TO LIFE:
    ERIKSON ON COPING WITH AGING  527

THE CENTRAL PROCESS: SOCIAL SUPPORT  527
    The Benefits of Social Support  528
    The Dynamics of Social Support  528
    The Social Support Network  529

THE PRIME ADAPTIVE EGO QUALITY AND THE
CORE PATHOLOGY  530
    Confidence  530
    Diffidence  530

APPLIED TOPIC: MEETING THE NEEDS OF THE
FRAIL ELDERLY  531
    Defining Frailty  531
    Supporting Optimal Functioning  532
    The Role of the Community  533
    The Role of Creative Action  533

CHAPTER SUMMARY  535

## ■ 16 UNDERSTANDING DEATH, DYING, AND BEREAVEMENT  536

MORTALITY AND PSYCHOSOCIAL
DEVELOPMENT  538

DEFINITIONS OF DEATH  539

THE PROCESS OF DYING  540
    CASE STUDY: TOO LATE TO DIE YOUNG  540
    The Good Death  542
        Hospice Care  543
        Euthanasia  543
    The Ethical Issues at the End of Life  544

DEATH-RELATED RITUALS  545
    Care of the Body  545
    Care of the Spirit  546
    Care of the Surviving Family, Friends, and
    Community  546
    HUMAN DEVELOPMENT AND DIVERSITY:
    THE AMISH WAY OF DEATH  547

GRIEF AND BEREAVEMENT  548
    Definitions  548
    Grief Work  549
    Five Patterns of Bereavement Among Widows  550
    Factors That Affect the Distress of Survivors  551
        Unacknowledged and Stigmatized Loss  551
    APPLYING THEORY AND RESEARCH TO LIFE:
    AMBIGUOUS LOSS  552

PSYCHOSOCIAL GROWTH THROUGH
BEREAVEMENT  553

CHAPTER SUMMARY  554

GLOSSARY  G-2

REFERENCES  R-2

CREDITS  C-2

NAME INDEX  I-2

SUBJECT INDEX  I-10

# Preface

WE ARE PLEASED to introduce the ninth edition of *Development Through Life: A Psychosocial Approach*. We have been thrilled over the years with the positive feedback we've received on the text, and are delighted about this new edition, which retains the features that students and faculty have praised, while reflecting the latest developments in the field. Psychosocial theory and the stage approach provide the core organizing framework. We have added a new chapter on death, dying, and bereavement at the request of many faculty who use the text. In keeping with our focus on positive aspects of development at each stage, we have attempted to present the end of life as a stimulus for new psychosocial growth for the dying person and for the survivors. Writing this chapter has expanded our own appreciation for the role of mortality in guiding meaning making.

We strengthened some of the emphases from the eighth edition by including the chapter on research methods, expanding our use of case studies and first person accounts, and enhancing the coverage of diversity by examining development across nations and among American ethnic groups. As always, we have updated the text carefully and thoroughly to reflect new theories, research, and applications. In this edition, we have taken new steps to demonstrate the usefulness of theory and research in human development for a critical understanding of real-world topics and social issues. More and more, research in our field involves carefully designed and controlled interventions that inform our understanding of risk, vulnerability, and resilience. We are learning how to intervene so that deficits can be overcome and more positive developmental trajectories can be supported. We believe that students who are educated about the science of human development can be strong advocates for optimal development in their families, schools, work settings, and communities.

## THE STAGE APPROACH

This edition provides a thorough chronological introduction to the study of human development from conception through very old age. The text treats physical, intellectual, social, and emotional growth in each of the 11 stages, emphasizing that development results from the interdependence of these areas at every stage. This strategy gives full attention to important developmental themes that recur in different stages of life. For each life stage, the process of development is linked to internal conflicts, changing self-awareness, and a dynamic social environment. As a result, students gain a sense of a multidimensional person, striving toward new levels of competence and mastery, embedded in multiple contexts.

## ADVANTAGES OF THE PSYCHOSOCIAL FRAMEWORK

Psychosocial theory provides an organizing conceptual framework that highlights the continuous interaction and integration of individual competencies with the demands and resources of culture. Development is viewed as a product of genetic, maturational, societal, and self-directed factors. Applying this integrated perspective to an analysis of human development has several advantages:

- Although the subject matter is potentially overwhelming, the psychosocial framework helps to identify and emphasize themes and directions of growth across the life span.
- The psychosocial framework helps readers assess the influence of experiences during earlier life stages on later development.
- The psychosocial framework clarifies how one's past, present, and expectations of the future are systematically connected to the lives of people who are older and younger. This perspective highlights issues of intergenerational transmission and the reciprocal influences of the generations.
- The framework offers a hopeful outlook on the total life course. Positive psychological capacities, such as hope, purpose, love, and caring, promote growth and help to clarify how a personal worldview develops. The promise of continuous growth in later adulthood and very old age validates the struggles of childhood, adolescence, and adulthood.
- The psychosocial perspective locates development within a framework of significant relationships. This helps students appreciate the idea that a sense of self and a sense of others emerge and mature together, fostering the simultaneous and complementary processes of autonomy and connection.

## THE LIFE-SPAN PERSPECTIVE

When we wrote the first edition of *Development Through Life*, we had just completed graduate study, we had two young children, and were in the midst of early adulthood. Now, at the publication of the ninth edition, we have celebrated the birth of two grandchildren, our three adult children are living in cities across the country and are embedded in their careers, and we are entering later adulthood.

The psychosocial, life-span perspective has been a valuable orienting framework for our scholarly work as well as our personal lives. It has provided insights into the birth and parenting of our three children; the death of our parents; the successes, disappointments, and transitions of our work lives; and the conflicts and delights of our relationship as husband and wife. The themes of this book have allowed us to anticipate and cope with the challenges of adult life, and to remain hopeful in the face of crises. We hope that the ideas presented in this text will provide these same benefits for you.

In addition to enhancing self-understanding, the life-span perspective is a means of comprehending the conflicts, opportunities, and achievements of central importance to people living through different stages than one's own. In this respect, it challenges our egocentrism. The life-span perspective assumes an interconnection among people at every period of life. This knowledge helps guide interactions with others so that they are optimally sensitive, supportive, and facilitative for growth at each life stage.

## EFFECTS OF CULTURAL AND HISTORICAL CONTEXTS

Studying development over the course of life requires sensitivity to ways societies change over time. The developing person exists in a changing cultural and historical context. Events since the eighth edition was published include the escalating war on terror; the invasion of Iraq and subsequent events, including democratic elections and ongoing violence; the Tsunami disaster in Southeast Asia; the death of Pope John Paul II; the reelection of a Republican president and Republican majorities in the United States Senate and House of Representatives; the loss of hundreds of thousands of jobs in the United States; and the continued escalation of the AIDS epidemic in Africa and China. These are just a few examples of the contexts in which development takes place that may dramatically alter people's lived experiences. Nothing could be more fascinating than trying to understand patterns of continuity and change over the life course within the context of a changing environment.

## EFFECTS OF TECHNOLOGY

Advances in technology continue to expand resources, alter patterns of communication, and influence the course of development. The mapping of the human genome expands the universe of possibilities for understanding the genetic components of life and for the maintenance and improvement of human health. Through medical interventions, about 50 percent of tiny babies weighing 500 to 750 grams can survive. Accurate, timely, and useful information is now available at our fingertips through the Internet. E-mail, cell phones, instant-messaging, and wireless Internet zones allow us to stay in touch with family members, coworkers, and friends in ways that were not possible a few years ago. Infants and toddlers are playing with interactive toys that respond to their touch or voice commands. Children in early school age use computers to play games, send messages, and find new information. In this edition of *Development Through Life*, we have highlighted examples of technology at each stage of life and provided discussions of its impact on development.

## EFFECTS OF POVERTY, DISCRIMINATION, AND OTHER FORMS OF SOCIETAL OPPRESSION

Numerous examples of the ways that poverty, discrimination, and various forms of societal oppression affect individual development are interwoven throughout the text. The expanding literature aids the further analysis of poverty by pointing out how it can influence development. At the same time, increased research on resilience illustrates the remarkable capacities for growth and adaptation at every period of life.

# ORGANIZATION

The following summarizes the basic organization of the text.

## INTRODUCING THE FIELD AND A CHAPTER ON RESEARCH: CHAPTERS 1–4

Chapter 1 describes the orientation and assumptions of the text and introduces the life-span perspective. Chapter 2 presents a detailed discussion of the positivist and qualitative approaches to the research process as it is applied to the study of human development. Chapter 3 introduces basic concepts of psychosocial theory, including an analysis of its strengths and weaknesses. Chapter 4 outlines significant ideas about change and growth from other theoretical perspectives. The presentation of each theory emphasizes its basic features, its implications for the study of human development, and its links to psychosocial theory.

## THE LATEST ON FETAL DEVELOPMENT AND GENETICS: CHAPTER 5

In Chapter 5, fetal development is presented, highlighting the bidirectional influences of the fetus and the pregnant woman within her social and cultural environments. Continued discoveries in the field of behavioral genetics have been included in this revision. We have emphasized research on the risks to fetal development associated with a pregnant woman's exposure to a wide range of substances, especially nicotine, alcohol, caffeine, other drugs, and environmental toxins. Poverty is discussed as a situation in which the risk increases for suboptimal fetal development. This chapter includes a detailed description of cultural differences in the way pregnancy and childbirth are conceptualized, providing a first model for considering the psychosocial process as it will unfold in subsequent chapters.

## GROWTH AND DEVELOPMENT FROM INFANCY TO VERY OLD AGE: CHAPTERS 6–15

Chapters 6 through 15 trace basic patterns of normal growth and development in infancy, toddlerhood, early school age, middle childhood, early adolescence, later adolescence, early adulthood, middle adulthood, later adulthood, and very old age. In these chapters we consider how individuals organize and interpret their experience, noting changes in their behavior, attitudes, worldview, and the coping strategies that they use in the face of changing environmental demands.

Each chapter begins with an examination of four or five of the critical developmental tasks of the stage. These tasks reflect global aspects of development, including physical maturation, sensory and motor competence, cognitive maturation, emotional development, social relationships, and self-understanding. We consider the psychosocial crisis of each stage in some detail. We also show how successfully resolving a crisis helps individuals develop a prime adaptive ego quality and how unsuccessful resolution leads to a core pathology. Although most people grow developmentally—albeit with pain and struggle—others do not. People who acquire prime adaptive ego qualities are more likely to lead active, flexible, agentic lives, and be resilient in the face of stressors. People who acquire core pathologies are more likely to lead withdrawn, guarded lives; they are more vulnerable to stressors resulting in greater risk of mental and physical health problems.

## APPLIED TOPICS AT THE END OF EACH CHAPTER

We conclude each chapter by applying research and theory to a topic of societal importance. These applied topics provide an opportunity for students to link the research and theory about normative developmental processes to the analysis of pressing social concerns. The flyleaf on the front cover of the book contains an overview of the basic tasks, crises, and applied topics for each stage of life.

## UNDERSTANDING DEATH, DYING, AND BEREAVEMENT: CHAPTER 16

The book closes with a new chapter—Understanding Death, Dying, and Bereavement—that brings special attention to end-of-life issues within a psychosocial framework. As with the developmental stage chapters, the topic illustrates the interaction of the biological, psychological, and societal systems as they contribute to the experiences of dying, grieving, and bereavement.

# NEW TO THIS EDITION

The ninth edition has retained the basic structure and positive developmental emphasis of previous editions. Many new sections bring greater clarity, elaboration, and a fresh way of thinking about a topic. The text has been completely updated. New research findings and recent census data have been integrated into the narrative.

## NEW CHAPTER 16: UNDERSTANDING DEATH, DYING, AND BEREAVEMENT

A new chapter on death, dying, and bereavement provides psychosocial analysis of numerous end-of-life topics, including definitions of death, the process of dying, death-related rituals, and grief and bereavement. The chapter emphasizes the role of culture in shaping ideas about death and expres-

sions of grief. We conclude the chapter with a discussion of the opportunities for psychosocial growth that are a result of bereavement and the considerations of one's own mortality.

## MORE ON THE ROLE OF DIVERSITY

This edition includes expanded coverage and examples of multiculturalism within the United States. New boxes entitled *Human Development and Diversity* provide more detail about individual and group differences, including a focus on culture, disabilities, sexual orientation, and ethnic identity.

## INCREASED USE OF CASE MATERIAL

We incorporate a great deal of case material including more first-person narratives, short vignettes, and links to illustrative cases in *Life-Span Development: A Casebook*. The case material helps to highlight the uniqueness of individual life stories. We have found this resource to be extremely useful in the classroom. Students relate to it, and it helps them appreciate their own lives and the lives of those who are close to them. Case material throughout the text illustrates the tension between understanding normative patterns of development and understanding individual life stories.

## INCREASED COVERAGE OF THE ROLE OF FATHERS

In several places throughout the life span we discuss the role and experience of fathers. In Pregnancy and Prenatal Development, we include a new box about a father's recollections of his daughter's birth; in Infancy, we feature new research on father-infant interaction and attachment, and we added a discussion on sensitive fathering; in Early Adolescence, we introduce a new box on teen fathers; and in Middle Adulthood, we present qualitative research on stepfathers.

## EXPANDED COVERAGE OF COGNITION

The ninth edition provides new information about cognition across the life span. In the chapter on theories, we incorporated a new box about the cognitive unconscious and a focus on the human mind and adaptive behavior; in Infancy, we explore new research on infants' understanding of the nature of objects and the ability to categorize objects; in Toddlerhood, we discuss pretense and young children's theory of the mind and how the brain adapts when children are bilingual; in Early School Age, we present new research on theory of mind; in Middle Childhood, we have extensively revised a discussion of concrete operational thought, and we include new research on children's literacy and mathematical problem solving; in Early Adolescence, we follow the changes in brain development that accompany new cognitive capacities and the links between emotion and cognition; in Early Adulthood, we discuss problem solving and conflict resolution in newly married couples; in Later Adulthood, we feature new research on memory and on expertise; and in Very Old Age, we offer a new discussion on executive functioning.

## NEW COVERAGE OF INTERGENERATIONAL RELATIONSHIPS

In addition to the longitudinal studies of individuals, a number of studies have recently reported findings about families over time. Some of the topics include the intergenerational transmission of divorce, the composition of multigenerational households, and ethnic differences in intergenerational relationships in families.

## FEATURES THAT SUPPORT LEARNING

Several features are included in the ninth edition that we expect will contribute to the learning process.

### BASIC CHAPTER PEDAGOGY

Each chapter begins with an outline and a list of objectives. These can be used to guide the reader to the main topics and help summarize basic ideas of the chapter. Glossary terms are presented in boldface to help introduce new concepts. Finally, each chapter ends with a chapter summary, which highlights main ideas in an integrative fashion, and with a set of questions entitled *For Further Reflection*. With these questions, we hope to encourage students to synthesize information across chapters, to link topics in the text to their own experiences, and to think about how they might relate ideas from the chapters to applied settings.

### BOXED FEATURES

Four types of boxed features are included to extend discussion on topics of special interest:

*Applying Theory and Research to Life* illustrates how new research and theory can be applied to concerns of daily social life.
*Technology and Human Development* provides examples of ways that technology enhances or, in some cases, adds new risks at different periods of life.
*Human Development and Diversity* presents a wide range of human differences that shape the nature of development at various stages of life.
*Case Studies* and accompanying thought questions encourage students to apply concepts from the chapter to real life experiences. The cases can be a focus for self-study or used in groups to foster discussion regarding the application of the main ideas in the chapter.

## ACKNOWLEDGMENTS

The works of Erik Erikson and Robert Havighurst have guided and inspired our own intellectual development. The combined contributions of these scholars have shaped the basic direction of psychosocial theory and have guided an enormous amount of research in human development. They directed us to look at the process of growth and change across the life span. They recognized the intimate interweaving of the individual's life story with a sociohistorical context, emphasizing societal pressures that call for new levels of functioning at each life stage. In their writing, they communicated an underlying optimism about each person's resilience, adaptability, and immense capacity for growth that finds new expression in the work of positive psychology. At the same time, they wrote with a moral passion about our responsibility as teachers, therapists, parents, scholars, and citizens to create a caring society. We celebrate these ideas and continue their expression in the ninth edition of *Development Through Life*.

We want to express our thanks to our many students, colleagues, and friends who shared their experiences and expertise. Through the years, our mentors, Bill McKeachie and Jim Kelly, have been unfailing sources of support and fresh ideas. Theirs are the voices of wisdom we count on, reminding us of the values of good scholarship and a generous heart. Our former students, now scholars in their own right, Brenda Lohman and Laura Landry Meyer, have offered valuable suggestions and encouragement. They made wonderful contributions to the supplements. In addition, they have been excellent collaborators on our life-span development case book. With each new edition, we turn to our children and their families to offer new observations, try out ideas, and talk over controversies. At each stage, they bring new talents and perspectives that enrich our efforts.

The ninth edition was produced under the guidance of a marvelous editor, Michele Sordi and her wonderful assistant, Jessica Kim. Their advice, encouragement, support, and vision have been instrumental in bringing this edition to fruition. We are very lucky to have had the benefit of their creative energy. In addition, we would like to express our appreciation to the other professionals at Wadsworth who have helped make this book possible: Emily Smith, production project manager; Vernon Boes, art director; Erik Fortier, technology project manager; Jennifer Keever, assistant editor; Dory Schaeffer, marketing manager; Tami Strang, advertising project manager; and Nicole Morinon, marketing assistant.

Finally, we acknowledge the thoughtful, constructive comments and suggestions of the following reviewers: Julie Cooper Altman, Adelphi University; Rosemary T. Hornak, Meredith College; David J. Johnson, Gannon University; Robert D. Johnson, Arkansas State University; Bonnie J. Kin, Georgia State University; Barbara Tremitiere, Penn State University–York; Michelle R. Dunlap, Connecticut College; and John Hotz, St. Cloud State University.

## NEW SUPPLEMENTS: PRINT, VIDEO, AND ELECTRONIC

*Development Through Life: A Psychosocial Approach*, ninth edition, is accompanied by a wide array of supplementary resources prepared for both the instructor and student.

### FOR THE INSTRUCTOR

**Instructor's Manual with Test Bank (0-495-03073-2)**
Written by Philip and Barbara Newman, Laura Landry-

Meyer, and Brenda Lohman, this manual contains chapter-specific outlines, teaching resources, discussion topics, and class projects. The test bank consists of approximately 100 multiple-choice questions, matching questions, short-answer questions, and essay questions for each chapter, all with page references. It also contains the Study Guide's test questions and answers. Each multiple-choice item is categorized based on type (factual, conceptual, definition, or application).

### ExamView® Computerized Testing (0-495-03074-0)

This easy-to-use tutorial system allows you to create, deliver, and customize printed and online tests and study guides in minutes. ExamView includes a Quick Test Wizard and an Online Test Wizard to guide instructors step by step through the process of creating tests. The tests appear on screen exactly as they will print or be displayed online. Using Exam-View's complete word processing capabilities, instructors can enter an unlimited number of new questions or edit questions included with ExamView.

## CLASSROOM PRESENTATION TOOLS FOR THE INSTRUCTOR

### Multimedia Manager Instructor's Resource CD-ROM: A Microsoft® PowerPoint® Link Tool (0-495-03075-9)

With the one-stop digital library and presentation tool, instructors can assemble, edit, and present custom lectures with ease. This CD-ROM contains ready-to-use PowerPoint lecture slides that include figures and tables from the text, videos, and animations. Instructors can use the material or add their own for a truly customized lecture presentation. This tool also contains an electronic Instructor's Manual with Test Bank.

### Wadsworth Developmental Psychology Video Library

Bring developmental psychology concepts to life with videos from Wadsworth's Developmental Psychology Library, which includes thought-provoking offerings from Films for Humanities, as well as other excellent educational video sources. This extensive collection illustrates important developmental psychology concepts covered in many life-span courses. Certain adoption conditions apply.

## FOR THE STUDENT

### Study Guide (0-495-03072-4)

Written by the authors of your textbook, with Laura Landry-Meyer and Brenda Lohman, the study guide is designed to improve mastery of the subject matter and to encourage students to take an active role in extending their learning through additional readings and observations. Each chapter of the study guide includes a review of the chapter outline and learning objectives, a pre-test and a post-test consisting of multiple-choice and true/false questions, sections with matching and short-answer questions, and "Suggestions for Further Observation and Study."

## INTERNET-BASED SUPPLEMENTS

### WebTutor™ Toolbox WebCT and Blackboard

Preloaded with content and available via a free access code when packaged with this text, WebTutor ToolBox pairs all the content of this text's rich Book Companion website with sophisticated course management functionality. You can assign materials (including online quizzes) and have the results flow automatically to your grade book. WebTutor ToolBox is ready to use as soon as you log on, or you can customize its preloaded content by uploading images and other resources, adding weblinks, or creating your own practice materials.

### InfoTrac® College Edition

With InfoTrac College Edition, instructors can stimulate discussions and supplement lectures with the latest developments in developmental psychology. Available as a free option with newly purchased texts, InfoTrac College Edition gives instructors and students four months of free access to an extensive database of reliable, full-length articles (not just abstracts) from hundreds of top academic journals and popular periodicals. In-text exercises suggest search terms to make the most of this resource.

### Book Companion Website

Visit the companion website at http://psychology.wadsworth.com/newman_newman9e, where you will find online resources for this book, including chapter-by-chapter quizzes, a glossary, flashcards, weblinks, and more! You can also visit Wadsworth Psychology Resource Center at http://psychology.wadsworth.com to access additional resources.

## LIFE-SPAN DEVELOPMENT: A CASE BOOK (0-534-59767-X)

This volume is not a supplement, but some instructors might want to add this to the reading list for their classes. Written by the authors of your textbook and Laura Landry-Meyer of Bowling Green State University, and Brenda Lohman of Iowa State University, this case book gives students an in-depth look at the forces that shape development. Each chapter of this case book uses lively, contemporary case studies to illustrate developmental transitions and challenges at every period of life. The chapters follow a consistent presentation, which includes an overview of developmental issues, two or three case scenarios, followed by pedagogical prompts to consider in a developmental analysis, a contextual analysis, and a psychosocial analysis. Chapters close with ideas for further research and study. The goal of the casebook is to stimulate critical thinking and the application of theory and research to authentic, real-world experiences.

# Brief Author Biographies

**Barbara M. Newman** (Ph.D., University of Michigan) is a professor in and chair of the Department of Human Development and Family Studies at the University of Rhode Island. She has also been on the faculty at Russell Sage College and The Ohio State University, where she served as department chair in Human Development and Family Science and as associate provost for Faculty Recruitment and Development. She teaches courses in life-span development, adolescence, family theories, and the research process. Also an active researcher, Dr. Newman's interests focus on parent-child relationships in early adolescence, factors that promote success in the transition to high school, the role of parenting as a stimulus to adult development through the process of revisitation, and the use of the cohort sequential design as an approach to the study of development. Her current research, funded by the University of Rhode Island's Research Foundation, is a short-term cohort sequential analysis of the role of family, peer, and school support in the transition to high school. For fun, Barbara enjoys reading, making up Project Bags for her grandchildren, taking walks along Narragansett Bay and Block Island Sound, and spending time with her family.

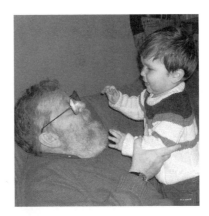

**Philip R. Newman** (Ph.D., University of Michigan) is an adjunct professor in the Department of Human Development and Family Studies at the University of Rhode Island. He has taught courses in introductory psychology, adolescence, social psychology, developmental psychology, counseling, and family, school, and community contexts for development. His research interests focus on group identity and alienation, the transition to high school for low-income, urban youths, and factors associated with retention for low-income, minority college students. He served as the director for Research and Evaluation of the Young Scholars Program at The Ohio State University and as the director of the Human Behavior Curriculum Project for the American Psychological Association. He is a fellow of the American Psychological Association, the Society for the Psychological Study of Social Issues (SPSSI), and the American Orthopsychiatric Association. For fun, Phil enjoys photography, reading mysteries, attending concerts and Broadway plays, and watching baseball. He home schooled his three children through elementary and middle school.

Together, the Newmans have worked on programs to bring low-income minority youths to college and to study the processes involved in their academic success. They are coauthors of 12 books and 11 articles in the field of human development. They met by the Mason Hall elevator at the University of Michigan, fell in love at first sight, and have been married for 39 years.

This edition of *Development Through Life* is dedicated to our grandchildren, Jakob and Max.

# CHAPTER 1

# THE DEVELOPMENT THROUGH LIFE PERSPECTIVE

*First Steps, 1943/Pablo Picasso/© 2005 Estate of Pablo Picasso/Artists Rights Society (ARS), New York./© Francis G. Mayer /Corbis*

*The study of human development reflects the interdependence of people at all ages. Children become adults; adults guide and nurture children. A person moves from the comfort of competence at each life stage in order to master the challenges of the next stage.*

■ ASSUMPTIONS OF THE TEXT

■ A PSYCHOSOCIAL APPROACH: THE INTERACTION
OF THE BIOLOGICAL, PSYCHOLOGICAL, AND
SOCIETAL SYSTEMS
The Biological System
The Psychological System
The Societal System
Overview of the Psychosocial Approach
CASE STUDY: ROSE

■ THE LIFE SPAN
Projections of Life Expectancy
Factors That Contribute to Longevity

■ CHAPTER SUMMARY

■ FURTHER REFLECTION

## CHAPTER OBJECTIVES

▶ *To introduce the basic assumptions that guide the organization of the text.*

▶ *To introduce the psychosocial approach to the study of development, including the interrelationship among the biological, psychological, and societal systems.*

▶ *To note historical changes in life expectancy and examine the implications of these changes for the study of development over the life span.*

PATRICK JONATHAN CARMICHAEL was born the son of a free man, who earned his way out of slavery in North Carolina before moving to Alabama and the Rump plantation. Carmichael attended Snowhill Institute, which was modeled after Booker T. Washington's Tuskegee Institute. It was here that the dream for his own school began. After graduating from high school, he taught for 5 years, then founded Purdue Hill Industrial High.

"The state put up just seventy-five dollars a year for expenses," Carmichael says. "Students paid tuition of twenty-five cents a year and paid in chickens or cans of syrup if they didn't have the money. You couldn't get a dime out of a state to build a Negro school back then. I'd write letters to people all over the country who I thought had a little charity about them to help us. I'd be the last man to put his light out because I'd be writing letters."

"He got twenty-five dollars a month," Carmichael's son adds. "He fed us kids by farming, getting up before dawn to work the fields, raise chickens and cattle and pigs. He had a big garden. All his earnings went back into the school. At night he'd write those letters to wealthy people in Boston or New York, trying to get a little money for the school. He was persistent. A little at a time. People in the area built the school. It started out as a one-room school with one teacher and eleven students and grew to a twelve-room school with two hundred and fifty students and ten teachers."

Patrick Jonathan Carmichael is now living with his son and daughter-in-law. He is 101 but has been with them for only the past few years. After retiring from his career in education in 1958, he lived alone on his farm until he broke his hip after going out to feed his cattle. He was 97.

"I didn't get along with my father when I was younger," says his son. "He was such a hard-working, disciplined man. Now it's different. It's like we're getting another chance. I have to take care of him, do

things for him like shave him. He needs me and we're developing more of a buddy relationship." (Heynen, 1990, p. 9. Patrick Jonathan Carmichael, born 1886, interviewed in 1987.)

Think for a moment about Patrick Jonathan Carmichael: his hopes, determination, sacrifices, family, accomplishments, and disappointments; the new challenges he must have faced as he retired from education, lived alone, and formed new, interdependent relationships with his son and daughter-in-law. Think of living 100 years—so many changes and so much to learn; so many losses and so many victories. What do we know of development through life? How can we conceptualize the dynamic development of individuals within the contexts of their societies, the period of history in which they grew up and entered adulthood, their families, their values and goals, and the obstacles they faced? How can we study patterns of change and growth in populations and still preserve an understanding of the intriguing uniqueness of individual lives? These are some of the challenging questions facing the discipline of human development.

The study of human development is puzzling. Our goal is to gain a more accurate understanding of how individuals make sense of their experiences, adapt to their environments, cope with challenges, and continue to develop from one period of life to the next. This process is as individual as each person's life story and is influenced by such factors as gender, ethnicity, socioeconomic status, sexual orientation, physical abilities and disabilities, and historical and social contexts. Even though each person's life is unique, common patterns of experience and meaning allow us to know and care for one another and contribute to one another's well-being. The life-span approach to human development strives to identify and account for patterns of transition and transformation from one period of life to another while recognizing both intergroup differences and individual variations within groups (Smith & Baltes, 1999).

This chapter provides a brief introduction to three topics

*Growth occurs at every stage of life. Within a large family, we have opportunities to observe family resemblances and individual differences; patterns of continuity from year to year as well as evidence of maturation and change.*

© Ariel Skelley/corbisstockmarket.com

that are central to the study of the life span. First, we outline our assumptions about human development that guide the orientation of the text. Second, we introduce the broad concept of a psychosocial approach to development. Third, we introduce data about life expectancy to start you thinking in a concrete way about the course of your life and the decisions you make that may directly influence your life story. ■

# ASSUMPTIONS OF THE TEXT

Our perspective on development through life makes the following five assumptions that are critical to the organization of this book:

1. *Growth occurs at every period of life, from conception through very old age.* At each period, new capacities emerge, new roles are undertaken, new challenges must be faced, and, as a result, a new orientation toward self and society unfolds. The concept of life-span development implies *plasticity*, a capacity for adaptive reorganization at the neurological, psychological, and behavioral levels.

2. *Individual lives show continuity and change as they progress through time.* An awareness of the processes that contribute to both continuity and change is central to an understanding of human development. *Continuity* refers to stability in characteristics from one period of life to another. It also refers to a sense of sameness over time built

on a history of memories, identity, and reflected self. *Developmental change* refers to patterns of growth and reorganization. Change may be attributed to biological maturation, systematic socialization, and to the interaction of these forces.

3. *We need to understand the whole person, because we function in an integrated manner.* To achieve such an understanding, we need to study the major developments in physical, social, emotional, and cognitive capacities and their interrelationships. We also need to study actions, the many forms of observable behavior. Each system serves as a stimulus for the others, with the overall purpose of enhancing the person's adaptive capacities.

4. *Behavior must be interpreted in the context of relevant settings and personal relationships.* Human beings are highly skilled in adapting to their environment. The meaning of a given behavior pattern or change must be interpreted in light of the significant physical and social environments in which it occurs.

5. *People contribute actively to their development.* These contributions take many forms, including the expression of tastes and preferences, choices and goals, and one's willingness to embrace or resist cultural and societal expectations. One of the most critical ways in which a person contributes to his or her development is through the creation of significant social relationships, which then form a context for social support and socialization. Some societies offer more opportunities for choice and promote a person's ability to mold the direction of development, whereas others have fewer resources, are more restrictive, or place less value on individuality (Veenhoven, 2000).

# A PSYCHOSOCIAL APPROACH: THE INTERACTION OF THE BIOLOGICAL, PSYCHOLOGICAL, AND SOCIETAL SYSTEMS

Erik Erikson (1963, p. 37) wrote that human life as the individual experiences it is produced by the interaction and modification of three major systems: the biological system, the psychological system, and the societal system. Each system can be examined for patterns of continuity and change over the life course. Each system shows evidence of adaptive capacities that respond to environmental demands. Each system can be modified by self-guided choices. The integration of the biological, psychological, and societal systems leads to a complex, dynamic portrait of human thought and behavior.

## THE BIOLOGICAL SYSTEM

The **biological system** includes all those processes necessary for the physical functioning of the organism (see Figure 1.1). Biological processes develop and change as a consequence of genetically guided maturation; environmental resources, such as nutrition and sunlight; exposure to environmental toxins; encounters with accidents and diseases; and lifestyle patterns of behavior, including daily exercise, eating, sleeping, and the use of drugs. In the case of Patrick Jonathan Carmichael, two examples of the influences of the biological system on his life experiences are his longevity and his physical strength. He lived a long time in good health. His uncommon hardiness, brought about by a combination of good genes, a life of rigorous exercise, and a healthy lifestyle, contributed to his ability to endure the physical demands of his life and to achieve many of his career goals, while still supporting his family. The experience of breaking his hip at an advanced age is another example of how changes in the biological system can modify the social and psychological systems.

The biological system changes over time, in part as a result of a genetically guided maturational process and in part as a result of interactions with the physical and social environment. Cultures differ in their support of physical growth and health, depending on the availability of adequate nutritional resources, the treatment of illness, and exposure to environmental toxins and hazardous conditions. A growing body of information is accumulating to assist people in making lifestyle choices that will increase their health and longevity.

## THE PSYCHOLOGICAL SYSTEM

The **psychological system** includes those mental processes central to a person's ability to make meaning of experiences

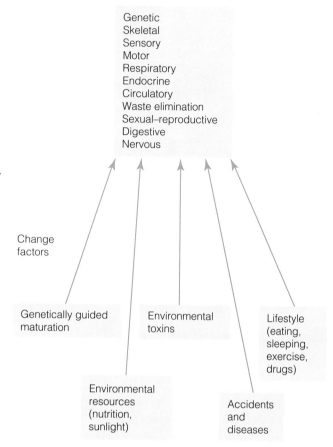

Genetic
Skeletal
Sensory
Motor
Respiratory
Endocrine
Circulatory
Waste elimination
Sexual–reproductive
Digestive
Nervous

Change factors

Genetically guided maturation

Environmental toxins

Lifestyle (eating, sleeping, exercise, drugs)

Environmental resources (nutrition, sunlight)

Accidents and diseases

**FIGURE 1.1**

The Biological System

and take action (see Figure 1.2). Emotion, memory, perception, problem solving, language, and symbolic abilities, and our orientation to the future—all require the use of psychological processes. In the case of Patrick Jonathan Carmichael, the influence of the psychological system can be appreciated when one considers his motivation, his persistence, his academic abilities, his ingenuity, his goals, and his sense of self-discipline. The psychological system provides the resources for processing information and navigating reality.

Like the biological processes, psychological processes develop and change over one's life span. Change is guided in part by genetic information. The capacity for intellectual functioning and the direction of cognitive maturation are genetically guided. A number of genetically transmitted diseases result in intellectual impairment and a reduced capacity for learning. Change also results from the accumulation of experiences and from encounters with various educational settings. The psychological processes are enhanced by numerous life experiences, such as playing sports, camping, traveling, reading, and talking with people. Finally, change can be self-directed. A person can decide to pursue a new interest, learn another language, or adopt a new set of ideas. Through self-insight, one can begin to think about oneself and others in a new light.

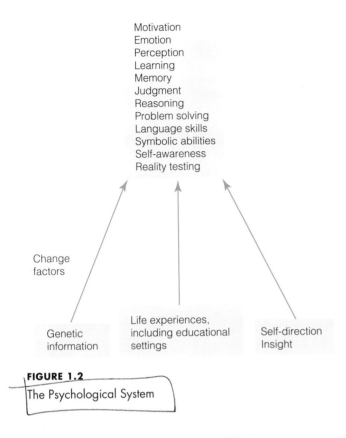

Motivation
Emotion
Perception
Learning
Memory
Judgment
Reasoning
Problem solving
Language skills
Symbolic abilities
Self-awareness
Reality testing

Change
factors

Genetic
information

Life experiences,
including educational
settings

Self-direction
Insight

**FIGURE 1.2**

The Psychological System

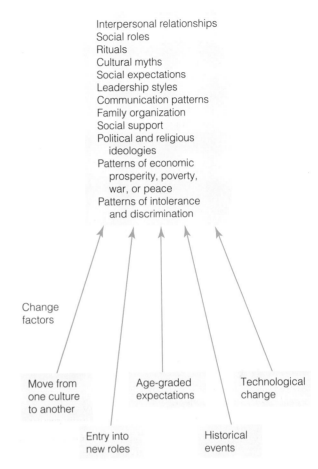

Interpersonal relationships
Social roles
Rituals
Cultural myths
Social expectations
Leadership styles
Communication patterns
Family organization
Social support
Political and religious
     ideologies
Patterns of economic
     prosperity, poverty,
     war, or peace
Patterns of intolerance
     and discrimination

Change
factors

Move from
one culture
to another

Entry into
new roles

Age-graded
expectations

Historical
events

Technological
change

**FIGURE 1.3**

The Societal System

## THE SOCIETAL SYSTEM

The **societal system** includes those processes through which a person becomes integrated into society (see Figure 1.3). Societal influences include social roles; social support; culture, including rituals, myths, and social expectations; leadership styles; communication patterns; family organization; ethnic and subcultural influences; political and religious ideologies; patterns of economic prosperity or poverty and war or peace; and exposure to racism, sexism, and other forms of discrimination, intolerance, or intergroup hostility. The impact of the societal system on psychosocial development results largely from interpersonal relationships, often relationships with significant others. The societal system is illustrated in the case of Patrick Jonathan Carmichael by the importance of Carmichael's educational experiences at the Snowhill Institute, the discriminatory practices that resulted in no state funding for Negro education, the involvement of other families in the community in encouraging education for their children, the philanthropic donations from benefactors outside the community, and the changing nature of his relationship with his son. Through laws and public policies, political and economic structures, and educational opportunities, societies influence the psychosocial development of individuals and alter the life course for future generations (de St. Aubin, McAdams, & Kim, 2004)

In this text, the role of culture is emphasized as it contributes to the pattern, pace, and direction of development. Cultures differ in their worldviews, including the emphasis

placed on collectivism or individuality, ideas about the major sources of stress and ways to alleviate stress, and beliefs about which groups are viewed as more powerful or more important than others (Morrison, Conaway, & Borden, 1994). Cultures differ in their emphasis on and belief in science, spirituality, and fatalism. They differ in their age-graded expectations, such as when a person is considered to be a child, an adult, or an elder. They differ in their definitions of morality, beauty, bravery, wealth, and other ideals that may define individual and group aspirations. As you read the text, you will encounter boxes entitled Human Development and Diversity, which provide examples of how norms of development might be viewed differently in different cultures or ethnic groups. We hope these examples will help sensitize you to the role of culture in defining what may be viewed as appropriate or normal behavior.

Societal processes change over one's life span. Entry into new roles brings new demands and behaviors. For example, in the United States, we expect children who are 5 years old to attend kindergarten and to have the social, physical, and emotional competencies to function in a large-group educational setting at this age. In Finland, although most children attend some form of child care program, they do not start

APPLYING THEORY AND RESEARCH TO LIFE

## Poverty

### CONDITIONS LEADING TO POVERTY

Since the 1960s, four major factors have contributed to the number of families living in poverty: (1) the decline in well-paying, blue-collar jobs; (2) large increases in single-mother households due to births to unmarried women and to divorce; (3) the erosion of the economic safety net for poor families, including the decline in cash transfers and benefits to families in the new welfare program, Transitional Assistance to Needy Families; and (4) the decline in the purchasing power of the minimum wage (Hernandez, 1993; Pavetti, 2000). Adjusted for inflation, the purchasing power of the minimum wage in 2004 ($5.15) is 24% less than it was in 1974 (Economic Policy Institute, 2004). Over the last decade, the percentage of children under age 18 living in poverty declined slightly, from 19.9% in 1990 to 15.6% in 2001 (U.S. Census Bureau, 2003).

Poverty is transitory for some families—as when a wage earner becomes unemployed and then finds new work—but persistent over the life course for others. For unmarried women who become mothers in adolescence, poverty is often a result of interrupted education, the inability to work full time (usually because

© Nathan Benn/CORBIS

*Poverty is a powerful characteristic of the societal system. Children growing up in poverty are exposed to stressors and hazards that can severely restrict development.*

of time needed to care for their children), and the low-paying jobs that are available to those with limited educational attainment. Furthermore, many of these women are growing up in families that are already living in poverty. Persistent poverty and exposure to poverty during infancy and early childhood are associated with greater vulnerability and more negative consequences to health, cognitive development, and school achievement than are single or later spells of poverty (McLoyd, 1998).

Divorce places many women and

---

elementary school until age 7. Most societies have age-graded expectations about the competencies that are desired and opportunities for participation in settings and roles that change for each stage of life.

Historical events—conditions of war or peace, being the victor or the vanquished, living in prosperity or poverty—influence how people in a given culture perceive themselves. For example, the conditions of World War II—forced military service, decreases in the availability of resources and the resulting system of rationing, the increased involvement of women in the labor market, the bombing of European cities, the unveiling of unprecedented human atrocities, the explosion of the first nuclear bomb over Japan—had a lasting impact on the values and ideology of the people who lived through that period (Elder, 1995).

### ■ THE PSYCHOSOCIAL IMPACT OF POVERTY

In thinking about the impact of societal factors on development, we want to highlight the context of poverty as a major obstacle to optimal development. Racism, sexism, ageism, homophobia, and discrimination against individuals with physical, intellectual, and emotional disabilities are other examples. However, under conditions of poverty, individuals have fewer options and less opportunity to escape or avoid these other societal deterrents. Poverty has potentially powerful and pervasive effects on the biological and psychological systems across the life span. In and of itself, poverty does not place inevitable limits on development. There are many instances, both famous and less well known, of children who grew up in poverty and achieved eminence (Harrington & Boardman, 2000). We need only think of the case of Patrick their children into poverty. In many instances, the family was already encountering financial strain, which is known to be one of the primary factors associated with divorce. However, following divorce, an estimated 27% of divorced women and their children fall below the poverty line (Chase-Lansdale, 1993). The level of poverty experienced by newly divorced women is aggravated by the failure of many fathers to pay child support (Smock & Manning, 1997). Poverty for these families is sometimes transitory, because many divorced women remarry or are able to find adequate employment after a year or two. However, in one study, 48% of respondents reported lower income even 5 years after the divorce (Thabes, 1997).

African American, Hispanic, and Native American families are overrepresented among those living in poverty, and their experiences of poverty are likely to be longer lasting. For individuals in these ethnic groups, the stresses associated with the chronic condition of poverty are linked with earlier exposure to health risks and higher exposure to environmental hazards. Higher incidences of health problems, greater challenges in achieving the developmental tasks of each life stage, and reduced life

expectancy are the result (Corcoran & Chaudry, 1997; Hayward, Crimmins, Miles, & Yang, 2000).

### FACTORS THAT MEDIATE THE IMPACT OF POVERTY

Although we are still a long way from fully understanding how some children escape its negative effects, we do know that many children who live in poverty continue to develop optimally. Some scholars have emphasized the notion of **resilience** as a characteristic of some children. Resilient children appear to have inner strengths that permit them to get the resources they need, to define their situation in a positive way, and to transcend their lives' challenges (Garmezy, 1991). These children are characterized by an easy, sociable temperament. They are active, seeking out stimulation and evoking responses from others. They are bright and able to solve problems readily. They usually have at least one supportive, loving relationship with a family member, and they have access to supportive contacts outside the family.

In addition to the resilience of children, other resources help parents to buffer the impact of poverty. Among low-income, single African American

mothers, for example, a higher level of education, the presence of an emotionally supportive social network, and strong religious beliefs all help reduce the negative effects of poverty (Kelly, Power, & Wimbush, 1992; Jayakody, Chatters, & Taylor, 1993; McLoyd, 1990). Different combinations of factors can provide family contexts that mediate the negative effects of poverty on children. The presence and involvement of a father or father figure is an important contribution to a child's resilience. However, in some families, even if a father is not present, other family members living in the household, such as grandparents, can provide support and help stabilize the family environment. In other families, mothers who have high self-esteem and high expectations for their children's success convey their support by providing early and continuous learning experiences for their children (Zhao, Brooks-Gunn, McLanahan, & Singer, 2000). Persistent poverty in a small child's life is a strong predictor of a wide variety of physical and mental health problems. Parents who are able to see their poverty as transitory and who take steps to move out of poverty may also differ with respect to their supportiveness and responsiveness to their children.

Jonathan Carmichael to recognize that many children flourish under conditions of meager family resources. In fact, some people choose to live very modest material lives in order to achieve other important goals. However, it is well documented that poverty increases the risks that individuals face, including risks associated with malnutrition, poor quality health care, living in a hazardous or dangerous neighborhood, and attending ineffective schools. Poverty is linked with reduced access to the basic resources associated with survival (Duncan, Brooks-Gunn, & Klebanov, 1994; Rank, 2000). Because of the complex and pervasive impact of poverty on development, we introduce it here as a fundamental societal theme. Issues related to the impact of poverty on patterns of development and family life will be addressed in more detail in subsequent chapters.

## OVERVIEW OF THE PSYCHOSOCIAL APPROACH

The psychosocial approach seeks to understand the internal experiences that are the product of interactions among biological, psychological, and societal processes. Changes in one of the three systems (biological, psychological, or societal) generally bring about changes in the others. As an example, consider the AIDS epidemic, a biological factor that has had a significant influence on the psychological and societal systems, including changing sexual practices, new approaches to sex education, modifications in health care and workplace practices, increased attention to the caregiving relationship within families, and new concerns about privacy. In Africa,

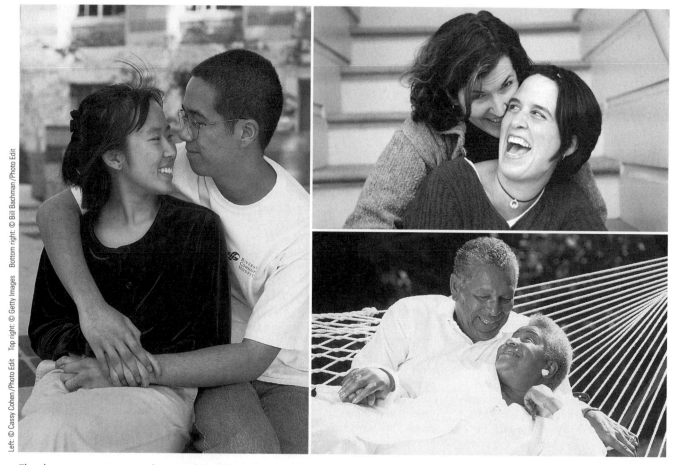

*The desire to experience a loving relationship remains strong throughout life. However, the self one brings to a loving relationship changes at each stage. How might experiences of love change from adolescence to early adulthood to later adulthood?*

large numbers of children are growing up without parents due to AIDS (Catalan, Sherr, & Hedge, 1997; Kalichman, 1998; Perloff, 2001).

From the psychosocial perspective, development results from the continuous interaction of the individual and the social environment. At each period of life, people spend much of their time mastering a unique group of psychological tasks that are essential for social adaptation within their society. Each life stage brings a normative crisis, which can be viewed as a tension between one's competencies and the new demands of society. People strive to reduce this tension by using a variety of familiar coping strategies and by learning new ones. A positive resolution of each crisis provides a new set of social abilities that enhances a person's capacity to adapt successfully in the succeeding stages. A negative resolution of a crisis typically results in defensiveness, rigidity, or withdrawal, which decrease a person's ability to adapt successfully in succeeding stages.

Throughout life, personal relationships occupy our attention. Some of these relationships are more important than others, but their quality and diversity provide a basis for the study of one's psychosocial development. As we progress through the stages of life, most of us develop an increasing ca-

pacity to initiate new relationships and to innovate in our thoughts and actions so as to direct the course of our lives.

The meaning we make of our experiences changes over the course of life. Think about the concept of love as an example. In infancy, love is almost entirely physical. It is the pervasive sense of comfort and security that we feel in the presence of our caregivers. By adolescence, the idea of love includes loyalty, emotional closeness, and sexuality. In adulthood, the concept of love may expand to include a new emphasis on companionship and open communication. The need to be loved and to give love remains important throughout life, but the self we bring to a loving relationship, the context within which the relationship is established, and the signs we look for as evidence of love change with age.

Meaning is created out of efforts to interpret and integrate the experiences of the biological, psychological, and societal systems. A primary focus of this meaning-making is the search for identity. Humans struggle to define themselves— to achieve a sense of identity—through a sense of connectedness with certain other people and groups and through feelings of distinctiveness from others. We establish categories that define whom we are connected to, whom we care about, and which of our own qualities we admire. We also establish categories that define those to whom we are not connected, those whom we do not care about, and those qualities of our own that we reject or deny. These categories provide us with an orientation toward certain kinds of people and away from others, toward certain life choices and away from others. The psychosocial perspective brings to light the dynamic interplay of the roles of the self and the other, the I and the We, as they contribute to the emergence of identity over the life course.

# CASE STUDY

## ROSE

*The interaction of the biological, the psychological, and the societal systems.*

Rose is a 60-year-old woman who has been having serious attacks of dizziness and shortness of breath as Thanksgiving approaches. Rose is usually active and energetic. In the past, she looked forward to entertaining her family, which used to include three married daughters, one married son, their spouses, and their children. However, her son has recently been divorced. Feelings between him and his ex-wife are bitter. Any attempts on Rose's part to communicate with her former daughter-in-law or her granddaughter are met with outbursts of hostility from her son. Although Rose is very fond of her daughter-in-law and her granddaughter, she knows that she cannot invite them to the family gathering without stirring up intense conflict with her son.

Rose's daughters suggest having the dinner at one of their homes in order to prevent further conflict. They hope this solution will take some of the pressure off their mother and ease the attacks. Rose agrees, but her attacks continue.

### ■ DISCUSSION

How are the biological, psychological, and societal systems involved in Rose's situation? The conflict is being expressed in the biological system through the symptoms of dizziness and shortness of breath. Psychological and societal demands may elicit responses from the biological system, as they commonly do in people under stress. Although the solution to the problem must be found in the psychological system, the biological system often alerts the person to the severity of the problem through the development of physical symptoms.

Rose's psychological system is involved in interpreting her son's behavior, which she views as forcing her to choose between him and her daughter-in-law and granddaughter. She might also use psychological processes to try to arrive at a solution to the conflict. So far, Rose has not identified any satisfactory solution. Although she can avoid the conflict most of the time, the impending Thanksgiving dinner is forcing her to confront it directly.

The psychological system includes Rose's self-concept as well as her emotional state. Through memory, Rose retains a sense of her family at earlier periods, when they enjoyed greater closeness. Having to face a Thanksgiving dinner at which she will feel angry at her son or guilty about excluding her daughter-in-law and her granddaughter places her in a fundamental conflict. The Thanksgiving meal is also a symbolic event, representing Rose's idea of family unity, which she cannot achieve.

The societal system influences the situation at several levels. First, there are the societal expectations regarding the mother role: Mother is nurturing, loving, and protecting. But Rose cannot be nurturing without sending messages of rejection either to her son or to her daughter-in-law and granddaughter. Second, social norms for relating to various family members after a divorce are unclear. How should Rose behave toward her son's former spouse? How should she relate to her grandchild if her son is no longer the child's custodial parent? Rose is confused about what to do. Third, the Thanksgiving celebration has social, religious, and cultural significance. This family ritual was performed in Rose's home when she was a child, and she has carried it through in her own home as an adult. Now, however, she is being forced to pass the responsibility for this gathering to her daughter before she is ready to do so and, as a result, Rose is likely to feel a special sense of loss. She will also lose the sense of family unity that she has tried to preserve.

### ■ CRITICAL THINKING AND CASE ANALYSIS

1. How does this case illustrate the interconnections among the biological, psychological, and societal systems?
2. Given what you know about the assumptions of psychosocial theory, how might Rose's stage of development influence her perceptions of this situation and her approach to coping with this conflict?
3. How might you frame a research question based on the information raised in this case study? (For example, how likely is it that parents experience health problems following their child's divorce?)
4. How do the assumptions of this text influence your approach to understanding the case of Rose?

# THE LIFE SPAN

The study of human development requires an analysis of the life span and a view of the periods of life that are embedded within it. How long does one expect to live? At what age is one considered to be adult? old? ancient? Answers to these questions, like so much of what we will discuss in this text, are found by considering a combination of biological, psychological, and societal factors. Life expectancy is a projection of the number of years one can expect to live. Think back to the case of Patrick Jonathan Carmichael, who was living alone and working on his farm until the age of 97. According

Table 1.1  Average Remaining Lifetime at Various Ages, 1900–2000

| AGE | 2000 | 1989 | 1978 | 1968 | 1954 | 1939–1941 | 1929–1931 | 1900–1902 |
|---|---|---|---|---|---|---|---|---|
| **At birth** | 77.0 | 75.3 | 73.3 | 70.2 | 69.6 | 63.6 | 59.3 | 49.2 |
| **65 years** | 18.0 | 17.2 | 16.3 | 14.6 | 14.4 | 12.8 | 12.3 | 11.9 |
| **75 years** | 11.4 | 10.9 | 10.4 | 9.1 | 9.0 | 7.6 | 7.3 | 7.1 |
| **80 years** | 8.7 | 8.3 | 8.1 | 6.8 | 6.9 | 5.7 | 5.4 | 5.3 |

Source: U.S. Census Bureau, 1984, 1992, 1997, 2000, 2003.

to population statistics, the life expectancy for someone born in 1900 was 49.2. Among Carmichael's cohort of African American men, the life expectancy was 32.5. If you consider African American men who reached the age of 65 in the 1950s, the additional life expectancy was 13.5 years. Patrick Jonathan Carmichael lived to be much older than the norm for his group. The task of mapping one's future depends on how long one expects to live. Naturally, for specific individuals, we can make only rough predictions. We know that some lives may be cut short by a disaster, an accident, or an illness. On the other hand, some people are exceptionally long lived.

Table 1.1 presents data on the average life expectancy of people in the United States during eight time periods. Look at the top row of the table, labeled "at birth." The average life expectancy of people born at the beginning of the 20th century was about 49 years. Over the course of the 20th century, we observe increasingly longer life expectancies. In the year 2000, people had a life expectancy at birth 27.8 years longer than they had in 1900.

You may be wondering how we can know about the life expectancy of people who were born in the year 2000. Not many years have passed to record deaths and life expectancy estimates for this group. The National Center for Health Statistics calculates life expectancy tables based on the number of deaths at each age for a particular year, information from the U.S. Census Bureau about the number of people who are alive at each age, and information from the Medicare program about the likelihood of dying among those 85 and older (Arias, 2002). So whereas the life expectancy information about people born in 1900 is based on the actual rates of death experienced by that group over time, the life expectancy projections for people born in 2000 are based on a summary of the death rates in the year 2000 for people at each age.

The next few lines in Table 1.1 show that people who reach an advanced age (65, 75, or 80) in each of the time periods have a longer life expectancy than the people who were born in those time periods. For example, a person born in 1900 could expect to live until age 49; but a person who was already 65 in 1900 could expect to live an additional 12 years to age 77. These data suggest that hazards during the early and middle years of life shorten the average life expectancy at birth. Infant mortality was a major factor in limiting life ex-

pectancy at the turn of the 20th century. Furthermore, many women died in childbirth, and respiratory diseases and heart disease were serious threats to life during the middle adult years. If one survived these common killers, one's chance for a long later life increased. Today, more and more adults are anticipating an extended period of what we refer to as "very old age"—75 and beyond.

Figure 1.4 provides a visual comparison of survival rates for the periods 1900–1902, 1949–1950, and 2000 (Arias, 2002). The curves show the percentage surviving at each age based on death registrations for those years. For the earliest cohort, there is a steep decline in survival in infancy and early childhood up to age 5 and then a gradual decline over the remaining years with few surviving past age 80. In comparison, the curve for the period 1949–1950 shows an improvement in survival for the first half of the life span, whereas the curve for the year 2000, which is almost rectangular in shape, shows improvement in survival during the last thirty years of life.

## PROJECTIONS OF LIFE EXPECTANCY

Table 1.2 shows life expectancy for the year 2000 and projected life expectancies for the periods 2005 and 2010 for men and women separately by race. The life expectancy of both men and women is expected to increase until the year 2010. Overall, men do not live as long as women. They die younger around the world as well as in various regions of the United States. The gap in life expectancy for U.S. men and women is slightly over 5 years for Whites and almost 7 years for Blacks. These projections appear fairly steady over the coming 10-year period; however, the difference is expected to increase again by the year 2050.

One question that has been raised is whether this increase in life expectancy can continue or whether there is an upper limit to the length of the life span. Many researchers have suggested that the primary diseases that resulted in mortality of infants and adults have already been brought under control. Increases in the life expectancy will be more modest over the coming 50 years, leading to an estimated life expectancy at birth of around 80 to 83 years in the United States.

As the life expectancy increases, it takes greater declines in

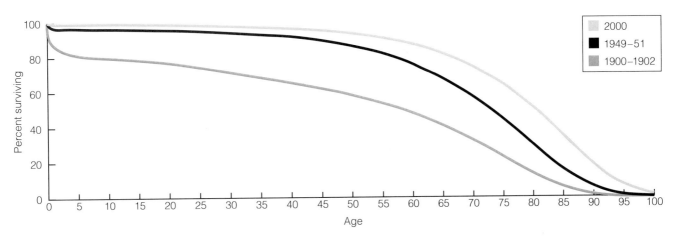

**FIGURE 1.4**

Percentage Surviving by Age: 1900–1902, 1949–1951, and 2000.

Source: Arias, 2002.

the death rate at every age to increase the life expectancy further. From this perspective, researchers argue that it is unlikely that there will be major improvements in the death rate of those under age 50 that would significantly add to their life expectancy. The conditions associated with death among older age groups are intimately linked to basic biological conditions of aging that, at present, are poorly understood. Many experts suggest that the best we can hope for is a healthier rather than a longer period of later life (Hayflick, 2000; Olshansky, Carnes, & Desesquelles, 2001).

Other scientists, many of whom are investigating the genetic bases of aging and longevity, are optimistic about substantial increases in longevity. Experiments with genetic engineering in flies, worms, and mice have been able to increase longevity in these species by 50%. Other research has found that imposing near-starvation dietary restrictions result in significant increases in longevity in mice. These studies may not have immediate relevance for humans, but they suggest paths for further investigation (Couzin, 2003; Kirkwood, 2001). Some futurists argue that there is no necessary limit to human longevity and that with the aging of each generation, there comes the possibility of new discoveries and new adaptations that will push longevity ahead (De Magalhaes, 2003).

**Table 1.2** Life Expectancy at Birth for the Year 2000 and Projections for 2005 and 2010 by Sex and Race

| RACE | 2000 MALE | 2000 FEMALE | 2005 MALE | 2005 FEMALE | 2010 MALE | 2010 FEMALE |
|---|---|---|---|---|---|---|
| **White** | 74.9 | 80.1 | 75.4 | 81.1 | 76.1 | 81.8 |
| **Black** | 68.3 | 75.2 | 69.9 | 76.8 | 70.9 | 77.8 |

Source: U.S. Census Bureau, 2003, Table 105, p. 83.

## FACTORS THAT CONTRIBUTE TO LONGEVITY

When you try to estimate your own life expectancy, you must consider projections for people in your country, region, and state, and in your age, educational, racial, and sex groups. Furthermore, research with identical twins has suggested that some components of longevity are genetically guided. People with long-lived ancestors are likely to be long lived themselves. Individual lifestyle factors are also associated with longevity.

Longitudinal studies of adults born between 1895 and 1919 who were studied in 1965 and again in 1984 (Guralnik & Kaplan, 1989) found that a variety of demographic, health, and lifestyle factors were associated with a high level of functioning in later life. These factors included having a fairly high family income; having no hypertension, arthritis, or back pain; being a nonsmoker; having normal weight; and consuming a moderate amount of alcohol. The last three factors in particular are influenced largely by personal decisions. Even hypertension and back pain are linked in part to lifestyle factors that are under a person's control. A growing body of research emphasizes the potential benefits of a well-balanced diet combined with the strategic use of vitamin and mineral supplements to slow the cellular damage associated with aging (Carper, 1995; Harman, Holliday, & Meydani, 1998; Rusting, 1992). Other research highlights the value of daily activity—even 20 to 30 minutes of exercise and movement—for promoting health and longevity (Brown et al., 2003).

Many of our most important life decisions are made with either an implicit or an explicit assumption about how long we expect to live. Our perception of our life expectancy has an impact on our behavior, self-concept, attitudes, and outlook on the future. For example, Colleen expects to live to be about 80 years old. She reasons that there is no rush about getting married because, even if she waits until she is 40, she

TECHNOLOGY AND HUMAN DEVELOPMENT

## The Role of Technology in the Study of Human Development

THROUGHOUT THIS BOOK, you will find boxes entitled Technology and Human Development. Technology that is relevant to human development encompasses many areas, including medical diagnostic equipment, such as magnetic resonance imaging (MRI), and amniocentesis, medications, and surgical procedures; reproductive technologies, such as in vitro fertilization; computers, including desktop, laptop, and handheld, and all the variety of software applications available through computers; communications technologies, such as telephone, television, radio, cell phones, faxes, paging devices, and cable; transportation technology, from scooters and tricycles to nuclear submarines and supersonic jets; weapons of all types; household technologies, such as stoves, refrigerators, freezers, microwave ovens, bread makers, coffee makers, and food processors; monitoring devices, including baby monitors, metal detectors, fire alarms, and security cameras; and the construction, manufacturing, and agricultural technologies necessary for specific areas of production.

*Technology* can refer to simple tools, such as a pencil or a shovel, or to complex integrated technologies, such as TERRA, NASA's Earth Observing System—a satellite with five types of remote sensors that are integrated to measure Earth's environment and changing climate. (You can find out more about TERRA by going to NASA's website, www.nasa.gov, and searching for TERRA.)

Sometimes it is hard to appreciate the role of technology in our lives, because much of it is so fully interwoven into our daily behavior. When you read reflections of adults who are over 75, their comments help bring our daily reliance on technology into perspective. They recall a childhood without televisions, cell phones, or computers; without frozen foods, jet airplane travel, or space exploration; with limited electrical equipment, few battery-operated devices, and no nuclear power or nuclear weapons. With each generation, technological innovations introduce new opportunities—and new handwringing about their potential negative impacts.

We hope that as you read about various technologies, you will take a critical stance toward their role in development. Not every innovation is appropriately designed or adapted for human use. Technologies, just like ideas, can be exploited to the advantage of some and the subordination of others. Technologies without ethics can become intrusive or oppressive. At the same time, the creation of new technologies reflects many of the prime adaptive ego qualities of human beings—hope, will, purpose, competence, care, and confidence. By including the boxes on Technology and Human Development, we not only highlight the many ways that technology may influence the direction of growth, but we celebrate the inventive spirit.

Within the text, frequent references to websites and online resources provide a recurrent reminder to the new world of learning without boundaries—one that is open, accessible, and available to anyone who has a computer and curiosity.

---

will still have 40 years of married life, and that is a long time to get along with one partner. In contrast, Tyrone expects to live to be about 25. Several of his older brothers' friends died of gunshot wounds, others died from drug overdoses, and some died in prison. He believes that he may as well take all the risks and have all the fun he can in life, because his time is short. Marie is celebrating her 90th birthday. She had expected to live to about age 75. Most of her friends and all her older siblings are dead. She is puzzled by the idea of having lived so long and sometimes wonders about the purpose of her long life.

As we look ahead, advances in medical technology and treatment coupled with improved support services for older adults can lead to higher standards of living and new levels of functioning in later life. On the other hand, inequities in the distribution of health care services and other societal supports may result in a growing disparity in the quality of later life for various segments of the population (Stahl, 1990).

Rachel Newman

*Age is relative, as is time. As the life span increases, the way we calculate our sense of maturity and aging changes. How old do you feel you are? In what way does your sense of being old depend on the situation?*

# Chapter Summary

This book presents the story of human development across the life span. The analysis is based on five assumptions: (1) Growth occurs at every period of life, from conception through very old age. (2) Individual lives show continuity and change as they progress through time. (3) We need to understand the whole person, because we function in an integrated manner. (4) Every person's behavior must be analyzed in the context of relevant settings and personal relationships. (5) People contribute actively to their development.

Psychosocial theory, which provides the organizing framework for the book, emphasizes interaction among the biological, psychological, and societal systems. As a result of maturation and change in each of these systems, individuals' beliefs about themselves and their relationships are modified. Although each life story is unique, we can identify important common patterns, allowing us to anticipate the future and to understand one another.

Demographic information about the life span stimulates thought about one's own life expectancy. In the United States, the average life expectancy increased by more than 50% during the 20th century. This dramatic change affects how each of us views our own future. We need to study human development in a constantly changing context. We can never be satisfied that the information from earlier periods will hold true for future generations.

# Further Reflection

1. How might people's own decisions and goals influence the course of their development?
2. What are some examples in your own experience of how the biological, psychological, and societal systems interact?
3. What are your own direct experiences with poverty? How might poverty influence the biological, psychologi-

cal, and societal systems and, thereby, influence the direction of development?
4. What are the critical settings in which development takes place? How do these settings change with age?
5. How does your culture influence your view of the life span? For example, what messages from your family, community, or ethnic group influence your sense of the distinctions between childhood, adolescence, adulthood, and old age?
6. What are your current thoughts about your life expectancy? What are you doing now to increase your chances of living a long, healthy life?
7. What are some examples of technological inventions that influence development? How is the direction or process of development altered because of these inventions?

# On the Web

**VISIT OUR WEBSITE**

Go to http://www.wadsworth.com/psychology to find online resources directly linked to your book.

# Casebook

For additional case material related to this chapter, see the case of "Mabel," in *Life Span Development: A Case Book,* by Barbara and Philip Newman, Laura Landry-Meyer, and Brenda J. Lohman, page 215. This case of a 93-year-old woman who is adapting to the physical changes of aging provides an opportunity to examine the interaction of the biological, psychological, and societal systems as they influence development in later life. It also introduces some of the challenges of coping successfully with extreme longevity.

# CHAPTER 2

# THE RESEARCH PROCESS

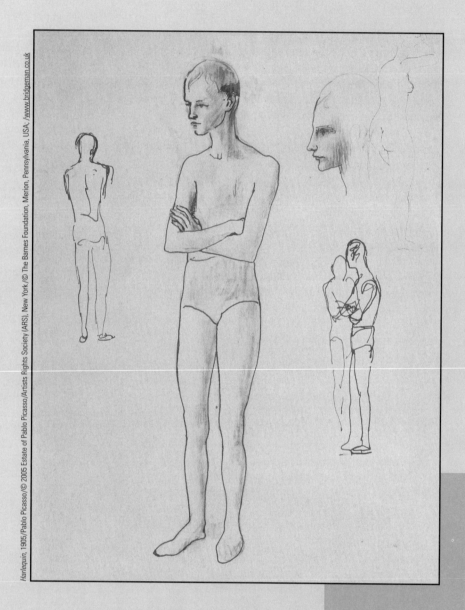

*Harlequin*, 1905/Pablo Picasso/© 2005 Estate of Pablo Picasso/Artists Rights Society (ARS), New York,/© The Barnes Foundation, Merion, Pennsylvania, USA,/www.bridgeman.co.uk

*Just as the artist explores ideas through experimentation with perspective, composition, shape, and color, the scientist explores theoretical relationships through the use of the scientific process.*

■ THE SCIENTIFIC PROCESS

The Positivist Approach to Research
The Qualitative Inquiry Approach to Research

■ RESEARCH DESIGN

Sampling
Research Methods

■ DESIGNS FOR STUDYING DEVELOPMENT

Retrospective Studies
Cross-Sectional Studies
Longitudinal Studies
Cohort Sequential Studies

■ EVALUATING EXISTING RESEARCH

■ ETHICS

■ CHAPTER SUMMARY

■ FURTHER REFLECTION

17

► *To define the scientific process, including the positivist and qualitative approaches to inquiry.*

► *To review issues in research design, including sampling, research methods, and designs for studying development.*

► *To consider the ethical guidelines for conducting research with human participants.*

REMARKABLE PROGRESS HAS been made over the past 100 years in bringing together observations, theories, and research to build a scientific knowledge base for the study of life-span development. In this chapter, we highlight basic principles of the scientific process from which much of our knowledge about development is derived. We describe the fundamental elements of the scientific process that lead to the gradual building of a systematic understanding of development. Scholars depend on this process to guide inquiry, a process that imposes constraints of logic, methodology, and ethics in hopes of building a sound, unbiased understanding of patterns and processes of development.

In approaching the challenges of conducting and interpreting research about development, remember that studies that summarize the responses or behaviors of groups of people will not necessarily account for the experiences of specific individuals. Similarly, the experiences of individuals will not necessarily be generalizable to larger groups. The study of life-span development is a quest for patterns of continuity and change over time and across historical eras. With this in mind, it is important to appreciate that patterns that might characterize the experiences of one cohort may not apply across historical periods. ■

# THE SCIENTIFIC PROCESS

The scientific process allows us to create a body of knowledge that contains procedures for ensuring that the information will be correct. Two major positions have been taken about how to approach the discovery of knowledge: *positivism* and *qualitative inquiry*, which is sometimes referred to as *postpositivism* or *phenomenology* (Denzin & Lincoln, 1998; Taylor & Bogdan, 1998).

*Positivism* approaches the study of human behavior by seeking causal relationships among factors, with the goal of trying to predict outcomes. Often, this approach applies statistical analyses to data gathered from many participants in order to test specific hypotheses. In the positivist approach, the research hypotheses guide decisions about the nature and size of the sample, the site(s) where data are collected, the methods of data collection, and the statistical procedures used to analyze the data.

*Qualitative inquiry* approaches the study of human behavior by trying to understand the meanings, motives, and beliefs that underlie a person's experiences. This approach emphasizes the individual's point of view and the subjective understandings that help account for a person's actions. Often this approach begins with examination of a *personal experience*, such as a parent's experience of caring for a child who has a developmental disability; a *process*, such as staff–parent communication in a neonatal unit; or a *unique phenomenon*, such as a near-death experience. Approaches to data collection may change as the study evolves, depending on the nature of the participants, the ideas that emerge, and the researcher's reactions and interpretations. Both positivism and qualitative inquiry strive to contribute to a new level of understanding of human behavior.

## THE POSITIVIST APPROACH TO RESEARCH

In this section, we describe the positivist research approach (see Figure 2.1). The research process usually begins with a puzzling idea or observation. The observer tries to figure out how to explain the observation and thinks about what leads to what—which events or conditions cause other events or conditions. In this process of searching for explanations, one develops a set of interrelated ideas to account for the observation. These ideas—often referred to as assumptions, hypotheses, or predictions—constitute a *theory*. The theory is not an end in itself, but a way to get going.

### ■ SCIENTIFIC OBSERVATION

The next step of the scientific process is to test the theory through systematic observation. A good theory contains specific predictions about cause and effect. After the predictions are stated, one must figure out how to test whether they are accurate. One must *operationalize* the concepts of a theory in order to test them. That is, one must translate an abstract concept into something that can be observed and measured.

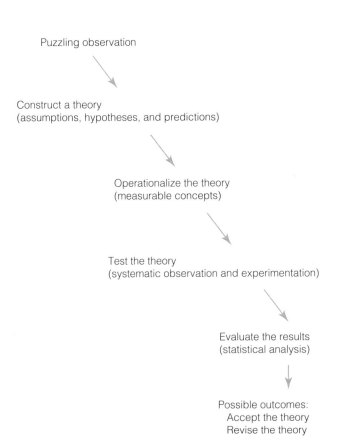

Puzzling observation

Construct a theory
(assumptions, hypotheses, and predictions)

Operationalize the theory
(measurable concepts)

Test the theory
(systematic observation and experimentation)

Evaluate the results
(statistical analysis)

Possible outcomes:
Accept the theory
Revise the theory
Reject the theory
Develop a new theory

**FIGURE 2.1**

The Scientific Process

Scientific observation is characterized by three essential qualities: It must be *objective*, *repeatable*, and *systematic* (Creswell, 1994). Objective observations accurately reflect the events that are taking place. They are not unduly influenced by what the observer expects or hopes to see. Suppose, for example, that you want an objective assessment of your child's talent for playing the guitar. You are unlikely to get objective feedback from friends or relatives. Because they know you and presumably would not like to insult you, they may be inclined to slant their answers to please you.

A more objective approach might be to include an audiotape of your child's guitar-playing with tapes of 10 other children. You would then ask another person to play the tapes for 10 people who do not know you or your child and ask each of them to rate the quality of musical ability demonstrated on each tape. You may or may not like the outcome, but at least your method would be more objective. It would reveal what other people think of your child's musical ability without being biased by any feelings about you or your child.

Social science research is always vulnerable to the theoretical biases and value orientations of the researchers. Certain practices of research design, sampling, and methodology are used to help overcome biases and build a higher level of objectivity into the process. However, many will argue that it is impossible to be entirely objective. One's orientation toward

framing research questions and interpreting the results are always influenced by cultural and historical contexts that shape the values, beliefs, and assumptions that guide the research process. That is why it is so important for the research carried out by one investigator to be repeatable.

If research is repeatable, then others could carry out a similar investigation and obtain the same results as the original investigator. In order for this to occur, the original investigator must carefully explain all the procedures used in the study, describe all the essential characteristics of the participants (e.g., age, sex, and social class background), and describe the setting or situation where the observations were made. As there are many ways that one group of participants might differ from another and many different ways that observations can be made, repeatability is an important part of building a body of social science knowledge.

Usually, a problem or process is investigated by an individual or research team, taking great care to make sure that observations are unbiased, orderly, carefully collected and recorded, and comprehensive. In order to ensure that the results of a study are accurate, the original researchers encourage other investigators to repeat the study to see if the same results are observed.

A systematic approach ensures that research is done in a careful, orderly way. Researchers have a framework of essential questions that they strive to answer based on what is already known and what certain theories predict. They approach research by having clear objectives, carefully defining the purpose of the research and the specific methods they will use to reach those objectives. Although some discoveries are made by accident, scientific research typically does not poke here and there at unrelated events.

Often the theory is not tested by the same person who develops it, because this person may have some personal investment in demonstrating that the theory is correct. The scientific process usually involves the ideas of more than one person. Sometimes, people with different points of view engage in debate, trying to refute positions they find flawed. At other times, two or more people work on different phases of theory building, experimentation, and evaluation.

If a theory is fruitful, many researchers working in independent groups will devise ways of extending and clarifying it. Working in this way, as a community of scholars, helps to ensure that a theory will not be confirmed simply because of the theorist's personal biases. For example, Erik Erikson was not the person who tested his own psychosocial theory. Many other researchers have devised strategies for operationalizing Erikson's concepts, thereby expanding our understanding of hope, identity, intimacy, generativity, and wisdom—to name a few—and clarifying the relationship of development in childhood and adolescence to adulthood and later life.

The final phase of the scientific process involves an *evaluation of the observations*. Statistical techniques help determine the likelihood that observations could have happened by chance. Observations that appear to be a result of chance do not confirm the theory. If the observations have a low probability of having occurred by chance, one says that they are statistically significant. If statistically significant results support the theory's predictions, one is likely to accept them as providing evidence for the theory. Nevertheless, scientists may continue to examine the propositions of the theory, involving new participants or new methods.

What if the results do not fit the theory's predictions? One approach is to reexamine the methods and design of the study. Perhaps the key concepts were not measured appropriately or the sample was biased in some way. When results of research are inconclusive or contrary to the predictions, scholars may try another research approach before revising the theory. But when several different studies fail to support the hypotheses, we tend to lose confidence in the entire structure of the theory. We may revise or discard the theory and begin to develop an alternative explanation for the observations.

In summary, in the positivist approach, the scientific process consists of creating a theory, testing it through research, and modifying, rejecting, or accepting it. If confirmed through the research process, a theory helps us interpret many observations about reality.

## THE QUALITATIVE INQUIRY APPROACH TO RESEARCH

Whereas the positivist perspective assumes that there is a "truth" that can be captured through the research process, the qualitative inquiry approach assumes that there are many versions of truth, depending on the informant and the context. Knowledge is not "out there" to be discovered; rather, it is invented, constructed, and continuously revised as one accumulates new information (Schwandt, 1998). The approach begins with a "beginner's mind." One looks at the world as if it were ripe for discovery. Theory typically emerges from the data, rather than guiding the methodology and data collection. When evidence is gathered that contradicts the theory, the theory is rejected or modified. Multiple methods are employed in order to learn as much as possible about the setting, the participants, and the contexts of behavior. In some instances, the observer's own experiences and beliefs are included as a guide to the meaningfulness of the observation. In other instances, the observer attempts to challenge his or her own point of view by gathering as many different perspectives about the process as possible. Because qualitative inquiry assumes that there is not one truth, all perspectives and insights are considered equally valid. A major emphasis is on interpretation, made possible by the close acquaintance of the researcher with the details and voices of the participants.

In the study of human development, both positivist and qualitative inquiry are applied, often as complementary approaches to the same issue. The idea is that generalizations and categories used in the positivist approach can be reframed or refined using data from qualitative inquiry. Assumptions from the positivist perspective may be challenged by observations made through qualitative inquiry. For example, many children who live in households that may be characterized as female-headed, single-parent families actually have fathers, uncles, and grandfathers who participate actively in their daily lives, and many children who live in households that may be characterized as two-parent families actually have little daily contact with their fathers. Categories and definitions that are assumed to be meaningful from a positivist perspective are often shown to be more ambiguous or diversely defined when considered through the qualitative lens.

# RESEARCH DESIGN

Regardless of whether the positivist or the qualitative approach is used, each empirical study needs to be designed. Research investigations are designed just as cars, bridges, and buildings are designed. Research design is often conducted in meetings where small groups of scholars try to think up the most appropriate approach for answering their questions. Scientists know that the information they gain from conducting research will be influenced by the characteristics of the participants who are involved in their study, the kind of data that are gathered, and the conditions under which the data are gathered. The principles of research design focus on the approach to selecting a sample, the methods used to gather information, the design for studying change, and the techniques used to analyze the data (Gliner & Morgan, 2000).

## SAMPLING

Sampling is the method for choosing participants who will be included in the study. The nature of the questions that are being addressed usually has implications for the best way to identify the sample. If the study is about some universal principle of development, it should apply to individuals from a wide variety of family and social backgrounds. For example, studies of normal language development should include children from various ethnic, racial, social class, and cultural backgrounds. One cannot argue for universal principles if the research has shown the processes or patterns to be true only for a homogeneous group of children.

Every sample is taken from a population. The population is the large group to which the findings of the research are intended to apply. There is no single, predetermined population; the relevant population depends on the purpose and scope of the research. The sample is a smaller subgroup of the larger population that will participate in the study. For example, the population of interest might be adolescents in the United States who graduate from high school but do not go on to college. Roughly 967,000 adolescents who graduated from high school in the spring of 2001 were not enrolled in any postsecondary school in the fall of 2001 (U.S. Census Bureau, 2003). No research study is likely to include all of those adolescents. So a sample is drawn that is expected to be rep-

*The generalizability of research depends heavily on the sampling process. Studies that focus on older adults often require interviewers who can meet face to face with participants in a variety of settings. What factors might limit the researcher's ability to sample older adults?*

resentative of the population. Under ideal conditions, the participants in any study of this population ought to have the same general characteristics (e.g., family income; race; gender; urban, suburban, or rural environment; and high school academic background) as the population from which the sample was selected. The sample and the population from which the sample is taken determine the generalizability of the research findings—the extent to which we can say with confidence that the observations made for this sample would apply to other groups. We must be careful not to assume that research findings based on one sample are generalizable for all ages, both sexes, all racial and ethnic groups, all social classes, or individuals from other cultures.

Five approaches to sampling are common in the research literature: *random samples*, *stratified samples*, *matched groups*, *volunteer samples*, and *qualitative sampling*. Each is described in more detail in the following sections. Each one has different implications for the generalizability of the findings (Henry, 1998).

## RANDOM SAMPLES

In a random sample, each person in a given population has an equal chance of being included. The researcher may ensure equal opportunity by putting each person's name on a

slip of paper and then choosing some of the slips blindly, or by selecting names from a list at random, using numbers produced by a random number generator. The Kaiser Family Foundation study of media use by infants, toddlers, and preschoolers discussed in Chapter 8 (Early School Age) is an example of a study that used a random sampling of households (Rideout, Vandewater, & Wartella, 2003). The study was a random, national telephone survey of families with children ages 6 months to 6 years old. The parent who spent the most time with the child was asked to complete the survey.

## STRATIFIED SAMPLES

In a stratified sampling approach, participants are deliberately selected from a variety of levels (*strata*) or subgroups within the population. For example, one study used a stratified, random sample to examine the care received from family members by African American and European American adults age 65 and older who lived in their own homes. The sample groups were selected in proportion to their numbers in the community. Within the African American and European American groups, participants were selected at random (Peek, Coward, & Peek, 2000).

## MATCHED GROUPS

The researcher can also select two or more groups of participants who are similar on many dimensions. In most studies using matched groups, participants in one group receive some type of treatment or participate in some type of experimental intervention that the participants in the other group do not receive or participate in. In other studies, the impact of a naturally occurring difference is examined. For example, a matched group design was used to study the impact of low birthweight on later middle school performance. At age 11, children who had weighed less than 750 grams at birth were compared to children who had weighed 750 to 1,400 grams, and to children of normal birthweight. The groups were matched on age, sex, and other background variables. The design allowed researchers to evaluate the long-term risks for very small babies (Taylor, Klein, Minich, & Hack, 2000).

## VOLUNTEER SAMPLES

Participants can be solicited by asking people directly, placing advertisements in newspapers or on bulletin boards, sending letters to teachers or parents asking for participants, or writing to professionals or groups of potential participants. Those who are included in the study are selected from among those who volunteer. Most studies that are conducted with students enrolled in introductory psychology courses involve volunteer samples. Although the students may be required to participate in research, they have a choice about which study they will volunteer for. In some sense, all research with human participants uses a volunteer sample. One cannot compel a person to participate in research.

## ■ THE QUALITATIVE APPROACH TO SAMPLING

The primary objective of the qualitative approach to sampling is to learn as much as possible from each informant. Researchers enter a setting with some general idea of questions they seek to understand. The strategy is to remain open to the information that is provided. Researchers may learn that they cannot get information about the question they started out with. For example, in a study of institutional wards for people with severe and profound retardation, Taylor (1987) wanted to know about residents' perspectives. However, many residents were nonverbal, and others were reticent to share their opinions. So Taylor shifted his attention to staff perspectives on the environment. Qualitative researchers emphasize that the informants should have the knowledge and experience that the researcher requires, be able to reflect and verbalize about the experiences, and be willing to participate in the study (Morse, 1998). The number of informants or settings in which research occurs is not decided in advance. Typically, the greater the depth and detail in each case, the fewer cases will be included. Additional cases are added as needed until the researcher believes that the variety of perspectives within a setting has been captured and the theoretical insights are well confirmed (Taylor & Bogdan, 1998).

## ■ STRENGTHS AND WEAKNESSES OF APPROACHES TO SAMPLING

What are some of the strengths and weaknesses of different approaches to sampling? Random sampling and stratified sampling are the most likely to ensure that a sample is *representative* of the population from which it is drawn. If each person in the population has an equal chance of being included in a study, then the outcome or results of the study ought to be equally likely to apply to those in the population who did not participate as to those who did. These sampling approaches are often used to provide statistical information about a population. They do not provide information about any specific person within the population. For example, the mean or arithmetic average income of a group of 100 people may not be the exact income of any single person in the group.

The use of matched samples allows one to examine the impact of naturally occurring events—such as unemployment, parental divorce, or low birthweight—that cannot be randomly assigned. By matching participants on a variety of background factors, such as IQ, family income, or birth order, one might be able to detect the impact of these events on emotional, social, or cognitive development. However, critics might argue that one cannot match groups perfectly, and one might omit an important variable for which there is no match. For example, in the study described earlier about the impact of low birthweight on school achievement, sibling order was not included in the match. Because we know that firstborns typically do better on tests of academic achievement than siblings born later, this factor might explain more about the outcome than birthweight.

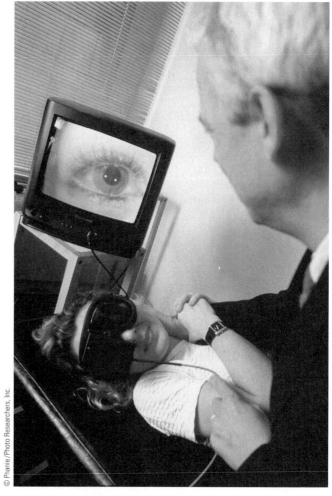

Phanie/Photo Researchers, Inc.

*Clinical samples often focus on children or adults who are undergoing a special, experimental treatment or who have undergone some unusual trauma. Without their participation, we could not learn about the potential benefits of new forms of treatment or intervention.*

The method that places the greatest limits on generalization is volunteer sampling. One never knows what type of person will volunteer to participate in social science research. Can you think of how reliance on volunteers may produce special problems? For example, imagine a study that promises to pay $25 to those who participate. People who volunteer to participate in this research may be especially in need of money. Sometimes, volunteers have more free time, are hoping to find some kind of help as a result of participating in the research, or have greater faith in science than those who choose not to volunteer.

Regardless of these difficulties, volunteer samples are widely used. Most of the studies cited in this textbook are based on volunteer samples. All studies involving observation, interview, or experimentation with children require formal consent from parents and could be classified as volunteer samples. Frequently, the only way to study a certain question is to ask for volunteers.

## TECHNOLOGY AND HUMAN DEVELOPMENT

# Observation Using Video Recording

THE TECHNOLOGY OF video recording has expanded the use of observational techniques for developmental research. A videotaped record can be reviewed over and over again. Several observers can watch a tape, stop it, and discuss what they saw. The same events can be observed from several points of view. For example, research on infants' responses to sweet and sour tastes uses video recording to document changes in facial expression. These images can be found in Chapter 6 (Infancy). Other studies use video recording to capture the dynamic quality of communication between mothers and infants. The sequence of coordination of attention followed by disengagement and then reconnection, called **synchrony**, means that the infant and caregiver move fluidly from one state to the next. When infants are paying attention to their caregivers, the caregivers attempt to stimulate them. As babies withdraw their attention, the caregivers learn to reduce stimulation and wait until the infants are ready to engage again (Tronick, 2003).

In research of this type, several observers might review the tapes, each one rating different aspects of the behavior. Videotaped records can also be slowed to frame-by-frame viewing, allowing for very detailed microanalysis of behavior. Facial expressions and motor sequences have been examined using this approach (Dekeyser, Verfaillie, & Vanrie, 2002). Videotaped records allow one to track the sequences of interaction, turn taking, and the formation of cycles of interaction among family members, which often occur too subtly or quickly to be captured by direct observation (Johnson, Cowan, & Cowan, 1999). In the development of case studies, video recordings can be used to document complex group interactions, reactions to new information, or changes in self-presentation and appearance over time (Walker, 2002).

Some of the research findings discussed in the text are based on **clinical samples**. This usually means that the participants have been involved in some type of treatment program or are on a waiting list to receive clinical treatment. These studies are especially important for understanding the causes of clinical conditions, the developmental paths or patterns that these conditions exhibit, or the impact of certain interventions on these conditions. Without voluntary participation, there would be no way to begin to document the effectiveness of treatment. At the same time, one must be cautious not to generalize findings from clinical studies to the population as a whole.

From a qualitative perspective, the best informants are those who willingly volunteer to share their experiences and reflect on them. If the informant is providing an authentic, open narrative, then insights can be drawn. Each informant's perspective is treated as one way of making meaning of the situation. The researcher's job is to try to build a complex picture of the topic by comparing the views of multiple informants.

## RESEARCH METHODS

A variety of methods has been used to study development. Each one has its strengths and weaknesses, allowing the investigator to focus on one set of behaviors at the expense of others. The choice of method must fit the problem under study. Six general categories of developmental research are described here: observation, case study, interviews, surveys, tests, and experimentation. These methods have all contributed to the discovery of knowledge, and as you read further in the text, you will find examples of each method. Some techniques—especially observation, case study, and interview—are more commonly used in qualitative inquiry as investigators try to uncover basic themes or dimensions of a problem. Other methods—especially observation using a predetermined coding scheme, experimentation, structured interviews, surveys, and tests—tend to be used in the positivist approach to the research process.

## ◼ OBSERVATION

One might argue that at the heart of all science is **observation**—taking note of events and trying to make sense of them (Adler & Adler, 1998). Direct observation of children in their home and school environments is one of the oldest methods for studying development (Kessen, 1965). Researchers have used mothers' diaries and observation logs to gather information about behavior in intimate settings that could not be known in any other way. Jean Piaget was guided by the observations of his own children in the formulation of his theory of cognition. Today, some researchers conduct observations in homes, schools, and day care centers where children typically spend their time. Others bring children and their families or friends into "homelike" laboratory settings, where they can watch children's behaviors under more constant and controlled physical conditions (Kochanska, Murray, & Harlan, 2000).

*In a naturalistic setting, observers can capture the flow of ongoing behavior and note the interactions among participants. Here, the observer watches as teacher and children engage in a reading lesson. The observer's presence does not appear to interfere with the children's interest and attention. What kinds of behaviors might be the focus of this observational study?*

© David Young-Wolff/PhotoEdit

**NATURALISTIC OBSERVATION.** Naturalistic observation refers to research in which behavior in a setting is carefully observed without any other kinds of manipulation. This type of observation provides insight about how things occur in the real world. In some instances, researchers go into a setting to observe the full range of interactions and behavior patterns. Based on their field notes, they begin to develop hypotheses or tentative explanations about the meaning of the behaviors. Then, they may test these hypotheses through more focused observation or through controlled experimentation. In other instances, researchers use observation to examine a specific behavior or relationship. They may be looking for different forms of peer aggression, patterns of social cooperation, or conditions that promote cross-gender interactions. In these cases, the observers limit the scope of their observations to behaviors that are relevant to their concerns.

**PARTICIPANT OBSERVATION.** A major methodological approach in qualitative inquiry is **participant observation**, in which the researcher actively engages in interactions with other members of a setting. This is done in order to gain a new understanding of how people in that setting experience the world or how the processes that take place in that setting might apply to broader issues such as socialization, control, or self-construction. To engage in this type of work, one must first obtain access to the setting and then gain the trust of the other people in the setting. Some participant observation takes place in public settings, such as parks, street corners, pool halls, or train stations, where the researcher can be accepted as a nonthreatening participant. Even in these situations, it may take time for people to interact with the observer or be willing to confide in him or her. In Elliot Liebow's (1967/2003) famous study of Black street-corner men, *Tally's Corner*, Liebow met his primary informant, Tally, while play-

ing with a puppy outside a carryout restaurant. The friendship he formed with Tally led to introductions to other men on the street.

The participant observer usually gathers data through field notes, which are made after an observational session. Over time, the skilled observer learns to retain information about the details of a session and to record it in a systematic way. This is a very demanding process; it may take several hours to summarize what was observed in a single hour in the field. In addition to the observations, the researcher tries to capture his or her own reactions to the situation, using personal feelings and responses as a way of empathizing with the participants. In a study of a mental institution, Taylor made the following field notes:

> O.C. [observer's comments]: Although I don't show it, I tense up when the residents approach me when they're covered with food or excrement. Maybe this is what the attendants feel and why they often treat the residents as lepers. (Taylor & Bogdan, 1998, p. 73)

One of the challenges in participant observation is to check out and confirm one's insights from observation by comparing them with information drawn from other sources. This is especially important the more involved one becomes in the setting and the more attached one grows to the participants. This confirmatory approach is called **triangulation**, and it can be achieved by looking at written documents about the setting, interviewing other informants, and sharing observations with other members of a research team. This is often done toward the end of the study, as the researcher is preparing to leave the field (Taylor & Bogdan, 1998).

**CORRELATION.** Observational studies lend themselves to an examination of correlation rather than causation. **Corre-**

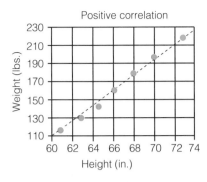

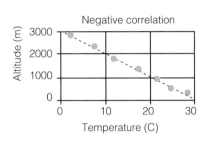

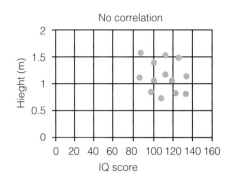

**FIGURE 2.2**

Patterns Reflecting Positive, Negative, and Zero Correlations

**lation** refers to a statistical analysis of the strength and direction of the relationships among variables. It reflects the degree to which knowing the value of one variable, such as popularity, allows one to predict the level of another variable, such as aggressiveness.

The correlation coefficient is a numeric index of the strength of relationship between variables that can range from a value of +1.0 to −1.0. Let us take as an example the correlation between popularity with peers and aggressiveness. If, as popularity increases, so does aggressiveness, the correlation is *positive* (between 0 and +1.0). If, as popularity increases, aggressiveness decreases, the correlation is *negative* (between 0 and −1.0). If there is no systematic relationship between aggressiveness and popularity, the correlation is close to 0 (see Figure 2.2). A correlation of .40 suggests that there is a positive relationship between aggressiveness and popularity, but that aggressiveness cannot be predicted entirely or even predominantly by knowing about a person's popularity.

A strong correlation between two variables shows only that there is an association between them. It does not provide information about causation. Knowing that aggression is negatively correlated with popularity does not necessarily mean that being aggressive causes children to be rejected by peers. It could be that some other factor, such as mistrust of others, accounts for both aggression and peer rejection.

**STRENGTHS AND LIMITATIONS OF THE OBSERVATIONAL METHOD.** Many scholars agree that direct observation is an ideal way to study behavior (Bakeman, 2000). It avoids the interpretive issues that are raised when one asks people to report on their behavior, and it allows for the documentation of patterns of behavior that may not have been anticipated by the investigator. For example, in studying patterns of dominance among children, one might assume that hitting is a form of dominance. However, in observing play behavior, one may find that certain kinds of hitting are a type of affectionate interaction rather than a mechanism for achieving dominance. Another strength of observation is the ability to allow participants' behaviors to guide the researcher's conceptualization. Rather than setting up a specific task

or group of questions and having people respond, the observer examines the full range of relevant behaviors and builds an interpretation of the meaning of the events from the patterns that have been observed.

Observational research also has weaknesses. It is often difficult to establish agreement among observers about exactly what occurred. Think about the times that you and a friend have been in the same situation but have entirely different reactions to what is happening or describe it very differently to a third party. Typically, two or more observers' codings of the same situation are compared to determine whether different observers rated the same event in the same way. This is called **interobserver reliability**. When interobserver reliability is high, one has confidence that all the observers are describing or coding the events in the same way. When interobserver reliability is low, the researchers must determine why and then correct the differences in observation techniques. This may result in changing the category scheme, so that it is easier to link each behavior with a category, or it may result in more training, so that the observers know more precisely how to code each behavior.

Another difficulty with the observational method occurs when so much activity is taking place that it is difficult to select specific behaviors or to code fast enough to keep up with the pace of activity in the setting. Some research focuses on a particular kind of behavior or behavioral sequence, such as helping behavior, peer rejection, or conflict. In naturalistic observation, one cannot be assured that the behavior of interest will take place during the observational period. Finally, some researchers fear that the presence of the observer or the introduction of audio recording or videotaping equipment, or even note taking, may change the nature of the behaviors that take place in the setting. Although there are techniques to limit the impact of the observer on the setting, this is always a concern in direct observation.

## ■ CASE STUDY

A case study is an in-depth description of a single person, family, social group, or social setting. The purpose of a case study may be to illuminate something very particular and interesting about the person or organization being studied, to illustrate a general principle by providing specific details, to examine a phenomenon that does not conform to theoretical predictions, or to stimulate theory development in an area that has not been investigated (Stake, 1998).

Some case studies document the lives of great individuals. In *Gandhi's Truth*, Erikson (1969) provided a psychosocial analysis of the life of Mahatma Gandhi. Erikson considered Gandhi's childhood, adolescence, and young adulthood as they contributed to his personality, his moral philosophy, and to the contradictions between his personal relationships and his role as a powerful social leader.

Case studies can also focus on social groups, families, and organizations. One of Anna Freud's most famous cases described the attachments that developed among a group of orphans who had lived together in a concentration camp during World War II (Freud & Dann, 1951). The study focused on the strong feelings the children had for one another and their strategies for maintaining their sense of connectedness once they were placed in a more normal social environment. The case illustrated a unique phenomenon—the intense emotional attachment of young children to each other—that had not been documented before.

Case studies can be based on a variety of sources of information, including interviews, therapy sessions, prolonged observation, diaries or journals, letters, historical documents, and talks with people who know the subject of the study. The researcher usually spends a great deal of time with the subject of the case, in conversation, observation, and gathering information from documents and informants in order to fully understand what is happening. In addition to gathering information, the researcher engages in ongoing reflection in order to reach a new depth of insight about the case.

**STRENGTHS AND LIMITATIONS OF THE CASE STUDY METHOD.** Case studies have the advantage of illustrating the complexity and uniqueness of the subject. They capture the interplay of complex, dynamic processes. Studies carried out with large samples often identify general principles, whereas case studies provide concrete examples of how these principles play out in the lives of specific individuals or groups. Some cases give the details of an experience that is rare and might not be captured in a large-scale study. Sometimes, the case study brings a problem to the attention of researchers, who then pursue it through other methods (Yin, 1994). Although case studies cannot provide the basis for broad generalizations, they can provide specific examples of instances where a broad generalization does not hold true. Throughout this book, you will find case study material that is intended to help you apply concepts from the text to specific examples and to serve as points of reflection about the relevance of human development content for understanding individuals' life stories.

Case studies have been criticized as unscientific. In the first place, they are obviously not representative of large groups of individuals. One must be cautious about generalizing the conclusions drawn from a case study to other individuals or groups. Moreover, if the information that provides the basis of the case study is gathered in a biased or subjective way, then the results or conclusions of the study will be of little worth. Of course, this criticism applies to any type of research. Finally, critics argue that there is no reliability in case studies. If different people were writing a case study on the same individual, they might come up with very different views of the events and their significance.

These limitations suggest that one must have a very clear idea of the study's purpose and a systematic approach to gathering information in order to conduct case studies that meet the standards of scientific observation. At the same time, vividly written, compelling case material has had a consistent impact in stimulating theory and research in the field of development. In some instances, the lucid recounting of case material is more convincing to policymakers than the results of studies based on large, national samples.

*John Glenn, a former astronaut and senator, has volunteered to participate in a case study of the effects of space on the aging process. Because of his unique background, long-term medical records are available that can be used to trace his physical health over a 50-year span.*

## ■ INTERVIEWS

Many case studies are based largely on face-to-face interviews. The interview method can also be used to gather data from large numbers of individuals and from people in clinical settings. Interviews can be highly structured, almost like a verbal survey, or very open ended, allowing the participant to respond freely to a series of general questions. There are at least three common uses of in-depth interviewing (Taylor &

## Piaget's Interview Method

PIAGET'S USE OF the interview method to elicit a young child's cognitive reasoning can be seen in two excerpts from his works. In the first, Piaget (1929, pp. 97–98) was exploring a 5-year-old child's understanding of dreams:

Where does the dream come from?
"I think you sleep so well that you dream."
Does it come from us or from outside?
"From outside."
What do we dream with?
"I don't know."
With the hands? With nothing?
"Yes, with nothing."
When you are in bed and you dream, where is the dream?
"In my bed, under the blanket. I don't really know. If it was in my stomach(!) the bones would be in the way and I shouldn't see it."
Is the dream in your head?
"It is I that am in the dream: it isn't in my head(!) When you dream, you don't know you are in the bed. You know you are walking. You are in the dream. You are in bed, but you don't know you are."

In the second excerpt, Piaget (1963, p. 283) was describing a 7-year-old child's understanding of class inclusion:

You present the child with an open box that contains wooden beads. The child knows they are all wooden because he handles them, touching each and finding that it is made of wood. Most of these beads are brown, but a few are white. The problem we pose is simply this: Are there more brown beads or more wooden beads? Let us call A the brown beads, B the wooden beads: Then the problem is simply that of the inclusion of A in B. This is a very difficult problem before the age of 7 years. The child states that all the beads are wooden, and that most of them are brown and a few are white, but if you

*In studies using a Piaget-style interview, children explain how they reach an answer and why they think their answer is correct. This provides insight into the reasoning behind correct and incorrect responses.*

ask him if there are more brown beads or more wooden beads he immediately answers, "There are more brown ones because there are only two or three white ones." So you say, "Listen, this is not what I am asking. I don't want to know whether there are more brown beads or more white beads, I want to know whether there are more brown beads or more wooden beads." And, in order to make it easier, I take an empty box and place it next to the one with the beads and I ask, "If I were to put the wooden beads into that box would any remain in this one?" The child answers, "NO, none would be left because they are all wooden." Then I say, "If I were to take the brown beads and put them into that box, would any be left in this one?" The child replies, "Of course, two or three white ones would remain." Apparently

he has now understood the situation, the fact that all the beads are wooden and that some are not brown. So I ask him once more, "Are there more brown beads or more wooden beads?" Now it is evident that the child begins to understand the problem, sees that there is indeed a problem, that matters are not as simple as they seemed at first. As we watch him we observe that he is thinking very hard. Finally he concludes, "But there are still more brown beads; if you take the brown ones away, only two or three white beads remain."

In studies using a Piagetian-style interview, children explain how they reached an answer and why they think their answer is correct. This provides insight into the reasoning behind correct and incorrect responses.

Bogdan, 1998). First, the life history or personal narrative allows the researcher to learn about a person's key life experiences and the meaning of those experiences. The researcher's role is to encourage the person being interviewed to cover all the important issues and to foster elaboration and reflection.

Second, through interviews, informants are asked to describe in detail events that occurred when the researcher was not present. This might be a historical event, a natural disaster, or the behaviors of a group to which the researcher does not have access. For example, a researcher may want to interview informants who have been members of a gang about the gang's initiation rites or practices. Third, interviews can be useful in gathering information from a number of people about a similar topic. For example, Harrington and Boardman (2000) interviewed 100 people whom they called "pathmakers"—people who achieved career success despite growing up in impoverished families and communities.

The success of the interview method depends heavily on the skill of the interviewer (Holstein & Gubrium, 1995). Interviewers are trained to be nonjudgmental as they listen to a participant's responses. They try to create **rapport** with the participant by conveying a feeling of trustworthiness and acceptance. The goal, especially in qualitative interviewing, is to create a conversational atmosphere where the person feels at ease to talk. In unstructured interviews, the interviewer must make use of this rapport to encourage the participant to say more about a topic and to share thoughts that may be private or personal. Matching the race and gender of the interviewer and the participant being interviewed has been found to help foster rapport and improve the quality of the data that are produced.

The interview method has traditionally been associated with clinical research; however, it is becoming a common method in the study of cognition and language as well. Piaget's structured interview technique (Piaget, 1929) provides a model for the investigation of conceptual development. The researcher who uses this technique asks a child a question (e.g., "Are clouds living or dead?"), and then follows up on the child's answer with questions about how the child arrived at his or her conclusion. In other studies, Piaget asked children to solve a problem, and then asked them to explain how they arrived at the solution. The child becomes an informant about his or her own conceptual capacities. This approach has been adapted in the study of moral development, interpersonal development, and positive, helping behavior.

**STRENGTHS AND LIMITATIONS OF THE INTERVIEW METHOD.** The interview method has the advantage of allowing individuals to contribute their own views on the topic being studied. They can tell the interviewer what is important to them, why they might choose one alternative over another, or what they think is wrong with the investigator's view of the situation. Interviews have the advantage of expediency when it might be difficult to gain access to a setting for observation or when one wants to gather information from a larger number of participants, rather than observing just a few.

There are also limitations to the interview method. Participants may present themselves in the way they want the interviewer to see them; when they do, they are said to be exhibiting a **self-presentation bias**. Research has suggested that young children's responses are especially vulnerable to influence by the interviewer. By smiling, nodding, frowning, or looking away, the interviewer can deliberately or inadvertently communicate approval or disapproval. There is a fine line between establishing rapport and influencing responses.

Another limitation of interviews is that people may not be aware of all the factors that influence their behaviors or deci-

sions. Thus, in asking people about their lives and why they behave as they do, one is limited to the person's level of sensitivity and insight into their own situation. Whereas one might see certain forces at work through participant observation, relying solely on interviews limits the researchers' access to contextual factors that may influence a person's behavior (Taylor & Bogdan, 1998).

## ■ SURVEYS AND TESTS

Survey research is a means of collecting specific information from a large number of participants. If people are to respond directly to surveys, they must be able to read and write, unless the survey questions are read to them. The survey method is, therefore, most commonly used with participants in middle childhood, adolescence, and adulthood. However, survey information about infants and toddlers is often collected from parents, child care workers, physicians, nurses, and others who are responsible for meeting the needs of young children. Thus, surveys have contributed a great deal to our knowledge about the way adults perceive the behaviors and needs of young children.

Survey methods can be used to collect information about attitudes ("Do you believe teachers should be permitted to use corporal punishment with their students?"), about current behaviors and practices ("How many hours per day do you watch television?"), about aspirations ("What do you hope to do when you graduate from high school?"), and about perceptions ("How well does your mother/father or son/daughter understand your views?").

Survey questions are prepared in a standard form, and the responses are usually coded according to a prearranged set of categories. In well-designed surveys, the questions are stated clearly and offer response choices that are not ambiguous or overlapping. In the most powerful surveys, the sample of respondents is carefully selected to be representative of the population under study. Surveys may be conducted by telephone, through the mail, on the Internet, in classrooms, at work, or in the participants' homes (Fowler, 1993).

*Tests* are often similar in form to surveys. They consist of groups of questions or problems that the person is expected to answer. Usually, tests are designed to measure a specific ability or characteristic. You are no doubt familiar with the kinds of tests typically given in school. You are presented with a group of items and asked to produce the correct answer or to select the correct answer from among several choices. Intelligence tests and achievement tests are of this nature. A researcher might give these tests along with some other measures in order to learn how intelligence relates to social life, emotions, or self-understanding.

Other tests are designed to measure a variety of psychological constructs, such as creativity, conformity, depression, and extroversion. Some tests are administered to assess whether a person has some form of mental illness, learning disorder, or developmental or physical disability.

Psychological tests must be reliable and valid to be useful. Tests are **reliable** when the results are consistent. A person

## The Use of the SAT in College Admissions

THE USE OF tests to determine school admissions and placement has come under serious attack. Some tests have been criticized for putting unfair emphasis on knowledge derived from a White, middle class, Eurocentric cultural perspective. Some tests have been criticized for putting at a disadvantage children whose first language is not English, or for being insensitive to different learning styles and modes of synthesizing information. A current controversy about the use of the *Scholastic Aptitude Test* (SAT) in college admissions is an example of this problem. The SAT I is described as an aptitude test that assesses a student's potential to do well in college, separately from his or her grades and specific content knowledge. In 2001, Dr. Richard Atkinson, the chancellor of the University of California raised questions about requiring the SAT I for all students applying to schools in the UC system (Cloud, 2001).

Three primary reasons were offered to de-emphasize these tests. First, African American and Hispanic students typically score lower on these tests than do European American students,

suggesting a built-in cultural bias to this approach to measuring aptitude for college learning. Second, students with financial resources can attend special courses to help improve their scores. Third, the tests are typically not as strong a predictor of college performance as are a combination of other factors, including high school grades, performance on achievement or advanced placement tests, evaluations of the rigor of the high school curriculum where students attended school, written essays, and, at some colleges, personal interviews (Lin, 2001).

Encouraging the university community to find another approach to admissions testing, Dr. Atkinson (Atkinson, 2001) made the following recommendations:

- The academic competencies to be tested should be clearly defined. There should be a demonstrable relationship between what is tested and what the student studied in high school. In other words, testing should be directly related to the required college preparatory curriculum.

- Students from any comprehensive high school in California should be able to score well if they mastered the curriculum.
- Students should be able to review their score and understand where they did well or fell short and what they must do to earn higher scores in the future.
- Test scores should help admissions officers evaluate the applicant's readiness for college-level work.

In 2004, the University of California announced a new admissions procedure for students entering in 2006. Students will take a new version of the SAT I, which focuses on writing and mathematics competences that are more reflective of the knowledge and skills that students are being encouraged to develop in a rigorous high school program. They will also be required to take two SAT II tests of their choice in areas such as history, English, mathematics, laboratory science, or a non-English language to demonstrate their readiness for college-level work (University of California, 2004).

---

who takes a reliable test on 2 consecutive days should get approximately the same score on both days, unless some deliberate training or intervention has been introduced between test sessions. There ought to be a positive correlation (between 0 and +1.0) between the two scores.

Tests are **valid** when they measure what they claim to measure. The people who design the tests have to define what it is they are trying to measure. They also have to provide evidence that their test really measures this construct (Ray, 1993). For example, if you are trying to measure self-esteem, you need to ask, "What do I mean by self-esteem?" and "What type of questions or tasks would provide evidence of self-esteem?" Consider the various tests that have been designed to measure intelligence in infants and very young children. The results of these tests are not very closely related to the results of tests of intelligence given in adolescence and adulthood (Slater, Carrick, Bell, & Roberts, 1999). In other words, correlations between intelligence tests given to infants and those given to the same individuals when they are older tend to be low (nearer to 0.0 than to +1.0 or −1.0). Why is this?

One explanation is that the infant tests are not really tests of broad, adaptive intelligence, but are measures of sensory processing and central nervous system coordination. As children get older, their symbolic capacities and acquired knowledge expand. As a result, they rely less on sensory processing and more on interpretation and experience to guide meaning-making and problem solving.

**STRENGTHS AND LIMITATIONS OF SURVEYS AND TESTS.** Surveys and tests have certain advantages that make them widely used in developmental research. They allow the comparison of responses by large groups of respondents. Surveys and tests have been designed to address a wide variety of topics. With a prearranged coding or scoring system, many tests can be administered and evaluated without the extensive training that is usually necessary with participant observation or interview methods.

This method also has limitations. Some surveys create attitudes where none existed before. This is referred to as the **reactive** nature of surveys. For example, you might ask sixth-grade children questions about their satisfaction with their school curriculum. The students may answer a lot of questions on this topic, even though they had not given much thought to the issue before. Thus, reading the questions and response options on a survey may help participants formulate their opinions (Wilson, LaFleur, & Anderson, 1996).

Another problem is the gap between answers to survey questions or scores on tests and actual behavior. Parents may respond to a survey by indicating that they allow their children to participate in family decisions, but when it comes to real family decisions, they may not give their children much voice. Some survey questions are more difficult for some respondents to answer accurately than others. For example, consider the following question: How often did you go for medical treatment over the past 6 months? It would be easier for a person who went only once to respond accurately and with confidence than for a person who went six or eight times (Mathiowetz, 1999).

### ■ EXPERIMENTATION

Experimentation is a method best suited for examining causal relationships. In an **experiment**, some variable or group of variables is systematically manipulated to examine the effect on an outcome. For example, in research on memory among older adults, which is discussed in Chapter 14 (Later Adulthood), the complexity of the material and the speed of presentation are varied in order to learn more about how these factors influence the ability of adults to recall information. The factor (or factors) that is manipulated by the experimenter is called the **independent variable**. The dimension of the participant's responses or reactions that is measured is

the **dependent variable** (Davis, 1995). The research is carried out to determine whether the independent variable or some combination of independent variables can produce a change in the dependent variable.

In some experiments, one group of participants has a certain set of experiences or receives information (usually referred to as a *treatment*) that is not provided to another group. The group that experiences the experimenter's manipulation is called the **experimental group**. The group that does not experience the treatment or manipulation is called the **control group**. Differences in behavior between the two groups are then attributed to the treatment. For example, in a study of academic performance in human development courses, students enrolled in a course would be randomly assigned to the experimental group, in which they are linked as a study group through e-mail, so they can contact one another, discuss questions from the course, and share their ideas. The other students, who are in the control group, do not receive this Internet support. Differences in course grades between the experimental and the control groups would be attributed to the Internet intervention.

In other experiments, the behavior of a single group of participants is compared before and after the treatment or across several treatments. Once again, systematic differences in behavior before and after the treatment are attributed to the experimental manipulation. In this case, each participant serves as his or her own control.

*Control* is the key to successful experimentation. The experimenter must exercise control in selecting the children or families who participate in a study. The participants must be able to bring equivalent competencies to the situation. If this condition is not met, one cannot assume that differences in behavior between groups are due to the treatment.

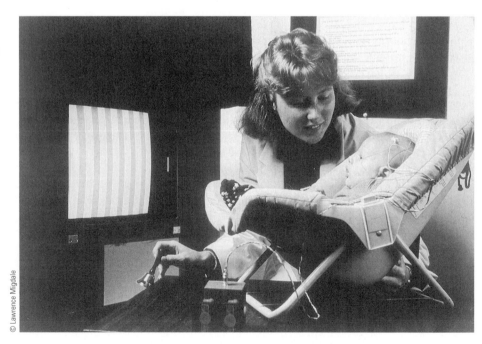

*The experimental method has been used widely to learn more about infants' visual and auditory abilities and their capacity to remember stimuli from one presentation to the next. As a parent, what would you want to know before deciding to give permission for your child to participate in experimental research?*

© Lawrence Migdale

Experimenters control the way a task is presented to the participants so that such factors as the ability to understand the instructions, the order of events, and the degree of comfort and familiarity with the setting do not interfere with the participants' behavior. Control ensures that changes in behavior do, in fact, result from the experimental manipulation.

Many studies in human development are **quasi-experimental**. This means that the treatment was not controlled by the experimenter but was the result of some pattern of life events (Wilson, 1995). Suppose we are interested in the impact of unemployment on conflict between married couples. We cannot (nor do we want to) cause some adults to lose their jobs while others remain employed. We can, however, compare couples of about the same age and social class who have experienced unemployment with couples who have not. In these studies, assignment to a "treatment" occurs as a result of real-world events. One would select participants for the study who are as much alike as possible in other respects, except for their encounters with unemployment. It is the task of the scientist to compare some of the consequences of this "treatment"—the experience of unemployment—and to address the limitations that are imposed on the results because of the way the individuals arrive in one group or the other to begin with.

**STRENGTHS AND LIMITATIONS OF THE EXPERIMENTAL METHOD.** The experimental method has the advantage of providing conclusions about causal relationships. If the results suggest that the participants' behavior changes only when something about the experimental situation changes, we can conclude that the manipulation has caused the changes in behavior. This is a very powerful statement, particularly as we search for explanations for how conditions that occur early in development might influence later outcomes.

Experiments also have limitations. Despite careful control, one cannot entirely rule out factors that can interfere with the impact of the treatment or that influence the respondents in ways that were not anticipated (Ray, 1993). For example, in a study of the impact of exposure to television violence, participants may have seen a televised documentary about the topic on the day before they came to participate in the research. In a study involving repeated observations, the participants might talk with each other about the study between testing sessions, thus influencing their responses. Any factor occurring outside the specific design of the study that influences the participants' responses is a threat to the **internal validity** or meaningfulness of the experiment.

Experiments may also be challenged on the basis of their **external validity**. We cannot be certain how applicable a controlled laboratory situation is to the real world. Would the behaviors that are observed in the laboratory also be observed at home, at school, or at work? For example, through studies of infant attachment (discussed in Chapter 6) we have learned that infants and young children do not behave the same way in the presence of their mothers as they do when their mothers are absent. Thus, experimental research conducted with children that does not allow their mothers to be present may produce behaviors that differ in quantity, quality, and sequence from the behavior that would be observed under conditions when the mothers are present.

Experimental studies tend to suggest that event A causes response B. In many domains of development, however, a multifaceted, reciprocal process promotes change. Think a moment about the development of *friendship*. A friendship depends on so many domains and on the fit or lack of fit along each domain for the two people. Friendships may be influenced by physical appearance, abilities, temperaments, intelligence, family background, whether others support the friendship or ridicule it, and so on. Friendships are sustained and promoted by continuous feedback and interaction among the friends rather than by one or two factors that could be said to promote or inhibit friendship. Experiments tend to suggest a unidirectional, causal explanation for behaviors that may be more accurately described using an interactional model.

Advantages and disadvantages of the five research methods are summarized in Table 2.1.

# DESIGNS FOR STUDYING DEVELOPMENT

The primary concern of developmental research is to describe and account for patterns of continuity and change over time. We want to know how individuals change over time and how groups of individuals who have been exposed to different life situations differ from one another as they age. This is a very challenging task, which requires strategies for considering changing individuals in changing environments. Four major research approaches have been created for examining development: *retrospective studies*, *cross-sectional studies*, *longitudinal studies*, and *cohort sequential studies*.

## RETROSPECTIVE STUDIES

A researcher engaged in a **retrospective study** asks the participants to report on experiences from an earlier time in their lives. Many early studies of childrearing used parents' recollections of their parenting techniques to evaluate their patterns of child care. Researchers who studied the effects of stress during pregnancy often asked women to recall their emotional state before, during, and after their child was born. Investigators of personality development use retrospective data by asking adolescent or adult subjects to recall important events of their childhood.

This approach produces a record of what a person has retained of past events. We cannot be certain that these events really occurred as they are remembered or, for that matter,

**Table 2.1**  Advantages and Disadvantages of the Methods of Developmental Research

| METHOD | DEFINITION | ADVANTAGES | DISADVANTAGES |
|---|---|---|---|
| **Observation** | Systematic recording of behavior. | Documents the variety of ongoing behavior; captures what happens naturally, without intervention. | Time consuming; difficult to achieve interrater agreement; requires careful training; observer may interfere with what would normally occur; difficult to capture and code full range of ongoing activity. |
| **Case study** | In-depth description of a single person, family, or group. | Focuses on complexity and unique experiences of individual; permits analysis of unusual cases. | Lacks generalizability; conclusions may reflect bias of investigator; hard to replicate. |
| **Interviews** | Face-to-face interaction in which each person can give a full account of his or her views. | Provides complex, first-person account; flexible method; allows access to the other person's own meaning. | Vulnerable to investigator bias; self-presentation bias; relies on participant's self-insight. |
| **Surveys and tests** | Standard questions administered to many participants. | Permits data collection from large samples; permits group comparisons of responses in standard form; requires little training; flexible. | Wording and way of presenting questions may influence responses; responses may not be closely related to behavior; tests may not be valid for certain groups. |
| **Experimentation** | Analysis of cause–effect relations by manipulation of some conditions while others are held constant. | Permits testing of causal hypotheses; permits isolation and control of specific variables; allows evaluation of treatment effects. | Laboratory findings may lack ecological validity; unable to control for all threats to internal validity; focuses on a unidirectional model of causality. |

whether they occurred at all. Piaget (1951) described a vivid memory from his second year of life:

> I was sitting in my pram, which my nurse was pushing in the Champs Elysées, when a man tried to kidnap me. I was held in by the strap fastened around me while my nurse bravely tried to stand between me and the thief. She received various scratches, and I can still see vaguely those on her face. (p. 188)

Thirteen years later, when Piaget was 15, the nurse joined a religious order. She wrote to his parents and returned a watch they had given her for protecting Jean from the kidnapper. She confessed that she had made up the story, even to the point of scratching her own face. Piaget believed he had created the visual memory from the story his parents had told him about the incident.

The passage of time may change the significance of certain past events in a person's memory. As we gain new levels of cognitive complexity or change our attitudes, we reorganize our memories of the past so as to bring them into line with our current level of understanding (Kotre, 1995). Sometimes, people claim to have recovered memories of past events that have been long forgotten or "repressed." It is difficult to determine the accuracy of these memories (Loftus, 1993). They may be entangled with current experiences or with ideas taken from books, movies, or conversations with others. They may be altered by the suggestion that something happened that actually did not, or by the suggestion that something did not happen that actually did. Because memory is so easily modified by suggestion, its usefulness in uncovering systematic data about the past is limited. However, retrospective data provide insight into how people make sense of their past and the role they give to past experiences in determining their present way of thinking. Studies that use the technique of life review provide insight into the way adults organize and structure key periods and events from their life history (McAdams et al., 1997).

## CROSS-SECTIONAL STUDIES

Studies that compare people of different ages, social backgrounds, or from different school or community settings are called **cross-sectional studies**. Such studies are quite common in research on child development. Investigators may compare children at different levels of biological maturity or different chronological ages to learn how a particular developmental domain changes with age. Most studies of cognitive development discussed in Chapter 9 (Middle Childhood), especially those that consider the shift from one type of reasoning to another, use the cross-sectional approach. They present children of different ages with the same kind of problems and then note differences in their approach to explaining and solving the problem. The main limitation of the cross-sectional method is that it measures group differences, not patterns of individual change over time. Often, however, these group differences are interpreted to suggest a pattern of development. With respect to studies on cognitive problem solving, the cross-sectional approach tells us that most 12-year-olds are more flexible in their reasoning than most 7-year-olds. It does not tell us how the same children actually change from the time they are 7 until they are 12, nor how the children who were most flexible at age 7 would perform at age 12 in comparison with those who were the least flexible.

## LONGITUDINAL STUDIES

A **longitudinal study** involves repeated observations of the same participants at different times. The time between observations may be brief, as from immediately after birth to 2 or 3 days after birth. Observations may be repeated over the entire life course, as in Leo Terman's longitudinal study of gifted children (Holahan, Sears, & Cronbach, 1995; Sears & Barbee, 1978; Terman & Oden, 1947, 1959).

Longitudinal studies have the advantage of tracking the course of development of a particular group of individuals. We can discover how certain characteristics of children in infancy or toddlerhood relate to those same characteristics when the individuals reach adolescence or adulthood. We can also learn whether certain qualities of childhood, such as intelligence or outgoingness, are related to overall social adjustment or life satisfaction in later years. Longitudinal studies permit us to trace intra-individual patterns over time—that is, how individuals change, for example, from the use of one-word expressions to two-word phrases. They also allow us to monitor changes in groups, for example, by comparing adults who have children in their early twenties to those who remain child free and looking at their economic or occupational attainment by midlife (Schaie, 1994).

Longitudinal studies may be difficult to complete, especially if they are intended to cover a significant time period, such as the years from childhood to adulthood. Over this span of time, participants may drop out of the study, the investigators may lose funding or interest in the project, or the methods may become outdated. Questions that once seemed important may no longer be seen as vital. Another limitation is that repeated interactions with the participants may influence their behaviors. In other words, participation in the study could itself become a factor in their development. One of the greatest limitations of longitudinal studies is that they focus on only one generation or cohort of participants. Imagine studying the academic achievement and occupational attainment of a group of children born in 1980. Historical and social factors that may influence the course of this group's development will be inextricably intertwined in the observations. One cannot tell if people growing up at other times in history would exhibit the pattern of changes that characterize this particular group.

## COHORT SEQUENTIAL STUDIES

A **cohort sequential design** combines the cross-sectional and the longitudinal approaches into one method of study (Schaie, 1965, 1992). Groups of participants, called *cohorts*, are selected because they are a certain number of years apart in age. For example, we might begin with three groups of adolescents who are 11, 14, and 17, respectively. Every 3 years,

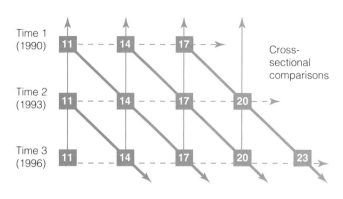

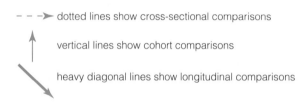

- - - → dotted lines show cross-sectional comparisons

↑ vertical lines show cohort comparisons

↘ heavy diagonal lines show longitudinal comparisons

**FIGURE 2.3**

The Cohort Sequential Design

these groups would be interviewed until the 11-year-olds have turned 17. Every 3 years, a new group of 11-year-olds would be added to the study. This combination of a longitudinal and a cross-sectional design is a powerful developmental research method. It produces immediate cross-sectional data, longitudinal data after 3 and 6 years, and a comparison of children who were the same age (11, 14, or 17) at three different times. This third comparison permits us to identify social and historical factors that may influence age-related differences. This comparison also allows us to control for the possible impact of repeated measurement on the participants. In Chapter 14 (Later Adulthood), you will read about the results of a cohort sequential study of adult intellectual ability.

Comparisons of cohorts over long periods of time provide a way of controlling for the many historical factors—such as access to schooling, health, medical treatment, and nutrition—that might influence intellectual performance, separating these factors from age-related changes. The elements of a cohort sequential design are shown in Figure 2.3.

## EVALUATING EXISTING RESEARCH

In addition to collecting new data, social scientists devote considerable scholarly effort to reviewing and evaluating existing research. As a student, you may be asked to review research findings on a topic of interest to you. You will probably

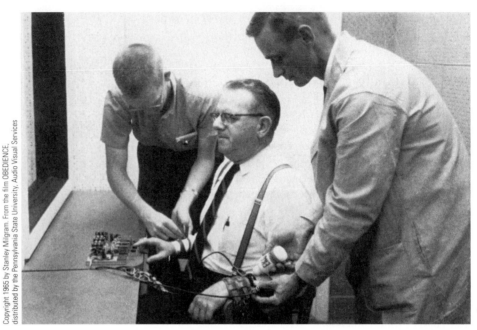

In the famous Milgram experiment, participants were deceived into believing they were causing physical harm to another person. One aspect of the deception was to involve research participants in connecting electrodes to the "learner." The distress the participants experienced in the experimental procedure led to important revisions in the code of ethical conduct in social science research.

Copyright 1965 by Stanley Milgram. From the film OBEDIENCE, distributed by the Pennsylvania State University, Audio Visual Services

rely on online databases, such as InfoTrac College Edition, EBSCOHOST, PsychInfo, or the Social Science Citation Index, to find books, book chapters, and journal articles relevant to your topic. These sources provide information from published sources, most of which have undergone a **peer review** process. This means that other professionals have read and critically evaluated the materials before they were published. You may also find information using Internet search engines. Internet resources are of a much more varied nature, including Web pages from professionals, reports of research institutes and centers, government documents, and ideas from teachers, students, and others who have opinions on the topic. The challenge in reviewing all this information is to apply a standard for judging its quality and validity as you formulate your own analysis of the topic.

Most researchers use this method of reading and reviewing the research of others to keep well informed about the research in their subject area. They analyze the work of others to generate new questions and to formulate well-founded conclusions about issues in their field of specialization. The study, analysis, and evaluation of current research literature constitute special skills in their own right.

# ETHICS

In conducting research with living beings, and especially with children, social scientists continually confront ethical questions. **Ethics** refers to principles of conduct that are founded on a society's moral code. As part of their professional socialization, researchers are obligated to maintain humane, morally acceptable treatment of all living study participants (American Psychological Association, 1992).

The ethical guidelines for research with humans encompass a variety of considerations. Because we are concerned about the right to privacy, the identities of individual participants must be kept confidential. They must not be coerced into participating in a research project, and their refusal to participate should have no negative consequences. If children in a classroom, for example, decide that they do not want to participate in a research project, or if their parents do not give permission for them to participate, they should not be shamed, given an undesirable alternate assignment, or given a lower grade.

Researchers must protect participants from unnecessary painful physical and emotional experiences, including shame, failure, and social rejection. Researchers must weigh the benefits of the new information they may discover in a particular study against the potential risks or harm to the participants. Two questions must guide the researcher's decisions:

1. How would you feel if you or one of your family members were a participant in this study?
2. Can the problem be studied in ways that do not involve pain, deception, or emotional or physical stress?

The American Psychological Association has published a guide for researchers titled *Ethics in Research with Human Participants* (Sales & Folkman, 2000). This guide provides advice to researchers about how to manage all aspects of the research process in order to avoid any conflict of interests and to maintain the trust and safety of participants. Participants have a right to know how their privacy will be preserved and what steps will be taken to ensure that responses or behaviors observed in the research will remain confidential. The guidelines require that participants be told about all aspects of the research that may influence their decision to participate. They must be free to withdraw from the study at any time. They are entitled to a full explanation of the study once it has been completed. When the participants are children, their parents must be given this information and must approve their children's participation.

Each university has an institutional review process that applies these or similar guidelines for the ethical conduct of research to proposals being prepared by faculty and students. Before a study can begin, the institutional review board considers the design of the study and its potential impact on participants. The investigators have to commit to a procedure of *informed consent*, so that participants are aware of the nature of the research, potential risks, conditions of confidentiality,

and their freedom to withdraw from the study at any time if they choose. Approval for the research is typically given for one year. The institutional review process includes a mechanism for ongoing evaluation of research that takes place over longer periods of time. Most schools, day care centers, hospitals, nursing homes, and other treatment centers have their own review procedures for determining whether they will permit research to be carried out with the people in their programs. Ethical guidelines are important in order to prevent exploitation of participants and to prevent unintended negative consequences of participation in research.

## Chapter Summary

The scientific process results in a body of knowledge that informs our understanding of human development. The research process may be guided by a positivist approach or by a qualitative inquiry approach. The former assumes that through careful scientific methods, specific hypotheses can be tested and causal relationships can be identified. The latter assumes that there are many truths and that the goal of research is to uncover the personal meanings of life experience. The two approaches lead to distinct research strategies.

How participants are selected for study is called sampling. Five methods are typically used to identify a sample: random sampling, stratified sampling, matched groups, volunteer sampling, and qualitative sampling. The way a sample is selected determines how generalizable the findings of the research will be.

The six principal research methods are observation, case studies, interviews, surveys, tests, and experimentation. Each method has its advantages and disadvantages, but all provide insights into continuity and change over the life span. Four designs for studying change are described: retrospective studies, cross-sectional studies, longitudinal studies, and cohort sequential studies. The method and design of research have a powerful effect on how the findings are interpreted.

No matter whether the approach to research is positivist or qualitative, the researcher must consider ethical guidelines in designing and carrying out the project. This means that the procedures and treatment of the participants must be guided by concerns for the participants' safety and for preserving a respectful, trusting relationship between the researcher and the participants.

## Further Reflection

1. How would you characterize the differences between the positivist and the qualitative approach to research?
2. What is the difference between scientific knowledge and knowledge gained through personal experience?

3. Try to form a researchable question about adjustment to college. What is the question? What are some ways to operationalize that question? (Translate the question into behaviors that can be observed or measured.) What research method might you choose to pursue this question? Why?
4. Consider a national survey on the well-being and life satisfaction of older adults using a stratified, random sample, and the case study of one individual, such as Patrick Jonathan Carmichael. What are the comparative strengths and weaknesses of these approaches to sampling?
5. How might the impact of the setting on behavior be taken into account in surveys, experiments, and observational research?
6. What kinds of ethical considerations might arise if you were conducting a study using participant observation as a method?

## On the Web

**VISIT OUR WEBSITE**

Go to http://www.wadsworth.com/psychology to find online resources directly linked to your book.

## Casebook

For additional case material related to this chapter, see the case entitled "Craig and Diane Try to Contribute to Science" in *Life Span Development: A Case Book*, by Barbara and Philip Newman, Laura Landry-Meyer, and Brenda J. Lohman, pp. 19–22. The case illustrates some of the considerations that parents may face in allowing their infant to be a participant in research and the ethical concerns that may need to be addressed with research involving infants.

# CHAPTER 3

# PSYCHOSOCIAL THEORY

*Psychosocial theory focuses on the ongoing interaction of the person and the social environment from infancy through very old age. Issues of childhood are revisited in every adult transition; and issues of adulthood are foreshadowed in each stage of childhood.*

■ WHAT IS A THEORY?

■ THE RATIONALE FOR EMPHASIZING
PSYCHOSOCIAL THEORY

■ BASIC CONCEPTS OF PSYCHOSOCIAL THEORY
Stages of Development
Developmental Tasks
Psychosocial Crisis
The Central Process for Resolving the Psychosocial Crisis
Radius of Significant Relationships
Coping Behavior
CASE STUDY: ERIK ERIKSON: A BIOGRAPHICAL
CASE STUDY OF PSYCHOSOCIAL DEVELOPMENT

■ EVALUATION OF PSYCHOSOCIAL THEORY
Strengths
Weaknesses
A Recap of Psychosocial Theory

■ CHAPTER SUMMARY

■ FURTHER REFLECTION

▶  *To define the general concept of theory and explain how one makes use of theory to increase understanding.*

▶  *To define the six basic concepts of psychosocial theory.*

▶  *To demonstrate how the concepts of psychosocial theory contribute to an analysis of basic processes that foster or inhibit development over the life span.*

▶  *To evaluate psychosocial theory, pointing out its strengths and weaknesses.*

IN THIS CHAPTER, we will define the general notion of theory and introduce the basic concepts of psychosocial theory that provide the integrating framework for our analysis of human development. In Chapter 4, we will discuss other theories that also account for growth and change. Some of those theories have provided the foundation on which psychosocial theory was based. Others complement psychosocial theory by clarifying the dynamic processes through which physical, intellectual, emotional, social, and self development take place. ■

# WHAT IS A THEORY?

A **theory** is a logical system of concepts that helps explain observations and contributes to the development of a body of knowledge. We all have our informal, intuitive theories about social life. For example, the adage, "The acorn doesn't fall far from the tree," is an informal theory, which predicts that children are going to grow up to behave a lot like their parents. A formal scientific theory is a set of interconnected statements, including assumptions, definitions, axioms, postulates, hypothetical constructs, intervening variables, laws, and hypotheses. The function of this set of interconnected statements is to describe unobservable structures, mechanisms, or processes and to relate them to one another and to observable events. For example, the explanation for why children resemble their parents is not directly observable. Theoretical concepts such as genetic inheritance, identification, modeling, or rewards and punishments are developed to help explain this resemblance.

A formal theory should meet certain requirements. It should be *logical* and *internally consistent*, with no contradictory statements. The hypothetical constructs should be translatable into *testable* hypotheses. The theory should be *parsimonious*, relying on as few assumptions, constructs, and propositions as possible. Finally, a theory should integrate previous research, and it should deal with a relatively large area of science (Miller, 2002). Most current developmental theories do not meet all these requirements of formal, scientific theories. However, they offer a language of constructs

and hypotheses that guide systematic inquiry and compare observations in order to build a body of knowledge.

In order to understand a theory, we must ask three questions:

1.  Which phenomena is the theory trying to explain? A theory of intellectual development may include hypotheses about the evolution of the brain, the growth of logical thinking, or the capacity to use symbolism. Such a theory is less likely to explain fears, motives, or friendship. Understanding the focus of the theory helps to identify its **range of applicability**. Although principles from one theory may have relevance to another area of knowledge, a theory is evaluated in terms of the behavior it was originally intended to explain.

2.  What assumptions does the theory make? Assumptions are the guiding premises underlying the logic of a theory. In order to evaluate a theory, you must first understand what its assumptions are. Charles Darwin assumed that lower life forms "progress" to higher forms in the process of evolution. Freud assumed that all behavior is motivated and that the unconscious is a "storehouse" of motives and wishes. The assumptions of any theory may or may not be correct. Assumptions may be influenced by the following:
    *   the cultural context that dominates the theorist's period of history;
    *   the sample of observations from which the theorist has drawn inferences;
    *   the current knowledge base of the field; and
    *   the intellectual capacities of the theorist.

3.  What does the theory predict? Theories add new levels of understanding by suggesting causal relationships, by unifying diverse observations, and by identifying the importance of events that may have gone unnoticed. Theories of human development offer explanations regarding the origins and functions of human behavior and the changes that can be expected in behavior from one period of life to the next.

A theory of development usually helps to explain how people change and grow over time, as well as how to account for continuity (Thomas, 1999). We expect a theory of human development to provide explanations about four questions:

1. What are the mechanisms that account for growth from conception through old age, and to what extent do these mechanisms vary across the life span?
2. What factors underlie stability and change across the life span?
3. How do physical, cognitive, emotional, and social functions interact? How do these interactions account for mixtures of thoughts, feelings, health states, and social relationships?
4. How does the social context affect individual development?

# THE RATIONALE FOR EMPHASIZING PSYCHOSOCIAL THEORY

We have selected **psychosocial theory** as an organizing framework for the text because of its range and scope. Psychosocial theory is not the only or the most widely accepted framework for studying human development; however, it combines three features that are not as clearly articulated or integrated in other theories:

1. Psychosocial theory addresses growth across the life span, identifying and differentiating central issues from infancy through old age. It also suggests that experiences of adolescence or adulthood can lead to a review and reinterpretation of earlier periods.
2. Psychosocial theory assumes that individuals have the capacity to contribute to their own psychological development at each stage of life. People have the ability to integrate, organize, and conceptualize their experiences in order to protect themselves, cope with challenges, and direct the course of their lives. Therefore, the direction of development is shaped by self-regulation as well as by the ongoing interaction of biological and societal influences.
3. Psychosocial theory takes into consideration the active contribution of culture to individual growth. At each life stage, cultural goals, aspirations, and social expectations and requirements make demands that evoke individual reactions. These reactions influence which of a person's capabilities will be developed further. This vital link between the individual and the culture is a key mechanism of development. Each society has its own view of the qualities that reflect maturity, qualities that are infused into the lives of individuals and help determine the direction of growth within the society.

One of the great theorists who identified and developed psychosocial theory was Erik H. Erikson. He initially was trained as a psychoanalyst. His theory was influenced by the

*At the Quinceañera, a 15-year-old Mexican American girl celebrates mass with her family. This ceremony illustrates one way that culture imparts new demands and expectations at critical developmental transitions. What might be the personal and social meaning of this rite of passage?*

© Bob Daemmrich/Stock Boston

work of many others, including Sigmund and Anna Freud, Peter Blos, Robert White, Jean Piaget, and Robert Havighurst, whose ideas you will encounter throughout this book. His wife, Joan, was an important intellectual influence as well. Erik and Joan collaborated on the formulation of the first presentation of psychosocial theory and its eight stages of development in 1950 (J. M. Erikson, 1988).

# BASIC CONCEPTS OF PSYCHOSOCIAL THEORY

Psychosocial theory presents human development as a product of the ongoing interaction between individual (*psycho*) biological and psychological needs and abilities on the one hand and societal (*social*) expectations and demands on the other hand. The theory accounts for patterns of individual development that emerge from a biopsychosocial process.

Psychosocial theory is linked to the term **psychosocial evolution**, a construct proposed by Julian Huxley (1941, 1942) to refer to the range of human abilities that allows us to gather knowledge from our ancestors and transmit it to our descendants. Childrearing practices, education, and modes of communication are examples of mechanisms that transmit information and ways of thinking from one generation to the next. At the same time, people devise new information, new ways of thinking, and new ways of teaching their discoveries to others. In this way, psychosocial evolution has proceeded at a rapid pace, bringing with it changes in technology and ideology that have allowed us to create and modify our physical and social environments.

Psychosocial theory, as we use it in this book, offers an organizational framework for considering individual development within the larger perspective of psychosocial evolution. The transmission of values and knowledge across generations requires the maturation of individuals who are capable of creating knowledge, symbolizing it, adapting it, and transferring it to others. At the same time, societies change, posing new challenges for adaptation. People change and grow, enhancing their potential for carrying their own and succeeding generations forward.

Psychosocial theory accounts for systematic change over the life span through six basic concepts: (1) stages of development, (2) developmental tasks, (3) psychosocial crises, (4) a central process for resolving the crisis at each stage, (5) a radiating network of significant relationships, and (6) coping—the new behavior people generate to meet new challenges. These concepts will be defined in the following sections. However, each concept includes stage-specific content that will be elaborated on in subsequent chapters.

## STAGES OF DEVELOPMENT

A **developmental stage** is a period of life that is characterized by a specific underlying organization. At every stage, some characteristics differentiate that stage from the preceding and succeeding stages. Stage theories propose a specific direction for development. At each stage, the accomplishments from the previous stages provide resources for mastering the new challenges. Each stage is unique and leads to the acquisition of new skills related to new capabilities (Davison, King, Kitchener, & Parker, 1980; Fischer & Silvern, 1985; Flavell, 1982; Levin, 1986; Miller, 2002).

The stage concept suggests areas of emerging competence or conflict that may explain a range of behaviors. You can verify the stage concept through reflection on your own past. You can probably recall earlier periods when you were very preoccupied by efforts first to gain your parents' approval, then to win acceptance by your peers, and later to understand yourself. Each of these concerns may have appeared all-encompassing at the time, but eventually each gave way to a new preoccupation. At each stage, you were confronted with a unique set of problems that required the integration of your personal needs and skills with the social demands of your culture. The end product was a new orienting mode and a new set of capabilities for engaging in interactions with others.

Erikson (1963) proposed eight stages of psychosocial development. The formulation of these stages can be traced in part to the stages of psychosexual development proposed by Freud and in part to Erikson's own observations and rich mode of thinking. Figure 3.1 shows the chart that Erikson produced in *Childhood and Society* to describe the stages of psychosocial development. The shaded boxes identify the main psychosocial ego conflicts of each stage. These ego conflicts produce new ego skills. In Erikson's original model, you will note that the periods of life are given names, such as oral-sensory or puberty and adolescence, but no ages. This approach reflects Erikson's emphasis on an individual timetable for development, guided by both biological maturation and cultural expectations.

The concept of the psychosocial stages of development is very good as far as it goes, but Erikson's road map seems in-

*The epigenetic principle assumes that it takes the entire life span, from the prenatal period through very old age, for all facets of human capacity to emerge. In later adulthood and very old age, grandparents transmit the wisdom of their generation to their grandchildren by teaching them stories, songs, customs, and beliefs.*

© Lawrence Migdale/Photo Researchers

| | 1 | 2 | 3 | 4 | 5 | 6 | 7 | 8 |
|---|---|---|---|---|---|---|---|---|
| 1. Oral–sensory | Basic trust vs. Mistrust | | | | | | | |
| 2. Muscular–anal | | Autonomy vs. Shame, doubt | | | | | | |
| 3. Locomotor–genital | | | Initiative vs. Guilt | | | | | |
| 4. Latency | | | | Industry vs. Inferiority | | | | |
| 5. Puberty and adolescence | | | | | Identity vs. Role confusion | | | |
| 6. Young adulthood | | | | | | Intimacy vs. Isolation | | |
| 7. Adulthood | | | | | | | Genera-tivity vs. Stagnation | |
| 8. Maturity | | | | | | | | Ego integrity vs. Despair |

**FIGURE 3.1**

Erikson's Model of the Psychosocial Stages of Development

Source: Erikson, 1963.

complete. Three criticisms of this "layout" of the life span have been raised. First, although the boxes in the figure look very even and comparable, each stage is actually of very different length. Second, the figure suggests discrete shifts from one stage to the next, when in fact the themes of these stages overlap (McAdams & de St. Aubin, 1992). The idea of life stages highlights qualitatively unique orientations toward oneself and others that dominate periods of the life span. Transitions from stage to stage are not instantaneous. Movement from one stage to the next is the result of changes in several major systems at roughly the same time. The new mixture of needs, capabilities, and expectations is what produces the new outlook at each stage.

Finally, if the idea of psychosocial evolution has validity—and we believe it does—new stages can be expected to develop as a culture evolves. We have identified 11 stages of psychosocial development, each with an approximate age range: (1) *prenatal*, from conception to birth; (2) *infancy*, from birth to 2 years; (3) *toddlerhood*, 2 and 3 years; (4) *early school age*, 4 to 6 years; (5) *middle childhood*, 6 to 12 years; (6) *early*

*adolescence*, 12 to 18 years; (7) *later adolescence*, 18 to 24 years; (8) *early adulthood*, 24 to 34 years; (9) *middle adulthood*, 34 to 60 years; (10) *later adulthood*, 60 to 75 years; and (11) *very old age*, 75 until death.

By discussing a prenatal stage, two stages of adolescent development, and very old age, we are adding three stages to those proposed by Erikson. This revision is a product of our analysis of the research literature, observations through research and practice, discussions with colleagues, and suggestions from other stage theorists.

The addition of these three new stages provides a good demonstration of the process of theory construction. Theories of human development emerge and change within a cultural and historical context. The differentiation of adolescence into two stages, for example, is a product of changes in the timing of onset of puberty in modern society, the expanding need for education and training before entry into the world of work, related changes in the structure of the educational system, and the variety of available life choices in work, marriage, parenting, and ideology.

**FIGURE 3.2**

The 11 Stages of the Life Span

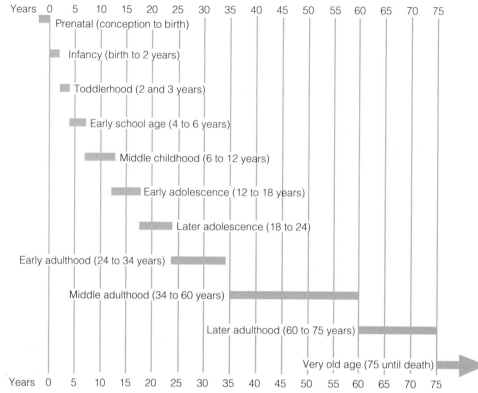

Figure 3.2 shows the 11 stages of psychosocial development as presented in this textbook. The age range given for each stage is only an approximation. Each person has his or her own timetable for growth. Differences associated with poverty, health, cultural group (e.g., differing rates of longevity) and exposure to environmental risks also lead to different timetables. The lengths of the stages vary, from the 9 months of the prenatal period to the roughly 26 years of middle adulthood.

Erikson (1963) proposed that the stages of development follow the **epigenetic principle**—a biological plan for growth that allows each function to emerge systematically until the fully functioning organism has developed. An assumption of this and other stage theories is that the stages form a sequence. Although one can anticipate challenges that will occur at a later stage, one passes through the stages in an orderly pattern of growth. In the logic of psychosocial theory, the entire life span is required for all the functions of psychosocial development to appear and become integrated. There is no going back to an earlier stage, because experience makes retreat impossible. In contrast to other stage theories, however, Erikson suggested that one can review and reinterpret previous stages in the light of new insight or new experiences.

Furthermore, the themes of earlier stages may re-emerge at any point. Through reflection and insight, a person can find new meaning or a new resolution to an earlier conflict. Joan Erikson reflects on the fluidity and hopefulness in this perspective:

This sequential growth . . . is now known to be more influenced by the social milieu than was in previous years considered possible. . . . Where a strength is not adequately developed according to the given sequence for its scheduled period of critical resolution, the supports of the environment may bring it into appropriate balance at a later period. Hope remains constant throughout life that more sturdy resolutions of the basic confrontation may be realized. (J. M. Erikson, 1988, p. 74–75)

The concept of life stages permits us to consider the various aspects of development, such as physical growth, social relationships, and cognitive capacities, at a given period of life and to speculate about their interrelation. It also encourages a focus on the experiences that are unique to each life period—experiences that deserve to be understood both in their own right and for their contribution to subsequent development. When programs and services are designed to address critical needs in such areas as education, health care, housing, and social welfare, the developmental stage approach allows the designers to focus on the needs and resources of the particular population to be served.

Despite the usefulness of a stage approach, one must avoid thinking of stages as pigeonholes. Just because a person is described as being at a given stage does not mean that he or she cannot function at other levels. It is not unusual for people to anticipate later challenges before they become dominant. Many children of toddler and preschool age, for example, play "house," envisioning having a husband or a wife and children. You might say that, in this play, they are anticipating the issues of intimacy and generativity that lie ahead. The experience of having a child—whether this occurs at age 18, 25, or 35—is likely to raise issues of generativity, even if the theory suggests that this theme is not in its peak ascendancy until middle adulthood (McAdams & de St. Aubin, 1998). Whereas some elements of each psychosocial theme can be observed at all ages, the intensity with which they are expressed at certain times marks their importance in the definition of a developmental stage. Erikson, Erikson, and Kivnick (1986) put it this way:

> The epigenetic chart also rightly suggests that the individual is never struggling only with the tension that is focal at the time. Rather, at every successive developmental stage, the individual is also increasingly engaged in the anticipation of tensions that have yet to become focal and in re-experiencing those tensions that were inadequately integrated when they were focal; similarly engaged are those whose age-appropriate integration was then, but is no longer, adequate. (p. 39)

As one leaves a stage, the achievements of that period are neither lost nor irrelevant to later stages. Important ego strengths emerge from the successful resolution of conflicts at every stage. Some of these strengths may be challenged or reorganized as events take place later in life that call into question the essential beliefs established in an earlier period. For example, the psychosocial conflict during early school age is initiative versus guilt. Its positive outcome, a sense of initiative, is a joy in innovation and experimentation and a willingness to take risks in order to learn more about the world. Once achieved, the sense of initiative provides a positive platform for the formation of social relationships and for further creative intellectual inquiry and discovery. However, experiences in a highly authoritarian school environment or in a very judgmental, shaming personal relationship may cause one to inhibit this sense of initiative or to mask it with a facade of indifference.

## DEVELOPMENTAL TASKS

At each stage of life, one faces new **developmental tasks** that contribute to increased mastery over one's environment. These tasks reflect areas of accomplishment in physical, cognitive, social, and emotional development, as well as development of the self-concept. Robert J. Havighurst, who first introduced the concept of developmental tasks, believed that human development is a process in which people attempt to learn the tasks required of them by the society to which they are adapting. These tasks change with age, because each society has **age-graded expectations** for behavior. "Living in a modern society is a long series of tasks to learn" (Havighurst, 1972, p. 2). The person who learns well receives satisfaction and reward; the person who does not suffers unhappiness and social disapproval.

Although Havighurst's view of development emphasizes the guiding role of society in determining which skills need to be acquired at a certain age, it does not totally ignore the role of physical maturation. Havighurst believed that there are **sensitive periods** for learning developmental tasks—that is, times when the person is most ready to acquire a new ability. Havighurst called these periods **teachable moments**. Most people learn developmental tasks at the time and in the sequence appropriate in their society. If a particular task is not learned during the sensitive period, learning it may be much more difficult later on.

The basic tasks we identify differ from those outlined in Havighurst's writings. Our choice of tasks is based on broad areas of accomplishment that have been identified by researchers as critical to psychological and social growth at each stage of life in a modern, technological culture. We recognize that the demands for growth may differ according to the orientation and complexity of a particular society. For example, in comparing gender role norms in Iran and the United States, Thomas (1999) pointed out that the legal minimum age for women to marry in Iran is 9 years and that at any age, Iranian women must have permission from their father or grandfather to marry. We have identified early adulthood—roughly ages 24 through 34—as the time when most people in the United States are focusing on exploring intimate relationships and making decisions about marriage. In the United States, women are free to marry without parental or family consent after age 18. Thus, the developmental task associated with establishing a commitment to an intimate partner would be present in both cultures, but the ages at which this task is usually addressed and the context for forming such a commitment differ from one society to the next. The tasks we present as central to successful adaptation at each stage of life in the United States are not necessarily the appropriate standards for maturation and growth in a developing country or in a traditional, tribal culture.

We believe that a relatively small number of major psychosocial tasks dominate a person's problem-solving efforts and learning during a given stage. As these tasks are mastered, new competencies enhance the person's ability to engage in more complex social relationships. We assume that successful cultures must stimulate behavior that helps its members learn what they need to know for both their own survival and that of the group.

Keep in mind that one is changing on several major levels during each period of life. Tasks involving physical, emotional, intellectual, and social growth, as well as growth in one's self-concept, all contribute to one's resources for coping with the challenges of life. Table 3.1 shows the developmental tasks we have identified as having major effects on the life experiences of most people in modern society and the stages during which each set of tasks is of primary learning value. There are 42 developmental tasks on the list. Whereas the infant is learning orientations and skills related to the first 5, a person at the early adulthood stage has already acquired skills related to 27 tasks from the previous stages. New learning

*Toddlerhood is a sensitive period for language development, when parent-child conversations are especially critical.*

may continue in these areas as well as in the 4 new developmental tasks faced by the young adult. This helps one appreciate that by the time people reach early adulthood, they have a considerable repertoire of competencies that can be used to cope with the challenges of life. A very old person has all the areas of previous learning to draw from while working on 3 new tasks.

## PSYCHOSOCIAL CRISIS

A **psychosocial crisis**, the third organizing concept of psychosocial theory (Erikson, 1963), arises because one must make psychological efforts to adjust to the demands of the social environment at each stage of development. The word *crisis* in this context refers to a normal set of stresses and strains rather than to an extraordinary set of events.

Societal demands vary from stage to stage. People experience these demands as mild but persistent guidelines for and expectations of behavior. They may be demands for greater self-control, further development of skills, or a stronger commitment to goals. Before the end of each stage of development, the individual tries to achieve a resolution, to adjust to society's demands, and at the same time to translate those demands into personal terms. This process produces a state of tension that the individual must reduce in order to proceed to the next stage. It is this tension state that produces the psychosocial crisis.

Mastery of the developmental tasks is influenced by the resolution of the psychosocial crisis of the previous stage, and it is this resolution that leads to the development of new social capabilities. These capabilities orient the person toward new experiences, a new aptitude for relationships, and new feelings of personal worth as he or she confronts the challenges of the developmental tasks of the next stage. In turn, the skills learned during a particular stage as a result of work on its developmental tasks provide the tools for the resolution of the psychosocial crisis of that stage. Task accomplishment and crisis resolution interact to produce individual life stories.

## PSYCHOSOCIAL CRISES OF THE LIFE STAGES

Table 3.2 lists the psychosocial crisis of each stage of development from infancy through very old age. This scheme, derived from Erikson's model shown in Figure 3.1, expresses the crises as polarities—for example, trust versus mistrust, and autonomy versus shame and doubt. These contrasting conditions suggest the underlying dimensions along which each psychosocial crisis is resolved. According to psychosocial theory, most people experience both ends of the continuum. The inevitable discrepancy between one's level of development at the beginning of a stage and society's push for a new level of functioning by the end of it creates at least a mild degree of the negative dimension. Even within a loving, caring family environment that promotes trust, an infant will experience some moments of frustration or disappointment that result in mistrust. The outcome of the crisis at each stage is a balance or integration of the two opposing forces. For each person, the relative frequency and significance of positive and negative experiences will contribute to a resolution of the crisis that lies along a continuum from extremely positive to extremely negative.

The likelihood of a completely positive or a completely negative resolution is small. Most individuals resolve the crises in a generally positive direction, supported by a combination of positive experiences and natural maturational tendencies. At each successive stage, however, the likelihood of a negative resolution mounts as the developmental tasks become more complex and the chances of encountering societal barriers to development increase. A positive resolution of each crisis provides new ego strengths that help the person meet the demands of the next stage.

To understand the process of growth at each life stage, we have to consider the negative as well as the positive pole of each crisis. The dynamic tension between the positive and negative forces respects and reflects the struggles we all encounter to restrain unbridled impulses, to overcome fears and doubts, and to look past our own needs to consider the needs

## Table 3.1  Developmental Tasks Associated with the Life Stages

| LIFE STAGE* | DEVELOPMENTAL TASKS |
|---|---|
| Infancy (birth to 2 years) | Maturation of sensory, perceptual, and motor functions |
| | Attachment |
| | Sensorimotor intelligence and early causal schemes |
| | Understanding the nature of objects and creating categories |
| | Emotional development |
| Toddlerhood (2 and 3) | Elaboration of locomotion |
| | Language development |
| | Fantasy play |
| | Self-control |
| Early school age (4 to 6) | Gender identification |
| | Early moral development |
| | Self-theory |
| | Peer play |
| Middle childhood (6 to 12) | Friendship |
| | Concrete operations |
| | Skill learning |
| | Self-evaluation |
| | Team play |
| Early adolescence (12 to 18) | Physical maturation |
| | Formal operations |
| | Emotional development |
| | Membership in the peer group |
| | Sexual relationships |
| Later adolescence (18 to 24) | Autonomy from parents |
| | Gender identity |
| | Internalized morality |
| | Career choice |
| Early adulthood (24 to 34) | Exploring intimate relationships |
| | Childbearing |
| | Work |
| | Lifestyle |
| Middle adulthood (34 to 60) | Managing a career |
| | Nurturing an intimate relationship |
| | Expanding caring relationships |
| | Managing the household |
| Later adulthood (60 to 75) | Accepting one's life |
| | Redirecting energy toward new roles and activities |
| | Promoting intellectual vigor |
| | Developing a point of view about death |
| Very old age (75 until death) | Coping with physical changes of aging |
| | Developing a psychohistorical perspective |
| | Traveling through uncharted terrain |

*We do not consider the concept of development tasks appropriate to the prenatal stage.

of others. The negative poles offer insight into basic areas of human vulnerability. Experienced in moderation, the negative forces result in a clarification of ego positions, individuation, and moral integrity. Although a steady diet of mistrust is undesirable, for example, it is important that a trusting person be able to evaluate situations and people for their trustworthiness and to discern cues about safety or danger in any encounter. In every psychosocial crisis, experiences at both the positive and the negative poles contribute to the total range of a person's adaptive capacities.

## Table 3.2 The Psychosocial Crises

| LIFE STAGE* | PSYCHOSOCIAL CRISIS |
| --- | --- |
| Infancy (birth to 2 years) | Trust versus mistrust |
| Toddlerhood (2 and 3) | Autonomy versus shame and doubt |
| Early school age (4 to 6) | Initiative versus guilt |
| Middle childhood (6 to 12) | Industry versus inferiority |
| Early adolescence (12 to 18) | Group identity versus alienation |
| Later adolescence (18 to 24) | Individual identity versus identity confusion |
| Early adulthood (24 to 34) | Intimacy versus isolation |
| Middle adulthood (34 to 60) | Generativity versus stagnation |
| Later adulthood (60 to 75) | Integrity versus despair |
| Very old age (75 until death) | Immortality versus extinction |

*We do not consider the concept of psychosocial crisis appropriate to the prenatal stage.

Why conceptualize life in terms of crises? Does this idea adequately portray the experience of the individual, or does it overemphasize conflict and abnormality? The term *crisis* implies that tension and conflict are necessary to the developmental process; crisis and its resolution are biologically based components of life experience at every stage. In fact, they are what drive the ego system to develop new capacities. "Growing pains" occur at every stage of life.

The term *psychosocial* draws attention to the fact that the psychosocial crises are, in part, the result of cultural pressures and expectations. Individuals will experience tension because of the culture's need to socialize and integrate its members. The concept acknowledges the dynamic conflicts between individuality and group membership at each period of life. The concept of *crisis* implies that at any stage, something can interfere with development and reduce one's opportunities to experience personal fulfillment.

The exact nature of the conflict is not the same at each stage. For example, few cultural limits are placed on infants. The outcome of the infancy stage depends greatly on the skill of the caregiver. At early school age, the culture stands in fairly direct opposition to the child's initiative in some matters by discouraging curiosity or questioning about certain topics, but offers abundant encouragement to initiative in others. In young adulthood, the dominant cultural push is toward the establishment of intimate relationships, yet an individual may

The attack on the World Trade Center on September 11, 2001, brought unforeseen crisis to thousands. At different developmental stages, people adapt in unique ways to crisis and loss. The impact of this crisis on the subsequent psychosocial development for the generations who experienced it is yet to be understood.

© Reuters NewMedia Inc./CORBIS

*Paul Drawing, 1923/Pablo Picasso/© 2005 Estate of Pablo Picasso/Artists Rights Society (ARS), New York/© Peter Willi /SuperStock*

*Paulo, Picasso's son, is shown in deep concentration as he sketches at his desk. Through imitation, a child takes ownership of actions and skills that he or she has observed among adults. It is little wonder that Paulo, surrounded by his father's ongoing artistic activity, would be drawn to imitate it.*

be unable to attain intimacy because of the lack of time to cultivate these relationships, competing pressures from the workplace, cultural norms against certain expressions of intimacy, or restrictions against certain types of unions.

As reflected in the epigenetic principle, the succession of crises occurs in a predictable sequence over the life course. Although Erikson did not specify the exact ages for each crisis, the theory hypothesizes an age-related progression, in which each crisis has its time of special ascendancy. The combination of biological, psychological, and societal forces that operate to bring about change has a degree of regularity within society that places each psychosocial crisis at a particular period of life.

In addition to these predictable crises, any number of unforeseen stresses may arise. Parents' divorce, the death of a sibling, victimization by violence, the loss of a job, and widowhood are examples of unforeseen life crises. The need to cope with them may overwhelm a person, particularly if several crises occur at the same time. The picture of predictable developmental stress that is emphasized in psychosocial theory must be expanded to include the possibility of unanticipated crises. Although these chance events may foster growth and new competencies, they may also result in defensiveness, regression, or dread. The impact of an unpredictable crisis will depend in part on whether the person is in a state of psychosocial crisis at the time (Cummings, Greene, & Karraker, 1991; Larson & Ham, 1993). For example, the unexpected death of a sibling might be exceptionally disruptive for someone who is also in a period of questioning related to personal identity, where matters of family loyalties and commitments to values and beliefs are unresolved.

The combination of predictable crises, unpredictable crises, and unique historical pressures may lead to the resurfacing of prior crises that require reorganization. For example, during early adulthood, when issues of intimacy versus isolation are salient, it is common to find a reworking of industry versus inferiority as well (Whitbourne, Zuschlag, Elliot, & Waterman, 1992). Young adults encounter the very concrete challenges of establishing themselves in the labor market and achieving self-sufficiency. The outcome of this reworking of an earlier crisis will depend in part on historical factors, such as the economic and materialistic orientation of the society as a specific age group enters early adulthood. It will also depend on additional individual factors—especially on whether the young adult has developed a clear commitment to occupational values during the earlier period of identity versus identity confusion. Thus, the psychosocial crises are not resolved and put to rest once and for all. Each crisis is played and replayed both during ongoing developmental changes and when life events challenge a balance that was achieved earlier.

## THE CENTRAL PROCESS FOR RESOLVING THE PSYCHOSOCIAL CRISIS

Every psychosocial crisis reflects some discrepancy between the person's developmental competencies at the beginning of the stage and new societal pressures for more effective, integrated functioning. How is the discrepancy resolved? What experiences or processes permit the person to interpret the expectations and demands of society and internalize them in order to support change? We have offered an extension of psychosocial theory by identifying a **central process** through which each psychosocial crisis is resolved. The central process, the fourth organizing concept of psychosocial theory, suggests a way that the person takes in or makes sense of cultural expectations and undergoes adaptive modifications of the self. The term *process* suggests a means by which the person recognizes new social pressures and expectations, gives these expectations personal meaning, and gradually changes. The process, unfolding over time, results in a new relationship between self and society.

For example, in toddlerhood, the psychosocial crisis raises the question of how children increase their sense of auton-

**Table 3.3** The Central Process for Resolving Each Psychosocial Crisis

| LIFE STAGE* | CENTRAL PROCESS |
| --- | --- |
| Infancy (birth to 2 years) | Mutuality with caregiver |
| Toddlerhood (2 and 3) | Imitation |
| Early school age (4 to 6) | Identification |
| Middle childhood (6 to 12) | Education |
| Early adolescence (12 to 18) | Peer pressure |
| Later adolescence (18 to 24) | Role experimentation |
| Early adulthood (24 to 34) | Mutuality among peers |
| Middle adulthood (34 to 60) | Person–environment fit and creativity |
| Later adulthood (60 to 75) | Introspection |
| Very old age (75 until death) | Social support |

*We do not consider the concept of central process appropriate to the prenatal stage.

omy without risking too many experiences that provoke a sense of shame and doubt. We suggest that *imitation* is the central process for psychosocial growth during toddlerhood (ages 2 and 3). Children expand their range of skills by imitating adults, siblings, television models, playmates, and even animals. Imitation provides toddlers with enormous satisfaction. As they increase the similarity between themselves and the admired members of their social groups through imitation, they begin to experience the world as other people experience it. They exercise some control over potentially frightening or confusing events by imitating elements of those occurrences in their play.

Movement toward a sense of autonomy in toddlerhood is facilitated by the child's readiness to imitate and by the variety of models available for observation. Through persistent imitative activity, children expand their self-initiated behavior and control over their actions. Repetitive experiences of this kind lead to the development of a sense of personal autonomy.

Imitating the behavior of others not only supports autonomy but helps to protect the toddler from too many experiences of shame and doubt. Behaviors that one observes in others—such as play activities that other children engage in, language use among family members, or daily habits like brushing teeth or washing hands—are usually in the range of acceptable and performable behaviors. Toddlers can see what happens to a person who is carrying out some behavior. If the consequences are favorable, the toddler can feel more confident about trying this behavior out. This does not work 100% of the time, but it is a fairly conservative approach to adding new actions to one's routine.

The central process for coping with the challenges of each life stage provides both personal and societal mechanisms for taking in new information and reorganizing existing information. It also suggests the means that are most likely to lead to a revision of the psychological system so that the crisis of that particular stage may be resolved. Each central process re-

sults in an intensive reworking of the psychological system, including a reorganization of boundaries, values, and images of oneself and others. Table 3.3 shows the central processes that lead to the acquisition of new skills, the resolution of the psychosocial crisis, and successful coping at each life stage.

## RADIUS OF SIGNIFICANT RELATIONSHIPS

The fifth organizing principle of psychosocial theory is the **radius of significant relationships** (Erikson, 1982, p. 31; see Figure 3.3). Age-related demands on individuals are communicated through their significant social relationships. For example, the law requires that all 6-year-olds go to school, but it is their parents who actually send them there. The law requires that people remain in school until they are 16, but it is their peers, teachers, parents, and the adolescents' own aspirations that encourage their continued attendance.

The demands exerted on a person by all elements of the social world make up the societal system. A person's ego includes a social processing system that is sensitive to social expectations. Initially, a person focuses on a small number of relationships. During childhood, adolescence, and early adulthood, the number of relationships expands, and the quality of these relationships takes on greater variety in depth and intensity. In later adulthood, the person often returns to a small number of extremely important relationships that provide opportunities for great depth and intimacy.

At each stage of life, this network of relationships determines the demands that will be made on the person, the way he or she will be taken care of, and the meaning that the person will derive from the relationships. The relationship network varies from person to person, but each person has a network of significant relationships and an increasing readiness to enter into more complex social life (Vanzetti & Duck,

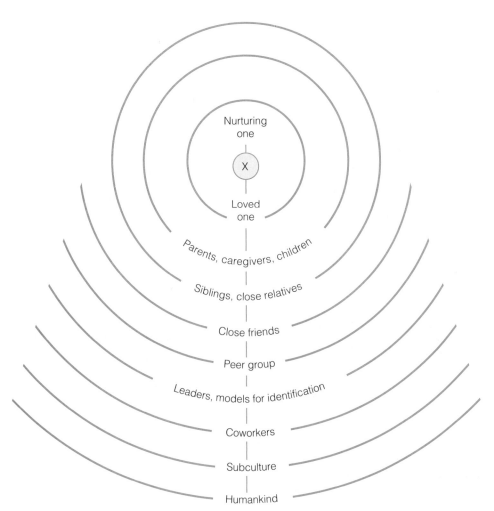

**FIGURE 3.3**
The Radius of Significant
Relationships

1996). The quality of these relationships and the norms for interaction are influenced by the nature of the specific social context.

## CONTEXTS OF DEVELOPMENT

One way of thinking about the impact of the societal system is to consider individuals as embedded in a kaleidoscope of changing, interconnected systems. Children are members of families. Parents and other relatives are members of other important work and community groups that can influence families. As they get older, children may become members of other institutions, such as child care programs, schools, religious groups, community clubs, or athletic teams. Communities are nested in cities, counties, states, and nations. An understanding of development requires insight into each level of social organization as well as across the culture as a whole. These organizations influence what is expected of each person, the roles they play, the activities they engage in, the resources available to meet these expectations, and the risks they may encounter.

The contexts of development embody social, economic, and historical factors. Events such as war, political revolution, famine, or economic collapse may temporarily alter the prevailing childrearing values, opportunities for education or employment, and the availability of resources. Furthermore, these events may increase exposure to violence and separation of family members or provide exposure to other unpredictable stressors that may disrupt the course of development. Family, culture, and ethnic group are three of the major contexts through which the radius of significant relationships is organized.

**FAMILIES.** All over the world, children are raised by small groups or families. Family is the universal primary social context of childhood. The family continues to be a meaningful context throughout life, especially as we think of the relationship of adults with their aging parents, the formation of new families in adulthood, and the lifelong connections among siblings. Historically, the term **family** has referred to a group of people, usually related by blood, marriage, or adoption. In contemporary U.S. society, however, people who view themselves as members of a family may have no legal relationship or shared ancestral bond. The psychosocial meaning of family continues to be defined as individuals who share a common destiny and who experience a sense of emotional

As a newborn, Max is the center of a radius of significant relationships, including his mother, grandmother, aunt, and uncles. For all these adults, Max has entered their radius of significant relationships.

© Philip Newman

intimacy. People in a family care about one another and take care of one another (McKenry & Price, 2000).

**CULTURE.**  **Culture** refers to the socially standardized ways of thinking, feeling, and acting that are shared by members of a society (Thomas, 1999). Culture includes the concepts, habits, skills, arts, technology, religion, and government of a people. It encompasses the tools and symbol systems that give structure and meaning to experience. In relation to human development, cultures have implicit theories about the stages of life, the expectations for behavior as one matures, and the nature of one's obligations to the older and younger members of the cultural group. A culture exerts influence directly through families as well as through other social organizations such as churches and schools. The United States, like other nations, has a culture that has a strong, unifying impact on its citizens. Within the United States, there are also noticeable regional cultural patterns marked by unique vocabulary and dialect, mannerisms, and styles of social interaction. Throughout this book, we will note the great differences in what life—including family life—is like in different cultures and note how the integration of person and culture produces distinctive personal experiences for individuals in various cultures.

**ETHNIC GROUPS.**  In addition to the common threads of culture that affect everyone who grows up or lives for a long time in the United States, there are also persistent subcultural forces that shape the daily lives of children and adults. The United States is a complex society made up of people from a vast array of cultures throughout the world. We call these groups **ethnic subcultures** or *ethnic groups*. People who belong to ethnic groups share socially standardized ways of

thinking, feeling, and acting with other members of their group. The subculture may or may not be in conflict with the mainstream culture of the United States. Much of the literature on human development in this country is based on observations of White, middle class participants of European ancestry. However, increasing attention is being given to the lifestyles, identity development, parenting practices, and family values of other ethnic groups, and we will give special attention to studies that highlight ethnic group comparisons where possible.

## COPING BEHAVIOR

**Coping behavior**, the sixth organizing concept of psychosocial theory, refers to the conscious, adaptive efforts that people use to manage stressful events or situations, and the emotions associated with these stressors (Somerfield & McCrae, 2000). Coping is a process that begins with an **appraisal** of the situation—what is the nature of this stressor, how much of a threat is it, how much time do I have to deal with this challenge, how much control do I have over the situation? Following the appraisal, one must enlist cognitive, affective, and behavioral strategies to manage the stress. Lazarus and Folkman (1984) distinguished between coping efforts that are targeted at changing something about the source of stress (*problem-focused coping*) and strategies that are targeted at managing or controlling one's emotions in the face of the stressor (*emotion-focused coping*). Often, these strategies are used together. Claire, who has taken a week of vacation, has returned to work to find a basket full of mail, 20 voice messages, and 80 e-mail messages. She still has her usual daily workload. She decides to take a short lunch and stay an hour late in order to catch up. At the same time, she tries to remain calm and think about the wonderfully relaxing time she had on her vacation so that she does not become depressed by this huge amount of work.

In order to understand how a person copes with a stressful situation, one must consider the nature of the stressor, how it is perceived by the person, and the range of resources that are available to address the situation (Lazarus, 2000; McCubbin & Patterson, 1982). The coping process depends on the specific stressful situation. One does not cope the same way if the house is on fire or if the baby has a high fever. The approach to coping also depends on the values, beliefs, and goals of the person or family involved and on how these values, beliefs, and goals lead to a particular interpretation of the stressor event. For example, in one family, the announcement that an oldest child decides to enlist in the military may be greeted with great joy and pride; in another family, that same announcement may be greeted with dismay and disappointment. Both families will worry about the child's safety and will experience the stress of the child's absence. However, the family's beliefs and goals will determine the meaning given to a child's decision to join the military.

Finally, individuals and families differ in the resources that are available to cope with a difficult situation. Resources include such things as social support, information, professional advice, financial resources, and a sense of humor. Fewer resources, or the lack of the appropriate resources, may impede the coping process.

Coping behavior is an important concept in psychosocial theory because it explains how unique and inventive behaviors occur. An important aspect of coping is the ability to redefine or *reappraise* the situation in a positive way. This suggests creating or re-emphasizing the meaning, values, and opportunities embedded in the stressful situation (Folkman & Moskowitz, 2000). For example, as Robert cared for his partner who had AIDS, he took special pleasure in routine, daily events like planning an enjoyable meal that they shared together. In the face of feelings of helplessness about the uncontrollable changes in his partner's condition, Robert also took steps to set attainable goals, like creating a video library of favorite movies that he and his partner could enjoy together. Thus, even while Robert was experiencing many negative emotions, he also found positive experiences in the context of the stress.

As a result of experiencing mastery and competence through coping, one builds a more positive expectation about being able to face new challenges. The positive consequences of coping help to sustain individuals during prolonged stressors. One can see how, over time, effective coping can contribute to the developmental process. In the face of threat, coping behavior allows the individual to develop and grow, rather than merely to maintain equilibrium or become disorganized.

In coping with life challenges, individuals create their own strategies, which reflect their talents, goals, and developmental abilities. Robert White (1974) suggested that effective coping is characterized by three important features: (1) the abil-

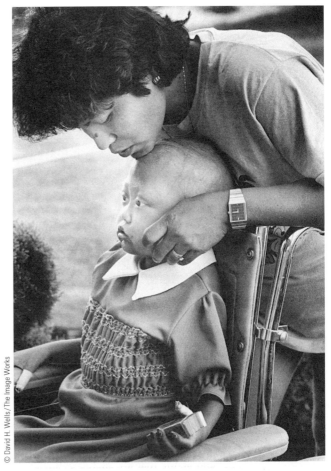

After a terrible accident, this child and her mother struggle to preserve the child's optimal level of functioning, find hope in small signs of improvement, and create innovative ways of solving innumerable social, financial, and medical problems. What are the coping resources that make it possible for this mother and child to remain proactive and optimistic?

ity to gain and process new information, (2) the ability to retain control over one's emotional state, and (3) the ability to move freely within the environment, preparing to engage or escape as necessary.

Think of the first day of kindergarten for a group of 5-year-olds. Some children are just sitting, shyly watching the teacher and the other children. Others are climbing all over the equipment and eagerly exploring the new toys. Still others are talking to the teacher or to the other children, finding out names, making friends, or telling about the bus ride to school. Each of these strategies can be understood as a way of gathering information while preserving a degree of autonomy and integrity in a new and potentially threatening environment. No one way is right, or even best, except as it serves the person by allowing access to information, freedom of movement, and some control over the emotions evoked by the new challenge.

An individual's characteristic style of coping is a dynamic process that changes in response to changing conditions. In research about how individuals cope with chronic pain, for

**Table 3.4** Prime Adaptive Ego Qualities

| LIFE STAGE | EGO QUALITY | DEFINITION |
|---|---|---|
| Infancy | Hope | An enduring belief that one can attain one's deep and essential wishes |
| Toddlerhood | Will | A determination to exercise free choice and self-control |
| Early school age | Purpose | The courage to imagine and pursue valued goals |
| Middle childhood | Competence | The free exercise of skill and intelligence in the completion of tasks |
| Early adolescence | Fidelity to others | The ability freely to pledge and sustain loyalty to others |
| Later adolescence | Fidelity to values | The ability freely to pledge and sustain loyalty to values and ideologies |
| Early adulthood | Love | A capacity for mutuality that transcends childhood dependency |
| Middle adulthood | Care | A commitment to concern about what has been generated |
| Later adulthood | Wisdom | A detached yet active concern with life itself in the face of death |
| Very old age | Confidence | A conscious trust in oneself and assurance about the meaningfulness of life |

Source: Based on Erikson, 1978.

example, participants were asked to make daily entries in a diary and were also prompted several times a day to respond to a set of questions about their appraisal of the situation, their mood, and their behaviors (Tennen, Affleck, Armeli, & Carney, 2000). Participants were most likely to use problem-focused strategies to cope with pain, or to use problem-focused and emotion-focused coping at the same time. However, as time went on, if the pain did not subside with the use of problem-focused strategies, they were likely to turn to emotion-focused solutions. In other words, the coping process was sensitive to the results of various strategies. If a person finds that active efforts to reduce pain are not working, then subsequent coping may shift to seeking spiritual or emotional support or trying to redefine the situation to make it more bearable.

According to psychosocial theory, at each stage of life, consistent efforts to face and cope with the psychosocial crisis of the period results in the formation of basic adaptive capacities, referred to as the **prime adaptive ego qualities**.

When coping is unsuccessful and the challenges of the period are not adequately mastered, individuals are likely to form maladaptive orientations referred to as **core pathologies**.

### ■ PRIME ADAPTIVE EGO QUALITIES

Erikson (1978) postulated prime adaptive ego qualities that develop from the positive resolution of the psychosocial crisis of a given stage and provide resources for coping with the next. He described these qualities as mental states that form a basic orientation toward the interpretation of life experiences. A sense of competence, for example, permits a person to feel free to exercise his or her wits to solve problems without being weighed down by a sense of inferiority.

The prime adaptive ego qualities and their definitions are listed in Table 3.4. These ego qualities contribute to the person's dominant worldview, which is continuously reformulated to accommodate new ego qualities (Markstrom, Sabino, Turner, & Berman, 1997). The importance of many of the

**Table 3.5** Core Pathologies

| LIFE STAGE | CORE PATHOLOGY | DEFINITION |
|---|---|---|
| Infancy | Withdrawal | Social and emotional detachment |
| Toddlerhood | Compulsion | Repetitive behaviors motivated by impulse or by restrictions against the expression of impulse |
| Early school age | Inhibition | A psychological restraint that prevents freedom of thought, expression, and activity |
| Middle childhood | Inertia | A paralysis of action and thought that prevents productive work |
| Early adolescence | Dissociation | An inability to connect with others |
| Later adolescence | Repudiation | Rejection of roles and values that are viewed as alien to oneself |
| Early adulthood | Exclusivity | An elitist shutting out of others |
| Middle adulthood | Rejectivity | Unwillingness to include certain others or groups of others in one's generative concern |
| Later adulthood | Disdain | A feeling of scorn for the weakness and frailty of oneself and others |
| Very old age | Diffidence | An inability to act because of overwhelming self-doubt |

Source: Based on Erikson, 1982.

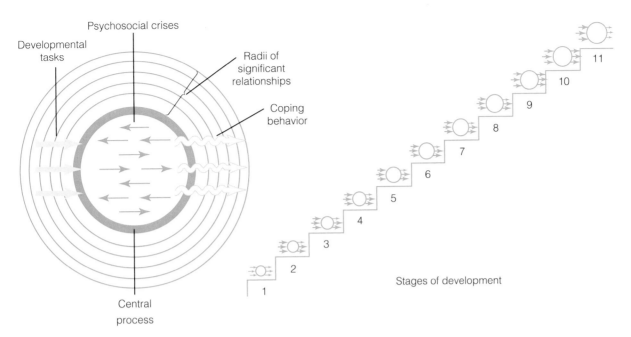

**FIGURE 3.4**

The Six Basic Concepts of Psychosocial Theory

prime adaptive ego qualities, including hope, purpose, competence, love, and wisdom, has been verified by research (Lopez & Snyder, 2003). For example, in interviews with people in very old age, Erikson and his colleagues found that those who were hopeful about their own future and that of their children were more intellectually vigorous and psychologically resilient than those not characterized by this orientation (Erikson et al., 1986). People with a hopeful attitude have a better chance of maintaining their spirits and strength in the face of crisis than people who are pessimistic. For both young and older adults, the ego strength of hope has been found to be a significant predictor of life satisfaction (Isaacowitz, Vaillant, & Seligman, 2003).

## ■ CORE PATHOLOGIES

Although most people develop the prime adaptive ego qualities, a potential core pathology or destructive force may also develop as a result of ineffective, negatively balanced crisis resolution at each stage (Erikson, 1982; see Table 3.5). The core pathologies also serve as guiding orientations for behavior. These pathologies move people away from others, tend to prevent further exploration of interpersonal relations, and obstruct the resolution of subsequent psychosocial crises. The energy that would normally be directed toward mastering the developmental tasks of a stage is directed instead toward resisting or avoiding change. The core pathologies are not simply passive limitations or barriers to growth. They are energized worldviews leading to strategies that protect people from further unwanted association with the social system and its persistent, tension-producing demands.

Figure 3.4 shows development as a building process that incorporates the six constructs of psychosocial theory. The structure grows larger as the radius of significant relationships expands and as the achievements of earlier stages are integrated into the behavior of the next stage of development.

# ■ CASE STUDY

## ERIK H. ERIKSON: A BIOGRAPHICAL CASE STUDY OF PSYCHOSOCIAL DEVELOPMENT

*Erik Erikson (1902–1994) illustrates the psychosocial perspective by describing the personal, family, and societal factors that contributed to his own identity crisis.*

There is first of all the question of origin, which often looms large in individuals who are driven to be original. I grew up in Karlsruhe in southern Germany as the son of a pediatrician, Dr. Theodor Homburger, and his wife Karla, née Abrahamsen, a native of Copenhagen, Denmark. All through my earlier childhood, they kept secret from me the fact that my mother had been married previously; and that I was the son of a Dane who had abandoned her before my birth. They apparently thought that such secretiveness was not only workable (because children then were not held to know what they had not been told) but also advisable, so that I would feel thoroughly at home in their home. As children will do, I played in with this and more or less forgot the period before the age of three, when mother and I had lived alone. Then her friends had been artists working in the folk style of Hans Thoma of the Black Forest. They, I believe, provided my first male imprinting before I had to come to terms with that intruder, the bearded doctor, with his healing love and mysterious instruments. Later, I enjoyed going back

*Erik H. Erikson and Joan Erikson, the parents of psychosocial theory*

and forth between the painters' studios and our house, the first floor of which, in the afternoons, was filled with tense and trusting mothers and children. My sense of being "different" took refuge (as it is apt to do even in children without such acute life problems) in fantasies of how I, the son of much better parents, had been altogether a foundling. In the meantime, however, my adoptive father was anything but the proverbial stepfather. He had given me his last name (which I have retained as a middle name) and expected me to become a doctor like himself.

Identity problems sharpen with that turn in puberty when images of future roles become inescapable. My stepfather was the only professional man (and a highly respected one) in an intensely Jewish small bourgeois family, while I (coming from a racially mixed Scandinavian background) was blond and blue-eyed, and grew flagrantly tall. Before long, then, I was referred to as "goy" in my stepfather's temple; while to my schoolmates I was a "Jew." Although during World War I, I tried desperately to be a good German chauvinist, I became a "Dane" when Denmark remained neutral.

At the time, like other youths with artistic or literary aspirations, I became intensely alienated from everything my bourgeois family stood for. At that point, I set out to be different. After graduation from the type of high school called a humanistic Gymnasium, . . . I went to art school, but always again took to wandering. . . . And in those days every self-respecting stranger in his own (northern) culture drifted sooner or later to Italy, where endless time was spent soaking up the southern sun and the ubiquitous sights with their grand blend of artifact and nature. I was a "Bohemian" then.

Source: Erikson, 1975.

## CRITICAL THINKING AND CASE ANALYSIS

As you think about this autobiographical case, consider the following questions:

1. Why did Erikson feel like a "stranger in his own culture"?
2. What are the biological, psychological, and societal factors that contributed to Erikson's identity crisis?
3. What factors from childhood appear to be influencing his experiences as an adolescent?
4. Who are the significant figures in Erikson's life, the radius of significant others, who influence his sense of how he should behave and who he should strive to become?
5. What factors might have contributed to Erikson's ability to cope with the challenges of this period of his life, eventually finding a direction and meaning to which he could commit his talent and energy?
6. Based on Erikson's account of his childhood and adolescence, how might his life experiences and his cultural context have influenced the nature and focus of his psychosocial theory?

# EVALUATION OF PSYCHOSOCIAL THEORY

Although we believe that psychosocial theory provides a useful theoretical framework for organizing the vast array of observations in the field of human development, we recognize that it has weaknesses as well as strengths. As a student of development, you must begin to form your own independent judgment of its usefulness and be alert to how the theory may influence your thinking. The strengths and weaknesses of psychosocial theory that are discussed in the following sections are listed in Table 3.6.

## STRENGTHS

Psychosocial theory provides a broad, integrative context within which to study life-span development (Hopkins, 1995; Kishton, 1994). The theory links the process of child development to the stages of adult life, individual development to the nature of culture and society, and the personal and historical past to the personal and societal future. Although many scholars agree that such a broad perspective is necessary, few other theories attempt to address the dynamic interplay between individual development and society (Miller, 2002).

The emphasis of psychosocial theory on ego development and ego processes provides insight into the directions of healthy development throughout life. The theory provides a framework for tracing the process through which self-concept, self-esteem, and ego boundaries become integrated into a positive, adaptive, socially engaged person (Hamachek, 1985, 1994). Emphasizing the normal, hopeful, and creative aspects of coping and adaptation, the theory has taken the study of development beyond the deterministic position of psychosexual theory or the mechanistic view of behaviorism,

## Table 3.6 Strengths and Weaknesses of Psychosocial Theory

| STRENGTHS | WEAKNESSES |
|---|---|
| The theory provides a broad, integrative framework within which to study the life span. | Explanations for the mechanisms of crisis resolution and the process of moving from one stage to the next need to be developed more fully. |
| The theory provides insight into the directions of healthy development across the life span. | The idea of a specific number of stages of life and their link to a genetic plan for development is disputed. |
| Many of the basic ideas of the theory have been operationalized using traditional and novel approaches to assessment. | The theory and much of its supporting research have been dominated by a male, Eurocentric perspective that gives too much emphasis to individuality and not enough attention to connection and social relatedness. |
| The concept of psychosocial crises, including the positive and negative poles of the crisis, offers a model for considering individual differences within a framework of normal development. | The specific ways that culture encourages or inhibits development at each life stage are not clearly elaborated. |
| The concept of the psychosocial crisis identifies predictable tensions between socialization and maturation. | |
| Longitudinal studies support the general direction of development hypothesized by the theory. | |

providing an essential conceptual framework for the emergence of positive psychology.

At one time, some argued that a weakness of psychosocial theory was that its basic concepts were presented in language that is abstract and difficult to examine empirically (Crain, 2000; Miller, 2002). However, over the past 20 years, such terms as hope, inhibition, autonomy, personal identity, intimacy, generativity, and integrity—to name a few—have been operationalized (Bohlin, Bengtsgard, & Andersson, 2000; Christiansen & Palkovitz, 1998; Kroger, 2000; Lopez & Snyder, 2003; Marcia, 2002; McAdams & de St. Aubin, 1998; Snyder, 2002). Concepts central to the theory—such as trust, autonomy, identity achievement, coping, well-being, social support, and intergenerational interdependence—have become thoroughly integrated into contemporary human development scholarship. Researchers have developed instruments to trace the emergence of psychosocial crises and their resolution in samples varying in age from adolescence to later adulthood (Constantinople, 1969; Darling-Fisher & Leidy, 1988; Domino & Affonso, 1990; Hawley, 1988; Waterman & Whitbourne, 1981; Whitbourne et al., 1992).

Unlike some other stage theories, psychosocial theory identifies tensions that may disrupt development at each life stage, providing a useful framework for considering individual differences in development. The positive and negative poles of each psychosocial crisis offer a way of thinking about differences in ego development at each stage of life as well as a model for considering cumulative differences across the life span. This matrix of crises and stages also provides a useful tool for approaching psychotherapy and counseling.

The concept of normative psychosocial crises is a creative contribution that identifies predictable tensions between socialization and maturation throughout life. Societies, with their structures, laws, roles, rituals, and sanctions, are organized to guide individual growth toward a particular ideal of mature adulthood. However, every society faces problems when it attempts to balance the needs of the individual with the needs of the group. All individuals face some strains as they attempt to experience their individuality while maintaining the support of their groups and attempting to fit into their society. Psychosocial theory gives us concepts for exploring these natural tensions.

Longitudinal research using psychosocial theory as a framework for studying patterns of personality change and ego development has found support for many of its basic concepts. Changes in psychological outlook that reflect the major themes of the theory—such as industry, identity, intimacy, and generativity—appear to emerge and become consolidated over time (Whitbourne et al., 1992). The box on the next page provides more details about one of these studies. There is also evidence of a preview of themes prior to their period of maximum ascendancy (Peterson & Steward, 1993) and evidence for the notion of revisitation through which adults are stimulated to rework and reorganize the resolutions of earlier issues (Shibley, 2000).

## WEAKNESSES

One weakness of psychosocial theory is that the explanations of the mechanisms for resolving crises and moving from one stage to the next are not well developed (Miller, 2002). The theory does not offer a universal mechanism for crisis resolution, nor a detailed picture of the kinds of experiences that are necessary at each stage if one is to cope successfully with the crisis of that stage. We have addressed this weakness by including the concepts of developmental tasks and a central process for each stage. The developmental tasks suggest some of the major achievements that permit a person to meet the social expectations of each stage. The central process identifies the primary mechanism through which the ego encounters societal expectations and integrates them into a revised sense of self. Using these two mechanisms, one can begin to clarify the process of movement from one stage to the next.

The specific number of stages and their link to a biologically based plan for development have been criticized. The nature

# Studying Psychosocial Development in Adulthood

ONE OF THE important contributions of psychosocial theory is the proposition that development continues through adulthood, with qualitatively unique characteristics emerging in a predictable pattern from later adolescence through very old age. Although this proposition may appear self-evident, the task of providing empirical evidence to support the idea is difficult. One of the challenges is that both individuals and society are changing over time, and we know that individuals are continuously adapting to changes in their social and historical context. In order to support the proposition of developmental change, one must try to separate the effects of historical time from development. The study described here provides an example of how this can be accomplished.

Researchers involved three cohorts of college students—those enrolled in 1966 (Cohort 1), those enrolled in 1977 (Cohort 2), and those enrolled in 1988 (Cohort 3)—in a study of psychosocial development (Whitbourne, Zuschlag, et al. 1992). For each group, students were asked to participate while they were enrolled in college. The two older groups were contacted as alumni to participate in the research again. Thus, the study was able to track changes in development from about age 20 through age 31 to age 42 for Cohort 1; from age 20 to age 31 for Cohort 2; and to compare these responses to Cohort 3 at about age 20 in 1988.

The study used a measure of psychosocial stages, the *Inventory of Psychosocial Development*, which was designed by Constantinople (1969) and expanded by Walaskay et al. (1983–1984) to measure the original eight stages of Erikson's theory. The scale includes 10 items for each psychosocial crisis, 5 for the positive pole and 5 for the negative pole. Each item is rated on a scale from 1 (*definitely most uncharacteristic of you*) to 7 (*definitely most characteristic of you*). Scores were

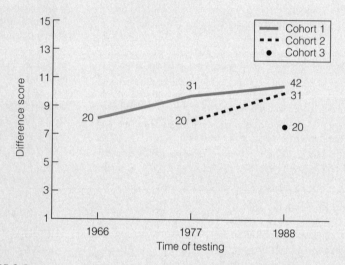

**FIGURE 3.5**

Scores on Stage 5 of the *Inventory of Psychosocial Development* by Year Tested and Cohort. Age at time of testing is indicated on the figure.

tabulated for each person at each time of measurement.

By including three different cohorts of participants, the design allowed researchers to study three questions:

1. Do people change in their resolution of the psychosocial crises over time?

2. Do groups of people who are at the same age at different periods of history look similar in their resolution of the crises?

3. If changes are found, are they consistent with Erikson's view of how personality ought to change?

The results of the study can be appreciated by examining Figure 3.5, which shows the three cohorts' scores on the *Inventory of Psychosocial Development*, Stage 5, identity versus role confusion. Participants in Cohorts 1, 2, and 3 were all at about the same level of development at age 20, regardless of the historical time when they were studied. Cohorts 1 and 2 both show significant changes in their scores from age 20 to 31. At age 31, respondents in Cohorts

1 and 2 were at about the same level of development. This result provides evidence that people do change in their resolution over time, and that the change is in the direction predicted by psychosocial theory. Similar pictures of significant age-related change independent of historical period were found for the stages of trust versus mistrust, industry versus inferiority, and intimacy versus isolation.

Scores for generativity versus stagnation and integrity versus despair were only measured in 1977 and 1988. Scores for generativity increased between the two times of measurement, but the change was not statistically significant. One real surprise in this study was that scores on the scale for Stage 8, integrity versus despair, declined between the period 1977 and 1988 for both Cohorts 1 and 2, and the scores for Cohort 3 were also quite low. These results suggested that a historical context effect may have been operating to increase feelings of meaninglessness and lack of moral anchor for all groups during the late 1980s.

and number of stages of life is arguably highly culturally specific. For example, in some societies, the transition from childhood to adulthood is swift, leaving little time or expectation for identity exploration. In many traditional societies, parents choose one's marital partner, there are few occupational choices, and one is guided toward one's vocation from an early age. Thus, although there is always a biological period of pubescence, there may be little experience of the psychosocial processes of adolescence (Thomas, 1999). In contrast, in our highly technological society, adolescence appears to be extended for some, especially as the age at first marriage is delayed and the complexity of preparing for and entering the labor market increases. As a reflection of this extension of modern adolescence, we have treated the period from puberty through about age 24 as two stages rather than one, each with its own psychosocial crisis and developmental tasks.

Along this same line of criticism, other human development scholars have taken a more differentiated view of the stages of adulthood and later life. In later life, health status, life circumstances, and culture interact to produce increasing variation in life stories. In a growing line of research, distinctions are being made between the "young-old" and the "old-old." These distinctions are sometimes based on health status and the person's capacity to manage tasks of daily life (Deeg, Kardaun, & Fozard, 1996).

In other research, distinctions are made on the basis of chronological age. For example, Leonard Poon has written extensively about the differences between centenarians (people who are 100 or more), octogenarians (people in their 80s), and sexagenarians (people in their 60s; Martin, Poon, Kim, & Johnson, 1996). Each cohort of older adults has been exposed to different historical crises, educational, health and occupational opportunities, and shifting societal values. Therefore, it is likely that the normative patterns used to describe development in adulthood and later life will become dated and need reexamination (Siegler, Poon, Madden, & Welsh, 1996).

We have addressed this concern in part by extending the traditional psychosocial stage approach to adulthood from three stages to four, adding a period called very old age. In the chapters on adulthood, we also address differences in lifestyle and life course that are attributable to historical and cultural trends. Nevertheless, the increasing life expectancy, accompanied by a longer period of healthy later life and the elaboration of lifestyles, makes it difficult to chart a normative life course from early adulthood into very old age.

In this book, you will also read about the important developmental issues of the prenatal period—a stage that Erikson's theory does not consider, but that clearly plays a central role in setting the stage for a lifetime of vulnerabilities and competencies. These revisions demonstrate the natural evolution of a theoretical framework as it continues to encounter new observations.

Finally, the psychosocial theory and related research have been criticized as being dominated by a male, Eurocentric, individualistic perspective that emphasizes **agency**—the ability to originate plans and take action—over connection and **communion**—the commitment to and consideration for the well-being of others (Bar-Yam Hassan & Bar-Yam, 1987; Gilligan, 1982/1993). The themes of autonomy, initiative, industry, and personal identity all emphasize the process of individuation. Critics have argued that ego development, separateness from family, autonomy, and self-directed goal attainment have been equated with psychological maturity, and that relatively little attention has been given to the development of interpersonal connection and social relatedness. These themes have been identified as central for an understanding of the psychosocial maturity of girls and young women. They also emerge in the study of collectively oriented ethnic groups—cultures in which maturity is equated with one's ability to support and sustain the success of the family or the extended family group rather than with one's own achievement of status, wealth, or recognition (Boykin, 1994; Josselson, 1987).

*All of these young people are in the stage of later adolescence. Some have reached the point of identity achievement; others have not. What determines whether a person moves from one developmental stage to the next?*

© Michael Newman/Photo Edit

Within the framework of psychosocial theory, the theme of connection is addressed directly through the first psychosocial crisis of trust versus mistrust in infancy, but then the thread is lost until early adolescence and early and middle adulthood, when group identity, intimacy, and generativity direct the focus back to the critical links that individuals build with others. The concept of the radius of significant relationships helps to maintain the perspective of the person interwoven in a tapestry of relationships, focusing especially on family and friends in childhood; on the family, peer group, love relationships, and close friends in early and later adolescence; and on intimate partners, family, friends, and coworkers in adult life. A basic premise of psychosocial theory is that the ego is taking shape in constant interaction with the community (Schlein, 1987).

To extend the theme of connection, the text elaborates on developing capabilities for social interaction and differences in socialization practices and outcomes for men and women in our society. A variety of social abilities, including empathy, prosocial behavior, interaction skills, and components of social cognition, are traced as they emerge in the context of family relationships, friendship, peer groups, and work. The text considers ethnic groups as well as broader social influences on development and the importance of a collective orientation toward responsibility in caring for children and creating a sense of community.

## A RECAP OF PSYCHOSOCIAL THEORY

At the beginning of this chapter, we discussed the three questions one must ask in order to understand a theory. Let us now answer these questions with respect to psychosocial theory:

*Which phenomena is the theory trying to explain?* Psychosocial theory attempts to explain human development across the life span—especially patterned changes in ego development, which is reflected in self-understanding, identity formation, social relationships, and worldview.
*What assumptions does the theory make?* Human development is a product of three interacting factors: biological maturation, the interaction between individuals and social groups, and the contributions that individuals make to their own psychological growth.
1. Growth occurs at every period of life, from conception through very old age.
2. Individual lives show continuity and change as they progress through time.
3. We need to understand the whole person, because we function in an integrated manner.
4. Every person's behavior must be analyzed in the context of relevant settings and personal relationships.
5. People contribute actively to their own development.
*What does the theory predict?*
1. There are 11 stages of development, which emerge in an ordered sequence. Issues of later stages can be previewed at an earlier time, but each issue has its period

of ascendance. It takes the entire life course, from the prenatal period through very old age, for all aspects of the ego's potential to be realized.
2. Developmental tasks are dictated by the interaction of the biological, psychological, and societal systems during each stage.
3. A normal crisis arises at each stage of development, and a central process operates to resolve this crisis. The resolution of the crisis at each stage determines one's coping resources, with a positive resolution contributing to ego strengths and a negative resolution contributing to core pathologies.
4. Each person is part of an expanding network of significant relationships that convey society's expectations and demands. These relationships also provide encouragement in the face of challenges.
5. Development will be optimal if a person can create new behaviors and relationships as a result of skill acquisition and successful crisis resolution during each stage of growth. Lack of development and core pathologies result from tendencies that restrict behavior (especially social behavior) in general and new behavior in particular. The mechanisms for positive and negative development are diagrammed in Figure 3.6.

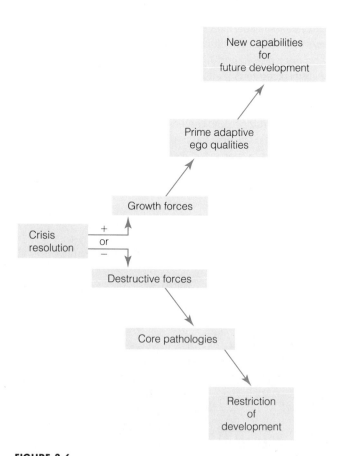

**FIGURE 3.6**

The Mechanism for Positive and Negative Psychosocial Development

# Chapter Summary

Psychosocial theory offers a life-span view in which development is a product of the interactions between individuals and their social environments. The needs and goals of both the individual and society must be considered in conceptualizing human development. Predictability is found in the sequence of psychosocial stages, the central process involved in the resolution of the psychosocial crisis at each stage, and the radius of significant relationships. Individuality is expressed in the achievement of the developmental tasks, in the balance of the positive and negative poles of each psychosocial crisis and the resulting worldview, and in the style and resources for coping that a person brings to each new life challenge.

Connectivity is achieved in the way the person learns to relate in a radius of significant others who make demands, convey social expectations, and offer social rewards. Over time, the person becomes engaged in increasingly complex social groups and institutions. A person's worldview at a particular age is a product of past identifications and the resolution of previous psychosocial crises, contemporary pressures and opportunities, and hopes for the future. In our society, there is great diversity in the outcomes of this psychosocial process and in the transmission of social expectations from one generation of adults to the next generation of children.

The basic concepts of psychosocial theory provide the framework for analyzing development across 11 life stages from the prenatal period through very old age. Each chapter from 5 through 15 is devoted to one life stage. Chapter 16 covers topics related to death and bereavement across the life span. With the exception of Chapter 5, on pregnancy and prenatal development, each life stage chapter starts with a discussion of the developmental tasks of that life stage. By tracing developments in physical growth, emotional growth, intellectual skills, social relationships, and self-understanding, you can recognize the interrelationships among all of these dimensions during each period of life.

In the second section of each chapter, we describe the psychosocial crisis of that life stage, accounting for the tension by examining the individual's needs and personal resources in light of the dominant societal expectations. In addition to defining the crisis, we conceptualize the central process by which it is resolved. The resolution of the crisis at each stage is tied to either new ego strengths or new core pathologies.

At the end of each chapter, we draw on the material we have discussed to analyze a topic that is of persistent concern to our society. These topics are controversial, and they may generate sentiment as they deepen understanding. We intend these sections to stimulate the application of developmental principles to real-world concerns.

Take a moment to study the table on the front leaf of the book. You can use this table as a guide to the major themes of the text. It may help you to see the connections among the topics in a chapter or to trace threads of continuity over several periods of life. You may also use this table in constructing a life map for yourself, which will reveal the levels of tension and the major psychosocial factors that are currently affecting your self-concept and your relationships with others.

# Further Reflection

Based on your understanding of psychosocial theory,
1. What is the focus or range of applicability of psychosocial theory? What is this theory about?
2. What role does the theory give to biological maturation and experience in guiding development? How do these factors interact?
3. What is the contribution of early life experience to later development?
4. How do the concepts of psychosocial theory help explain how a person moves from one stage of life to the next?
5. What is coping? How does it fit into the process of development over the life course? Can you describe an example of your own coping behavior as you faced a new or demanding situation in the past few months?
6. How might people at different psychosocial stages differ in the ways they are affected by a similar stressor such as unemployment?

# On the Web

**VISIT OUR WEBSITE**

Go to http://www.wadsworth.com/psychology to find online resources directly linked to your book.

# Casebook

For additional case material related to this chapter, see the case of "Ayesha and the Dinosaurs" in *Life Span Development: A Case Book*, by Barbara and Philip Newman, Laura Landry-Meyer, and Brenda J. Lohman, page 100. This case of an engaging 10-year-old illustrates ways in which the psychosocial strengths of trust, autonomy, initiative, and industry come together to support effective problem solving. The case provides an opportunity to discuss the usefulness of the central concepts of psychosocial theory for guiding understanding about positive development.

# CHAPTER 4

# MAJOR THEORIES FOR UNDERSTANDING HUMAN DEVELOPMENT

*Portrait of Ambroise Vollard, 1910/Pablo Picasso/© 2005 Estate of Pablo Picasso/Artists Rights Society (ARS), New York,/© Bridgeman Art Library, London /SuperStock*

*Cubism is like theoretical painting. It moves beyond the surface to reveal the elements of which the subject is composed. Theories provide ways of understanding behavior by introducing structures and processes that are not immediately observable.*

■ THE THEORY OF EVOLUTION

Implications for Human Development
Links to Psychosocial Theory

■ PSYCHOSEXUAL THEORY

Implications for Human Development
Links to Psychosocial Theory

■ COGNITIVE DEVELOPMENTAL THEORY

Basic Concepts in Piaget's Theory
Implications for Human Development
Vygotsky's Concepts of Cognitive Development
Implications for Human Development
Links to Psychosocial Theory

■ THEORIES OF LEARNING

Classical Conditioning
Operant Conditioning
Social Learning Theory
Cognitive Behaviorism
Summary of the Learning Theories
Links to Psychosocial Theory

■ CULTURAL THEORY

Implications for Human Development
Links to Psychosocial Theory

■ SOCIAL ROLE THEORY

Implications for Human Development
Links to Psychosocial Theory

■ SYSTEMS THEORY

Implications for Human Development
Links to Psychosocial Theory
CASE STUDY: JACK MANASKY
AND HIS DAUGHTER MARILYN

■ CHAPTER SUMMARY

■ FURTHER REFLECTION

▶  *To review the basic concepts of seven major theories that have guided research in the study of human development. These theories include evolutionary theory, psychosexual theory, cognitive developmental theory, theories of learning, cultural theory, social role theory, and systems theory.*

▶  *To examine the implications of each theory for the study of human development.*

▶  *To clarify the links between each of these theories and psychosocial theory.*

IMAGINE THAT YOU are taking a road trip across the country. To plan your route and find your way, you might want a map of the United States that indicates the major highways and the location of urban centers and scenic areas. However, you will probably want to get more detailed maps of the states you will visit. Once you arrive at a city, or a state or national park, you will need tourist maps showing the historic sites, shopping areas, hotels, and walking trails, so that you can enjoy each spot to its fullest.

With respect to this book, psychosocial theory is like the map of the United States: It provides a broad, conceptual umbrella for the study of human development. However, we need other theories to explain behavior at different levels of analysis. The theories presented in this chapter are like the maps of states, cities, and special scenic areas. They guide research and thinking in specific areas of human development. This chapter does not provide comprehensive coverage of all theories of human development, but a group of theories selected for their significant impact in guiding research and intervention. Many theories presented here continue to be evaluated and challenged by researchers as new and competing ideas about human behavior emerge.

First, we present the parent *theory of evolution* to provide the large picture of species change over long time periods. Evolutionary theory places the study of individual development in the context of the history of the species. A forerunner of psychosocial theory, *psychosexual theory* explains the relationship of mental activity to changing needs, wishes, and drives, with a particular focus on the role of sexual and aggressive needs. *Cognitive theory* describes the maturation of capacities for logical thought. *Learning theory*, *cultural theory*, *social role theory*, and *systems theory* each introduce mechanisms that explain how the environment makes its unique impact on the person and guides the content and direction of growth. The use of a family of theoretical perspectives helps to maintain flexibility in interpreting behavior and facilitates our understanding of the integration of individuals and social systems.

In each section, a brief explanation of the theory and a few major constructs are presented, along with an analysis of the theory's contributions to the study of development and links to psychosocial theory. In subsequent chapters, additional ideas from many of the theories will be presented as they relate to specific topics. ■

# THE THEORY OF EVOLUTION

The theory of evolution explains how diverse and increasingly more complex life-forms come to exist. Evolutionary theory assumes that the natural laws that apply to plant and animal life also apply to humans. The law of **natural selection** explains how, over generations, species gradually change to respond to changing environmental conditions (Darwin, 1859/1979). The law of natural selection claims that behavior is adapted to the environment in which it occurs. Natural selection operates at the level of genes that are passed, via an organism's reproductive process, from one generation to the next. Reproductive success, sometimes called **fitness**, varies among members of a species (Archer, 1991).

Every species produces more offspring than can survive to reproduce, because of limitations of the food supply and natural dangers. Darwin observed that there was quite a bit of variability among members of the same species in any given location. Some individuals were better suited than others to their immediate environment and, thus, were more likely to survive, mate, and produce offspring. These offspring were also more likely to have characteristics appropriate for that location. Over time, those members of the species that had the selective advantage would be more likely to survive and reproduce, thus passing their genetic characteristics on to future generations. If the environment changed (e.g., in climate), only certain variations of organisms would survive, and again species would evolve. Forms of life that failed to adapt would become extinct. Thus, in the context of changing environmental conditions, the variability within a species ensures the species' continuation or its development into new forms. Darwin viewed evolutionary change as taking place slowly and incrementally as individual organisms adapt and populations with similar adaptive characteristics come to dominate an environment or **ecological niche**.

The concept of **inclusive fitness** was later added to the theory of natural selection (Hamilton, 1964). This idea suggests that fitness is not only determined by an individual's own success in passing genes along to the next generation through reproduction. A characteristic can be selected if the genes are passed along to the next generation by promoting the survival and reproductive success of others who carry those genes. In human groups, behaviors that support one's family members or that make it possible for one's kin to be more attractive in the mating process would be considered examples of inclusive fitness. This concept highlights the adaptive advantage of supportive kin networks that selectively direct their resources toward members of their family, kinship network, tribe, or ethnic group.

Two subspecialties that have emerged from evolutionary theory are *ethology* and *evolutionary psychology*. **Ethology** is the study of the functional significance of expressive behavior in its social context from an evolutionary perspective (LaFreniere, 2000). This means that ethologists focus on describing the unique adaptive behaviors of specific species, such as mating, caregiving, play, or strategies for obtaining resources. They are especially interested in behaviors that appear to be spontaneous and that provide some type of adaptive advantage. An example is the infant's smile. Smiles occur early in the postnatal period. They function as a powerful signal that evokes a caregiving response. Over time, the infant's smile takes on a more complex meaning within the social context. Yet it begins as an unlearned behavior that has important survival value Through comparisons among species, the study of the conditions that evoke and maintain adaptive behaviors helps to clarify the role of behavior in the long-term survival of the species (Charlesworth, 1992).

**Evolutionary psychology** is the study of the long-term, historical origins of behavior. Whereas ethology focuses on analyzing adaptive behavior patterns across species, evolutionary psychology draws on principles of evolution to understand the human mind. "The mind is a set of information-processing machines that were designed by natural selection to solve adaptive problems faced by our hunter-gatherer ancestors." (Cosmides & Tooby, 1997).

This focus takes us to a time when humans lived in small, nomadic groups, traveling from place to place to find sources of food and trying to protect themselves from the dangers of predatory animals, weather, illness, and other humans. This way of life existed for more than two million years, during which various human species (along with their human minds) emerged. From this perspective, the human mind is highly adapted to solve the problems faced by these human ancestors, but it may not be well adapted to solve the new problems that have emerged in our recent industrial and postindustrial way of life.

From an evolutionary perspective, any behavior can be assessed by asking a few basic questions: What behavior is necessary to achieve a goal? How much energy is needed to achieve the goal? When should the organism stop the activity? What should the organism do next? These questions suggest that the organism has to recognize the nature of a problem and bring to bear the best "tool" needed to solve the problem (Neese, 2001). There are start-up costs to beginning any new behavior, so the most adaptive responses will contribute to long-term fitness. Once a behavior has been started, the organism has to assess how hard and how long to persist at the task. There is risk in putting too much energy into one problem and ignoring other important tasks.

## IMPLICATIONS FOR HUMAN DEVELOPMENT

Evolutionary theory assumes that human beings arrived at their current forms through a long process of natural selection. Most scholars agree that the human species began in Africa about two million years ago with *Homo erectus* and that modern humans, *Homo sapiens*, have been traveling across Africa, Europe, and Asia for about 100,000 years (Balter, 2001). Thus, one must conclude that the genome of contemporary human beings and its expression in basic biological features—such as the development of the brain, bipedalism, the capacity for coordinated movement, the nature of infant instincts, and the sensory and perceptual systems—are a result of their adaptive advantage over a long time and across multiple environments (Gray, 1996). With its focus on reproductive success, evolutionary theory highlights three phases of the life history: (1) healthy growth and development leading up to the reproductive period; (2) success in mating and the conception of offspring; and (3) the ability to parent offspring so they can survive, reach reproductive age, and bear offspring of their own (Charlesworth, 1992).

Humans are most vulnerable during infancy and childhood. Children require nurture and care in order to survive to reproductive age. Biological capacities and the environments in which they can be expressed operate together to produce behavior. A genetic plan, shaped through hundreds of generations, guides infants' predispositions, capacities, and sensitivities. Evolutionary theory points out that infants come into the world with a range of innate capacities and potentials. They are able to establish social contact, organize information, and recognize and communicate their needs. At the same time, these innate capacities are expressed in specific contexts. The quality of parenting, adequacy of resources, and competition for resources with other siblings are examples of environmental factors to which infants must adapt. Childhood experiences shape the future of the human species by providing the context for the establishment of attachments, meaningful social competence, and problem-solving capacities. These in turn have a bearing on an individual's behavior in adulthood—particularly the ability to form intimate relationships and to parent offspring.

© Mark Newman / Tom Stack and Associates

*From an evolutionary perspective, the attachment behavioral system is central to the offspring's survival. Adults have strategies for monitoring and protecting their young, and infants have capacities for alerting their caregivers when they are frightened or upset. What behaviors in human infant–mother pairs help them stay connected in times of distress?*

In adolescence and adulthood, the evolutionary focus shifts to emerging reproductive capacities—the ability to find a mate, to reproduce, and to rear one's young so that they can reach their own reproductive age. With advanced age, the forces of selection weaken. Because early humans died at a relatively young age due to predators, diseases, and environmental hazards, the selective advantage of characteristics that might be noticeable in later life was not preserved. As a result, the genome does not guide the direction of development to preserve high levels of functioning in later life as it so clearly does in infancy, childhood, and the transition through puberty to reproductive adulthood (Baltes, 1997). More rests on culture, lifestyle, and social resources to support successful aging.

The evolutionary perspective draws attention to the interconnection between an individual's life history and the long-range history of the species. Principles of natural selection operate slowly over generations. However, the reproductive success of individuals over the course of their own life span determines whether their genetic material continues to be represented in the larger population. Many general areas of human behavior are functionally relevant to the successful survival and fitness of individuals and groups (Charlesworth, 1992). They include the following:

- Reproductive strategies, such as having few or many sex partners; or early or later entry into sexual activity.
- Infant immaturity, requiring prolonged care.
- Infant–caregiver attachment.
- Parent–child conflicts and sibling rivalry.
- Peer group formation and functions, especially cooperation, competition, dominance, and submission.
- Pair bonding and mate selection.
- Helping behavior and altruism.
- Learning as adaptive behavior.
- Individual creation and modification of the environment.
- Social evolution and the elaboration of rites, rituals, and religions.

The evolutionary perspective directs attention to the importance of variability for a species' survival. Although theories of development typically focus on general patterns of continuity and change across individuals, evolutionary theory prompts one to attend to the importance of individual differences in the study of development. These differences help explain how the human species adapts successfully across a wide variety of environmental conditions.

## LINKS TO PSYCHOSOCIAL THEORY

Evolutionary theory is the larger framework within which broad issues of individual adaptation, species adaptation, and species survival are considered. Erikson drew heavily on concepts first introduced in Huxley's (1942) theory of **psychosocial evolution**. Huxley studied the processes through which human beings influenced their own adaptation. He focused on the creation of new information and the invention of strategies for communicating that information from one generation to the next. Evolutionary theory and its offspring, evolutionary psychology, typically point to behaviors that have a genetic underpinning, having emerged as a result of their adaptive advantage over thousands of years in the early hunting and gathering period of human evolution. Psychosocial evolution, in contrast, suggests a process through which contemporary patterns of knowledge gathering and transmission may alter behavior and transform or override these genetically guided patterns.

Psychosocial theory translates the idea of species adaptation to the individual level through the concepts of the psychosocial crisis and coping. Individuals encounter a necessary developmental struggle between their own traits and capacities and the requirements and demands of the environment. Each generation within a society faces similar challenges to cycle critical resources to the young, to nurture competence and a capacity for caring in the new generation of adults, and to inspire younger generations with hope and anticipation about the prospects of growing old. Within cultural groups, rites and rituals serve to protect and preserve resources, direct the rearing of children, and assist individuals through key transitions. Groups that adapt successfully are those that effectively cycle resources, help new members, and pass along information that will help individuals cope with future challenges.

One unique aspect of the human species is our ability to modify the environment in significant ways. We not only adapt to the environment, but we also alter it to suit our needs. Many of these modifications of the environment increase the chances that individuals within the group will survive; however, some modifications introduce grave risks. Psychosocial theory indicates a direction of individual growth in which the adults of a society use their competence and power to ensure the safety and well-being of future generations.

# PSYCHOSEXUAL THEORY

Evolutionary theory emphasized the critical role of sexual reproduction in the survival or extinction of species. Freud's (1933/1964) psychosexual theory focused on the contribution of biologically based, instinctual drives—especially sex and aggression—for personality development. Freud distinguished between the impact of sexual drives on mental activity and their effect on reproductive functions. Drawing largely on material from therapeutic sessions with his patients, Freud recognized the profound influence of sexuality on mental activity. Furthermore, he came to believe that very young children had strong sexual drives. He argued that although children are incapable of reproduction, their sexual drives operate to direct aspects of their fantasies, problem solving, and social interactions.

The most enduring contribution of psychosexual theory is its identification of domains of consciousness, referred to as the *conscious*, the *preconscious*, and the *unconscious*. Many explanations for seemingly irrational behavior can be found by analyzing the conflicting sexual and aggressive needs, fears, and wishes that are housed in the unconscious. Over the past 30 years, scholarly interest in cognitive processes has resulted in renewed attention to the notion of the **cognitive unconscious**—the range of mental structures and processes that operate outside awareness but play a significant role in conscious thought and action (Kihlstrom, 1987). Just as Freud argued, it is becoming evident that conscious thought accounts for only a small proportion of our capacities to identify, analyze, recall, and synthesize information.

Psychosexual theory describes three basic structures of the personality: the **id** (the sexual and aggressive impulses), the **ego** (reality-oriented functions), and the **superego** (the moral, ethical principles). As the ego develops, the child becomes increasingly adept at satisfying id impulses in ways that are socially acceptable and do not offend the moral and ethical content of the superego. Maturation and mental health rest on the ability of the ego to control and satisfy drive forces without violating the internalized moral sanctions of the culture.

Frequently, id impulses become so strong that they threaten to overwhelm the ego. For example, a man may find himself extremely jealous of the time his wife is spending with their infant. He may have strong, hostile feelings toward the infant or his wife—feelings he believes are unacceptable. Under these conditions, Freud argued, defense mechanisms come into play to protect the ego from painful thoughts and feelings, including guilt and anxiety.

*Freud's patients visited him in his office in Vienna, surrounded by cultural artifacts that were sources of stimulation to his own thinking. Central to the office was the famous couch. Freud invented the technique of free association as a way to gain insight into the unconscious.*

Stock Montage

## The Cognitive Unconscious

THE IDEA OF the **unconscious** suggests that there are mental processes at work of which we are not aware. Freud used dreams and slips of the tongue as two sources of evidence about the activities of the unconscious. The challenge to contemporary researchers is to find ways of "observing" unconscious mental activity outside the context of psychotherapy.

Research by Siegler and Stern (1998) was designed to explore the existence of mental processes that occur outside of awareness, particularly processes that are involved in problem solving. To investigate this possibility, they gave second graders a set of math problems to solve that involved inversion. The problems are of the type $A + B - B = A$. These problems can be solved mathematically by adding A and B and then subtracting B. They can also be solved through *insight*, by realizing that the answer is always the first number, A. Children were asked to solve these problems and then to explain how they solved them. The time it took to solve the problems was also measured. It took the children 8 seconds or longer to solve the problems through computation—and 4 seconds or less to solve them through insight.

The children were timed to see how long it took them to solve the problems, and they were interviewed to find out how they solved the problems. No less than 90% of the children discovered the unconscious insight before they were able to explain the insight verbally. That is, from the speed of their responses, it was clear that they were using the shortcut, even though in their verbal report they said they were using computation to solve the problem. The use of the unconscious insight affected the time to solve the problem immediately. There was an abrupt switch from an average response time of 12 seconds to an average response time of 2.7 seconds. After three or four trials in which the children used the unconscious strategy, many of them reported using the shortcut as a strategy for solving the problem. However, not all the children who used the shortcut were able to verbalize it as a strategy (Siegler, 2000). This line of research suggests that the unconscious includes resources for analyzing information and making discoveries that can influence behavior even though the person cannot verbally report about them. It demonstrates the active role of the unconscious in organizing meaningful thoughts.

**Defense mechanisms** include a variety of mental "tricks" that recast or distort the feelings so that they are more acceptable, or bury them so that they are removed from consciousness (Cramer, 2000). *Repression* is a global defense in which the feelings and thoughts are simply pushed into the unconscious. *Denial*—claiming that the feelings or the experience never happened—and *projection*—placing the blame for the feelings onto someone else—are two of the more common, immature defense mechanisms. At moments of heightened emotionality or threat, everyone uses some form of defense to help preserve some semblance of control. However, the use of defense mechanisms to manage anxiety over a long time can be destructive to reality testing and to forward movement in adapting to the new, altered reality.

Psychosexual theory describes five stages of development: the *oral, anal, phallic, latent,* and *genital* stages. At each stage, the focus of conflict around the expression of sexual and aggressive impulses changes. The stages reflect shifts in the body areas where pleasure is experienced and shifts in the orientation to self and social relationships.

In adolescence, a resurgence of sexual and aggressive energy challenges many of the ego's earlier coping strategies. The ego must find new ways to express and modify impulses. An essential aspect of this process is thought to be the separation of ego from earlier figures of attachment and investment of energy in the self as well as in new social relationships.

*Self Portrait, 1903/Pablo Picasso/© 2005 Estate of Pablo Picasso/Artists Rights Society (ARS), New York*

*In each of us, the id is the source of instincts and impulses. At age 22, Picasso drew this devilish caricature of himself, suggesting his impulsive, primate nature.*

## IMPLICATIONS FOR HUMAN DEVELOPMENT

Psychosexual theory emphasizes the importance of the tension between interpersonal demands and intrapsychic demands in shaping personality. The ego develops skills for dealing with the realities of the interpersonal world. It also develops skills for satisfying personal needs and for imposing personal standards and aspirations about the way these needs are satisfied. The expectations of others—particularly parents—are internalized and given personal meaning in the formation of the superego. By developing this idea, Freud was able to show how a child translates the demands of the interpersonal world into his or her own personal way of functioning. At the same time, new demands and experiences continue to play a role in the development of personality. Freud focused on the effects of sexual impulses on personal and interpersonal life throughout adulthood.

One of the major early contributions of psychosexual theory was the identification of the influence of childhood experiences on adult behavior. Freud argued that the basic dynamics of personality are established by the age of 6 or 7. Psychosexual theory was unique in its focus on stages of development, family interactions, and unresolved family conflicts as explanations for ongoing adult behavior. The emphasis Freud gave to the importance of parenting practices and their implications for psychosexual development has provided one of the few theoretical frameworks for examining parent–child relationships. Many of the early empirical studies in developmental psychology focused on issues that derived from Freud's theory, such as childrearing and discipline practices, moral development, and childhood aggression.

The psychosexual approach recognizes the importance of motives, emotions, and fantasies that guide behavior. Within this framework, human behavior springs at least as much from emotional needs as from reason. The psychosexual theory suggests that unconscious motives and wishes explain behaviors that otherwise might not make sense. Many domains of mental activity—including fantasies, dreams, primary process thoughts and symbols, and defense mechanisms—influence how individuals make meaning from their experiences. Through the construct of the unconscious, Freud provided a means for explaining thoughts and behaviors that appear irrational, self-destructive, or contradictory. The idea that development involves efforts to find acceptable outlets for strong, often socially unacceptable impulses still guides therapeutic intervention with children, adolescents, and adults.

Another critical contribution is Freud's recognition of the role of sexual impulses during childhood. Freud believed that a sexual relationship with a loving partner is important for healthy adult functioning. Sexual impulses have a direct outlet in behavior during adult life. However, Freud argued that children also have needs for sexual stimulation and satisfaction, but have no acceptable means to satisfy those needs. Today, we are more aware of a child's need for hugging, snuggling, and physical warmth with loving caregivers, but most adults still find it difficult to acknowledge that young children have sexual impulses. Childhood wishes and needs, bottled up in the unconscious, guide behavior indirectly through symbolic expression, dreams, or, in some cases, the symptoms of mental disorders. We need only look at a daily newspaper to recognize that the acceptance and expression of sexual impulses continue to be points of conflict in modern society. Controversies over sexual dysfunction, sexual abuse, rape by strangers and acquaintances, sexual harassment in the workplace, sexually transmitted diseases, contraception, abortion, infidelity, and homophobia reveal the difficulties that Americans have in dealing with the expression of sexual impulses.

## LINKS TO PSYCHOSOCIAL THEORY

Both psychosexual theory and psychosocial theory are stage theories that address basic, qualitative changes in self-understanding and social orientation. Erikson, having been trained in psychoanalysis under Anna Freud and mentored by Sigmund Freud and other members of the Analytic Institute, readily acknowledged his intellectual ties to Freud's psychosexual theory. Freud and Erikson both posited five stages from infancy through adolescence. Psychosexual theory deals with conflicts that the child experiences in satisfying his or her basic needs and impulses, especially sexual and aggressive impulses, within socially acceptable boundaries. Psychosocial theory expands this view by considering the broad range of social demands and social expectations that confront children at each point in development as well as the wide variety of competencies and social resources that children have for meeting those demands.

Of particular note is the difference between how Freud and Erikson conceptualized the period of middle childhood. Freud referred to this time as *latency*, suggesting that it was a time of relative quiet with respect to sexual and aggressive drives, when no new personality characteristics were emerging. Erikson saw these years as a time of critical focus on ego skills and mastery, highlighting expectations for children during the period from ages 6 to 12 to begin developing competence in culturally valued skills and knowledge.

Both psychosocial theory and psychosexual theory describe characteristics and functions of the ego system. However, psychosocial theory goes beyond childhood and adolescence, suggesting the direction for ego development in early, middle, and later adulthood. Psychosocial theory gives a greater role to the individual in guiding and shaping the direction of his or her development through the use of coping strategies that redefine conflicts and identify new resources.

Sexual impulses and needs are central to the psychosexual analysis. In the psychosocial framework, sexual behavior is considered within the broader context of social relations.

Gender role development, sexual relationships, gender identity, intimacy, marriage, and nurturing the intimate relationship are all elements of psychosocial development that are addressed as the product of a complex synthesis of thoughts, wishes, behaviors, and social expectations at various stages of life.

In this respect, psychosocial theory has more in common with the interpersonal, **relational paradigm** that has emerged and consolidated within psychoanalytic thought over the past 70 years (Borden, 2000). Theorists such as W. R. D. Fairbairn, Melanie Klein, Harry Stack Sullivan, Donald Winnicut, and Heinz Kohut have been forerunners in this perspective. They stressed that humans have basic needs for connection, contact, and meaningful interpersonal relationships throughout life. According to this view, the self is formed in an interpersonal context and emerges through interactions with others. The path toward maturity requires that the person achieve a sense of vitality, stability, and inner cohesiveness, which are formulated through interpersonal transactions. In the relational perspective, psychopathology or dysfunction arises when a person internalizes rigid, rejecting, or neglectful relational experiences and then uses these internalizations to anticipate or respond to real-life social encounters. Because the internalized relational pattern is familiar and well learned, the person is reluctant to give it up even if it leads to feelings of isolation, anxiety, or self-loathing (Messer & Warren, 1995).

Psychosexual theory suggests that basic issues of personal development are in place by adolescence. The results of this development are then played out for the remainder of adult life in a person's defensive style, fixations, typical sexual behavior and sexual fantasies, and the strategies for sublimating sexual and aggressive impulses. In contrast, psychosocial theory assumes that development goes on throughout life. The skills resulting from accomplishing new developmental tasks are learned, and new social abilities are achieved. The radius of significant relationships expands, bringing new expectations and new sources of social support. As new conflicts arise, they stimulate new growth, and new ego qualities emerge as a result of successfully coping with each new challenge.

# COGNITIVE DEVELOPMENTAL THEORY

**Cognition** is the process of organizing and making meaning of experience. In psychosexual theory, this function was assigned to the ego. Interpreting a statement, solving a problem, synthesizing information, critically analyzing a complex task—all of these are cognitive activities. Cognitive developmental theory focuses specifically on how knowing emerges and is transformed into logical, systematic capacities for reasoning and problem solving. Perhaps the most widely known

and influential of the modern cognitive theorists is Jean Piaget. His concepts provide the initial focus of this section. Recent interest in the social framework within which cognition develops has been stimulated by the work of L. S. Vygotsky. Several of his important contributions, introduced toward the end of this section, complement and expand the developmental perspective on how cognition emerges and changes over the life course.

## BASIC CONCEPTS IN PIAGET'S THEORY

According to Piaget, every organism strives to achieve equilibrium. **Equilibrium** is a balance of organized structures, whether motor, sensory, or cognitive. When structures are in equilibrium, they provide effective ways of interacting with the environment. Whenever changes in the organism or in the environment require a revision of the basic structures, they are thrown into disequilibrium (Piaget, 1978/1985). Piaget focused on how equilibrium is achieved with the environment through the formation of schemes (the structure or

© Elizabeth Crews

*Experimentation with a string is an example of sensorimotor exploration. This infant is discovering the properties of the string through tactile, visual, and motor strategies. What are some examples of sensorimotor exploration that you continue to use as an adult?*

**FIGURE 4.1**

Adaptation = Assimilation + Accommodation

organization of action in thought) and operations (the mental manipulation of schemes and concepts) that form systematic, logical structures for comprehending and analyzing experience, and on how equilibrium is achieved within the schemes and operations themselves.

Equilibrium is achieved through **adaptation**—a process of gradually modifying existing schemes and operations in order to take into account changes or discrepancies between what is known and what is being experienced (see Figure 4.1). Adaptation is a two-part process in which the continuity of existing schemes and the possibility of altering schemes interact. One part of adaptation is **assimilation**—the tendency to interpret new experiences in terms of an existing scheme. Assimilation contributes to the continuity of knowing. The second part of adaptation is **accommodation**—the tendency to modify familiar schemes in order to account for new dimensions of the object or event that are revealed through experience.

Piaget hypothesized that cognitive development occurs in four stages, each of which is characterized by a unique capacity for organizing and interpreting information. At each new stage, competencies of the earlier stages are not lost but are integrated into a qualitatively new approach to thinking and knowing. The essential features of these stages are introduced here. They will be discussed in greater detail in subsequent chapters.

The first stage, **sensorimotor intelligence**, begins at birth and lasts until approximately 18 months of age. This stage is characterized by the formation of increasingly complex sensory and motor schemes that allow infants to organize and exercise some control over their environment.

The second stage, **preoperational thought**, begins when the child learns a language and ends about age 5 or 6. During this stage, children develop the tools for representing schemes symbolically through language, imitation, imagery, symbolic play, and symbolic drawing. Their knowledge is still very much tied to their own perceptions.

The third stage, **concrete operational thought**, begins about age 6 or 7 and ends in early adolescence, around age 11 or 12. During this stage, children begin to appreciate the logical necessity of certain causal relationships. They can manipulate categories, classification systems, and hierarchies in groups. They are more successful at solving problems that are clearly tied to physical reality than at generating hypotheses about purely philosophical or abstract concepts.

The final stage of cognitive development, **formal operational thought**, begins in adolescence and persists through adulthood. This level of thinking permits a person to conceptualize about many simultaneously interacting variables. It allows for the creation of a system of laws or rules that can be used for problem solving. Formal operational thought reflects the quality of intelligence on which science and philosophy are built.

At the start of each new stage, the child experiences a type of egocentrism or limitation in point of view. With experience, children gain new objectivity about their perspective and are able to step back from the situation and see it more flexibly.

## IMPLICATIONS FOR HUMAN DEVELOPMENT

Piaget's theory has had an enormous influence on our understanding of cognition and the way we think about the reasoning capacities of infants and young children. Six implications of the theory for the study of child development are discussed here. First, the theory suggests that cognition has its base in the biological capacities of the human infant—that knowledge is derived from action. For example, infants learn about the features of objects by grasping and sucking on them. Knowledge is constructed rather than passively absorbed. Children as well as adults select, explore, and experiment with objects and later with ideas. They create their knowledge through this active engagement.

As the knower changes, so does what is known. For example, an infant may know a ball through its touch, how it feels in the hand or mouth, through its appearance, and through its response to the infant's actions. A toddler may become aware of the functions of a ball by kicking, throwing, rolling, and bouncing it. At later ages, children understand more about the physical properties of a ball and can link it to other shapes and categories of objects. With each more advanced level of motor, symbolic, and interpersonal capacity, the knower creates a new meaning of objects, people, and the interactions among them. Because of natural interest and through exposure to a wide range of materials, stimuli, and experiences, infants and young children "teach themselves" a great deal of what they know. This perspective has been integrated into instructional strategies in which children are encouraged to construct meaning through direct experience. Through free exploration, which typically requires the coordination of perspectives and the manipulation of interconnected elements, an understanding of the integration of coordinated factors is naturally acquired (Kamii, 1985, 1994).

Second, discrepancies between existing schemes and contemporary experiences promote cognitive development. Encounters with all types of novelty—especially experiences that are moderately distinct rather than widely different from what is already known—are important for advancing new ideas and new ways of organizing thought. Extending this idea, encounters with differences in opinion through discussion and reading are just as important in adolescence and adulthood as encounters with different types of sensory materials in infancy and toddlerhood.

Third, infants have the capacity for thinking and problem solving. Although infants do not make use of symbolic strategies, they are able to establish certain logical connections between means and ends that guide their problem-solving efforts.

Fourth, infants, toddlers, and school-age children think in different ways, and the ways they think are different from the ways adults think. This does not mean that their thinking is unorganized or illogical, but the same principles of logic that typically govern adult thought do not govern the thinking of young children.

Fifth, beginning with the period of concrete operations, children can approach problems using many of the principles that are fundamental to scientific reasoning. They can also begin to reason about their reasoning—introducing the importance of **metacognition**, or the many strategies used to guide the way we organize and prepare ourselves to think more clearly and effectively.

Sixth, thinking about the social world is regulated by many of the same principles as thinking about objects in the physical world. As we learn about the principles that govern objects and physical relationships, we are also learning about ourselves and others.

## VYGOTSKY'S CONCEPTS OF COGNITIVE DEVELOPMENT

Piaget's focus on cognitive development emphasized a process in which individuals investigate, explore, discover, and rediscover meaning in their world. Although Piaget acknowledged the significance of social factors—especially parents and peers—in the cognitive process, his theory focused on individuals in interaction with their environment. In contrast, Vygotsky argued that development can only be understood within a social framework. Vygotsky (1962, 1978) proposed that the study of cognitive development must take as its unit of analysis the *person in activity in a setting*. The person and the culture are intricately interwoven through the process of social interaction. New levels of understanding begin at an interpersonal level as two individuals, initially an infant and an adult, coordinate their interactions. Eventually, interpersonal collaboration becomes internalized to make up the child's internal mental framework. Through continuous interaction with others, especially adults and older children, a child revises and advances his or her levels of understanding.

> New understanding, gained through collaboration, is a product of the child's original understanding, the partner's different understanding, the child's difficulties with the task and the ways they are expressed in the course of their interaction, the partner's response to those difficulties, and so on. Since this process evolves over time, and each person's responses depend on what the other has previously done or said, the outcome is one that cannot be attributed to either one or the other. The unit of analysis extends beyond the individual. (Tudge & Winterhoff, 1993, p. 76)

Three of the central concepts in Vygotsky's theory are introduced here: (1) culture as a mediator of cognitive structuring, (2) movement from the intermental to the intramental, and (3) the zone of proximal development.

### CULTURE AS A MEDIATOR OF COGNITIVE STRUCTURING

Vygotsky argued that cognitive development can only be understood in the context of culture. Think for a moment about the many ways that culture shapes the content of thought and the processes through which ideas are developed.

*Vygotsky's theory emphasizes the social context of cognitive development. Children often learn by interacting with older siblings who can answer their questions and show them how to solve problems.*

A simple conversation between a mother and a child or a situation in which a grandparent is trying to instruct a young child includes layers of cultural beliefs and strategies—beliefs about what children think about, the skills they are encouraged to attain, the sources of information that are available to them, the ways information is shared, the kinds of activities that children, adolescents, and adults are permitted to engage in, and the limits that are placed on a child's participation in certain settings. (Miller, 2002)

Of the many elements of culture that shape cognition, one that was of special interest to Vygotsky was the idea of tools and signs as human inventions that shape thought. Technical tools such as plows, cars, weapons, and signs—sometimes referred to as *psychological tools*—like symbolic systems, counting systems, and strategies for remembering, modify the person's relationship to the environment. Through the use of tools, humans change the way they organize and think about the world. Vygotsky viewed tools as a means through which the human mind is shaped and modified over the course of history.

## ◼ MOVEMENT FROM INTERMENTAL TO INTRAMENTAL

Perhaps contrary to common sense, Vygotsky argued that high-level mental functions begin in external activity that is gradually reconstructed and internalized. He gave the example of *pointing*. Vygotsky claimed that initially, an infant will reach toward an object that is out of reach, stretching the hand in the direction of the object and making grasping motions with the fingers. This is a movement directed to the object. As soon as the caregiver recognizes that the child wants the object and is able to satisfy the child's request, the child

begins to modify the reaching and grasping motion into a socially meaningful gesture—pointing. The caregiver's understanding of the gesture and the *intermental* coordination between caregiver and infant result in an *intramental* process for the infant—an understanding of the special relationship between the desired goal, the caregiver as mediator, and pointing as a meaningful sign.

## ◼ THE ZONE OF PROXIMAL DEVELOPMENT

Taking the idea of internalization further, Vygotsky offered the concept of the **zone of proximal development** to explain how learning and development converge. The zone of proximal development is "the distance between the actual developmental level as determined by independent problem solving and the level of potential development as determined through problem solving under adult guidance or in collaboration with more capable peers" (Vygotsky, 1978, p. 86).

We have all experienced situations in which we were able to solve a task only with the assistance and advice of someone else. The typical efforts of parents to help a child put together a jigsaw puzzle by suggesting strategies, like selecting all the straight-edged pieces first to make the border, or sorting the many pieces into those with a similar color, are examples of how learning takes place within the zone. Vygotsky suggested that the level of competence a person can reach when taking advantage of the guidance of others reflects the functions that are in the process of maturation, as contrasted to those that have already matured. Learning within the zone of proximal development sets into motion the reorganization and internalization of existing developmental competencies, which then become synthesized at a new, higher intramental level.

## IMPLICATIONS FOR HUMAN DEVELOPMENT

Vygotsky's theory suggests that the boundaries between the individual and the environment are much less clear than one might infer from most other theories of human development. In fact, Vygotsky directs attention to the guiding role of social interaction and culture in shaping and orienting cognition, thus bringing the study of cognitive development into much greater harmony with the concepts of psychosocial theory than are seen in Piaget's theory.

Several specific implications of Vygotsky's work can be inferred (Davydov, 1995). First, the mental structures and functioning of people raised in a specific culture will be different from those of people raised in other cultures, just as the thinking of a toddler is different from the thinking of an adult. In comparison to Piaget, who viewed the emergence of logical thought as largely a universal process, Vygotsky considered the nature of reasoning and problem solving as culturally created. Because of the way in which intermental experiences and networks structure intramental events, one's family and others who influence and control the structure of early learning and problem-solving experiences will have a strong influence on the structure of one's thinking. For example, Levy (1996) compared concepts of learning and intelligence in a Tahitian and a Nepalese community. The Tahitians believed that children learn primarily through play, imitation, trial and error. Adults do not do much to instruct young children, assuming that they will learn most things by themselves. This is a very Piagetian point of view. In contrast, the Nepalese adults believed that children needed direct instruction in every area or risk the formation of "bad character." Without this guided instruction, the Nepalese thought that children could not achieve mastery. In the Nepalese community, learning and intelligence were viewed as resulting from the internalization of the community's knowledge.

A second implication of Vygotsky's work is that individuals can promote their own cognitive development by seeking interactions with others who can help draw them to higher levels of functioning within their zone of proximal development. Piaget considered encounters with discrepancies or disequilibrium, and the process of adaptation as the primary explanations for cognitive growth. Vygotsky added the notion that development can be facilitated through interactions with more skillful play companions or collaborators.

## LINKS TO PSYCHOSOCIAL THEORY

Both cognitive developmental theory and psychosocial theory focus on development as a product of ongoing interactions between the individual and the environment. For both theories, psychological development is a product of dis-

crepancies, referred to as *disequilibrium* in cognitive developmental theory and as *psychosocial crises* in psychosocial theory. Piaget's theory, like psychosocial theory, proposes a set of stages of development, with each stage growing from and integrating the achievements of earlier stages. Piaget considered development in four stages that covered the period from infancy through adolescence. Erikson described these same years in five stages, drawing a greater distinction in functioning between early and middle childhood than did Piaget. Although contemporary scholars are addressing issues of changes in cognitive functioning in adulthood, Piaget's theory does not offer any hypotheses about the qualitative changes that might follow the period of formal operational reasoning, whereas psychosocial theory makes clear predictions about the direction of ego development in early, middle, and later adulthood.

Piaget's focus, as well as Vygotsky's, is on the cognitive domain—especially on the process of knowledge acquisition and logical reasoning. The meaning a person makes of a situation depends largely on the stage of mental development attained. Feelings, social relationships, and self-understanding are viewed as cognitive schemes that are constructed with the same logic that the person applies to the understanding of objects. In psychosocial theory, cognitive development is referred to as ego development—an understanding of how the self emerges and shapes a personal identity with goals, values, beliefs, and strategies for achieving goals within the constraints of the society. Ego development involves planning, making decisions, coping with challenges, and facing the future with a sense of purpose.

However, psychosocial theory considers the emotional domain as a pervasive filter through which a person organizes and interprets experience. The nature of the resolution of each psychosocial crisis guides a person's ability to adapt and mature within society. As a psychotherapist, Erikson was aware of the many instances when one's reasoning abilities and problem-solving skills are disrupted by strong emotional conflicts, unconscious wishes and fears, and conflicting social demands. He highlighted the array of outlooks and coping strategies—such as trust and mistrust, or hope and withdrawal—that determine the direction of psychological development. For example, feelings of hope or hopelessness will influence a person's willingness to engage in new learning situations with interest and enthusiasm or with caution and apprehension. The nature of one's cognition during a period of life will be influenced by one's psychosocial orientation. *+ cog + emotional intertwined*

Vygotsky's theory provides an important link between Piaget's emphasis on the maturation of logical reasoning and psychosocial theory's emphasis on the maturation of self in society by emphasizing the interpersonal nature of cognition. The idea of a zone of proximal development relates closely to the construct of the radius of significant relationships, capturing the unique interpersonal and cultural context of all aspects of knowing, whether it is knowing about the logic of the physical world or about the logic of relationships.

# THEORIES OF LEARNING

Learning theorists have proposed mechanisms to account for the relatively permanent changes in behavior that occur as a result of experience. The reason why humans have such an extensive capacity to adapt to changes in the environment is that they are so well equipped to learn. Four theories of learning that have made significant contributions to the study of human development are reviewed here: (1) classical conditioning, (2) operant conditioning, (3) social learning, and (4) cognitive behaviorism.

## CLASSICAL CONDITIONING

The principles of **classical conditioning**, sometimes referred to as *Pavlovian conditioning*, were developed by Ivan Pavlov (1927/1960). Classical conditioning highlights the types of learning that occur when events take place close together in time and thereby acquire similar meaning. In much of his work, Pavlov used the salivary reflex as the response system. He carried out an extensive body of research in an effort to understand the conditions under which stimuli in the environment other than food would elicit or inhibit salivation.

The model for classical conditioning is shown in Figure 4.2. The four basic elements in a classical conditioning experiment are the *neutral stimulus* (NS), the *unconditioned stimulus* (US), the *unconditioned response* (UR), and the *conditioned response* (CR). Before conditioning, the bell is a neutral stimulus (NS). It elicits a response of interest or attention, but nothing more. The sight and smell of food are unconditioned stimuli (US) that elicit salivation, the unconditioned response (UR). No learning is required for the smell of food to evoke salivation. During conditioning trials, the bell is rung shortly before the food appears. The dog is said to have been *conditioned* when it salivates to the sound of the bell even before the food is presented. The bell, therefore, comes to control the salivation response; it becomes a *conditioned stimulus*. The bell is no longer neutral—it has meaning as a signal for food. Salivation that occurs in response to the bell alone is called the conditioned response (CR). You may be able to relate to this form of learning by thinking of your own reaction when you look at your watch or at the clock and realize that it is approaching dinner time. Often, just knowing that it is nearing the time when you usually eat is a stimulus for feeling hunger pangs.

Conditioning does not take place randomly between any two events linked in time. A conditioned response is established to the degree that there is a *meaningful* relationship between the NS and the US. Usually NS and US must occur together many times before conditioning is established. Furthermore, the NS itself is not totally neutral. A visual stimulus such as a colored light will prompt visual orienting, for

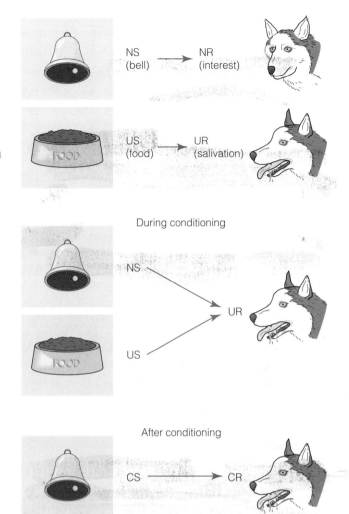

NS = Neutral stimulus    UR = Unconditioned response
NR = Neutral response    CS = Conditioned stimulus
US = Unconditioned stimulus    CR = Conditioned response

**FIGURE 4.2**

Classical Conditioning. Before conditioning, the bell is a neutral stimulus that evokes interest but no other response. After several pairings of the bell and food, the bell becomes a conditioned stimulus that evokes the conditioned salivation response.

instance, whereas an auditory stimulus may simply increase attention or arousal. In a conditioning experiment, the learner builds many associations simultaneously. Although the focus of a particular experiment may be on establishing a link between one NS and one US, the learner will build links among many elements of the environment—its visual, auditory, and olfactory components, including the US. Pavlovian conditioning provides a model for understanding how multiple associations can be established and triggered in the process of concept formation, memory, and problem solving (Lavond & Steinmetz, 2003).

## ■ IMPLICATIONS FOR HUMAN DEVELOPMENT

Classical conditioning accounts for a great deal of the associational learning that occurs throughout life. When a specific symbol is paired with an image, emotional reaction, or object, that symbol takes on new meaning. The associations that are made through classical conditioning may involve labels and concepts, but they do not necessarily require language skills. During infancy and toddlerhood, a variety of positive and negative emotional reactions are conditioned to people, objects, and environments as the child develops new associations. Your reactions to the taste of a certain type of food or the feel of a particular material may be the result of conditioned learning that has persisted until adulthood. Similarly, *fears* can be the results of classical conditioning. Fear can be conditioned to a specific cue, such as a sound, light, or smell, which signals the onset of a painful experience. It can also be conditioned to the context in which the painful event occurred (Godsil, Quinn, & Fanselow, 2000). Many people recall at least one frightening experience from childhood, such as nearly drowning, being beaten, or falling from the top of a slide. The association of fear or pain with a specific target may lead to systematic avoidance of that object for the rest of one's life.

## OPERANT CONDITIONING

**Operant conditioning** emphasizes the role of repetition and the consequences of behavior in learning. In this type of learning process, behaviors are strengthened when they are followed by positive consequences and weakened when they are followed by negative consequences. B. F. Skinner, one of the best-known American learning theorists, developed many of the principles of operant conditioning. Skinner's (1938) work focused on the modification of voluntary behaviors as a result of the consequences of those behaviors. In the traditional operant conditioning experiment, learning takes place as a result of a connection between a desired *response* (R) and a *stimulus consequence* (S). The researcher selects a response in advance (e.g., pushing a bar or pecking on a lighted button) and then waits until the subject makes the desired response (or at least a partial response). Then the experimenter presents a stimulus consequence called a *reinforcement*. **Reinforcement** is operationally defined as any stimulus that makes a repetition of the desired response more likely.

There are two kinds of reinforcers. Some, such as food and smiles, increase the rate of response when they are *present*. These are called **positive reinforcers**. Giving a child a big smile or a hug when he or she picks up his toys is an example of positive reinforcement. Other reinforcers, such as electric shock, increase the rate of response when they are *removed*. These are called **negative reinforcers**. Suppose a mother gets upset whenever she hears her baby cry. She may try a number of things to stop the crying—rocking, feeding, talking, or

Smiling is an important positive reinforcement. The adult's smile encourages the child, and the child's laughter keeps the adult engaged in the dialogue. What are some other examples of how social behavior serves as a positive reinforcement?

changing the baby's diapers. If one of these behaviors leads to an end to the noise, it is reinforced; the mother is more likely to try that behavior again the next time. The baby's cry is a negative reinforcer because when it stops, the specific caregiving response is strengthened. (The mother's caregiving response may in turn become a positive reinforcer from the baby's perspective.)

In many instances, the behavior to be learned is one that has never been performed before. How can you be reinforced for making a complex response if you have never done it? One means of developing a new complex response is *shaping* (Davey & Cullen, 1988). The response is broken down into its major components. At first, a response that is only an approximation of one element of the behavior is reinforced. Gradually, new elements of the behavior are added, and a reinforcement is given only when two or three components of the desired response are linked together. Once the person makes a complete response, earlier approximations are no longer reinforced. Parents often use the shaping process to teach their young children such complicated behaviors as table manners, toilet use, and care of their belongings.

Within the field of operant conditioning, research has been devoted to understanding which conditions of learning result in the strongest, longest lasting habits. **Schedules of reinforcement** refer to the frequency and regularity with which reinforcements are given. A new response is conditioned rapidly if reinforcement is given on every learning trial. This schedule is called **continuous reinforcement**. Responses that are established under conditions of continuous reinforcement are very vulnerable to **extinction**—that is, if the reinforcement is removed for several trials, response performance deteriorates rapidly.

Some schedules vary the amount of time or the number of trials between reinforcements. This procedure is called **intermittent reinforcement**. The learner responds on many occasions when no reinforcement is provided but does receive reinforcement every once in a while. Such schedules result in the most durable learning. Intermittent reinforcement lengthens the time an operant behavior remains in the learner's repertoire after reinforcement has been permanently discontinued (Ferster & Culbertson, 1982; Shull & Grimes, 2003).

An intermittent reinforcement schedule is probably most like real life. It would be very difficult for anyone to learn a behavior if every instance of it had to be reinforced. A child often exhibits a new response when no observers are present, when teachers are attending to other matters, or in the context of other behaviors that are followed by a negative consequence. Research on operant conditioning demonstrates that conditions of intermittent reinforcement are precisely those under which the longest lasting habits are formed.

Positive and negative reinforcement are commonly associated with trying to build up or increase the likelihood of a behavior. Operant conditioning also has concepts associated with damping out or reducing the frequency of behavior: extinction and punishment. **Extinction** is a process in which an expected reinforcement no longer occurs following the behavior. When we advise parents to "ignore" undesirable behavior, we are suggesting the use of extinction as a means of eliminating the behavior. Theoretically, if the tendency to behave in a specific way can be strengthened through reinforcement, it can be weakened when no reinforcement takes place.

**Punishment** refers to a noxious stimulus that follows an undesirable behavior. In experiments with animals, a behavior might be punished by administering an electric shock to the floor of the cage after the animal presses a bar or pecks at a light. After a few trials, the animal will no longer press the bar. However, Skinner argued that punishment did not work any more quickly than extinction and often was accompanied by undesired side effects. For example, a child who is punished at school for a specific behavior may develop a resistance to attending school altogether. Some students find the concepts of negative reinforcement and punishment confusing. One way to distinguish the two is to think of negative reinforcement as *taking away* a stimulus consequence in order to *increase* a response, whereas punishment *gives* a stimulus consequence in order to *decrease* a response.

## IMPLICATIONS FOR HUMAN DEVELOPMENT

The principles of operant conditioning apply whenever the environment sets up priorities for behavior and conditional rewards or punishments for approximating a desired behavior. People change whenever their operant behaviors adapt to changes in environmental contingencies. The environment controls the process of adaptation through the role it plays in establishing and modifying contingencies (Skinner, 1987). Behavior can be modified in the desired direction as long as the person who is guiding the conditioning has control over the distribution of valued rewards. These principles are especially applicable to the learning that takes place during toddlerhood (ages 2 and 3) and early school age (4 to 6). Children at these ages are unlikely to be able to consider the existing framework of reinforcement. Once individuals analyze a reinforcement schedule, they may choose to adapt to it, resist it, or redefine the environment in order to discover new sources of reinforcement.

Operant conditioning occurs throughout life. Although one typically thinks of adults establishing the reinforcement schedules that shape the behavior of children, it is clear that a child's behavior is often a reinforcement for an adult. A child's smile or laugh, enthusiasm, or attention are reinforcements that modify a parent's or teacher's behavior. Negative reinforcement is a process that is often used to account for moral behavior. In a well-socialized person, anxiety and guilt build up in anticipation of performing some socially unacceptable behavior. By resisting the temptation to perform the misbehavior, the anxiety and guilt are reduced. Thus, restraint or social control is negatively reinforced.

Operant conditioning provides the theoretical and experimental framework for *applied behavioral analysis*, an intervention that uses systematic behavioral strategies to assist people who have severe behavior problems, including aggressive disorders and autism. Applied behavioral analysis begins with careful observation and analysis of disruptive behaviors. Then a very specific set of behavioral objectives are identified, and the behavior is broken down into simple components that can be shaped through systematic reward. The application of consistent principles of operant conditioning creates a more predictable, supportive environment, in which the child can learn new behaviors and feel the satisfaction of mastery. Regular recording of behaviors is part of this intervention with the goal of providing experimental evidence of behavior change (Foxx, 2001; Frea & Vittimberga, 2000).

## SOCIAL LEARNING THEORY

The concept of **social learning** evolved from the awareness that much learning takes place as a result of observing and imitating other people's behavior (Bandura & Walters, 1963). Changes in behavior can occur without being linked to a specific pattern of positive or negative reinforcement. They

© Elizabeth Crews

*Social learning theory emphasizes the role of observation and imitation as means of learning new behaviors. Can you think of a new response that you recently learned through imitation?*

can also occur without numerous opportunities for trial-and-error practice. A person can watch someone perform a task or say a new expression and imitate that behavior accurately on the first try.

Early research in social learning theory was devoted to identifying conditions that determine whether or not a child will imitate a model (Bandura, 1971, 1977, 1986). Children have been found to imitate aggressive, altruistic, helping, and stingy models. They are most likely to imitate models who are prestigious, who control resources, or who are themselves rewarded. Bandura and Walters (1963) suggested that children not only observe the behaviors carried out by a model, but they also watch what happens to the model. When the model's behavior is rewarded, the behavior is more likely to be imitated; when the model's behavior is punished, the behavior is more likely to be avoided. When naughty behaviors go unpunished, they too are likely to be imitated. This process is called **vicarious reinforcement**. Through observational learning, a child can learn a behavior and also acquire the motivation to perform that behavior or to resist performing that behavior depending on what is learned about the consequences linked to that behavior. Thus, observational learning can hold the key to self-regulation and to the internalization of standards for resisting certain behaviors as well as for enacting behaviors (Grusec, 1992).

Recent directions in social learning theory have taken an increasingly cognitive orientation, sometimes referred to as **social cognition** (Bandura, 1989, 1991). Through observational learning, the child becomes acquainted with the general concepts of the situation as well as with the specific behaviors. Direct reinforcement or nonreinforcement provides one type of information about how to behave in a certain situation. Moreover, people watch others, learn about the consequences of their actions, and remember what others have told or shown them and what they have read or learned about the situation. Over time, one forms a symbolic representation for the situation, the required behaviors, and the expected outcomes. A worker may learn that with one type of supervisor, it is appropriate to ask lots of questions and offer suggestions for ways of solving problems, whereas with another supervisor, it is better to remain quiet and try not to be noticed. The rules for behavior in each setting are abstracted from what has been observed in watching others, what happened following one's own behavior in the past, and what one understands about the demands in the immediate situation. The culmination of this learning process is what Bandura (2000) referred to as **efficacy**, including planning intentional actions, guiding and directing one's own behaviors toward a goal, and reflecting on one's actions to assess their quality, impact, and purpose.

## ■ IMPLICATIONS FOR HUMAN DEVELOPMENT

The principles of social learning theory are assumed to operate in the same way throughout life. The concept of social learning highlights the relevance of models' behavior in guiding the behavior of others. These models may be parents, older siblings, peers, entertainment stars, or sports heroes. Because new models may be encountered at any life stage, new learning through the process of observational learning is always possible. Exposure to a certain array of models and a certain pattern of rewards or punishments results in the encouragement to imitate some behaviors and to inhibit the performance of others. The similarity in behavior among people of the same age reflects their exposure to a common history of models, rewards, and punishments. Recognition of the potential impact one has as a model for others—especially in the role of parent, teacher, clinician, counselor, or supervisor—ought to impart a certain level of self-conscious monitoring about the behaviors one exhibits and the strategies one employs in the presence of those who are likely to perceive one as a model for new learning.

## COGNITIVE BEHAVIORISM

One objection that has been raised frequently against classical and operant conditioning as theories of learning is that they have no language or concepts to describe the events that occur in the learner's mind. Cognitive behaviorists study the many internal mental activities that influence behavior. Edward Tolman (1932/1967, 1948) introduced the notion of a **cognitive map**—an internal mental representation of the learning environment. According to Tolman, individuals who perform a specific task in a certain environment attend primarily to that task, but they also form a representation of the rest of the setting. The cognitive map includes expectations about the reward system in operation, the existing spatial relationships, and the behaviors accorded the highest priority. An individual's performance in a situation represents only part of the learning that has occurred. The fact that people respond to changes in the environment indicates that a complex mental map actually develops in this situation.

According to Walter Mischel (1973, 1979; Mischel & Shoda, 1995), six types of cognitive and affective factors mediate a person's behavior in a situation and account for continuity in how people respond across situations: encodings; expectancies and beliefs; affects (feelings and emotional responses); goals and values; competencies; and self-regulatory plans (see Figure 4.3). **Encodings** refer to constructs the person has about the self, the situation, and others in the situation. **Expectancies** refer to cognitive assessments about one's ability to perform, ideas about the consequences of one's behavior, and the meaning of events in one's environment. These expectancies are formed largely on the basis of past learning in similar situations or generalized across similar situations. Mischel has pointed out that the situations may not be the same physically, but they must share some degree of affective similarity. For example, being a newcomer in a social

situation may be associated with expectancies, even though the exact situation may differ from one context to another.

**Affects** are the feelings and emotional reactions or physiological responses that are associated with a situation. Feelings of anger, fear, arousal, excitement, or jealousy might interact with expectancies and encodings to guide behavior. **Goals** and **values** are related to the relative importance one places on the outcomes of situations. One person may value high levels of task performance, whereas another may value success in social situations. One's behavior in a situation is influenced by how one values its possible outcomes. **Cognitive competencies** consist of knowledge, skills, and abilities.

**Self-regulatory plans** are strategies for achieving one's goals, including techniques for managing internal emotional states, creating a plan, and putting the plan into action. In comparison to the notion of classical or operant conditioning, self-regulation focuses on how one leaves the realm of stimulus control in order to gain control over behavior. Self regulation is especially important in situations where temptations, frustrations, or self-doubt threaten to pull one away from important goals (Mischel & Ayduk, 2002). As people become increasingly aware of the effects of stimuli on their behavior, they can learn to overcome, channel, or eliminate those influences that tempt them to abandon their goals.

## ◼ IMPLICATIONS FOR HUMAN DEVELOPMENT

Cognitive behaviorism suggests that through the full range of learning processes, including classical conditioning, operant conditioning, and observational learning, the learner acquires cognitive structures that influence his or her subsequent learning and performance. The learner acquires an outlook on the learning situation. This outlook influences the learner's feeling of familiarity with the task, motivation to undertake the task, optimism about performing the task successfully, and strategies for approaching the task. In addition to everything a parent, teacher, or supervisor might do to structure a learning environment, one must always take into account the outlook that the learner brings to the task. Differences in expectancies, self-control strategies, values, and goals all influence the way individuals approach a learning situation.

## SUMMARY OF THE LEARNING THEORIES

All four of the learning theories contribute insights into human behavior (see Table 4.1). Classical conditioning can account for the extensive network of associations that are formed between symbols and stimuli, the enduring emotional reactions to one's environment, and the organization of learning associated with reflexive patterns. Operant conditioning emphasizes the acquisition of behavioral patterns on the basis of their consequences. Social learning theory adds the important element of imitation. People learn new behaviors by

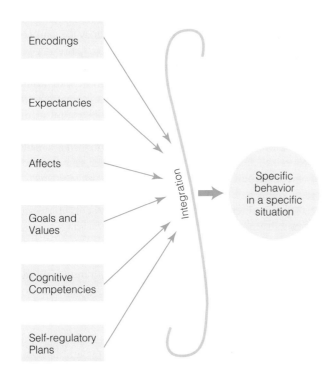

**FIGURE 4.3**

The Six Cognitive and Affective Dimensions that Influence Behavior

**Table 4.1**   Summary of the Processes in Four Theories of Learning

| CLASSICAL CONDITIONING | OPERANT CONDITIONING | SOCIAL LEARNING | COGNITIVE BEHAVIORISM |
|---|---|---|---|
| When two events occur very close together in time, they acquire similar meanings and produce similar responses. | Responses that are under voluntary control can be strengthened or eliminated, depending on the consequences associated with them. | New responses can be acquired through the observation and imitation of models. | In addition to new responses, the learner acquires a mental representation of the situation, including expectations about rewards and punishments, the kinds of responses that are appropriate, and the physical and social settings in which they occur. |

watching others. Through social learning, individuals develop an understanding of the social consequences of behavior, leading to new patterns of behavioral expression and self-regulation. Finally, cognitive behaviorism suggests that a complex set of expectations, goals, and values can be treated as behavior and can influence performance. Although information or skills can be learned, they will not be expressed in behavior unless expectations about the self and the environment justify their enactment. This perspective highlights a person's capacity to guide the performance of new learning.

## LINKS TO PSYCHOSOCIAL THEORY

The learning theories and psychosocial theory operate at different levels of abstraction. The learning theories provide insight into the laws that govern many of the basic mechanisms of adaptation. Psychosocial theory assumes that growth and change continue throughout the life span; however, the theory does not attempt to account for the exact processes by which new behaviors, new coping strategies, or new ego strengths are acquired. The learning theories provide explanations for the ways in which the patterns of daily events might shape the direction of adaptation and growth. They offer insight into the processes through which society's rules, norms, and customs become internalized and translated into habits, preferences, and expectations, which become generalized across common situations. The learning theories emphasize the significance of the immediate environment in directing the course of growth and also help to explain why habits or patterns of behavior may be difficult to change, even when they appear to be dysfunctional. These theories speak less to the construction of meaning, the nature and organization of needs and goals, or the direction of development as the changing person interacts with a changing society over the life span.

## CULTURAL THEORY

The concept of *culture*, although defined in a variety of ways by anthropologists, political scientists, sociologists, and psychologists, refers here to the learned systems of meanings and patterns of behaviors that are shared by a group of people and transmitted from one generation to the next. **Physical culture** encompasses the objects, technologies, structures, tools, and other artifacts of a culture. **Social culture** consists of norms, roles, beliefs, values, rites, and customs (Herkovits, 1948; Triandis et al., 1980; Triandis, 1994; Rohner, 1984; Betancourt & Lopez, 1993).

Culture has been described as a **worldview**—a way of making meaning of the relationships, situations, and objects encountered in daily life. Basic ideas, such as whether people are considered to be in control of nature or a part of nature, who is included in the definition of family, what characteristics are considered signs of mental health or mental illness, which acts are construed as hostile or nurturing, which aspects of the environment are considered dangerous or safe—all these and many other mental constructions are shaped by culture (Kagitcibasi, 1990). Culture guides development, not only through encounters with certain objects, roles, and settings, but also through the meanings linked to actions.

The principle of **cultural determinism**, introduced by Ruth Benedict (1934/1950), suggests that the individual's psychological experiences are shaped by the expectations, resources, and challenges posed by one's specific cultural group. Similar to the learning theories, cultural determinism suggests that individuals' behaviors are shaped through **enculturation**, in which culture carriers teach, model, reward, punish, and use other symbolic strategies to transmit critical practices and values. Two theoretical constructs that allow one to compare cultures are presented here: continuity and discontinuity, and individualism and collectivism.

The extent to which development is viewed as distinct stages of life depends on the degree to which socialization within a culture is characterized by continuity or discontinuity. **Continuity** is found when a child is given information and responsibilities that apply directly to his or her adult behavior. For example, Margaret Mead (1928/1950) observed that in Samoan society, girls of 6 or 7 years of age commonly took care of their younger siblings. As they grew older, their involvement in the caregiving role increased; however, the behaviors that were expected of them were not substantially changed. When there is continuity, development is a gradual, fluid transformation, in which adult competencies are built directly on childhood accomplishments.

Kwanzaa was created to strengthen the cultural identity of the African American ethnic group. Family members participate in rituals that highlight a common ancestry and shared cultural values.

© Tom Wilson/Getty Images

**Discontinuity** is found when a child is either barred from activities that are open only to adults or is forced to "unlearn" information or behaviors that are accepted in children but considered inappropriate for adults. The change from expectations of virginity before marriage to expectations of sexual responsiveness after marriage is an example of discontinuity.

Cultures that have discrete, age-graded expectations for people at different periods of life produce a pattern of development in which age groups have distinct characteristics and appear to function at different skill levels. These societies are marked by public ceremonies, graduations, and other *rites of passage* from one stage to the next.

The dimensions of *individualism* and *collectivism* provide another lens for comparing cultures (Triandis, 1990, 1995, 1998). **Collectivism** refers to a worldview in which social behavior is guided largely by goals that are shared by a collective, such as a family, tribe, work group, or political or religious association. Group solidarity is valued. The ingroup creates norms, goals, and beliefs that are enculturated and endorsed by its members. When conflicts arise between group goals and personal goals, a person is expected to act in the best interest of the group. **Individualism** refers to a worldview in which social behavior is guided largely by personal goals, ambitions, and pleasures, which may or may not coincide with the interests of the group. Competition and personal achievement are valued. When conflicts arise between group and personal goals, it is considered acceptable and perhaps expected that personal goals will come first.

Cultures can be described as relatively more collectivist or individualist. Typically, societies marked by great complexity, affluence, social mobility, and cultural diversity tend to be more individualist in their worldview. People within cultures can also be described as adhering to more individualist or

collectivist values. Thus, not everyone in a collectivist culture equally endorses the collectivist worldview. Subgroups within a society may differ in how much their values reflect the dominant individualist or collectivist orientation of the larger society.

## IMPLICATIONS FOR HUMAN DEVELOPMENT

According to the concept of cultural determinism, culture is more important than biology in determining whether various stages of development will be experienced as stressful or calm. This concept is illustrated by the ways in which different cultures mark an adolescent girl's first menstruation (Mead, 1949/1955). In some societies, people fear menstruation and treat the girl as if she were dangerous to others. In other societies, she is viewed as having powerful magic that will affect her own future and that of the tribe. In still others, the perceived shamefulness of sex requires that the menstruation be kept as secret as possible. The culture thus determines how a biological change is marked and how the transition will be perceived.

Societies vary in the extent to which they expect people to make significant life decisions during each life period and in the range of choices they make available. American adolescents are expected to make decisions regarding sex, work, politics, religion, marriage, and education. In each of these areas, the alternatives are complex and varied. As a result, adolescence is prolonged, and the risk of leaving this period without having found a solution to these problems is great. In cultures that offer fewer choices and provide a clearer path

**HUMAN DEVELOPMENT AND DIVERSITY**

## Implications of Individualism and Collectivism for Parenting Practices

THE CONSTRUCTS OF individualism and collectivism refer to two different value systems that characterize a culture. Individualism encourages and celebrates individual accomplishments and self-expression; collectivism encourages and celebrates interdependence and the strength of the community. Every society requires some blend or balance between these two perspectives. In order to survive, a group must be able to support both the *I* and the *We*, the individual person and the group. However, as one interacts with people from different cultural backgrounds, it is helpful to be aware of the dominant orientation toward either individualism or collectivism in order to achieve greater insight into the person's likely motivations, goals, and sense of moral obligation. Table 4.2 summarizes the features of these two orientations (Trumbull, Rothstein-Fisch, & Greenfield, 2000).

These contrasting values have implications for the behaviors that parents value and the way they interact with their children. Individualist cultures encourage more independent play. They foster a child's autonomy and self-expression by allowing greater physical distance between the child and the caregiver, asking the child his or her opinions, and allowing children to have a voice in decision making.

**Table 4.2** A Comparison of Individualism and Collectivism

| INDIVIDUALISM | COLLECTIVISM |
|---|---|
| Fosters independence | Fosters interdependence |
| Values individual achievement | Values group success |
| Promotes self-expression | Promotes adherence to norms |
| Values individual thinking | Values group consensus |
| Associated with egalitarian relationships | Associated with hierarchical roles and respect for elders |
| Understanding the physical world as knowable apart from its meaning for human life | Understanding the physical world in the context of its meaning for human life |
| Associated with private property and individual ownership | Associated with shared property and group ownership |

Children are praised for doing things on their own and moving toward self-reliance. In both subtle and specific ways, children in individualist cultures are encouraged to compete with each other and to feel pride in their individual achievements.

Children in collectivist cultures are kept closer to their parents or caregivers during infancy. They are more likely to be nurtured through longer periods of breastfeeding, carried or held closely during infancy, and socialized through gentle encouragement and indulgences well into child-

hood. Families in collectivist cultures usually include extended kinship groups that all play an active role in a child's comfort, socialization, and care. Children are taught to be respectful of their elders and to show deference for adults' opinions and decisions. A strong value for sharing and cooperation leads to encouragement for children to share their belongings and to learn from one another. Children are praised for behaviors that evidence responsibility for others, a sense of duty, and commitment to the family (Greenfield & Suzuki, 1998).

from childhood to adulthood, adolescence may be brief and relatively free of psychological stress.

The study of development must be approached with an appreciation for the cultural context. Cultural expectations about the timing for entry into and completion of certain life tasks, such as schooling, work, marriage, childbearing, and political and religious leadership, influence the tempo and tone of one's life history. Cultures also vary in the personal qualities they admire and those they consider inappropriate or shameful. A society's standards of beauty, leadership, and talent determine how easily an individual can achieve status within it.

One of the criticisms of scientific knowledge about development is that it lacks the diversity of cultural contexts. If we accept the idea of cultural determinism, we must agree that

development can only be fully understood by taking into consideration the particular ecological and cultural context in which it occurs. Much of what is known about development is based on a small sample of the peoples of the world. Advances in the social sciences in the United States, Canada, Japan, Australia, and Europe have not been matched by the study of development in less economically developed nations in Africa, Latin America, and Asia. Thus, attempts to identify and establish universal principles of development must be tempered by the realization that our scientific observations do not yet reflect the variation in cultural environments that guide the socialization process and the paths to maturity and aging (Nsamenang, 1992).

Cultures not only differ from one another, but some societies are more culturally diverse than others. With increased global travel, migration, global communication systems, and opportunities to study or work in other cultures, most contemporary societies are becoming more culturally diverse than in the past. This means that there may be tensions between dominant and minority cultures as well as conflicts among **ethnic groups**. The relative contribution of ethnic group influences to a person's development depends on the intensity of the family's loyalty to the group, the balance of time spent with members of one's own ethnic group and with members of other cultural groups, and the way the group is viewed or treated within the larger society (Phinney, 1996a). In studying patterns and processes of development, we must keep in mind that people of various ethnic groups may have unique views on such issues as appropriate child behavior and successful maturity, the nature of gender roles, and the proper balance between individual achievement and responsibility to family and community.

## LINKS TO PSYCHOSOCIAL THEORY

Psychosocial theory is based on the assumption that culture contributes fundamentally to individual development. Erikson argued that basic cultural values regarding generosity, self-control, independence, or cooperation could be interpreted from infant caregiving practices. Just as evolutionary theory asserts that adaptation is a product of the interaction between the organism and the physical environment, psychosocial theory assumes that individual development is a product of continuous interaction between the developing person and the demands and resources of the cultural environment.

Ruth Benedict's view was that the degree to which development appears stagelike depends on the continuity or discontinuity of the society. In contrast, psychosocial theory gives a greater role to biological maturation as a stimulus for stage change. However, the content of the stages is derived from the view that all cultures must be able to adapt to changes in economic, environmental, and intercultural conditions. Stages of individual development are interwoven with the ability of the society to adapt and continue. Psychosocial theory suggests, for example, that the way trust is established will differ from one culture to the next, but that all societies have mechanisms for building levels of trust and mistrust during the period of infancy. The psychosocial stages emerge as a product of the changing person and the mechanisms of socialization within each culture that call them forth.

# SOCIAL ROLE THEORY

Another approach to thinking about the effect of the environment on development has been suggested by social psychologists such as Orville Brim (1966) and sociologists such as Talcott Parsons (Parsons & Bales, 1955). They traced the pro-

The social role of "healer" can be found in most cultures. Although the costumes and techniques may differ, healers typically have access to knowledge not shared by most of the people in the society. What are some of the role expectations associated with healers in our society?

cess of socialization and personality development through the person's participation in increasingly diverse and complex *social roles*. A **social role** is any set of behaviors that has a socially agreed-upon function and an accepted code of norms (Biddle, 1979; Biddle & Thomas, 1966; Brown, 1965). The term *role* was taken from the context of the theater. In a play, actors' behaviors are distinct and predictable because each actor has a part to play and follows a script. You will recall this metaphor from Shakespeare's analysis in *As You Like It*, "All the world's a stage, / and all the men and women merely players. / They have their exits and their entrances, / and one man in his time plays many parts" (Act 2, scene 7).

Role theory applies this same framework to social life (Biddle, 1986). The three elements of concern to role theory are the patterned characteristics of social behavior (*role enactment*), the parts or identities a person assumes (*social roles*), and the scripts or shared expectations for behavior that are linked to each part (*role expectations*).

Social roles serve as a bridge between the individual and the society. Every society has a range of roles, and individuals learn about the expectations associated with them. As people enter new roles, they modify their behavior to conform to these role expectations. Each role is usually linked to one or more related or *reciprocal* roles. The student and the teacher, the parent and the child, and the salesperson and the customer are reciprocal roles. Each role is partly defined by the other roles that support it. The function of the role is determined by its relation to the surrounding role groups to which it is allied.

Four dimensions are used to analyze the impact of social roles on development: the *number* of roles a person occupies; the *intensity* of role involvement, or how deeply the person identifies with the role; the amount of *time* the role demands; and the extent to which the expectations associated with each role are either highly *structured* or *flexible* and open to improvisation.

## IMPLICATIONS FOR HUMAN DEVELOPMENT

All cultures offer new roles that await individuals as they move from one stage of life to another. Some of these roles may be directly associated with age, such as the role of a high school student. Other roles may be accessible only to those of a certain age who demonstrate other relevant skills, traits, or personal preferences. In many elementary schools, for example, the fifth-grade students become eligible to serve in the role of crossing guard to help the younger children get across the streets near the school. Families, organizations, and the larger community have implicit theories of development that determine what role positions open up for individuals in each age group. Some of the most important life roles persist across several stages, including child, parent, and sibling. The expectations for role performance remain the same in some respects, but change in others. We can begin to see how social roles provide consistency to life experiences and how they prompt new learning.

Involvement in personal relationships and social groups contributes to the formation of one's **social identity**—that aspect of the self-concept that is based on membership in a group or groups and on the importance and emotional salience of that membership (Tajfel, 1981). Some of these role relationships are personal—based on family, friendship, or intimate relationships. Others are political, religious, or ethnic. Some aspects of one's social identity may be associated with a stigmatized group, such as being homeless, unemployed, or on welfare (Deaux, Reid, Mizrahi, & Ethier, 1995). In modern societies, people are members of many groups and form complex social identities, in which many roles and their varying meanings and values are balanced and synthesized. Understanding a person's social identity helps account for which groups a person may view as "ingroups" and "out-

groups," why a person might discriminate against certain outgroups, or how a person's views of fairness and justice may be shaped (Simon & Klandermans, 2001).

## LINKS TO PSYCHOSOCIAL THEORY

Role relationships provide a central mechanism through which the socialization process takes place. In psychosocial theory, one might think of the radius of significant relationships as an interconnected web of reciprocal roles and role relationships through which the expectations and demands of society make themselves known. The idea of reciprocity in roles is closely linked to the concept of interdependence of people at different psychosocial stages. The capacity of adults to resolve the crises of their life stages and to achieve new ego strengths is intricately linked to the ability of children and youth to flourish and grow. Social role theory helps clarify why this is so important, as children and adults occupy many reciprocal roles.

In the following chapters, we describe a number of life roles especially related to family, school, and work. As the number of roles increases, individuals must learn some of the skills of role playing, role differentiation, and role integration. The developmental crisis of later adolescence (individual identity versus identity confusion) emphasizes the challenge of being able to integrate several diverse roles in order to preserve a sense of personal continuity. With each new role, one's self-definition changes and one's potential for influencing the world increases.

# SYSTEMS THEORY

Systems theories attempt to describe and account for the characteristics of systems and the relationships among the component parts found within the system (Sameroff, 1982). Systems theories take the position that the whole is more than the sum of its parts. Any system—whether it is a cell, an organ, an individual, a family, or a corporation—is composed of interdependent elements that share some common goals, interrelated functions, boundaries, and an identity. The system cannot be wholly understood by identifying each of its component parts. The processes and relationships of those parts make for a larger, coherent entity. The language system, for example, is more than the capacity to make vocal utterances, use grammar, and acquire vocabulary. It is the coordination of these elements in a useful way in a context of shared meaning. Similarly, a family system is more than the sum of the characteristics and competencies of the individual family members.

A system cannot violate the laws that govern the functioning of its parts, but at the same time it cannot be explained solely by those laws. Biological functioning cannot violate the

## Role Strain and Parenthood

A RECURRING THEME in the literature on parenthood is the experience of role strain. **Role strain** is defined as a sense of difficulty in meeting perceived role expectations or balancing competing role demands (Biddle, 1986). Each of the four dimensions of social roles may contribute to parental role strain. When parenting is added to other adult roles, especially those of worker and spouse, the demands of the new role may seem overwhelming. Because the parent role has great intensity, the sense of involvement in all the behaviors associated with the role intensifies, and so does anxiety about failure to meet the expectations of the role. First-time parents especially may have little confidence in their ability to fulfill their roles, and the level of worry associated with the role rises accordingly.

The parent role takes a lot of time. Most first-time parents underestimate how much time infants and toddlers require. When new parents, especially mothers, reflect on the time they spend in a variety of social roles, they point to the parent role as more time consuming than any other role, now or in the past.

Role strain linked with parenting is related to the structure of the role. Some adults have a very clear set of ideas about how they should enact their parent role, but many are unsure. Husbands and wives are likely to differ in their views on childrearing techniques. These differences require time to resolve. Because of the hardships or distress they recall from their own childhoods, many adults do not want to raise their children the way they were raised themselves. They have to learn a new script for this role.

There are at least four ways to minimize the role strain associated with the parent role (Bornstein, 2002; Cowan & Cowan, 1988; Newman, 2000):

1. Parents need to focus on a small number of expectations for their parenting role and focus on finding pleasure in meeting those expectations rather than worrying about the many expectations that are not being met.
2. The ability to delegate role responsibilities can reduce role strain. Parents who can hire others to help with some of the parenting responsibilities or who can turn to family members or friends for help will experience less role strain than those who are solely responsible for the parenting role. Couples who can flexibly alter and share household responsibilities in response to the demands of parenting will experience more satisfaction and less strain.
3. The ability to integrate several aspects of the role in one activity can reduce role strain. Some parents become quite inventive about ways to maintain contact with their infant and still carry out their household chores and other work and also have time with each other.
4. Role strain is reduced when partners reach consensus about their parent roles. New parents who have resolved their differences regarding childrearing philosophy, child care activities, and the division of household responsibilities experience less role strain and a higher level of marital satisfaction than those who continue to have opposing views on these issues.

---

laws of physics and chemistry, but the laws of physics and chemistry cannot fully explain biological functioning. Similarly, children's capacities for cognitive growth cannot violate the laws of biological functioning, but biological growth does not fully explain the quality of thought.

Individuals, families, communities, schools, and societies are all examples of open systems. Ludwig von Bertalanffy (1950, 1968) defined **open systems** as structures that maintain their organization even though their parts constantly change. Just as the water in a river is constantly changing but the river itself retains its boundaries and course, so the molecules of human cells are constantly changing while the various biological systems retain their coordinated functions.

Systems change in the direction of adjusting to or incorporating more and more of the environment into themselves, in order to prevent disorganization as a result of environmental fluctuations (Sameroff, 1982). *Adaptation*—whether the concept is articulated by Darwin, Piaget, Skinner, or Bandura—seems to be a fundamental process. Ervin Laszlo

(1972) described this property of an open system as **adaptive self-regulation**. A system uses **feedback mechanisms** to identify and respond to environmental changes. The more information about the environment the system is capable of detecting, the more complex these feedback mechanisms must be. When the oxygen level of the environment is reduced, for example, you tend to grow sleepy. While you sleep, your breathing slows, and you use less oxygen. Some of these adjustments are managed unconsciously by the organization of biological systems. Others are managed more deliberately by efforts to minimize the effects of environmental changes. Most systems have a capacity for storing or saving resources so that temporary shortages do not disrupt their operations.

When open systems are confronted by new or changing environmental conditions, they have the capacity for **adaptive self-organization**. The system retains its essential identity by creating new substructures, by revising the relationships among components, or by creating new, higher levels of organization that coordinate existing substructures.

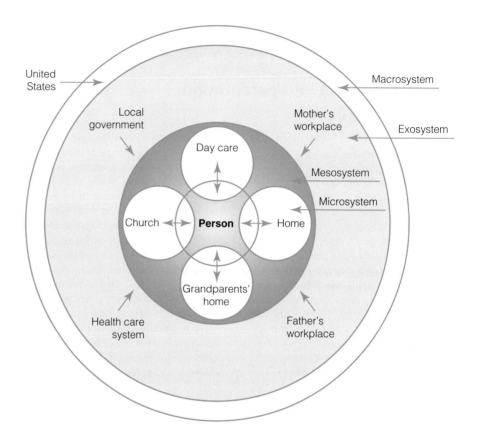

Specific examples of microsystems and systems in the exosystem are given, but many other systems could be shown. Arrows in the mesosystem show a two-way, or bidirectional influence; arrows in the exosystem are unidirectional, because the developing person does not participate in those settings. The person, the microsystems, and the relationship among systems change over time.

**FIGURE 4.4**

A Topography of the Relationship Among Systems

Source: Adapted from Bronfenbrenner, 1979.

From the systems perspective, the components and the whole are always in tension. What one understands and observes depends on where one stands in this complex set of interrelationships. All living entities are both parts and wholes. A person is a part of a family, a classroom or workgroup, a friendship group, and a society. A person is also a whole— a coordinated, complex system composed of physical, cognitive, emotional, social, and self subsystems. Part of the story of human development is told in an analysis of the adaptive regulation and organization of those subsystems. Simultaneously, the story is told in the way larger systems fluctuate and impinge on individuals, forcing adaptive regulation and reorganization as a means of achieving stability at higher levels of system organization.

In an effort to elaborate and clarify the interlocking system of systems in which human behavior takes place, Urie Bronfenbrenner (1979, 1995, 1999) offered the following topography of the environmental structure (see Figure 4.4):

A **microsystem** is a pattern of activities, roles, and interpersonal relations experienced by the developing person in a given setting with particular physical and material characteristics.

A **mesosystem** comprises the interrelations among two or more settings in which the developing person actively participates (e.g., for a child, the relations among home,

school, and neighborhood peer group; for an adult, among family, work, and social life).

An **exosystem** refers to one or more settings that do not involve the developing person as an active participant, but in which events occur that affect—or are affected by—what happens in the setting containing the developing person.

The **macrosystem** refers to consistencies in the form and content of lower order systems (micro-, meso-, and exo-) that exist, or could exist, at the level of the subculture or the culture as a whole, along with any belief systems or ideology underlying such consistencies (Bronfenbrenner, 1979, pp. 22, 25, 26).

The **chronosystem** refers to time (Bronfenbrenner, 1995). Both the individual and the systems in which that person is embedded change over time. What is more, the relationships among the systems change over time. Some of these changes are patterned, developmental transformations, such as the change in a child's capacity for coordinated movement and voluntary, goal-directed action. Other changes are societal, such as a community decision to restructure a school system from an elementary (Grades K–6), junior high (Grades 7–9), and high school (Grades 10–12) system to an elementary (Grades K–5), middle school (Grades 6–8), and high school (Grades 9–12) system. Finally, some changes reflect

*The neighborhood is a microsystem. Children adapt their play to the physical characteristics of their neighborhoods. How might adaptive regulation differ for children who grow up in these two communities?*

the decline or improvement of resources in a setting, as when a neighborhood becomes transformed through urban development.

Bronfenbrenner argued that development is influenced directly by the interactions that take place within a single microsystem, such as the family, and by the similarities and differences in patterns of interaction that occur across the various systems in which the person functions (the mesosystem). Events in other, adjoining systems—such as decisions in the workplace that affect the parent's work schedule or decisions in city government that affect resources for the local schools—also have an impact on development even though the child does not participate directly in these settings. Furthermore, the roles, norms, and resources within settings as well as the interrelationships among systems have a unique pattern of organization and reflect an underlying set of beliefs and values that differ from one culture or ethnic group to the next. These cultural characteristics are transmitted to the developing person.

## IMPLICATIONS FOR HUMAN DEVELOPMENT

Systems theory has been applied to the study of the life span through *developmental systems theory* (Lerner, Dowling, & Roth, 2003). This perspective emphasizes the ongoing interaction and integration across many levels of the human organism from the genetic to the behavioral level, within the nested contexts of the person, family, community, and culture, to consider both continuity and change over individual and historical time. *Plasticity*, the capacity for change, is at the heart of this approach. The *person in the setting* is the focus of analysis. The challenge to developmental systems theory

is to understand the reciprocal regulation of the person and the environment over time. How is the person shaped and defined by the contexts in which he or she functions? How does the person influence these contexts to foster more optimal environments for growth (Bronfenbrenner, 2004)?

Systems theory has also been applied to the analysis of family functioning. Family systems theories focus on how families establish and maintain stable patterns of functioning. Families are viewed as emotional units identifiable by certain boundaries and rules (Broderick, 1993). The **boundaries** of the family determine who is considered to be a family member and who is an outsider. They influence the way information, support, and validation of the family unit are sought and the way new members are admitted into the family. Some families have very strict **rules** that maintain a narrow boundary around the family. Few sources of information or contact are admitted. Other families extend the sense of belonging to a wide range of people who bring ideas and resources to the family system.

Family systems are maintained by patterns of communication (Vogl-Bauer, 2003). Positive and negative *feedback loops* operate to stabilize, diminish, or increase certain types of interactions. For example, a feedback loop is positive when a child offers a suggestion and a parent recognizes and compliments the child on that suggestion. As a result, the child is encouraged to continue to offer suggestions, and the parent comes to view the child as someone who has valuable suggestions to offer. A feedback loop is negative if a parent ignores the child's suggestions or scolds the child for making them. The child is less likely to make further suggestions, and the parent's view of the child as someone who has no valuable ideas to offer is confirmed. Many positive and negative feedback loops operate in families to sustain the qualities of the system, such as the power hierarchy, level of conflict, and balance between autonomy and dependence among the members.

One of the most commonly noted characteristics of family systems is the **interdependence** of the family members. Changes in one family member are accompanied by changes in the others. Imagine for a moment that family members are standing in a circle and holding a rope. Each person is trying to exert enough tension on the rope to keep it tight and preserve the circular shape. The amount of tension each person must exert depends on what every other person is doing. Now imagine that one member of the family lets go of the rope and steps away. In order to retain the shape and tension of the rope, everyone else has to adjust his or her grip. Letting go of the rope is an analogy for many kinds of changes that can occur in a family—a parent becomes ill, a child goes off to college, or a parent takes on a demanding job outside of the home. The system adjusts by redefining relationships, modifying patterns of communication, and adjusting its boundaries. The members and their interdependencies change. Similar adjustments must be made if a member is added to the family system or when the system undergoes some other major transition.

The systems theory perspective offers an especially productive approach to clinical problems. A person who has been identified as dysfunctional is treated not as a lone individual but as part of a family system. From a systems theory perspective, the assumption is that the person's problems are a product of the interactions among family members. The only way to bring about changes in that person's functioning is to alter the functioning of the *other* members of the system as well. If the person is "underfunctioning"—that is, acting irresponsibly, not communicating, not performing at his or her level of capability, withdrawing, or acting impulsively— one assumes that others in the family are "overfunctioning"— that is, assuming many of the person's roles and responsibilities in order to "take up the slack." The dysfunctional behavior is maintained because it is a component of an emotional unit. In other words, the dysfunction belongs neither to the person nor to the other family members but to the particular interdependence among the family members that operates to preserve the viability of the family system as a whole (Bowen, 1978).

By definition, family systems are also interdependent with adjacent systems. Thus, the understanding of families requires an analysis of the resources and demands of other social systems that impinge on families and of the opportunities that families have for influencing adjoining systems. A woman who is experiencing an extremely demanding, stressful, and sexist work environment, for example, may be constantly tired, tense, and irritable in her behavior toward her family members. She may bring home the resentments from work in the way she treats and expects to be treated by the men and women in her family. If the job is important to her and her family, no one may be willing to acknowledge the disruptive impact that the work setting is having on family life. Family violence, the effects of unemployment on families, participation of mothers in the labor force, child care, and the role of parents in their children's schooling are all being examined from a systems perspective.

## LINKS TO PSYCHOSOCIAL THEORY

Psychosocial theory embraces the basic assumption of systems theory—that an understanding of development requires an analysis of the person embedded in a number of interrelated systems. Systems theory predicts that systems change through adaptive self-regulation and adaptive self-organization. The direction of this change is not necessarily patterned, except that it is expected to move in the direction of creating new, higher levels of organization to coordinate newly developed substructures. The nature of change is a product of efforts to retain a sense of system identity and boundaries in the face of multiple demands and shifts in environments. According to psychosocial theory, however, change is patterned. With expanding cognitive capacities and the resolution of each new psychosocial crisis, a person is propelled into increasingly complex social systems and encounters new stimulation for growth through participation in a greater variety of social relationships. At each new stage, individuals develop new coping skills and devise strategies for new levels of participation in the social system. Eventually, they create innovative approaches for modifying the social system itself.

# CASE STUDY

## JACK MANASKY AND HIS DAUGHTER MARILYN

*Jack Manasky has been widowed for six years. He still writes letters to his beloved wife Anna, keeping her up to date on the events of his life. In this small episode, a lot is revealed about Jack's life, his sense of self, and his relationship with his adult daughter:*

Dear Anna,

I am writing this from a coffee shop. My seat is by the window. Why, you are thinking, am I sitting in a coffee shop when I have a perfectly good house to sit in? Okay, I will tell you.

Marilyn, our dear daughter, may she have a long and wonderful life, this dear child of ours who is no longer a child, decided last month to cure me. Cure me of what, I do not know. I did not ask. One day she came in. A day no different from any other. I was sitting in the living room watching the television news.

Marilyn went into the kitchen to empty her grocery bags. "Dad," she said. "I bought you new coffee. It's decaffeinated."

"What does this mean, decaffeinated?" I asked. This I said from my chair, why should I walk into the kitchen?

"Unleaded, Dad. You shouldn't be drinking regular coffee. It's a diuretic."

By this time she was standing in the doorway of the kitchen, folding her paper bag. "It means it takes too much water out of you. You're too old for that."

Nu? Decaffeinated. Diuretic. Too much water. Let her do what she wants. What did I care?

I forgot about it. The next day, I got up, I fed the birds, read the newspaper, and drank my coffee. No big deal. But that afternoon, a headache. And what a headache, loud, pounding, I could not think. This was not so new to me. Headaches. They come, they go. But this one, it was different. The next day, it was still with me. And the next day also. Like a black cloud, it filled my head with thunder, everywhere I went.

When Marilyn came on the third day, I remembered. "Marilyn," I said, "this decaffeinated coffee, however you call it, it is killing me."

"Ha, ha," she laughed. "It's not killing you, Dad. It's good for you."

"It's murdering me. Go, buy me some coffee. Or tomorrow you will be pouring this decaffeinated coffee on my grave."

"Dad," she said. "You have a headache? You'll get over it. It's not the decaf that's giving it to you. It's from no caffeine. It'll stop soon." She laughed again, and then she was gone. This is what she does. Comes into my house, checks things off her list, and then disappears.

I sat down. "Okay." I said to the floor. "I will buy my own coffee."

Source: From "Starboys" by Elissa Goldberg in *Families in Later Life: Connections and Transitions*, by Alexis J. Walker et al., pp. 250–251. Copyright 2001 Pine Forge Press.

## ■ CRITICAL THINKING AND CASE ANALYSIS

Consider what each of the theories discussed in this chapter might have to offer in helping to understand this interaction between an aging, widowed father and his adult daughter.

## ■ EVOLUTIONARY THEORY

1. How can evolutionary theory account for Marilyn's motivation to care for her aging father? What aspect of fitness is enhanced when children use their resources to support their parents' longevity and well-being?

2. Psychosocial evolution is typically viewed as the flow of knowledge from the older to the younger generation. How does this case modify that perspective?

## ■ PSYCHOSEXUAL THEORY

3. How can psychosexual theory account for Marilyn's motivation to care for her aging father?

4. How can psychosexual theory account for Jack's coping strategy of writing letters to his deceased wife?

5. If Jack watches television news as part of his daily routine, why doesn't he know about decaffeinated coffee? What

defense mechanisms might he be using to block out information about the negative effects of coffee on health?

## ■ COGNITIVE DEVELOPMENTAL THEORY

6. How would you characterize Marilyn's level of cognitive reasoning as she tries to modify her father's coffee-drinking behavior?

7. How would you characterize Jack's level of cognitive reasoning about the relationship of his headaches to the new coffee?

## ■ LEARNING THEORIES

8. How do the learning theories explain the establishment of a pattern or routine of behavior such as the one Jack describes—feed the birds, read the newspaper, drink a cup of coffee?

9. What is the importance of these behavior patterns for Jack?

10. What principles of learning theory could help Marilyn be more effective in altering her father's behavior?

## ■ CULTURAL THEORY

11. What can you detect from this case about the cultural norms for the relationship of an adult daughter and an aging father?

12. Can you describe a cultural context in which Jack and Marilyn might have a very different type of relationship and a different style of interaction?

13. How is the U.S. cultural value of independence and individualism expressed in the case?

## ■ SOCIAL ROLE THEORY

14. How is Marilyn defining her role as an adult child of a widowed father?

15. How is Jack defining his role as Marilyn's father?

16. What role does Anna, Jack's deceased wife, play in Jack's life?

## ■ SYSTEMS THEORY

17. How would you evaluate the feedback mechanisms between Jack and Marilyn and their impact on each other's behavior?

18. How would you describe the interactions among the biological, psychological, and societal systems in this case?

19. How might macrosystem values and resources regarding health and nutrition be influencing Marilyn's behavior toward her father?

20. At the end of the case, Jack says, "Okay, I will buy my own coffee." Which concepts presented in this chapter best explain a person's decision to change his or her behavior in order to achieve a new goal?

# Chapter Summary

The seven theoretical perspectives we have reviewed take distinct approaches to continuity and change across the life span. Evolutionary theory provides a framework for understanding individual development within the broad perspective of the biological evolution of the human species. Although a life span of 85 or 90 years may seem long, it is but a flicker in the millions of years of biological adaptation. Evolutionary theory highlights the genetically governed aspects of growth and development. The environment provides the specific conditions that require adaptation. However, adaptive change can occur only if it is supported by the genetically based characteristics of the organism. The basic mechanism that accounts for species change over many generations is natural selection.

Ethology, the study of evolutionarily significant behaviors, provides a systematic approach to analyzing reproductive practices, caregiving behaviors, strategies for obtaining resources, and other behaviors that contribute to individual and species survival. Evolutionary psychology focuses on understanding the human mind in terms of the problems of survival it has been shaped to solve.

According to psychosexual theory, development follows a biologically determined path in which patterns of social relationships change as a result of emerging sexual impulses and the sexualization of body zones. Culture plays a major role in establishing the taboos and acceptable patterns of sexual gratification that lead to conflicts, fixations, and strategies for sublimation. The content of the unconscious—including sexual impulses, wishes, and fears—guides behavior and gives it meaning. Psychosexual theory emphasizes the years of infancy and childhood as those in which basic personality patterns are established. It also identifies the family, especially the parent–child relationship, as the primary context within which conflicts related to the socialization of sexual impulses are resolved. In contemporary psychoanalytic theory, interpersonal needs and the relational context of ego development are highlighted in contrast to the drive-based perspective of traditional psychosexual theory.

Cognitive developmental theories focus on the etiology of rational thought and the capacity for scientific reasoning. Piaget's cognitive theory, like psychosexual theory, views development as the product of a biologically guided plan for growth and change. The elements that make cognitive growth possible are all present in the genetic information that governs the growth of the brain and nervous system. However, the process of intellectual growth requires interaction with a diverse and responsive environment. Cognitive development is fostered by the recognition of discrepancies between existing schemes and new experiences. Through the reciprocal processes of assimilation and accommodation, schemes are modified and integrated to form the basis for organizing and explaining experience. The child is viewed as actively constructing knowledge through sensory, motor, and representational exploration.

Vygotsky's contribution to cognitive theory places the development of higher mental processes in a dynamic social context. Although thinking and reasoning are dependent on biologically based capacities, the way in which mental activity is organized reflects unique characteristics of the social context, especially as culture is transmitted through language, tools, and social relationships.

Learning theories focus on the mechanisms that permit individuals to respond to their diverse environments and the changes in thought and behavior that accompany changes in the environment. Behavior can be shaped and modified by systematic changes in environmental conditions. According to learning theorists, human beings have an especially flexible behavioral system. No assumptions are made about universal stages of growth. As conditions in the environment change, response patterns also change. Similarity among individuals at a particular period of life is explained by the fact that they are exposed to similar environmental conditions, patterns of reinforcement, and models. Consistent contingencies between behaviors and their consequences result in the formation of cognitive expectations as well as behaviors.

Cultural theory, like the learning theories, emphasizes the role of the environment in directing the course of development. Within this framework, the significance of biological maturation depends on the interaction between the individual and the social context. The possibilities for cultural variation are enormous. What we define as the normal or natural pattern and tempo of change in competence, roles, and status depends largely on the way a society recognizes and treats individuals of different ages, sexes, and degrees of kinship.

Social role theory suggests that learning is organized around key social functions called roles. As people enact roles, they integrate their behavior into meaningful units. Meaning is provided by the definition of the role and by the expectations of those in reciprocal roles. Development is a product of entry into an increasing number of complex roles over the life span. As children acquire and lose roles, they change their self-definitions and their relationships with social groups. Most societies define roles that are linked with gender, age, marital status, and kinship. These roles provide patterning to the life course. However, the patterns are understood to be products of the structures and functions of the society rather than of genetic information.

Systems theory emphasizes the multidimensional sources of influence on individuals and the simultaneous influence of individuals on the systems of which they are a part. Each person is at once a component of one or more larger systems and a system unto him- or herself. One must approach the study of development from many angles, identifying the critical resources, the flow of resources, and the transformation of resources that underlie an adaptive process of reorganization and growth. This perspective has been applied to an analysis of families and family change as well as to individual development over the life span.

## Further Reflection

1.  Imagine that you had to explain development to a new parent. What mechanisms or processes do the seven theories offer to explain how children grow up and change from infancy into adulthood?
2.  Which of the theories is most like your own beliefs about development? Which is least like your own beliefs? Why?
3.  In what ways do the theories overlap? Give some examples of ways that two or more of the theories use different words or terms to explain basically the same thing.
4.  In what ways do the theories offer something unique to the understanding of development? Give some examples of ways in which one or two of the theories contribute something that does not seem to be included in the others.
5.  Psychosocial theory assumes that development is a product of the interactions among the biological, psychological, and societal systems. Try to identify the role of these three systems in each of the theories discussed in this chapter.
6.  What are the implications of each theory for the educational environment for young children, adolescents, college students, or adult learners? If you were in charge of creating a learning environment, which theory or combination of theories would you draw on to guide your planning and your interaction with students?

## On the Web

**VISIT OUR WEBSITE**

Go to http://www.wadsworth.com/psychology to find online resources directly linked to your book.

## Casebook

For additional case material related to this chapter, see the case of "A School Debate," in *Life Span Development: A Case Book*, by Barbara and Philip Newman, Laura Landry-Meyer, and Brenda J. Lohman, page 13. This case focuses on the opinions of teachers and the school principal at a middle school about how to increase school attendance and reduce student tardiness. The varying suggestions reflect the application of different theories of human development to the solution of an important real-world problem. The case provides practice in linking theoretical ideas about causes of behavior to potential strategies for intervention.

# CHAPTER 5

# THE PERIOD OF PREGNANCY AND PRENATAL DEVELOPMENT

*The Dream, 1932/Pablo Picasso/Artists Rights Society (ARS), New York/SuperStock*

*The period of pregnancy involves intricate inter-actions between the developing fetus and the pregnant woman. The pattern of fetal development is guided largely by genetic factors, but the pregnant woman's health, social support, and emotional well-being can have substantial impact on fetal growth.*

■ **GENETICS AND DEVELOPMENT**

Genes and Chromosomes as Sources of Genetic Information
The Laws of Heredity
Genetic Sources of Individual Differences
Genetic Technology and Psychosocial Evolution
Evaluating the Contribution of Genetic Factors to Behavior

■ **NORMAL FETAL DEVELOPMENT**

Fertilization
Development in the First Trimester
Development in the Second Trimester
Development in the Third Trimester

■ **THE BIRTH PROCESS**

Stages of Labor
Cesarean Delivery
Infant Mortality

■ **THE MOTHER, THE FETUS, AND THE PSYCHOSOCIAL ENVIRONMENT**

The Impact of the Fetus on the Pregnant Woman

CASE STUDY: A FATHER'S RECOLLECTIONS ABOUT HIS DAUGHTER'S BIRTH

The Impact of the Pregnant Woman on the Fetus

■ **THE CULTURAL CONTEXT OF PREGNANCY AND CHILDBIRTH**

Reactions to Pregnancy
Reactions to Childbirth

■ **APPLIED TOPIC: ABORTION**

The Legal Context of Abortion in the United States
The Incidence of Legal Abortions
The Psychosocial Impact of Abortion

CASE STUDY: KAREN AND DON

■ **CHAPTER SUMMARY**

■ **FURTHER REFLECTION**

► To describe the biochemical basis of genetic information and the process through which it is transmitted from one generation to the next.

► To identify the contributions of genetic factors to individuality through their role in controlling the rate of development, their contributions to individual traits, and the genetic sources of abnormalities.

► To trace fetal development through three trimesters of pregnancy, including an understanding of critical periods when normal fetal development can be disrupted.

► To describe the birth process and factors that contribute to infant mortality.

► To analyze the reciprocity between the pregnant woman and the developing fetus, focusing on ways in which pregnancy affects a childbearing woman and expectant father and on basic influences on fetal growth, such as maternal age, drug use, nutrition, and environmental toxins.

► To examine the impact of culture on pregnancy and childbirth.

► To analyze abortion from a psychosocial perspective, including the legal context, its social and emotional impact on women, and men's views.

WHEN DOES AN individual's life story begin? At birth? At conception? At the birth of his or her parents? We are each linked back in time, through a lifeline comprising our ancestry, our culture, and our genetic makeup. This chapter begins the story at the molecular level of genes and chromosomes, moves to the biological maturation of the fetus during the prenatal period, and then expands the view of early development by considering the psychosocial and cultural contexts of the period of pregnancy.

Genetic factors guide the tempo of growth and the emergence of individual characteristics. As the human fetus grows, sensory and motor competencies emerge. The psychosocial environment provides both resources for and challenges to healthy development. Cultural attitudes toward pregnancy and childbirth, poverty and the associated stressors, support from the child's father and other significant family members, maternal nutrition, and exposure to toxins or drugs are among the factors that affect fetal growth. ■

# GENETICS AND DEVELOPMENT

Variability, which is so essential for human survival, is guaranteed, in part, by the complexity of the human *genome* (all the genetic material in the chromosomes of a human being) and the mechanisms for genetic inheritance. Over the past few years, there have been monumental accomplishments in the field of genetics. In 2003, the Human Genome Project was completed, mapping 99% of the gene-containing regions

of the human chromosomes to a high degree of accuracy. Genetic mapping involves identifying the molecular structure and specific location of each gene on a specific chromosome. An excellent source of information and links about the results, ethics, and future directions of genomic research can be found on the World Wide Web at www.doegenomes.org, the U.S. Department of Energy Human Genome Project.

In this section, we briefly review the biology of genetics and the laws that govern the transmission of genetic information from one generation to the next. As parents, teachers, and human service professionals, we are encouraged to value and respond to human diversity. The growing knowledge about human genetics provides a foundation for appreciating the biological basis of this diversity.

## GENES AND CHROMOSOMES AS SOURCES OF GENETIC INFORMATION

When we talk about inherited characteristics, we are really referring to two different kinds of heredity. The first includes all the genetic information that comes to us as members of the human species. This is called the **gene pool**. Most inherited genetic information is shared by *all* human beings, such as patterns of motor behavior (e.g., walking upright), brain size, and body structure, including the proportional size of the head, torso, and limbs. Two of the most relevant of these species-related characteristics are the readiness to learn and the inclination to participate in social interaction.

The second kind of heredity consists of characteristics that have been transmitted through a specific *ancestry*. Hair color, skin color, blood group, and height result from the genetic in-

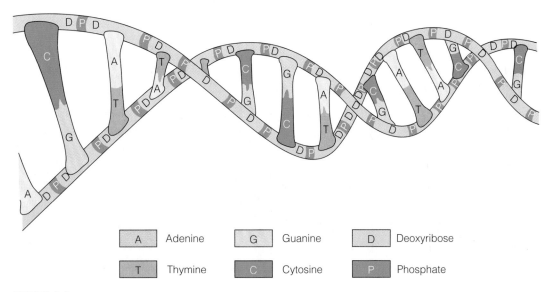

| A | Adenine | G | Guanine | D | Deoxyribose |
| T | Thymine | C | Cytosine | P | Phosphate |

**FIGURE 5.1**

Diagram of a Small Part of a DNA Molecule. The biochemical basis of genetic information is the DNA (deoxyribonucleic acid) molecule, which has the shape of a double helix (i.e., it looks somewhat like a twisted rope ladder). The sides of this ladder comprise alternating units of sugar (deoxyribose) and phosphate, and its rungs are made up of pairs of nitrogen bases (so named because they contain the element nitrogen as well as hydrogen and carbon). The four nitrogen bases involved are adenine (A), guanine (G), cytosine (C), and thymine (T). They are often referred to by their initial letters, and A, G, C, and T are called the genetic alphabet.

formation passed on from one generation to the next. Given all the shared information that is carried in the genome, these individual differences amount to only 0.1% of all the DNA (McGuffin, Riley, & Plomin, 2001). Genetic information links each new person to the human species in general and also to a specific genetic ancestry.

**Chromosomes**, the long, thin strands of genetic material located in the cell nucleus, are formed from chains of DNA molecules (see Figure 5.1). Most single **genes** are composed of a piece of DNA that codes for the production of one protein and occupies a specific place on a chromosome (see Figure 5.2). It was once believed that human beings had between 100,000 and 140,000 functional genes distributed along the 23 pairs of chromosomes; the recent estimate based on genome mapping places the number of functional genes between 30,000 and 35,000 (Venter et al., 2001; U.S. Department of Energy Office of Science, 2004). The functions of about 50% of the identified genes are not yet known. The important work of the genes is to produce proteins, which then guide cellular formation and functioning. Only about 2% of the genome actually codes for proteins.

One common misconception is that there is one gene for specific traits such as sociability, intelligence, or criminality. McGuffin, Riley, and Plomin (2001) have pointed out that

single genes do not determine most human behaviors. Only certain rare disorders such as Huntington's disease have a simple mode of transmission in which a specific mutation confers the certainty of developing the disorder. Most types of behavior have no such clear-cut pattern and de-

pend on interplay between environmental factors and multiple genes. (p. 1232)

In each chromosome pair, one chromosome comes from the father and one from the mother. As you can see in Figure 5.2, the chromosome pairs differ in size. In 22 pairs of chromosomes, both members are similar in shape and size. They also contain the same kinds of genes. The 23rd pair of chromosomes is a different story: Female humans have two X chromosomes, and male humans have one X and one Y chromosome. The X and Y notation is used because these chromosomes differ in shape and size (the X chromosome is longer than the Y chromosome; see the last pair in Figure 5.2). There are very few similarities in the genes present on the X and Y chromosomes.

## THE LAWS OF HEREDITY

The laws that govern the process by which genetic information is transmitted from parent to offspring were discovered by Gregor Mendel (1866), a monk who studied the inherited characteristics of plants, particularly garden peas. His laws were formulated long before the discovery of the biochemical substances that compose genes and chromosomes.

### ALLELES

In the 22 pairs of identical chromosomes, each gene has at least two possible states or conditions, one on each chromosome in the pair. These alternative states are called **alleles**.

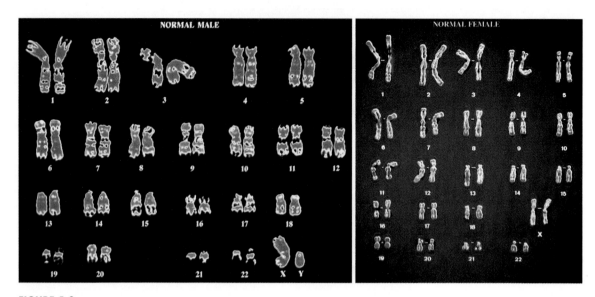

**FIGURE 5.2**

The 23 Pairs of Chromosomes in a Normal Male (left) and Female (right) Human

Whatever the allelic state of the gene from one parent, the other parent's allele for that gene may be either the same or different. If both alleles are the same, the gene is said to be **homozygous**. If the alleles are different, the gene is **heterozygous**.

## GENOTYPE AND PHENOTYPE

The genetic information about a trait is called the **genotype** (e.g., the genetic information that encodes skin color). The observed characteristic (e.g., one's actual skin color) is called the **phenotype**. The expression, "There is more here than meets the eye," suggests the difference between genotype and phenotype. What you see is not necessarily what you get.

Genotype can influence phenotype in three different ways. First, the differences in the allelic states of several genes sometimes result in a **cumulative relation**, in which more than one pair of alleles influences the trait. An example of this kind of relation is the genetic contribution to height. A person who receives mostly "tall" alleles of different genes will be tall; a person who receives mostly "short" alleles of different genes will be short. Most people receive a mix of "tall" and "short" alleles and are of average height.

Second, the differences between alleles may result in **codominance**, in which both genes are expressed in the new cell. An example of codominance is the AB blood type, which results from the joining of an A blood-type allele from one

*About 70% of people of European ancestry can roll up the sides of their tongue to form a tube; 30% cannot do this. In the 1940s this capacity was thought to be an inherited trait, although some people were able to learn to do it. However, in the 1950s, studies showed that about 30% of monozygotic twins were discordant for the trait, meaning that one twin could do it and the other could not. This has shed doubt on the notion of tongue rolling as a genetic marker.*

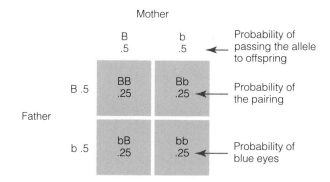

Note: Whenever B allele is present, eyes will be brown.

**FIGURE 5.3**

Probability of Heterozygous Brown-Eyed Parents Producing Blue-Eyed Offspring

parent and a B blood-type allele from the other parent. This blood type is not a mixture of A and B, nor is A subordinate to B or B to A; instead, a new blood type, AB, is formed.

Third, differences in the allele states of a gene may result in a **dominance** relation. Dominance means that if one allele is present, its characteristic is always observed whether the other allele of the pair is the same or not. The allele that dominates is called the *dominant* allele. The other allele that is present, but whose characteristic is masked by the dominant allele, is called the *recessive* allele. Eye color is the result of a dominance relation. The allele for brown eyes (B) is dominant over the allele for blue eyes (b). The probability that the recessive trait of blue eyes will emerge in the offspring of two heterozygous parents is illustrated in Figure 5.3. The possible combinations of the gene related to brown or blue eye color are BB, Bb, bB, and bb. Only one combination, bb, which will occur on the average in only 25% of the offspring, results in a child with blue eyes. The other three genotypes result in one phenotype—brown eyes.

## ■ SEX-LINKED CHARACTERISTICS

Certain genetic characteristics are said to be **sex-linked** because the gene for the specific characteristic is found on the sex chromosomes (X and Y). The female ova carry only X chromosomes. Half of the male sperm carry Y chromosomes, and half carry X chromosomes. Male children can be produced only when a sperm carrying a Y chromosome fertilizes an egg, and the result is an XY combination in the 23rd chromosome pair. All sperm carrying X chromosomes will produce female children.

Sex-linked traits are more likely to be observed in male offspring, even though they may be present in the genotype of female offspring. You will understand this more readily if you visualize the XY chromosome pair. When a trait is carried on the Y chromosome, it will be inherited and transmitted only by male offspring, because only male offspring have the Y chromosome. Interestingly, the Y chromosome is quite small,

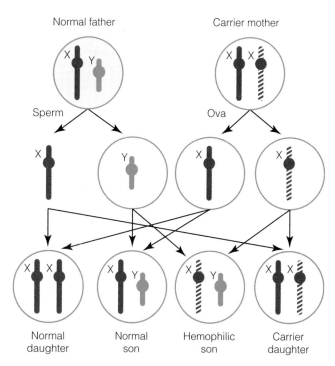

**FIGURE 5.4**

Sex-Linked Inheritance of Hemophilia. The allele for hemophilia is carried on the X chromosome. If the allele is either heterozygous or homozygous for the dominant trait (normal blood clotting), a female child will have normal blood-clotting capabilities. Only if she is homozygous for the recessive trait (a very rare occurrence) will she be hemophilic. A male child, on the other hand, has only one allele for the clotting gene, which he inherits from his mother. If that allele is dominant, his blood will clot normally, but if it is recessive, he will be hemophilic.

Source: From "The Molecular Genetics of Hemophilia" by R. M. Lawn and G. A. Vehar, 1986, *Scientific American, 254*, p. 50. Copyright © 1986. All rights reserved.

and few exclusively Y-linked traits have been identified. One of the few key genes that has been located on the Y chromosome is SRY, which is responsible for setting into motion the differentiation of the testes during embryonic development. Once the testes are formed, they begin to produce hormones that account for further differentiation of the male reproductive system.

Sex-linked traits that are carried on the X chromosome are more likely to be observed in male offspring than in female offspring, because male children do not have a second X chromosome to offset the effects of an X-linked trait. Hemophilia A, the most common type of hemophilia, is an example of such a sex-linked trait. Individuals with hemophilia lack a specific blood protein that causes their blood to clot after receiving a wound (ADAM, 2004). The allele for hemophilia is a recessive trait carried on the X chromosome; however, it is most likely to affect men (see Figure 5.4). Half (50%) of the male offspring of female carriers have the disease, and 50% of their female offspring are carriers. All female children of a man with hemophilia are carriers of the trait. This disease affects approximately 1 in 5,000 men.

Other genes are expressed exclusively in one sex but are not found on the sex chromosomes per se. For example, the genes for male beard development and female breast development are not located on the sex chromosomes. However, these characteristics will emerge only in the presence of the appropriate hormonal environment, which is directed by the sex chromosomes.

## GENETIC SOURCES OF INDIVIDUAL DIFFERENCES

The study of genetics reveals that individual variability is due to more than the many variations in environment and experience that confront a growing person. Variability is built into the mechanism of heredity. Each adult couple has the potential for producing a great variety of genetically distinct children. Three areas in which genetic determinants contribute to individual variability are *rate of development, individual traits,* and *abnormal development.*

### ■ GENETIC DETERMINANTS OF RATE OF DEVELOPMENT

Genes regulate the rate and sequence of maturation. The concept of an epigenetic plan for growth and development is based on the assumption that a genetically guided system promotes or restricts the growth of cells over the life span. Genetic factors have been found to play a role in behavioral development, including the onset of various levels of reasoning, language, and social orientation.

Evidence of the role of genetics in guiding the rate and sequence of development has been provided by studies of identical twins (who have the same genotype). The rates at which identical twins develop are highly correlated, even when those twins are reared apart. A number of characteristics— including the timing of the acquisition of motor skills, personality development, changes in intellectual capacity among aged twins, and the timing of physical maturation—show a strong genetic influence (Bouchard & Pederson, 1999).

Genes can be viewed as internal regulators that set the pace for maturation. They signal the onset of significant developmental changes throughout life, such as growth spurts, the eruption of teeth, puberty, and menopause. They also appear to set the limits of the life span. A small number of genes influences how many times the cells of a specific organism can divide and replicate (Marx, 1988). Research on three different animal species—fruit flies, worms, and mice—has shown that when the most long-lived of a species are bred, the offspring live longer than average (Barinaga, 1991).

Differences in the rate of development contribute to our understanding of psychosocial growth. Differences in age at crawling or walking, for example, bring children into contact with new aspects of their environments and provide them with changing capacities at different chronological ages. Thus, the genetic processes that regulate readiness for certain kinds of growth and vulnerabilities to particular kinds of stress contribute to systematic differences among individuals. For example, adult expectations for the accomplishment of such specific tasks as toilet training, getting dressed without help, and learning to write interact with the child's developmental level. Disappointment may be conveyed to developmentally "late" children, and pride and approval may be conveyed to developmentally "accelerated" children.

### ■ GENETIC DETERMINANTS OF INDIVIDUAL TRAITS

Genes contain specific information about a wide range of human characteristics, from eye color and height to the ability to taste a particular substance called phenylthiocarbamide (which to tasters is bitter, but to nontasters has no taste at all). Some characteristics are controlled by a single gene. However, most significant characteristics, such as height, weight, blood group, skin color, and intelligence, are guided by the combined action of several genes. When multiple genes are involved in the regulation of a trait, the possibilities for individual differences in that trait increase. Because many characteristics are regulated by multiple genes, the variety of human phenotypes is enormous.

Genetic factors also play a substantial role in individual differences in personality (Borkenau, Riemann, Angleitner, & Spinath, 2001; Loehlin, 1992; Plomin, 1990, 1994). Traits such as *sociability* (a tendency to be outgoing), *inhibition* (a tendency to be cautious and socially shy or withdrawn), and *neuroticism* (a tendency to be anxious and emotionally sensitive) are pervasive dimensions of personality that appear to have strong genetic components. Research on the biological basis of sexual orientation suggests that genes may influence the development of the part of the brain that guides sexual behavior (LeVay, 1991). Identical twins are more likely to have the same sexual orientation than are fraternal twins or adoptive siblings (Bailey & Pillard, 1991, 1994). Even in rather specific areas of personality, such as political attitudes, aesthetic preferences, and sense of humor, identical twins show greater similarity than fraternal twins, even when the identical twins are reared apart from each other.

Extending the analysis of the impact of genetics on individual differences, Sandra Scarr (1992) suggested at least three ways in which genetic factors influence the environment of individuals. First, most children are raised by their parents in environments created by their parents. Thus, children receive both their genes and their home environment from a common genetic source—their parents. As an example, a parent who is temperamentally sociable is more likely than a withdrawn or timid parent to have lots of people at the house, to enjoy the companionship of others, and therefore to expose his or her children to more companionable adults.

Second, people draw out responses from others that are related to their own personality characteristics. Thus, broad, genetically based aspects of one's individuality will affect the kinds of social responses one receives from others, including

**Table 5.1**  Examples of Genetic and Chromosomal Disorders

**GENETIC DISORDERS**

**Autosomal dominant gene**

*Huntington's chorea:* Rapid, jerky, involuntary movements; deterioration of muscle coordination and mental functioning. Symptoms usually do not appear until age 35–50. Caused by genetic defect on chromosome 4.

*Marfan's syndrome:* Elongated fingers; deformed chest and spine; abnormal heart. Tendons, ligaments, and joint capsules are weak.

**Autosomal recessive gene**

*Albinism:* Hair, skin, and eyes lack the pigment melanin. Often accompanied by visual problems and a susceptibility to skin cancer.

*Cystic fibrosis:* Certain glands do not function properly. The glands in the lining of the bronchial tubes produce excessive amounts of thick mucus, which leads to chronic lung infections. Failure of the pancreas to produce enzymes necessary for the breakdown of fats and their absorption from the intestines leads to malnutrition. Sweat glands are also affected. Often fatal by age 30. Caused by missing base pairs on chromosome 7.

*Sickle-cell anemia:* Malformation of red blood cells reduces the amount of oxygen they can carry. Results in fatigue, headaches, shortness of breath on exertion, pallor, jaundice, pain, and damage to kidneys, lungs, intestine, and brain.

*Tay-Sachs disease:* Absence of a certain enzyme results in the buildup of harmful chemicals in the brain. Results in death before age 3.

**X-linked recessive gene**

*Color blindness:* Defect of light-sensitive pigment in one or more classes of cone cells in the retina of the eye and/or an abnormality in or reduced number of cone cells themselves. The two common types are reduced discrimination of light wavelengths within the middle (green) and long (red) parts of the visible spectrum.

*Hemophilia:* Absence of a blood protein (factor VIII) reduces effectiveness of blood clotting. Severity of disorder varies. Bleeding episodes likely to begin in toddlerhood.

**CHROMOSOMAL DISORDERS**

**Autosomal abnormality**

*Down syndrome:* Additional 21st chromosome; also called *trisomy 21*. The excess chromosome results in physical and intellectual abnormalities, including IQ in the range of 30–80; distinctive facial features, heart defects, intestinal problems, hearing defects; susceptibility to repeated ear infections. Tendency to develop narrowing of the arteries in adulthood, with attendant increase in risk of heart disease.

**Sex-chromosome abnormalities**

*Turner's syndrome:* Usually caused by a lack of one X chromosome in a girl; sometimes one of two X chromosomes is defective; occasionally some base pairs are missing on an X chromosome. These abnormalities result in defective sexual development and infertility, short stature, absence or retarded development of secondary sex characteristics, absence of menstruation, narrowing of the aorta, and a degree of mental retardation.

*Klinefelter's syndrome:* One or more extra X chromosomes in a boy. This abnormality results in defective sexual development, including enlarged breasts and small testes, infertility, and often mental retardation.

Source: Based on information provided in Clayman, 1989.

one's parents. Third, as people mature and become increasingly assertive in selecting certain experiences and rejecting others, their own temperaments, talents, intelligence, and level of sociability will guide the kinds of environments they select, strengthening certain genetic predispositions while dampening others.

# GENETIC DETERMINANTS OF ABNORMAL DEVELOPMENT

In addition to characteristics such as physical appearance, temperament, talent, and intellectual capacity, a wide variety of abnormalities, or *anomalies*, have a genetic cause. The most dramatic anomalies result in a spontaneous abortion of the fetus early in the pregnancy. Approximately 15–20% of recognized pregnancies end in first-term spontaneous abortion (Geyman, Oliver, & Sullivan, 1999). The majority of these early-term spontaneous abortions are due to chromosomal

abnormalities in the fertilized **zygotes** (the developing organism formed from the father's sperm and the mother's egg).

Of those infants who survive the neonatal period, an estimated 3–5% of newborns have one or more major recognizable anomalies (Cunningham et al., 2001). The incidence of anomalies increases to 6–7% as some disorders are diagnosed later in childhood. Some birth defects are linked to a specific chromosome or to a single gene. Other birth defects are linked solely to environmental factors, such as drugs, medications, and fetal and maternal infections. Most malformations, however, result from the interaction of genetic vulnerabilities and environmental hazards, or are of unknown origin (Moore, 1993).

Examples of genetic and chromosomal disorders are listed in Table 5.1. The disorders are presented in two broad categories: those associated with specific genes and those associated with chromosomal abnormalities. Within those categories, some disorders are found on 1 of the 22 pairs of

**autosomal** chromosomes (chromosomes other than the sex chromosomes), and others are on one of the sex chromosomes. There are now 1,100 genes for which at least one disease-related mutation or alternate allele has been identified using the map-based approach to gene discovery. However, many diseases are thought to involve multiple genes in some form of interaction. What is more, many diseases that have an identified genetic basis—such as hypertension, schizophrenia, or coronary artery disease—are expressed in certain environments, including the prenatal environment, and not in others (Peltonen & McKusick, 2001).

Certain genetic diseases are linked directly to our ancestry; therefore, their incidence is higher in certain populations than in others (Thompson, McInnes, & Willard, 1991; Emery & Mueller, 1992). For example, Tay-Sachs disease is present in 1 out of 3,900 infants born to Ashkenazi Jews (Jews who settled in Eastern Europe) but only in 1 out of 112,000 other U.S. infants. Thalassemia, a disease involving faulty production of hemoglobin (which carries oxygen in the blood), is found most often in people of Mediterranean, Middle Eastern, and Southeast Asian origins. The variety of genetic abnormalities serves to broaden the range of individual variability. Many of these irregularities pose a challenge both to the adaptive capacities of the affected person and to the caregiving capacities of the adults involved.

## GENETIC TECHNOLOGY AND PSYCHOSOCIAL EVOLUTION

Psychosocial evolution has typically been differentiated from biological evolution in that change is accomplished by social mechanisms rather than incorporated in the genetic structure. As a result of scientific knowledge, however, we are entering an era when it is possible to intervene to influence the genotype. One such intervention is **genetic counseling**. Individuals and couples with a family history of a genetic disease—or who for some other reason worry about the possibility of transmitting a genetic disease to their children—can have a blood test to identify genes that may result in the inherited disorder. The locations of the genes that account for such abnormalities as Tay-Sachs disease, sickle-cell anemia, Duchenne muscular dystrophy, and cystic fibrosis have been identified. Couples who have reason to believe that they may carry genes for one of these diseases can be advised about the probability of having children who may be afflicted (Somerson, 1997; Horowitz, Sundin, Zanko, & Lauer, 2001). If significant numbers of the carriers of genetic diseases decided not to reproduce, the incidence of these diseases in the population would decline over time. Thus, a psychosocial intervention would modify the gene pool.

### ETHICAL CONSIDERATIONS

Gene transfer; the patenting of new life forms created through genetic engineering; genetic fingerprinting, which is used to help identify criminal suspects; and, most recently, cloning

*Successful mapping of the human genome promises to expand our understanding of the genetic basis of human behavior and disease.*

© Roger Tully/Getty Images

from an adult mammal are some of the topics that are raising new ethical concerns. There is a general consensus that the use of gene therapy to treat serious diseases such as cystic fibrosis or cancer is ethical. There is less agreement about the use of intervention to alter the genetic code at the level of the zygote or to attempt to introduce genes intended to enhance aspects of normal development in humans. Even the advances in identifying genetic markers for specific diseases can lead to ethical dilemmas. Individuals are turning down the opportunity to be tested for possible genetic diseases for fear that they will be denied health insurance, life insurance, or employment (Beardsley, 1996).

The possibility of reproducing genetically identical clones from human tissue has stirred the conscience of the religious, political, and medical communities. Is it ethical to clone human genes so that great scholars, scientists, and artists can walk the Earth again? Should cloning become an approved technology for coping with infertility? Recently, the debate has extended to include human stem cell research. Through a procedure called **nuclear transplantation**, the nucleus of an egg cell, which contains its DNA, is removed and replaced with the DNA from an adult cell. If this egg, with its new

DNA, undergoes cell division and survives for several days, it produces embryonic stem cells. These cells have the potential to develop into any type of organ in the body. Thus, they can be injected in a person with a debilitating disease to replace dead or infected tissues. Because the DNA comes from the person's own healthy cells, there is less risk that the body will reject these stem cells.

This same procedure, nuclear transplantation, can be used for reproductive cloning. Once the donor DNA is injected into an egg cell and the cell begins to divide, it can be implanted into a uterus. If the implant survives, it would develop into a fetus with the same DNA as the donor. Although there is strong public opposition to the cloning of humans, there is growing support for stem cell research. Laws banning scientific research into human nuclear transplantation have been debated in Congress, thereby moving the dialogue beyond the scientific and medical merit and safety of these procedures and into the world of politics and public opinion (American Association for the Advancement of Science, 2003; Jaenisch & Wilmut, 2001).

## EVALUATING THE CONTRIBUTION OF GENETIC FACTORS TO BEHAVIOR

Accomplishments in mapping the human genome still leave us with critical questions about how genes and the environment interact to influence behavior. Genes cannot be expressed without an appropriate environment, including the biological environment at the cellular level and the physical and social environments at the larger systems level. For example, a human being needs to breathe oxygen. If an infant is deprived of oxygen in the prenatal period or during the birth process, his or her genetic potential for intelligence will not be observed in behavior. What is more, individuals and their environments are in a state of dynamic interaction and change, each modifying the other (Rose, 2001).

### GENETICS AND INTELLIGENCE

One area that has received considerable attention is the relative contributions of genetic and environmental factors to intelligence. To what extent is a person's intelligence "set" by hereditary factors? To what extent is it a product of experience? Intelligent behavior requires the successful integration of both (Plomin, 1990). It relies on the structure of the central nervous system and the sense receptors, which are products of genetically guided information. However, the healthy functioning of these systems requires adequate nutrition, rest, and freedom from disease—conditions that vary with the environment. Intelligent behavior builds on experiences with diverse stimuli, social interactions, and schooling—all elements of the physical and social environment.

The influence of genetic factors on intelligence may be observed in two ways. First, specific genetic irregularities can

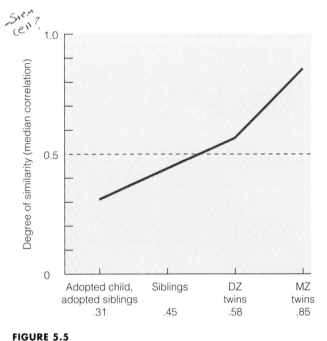

**FIGURE 5.5**

Similarity in Intelligence Among Siblings at Four Levels of Relationship

Source: From "Familial Studies of Intelligence: A Review," by T. J. Bouchard and M. McGue, 1981, *Science, 212*, 1055–1059. Copyright © 1981 AAAS. Reprinted by permission.

cause degrees of mental retardation. Two examples are Down syndrome and Turner's syndrome (see Table 5.1 for descriptions). These and many other genetic diseases play an indisputable role in restricting intellectual potential.

A second approach to understanding the influence of genetics on intelligence is through the study of family relationships. Family members may be related closely or distantly. The closer the relatives, the more similar their genetic makeup. If intelligence is influenced by genetics, close relatives should be more similar in intelligence than distant relatives.

Figure 5.5 shows the degree of similarity found in more than 100 studies of intelligence in siblings at four different degrees of relationship. Similarity in intelligence increases with the degree of genetic relatedness. The high similarity in intelligence of identical, monozygotic (MZ) twins gives striking evidence of the contribution of genetics to intelligence. Fraternal, dizygotic (DZ) twins who share the same prenatal, home, and childrearing environments show much less similarity than do MZ twins and not much more than "ordinary" siblings. An overview of studies that have attempted to evaluate the contribution of genetic factors to cognitive ability suggests that genetics accounts for 50% of the variance, shared environmental factors account for 33% of the variance, unshared environmental factors account for 17% of the variance, and measurement error accounts for 10% of the variance in intelligence (Gottesman, 1997). Thus, the evidence supports the significant role of both genetic and environmental factors in shaping the capacity for complex thinking and cognitive performance.

**FIGURE 5.6**

Hypothetical Reaction Range
of Intelligence for Three Genotypes

Source: Adapted from "Genetic Aspects of Intelligent Behavior," by I. Gottesman, in N. Ellis (Ed.), *Handbook of Mental Deficiency*, p. 255. Copyright © 1963 McGraw-Hill. Reprinted by permission.

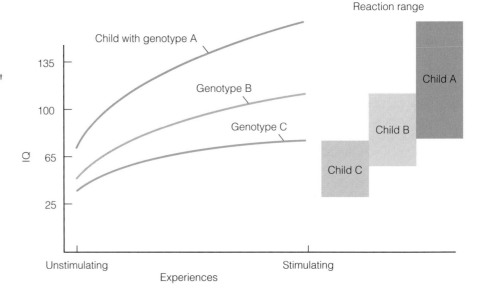

## ■ THE REACTION RANGE

One way to conceptualize the influence of genetics on behavior is to view the genotype as establishing a **reaction range**— that is, a range of possible responses to environmental conditions, the limits of which are determined by one's genotype. Under similar environmental conditions, genetic differences are most likely to be expressed; however, when environmental conditions vary, the advantages of one genotype over another may be masked by the adversities or opportunities of the environment. Figure 5.6 shows the hypothetical reaction ranges of three children with respect to intelligence. Child A has greater genetic potential for intelligence than Child B, who has greater potential than Child C. When all three children are in nonstimulating environments, their IQs develop at the lower end of their potential range. When all three children are in stimulating environments, their IQs develop to-

ward the upper end of their potential range. If the three children are in different environments, their differences in genetic potential may be masked by the way the environments act on this potential. If Child B and Child C are in stimulating environments and Child A is in an nonstimulating environment, Child B may have the highest measured IQ, and the IQs of Children C and A may be lower and very similar. Each child's intellectual ability can be expressed as a range that is a product of the interaction of genetic potential and environment.

The concept of the reaction range can be seen clearly in the outlook for children with Down syndrome (Cody & Kamphaus, 1999; Laws, Byrne, & Buckley, 2000). This condition, which occurs in 1 of every 700 live births, is the most common genetic cause of mental retardation in the United States. In the early part of the 20th century, children born with Down syndrome had a life expectancy of 9 years. Today, the

*Even though children with Down syndrome have mild to moderate disabilities, they also have many talents and abilities. They benefit enormously from early intervention services, including physical, speech, and developmental therapies. Children with Down syndrome enjoy and benefit from social interactions with their typically developing peers.*

life expectancy of a child with Down syndrome is 30 years, and 25% of individuals with Down syndrome live to age 50. Medical care, early and constant educational intervention, physical therapy, and a nurturing home environment have significant positive results for children with Down syndrome. Participation in a mainstreamed classroom environment has been shown to have significant benefits for these children's vocabulary, grammar, and certain memory skills. Under optimal conditions, individuals with Down syndrome are able to achieve a moderate degree of independence and to participate actively in the life of their schools, communities, and families.

# Normal fetal development

Genetic information guides the production of proteins, the formation of body structures, and their interrelated functions. The following description takes us from the cellular level of fertilization to the elaboration of physical and sensory capacities over the three trimesters of pregnancy.

## FERTILIZATION

One normal ejaculation contains several hundred million sperm. This large number is necessary to ensure fertilization, because most sperm die on the way through the vagina and the uterus. Each microscopic sperm is composed of a pointed head and a tail. The head contains the genetic material necessary for reproduction. The tail moves like a whip as the sperm swims through the cervix and uterus and into the fallopian tubes. Swimming at the rate of 1 inch every 8 minutes, sperm may reach the egg in as little as 30 minutes, but the journey usually takes about 6 hours; sperm can stay alive in the uterus for up to 5 days.

In contrast to a man, who produces billions of sperm in a lifetime, a woman ordinarily releases just one ovum, or egg, each month, midway through the menstrual cycle. In a lifetime of approximately 40 fertile years, during which she can be expected to have two children, the average woman releases approximately 450 eggs. Each woman is born with her complete supply of eggs.

Like the sperm, the ovum is a single cell that contains genetic material. In comparison with body cells, the ovum is quite large (0.12 millimeters), about the size of the period at the end of this sentence. When the ovum is mature, it is encased in a sac of fluid and floats to the surface of the ovary. The sac ruptures and releases the ovum into one of the two fallopian tubes. Millions of feathery, hair-like structures in the fallopian tube sweep around the ovum and gently move it toward the uterus.

Only one sperm can enter the egg. As the first sperm passes through the egg's cell membrane, a rapid change in the membrane's chemistry effectively locks out other sperm. If the ovum is not fertilized within the first 24 hours of its maturity, it begins to disintegrate and is shed along with the lining of the uterus in the next menstrual period.

Once inside the egg cell, the sperm loses its tail, and the head becomes a normal cell nucleus. The egg cell also goes through a final change in preparation for fertilization. The gametes (egg and sperm cells) contain only one of each chromosome, rather than the full set of 23 pairs. When the cell nuclei of the sperm and the ovum meet in the egg cytoplasm, their separate chromosomal material is integrated into a single set of 23 pairs of chromosomes. At this moment, all the information necessary to activate growth is contained in a single cell.

## ■ TWINS

The cell produced when the sperm has fertilized the egg is referred to as a **zygote**. The zygote travels down the fallopian tube and divides as it travels toward the uterus without growing larger. After about a week, this mass of cells implants in the uterus. Occasionally, this growing mass of cells divides in two and separates, forming two individuals with the same

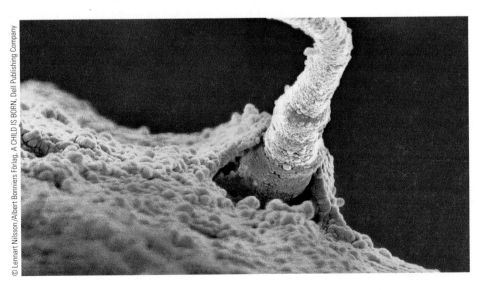

*When the sperm breaks through the lining of the egg, a biochemical reaction takes place that prevents other sperm from entering the cell.*

© Lennart Nilsson/Albert Bonniers Förlag, A CHILD IS BORN, Dell Publishing Company

*Identical twins have the same geno-type; fraternal twins are no more alike genetically than other siblings. However, both kinds of twins share the same prenatal environment.*

© Syracuse Newspapers/Lisa Kratz/The Image Works

chromosomal composition. These individuals are referred to as **monozygotic** (MZ) twins, because they come from a single zygote. They are always of the same sex, and they are strikingly similar in physical appearance, a characteristic leading to the alternative term **identical twins**.

**Fraternal twins** occur as a result of multiple ovulations in the same cycle. Each egg develops separately in the ovary, is shed and fertilized individually, and develops separately in the uterus. The result is **dizygotic** (DZ) twins—that is, two-egg twins. Actually, these twins are litter mates and may be of different sexes. Genetically, they bear no more resemblance to one another than other children of the same parents. However, they share the same prenatal environment and a more common parenting environment than do most siblings who are born one or more years apart. Approximately 33 in 1,000 live births are multiple births, most of them twins. The ratio of multiple births is notably higher among mothers over age 30, possibly because older mothers are more likely to be using some type of fertility therapy (Martin et al., 2003).

## ■ INFERTILITY AND ALTERNATIVE MEANS OF REPRODUCTION

**Infertility**, or the inability to conceive, can result from problems in the reproductive system of the man, the woman, or both. The risk of infertility increases with age and is associated with exposure to toxins, including cigarette smoke, pesticides, chemical solvents, and fumes from anesthesia (Sinclair & Pressinger, 2001). Research on the emotional impact of infertility suggests that it is a major source of stress. The discovery of infertility may force a couple to reassess the meaning and purpose of their marriage. It may raise doubts in the couple about their self-worth; it often disrupts their sat-

isfaction with their sexual relationship; and it often isolates them because of the difficulty of discussing this personal family problem with others (Haynes & Miller, 2003).

> I have been trying to conceive for two years. Each month, at ovulation, I am so sure this will be "the month." And then, like clockwork, my period comes and I spend at least a day feeling depressed. Sex has even become a chore for both me and my partner. This whole infertility roller-coaster is definitely hurting our relationship and sex life. Well-meaning friends tell me it will happen when the time is right, but I don't know how to help our relationship in the meantime. (Peterson, 2001)

When couples perceive similar levels of distress and are able to communicate with each other about it, they report higher levels of marital satisfaction (Peterson, Newton, & Rosen, 2003). However, it is not uncommon for husbands and wives to have different reactions to infertility and different levels of distress about it, which results in more strained marital relationships. The stressors associated with infertility may go on over a long period. Some couples undergo treatments for years before conceiving or giving up on their hopes for a biologically related child (Savitz-Smith, 2003).

In addition to the emotional costs of treatment, there are tremendous financial costs, ranging from $10,000 to $100,000, most of which is not covered by insurance. What is more, many procedures are unsuccessful. During one year of unprotected sexual relations, 90% of healthy couples achieve pregnancy. Data from 384 U.S. clinics reporting to the National Center for Chronic Disease Prevention and Health Promotion in 2001 are presented in the Box on Reproductive Technologies. For women under age 30, about 40% of artificially assisted cycles resulted in pregnancy, and 35% resulted in live births, including multiple births. At older ages, the percentages decline. Only 23% of cycles involving women over the age of 40 resulted in pregnancy, and 16% resulted in live births (Centers for Disease Control and Prevention, 2003). Over time, the impact of infertility becomes increasingly stressful, leading to high levels of depression as various alternatives are tried and fail (Domar et al., 2000). For more information about infertility and reproductive technologies, you may want to visit the International Council on Infertility Information Dissemination Web site at www.inciid.org.

**ETHICAL CONSIDERATIONS.** Assisted reproductive technologies (ARTs) have raised legal and ethical questions (Elmer-Dewitt, 1991; Lemonick, 1997). The husband of a woman who is planning to be artificially inseminated must consent to the procedure and agree to assume legal guardianship of the offspring. The lack of official guidelines for screening donors raises the issue of who should be responsible if a child resulting from artificial insemination has a severe genetic anomaly. Another concern being raised is what the sperm donor's rights are to a relationship with his offspring. In 1983, a California man was granted weekly visitation rights to a child who had been conceived with his sperm.

In the widely publicized case of Baby M., William and Elizabeth Stern paid Mary Beth Whitehead $10,000 to be a surrogate mother. Baby M. was conceived with Ms. Whitehead's egg and Mr. Stern's sperm. After the birth, Ms. Whitehead decided that she wanted to keep the baby. In ensuing court battles, the New Jersey Supreme Court decided that the contract between the couple and Ms. Whitehead was void and that it was illegal to pay a woman to bear a child for someone else. Nonetheless, the court granted custody of the child to the Sterns, arguing that they could provide the child with a more stable home environment. The court rejected the right of Elizabeth Stern to adopt the baby and supported Ms. Whitehead's right of continued visitation as the genetic and gestational mother (Lacayo, 1988; Silverman, 1989).

To avoid the problems in the Stern/Whitehead case, John and Luanne Buzzanca paid Pamela Snell to be a surrogate mother for a baby conceived through in vitro fertilization from anonymous donors. Before the baby was born, John divorced Luanne. When Luanne later filed for child support, the judge ruled that John was in no legal sense the father and that Luanne was not the legal mother although she is raising Baby J. (Foote, 1998).

As a result of fertility intervention, a 63-year-old postmenopausal woman gave birth. She is reported to be the oldest birth mother on record (Kalb, 1997). Ethical considerations have been raised about the use of medical technology to keep the birth window open at this advanced age. Concerns focus on the medical complications associated with pregnancy in older women and on whether older men and women can sustain effective parenting as their children move into adolescence while they enter later adulthood.

Finally, questions are raised about the limits that should be placed on the production and use of embryos in vitro.

Should we permit scientists to produce embryos from frozen sperm and egg cells for purposes other than implantation? Thousands of frozen embryos are held in various medical and laboratory facilities in the United States. Research on embryos is important for further understanding of the expression of genetic diseases, for understanding the factors associated with miscarriages, and for improving reproductive technologies. Different countries and states within the United States differ in their laws governing the use, preservation, and ownership of embryos produced through ART. Ethical and legal questions are being raised about the rights of parents to determine the fate of these embryos, the embryos' rights to protection and inheritance, and the responsibility of institutes and laboratories to ensure the proper use of the embryos.

On an encouraging note, longitudinal studies have reported the positive quality of parenting and positive developmental outcomes for children conceived through artificial insemination and in vitro fertilization (Golombok, Cook, Bish, & Murray, 1995; Golombok, MacCallum, & Goodman, 2001). Families with children conceived through alternative reproductive technologies were compared with families with naturally conceived and adopted children. In general, parents of children conceived through both types of assisted reproduction showed more warmth and involvement with their children, higher levels of interaction, and lower levels of stress than the parents of children who were conceived naturally. Parents of adopted children typically scored in between the levels of the other two groups. For families who remained in the study through their child's adolescence, there were no significant differences among the groups of children with respect to social and emotional development. Other research has supported the positive developmental trajectory for mother–infant relationships for infants conceived through in vitro fertilization (Gibson, Ungerer, McMahon, Leslie, & Saunders, 2000).

## DEVELOPMENT IN THE FIRST TRIMESTER

The period of pregnancy—typically 40 weeks after the last menstrual period, or 38 weeks from ovulation—is often conceptualized in three 3-month periods called *trimesters*. Perhaps because development is so rapid and dramatic during the first trimester, it is divided further into the *germinal period*, the *embryonic period*, and the *fetal period*. Each trimester brings changes in the status of the developing fetus and its supporting systems. These changes are summarized briefly in Table 5.2 (Moore & Persuad, 1998). You can visit http://www.w-cpc.org/fetal.html to watch a brief animated film of the process of fetal development. The pregnant woman also experiences changes during the trimesters. In the first trimester, many women are not certain that they are pregnant. By the last trimester, though, the woman is usually certain, and so is everyone else!

TECHNOLOGY AND HUMAN DEVELOPMENT

# Reproductive Technologies

ROUGHLY 2.3 MILLION couples seek help for infertility in the United States each year (Begley, 1995). Problems of infertility increased 25% from 1988 to 1995, stimulating new and expanding research into reproductive technologies (Lemonick, 1997). Some remarkable alternatives have been developed for couples who are unable to conceive. With each of these procedures comes new challenges in how to conceptualize men's and women's reproductive functions and their implications for family formation.

Much of the data about reproductive technology focuses on strategies for artificially fertilizing ova and transferring them to the uterus for the prenatal period. Figure 5.7 shows the results of assisted reproductive technology (ART) cycles in 2001 that used fresh (as opposed to frozen) nondonor eggs or embryos. This means that the egg was harvested from the woman who was trying to become pregnant, fertilized, and then, if the fertilization was successful, transferred to the uterus.

The number of ART cycles increased by 66% from 1996 to 2001, and the number of live babies born who were conceived using ART increased by 94%. These figures indicate improved techniques for supporting pregnancies following conception through ART (Centers for Disease Control and Prevention, 2003). Many websites are available for advice, exchange of information, and encouragement to individuals who are using or thinking about using these new technologies. The following list describes reproductive technologies in use today.

## ARTIFICIAL INSEMINATION

This is an old form of reproductive technology that is commonly used in animal husbandry and more recently has been applied to human fertilization. Sperm that have been donated and frozen are injected into a woman at the time of her ovulation. The most successful approach is to inject the sperm directly into the uterus (IUI, *intrauterine insemination*), thus bypassing the potentially destructive cervical environment.

Typically, the male partner is the source of the sperm; however, this is not necessary. Some sperm banks keep the donors' characteristics on file, which enables the woman to select the sperm of a donor whose features she desires in her offspring. Other banks blend sperm, so that the recipient cannot trace the donor's identity. In one recent case, a woman froze her husband's sperm and was able to conceive his child using artificial insemination after his death. Success rate: 15–20% per cycle using IUI (Peris, 2000).

## FERTILITY DRUGS

The administration of fertility drugs usually results in the release of multiple eggs at a cycle, increasing the chances that one egg will be fertilized. In about 20% of cases, multiple births result. The birth of the McCaughey septuplets in 1997 was a result of the use of the fertility drug Metrodin. Most other assisted reproductive technologies begin with this step (i.e., using some form of medication to stimulate the ovaries to produce eggs). If this is successful, decisions must be made about how many eggs to fertilize and how many embryos to transfer to the uterus.

## IN VITRO FERTILIZATION (FERTILIZATION IN AN ARTIFICIAL ENVIRONMENT)

Eggs are removed from the ovary and placed in a petri dish inside an incubator. Then a few drops of sperm are added to the dish. If the eggs are fertilized and the cells begin to divide, they are implanted in the uterus for subsequent development. Typically, two or three embryos are transferred at once in hopes that at least one will implant and mature. Success rate for women under age 35 ranges from 37% per cycle with nondonor eggs to 42% with donor eggs.

## INTRACYTOPLASMIC SPERM INJECTION

A modification of in vitro fertilization in which a sperm is injected directly into

---

## ■ THE GERMINAL PERIOD

After fertilization, the egg begins to divide. At this time, the cell material is referred to as a **zygote** until implantation. The first series of cell divisions does not increase the mass of the cells, nor do the cells take on specialized functions; rather, the cell material is redistributed among several parts. When implantation is successful, by the sixth day after fertilization, the egg makes contact with the lining of the uterus and begins to attach itself there. At this point, the cells are referred to as an **embryo**. Sometimes, the egg does not reach the uterus but attaches itself to the fallopian tube or even to some area of the intestine. The embryo may grow in these locations until the organ ruptures.

## ■ THE EMBRYONIC PERIOD

The 3 weeks following implantation are devoted primarily to elaboration of the supportive elements that will house the embryo. An **amniotic sac** surrounds the embryo and fills with a clear, watery fluid. This fluid acts as a cushion that buffers the embryo and permits it to move about and change position.

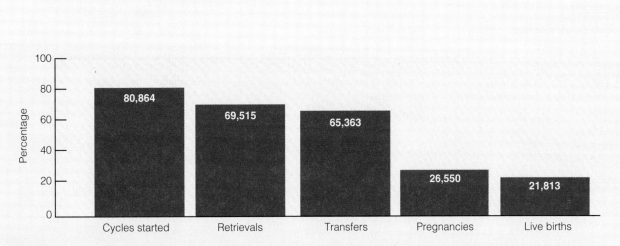

**FIGURE 5.7**

Outcome of Assisted Reproductive Technology Cycles Using Fresh, Nondonor Eggs or Embryos, by Stage: 2001

the egg. This procedure is used when there is a very low sperm count or non-motile sperm. Embryos produced by in vitro fertilization can be frozen for future use if the initial pregnancy does not go full term. Success rate: 50%.

**GAMETE INTRAFALLOPIAN TRANSFER (GIFT)**

Eggs and sperm are transferred into a woman's fallopian tubes. Fertilization takes place as it normally would, within the woman's reproductive system. These eggs and sperm may come from the couple or from other donors. Thus,

the fetus may be genetically related to the man or the woman in the couple or to neither. Success rate: 28%.

**IN VIVO FERTILIZATION (FERTILIZATION IN A LIVING BODY)**

Partners involve another woman in the conception. The second woman, who has demonstrated her fertility, is artificially inseminated with the man's sperm. Once an embryo has formed, it is transferred to the first woman's uterus, which becomes the gestational environment. The child is therefore genetically related to the man but not to the woman.

**SURROGATE MOTHER**

Typically, sperm from an infertile woman's husband are injected into the surrogate mother during the time of her monthly ovulation. The surrogate mother bears the child and returns it to the couple at birth. In one remarkable case, a woman agreed to be the surrogate mother for her own daughter who wanted a child but was born without a uterus. At age 42, this mother gave birth to twin grandchildren (Elmer-Dewitt, 1991).

Once the embryo is firmly implanted in the uterus, special cells in the placenta produce a hormone that maintains the uterine lining. This hormone is excreted through the kidneys, so a urine sample can be evaluated to determine its presence. Home pregnancy tests are based on the detection of this hormone in a small drop of urine, and are accurate 1 or 2 days after implantation. A large number of pregnancies are spontaneously aborted in these early weeks, usually as a result of some major abnormalities of the embryo (Winston & Handyside, 1993).

The **placenta** is an organ that is newly formed with each

pregnancy and is expelled at birth. Nutrients necessary for the embryo's growth pass through the placenta, as does the embryo's waste, which then passes into the mother's blood. Thus, the placenta is an exchange station at which adult material is synthesized for the embryo's use and foreign materials harmful to the embryo's development can be screened out. However, this screening is imperfect. Even though the mother's blood and the embryo's blood are separated by independent systems, the placenta permits the two systems to come close enough that oxygen and nutrients from the mother's blood can enter the fetal system and waste products from the

**Table 5.2** Major Developments in Fetal Growth During the Three Trimesters

| FIRST TRIMESTER | SECOND TRIMESTER | THIRD TRIMESTER |
|---|---|---|
| Fertilization | Sucking and swallowing | Nervous system matures |
| Growth of the amniotic sac | Preference for sweet taste | Coordination of sucking and swallowing |
| Growth of the placenta | Skin ridges on fingers and toes | Mechanisms for regulating body temperature |
| Emergence of body parts | Hair on scalp, eyebrows, back, arms, legs | More efficient digestion and excretion |
| Differentiation of sex organs | Sensitivity to touch, taste, light | Degeneration of the placenta toward the end of the ninth month |
| Initial formation of central nervous system | Sucks thumb | |
| Movement | 6-month average size: 10 inches, 2 pounds | 9-month average size: 20 inches, 7 to 7½ pounds |
| Grasp reflex | | |
| Babinski reflex | | |
| Heartbeat | | |
| 3-month average size: 3 inches, about ⅖ ounce | | |

fetal system can be removed. In the process, certain substances in the mother's system may affect the fetal system.

Agents that can produce malformations in the fetus while the tissues and organs are forming are referred to as **teratogens**. Teratogens have a wide variety of forms, such as viruses; medicines, alcohol, and other drugs that a pregnant woman takes; and environmental toxins. During the first trimester—especially weeks 3 through 9—the embryo is particularly sensitive to the disruptive influences of teratogens (see Figure 5.8).

In the third and fourth weeks, the embryo's cells differentiate rapidly, taking on the specialized structures that will permit them to carry out their unique functions in the body. Similar cells are grouped into tissues that gradually emerge as body organs. The first essential changes include the establishment of the body form as an elongated cylinder and the formation of the precursors of the brain and the heart. The neural tube, which is the structural basis of the central nervous system, begins to take shape at the end of the third week after conception. Cells in the neural tube are produced at the miraculous rate of 250,000 a minute over the first 5 weeks, as the tube is differentiated into five bulges that are the forerunners of the major subdivisions of the brain. The central nervous system begins to develop early in the prenatal period and continues to develop throughout childhood and adolescence. Most of the neurons that will make up the cerebral cortex are produced by the end of the second trimester. By birth, the infant's brain contains roughly 100 billion neurons, ready to be linked and organized into networks as the infant responds to environmental stimulation and patterned experience (Nash, 1997; Aoki & Siekevitz, 1988). By the end of the fourth week, the head, the upper trunk, and the lower trunk are visible, as are the limb buds and the forerunners of the forebrain, midbrain, hindbrain, eyes, and ears. The embryo has increased 50 times in length and 40,000 times in weight since the moment of fertilization.

By the end of the second month, the embryo looks quite human. It weighs about 2.25 grams and is about 28 millimeters (1 inch) long. Almost all the internal organs are formed, as are the external features of the face, limbs, fingers, and toes. At 8 weeks, the embryo will respond to mild stimulation. The embryonic period ends about 10 weeks after the last menstrual period—most of the essential structures are formed by this time. The term **fetus** is used from this point until birth.

## ■ THE FETAL PERIOD

In the third month, the fetus grows to 3 inches, and its weight increases to 14 grams. The head is about one third of the total body length. During this month, the fetus assumes the

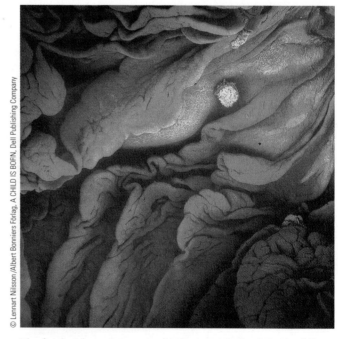

The fertilized egg begins to divide as it travels along the fallopian tube toward the uterus.

© Lennart Nilsson/Albert Bonniers Förlag, A CHILD IS BORN, Dell Publishing Company

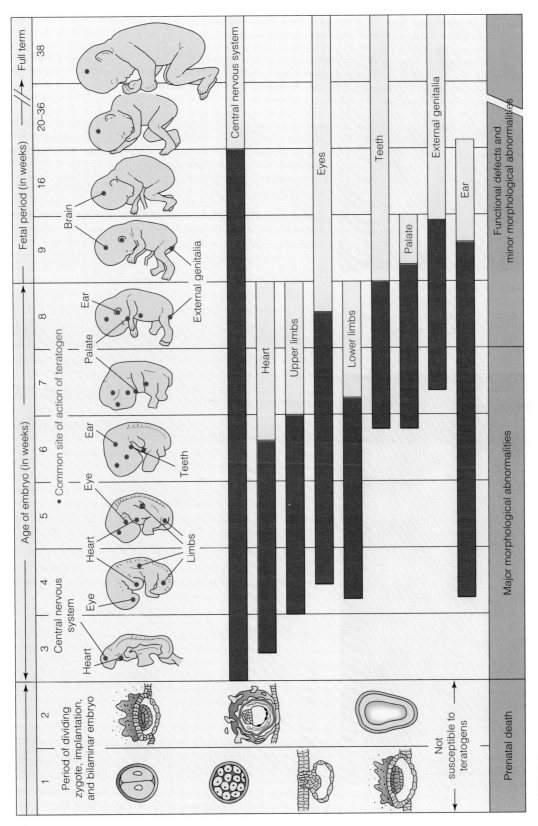

**FIGURE 5.8**

Critical Periods in Prenatal Development. During the first 2 weeks of development, the embryo is usually not susceptible to teratogens. During these predifferentiation stages, a substance either damages all or most of the cells of the embryo, resulting in its death, or damages only a few cells, allowing the embryo to recover without developing defects. Dark bars denote highly sensitive periods for particular organs or organ systems; light bars indicate stages that are less sensitive to teratogens. Severe mental retardation may result from the exposure of the embryo or fetus to teratogenic agents, such as high levels of radiation, from the 8th to the 16th week.

Source: From *The Developing Human: Clinically Oriented Embryology*, 4th ed., by K. L. Moore. Copyright © 1993 by W. B. Saunders. Reprinted by permission.

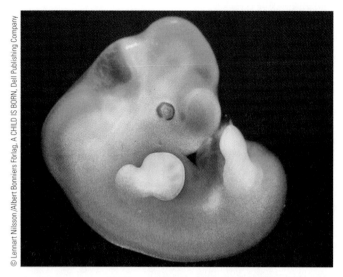

*At 5½ weeks, cell differentiation has resulted in an embryo that is about 0.4 inch (1 cm) long. Emerging shapes of the head, arm, and fingers are visible. Many women are not even sure about their pregnancy at this point in fetal development.*

*At 8 weeks, the fingers are clearly differentiated and the hand is distinct from the forearm. Reflexes sometimes guide the hand toward the face. The fetus is encased in the amniotic sac.*

*fetal position*, arms curled up toward the face and knees bent in to the stomach. The eyelids are fused.

A dramatic change takes place in the sex organs during this period. All embryos go through a bisexual stage, during which no sex-linked characteristics can be discerned. Both female and male embryos have a surface mass that becomes the testes in male fetuses and eventually deteriorates in female

fetuses, when new sex cells grow to form the ovaries. Both male and female embryos have two sets of sex ducts. In male fetuses, the sperm ducts develop and the female ducts dissolve. In female fetuses, the fallopian tubes, the uterus, and the vagina develop, and the other ducts degenerate. Finally, both male and female embryos have a conical area that is the outlet for the bladder duct. When the male testes develop, this area forms into the penis and scrotum. In female fetuses, it remains to form the clitoris, which is surrounded by the genital swellings of the labia majora.

Differentiation of the male and female genitalia is guided by genetic information. In the presence of the "maleness" gene, SRY, the undifferentiated embryonic tissue is transformed into the testes. The testes then produce hormones that facilitate the further elaboration of male genitalia and internal reproductive structures. Genes carried on the X chromosome are thought to guide the formation of the ovaries (Crooks & Bauer, 1996).

The genetic factors that produce the differentiation of the fetus as male or female appear to influence more than the formation of the reproductive organs and the production of hormones. Research on the organization and structure of the brain suggests that during fetal and early postnatal development, sex hormones direct male and female brains along slightly different paths. Three areas of the brain—the hypothalamus, amygdala, and hippocampus—have been studied as potential sites for sex differences in structure that may relate to some of the functional areas in which men's and women's problem-solving and cognitive skills differ (Kimura, 1992).

The 3-month-old fetus moves spontaneously and has both a grasp reflex and a Babinski reflex, in which the toes extend and fan out in response to a mild stroke on the sole of the foot. When an amplified stethoscope, called a Doppler, is placed on the mother's abdomen, the fetal heartbeat can be heard through the uterine wall by the expectant parents as well as the physician and nurse. For expectant parents, listening to the fetal heartbeat is one of the first experiences that transforms the fetus from something abstract and remote to a concrete, vital reality.

## DEVELOPMENT IN THE SECOND TRIMESTER

During the second trimester, the average fetus grows to 10 inches and increases in weight to almost 2 pounds. The fetus continues to grow at the rate of about an inch every 10 days from the fifth month until the end of the pregnancy. During this trimester, the uterus itself begins to stretch and grow. It rises into the mother's abdominal cavity and expands until, by the end of the ninth month, it is pushing against the ribs and diaphragm. The reality of a growing life becomes more evident to the pregnant woman during this trimester as she observes the changes in her body and experiences the early fetal movements, called **quickening**. These movements first feel like light bubbles or twitches; later, they can be identified as the foot, elbow, or fist of the restless resident.

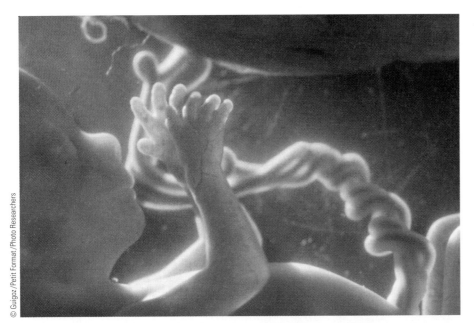

*At 16 weeks, the fetus is about 6.4 inches (16 cm) long and is clearly recognizable as a human child. The fetus has assumed what is known as the "fetal position"—arms curled up near the head and legs bent in toward the stomach—a position that remains part of the human behavioral repertoire throughout life.*

© Guigoz/Petit Format/Photo Researchers

During the fourth month, the fetus begins to suck and swallow. Whenever the fetus opens its mouth, amniotic fluid enters and cycles through the system. This fluid provides some nutrients in addition to those absorbed through the placenta. The 4-month-old fetus shows some preference for a sweet taste: If sugar is introduced into the amniotic fluid, it will swallow the fluid at a faster rate.

In the fifth month, the skin begins to thicken, and a cheesy coating of dead cells and oil, the *vernix caseosa*, covers the skin. The individuality of the fetus is marked by the pattern of skin ridges on the fingers and toes. Hair covers the scalp, eyebrows, back, arms, and legs.

The sensory receptors of the fetus are well established by the end of the sixth month. The fetus is sensitive to touch and may react to it with a muscle movement. It will also stick out its tongue in response to a bitter taste. Throughout the sixth month, the nostrils are plugged by skin cells. When these cells dissolve, the nose fills with amniotic fluid; thus, the sense of smell is probably not functional until birth.

The external ear canal is filled with fluid, and the fetus

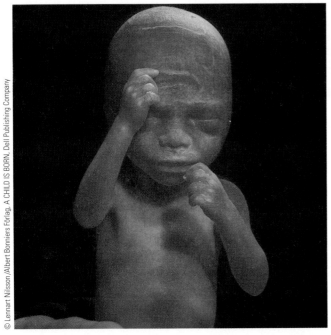

© Lennart Nilsson/Albert Bonniers Förlag, A CHILD IS BORN, Dell Publishing Company

*At 23 weeks, the fetus is about 12 inches (30 cm) long, still small enough to have room to swim about in the expanding uterus. As any pregnant woman will tell you, the fetus is active at this stage, kicking, grasping, waving its arms, and turning over.*

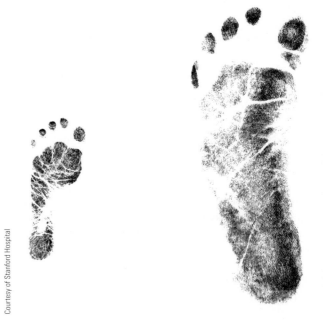

Courtesy of Stanford Hospital

*These are the birth footprints of a baby born prematurely at 23 weeks, and one born at a full 40-week gestational age.*

## Looking in on the Fetus

MOST EXPECTANT PARENTS worry about whether their baby is developing normally. Today, many of these worries can be minimized through technologies that allow the evaluation of fetal development during the early months of pregnancy. Several of these techniques are associated with some risk and should not be used without ample justification. However, especially in high-risk pregnancies, monitoring fetal development may lead to interventions that will save lives if problems do exist and that will reduce the stress associated with unfounded worry. Four monitoring strategies are described here (Cunningham et al., 2001).

### ELECTRONIC FETAL HEART RATE MONITORING

Rather than listen to the fetal heart rate periodically by stethoscope, birth attendants can monitor it continuously with electronic equipment that is painlessly attached to the pregnant woman's abdomen. This technique is especially useful in detecting any disruption in the fetal oxygen supply during labor.

### ULTRASOUND

Based on submarine sonar technology from World War II, ultrasound uses re-

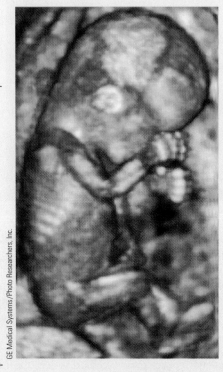

GE Medical Systems/Photo Researchers, Inc.

flected sound waves to produce a visual image of the fetus. Ultrasound can be used to date the pregnancy more precisely, to diagnose multiple pregnancies, and to detect fetal malformations. Re-

cent advances in ultrasound technology provide new, detailed three-dimensional images of fetal development. The website at Amazingpregnancy.com offers week by week 3-D images of fetal growth, including images of twins and triplets.

### AMNIOCENTESIS

In this procedure, about 20 cubic centimeters of amniotic fluid are withdrawn from the uterus. This procedure is sometimes performed in the 16th week of pregnancy to evaluate fetal cells for chromosomal defects or enzyme disorders. Later in pregnancy, fetal cells can be evaluated for the maturation of the lungs. Thus, serious respiratory disorders can be prevented by delaying cesarean deliveries until the lungs are adequately developed.

### FETOSCOPY

The fetus can be examined directly and its blood sampled through a fiber optic lens inserted into the uterus. This technique permits the diagnosis of genetic disorders, especially blood diseases that cannot be detected in amniotic fluid, which in some cases can be treated surgically and medically before birth.

does not tend to respond to sound until the eighth or ninth month; however, the semicircular canals of the inner ear are sensitive to stimulation. The nerve fibers that connect the retina to the brain are developed by 6 months, and infants born prematurely at this time respond to light.

At 25 weeks, the fetus functions well within its uterine environment. It swallows, digests, excretes, moves about, sucks its thumb, rests, and grows. However, the nervous system, which begins to develop at 3 weeks, is still not mature enough to coordinate the many systems that must function simultaneously to ensure survival. Whereas the 22-week-old fetus has almost no chance to survive outside the uterus, the outlook for a 24-week-old fetus is anywhere from 50% to 90%, depending on the quality of the intensive care and the birth conditions (Brazy, 2001). By 30 weeks, survival outside the uterus is almost certain.

## DEVELOPMENT IN THE THIRD TRIMESTER

In the last trimester, the average fetus grows from 10 to 20 inches and increases in weight from 2 to 7 or 7½ pounds. These increases in body size and weight are paralleled by a maturation of the central nervous system. Studies of 36- to 39-week-old fetuses have found that they are sensitive to changes in low-pitched musical notes, to pulsing as compared to continuous sounds, and to changes in speech sounds (Cheour-Luhtanen, Alho, Sainio, Rinne, & Reinikainen, 1996; Groome et al., 2000; Lecanuet, Graniere-Deferre, Jacquet, & DeCasper, 2000). In one study, pregnant women recited a children's rhyme aloud every day from the 33rd through the 37th week of fetal development. Monitoring of the fetal heart rate provided evidence that the fetuses recognized a tape recording of the familiar rhyme in comparison to unfamiliar rhymes. All this evidence supports the notion that a fetus experiences its mother's speech sounds during the third trimester and becomes familiar with the sound of her voice (DeCasper et al., 1994; DeCasper & Spence, 1986; Spence & DeCasper, 1987).

The advantages that a full-term fetus has over a premature, 28-week-old fetus include: (1) the ability to begin and maintain regular breathing; (2) a stronger sucking response; (3) well-coordinated swallowing movements; (4) stronger peristalsis and, therefore, more efficient digestion and waste excretion; and (5) a more fully balanced control of body temperature.

The full-term fetus has been able to take advantage of minerals in the mother's diet for the formation of tooth enamel. As the placenta begins to degenerate in the last month of pregnancy, antibodies against various diseases that have been formed in the mother's blood pass into the fetal bloodstream. They provide the fetus with immunity to many diseases during the first few months of life.

The uterus cannot serve indefinitely as the home of the fetus. Several factors lead to the eventual termination of the fetal–uterine relationship. First, as the placenta degenerates, antibodies that form in both the mother's and the fetus's blood would destroy the blood of the other. Second, because the placenta does not grow much larger than 2 pounds, the fetus, as it reaches its maximum size, cannot obtain enough nutrients to sustain life. Third, the fetal head cannot grow much larger than the pelvic opening without endangering the brain in the birth process. Even though soft connecting membranes permit the skull plates to overlap, head size is a factor that limits fetal growth.

Late in pregnancy, the fetal brain begins to produce hormones that increase the production of estrogen in the placenta. This, in turn, leads to a shift from mild to strong uterine contractions, which result in dilation of the cervix, rupture of the amniotic sac, and delivery (Nathanielsz, 1996). The approximate time from conception to birth is 38 weeks. However, there is a great deal of variability in the duration of pregnancies and in the size of full-term infants, even infants born to the same mother.

# THE BIRTH PROCESS

Birth is initiated by involuntary contractions of the uterine muscles, commonly referred to as **labor**. The length of time from the beginning of labor to the birth of the infant is highly variable. The average time is 14 hours for women undergoing their first labor (*primiparae*) and 8 hours for women undergoing later labors (*multiparae*).

The uterine contractions serve two central functions: *effacement* and *dilation*. **Effacement**, or thinning, is the short-

ening of the cervical canal. **Dilation** is the gradual enlargement of the cervix from an opening only millimeters wide to one of about 10 centimeters—large enough for the baby to pass through. Effacement and dilation occur without deliberate effort by the mother. Once the cervix is fully enlarged, the mother can assist in the birth by exerting pressure on the abdominal walls of the uterus. The baby, too, helps in the birth process by squirming, turning its head, and pushing against the birth canal.

## STAGES OF LABOR

The medical profession describes three stages of labor. The first stage begins with the onset of uterine contractions and ends with the full dilation of the cervix; this is the longest stage. The second stage involves the expulsion of the fetus. It begins at full dilation and ends with the delivery of the baby. The third stage begins with delivery and ends with the expulsion of the placenta. This stage usually lasts 5 to 10 minutes.

These three stages of labor do not precisely parallel the personal experience of childbirth. For example, although the expulsion of the placenta is considered a unique stage of labor in the medical model, it is rarely mentioned in women's accounts of their birth experiences. On the other hand, many of the signs of impending labor that occur in the last weeks of pregnancy are often included in women's accounts of labor.

In terms of the psychological adaptation to the birth process, labor can be viewed as having five phases: (1) early signs that labor is approaching; (2) strong, regular uterine contractions, signaling that labor has begun and generally accompanied by a move from the home to the hospital or birthing center; (3) the transition phase, during which contractions are strong, rest times between contractions are short, and women experience the greatest difficulty or discomfort; (4) the birth process, which allows the mother's active participation in the delivery and is generally accompanied by a move from the labor area to the more sterile delivery room; and (5) the postpartum period, which involves the initial interactions with the newborn, physiological changes that mark a return to the prepregnant state, and the return home. The significant events of these phases are summarized in Table 5.3.

## CESAREAN DELIVERY

Sometimes a normal, spontaneous vaginal delivery would be dangerous to the mother or the newborn (Cunningham et al., 2001). One alternative is to remove the baby surgically through an incision in the uterine wall. The procedure, called a *cesarean section*, may have gotten its name from an 8th-century BC Roman law, *lex cesarea*, which required that in the case of the death of a pregnant woman, a postmortem operative delivery would be performed, so that the mother and child could be buried separately (Sehdev, 2004). Until as late

**Table 5.3** Significant Events of the Five Stages of Labor

**Phase 1: Early signs that labor is approaching**
1. Lightening (about 10 to 14 days before delivery). The baby's head drops into the pelvic area.
2. Release of the plug that has kept the cervix closed.
3. Discharge of amniotic fluid.
4. False labor: irregular uterine contractions.

**Phase 2: Onset of labor**
1. Transition from home to hospital or birthing center.
2. Strong, regular contractions 3–5 minutes apart.

**Phase 3: Transition**
1. Accelerated labor, with contractions lasting up to 90 seconds and coming 2 or 3 minutes apart.
2. Some sense of disorientation, heightened arousal, or loss of control.

**Phase 4: Birth**
1. The baby's head presses down on the bottom of the birth canal.
2. The mother experiences a strong, reflexive urge to push to expel the baby.
3. The mother typically is moved from a labor area to a more sterile delivery room.

**Phase 5: Postpartum period**
1. Mother and infant have initial contact.
2. Placenta is expelled.
3. Rapid alteration of the hormone system to stimulate lactation and shrink the uterus.
4. Mother and infant engage in early learning behaviors; infant attempts to nurse; mother explores infant and begins to interpret his or her needs.
5. Return to the home and introduction of the newborn into the family setting.

as the 17th century, infants might be saved through the cesarean section but the operation was usually fatal to mothers.

The incidence of cesarean deliveries in the United States increased from 5.5% of births in 1970 to 22% in 1999 (U.S. Census Bureau, 2003). Cesarean deliveries may be planned or unplanned. The procedure may be used if labor is severely prolonged and the fetus appears to be at risk due to lack of oxygen. It may also be used when the infant is in the breech position (feet or buttocks first rather than head first) or if the mother's pelvis is too small for the infant's head to pass through. Physicians often recommend a repeat cesarean if the woman has delivered by cesarean section before. The rate of cesarean deliveries is higher for mothers age 30 and older than for younger mothers.

The cesarean delivery makes childbirth a surgical procedure, requiring anesthetics, intravenous feeding of the mother, and a prolonged recovery period. Although the procedure undoubtedly saves many infants and mothers who would not survive vaginal childbirth, there is some concern that it is being misused for the convenience of health professionals or busy mothers who want to be able to schedule deliveries and thus avoid waiting for the unpredictable onset of labor. *Healthy People 2000*, the U.S. Public Health Service goal statement, called for a reduction of the national cesarean rate to 15% (Healthy People, 1990)—a goal implying that a sub-

stantial number of the current cesarean procedures are not required.

## INFANT MORTALITY

The *infant mortality rate* is the number of infants who die during the first year of life per 1,000 live births during that year. In 2002, the U.S. rate was estimated at 7.0 deaths per 1,000 live births—up from 6.8 in 2001. This was the first increase in the U.S. infant mortality rate since the 1960s. Increases in multiple births, low birthweight (under 2,500 grams), and premature births (less than 37 weeks) are all associated with this increase in infant mortality (Kochanek & Martin, 2004). The rate for Black babies in the United States in 2001—14 deaths per 1,000 live births—was higher than the infant mortality rates in countries such as Chile, the Czech Republic, Cuba, and Poland, which are considered economically emergent nations (U.S. Census Bureau, 2003).

Roughly two thirds of infant deaths occur during the first month after birth. Most of these deaths result from severe birth defects, premature birth, or *sudden infant death syndrome* (SIDS), in which apparently healthy babies are put to bed and are later found dead with no clear explanation, even after autopsy (Willinger, James, & Catz, 1991).

## The Impact of Cesarean Delivery

WHAT IS THE impact of a cesarean delivery on the newborn and the parents? In the short run—that is, within 5 minutes after birth—babies delivered by cesarean section are more likely to show signs of risk than babies delivered vaginally. This difference holds for babies who are delivered by repeat cesarean section and who therefore are not at risk in other ways (Burt, Vaughan, & Daling, 1988). However, long-term follow-ups of babies delivered by cesarean section have found no effects on the child's IQ or standardized math and verbal test scores (Entwisle & Alexander, 1987).

The effects of cesarean delivery on parents have been summarized in a meta-analysis of 48 separate studies on the psychosocial correlates of cesarean childbirth (DiMatteo et al., 1996). Comparisons were made for mothers who delivered through cesarean section and those who delivered vaginally. Mothers who delivered through cesarean section experienced a longer delay in making their first contact with their infant. When they did make contact, mothers who had a cesarean section evaluated their babies less positively while they were in the hospital. Mothers undergoing cesarean deliveries were less satisfied overall with their delivery experience. However, there was no difference among groups of mothers in their level of postpartum anxiety or their confidence in their ability to parent.

Mothers who experienced cesarean delivery reported greater fatigue than other mothers, even up to 2 months postpartum. However, they did not differ from other mothers in their level of functioning after 2 months, their anxiety or sense of stress at home, or the time until they returned to work. They were less likely to breastfeed. However, those who did breastfeed nursed their babies for just as long as other mothers.

Other research has considered the longer term impact of the cesarean delivery for mother–infant interactions. Mothers who delivered by planned or unplanned cesarean were no different from mothers who delivered vaginally in the quality of mother–infant interactions or mothers' positive feelings toward their infants at 4 and 12 months after birth (Durik, Hyde, & Clark, 2000).

---

Infant mortality rates are influenced by many factors, including: (1) the frequency of birth complications; (2) the robustness of the infants who are being born, which is influenced by their prenatal nutrition and degree of exposure to viruses or bacteria, damaging X rays, drugs, and other teratogens; (3) the mother's age; and (4) the facilities that are available for prenatal and newborn care. One fourth of infant deaths result from complications associated with low birthweight. If the conditions leading to prematurity could be altered, the U.S. infant mortality rate would be significantly improved (Kocohanek & Martin, 2004).

Infant mortality rates vary from one country and region of the world to another. In 2002, the infant mortality rate in Japan was 3.3, but in that same year, the infant mortality rate in 12 other countries of the world was more than 90. The United States, with all its resources and advanced technology, in fact ranks behind other industrialized countries, including Australia, Belgium, Canada, France, Germany, Greece, Japan, the Netherlands, Spain, and the United Kingdom. Within the United States, regional infant mortality rates range from a low of 3.8 per 1,000 in New Hampshire to a high of 10.7 per 1000 in Delaware (U.S. Census Bureau, 2003).

The density of low-income populations, availability of educational materials on the impact of diet and drugs on the developing fetus, and adequacy of medical facilities for high-risk newborns all contribute to the regional variations in infant death rates among populations of different incomes. Children conceived in poverty are at the greatest risk of infant mortality. Their mothers receive poorer quality prenatal care and are exposed to more dangerous environmental and health factors during the prenatal period than are mothers of children conceived in more advantaged families. The chances that any one infant will survive the stresses of birth depend on the convergence of biological, environmental, cultural, and economic influences on his or her intrauterine growth, delivery, and postnatal care (Dole et al., 2004).

## THE MOTHER, THE FETUS, AND THE PSYCHOSOCIAL ENVIRONMENT

The course and pattern of prenatal development are guided by genetic information that unfolds in the context of the pregnant woman's biopsychosocial environment. A woman's health, her attitudes toward pregnancy and childbirth, her lifestyle, the resources available to her during her pregnancy, and the behavior demanded of her by her culture all influence her sense of well-being. Many of these same factors may directly affect the health and growth of the fetus. In the next section, we discuss the impact of the fetus on the pregnant woman, including how the pregnancy might affect the infant's father and his relationship to the mother. The subsequent section focuses on the impact of the pregnant woman on the

*Depending on their health, the type of work they do, and the support of family and workplace colleagues, some women can continue to work well into the last trimester of their pregnancy.*

© Michael Krasowitz/Getty Images

fetus and the many factors that contribute to the quality of the intrauterine environment.

## THE IMPACT OF THE FETUS ON THE PREGNANT WOMAN

Consider some of the ways in which a fetus influences a pregnant woman. Pregnancy alters a woman's body image and her sense of well-being. Some women feel especially vigorous and energetic during much of their pregnancy; others experience distressing symptoms, such as nausea, backache, swelling, headache, and irritability. Some women say they have difficulty remembering things during their last trimester. Although changes in the hormonal environment might be able to account for some of these symptoms, others are probably brought about by the convergence of physical, cognitive, and emotional changes of pregnancy (Buckwalter et al., 1999). In some cases, pregnancy is accompanied by serious illnesses that threaten the mother's health.

### ■ CHANGES IN ROLES AND SOCIAL STATUS

Women who become pregnant may be treated in new ways by people close to them and by the broader community. Usually, fathers become more concerned for and supportive of their pregnant partners, and pregnant women may also be viewed in a new light by their peers. In some communities, adolescent girls who become pregnant feel ashamed or guilty. In others, becoming pregnant during adolescence is viewed by the peer group as an accomplishment, a sign of maturity. At work, women who become pregnant may be given fewer responsibilities or may be passed over for promotions. In business settings, pregnancy may be viewed as an annoyance,

something that is likely to interfere with productivity and is, at best, to be tolerated.

Within the family, a pregnant woman is likely to be treated with new levels of concern and care. Her pregnancy affects her partner, her parents and siblings, her previous children, and her partner's family. By giving birth to a first child, a woman transforms her mother and father into grandparents and her brothers and sisters into uncles and aunts. Moreover, pregnancy may strengthen the gender identity of the baby's mother or father. Just as infertility threatens one's gender identity, becoming pregnant may be viewed as confirmation of a woman's femininity and a man's virility in impregnating her (Heitlinger, 1989).

In some societies, pregnancy and childbirth confer special status on a woman. In Japan, for example, traditional values place motherhood above all other women's roles. "Only after giving birth to a child did a woman become a fully tenured person in the family" (Bankart, 1989). When they become mothers, Japanese women begin to have an impact on government, community, and public life as the people who are specially responsible for molding and shaping the next generation. For Mexican American women, childbearing is likely to be viewed within a broad religious context. "It is considered the privilege and essential obligation of a married woman to bear children, but children come 'when God is willing'" (Hahn & Muecke, 1987). Despite their difficult economic and social conditions, women who are Mexican immigrants in the United States have relatively fewer low-birthweight babies than mothers from other low-income groups. One explanation for this is that pregnancy brings forth substantial family support, which buffers the pregnant woman from the adverse effects of poverty (Sagrestano, Felman, Killingsworth Rini, Woo, & Dunkel-Schetter, 1999; Sherraden & Barrera, 1996).

## The Doula or Birth Companion

THE IDEA OF having a supportive companion available to women during childbirth has been formalized in the role of *doula*. The term doula comes from a Greek word for handmaiden, referring to the primary servant for the woman of the household. Before the introduction of hospital deliveries, most cultures had a role for a close female companion who accompanied a woman during childbirth. The contemporary doula is trained to offer information as well as physical and emotional support during labor, delivery, and the early weeks following childbirth. Her role is to remain at the side of the laboring mother to help her have a safe, reassuring childbirth experience. She does not take the place of the midwife, obstetrician, nurses, or the mother's partner (Doulas of North America, 1998).

The contribution of companion support to reducing complications during labor and delivery was studied with a group of Guatemalan women (Sosa, Kennell, Klaus, Robertson, & Urrutia, 1980). The hospital normally did not permit any visitors to remain with an expectant woman in the maternity ward. Each woman in this study, however, was assigned a companion who stayed with her until delivery, talking to the woman, holding her hand, rubbing her back, and providing encouragement during labor. These mothers had fewer complications during labor than a group of women who had no companion, and their babies showed fewer signs of fetal distress. The mean length of labor was more than 10 hours shorter for those women who had a companion than for those who were alone.

A review of 15 studies involving more than 12,000 women examined additional empirical support for the contribution of the doula in childbirth (Hodnett, 2003). The studies were conducted in Australia, Belgium, Botswana, Canada, Finland, France, Greece, Guatemala, Mexico, South Africa, and the United States, under very different hospital conditions. All of the studies contrasted the childbirth experiences of women who did and did not have a supportive companion available during labor and delivery. Mothers who were accompanied by a supportive companion had shorter labors and fewer obstetrical difficulties. The presumption is that a woman who is attended by a doula has lower levels of anxiety, thus reducing the release of neurotransmitters that might contribute to obstetrical difficulties and neonatal distress (Corter & Fleming, 2002). The presence of a doula is especially valuable in cases, as in the Guatemalan study, where women would ordinarily labor alone with just the presence of the medical staff. To find out more about doulas and their role as birth companions, visit www.DONA.org.

## CHANGES IN THE MOTHER'S EMOTIONAL STATE

Pregnancy is the 12th most stressful life change in a list of 43 life events in the *Social Readjustment Rating Scale* (Holmes & Rahe, 1967). Thus, it is no surprise that mothers and fathers have strong emotional reactions to pregnancy. The woman's attitude toward her unborn child may be pride, acceptance, rejection, or—as is usually the case—ambivalence. In most normal pregnancies, women experience anxiety and depression as well as positive feelings of excitement and hopefulness. The normal physical changes during the gestational period include symptoms that are often associated with depression, such as fatigue, sleeplessness, slowed physical movement, preoccupation with one's physical state, and moodiness (Kaplan, 1986). Moreover, throughout the pregnancy, the expectant woman has recurring worries and fears about the childbirth experience, whether the baby will be healthy, her own well-being, and the health and well-being of her family. These fears may be accentuated if the woman has heard about problems with childbirth from friends and relatives. In one study, women who had attended childbirth classes were interviewed 4 weeks after they gave birth. Thirty-four percent of the women reported that their childbirth experience was traumatic, including many who had symptoms of post-traumatic stress disorder (Soet, Brack, & Dilorio, 2003). Among women who have had previous pregnancies, worries may focus on recollections about the difficulties of delivery and the health and care of the new baby (Melender, 2002). Some women receive troubling information during an ultrasound screening about possible fetal abnormalities. This information adds to anxiety during pregnancy (Brisch et al., 2003).

Certain psychosocial factors are associated with increased anxiety and depression during pregnancy, including exposure to stressors, the absence of a supportive partner, and experiencing an unwanted pregnancy (Kalil, Gruber, Conley, & Sytniac, 1993). In a study of low-income African American and European American women, depression was high early in the pregnancy and declined in the months following the birth of the child, as the women coped successfully with their pregnancy. Self-esteem, which was higher for the African American women in the study, was associated with lower levels of initial prenatal depression. For both African American and European American women, the women who showed the greatest drop in depression over the pregnancy had relatively more financial resources, more social support, and fewer other life stressors (Ritter, Hobfoll, Lavin, Cameron, & Hulsizer, 2000).

Some level of maternal anxiety may be appropriately adaptive as a woman prepares to experience labor and delivery and to make the many changes necessary to care for a newborn. However, it is possible that strong emotional reactions—such as prolonged anxiety or depression—may influence the fetal environment directly through the secretion of maternal hormones that cross the placental barrier. Research with animals has demonstrated that mothers' exposure to stress during pregnancy does have long-term negative consequences for learning, motor development, and adaptive behavior in offspring. A review of existing literature suggests that among humans, prenatal stress is associated with higher rates of spontaneous abortion, preterm labor and delivery, and growth delay among babies (Mulder et al, 2002). Current studies consider the relationship between stress-related changes in endocrine levels during pregnancy and motor development, cognitive development, and immune functioning in babies. Research is focusing on ways in which stress-induced physiological changes in the mother might influence fetal nervous system development (Field et al., 2003; DiPietro, 2004). The relationships between extreme prenatal stress and fetal or newborn cognitive and behavioral outcomes in humans are still considered tentative. The evidence is clearer that a mother's emotional state during pregnancy is related to her experiences during labor and her later parenting behaviors.

A woman's feelings about her femininity, her attitudes toward the unborn child, and her psychological stability are associated with difficulties experienced during pregnancy and labor. Women who have more stable personalities and a positive orientation toward pregnancy react more favorably to the stresses of labor. Anxious, irritable women are more likely to have longer labors and more complications during labor and delivery. During labor and delivery, women who are more fearful of childbirth and who believe that the outcomes of childbirth are outside their own control are more likely to request epidural anesthesia than are women who had a low fear of childbirth and wanted to participate actively in the childbirth process (Heinze & Sleigh, 2003).

The mother's emotional state during pregnancy has an impact beyond the events of childbirth. Women who experience notable depression during pregnancy are more likely to continue feeling depressed after giving birth and are more likely to have additional depressive symptoms in the 5 years following childbirth. Clinicians who focus on the etiology of depression in women emphasize that the period of pregnancy and childbirth should be a time for preventive intervention (Le, Munos, Ippen, & Stoddard, 2003).

## ■ FATHERS' INVOLVEMENT DURING PREGNANCY AND CHILDBIRTH

In the first trimester, fathers are able to hear the fetal heartbeat amplified through the Doppler. Through the use of ultrasound, fathers are able to visualize the developing fetus. During the second trimester, a father is able to make contact with his unborn child as he places his hand on his partner's abdomen and feels the life and movement within. For many men, this is a time of great joy, as the prospect of fatherhood becomes more than abstract empathy with his partner's experiences. Investment in the new life begins to increase as the reality of the fetus becomes more concrete. These times can provide the basis for a new kind of intimacy for the expectant couple as they begin to talk about their plans and hopes for the child, share their feelings about the pregnancy and upcoming birth, and explore their feelings related to assuming responsibility for the care and protection of their child.

Sometimes, however, the first movements of the fetus stimulate a negative reaction in the father. In a longitudinal study of men during their partner's pregnancy and 8 weeks after birth, men living in stepfamilies had higher levels of depression both before and after the birth than did men in more traditional families (Deater-Deckard, Pickering, Dunn, & Golding, 1998). A father's depression may, in turn, have a negative effect on the mother, leaving her depressed and aware that she is without the support she was expecting. Some men are not comfortable with the physical events of pregnancy, and they try to deny them by turning away from the mother. They do not want to feel the fetus's movements and are extremely uneasy or embarrassed by the pressure to understand the details of the female anatomy. Some men think that the fetus and then the baby threaten their own position with the mother, and they feel resentful and competitive toward the woman and the unborn infant. In some families, this resentment may lead to violence. For example, one study of low-income, urban women found that 38% had experienced violence from their male partner during their pregnancy (O'Campo et al., 1995).

Some men worry about the economic ramifications of the impending birth. If they are unemployed or underemployed, they may worry about money, have low confidence, feel they are not worth much, or be fearful that the mother's income will decrease. Some of these men may become more distant from the mother, increasing feelings of isolation rather than intimacy. Emotions associated with isolation, including feeling more anxious and depressed, can have a negative impact on the fetus as well as on the mother. As discussed earlier, these emotions can increase the difficulties of pregnancy, the birth itself, and the early months of parenting—difficulties that can have strong negative effects on establishing a healthy parent–child relationship (Field et al., 1985; Field et al., 1990).

The many different types of relationships that are possible between the mother and her partner have implications for both the emotional state of the mother during pregnancy and the psychosocial development of the child. Research supports the idea of continuity between the quality of the relationship between the partners during the prenatal period and the quality of their parenting in the early years of childhood. This continuity in turn has implications for the child's growth and development. Partners who show high levels of negative in-

*Fathers are becoming increasingly involved in supporting their partner's pregnancy and delivery. This support is both an important aspect of identification with the father role, and a great emotional comfort to the mother.*

© Lawrence Migdale/Stock Boston Inc./Picturequest

teraction or detachment during the prenatal period may have trouble providing an emotionally secure environment for their newborn child.

> Couples characterized by positive mutuality, partner autonomy, and the ability to confront problems and regulate negative affect are responsive to the needs of their infants, promote their autonomy, and have more secure and autonomous children, as seen throughout the first four years of life. (Heinicke, 1995, p. 295)

Trends in the United States have shifted dramatically toward greater involvement of fathers during labor and delivery (Shapiro, Diamond, & Greenberg, 1995). Expectant fathers often attend childbirth classes to learn to assist their partners during the delivery. The father's presence during labor and delivery is typically a great comfort to the pregnant woman. When the father is present, women tend to have shorter labors, report experiencing less pain, use less medication, and feel more positive about themselves and their childbirth experience (Grossman et al., 1980; Woollett & Dosanjh-Matwala, 1990). Fathers also describe their participation in the birth as a peak experience. First-time fathers interviewed about their childbirth experiences reported both positive and negative feelings. These fathers felt that they were most helpful to their wives during labor, and they found the birth experience to be extremely powerful (Nichols, 1993). Negative experiences for men during childbirth occur when they are unsure what their role is during the delivery or when hospital personnel treat them rudely, as a disruption, or fail to provide them with the information they want during the labor and delivery process (Johnson, 2002).

# ■ CASE STUDY

## A FATHER'S RECOLLECTIONS
## ABOUT HIS DAUGHTER'S BIRTH

*The sentiments of frustration and joy are captured in this description of a father's experiences during labor and delivery. The text was taken from a bulletin board discussion about fathers' views of whether they should be present at their child's birth on Blacknet.com, a place for dialog and communication within the Black community of the United Kingdom.*

Gonna remenise about when my first child was born, I remember being dragged out of work on a Wednesday am because my then wife had gone into labour. Someone however forgot to inform me that women needed to dialate. geeez.

So after rushing to Guys hospital I'm told Baby not ready. Anyway I'm waiting for said wife to get big enough so to speak. All flippin day, All day man watching the paint dry.

I was like Donkey in Shrek 2 'Are we there yet?' every five minutes, then night falls I think ok, maybe it will be a night birth. Oh nooo, nooo such luck.

So here am i holding my wifes hand, or was that her squeezing the blood out of my hand. hmmm yes that was it. I'm giving the *'i'm in control mans'* talk you know *'come on darling its ok, breath breath'* My girl is in full contractions now about 20 mins apart. So the top half of me is trying to be firm and calm, the bottom half is trying hard not to piss mi pants.

Then the nurse mentioned Epidural, oh my days I know i nearly passed out at the sight of the needle going into the spinal column, all the while that wretch is screaming blue murder in the next room. *'get it out'*.

Anyway after waiting ALL day (do I still sound vex?) and ALL night with a hardback chair for a bed, you know I'm happy right? . . . next thing I know doctor come in approx 8:40 am ish. *'ok lets do it'*. Next thing I know they pull out these stirrups out of nowhere and got my wife with both legs in the air like she's riding an invisable horse whilst lying on her back.

Then a whole heap of student doctors and nurses come into the room, and I mean a whole heap. So here's the wife with legs up in the air, fanny out of door, and all these strangers peering right up it. Now you know man is about to cuss right.

Anyway before I could get into it, baby starts to be delivered and out she pops, 9 am in the morning. she pops out. can't describe how i felt but it was as close to perfection as i will ever get. bonded with her and we've been close not matter what 21 years later.

Source: Kunjufu (2004).

## ■ CRITICAL THINKING AND CASE ANALYSIS

1. Given all the stress of the situation, what might account for the very positive feelings reported by Kunjufu at the moment of birth?

2. What are some different roles that men can play during the childbirth process? What roles is Kunjufu playing?

3. What might be some reasons that men do not want to be present during labor and delivery?

4. How do hospital personnel influence the experiences of fathers during childbirth?

5. How might childbirth preparation classes influence the experiences of fathers during childbirth?

## THE IMPACT OF THE PREGNANT WOMAN ON THE FETUS

Among the factors that influence the fetus's development are the mother's age, use of drugs during pregnancy and delivery, exposure to environmental toxins, and diet. The quality of a pregnant woman's physical and emotional health before and during pregnancy is linked to her own knowledge about and preparation for pregnancy as well as to her culture's attitudes and practices associated with childbearing. One of the most harmful influences of the psychosocial environment on fetal development is poverty. Embedded in the conditions of poverty are many of the individual factors associated with suboptimal prenatal development.

## ■ THE IMPACT OF POVERTY

Perhaps the most powerful psychosocial factor that influences the life chances of the developing fetus is poverty. Women living in poverty are likely to experience the cumulative effects of many of the factors associated with infant mortality and de-

velopmental vulnerabilities (Kotelchuck, 1995). Poverty is directly linked to poor prenatal care. Women who live in poverty are likely to begin having babies at an earlier age and to have repeated pregnancies into their later adult years—practices that are associated with low birthweight. Women who have had little education are less likely to be aware of the risks of smoking, alcohol, and drug use for their babies and are more likely to use or abuse these substances. Women living in poverty are less likely to have been vaccinated against some of the infectious diseases (e.g., rubella) that can harm the developing fetus. Poverty is linked with maternal malnutrition, higher instances of infection, and higher rates of diabetes and cardiovascular disease, which are all linked to the infant's low birthweight and physical vulnerability (Cassady & Strange, 1987).

Many of the risks that face infants born to women who live in poverty are preventable. A well-organized, accessible system of regional medical care facilities combined with an effective educational program on pregnancy and nutritional support can significantly improve the health and vigor of babies born to women in poverty (Swyer, 1987). One of the central themes in delivering effective prenatal and continuing services to women in poverty is the establishment of a caring relationship between the woman and the health care provider. This caring relationship provides emotional support to the woman, encouraging her to feel valued as a client, as a mother, and as an adult in the community (Barnard & Morisset, 1995).

A systematic evaluation of a program of coordinated maternity care for women on Medicaid in North Carolina demonstrated that a comprehensive prenatal care program improves birth outcomes even in a high-risk population (Buescher, Roth, Williams, & Goforth, 1991). This kind of coordination involves more than providing prenatal checkups and information about health care during pregnancy. It recognizes the complex challenges that face women in poverty, including violence, hazardous living conditions, poor quality services, and unstable or disruptive social relationships (McAllister & Boyle, 1998). Effective interventions must include nonmedical support services, such as making sure the woman has access to food stamps; is part of the Women, Infants, and Children (WIC) food program; has the transportation needed for prenatal and postnatal health care appointments; and receives housing assistance or job training as necessary. Furthermore, resources must be provided to care for, educate, and support children whose intellectual, physical, and emotional capabilities have been restricted before birth by their mothers' poverty. The life chances and quality of survival of infants born in poverty are a reflection of the value that a society places on social justice.

## ■ MOTHER'S AGE

The capacity for childbearing begins about 1 to 1½ years after menarche (the beginning of regular menstrual periods) and normally ends at the climacteric, or menopause (the end-

**HUMAN DEVELOPMENT AND DIVERSITY**

## Psychosocial Factors Linked to Preterm Births for African American and European American Women

THE RATE OF preterm and low-birthweight babies has risen substantially from the mid-1980s to 2002. Roughly 12% of all U.S. births are less than 37 weeks of gestational age, and close to 8% have low birthweight (under 2,500 grams). Preterm births and low birthweight are major causes of infant mortality (Martin et al., 2003). Research about the causes of preterm births typically focuses on genetic, physiological, psychological, and behavioral factors. Much of this research has found that even when taking into account differences in income, education, health behaviors, and access to prenatal care, African American women have a higher risk for preterm births than European American women.

Researchers in North Carolina conducted a study to determine whether psychosocial factors such as stressors experienced during pregnancy, social support from the baby's father, perceptions of racial or gender discrimination, perceived neighborhood safety, and strategies for coping with stress might help predict preterm births (Dole et al., 2004). The investigators examined the hypothesis that African American and European American women differ in the kinds of environmental stressors they are exposed to and in the way they cope with these stressors,

and that these differences might help account for their different rates of preterm births.

Data were gathered from more than 1,800 pregnant women, 38% of whom were African American. The study examined which psychosocial factors were the best predictors for preterm delivery in the two groups when controlling for age, parity (number of previous pregnancies), education, marital status, household income in relation to the number of adults and children in the household, prepregnancy body mass, and prenatal care.

European American women were more at risk for preterm births when

- they reported a large number of negative life events during pregnancy;
- they were not living with a partner;
- they used escape or avoidance as a strategy for coping with problems;
- they reported living in a dangerous neighborhood.

African American women were more at risk for preterm births when

- they reported using distancing as a strategy to cope with problems;
- they reported high levels of racial discrimination;

- they reported high levels of gender discrimination;
- they reported high pregnancy-related anxiety.

Not only is the nature of the psychosocial environment different for African American and European American women in North Carolina, but they experience different vulnerabilities to stress. For example, even though more African American than European American women lived in dangerous neighborhoods, this factor was a significant predictor of having a preterm infant for European American women, but not for African American women. More African American than European American women reported high levels of racial discrimination, and those who did were at greater risk for a preterm delivery. Escape and avoidance were high-risk coping strategies for European American women; distancing was a high-risk strategy for African American women. The implications of this research are that programs designed to prevent preterm births need to examine the psychosocial contexts of the participants and take into consideration racial and cultural differences, including different perceptions of stressors and resources that help women cope with those stressors.

---

ing of regular menstrual periods). Thus, a woman is potentially fertile for about 35 years of her life. Pregnancy and childbirth can occur at various times during this period. The effects of childbirth on the physical and psychological well-being of a mother vary with her age and emotional commitment to the mother role. Similarly, these factors also contribute significantly to the survival and well-being of her infant. In later chapters, we will discuss the psychosocial consequences of childbearing for adolescents and adults. Here we simply point out that the quality of prenatal care and the degree of risk during childbirth are associated with the age of the mother during pregnancy (see Figure 5.9).

Women between the ages of 16 and 35 tend to provide a better uterine environment for the developing fetus and to give birth with fewer complications than do women under 16 or over 35. Particularly when it is their first pregnancy, women over 35 are likely to have a longer labor than younger women, and the labor is more likely to result in the death of either the infant or the mother. As expected, the two groups with the highest probability of giving birth to premature babies are women over 35 and those under 16 (Schuster, 1986).

Premature children of teenage mothers are more likely than those of older mothers to have neurological defects that will influence their coping capacities. Also, mothers under 16

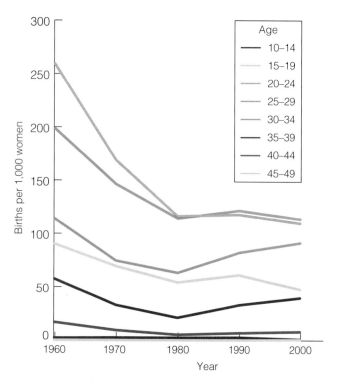

**FIGURE 5.9**

Live Birthrates by Age of Mother, 1960–2000

Source: U.S. Census Bureau, 1986, 1989, 1992, 2003.

tend to receive less adequate prenatal care and to be less bio-logically mature. Young mothers are likely to engage in other high-risk behaviors including alcohol and drug use that have negative consequences for fetal development (Cornelius, 1996; Cornelius, Goldshmidt, Taylor, & Day, 1999). Evidence suggests that good medical care, nutrition, and social support improve the childbirth experiences of adolescent mothers who are over 16. However, the physical immaturity of those under 16 puts the mother and the infant at greater risk even with adequate medical and social supports (Osofsky, Hann, & Peebles, 1993; Roosa, 1984).

A primary risk for infants of mothers who are over 40 is Down syndrome (Moore, 1993). It is hypothesized that the relatively high incidence of Down syndrome in babies born to older women is the result, in part, of deteriorating ova. How-ever, older women are also likely to have male partners who are their age or older. Even though new sperm are produced daily, some evidence suggests that among older men, the rate of genetically defective sperm increases. Thus, aging in one or both partners may contribute to the increased incidence of Down syndrome in babies born to older women. These explanations are not entirely satisfactory, however, because older women who have had multiple births are not as likely to have a baby with Down syndrome as are women who have their first child at an older age. What is more, many babies with Down syndrome are born to women who are under 35. It is likely that in some cases, Down syndrome is a result of

errors that occur during cell division and that in others, it is a result of a genetically transmitted condition.

Figure 5.9 shows the rate of live births to women in the age range from 10 to 44 between 1960 and 2000. In every age range except the youngest, fewer women are having babies to-day than in the 1960s. Two other observations about the data presented in this figure are relevant to our understanding of the timing of childbearing in adult life. First, since 1960 the trend has shifted from a higher birth rate in the period from age 20 to 24 to a more equal birth rate during the full decade of the 20s. Second, in comparison to the 1980s, the current trend shows an increased rate of childbearing for women dur-ing their 30s and early 40s.

## ◼ MATERNAL DRUG USE

The range of drugs used by pregnant women is enormous. Iron, diuretics, antibiotics, hormones, tranquilizers, appetite suppressants, and other drugs are being either prescribed for or taken voluntarily by pregnant women. Furthermore, women influence the fetal environment through their volun-tary use of such drugs as alcohol, nicotine, caffeine, marijuana, cocaine, and other narcotics. Studies of the effects of specific drugs on fetal growth suggest that many drugs ingested by pregnant women are in fact metabolized in the placenta and transmitted to the fetus. What is more, although the impact of a specific dosage of a drug on the pregnant woman may be minimal, the impact on the fetus may be quite dramatic. Male-mediated effects of drugs on fetal development are also documented but less well publicized. Drug abuse among men may produce abnormalities of the sperm that can account for birth defects in their offspring (Pollard, 2000).

In reviewing the following sections about the impact of drugs on fetal development, two principles must be consid-ered. First, evidence suggests that genetic predisposition may make some developing fetuses more vulnerable than others to the negative effects of certain drugs or toxins. Data on this genetic variability were derived from animal studies, because animals are more likely to have large litters of offspring, some of which show greater resilience to the presence of prenatal teratogens than others (Vorhees & Mollnow, 1987). Second, most teratogens do not have an all-or-none impact on the central nervous system. The consequence to the fetus of ex-posure to teratogens varies by the dosage, the duration, and the timing of exposure.

**NICOTINE.** Babies born to mothers who smoke throughout their pregnancy weigh an average of 200 grams less than those born to nonsmoking mothers. Women who smoke are at greater risk for miscarriages, stillbirths, and preterm deliv-eries. Neurological examinations of babies exposed to nico-tine during the prenatal period showed decreased levels of arousal and responsiveness at 9 and 30 days after birth (Fried, Watkinson, Dillon, & Dulberg, 1987). Infants of smokers have a three to four times greater risk of sudden infant death before 2 months of age (Pergament, 1998).

*Both of these children show the facial characteristics of fetal alcohol syndrome: eyes widespread, with an epicanthic fold; short nose; small midface and thin upper lip.*

**ALCOHOL.** The evidence is conclusive that alcohol is a teratogen. Prenatal exposure to alcohol can disrupt brain development, interfere with cell development and organization, and modify the production of neurotransmitters, which are critical to the maturation of the central nervous system (Sokol, Delaney-Black, & Nordsstrom, 2003). The complex impact of alcohol on fetal development has been given the name **fetal alcohol syndrome** (Abel, 1984). Fetal alcohol syndrome is associated with disorders of the central nervous system, low birthweight, and malformations of the face, eyes, ears, and mouth. The risk of fetal alcohol syndrome for infants born to women who drink heavily—that is, 1.5 ounces or more of alcohol a day—is 30–50%. Even moderate daily alcohol use can produce some of these symptoms, especially if it is combined with malnutrition. At a rate of 1 to 3 infants affected per 1,000 live births, fetal alcohol syndrome is the greatest source of environmentally caused developmental disruption in the prenatal central nervous system (Vorhees & Mollnow, 1987).

Fetal exposure to alcohol disrupts verbal and visual learning. In a longitudinal study of the effects of prenatal exposure to alcohol, children born to mothers who consumed 1.5 ounces of alcohol (one average-strength drink) daily during pregnancy showed significantly lower IQ scores at age 4 than did children whose mothers used little or no alcohol (Streissguth, Barr, Sampson, Darby & Martin, 1989). Alcohol use was a significant predictor of reduced IQ scores even when many other factors—the mother's educational level, the child's birth order, the family's socioeconomic level, the child's involvement in preschool, and the quality of the mother–child interaction—were taken into account. In other words, the many environmental variables that are known to have a positive effect on a young child's intellectual functioning did not compensate for the disruption in development of the central nervous system associated with exposure to alcohol during pregnancy. We emphasize the risks associated with pre-

natal exposure to alcohol because it is so widely used in American society and because even what many adults consider to be a "safe" or socially acceptable amount of alcohol during pregnancy can have a negative effect on the fetus.

**CAFFEINE.** Caffeine freely crosses the placenta. It is commonly consumed in coffee, certain sodas, and tea. Heavy caffeine consumption—defined in one study as more than 300 milligrams, or roughly three cups of coffee per day—is associated with an increased risk of low birthweight, and there is a modest relationship to prematurity. Infants born to women who reduced the amount of caffeine they drank after the sixth week of pregnancy showed no ill effects associated with early caffeine consumption (Fenster, Eskenazi, Windham, & Swan, 1991; McDonald, Armstrong, & Sloan, 1992).

**NARCOTICS.** The use of narcotics, especially heroin and cocaine, as well as methadone (a drug used in the treatment of heroin addiction), has been linked to increased risks of birth defects, low birthweight, and higher rates of infant mortality (Howell, Heiser, & Harrington, 1999). Infants who have been exposed prenatally to opiates, cocaine, and methadone show a pattern of extreme irritability, high-pitched crying that is evidence of neurological disorganization, fever, sleep disturbances, feeding problems, muscle spasms, and tremors (Bard et al., 2000). These babies are at high risk for sudden infant death syndrome. Longer range studies found that some children who were exposed to addictive drugs in the prenatal period continued to show problems with fine-motor coordination, had difficulty focusing and sustaining their attention, and, perhaps as a result, had more school adjustment problems.

The longer term impact of prenatal drug exposure varies. Many women who use cocaine also drink alcohol and are malnourished and often exposed to violence and to sexually transmitted diseases. Thus, the impact of cocaine alone is dif-

**HUMAN DEVELOPMENT AND DIVERSITY**

## AIDS and Mother-to-Child Transmission

BY THE END of 1999, an estimated 15.7 million women and 1.3 million children were infected with HIV (human immunodeficiency virus) worldwide. Almost all these children under the age of 10 were infected by their mothers, and most of them live in developing countries in Africa and Asia. Children born to untreated HIV-positive mothers have about a 25% chance of developing the disease. The chances of transmitting HIV increase to 45% when mothers breastfeed—a practice that is very common in developing countries (Bassett, 2001; Rosenfield & Figdor, 2001).

In North America and Europe, the transmission of HIV from mother to infant has decreased dramatically due to the availability of drugs administered to the mother for a few weeks—or once while the mother is in labor—and to the infant within 3 days of birth. However, in the developing countries of Africa and Asia, where the disease is a raging epidemic,

these effective treatments are almost never available. What accounts for this failure?

Four issues prevent the translation of what is known as best practice to what is actually done in developing countries:

1. The costs of the medication to prevent mother-to-infant transmission are enormous for poor countries.
2. Voluntary counseling and testing are the cornerstones of prevention and intervention, but many women are reluctant to be tested for HIV due to the stigmatizing nature of the disease. Even though most women are infected by their husbands, the testing is done on women, and they are blamed for bringing HIV into their families. Women who test positive may risk being abandoned by their husbands, thus losing the support of their families even as they face the future of their illness.

3. The risk of transmission of HIV through breastfeeding continues even with the drug treatment. In order for women to give up breastfeeding, they need to be assured of safe water supplies and adequate availability of formula. Otherwise, the children will die of diarrhea and malnutrition.
4. The treatment does not benefit the HIV-infected women but prevents the spread of the disease to infants. As a result, although the infants may be spared the disease, they are highly likely to become orphans of infected fathers and mothers.

This example illustrates the broad issues underlying the topic of the influence of the mother on fetal development. The care of mothers is essential to the well-being of the developing fetus, and the cultural, societal, and family contexts figure prominently in the care of mothers.

---

ficult to assess (Pollack, 2000). In one study, about one third of the babies exposed prenatally to cocaine showed deficits in tests of motor or mental development during infancy; the others scored in the normal range (Cosden, Peerson, & Elliott, 1997). Of course, it is difficult to separate the direct prenatal effects of these drugs on the nervous system from the effects after birth that are associated with being parented by a drug-using mother (Tyler, Howard, Espinosa, & Doakes, 1997). One study focused on the caregiving environment of 2-year-old children who had been prenatally exposed to cocaine. Those who were in nonparental caregiving environments were doing much better at age 2 with respect to physical development, cognitive and language skills, and social and emotional functioning than those who continued in the care of their cocaine-using birth mothers (Brown et al., 2004).

Because of the widespread abuse of cocaine, some law enforcement officials are arresting and charging women who have exposed their unborn infants to these harmful and illegal substances. In 1997, a woman in South Carolina was charged with murder by child abuse when it was determined that her smoking crack cocaine was responsible for the death of her unborn child ("Crack-Using Woman," 1997). State laws have been passed that allow criminal charges to be filed

against women who give birth to babies who have illegal substances in their blood. Several states have tried taking babies away from these mothers, but this action poses an extremely difficult ethical dilemma. Those who oppose such actions argue that alcohol use, smoking, and other forms of maternal behavior also have known negative effects on the developing fetus. Should women who use these legal substances also be charged with child abuse? What is more, can society ensure that the babies taken from these mothers and placed in foster care will do better than they would have done in the care of their birth mothers? On the other hand, some argue that the state has the responsibility to protect the well-being of the unborn child, especially during the third trimester when the fetus has reached the point of viability. According to this view, actions that result in harm or death to the fetus ought to be considered child abuse and prosecuted as such (Pollack, 2000).

**PRESCRIPTION DRUGS.** Some drugs are administered to women during pregnancy as part of the treatment of a medical condition. The tragic outcome of the use of thalidomide for the treatment of morning sickness in the 1960s alerted society to the potential danger of certain chemicals to the fetus, particularly during the period of fetal differentiation and growth in the first trimester. Thalidomide taken during the 21st to 36th days after conception can cause gross deformities of the baby's limbs.

Some drugs are administered to help sustain the pregnancy. Others are used to help control medical conditions, such as epilepsy or AIDS. Studies examining the dose and timing of these drugs suggest that they can have temporary or long-term consequences for neurological development, motor behavior, and personality (Rovet et al., 1995). The effects of some kinds of drugs may persist for a long time after birth, either by directly altering the central nervous system or by influencing the pattern of caregiver–infant interactions.

**OBSTETRIC ANESTHETICS.** The study of the effects on the newborn of drugs used during delivery provides further evidence of the infant's dependence on the immediate environment. Initially, pain-relieving drugs were used for the benefit and convenience of pregnant women and their physicians, and their effects on the newborn were not noticed. However, evidence suggests that the type, amount, and timing of anesthetic use in delivery are all factors that may induce neonatal depression and affect the coping capacities of newborns. The use of anesthetic drugs during delivery has been found to interfere with the infant's ability to habituate to a stimulus (i.e., to stop responding after repeated presentations of the stimulus), to reduce the infant's smiling and cuddliness, and to reduce alert responses to new stimuli. Furthermore, the relationship between drug use and some infant behavior has been observed to last as long as 28 days (Stechler & Halton, 1982; Naulty, 1987).

## ENVIRONMENTAL TOXINS

As increasing numbers of women enter the workforce and assume nontraditional work roles, concern about the hazards of work settings for fetal development continues to grow. In an Allied Chemical plant, fears that fluorocarbon 22 might cause fetal damage led to the layoff of five female workers. Two of these women chose to be sterilized in order to hold their jobs (Bronson, 1979). Wives of men who are employed in hazardous environments may also experience higher rates of miscarriage, sterility, and birth defects in their babies. In one study, fathers' exposure to specific solvents and chemicals at work was linked to higher rates of spontaneous abortions among their wives (Lindbohm et al., 1991). Recent research links men's workplace exposure to lead to reduced sperm count, sperm motility, and sperm concentration, resulting in negative consequences for fertility. Paternal exposure to lead is also associated with low-birthweight babies (Alexander et al., 1996; Min, Correa-Villasenor, & Stewart, 1996).

The workplace is not the only setting in which pregnant women may be exposed to environmental toxins. Women who regularly ate a large amount of polluted fish from Lake Michigan for 6 years before they became pregnant had infants who showed certain memory deficits at 7 months of age (Jacobson, Fein, Jacobson, Schwartz, & Dowler, 1985). Although the level of these toxins—industrial waste products found in air, water, and soil—had no measurable effects on the mothers, it was high enough to influence central nervous system functioning in the fetuses. This finding makes it clear that all communities must be sensitive to the quality of their water, air, and soil. Each new generation depends on its predecessors for protection from these environmental hazards.

## MOTHER'S DIET

The notion that no matter what the pregnant woman eats, the fetus will get what it needs for growth is simply not true. Providing adequate nutrition for fetal development requires both a balanced diet for the mother and the capacity to transform nutrients into a form that the fetus can ingest (which the placenta takes care of; Lindblad, 1987).

Experimental research on the effects of maternal malnutrition on fetal development has been conducted primarily with rats. The impact of prenatal malnutrition on rats shows that when the mother is malnourished, fewer nutrients cross the placenta. The fetal brain receives comparatively more of the limited nutritional resources than the other organs; however, the central nervous system is disrupted. The consequences, for those fetuses that survive, include delayed skeletal development, impaired reflexes, and cognitive deficits (Galler & Tonkiss, 1998; Lukas & Campbell, 2000). Many experts assert that for humans, prenatal malnutrition, depending on its timing and severity, has an irreparable impact on central nervous system development and, as a result, on intellectual performance (Morgane et al., 1993). However, this assertion is difficult to demonstrate experimentally.

Most of the data on the effects of malnutrition on human fetal growth have come from studying the impact of disasters and crises—such as famines, wars, and extreme poverty—on pregnant women. For example, several studies examined the impact of the Dutch Hunger Winter of 1944–1945, when the German army blockaded food supplies to the Netherlands. In a study of men born in the famine region during that period, 21% were exposed to severe prenatal malnutrition for one or more trimesters. Malnutrition is inferred from the baby's low birthweight in comparison with his or her gestational age (the age of the fetus from the time of conception until birth). Babies who are small for their gestational age have a higher mortality rate, more complications during postdelivery care, and a higher risk of mental or motor impairment than do babies who are of average weight for their gestational age (Cassady & Strange, 1987). Prenatal malnutrition has an impact on the normal growth of all organs, normal organ functions, and the normal development of the central nervous system. Behavioral disorders, learning disabilities, and certain forms of mental illness have been linked to prenatal malnutrition (Morgane et al., 1993; Neugebauer, Hoek, & Susser, 1999).

A child may be malnourished during pregnancy, after birth, or both. Although some growth retardation is hypothesized to occur if a fetus is malnourished, the most severe impact on growth occurs when resources are inadequate both before and after the child is born. This is the case in many poverty-stricken areas of the world. When prenatal malnutrition is followed by postnatal malnutrition and disease, it is impossible to study the effects of prenatal malnutrition alone.

A pregnant woman's diet can be successfully modified to increase the newborn's weight. Diet supplements that are rich in protein and high in calories appear to have the most positive impact (Sigman, 1995). The rate of infant mortality declined 69% for the babies born to Guatemalan women who were given a protein-enriched supplement (Brown & Pollitt, 1996). In Mexico, a longitudinal study compared children born to women who had received nutritional supplements with those who had not, when the children were 12 and again at 18. Those without the supplement had a longer, slower period of cognitive maturity, some still showing gains at age 18. However, the prenatally undernourished children never performed at the level of those whose mothers received a supplement, even at age 18 (Chavez, Martinez, & Soberanes, 1995).

In order for prenatal nutritional intervention to have the greatest impact, it must be coupled with efforts to reduce the continued effects of poverty after birth. Children who are at risk for malnutrition are likely to experience more illness, lethargy, and withdrawal; delayed physical growth; and, in consequence, delayed intellectual growth. On the other hand, some of the negative effects of malnutrition can be offset if infants are adequately nourished after birth (Tanner, 1990). These infants show increased activity, make greater demands on their environment, and prompt more active caregiving responses (Brazelton, 1987a). This pattern of interaction may offset the initial deficits resulting from an inadequate prenatal nutritional environment.

# THE CULTURAL CONTEXT

Julan is a Hmong, now living in Australia. She has just had a baby, and she and her family are preparing for the soul-calling ceremony on the third day after the baby's birth. Once completed, she will feel that she has done what is needed to protect the baby and link it to its living as well as its supernatural world. The Hmong believe that each of us has three souls—one that enters the body when the infant is conceived, one that enters as the baby takes its first breath during childbirth, and one that enters on the third day after birth. The soul-calling ceremony secures these souls in the infant's body and thus ensures the baby's well-being (Rice, 2000).

In order to appreciate the events surrounding the birth of a child, one must understand some of the idiosyncrasies in a culture's approach to pregnancy and birth. The beliefs, values, and guidelines for behavior regarding pregnancy and childbirth have been referred to as the **birth culture** (Hahn & Muecke, 1987; Scopesi, Zanobini, & Carossino, 1997). The

decision to have a child, the social and physical experiences of pregnancy, the particular style of help that is available for the delivery of the child, and the care and attitudes toward both mother and baby after delivery are all components of the birth culture. Not everyone in a cultural group adheres to the full script of the birth culture, but at the very least, these guidelines are part of the mythology or lore that surfaces as a woman and her partner experience the events of pregnancy.

Information about approaches to pregnancy and childbirth in traditional cultures are drawn primarily from the Human Relations Areas Files (Murdock & White, 1969) and from Ford's (1945) comparison of reproductive behavior in 64 cultures. In most traditional societies, men and nontribal women are not allowed to observe delivery. Furthermore, many of the events related to conception and delivery are considered too personal or private to discuss with outsiders. Thus, the data on childbearing practices are not complete. Comparisons across cultures serve only to place the American system in a cultural context.

## REACTIONS TO PREGNANCY

Many cultures share the assumption that the behavior of expectant parents will influence the developing fetus and the ease or difficulty of childbirth. Of the 64 cultures studied by Ford (1945), 42 prescribed certain behaviors for expectant parents and prohibited others. Many such restrictions were dietary.

> Among the Pomeroon Arawaks, though the killing and eating of a snake during the woman's pregnancy is forbidden to both father and mother, the husband is allowed to kill and eat any other animal. The cause assigned for the taboo of the snake is that the little infant might be similar, that is, able neither to talk nor to walk. (Roth, 1953, p. 122)

In many Asian, Mediterranean, and Central and South American cultures, pregnancy is believed to be affected by the balance of "hot" and "cold" foods in a woman's diet. Pregnant women are advised to avoid both very "hot" foods, such as chili peppers and salty or fatty foods, and very "cold" foods, such as acidic, sour, or cold fresh foods (Hahn & Muecke, 1987).

A culture's view of pregnancy determines the kinds and severity of the symptoms associated with it, the types of treatment or medical assistance sought during pregnancy, and the degree to which pregnancy is responded to as a life stressor. Attitudes toward pregnant women can be characterized along two dimensions: (1) solicitude versus shame, and (2) adequacy versus vulnerability (Mead & Newton, 1967).

### SOLICITUDE VERSUS SHAME

**Solicitude** toward the pregnant woman is shown in the care, interest, and help of others. For example, it is said among Jordon villagers that "as people are careful of a chicken in the egg, all the more so should they be of a child in its mother's

## Couvade

SOME CULTURES OBSERVE the formal practice of **couvade**, in which the expectant father takes to his bed and observes very specific taboos during the period shortly before birth. Among the Arapesh of New Guinea, childbearing is believed to place as heavy a burden and drain of energy on the father as on the mother. Some cultures believe that by following the ritual of couvade, fathers distract the attention of evil spirits, so that the mother and baby can go through the childbirth transition more safely (Helman, 1990).

Even in groups that do not practice the ritual of couvade, it is common to find expectant fathers experiencing some couvade symptoms, such as general fatigue, stomach cramps, nausea, dizziness, or backache. Symptoms often begin toward the end of the first trimester, are noticeable again toward

the end of pregnancy, and end with childbirth (Klein, 1991).

> Couvade is a crisis of faith—the faith a man has in his ability to face the unknown. As the wife increaseth, the husband decreaseth. In his despair, he is at the bottom of the barrel of his manhood. There he gropes for something new in his composition to help him to cope; and what he finds is something very, very old—an ancient technique to help man survive this very normal but very upsetting ordeal.
>
> Ancient tools, ancient tricks, ancient masks. What he discovers is that modern man and ancient man, different as button-down and buckskin, are quite alike in one respect—they both value their security, and are both threatened when their manly armor starts to crack." (Finley, 1984)

Trethowan (1972), one of the first to document the nature and extent of

couvade symptoms in the normal population, suggested that these physical symptoms are the product of a man's emotional ambivalence toward his wife during her pregnancy. The expectant father may experience empathy and identify with his wife's pregnant state. At the same time, he may experience some jealousy of his wife, resentment of the loss or potential loss of intimacy in their relationship, repulsion by his wife's physical appearance, or some envy of his wife's ability to bear a child. These psychological conflicts, many of which are probably unconscious or unexpressed, are amplified by an expectant father's conscious worries about the health and well-being of his wife and their baby. The combination of these stresses may produce the couvade syndrome.

womb" (Grandquist, 1950). As the Chagga in Africa say, "Pay attention to the pregnant woman! There is no one more important than she" (Guttmann, 1932).

At the other end of this spectrum are the cultures that keep pregnancy a secret as long as possible. This custom may stem from a fear that damage will come to the fetus through supernatural demons or from shyness about the sexual implications of pregnancy.

Societies that demonstrate solicitude increase the care given to the pregnant woman and fetus. These attitudes emphasize the importance of birth as a mechanism for replenishing the group, and additional resources are likely to be provided to the pregnant woman. By keeping the pregnancy a secret, cultures that instill a sense of shame in the woman do not promote the health of the mother or the fetus and may not encourage couples to have children.

### ADEQUACY VERSUS VULNERABILITY

In many societies, pregnancy is a sign of sexual prowess and a means of access to social status. Some cultures do not arrange a wedding until after the woman has become pregnant. In a polygynous family—one in which a man has more than one wife—the pregnant wife receives the bulk of her husband's attention and may prevent her husband from taking an additional wife (Grandquist, 1950). In some cultures, women

are considered more attractive after they have borne children. "Thus, the Aymara widow of South America with many children is regarded as a desirable bride" (Tichauer, 1963). "Lepcha men consider that copulation with women who have borne more than one child is more enjoyable and less exhausting than with other adult women" (Gorer, 1938).

The other end of this continuum is the view that child-making is exhausting, pregnant women are vulnerable, and women grow more frail with each pregnancy. Among the Arapesh of New Guinea (Mead, 1935), pregnancy is tiring for both men and women. Once menstruation stops, the husband and the wife believe that they must copulate repeatedly in order to provide the building materials for the fetus's semen and blood.

Many cultures teach that during pregnancy, the woman and the fetus are more readily exposed to evil spirits. In several cultures, the forces of life and death are thought to be engaged in a particularly intense competition for the mother and the fetus around the time of delivery.

Solicitude versus shame and adequacy versus vulnerability are two dimensions that create a matrix within which the birth culture of any society or subculture can be located. Within this framework, pregnancy may be viewed as a time of great rejoicing or extreme shame, of feeling sexually powerful or extremely vulnerable. One might describe the U.S. medical birth culture, for example, as being characterized by

## HUMAN DEVELOPMENT AND DIVERSITY

### Taegyo (Fetal Education)

THE FOLLOWING DESCRIPTION of Korean prenatal care practices was written by a Korean woman who delivered her first child in Korea and her second in the United States while her husband was in graduate school. She struggled with her own ambivalence about whether the traditional Korean practices were restrictive superstitions or valuable wisdom. Writing this research paper about her own culture helped her clarify the place of traditional practices in her modern world.

Taegyo has a long history. I could easily find its history and the contents transmitted from generation to generation through literature and folklore on several Korean websites. Taegyo dates from the Koryo dynasty (918–1392 A.D.) in Korea. The old Korean literary works, such as Taegyohunnyo, Taegyosingi, Kyuhabchongseo, and

Donguibogam provide mental and attitudinal guides for pregnant women. The most important point is the behavior of pregnant women; there are guides for maintaining the emotional stability of pregnant women, including having good carriage; guides for clothes, for promoting pregnant women's health, the prohibition of certain foods and medicines, and so on. In addition, paternal Taegyo has been considered important from old traditional times until now because it is believed to significantly influence the physical and psychological condition of the baby as well.

According to Taegyosingi, which was written in the Chosun dynasty (1392–1910) and became the foremost guide for fetal education, pregnant women need peaceful and comfortable surroundings and special care from other family members.

It also recommends that pregnant women read good literature, follow the teaching of sages, look at good pictures, listen to good stories, and eat beautifully shaped foods with vivid colors. There are also many prohibited points: not to sleep with your husband; not to take any medications without caution; not to sit in cold or dirty places; not to go outside when it is dark, windy, or rainy; not to wash with cold water; not to sleep on your stomach; not to sleep after eating too much; not to whisper; not to lie or deceive; not to use abusive language. These prohibitions are based on the belief that the fetus feels exactly what the mother feels; thus pregnant women should be careful in everyday life, and listen and speak good things and behave and think properly.

Source: Kim (2002).

solicitude and vulnerability. Pregnant women are usually treated with increased concern and care and are often placed in a medical system that increases their sense of dependency. Attitudes in the workplace also contribute to the sense of vulnerability when pregnancy is viewed as incompatible with serious dedication to the job.

In the United States, both men and women apply expectations of the "sick role" to pregnant women. This idea includes the view that pregnant women should not exert themselves and are excused from certain obligations; that they need special care and should seek out medical expertise to meet these health care needs; that they should do whatever is necessary to comply with the health recommendations of experts; and that their moodiness, irritability, or other symptoms are forgiven because these symptoms are attributed to their pregnant state (Myers & Grasmick, 1990).

## REACTIONS TO CHILDBIRTH

Childbirth is an important event in most societies, marked by the presence of specially designated attendants, a specified location, and certain ceremonies and rituals intended to support the miraculous emergence of the newborn into the society. In traditional societies, the delivery is usually attended by two or more assistants with specific assigned roles. Traditional birth attendants are found in all areas of the world.

They are usually women who have had children themselves and who are respected members of their community. In Jamaica, the nana, or midwife, is one of the key figures in the village. She is called on to assist in many family crises. During pregnancy and childbirth, the nana provides assistance in the many rituals and taboos that mark the rebirth of the woman as a mother, and she usually cares for the mother and the infant until the ninth day after birth (Kitzinger, 1982).

In most traditional cultures, childbirth takes place in a familiar setting, either at home or in a nearby birthing hut. If the birth takes place at home, a woman may be separated from others by a curtain for privacy, but she knows that her family members are close at hand. Women typically give birth standing, squatting, or sitting and reclining against something or someone. The Western birth custom of lying on one's back with one's feet propped up in the air has no counterpart in traditional birth cultures, nor are women expected to be moved from one setting or room to another during the phases of labor (Helman, 1990). That appears to be a ritual reserved for women in modern, industrialized societies.

Views about the birth itself range from an extreme negative pole, where birth is seen as dirty and defiling, to an extreme positive pole, where it is seen as a personal achievement. The view of childbirth as a normal physical event is the midpoint on this continuum.

When birth is viewed as dirty, as it is by the Arapesh of New Guinea and the Kadu Gollas of India, the woman must go to an area away from the village to deliver her child. Many cultures, such as that of the ancient Hebrews, require extensive purification rituals after childbirth. Vietnamese villagers believe that mothers should not bathe or shampoo their hair for a month after giving birth, so that the baby will not "fall apart," and that the new mother must not have sexual intercourse for 100 days (Stringfellow, 1978).

A slightly more positive orientation toward childbirth is to identify it as a sickness. This view causes a pregnant Cuna Indian woman to visit her medicine man for daily medication. The midpoint of this spectrum—what we might most appropriately describe as "natural childbirth"—is a setting in which the mother delivers her baby in the presence of many members of the community, without much expression of pain and with little magic or obstetrical mechanics. Clark and Howland (1978) described childbirth for Samoan women as follows:

> The process of labor is viewed by Samoan women as a necessary part of their role and a part of the life experience. Since the baby she is producing is highly valued by her culture, the mother's delivery is also commendable and therefore ego-satisfying. Pain relief for labor may well present the patient with a conflict. She obviously experiences pain as demonstrated by skeletal muscle response, tossing and turning, and fixed body positions, but her culture tells her that she does not need medication. It is the "spoiled" palagi [Caucasian] woman who needs pain-relieving drugs. Moreover, the culture clearly dictates that control is expected of a Samoan woman, and no overt expressions of pain are permissible. (p. 166)

At the most positive end of the scale, birth is seen as a proud achievement. Among the Ila of Northern Zimbabwe, women attending childbirth were observed to shout praises of the woman who had a baby. They all thanked her, saying, "I give thanks to you today that you have given birth to a child" (Mead & Newton, 1967, p. 174).

A similar sentiment is expressed in Marjorie Karmel's (1983) description of the Lamaze method of childbirth:

> From the moment I began to push, the atmosphere of the delivery room underwent a radical transformation. Where previously everyone had spoken in soft and moderate tones in deference to my state of concentration, now there was a wild encouraging cheering section, dedicated to spurring me on. I felt like a football star, headed for a touchdown. (pp. 93–94)

The American view of childbirth seems to be evolving toward an emphasis on safety for mother and child, and toward building a sense of competence in the mother and the father as they approach the care of their newborn (Sameroff, 1987). In comparison with the medical practices of the 1940s and 1950s, there is now less use of obstetrical medication during childbirth, greater involvement of fathers or other birth coaches during labor and delivery, and more immediate contact between infants and their parents. There are more op-

The modern U.S. birth culture favors less use of obstetrical medication so that the mother is awake, the father is involved, and the medical staff are part of the support group.

© Christopher Bissell/Getty Images

portunities for the baby to spend much of the day with the mother and for siblings to visit. Hospital stays are typically shorter.

At the same time, women are taught that the best way to promote the healthy development and safe delivery of their child is to make early and regular visits to their obstetrician during the prenatal period, to attend childbirth instructional classes, to observe restrictions in diet and use of drugs, and to avoid exposure to certain environmental hazards that may harm the fetus. Midwifery and birthing centers have been slow to develop in the United States, and most physicians strongly urge their patients to deliver their children in a hospital. What is more, the use of elective cesarean deliveries contradicts the view of childbirth as a natural event. Some argue that the birth culture in the United States is created to reinforce the values of science and technology in the face of an event that is at heart natural, personal, and communal (Davis-Floyd, 1990).

It is reasonable to speculate that events at the time of the birth influence the mother's feelings about herself and her parenting ability. Efforts by the community—especially family members, close friends, and health care professionals—to foster a woman's competence in and control of parenting and to express care and support for her seem to promote a woman's positive orientation toward herself and her mothering role. On the other hand, messages of social rejection, doubts about a woman's competence, and attempts to take away control or to isolate the mother from her infant or her social support system may undermine the woman's self-esteem and interfere with her effectiveness as she approaches the demanding and exhausting task at hand (Dunkel-Schetter, Sagrestano, Feldman, & Killingsworth, 1996).

The population of the United States is increasingly diverse, and attention must be given to understanding the variety of cultural norms affecting the pregnant woman and her family support system. For example, research on the birth settings in hospitals in the United States, Germany, France, and Italy found that each country had a somewhat different focus on the woman's ability to have control over the birth process, the types of emotional and technical support provided, the availability of childbirth preparation classes, and the focus given to mother–child and father–child bonding in each setting (Scopesi, Zanobini, & Carossino, 1997). Other studies of immigrants giving birth in a new country emphasize problems of communication between women, their families, and the childbirth professionals that undercut the woman's sense of confidence and control. Immigrant women are especially distressed by behaviors that they perceive to be unkind, rushed, or unsupportive during their labor and delivery (Small, Rice, Yelland, & Lumley, 1999). Efforts are needed to interpret the key elements of the birth culture for women who are not familiar with it, so that they may understand and possibly reinterpret those aspects that appear disrespectful or threatening.

## APPLIED TOPIC

# ABORTION

**ABORTION** IS THE termination of a pregnancy before the fetus is able to live outside the uterus. Each year, thousands of pregnancies are terminated through spontaneous abortion, usually referred to as **miscarriage**. However, the focus of this section is on the *voluntary* termination of pregnancy. In obstetrical practice, abortions are induced differently before and after 12 weeks of gestation. Before 12 weeks, the pregnancy is aborted by dilating the cervix and then removing the contents of the uterus by suction with a vacuum aspirator or by scraping out the uterus. After 12 weeks, abortion can be induced by the injection of a saline solution or of prostaglandin, which stimulates labor. The fetus also may be removed surgically by a procedure similar to a cesarean section (Cunningham et al., 2001).

A nonsurgical approach to abortion was developed in France in 1988 with the drug RU-486, now called mifepristone, that interrupts pregnancy by interfering with the synthesis and circulation of progesterone (Baulieu, 1989). When combined with doses of prostaglandin, it is found to be 92% effective if taken within the first 49 days after the last menstrual period. It causes the uterine lining to slough off, so there is no need for vacuum aspiration or surgical intervention (Planned Parenthood, 2000). Administration of mifepristone typically requires several clinic visits. If expulsion is not complete by the third visit, a surgical abortion is required. Studies find that 1 woman out of 100 using the drug is still pregnant at 12 days, and 2 to 4 out of 100 have had incomplete abortions ("How RU-486 Works," 1997). The drug was approved by the FDA in the United States in 2000 to be prescribed by a physician who can make a referral to a hospital or surgeon should a surgical abortion be required ("Congress and RU-486," 2001). Many physicians who would not perform surgical abortions on moral grounds say that they would be willing to prescribe and monitor the use of RU-486 for women who requested it (Rosenblatt, Mattis, & Hart, 1995).

*The abortion controversy continues to highlight the social, political, religious, and cultural significance of the prenatal period. What do you see as the eventual resolution of this controversy in the United States?*

© Brendan Smialowski /AFP/Getty Images

## THE LEGAL CONTEXT OF ABORTION IN THE UNITED STATES

At the heart of the abortion controversy in the United States is the conflict between society's responsibility to protect the rights of a woman and its responsibility to protect the rights of an unborn child. On one side are those who insist that a woman has the right to privacy and the right to choose or reject motherhood. On the other side are those who seek to protect the rights of the unborn fetus, which is incapable of protecting its own interests. Some argue that this is a false dichotomy and that we cannot truly separate the well-being of mother and unborn fetus.

A major point requiring definition in the abortion controversy is the developmental age at which the embryo is considered an individual and thus entitled to protection by the state. In 1973, in the case of *Roe v. Wade*, the U.S. Supreme Court proposed a developmental model to address that issue. The court supported the division of pregnancy into three trimesters and considered abortion a woman's right in the first trimester, guarded by the U.S. Constitution's protection of privacy. The court said that in the second trimester, some restrictions could be placed on access to abortion because of its risk to the mother; however, the fetus's rights were still not an issue during this period. In the final trimester, when the fetus was regarded as having a good chance of surviving outside the uterus, states could choose not to permit abortion. This ruling endorsed a woman's right to full control over the abortion decision until the fetus reached a point of developmental **viability**. At that point, the Court ruled, society's responsibility to the unborn child outweighs the woman's right to freedom and privacy.

In the years since the *Roe v. Wade* decision, the Supreme Court has ruled unconstitutional the state laws that tried to regulate abortions. However, by the year 2001, the states had a wide range of regulations, some permitting and others prohibiting restrictions of various types. The main areas where restrictions have been imposed are as follows: abortion reporting requirements; clinic access; parental involvement; mandatory delay and state-directed counseling; restrictions on insurance coverage of abortion; state funding of abortion for Medicaid recipients; "partial-birth" abortion bans; and restrictions on later abortions. For details about the restrictions that apply in each state, visit the website of the Allan Guttmacher Institute, www.guttmacher.org.

In general, courts have ruled that states ought not to impose an undue burden on a woman by placing major obstacles in her way if she seeks an abortion before the fetus has reached viability. However, many states require counseling and informed consent, often with a mandatory waiting period, before the abortion can be performed. Restrictions also focus on the requirement for minors to get parental consent before having an abortion. Most states require reporting from physicians who perform abortions. At present, women are not required to have the consent of their husbands or the child's father before having an abortion.

## THE INCIDENCE OF LEGAL ABORTIONS

The number of reported legal abortions in the United States increased dramatically after the *Roe v. Wade* decision, from 745,000 in 1973 to 1,554,000 in 1980 (U.S. Census Bureau, 1999). Since then, the trend has been a decline in the number of abortions and in the ratio of abortions to live births. A report from the Alan Guttmacher Institute placed the number of abortions in 2000 at 1.31 million, with an abortion ratio of 24.5 abortions per 100 live births and abortions, which is the lowest abortion ratio in the U.S. since 1974 (Finer & Henshaw, 2003). This decline is attributed to the interaction of a number of factors, including changes in attitudes toward abortion, decline in access to abortion clinics, more effective contraceptive use, and a resulting decline in the number of unwanted pregnancies. The public controversy and acts of violence at abortion clinics have had an impact on the number of facilities that perform abortions and on the training of physicians. One report found that first-trimester abortion education is a routine part of the training in only 46% of obstetrics and gynecology residency programs. More than 80% of U.S. counties do not have abortion facilities (Golmand et al, 2004).

Some of the characteristics of U.S. women who had legal abortions in 1999 are summarized in Table 5.4. The data suggest that women who have abortions come from a diversity of socioeconomic, family, and cultural contexts and that they have different reasons for having an abortion. The age group from 20 to 24 years old had the highest rate of abortions (32% of all abortions), followed by those from 25 to 29 (23% of all abortions) and 15 to 19 (18% of all abortions). White women had 56% of all legal abortions. Most of the abortions were performed on unmarried women, with the majority having no prior abortions. Still, 20% of women had experienced two or more abortions, suggesting that some women used it as a method of birth control.

## THE PSYCHOSOCIAL IMPACT OF ABORTION

What do we know about the impact of abortions on women? Are abortions medically risky? How do women cope emotionally with the experience of abortion? In 1965, 20% of all deaths associated with pregnancy and childbirth were linked to abortion. Since the legalization of abortion, abortion-related deaths have decreased by more than 50%. In 1989, maternal deaths associated with legal abortions were 0.8 per 100,000; maternal deaths associated with pregnancy and childbirth were 8 per 100,000 (U.S. Bureau of the Census,

**Table 5.4**  Legal Abortions in the United States: Selected Characteristics, 1999

| | |
|---|---|
| **Total legal abortions in 1999:** | 1,315,000 |
| **Abortion ratio** (no. of abortions per 1000 abortions and live births): | 246 |

**Age of women having abortions (%)**

| | |
|---|---|
| Under 15 | 1 |
| 15–19 | 18 |
| 20–24 | 32 |
| 25–29 | 23 |
| 30–34 | 14 |
| 35–39 | 8 |
| 40 and over | 3 |

**Marital status of women having abortions (%)**

| | |
|---|---|
| Married | 19 |
| Unmarried | 81 |

**Race of women having abortions (%)**

| | |
|---|---|
| White | 56 |
| Black and other | 44 |

**Number of prior live births for women having abortions (%)**

| | |
|---|---|
| None | 41 |
| 1 | 28 |
| 2 | 20 |
| 3 | 18 |
| 4 or more | 4 |

**Number of prior induced abortions (%)**

| | |
|---|---|
| None | 52 |
| 1 | 28 |
| 2 or more | 20 |

**Weeks of gestation at time of abortion (%)**

| | |
|---|---|
| Less than 9 weeks | 57 |
| 9–10 weeks | 21 |
| 11–12 weeks | 11 |
| 13 weeks or more | 12 |

Source: U.S. Census Bureau, 2003, Table 103.

1992). Legal abortion, especially before 12 weeks, was 10 times safer physically than carrying a pregnancy to term.

Although the physical risks of abortion are less than those associated with childbirth, this still leaves unanswered questions about the emotional or psychological risks. In 1987, President Reagan asked Surgeon General C. Everett Koop to evaluate the impact of abortion on women's physical and mental health. If abortions were found to be associated with increased rates of physical or mental illnesses, this could provide a scientific basis for framing public health policies limiting access to abortions. After an extensive evaluation of roughly 250 studies, Surgeon General Koop reported that "the scientific studies do not provide conclusive data about the health effects of abortion on women" (Holden, 1989, p. 730). Of the studies included in Koop's review that focused on the psychological impact of abortion, most were so seriously flawed methodologically that their results could not be used to support either side of the abortion debate (Wilmoth, 1992).

# CASE STUDY

## KAREN AND DON

*The decision about giving birth to an infant with severe genetic anomalies.*

A young couple, whom we will call Karen and Don, wanted to start a family but were troubled by a puzzling coincidence. A few years before, Don's sister had given birth to a daughter with abnormalities that matched a pattern in Don's younger brother: a heart defect, a double thumb, a club foot, and severe mental retardation. One child like this in the family could be attributed to "accident" or "fate," thought the couple, but two could not.

Karen and Don went to a human genetics clinic and began a process of discovery. With the help of a counselor, they constructed a family tree, . . . identified potential carriers of the disorder in Don's family, and persuaded them to get a blood test. Don's test confirmed the young couple's worst fear: He was a carrier and potential children were at risk. . . .

The impact of these discoveries on Don's family was profound. When blood testing revealed that his mother was not a carrier, she was relieved of a burden of guilt she had secretly carried for years. She had always thought that she was the cause of her son's and her granddaughter's abnormalities. The same information implicated Don's father; his reaction to it can be gauged by his refusal to have a blood test. Don's sister, who had just given birth to a normal child, had a tubal ligation. Don himself fell into guilty silence. Not only was he the carrier of a genetic defect; he was disappointing his wife, who desperately wanted to have a baby. He thought of artificial insemination, rejected the idea, and came close to abandoning altogether the idea of having children. Then, suddenly and surprisingly, after beginning to look into adoption, Karen discovered she was pregnant. . . .

Now the process of discovery was extended one generation down, as Karen underwent amniocentesis to determine the status of her unborn fetus. . . . Karen's mother. . . . would not tolerate abortion. "She kept saying, 'There is no way that you will terminate your pregnancy if you get bad news. There is just no way.' She didn't tell anyone I was pregnant." . . . A process of intervention began for Karen and Don when amniocentesis revealed that theirs was to be a child with severe abnormalities. "Maybe I should go ahead and have the child," she remembered thinking, "because it could be the only one I'll ever have." But they had already decided under what conditions they would terminate their pregnancy. "If the fetus had been a carrier, then we were going to go ahead and go full term and have the child. But we did not want to have a child that we knew would have physical deformities and be mentally retarded." They had to inform their families of their intentions, and that included Karen's mother. "When we called and said, 'It's bad news and I'm terminating the pregnancy,' she just couldn't believe it."

Karen's abortion was no easy matter for her. "It's not like I just lost the baby, I had a miscarriage. I willfully went in and terminated a pregnancy, and it was hard for people to deal with it. Some people think it was the kind of thing . . . you go in and you're knocked out and you wake up and you're not pregnant anymore. And that's not the way it was at all. They induced labor, and I was in labor for ten hours, and I delivered a child. I was awake. My mother called to find out how I was doing afterward, but then dropped the subject. When I went back to work, everyone acted like things should be normal, like nothing had ever happened, and I was definitely mourning."

Source: "Intergenerational Buffers: The Damage Stops Here," by J. Kotre and K. B. Kotre, pp. 367–389, in D. P. McAdams & E. de St. Aubin (Eds.), *Generativity and Adult Development: Psychosocial Perspectives on Caring for and Contributing to the Next Generation.* Copyright © 1998 American Psychological Association. Reprinted by permission.

### ■ CRITICAL THINKING AND CASE ANALYSIS

1. Try to put yourself in the roles of the main characters in this case: Karen, Don, Karen's mother, Don's mother, Don's father. How might you react?
2. How does technology enter into the case?
3. How are the biological, psychological, and societal systems involved in understanding the issues faced by Karen and Don?
4. How might Karen and Don's marital relationship be influenced by these experiences?
5. What are the ethical considerations in this case?
6. In what ways do cultural issues related to pregnancy, childbirth, and abortion come into play in this case? How might a couple living in a different cultural context approach this situation differently?

The typical emotional reactions of women who have had abortions are relief at having taken control over one's situation by ending an unwanted pregnancy, and regret over the loss (Elias, 1998; Lemkau, 1988; Zucker, 1999). In a study of more than 400 women 2 years after they had an abortion, 70% felt they had made the right decision. Especially when the pregnancy was unwanted and the abortion is performed within the first 12 weeks, women generally resolve any negative feelings and thoughts they may have had soon after the abortion (Adler et al., 1990). However, roughly 30% of women experience some emotional distress as they look back on their decision (Bradshaw & Slade, 2003).

Several factors are associated with a positive abortion outcome (Alter, 1984; Miller, 1992). Women who have an androgynous gender identity—that is, a flexible view of both masculine and feminine characteristics—report less sense of loss, less anxiety, fewer physical symptoms, and fewer

thoughts about death than other women (androgyny is discussed further in Chapter 10). These women tend to have a less traditional gender role orientation and expect to find a variety of sources of satisfaction in their lives in addition to or instead of childrearing.

Another factor related to postabortion adjustment is a woman's views about the acceptability of abortion within the cultural context of her family's and community's beliefs (Wang & Buffalo, 2004). Not surprisingly, women who believe that abortion is an acceptable solution to an unwanted pregnancy and that abortion is also acceptable to their friends, family, and partner are less likely to experience strong feelings of regret or emotional upset following an abortion. Religious beliefs, childbearing motives, and the woman's awareness of community opinions influence her own attitudes toward abortion.

Even though abortions can be associated with positive feelings of having taken control of one's destiny, one must not overlook the negative reactions that some women face. For women whose support systems do not sanction abortion, the decision to have an abortion is likely to be associated with strong negative emotions. Lemkau (1988) reviewed clinical cases in which abortion produced strong, unresolved negative emotions. Sometimes, when a genetic anomaly is discovered in the fetus, abortion is performed late in pregnancy. A woman who has already become attached to the fetus grieves for her loss. In other second-trimester abortions, the ambivalence that caused the delay in the decision to have an abortion is exaggerated by the physical discomfort associated with a later abortion. Some women discover that they are unable to conceive after an abortion, and guilt, anger, and regret surface. Women who are divorced, separated, or widowed at the time of an abortion appear to be more vulnerable to strong negative emotional reactions (Speckhard & Rue, 1992).

### ■ MEN'S REACTIONS TO ABORTION

Although abortion is often construed as a "women's issue," women and their unborn babies are not the only people affected by the abortion decision. In 1976, the Supreme Court ruled that a woman did not need the consent of her husband or the child's father to have an abortion, overruling a previous requirement of the father's consent that had been legislated in 12 states (Etzioni, 1976). Since that decision, the Supreme Court has supported a woman's independence from her husband or a child's father with regard to reproductive decision making. However, questions about the legal rights of fathers to determine the fate of their unborn children are still being raised, and the laws will probably continue to be challenged as fathers become increasingly committed to participation in parenting.

Not much is known about men's reactions to their partners' abortions. Shostak and McLouth (1985) interviewed 1,000 men who had accompanied women to abortion clinics across the United States. Of these men, 93% said they would alter their birth-control methods as a result of the experience;

83% believed that abortion was a desirable way of resolving the pregnancy problem. Many of these men expressed anxiety, frustration, and guilt in relation to the unwanted pregnancy and the abortion. Recent studies suggest that men, especially adolescent fathers, may experience feelings of anxiety, anger, and moral conflicts about abortion. Young men feel that they need to "be strong" for their girlfriends, even if they are feeling their own sense of confusion or loss. Just as for women, the response of men is embedded in their value system and in their relationship with the baby's mother. For young fathers, issues of secrecy and consideration for the girlfriend may prevent them from seeking support for their own feelings (Holmberg & Wahlberg, 2000; Maloy & Patterson, 1992; Thomas & Striegel, 1994–1995). More research is needed to learn how fathers' reactions to and attitudes about abortion contribute to the abortion decision and how abortion experiences affect a man's future approach to sexual relationship and paternity.

The debate surrounding the legalization and availability of abortion services is an excellent example of a psychosocial controversy. Embedded in this controversy are key human development issues: When does human life begin? When is a fetus viable—that is, capable of life outside the uterus? What is the society's responsibility to unborn children? To women of childbearing age? What is the impact of an abortion on a woman's physical health, psychological well-being, and future childbearing? What is the impact of bearing and rearing an unwanted child on a woman's physical health and psychological well-being? What is the impact of being an unwanted child? What are the rights of fathers with respect to a woman's decision to have an abortion? What are the rights and responsibilities of parents in regard to an adolescent's abortion? The politicization of the abortion controversy often overshadows the personal dilemmas that face women and men as they confront this difficult decision.

# Chapter Summary

A fetus develops in a psychosocial context—genetic inheritance links each new infant both to a specific ancestry and to the evolutionary history of the species. Genetic factors contribute to the rate of development and to the pattern of individual characteristics. Many personal competencies and abnormalities have their origins in the pattern of genetic information provided at fertilization. Our understanding of the biochemical basis of genetics and the completion of the Human Genome Project are leading to the development of new technologies that may one day result in the ability to correct genetic abnormalities or to modify the genotype. These advances pose new psychosocial dilemmas and require that the public become better educated in such areas as science, human development, and ethics.

The 9 months of fetal development involve a rapid differentiation of body organs and a gradual integration of survival functions, especially the ability to suck and swallow, the regulation of breathing and body temperature, and the maturation of the digestive system. Sense receptors are prepared to respond to stimulation long before they are put to use. The central nervous system, which begins to take shape in the third and fourth weeks after conception, continues to develop and change throughout the prenatal period and into childhood and adolescence.

During pregnancy, the mother and the fetus are interdependent. Pregnancy affects a woman's social roles and social status and influences how people treat her and what resources become available to her. A woman's physical well-being and emotional state along with her attitude toward her pregnancy and her developing attachment to her unborn child set the stage for the quality of her parenting after the child is born.

Characteristics of the mother, her lifestyle, and her physical and cultural environment all influence fetal development. Of special concern are the mother's age, any drugs she takes during her pregnancy, her exposure to certain diseases and environmental toxins, the use of anesthetic drugs during delivery, and the mother's diet. A specific social concern is the impact of poverty on fetal development. Infants conceived by women living in poverty are exposed to the cumulative effects of many of the environmental hazards that are known to result in low birthweight and congenital abnormalities.

The experiences of pregnancy and childbirth are embedded in a cultural context. The birth culture provides a set of guidelines for behavior and attitudes toward and beliefs about restrictions on the woman's activities, the availability of resources, and the treatment of a pregnant woman by others. A matrix of orientations toward pregnancy reflects solicitude versus shame and adequacy versus vulnerability. Most birth cultures can be located within this matrix.

Several factors involved in the prenatal period converge in the issue of abortion. The decision to abort reflects the mother's attitude toward childbirth; her criteria for a healthy, normal child; her age and economic resources; and her access to a safe means of ending the pregnancy. The decision about abortion also reflects the culture's attitudes about the moral implications of ending a life after conception and the legal principles about when the fetus itself has a right to society's protection. Finally, the decision to abort is related to the safety, accessibility, and expense of the procedure.

The stage is now set to consider the remaining life stages in a psychosocial context. We have discussed the emergence of a child into an existing family, community, and cultural network. The challenges to growth at every life stage reflect the balance between the unique talents and resources that a person offers and the barriers, expectations, and resources that he or she confronts in the environment.

# Further Reflection

1. What do you know about your genetic makeup? How would you find out more if you were interested?

2. Where do you stand on the relative contribution of genetics and environment to human behavior? How do genetics and environment contribute to areas of human functioning such as intelligence, creativity, leadership, or sense of humor?

3. If you were to face the challenge of infertility, how might you cope? What alternatives would you be willing to consider? Childlessness, adoption, fertility drugs, artificial reproductive technologies? How important is it to you to have genetically related offspring?

4. Suppose your work exposed you to environmental toxins that might have a negative impact on your unborn child. What would you do?

5. Pregnancy is a powerfully gendered experience. As a man or woman, what do you imagine is the experience of pregnancy for the opposite sex?

6. What are your experiences with the cultural rituals, practices, and beliefs of the period of pregnancy? What "superstitions" or rituals have you encountered associated with pregnancy?

7. How do you distinguish abortion as a legal issue and as a topic in the study of human development? How much do you rely on science and technology to help inform your views about abortion?

# On the Web

**VISIT OUR WEBSITE**

Go to http://www.wadsworth.com/psychology to find online resources directly linked to your book.

# Casebook

For additional cases related to this chapter, see the case of "Lonita and Tano" in *Life Span Development: A Case Book*, by Barbara and Philip Newman, Laura Landry-Meyer, and Brenda J. Lohman, pp. 32–37. This case introduces the challenges of supporting a healthy pregnancy for a new immigrant couple with few financial resources.

# CHAPTER 6

# INFANCY (FIRST 24 MONTHS)

*Mother and Son on the Seashore*, 1921/Pablo Picasso/© 2005 Estate of Pablo Picasso/Artists Rights Society (ARS), New York /SuperStock

*Through a process of mutual adaptation, mother and infant establish a pattern of meaningful interactions and build the foundation for trust.*

■ NEWBORNS

■ DEVELOPMENTAL TASKS

The Development of Sensory/Perceptual and Motor Functions
CASE STUDY: THE COTTON FAMILY
Attachment
Sensorimotor Intelligence and Early Causal Schemes
Understanding the Nature of Objects and Creating Categories
Emotional Development

■ THE PSYCHOSOCIAL CRISIS: TRUST VERSUS MISTRUST

Trust
Mistrust

■ THE CENTRAL PROCESS FOR RESOLVING THE CRISIS:
MUTUALITY WITH THE CAREGIVER

Coordination, Mismatch, and Repair of Interactions
Establishing a Functional Rhythm in the Family
Parents with Psychological Problems

■ THE PRIME ADAPTIVE EGO QUALITY
AND THE CORE PATHOLOGY

Hope
Withdrawal

■ APPLIED TOPIC: THE ROLE OF PARENTS

Safety in the Physical Environment
Fostering Emotional and Cognitive Development
Fathers' and Mothers' Parental Behavior
Parents as Advocates
The Importance of Social Support

■ CHAPTER SUMMARY

■ FURTHER REFLECTION

▶ *To identify important milestones in the maturation of the sensory and motor systems, and to describe the interactions among these systems during the first 2 years of life.*

▶ *To define social attachment as the process through which infants develop strong emotional bonds with others, and to describe the dynamics of attachment formation during infancy.*

▶ *To describe the development of sensorimotor intelligence, including an analysis of how infants organize experiences and conceptualize causality.*

▶ *To examine how infants understand the properties of objects, including the sense that objects are permanent, that they have unique properties and functions, and that they can be categorized.*

▶ *To examine the nature of emotional development, including emotional differentiation, the interpretation of emotions, and emotional regulation.*

▶ *To analyze the factors that contribute to the resolution of the psychosocial crisis of trust versus mistrust, including the achievement of mutuality with the caregiver and the attainment of a sense of hope or withdrawal.*

▶ *To evaluate the critical role of parents and caregivers during infancy, with special attention to issues of safety in the physical environment; optimizing cognitive, social, and emotional development; and the role of parents and caregivers as advocates for their infants with other agencies and systems.*

INFANCY IS A stage of strikingly rapid development. During the first year of life, the infant's birthweight almost triples. (Imagine if your weight tripled within 1 year at any other time in your life!) The baby seems to grow before your very eyes. Parents will remark that they go to work in the morning, and their baby seems to have changed by the time they return in the evening. Along with this extraordinary rate of physical growth comes a remarkable process of increased control and purposefulness, leading to the integration of simple responses into coordinated, patterned behavior. By the age of 2, the fundamentals of movement, language, and concept formation can be observed. Most infants are marvelously flexible, capable of adapting to any of the varied social environments into which they may be born.

As families in the United States have become smaller, we have seen a change in the emphasis that society places on infancy. Each child is taken much more seriously. Safety concerns have prompted laws about car seats for infants, guidelines for putting babies to sleep on their back or side, and the widespread use of monitors in the baby's room to catch signs of infant distress. The medical community is devising complex technologies for saving the lives of babies who are born weighing 1,000 grams (32 oz.) or less. The psychological community is giving attention to infant temperament and to the early origins of personality, focusing on

individual differences among infants from the very first weeks of life. A growing "baby industry" offers special equipment, foods, toys, books, and other paraphernalia intended to enrich the infant's sensory, perceptual, and motor development and to support the parent–infant bond. Furthermore, parents take classes, read books and magazines, and join support groups so that they can "get it right the first time."

The story of development during infancy requires that one keep in mind a strong, genetically guided pattern of growth and development in continuous interaction with a complex and changing social and physical environment (Plomin, De-Fries, Craig, & McGuffin, 2003). The mother's personality, the father's involvement in child care, cultural beliefs surrounding childrearing practices, and poverty or economic strain that affect the parents' psychological well-being are all factors that influence a child's vulnerability or resilience (Plomin & McClearn, 1993). As the infant's capacities change, they bring him or her into interaction with new facets of the environment. As daily experiences take place, they shape the infant's neural pathways into patterns of thought and behavior (Coll, 2004).

From the perspective of psychosocial development, five major developmental tasks are especially critical during infancy:

- establishment and coordination of the sensory, perceptual, and motor systems
- formation of an attachment to at least one person
- elaboration of the sensorimotor intellectual system
- initial understanding of the nature of objects and creation of categories for organizing the physical and social world
- differentiation of the emotional system

This chapter begins with a description of the physical status of the newborn and then discusses each of the five developmental tasks. The psychosocial crisis of infancy—trust versus mistrust—is explored as a way of conceptualizing the foundational orientation toward self and society. The chapter closes with an examination of the key roles that parents and caregivers can play in providing the environmental supports that promote optimal development in the infant and lay the foundation for future growth. ∎

# Newborns

In the United States, the average full-term baby weighs 3,300 grams (7 to 7.5 pounds) and is 51 centimeters (20 inches) long. Boys are slightly heavier and longer than girls. At birth, girls' nervous systems and bones are about 2 weeks more mature than boys'.

In the first minute after birth, and then again at 5 minutes, the newborn's life signs are evaluated using the **Apgar scoring method,** named for its originator, Virginia Apgar (see Table 6.1). Five life signs are scored on a scale from 0 to 2: heart rate, respiratory effort, muscle tone, reflex irritability, and body color. A score of 7 to 10 means the infant is in good condition. Scores of 4 to 6 mean the infant is in fair condition and may indicate the need for the administration of supplemental oxygen. Scores of 0 to 3 suggest an extremely poor condition and the need for resuscitation. Even among the infants who score 7 to 10, those with scores of 7 or 8 show less efficient attention and poorer cognitive processing than the higher scoring infants. The most important use of the Apgar scoring

method is for evaluating the need for immediate intervention rather than as a means of assessing subsequent development (American Academy of Pediatrics, 1996). The Apgar score does not explain the source of the difficulty, but it provides an indication that some level of intervention is needed.

Babies differ in their physical maturity and appearance at birth. Differences in physical maturity have distinct consequences for the capacity to regulate survival functions such as breathing, digesting, waking, and sleeping. Infants who weigh less than 2,500 grams (about 5 pounds 8 ounces) are called **low-birthweight babies**. Low birthweight may result from prematurity (i.e., being born before the full period of gestation). It may also result from the mother's inadequate diet, smoking, or use of drugs, as discussed in Chapter 5. These factors tend to lower the fetus's weight for a given gestational age. Babies who are **small for their gestational age (SGA)** are at greater risk for health problems than those who are born prematurely but are of average weight for their gestational age.

Many interventions have been devised to improve the care of very small babies. Management of their breathing, temperature regulation, monitoring of heart rate, creation of appropriate stimulation and nurturant care in the hospital all contribute to improving the chances for survival. The box about Very Small Babies (p. 138) discusses some of the risks for developmental disabilities among babies weighing less than 1,500 grams. Renewed efforts are needed to determine the causes of low birthweight, and to prevent as many preterm births as possible (Holzman & Paneth, 1998).

# Developmental Tasks

## THE DEVELOPMENT OF SENSORY/PERCEPTUAL AND MOTOR FUNCTIONS

During the first months of life, the sensory/perceptual system—vision, hearing, taste, smell, touch, motion sensitivity, and responsiveness to internal cues (*proprioception*)—is

**Table 6.1** The Apgar Scoring Method

| | Score | | |
|---|---|---|---|
| SIGN | 0 | 1 | 2 |
| **Heart Rate** | Absent | Slow (less than 100 beats/minutes) | More than 100 beats/minute |
| **Respiratory Effort** | Absent | Slow or irregular breathing | Good crying, strong breathing |
| **Muscle Tone** | Flaccid or limp | Weak; some flexion of extremities | Active motion, strong flexion of extremities |
| **Reflex Irritability** | No response | Weak cry, grimace, cough, or sneeze | Vigorous cry, grimace, cough, or sneeze |
| **Color** | Blue, pale | Body pink, extremities blue | Completely pink |

Source: Apgar, 1953.

## TECHNOLOGY AND HUMAN DEVELOPMENT

# Very Small Babies

MANY BABIES ARE born before they are fully developed. Modern technology has pushed back the boundary of fetal viability to about 24 weeks of gestational age, or a weight of about 500 grams (slightly more than 1 pound). These tiny babies, not much bigger than the palm of your hand, receive weeks of round-the-clock care in their struggle to survive. In the United States, 49% of babies with birthweights between 500 and 750 grams survive (NICHD, 2004).

What do we know about the developmental progress of these very small babies? Very-low-birthweight babies are clearly different from full-term babies. They are less physically attractive; they have higher pitched, unpleasant cries; they are more easily overstimulated and more difficult to soothe; and they are less able to establish rhythmic patterns of social interaction. Because of the aversive and ambiguous meaning of their cries, mothers of very low-birthweight babies are more likely to withdraw or become distressed rather than respond with appropriate soothing (Worchel & Allen, 1997). What is more, during the first weeks and months of life, parental contact takes place in the intimidating environment of the hospital, where the babies are usually hooked up to monitors, have one or more tubes in their bodies, and are going through periodic physical crises in the struggle for survival.

In this context, the process of attachment formation appears to face significant challenges. Parents find it hard to synchronize their parenting activities with the activities of their babies. They perceive their babies as difficult and find that they receive few cues of satisfaction or responsiveness from them. In other words, the establishment of a sense of reciprocity between parent and low-birthweight infant is more difficult

in the early months of life (Levy-Shiff, Sharur, & Mogilner, 1989).

Depending on the health and robustness of the infants, and with the appropriate parental responsiveness, approximately 65% of parents and low-birthweight babies are able to establish a framework of secure, trusting interactions by the end of the child's infancy, just as do parents and full-term infants (Goldberg & DiVitto, 1995). However, in a study of very low-birthweight babies (average weight 955 grams), significantly fewer preterm babies had secure attachments at 19 months than the comparison group of full-term babies. In fact, the percentage of very small babies who showed a secure attachment *declined* from 14 to 19 months. One explanation for this decline is that the disruptive effects of prematurity accumulate during the second year of life, introducing more anxiety among caregivers and greater difficulty in achieving mutuality in the infant–caregiver relationship (Mangelsdorf et al., 1996).

Extremely low-birthweight infants are at risk for problems in subsequent cognitive development. Infants who are born weighing less than 1,500 grams are likely to suffer serious brain hemorrhages. Moreover, their undeveloped lungs cannot deliver an adequate supply of oxygen to the brain. Chronic lung disease, frequently associated with prematurity, results in breathing problems, feeding difficulties, lung infections, and disrupted flow of oxygen (Singer, Davillier, Bruening, Hawkins, & Yamashita, 1996). These insults to the nervous system have an impact on a variety of information-processing skills that can be measured in newborns.

High-risk, preterm infants show deficits in measures of regulation of

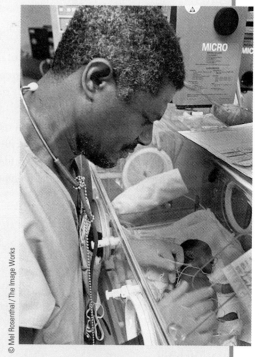

© Mel Rosenthal / The Image Works

*Hours of intensive care combined with new medical technologies increase the life chances for very tiny babies. Yet many of them are at high risk for developmental disabilities associated with their extremely low birthweight and related physical immaturity.*

arousal and attention, visual recognition of familiar stimuli, and reactivity to novel stimuli (DiPietro, Porges, & Uhly, 1992; Rose, Feldman, & Wallace, 1992). In a Dutch study, more than 1,300 very low-birthweight babies born in 1983 were studied into adolescence. About 10% had very serious abnormalities. However, another 40% had an accumulation of developmental disabilities and behavioral and learning difficulties that accumulated over time to impede their ability to function independently (Walther, den Ouden, & Verloove-Vanhorick, 2000).

developing rapidly and appears to function at a more advanced level than the motor system. Because most muscle movements are not under the infant's voluntary control in the early days and months of life, researchers have had to apply considerable ingenuity to study infants' sensory/perceptual

competencies. How can you know if an infant detects the difference between the color red and the color orange, or between the mother's voice and the voice of a stranger? We cannot simply ask an infant to point to a circle or press a button to respond to a certain change in color or image. Behaviors such as gazing time, changes in heart rate, strength or frequency of sucking, facial action, head turning, and habituation are used as indicators of infants' interest or change in response to stimuli.

**Habituation** means that the infant's response decreases after each presentation of an identical stimulus (Bornstein, 1992). Habituation allows the infant to shift attention to new aspects of the environment as certain elements become familiar. When a new stimulus is presented, such as a new level of loudness, or the same tone presented to a different ear, the infant shows an increase in alert responsiveness. Habituation is one of the most primitive forms of learning and is observed in many other mammalian species.

Habituation is a means of determining whether an infant can discriminate between two different stimuli. The researcher first habituates the infant to one stimulus; then a second stimulus is presented. Signs of renewed interest or alertness, measured by changes in heart rate, gazing time, or eye movements, are taken as evidence that the infant has detected a difference between the two stimuli. If the infant shows no new signs of interest or responsiveness, this is taken as evidence that the differences between the two stimuli were too slight to be perceived.

For example, 16 newborns who were 48 hours old were habituated to a two-dimensional image of a normal face or a "scrambled" face (eyes on the bottom of the oval, nose at the top with the eyebrows). The face was moved slowly along a bar from the midline to the right and then to the left. Fixation time was measured until the baby's looking time decreased by 60% from the level of the first three trials. Then the new stimulus was introduced. No matter whether the babies were initially habituated to the normal or to the scrambled face, they all showed an increase in fixation or looking time when the novel face was presented. Habituation was a sensitive technique for demonstrating newborns' ability to tell the difference between a normal and a scrambled face (Easterbrook, Kisilevsky, Muir, & Laplante, 1999). Similar findings have been observed in infants' responses to patterns of musical notes, phonetic sounds, and complex shapes. These studies support the notion that young infants are capable of forming and retaining a scheme for sensory experiences against which they can compare new events.

## ■ SENSORY/PERCEPTUAL DEVELOPMENT

Most infants are born with intact sensory organs and a well-formed brain. The infant's brain contains about 100 billion neurons, or nerve cells, which are already connected in pathways that are designed to execute definite functions. The fundamental organization of the brain does not change after birth, but details of its structure demonstrate **plasticity** (Johnson, 1999; Nash, 1997; Singer, 1995). During the first 3 years, the brain triples in weight and creates about 1,000 trillion connections among the neurons. Then the pathways are gradually pruned. Each sensory capacity is associated with an area of the cortex that links sensations with memories of similar sensations and, over time, with an emerging meaning of the sensory array. As a result of early experience, sights, smells, sounds, tastes, touches, and postures activate and strengthen specific neural pathways, whereas other pathways fall into disuse. Thus, the infant's interaction with the immediate stimulus environment begins to shape the organization of neural connections, creating very early patterns of familiarity and meaning (Brierley, 1993).

To see a map of the sensory and motor areas of the brain and how they relate to the infant's emerging capacities, visit the following website: http://www.babycenter.com/general/baby/babydevelopment/6752.html. At this site, you can further explore each area of sensory and motor development, including the typical pattern of development in infancy, suggestions for how caregivers can foster optimal development, and how to recognize potential abnormalities.

It would be difficult to review the full range and detail of sensory capacities that emerge and develop during infancy. Maturation in these domains is breathtaking. Our discussion focuses on those abilities that permit infants to participate in and adapt to their social environment. From birth, sensory/perceptual capacities are vital resources that help infants establish emotional links with their caregivers, gather information about their environment, and cope with sources of stress. Although we provide information on each of the sensory modalities, it is important to realize that they typically function together in a bimodal or multimodal system. Infants not only hear their caregivers, but they see, smell, and touch them. Voices are normally associated with faces; tastes are linked to smells and textures. Sensory meaning-making takes place with the benefit of information from multiple sources.

**HEARING.** You may be surprised to learn that hearing rather than vision is the sense that provides the very earliest link between the newborn and his or her mother. Research has confirmed that the fetus is sensitive to auditory stimulation in utero (Aslin, 1987; De Casper & Spence, 1986). Before birth, the fetus hears the mother's heartbeat. This sound continues to be soothing to the infant in the days and weeks after birth. Newborns show a preference for the sound of their mother's voice over the voice of an unfamiliar woman (De Casper & Fifer, 1980). They also show a preference for the sound of melodies that their mother sang during the pregnancy and even for the sound of prose passages she read during the prenatal period. One must assume that an infant's indication of preference for these auditory stimuli is based on familiarity with the sounds from exposure in utero.

Young infants can distinguish changes in the loudness, pitch, duration, and location of sounds (Kuhl, 1987). Many of these capacities are present among newborns but become increasingly sensitive by 6 months. Infants can use sounds to locate objects in space. In one study, babies ages 6 to 8 months were placed in a darkened room. Objects that made sounds were located within reach and out of reach, and off to the right or left of midline. The babies made reaching motions in the correct direction of the sounds, and they made more efforts to reach objects that sounded as if they were within reach than to reach objects that sounded out of reach

*Even in the first days of life, a new-born is taking in sensory information about his mother's face, the sound of her voice, her scent, and the way it feels to be cuddled in her arms.*

(Clifton, Perris, & Bullinger, 1991). In another study, infants ages 4 to 6 months were exposed to a "looming" sound, which appeared to come closer or recede from them at a slow or rapid pace. When the sound loomed toward them quickly, the babies leaned back in a defensive strategy to escape the anticipated threat. This suggests that infants have the ability to use auditory information to detect relative speed and distance (Freiberg, Tually, & Crassini, 2001).

The human voice is one of the earliest stimuli to evoke an infant's smile; infants appear to be particularly sensitive to language sounds (Benasich & Leevers, 2003). Very young babies are able to differentiate basic sound distinctions used in human speech throughout the world. Infants from all language environments are able to perceive and distinguish among the speech sounds that could be used in one or more of the world's languages. By 6 months of age, however, infants prefer to listen to sequences of words spoken in the mother's language rather than in a foreign language, especially if the two languages differ in their overall tone, pauses, and rhythm (Sansavini, Bertoncini, & Giovanelli, 1997). During the second 6 months of life, after exposure to a native language, the infant's ability to make some sound distinctions declines. Speech perception becomes more tied to the native language as infants begin to attach meaning to certain sound combinations, indicating a reorganization of sensory capabilities as the child learns to listen to people speaking a particular language (Bornstein, 1995; Werker & Tees, 1999). This is an example of the plasticity referred to earlier—a fine-tuning of the neural network as a result of experience.

**VISION.** Infants respond to a variety of visual dimensions, including movement, color, brightness, complexity, light–dark contrast, contours, depth, and distance (Slater & Johnson, 1998). The vast majority of research on sensory development in infancy has concentrated on assessing the acuity or sensitivity of vision. Visual behaviors also offer a way to assess the infant's cognitive capacities. For instance, the time an infant takes to scan an object and the length of time spent fixating on a novel object are indications of infant intelligence. Shorter fixation time indicates greater speed and efficiency in neural processing (Colombo, Mitchell, Coldren, & Freeseman, 1991; Jacobson et al., 1992).

**Visual acuity** improves rapidly during the first 4 months. Pattern and movement perception mature as well. By 2 months, infants form an expectation of a visual sequence. As they watch a pattern of events, they show evidence of anticipating the next event in the sequence (Aslin, 1987; Canfield & Haith, 1991). Three-month-old infants respond to wavelengths of light as though they perceive distinct hues of blue, green, yellow, and red (Aslin, 1987; Bornstein, Kessen, & Weiskopf, 1976; Teller & Bornstein, 1987). Four-month-old babies perceive objects as adults would, although they do not have the same set of cognitive associations with them that imply specific functions or categories. They recognize shapes and detect complex patterns of motion such as human walking. Infants are born with a variety of skills for detecting visual stimuli, which matures rapidly into the coordination of visual perception. However, the process of visual cognition—that is, understanding the nature of objects and their physical properties—requires further experimentation (Johnson, 2003).

**FACENESS.** The human face and "faceness" in general have special appeal for newborns (Nelson, 2001). Infants show preference for face-like stimuli. In the early weeks following birth, infants have optimal focus on objects that are about 20 cm away—approximately the distance between the mother's face and her baby cradled in her arms. Newborns can shift

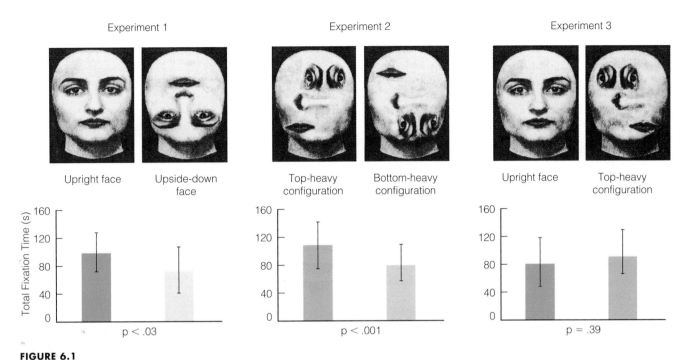

**FIGURE 6.1**

Stimulus Pairs from Three Experiments on Infants' Preference for Top-Heavy Configurations. For each experiment, the total fixation time toward each stimulus is shown along with the *p* value for comparison between the two stimuli.

Source: Cassia, Turati, & Simion, 2004.

focus to scan and keep track of a moving target, but not as easily and smoothly as older babies. Young infants focus their attention on the contours or external borders of objects rather than on the internal details. Thus, if you were holding a young baby, the child might appear to be staring at your hairline or your chin rather than at your mouth. Faces have many of the properties that infants prefer. The hairline is a type of contour; the eyes provide a light–dark contrast; and the facial expressions provide a changing, moving stimulus.

An experiment with newborns who were 25 to 73 hours old demonstrated that one of the features of a face that is important to babies is the "top-heavy" configuration of the features (Cassia, Turati, & Simion, 2004). Figure 6.1 shows the comparisons that support this conclusion. Fixation time to the stimulus pairs of faces was used as evidence of preference. In Experiment 1, babies preferred the upright to the upside-down face. In Experiment 2, babies preferred the top-heavy scrambled face to the bottom-heavy scrambled face. In Experiment 3, there was no difference in preference between the normal upright face and the top-heavy scrambled face. The results of the three studies together provide evidence of the importance of this aspect of faceness in capturing a newborn's attention. By 6 or 7 months of age, infants treat faceness as a special visual category, showing surprise when facial features are disorganized or upside down (Catherwood, Freiberg, Green, & Holt, 2001; Cohen & Cashon, 2001).

In addition to the form, shape, and movement of the human face, certain facial expressions appear to have meaning to very young babies. One- and two-day-old babies are able to discriminate and imitate the happy, sad, and surprised expressions of a live model (Field, Woodson, Greenberg, & Cohen, 1982). This very early capacity for imitation wanes and is replaced between the ages of 1 and 2 months with a voluntary capacity for imitation of facial expressions when the model is not present. Some time between 4 and 7 months, infants are able to recognize and classify some expressions such as happiness and anger (Caron, Caron, & MacLean, 1988; Ludemann, 1991; Nelson, 1987).

Lack of motion in an adult face has a disturbing effect on infants. When adults pose with a still face, babies stop looking at the adult and, in some cases, begin grimacing or showing other signs of discomfort. This reaction suggests that infants anticipate a certain normal sequence of facial movements in a human interaction. Thus, the absence of facial movements is not simply noted as novel but distressing (Muir & Lee, 2003).

Some 2-day-old infants discriminate between their mother's face and the face of a stranger (Field, Cohen, Garcia, & Greenberg, 1984). By 3 months, almost all infants can distinguish a parent's face from that of a stranger (Zucker, 1985). These visual perceptual skills illustrate the highly developed capacities for orienting toward social stimuli that permit infants to participate readily in the social context on which their survival depends.

Of course, sights and sounds typically go together. When people speak, their mouths change shape and their faces move. By 3 months of age, infants can recognize familiar voice–face associations. They show surprise when a familiar

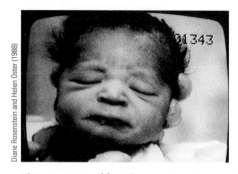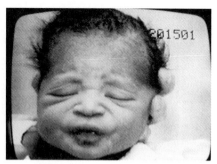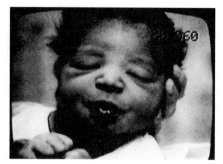

*This sequence of facial expressions in a newborn was elicited by a sweet solution. The initial negative grimace is followed by relaxation and sucking.*

face is paired with an unfamiliar voice (Brookes et al., 2001). By 4½ months, they can imitate the facial expressions associated with specific spoken sounds—making different faces for the /i/ sound and the /a/ sound (Patterson & Werker, 1999). So while babies are making sense of their visual environment, they are also using vision as a source of information about language and communication.

**TASTE AND SMELL.** Newborns can differentiate sweet, sour, bitter, and salty tastes. Facial responses to salty, sour, and bitter solutions share the same negative upper and mid-face response but differ in the accompanying lower face actions: The lips purse in response to a sour taste, the mouth gapes in response to a bitter taste, and no distinctive lower facial reaction is seen in response to a salty taste. Two hours after birth, an infant's facial responses to a sweet taste (sucrose) are characterized primarily by relaxation and sucking. Sucrose has an especially calming effect on newborns and appears to reduce pain. In one experiment, newborns 1 to 3 days old who were undergoing circumcision or were having their heel pricked for a blood test for phenylketonuria cried much less when they were given a small sucrose solution to suck (Blass & Hoffmeyer, 1991). The calming effect of sweet-tasting substances has been observed in both preterm and full-term infants (Smith & Blass, 1996). It is likely that the normal taste of milk, which includes this sweet flavor, has the combined effect of releasing natural opioids, thereby raising the pain threshold, and reducing heart rate and activity level, thereby conserving energy.

Breastfed babies are particularly sensitive to their mothers' body odors (Cernoch & Porter, 1985). One study found that 7-day-old babies could use the sense of smell to distinguish their own mothers' nursing pads from those of other mothers (MacFarlane, 1975). The mother's odor may play an important role in stimulating early mother–infant interactions (Porter, Balogh, & Makin, 1988).

**TOUCH.** The skin is the largest sensory organ and the earliest to develop in utero. A variety of evidence from animal and human research suggests that touch plays a central role in development. Gentle handling, including rocking, stroking, and cuddling, all have soothing effects on a baby. **Swaddling**—the practice of wrapping a baby snugly in a soft blanket—is a common technique for soothing a newborn in many cultures. One of the effective techniques for caring for low-birthweight babies is to introduce regular gentle stroking, rocking, and other forms of soothing touch.

Touch is an active as well as a passive sense; babies use it to explore objects, people, and their own bodies. *Sucking* is one of the earliest coping strategies infants use to calm themselves (Blass & Ciaramitaro, 1994). Sucking and mouthing are early forms of exploratory touch. Babies can recognize the qualities of objects from the way they feel in their mouths—nubbly or smooth, chewy and flexible or rigid (Rose & Ruff, 1987). For older infants, most tactile information comes through touching with the hands and bringing objects to the face in order to take a closer look or to explore them with the mouth. By 5 or 6 months of age, infants can use their hands for the controlled examination of objects. They finger surfaces to explore small details and transfer objects from one hand to the other to detect corners, shapes, and the flexibility of surfaces as well as the object's size, temperature, and weight (Bushnell & Boudreau, 1991).

**THE INTERCONNECTED NATURE OF SENSORY/ PERCEPTUAL CAPACITIES.** The sensory/perceptual capacities function as an interconnected system to provide a variety of sources of information about the environment at the same time (Calvert, Spence, & Stein, 2004). Consider the situation when an infant is being nursed. At first, the mother guides the baby toward her breast, but the baby makes use of visual, tactile, olfactory, and kinesthetic cues to find and grab hold of the nipple. If the baby is very hungry, he or she may close his or her eyes in order to concentrate exclusively on bursts of sucking behavior, coordinating sucking and swallowing as efficiently as possible. But as the initial swallows of milk satisfy the strong hunger pangs, the baby pauses to take in other aspects of the situation. He or she may gaze at the contours of the mother's face, playfully lick the milk dripping from the mother's breast, smell the milk's fragrance and taste its special sweet taste, and listen to the sound of the mother's voice offering comfort or inviting conversation. The baby may reach up to explore the mother's skin or relax in the comfort of the mother's gentle embrace. All the sensory information

*Sucking and mouthing are important ways of exploring objects in the environment. Fists and toes are the first easy targets.*

© Philip Newman

becomes integrated to create familiarity with this scheme, including a growing recognition of the mother and a rich mixture of sensory impressions associated with this special situation in which hunger is satisfied.

## ■ MOTOR DEVELOPMENT

At birth, an infant's voluntary muscle responses are poorly coordinated. Most early motor responses appear to be **reflexive**, meaning that a specific stimulus will evoke a particular motor response without any voluntary control or direction. Many of these built-in responses help infants to survive and lead them to develop more complicated sequences of voluntary behavior. The sucking reflex is a good example. At birth, inserting something in an infant's mouth produces a sucking reflex. This helps infants gain nourishment relatively easily before sucking behavior is under their control. Before long, infants become skillful at controlling the strength and sensitivity of sucking behavior. They use sucking and mouthing as strategies for tactile exploration. Infants have been shown to use their mouths to explore objects that they can then identify visually, thus transferring information from the tactile sense to the visual sense (Gibson & Walker, 1984; Meltzoff & Borton, 1979).

Table 6.2 describes a number of common infant reflexes, the evoking stimulus, and the response. Infant reflexes include sucking, grasping, rooting (turning the head in the direction of the cheek that is stroked), coughing, and stepping. With time, many of these behaviors make a transition from an *involuntary* to a *voluntary* behavior. In the process, infants may lose a response before they regain control over simple movements. Then they blend several of these new voluntary movements into increasingly coordinated and complex patterns of behavior (Fentress & McLeod, 1986). For example, very young infants can support their full weight through the strength of their grasping reflex. When propped in an infant seat, they will reach and grasp reflexively at an object, reaching their target about 40% of the time. At 4 weeks of age, this reflexive reaching behavior seems to disappear, but by 5 months it is replaced by voluntary reaching, accurate grasping, clutching, and releasing (Bower, 1987).

**REACHING AND GRASPING.** The transition from involuntary to voluntary reaching and grasping results from genetically guided maturation coupled with repeated exploration. Infants practice controlled, coordinated muscle movements, guided by visual and auditory cues—particularly cues about size, distance, and direction. In the following example, a 2-month-old girl gains control of her hands and fingers:

> She has discovered her hands, stares at them many times a day for three or four minutes at a time, watches them as she wiggles fingers, extends and flexes them, rotates wrists. She also clasps her hands together and stares at them out in front of her at arm's length (Church, 1966, p. 7).

Voluntary reaching begins as the child tries to make contact with objects on the same side of the body as the outstretched hand. By 4 months, babies will reach for objects placed on the same side, the opposite side, or in the middle of the body. By this age, babies have also become skilled in using both hands to hold an object, so they are more able to keep the object close enough to investigate. They may shift from exploring with their fingers to sucking and biting to find out more about the object (Rochat, 1989). Between 5 and 7 months, babies become increasingly accurate at reaching and grasping a moving object, alternating hands to intercept an object by anticipating the direction of its movement (Robin, Berthier, & Clifton, 1996).

By 12 months, babies have mastered the pincer grasp, using their index finger and thumb to pick up tiny things, such

**Table 6.2** Some Infant Reflexes

| REFLEX | EVOKING STIMULUS | RESPONSE |
|---|---|---|
| **Reflexes that facilitate adaptation and survival** | | |
| Sucking reflex | Pressure on lips and tongue | Suction produced by movement of lips and tongue |
| Pupillary reflex | Weak or bright light | Dilation or constriction of pupil |
| Rooting reflex | Light touch to cheek | Head movement in direction of touch |
| Startle reflex | Loud noise | Similar to Moro reflex (below), with elbows flexed and fingers closed |
| Swimming reflex | Neonate placed prone in water | Arm and leg movement |
| **Reflexes linked to competences of related species** | | |
| Creeping reflex | Feet pushed against a surface | Arms and legs drawn under, head lifted |
| Flexion reflex | Pressure on sole of foot | Involuntary bending of leg |
| Grasp reflex | Pressure on fingers or palm | Closing and tightening of fingers |
| Moro reflex | Infant lying on back with head raised—rapidly release head | Extension of arms, head thrown back, spreading of fingers, crossing arms across body |
| Springing reflex | Infant held upright and slightly forward | Arms extended forward and legs drawn up |
| Stepping reflex | Infant supported under the arms above a flat surface | Rhythmical stepping movement |
| Abdominal reflex | Tactile stimulation | Involuntary contraction of abdominal muscles |
| **Reflexes of unknown function** | | |
| Achilles tendon reflex | Blow to Achilles tendon | Contraction of calf muscles and downward bending of foot |
| Babinski reflex | Mild stroke on sole of foot | Fanning and extension of toes |
| Tonic neck reflex | Infant on back with head turned to one side | Arm and leg on side toward which head is facing are extended, other arm and leg flexed |

as string and thread, pieces of dry cereal, and spaghetti noodles. With this advance, they can also manipulate things by lifting latches, turning knobs, and placing small things inside bigger things and trying to get them out again. These motor skills provide new information about how objects work and how they relate to one another. The development of fine motor skills contributes to the infant's sense of mastery and can be a source for positive emotions. At the same time, they may cause new conflicts between the baby and the caregiver, who knows that tiny things that shouldn't are going to go into the mouth, and objects that ought to be left alone are going to be touched, moved, and manipulated.

**MOTOR SEQUENCE.** Motor skills develop as a result of the physical growth and maturation of bones, muscles, and the nervous system in the context of varied environmental opportunities. Figure 6.2 shows the normal sequence of development of motor and movement skills during the first year of life; however, babies vary in the sequence and rate at which they acquire these skills. Individual children grow in spurts, interspersed with times of slow growth and some periods of regression (Fischer & Rose, 1994). Usually, however, during the first 12 months, babies begin to hold their heads up and roll over by themselves; they learn to reach for things and grasp them; they sit, crawl, stand, and walk. Parental expectations seem to influence the timing of the onset for some of

these milestones (Hopkins & Westra, 1990). During the second year, walking becomes increasingly steady; crawling may be used for play but is no longer the preferred method for locomotion. Babies explore stairs, climbing up and down using a variety of strategies. They start to slide or jump down from modest heights. Each of these accomplishments requires practice, refinement, struggle, and finally, mastery.

**THE CONTRIBUTIONS OF NATURE AND NURTURE IN MOTOR DEVELOPMENT.** Motor development provides an excellent illustration of the interaction between the genetically guided plan for growth and the contributions of experience. The unfolding of motor capacities is guided by genetics, beginning as it does with the presence of a wide range of reflexive responses that are "hardwired," so to speak, into the infant's neurological system. At the same time, within this plan, one observes both individual and group differences. Not only are babies different from one another at birth, but they also show different rates of motor advancement. For example, one study examined how babies adapted their locomotor strategy for going down a slope. Thirty-one infants, all 14 months old, were recruited for the study. Even though they were all the same age, their prior experience with walking ranged from 10 days to 137 days (Adolph & Eppler, 2002). Cultures differ in the opportunities they provide for motor exploration, yet the emergence of bipedalism is a uni-

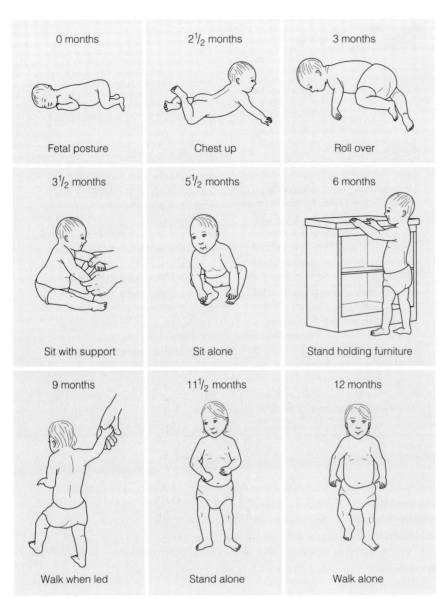

**FIGURE 6.2**

A Typical Sequence of Motor Development and Locomotion in Infancy

Source: From W. K. Frankenberg and J. B. Dodds (1967). "The Developmental Screening Test," *Journal of Pediatrics*, 71, 181–191.

versal characteristic of human children (see box on Zinacanteco Childrearing).

Although the normative pattern of motor development suggests a preprogrammed sequence of stages that is heavily guided by genetics and neural structures, research on the process of motor development has challenged this assumption. Researchers now regard the regularities in motor behavior as the result of a dynamic process of exploration in which infants coordinate their physical actions with the demands and opportunities of the situation. The combination of a maturing central nervous system, growth in strength and coordination, opportunities for various types of movement, and the emergence of cognitions to understand and anticipate actions underlies an ongoing process of self-correcting, adaptive movement (Rutkowska, 1994).

Perception and action work hand in hand, giving the infant information about the physical properties of the situation and feedback about the consequences of a specific motor strategy. Over time and with practice in similar situations, the infant discovers the combination of action, intensity, direction, and speed that will create the desired outcome. With additional practice, this pattern then becomes most likely and increasingly efficient (Thelen, 1995).

Consider Brad's efforts to crawl. He is placed face down in the middle of a brightly colored blanket. His mother kneels at the edge of the blanket and dangles a favorite stuffed bear. She smiles and says encouragingly, "Come on, Brad, come get Teddy." Brad looks intently, reaches toward the bear and, by kicking and squirming, manages to move forward. This snakelike movement is Brad's first accomplishment en route to well-organized crawling. Before he masters crawling, however, he must learn to raise himself on his knees, coordinate his hand and leg movements, and propel himself forward rather than backward.

## HUMAN DEVELOPMENT AND DIVERSITY

## Zinacanteco Childrearing

ALONG WITH INDIVIDUAL differences in motor development and activity level, there are cultural differences in childrearing practices that encourage certain types of motor behavior and restrict others. The following cross-cultural example illustrates this point. Among the Zinacantecos of southeastern Mexico, the newborn infant is draped in a long skirt held in place by a belt or wrap.

> Then the newborn is wrapped in additional layers of blankets to protect him from "losing parts of his soul." This swaddling acts as a constant suppressant to motor activity. . . . Infants' faces are covered except during feedings, especially during the first three months, to ward off illness and the effects of the "evil eye" (Brazelton, 1977, p. 155).

Among the Zinacantecos, babies are rarely on the floor. Rather, they are held in the mother's lap, in her arms, or carried on her back. Mothers use breastfeeding as a frequent quieting strategy. They respond to any signs of restlessness or crying by offering the breast. In comparison to many U.S. parents, the Zinacanteco mothers rarely urged their babies to perform new motor behaviors and showed no special recognition or excitement when a new behavior was accomplished.

Zinacanteco babies are quieter and less demanding than typical U.S. babies. Most of those evaluated in this study lagged behind U.S. babies by 1 month in motor development. Despite a very restrictive environment for motor development, they all showed about the same pattern of motor skill

acquisition over the first year as did the U.S. infants.

This example illustrates how culture and the epigenetic process operate together. The human genetic plan supports walking as an emerging stage of motor development across cultures, and caregivers in different cultures share certain behaviors that support safe walking. However, the childrearing practices of the Zinacanteco instill two culturally valued characteristics: restrained movement, and a tendency to observe and respond rather than to initiate behaviors. These qualities, transmitted from one generation to the next through consistent childrearing practices, provide a source of continuity in cognition and behavior from infancy into adulthood (Greenfield & Childs, 1991).

---

Most babies reach a point when they rock in a stationary position on all fours before they can crawl. In repeated observations of 15 infants as they made the transition to crawling, a key precursor was found to be the establishment of a strong hand preference. When infants fell from a seated position onto their hands, they tended to fall onto their nonpreferred hand, so that the preferred hand was available to reach out and begin crawling. Confidence in being able to maintain one's body weight on one arm and two legs while reaching out with the preferred hand is part of the motor sequence necessary for forward crawling (Goldfield, 1989). Crawling, which tends to be regarded as natural and easily performed in infancy, is in fact achieved by long and patient effort in the coordination of head and shoulder movement, reaching, and kicking. As the baby changes from crawling to walking, new strategies for navigating the environment have to be invented.

Infant motor behavior requires flexibility because of the rapid change in physical size and strength and the variety of contexts for movement. Infants gain greater motor control with each postural status from sitting and crawling to standing and walking. At the same time, each new motor capacity permits the exploration of a more varied environment. As a result, infants have to be able to make immediate assessments of the relationship between their physical abilities and the environmental conditions in order to decide whether to avoid action, take familiar actions, or try to invent some new,

adapted action. The evidence for this flexibility can be seen as babies experiment with descending slopes and slides. Some try going headfirst and then slide backwards; others try to go down with a crab-like crawl and then switch over to their bottoms, and still others won't go down at all (Adolph & Eppler, 2002).

## ■ TEMPERAMENT

**Temperament** is a theoretical construct that refers to relatively stable characteristics of response to the environment and patterns of self-regulation (Putnam, Sanson, & Rothbart, 2002; Thomas & Chess, 1980). Temperament is a significant source of individual differences that emerges from a combination of genetic, environmental, and socially constructed factors. Theorists have offered different views about the specific features of temperament and what accounts for the stability of these features. However, they all tend to agree on two aspects of temperament: (1) a primary feature of temperament is the child's positive or negative reaction to environmental events; and (2) the stability of this reaction leads to a patterned reaction by others (Vaughn & Bost, 1999).

In early work on this construct, Escalona (1968) focused on individual differences among infants in the permeability of the boundary between the self and the stimulus environment and on the differential sensitivity of the infant to various sense

**Table 6.3** Three Types of Infant Temperament

| TYPE | DESCRIPTION | % OF TOTAL SAMPLE |
|---|---|---|
| Easy | Positive mood, regular body functions, low or moderate intensity of reaction, adaptability, positive approach rather than withdrawal from new situations | 40 |
| Slow to Warm up | Low activity level, tendency to withdraw on first exposure to new stimuli, slow to adapt, somewhat negative in mood, low intensity of reaction to situations | 15 |
| Difficult | Irregular body functions, unusually intense reactions, tendency to withdraw from new situations, slow to adapt to change, generally negative mood | 10 |

Source: From "The Origin of Personality," by A. Thomas, S. Chess, and H. Birch, 1970, *Scientific American, 223,* 102–109.

modalities. Differences in motor behavior have been assessed along dimensions such as activity level, soothability, reactivity to stimuli, calm and fluid movement versus spastic and jerky movement, and cuddliness (Brazelton, Nugent, & Lester, 1987). Thomas, Chess, and Birch (1970) rated newborn infants on nine temperamental qualities: activity level, rhythmicity, approach/withdrawal, adaptability, intensity of reaction, threshold of responsiveness, quality of mood, distractibility, and attention span and persistence. These dimensions are closely linked to the sensorimotor system and to the adaptive mechanisms that infants have for orienting to and withdrawing from stimulation.

Based on their research, Thomas, Chess, and Birch were able to classify infants into three temperamental groupings: *easy, slow to warm up,* and *difficult.* Table 6.3 summarizes the characteristics of each of these temperaments and the percentages of the sample that could be clearly identified as one of the three categories. Roughly 35% of the sample could not be classified.

Three aspects of temperament, including activity level, sociability, and emotionality, are thought to be influenced largely by genetic factors (Braungart, Plomin, DeFries, & Fulker, 1992; Buss & Plomin, 1984, 1986; Goldsmith et al., 1987; Goldsmith & Campos, 1986; Thomas & Chess, 1977, 1986; Wilson & Matheny, 1986). These dimensions—especially emotionality and activity level—show modest stability over adjacent periods of infancy and toddlerhood (Bates, 1987; Calkins & Fox, 1992).

Another view of temperament considers two basic dimensions: reactivity and self-regulation (Rothbart, 1991; Rothbart & Derryberry, 1981). **Reactivity** is the child's threshold for arousal, which could be evidenced at the physiological, emotional, or motor level. Children who have a low threshold for reactivity may get very excited with just a small amount of stimulation; in the face of a new situation, they may get very anxious where less reactive children would remain calm. Reactivity might be thought of as a child's likelihood of becoming distressed. **Self-regulation**, sometimes referred to as *behavioral inhibition,* can be thought of as a continuum from

bold or brazen to inhibited and cautious. The two dimensions function together to shape children's typical reactions to environmental stimulation and their ability to inhibit or express these reactions at an emotional or behavioral level.

A child's temperament influences the tone of interactions, the frequency with which interactions take place, the way others react to the child, and the way the child reacts to the reactions of others. Highly active, sociable children are likely to initiate interactions and to respond positively to the attention of others. More passive, inhibited children will be less likely to initiate interactions and may withdraw when other children or adults direct attention to them. Many studies emphasize the relevance of the fit or match between the parent's temperament and that of the child (Plomin, 1990). Consider the role of temperament in the case study on the Cotton Family.

Although temperament shows some consistency over the period of infancy and toddlerhood, it is only modestly stable over longer periods of time, depending on culture, measurement techniques, and methods of analysis. Measures of temperament in infancy do not correlate all that highly with measures in the early and middle school years. In all likelihood, temperamental characteristics are modified as they come into contact with socialization pressures at home and at school, as well as with new internal capacities to regulate behavior. For example, Thomas and Chess (1977, 1986) found that when parents were calm and allowed their difficult children to adapt to novelty at a leisurely pace, the children grew more comfortable and had an easier time adapting to new routines. However, if parents were impatient and demanding, then their difficult children remained difficult and had a hard time adjusting to new situations as they grew older.

A growing body of research has expanded the idea proposed by Thomas and Chess that child outcomes are a product of child temperament and parenting strategies. A few examples of this kind of interaction follow:

• Infants with difficult temperament are at risk for behavior problems when their mothers are unpredictable and harsh, but not when their mothers are responsive and warm (Sanson, Oberklaid, Pedlow, & Prior, 1991)

- Children who are fearful are more likely to be inhibited with their peers when their mothers are overprotective, but more confident with their peers when their mothers are reassuring and supportive of the child's autonomy (Rubin, Hastings, Stewart, Henderson, & Chen, 1997).

- Parental use of harsh punishment is not predictive of aggressive behavior for children who are flexible and low in reactivity, but is strongly linked to aggressiveness among children who are inflexible and highly reactive (Patterson & Sanson, 1999).

These and other findings are creating a complex picture of the interaction of child temperament and parenting style for child outcomes.

# CASE STUDY

## THE COTTON FAMILY

*Nancy and Paul Cotton are a professional couple who gave birth to their first child, Anna, after they had been married for 7½ years.*

Nancy said, "We wanted a baby but couldn't decide when to have one. Finally we realized that we could not control everything, or time things perfectly. No one can predict the future. So we finally decided to go ahead and have a child as soon as possible. . . . We were both privileged, lucky, and had lived well. By the time we had Anna, I was thirty-three, and our marriage and careers were established. We felt secure.

"Being an optimistic person, I guess I expected nirvana. Anna was difficult to deliver, and breastfeeding was a nightmare. Every time she nursed, it hurt. But I didn't want to miss the opportunity. I was so determined. I used a stopwatch to make sure Anna got enough milk, and I gave her a pacifier for recreation. When she was five weeks old, I went off to our summer house on Martha's Vineyard. I wondered if it was the right decision because there was less in the way of family and friends for support. But we worked things out together that summer. She was energetic from the first, and I was constantly sleep-deprived, but we were oh! so close. I found ways to make it easier for us. I found a babysitter to give me an afternoon break; I used the "Swyngomatic" so that I could eat a warm supper every once in a while, and I learned to give Anna pacifiers or bottles to soothe herself."

Paul interjected: "She was like a miracle to me. She was fabulous! Miraculous! She even looked like me. I did as much for her as Nancy did, not out of guilt, but because I couldn't keep my hands off her. I took her with me everywhere when I was off work. At the Stop-and-Shop, all the ladies crowded around me, 'How do you do it? You're so good with her!'" As he talked of Anna, his cheeks flushed, his whole body actively described the dramatic and exciting time they had together. "I learned all

about babies from her. I can bathe a kid faster than anyone in the world."

"I went back to work when Anna was three months," said Nancy. "I found full-time help. That way, I could enjoy her when I was home and get away when I needed to. I am a high-activity person, so I could understand a high-activity child like Anna. We could cycle together. I've never felt a bit of anxiety or ambivalence about her. I feel as if I've known her from the very first.

"Anna fit," said Nancy. "From the time she was born, we'd pick her up and just go. As you can see, going is pretty important in our family, and Anna thrived on it. We were not the only ones who enjoyed her; my own mother thought she was fabulous. She took care of her part-time after I went back to work. I had a chance to see my mother be loving and kind, a good mother to Anna. It was like reliving my own childhood—another kind of miracle. You see, I'd had a sister, Ginny, who had died. Anna gave my mother an opportunity to heal the pain of Ginny's death. This was true for me, too. We called her Anna Virginia after this sister. Ginny had a devastating mental illness. Ginny's spirit, intelligence, and humor seemed to live again in Anna, but without the shadow of vulnerability."

Source: From *What Every Baby Knows*, by T. B. Brazelton, pp. 11–13. Copyright © 1987 Addison-Wesley. Reprinted by permission.

## ■ CRITICAL THINKING AND CASE ANALYSIS

1. How would you describe Anna's temperament? What problems might the Cotton family have faced if Anna had been a more passive, reserved, and inhibited child?

2. In what ways was Anna being expected to adapt to the Cotton family lifestyle?

3. What are some of the challenges Nancy and Paul faced as new parents? How did they cope with these challenges?

4. How would you describe Paul's enactment of the father role?

5. How would you describe Nancy's enactment of the mother role?

6. Anna seems to be influencing the well-being of her mother, father, and her grandmother. What impact does Anna have on each of these family members?

# ATTACHMENT

Have you ever wondered how feelings of love and connectedness form between babies and their caregivers? At birth, an infant could be taken home from the hospital by any adult and be perfectly content. The newborn baby has not yet clearly differentiated his or her parents from others. Yet by the end of the first year of life, babies not only know their caregivers but also have very strong emotional preferences for these adults over all others. **Attachment** is the process through which people develop specific, positive emotional bonds with others. John Bowlby proposed the notion of the **attachment behavior system** as an organized pattern of in-

**Table 6.4** Five Stages in the Development of Attachment

| STAGE | AGE | CHARACTERISTICS |
|---|---|---|
| 1 | Birth to 3 months | Infant uses sucking, rooting, grasping, smiling, gazing, cuddling, crying, and visual tracking to maintain closeness with caregivers. |
| 2 | 3 to 6 months | Infant is more responsive to familiar figures than to strangers. |
| 3 | 6 to 9 months | Infant seeks physical proximity and contact with objects of attachment. |
| 4 | 9 to 12 months | Infant forms internal mental representation of object of attachment, including expectations about the caregiver's typical responses to signals of distress. |
| 5 | 12 months and older | Child uses a variety of behaviors to influence the behavior of the objects of attachment in ways that will satisfy needs for safety and closeness. |

fant signals and adult responses that lead to a protective, trusting relationship during the very earliest stage of development. The nurturing responses of the caregiver form a corresponding behavioral system referred to as **parenting** or **caregiving** (Ainsworth, 1985; Bowlby, 1988).

The construct of attachment introduced a perspective for understanding infant–caregiver interactions that highlights the active, social orientation of the infant in a behavioral system that is designed to protect the infant from harm. Many of the sensory and motor competencies described earlier in this chapter contribute to an infant's ability to establish a vivid mental scheme of the caregiver and to stimulate caregiving behaviors.

Certain patterns of caregiver–infant interaction in the first months of life contribute to the formation of attachment. One of the most significant of these is **synchrony** of interaction (Isabella & Belsky, 1991). Parent–infant pairs that show positive attachment relations at 1 year are characterized in the early months by interactions that are rhythmic, well timed, and mutually rewarding. When the caregiver is unresponsive to the infant's signals of distress, overly intrusive when the infant is calm, or underinvolved, a less positive attachment is formed. In addition to the quality of interactions, the quantity of interaction also plays a key role in establishing the infant's confidence about the caregiver's capacity to protect and comfort (Cox, Owen, Henderson, & Margand, 1992).

Evidence that an attachment has been formed is seen in at least three behaviors. First, infants try to maintain contact with the object of attachment (Ainsworth, 1973). Second, infants show distress when the object of attachment is absent (Schaffer & Emerson, 1964). Third, infants are more relaxed and comfortable with the object of attachment and more fretful with others (Bronson, 1973).

## ■ THE DEVELOPMENT OF ATTACHMENT

The attachment system emerges as caregivers provide protection from potential dangers and stressors while allowing the infant opportunities to learn the skills needed to function in-dependently. One can think of attachment as a lifelong developmental system in which people use increasingly complex physical, cognitive, and communicative strategies to form strong emotional bonds that will protect them from real or perceived threats. Attachment theorists have described a sequence of stages in the formation of the attachment relationship, much of which takes place during the first 12 months of life (Ainsworth, 1973, 1985; Bowlby, 1969/1982; Marvin & Britner, 1999; see Table 6.4).

In the first stage, during the first 3 months of life, infants engage in a variety of behaviors, including sucking, rooting, grasping, smiling, gazing, cuddling, crying, and visual tracking, which serve to maintain closeness with a caregiver or bring the caregiver to the infant. However, these behaviors do not appear to be aimed at a specific person. Through these contacts, babies learn about the unique features of their caregivers. Caregivers and infants experience repeated interactions, which result in the formation of predictable patterns. Infants begin to internalize rhythmic patterns of interaction, which become a foundation for expectations about interpersonal communication.

In the second stage, from about 3 to 6 months, an infant's attachment is expressed through preferential responsiveness to a few familiar figures. Infants smile more at the familiar person than at a stranger, show more excitement at that person's arrival, and appear to be upset when he or she leaves. During this phase, babies initiate more interactions toward the familiar caregiver and are able to control the interaction by linking a chain of behaviors into a more complex sequence. In Stage 1, for example, the baby may look intently at the primary caregiver. In Stage 2, the baby looks intently, reaches toward the caregiver's face, and pulls his or her hair.

In Stage 3, from about 6 to 9 months, babies seek physical proximity with the objects of attachment. The ability to crawl and to coordinate reaching and grasping contribute to greater control over the outcomes of their actions. In this phase, babies experiment with an optimal distance from the caregiver. They may crawl away, look back, and then, depending on the caregiver's perceived availability, crawl back to the caregiver

*Close, physical contact during nursing pro-
vides infants with a combination of sensory
stimuli, sight, sound, smell, and touch that
contribute to the formation of an early
scheme for their mother.*

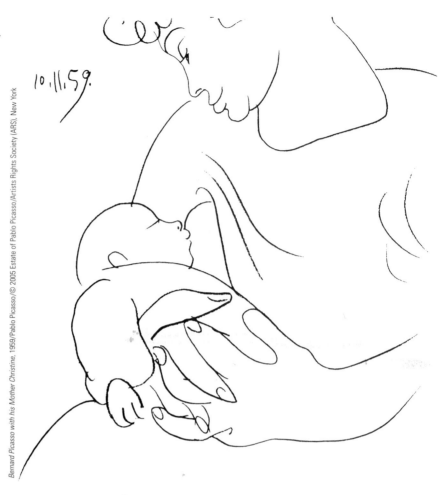

or smile and continue exploring. If the caregiver is preoccupied or out of sight, the baby may cry to bring the caregiver
closer or to reestablish contact.

In Stage 4, from about 9 to 12 months, babies form the
first internal representation of their caregivers. This internal
representation provides the first robust working model of an
attachment relationship. Specific characteristics of a caregiver
and expectations about how the caregiver will respond to the
infant's actions are organized into a complex **attachment
scheme**—the internal mental representations of the anticipated responses of a caregiver.

In Stage 5, in toddlerhood and later, young children use
a variety of behaviors to influence the behavior of their parents and other objects of attachment in order to satisfy their
own needs for closeness. Children may ask to be read to, cuddled at bedtime, and taken along on errands. These and other
strategies produce caregiver behaviors that will satisfy a
child's continuing needs for physical contact, reassurance,
closeness, and love.

Bowlby described a new and important capacity that
emerges in this stage: **goal-corrected partnership**. As children become aware that other people have their own separate
points of view, they begin to include the other person's needs
and goals into their plans. Toddlers and early school-age children begin to find more flexible and adaptive ways to main-

tain proximity and to seek reassurance. They are able to manage negotiated separations more easily. So when a mother
tells her 3-year-old to wait in the car with grandma for a few
minutes while she finishes her shopping, the child is able to
do this without much distress.

As children mature, they begin to conceptualize new risks
and threats to their security. They may initiate new strategies
for maintaining closeness to the objects of their attachment.
Especially when they are undergoing unusual stress, as in
times of illness, divorce, or rejection, children of any age may
try to activate the attachment system by sending signals that
will result in comforting and closeness.

**STRANGER ANXIETY.** During the second half of the first
year, two signs of the child's growing attachment to a specific
person are observed: stranger anxiety and separation anxiety.
**Stranger anxiety** is the baby's discomfort or tension in the
presence of unfamiliar adults. Babies vary in how they express their protest to strangers and in how intensely they react (Rieser-Danner, 2003). They may cling to their parents,
refuse to be held, stiffen at the stranger's touch, or merely
avert their eyes from the stranger's face.

The baby's response to a stranger depends on specific dimensions of the situation, including how close the mother is,
how the stranger approaches the baby, and how the mother

*With Dad nearby, Jakob can begin to explore this new environment and return to his secure base as needed.*

responds to the stranger (Keltenbach, Weinraub, & Fullard, 1980). For example, if a mother speaks in a positive tone of voice to her baby about a stranger, the baby's response to the stranger is likely to be positive (Feinman & Lewis, 1983). The baby's response will also be influenced by the amount of prior experience with unfamiliar adults. Normally, wariness of strangers is considered a positive developmental sign—that is, babies are able to detect the differences between their parents and adults they do not know. Of course, wariness of strangers continues to be expressed throughout life. In fact, one often sees stronger expressions of suspiciousness or fear among adults encountering strangers than among babies.

**SEPARATION ANXIETY.** At about 9 months, infants give another indication of the intensity of their attachment to their parents by expressing rage and despair when their parents leave. This reaction is called **separation anxiety**. Separation can evoke two different kinds of behavior. Under some conditions, separation from the caregiver will stimulate attachment behaviors—especially efforts to find the caregiver and regain physical contact (Ainsworth, Bell, & Stayton, 1971). Separation can also evoke protest, despair, or detachment, depending on the length of the separation (Bowlby, 1960; Robertson & Robertson, 1989).

The baby's response to separation depends on the conditions. Infants are less distressed when mothers leave them alone in a room at home than when they do so in a laboratory (Ross, Kagan, Zelazo, & Kotelchuck, 1975). They are less

likely to protest if the mother leaves the door to the room open than if she closes the door as she leaves. Separation from the mother for periods of 30 minutes has been identified as a distinct source of stress for babies 9 months of age and older. Neurological and biochemical evidence of stress, including increases in adrenocortical activity and concentrations of cortisol in the saliva, were associated with 30 minutes of separation from the mother in a laboratory situation (Gunnar, Larson, Hertsgaard, Harris, & Brodersen, 1992; Larson, Gunnar, & Hertsgaard, 1991). The impact of stressful separations can be seen in the disruption of basic physical patterns, especially sleep disturbances, and in regression to more immature forms of play behavior, aimless wandering, and altered interactions with peers and teachers in the childcare setting (Field, 1991).

Babies' responses to separation may also be related to their temperament (Gunnar et al., 1992; Gunnar, Mangelsdorf, Larson, & Hertsgaard, 1989; Izard, Haynes, Chisholm, & Baak, 1991). Babies who have a strong negative reaction to uncertainty, those who are especially distressed when they are confined or prevented from attaining a goal, and those who are upset by novelty or who tend to withdraw from it may find the experience of separation more stressful than others. Unique strategies of caregiving might be needed to buffer these babies from the stressful impact of separation.

A baby's responses to separation and reunion have been used as key behavioral indicators of attachment quality. Babies who are described as having an insecure attachment are more distressed when they are separated from their mothers, and the mothers appear to be less responsive in calming their babies following separation (Harel & Scher, 2003)

Over time, babies become more flexible in response to parents' temporary departures. Young children learn to tolerate brief separations. At 2 years of age, children are able to use a photograph of their mother to help sustain their adaptation to a new setting in the mother's absence (Passman & Longeway, 1982). By the age of 3, children may even look forward to a night with a babysitter or an afternoon at grandfather's house. Once the attachment is fully established, children can comfort themselves by creating mental images of their parents and by remembering their parents' love for them. During infancy, however, the parents' physical presence remains a focal point of attention and concern.

### ■ FORMATION OF ATTACHMENTS WITH MOTHER, FATHER, AND OTHERS

Most infants have more than one caring person with whom they form an attachment. Most commonly, the first object of attachment is the mother, but fathers, siblings, grandparents, and child care professionals also become objects of attachment. Several factors have been identified as important for predicting which people will form the infant's hierarchy or radius of significant attachment figures (Cassidy, 1999; Colin, 1996):

1. The amount of time the infant spends in the care of the person.
2. The quality and responsiveness of the care provided by the person.
3. The person's emotional investment in the infant.
4. The presence of the person in the infant's life across time.

Infants tend to have the same type of attachment with their fathers and their mothers, but these relationships are established independently and depend on the time spent together and the quality of their interactions (Fox, Kimmerly, & Schafer, 1991). Early studies found that babies tended to have playful interactions with their fathers—smiling, laughing, and looking—and comforting, stress-reducing interactions with their mothers (Lamb, 1976). Recent studies confirm that infants experience positive emotions as they play with their mothers and fathers. However, the intensity and rhythm of the experiences seem to differ. In mother–infant interactions, babies seem more calm, and their happy expressions are part of a social dialogue. In father–infant interactions, the babies are more excited, showing sudden bursts of laughter and activity (Feldman, 2003). In a study of 126 firstborn sons, 60% were found to have secure attachments with their fathers at 13 months of age (Belsky, 1996).

In Israel, kibbutz-reared infants showed great similarity between their attachment to their fathers and to their specially trained caregiver (called *metapelet*). However, there was no consistent pattern of similarity in the quality of their attachments to mother and father and to mother and metapelet

(Sagi et al., 1985). In subsequent research, when these kibbutz-reared children were 5 years old, the quality of their infant attachment to the metapelet was a significant predictor of their socioemotional development as observed in school and at free play in their dormitory (Oppenheim, Sagi, & Lamb, 1988). In the Israeli case, where there are multiple caregivers, it has also been observed that when one attachment relation is negative, it can negatively influence other attachment relations. For example, in a study of more than 750 Israeli infants, those who experienced poor quality care in center-based settings were also more likely to develop insecure attachments with their mothers (Sagi et al., 2002)

This research suggests that in the Israeli case, the combined contribution of multiple secure attachments, rather than the mother–infant relationship alone, is the best predictor of subsequent social competence (Sagi & van IJzendoorn, 1996). Exactly how infants synthesize the internal representations of various attachments is not well understood. Possibly, the distinct relationships have relevance for different interpersonal domains or become central as individuals assume a variety of social roles (Bretherton, 1985; Bridges, Connell, & Belsky, 1988).

### ■ PATTERNS OF ATTACHMENT

It is important to distinguish between the presence of an attachment and the quality of that attachment. According to attachment theory, if an adult is present to interact with the infant, an attachment will be formed. However, individual differences emerge in the quality of that attachment, depending on the accumulation of information the infant gathers over many instances when the infant is seeking reassurance, comfort, or protection from threat (Weinfield, Sroufe, Egeland, & Carlson, 1999). The adults' acceptance of the infant and their ability to respond to his or her varying communications are important to forming a secure attachment. The caregivers' patterns of expressing affection and rejection will influence how well babies can meet their strong needs for reassurance and comfort.

**THE STRANGE SITUATION.** Differences in the quality of attachment have been highlighted by observations of babies and their caregivers in a standard laboratory procedure called the **strange situation** (Ainsworth, Blehar, Waters, & Wall, 1978; Bretherton, 1990). During an approximately 20-minute period, the child is exposed to a sequence of events that are likely to stimulate the attachment system (see Table 6.5). The situation introduces several potentially threatening experiences, including the presence of a stranger, the departure of the mother, being left alone with a stranger, and being left completely alone—all in the context of an unfamiliar laboratory setting. During this sequence, researchers have the opportunity to make systematic observations of the child's behaviors, the caregiver's behaviors, and the characteristics of their interactions, and to compare these behaviors across varying segments of the procedure.

**Table 6.5** The Strange Situation Laboratory Procedure

| EPISODE | DURATION | PARTICIPANTS* | EVENTS |
|---------|----------|---------------|--------|
| 1 | 30 sec. | M, B, O | O shows M and B into the room, instructs M on where to put B down and where to sit; O leaves. |
| 2 | 3 min. | M, B | M puts B down close to her chair, at a distance from the toys. She responds to B's social bids but does not initiate interaction. B is free to explore. If B does not move after 2 minutes, M may take B to the toy area. |
| 3 | 3 min. | M, B, S | This episode has three parts. S enters, greets M and B, and sits down opposite M without talking for 1 minute. During the 2nd minute, S engages M in conversation. S then joins B on the floor, attempting to engage B in play for 1 minute. At the end of this episode, M leaves "unobtrusively" (B usually notices). |
| 4 | 3 min. | B, S | S sits on her chair. She responds to B's social bids but does not initiate social interaction. If B becomes distressed, S attempts to comfort B. If this is not effective, M returns before 3 minutes are up. |
| 5 | 3 min. | M, B | M calls B's name outside the door and enters (S leaves unobtrusively). If B is distressed, M comforts B and tries to reengage B in play. If B is not distressed, M goes to sit on her chair, taking a responsive, noninitiating role. At the end of the episode, M leaves, saying, "Bye-bye; I'll be back." |
| 6 | 3 min. | B | B remains alone. If B becomes distressed, the episode is curtailed and S enters. |
| 7 | 3 min. | B, S | S enters, comforting B if required. If she cannot comfort B, the episode is curtailed. If B calms down or is not distressed, S sits on her chair, taking a responsive role as before. |
| 8 | 3 min. | M, B | M returns (S leaves unobtrusively). M behaves as in episode 5. |

*O = observer; M = mother; B = baby; S = stranger.

Source: Data from I. Bretherton, "Open Communication and Internal Working Models: Their Roles in the Development of Attachment Relationships." R. Dienstbier & R. A. Thompson (eds.), *Nebraska Symposium on Motivation, 1988: Socioemotional Development, 36*, 60–61.

**FOUR PATTERNS OF QUALITY OF ATTACHMENT.** Four patterns of attachment behavior have been distinguished using the strange situation methodology: (1) secure attachment, (2) anxious-avoidant attachment, (3) anxious-resistant attachment, and (4) disorganized attachment.

Infants who have a **secure attachment** actively explore their environment and interact with strangers while their mothers are present. After separation, the babies actively greet their mothers or seek interaction. If the babies were distressed during separation, the mothers' return reduces their distress, and the babies resume exploring the environment. Infants who show an **anxious-avoidant attachment** avoid contact with their mothers after separation or ignore their efforts to interact. They show less distress at being alone than other babies. Infants who show an **anxious-resistant attachment** are very cautious in the presence of the stranger. Their exploratory behavior is noticeably disrupted by the caregiver's departure. When the caregiver returns, the infants appear to want to be close to the caregiver, but they are also angry, so that they are very hard to soothe or comfort. In the **disorganized attachment**, babies' responses are particularly notable in the reunion sequence. The disorganized babies have no consistent strategy for managing their distress. They behave in contradictory, unpredictable ways that seem to convey feelings of extreme fear or utter confusion (Belsky, Campbell, Cohn, & Moore, 1996).

When observed at home, babies who have a secure attachment cry less than other babies (Ainsworth, 1985; Tracy & Ainsworth, 1981). They greet their mothers more positively on reunion after everyday separations and respond more cooperatively to their mothers' requests. One can sense that securely attached babies have a **working model** of attachment in which they expect their caregiver to be accessible and responsive.

Mothers of babies who were characterized as anxious-avoidant seem to reject their babies. It is almost as if they were angry at their babies. They spend less time holding and cuddling their babies than other mothers, and more of their interactions are unpleasant or even hurtful. At home, these babies cry a lot, they are not readily soothed by contact with the caregiver, and yet they are quite distressed by separations.

Infants who are characterized as anxious-resistant have mothers who are inconsistent in their responsiveness. Sometimes, these mothers ignore clear signals of distress. At other times, they interfere with their infants in order to make contact. Although these mothers enjoy close physical contact with their babies, they do not necessarily do so in ways appropriate to the baby's needs. The result is the formation of an internal working model of attachment that is highly unpredictable. These babies try to maintain proximity and to avoid unfamiliar situations that increase uncertainty about accessibility to their caregiver.

Observations of mothers and infants who are described as having a disorganized attachment highlight two different pat-

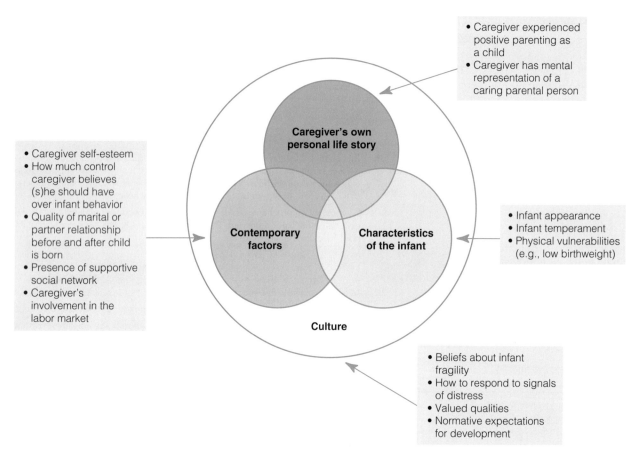

• Caregiver experienced positive parenting as a child
• Caregiver has mental representation of a caring parental person

• Caregiver self-esteem
• How much control caregiver believes (s)he should have over infant behavior
• Quality of marital or partner relationship before and after child is born
• Presence of supportive social network
• Caregiver's involvement in the labor market

• Infant appearance
• Infant temperament
• Physical vulnerabilities (e.g., low birthweight)

Caregiver's own personal life story

Contemporary factors

Characteristics of the infant

Culture

• Beliefs about infant fragility
• How to respond to signals of distress
• Valued qualities
• Normative expectations for development

**FIGURE 6.3**

Factors Contributing to Caregiver Sensitivity

terns. Some mothers are negative, intrusive, and they frighten their babies in bursts of intense hostility. Other mothers are passive and helpless, rarely showing positive or comforting behaviors. These mothers appear to be afraid of their babies, perhaps not trusting their own impulses to respond appropriately (Lyons-Ruth, Lyubchik, Wolfe, & Bronfman, 2002).

In U.S. samples, about two thirds of the children tested have been characterized as securely attached. Of the remainder, more children fall into the anxious-avoidant category than into the anxious-resistant category (Ainsworth et al., 1978). Only a small percentage of infants show the disorganized pattern (Carlson, Cicchetti, Barnett, & Braunwold, 1989; Radke-Yarrow, Cummings, Kuczynski, & Chipman, 1985; van IJzendoorn et al., 1992). Research has suggested links between the disorganized attachment and serious mental health problems in later childhood and beyond, including depression, borderline personality, and dissociative reactions (Lyons-Ruth et al., 2002; Fonagy, 2003).

## ■ PARENTAL SENSITIVITY AND THE QUALITY OF ATTACHMENT

How can we account for differences in the quality of the attachment? Early work on the formation of a secure attachment argued that a cornerstone in this process was maternal

sensitivity (Ainsworth et al., 1978). **Sensitivity** is generally defined as attentiveness to the infant's state, accurate interpretation of the infant's signals, and well-timed responses that promote mutually rewarding interactions (Isabella et al., 1989). A sensitive caregiver is not only able to recognize the infant's emotional state, but to empathize with it and to make an appropriate response. A parent might recognize that his or her infant is distressed but be too busy or preoccupied to respond or to provide effective comfort (Leerkes, Crockenberg, & Burrows, 2004). Mothers who are psychologically available, responsive, consistent, and warm in their interactions with their babies—especially during the first 6 months of the baby's life—are found to be most successful in establishing a secure attachment relationship that can be measured by the time the baby is 12 months old (Braungart-Rieker, Garwood, Powers, & Wang, 2001).

Four general factors come into play in producing the kind of sensitivity that underlies secure attachments: (1) cultural and subcultural differences, (2) the caregiver's personal life story, (3) contemporary factors, and (4) characteristics of the infant (see Figure 6.3).

**CULTURAL AND SUBCULTURAL DIFFERENCES.** Cultural and subcultural differences are integrated into one's mental representation of a parent or caregiver. The culture's beliefs about infants, including how fragile or vulnerable they are, how best to help infants cope with distress, and what skills or temperamental qualities are most valued, are likely to shape a caregiver's practices (Coll, 1994). For example, Japanese mothers keep close, continuous proximity to their infants. Separations are infrequent, and infants are expected to monitor their mothers' reactions in order to assess people and objects in the environment. Japanese mothers subtly direct their infants' play behavior through gestures and facial expressions. Independent play is not especially valued, and the idea that children would handle separation and reunion with the mother with little distress is not expected by Japanese caregivers (Okimoto, 2001).

The study of attachment-related responses across U.S. ethnic subgroups is limited. However, some examples suggest how a cultural worldview influences the pattern of parental responsiveness and sensitivity. In a comparison of European American, African American, and Cuban American mothers' perceptions of infant crying and related responses, the African American mothers were least likely to perceive their babies' cries as urgent or distressing (Zeskind, 1983). In line with this perception, they were least likely to cuddle their babies. The Cuban American mothers were most likely to soothe their babies with a pacifier and by cuddling and responding quickly to their babies' cries. In another study comparing European American and Puerto Rican mothers reactions to their infants in the strange situation, the European American mothers focused on behaviors such as autonomy, self-control, and activity, which support cultural values of independence. The Puerto Rican mothers focused on their infants' affection, respectfulness, proximity seeking, and responsiveness, which support cultural values of respect for authority and family relatedness (Harwood, 1992; Zayas & Solari, 1994). These comparisons suggest distinct normative patterns of caregiving in different cultural groups (Keller et al., 2004).

THE CAREGIVER'S PERSONAL LIFE STORY. Aspects of the caregiver's personal life story contribute to being able to serve as a secure base for a child. Adults who recall their own parents as accepting, responsive, and available are more likely to be able to transmit those qualities as they enact the caregiver role. Adults who have experienced early loss or disruption of an attachment relationship have more difficulty providing a secure base for their offspring (Belsky, 1996; Fonagy, Steele, & Steele, 1991). Studies suggest that the internal working model of an attachment relationship may be transmitted across generations, with mothers and fathers drawing on the model of an attachment they formed as infants and young children, which then guides their perceptions of infant cues and their own responses (Bornstein, 2002; George & Solomon, 1999).

CONTEMPORARY FACTORS. Contemporary factors can influence the ability of an adult to provide a secure base for attachment. For example, some mothers experience high levels of postnatal depression. Depressed mothers are likely to be less attuned to their infants' signals, less playful, less verbally stimulating, more irritable, and generally less enthusiastic and happy as they interact with their infants (Edhborg, Lundh, Seimyr, & Widstroem, 2001). The role of the child's father, and the relationship between the mother and father or the caregiving partners are especially central. A partner who is supportive, involved in caregiving, and reassuring about meeting the challenges of parenting a newborn provides a context in which even mothers who have had insecure attachments themselves can thrive. On the other hand, some relationships are characterized by conflict and poor communication, in which the partner may even compete with the infant for the mother's care or impede the mother's efforts to care for her infant (Cowan, Cohn, Cowan, & Pearson, 1996). Other contemporary factors that influence the caregiver's sensitivity to the infant include the caregiver's self-esteem, the degree of control the caregiver believes he or she should have over the infant's behavior, the presence of a supportive social network that validates the person's caregiving efforts, the person's involvement in the labor market, and financial worries (George & Solomon, 1999; Jacobson & Frye, 1991).

INFANT CHARACTERISTICS. The quality of attachment can also be influenced by the characteristics of the infant. Infants born with physical abnormalities are more likely to evoke responses of rejection or neglect from caregivers (Langlois, Ritter, Casey, & Sawin, 1995). Physical conditions such as colic can test the parents' commitment to caregiving and create a cycle of anxiety and fearfulness. Babies with colic may not find comfort in their caregivers' efforts to soothe them, and caregivers may not experience a sense of efficacy in their ability to calm their child.

Certain aspects of the infant's temperament—especially fearfulness, sociability, and the intensity of negative emotions—may influence the way the attachment relationship is established (Izard et al., 1991). Studies have shown that temperament influences the kinds of caregiver responses that are most likely to create an internal sense of security or insecurity. Infants who are irritable are often difficult for parents to respond to. Over time, some parents may respond to difficult infants harshly or by withdrawing. These behaviors may produce an insecure attachment for the infant (Putnam, Sanson, & Rothbart, 2002).

## ■ THE RELEVANCE OF ATTACHMENT TO LATER DEVELOPMENT

The nature of one's attachment and the related internal working models of attachment influence expectations about the self, others, and the nature of relationships (Shaver, Collins, & Clark, 1996). What is more, the formation of a secure attachment relationship is expected to influence the child's ability to explore and engage the environment with confidence, knowing that the protective "other" is near at hand. Children who experience a secure attachment are less likely to be exposed to uncontrollable stress. They experience rhythmic, meaningful, and predictable interactions that contribute to their social competences. As a result, they are *hopeful* about their ability to form positive relationships with others (Weinfield et al., 1999).

Long-term benefits of a secure attachment have been documented. Secure attachments in infancy have been associated with positive adaptive capacities when the child is 3 to 5 years old. Securely attached infants become preschoolers who show greater resilience, self-control, and curiosity (Vaughn, Egeland, Sroufe, & Waters, 1979). In contrast, infants who have a disorganized attachment are very hostile, aggressive preschoolers.

A new clinical diagnosis—**reactive attachment disorder**—has been linked to serious disturbances in infant attachment. Two expressions of this disorder have been described: **inhibited type**, in which the person is very withdrawn, hypervigilant in social contacts, and resistant to comfort; and **uninhibited type**, in which the person shows a lack of discrimination, being overly friendly and attaching to any new person (DeAngelis, 1997).

From a life-span perspective, the quality of the attachment formed in infancy influences the formation of later relationships (Ainsworth, 1989). Children who have formed secure attachments are likely to find more enjoyment in close peer friendships during their preschool years. In an analysis of the results of more than 60 studies of the relationship of parent–child attachment and peer relations, the quality of attachment with the mother was consistently predictive of the quality of close peer friendships well into middle school and early adolescence (Schneider, Atkinson, & Tardif, 2001). Children who have secure attachments are more likely to attribute positive intentions to peers, whereas children with anxious attachments are more likely to view peers with wariness.

A growing body of work indicates stability in attachment orientation from infancy to adulthood. In one longitudinal study, 50 infants who were assessed in the strange situation at 12 months were assessed again with the *Berkeley Adult Attachment Interview* at age 20 (Waters et al., 2003). Over this 20-year period, the same secure or insecure attachment style was observed in 72% of the participants. Exposure to negative life events such as parental loss, parental divorce, or severe parental illness was associated with change in classification for some, but not all of the participants.

The attachment construct has been used to help explain the nature of adolescent and adult love relationships. Romantic relationships can be characterized along many of the same dimensions as infant attachments, including the desire to maintain physical contact with the loved one, increased disclosure and responsiveness to the loved one, the effectiveness of the loved one in providing comfort and reassurance that reduce distress, and an element of exclusiveness or preferential response to the loved one (Hazan & Shaver, 1987).

Fears about loss and abandonment, born from anxious-avoidant attachments, are likely to result in anxiety about one's contemporary romantic relationships:

I had a real problem trusting anyone at the start of any relationship. A couple of things happened to me when I was

© Michael Newman / Photo Edit

*The attachment construct continues to be evident in adult, loving relationships. This mother and daughter enjoy physical closeness, comfort each other, and look to each other for reassurance in times of stress.*

young, which I had some emotional difficulties getting over. At the start of our relationship, if P. had been separated from me, I would have been constantly thinking: "What was he doing?"; "Was he with another girl?"; "Was he cheating on me?"; all that would have been running through my head. (Feeney, 1999, p. 365)

People with insecure attachments tend to be more coercive and mistrustful, thus pushing their partners away. They may have special difficulty establishing and maintaining romantic relationships as they move from childhood friendships into the more demanding expectations of sexual intimacy and disclosure in adolescent and adult relationships (Tracy, Shaver, Albino, & Cooper, 2003). The contribution of attachment orientation to intimate relationships will be discussed further in Chapter 12 (Early Adulthood).

The parenting relationship can also be understood as an elaboration of the attachment representation. Adults who have experienced a secure attachment in their own infancy are more likely to be able to comfort and respond to their children. Adults whose childhood attachments were unpredictable or even hostile are more likely to have difficulty coping successfully with young infants' needs (George & Solomon, 1999; Ricks, 1985). For example, in an observational study, parents were observed while their infants were having inoculations. Those parents who had an avoidant attachment style were less responsive to their infants' distress in this context (Edelstein et al., 2004).

It would be a mistake to assume that the quality of adult love relationships or parental behavior is determined solely by the quality of childhood attachments. Many experiences, new relationships, and new learning intervene to modify the attachment representation and to expand one's capacity to love another person after infancy. However, a growing body of work links the quality of early attachments with a person's orientation to and capacity for social relationships within the context of friendships, intimate relationships, and parent–child relations.

The formation of an attachment relies on both social and cognitive capacities that emerge in infancy. Infants use their sensory and motor capacities to explore and interact with their caregiver. The fact that the caregiver becomes a unique "other" for the infant is evidence of the baby's use of sensorimotor intelligence to form a meaningful scheme. Other sensory and motor schemes emerge as well, providing increasingly complex and organized structures through which infants make meaning of their social and physical world.

## SENSORIMOTOR INTELLIGENCE AND EARLY CAUSAL SCHEMES

What is sensorimotor intelligence? Think for a moment of a familiar experience, such as tying your shoelaces. The pattern of tying the shoelace unfolds with little, if any, language involved. In fact, the task of explaining to a young child how to tie a shoelace is particularly difficult because very few words or concepts are part of the process. This kind of motor routine is an example of **sensorimotor intelligence**. When infants begin to adapt their sucking reflex to make it more effective, or when they use different techniques of sucking for the breast and the bottle, they are demonstrating sensorimotor intelligence. The familiar scheme for sucking is modified so that it takes into account the special properties of the breast and the bottle, depending on the situation.

### ■ HOW INFANTS ORGANIZE THEIR EXPERIENCES

According to Piaget's (1970) theory of cognitive development, the chief mechanism governing the growth of intelligence during infancy is **sensorimotor adaptation**. From the very earliest days of life, infants use their reflexes to explore their world. At the same time, they gradually alter their reflexive responses to take into account the unique properties of

objects around them. Infants do not use the conventional symbolic system of language to organize experience. Rather, they form concepts through perception and direct investigation of the environment. The notion of sensorimotor intelligence, then, encompasses the elaboration of patterns of movement and sensory experiences that the child comes to recognize in association with specific environmental events.

According to an emerging view, sometimes referred to as the *Theory theory*, infants form theories about how their world operates and modify them as new information is gathered. The infant starts out with some basic sensory, motor, and cognitive organizational structures. For example, 3½-month-old infants were shown an object being lowered into a container that had either a wide opening or no opening at the top. They looked significantly longer at the figure with no opening, suggesting that by this young age, they already have a scheme or expectation about how one object contains another (Hespos & Baillargeon, 2001).

With each new challenge, a process of adaptation results in the revision of basic schemes to better predict and interpret experience (Gopnik & Meltzoff, 1997). For example, Ruby, who is 12 months old, may be surprised and upset when her grandmother scolds her as she reaches for a shiny glass bowl on the table. Grandmother knows that the bowl will break if Ruby pushes it off the table. By 16 months, Ruby warily watches her grandmother's face as she reaches for the bowl and may withdraw her hand if she sees Grandma frown or hears the sharp "No!" that has come to be associated with "Don't touch." Ruby has developed a theory that she should not touch the bowl, which she cautiously tests by reaching for it and watching for the response.

One of the most important components of sensorimotor intelligence is the capacity to anticipate that certain actions will have specific effects on objects in the environment. Infants develop an understanding of **causality** based largely on sensory and motor experience. Babies discover that if they cry, Mama will come to them; if they kick a chair, it will move; and if they let go of a spoon, it will fall to the floor. These predictable sequences are learned through repetition and experimentation. The predictability of the events depends on the consistency with which objects in the world respond as well as on the child's initiation of the action. Babies learn to associate specific actions with regularly occurring outcomes. They also experiment with their own actions to determine the variety of events that a single behavior may cause. Eventually, they are able to work backward: They can select a desirable outcome and then perform the behavior that will produce it.

### ■ THE DEVELOPMENT OF CAUSAL SCHEMES

The achievement of complex, purposeful, causal behaviors develops gradually during the first 2 years of life. This achievement requires that infants have an understanding of the properties of objects in their environment and a variety of strategies for manipulating those objects. Research has shown that infants form expectations about how objects function in

**Table 6.6**  Six Phases in the Development of Sensorimotor Causality

| PHASE | APPROXIMATE AGE | CHARACTERISTIC | EXAMPLE |
|---|---|---|---|
| 1. Reflexes | From birth | Reflexive responses to specific stimuli | Grasp reflex |
| 2. First habits | From 2nd week | Use of reflexive responses to explore new stimuli | Grasp rattle |
| 3. Circular reactions | From 4th month | Use of familiar actions to achieve new goals | Grasp rattle and make banging noise on table |
| 4. Coordination of means and ends | From 8th month | Deliberate use of actions to achieve new goals | Grasp rattle and shake to play with dog |
| 5. Experimentation with new means | From 11th month | Modifications of actions to reach goals | Use rattle to bang a drum |
| 6. Insight | From 18 months | Mental recombination of means and ends | Use rattle and string to make a new toy |

Source: Adapted from Piaget and Inhelder, 1969.

specific conditions (Baillargeon, 2004). For example, one object can fit inside another, but not if the second object has no opening. Another expectation is that an object can be hidden behind another larger object. Over time, infants become aware of the relevant variables that operate in a specific physical context. For example, a tall object cannot completely fit inside a shorter container. Infants appear to learn about the relationship of objects under specific conditions, but they do not generalize from one type of event to another. Therefore, they must be able to explore and experiment with objects in order to select the most effective strategies for coordinating actions to achieve specific goals.

The dynamic process of establishing a complex causal scheme is illustrated in a study of the emergence of the use of a spoon as a tool for eating (Connolly & Dalgleish, 1989). The infants were observed once a month for 6 months in their home during a meal time. At first, actions involving the spoon appeared to focus on exploration of the spoon itself. The infants banged the spoon, sucked it, or rubbed it in their hair. Then the babies showed an understanding of the purpose of the spoon as a tool by repeating the action sequence of dipping the spoon in the dish and bringing it to the mouth. However, no food was on the spoon. In the third phase, babies began to integrate the function and the action by loading the spoon with food and then bringing it to the mouth. During this phase, they made so many errors that very little food actually got to the mouth via the spoon. Finally, babies were able to coordinate the action and the function by using the other hand to steady the bowl, altering the angle of the spoon, picking up food they had dropped, and devising other strategies to enhance the function, depending on the type of food involved. Here we see a demonstration of how one complex motor behavior becomes part of a problem-solving action sequence during the sensorimotor period of development.

Piaget and Inhelder (1966/1969) described six phases in the development of causal schemes (see Table 6.6). Subsequent research and related theoretical revisions have confirmed these levels of cognitive development (Fischer & Silvern, 1985). In Phase 1, *reflexes,* cause and effect are linked

through the involuntary reflexive responses. The built-in stimulus-response systems of key reflexes are viewed as the genetic origin of intelligence. Babies suck, grasp, and root in response to specific types of stimulation. Piaget viewed these reflexes as adaptive learning systems. In detailed observations of his youngest child, Laurent, he noted daily changes in sucking behavior during the first month of life. Laurent became increasingly directed in groping for the breast, forming early associations between those situations in which he would be fed and those in which he would not (Gratch & Schatz, 1987; Piaget, 1936/1952).

In the second phase, *first habits,* the reflexive responses are used to explore a wider range of stimuli. Babies explore toys, fingers, parents' noses, and blankets by sucking on them. Gradually, they discover the unique properties of objects and modify their responses according to the demands of the specific objects. The fact that a baby can satisfy his or her own need to suck by bringing an object to the mouth is a very early form of purposive causal behavior.

The third and fourth phases involve coordination of means and ends, first with familiar situations and then with new ones. In the third phase, *circular reactions,* babies connect an action with an expected outcome (Wentworth & Haith, 1992). They shake a rattle and expect to hear a noise; they drop a spoon and expect to hear a noise when it hits the floor; they pull Daddy's beard and expect to hear "ouch." They do not understand why a specific action leads to the expected outcome, but they show surprise when the expected outcome does not follow.

In the fourth phase, *coordination of means and ends,* infants use familiar actions or means to achieve new outcomes. They may shake a rattle to startle Mommy or pull Daddy's beard to force him to look away from the television set. The means and the outcomes have become quite distinct. There can be no question about the purposiveness of behavior at this point. At this stage, coordination of means and ends are closely tied to a specific context. For example, a baby may know how to make certain kicking motions to move a mobile or to get a toy to jiggle in the crib. But in another room with the same toy, the baby may not make the same connection. This may explain why babies perform less competently in the laboratory environment than they do at home. Many causal strategies that become part of a baby's daily repertoire are supported by the context of a familiar environment (Rovee-Collier, Schechter, Shyi, & Shields, 1992).

The fifth phase, *experimentation with new means,* begins as children experiment with familiar means to achieve new goals. When familiar strategies do not work, children will modify them in light of the situation. One can think of this stage as sensorimotor problem solving. Children will try to reach a drawer by standing on a box, fix a broken toy with a string, or make a gift by wrapping a toy in a piece of tissue.

The last phase in the development of sensorimotor causality, *insight,* involves mental manipulation of means–end relationships. Instead of actually going through a variety of physical manipulations, children carry out trial-and-error problem-solving activities and planning in their minds, anticipating outcomes. They can sort out possible solutions and reject some without actually having to try them. The result is insight: Mental experimentation brings the child to the best solution, which is the only one necessary to enact.

The capacity to perceive oneself as a causal agent and to predict the outcome of one's actions are essential to the development of a sense of competence, which involves investigation of the environment, directed problem solving, and persistence toward a goal. Furthermore, adults' abilities to formulate a plan, execute it, and evaluate its outcome depend on these skills.

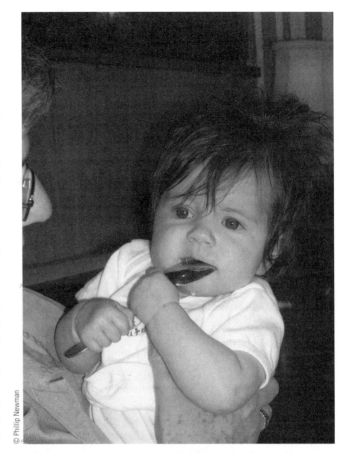

*Through mouthing, Josie is gathering information about a spoon.*

## UNDERSTANDING THE NATURE OF OBJECTS AND CREATING CATEGORIES

Babies are active explorers of their environment (Bruner, 2001). From birth, they try to make direct sensory contact with objects. They reach for, grasp, and mouth objects. They track objects visually, altering their gaze to maintain contact with them. Certain combinations of mouthing, looking at, and manipulating objects have been categorized as a type of examining behavior that provides infants with a scheme for gathering information about novel objects (Ruff, Saltarelli, Capozzoli, & Dubiner, 1992). As products of this active engagement with the object world, two related but independent aspects of infant intelligence develop: an understanding of the nature of objects, and the ability to categorize similar ones.

### ■ THE NATURE OF OBJECTS

Through looking, manipulating, and examining, infants establish that objects have basic properties. In the discussion of vision, we pointed out that very young babies recognize the contours of objects and that by 4 months, they seem to perceive objects just as adults would. That is, babies see objects as separate from each other, defined by boundaries, taking up

space, having depth, and having certain attributes of weight, color, malleability, texture, and the capacity to contain something else or not. All of these properties influence the types of actions that infants use to explore the objects and the ways they are eventually woven into other actions (Xu, 2003).

**OBJECT PERMANENCE.**  Piaget (1954) argued that understanding the properties of objects was one of the foundations of logical thought. One of the most carefully documented of these properties is **object permanence**—the concept that objects in the environment are permanent and do not cease to exist when they are out of reach or out of view. A permanent object retains its physical properties even when it cannot be seen.

Piaget suggested that initially, the infant is aware of only those objects that are in the immediate perceptual field. If a 6-month-old girl is playing with a rattle, it exists for her. If the rattle drops out of her hand or is taken away, she may show some immediate distress but will not pursue the rattle. The attainment of the concept of the permanent object frees children from reliance only on what they can see. The ability to hold the image of an object in the mind is a critical step in the emergence of complex representational thinking.

Piaget suggested that the capacity to understand that objects continue to exist requires a level of representational or symbolic thinking, which would permit an infant to hold the idea of the object in mind while it was hidden. It also requires a combination of sensorimotor capacities that permit the infant to become actively engaged in reaching, tracking, and uncovering hidden objects and learning about the spatial properties of objects in the environment. Thus, according to Piaget, the first real evidence that infants have the ability to pursue a hidden object could not really be observed much before 8 or 9 months of age, when babies begin to crawl; and the full confidence in an object's permanence could probably not emerge much before 16 to 18 months, when infants have access to representational thinking. By this age, infants can imagine various movements and displacements of objects without actually viewing them.

A growing body of research has focused on what infants know and expect about objects well before they can crawl or pursue objects through space. In a series of experiments, Renée Baillargeon has tried to determine how infants evaluate objects that are hidden from view. One of the features of her experiments is that she has cleverly deleted the motor search component. Most of her experiments use habituation in pretest conditions and a change in looking time as evidence for infants' reactions to an unexpected outcome. Even at very early ages, before infants can search for and retrieve objects, they appear to have a memory of the locations of objects and can anticipate that they take up space. Infants as young as 4 months were able to retain the image of an object as it disappeared behind a screen and showed surprise when the object emerged from the screen when it ought to have been blocked (Baillargeon & DeVos, 1991). Baillargeon's studies demonstrate that infants can follow an object through at least three different ways of hiding it: by placing the object in a container; by moving the object behind a screen; or by covering the object (Baillargeon, 2004).

Young infants have a well-developed sense of objects as distinct, permanent structures that will be set into motion when they are pushed, knocked, or in some other way "launched" by another object. They also expect that, once in motion, an object will follow a prescribed trajectory (Belanger & Desrochers, 2001). The infant's ability to anticipate an object's trajectory behind a screen is an early step in a sequence of abilities that will eventually produce the complex search process that Piaget described (Wilcox, Schweinle, & Chapa, 2003).

OBJECT PERMANENCE AND ATTACHMENT.   The process through which infants establish a scheme for objects as permanent and subject to all the laws of nature is closely linked to their understanding of themselves and their relationships with others. Each step taken to analyze and organize the object world provides insight about one's self as well as about others (Tyson, 1996).

The scheme for the permanent object applies to both humans and inanimate objects. One reason why babies experience separation anxiety is that they are uncertain whether a person to whom they are attached will continue to exist when that person is out of sight or inaccessible. Once the infant has a clear understanding of object permanence, the fear that a loved caregiver may vanish when he or she leaves the house is reduced. Interestingly, some qualities of maternal care are associated with the emergence of object permanence during the first 7 months of life. The babies of mothers who communicate with them frequently, who express positive feelings toward them, and who actively stimulate their achievements are more likely to apply the scheme of permanence to people as well as things (Chazan, 1981). The growth of attachment and the achievement of object permanence are mutually enhancing.

## ■ THE CATEGORIZATION OF OBJECTS

Physical objects have four basic properties:

1. Objects have a location, and a path and speed of motion.
2. Objects have mechanical properties that include how they move and their relation to other objects.
3. Objects have features, such as their size, shape, and color.
4. Objects have functions; this is what objects do or how they are used (Wilcox, Schweinle, & Chapa, 2003).

As infants explore and experiment with objects, they begin to devise schemes for grouping objects together. They modify these schemes to add new items to the category and to differentiate one category from another. Categories can be based on the physical properties of objects, such as "smooth" and "rough," or on the functions of objects, as in "something to sit on" and "something to dig with." The classification of objects and events into categories is one method infants have of coping with the vast array of new experiences that they encounter.

**Categorization** is a fundamental element of information processing. By treating certain individual objects as similar because they belong to the same basic grouping, like two individual red blocks or two wiggly goldfish, the potential amount of information to process is reduced (Rosch, 1978; Younger, 1992). If an item is classified as a member of a category, then all the information that has been accumulated regarding that category can automatically be applied to the specific object. This process aids in the storage and recall processes of memory, in reasoning and problem solving, and in the acquisition of new information. Classification of objects into categories is a cognitive capacity that becomes increasingly sophisticated over the childhood years.

As we pointed out earlier in the chapter, one of the early categories that has special meaning for infants is "faceness." By 6 months of age, infants attribute clear expectations to faces. They expect faces to be organized in a certain pattern and to move and respond in special ways (Nelson, 2001). Six-month-old infants can categorize faces as attractive or unattractive (Ramsey et al., 2004).

A second related category that appears early in infancy is the distinction between people and inanimate objects

(Ellsworth, Muir, & Hains, 1993; Rakison & Poulin-Dubois, 2001). Infants have been observed to smile, vocalize, and become more active when interacting with people as compared to things. By 3 months of age, infants show their ability to categorize stimuli as people or things by smiling almost exclusively at people. Infants may look with equal interest at inanimate objects, especially novel ones, but their smiles are reserved for people. This distinction between the social and the nonsocial realm can be considered a **foundational category**. It provides evidence for the unique role of social relationships in the process of adaptation and growth. From this basic distinction between a person and a thing, many further categories, such as father and mother, familiar and stranger, or adult and child, emerge that begin to differentiate the infant's social world.

Research on infant categorization skills typically involves sorting objects into groups. Using a habituation-type methodology, the earliest form of categorization can be observed. When 4½-month-old babies see an object alone, and then placed next to a different object, they respond in a way that indicates their recognition that the two objects are different (Needham, 2001). Using visual silhouettes, 3- and 4-month-old babies were able to distinguish between images of cats and dogs, primarily through a comparison of the information in the shape and features of the silhouette heads (Quinn, Eimas, & Tarr, 2001). Thus, at very early ages, infants are able to differentiate and group people and objects in their environment.

The categorization process advances over the first year, as objects are linked to concepts and functions. By 15 months, babies will touch all the objects that belong to one category and then touch all the objects in another category. By 18 months of age, children can perform multidimensional categorization tasks (e.g., sorting eight objects, such as four brightly colored yellow rectangles and four human-shaped plastic figures, into two distinct groups; Gopnik & Meltzoff, 1987, 1992). This kind of sorting does not require the ability to give names to the objects. However, by 20 months, infants will use both visual cues and names to categorize objects. The larger the infant's vocabulary, the more likely the baby is to use names to help group objects together (Nazi & Gopnick, 2001). Thus, categorizing and naming appear to be closely linked. By the close of the second year of life, babies know that objects have certain stable features, that some objects "belong" with others, and that objects have names. With these achievements, infants impose a new degree of order and predictability on their daily experiences.

## EMOTIONAL DEVELOPMENT

Emotions, like fear, sadness, anger, and joy, are part of a complex set of interconnected feelings, thoughts, and behaviors. Plutchik (2001) conceptualized emotions as part of a feedback system (see Figure 6.4). A stimulus—which could be an internal experience, such as pain, or an external stimulus, such as a looming object—is perceived and given some meaning. The meaning is associated with a feeling or emotion and with its accompanying physiological state. These combine to create an impulse for action that, if expressed, is observed in behavior. The behavior has some impact on the feeling state and the meaning of the situation. If the initial stimulus is perceived as a threat, then fear is aroused, with its accompanying physical components, including a rise in adrenaline, increased heart rate, and an impulse to flee or freeze. If the impulse to flee is acted on, and the threat is reduced, the feeling of fear declines as well.

According to Charles Darwin (1872/1965), one contribution of emotions to species survival is the ability to communicate the perceived situation to others. For example, if one animal perceives a threat and begins to shriek or run, others will interpret the behavior as a response to threat and will be alerted to the danger. The expression of some emotions, such as sadness and joy, often brings people together. The expression of others, such as anger and disgust, may increase the distance between people.

Because of their essential role in survival and social interaction, emotions have become an important focus of study in infant development. Emotional development during infancy can be understood along four dimensions. First, new emotions emerge over the period of infancy and become differentiated along dimensions of intensity—from anger to rage or from wariness to anxiety. Second, with cognitive maturation, a child interprets events differently. New emotions may become attached to familiar situations. An experience that may once have caused wariness, such as a new toy or a loud noise, may become a source of excitement or joy as the child gains a new understanding of the situation. Third, children develop strategies for regulating their emotions, so that they are not overwhelmed by emotional intensity. Fourth, emotions serve as a channel for adult–infant communication.

## ▪ EMOTIONAL DIFFERENTIATION

Emotions gradually become differentiated during the first 2 years of life. Peter Wolff (1966) described seven states of arousal in newborn infants. Each is characterized by a distinctive pattern of respiration, muscle tone, motor activity, and alertness (see Table 6.7). In these states, one observes the earliest differentiation among distress (*crying*), interest (*alert inactivity*), and excitement (*waking activity*). A newborn's state of arousal will influence his or her capacity to respond to the environment. Changes in arousal state also serve to cue responses from caregivers. Crying usually brings an effort to comfort or soothe. Visual alertness is likely to prompt social interactions. Parents try to interact with their infants, achieve eye contact, and initiate nonverbal exchanges during the alert phases (Tronick, Als, & Brazelton, 1979).

Crying is an especially important emotional expression that contributes to the infant's survival. Until about 6 or 7 months of age, the infant's mobility is quite limited. The cry is one of the primary signals available that will bring the

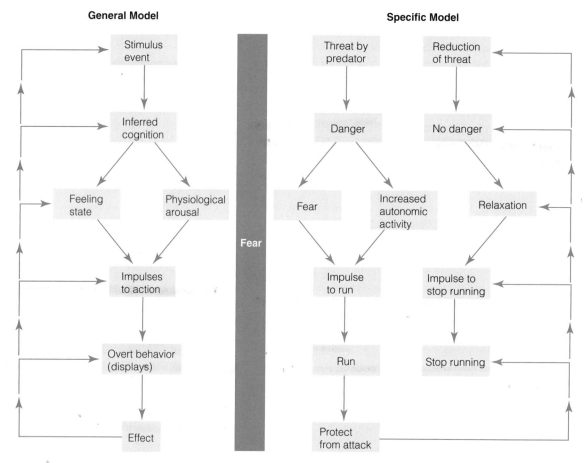

**FIGURE 6.4**

The Feedback System of Emotions. Feedback loops in emotion show how sensory information is evaluated and translated into action or some other outcome that normalizes the relationship between the individual and the triggering event. The inner state perceived as fear may arise from a threat that is perceived as "danger"; the fear triggers an impulse to flee, which results eventually in a reduction of the threat.

Source: Plutchik, 2001.

Table 6.7  States of Arousal in Newborns

| AROUSAL STATE | DESCRIPTION |
|---|---|
| Regular sleep (RS) | Full rest; low muscle tonus, low motor activity; eyelids firmly closed and still; even, regular respiratory rhythm, about 36 breaths per minute. |
| Irregular sleep (IS) | Slightly greater muscle tonus; gentle motor activity; frequent facial grimaces and smiles; occasional rapid eye movement; irregular respiration, about 48 breaths per minute. |
| Periodic sleep (PS) | Intermediate between RS and IS; bursts of rapid, shallow breathing alternate with bursts of deep, slow breathing. |
| Drowsiness (D) | More active than RS but less active than IS or PS; eyes open and close; eyes, when open, are dull and glazed and may roll upward; respiration variable but of higher frequency than during RS. |
| Alert inactivity (AI) | Slight activity; face relaxed; eyes open and "bright"; respiration constant and more rapid than in RS. |
| Waking activity (WA) | Frequent, diffuse motor activity; vocalizations; skin flushed when active; irregular respiration. |
| Crying (C) | Vigorous, diffuse motor activity; facial grimaces; skin red; eyes open or partially closed; crying vocalization. |

Source: Adapted from Wolff, 1966.

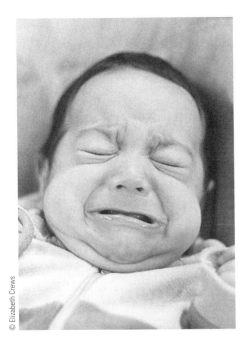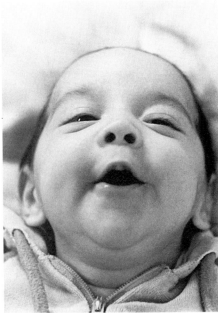

At 10 weeks of age, a baby's expression of emotion through cooing and crying provides distinct, easily interpreted messages that cue caregivers to the baby's inner state.

© Elizabeth Crews

caregiver into proximity with the infant. Infant cries vary in pitch as well as in tempo and duration. Mothers report that infants cry more in the late afternoon and early evening, often just as they are preoccupied with tasks of meal preparation (McGlaughlin & Grayson, 2001).

Adults have measurable emotional reactions to infant crying, including changes in heart rate, breathing, and perspiration, which indicate that the cry serves as a stressor (Brewster, Nelson, McCanne, Lucas, & Milner, 1998). Studies from laboratory and natural field settings and across cultures suggest that high-pitched cries are considered more upsetting to the caregiver and are treated as a signal of a more urgent need than are low-pitched cries. Moreover, information is contained in the pauses between cries. Cries that involve shorter pauses between crying sounds are perceived by adults as more arousing and unpleasant (Zeskind, Klein, & Marshall, 1992).

A broader pallet of emotions emerges gradually from the basic states of arousal and distress. The differentiation of emotions follows a regular pattern, as Table 6.8 suggests. This table describes age-related changes for three dimensions of emotion: *pleasure–joy*, *wariness–fear*, and *rage–anger*. Emotional responses during the first month are closely tied to the infant's internal state. Physical discomfort, arousal, pain, and changing tension in the central nervous system are the major sources of emotions. During the period from 1 to 6 months, emotions begin to be tied more to a separation of self and environment. Babies smile at familiar faces; they show interest in and curiosity about novel stimuli. They express rage when nursing is disrupted or when they are prevented from viewing an activity they have been intently watching.

The period from 6 to 12 months reflects a greater awareness of the context of events. Emotions of joy, anger, and fear are tied to a baby's ability to recall previous experiences and

to compare them with an ongoing event. These emotions also reflect a baby's ability to exercise some control over the environment and frustration when goals are blocked. At this age, the distinctions among some of the negative emotions, such as anger, fear, and sadness, may be difficult to detect by someone who is not familiar with the child (Camras, Malatesta, & Izard, 1991). By the end of the first year, the extent of an infant's negative emotions such as irritability and fear appear to be influenced by their caregiver's depression and anxiety. Positive emotions are not as clearly tied to the caregiver's characteristics (Pauli-Pott, Mertesacker, & Beckman, 2004).

Emotions that are observed during the second year of life—especially anxiety, pride, defiance, and shame—suggest an emerging sense of self. Infants recognize that they can operate as causal agents. They also begin to respond to the emotions of others. They can give love to others through hugs, kisses, and tender pats. They can share toys, comfort another distressed infant, and imitate another person's excitement. In becoming a more distinct being, an infant achieves a new level of awareness of the capacity to give and receive pleasure as well as the vulnerability of self and others.

The dimension of wariness-fear becomes more differentiated during the second year. The theme of *anxiety* was introduced in the discussion of attachment, pointing out the emergence of stranger anxiety at about 6 months and separation anxiety at about 9 months. Anxiety of a more nonspecific form begins to be observed during the second year. Babies begin to anticipate negative experiences and express fear of objects or events that have been associated with negative experiences in the past. The construct of anxiety is included as a major dynamic in describing patterns of attachment, especially in relationships characterized by potentially rejecting or unpredictable caregivers.

**Table 6.8** Age-Related Changes in Emotional Differentiation

| MONTH | PLEASURE-JOY | WEAKNESS-FEAR | RAGE-ANGER |
|---|---|---|---|
| 0–3 | Endogenous smile; turning toward | Startle/pain; obligatory attention | Distress due to covering the face, physical restraint, extreme discomfort |
| | | | Rage (disappointment) |
| 3 | Pleasure | | |
| 4–5 | Delight; active laughter | Wariness | |
| 7 | Joy | | |
| 9 | | Fear (stranger aversion) | Anger |
| 12 | Elation | Anxiety; immediate fear | Angry mood, petulance |
| 18 | Positive valuation of self | Shame | Defiance |
| 24 | Affection | | Intentional hurting |
| 36 | Pride, love | | Guilt |

Note: The age specified is that of neither the first appearance of the affect in question nor its peak occurrence; it is the age at which the literature suggests the reaction is common.

Source: From "Socioemotional Development," by L. A. Sroufe, in *Handbook of Infant Development*, J. D. Osofsky (Ed.), pp. 462–516. Copyright © 1979 John Wiley & Sons, Inc.

## EMOTIONS AS A KEY TO UNDERSTANDING MEANING

An infant's emotional reactions provide a channel for determining the meaning the child is giving to a specific situation. Often, these reactions are studied by the systematic coding of facial expressions. One example of how emotions provide a window on meaning comes from a study of infants in an operant conditioning experiment. Infants at ages 2, 4, and 6 months were observed while they learned an operant arm-pulling task. A string was attached to the infant's wrist. When the string was pulled, it activated a switch that turned on a color slide of an infant smiling accompanied by the sound of children singing the *Sesame Street* theme song. During the learning phase, pulling the string produced the visual and auditory stimulus. During the extinction phase, nothing happened when the string was pulled.

Even as young as 2 months old, the babies' expressions changed from interest and enjoyment during the learning phase to anger and sadness during the extinction phase. The findings were interpreted to illustrate that infants' anger is associated with violation of their expectations and that expressions of interest and enjoyment are associated with learning and increased control (Sullivan, Lewis, & Alessandri, 1992). The discussion of infant smiling in Applying Theory and Research to Life: The Meaning of an Infant's Smile provides further evidence of the link between emotional expression and meaning.

## THE ABILITY TO REGULATE EMOTIONS

**Emotional regulation** refers to a variety of processes that allow infants to control the intensity of their emotional state and reduce feelings of distress. These abilities, which mature over the first 2 years of life, have important implications for

a child's successful social participation in preschool and later childhood (Calkins, 2004). Infants develop a range of techniques for coping with intense emotions, both positive and negative. Even newborns have some strategies for reducing the intensity of distress, such as turning the head away, sucking on the hands or lips, or closing the eyes. As infants gain new motor coordination and control, they can move away, distract themselves with other objects, or soothe themselves by rocking, stroking, or thumb sucking (Kopp, 1989). However, one surely has observed many instances when infants are not able to regulate the intensity of their emotions. Researchers who work with infants will tell you of the number of babies who had to be eliminated from their study because they simply could not be calmed enough in the experimental procedure to attend to the task.

One of the most important elements in the development of **emotional regulation** is the way caregivers assist infants to manage their strong feelings (Kopp, 1989; Tronick, 1989). Caregivers can provide direct support when they observe that a child is distressed. They may cuddle, hug, rock, or swaddle a baby. They may offer food or a pacifier to the baby or nurse her as a means of comfort. Through words and actions, the caregiver may help a child interpret the source of the stress or suggest ways to reduce the stress.

Concern has been focused especially on babies who show intense negative emotionality early in infancy. Babies who show high levels of motor activity and who cry a lot at 4 months of age have been found to show high levels of wariness, fearfulness, and shyness at later ages (Park, Belsky, Putnam, & Crnic, 1997). These babies tend to be at risk for subsequent behavior problems. Studies have been directed toward analyzing individual differences in negative emotionality and the family characteristics that might be associated with changes in negativity over the first year of life (Calkins & Howse, 2004; Pauli-Pott et al., 2004). In one such study in

## The Meaning of an Infant's Smile

THE INFANT'S SMILE is a social treasure. Parents and grandparents may go to great lengths to bring out this sweet expression. Yet researchers have discovered that an infant's smile can have a wide variety of meanings and can be produced in response to many stimuli.

The earliest smiles, observed during the first month of life, may occur spontaneously during sleep or in response to a high-pitched human voice. Gentle tactile stimulation—touching, tickling, and rocking—can produce these early smiles. A baby's first smiles are not a true form of social communication, although they are likely to produce positive feelings in the adult caregiver (Wolff, 1963, 1987).

*Social smiles* begin to be observed at about 5 weeks of age. These smiles are first produced in response to a wide range of stimuli: familiar faces and voices (especially the mother's), strangers, and nonhuman objects. Games such as tickle and peekaboo bring on open-mouth smiles and laughter. The social smile conveys both recognition of familiarity and an invitation to further communication or interaction. By 4 months of age, infants smile more when the pattern of interaction is organized and pre-

dictable than when it is random and unfamiliar (Rochat, Querido, & Striano, 1999).

The *cognitive smile* develops alongside the social smile. Infants smile in response to their own behaviors, as if they were expressing satisfaction with their accomplishments or self-recognition. In a study of infants over the period from 7 to 20 weeks, babies were observed to show the "coy" smile—smiling while averting their gaze—when they were successful in getting attention or renewing attention from an adult (Reddy, 2000). At 3 months, babies smile in response to events that are moderately familiar, as if expressing pleasure in understanding the situation (Kagan, 1984). Infants also smile elaborately when they are able to make something happen, as when they wiggle a mobile or hear a bell jangle when they kick their feet (Cicchetti & Schneider-Rosen, 1984). These *mastery smiles* do not appear to have a social intention. By 8 months, infants smile when they are able to grasp a new concept (Kagan, 1984).

In the second year of life, smiling is associated with a primitive form of humor. Babies smile when they recognize an incongruity, such as seeing their

*The mastery smile!*

mother drinking from a baby bottle or crawling on her hands and knees. These smiles suggest that the baby appreciates something about the discrepancy between what is being presented and what is normally observed (Cicchetti & Schneider-Rosen, 1984).

Babies smile in a variety of contexts. The conditions that evoke smiles change as the baby matures. Thus smiles, like other emotional expressions, should be interpreted in relation to the infants' existing schemes and goals.

volving 148 babies and their parents, characteristics of the mothers and the fathers were examined separately to learn what might lead to increased negativity in the infants from 3 months to 9 months of age. In addition to the direct quality of interactions between the mother–infant and father–infant pairs, researchers found that high levels of marital dissatisfaction on the part of the mother or the father and the father's emotional insensitivity were tied to increases in the infant's negativity. This is significant because it suggests that the emotional climate of the parental system is communicated in ways that an infant can perceive as early as 3 to 9 months of age (Belsky, Fish, & Isabella, 1991).

Caregivers' approaches to infant emotional regulation vary with the culture (Kitayama, Karasawa, & Mesquita, 2004). In some cultures, caregivers regulate emotions by preventing a child from being exposed to certain arousing situations. Japanese mothers, for example, try hard to prevent their children from being exposed to anger by avoiding frustrating them.

Furthermore, parents rarely express anger to their young children, especially in public. Thus, Japanese parents try to regulate anger by minimizing the child's experiences with it (Miyake, Campos, Kagan, & Bradshaw, 1986). Cultural values influence how mothers respond to infants' distress and what they teach their babies about how to regulate feelings of wariness, fear, and anxiety.

Infants achieve emotional regulation by observing emotional reactions of others (Campos, Campos, & Barrett, 1989). Children observe anger, pride, shame, or sadness in others, often in response to their own emotional expressions. For example, Connie stumbles and falls in trying to take a step on her own. She looks up at her mother. If her mother looks upset and frightened, Connie may begin to cry. On the other hand, if her mother laughs or speaks to her in a comforting tone, Connie may get up and try again. Children can be distracted from their sadness by seeing laughter and joy in someone else. Through empathy, they can reduce their angry

*Emotions provide a channel of communication before speech and language. The exchange of playful laughing and smiling is an early form of conversation.*

© Myrleen Ferguson Cate/Photo Edit

feelings toward someone else by seeing how sad or frightened the other person is.

As children understand the consequences or implications of a situation, they have new motives for regulating or failing to regulate their emotions. Children may extend or expand their signals of distress if they think they will help them achieve their goals, such as special attention or nurturing. Children may try to disguise their distress if they think it will provoke additional pain. Emotional regulation, like emotional signaling, takes place in an interpersonal context.

## ■ EMOTIONS AS A CHANNEL FOR ADULT–INFANT COMMUNICATION

Emotions provide a two-way channel through which infants and their caregivers can establish **intersubjectivity**. An infant has the capacity to produce a range of emotional expressions, including fear, distress, disgust, surprise, excitement, interest, joy, anger, and sadness. Parents and other caregivers rely on the facial, vocal, and behavioral cues related to these emotions as ways of determining an infant's inner states and goals and responding to them. Babies in turn can also detect and differentiate the affective expressions of others. Young infants can differentiate facial expressions of fear, anger, happiness, sadness, and surprise. In cycles of interaction, responsive caregivers monitor changes in a baby's affect as a way of determining whether their interventions are effective (Meins, 2003).

Think of a 6-month-old baby who wants a toy that is out of reach. The baby waves her arms in the direction of the toy, makes fussy noises, and looks distressed. As her father tries to figure out what the baby wants, he watches her expressions in

order to discover whether he is on the right track. Parents who are attuned to this form of communication are more likely to help babies to achieve their goals, and babies are more likely to persist in attempts to communicate because they have experienced success in such interactions. Through a shared repertoire of emotions, babies and their caregivers are able to understand one another and create common meanings. Thus, emotional expression becomes a building block of trust (Trevarthen & Aitken, 2001).

**SOCIAL REFERENCING.** One of the most notable ways that infants and adults have of co-constructing their reality is the mechanism of **social referencing**. Under certain circumstances, infants make use of the emotional responses of another person to guide their own behavior. They often use their mothers as a *social reference*, but other adults can serve this function as well (Hornik & Gunnar, 1988; Klinnert, Emde, Butterfield, & Campos, 1986; Walden & Ogan, 1988). As infants approach an unfamiliar adult, an ambiguous situation, or a novel object, they look to their mother and use her facial expression or verbal expressions as a source of information about the situation. If the mother expresses wariness or a negative emotion, the infant is more likely to withdraw or to explore with caution. On the other hand, if the mother expresses a positive emotion, the infant is more likely to approach the situation or the unfamiliar person with confidence. By 12 months of age, infants consistently use this mechanism to try to appraise an ambiguous situation (Rosen, Adamson, & Bakeman, 1992).

Social referencing illustrates how members of a cultural group build a shared view of reality during infancy. Infants actively request information by looking to their mothers or other adults. The adult's expression, either positive or negative, cues the infant about whether to approach or withdraw. Infants reduce their uncertainty and begin to appraise their world in the context of the emotional responses of their caregivers. You can probably imagine the wide range of objects and situations that can be evaluated through this mechanism. Foods, toys, people, animals, sounds, plants, objects of all sorts can be discerned as positive and approachable or negative and a cause for wariness. Depending on the cultural outlook, infants in different societies will begin to categorize their experiences differently based in part on these early appraisals derived from social referencing.

# THE PSYCHOSOCIAL CRISIS: TRUST VERSUS MISTRUST

The term *psychosocial crisis* refers to a state of tension that occurs as a result of the developmental needs of the individual and the social expectations of the culture. At each stage of life, the crisis is expressed as a struggle between the positive and the negative poles of a critical dimension. In infancy, the specific nature of the crisis—trust versus mistrust—focuses on the fundamental nature of an infant's sense of connection to the social world.

## TRUST

In adult relationships, **trust** refers to an appraisal of the availability, dependability, and sensitivity of another person (Mikulincer, 1998). Trust emerges in the course of a relationship as one person discovers those traits in another person. As the level of trust grows, the partners may take some risks by disclosing information or feelings that may lead to rejection. Relationships that endure through periods of risk grow in feelings of trust. However, trust is more than a summary of the past: It is a faith that the relationship will survive in an unpredictable future. This faith begins in infancy. A trusting relationship links confidence about the past with faith about the future.

For infants, trust is an emotion—an experiential state of confidence that their needs will be met and that they are valued. Trust is inferred from the infant's increasing capacity to delay gratification and from the warmth and delight that are evident in interactions with family members. The sense of trust expands from immediate figures in the social environment to the supportiveness and responsiveness of the broader social and physical world. Infants also learn to trust their sensory systems in processing stimulation from the environment. In this function, the sense of trust extends to learning to trust oneself.

The sense of basic trust is related to but not identical to Bowlby's concept of attachment. Attachment refers to the behavioral system that ensures safety and security for the infant. Over time, the internal representation of the attachment relationship generalizes to other dyadic (paired) relationships, especially where issues of intimacy and protection are relevant. Trust is a broader construct. Within the framework of trust, infants not only establish an assessment of the central social figures in their world as trustable or untrustable, but they also achieve a sense of their own value and trustworthiness. Over time, a basic sense of trust expands to a global optimism about how one expects to be treated by others and about one's ability to cope with life's challenges. Trust is an integrating force that helps synthesize emotions, cognitions, and actions under conditions of uncertainty, allowing the person to pursue goals with a belief that things will work out well.

## MISTRUST

During infancy, experiences of **mistrust** can arise from at least three sources: infant wariness, lack of confidence in the caregiver, and doubt in one's own lovableness. First, wariness, one of the earliest infant emotions, is linked initially to at least two infant reflexes, the "startle" response in reaction to loud noises and the Moro reflex in response to sudden loss of support. All infants are prewired neurologically to be alert to certain environmental dangers. Two of the caregiver's functions are to minimize the infant's exposure to stimuli that evoke these reflexes, and to comfort and reassure the infant after exposure to threatening stimuli.

Second, babies can lack confidence in the good intentions of others. Some caregivers are unable to differentiate the infant's needs or respond appropriately to them. Others are indifferent or unusually harsh. Under these conditions, seeds of doubt may grow about the trustworthiness of the environment.

Third, babies experience the power of their own rage. In some children, self-regulatory abilities are poorly developed, which leads to frequent outbursts of negativity and frustration. They can learn to doubt their own lovableness as they encounter the intensity of their own capacity for anger.

Most parents also contribute to experiences of mistrust because they inevitably make some mistakes in responding to their infant's signs of distress, particularly when the baby is young. They may first try the bottle and, if the crying continues, they may change the diaper, give water, move the baby to another room, or put the baby to bed—trying a variety of things until something works. Over time, however, sensitive caregivers learn to interpret their child's signals correctly and to respond appropriately, thereby fostering the infant's sense of trust in the environment.

Feelings of doubt or anxiety about the bond of trust are more common than may have been expected. About one third of American infant–mother pairs who have been systematically observed show evidence of an insecure attachment.

*Lilly expresses her wariness as her father gives her over to the nanny. The intensity of her protest reflects the discomfort of being placed in the care of a stranger.*

© Spencer Grant/Photo Edit

Cross-cultural research provides further evidence that a significant proportion of infants have difficulty deriving emotional comfort or security from their caregivers (Posada et al., 1995; van IJzendoorn & Kroonenberg, 1988; van IJzendoorn & Sagi, 1999).

In addition to the mistrust that emerges in the context of inconsistent, unresponsive, or harsh caregiving, there are many cases in which the mother–infant relationship is disrupted. This can happen in conditions of war, parental imprisonment, parental death due to disease or accident, or lengthy hospitalization. In all of these situations, an infant is at risk for experiencing a strong sense of mistrust.

Mistrust may manifest itself in the infant by withdrawal from interaction and by symptoms of depression and grief, which include sobbing, lack of emotion, lethargy, and loss of appetite (Field et al., 1988). It may also be revealed later on in development in the expressions of interpersonal distress observed in the angry, anxious, and resistant behaviors of children with insecure attachments or in the inability to form close, satisfying relationships with others as adolescents and adults. Mistrust may provide a foundation for the emergence of a negative scheme about the self—a scheme that is elaborated over time by defining the self with a cluster of closely related, negative attributes such as cautiousness, nervousness, or introversion (Malle & Horowitz, 1995).

All infants experience some aspects of mistrust, either as a result of mismatches between their needs and the caregiving strategies they receive or as a product of their own difficulties in modulating strong feelings of wariness or anger. Thus, the resolution of the crisis in the direction of trust reflects a real psychological achievement, in which infants are able to minimize their wariness of the environment and to regulate their own inner passions.

Over the life span, the sense of trust is transformed and matures into an inner framework for the understanding of life. Among older adults who have a strong sense of trust, many of life's disappointments and complexities are minimized by a growing religious faith. Their basic sense of trust evolves into a powerful belief in a great source of goodness and love in the universe, a force that can transcend the pain of daily tragedies and give integrity and meaning to their dying as well as to their living (Erikson et al., 1986).

# THE CENTRAL PROCESS FOR RESOLVING THE CRISIS: MUTUALITY WITH THE CAREGIVER

To resolve the crisis of trust versus mistrust, an infant must establish a feeling of **mutuality** with a caregiver. Mutuality is a characteristic of a relationship. Initially it is built on the consistency with which the caregiver responds appropriately to the infant's needs. The caregiver comes to appreciate the variety of an infant's needs, and the infant learns to expect that his or her personal needs will be met. Within families, the establishment of mutuality differs with each child, depending on infant characteristics and parental responses (Deater-Deckard & O'Connor, 2000).

An infant influences the responses of a caregiver in many ways. Infants' irritability and soothability contribute to the kinds of responses that adults make. Infants can reject or end an interaction by fussing, becoming tense, crying, or falling asleep. They can maintain an interaction by smiling, cooing, snuggling comfortably, or maintaining eye contact. Techniques of comforting do not call forth the same responses from all babies (Campos, 1989). A pacifier helps comfort some babies, whereas others respond to being wrapped snugly in a warm blanket.

An infant and a caregiver learn to regulate the amount of time that passes between the expression of a need and its satisfaction. Bell and Ainsworth (1972) observed mothers' responses to infant crying during the first year of life. Over the course of the year, the infants' crying decreased, and the mothers tended to respond more quickly to their cries. This finding suggests a process of mutual adaptation by mothers and infants. Some mothers came quickly and ignored few cries. Other mothers waited a long time and ignored much of the crying. The longer mothers delayed in responding to their infants' cries, the more crying the infants did in later months. Babies whose mothers responded promptly in the first 6 months of life cried less often in the second 6 months.

## COORDINATION, MISMATCH, AND REPAIR OF INTERACTIONS

The study of mutuality with the caregiver has focused in some detail on patterns and rhythms of social interaction, especially coordination, matching, and synchrony (Tronick, 2003). **Coordination** refers to two related characteristics of interaction: matching and synchrony. **Matching** means that the infant and the caregiver are involved in similar behaviors or states at the same time. They may be playing together with an object, cooing and smiling at each other, or fussing and angry at each other. **Synchrony** means that the infant and caregiver move fluidly from one state to the next. When infants are paying attention to their caregivers, the caregivers attempt to stimulate them. As babies withdraw attention, the caregivers learn to reduce stimulation and wait until the infants are ready to engage again. Normally, mother–infant interactions become increasingly coordinated (Isabella & Belsky, 1991; Tronick & Cohn, 1989). This does not mean that most of the interactions are coordinated. In fact, especially when babies are very young, matched interactions appear to become mismatched rather quickly.

A mother and infant may be engaged in a period of cooing and laughing. The mother makes a funny noise, the baby reacts by cooing and laughing, then the mother makes the noise again and the baby laughs. On the third try, the mother cannot get the baby to make eye contact. She may try shifting the baby to another position or making the noise at a different pitch, but the baby looks away and squirms. The game is over; the connection is temporarily broken.

Why is mother–infant communication so frequently disrupted? The explanation may lie partly in the infant's inability to sustain coordinated communication, partly in a rapid shift of need states, and partly in the inability of adults to sustain long periods of nonverbal communication. In normal mother–infant pairs, however, periods of **mismatch** are usually followed by **communication repairs**, so that infants and mothers cycle again through points of coordination in their interactions.

At a theoretical level, this process of coordination, mismatch, and repair can be viewed as a building block for mutuality. Infants and caregivers gain confidence in their ability to communicate. Infants have many opportunities to experience the satisfaction of shared communication and the sense of being embedded in a responsive social environment. They also experience frequent recovery from a mismatched state to a state of effective communication, so that they can be hopeful about the ability to make these repairs in the future.

## ESTABLISHING A FUNCTIONAL RHYTHM IN THE FAMILY

The match or mismatch between an infant's rhythms and the family's rhythms is an important factor in the overall adjustment of a family to a new baby (Sprunger, Boyce, & Gaines, 1985). Some babies are quite predictable; the timing of their sleeping, eating, playtime, and even fussy periods follows a clear pattern. Other babies are much less regular. All babies are changing rapidly during the first 24 months of life, so daily patterns are bound to change, and families must make frequent adjustments in order to continue to meet the infant's needs.

In American culture, by the end of the first year of life, babies are typically expected to modify their schedule of needs so that they sleep when the rest of the family sleeps, play when the rest of the family is awake, and eat three or at most four times a day, generally when the other family members eat. During the second year of life, the demands of parenting change. Babies become more mobile and have new capacities to initiate activities. Their attention span increases, they have new requirements for stimulation, and they have new areas of wariness and resistance—things they don't want to do (like take a nap) or people they don't want to be with (like a certain baby-sitter). These and other changes require adaptation on the part of parents in order to sustain the mutuality that had been achieved or to rectify problems in attachment and trust that may now be evident (Heinicke & Guthrie, 1992). The stable feature in mutual relationships is the caregiver's effort to be responsive to the child's changing capacities and needs, and the child's ongoing monitoring of and responsiveness to the caregiver's cues (Masur & Turner, 2001; Robinson & Acevedo, 2001).

## Is There a Critical Period for Attachment?

A CRITICAL PERIOD is a time of maximal sensitivity or readiness for the development of certain skills or behavior patterns. The particular skill or behavior pattern is not likely to emerge before the onset of the critical period, and it is extremely difficult if not impossible to establish once the critical period has passed. The successful emergence of any behavior that has a critical period for development depends on the coordination of the biological readiness of the organism and environmental supports (Scott, 1987).

Konrad Lorenz (1935, 1937/1961) was one of the first ethologists to compare the critical periods in physical development and those in behavioral development. Lorenz described a process of social attachment among birds that he called **imprinting**. In this process, the young bird establishes a comparatively permanent bond with its mother. In her absence, however, the young bird will imprint on other available targets, including a model of its mother or a human being. For birds, the onset of the critical period coincides with the time at which they are able to walk and ends

Konrad Lorenz inadvertently became the target of imprinting for these geese. They followed him as if he were their mother.

when they begin to fear strangers. After this point, no new model or species can be substituted as a target for imprinting.

Soon after a baby's birth, the parent's attachment to the baby becomes quite specific; the parent would not be willing to replace his or her own baby with any other baby of similar age. Is there a time when infants are most likely to form such an attachment to the primary caregiver? Is there a point after which such attachments cannot be

## PARENTS WITH PSYCHOLOGICAL PROBLEMS

The importance of reciprocal interactions in building trust and hope during infancy is highlighted by studies of parents with psychological problems. Sensitivity to an infant's emotional states, the ability to respond appropriately to an infant's needs, and the quality of common, daily interactions can all be impaired by family risk factors. Studies of parents who are experiencing marital discord, who have been victims of child abuse or neglect, who are depressed, or who are mentally ill suggest that the interactional cycles of these parents and their children lack synchrony (Rutter, 1990). For example, in a comparison of mothers who had been maltreated as children and those who had not, the maltreated mothers were less involved with their children during play, made use of fewer strategies to direct their children's activities, and used a more negative tone with their children (Alessandri, 1992).

Other research has compared interactions between depressed and nondepressed mothers and their infants. The depressed mothers were found to be unresponsive, emotionally unavailable, and unable to sustain smooth communication with their babies. Depressed mothers were less likely to show animated, positive facial expressions. Typical efforts at fostering an infant's emotional regulation, commonly observed in nondepressed mothers—such as introducing stimulating toys and games, touching and talking, and the efforts at reducing arousal through appropriate soothing and comforting—were not common in depressed mothers. For their part, the infants of depressed mothers had few expressions of interest, showed more sad and angry expressions, showed less ability to match a happy face with a happy vocal expression, and were less able to regulate their emotions. Interactions between the mothers and infants appeared to be stressful and mutually unsatisfying (Field, 2002). See the box on Distressed Mothers (p. 172) to learn more about an approach to intervention.

formed? The most direct way to examine this question would be to separate an infant from his or her mother and observe the consequences in the infant's ability to establish a bond with a new caregiver. Because such experimentation would be unethical, however, evidence to address these questions has been drawn from real-life situations in which the mother–infant relationship has been disrupted.

Leon Yarrow (1963, 1964, 1970) observed 100 infants who were shifted from foster mothers to adoptive mothers. The infants who were separated from their foster mothers at 6 months or earlier showed minimal distress. They did not express prolonged anger or depression over the separation if their physical and emotional needs continued to be met. In contrast, all the infants who were transferred from foster mothers to adoptive mothers at 8 months or older showed strong negative reactions, including angry protest and withdrawal. These infants found the disruption of their earlier relationships very stressful.

Later research by John Bowlby (1980) focused on adolescents who

had moved repeatedly from one foster home or institution to another. These children never had an opportunity to form an enduring, loving relationship with a caring adult. As adolescents, they were described as *affectionless* and unable to form close relationships with others. Recent studies have confirmed that children who spend their infancy in institutions where the turnover in caregivers is high show disruptions in social functioning, including indiscriminate friendship formation, difficulty in forming close relationships, and difficulty in finding emotional support from peers (Rutter, 1995). From these real-world examples of disruption in the mother–infant relationship, we can say that a critical period for attachment must begin at about 6 months of age.

When might this period be over? The quality of the attachment relationship is established well before 24 months. Longitudinal studies have reported consistency in the quality of attachment from 12 to 18 months, from 12 to 20 months, and from 12 months to 6 years (Main, Kaplan, & Cassidy, 1985). Is there really a closing-off point—a time

after which a secure attachment can no longer be established? If there is no opportunity to form a consistent relationship with a loving adult, as in the case of the adolescents Bowlby studied, no attachment will be formed. In a study of children who spent their first years of life in an institution where the quality of care was good but staff turnover was high, children who were adopted at age 2 were able to form secure attachments to their adoptive parents. However, at later observations at ages 8 and 16, the children showed evidence of difficulty in peer relations similar to the children who remained in the institution (Hodges & Tizard, 1989). Lack of continuity in caregiving during infancy, such as might occur in institutional care or in shifts from one foster home to the next, is likely to produce long-lasting disruptions in relationship formation, even if a secure attachment with a caregiver is formed at a later time.

# THE PRIME ADAPTIVE EGO QUALITY AND THE CORE PATHOLOGY

## HOPE

Erikson (1982) has argued that the positive resolution of the psychosocial crisis of trust versus mistrust leads to the adaptive ego quality of *hope*. As you will recall from Chapter 3, the prime adaptive ego qualities shape a person's outlook on life in the direction of greater openness to experience and information, greater capacity to identify a variety of pathways to achieve one's goals, more willingness to assert the self and to express one's wishes and views, and a positive approach to the formation of close relationships. Even in the face of difficulties and stressful life events, these qualities contribute to higher levels of functioning and well-being (Peterson & Seligman, 2003).

As the first of the prime adaptive ego qualities, **hope** pervades the entire life story. It is a global cognitive orientation that one's goals and dreams can be attained and that events will turn out for the best. As Erikson described it, "Hope bestows on the anticipated future a sense of leeway inviting expectant leaps, either in preparatory imagination or in small initiating actions. And such daring must count on basic trust in the sense of a trustfulness that must be, literally and figuratively, nourished by maternal care and—when endangered by all-too-desperate discomfort—must be restored by competent consolation" (1982, p. 60).

Hopefulness combines the ability to think of one or more paths to achieve a goal with a belief in one's ability to move along that pathway toward the goal (Snyder, Cheavens, & Sympson, 1997). The roots of hopefulness lie in the infant's understanding of the self as a causal agent. Each time a baby takes an action to achieve an outcome, the sense of hope grows. When babies encounter obstacles or barriers to their goals, sensitive caregivers find ways to remove the

## Fostering Mutuality Among Distressed Mothers and Their Infants

THE RESULTS OF an early intervention study with mother–infant pairs assessed as having anxious attachments help clarify those aspects of mutuality that may be most amenable to repair. The study involved 100 Spanish-speaking mothers who had recently emigrated from Mexico or Central America to the United States and their 12-month-old babies (Lieberman, Weston, & Pawl, 1991). These families were considered to be at risk for attachment disturbances because the combination of poverty, unemployment, and sudden cultural transition increased both anxiety and depression among the mothers. The mother–infant dyads were assessed using a home visit and observation in the strange situation. Of those who could be clearly classified, 34 anxious dyads were placed in the experimental intervention program, 25 anxious dyads were in the anxious control group, and 34 secure dyads were in a second, secure control group. The intervention involved weekly home visits with a trained intervener over the second year of life.

The interveners' efforts focused on two themes. First, they tried to encourage the mother's ability to express her own feelings, including her longings for security, concerns for protection and safety when she was a child and in the present, and negative feelings of self-doubt and anger toward others, including the child and the intervener. Second, they tried to provide developmentally relevant information about the child, including observations about the child's temperament, observations about age-appropriate opportunities to foster exploration, and strategies for negotiating mother–infant conflicts that would help restore synchrony.

The impact of the intervention was assessed at 24 months using videotapes of a 1½-hour laboratory session. The session included free play with mother

*When mothers are depressed, they are less psychologically available for reciprocal interactions. This baby is trying to get her mother's attention, but her mom, although physically present, seems to be in a world of her own.*

and baby, play with a female stranger while the mother was present, child-directed play while the adults were unavailable, separation from the mother while the stranger remained in the room, reunion with the mother when the stranger left the room, and snack with mother, child, and observer.

Mothers in the experimental anxious attachment group showed significantly greater levels of empathy toward their children during this laboratory session than did the anxious controls. These mothers also initiated more interactions with their babies. The children showed fewer angry, avoidant, and resistant behaviors than did the anxious controls. Upon reunion after the brief separation, the mothers and children in the experimental group showed more evidence of eagerness and readiness to resume interaction than did the anxious controls. There were no significant differ-

ences between the intervention group and the securely attached controls on any of the behavioral measures at 24 months, suggesting that the intervention was effective in repairing the attachment system to the point that the initially anxious group was behaving very much like the secure group in the laboratory situation.

The results of this study suggest that interventions that engage the mother and support her emotional involvement in the parenting process can have a beneficial impact on the emotional development of the child. The intervention contributes to the mother's greater self-acceptance and reduced frustration, as well as her increased empathy for the child's needs and developmental level. These changes lead to the child's improved capacity to regulate his or her behavior in harmony with a more predictable, responsive partner.

*Using all her problem-solving skills and motor coordination, this baby is surging forward toward independence by clambering out of her playpen. Hopefulness allows babies to set new goals and take new risks.*

obstacles or lead them along a new path toward the goal. The infant's sense of self as a causal agent combined with the caregiver's sensitivity create the context for the emergence of hope.

Research with adults shows that people who have a hopeful, optimistic outlook about the future have different achievement beliefs and emotional reactions in response to actual achievement than do people who have a pessimistic outlook (Dweck, 1992; Norem & Cantor, 1988). People who have higher levels of hopefulness undertake a larger number of goals across life areas and select tasks that are more difficult. Hopefulness is generally associated with higher goals, higher levels of confidence that the goal will be reached, and greater persistence in the face of barriers to goal attainment, thus leading to higher overall levels of performance (Snyder, 2002). Feelings of hope help people deal with their most difficult challenges, including serious illness, injury, bereavement, and facing the end of life (Sullivan, 2003).

Within the psychosocial framework, hope provides the platform from which very young children take certain "leaps of faith." When an infant overcomes doubts and hesitancy in taking a first independent step, you see the dividend of hope. When a toddler clambers over the bars of her crib and lets herself drop several inches to the floor, you see the dividend

of hope. As a parent, when you give your adolescent the keys to the car and watch as he or she drives off alone, you see the dividend of hope. Without hope, neither the individual nor the society could bear the weight of uncertainty in our changing world. With hope, individuals can envision a better society and come together in actions to reach the collective good (Braithwaite, 2004).

## WITHDRAWAL

As a core pathology, **withdrawal** refers to a general orientation of wariness toward people and objects. This is especially disturbing because, during infancy, healthy development is a pattern of outward motion, extension, and increasing engagement with the social and physical worlds. Infants typically reach and grasp, crawl, stand, and walk. They explore through gazing, mouthing, and manipulating objects. Their behavior is typically characterized by interest in novelty, joy in learning, and frustration at encountering barriers to goal achievement. Over the first year, babies become increasingly connected to significant figures in their social world, following them about, devising strategies to engage them in interaction, and looking to them for consolation when they are distressed.

Infants who are characterized by withdrawal may show evidence of passivity, lethargy, and neutral or negative affect. They are not readily engaged in social interaction and do not show the signs of self-directed exploration that are typical of most healthy infants. Withdrawal may have some of its roots in genetically determined temperamental characteristics. Some babies have a very low threshold for pain. They are highly sensitive to sensory stimulation and recoil from the kinds of handling that other babies find comforting or pleasurable. Some babies are more passive than others, requiring little in the way of stimulation and showing less evidence of exploratory behavior than active babies.

One of the earliest descriptions of withdrawal in infancy was provided by Rene Spitz's (1945, 1946) analysis of children who had been institutionalized before 1 year of age. The babies who suffered the most had been placed in a foundling home in which eight babies were cared for by one nurse. These babies went through a phase of initial rage, followed by a period of physical and emotional withdrawal. They lay passively in their cribs, showing limited motor exploration and little emotionality. Furthermore, they rarely smiled or showed excitement. The babies' babbling and language were extremely delayed. They deteriorated physically. Their measured developmental level dropped substantially over a year's time. These babies suffered from a combination of a loss of their attachment figure, a lack of meaningful social interaction, and an absence of appropriate sensory stimulation—all of which produced what Spitz called *anaclitic depression*.

Not all instances of withdrawal are as severe as the anaclitic depression syndrome. However, a growing literature focuses on the links between disrupted mother–infant interaction and subsequent social withdrawal (Gerhold et al., 2002). Temperamental factors including behavioral inhibition and a low threshold for sensory stimulation, an anxious-avoidant attachment, and a lack of contingent, responsive caregiving can combine to produce mistrust and the formation of the core pathology of withdrawal. Social withdrawal can become such a severe social deficit that it interferes with adaptive functioning and requires clinical treatment (Calkins & Fox, 2002).

APPLIED TOPIC
# THE ROLE OF PARENTS

PARENTS HAVE AN enormous responsibility for their children's physical and psychosocial growth. We have portrayed infants as active, adaptive, and eager to master the environment. At the same time, the immaturity of human infants at birth necessitates a long period of dependence on adults. The few instinctive behaviors of human infants in comparison with the infants of other species is compensated for by their enormous capacity to learn. For this potential to be realized, infants must rely on their parents to maintain their health, provide stimulation, and protect them from danger. During the period of dependence, infants become entwined in complex social systems and develop strong emotional bonds with their caregivers. The quality of these early relationships provides infants with mental representations that guide their later development of friendships, intimacy, and relationships with their own children.

Infancy, just like pregnancy and childbirth, is culturally constructed. Despite the powerful, genetically guided plan for development, the content of experience and the way the period of infancy is viewed depend on cultural traditions, beliefs, and technologies. Some of the ways that culture defines infancy include the infant's sleeping arrangements; the choice of clothing; the choice of the infant's name and the naming process; the selection of foods; and access to nursing from mothers and other lactating women (Valsiner, 2000). Parents transmit the culture through their care, and by enacting certain rituals and practices, they introduce and integrate their infant into the cultural community.

## SAFETY IN THE PHYSICAL ENVIRONMENT

One of the central responsibilities that parents face is to ensure infants' survival by protecting them from environmental dangers. The ecology of home and neighborhood, including the society's degree of modernization, influences the kinds of dangers to which infants are exposed and the kinds of practices that families and cultures invent to protect their offspring. In addition to physical risks, some dangers are linked to superstitions, religious beliefs, and matters of the spirit world. In many parts of the world, parents take special precautions to prevent their infants from coming under the influence of an "evil eye." The eye gaze may be viewed as a vehicle through which a person may deliberately or inadvertently transmit harmful feelings of jealousy, revenge, or unbridled pride (Galt, 1991).

*Infancy is culturally constructed. Cora rises early each morning, ties her infant to her back, and walks to the market to sell flowers. She expects her baby to be calm and quiet while she earns her living.*

© Oliver Benn/Getty Images

## TECHNOLOGY AND HUMAN DEVELOPMENT

# Infant Safety

AS WE POINTED out early in this chapter, medical technologies are saving the lives of many low-birthweight infants who would have died in earlier times. However, as societies become more technologically advanced, infants are exposed to new risks. Some of the technologies that have contributed most to modernization and the quality of life, such as automobile travel and electricity in the home, also present serious challenges for infant safety.

### CAR SEATS

All 50 states have child restraint laws to protect children during automobile travel. The regular seat belts that are installed with cars are not adequate to protect small children. As a result, various types of car safety seats have been created. Properly installed child safety seats can reduce the risk of death in auto accidents by 71%. However, when vehicles have been stopped and checked, 85% of child safety seats are found to be improperly installed. There are a variety of resources on the Web, training programs, and safety check locations to guide the proper installation of child safety seats. These seats must be properly anchored into the back seat. For infants up to 1 year of age and 20 pounds weight, the seats must be facing backward, and installed at an angle. The harness must fit snugly around the chest, not too tight at the neck or the abdomen. As children grow, the seats may be turned to face forward, and the anchoring, harness, and fit all have to be adjusted (Cincinnati Children's Hospital Medical Center, 2004).

### SAFETY IN THE HOME

The website on Wellness from the Cincinnati Children's Hospital Medical Center (1998) offers the following suggestions for infant safety in the home. Many of these suggestions are linked to the range of technologies that are part of the infant's home environment, including the crib, toys, cleaning products, medicines, electrical outlets, and telephone cords.

- Remove any strings that are on the bottom of the sleeping gowns. Strings can stop your baby's circulation if they become wrapped around the baby's neck and toes.
- Keep objects that may be swallowed, such as marbles, plastic bags, toys with buttons, and balloons, away from your baby.
- Crib spindles should be no more than 2⅜ inches apart. Drop sides should lock securely in place when raised or lowered. Crib pads should be used to keep baby's arms and legs from poking between the spindles.
- Crib toys should be safe and not have parts that can be chewed off and swallowed. Place toys in the crib. Tying the toys to the crib is dangerous. The baby's neck, fingers or toes could become tangled in the string.
- If your baby uses a pacifier, hold it in his or her mouth or gently prop it with a folded diaper. Tying the pacifier around the baby's neck, to his or her clothes, or to his or her bed is dangerous.

- Leaving a bucket of water and your baby alone in a room is dangerous. He or she could fall into the bucket headfirst and not be able to get out of the bucket.
- Once your baby begins to crawl and move around, put away breakable or valuable objects that he or she can reach. Close stairway doors, or use safety gates at the top and bottom of stairs.
- When your baby is crawling or walking, a lollipop, toothbrush, spoon, stick, or any long-handled object is dangerous. If he or she falls while the object is in his or her mouth or near the eyes, it could cause serious injury.
- Move cleaning products and medicines from your baby's reach or put safety locks on all lower cupboards. Remove any household plants (80% of all reported accidental poisonings involve children between the ages of 10 and 30 months).
- Cover unused electrical outlets with safety plugs. Hide electrical cords under rugs or behind furniture. Repair any frayed electrical cords. Keep your baby away from unused telephone jacks and disconnected telephone cords.

There are many new technological innovations that parents of infants can take advantage of. Some of these innovations pose risks to infants, but then new technologies are often invented to reduce or prevent the risks.

The presence of dangers or risks in the environment usually elicits some effort to restrict a child's movement through swaddling, carrying the baby in a sling, or placing the baby in a playpen. Because of concern about dangers, caregivers also invoke certain prohibitions, such as telling the child, "No, don't touch that," or pulling the child away from something dangerous. As infants become more mobile in the second half of their first year, the need to introduce prohibitions and to monitor exploratory activities increases. Depending on the cultural values concerning independent exploration, caregivers may heighten their restrictions and prohibitions or may try to modify the environment to permit safe, unrestricted exploration.

Certain childrearing practices arise from a desire to protect young children from known dangers. For example, Robert LeVine (1977) described the practice of many African cultures of carrying infants 18 months and older on the back, even though they were able to walk around. This practice was used to prevent toddlers from getting burned on the open cooking fires at an age when they were mobile enough to walk or stumble into the fire and yet not old enough to know how to inhibit their movements. Other hazards in the neighborhood, such as falling off steep cliffs or into lakes, rivers, or wells, prompted this same carrying behavior.

In industrialized countries, infants face different types of hazards, such as electrical outlets, steep stairs, and open containers of insecticides, cleaning agents, and other poisons. See the box on Infant Safety (p. 175) for a discussion of how technologies can introduce new hazards. Many American families protect babies from these dangers by putting gates at a doorway or at the top of a stairway, or by placing an infant in a crib or playpen to restrict her or his exploration. In other homes, the strategy is to baby-proof the home by removing as many known dangers as possible so that the baby has maximum freedom for exploration. These two different strategies reflect two different values concerning childrearing—both with the same goal of providing maximum safety and protection from danger. In the former case, parents try to preserve their adult environment. Children must modify their behavior in order to fit into the home. In the latter case, parents modify the environment to accommodate the baby's developmental needs.

## FOSTERING EMOTIONAL AND COGNITIVE DEVELOPMENT

Another component of the parents' role during infancy is their ability to promote emotional and cognitive development. Much of the behavior that appears to be important in the development of strong emotional bonds between infants and parents is also central to the fostering of intellectual growth.

If you have ever observed a child and a parent in a novel environment, such as a doctor's office, you may have seen an example of this dual function. The positive emotional attachment to the parent provides a basis for a wide range of cognitive skills. The parent serves as an island of safety and reassurance from which the child can explore. The child first moves out into the environment and then returns to the parent. The next time, the child may wander a bit farther, exploring magazines, couches, or other children before once again returning to the parent. One may even see the child leave the room and wander into the hallway or into an empty examining room, eventually returning (if not first retrieved by a watchful nurse) to the parent's side. Parents can appreciate the benefit of the trust and confidence they have built with their infants as they encourage exploration, introduce their infants to new and unfamiliar objects, and support the infants' efforts to master difficult motor tasks. Trust in a human relationship serves to generate trust in the broader environment. Once children trust the bond between themselves and their parents, the parents can use that confidence to encourage an open, exploring attitude toward the unfamiliar (Landry, Smith, Swank, Assel, & Vellet, 2001).

Another way that parents foster both emotional and intel-

lectual growth is by structuring the stimulus environment to suit the infant's developmental level (Bornstein, 2002). Parents need to recognize the infant's perspective in providing toys, sounds, and visual stimulation. Part of the parents' function is to initiate interactions and not just respond to their infants' demands for attention. Parents need to create what they perceive to be a suitable environment—one that allows a variety of experiences, a reasonable amount of challenge, and adequate opportunities to experience success. Furthermore, parents should be attuned to their infants developing skills and alter the environment appropriately. As their children mature, parents must provide more complex stimuli, more opportunities for autonomy, and more encouragement for tolerating frustration. By providing experiences that are attuned to the infant's level of cognitive functioning, parents are also supporting emotional satisfaction, confidence, and joy.

Parents use a variety of methods to help their infants regulate their emotions. Through physical and verbal play, they increase the baby's arousal and orient the baby toward objects in the environment. Through soothing and comforting, they help their infants regain a calm state after distress. As babies mature, parents increase their use of language to guide behavior and provide new problem-solving strategies. Infants are constantly watching their parents, observing the parents' emotional reactions as well as their novel behaviors. As a negative example, infants of depressed mothers become passive and inhibited in their reactions to the environment as they observe their mothers' passive or angry depressive symptoms.

## FATHERS' AND MOTHERS' PARENTAL BEHAVIOR

Do fathers and mothers differ in how they enact the parent role with infants? As we noted earlier, babies form strong attachments to their fathers as well as to their mothers. Fathers may be just as involved in and sensitive to their babies' needs as mothers. However, the daily interactions between mothers and their babies and those between fathers and their babies are distinct. In a study of more than 1,500 children in U.S. two-parent families, children spent an average of 1.4 hours on weekdays with their fathers, and 3.3 hours on weekends. Mothers were the primary caregivers of infants and young children during the week, but fathers took on a more equal role on the weekends (Yeung, Sandberg, Davis-Kean, & Hofferth, 2001). A greater proportion of the time that mothers spend with their babies is devoted to caregiving. Fathers, who spend less time overall with their babies, tend to focus more on play—especially physical play. When mothers play with their babies, the play tends to be with words or with toys, as opposed to rough-and-tumble activity (Laflamme et al., 2002).

Mothers more frequently respond to their babies, express affection, and follow up on behavior their babies initiate. They are also likely to be more accepting of their child's behavior and to emphasize and value emotional expressiveness. Fathers are more likely to disregard babies' cues and to direct

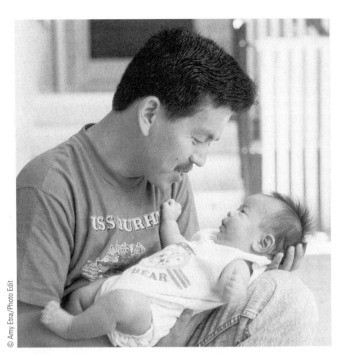

*The more involved a father is in his infant's care, the more accurate he is in reading the baby's signals.*

their attention to new targets. They are more likely to emphasize control and discipline (Rosen & Rothbaum, 1993). At home, fathers are likely to continue their leisure activity, such as reading or watching television, in the presence of their babies, whereas mothers are likely to interact with their babies.

The quality of interaction between fathers and infants depends heavily on the context. When mothers are present, for example, fathers interact less with their babies. When fathers are alone with their babies, they are more engaged and sensitive play companions. When fathers are not overly stressed at work, have strong positive identification with their own fathers, and are in satisfying, harmonious marriages, they achieve greater levels of intersubjectivity with their babies. Fathers of male infants tend to interact more with them than fathers of female infants (Goldberg et al., 2002). Fathers become more effective parents the more they understand the complexity and sophistication of infant competencies.

## PARENTS AS ADVOCATES

In addition to providing care themselves, more and more parents are responsible for arranging supplemental care for their infants. As a result, parents become advocates for their child. Parents must review the child care services available to them and select a setting that will meet their infant's needs and accommodate their work requirements and economic resources. Family day care, in-home babysitting, and center-based care are three common alternatives.

To function as advocates for their children, parents may have to engage in an unfamiliar kind of thinking. They may even feel unqualified to make the kinds of judgments required. For example, parents must evaluate the competence and motivation of the adults who will care for their child. They must estimate how successful these caregivers will be in meeting their child's needs for security and stimulation. And they must consider the degree to which alternative caregivers reflect their own parental values, beliefs, and strategies.

Even when pressures to continue a caregiving arrangement are very strong, parents must be able to assess its impact on their children. They must try to judge whether their children are in the kind of responsive, stimulating environment that will enhance their development. In the best situations, alternative care settings actually complement a parent–infant relationship. In the worst settings, infants may be neglected and abused. It is essential for parents to maintain communication with the alternative caregivers, to assess the quality of the care, and to intervene promptly when necessary to ensure their infant's well-being.

Another situation in which parents serve as advocates for their infants occurs when the children have some type of chronic illness, developmental delay, or special physical needs. These children may require coordinated health care, therapeutic interventions, mental health services, and educational supports. Most states have early intervention programs to support parents and help them understand the nature, prognosis, and treatment of the infant's condition. Early intervention case managers help build a bridge between parents and physicians or other health professionals. They also assist in the identification of appropriate community resources. However, the parents are ultimately responsible for making sure that the services match the child's changing needs.

## THE IMPORTANCE OF SOCIAL SUPPORT

The infant's physical, cognitive, social, and emotional development are fostered through the loving care of mothers, fathers, other family members, and community caregivers who are able to create supportive relationships with one another and with the infant. Infant mental health and optimal development are intimately entwined with the mental health of caregivers (Weatherston, 2001). A variety of contextual factors play a part in parents' ability to promote their child's optimal development. Adults who had difficult experiences with their own caregivers may come to the parental role with special challenges. They may not have experienced the comfort, responsiveness, or appropriate stimulation that are essential for effective parenting. Some factors, however, help to make up for these deficits. The quality of one's intimate relationship with a loving partner is important in sustaining positive parent–child relationships (Simons, Lorenz, Wu, & Conger, 1993). Couples who experience mutuality and trust in their own relationship are better able to create a predictable, supportive, and caring family environment for their children.

Sources of social support beyond the intimate partner may also enhance one's effectiveness as a parent. This support may

**Table 6.9** Optimizing an Infant's Development

Spend time with the child; be available when the child needs you.

Provide warmth and affection; express positive feelings toward the baby in many ways—verbally, through touching and hugging, and through playful interactions.

Communicate often, directly with the child; engage the child in verbal interaction.

Provide stimulation.

Encourage the child's active engagement in and exploration of the environment.

Help the child understand that he or she causes things to happen.

Help the child engage in directed problem solving.

Encourage the child to persist in efforts to reach a goal.

Keep things predictable, especially when the infant is very young.

Guide language development by using words to name, sort, and categorize objects and events.

Accept the child's efforts to achieve closeness.

Be sensitive to the child's state; learn to interpret the child's signals accurately; time your responses appropriately.

Find effective ways to soothe and comfort the child in times of distress.

Help the child interpret sources of distress and find ways to regulate distress.

Minimize the child's exposure to intensely negative, hostile, and frightening events.

Be aware of the visual and auditory cues you send when you interact with the child.

Pay attention to how the child is changing over time.

Monitor the child's emotional expressions to evaluate the success of specific actions and interventions.

come from the child's grandparents and other family members, friends, and health care and mental health professionals (Bornstein & Tamis-LeMonda, 2001). The effective use of a social support network ensures that adults will not be isolated as parents, and that others will be available to help the parents identify and interpret childrearing problems. Often, the help is very direct—for example, child care or sharing of clothes, playthings, and furniture. Support may also take the form of companionship and validation of the importance of the parental role. However, evidence suggests that social support cannot fully compensate for the lack of partner support or for the stresses on parenting caused by economic pressures that prevent parents from meeting basic life needs (Simons et al., 1993).

In reviewing this chapter, you can begin to appreciate the demanding nature of the parents' role in promoting optimal development during their baby's infancy. The elements of effective parenting that we have identified or implied are listed in Table 6.9. As a parent, one must rely heavily on one's own psychological well-being and on the encouragement of one's spouse, caring friends, and family to sustain the ego strengths and emotional resources necessary to the task.

The way parents conceive of their role has a major influence on the direction and rate of their infants' development. Parenting also allows adults opportunities for creative problem solving, empathy, physical closeness, and self-insight. Enacting the parent role makes considerable physical, cognitive, and emotional demands, but attachment to a child also promotes the parent's own psychosocial development. These contributions to adult development are described further in Chapters 12 (Early Adulthood) and 13 (Middle Adulthood).

# Chapter Summary

Although the genetic plan plays a major role in guiding physical and sensory/perceptual maturation during infancy, there is considerable evidence for plasticity in neurological development as an infant's sensorimotor system interacts with the social and physical environment. During infancy, a child rapidly develops sensory and motor skills, social relationships, and emotional and conceptual skills. Babies are born with

the capacity to perceive their environment and to evoke responses from their caregivers. In this sense, they are not helpless.

During the first year, infants' voluntary motor functions mature rapidly. A social attachment forms between the infant and the primary caregiver, creating the basic mental representation for subsequent intimate relationships. Sensorimotor intelligence begins with the use of motor and sensory capacities to explore and understand the environment. Of the many schemes that are established during this period, the emergence of an increasingly complex sense of causal relationships, the establishment of the concept of object permanence, and the formation of categories of objects are achievements that impose order and predictability on experience. Emotions are an early and continuous means of achieving intersubjectivity between infants and their caregivers. Emotional regulation provides a critical underpinning for subsequent cognitive functioning and social competence.

The establishment of trust between the infant and the caregiver is significant in both intellectual and social development. Through repeated interactions with caregivers, the infant develops a concept of the adult as both separate and permanent. Parental sensitivity is an underlying factor in determining the quality of attachment. Factors that appear to influence sensitivity are the adult's past experiences, including the way he or she was cared for as a young child; contemporary factors that influence the caregiver's well-being, self-esteem, and emotional availability, such as the quality of the parental dyad and experiences at work; and characteristics of the infant. Once established, the trusting relationship between the infant and the caregiver becomes a source of security for the infant's further explorations of the environment and a framework for future close relationships. Trust serves as a basis for an orientation toward hopefulness.

Infants are skilled at adapting to their environment, but they cannot bring about major changes in it. Parents and other caregivers are ultimately responsible for structuring the environment so that it is maximally suited to the infant. These adults are also the sources of the responsiveness, sensitivity, acceptance, and warmth that create an atmosphere conducive to the establishment of trust.

## Further Reflection

1. What are some examples of how hearing and vision work together to help infants form schemes about their world?
2. What is the possible evolutionary basis of the attachment behavioral system? How might contemporary life events threaten to disrupt this system?

3. What are some ways that caregiving practices can nurture the infant's ability to develop causal schemes?
4. How might differences in temperament modify the kind of caregiving a baby receives?
5. What does it mean to say that meaning is co-constructed in infancy? How do infants and caregivers use emotional communication to create meaning?
6. How might life conditions such as poverty, the dual-career family, single parenting, or having a very low-birthweight baby influence the role of parents as advocates during infancy?
7. What role might the sense of trust and the ego strength of hope have for the enactment of life roles such as friend, teacher, supervisor, political or spiritual leader?
8. What are some examples of how infants influence and even enhance the lives of their family members?

## On the Web

### VISIT OUR WEBSITE

Go to http://www.wadsworth.com/psychology to find online resources directly linked to your book.

## Casebook

For additional case material related to this chapter, see the case of "Marcie and Mom" in *Life Span Development: A Case Book*, by Barbara and Philip Newman, Laura Landry-Meyer, and Brenda J. Lohman, pp. 54–55. The case offers a starting point for discussing a common parenting routine—bedtime—and how infant temperament, mother's parenting style, and context interact to create a parenting environment.

# CHAPTER 7

# TODDLERHOOD (AGES 2 AND 3)

*Paul as Harlequin, 1924/Pablo Picasso/© 2005 Estate of Pablo Picasso/Artists Rights Society (ARS), New York/© Peter Will/SuperStock*

*Picasso painted his first son, Paulo, as Harlequin when Paulo was three. The Harlequin role was one that both father and son enjoyed—a fantasy linked to the magic and mystery of circus life that Picasso had detailed so carefully 20 years earlier.*

CASE STUDY: ALICE WALKER GOES TO THE FAIR

■ DEVELOPMENTAL TASKS
Elaboration of Locomotion
Language Development
Fantasy Play
Self-Control

■ THE PSYCHOSOCIAL CRISIS:
AUTONOMY VERSUS SHAME AND DOUBT
Autonomy
Shame and Doubt

■ THE CENTRAL PROCESS: IMITATION

■ THE PRIME ADAPTIVE EGO QUALITY
AND THE CORE PATHOLOGY
Will
Compulsion

■ THE IMPACT OF POVERTY ON PSYCHOSOCIAL
DEVELOPMENT IN TODDLERHOOD

■ APPLIED TOPIC: CHILD CARE
The Impact of Child Care on Intelligence and Academic Achievement
The Impact of Child Care on Social Competence
The Impact of Child Care on Peer Relations
Directions for the Future of Child Care in the United States

■ CHAPTER SUMMARY

■ FURTHER REFLECTION

## CHAPTER OBJECTIVES

▶ *To describe the expansion of motor skills during toddlerhood, indicating their importance for the child's expanding capacity to explore the environment and to experience opportunities for mastery.*

▶ *To document accomplishments in language development and describe the influences of interactive experiences and the language environment for gaining communicative competence.*

▶ *To describe the development of fantasy play and its importance for cognitive and social development.*

▶ *To examine the development of self-control, especially impulse management and goal attainment, highlighting strategies young children use to help regulate their actions.*

▶ *To analyze the psychosocial crisis of autonomy versus shame and doubt, to clarify the central process of imitation, and to describe the prime adaptive ego strength of will and the core pathology of compulsion.*

▶ *To conceptualize the impact of poverty on development in toddlerhood.*

▶ *To apply a psychosocial analysis to the topic of child care, emphasizing the impact of the nature and quality of care on development during toddlerhood.*

TODDLERS SEEM TO bubble with unpredictable, startling thoughts and actions that keep adults in a state of puzzled amazement. Toddlers are extremely busy—talking, moving, fantasizing, and planning all the time. Their outpouring of physical activity—its vigor, constancy, and complexity—is remarkable. Equally impressive is the flood of cognitive accomplishments, especially language production and unique forms of playful fantasy.

Building on a foundation of trust and optimism formed during infancy, toddlerhood brings a flowering of the sense of personal autonomy, an enjoyment and confidence in doing things for oneself and expressing one's will. The successful blending of these two basic capacities for trust and autonomy provides a strong, protective shield for the young child's ego system. From this foundation, children are able to venture into satisfying and meaningful social relationships, engage in playful problem solving, and face their future with an outlook of hopefulness and assertiveness.

The chances for such a positive conclusion to the period of toddlerhood rest largely on the quality of the home environment. Toddlers, with their high energy level, improbable ideas, impish willfulness, and needs for mastery, run headlong into the full range of limits in their physical and social environment. Parenting during toddlerhood is like paddling a canoe through the rapids. It requires vigilance, good communication between the bow and the stern, flexibility, and a certain *joie de vivre* that keeps the whole trip fun. A child's

cognitive and social development during this period of life can be facilitated by the parents' own ego development, their style of parenting, and the quality of their relationship (Miller, Cowan, Cowan, Hetherington, & Clingempeel, 1993). The degree to which discord and conflict introduce stress into the lives of parents brings special risk for some toddlers.

The developmental tasks of toddlerhood—expanded locomotion, language and communication skills, fantasy play, and self-control—all contribute to the child's emerging independence within the boundaries of the social group. Some theorists refer to this as the first individuation process (Blos, 1979; Mahler, Pine, & Bergman, 1975). Obviously, 3-year-olds are not ready to set out for life alone in the big city. But they are ready to express independent thoughts, exercise some control in making choices, and do some things independently. The psychosocial crisis during this period of life—autonomy versus shame and doubt—refers to the child's struggle to establish a sense of separateness without disrupting the bonds of affection and protection that are critical to a young child's physical survival and emotional connection to the family. In many cultures, expectations for autonomy are brought about by the birth of the next child, requiring the toddler to achieve new levels of self-sufficiency. Typically, this takes place with the support of older siblings, neighboring children, and extended family members who model and encourage new levels of mature behavior (Edwards & Liu, 2002). ∎

# CASE STUDY

## ALICE WALKER GOES TO THE FAIR

*It is unusual to find first-person recollections of the period of toddlerhood. In this selection, Alice Walker, Pulitzer Prize-winning novelist and poet, shares an early memory.*

It is a bright summer day in 1947. My father, a fat, funny man with beautiful eyes and a subversive wit, is trying to decide which of his eight children he will take with him to the county fair. My mother, of course, will not go. She is knocked out from getting most of us ready: I hold my neck stiff against the pressure of her knuckles as she hastily completes the braiding and then the beribboning of my hair. My father is the driver for the rich old White lady up the road. Her name is Miss Mey. She owns all the land for miles around, as well as the house in which we live. All I remember about her is that she once offered to pay my mother thirty-five cents for cleaning her house, raking up piles of her magnolia leaves, and washing her family's clothes, and that my mother—she of no money, eight children, and a chronic earache—refused it. But I do not think of this in 1947. I am two and a half years old. I want to go everywhere my daddy goes. I am excited at the prospect of riding in a car. Someone has told me fairs are fun. That there is room in the car for only three of us doesn't faze me at all. Whirling happily in my starchy frock, showing off my biscuit-polished patent leather shoes and lavender socks, tossing my head in a way that makes my ribbons bounce, I stand, hands on hips, before my father. "Take me, Daddy," I say with assurance; "I'm the prettiest!"

Later, it does not surprise me to find myself in Miss Mey's shiny black car, sharing the back seat with the other lucky ones. Does not surprise me that I thoroughly enjoy the fair. At home that night I tell the unlucky ones all I can remember about the merry-go-round, the man who eats live chickens, and the teddy bears, until they say: "That's enough baby Alice. Shut up now, and go to sleep."

Source: From "Beauty: When the Other Dancer Is the Self," by A. Walker, pp. 257–258. In H. L. Gates, Jr. (ed.), *Bearing Witness: Selections from African-American Autobiography in the Twentieth Century.*

## ■ CRITICAL THINKING AND CASE ANALYSIS

1. What is the spirit of toddlerhood that is captured in this case?
2. How does the case relate to the tasks of locomotion, language, fantasy play, and self-control?
3. What aspects of Alice's self-concept appear to be forming in this episode?
4. What images of her mother and father are being established at this age?

# DEVELOPMENTAL TASKS

The use of the word *toddler* to describe development for 2- and 3-year-olds is in itself a clue to the important part that locomotion plays. In fact, it is only during the first year of this stage that the child actually toddles. By age 3, the child's walk has changed from the precarious, determined, half-humorous toddle to a more graceful, continuous, effective stride. Removal of diapers probably plays an important role in the progress of a child's walk. When toddlers no longer have a large wad of padding between their legs, they quickly make the transition from ugly duckling to swan. Of course, their physical development, including changes in the shape and strength of leg muscles, contributes significantly to this transformation (Clark & Phillips, 1993).

## ELABORATION OF LOCOMOTION

Locomotion plays a central role in the toddler's psychosocial development, facilitating the transformation of ideas into action and prompting new types of interactions with the social and physical environment. As locomotor skills develop, the child has new ways of remaining close to the object of attachment, new avenues for investigating the environment, and new strategies for coping with stressful situations. Growth in locomotion and cognition go hand in hand. An understanding of space, distance, and the relationship of one place to the next expand as children maneuver through their environment (Gibson & Pick, 2002). Locomotor skills also figure prominently in the elaboration of play during this period. To the extent that coping involves the ability to maintain freedom of movement under conditions of threat, the locomotor skills acquired during toddlerhood provide a fundamental arsenal of lifelong strategies for "fight" or "flight." Advanced locomotor skills may also increase conflicts with caregivers, introducing new struggles of willfulness and new parental constraints (Biringen, Emde, Campos, & Appelbaum, 1995).

When Ellen was about 2½ years old, she enjoyed watching her older brother climbing up a tree in the neighbor's yard. She would beg her brother to lift her up so she could get into the tree with him. One afternoon, Ellen's brother lifted her into the tree and then ran off to play with a friend. Ellen tried to get down from the tree, but she got her foot stuck in a crack between the branches. She cried and yelled until her mom came to get her. Ellen's mom scolded her for being in the tree and warned her never to go up there again. But the next afternoon, Ellen was back trying to figure out how to climb into the tree on her own.

From this example, one can see that when locomotor skills occur early in a developmental period, before the maturation of verbal and cognitive competence, toddlers may find

**Table 7.1**  Changes in Gross Motor Skills During Toddlerhood and Early School Age

| AGE | WALKING AND RUNNING | JUMPING | HOPPING | THROWING AND CATCHING | PEDALING AND STEERING |
|---|---|---|---|---|---|
| 2–3 years | Walks more rhythmically; opposite arm–leg swing appears. Hurried walk changes to true run. | Jumps down from step. Jumps several inches off floor with both feet, no arm action. | Hops 1 to 3 times on same foot with stiff upper body and nonhopping leg held still. | Throws balls with forearm extension only; feet remain stationary. Awaits thrown ball with rigid arms outstretched. | Pushes riding toy with feet; does little steering. |
| 3–4 years | Walks up stairs, alternating feet. Walks downstairs, leading with one foot. Walks in a straight line. | Jumps off floor with co-ordinated arm action. Broad jumps about 1 foot. | Hops 4 to 6 times on same foot, flexing upper body and swinging nonhopping leg. | Throws ball with slight body rotation but little or no transfer of weight with feet. Flexes elbows in preparation for catching; traps ball against chest. | Pedals and steers tricycle. |
| 4–5 years | Walks downstairs, alternating feet. Runs more smoothly. Gallops and skips with one foot. | Improved upward and forward jumps. Travels greater distance. | Hops 7 to 9 times on same foot. Improved speed of hopping. | Throws ball with increased body rotation and some transfer of weight forward. Catches ball with hands; if unsuccessful, may still trap ball against chest. | Rides tricycle rapidly, steers smoothly. |
| 5–6 years | Increased speed of run. Gallops more smoothly. True skipping appears. | Jumps off floor about 1 foot. Broad jumps 3 feet. | Hops 50 feet on same foot in 10 seconds. Hops with rhythmical alternation (2 hops on one foot and 2 on the other). | Has mature throwing and catching pattern. Moves arm more and steps forward during throw. Awaits thrown ball with relaxed posture, adjusting body to path and size of ball. | Rides bicycle with training wheels. |

Source: From *Infants, Children, and Adolescents*, by L. E. Berk, p. 299. Published by Allyn and Bacon, Boston, MA. Copyright © by Pearson Education.

themselves at odds with caregivers who must limit locomotion to protect the child's safety and to secure the safety of other people and objects in the environment.

Difficulties encountered by engineers and inventors in trying to duplicate human locomotor skills with robots have demonstrated just how intricate and exquisite are the toddler's accomplishments (Meghdari & Aryanpour, 2003). The possibility that lifelong movement patterns are acquired during these 2 years extends our appreciation of toddlers' locomotor accomplishments. Qualitative changes in locomotive behavior are not simply a result of maturation of the cerebral cortex. Changes in body weight and muscle mass, combined with new capacities to coordinate feedback from the limbs and to judge the amount of effort needed to achieve a motor goal, are all components in what appears to be a regular progression in motor behavior (Kalverboer, Hopkins, & Geuze, 1993). Some landmarks of motor development that are reached from ages 2 to 6—walking and running, jumping, hopping, throwing and catching, pedaling and steering—are described in Table 7.1. The development and perfection of these skills depends on opportunity and encouragement as well as on the maturation of the cognitive and motor systems (Williams & Abernathy, 2000).

As walking becomes a more comfortable form of locomotion, new skills are added to the child's repertoire. Running and jumping are the first to emerge. By the age of 4, children are likely to leap from stairways, porches, or ladders. They have begun to imagine what it might be like to fly. Jumping is their closest approximation to flying. Evidence suggests that the underlying structure of the jumping pattern remains stable throughout childhood and into adulthood (Clark, Phillips, & Petersen, 1989). The child's delight in exploring jumping behavior may be the result of the acquisition of a fundamental movement pattern that fills the child with a basic sense of mastery as well as a sense of lifelong possibilities.

Children's running abilities become more elaborated all through toddlerhood. In films used to study the emergence of running, it appears that for toddlers, running and walking are very much alike, with little increase in velocity and little or no "flight" (the time when both feet are off the ground) in running. At the beginning, toddlers appear to be running because they are moving a bit faster, but their action is not similar to adult running. Over time, however, the movements smooth out as flight time and velocity increase (Whitall & Getchell, 1995).

*Toddlerhood brings tremendous advances in locomotion as children enjoy walking, running, jumping, and hopping. Leaping from steps, walls, chairs, and benches is almost like flying!*

At first, youngsters may run for the sake of running. They practice the art over and over again. Later in toddlerhood, running changes from a kind of game in itself to a valuable component of many other games. The absolute speed of toddlers is limited by their somewhat precarious balance and short legs. This does not discourage them, however, from devoting a great deal of time and energy to running. The goals of mastery and getting to new places for exploration are too strong to dampen their enthusiasm.

Toddlers are often exposed to a wide variety of other forms of locomotion, such as swimming, skiing, skating, sledding, and dancing. Children seem eager to use their bodies in a variety of ways, and they learn quickly (Williams & Abernathy, 2000). As their physical coordination improves, children engage in a new repertoire of large-muscle activities: climbing, sliding, swinging, pounding, digging, and rough-and-tumble play. These forms of physical activity provide an important source of information about the physical self. They offer an avenue for mastery, and they are also the basis for a lot of fun. Toddlers enjoy their bodies and are generally joyful when in the midst of physical play. Thus, physical activity contributes in an essential way to the toddler's self-concept. Children who lack muscle strength or coordination experience strong feelings of frustration as they struggle to keep their balance, throw or catch a ball, or use their hands and feet to perform new tasks.

# LANGUAGE DEVELOPMENT

## SEMIOTIC THINKING

Jean Piaget (1970) described the years from about 2 to 5 or 6 as the stage of **preoperational thought**. This is a transitional period during which the schemes that were developed during infancy are represented internally. The most significant achievement of this new stage of cognitive development is the capacity for **semiotic** or *representational* thinking—understanding that one thing can stand for another. In semiotic thinking, children learn to recognize and use symbols and signs. **Symbols** are usually related in some way to the object for which they stand. The cross, for example, is a symbol of Christianity. In pretend play, a scarf or a blanket may be a symbol for a pillow or a dress. **Signs** stand for things in a more abstract, arbitrary way. Words are signs; there is no direct relation between the word *dog* and the animal to which the word refers, yet the word stands for the object. For adults, it seems natural to use matchsticks or little squares of cardboard to represent people or buildings, but for children, the idea that a stick may be a car or a horse is a dramatic change in thinking that emerges gradually during the preoperational period.

Symbolization brings enormous flexibility to human thought. The symbol embodies an idea of something separate from the thing itself. With the elaboration of various types of symbols, children can begin to recount events apart from the situation in which they occurred. They can invent worlds that never existed.

Children acquire five representational skills that allow them to manipulate objects mentally rather than by actual behavior: (1) imitation in the absence of the model, (2) mental images, (3) symbolic drawing, (4) symbolic play, and (5) language. Representational skills allow children to share their experiences with others and to create imagined experiences. These skills also free children from communicating only through gestures and opens up opportunities to communicate about the past or the future as well as the present (Nelson, 1999). Children can express relationships they may have known in the past by imitating them, drawing them, talking about them, or acting them out in fantasy. They can also portray events and relationships that they wish would occur or that they wish to alter. In this and the following sections, we focus on two of these representational skills, language and fantasy play, which are among the most notable achievements of toddlerhood and are foundational for psychosocial development across the life span.

## COMMUNICATIVE COMPETENCE

In the process of language development, children acquire **communicative competence**: They become adept at using all the aspects of language that permit effective participation in the language environment of their culture (Kuczaj & Hill,

## TECHNOLOGY AND HUMAN DEVELOPMENT

# How the Brain Processes Language

BRAIN DEVELOPMENT AND language capacity are intimately related. From birth to age 3, the brain increases in weight from 400 to 1,100 grams, and trillions of neural connections are formed. Furthermore, myelination increases, continuing beyond infancy and toddlerhood well into adolescence. Myelination contributes to the speed of neural firing. Thus, over the period of infancy and toddlerhood, the brain is working extremely hard, forming neural connections (*synapses*) and responding with increasing speed.

With the use of positron emission tomography (PET) and functional magnetic resonance imaging (fMRI), one can observe different areas of activity in the brain related to varying language activities including speaking, seeing, and hearing words. PET is a technique that begins with the injection or inhalation of a radioactive material. As this material is metabolized in the brain, gamma rays are emitted and recorded. Using PET technology, one can discern which area of the brain is active during a particular type of activity, such as hearing or reading language. In fMRI, brain areas with more blood flow and more oxygenated blood show up better on the MRI. The fMRI takes advantage of this by comparing the brain at rest with the brain as the person performs a series of tasks. The areas of the brain that become more visible following the task are assumed to have been activated by the task (Gregg, 2004). To learn more about how fMRI can pro-

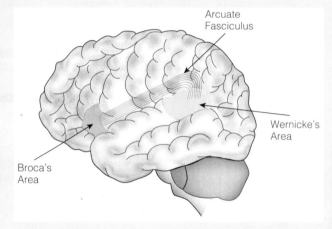

**FIGURE 7.1**

Three Areas of the Brain That Are Intimately Related to Speech: Broca's Area, Wernicke's Area, and the Arcuate Fasciculus, a Bundle of Nerve Fibers That Connects the Two. Damage to these areas leads to a loss of the ability to speak, called *aphasia*. Damage to Broca's area results in an inability to produce speech, but language comprehension remains functional. Damage to Wernicke's area does not affect the ability to produce language, but understanding is lost. People with Wernicke's aphasia can produce words clearly, but they do not make sense. People who have damage to the arcuate fasciculus can understand language, but their speech does not make sense, and they cannot repeat words.

duce immediate 3-D images of brain activity during a task, visit the website of the Pittsburgh Supercomputer Center (http://www.psc.edu/science/), where there is a description of technology that links MRI with the high-speed Cray T3E supercomputer.

Research confirms that linguistic competence—especially the ability to produce and understand verbal material—typically becomes focused in the left hemisphere of the brain during toddlerhood. However, various neuroimaging studies have demonstrated that many regions of the brain are involved in language production and comprehension (Gernsbacher & Kaschak, 2003; see

Figure 7.1). In infancy, both hemispheres are involved in language perception. By the end of the third year, toddlers process most information related to grammar in the left hemisphere (Brownlee, 1998). Language production capacities of the brain demonstrate remarkable plasticity. In a comparison of children who had congenital left hemisphere damage with adults who had left hemisphere injuries, the children scored much higher than the adults on measures of spontaneous speech, suggesting that other areas of the brain had taken over many of these functions (Bates et al., 2001).

Furthermore, speech is different from other cognitive functions related to communication, such as language comprehension or symbolizing an idea by drawing a picture. In a condition called *aprosodia*, people have difficulty talking about their emotions when there is damage to the area of the right hemisphere that mirrors the area of the left hemisphere that is used for language. Studies involving deaf users of sign language compared to hearing participants who use spoken language have provided evidence that injury to the left hemisphere can result in a form of language aphasia. For the deaf, this injury does not interrupt the capacity to make other types of gestures, confirming that language functions are differentiated from other symbolic and motor functions that might be involved in the communicative process (Corina, Vaid, & Bellugi, 1992).

2003). This includes producing the sounds of the language; understanding the system of meanings, the rules of word formation, and the rules of sentence formation; developing a rich vocabulary; making adjustments to the social setting that are necessary to produce and interpret communication (*pragmatics*); and acquiring the ability to express thoughts in written as well as oral form. Through the achievement of communicative competence, children become increasingly integrated into their culture. They learn the expressions, tones of voice, and gestures that link them intimately to the language environment of their home and community. They learn when to speak and when to remain silent; how to approach communication with peers, parents, and authority figures. They learn the terms applied to kin, close friends, acquaintances, and strangers; the words that are used to disparage or devalue; and the words that are used to recognize and praise. If nurturing is the primary vehicle for cultural socialization in infancy, communication is the primary vehicle in toddlerhood.

Communicative competence begins during infancy and develops across the entire life span. Vocabulary, grammar, and pragmatics continue to be refined as one engages in formal schooling and enters a wider range of social settings where specific words, expressions, and styles of interaction are in use. But toddlerhood appears to be the time of a dramatic expansion in verbal competence, when remarkable achievements are made in an exceptionally brief period. The following discussion of language and communication is divided into two major sections: (1) language milestones and (2) the language environment. The first section outlines the pattern of communication accomplishments of infancy and toddlerhood, including the expanded use of words with meaning, the formation of two-word sentences, more complex sentence formation, and grammar. Important physiological structures support this emerging competence. The second section identifies factors in the psychosocial environment that help facilitate and optimize communicative competence.

The text provides an overview of patterns of accomplishment in language and communication from infancy through about age 4. At the outset, however, it is important to recognize the wide variability in the development of communicative skills. Certain sequences or *developmental milestones* appear to be quite common among children from many language environments. For example, communicative gestures precede the production of spoken words, and the production of a substantial vocabulary of spoken words precedes the linking of words into two-word sentences. But the timing of the onset of these various abilities and their rate of growth varies from child to child. For example, in a large national study of infant/toddler language, word production for 12-month-old infants ranged from the 90th percentile, who used 26 words or more, to the 10th percentile, who produced no words (see Figure 7.2). By 16 months of age, those in the 90th percentile were using 180 words, and those in the 10th per-

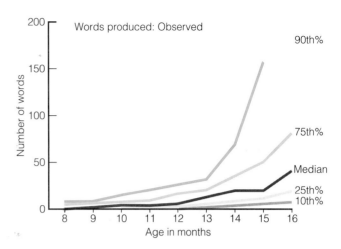

**FIGURE 7.2**

Word Production from 8 to 16 Months

Source: From "Variability in Early Communicative Development," by L. Fenson et al., 1994, *Monographs of the Society for Research in Child Development, 59*(5), 38. Copyright © 1994 The Society for Research in Child Development, Inc. Reprinted by permission.

centile produced 10 words or less (Fenson et al., 1994). All these children were healthy, normal children, with no known history of developmental delay, prematurity, or genetic disease. As you read about modal or typical patterns, try to remember that these patterns disguise important variations.

## ■ COMMUNICATION ACCOMPLISHMENTS IN INFANCY

Research on language development has focused on the forerunners of language competence that are present from birth through the first 2 years of life. Thought and language seem to travel independent courses that typically intersect during the second year of life (Molfese, Molfese, & Carrell, 1982). Before that time, one can distinguish meaningful communication that does not require speech, such as pointing and gesturing, and vocalizations that are not meaningful, such as babbling and cooing. However, a rare genetic disease, Williams syndrome, suggests that the capacities for language and cognition are distinct. Children with Williams syndrome are typically very talkative and sociable; they develop a large vocabulary and speak in grammatically correct sentences. Although their speech indicates some developmental abnormalities, it is much further advanced than their other cognitive functions. For example, children with Williams syndrome may have difficulty with tasks that are easy for most middle school-age children, like tying their shoes, subtracting 2 from 4, or writing their street address (Schultz, Grelotti, & Pober, 2001). This genetic condition forces one to think about language competence separate from other cognitive abilities. Of course, one does not have to go to the extreme of people with Williams syndrome to find examples of people whose speech seems disconnected from their ability to think and reason.

**LANGUAGE PERCEPTION.** Infants are able to recognize sounds and differentiate between sound combinations long before they are able to produce language or understand word meaning. This capacity to recognize language sounds, including the phonetic combinations of letters and words and the intonation of words and sentences, is called **language perception** (Tsao, Liu, & Kuhl, 2004). Young infants are able to hear and distinguish among the major language sounds used in natural language. By 5 months of age, infants are able to differentiate words that emphasize the first syllable, like *father*, and words that emphasize the second syllable, like *begin*. By this age, they also recognize the sound of their own name (Mandel, Jusczyk, & Pisoni, 1995; Weber, Hahne, Friedrich, & Friederici, 2004).

**BABBLING.** **Babbling**, initially characterized by sounds used in many languages, begins to reflect the sounds and intonation infants are most likely to hear. Sounds they do not hear drop out of their babbling and, at about this same time, their capacity to differentiate among language sounds not found in their native language diminishes (Bates et al., 1987). This environmental shaping of language competence provides another example of the plasticity of brain functions, discussed in Chapter 6 (Infancy). Some networks grow and become strengthened by experience, whereas others wither and are absorbed into the neural mass.

Babbling begins to take on a special character, connecting consonants and vowels and repeating these combinations, when the baby is around 6 to 10 months. Although parents may eagerly receive this type of babbling as evidence of first words (i.e., *baba*, *mama*, *dada*), there is debate about whether these repetitions of babbling sounds have a symbolic value.

One sound that is especially important in the parenting process is "Mama." The infant word for mother has many similarities across hundreds of language groups. In a study of "Mama" sounds, a pediatrician asked 75 parents of newborns in his practice to listen for *mama* sounds (Goldman, 2001). If they heard one, he asked them to note the infant's age; the circumstances of the sound (time of day, etc.); if they could determine whether the infant wanted something, and if so, what; and if the sound was directed at anyone, to whom it was directed. Of the 75 parents, 52 spoke only English. Other languages included Spanish, Hindi, Italian, Russian, Hebrew, Ibo, Chinese, and some combination of Spanish and Greek or Italian. Fifty-five of the parents heard a *mama* sound, often as part of a cry. Thirty-two infants made the *mama* sound for the first time in the first 2 months of life. It became more distinct and more of a whine or call as it was repeated over the first 6 months. For those babies who made *mama* sounds, the sound was interpreted as an indication of wanting—especially wanting to be picked up, wanting attention, or wanting to be taken out of the crib or infant seat and entertained. An impli-

cation of this research is that by 2 months, many infants have the ability to use a noncrying vocalization to serve as a call that brings caregiver attention.

**COMMUNICATION WITH GESTURES.** By 8 months, infants also use sounds like grunting and whining in combination with gestures to achieve a goal. Thus, sounds combined with gestures and looks in a certain direction become part of purposeful communication—trying to get the caregiver to reach a cookie or get a certain toy off the shelf. A common first gesture is to raise the arms up toward the caregiver in a desire to be picked up (Fenson et al., 1994). Sounds may also be used to express emotion or to get someone's attention. When Jakob was about 14 months, he used the gesture of shaking his hands to signal that he was all done with his food. This was much preferred to having him throw the food on the floor!

Three other communicative strategies emerge at about 9 to 11 months. Infants begin to seek adult interest and attention by *showing* them objects and thereby initiating an interaction.

© David Young-Wolff / Photo Edit

*Gestures, such as pointing, are forms of preverbal communication.*

Soon after showing, the infant begins *giving objects*. Adults who are willing to engage in this type of exchange will find the baby bringing them a whole variety of toys, utensils, and pieces of dirt or dust for inspection. Following giving, a common next key gesture is *pointing*. There is some debate about whether pointing is a form of reaching or a way of getting an adult's attention to notice an object. In either case, it is an example of an infant's initial ability to establish a shared reference point with respect to some object in the environment. The role of gestures in establishing intersubjectivity is an excellent example of the interdependence of motor, social, and psychological systems as they combine to support language development (Iverson & Thelen, 1999).

**EARLY GRAMMAR.** **Grammar** refers to rules that guide the combination of words and phrases in order to preserve meaning. In English, for example, sentences are usually formed from nouns (people, places, or things) or noun phrases, followed by verbs (actions) or verb phrases (e.g., "The girl reads the book."). Certain cues about the way words are used in a sentence or their order in a sentence convey their meaning. For example, the word "the" is a signal that a noun will follow.

By 7–8 months of age, infants show the ability to recognize the specific regularities in spoken speech and to detect rules about the combination of language sounds. For example, babies were exposed to a long string of nonsense syllables for 2 minutes. In this string, certain sounds were always followed by other sounds. For example, *pa* was always followed by *biku*. In the test situation, babies recognized the difference between a sound combination that was used frequently in the string of sounds, such as *pabiku*, and a combination that was used very infrequently (Saffran, Aslin, & Newport, 1996). In other studies, babies were habituated to 2 minutes of a grammar in which sentences followed an ABA form, such as *ga ti ga*, or a grammar that followed the ABB form, such as *ga ti ti*. In the test situation, babies recognized the difference between the grammar to which they were habituated and an inconsistent grammar made up of entirely different sounds (Marcus, 2000). Thus, long before babies can produce words, word phrases, or grammatically correct sentences, they are gathering information about the rules that hold sounds and phrases together in order to make meaning.

**FIRST WORDS.** From infancy to toddlerhood, one of the most significant changes that takes place is that **words** emerge as more salient than gestures as a way to refer to objects (Namy & Waxman, 2002). Around the age of 8 months, infants understand the meanings of some individual words and phrases (Fenson et al., 1994; Harris, 1992). This ability to understand words, called **receptive language**, precedes **language production**, the ability to produce spoken words and phrases. You can direct a baby's glance by saying, "Look at the flowers," or "Do you want candy?" At this age, babies can go through their paces in the ever delightful game of "point

to your nose, eyes, ears," and so on, The number of words infants understand increases rapidly after 12 months. According to one analysis, 16-month-olds have a receptive vocabulary of between 92 and 321 words (Fenson et al., 1994).

One of the first significant events in the development of language production is the *naming of objects*. With repetition, a sound or word becomes associated with a specific object or a set of related objects. For example, a child may say *ba* whenever she sees her bottle. If she is thirsty and wants her bottle, she may try saying *ba* in order to influence her caregiver to produce the bottle. Gestures, actions, and facial expressions often accompany the baby's word and help establish its meaning in the caregiver's mind. If the baby's word has meaning to the caregiver and serves to satisfy the baby's needs, it will probably be retained as a meaningful sign. The word *ba* may come to mean "bottle" and other liquids the child wishes to drink, such as juice, water, or milk.

The important characteristic of first words is their shared meaning. Even though *ba* is not a real word, it functions in the same way that any noun does—it names a person, place, or thing. These single-word utterances accompanied by gestures, actions, vocal intonation, and emotion are called **holophrases**. They convey the meaning of an entire sentence. For example, saying "ba, ba" in a pleading tone while pointing to the refrigerator and bouncing up and down conveys the meaning "I need a bottle," or "Get me the bottle." Gradually, the child discovers that every object, action, and relationship has a name.

Young children first talk about what they know and what they are interested in. Common first words include important people (*Mama, Dada,* names of siblings), foods, pets, toys, body parts (*eye, nose*), clothes (*shoe, sock*), vehicles (*car*), favorite objects (*bottle, blanket*), other objects in the environment (*keys, trees*), actions (*up, bye-bye*), yes, *no, please, down, more,* pronouns (*you, me*), and states (*hot, hungry*). Lois Bloom (1993) has suggested that a "principle of relevance" guides the early acquisition of new words. Babies pay special attention to words and expressions that are most closely linked with what they are doing and thinking about at the time. For that reason, the actual vocabulary that is acquired during infancy is quite idiosyncratic, reflecting the themes and experiences of each child's everyday life.

## ■ COMMUNICATIVE COMPETENCE IN TODDLERHOOD

Language development in toddlerhood brings rapid acquisition of a wide-ranging vocabulary and the initial use of a primitive grammar that is quickly transformed into the grammar of the spoken language.

**VOCABULARY.** During the period from 12 to 16 months, infants make significant progress in learning the names of objects and applying them to pictures or real examples. There is a rapid expansion of vocabulary during these 4 months from few or no spoken words to about 26. Sometime around 18 months, the child acquires a large number of new words, and vocabulary continues to expand at a rapid rate throughout the toddler and early school years (Rice, 1989). The average toddler of 30 months has a spoken vocabulary of about 570 words. In order to accomplish this feat, children seem to *fast-map* new meanings as they experience words in conversation. To **fast-map** is to quickly form an initial, partial understanding of a word's meaning. It is an information-processing technique in which children relate the new word to the known vocabulary by linking it to the known word storage space and to concepts that are already well understood. The child has to hear the new word only a few times in a context that makes its meaning clear. Thus, without direct word-by-word tutoring, children accumulate numerous samples of their culture's language from the speech they hear and attach a minimally satisfactory definition to each word or phrase. This vocabulary burst is associated with speed of processing in word recognition. Young children who recognize words with greater speed also seem to have a greater vocabulary. The relationship between these two factors is not fully understood (Fernald, Swingly, & Pinto, 2001).

The early phase of vocabulary development seems to focus on broad semantic categories—animals, cars, fruits, clothes, and so on. New words, particularly nouns, are treated like the name of a category of things rather than of only one specific object or a part of it. For example, when a child learns the word *cup*, it is used to refer to all objects that have the general shape and function of a cup. A much slower process of vocabulary development occurs as children and adults learn the distinctions among words within categories (McDonough, 2002). You may have a very good idea about the distinction between annual and perennial flowering plants, but you may not know the difference between the many types of each group and how to recognize them. In fact, building a vocabulary of subcategories may become an entire field of study, such as botany or zoology, in which the types and subtypes of a larger category are identified, classified, and named.

**TWO-WORD SENTENCES.** At 16 months of age, few children make two-word sentences, but by 30 months almost all children make them (Fenson et al., 1994). These two-word sentences are referred to as **telegraphic speech**. Children merge two words into phrases that are essential to communicate what they intend to say. Just as in a telegram, however, other words—verbs, articles, prepositions, pronouns, conjunctions—are left out. A child will say, "my ball," "more juice," and "Daddy gone." Before this point, children tend to utter single words accompanied by gestures and actions. By stringing two words together, they convey more meaning through verbal communication and rely less heavily on gestures and actions. The acquisition of telegraphic speech allows a child to make fuller use of the symbolism inherent in language to communicate meaning (Powers, 2002).

Children are quite innovative in using two-word sentences. They continue to understand more than they are able to say,

but they appear to use their limited number of words and the newfound ability to combine them to get their point across. Children may convey different meanings with the same sentence. "Daddy go," for example, may be used to tell someone that Daddy has left, or it may be used to tell Daddy to leave. Children often indicate their meanings by tone of voice or by the words they stress. The use of two-word sentences is characteristic of toddler-age language learners in many cultures (Messer, 2000).

Martin Braine (1976) analyzed the first word combinations spoken by children in English, Samoan, Finnish, Hebrew, and Swedish. His goal was to identify the kinds of rules or patterns that governed these early combinations. Ten patterns of word combination were embedded in those early language samples:

1. Making reference to something: See +X (*see mother*)
2. Describing something: Hot +X (*hot stove*)
3. Possession: X has a Y (*Billy has a bottle*)
4. Plurality: Two +X (*two dogs*)
5. Repetition or other examples: More +X (*more up*)
6. Disappearance: All gone +X (*all gone milk*)
7. Negation: No +X (*no sleep*)
8. Actor–action relations : Person +X (*Daddy sleep*)
9. Location: X +here (*Grandma here*)
10. Requests: Have +X (*have it, ball*)

Braine found that although he could identify some common patterns of word combinations, they were not guided by the grammatical categories of the spoken language but by the meanings that the child wished to express and by the variety of objects, people, and interactions in the immediate environment. The patterns of word combinations used by some children did not overlap at all with those used by other children in the same culture.

Early language is closely tied to the representation of sensorimotor schemes—the activities that dominate the child's life, such as eating, sleeping, playing games with mommy or daddy or the siblings, going places, coming back home, and so on. It expresses the properties and relationships of the objects and people that are important in a child's life. Language use emerges within a larger communication system and reflects a child's cognitive capacities. At the same time, it reflects the perceptual and functional characteristics of the environment. Vocabulary and grammar grow hand in hand; as toddlers learn more words, they use them in combination to express more complex ideas. The kinds of objects and relationships that are central to daily life influence the content and complexity of a child's early language (Bates & Goodman, 2001).

**GRAMMATICAL TRANSFORMATIONS.** By combining words according to the set of rules of grammar for a given language, a person can produce a limitless number of messages that can be understood by another person. Remarkably, by the age of 4, children appear to be able to structure their sentences using most of these rules without any direct instruction. Consider the difference in meaning between "The boy hit the ball" and "The ball hit the boy." The simple matter of word order in a sentence is critical for preserving meaning. The basic format of an English sentence—noun phrase followed by verb phrase—is a central part of its grammar. In order to ask a question or produce a negative sentence, the speaker transforms this word order according to a specific set of rules (e.g., "You are going" versus "Are you going?"). The addition of certain inflections and modifiers conveys information about time, possession, number, and relation. As children learn the grammatical transformations of their language, they become much more effective in conveying exactly what they have in mind.

A surprising observation is that children use correct transformations for the past tenses of irregular verbs (*went*, *gave*, *run*) before they use correct inflections of regular verbs (*talked*, *walked*, *jumped*). It appears that children first learn the past tenses of irregular verbs through rote memory. Once they learn the rule for expressing the past tense by adding *-ed*, they occasionally **overregularize** this rule and begin making errors in the past tense. Thus, a 2-year-old is likely to say "I ran fast," but a 3-year-old may say "I runned fast." According to a model proposed by Gary Marcus, children recognize and have a symbolic category for words that are verbs. They establish a default rule: "To form the past tense, add *-ed* to any word that can be categorized as a verb." They also memorize the past forms of the irregular verbs as they encounter them. When an irregular verb is required, its irregular past tense form is always used if the child can recall it. However, if the child cannot recall the past tense, or if the word is novel, the default rule is called into play. In a study of preschoolers, the rate of overregularization was 4.5%. This fell to 2.5% for first-graders and 1% for fourth-graders, suggesting that as a child's vocabulary grows, the need to apply the default rule to unfamiliar verbs declines (Marcus, 1996).

The grammatical errors that young children make alert us to the fact that they are working to figure out a system of rules with which to communicate meaning. It is unlikely, however, that these errors result from imitation of adult speech. Children say such things as "My do it" or "Dose mines." They have certainly not copied those expressions from adults; rather, these errors suggest the beginning of a grammar that becomes more specialized and accurate as children acquire the opportunity to match their speech to that of others. One can "catch" toddlers in the act of building their grammar by listening to them revise their own speech. From the age of 2 to 4, as their grammar matures, toddlers will pause in mid-sentence and revise their speech to make a more complex or complete expression. Aware of linguistic alternatives, they stop to select one that best expresses their thoughts in a specific language environment (Rispoli, 2003).

The milestones in language development during the first 4 years of life are summarized in Table 7.2. During the first year of life, babies are highly sensitive to spoken language. They use vocalization in a playful way as a source of sensory stimulation. Gradually, babies produce vocalizations that im-

itate spoken language. In the second year, babies understand words and phrases. They develop a vocabulary and begin to form two-word phrases. During the third year, language is definitely used to communicate ideas, observations, and needs. Comprehension of spoken language seems almost complete. Some of their speech may not be easily understood by people outside the family, partly because they are unable to produce clear phonetic sounds and also because their knowledge of adult grammar is limited. During the fourth year, most children acquire an extensive vocabulary. They can create sentences that reflect most of the basic rules of grammar. Their language is a vehicle for communicating complex thoughts that are usually understood by children and adults outside the family. They can use their communicative skills to participate in social exchanges with other children, talk about their experiences, make plans, and resolve conflicts.

## ■ LANGUAGE DEVELOPMENT BEYOND TODDLERHOOD

Although the fundamentals of language are well established by age 4, there are still some things that toddlers cannot achieve with language. For example, Mary may raise a fuss about wanting the biggest piece of cake. If you allow her to make a choice, she selects a piece with lots of frosting. Clearly, the word *biggest* is not being used correctly. Even though Mary is able to memorize and repeat the words *big*, *bigger*, and *biggest*, she does not yet fully understand the concept to which they refer. Other observations suggest that 2- and 3-year-olds have difficulty using verbal instructions to control or guide their behavior (Tinsley & Waters, 1982). They may be able to tell themselves to "stop" or "go slow," but these commands are not effective in slowing them down. Both of these examples demonstrate that toddlers' language development can be somewhat misleading. One may assume that children fully understand the more abstract meaning of the words they use, but in fact their language continues to be very idiosyncratic throughout toddlerhood.

As the process of fast-mapping implies, children may add a word to their vocabulary without understanding the several meanings that this word has in different contexts. During the periods of early and middle childhood, considerable time and attention is devoted to exploring vocabulary, correcting some meanings that were incorrectly learned, and expanding the full range of meanings and underlying concepts that are linked to the many words that were acquired so rapidly during toddlerhood. One estimate is that the reading vocabulary or comprehension of dictionary entries of a 10-year-old child is close to 40,000 words, with another 40,000 proper names, places, and expressions unique to the child's own family, neighborhood, and cultural group (Anglin, 1993).

Important language functions develop more fully during early and middle childhood (Dickinson & Tabors, 2001). As their understanding of the self and the social environment expand, older children use language to plan a problem-solving

**Table 7.2** Milestones in Language Development

| AT THE COMPLETION OF: | VOCALIZATION AND LANGUAGE CHARACTERISTICS |
| --- | --- |
| 12 weeks | Markedly less crying than at 8 weeks; when talked to and nodded at, smiles, followed by squealing-gurgling sounds usually called cooing, that is vowel-like in character and pitch-modulating; sustains cooing for 15–20 seconds. |
| 16 weeks | Responds to human sounds more definitely; turns head; eyes seem to search for speaker; occasionally some chuckling sounds. Recognizes the sound of his/her name. |
| 20 weeks | The vowel-like cooing sounds begin to be interspersed with consonantal sounds; acoustically, all vocalizations are very different from the sounds of the mature language of the environment. |
| 6 months | Cooing changing into babbling resembling one-syllable utterances, neither vowels nor consonants have very fixed recurrences; most common utterances sound somewhat like ma, mu, da, or di. |
| 8 months | Reduplication (or more continuous repetition) becomes frequent; intonation patterns become distinct; utterances can signal emphasis and emotions. Produces meaningful gestures like wanting to be picked up, showing, or giving. Understands some words and phrases. |
| 10 months | Vocalizations are mixed with sound play such as gurgling or bubble blowing; appears to wish to imitate sounds, but the imitations are never quite successful; expansion in comprehension of words. |
| 12 months | Identical sound sequences are replicated with higher relative frequency of occurrence and early word production (mama or dada); understands about 50 words and simple commands (e.g., "Show me your eyes."). |
| 16 months | Has a definite repertoire of about 40 words (the top 90th percentile has 180 word vocabulary); still much babbling but now of several syllables with intricate intonation pattern; no pattern; words may include items such as thank you and come here, but there is little ability to join items into spontaneous two-word phrases; understanding is progressing rapidly. |
| 24 months | Vocabulary of more than 300 items (some children seem to be able to name everything in the environment); begin spontaneously to join vocabulary items into two-word phrases; all phrases appear to be own creations; definite increase in communicative behavior and interest in language. |
| 30 months | Continuing increase in vocabulary with more than 550 words; many new additions every day; no babbling at all; utterances have communicative intent; frustrated if not understood by others; utterances consist of at least two words, many have three or even five words; use of linguistic suffixes for possession, plural, and past tense; frequent use of irregular plural noun (foot/feet) and irregular verbs; intelligibility is not very good yet by those unfamiliar with the child's speech. |
| 3 years | Vocabulary of some 1000 words; about 80% of utterances are intelligible even to strangers; grammatical complexity of utterances is roughly that of colloquial adult language, although mistakes still occur. |
| 4 years | Language is well established; deviations from the adult norm tend to be more in style than in grammar. |

Source: Adapted from Lenneberg, 1967, and Fenson et al., 1994.

strategy, guide a complex series of motor activities, or identify the relationships among objects. Vocabulary expands, and words are used more frequently in the ways they are used in adult speech. Children learn the patterns of "polite" speech as well as slang. Depending on the nature of their conversational partners at home and school, their sentences become more complex, including conditional and descriptive clauses. The irregular verbs and nouns are learned and used correctly. As children attend school, they learn to conceptualize the grammatical structure of their language.

Beyond the formal elements of vocabulary, grammar, reading, and writing, language becomes a vehicle for creative expression. Children write poems, essays, and stories. They begin to use sarcasm, puns, and metaphors to elaborate their speech. They create secret codes with their special friends. Children make up riddles and jokes, put on plays and puppet shows, work on school newspapers, and leave enigmatic or corny messages in their friends' yearbooks.

Language plays a critical role in the resolution of subsequent psychosocial crises, especially the establishment of group identity, intimacy, and generativity. It is primarily through the quality of one's spoken language that one achieves the levels of disclosure that sustain friendship and subsequent intimate relationships. Language also serves as a mechanism for resolving conflicts and for building a sense of cohesiveness within groups, whether of friends, coworkers, or family members.

## ■ THE LANGUAGE ENVIRONMENT

In this section, we focus primarily on the nature of the interaction between toddlers and their caregivers, with some attention to the issue of bilingualism and the relationship of the language environment at home and school. Language is a cultural tool, a means for socializing and educating young children. It is one of many inventions for creating a sense of group identity and for passing the mythology, wisdom, and values of the culture from one generation to the next. Language is a part of the psychosocial environment. Competence in the use of language solidifies the young child's membership

*Toddlers can use their language to enhance play and foster cooperation.*

© Laura Dwight/Photo Edit

in the immediate family and in the larger cultural group. Although there is strong evidence for genetically based origins of the capacity for language learning, the specific content and tone of a child's communication is strongly influenced by the language environment. In many industrialized cultures, children are separated from the world of adult work. Special educational settings are created to prepare children for the tasks of adulthood, and adults interact with children in specific ways that differ from their interactions with other adults. In other cultures, children are present in the midst of ongoing adult activities. Children are encouraged to become active listeners and observers, gradually participating in conversations and work as their abilities permit. Thus, the nature of the interactive language environment, the expectations for children to participate, and the kinds of communications that children are likely to engage in can vary based on the broad cultural orientation about the place and role of children in the larger society (Rogoff & Angelillo, 2002; Rogoff, Paradise, Arauz, Correa-Chavez, & Angelillo, 2003).

**INTERACTION AND LANGUAGE DEVELOPMENT.** Probably the most important factor that caregivers contribute to cognitive growth is the opportunity for interactions. Brain development in infancy and toddlerhood is stimulated by exposure to adult language through conversation, "baby talk," and reading aloud. An interactive human being can respond to a child's questions, provide information, react in unexpected ways and surprise the child, explain plans or strategies, and offer praise or criticism. The frequency and quality of parent–child interactions are closely associated with children's social and cognitive competence (Hart, Newell, & Olsen, 2003).

The causal relationship between child competence and frequency of parent–child interaction is still a matter of some controversy. Consider these three different explanations:

1. Parents and their offspring may share a genetic predisposition for verbal competence, which is evident in the frequency of parent–child interaction and in the early acquisition of verbal skills.
2. Parents who interact frequently with their children provide a rich array of verbal stimuli and thereby promote high levels of verbal comprehension and production.
3. Children who are more verbally competent stimulate more interaction from their caregivers, which then establishes a more active and diverse verbal environment.

Over time, research will no doubt clarify the nature of these relationships.

Certain characteristics of a language partner have been shown to facilitate a child's language acquisition and communication skills (Singh, Morgan, & Best, 2002; Snow, 1984). When talking to infants and young children, adults tend to speak in a high pitch, use shorter sentences, speak slowly, use attention-getting strategies, and speak in a friendly, positive tone. They modify their speech so that they are more likely to be understood by using simplified, redundant speech that corresponds to the child's level of comprehension and interest (Mitchell, 2001). Even older children will modify their speech when interacting with toddlers to hold their attention and guide their behavior (Rice, 1989):

1. They simplify utterances to correspond with the toddler's interests and comprehension level.
2. They emphasize the here and now.
3. They use a more restricted vocabulary.
4. They do a lot of paraphrasing.
5. They use simple, well-formed sentences.
6. They use frequent repetitions.
7. They use a slow rate of speech with pauses between utterances and after the major content words.

## HUMAN DEVELOPMENT AND DIVERSITY

### Bilingualism

YOUNG BILINGUAL CHILDREN are adept at switching from one language to another as the conversational situation demands. In one study of bilingual Hispanic children in Miami, Florida, the children had access to a non-overlapping vocabulary in Spanish and English. In this instance, knowing the two languages actually expanded the concepts they could use to express their thoughts in comparison to children who spoke English or Spanish only (Umbel, Pearson, Fernandez, & Oller, 1992).

Code switching begins at a very early age. In a study of a bilingual English-Portuguese infant at play with his mother and father, the child switched languages to fill in the gaps in his vocabulary. If he did not know the word for something in one language, he used the other. Similarly, his parents switched codes in order to provide language that was the best match with the child's level of understanding. Thus, bilingual families can use their language environment to the child's advantage, providing alternative communication strategies to improve communication and understanding (Nicoladis, 1998; Nicoladis & Secco, 2000).

How do bilingual individuals prevent one language from interfering with another? Research using functional magnetic resonance imaging

The teacher, who speaks Spanish and English fluently, helps students become bilingual by encouraging them to use both languages to express their ideas.

(fMRI) explored the process by which bilingual individuals inhibit one language while drawing on another. In this research, individuals who were bilingual from infancy were compared to those who were monolingual. Participants were asked to press a button when they saw a word in one language, but not to press the button when they saw words in another language or "pseudowords." In this type of task, the bilinguals avoided encoding the meaning of the nontarget words. None of the brain areas that are associated with word frequency or meaning were activated when the nontarget words were displayed. Instead, bilinguals had adapted a distinct path from sound properties of the words to meaning only for the target words (Rodriguez-Fornells, Rotte, Heinze, Nosselt, & Munte, 2002). The implication is that early bilingualism stimulates additional plasticity in brain organization and function to accomplish tasks that require language separation.

These characteristics of caregiver speech are not universal; rather they reflect cultural norms for addressing toddlers. They are most typically observed in European American, middle class, Western societies. In one cross-cultural analysis, for example, it was observed that African American adults in the rural South did not simplify or censor their speech for young children (Heath, 1989). They frequently did not address children directly, but expected the children to hear what they said and to interrupt if they had something to add. Adults and children directed one another's behavior with specific commands. It was just as acceptable for a toddler to command an adult as the other way around. Adults teased children, especially in the presence of others, in order to give the children a chance to show off their quick wit and to prac-

tice assertiveness. Within this language environment, children have the opportunity to hear a variety of opinions, gather information that extends their direct experience, and observe shifts in language tone and style that accompany changes in the topic or purpose of the conversation. This example illustrates the variation in communication styles that characterize American families, producing substantial differences in the language-learning environments of the home.

Other research describes variations in the nature and amount of parent–child interaction that takes place during a typical day. In one longitudinal study, 40 families (15 Black and 25 White) were observed once per month over 2½ years (Hart & Risley, 1992). The observations covered the period shortly before, during, and after the child was learning to talk. The number of words spoken to a child in an hour varied from 232 to 3,606; the percentage of time that parents were in the same room as the child ranged from 38% to 99%; and the average number of times that parents and children took turns in an interaction ranged from 1.8 to 17.4.

This observational study found that the quality of a parent's speech toward the child was positively related to the child's IQ at 37 months of age. The study also found a systematic relationship between the quality of a parent's speech toward the child and the family's socioeconomic status. Children in lower socioeconomic status families experienced less time with their parents, fewer moments of joint play, and exposure to fewer words. Children were less likely to have their speech repeated or paraphrased by their parents, less likely to be asked questions, and more likely to experience prohibitions placed on their behavior. Those parents who were most likely to place prohibitions on their child's activities during this age period were less likely to listen intently to their child's speech, repeat what the child had said, or ask the child questions. Other studies have emphasized that it is not socioeconomic status per se that influences language development. Within socioeconomic groups, the more children experience responsive and stimulating interactions with caregivers in the home, the further advanced their language abilities by age 3 (Roberts, Burchinal, & Durham, 1999).

In learning vocabulary, children appear to be sensitive to the competence of their language partners. For example, in one study, 3- and 4-year-olds participated in an experiment where the experimenter appeared to be either knowledgeable and confident or uncertain about the name for a given toy. In the confident situation, the experimenter said things like: "I know right where my friend left her *blinket*." In the uncertain situation, the experimenter said, "I'd like to help my friend, but I don't know what a *blinket* is." Even though the children in both situations learned how the toy worked, they only used the name of the toy if the experimenter appeared confident (Sabbagh & Baldwin, 2001). The implication of this work is that by age 3, children are able to assess the expertise and confidence of the language partner before incorporating words into their vocabulary.

### SCAFFOLDING AND OTHER STRATEGIES FOR ENHANCING LANGUAGE DEVELOPMENT.

The process of language learning involves a pattern of mutual regulation and upward **scaffolding**. Children try to match the verbal expressions used by adults, both in pronunciation and in selection of words (Nelson, 1973). Sometimes a child may be misunderstood because the child's pronunciation is so discrepant from the real word (*ambiance* for *ambulance*; *tommick cake* for *stomach ache*). At the same time, adults may use simplification or some other strategy to make sure they are being understood. Through frequent interactions, adults encourage language development by establishing a good balance between modifying their speech somewhat and modeling more complex, accurate speech for their children. Verbal scaffolding can provide children with more complex ideas about the coordination of actions as well as strategies for using language to plan and achieve complex goals. Scaffolding is closely related to Vygotsky's idea of the zone of proximal development. By interacting with a more verbally competent adult or peer, children are able to acquire new terms and new ways of linking actions and outcomes that can then enhance their own independent problem solving (Gregory, Kim, & Whiren, 2003; Landry, Miller-Loncar, Smith, & Swank, 2002).

Adults make use of several strategies to clarify a child's meaning when the speech is unclear. One is **expansion**, or the elaboration of the child's expressions:

CHILD: Doggie wag.

PARENT: Yes, the dog is wagging her tail.

Another strategy is **prompting**, often in the form of a question. Here the parent urges the child to say more:

CHILD: More crackel.

PARENT: You want more what?

In both of these interactions, the adult is helping the child to communicate more effectively by expanding on or asking the child to elaborate on something of interest to him or her. The kinds of sentences that parents use help children see how they can produce new sentences that are more grammatically correct and therefore more meaningful to others.

### READING AND LANGUAGE GAMES.

Socially interactive rituals, such as telling stories, playing word games, verbal joking and teasing, and reading books together, also seem to enhance language development, especially by building vocabulary and preparing children to use language comfortably in social situations. Reading aloud has been identified as an especially important language activity, not only in preparation for literacy, but also for expanding a child's language skills (Crain-Thoreson & Dale, 1992; Hammer, 2001; Valdez-Menchaca & Whitehurst, 1992). During toddlerhood, an adult may start out by reading picture books and asking the child questions about the pictures. The adult may try to relate the picture to some event in the child's life or ask the children to tell something they notice about the pictures. Thus, just as in scaffolding with respect to language, reading along with an experienced reader can scaffold the child's literacy skills (Verhoeven, 2001). Over time, the child becomes more and more the storyteller, while the adult listens, encourages, and expands the tale. Some books are read aloud so often that the toddler begins to "read" them from memory or retell the story in her own words from the pictures.

As children enter early school age, this type of ritualized reading activity provides a framework for the child's concept of what it means to be a reader. Reading aloud introduces the notion that printed letters make up words; that stories usually have a beginning, middle, and end; and that printed words and spoken words are similar in some ways. Experiences

*The reading activities that parents and toddlers share are an important part of literacy. By reading aloud and talking about pictures, parents create the environment within which their children eventually think of themselves as readers.*

© Elizabeth Crews

handling books, becoming aware of the link between letters and their sounds, beginning to recognize printed words, and practicing the actions associated with reading all contribute to early reading proficiency (Hammill, 2004). Depending on the context in which children read, they may also realize that you can learn things from printed words that you cannot always know from the pictures. They discover that reading is a way to learn about the world beyond what you can know through direct experiences.

Children and parents often engage in language games that expand the child's use of words and phrases. These games are usually part of ongoing family life. They are introduced not as a separate activity but as an extension of a related activity. The quality of toys, social games, and conversation between mothers and their infants predicts the level of the child's language development at ages 2 and 3 (Lacroix, Pomerleau, Malcuit, Seguin, & Lamarre, 2001). As an example, one mother described one of her 3½-year-old son David's spontaneous games that began to build the bridge from speech to literacy. As the game developed, the object was for David to point to road signs as he rode with his mother to nursery school and for her to read as many of the signs as possible while they were driving along. David had created this game, and his mother played along willingly (Hoffman, 1985):

> On the way to nursery school, David said, "Let's talk about signs! What does that sign say?" I answered, "Right turn signal."
>
> David proceeded with, "And what does that yellow and red shell say?"
>
> I answered him, "It says 'Shell'—that's a gasoline station."
>
> He asked, "Does it have seashells in it?"
>
> I answered, "No."
>
> We proceeded to read signs. I read the majority as he requested. However, David read "Speed Limit 35," "Bike Route," and "No Parking Any Time." When we came to "No

Parking This Side of Street," he thought it was "No Parking Any Time."

These were the signs that I was able to read as he requested while I was driving. They were not the only ones on the route.

| | |
|---|---|
| Speed Limit 40 | Watch Children |
| Bike Route (2 times) | No Parking Any Time |
| Speed Limit 35 | (20 times) |
| (12 times) | Signal Ahead (3 times) |
| No Turn on Red (3 times) | School Speed Limit (2 times) |
| No Littering | No Parking on This Side of |
| Driveway | Street (7 times) |

With the achievement of language skills, children and their caregivers begin to explore a vast array of topics through spoken language. They explore their needs—hunger, thirst, sleepiness, and companionship. They travel along the paths of emotions such as anger, sadness, delight, pride, and shame. They talk playfully with one another, examining new objects, discussing kinship relations, and creating fantasies. Furthermore, adults and children talk about philosophical and moral questions like lying, helping, "what ifs," and the question "how would you feel if it happened to you?" As children speak from their own inner world, revealing their own point of view, parents begin to know and appreciate their children's concerns and needs in a new way. Similarly, children begin to hear and understand their family's talk in a new way. They can question what they do not understand and expand what they know through family talk.

One area that has received special attention is the role of family conversation about feelings and its relation to a child's ability to express feelings and to identify feelings in others. Children's use of words to refer to feelings and to describe emotions increases notably at 3 and 4 years of age. At this same time, children become more skilled at recognizing feelings in others and in understanding how a person might feel in a certain situation (Brown & Dunn, 1992). Toddlers who

*Cindy hopes that by talking with her son now about his feelings she will build a strong basis for communication in the years ahead when their conflicts may be more difficult.*

have frequent experiences of talking with their mothers when they are in distress or conflict appear to be more effective at the age of 6 in understanding the point of view of others and in anticipating others' needs (Dunn, Brown, & Beardsall, 1991). Children who grow up in families that are open to identifying and talking about emotions are more likely to carry on this kind of talk at later ages and to show sensitivity to others in relationships outside the family (Jenkins, Turrell, Kogushi, Lollis, & Ross, 2003).

## FANTASY PLAY

Fantasy play and language are contrasting forms of representation (Copple, 2003). In acquiring language, children learn to translate their thoughts into a commonly shared system of signs and rules. For language to be effective, children must use the same words and grammar as the older members of the family, discovering how to translate their thoughts into existing words and categories. Fantasy serves almost the opposite function. In fantasy, children create characters and situations that may have a very private meaning. There is no need to make the fantasy comprehensible to an audience. There are probably many times when children have strong feelings but lack the words to express them. They may be frustrated by their helplessness or angry at being overlooked. They can express and soothe these feelings in the world of imagination, even though the feelings may never become part of a shared conversation (Erikson, 1972).

The worlds of make-believe, poetry, fairy tales, and folklore—the domains we often associate with childhood—open up to the toddler as the ability for symbolization expands. Pretend play is not possible without semiotic thinking;

it underlies the capacity for imagination, for allowing objects and people to take on new identities and new meaning.

## ▪ THE NATURE OF PRETEND PLAY

During infancy, play often consists of the repetition of a motor activity. Infants delight in sucking their toes or dropping a spoon from the high chair. These are typical **sensorimotor play** activities. Toward the end of infancy, sensorimotor play includes the deliberate imitation of parental acts. Children who see their mothers washing the dishes may enjoy climbing up on a chair and getting their hands wet, too. At first, these imitations occur only when they are stimulated by the sight of the parent's activity. As children enter toddlerhood, they begin to imitate parental activities when they are alone. A vivid mental image of an action permits them to copy what they recall instead of what they see. This is the beginning of **symbolic play**. Before the period of preoperational thought, children do not really pretend because they cannot let one thing stand for something else. Once the capacity for symbolic thought emerges, children become increasingly flexible in allowing an object to take on a wide variety of pretend identities.

Two-year-olds appear to be able to understand the context of a pretend situation. Using pretend props, they can pretend to feed a hungry animal or give a drink to a thirsty animal. They can assign a pretend function to a substitute prop, treating a wooden block as if it were a banana or a piece of cake. And they can follow through with the consequences of a pretend situation, like pretending to wipe up pretend spilled tea with a towel (Harris & Kavanaugh, 1993). These young children can construct a make-believe world, in which objects are assigned a pretend meaning (toy blocks can be bananas) and words are used in pretend ways ("feed the monkey a banana" is acted out by putting a toy block up to the mouth of a toy monkey).

## THE CAPACITY FOR PRETENSE

Pretense, whether through symbolic play, symbolic drawing, or telling make-believe stories, requires that children understand the difference between pretend and real (Kavanaugh & Engel, 1998). A child's ability to pretend provides insight into his or her "theory of mind." For example, in a game of doctor, children realize that someone is acting "as if" he or she were sick and had a bad tummy ache. They know that they and the other players are not really sick. Sometimes, adults wonder whether children can in fact distinguish between reality and pretense. The line between make-believe and reality may become blurred for all of us. At times, adults can encounter such confusion when watching television. Which televised images are pretend and which are real? Are the images and messages used to advertise products real or pretend? Is a television news story real or pretend? Are dramatic reenactments of historical events real or pretend?

In simplified situations, children as young as 2 can tell when someone is pretending and can follow the transformations in a pretend sequence (Rakoczy, Tomasello, & Striano, 2004; Walker-Andrews & Harris, 1993). For example, an investigator might tell a child that she is going to fill two bowls with cereal, and then pretend to fill the bowls. Then the investigator pretends to eat all of the cereal in her bowl, saying something at the end to indicate that all the cereal is gone. She then asks the child to feed a doll its cereal. Many 2-year-olds and most 3-year-olds can follow this type of scenario, selecting the bowl that is still full of pretend cereal and feeding it to the doll.

Studies about pretense lead to further speculations about what toddlers understand about someone else's mental state. For example, some research focuses on what toddlers think is going on in someone else's mind as they are pretending. In judging whether someone else is pretending or not, toddlers tend to focus on the way the person is acting and the context of the situation rather than on what the person's intentions might be. Toddlers are quite accurate about judging when someone is engaging in make-believe or in a realistic activity, but they may not be able to tell you what the person is thinking about (Ganea, Lillard, & Turkheimer, 2004; Rosen, Schwebel, & Singer, 1997; Sobel, 2004).

Toddlers know the difference between what an object really is and what someone is pretending that it is (Flavell, Flavell, & Green, 1987). For example, 3-year-olds understand that a sponge is really a sponge, but they can pretend it is a boat floating in the water or a car driving along the road. Three-year-olds also understand the difference between knowing something and pretending something. If they see a rabbit, they know it is real, but they also know that they do not have to have seen a rabbit in order to imagine one. However, compared with older children, 3-year-olds are more convinced that imagination reflects reality. If they imagine something,

like a fire-breathing dragon or a horse with wings, they think it may actually exist. In contrast, 4-year-olds understand that something that is imagined may not have a counterpart in reality (Woolley & Wellman, 1993).

## CHANGES IN FANTASY PLAY DURING TODDLERHOOD

Toddlers can direct their play in response to mental images that they have generated by themselves. At first, their symbolic play is characterized by the simple repetition of familiar activities. Pretending to sweep the floor, to be asleep, to be a dog or a cat, and to drive a car are some of the early play activities of toddlers. Fantasy play changes in four ways during toddlerhood (Lucariello, 1987; Tamis-LeMonda, Uzgiris, & Bornstein, 2002):

1. The action component becomes more complex as children integrate a sequence of actions.
2. Children's focus shifts from the self to fantasies that involve others and the creation of multiple roles.
3. The play involves the use of substitute objects, including objects children only pretend to have, and eventually the invention of complex characters and situations.
4. The play becomes more organized and planned, and play leaders emerge.

First, children combine a number of actions in a play sequence. From pretending to sweep the floor or take a nap, they devise strings of activities that are part of a complex play sequence. While playing firefighter, children may pretend to be the fire truck, the hose, the ladder, the engine, the siren, the people being rescued, and the firefighters. All the elements of the situation are brought under the children's control through this fantasy enactment.

Second, children become increasingly able to include others in their play and to shift the focus of the play from the self to the others (Howes, 1987; Howes, Unger, & Seidner, 1989). One can see a distinction here between solitary pretense, social play, and social pretend play. Children engaged in **solitary pretense** are involved in their own fantasy activities, such as pretending that they are driving a car or giving a baby a bath. Children engaged in **social play** join with other children in some activity. They may dig together in the sand, build with blocks, or imitate each other's silly noises. In **social pretend play**, children have to coordinate their pretense. They establish a fantasy structure, take roles, agree on the make-believe meaning of props, and solve pretend problems. That 2- and 3-year-olds can participate in this type of coordinated fantasy play is remarkable, especially given their very limited use of language to establish and sustain coordination.

Third, fantasy play changes as children become more flexible in their use of substitute objects in their play. Fantasy play begins in the areas closest to children's daily experience. They use real objects or play versions of those objects as props in their pretense. For example, they pick up a toy telephone and pretend to call Grandma, or they pretend to have a picnic with toy cups and plates and plastic foods. But as

## TECHNOLOGY AND HUMAN DEVELOPMENT

### Children's Toys

OVER TIME, CHILDREN'S toys have reflected the technological innovations of the society. Since the 1600s, children have ridden wooden hobby horses, carved to size, and often painted with the saddle and gear used at the time. In most cultures, dolls are available, made of corn husks, rags, wood, or animal skins. By the 18th century, fancy dolls made of porcelain could be dressed in the fashion of the period.

Toward the end of the 19th century, some of the more innovative toys used springs and keys to wind, so the toys could produce a mechanical action. Wind-up toys might be cars or carriages that move, walking dolls, or merry-go-rounds that spin around. The famous mechanical banks included a spring action in which a coin was deposited in the slot by pulling back on a lever.

With the invention of electricity, electric trains became a favorite for children and adults. Train sets could recreate certain models of engines and types of cars. On electrified tracks, trains could follow a variety of routes, encountering model villages, passing under bridges or through tunnels, and shifting from one set of tracks to the other.

© Big Cheese Photo/SuperStock

*Interactive computer games are fascinating for young children and help pass the time on long road trips.*

In the mid-20th century, toys became battery operated. With the flick of a switch, dolls could talk, cars could move, and pretend ovens could light up. Following the battery-operated phase came remote-control toys that could be operated using radio waves. Toy cars, boats, or airplanes could be manipulated at a distance using remote-control panels.

With the miniaturization of information on computer chips, battery-operated toys have become increasingly complex and, in some cases, interactive. Toys have many features, including sounds, lights, and movement. For example, the Little Tikes Cookin' Fun Interactive Kitchen has the following description:

This unique kitchen plays along with children by recognizing and responding to individual foods placed on the burner. Other deluxe features include a microwave that makes three cooking sounds and has a lighted countdown timer. When kids turn on the faucet, they'll hear running water, and when they "wash" the dishes, a motion sensor triggers dish and silverware sounds. Features realistic house details on the outside, plus a pretend coffee maker, dishwasher, refrigerator, oven, sink and 13 accessories. (KB Toys, 2004)

---

they develop their fantasy skills, these props are no longer essential. Children can invent objects, create novel uses for common objects, and sometimes pretend to have an object when they have nothing (Boyatzis & Watson, 1993). Despite these remarkably inventive capacities to impose meaning on neutral objects, children's toys have become increasingly more realistic, reflecting the nature of modern technology. Whereas experts in early childhood education continue to recommend the use of flexible, open-ended play materials for young children, toy makers appear to be enthusiastic about producing "realistic" play materials.

Play moves away from common daily experiences to invented worlds based on stories, television programs, or purely imagined characters and situations. Children may take the roles of characters with extraordinary powers. They may pretend to fly, become invisible, or transform themselves into other shapes with the aid of a few secret words or gestures. Their identification with a particular fantasy hero or heroine

may last for days or even weeks as they involve the characters of the story in a variety of fantasy situations.

Fourth, fantasy play becomes more planned and organized. The planning emerges as children try to coordinate their pretend play with other players. It is also a product of a new realization of what makes pretend play most fun, and of the desire to make sure that those components are included in the play. In a preschool or day care group, certain children are likely to take the lead in organizing the direction of fantasy play. They may set the play in motion or give it direction by suggesting the use of certain props, assigning roles, or working out the context of the play. In this example, a child demonstrates this kind of leadership:

STUART (climbing up on a tractor tire): This will be our shark ship, OK? Get on quick, Jeremy! The sharks will eat you!

JEREMY: No! This is my police helicopter!

STUART: Well, OK. We're police. But we need to chase the sharks, OK? I see the sharks way down there! Come on!

JEREMY: OK. Let's get 'em! (They both make helicopter noises and swat at make-believe sharks with plastic garden tools.) (Trawick-Smith, 1988, p. 53)

Some theorists distinguish symbolic role playing from games with rules, implying that the latter are guided by a formal set of mental operations that constrain play, whereas the former is open and flexible. However, it is clear that pretend play operates within a rule-bound structure (Harris & Kavanaugh, 1993; Vygotsky, 1978). In order to coordinate symbolic play with a partner, children have to come to some mutual understanding about the situation, props, characters, and plot. The players have to limit their behavior in ways that conform to the unspoken or latent rules of the pretense. For example, if the children decide that certain leaves are the pretend food, then no one can use the leaves as bricks to build a house or as hats. If one player is supposed to be the mommy, that player has to act like the mommy and not like the baby. In games with rules, the rules are more readily spelled out, but in both types of play, part of what makes it fun is to function within the boundaries of certain kinds of constraints.

Dramatic role playing, in which a child takes on the role of another person or creates a fantasy situation, increases steadily from the ages of 3 through 5. By the age of 6, however, children become involved in games with rules. They may use their fantasy skills during play by making up new games or new rules rather than by engaging in pretend play. If one is looking for the experts in diversified, elaborated fantasy, observe 4- and 5-year-olds.

### ■ THE CONTRIBUTIONS OF FANTASY PLAY TO DEVELOPMENT

Fantasy play is not simply a diversion. Children use fantasy to experiment with and understand their social and physical environments and to expand their thinking (Pellegrini & Bjorklund, 2004). Views of the importance and value of fantasy play vary widely. Piaget (1962) emphasized the assimilative value of play. He believed that through fantasy and symbolic play, children are able to make meaning of experiences and events that are beyond their full comprehension. Fantasy play is a private world to which the rules of social convention and the logic of the physical world do not necessarily apply. From this perspective, fantasy play frees the child from the immediacy of reality, permitting mental manipulations and modifications of objects and events.

Vygotsky (1978) saw fantasy play quite differently. He argued that

play creates a zone of proximal development of the child. In play a child always behaves beyond his average age, above his daily behavior; in play it is as though he were a head taller than himself. As in the focus of a magnifying glass, play contains all developmental tendencies in a condensed form and is itself a major source of development. (p. 102)

Vygotsky used the term **zone of proximal development** to refer to a range of potential performance. When trying to assess a child's developmental level, it is important to understand not only what the child already knows and can already perform, but also the domains that are "in progress," so to speak—the areas that are emerging as new fields of mastery. Normally adults—especially parents and teachers—and more advanced peers promote development by engaging children in activities and problem-solving tasks that draw children into their zone of proximal development—the new directions along which their capacities are moving. However, in play, Vygotsky saw a cognitive process that in and of itself captures a foreshadowing of the child's next higher level of functioning. In pretend play, children address areas where they do not yet feel competent in their lives and try to act as if they were competent. They set rules for their performance, and they commit themselves to function according to them. So if a child is pretending to be a good mother, she brings forward all the ideas she has about how to be a good mother and applies them to the pretend situation. Similarly, if a child is pretending to be a superhero, she imposes all the rules of power, goodness, and helpfulness that she knows of and tries to limit her actions to those rules. Vygotsky regarded fantasy play as a window into the areas of competence that the child is striving to master but are still out of reach.

Erikson (1972) considered play vital in promoting personality and social development. He valued play as a mechanism for dramatizing the psychological conflicts that children are struggling with, such as angry feelings toward their siblings or parents, or jealousy over a friend's new toys. According to Erikson, the play often not only represents the problem but also offers a solution, so that children experience some new sense of resolution and a reduction in the tension associated with the conflict. Symbolic play provides a certain flexibility or leeway in structuring the situation and, at the same

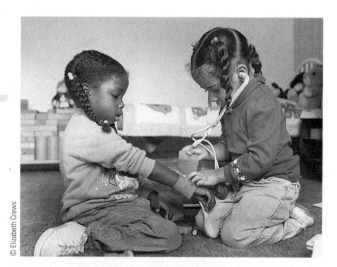

*One of the favorite forms of social pretense is "doctor." With the use of a few props, friends can explore the fascinating realm of illness, healing, comforting, and advising. Patient–doctor play allows children to gain mastery over an area of great concern and uncertainty.*

© Elizabeth Crews

## Imaginary Companions

PROBABLY THE MOST sophisticated form of symbolic play is the creation of an imaginary friend (Singer, 1975). An imaginary friend, which may be an animal, a child, or some other creature, springs complete in concept from the mind of the child. It occupies space. It has its own personality, which is consistent from day to day. It has its own likes and dislikes, which are not necessarily the same as those of its creator. Although not all children who have imaginary companions disclose this information to adults, some studies have shown that as many as 65% of toddlers have imaginary companions, and some children have more than one (Singer & Singer, 1990).

The prevalence of imaginary companions may be greater than one might have guessed. In one study in the United Kingdom, 1,800 children were asked about past or present experience with imaginary companions. Roughly 46% said they had one (Pearson et al., 2001). When parents were surveyed about their children, those with imaginary companions were more likely to be firstborn or only children, were judged by parents to be very imaginative in other aspects of their play, and to enjoy magical or fantasy play as compared to other forms of play. Children who have imaginary companions also tend to have more extensive language competence, which is observable in their ongoing conversations with their invisible friend (Bouldin & Pratt, 1999; Gleason, Sebanc, & Hartup, 2003).

In one study, investigators invited children who had imaginary companions to come to the laboratory and play with their companions (Taylor, Cartwright, & Carlson, 1993). The children seemed willing to talk about their companions, and they thought the investigators would be able to see and touch their companions just as they could. For most of the children, the companions remained consistent for 6 months and retained an active role in the child's fantasy life.

Several functions are served by an imaginary friend: It takes the place of other children when there are none around; it serves as a play companion for pretend play; it serves as a confidant for children's private expression; and it is often involved in their efforts to differentiate between right and wrong. Children can distinguish the social relationship they have with their imaginary companion from the relationships they have with parents, siblings, and best friends. Imaginary companions and real friends are viewed as similar in many ways, but children are more likely to comfort and nurture their imaginary friend than their real friend (Gleason, 2002).

---

time, imposes some limits so that children may experience a new mastery of issues that are perplexing or overwhelming in real life.

Pretend play is a form of representational thought—a way that children experiment with the relationships of objects and social roles. For children who have some forms of language delay, observations of their pretense provides insight into their cognitive capacities (Butterfield, 1994). Research suggests that pretend play actually fosters cognitive, emotional, and social development. Children who have well-developed pretending skills tend to be well liked by their peers and to be viewed as leaders (Ladd, Price, & Hart, 1988). This is a result of their advanced communication skills, their greater ability to take the point of view of others, and their ability to reason about social situations. Children who have been encouraged in a playful, imaginative approach to the manipulation and exploration of materials and objects through fantasy show more complex language use and more flexible approaches to problem solving (Burke, 1987). Children who have frequent opportunities for pretend play—especially with a more experienced play partner—are better able to express their feelings, show higher levels of empathy, and are more aware of their emotional states (Galyer & Evans, 2001; Lindsey & Colwell, 2003).

The importance of fantasy play in the full social, intellectual, and emotional development of young children cannot be underestimated. Some parents and teachers want to define a young child's cognitive growth in terms of the acquisition of words and concepts that seem relevant to the "real world." They emphasize the importance of learning numbers and letters, memorizing facts, and learning to read. However, research on cognitive development suggests that gains in the capacity for symbolic thought provide the essential underpinnings of subsequent intellectual abilities, such as abstract reasoning and inventive problem solving.

### ■ THE ROLE OF PLAY COMPANIONS

Cognitive developmental theory emphasizes the normal emergence of representational thought and symbolic play as the natural outcome of cognitive maturation during toddlerhood. However, the quality of that play as well as its content depends in part on the behavior of a child's play companions. Consider the following incident:

In a university preschool where college students were having their first supervised experience as teachers of young children, a child of 3 made a bid for some pretend play with a student teacher. The child picked up the toy telephone and made ringing noises. The student teacher picked up another phone and said, "Hello." The child asked, "Is Milly there?" The student teacher said, "No," and hung up the phone. Rather than extending the pretense into a more elaborate social pretend situation by saying something like

"Who is calling?" or pretending to put Milly on the phone, the student teacher brought the scenario to a close.

As play companions, parents, siblings, peers, and child care professionals can significantly enrich a child's fantasy play. Play companions can elaborate a child's capacity for fantasy, legitimize fantasy play, and help the child to explore new domains of fantasy. Research has shown that when mothers are available as play companions, the symbolic play of their 2-year-old children is more complex and lasts longer (Slade, 1987; Tamis-LeMonda, Uzgiris, & Bornstein, 2002). When adults are trained to engage in and encourage pretend play with toddlers, the toddlers show a higher level of ability to coordinate their responses with those of the adults. From age 16 to 32 months, toddlers become increasingly skillful in directing an adult's behavior and negotiating changes in kinds of play (Eckerman & Didow, 1989). Early and frequent opportunities to pretend with older siblings as well as with parents contribute to a young child's ability to understand other people's feelings and beliefs. As toddlers experiment with pretend roles, construct fantasy situations, and manipulate objects with a play companion, they are forced to establish new channels of shared meaning, thus fostering a new degree of awareness about self and others (Youngblade & Dunn, 1995).

In child care settings, the availability of a consistent group of age-mates results in more complex, coordinated play. In contrast, children who have had many changes in their child care arrangements are less likely to engage in complex social pretend play with other children (Howes & Stewart, 1987). Because toddlers rely so heavily on imitation and nonverbal signals to initiate and develop their social pretend play, the more time they have together, the more complex their fantasy play will be (Eckerman & Didow, 1996).

The importance of pretense and the way pretend play is nurtured depends in part on the meaning it is given in one's culture. For example, among the Ijaw of Nigeria, children under 5 are thought to have a special link with the female creator spirit (Leis, 1982). Adults may watch a young child playing alone, interacting with imaginary companions by giving out pretend food, or speaking to them in a happy tone. Rather than dismissing this activity as child's play, the adults believe that the child is interacting with the spirit world and will take care not to disrupt the activity. An Ijaw woman who wants to become pregnant might try to appeal to a small child, hoping that if she is kind to the child, the child will use his or her special link to the spirit world to help bring about the pregnancy (Valsiner, 2000). The nature and role of imaginary companions may be tolerated by U.S. families, but among scholars of child development, they are considered evidence of advanced symbolic representation, an emerging sense of self, and a strategy for achieving new levels of self-control.

## SELF-CONTROL

Do you ever find that you roll over for 10 more minutes of sleep even when you know you should get out of bed? Do you let your mind wander when you need to be paying attention? Do you go for that extra helping of cake when you are trying to lose five pounds? These are just a few examples of lapses in self control. Self-regulation is frequently noted as a marker of maturity—the ability to control impulses, direct action toward a goal, express and inhibit the expression of emotions, and resist temptation are all evidence of this capacity (Heatherton, 2000). Over time, self-control becomes a foundation for moral behavior. For toddlers, self-control is the ability to comply with a request, modify behavior according to the situation, initiate or postpone action, and behave in a socially acceptable way without having to be guided or directed by someone else (Kopp, 1982). These abilities reflect a growing sense of selfhood.

## ■ LANGUAGE AND FANTASY AS STRATEGIES FOR CONTROLLING IMPULSES

Language and fantasy are children's most useful tools for managing impulses. Talking about feelings and needs enables adults to help children understand more about their emotions and to help them devise strategies for self-regulation. Thompson (1990) identified four ways that caregivers use talking about emotions to help young children gain control. First, parents articulate the family or cultural rules of emotional expression: "Don't get so excited; calm down!" or "Stop that fussing; big boys don't whine and cry!" These lessons give young children an idea about the acceptable levels of impulses or emotional intensity and about the types of emotions that need to be regulated.

Second, adults help modify the intensity of emotions through reassuring or distracting talk. They may try to distract a child who is worried about getting an injection, or try to convince the child that the shot won't hurt or that it will be just a little sting. They may try to comfort a sobbing child by talking about some happy event that will distract the child from his or her troubles.

Third, adults give children ideas for ways to manage their impulses. They might help by suggesting that the child think of pleasant times from the past or by singing a cheerful song. Adults teach children superstitions, rituals, and stories about how people handle their strong feelings.

Fourth, children listen and imitate adults who talk about their own strong emotions and impulses. The development of symbolic imagery allows children to create imaginary situations in which disturbing problems can be expressed and resolved. Through fantasy play, toddlers can control situations that are far beyond their real-world capacities (Singer & Singer, 1990). They can punish and forgive, harm and heal, fear and conquer fear—all within the boundaries of their own imagination. Children can use the context of pretense to manage strong feelings and to preserve their emotional control (Galyer & Evans, 2001). When Robbie feels bad about something, he says, "Superheroes don't cry." He is making use of fantasy and language to control his emotional state. When children are asked to resist temptation, they use a variety of verbal strategies, including talking quietly to themselves and singing songs to distract themselves (Mischel, Shoda, &

## The Control of Angry Feelings

THE EXPRESSION OF anger, which is important to the child's development of a sense of autonomy, typically generates tension between parents and children (Wenar, 1982). Toddlers get angry for many reasons, including inability to perform a task, parental restrictions on behavior, and peer or sibling rivalry. As toddlers become increasingly involved in directing the outcomes of their activities, they get angry when someone interrupts them or offers unrequested assistance (Bullock & Lutkenhaus, 1988). Toddlers are likely to get angry when they are tired, or when they are forced to make a transition from something they are enjoying to something someone else wants them to do. Furthermore, some children are temperamentally more aggressive than others.

Children rely on their parents as models for learning how to express and control anger. The times when parents are angry are very important. Children learn as much or more about the expression of anger from watching their parents when they are angry as they do from verbal explanations or punishment (Bandura, 1977). Children are sensitive to angry expressions directed toward them through both verbal and nonverbal behavior. In some parent–child dyads, anger is a dominant theme in the parenting interactions (Aber, Belsky, Slade, & Crnic, 1999). Parents who are angry

and abusive toward their children provide a model for the imitation of angry behavior. Children are also sensitive to anger between their parents, even when it is not directed at them. Parents' hostility to each other, expressed through quarrels, sarcasm, and physical abuse, increases children's sensitivity to anger and is closely related to disturbances in development (Cummings, Pellegrini, Notarius, & Cummings, 1989).

Not all parenting efforts are directed at inhibiting the expression of anger. In an ethnographic study of the socialization of anger and aggression, three 2-year-old girls and their mothers from a working class neighborhood of Baltimore were studied in detail. The mothers considered assertiveness and self-defense essential to survival in their neighborhood. Along with socialization strategies that focused on controlling inappropriate aggression, the mothers found many ways to model aggressiveness as they talked to others in the girls' presence and to reward certain displays of toughness and assertiveness in the girls' behavior (Miller & Sperry, 1987).

Children who can express anger and not lose control make tremendous gains in the development of autonomy. Anger at and conflict with parents give toddlers evidence that they are indeed very separate from their parents and that the separateness, although painful, is legiti-

mate. Children who are severely punished or ridiculed for their anger are left in a state of doubt. They see models for the expression of anger in the way their parents respond to them, and yet they are told that anger is not appropriate for them. The goal in the socialization of angry feelings is to help children find legitimate expressions of anger without hurting themselves or others. Between ages 2 and 5, the frequency of angry, aggressive behaviors declines as children develop effective strategies for self-control (Cummings et al., 1989).

Several strategies help young children manage or reduce the intensity of their anger (Berkowitz, 1973; Thompson, 1990):

- ignoring aggression
- providing brief "time-out" periods in a nearby quiet area until the emotion has subsided
- arousing feelings that are incompatible with anger, especially empathy for the victim
- minimizing exposure to stimuli that arouse aggressive impulses
- explaining the consequences of aggressive actions for the other person
- explaining the circumstances that may have led to the initial feelings of anger or frustration

Rodriguez, 1989). Toddlers who can talk to themselves may be able to control their fears, modify their anger, and soften their disappointments. They may repeat their parents' comforting words, or they may develop their own verbal strategies for reducing pain and suffering.

## ■ CONTROL OF IMPULSES

Early in infancy, self-control is usually understood as the infant's ability to prevent disorganization brought on by overstimulation and to recover from emotional distress. Babies have a variety of internal regulating strategies (Kopp, 1982). For example, by sucking or rocking, babies can soothe themselves. They can also resist overstimulation by turning away, crying, or going to sleep.

During toddlerhood, self-control develops in two directions: control of impulses and self-regulated goal attainment, which is discussed later in this chapter. First, children improve their ability to modify and control their impulses. The case of Colin illustrates how toddlers may fall prey to their impulses. Sometimes, they simply cannot interrupt an ongoing action, even one they know is inappropriate. Colin, age 2 years 9 months, is just starting nursery school:

In his relations with children, Colin progressed quickly from a quiet, friendly, watching relationship on the first few days to actively hugging the other children. The hugging seemed to be in an excess of friendliness and was only mildly aggressive. Having started hugging, he didn't know how to stop, and usually just held on until he pulled the child down to the floor. This was followed very closely by

*It takes a lot of self-control for Anna to cope with the baby's screaming. She holds her ears, grits her teeth, and shakes her leg rather than give the baby a wallop.*

© Elliott Erwitt/Magnum Photos

hair pulling. He didn't pull viciously, but still held on long enough to get a good resistance from the child. He grabbed toys from others. When stopped by an adult from any of these acts, he was very responsive to reason, would say, smiling, "I won't do it any more," would tear around the room in disorganized activity, and then return to hugging or pulling hair. (Murphy, 1956, pp. 11–12)

From age 2 to 3, children are increasingly able to modify and control their impulses and withstand delays in gratification. They also become more willing to modify their behavior because they do not wish to cause distress to others. The ability to regulate or restrain behavior is a product of changing cognitive, social, and emotional competencies. Children become increasingly sensitive to the negative consequences of impulsive acts. At the same time, they develop new strategies to help manage feelings of frustration, such as distracting themselves and redirecting their attention to some alternative activity or toy, creating a pretend scenario in which they soothe themselves through a fantasy character, using some physical soothing or comforting strategy like thumb sucking or cuddling with a blanket, and seeking comfort or distraction from a parent or play companion (Grolnick, Bridges, & Connell, 1996; Zahn-Waxler, Radke-Yarrow, Wagner, & Chapman, 1992).

**INCREASING SENSITIVITY TO THE DISTRESS OF OTHERS.** Toddlers can observe and empathize with distress expressed in others, both children and adults. Moreover, they begin to understand when they have been the cause of someone else's distress (Zahn-Waxler, Radke-Yarrow, et al., 1992; Zahn-Waxler, Robinson, & Emde, 1992). Often, the socialization environment helps to focus toddlers' attention on

these instances when parents or teachers point out their actions and the consequences. The following observation from a study of family interaction shows how a conversation about negative consequences and a child's concern over his mother's distress contributed to the self-regulation of impulses:

> Danny is 33 months old. He and his mother are at the sink washing dishes. Danny blows a handful of suds at his mother and some gets in her eyes. Danny is laughing at this new game.
>
> M: No! Nuh uh, Danny. Danny you got it in my eye. (mild negative affect)
>
> Danny stops laughing.
>
> M: Don't do that in my eye, OK? It hurts to get soap in your eye.
>
> D: (very serious) I won't. (Brown & Dunn, 1992, pp. 347–348)

**DISCIPLINE STRATEGIES AND IMPULSE CONTROL.** In toddlerhood, the immediate aim of discipline is to achieve compliance (Kochanska, Aksan, & Koenig, 1995). A parent typically wants children to stop doing something ("Don't touch those figurines; they might break") or to do something ("Help me put the toys away now, it's time to go to bed"). If the child complies, a parent might respond positively by smiling, patting the child or giving a hug, or complimenting the child for being good, helpful, or obedient. If the child does not comply, a parent may try some form of distraction or offer some choice ("You can help clean up now or in 5 minutes"). But if compliance is not forthcoming, some type of discipline is likely to ensue.

Discipline practices have been described in three general categories (Hoffman, 1977):

1. **Power assertion**: Physical punishment; shouting; attempts to physically move a child or inhibit behavior; taking away privileges or resources; or threatening any of these things.
2. **Love withdrawal**: Expressing anger, disappointment, or disapproval; refusing to communicate; walking out or turning away.
3. **Inductions**: Explaining why the behavior was wrong; pointing out the consequences of behavior to others; redirecting behavior by appealing to the child's sense of mastery, fair play, or love of another person.

In addition to these three general categories of discipline techniques, parental modeling and reinforcement of acceptable behaviors are significant in the development of internal control (Maccoby, 1992). In order to correct their behavior, children must know what acts are considered appropriate as well as how to inhibit their inappropriate acts. Modeling and reinforcement aid children in directing their behavior; discipline serves to inhibit or redirect it.

The manner in which the discipline is carried out over time is associated with child outcomes, especially increases in compliance, prosocial behavior, and the eventual internalization of moral standards; or increases in noncompliance, aggressiveness, and low levels of moral reasoning. Three features of the approach to discipline appear to be important (O'Leary, 1995):

1. The discipline should be immediate or as close in time to the situation as possible. Laxness in discipline, such as laughing at an undesirable behavior, waiting too long to respond, reprimanding the child sometimes but not at other times for the same misconduct, or inadvertently rewarding a child for misconduct are all practices that are likely to increase rather than decrease the undesired behavior.
2. The discipline should be appropriately firm, but not overreactive. The response to noncompliance should be coordinated with the child's behavior, focusing on expressing concern for the harm that was done, engaging the child in talking about how to repair the situation, and setting the stage for what the child might do next (Edwards & Liu, 2002). Practices that are intensely harsh, abusive, or cruel, whether they involve physical or emotional intensity, are associated with increases in problem behaviors. The infrequent use of power-assertive punishment in an overall context of a warm, nurturing relationship may prove effective in fostering compliance. However, intense and frequent harsh punishment is associated with a variety of maladaptive consequences for children (Weiss, Dodge, Bates, & Petit, 1992).
3. The discipline for a toddler should be brief. It is important to make sure that the toddler understands what the misbehavior was and why it was wrong, but the explana-

tion should be concise and presented at the toddler's level of understanding. Punishment involving love withdrawal is especially likely to be carried on too long. The parent should make sure the toddler knows when she or he is back in the parent's "good graces," and not let the child spend hours thinking the parent is still angry.

**INDIVIDUAL DIFFERENCES IN THE ABILITY TO CONTROL IMPULSES.** The ability to delay gratification varies with the individual. At least three factors are associated with differences in the ease or difficulty that children have in controlling their impulses (see Figure 7.3). First, toddlers differ in their capacity to empathize with the distress of others. Empathy itself appears to have a genetic as well as an environmental basis. In a study of identical and fraternal twins who were 2 years old, the identical twins showed greater similarity in their emotional concern about and response to others' distress than did the fraternal twins. Moreover, mothers who showed a stronger concern for others in their childrearing strategies had children whose empathy was more fully developed. Furthermore, girls were observed to be more empathic than boys (Zahn-Waxler, Robinson, et al., 1992). Individual differences in sensitivity to the distress of others lead to differences in how upset a child might be by finding that his or her behavior had caused someone suffering and in how willing the child may be to curb that behavior in the future.

Second, differences in temperament affect self-control. Children who are more aggressive, active, or socially outgoing may experience more situations in which their actions are viewed as disruptive or in need of control. In contrast, children who are more socially inhibited, withdrawn, or passive may encounter fewer expectations to curb or restrict their behavior (Kochanska & Radke-Yarrow, 1992). The temperamental characteristic described as **effortful control** refers to a child's ability to suppress a dominant response and perform a subdominant response instead. For example, even when Riley wants to shout out loud, he can talk in a whisper because he sees that grandpa is napping and does not want to

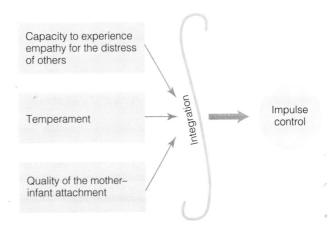

**FIGURE 7.3**

Factors Associated with the Ability to Control Impulses

wake grandpa. Infants who are less emotionally intense in their expressions of anger or joy, and who are more cautious in a novel situation, have been found to have greater effortful control in toddlerhood (Kochanska & Knaack, 2003).

Effortful control reflects an ability to slow down one's actions on request, suppress a movement in response to instructions, and override the tendency to respond to a global display and pay close attention to the details in a stimulus (Kochanska, Murray, & Coy, 1997). One measure of effortful control requires a child to move a toy turtle and a toy rabbit along a curved path toward a barn. Effortful control was demonstrated in the child's ability to move the rabbit quickly and the turtle slowly along the same path. Longitudinal evidence suggests that effortful control in toddlerhood provides a basis for the formation of conscience and moral development in the early school-age period. It allows the young child to respond more easily to parental requests and to interrupt or suppress undesirable behaviors (Kochanska, Murray, & Harlan, 2000).

Third, the capacity for self-regulation may depend on the quality of the mother–infant attachment. Children who lack attachment security are more likely to exhibit irritability, avoidance, resistance, and aggressiveness as preschoolers (Teti, Nakagawa, Das, & Wirth, 1991). They have more difficulty calming themselves and reducing the intensity of their impulses. In contrast, sensitive caregiving, in which the mother and toddler are able to coordinate their interactions to sustain longer periods of mutually responsive interaction, is associated with an enhanced capacity for self-regulation. Toddlers who experience this rhythmic coregulation are better able to distract themselves and deliberately guide their attention away from tempting objects that they are not allowed to touch (Raver, 1996).

Since the early 1960s, Walter Mischel and his colleagues have investigated the process by which children **delay gratification**. To delay gratification, a child must exert willpower in order to resist a strong immediate pull or temptation. This requires shifting attention or distancing oneself from the immediate situation and redirecting attention or action in order to achieve a different goal (Mischel & Ayduk, 2002). For example, when they were at the zoo, Kelly asked for ice cream. Her mother said she could either have ice cream now or go to McDonalds for dinner when they left the zoo. Kelly agreed to wait and go to McDonalds. At age 4, children who delay gratification longer tend to be more intelligent, more likely to resist temptation, demonstrate greater social responsibility, and have higher achievement strivings.

According to Mischel's research, a 4-year-old's ability to use self-regulatory strategies to delay gratification has enduring effects. More than 10 years later, children who had waited longer in an experimental situation that required a self-imposed delay of gratification at age 4 were described by their parents as socially and academically more competent than their peers. Their parents rated these children as more verbally fluent and able to express ideas, using and responding to reason, and more competent and skillful. These children

were more attentive and able to concentrate, plan, and think ahead, and they were also seen as better able to cope with frustration and resist temptation (Mischel et al., 1989; Morf & Mischel, 2002).

Other longitudinal studies have supported the strong link between early evidence of self-control and subsequent socialization. Children who are able to regulate their emotional reactions and resist temptations in toddlerhood are less likely to violate parental rules, they are more planful as they approach new tasks, and as a result, they are more likely to be successful in school settings where cooperation and compliance are highly valued (Rothbart, Ahadi, & Evans, 2000).

## ■ SELF-REGULATED GOAL ATTAINMENT

The second sense in which self-control develops has to do with toddlers' feelings that they can direct their own behavior and the behavior of others to achieve intended outcomes (Messer, Rachford, McCarthy, & Yarrow, 1987). During infancy, children become increasingly aware of themselves as causal agents. They make things happen. In toddlerhood, children become much more assertive about their desire to initiate actions, persist in activities, and determine when these activities should stop.

Benjamin at 27 months, 17 days:

When I put him to bed tonight he bellowed at the top of his lungs for a good five minutes from sheer rage that I wouldn't let him get down on the floor and go on playing with his car. What he wants and doesn't want he can be very noisy about—but he can also obviously be rather confused as to what he does want. . . . This is especially true in the afternoon after his nap. He may wake up demanding a ride or a walk. By the time he gets downstairs, it has switched to "Want to pway bwocks." (Church, 1966, p. 157)

Toddlers' sense of **agency**—their view of themselves as the originators of action—expands to include a broad array of behaviors. Children want to participate in decisions about bedtime, the clothes they wear, the kinds of foods they eat, and family activities. They want to do things they see their parents and their older siblings doing. Their confidence in their own ability to handle very difficult tasks is not modified by a realistic assessment of their own skills. According to toddlers, "Anything you can do, I can do better." When they have opportunities to do some of these new and complex things and they succeed, they gain confidence in themselves and their abilities. Toddlers feel themselves to be valuable members of the family as they contribute to routine household tasks. Their feelings of confidence and value are matched by the acquisition of a wide variety of complex, coordinated skills.

**SPEECH AND GOAL ATTAINMENT.** Vygotsky (1978) argued that speech plays a central role in self-directed goal attainment and practical problem solving. He described the problem-solving behaviors of toddlers as involving both

*In toddlerhood, children begin to develop self-reliance. Maria can wash her hands by herself, just one of many areas where she is gaining confidence about guiding her own behavior.*

speech and action. Toddlers use what was described by Piaget (1952) as *egocentric speech* to control and direct their behavior. The speech is considered egocentric because it is not intended to communicate with anyone else and often doesn't make sense to anyone else. Vygotsky (1978) suggested that egocentric speech, or speech turned toward the self, and actions are part of the same problem-solving function. The more difficult the problem, the more speech is necessary for the child to find a solution. "Children solve practical tasks with the help of their speech, as well as their eyes and hands" (p. 26).

Speech gives children a new degree of freedom, flexibility, and control in approaching tasks and working toward a goal. They can use words to call to mind tools that are not visible. They can plan steps toward a goal and repeat them to guide their actions. They can use words like *slowly, be careful,* or *hold tight* to control their behavior as they work on a task. Language skills and self-control operate together to help children inhibit negative emotions and disruptive behavior during times of frustration (Lynam & Henry, 2001).

The kind of speech that guides problem solving emerges from the social speech that characterizes children's interactions with adults. Often, when young children try to figure out how to work something or how to get something that is out of reach, they turn to adults for help. Vygotsky suggested that the kind of talk that adults use as they guide young children is then used by the children themselves to support and guide their own behavior. He referred to this process as the *internalization of social speech* and suggested that through this mechanism, children's social environment shapes their thinking, planning, and problem solving. In a sense, a child's capacity for self-directed goal attainment depends largely on what he or she has taken in of the spoken, practical advice and guidance given by adults and older peers who have tried to help the child solve problems in the past.

We have considered two rather different phenomena under the developmental task of self-control. Children's ability to control their impulses is closely linked to the psychoana-lytic concept of delay of gratification, as Freud (1905/1953) used it to describe development during the oral and anal stages. Self-directed goal attainment, sometimes referred to as agency, is a general motivation that accounts for children's efforts to increase their competence through persistent investigation and skillful problem solving (Harter, 1982; White, 1960). Both abilities foster toddlers' growing awareness of themselves. To function effectively as family members, toddlers must feel confident in their ability to control the inner world of their feelings and impulses and the outer world of decisions and tasks. As toddlers discover that they can tolerate stress, express or withhold their anger as appropriate, and approach difficult tasks and succeed at them, they also lay claim to a growing definition of selfhood.

Toddlerhood is an important time in the development of a person's sense of self-efficacy—the conviction that one can perform the behaviors demanded by a specific situation (Bandura, 2000). The more toddlers can do by themselves, the more confidence they will have in their ability to control the outcomes of their actions and achieve their goals. Over time, the sense of self-control that is formed during toddlerhood is integrated into adult capacities to overcome obstacles to achieve important goals and to engage in acts of generosity and kindness even when these acts conflict with their own immediate needs.

# THE PSYCHOSOCIAL CRISIS: AUTONOMY VERSUS SHAME AND DOUBT

During toddlerhood, children become aware of their separateness. Through a variety of experiences, they discover that their parents do not always know what they want and do not always understand their feelings. In early toddlerhood, children use rather primitive devices to explore their independence. They may say "no" to everything offered to them whether they want it or not. This is the period that people often refer to as the *terrible twos*. Toddlers seem very demanding and insist on having things done their own way.

## AUTONOMY

The positive pole of the psychosocial crisis of toddlerhood is **autonomy**. During this period of life, autonomy refers to the ability to behave independently—to perform actions on one's own. In most cultures, expectations for autonomy are expressed as encouragement for children to perform daily tasks such as dressing and feeding themselves, playing alone or with peers, and sleeping apart from parents. The exact list of expectations and the age at which these behaviors are to be accomplished varies from one society to the next. Within U.S. society, pressures for autonomy are often expressed in early expectations for skill acquisition and verbal expressiveness. Children do not just prefer to do most things on their own, they *insist* on it. Once children begin to work on a task, such as putting on pajamas or tying shoelaces, they will struggle along, time after time, until they have mastered it. They may adamantly reject help and insist that they can manage on their own. They will allow someone else to help them only when they are sure that they can progress no further by themselves.

In many non-Western cultures, *interdependence* rather than independence is the valued goal of socialization. Children are likely to experience pressures toward autonomy with the birth of a sibling. Rather than pressing for separateness and distance from the caregiver, toddlers may hover near their mother, distressed at her new lack of availability. Through guidance from older siblings and peers, young children learn to participate in the ongoing activities of the household, watching intently, imitating others, and contributing as they can to daily tasks. Within this cultural context, expectations for autonomy may emphasize the ability to demand less of the mother, to become sensitive to the needs of others, and to function cooperatively with peers (Edwards & Liu, 2002; Harkness & Super, 1995).

The establishment of a sense of autonomy requires not only tremendous effort by the child but also extreme patience and support from the parents. Toddlers' demands for autonomy are often exasperating. They challenge their parents' good sense, goodwill, and good intentions. Parents must learn to teach, cajole, absorb insults, wait, and praise. Sometimes, they must allow their children to try things that the children may not be able to do. By encouraging their children to engage in new tasks, parents hope to promote their sense of competence.

In the development of autonomy, toddlers shift from a somewhat rigid, nay-saying, ritualized, unreasonable style to an independent, energetic, persistent one (Erikson, 1963). The behavior of older toddlers is characterized by the phrase "I can do it myself." They are less concerned about doing things their own way and more concerned with doing them on their own. Toddlers demonstrate an increasing variety of skills. Each new accomplishment gives them great pride. When doing things independently leads to positive results, the sense of autonomy grows. Toddlers begin to create an image of themselves as people who can manage situations competently and who can satisfy many of their own needs. Children who have been allowed to experience autonomy should, by the end of toddlerhood, have a strong foundation of self-confidence and feelings of delight in behaving independently.

## SHAME AND DOUBT

Some children fail to emerge from toddlerhood with a sense of mastery. Because of their failure at most attempted tasks or because of continual discouragement and criticism from parents, or most likely because of both, some children develop an overwhelming sense of shame and self-doubt. This is the negative resolution of the psychosocial crisis of toddlerhood (Erikson, 1963). **Shame** is an intense negative emotion that focuses on a negative evaluation of the self. Often it is accompanied by a sense of having been exposed or ridiculed and made to feel inferior to others. Feelings of shame do not have to occur in the presence of an audience; however, they usually involve at least an imagined notion of how one's behavior might look to others (Tangney, 2001).

One source of shame is social ridicule or criticism. You can probably recall feelings of shame for having spilled your milk or having lost your jacket. One of the earliest experiences of shaming is typically linked to toilet training. Shame generally originates in an interpersonal interaction in which you feel that you have violated a valued social standard or in which you have been embarrassed or ridiculed for behaving in a stupid, thoughtless, or clumsy way (Tangney, Wagner, Fletcher, & Gramzow, 1992). When you are shamed, you feel small, ridiculed, and humiliated. Some cultures rely heavily on shame coupled with opportunities for restitution as a means of social control. Children in these cultures grow up with a strong concern about how their behaviors might reflect on their family or result in disrupting the social bond with their community. One of their greatest fears is to be publicly accused of immoral or dishonorable actions that would bring disgrace to their family (Scheff, 2003).

Internal conflict is another source of shame. As children construct an idea of what it means to be a good, decent, capable person, they build a mental image of an ideal person. Children feel shame when their behavior does not meet the standards of their ideal, even though they have not broken a rule or done anything naughty. In general, shame is associated with feelings that the "whole self" is bad or worthless. It makes one want to disappear from the eyes of others.

Shame is extremely unpleasant. In order to avoid it, children may refrain from all kinds of new activities. Children who feel shame lack confidence in their abilities and expect

## HUMAN DEVELOPMENT AND DIVERSITY

## Toilet Training

EVERY HUMAN CULTURE has some mechanism to remove waste products from close proximity to the social group. The effort to teach children how to dispose of human waste in a culturally appropriate fashion is the focus of what we in the United States refer to as *toilet training* or *potty training*. Any approach to this task reflects a combination of technology, beliefs, and practices. One of the basic issues is whether one believes that the regulation of this training should be left to the child, drawing on a sense of developmental readiness, or left in the hands of the "trainers," which usually suggests a training program (Valsiner, 2000).

In Freud's psychoanalytic theory, toilet training symbolized the classic psychological conflict between individual autonomy and social demands for conformity. In this particular conflict, children are destined to lose (White, 1960). They must subordinate their autonomy to expectations for a specific routine regarding elimination. In the United States, the contemporary approach to this dichotomy between autonomy and conformity is advocated by the American Academy of Pediatrics (1999). Their advice about toilet training combines waiting until the child is ready with introducing toileting in a guided, systematic fashion:

*Autonomy/Readiness*: "Chances are, toilet training won't be very successful until your child is past the extreme negativism and resistance to it that occurs in early toddlerhood. He must want to take this major step. He'll be ready when he seems eager to please and imitate you, but also wants to become more independent. Most children reach this stage sometime between 18 and 24 months, but it is also normal for it to occur a little later."

*Spencer is able to relax on a potty just his size, taking advantage of a few quiet moments for reading as he develops his toilet habits.*

*Conformity/Training*: "The best way to introduce your toddler to the concept of using the toilet is to let him watch other family members of his sex. . . . For the first few weeks, let him sit on the potty fully clothed while you tell him about the toilet, what it's for and when to use it. Once he sits on it willingly, let him try it with his diaper off. Show him how to keep his feet planted solidly on the floor, since this will be important when he's having a bowel movement. Make the potty part of his routine, gradually increasing from once to several times each day."

The experts suggest starting with bowel training, and then moving on to urinating in the potty by allowing the

child to play near the potty, dropping the contents of the dirty diaper in the potty so the child sees the connection, reminding the child to use the potty when needed, but not to show disappointment when he or she misses or forgets. Patience, reassurance, and praise are suggested while the caregiver encourages increasing compliance with toileting practices.

This approach, which you may find extremely sensible and "right," can be contrasted with the practices of the Digo, a group living in coastal Kenya and Tanzania. The Digo live in huts with mud floors. The smell of urine mixed with the mud is extremely unpleasant and difficult to remove. So the Digo are eager to have their infants urinate out of the hut as early as possible. Training begins at 2 to 3 weeks of age. The caregiver sits on the ground outside the hut with feet outstretched and places the baby in the appropriate position for urinating. The baby is placed on the caregiver's feet, facing away from the caregiver but supported by the caregiver. While in this position, the caregiver makes a low sound ("shuus") which serves as a conditioned stimulus for urination. This is repeated frequently, day and night, until the baby urinates in this position following the sound. When this happens, the baby is rewarded with breastfeeding. By the age of 4 to 5 months, Digo babies are trained to urinate only in the culturally approved position and setting (De Vries & De Vries, 1977). In contrast to the recommendations of the American Academy of Pediatrics, this approach places a strong emphasis on training and shows a perception of readiness that is much earlier than that held in U.S. and other Western cultures.

to fail at what they do. The acquisition of new skills becomes slow and painful when feelings of self-confidence and worth are replaced by constant doubt. Children who have a pervasive sense of **doubt** feel comfortable only in highly structured and familiar situations, in which the risk of failure is minimal. As college students, young people who have high levels of shame were also characterized by high levels of resentment, irritability, anger, suspiciousness, and a tendency to blame others (Kaufman, 1989; Lewis, 1987). Because of its relationship to humiliation and self-denigration, people who respond to situations with strong feelings of shame are less likely to experience empathy for the victim, and more likely to respond with anger. Their self-loathing is quickly redirected to direct or displaced aggression (Tangney & Dearing, 2002).

All children experience some failures amid their many successes. In the process of achieving a new level of separateness, children may discover that they have harmed a loved one, broken a treasured toy, or wandered too far away and become separated from the caregiver at a crowded store or an unfamiliar park. Toddlers often exhibit periods of ambivalent dependency alternating with what appears to be unrealistic self-assurance as they try to establish a comfortable level of individuation from the loved one. The successful outcome to this process requires flexibility and warmth on the part of caregivers who accept and welcome the emerging selfhood of their child while building support for appropriate levels of self-control (Edwards, 1995).

# THE CENTRAL PROCESS: IMITATION

The primary mechanism by which toddlers emerge as autonomous individuals is **imitation**. Although imitation requires the presence of active models, its outcome is a shift of the action from the model to the imitator. In other words, once toddlers succeed in imitating a certain skill, that skill belongs to them, and they can use it for any purpose they like. Toddlers seem driven to imitate almost everything they observe, including their parents' positions at the toilet. Toddlers' vocabularies expand markedly through their imitation of the words they hear in adult conversations, on television, and in stories. Their interest in dancing, music, and other activities stems from imitation of parents and peers. When one child in a play group makes a funny noise or performs a daring act, other children appear to be compelled to re-create this novel behavior.

The imitative behavior of toddlers is different from the socially induced conformity observed in older children. Toddlers are not aware of a great many social norms and therefore feel little pressure to conform to them. Their imitative behavior is really a vehicle for learning. Every act becomes their own, even if it has been inspired by others. The primary

motivation for imitation during toddlerhood is the drive for mastery and competence.

Jess liked to imitate adult tasks. When his mother cleaned the house, he followed her with a cloth, trying to dust the tables. When Mark (*Jess's older brother*) fed the dog, Jess helped him by getting the dog's dish. When his father shaved in the morning, Jess took a toothbrush to imitate his father with lathering and shaving motions. He was learning to brush his teeth, even though his span of attention was short at this job and the cleansing ineffective. (Brazelton, 1974, pp. 139–140)

In studies of imitation in the home environment, toddlers show an impressive pattern of imitating their parents' household, self-care, and caretaking activities. They show increasing interest in imitating behaviors that are socially meaningful and valued. These observations have led researchers to suggest that imitation is critical in satisfying toddlers' need for social competence (Kuczynski, Zahn-Waxler, & Radke-Yarrow, 1987). Through imitation, toddlers also derive pleasure from the similarity they perceive between themselves and their model. This perceived similarity is a secondary benefit of the imitative process (Kagan, 1958).

Imitation is also a means of participating in and sustaining social interactions and advancing social cognition (Meltzoff, 2002). In a peer setting, imitation emerges as a dominant strategy for children to coordinate their behaviors with those of other toddlers. Before verbal communication becomes a truly useful tool for establishing or maintaining social contact, toddlers imitate one another. Through imitation, toddlers can feel connected to one another and begin to invent coordinated games (Eckerman, Davis, & Didow, 1989). With increasing cognitive maturity, children select imitation behaviors that have relevance to their own needs for mastery, nurturance, and social interaction. Imitation advances empathy. By watching and repeating the actions of others, toddlers begin to gain insight into the other person's experiences and emotional state.

The emphasis on imitation highlights the central role of culture at this period of life. In many cultures, adults orient young children toward important tasks and expect them to watch and learn in a process of imitation and shared problem solving (Rogoff, Mistry, Goncu, & Mosier, 1993). Children are surrounded by daily events that provide models for imitation, which reflect the culture of their families and communities. Toddlers rapidly accumulate the vocabulary of speech and action that belongs to their cultural group. How visitors are greeted when they arrive at the home; how adults groom themselves, dress, and speak to one another; how household tasks and chores are performed; how older children amuse themselves; how young people and older people treat each other—the thousands of words, gestures, and rituals of daily life make up the culture absorbed by watchful toddlers as they arm themselves with the resources to press toward autonomy.

# THE PRIME ADAPTIVE EGO QUALITY AND THE CORE PATHOLOGY

## WILL

Erikson et al. (1986) identified the prime adaptive ego quality that emerges through the successful resolution of the psychosocial crisis of toddlerhood as **will**—the capacity of the mind to direct and control action. It is closely linked to the idea of self-directed goal attainment. Will is the inner voice, focusing attention, encouraging, and urging one on, especially in the face of obstacles. It provides the psychological energy that allows people to press harder in competition, work to surpass previous achievements, and reach for new goals. In the face of disability, it is the force that urges the person to make peace with the loss and focus on alternate goals. In the face of crisis, people often refer to their will to survive or their will to live as the fundamental strength that kept them looking for new solutions or that prevented them from giving up hope. In older people who experience potentially spirit-crushing, painful losses or disabilities, will is the force that provides buoyancy as they learn to accept their decline, look for areas of continued mastery, and reflect nostalgically on past achievements.

Sometimes, we think of will in a negative way, as associated with stubbornness or overbearing dominance, that is, "bending to someone's will." But the meaning of will in the psychosocial context refers to the sense of inner determination and purpose that permits a person to set goals freely and make persistent efforts to achieve them. It reflects the positive connotation of the term *willpower*, the ability to sustain effort and delay gratification in order to achieve a long-term goal (Mischel & Ayduk, 2004). Will leads to a positive belief in oneself as someone who can make things happen. When you see a child struggling to carry a heavy box or drag a wagon filled with toys up a steep hill, you see will in action. When you watch an older child chew and twist a pencil trying to figure out a tough math problem, you see will in action. And when you go to the high school swimming pool at 6 in the morning and see students working out or swimming laps to get ready for an upcoming meet, you see will in action.

## COMPULSION

Will provides a voluntary energy and focus to action. In contrast, **compulsions** are repetitive behaviors that are motivated by impulse or by restrictions on the expression of it. They are nonspontaneous and unchanging. Compulsions are a close relative to the *ritualization* that is developed in toddlerhood. Children at this stage typically devise some well-ordered **rituals**, especially around important transitions such as going to bed, getting dressed, and leaving the house (Albert, Amgott, Krakow, & Marcus, 1977). They insist that these rituals be followed precisely and threaten to become extremely angry if the rituals are violated. Rituals represent efforts to bring control and order to the environment. They are often associated with fears, such as fear of strangers or separation from loved ones for younger children, or fears of environmental threats such as burglars or illness in somewhat older children (Evans, Gray, & Leckman, 1999). Rituals help provide feelings of sameness and continuity during changes in setting or state that may threaten toddler's feelings of selfhood.

Benjamin at 27 months, 17 days:

> His bedtime rituals are changing but still evident. He must be read to—as many books as the reader will stand for—and his music-box must be wound up. And I don't think he knows it's even possible to sleep any way except on the stomach. But he doesn't ask for his three old favorite stories to be told to him any more (thank heaven) and he doesn't always ask to be sung to—sometimes he wants one of three or four particular songs, but by no means always. (Church, 1966, p. 159)

Toddlers' rituals usually do not repeat adult ways of doing things; thus, they are not mere imitations of adult rituals.

Will reflects an inner determination to persist toward a goal. Cody shows his will as he drags the beach equipment out to the family spot.

© Robert Brenner/Photo Edit

Their rituals, however, like those of adults, serve the important psychological function of bringing order and a sense of mastery to the unknown or the unpredictable. This in turn provides a feeling of security as toddlers pursue well-learned behaviors that work and may also have private symbolic meaning. In comparison to adaptive rituals that actually provide a sense of comfort and relief from uncertainty, compulsions must be carried out again and again, never adequately resolving the anxiety that motivates them.

**Obsessions** are persistent, repetitive *thoughts* that serve as mechanisms for binding anxiety. *Compulsions* are repetitive, ritualized *actions* that serve the same function. The idea of binding anxiety means that the person feels that the thoughts or behaviors reduce some other source of distress. For instance, a person with a compulsive neurosis may become committed to repeated handwashing to rid the self of uncleanness. The compulsive handwasher "scrubs his hands in tortured solitude, until they become raw, and yet he never feels clean" (Erikson, 1977, p. 78). Over time, a neurosis may become very disruptive to daily life because it takes a lot of time, makes it hard to concentrate on tasks, and the person feels a loss of control.

In a sense, people who suffer from obsessions and compulsions have a damaged will. Their ability to willfully direct their thoughts and actions toward a goal is impaired. Rather, they feel that their thoughts and actions are being controlled by some powerful force outside their voluntary control. It is not the same as a hallucination. People with compulsions or obsessions do not think that someone from outer space or some voice from the spirit world is telling them what to do. They recognize the directive as coming from their mind, but not from their will.

Compulsions represent the ego's attempts to provide some structure to reality, but they do not work to promote further development because they are not meaningful (Erikson, 1982). The experience of the doubt-filled, shame-ridden person tends to be continuously unpleasant, uncertain, and sometimes tortuous. Life is enacted around carefully orchestrated patterns of meaningless, compulsive behaviors.

# THE IMPACT OF POVERTY ON PSYCHOSOCIAL DEVELOPMENT IN TODDLERHOOD

The Children's Defense Fund (2003) reported that 12.1 million or nearly 17% of U.S. children under the age of 18 live in poverty according to federal standards. This means that, if they lived in a three-person family, the family's annual income was $14,348 or less. In fact, this is much less than it costs to meet basic needs for housing, food, transportation, health care, and child care expenses. The United States has the distinction of the highest child poverty rate among 17 developed countries, with more than 13 million children suffering from food insecurity. These children do not consistently have access to food and may have to eat substandard food, inadequate meals, skip meals, or get their food from food pantries and shelters (Children's Defense Fund, 2003; Lott & Bullock, 2001).

Poverty is often associated with conditions that are disruptive to optimal development, including poor nutrition, inadequate health care, limited parental education, unstimulating parent–child interactions, and harsh punishment (Ramey, Campbell, & Ramey, 1999). Economic hardship produces emotional distress among parents, which is likely to result in harsh, neglectful, or erratic parent–child interactions (McLoyd, 1990). Mothers living in poverty are more likely than more affluent mothers to use power assertion and physical punishment as a form of discipline. Studies of the relationship of poverty to parenting practices and children's mental health have found that the amount of spanking parents use is directly related to the family's current level of poverty. This pattern has been observed in Black, Hispanic, and non-Hispanic White families. Furthermore, the more likely parents are to use spanking and harsh discipline—especially when it is used without accompanying emotional support or warmth—the more likely their children are to show signs of emotional distress (depression, fearfulness, and crying) and externally directed behaviors such as arguing, disobedience, destructiveness, and impulsiveness (Conger et al., 2002; McLeod & Shanahan, 1993; McLoyd & Smith, 2002).

Parents living in poverty tend to emphasize obedience and are less likely to use reasons and explanations in their discipline practices. They are less likely to reward their children through praise and encouragement and less likely to ask their children for their ideas and opinions. In general, parents living in poverty have been characterized as less sensitive to their child's needs and less emotionally supportive. This approach to parenting may be due in large part to the emotional distress created by the conditions of poverty. Frustration and anger at poverty may give way to feelings of worthlessness, victimization, and loss of control. These factors are often associated with both physical and mental health problems that can be expressed in pessimism, loss of hope, depression, drug and alcohol abuse, and psychosomatic ailments (McLoyd, 1990).

Another explanation for the use of harsh parenting that emphasizes obedience is the fact that poor families are more likely to live in high-risk neighborhoods, where children are likely to be exposed to violence (Ceballo & McLoyd, 2002). As a result, parents in poverty worry more about their children's safety and may be more emotionally reactive when children defy their authority.

From a psychosocial perspective, one might ask how poverty influences the developmental tasks of toddlerhood—the elaboration of locomotion, the experiences of fantasy and

These Iranian children live in a neighborhood that has experienced prolonged poverty. They play in the streets where they come into contact with trash, pollutants, and crumbling buildings. They also face inadequate shelter, malnutrition, and lack of health care.

play, learning language, and the development of self-control. How do the conditions of poverty affect the expression of autonomy or the experiences of shame and doubt?

Current literature does not address these questions directly. Despite wide social interest and extensive policy debates regarding the needs of children who live in poverty, little research has focused on the consequences of poverty for specific developmental tasks. Toddlers are probably not directly aware of their poverty status. In comparison to older children who might understand from watching television, reading the newspaper, or interacting with other children in school that they are in a relatively impoverished situation, toddlers are not likely to have any comparative perspective. They assume that what they experience from day to day is what most everyone experiences. Toddlers probably do not feel shame about being poor, nor do they define themselves in this way. Poverty probably does not produce the same level of frustration and anger for toddlers as it does for adolescents or adults.

However, toddlers suffer the direct effects of poverty. Two major consequences of poverty are poor health and inadequate nutrition. A national study found that children from families with incomes below the poverty level were three times more likely to be in poor health than were children from families with incomes above $35,000. Many children from low-income families have no regular source of health care and have not been immunized for measles and other infectious diseases. Repeated bouts of illness combined with poor nutrition detract from a child's energy. The combination of malnutrition and illness has multiple consequences,

including the possibility of structural brain damage, lethargy, delayed physical growth, and, as a result, minimal exploration of the environment. All these factors taken together produce what has been observed as delayed psychomotor and cognitive development in toddlerhood (Brown & Pollitt, 1996; Pollitt, 1994). Poor health in childhood has a lasting impact on adult health (Halfon, Inkelas, & Hochstein, 2000).

Other aspects of poverty may interfere with the achievement of developmental tasks. Living in especially crowded conditions with many other children and adults may result in limited exploration; moreover, many poor neighborhoods lack safe play spaces in or near the home (Bradley et al., 1994). Lack of access to a variety of play materials may have a negative impact on language development as well as symbolic play. Crowding may also make it difficult for toddlers to have the private, uninterrupted space or permission for fantasy. On the other hand, some children may make use of fantasy to block out some of the more negative or troubling aspects of their environment or use fantasy to create an inner space where their situation is less stark. Language development may be deterred if parents or caregivers do not interact much with their toddlers, if they tell their children what to do rather than involve them in discussion, or if they consistently tell their children to be quiet and not to speak. Harsh parenting has been found to interfere with the development of self-regulation. If parenting is chaotic and unpredictable, or if the levels of anger and aggression in the home are high, children may find it difficult to organize or direct their behavior in any systematic way.

# CHILD CARE

EVERY PERSON WHO expects to combine parenting and employment or schooling must give some thought to how to provide child care during his or her absence. In the United States, child care arrangements constitute a highly diverse market, especially when compared with kindergarten through 12th-grade public education (Holloway & Fuller, 1992). Child care in the United States is covered by minimal federal and state regulations. Thus, children are in the care of a wide range of caregivers with varying types of education and training, from no specific background and training at all to bachelor's and master's degrees.

Table 7.3 summarizes the child care arrangements for children under 6 who have not yet entered kindergarten. In 2001, 74% of children were involved in some type of nonparental care. This is an increase from 69% in 1991. The largest group, 56.4%, was in center-based care, which includes day care centers, Head Start programs, preschool, prekindergarten, and other early childhood programs (U.S. Census Bureau, 2003). Arrangements vary by race/ethnicity and household income. Households with higher incomes ($50,000 or more) are more likely to make some type of nonparental arrangement for their children and are most likely to use center-based programs. Hispanic families are less likely to make nonparental arrangements than other racial/ethnic groups. African American families are more likely to involve relatives in the care of their children.

Child care arrangements reflect a variety of philosophies about the care of young children, wide differences in curriculum, and a wide range of physical settings. The *laissez faire* approach to the care of toddlers seems to reflect a cultural belief that the nurturance and socialization of young children is primarily the responsibility of the family, whereas the schooling

**Table 7.3** Patterns of Child Care in the United States: 1991–2001

| CHARACTERISTIC | Children | | Type of nonparental arrangement[1] | | | |
| | NUMBER (1,000) | % DISTRIBUTION | IN RELATIVE CARE | IN NONRELATIVE CARE | IN CENTER-BASED PROGRAM[2] | WITH PARENTAL CARE ONLY |
|---|---|---|---|---|---|---|
| 1991, total | 8,428 | 100.0 | 16.9 | 14.8 | 52.8 | 31.0 |
| 1995, total | 9,232 | 100.0 | 19.4 | 16.9 | 55.1 | 25.9 |
| 2001, total | 8,551 | 100.0 | 22.8 | 14.1 | 56.4 | 26.1 |
| **Age:** | | | | | | |
| 3 years old | 3,795 | 44.4 | 23.6 | 14.7 | 42.8 | 33.8 |
| 4 years old | 3,861 | 45.1 | 22.5 | 13.6 | 65.9 | 20.4 |
| 5 years old | 896 | 10.5 | 20.9 | 13.1 | 73.0 | 18.0 |
| **Race-ethnicity:** | | | | | | |
| White, non-Hispanic | 5,313 | 62.1 | 19.6 | 16.5 | 59.1 | 25.3 |
| Black, non-Hispanic | 1,251 | 14.6 | 36.7 | 8.5 | 63.1 | 15.1 |
| Hispanic | 1,506 | 17.6 | 22.8 | 11.3 | 39.9 | 39.0 |
| Other | 482 | 5.6 | 22.8 | 10.8 | 61.8 | 23.7 |
| **Household income:** | | | | | | |
| Less than $10,001 | 951 | 11.1 | 37.1 | 6.2 | 45.6 | 30.5 |
| $10,001 to $20,000 | 1,156 | 13.5 | 23.5 | 10.8 | 50.6 | 32.3 |
| $20,001 to $30,000 | 1,134 | 13.3 | 24.3 | 10.4 | 49.3 | 32.4 |
| $30,001 to $40,000 | 978 | 11.4 | 24.5 | 12.6 | 48.9 | 32.2 |
| $40,001 to $50,000 | 822 | 9.6 | 21.9 | 15.2 | 42.9 | 36.4 |
| $50,001 to $75,000 | 1,724 | 20.2 | 20.7 | 18.6 | 62.3 | 20.9 |
| $75,001 or more | 1,788 | 20.9 | 15.3 | 18.6 | 75.1 | 12.8 |

[1] Columns do not add to 100.0 because some children participated in more than one type of nonparental arrangement.

[2] Center-based programs include day care centers, Head Start programs, preschools, prekindergarten, and nursery schools.

Source: U.S. Census Bureau. (2003), *Statistical abstract of the United States: 2003*, Table No. 577.

of children over the age of 5 is a public concern. However, most early childhood experts will agree that there are markers of quality care that have an impact on children's daily experiences as well as on their long-term cognitive, emotional, and social development. These markers include advanced training in the field of child development and early childhood education for the caregivers; a small caregiver-to-child ratio and smaller group size; a safe, clean, environment; and sensitive, developmentally appropriate interactions between caregivers and children (Honig, 2002).

Because of the growing national need for child care and the wide choice of child care arrangements, parents, educators, and policymakers are asking such critical questions as, "How does day care influence the development of young children?" "What is our obligation to ensure quality day care for the children of working parents?" "What is our obligation as a society to meet the health, nutrition, and safety needs of the children of poor parents?"

Assessments of child care's effects on young children generally focus on intellectual abilities, socioemotional development, and peer relations. Research has tended to emphasize the impact of child care on the children of families living in poverty, because they are at a higher risk for school failure, illiteracy, and subsequent minimal employment or unemployment, even though they are less likely to be enrolled in center-based care than families with more resources. Many studies focus on Head Start—a federally funded early childhood program that has a complex mission, including education, health, mental health, and family support. However, until recently, Head Start was structured as a preschool enrichment program rather than full day care. Not all child care programs have the same educational emphasis or developmental curriculum as Head Start. Many studies that investigate the impact of child care do not systematically control for the differences in program focus, services, and hours of service that exist among public and private day care and preschool programs.

## THE IMPACT OF CHILD CARE ON INTELLIGENCE AND ACADEMIC ACHIEVEMENT

Increasingly, researchers agree that the effect of quality day care on toddlers is positive but modest (Azar, 1997). The research literature is still developing, and many questions are still unanswered, but data from model programs show that quality day care contributes to intellectual achievement, as reflected in higher IQ scores, both during the preschool years and during the first grade (Burchinal et al., 2000). Because of the questionable validity of IQ scores for very young children and for children from various racial and ethnic subgroups, the focus on IQ as an indication of program impact may be

inadequate. Thus, recent studies have focused on more specific competencies such as language ability, cognitive problem solving, and motivation for school and school achievement as evidence of the long-term impact of child care on intellectual development.

The National Institute of Child Health and Human Development (NICHD) is carrying out a longitudinal study of the effects of early child care (Owen, 1997; National Institutes of Health, 2000). The primary aim of the study is to learn what impact child care has on developmental outcomes above and beyond the influence of family and home environment. In this study, 1,300 children under 1 month of age and their families were identified as participants from 10 sites across the United States. The study, initiated in 1991, followed up the children until age 7. Families varied by race, income, family structure, mother's education and employment status, and the number of hours children spent in nonparental care. The kinds of care included that given by grandparents and other relatives, by a nonrelative in the home, in a home-based setting, and in a center. The quality of care was measured with a focus on caregiver interactions that are expected to promote positive emotions, social competence, and cognitive and language skills. Overall, the results to date indicate an important link between quality care and children's subsequent development:

> Positive care giving is measured by observing and documenting the frequency of interaction, and then rating the quality of the interaction. The child care settings were also measured both in terms of their "regulable" characteristics, or guidelines recommended by governments, such as group size, child/adult ratio, and physical environment; and of the care giver's characteristics, such as formal education, specialized training, child care experience, and beliefs about child rearing.

> The research team found that child care situations with safer, cleaner, more stimulating physical environments and smaller group sizes, lower child/adult ratios, and care givers who allowed children to express their feelings and took their views into account, also had care givers who were observed to provide more sensitive, responsive, and cognitively stimulating care—quality of care that was expected to be associated with better developmental outcomes for children. (Retrieved July 29, 2001, from http://www.nichd.nih.gov/publications/pubs/early_child_care.htm)

For more detailed information about this national longitudinal study, visit the NICHD website at http://secc.rti.org/

Current findings from this research suggest that family variables, including income, mother's vocabulary, home environment, and the way mothers stimulate their babies to promote cognitive growth, were *more important* predictors of the child's cognitive development than the quality of child care. However, after all these family factors were taken into account, the quality of language stimulation directed to the child in the child care setting made a significant additional contribution to children's language and cognitive competence measured at ages 2 and 3 (NICHD Early Child Care Research Network, 2002).

Children in higher quality care had higher scores on measures of infant development and school readiness. After controlling for quality of child care settings, the research found that children who did not attend any type of formal child care and were cared for at home performed just as well as those who attended quality care programs. Those who were cared for in family day care in their infancy performed better at age 3 than did those in other types of non-family care (National Institutes of Health, 2000).

In addition to test score benefits, children who have participated in model programs and Head Start are less likely to be placed in special education classrooms or to be held back a grade. These advantages are of significance in thinking about the trade-off in costs and benefits of providing early educational experiences to children at risk of school failure (Haskins, 1989).

The Perry Preschool Project, a model program that has carried out extensive longitudinal research on its participants, has seen a number of indications of academic success. In the mid-1960s, 123 African American children from very low-income families were selected to participate in this program. They were randomly assigned to a quality preschool intervention or to no preschool. At age 19, children who had attended a quality preschool program had higher grades, fewer failing grades, a more positive attitude toward school, and a higher literacy rate than a comparable group of young adults living in poverty who had not participated in a quality child care program (Schweinhart & Weikart, 1988). Most (95%) of those who had participated in the study were re-interviewed at age 27. The group that had the preschool experience continued to show evidence of the benefits of their early childhood education. Those who had attended the quality preschool were 30% more likely to have graduated from high school or received their GED. They were four times more likely to be earning $2,000 or more per month, and three times more likely to own their own homes (High/Scope, 2003).

## THE IMPACT OF CHILD CARE ON SOCIAL COMPETENCE

Quality care is also associated with higher levels of social competence, self-esteem, and empathy. Children who interact positively with adults in their day care settings are more likely to continue to interact positively and comfortably with their teachers and classmates in the elementary grades (Vandell, Henderson, & Wilson, 1988). Some studies have found that children with more hours of child care experience are less compliant with their parents' wishes than children who have not been in day care. The study conducted by NICHD helps explain these findings. The more time children spent in nonmaternal care, the less responsive mothers were to their children at ages 15 and 36 months, and the less affectionate the child was to the mother at 24 and 36 months (NICHD Early Child Care Research Network, 2002; Owen, 1997). These findings were strongest for children who were in low-quality care for the longest time periods. One might infer that mothers who are separated from their children for long peri-

*Social competence is enhanced in quality child care through experiences in taking turns, helping, sharing, and coordination of pretend play.*

© David Young-Wolff/Photo Edit

ods each day become less attuned to their children's cues and less effective in establishing an effective communicative rhythm. At the same time, children who are exposed to low-quality alternative care do not have the support for effective self-control and communicative competence that are experienced in higher quality settings.

Few of the evaluations of model programs or Head Start have addressed long-term social consequences. However, results from the Perry Preschool Project showed that by age 19, fewer of the children studied had committed delinquent acts or had been processed by the courts, fewer had been on welfare, and more had been employed (Barnett, 1996). In the follow-up at age 27, those who had been enrolled in the quality preschool program were less likely to have been arrested for drug dealing, men had been married longer, women were more likely to be married and less likely to have had a child out of wedlock (High/Scope, 2003).

## THE IMPACT OF CHILD CARE ON PEER RELATIONS

Quality child care also has an impact on peer relations. Children benefit from opportunities to interact with a variety of peers in settings where adults are readily available to help them make choices and resolve differences. The quality and complexity of social play are especially enhanced when children remain in the same child care setting rather than moving from one arrangement to another. In stable conditions, toddlers, whose verbal skills are limited, expand their strategies for coordinating their play with others and for exploring shared fantasies. Children who are growing up in difficult and impoverished life circumstances are especially likely to benefit from stable, consistent caregiving practices, where they can form a secure attachment to the caregivers and experience calm, friendly interactions with peers (Ritchie & Howes, 2003). Long-term benefits for peer relations were observed for the participants of the Perry Preschool Project when, at age 19, they were more likely to report that they provided help to their friends and family than were comparison participants, but they were less likely to volunteer without pay for community service (Schweinhart & Weikart, 1988).

As Head Start is more comprehensive than most preschool or child care programs, it is worthwhile to consider its additional benefits for children (Zigler & Styfco, 2004). In 30 studies that reported on the health impact of Head Start, the data showed that participating children are more likely to get a wide variety of examinations and assessments covering medical and dental health, speech and hearing, vision, and nutrition. All of these opportunities allow a direct response to young children's physical needs when their parents may not be aware of emerging problems or are unsure how to address them. Because Head Start provides meals, young children in the program have a much higher daily nutritional intake than similar children who are not in the program. Thus, Head Start succeeds in bringing to young children essential benefits that they are not receiving through their families.

As an additional benefit, Head Start has had a positive impact on families and communities. An estimated 30,000 parents and community members have been involved in some form of training and career development. Head Start has created an estimated 76,000 jobs, the majority of which are held by minority members in the communities where the programs are located. These benefits empower adults to influence the quality of education in their communities and broaden their understanding of the educational process (Haskins, 1989; Holloway & Fuller, 1992).

## DIRECTIONS FOR THE FUTURE OF CHILD CARE IN THE UNITED STATES

The United States faces a critical gap between the demand for *affordable, quality* child care and its availability. Although the number of child care settings appears to be ample, those that meet the standards of high quality are comparatively scarce. For example, about 31,000 children 4 years old and younger were treated in U.S. hospital emergency rooms for injuries in child care and school settings in 1997; 8,000 of these injuries occurred from falls on playgrounds. In a study conducted by the U.S. Consumer Product Safety Commission in 1998, 220 licensed child care settings were evaluated for the presence of possible safety hazards. The safety hazards monitored in this study included unsafe cribs, soft crib bedding, improper playground surfacing, poorly maintained playground surfacing, absence of child safety gates at the top of stairs, loops hanging from the window blind cords, drawstrings around the necks in children's clothing, and recalled children's products. The study reported that two thirds of the settings showed at least one of these hazards (Consumer Product Safety Commission, 1999).

Concern about the need for affordable, quality child care is expressed by parents who are in the labor market as well as by those who would like to be in the labor market. The United States now has a national parental-leave policy, so that parents can take time off to care for their newborns without risking the loss of their jobs. But concerns about child care continue throughout toddlerhood and well into the elementary school years, when children need adult supervision before and after school hours. Services for certain groups, including children with disabilities, those whose parents have evening work schedules, children who are ill, and those who need year-round programs, are in short supply. Furthermore, the supply of quality centers is unevenly distributed, so that many families in low-income communities do not have access to quality care (Fuller, Kagan, Caspary, & Gauthier, 2002).

Changes in national welfare policies place new pressures on the need for affordable, quality child care services. In the past, for example, Head Start programs, which have been an important resource to children in low-income families, have not offered full day care. However, as mothers of young children who were previously receiving welfare benefits are required to enter the labor market, they need to find full day care for their children. Consider the dilemma of a woman who was trying to locate quality care for her child:

> I called child care agencies. . . . And I interviewed all the people they [the state] gave me with licenses. I sat in some

of the places for quite a while. I saw drugs being sold in and out of those places. I found one place I thought my daughter would be secure. She was sexually abused. I think that was the thing that really gave it to me then: I quit my job and went fully back on the welfare system. (Scarbrough, 2001, p. 267)

Quality, affordable child care is one of the primary resources that single parents rely on in order to stay off welfare. Without some form of child care subsidy, women cannot support themselves and their families on what they are typically able to earn in jobs that pay a minimum wage.

## Chapter Summary

The developmental tasks of toddlerhood support children's ability to find order and consistency in their world and to express the self. Locomotive skills heighten toddlers' sense of mastery and expand their boundaries of experience. Language is both a tool for the expression of feelings and concepts and a primary mechanism of socialization. Toddlers' use of language gives us clues to their cognitive development and their needs. Through language, children influence others, gain access to worlds of information, and learn new strategies for the control and expression of their impulses. The emergence of fantasy provides toddlers with an internal, personal form of symbolic representation. Fantasy allows a pseudomastery in which barriers are overcome and the limitations of reality are less important. Conflicts can be acted out and pretend solutions can be found. Fantasy may be enhanced by language, but it thrives even in the absence of words. Efforts at self-control—both impulse regulation and self-directed goal attainment—begin in toddlerhood and continue through life.

The psychosocial crisis of autonomy versus shame and doubt reflects the child's needs for self-expression and mastery. Young children develop individuality by exercising the skills that develop during toddlerhood. Self-doubts result from repeated ridicule, shame, and failure. The adaptive ego quality of will, directly linked to self-directed goal attainment, emerges in a positive resolution of this crisis. In the context of shame and doubt, the child is likely to rely more and more on compulsive, ritualized behaviors.

Autonomy and individuation ordinarily emerge in the context of the parent–child relationship. Toddlers are avid observers, imitating and incorporating parental behaviors and values into their own routines. Parental interaction, acceptance, and discipline all contribute to a child's emerging sense of individuality. However, living in poverty increases the likelihood that parents will be psychologically unavailable

or will use harsh, restrictive disciplinary strategies that produce shame or unexpressed rage in their young children.

Increasing numbers of young children are being cared for in group settings. The impact of child care depends heavily on the quality of the personnel, the nature of the program, and an appropriate physical environment. Many studies suggest that quality child care contributes to the toddler's optimal development. A major concern, however, is the availability of affordable, quality care to those families that need it.

## Further Reflection

1. What do you recall from your childhood about the emergence of locomotor activities? In what ways do motor skills continue to contribute to your sense of autonomy and mastery as an adult?
2. Reflect on the words *language*, *thought*, and *speech*. What are the differences among these three? How are they interconnected?
3. How does the capacity for pretense contribute to development in childhood? How would you evaluate our contemporary U.S. society with respect to the value it places on fantasy play in childhood? In adulthood?
4. Why is self-control emphasized as a primary developmental task in toddlerhood? How does it relate to the theme of autonomy versus shame and doubt? How do individual differences in self-control play out in later stages of childhood and adolescence?
5. How does culture influence the expression of the psychosocial crisis of autonomy versus shame and doubt? What are the societal forces that foster the sense of autonomy in toddlerhood? What are the forces that create a sense of shame and doubt?
6. Imagine that you have to decide about child care arrangements for your child. Given what you have read

about the developmental tasks and the psychosocial crisis of toddlerhood, what are some of the features of the child care arrangement that would be most important in your decision?

## On the Web

### VISIT OUR WEBSITE

Go to http://www.wadsworth.com/psychology to find online resources directly linked to your book.

## Casebook

For additional case material related to this chapter, see the case of "Little Raymond" in *Life Span Development: A Case Book*, by Barbara and Philip Newman, Laura Landry-Meyer, and Brenda J. Lohman, pp. 77–80. The case illustrates ways in which a toddler uses language and fantasy to cope with frustration when Mom's boyfriend interferes with his play.

# CHAPTER 8

# EARLY SCHOOL AGE (4–6 YEARS)

*Claude in Blue*, 1950/Pablo Picasso/© 2005 Estate of Pablo Picasso/Artists Rights Society (ARS), New York

*Starting school brings an expansion of the child's social world: encounters with new adults and peers, new social norms, higher expectations, and new information. Each of these changes has an effect on the child's self-concept.*

220

■ DEVELOPMENTAL TASKS

Gender Identification

CASE STUDY: GENDER IDENTIFICATION
IN EARLY CHILDHOOD

Early Moral Development

CASE STUDY: EARLY LEARNING ABOUT OBEDIENCE

Self-Theory
Peer Play

■ THE PSYCHOSOCIAL CRISIS: INITIATIVE VERSUS GUILT

Initiative
Guilt

■ THE CENTRAL PROCESS: IDENTIFICATION

■ THE PRIME ADAPTIVE EGO QUALITY
AND THE CORE PATHOLOGY

Purpose
Inhibition

■ APPLIED TOPIC: SCHOOL READINESS

Defining Readiness
Measuring Kindergarten Readiness
Obstacles to School Readiness
Who Is Responsible for Meeting the Goal for School Readiness?

■ CHAPTER SUMMARY

■ FURTHER REFLECTION

## CHAPTER OBJECTIVES

▶ *To describe the process of gender identification during early school age and its importance for the way a child interprets his or her experiences.*

▶ *To describe the process of early moral development, drawing from theories and research to explain how knowledge, emotion, and action combine to produce internalized morality.*

▶ *To analyze changes in the self-theory, with special focus on the theory of mind and self-esteem during the early-school-age years.*

▶ *To explore the transition to more complex group play and the process of friendship development in the early school-age years.*

▶ *To explain the psychosocial crisis of initiative versus guilt, the central process of identification, the prime adaptive ego function of purpose, and the core pathology of inhibition.*

▶ *To analyze the construct of school readiness, its relation to the developmental tasks of early school age, and the obstacles that may prevent children from being able to adapt and learn in the school environment.*

THE PERIOD OF *early school age* brings children face to face with new and complex socialization forces. By the age of 6, virtually all children in the United States are enrolled in school. Children today are encountering school or school-like experiences at earlier ages than in the past. In 2001, 52% of 3- and 4-year-olds were enrolled in school, an increase from 20% in 1970 (U.S. Census Bureau, 2003). Thus, it has become *normative* for children to be enrolled in some type of schooling before the age that the law requires. School brings new information and experiences, new opportunities for success and failure, and new settings for peer group formation. School is a new source of influence on the child beyond the family. Beliefs and practices followed at home may come under scrutiny and be challenged by teachers or classmates. Parents' personal hopes and aspirations for their children may be tempered by the reality of the children's school performance.

Most early-school-age children exhibit wide-ranging curiosity about all facets of life. "How does this work?" "Why is that the rule?" "Why can't I do that?" The child's self-concept is transformed in coordination with his or her exposure to new socialization voices. In addition to family and school, the peer group, neighborhood, and television all influence children's self-concept during early school age. Once children become aware of alternatives to their own families' rules and patterns, they begin to question familiar notions. The press toward *independence of action* seen in the toddler is now accompanied by a new *independence of thought* in the early-school-age child. ■

# DEVELOPMENTAL TASKS

During the early-school-age period, between the ages of 4 and 6, children are constructing a broad overview of how their interpersonal world is structured and where they fit in. They are devising a scheme for self in society. Because children's life experiences are limited and because they are still highly impressionable, the nature of this initial worldview is likely to be very compelling, permeating their outlook in the years ahead. The lessons from early childhood about what it means to be a good person, to be a "good" boy or girl, man or woman, to be cherished or despised are established at a deep emotional and cognitive level. These ideas are intertwined with feelings of being safe, loved, and admired or neglected, rejected, or abused. As a result, the basic beliefs about oneself and others that are formed at this time are often difficult to review or revise.

In this chapter, four developmental tasks are discussed that contribute to the child's capacity to construct a worldview. The topic of **gender identification** includes a discussion of the physical, cognitive, emotional, and social domains as they become integrated into an early scheme for thinking of oneself as male or female. Issues of right and wrong surface constantly as a result of the child's newly acquired abilities for independent thought and exposure to a much wider range of social influences. These experiences provide the basis for early **moral development**. Understanding and experiencing the self expands markedly during early school age. This developmental task centers on the acquisition of a personal **self-theory** that becomes increasingly complex because it is being

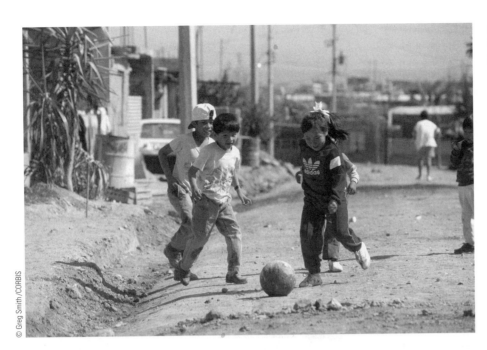

*In early school age, children's worlds expand as they spend more time with playmates in their neighborhood.*

stimulated by expanding social influences. Accompanying the development of the self-theory is the development of a set of complex feelings about the self called *self-esteem*. A fourth area involves new levels of participation in **peer play**. Through the process of learning the rules and playing cooperatively with others, children begin to form meaningful friendships and mental representations of ways of participating in groups.

## GENDER IDENTIFICATION

Every human society has patterns of organization based partially on **gender**. Male and female individuals are often assigned different roles, engage in different tasks, have access to different resources, and are viewed as having different powers and attributes. The specific content of these gender roles varies widely from one culture to another. As children form their concept of gender identity, they must integrate their own physical experiences, knowledge, and observations with the socialization messages coming to them from parents, siblings, peers, and other salient voices of the culture.

## CASE STUDY

### GENDER IDENTIFICATION IN EARLY CHILDHOOD

*Lee, a mother of six children, recalls with warmth and humor her early childhood years growing up in New Mexico in the 1920s and 1930s.*

I was born in the southern part of New Mexico in Ruidoso. The town was up in the pines in the mountains and was mostly just a main street that followed the river. There was a meadow on one side of the river with a lot of Indian arrowheads and shards and the biggest grasshoppers in the world. I used to go catch grasshoppers and find arrowheads, and my cousin Bob and I would wander around by ourselves.

My father was a carpenter and my mother had planned to be a nurse until she stopped and got married. I think my father must have really wanted a son because I was quite a tomboy and grew up as his only son. I helped him dig and move rocks instead of learning how to cook and sew. We had a large family, uncles and aunts and a grandmother and great aunt, with houses right next to each other and big, traditional holiday dinners with everybody there.

My cousin Bob was two years younger than I was and we were inseparable. . . . He was a rough, tough little kid. We ran around without coats in the winter and hardly ever got sick, and he and I grew up together. It was almost like two boys because we used to go to the river and fish with our hands and churn the fish over a little fire and try to eat it. We just grew up like little wild things. My parents expected me to be on the premises by nightfall, but that was about it. We played cowboys and Indians with the other kids in the neighborhood, and we never played with girls at all; they were really something to be scorned. But he was allowed to cuss and have good tantrums that I wasn't allowed to have.

My mother always provided books and she would tell stories about Huckleberry Finn. The river in our town was much too small for a raft; it was rocky and was just a stream, but we'd pretend rafts and imagine running away. One time I got tied up on an Indian raid and left there, and I was too stubborn to call for help, so I was there past supper time and my mother found me and brought me in.

I was always tearing up my clothes, and my mother was always tearing me up about that. I think she would have liked to have a daughter. It wasn't until my sister Barbara was born that she had a daughter. Barbara had long curls and was pretty feminine. That way mother had the daughter to play with and daddy had the son and everything was all right.

Source: Excerpt from *Dignity: Lower Income Women Tell of Their Lives and Struggles,* by F. L. Buss, pp. 173–173. Copyright © 1985 University of Michigan Press.

## ■ CRITICAL THINKING AND CASE ANALYSIS

1. What aspects of the formation of gender identification are captured in this narrative?
2. What are the salient images of mother and father that Lee may have identified with?
3. What role might the rural, small-town environment have played in Lee's experiences of gender identification in early childhood?
4. How much of Lee's preference for rough-and-tumble play do you attribute to her desire to be "the son" for her father? How much do you attribute to her temperament and other aspects of her personality?
5. From what you have read, and drawing on your own experiences, how might Lee's gender identification at this period of her life influence her later relationships with male and female peers, and her capacity to form intimate relationships in later adolescence or early adulthood?

## ■ INDIVIDUAL DIFFERENCES VERSUS CONSTRUCTIVISM

The debate about gender is not whether gender differences exist but rather how to explain them. Two perspectives on this topic are the view that gender differences are a result of *individual differences* between boys and girls, and the view that gender differences are *constructed* in specific interpersonal contexts as a product of the social situation and cultural expectations for behavior (Bohan, 1993; Thompson, 1993). The **individual differences** perspective suggests that gender differences reside within the individual as persistent, internal attributes. Whether the differences are a result of biology, socialization, or an interaction between the two, this perspective suggests that differences between boys and girls are stable characteristics that individuals bring to various situations.

The research about sex differences in the organization of the brain is an example of this perspective. Male brains have more white matter—that is, the long fibers that help transmit information from the brain to the body—and less gray matter—where information is processed—than female brains (Gur et al., 1999). Furthermore, the bundle of nerves that connects the right and left hemispheres is thicker in female brains than in male brains, allowing information to cross between the two parts of the brain more quickly in girls. The exact relationship between brain structure and behavior is not fully understood (Kelly, Ostrowski, & Wilson, 1999).

Some researchers believe that these differences help account for the fact that girls speak earlier and have an easier time learning language and communication skills than boys. In comparison, boys show greater competence and enjoyment in gross motor activity.

There is also some evidence that the way the brain processes emotion differs in girls and boys. For boys, emotions are processed in the limbic system, which is a primitive area of the brain and more likely to be linked to action. For girls, emotions are processed in an area of the brain close to the speech center, making it easier for girls to talk about their emotional reactions. Boys actually have more intense reactions to emotionally arousing stimuli, but they are less likely to express their feelings. For example, when boys and girls were put in a room where they could hear a baby crying, the boys showed a greater increase in heart rate and more physical signs of stress than the girls (Mulrane, 2001).

The **constructivist** perspective suggests that gender differences are a product of particular interactions that have a socially agreed-upon, gender-related meaning. In this view, the specific behaviors that are described as masculine or feminine depend largely on the situation, including expectations that people will behave in gender-appropriate ways. For example, in a study of social interaction between pairs of toddlers (Jacklin & Maccoby, 1978; Maccoby, 1990), one variable measured was the amount of time one partner stood watching while the other child played with the toys. Standing by and watching was a behavior that the researchers called *passive*. In same-sex pairs, girls were rarely passive, but in mixed-sex pairs, the girl frequently stood watching while the boy played with the toys. This kind of finding is replicated at older ages, showing that girls and boys, men and women, interact in stereotypically gender-defined ways, particularly when they are observed in public settings and in mixed-sex groups.

We cannot resolve the debate about whether gender differences are traits located in individuals or constructed by the way individuals interact. As discussed earlier, both views have merit and evidence to support them. Because cultures tend to intervene very early to assess a child's biological sex and impart the related gender expectations, it is difficult to know how much of behavior is constructed and how much is a result of individual differences. The most useful approach to evaluating these positions appears to be one in which behavior in same-sex groups is compared to behavior in mixed-sex groups, or where behavior in private is compared to socially observable behavior (Aries, 1998).

In this and other discussions of gender identification, you will want to differentiate among three concepts: sex, gender, and sexual orientation. **Sex** refers to biologically linked features or distinctions that are determined by chromosomal information. An infant's external genitalia are typically used as the evidence to determine sex. In most cases, the chromosomes and the hormones that are produced in the prenatal period converge to produce an unambiguous sex. However, there are exceptions of chromosomally male (XY) individuals who have undeveloped male genitalia and are identified as female at birth; and chromosomally female (XX) individuals who have hormonal imbalances that result in the appearance of male genitalia (Crooks & Bauer, 2005). **Gender** refers to the integrated cognitive, social, and emotional schemes associated with being male or female. In childhood, gender includes coming to see oneself as a boy or girl in one's family, friendship group, and community, and also sensing how well one meets the social expectations for a boy or girl. **Sexual orientation** refers to one's preference for sexually intimate partners. The three common sexual orientations discussed in the literature are *heterosexual*, *homosexual*, and *bisexual*. Sexual orientation is not a primary topic of discussion in this chapter.

Our goal in the discussion that follows is to understand how young children begin to conceptualize gender as a dimension of their self-concept, an organizing principle of social life, and a guide to their behavior. We do not expect a lifetime's work on gender identity to have been completed by 6 years of age. During this period, however, significant conceptual and emotional changes give gender greater clarity and highlight the relevance of one's gender in each child's overall self-concept. The four components of gender identification that are included are (1) understanding the concept of gender; (2) learning gender role standards and stereotypes; (3) identifying with parents; and (4) forming a gender preference.

## ■ UNDERSTANDING GENDER

Understanding one's gender involves four components that emerge in a developmental sequence from toddlerhood through early school age (Kohlberg, 1966; Martin, Ruble, & Szkrybalo, 2002): (1) applying the correct gender label to themselves and others, (2) understanding that gender is stable, (3) understanding gender constancy, and (4) understanding the genital basis of gender (see Figure 8.1). According to this analysis, children construct the meaning of gender, including the stability and constancy of their own gender and the gendered nature of their society, in much the same way that they form other cognitive schemes such as object permanence, which was discussed in Chapter 6 (Infancy) or conservation of matter, which will be discussed in Chapter 9 (Middle Childhood).

The correct use of **gender labels** is the earliest component of gender identification to be achieved. The categorization of people as male and female is a natural category, much like the distinction between the familiar person and the stranger or between people and inanimate objects, as discussed in Chapter 6. Even before the abstract categories *male* and *female* are understood, children learn to refer to themselves as boys or girls by imitating their parents. From infancy, parents make continual reference to a child's gender in such statements as "That's a good boy" or "That's a good girl."

By the age of 2½, children can accurately label other children as boys or girls, and by the age of 3, they can accurately sort photographs of boys and girls. They can also apply gender labels such as *Mommy* and *Daddy*, *brother* and *sister*, and *boy* and *girl* accurately (Thompson, 1975; Leinbach & Fagot, 1986). Once they know these labels, children seek out cues to help them make these distinctions correctly, like hair style, clothes, or body shape. Their attention is directed to the differences between male and female individuals.

Understanding **gender constancy** appears to emerge somewhat later, usually between ages 4 and 7 (Serbin,

1. Correct use of the gender labels.

2. Gender is stable.

3. Gender is constant.

4. Gender has a genital basis.

**FIGURE 8.1**

Four Components of the Concept of Gender

Powlishta, & Gulko, 1993; Levy, 1998). Understanding the genital basis of gender provides a fundamental context for understanding that gender is constant. In research involving 3-, 4-, and 5-year-olds, the majority of children who understood the genital differences between the sexes could also tell that a child's sex did not change simply because the child was dressed up to look like a member of the opposite sex. These young children understood that sex is a constant feature of a person, no matter how the person is dressed or whether the hair is long or short. In contrast, the majority of the children who had no knowledge of genital differences were unable to respond correctly to questions about constancy (Bem, 1989).

## ■ GENDER ROLE STANDARDS

**Gender role standards** are cultural expectations about appropriate behavior for boys and girls and for men and women. One might consider these *sex stereotypes*. If you had no information about a person other than whether the person was male or female, what qualities would you attribute to that person? How would you expect the person to behave? For young children, this usually means the kinds of toys, clothes, and activities that would be preferred by boys or girls.

In research on gender role standards, children are asked to identify whether certain activities, occupations, or traits are more frequently associated with male individuals, female individuals, or both. For example, in the *Sex-Role Learning Index*, children are shown drawings of 20 objects traditionally associated with gender roles, 10 for the male gender role (such as a hammer, a shovel, and a fire helmet) and 10 for the female gender role (such as an iron, a stove, and dishes). By age 7, most children make a perfect score on this type of test, illustrating that they know how their society links a person's sex to activities or occupations (Beere, 1990; Serbin et al., 1993; Levy, 1998). Knowledge of gender-typed personality traits, such as gentle and affectionate or adventurous and self-confident, emerges somewhat later. In one study of more than 550 children, sixth-graders answered about 90% of these types of questions correctly (Serbin et al., 1993).

An early-school-age child's knowledge about gender role standards shapes the child's preferences and behaviors. For example, once children identify certain toys as more appropriate for girls and others as more appropriate for boys, their own toy preferences are guided by these standards. Conversely, when they like a toy that is not obviously sex-stereotyped, they are inclined to think that other children of their sex would like that toy as well (Martin, Eisenbud, & Rose, 1995). One consequence of this gender-typed thinking is that it limits a child's willingness to play with certain toys and games, and therefore reduces the child's opportunities to learn from a variety of play experiences.

The nature of parental influences on children's gender role stereotyping is very complex (Turner & Gervai, 1995). Some parents believe that boys should be assertive and fight for their rights. Others believe that boys should think carefully about what is right and wrong and guide their actions by rea-

son rather than by impulsive aggression. Each of these sets of parents has a conception of male attributes that is communicated to their sons by a variety of means over a long period. The toys that parents give their children, the experiences to which they expose them, and the activities in which they encourage their children's participation all reflect some dimensions of the parents' gender role standards. By the time children reach school age, they have been encouraged to adopt those standards and disciplined for what their parents have viewed as gender-inappropriate behavior. Young girls may be shamed for their assertiveness by being told that they are acting "bossy," and young boys may be warned to "stop acting like a sissy."

As the cognitive underpinnings related to the concept of gender mature, children form **gender schemes**, or personal theories about cultural expectations and stereotypes related to gender. Children look for clues about gender, seeking information from their social environment about what activities they should or should not engage in ("Boys don't dance," "Girls don't play with trucks"), whom they should play with, and what information is especially relevant for them as boys or girls. They use this information to organize their perceptions, focus their attention, and interpret information in such a way as to be consistent with their gender scheme (Levy, Barth, & Zimmerman, 1998; Martin & Ruble, 2004).

For boys, gender schemes play a role in the recollection of behavior from as early as age 2 (Bauer, 1993). By the kindergarten years, both boys and girls recall information that is consistent with their gender stereotypes better than information that is counter to the stereotype or that is more relevant to the opposite sex (Liben & Signorella, 1993). Among children between the ages of 5 and 12, the greater their knowledge of gender role standards, the greater their preference for same-sex peers and for gender-typed adult activities and occupations (Serbin et al., 1993).

Not all children are equally rigid in applying gender role standards to themselves or to others. Flexibility in the application of gender role standards to oneself and others appears to be influenced by both cognitive factors and socialization. Children learn the stereotypes and expectations related to their own gender before learning the expectations for the opposite gender (Martin, Wood, & Little, 1990). Preschool-age children are likely to see gender role transgressions (e.g., boys playing with dolls or girls pretending to be firefighters) as more permissible than are older children, ages 6 and 7 (Smetana, 1986; Lobel & Menashri, 1993). In particular, young children who have more advanced abilities to differentiate between moral norms (e.g., telling the truth) and social norms (e.g., saying "please" and "thank you") are also less stereotyped in their play activities and toy choices (Lobel & Menashri, 1993). Among 5- to 10-year-olds, training in multiple classification skills (sorting objects into more than one category) is associated with more egalitarian, less stereotyped responses to gender-related tasks (Bigler & Liben, 1992).

Variations in family environment and socialization influence children's thinking about gender role norms. Girls are

*Although early-school-age children are familiar with gender stereotypes, they are also likely to be flexible in their gender-role play.*

generally more flexible about gender roles than boys. Young boys whose fathers live in the home typically have an earlier knowledge of gender-typed roles. However, if these fathers participate in nontraditional activities in the home, the boys' gender role knowledge is delayed. Children whose mothers perform nontraditional tasks develop a more flexible attitude, seeing more activities and occupations as appropriate for both men and women (Serbin et al., 1993).

### ■ IDENTIFICATION WITH PARENTS

The third component of gender identification involves parental identification. **Identification** is the process through which one person incorporates the values and beliefs of another. To identify with someone is not to become exactly identical to that person, but to increase one's sense of allegiance and closeness to him or her. Through the process of identification, ideals, values, and standards of the family and community are internalized so that they become a part of the individual's own belief system. During early school age, most children admire and emulate their parents. They begin to internalize their parents' values, attitudes, and worldviews. Children identify with both parents, not just with the parent of the same sex. However, same-sex parental identification can include important information about gender. For example, in a study of maternal identification, self-esteem, and body image, Hispanic and European American girls whose mothers had high self-esteem also had high self-esteem. Girls who wanted to be like their mothers had higher self-esteem and more positive feelings about their physical appearance and body image than the girls who did not want to be like their mothers (Hahn-Smith & Smith, 2001).

Individual differences in children's gender-typed prefer-

ences in toys and play activities as well as their gender role knowledge are linked to parental attitudes and behaviors. Parents who have more traditional gender-typed attitudes tend to have children who are more stereotyped in their play preferences and whose knowledge of sex stereotypes develops at a younger age (Fagot & Leinbach, 1989; Weinraub et al., 1984). Parents can make deliberate efforts to encourage more flexibility in gender role conceptualization and preferences by deliberately modeling counterstereotyped activities—fathers making dinner; mothers mowing the lawn. Parents can also balance their children's play activities so that both boys and girls have opportunities for independent play that does not require collaboration (e.g., playing with toy trucks and cars on a track) and opportunities for cooperative, social-relational play (e.g., playing pretend school with "teachers" and "students" [Leaper, 2000]).

Parents devise their beliefs and parenting practices out of a strong, internalized cultural script about gender. So even if they endorse gender flexibility, they may not be able to carry through entirely with their beliefs. For example, many studies focus on how parents talk to their children. The results of this work suggest that mothers are generally both more supportive and more negative with their children—that is, more expressive—whereas fathers are more directive, or task oriented. Furthermore, daughters receive more verbal interaction than do sons, especially from mothers. Finally, fathers are more assertive than mothers, and children are more assertive with their mothers than with their fathers (Leaper, Anderson, & Sanders, 1998). Thus, the family environment is *gendered* through patterns of communication that give children different role models for the behavior of mothers and fathers and provide boys and girls with opportunities to develop different approaches to social interaction.

In addition to the enactment of scripts for how to interact, most adults have deeply held standards about how men and women, boys and girls ought to behave. Consider the following:

> [A family] with three children (5-year-old Dan, 7-year-old Lyle, and 3.5-year-old Amy) in which the mother had always believed that her children should be exposed to all types of experiences, with no distinction indicated between "boy's kind" and "girl's kind." She encouraged her older son's play with dolls. . . . The boys were not allowed to play "aggressive" sports (American football) and were redirected by parents towards ballet and soccer. Yet the mother herself reported being "taken to the limits":

> . . . watching her [the mother] play with Amy, the mother was painting Amy's fingernails, Dan asked his mother to paint his fingernails too. "I could only bring myself to paint two [nails]. I knew it was ridiculous, but it just bothered me." (MacKain, 1987, p. 120)

This example illustrates how strongly internalized the standards about gender distinctions can be. Even for parents who want to minimize gender distinctions, some prohibitions or constraints are difficult to disregard (Valsiner, 2000).

The contribution of parental identification to a child's gender identity is not all that well understood (Fagot, 1995). On balance, mothers spend much more time than fathers in the care and rearing of young children. Thus, much of what children learn about the male role is likely to be interpreted through interactions with their mothers, and by watching their mothers and fathers, other male companions, or observing men on television. In a study of 3- to 6-year-olds in which the fathers were the primary caregivers, children had higher levels of a sense of internal control and scored higher on verbal ability than children in more traditional families. However, there were no differences in the children's gender identification between traditional and father-caregiver families (Radin 1982, 1988). In a follow-up study, when the children were adolescents, the children who had experienced primary care by their fathers endorsed more nontraditional employment arrangements and role sharing by men and women. They also were more favorable about nontraditional child care arrangements where fathers spent more time caring for their young children (Radin, 1993). Thus, based on findings from this research program, the impact of father involvement on gender identity was more evident as the children got older, rather than during early childhood. The box on Children Raised by Gay or Lesbian Parents (p. 229) illustrates the lack of a clear link between parental identification and sexual orientation.

## ■ GENDER PREFERENCE

The fourth component of gender identification is the development of a personal preference for the kinds of activities and attitudes associated with masculine or feminine roles. Preferences for gender-typed play activities and same-sex play com-

panions have been observed among preschoolers as well as older children (Hoffmann & Powlishta, 2001). The attainment of these preferences is a more complex accomplishment than might be imagined. In fact, one's gender role preference may fluctuate considerably throughout life (Maccoby, 2002).

**Gender preference** depends primarily on three factors. First, the more closely one's own strengths and competencies approximate the gender role standards, the more one will prefer being a member of that sex. Some researchers who write about the childhood recollections of gay men report experiences of gender nonconformity. These men remember feeling different from their male age-mates, like outsiders or imposters, or being admonished by their parents to act more like a "boy" (Beard & Bakeman, 2000; Isay, 1999). Both boys and girls can have experiences, like those described by Lee in the case study on Gender Identification in Early Childhood, when their personal preferences for play behavior do not seem to fit with the cultural standards or stereotypes for their sex.

Second, the more one likes the same-sex parent, the more one will prefer being a member of that sex. These two factors begin to have a significant impact on a child's gender preference as his or her self-concept becomes more clearly differentiated. As children enter school and are exposed to the process of evaluation, they begin to have a more realistic sense of their unique qualities. As they acquire this self-reflective ability, they can appreciate the similarities and discrepancies between (1) self and the gender role standard and (2) self and the same-sex parent.

The third determinant of gender preference consists of environmental cues as to the value of one sex or the other. The cues may emanate from the family, ethnic and religious groups, the media, social institutions (such as the schools), and other culture carriers. Many cultures have traditionally valued men more than women and have given men higher status. For example, among Japanese immigrants who came to the United States between the 1890s and early 1900s, a strong value was the commitment to a hierarchical and male-head-of-household view of the family (Ishii-Kuntz, 1997):

> The Issei (*first generation immigrant families*) customarily designated their eldest son the successor to the family business. . . . Accordingly, the eldest Nisei (*second generation*) son usually received special treatment and privileges from his parents. In many Issei families, he was the second to be served at meals, after his father, and he was generally indulged by his mother. . . . Younger siblings were instructed to obey his directions, and even older sisters were expected to defer to him. (Ishii-Kuntz, 1997, p. 138)

To the extent that such culturally determined values are communicated to children, boys are likely to establish a firmer preference for their sex group, and girls are likely to experience some ambivalence toward if not rejection of their sex group. In other words, it is easier to be happy and content with oneself if one feels highly valued than if one feels less valued.

# Children Raised by Gay or Lesbian Parents

A GROWING NUMBER of gay and lesbian couples are rearing children. In most cases, the children were conceived in heterosexual marriages. Then one parent established a lesbian or gay relationship and continued to raise the child. Some lesbian couples have children conceived through artificial insemination, and both lesbian and gay couples have assumed the parent role through adoption (Bailey, Bobrow, Wolfe, & Mikach, 1995; Flaks, Ficher, Masterpasqua, & Joseph, 1995). The emergence of this unique family structure provides an opportunity to better understand the process of gender role socialization and the development of sexual orientation. Many questions about childrearing environments and child outcomes can be posed. Do parents who have a homosexual orientation differ from heterosexual parents in their parenting strategies or parental role behaviors? How relevant is a parent's sexual orientation in shaping a child's gender role identification?

Research has just begun to address some of these issues. Several studies have reported that when compared to heterosexual couples, lesbian couples exhibit more sensitive parenting and more egalitarian role relationships. Open disclosure of the lesbian relationship, the ability to maintain ties with the rest of the child's family, and a perception that the partners share equally in the tasks associated with household and child care all contribute to the child's emotional well-being (Patterson, 1995). In general, studies of the well-being and cognitive and emotional adjustment of children growing up with lesbian mothers find no differences between these children and those growing up in heterosexual families (Fitzgerald, 1999). The children have gender role preferences that are very similar to those of children growing up in heterosexual

families (Patterson, 1992; Flaks et al., 1995).

One study reviewed findings from 23 studies of children of lesbian and gay parents (Anderssen, Amlie, & Ytteroy, 2002). Of these studies, most were conducted in North America, but 4 focused on European samples. 20 studies reported on children of lesbian mothers; 3 on children of gay fathers. The results of these studies were discussed in terms of seven outcomes: emotional functioning; sexual preference; stigmatization; gender role behavior; behavioral adjustment; gender identity; and cognitive functioning. Not all studies measured all of these variables, and even when studies focused on common outcomes, they used a variety of methods to measure the same variables. The studies of children of gay fathers only focused on sexual preferences and stigmatization.

Despite the variations in approaches to sampling, measurement, and design, the studies reported quite similar results. Children of lesbian mothers did not differ from other children with respect to emotional or behavioral problems; gender identity; gender role behavior; or cognitive functioning. Children's sexual preference was not related to their parents' sexual orientation. There was some greater sensitivity to stigmatization among children of lesbian and gay parents, with children in some studies reporting being teased about being gay or lesbian. Also, children gave more thought to whom they would tell about their parents' sexual orientation. However, these experiences were not associated with higher rates of emotional or behavioral difficulties. The authors concluded that the research, with its many flaws, does provide a picture of general similarity between children reared in gay or lesbian families and those reared by heterosexual families.

The results suggest that the sexual

*Research suggests that the sexual orientation of parents is not a powerful predictor of their child's gender identification or future sexual orientation.*

orientation of parents is not a powerful predictor of a child's gender identification or of his or her future sexual orientation. Future research might focus more on the unique nature and experience of children growing up in gay and lesbian families, with a particular need to include more studies of gay fathers and their approaches to parenting. Rather than examining vulnerabilities or potential deficits in comparison to children raised in heterosexual families, future research might shed new light on the approaches to gender socialization and the interpersonal worldview that emerge in this family form.

**Table 8.1** Dimensions of Gender Role Identification

| DIMENSION | GENDER ROLE OUTCOME |
|---|---|
| Developing an understanding of gender | I am a boy; I will grow up to be a man. |
| | I am a girl; I will grow up to be a woman. |
| Acquiring gender role standards | Boys are independent; they play with trucks. |
| | Girls are interpersonal; they play with dolls. |
| Identifying with the same-sex parent | I am a lot like Daddy. I want to be like him when I grow up. |
| | I am a lot like Mommy. I want to be like her when I grow up. |
| Establishing a gender role preference | I like being a boy. I'd rather be a boy than a girl. |
| | I like being a girl. I'd rather be a girl than a boy. |

Some families develop a strong preference regarding the sex of an expected child. In a longitudinal study of Swedish children from birth to age 25, the parents' prenatal preferences for a son or daughter were related to perceived problems in the mother–child and father–child relationships (Stattin & Klackenberg-Larsson, 1991). Mothers' perceptions of problems in the parent–child relationship—especially the relationship between fathers and their nonpreferred daughters—were significantly related to the fathers' disappointed hopes for a son.

Looking back on their relationship with their parents at age 25, nonpreferred daughters were especially likely to note problems, saying that their mothers did not have time for them, their fathers were stricter with them and had less time for them, and their relationships with their fathers were, in general, worse than the relationships described by preferred daughters. Research among families in India found that mothers' preferences for sons were positively correlated with their sons' IQ scores and negatively correlated with their daughters' IQ scores (Raina, Malhi, Malhotra, & Jerath, 2003).

These kinds of studies suggest that parental preference for one sex over the other can influence the quality of parent–child interactions and the resources, interactions, and opportunities available to boys and girls as they are growing up. One implication for gender development is that children may know their sex and the behaviors that are expected of members of that sex, and yet wish they were a member of the opposite sex.

Table 8.1 summarizes the four components of the acquisition of gender identification: (1) developing an understanding of gender, (2) learning gender role standards, (3) identifying with parents, and (4) establishing a gender preference. What was once viewed as a predominantly biological process of sex role differentiation is now viewed as a product of the interaction of biological, cognitive, and social factors. The outcome of the process for an individual child depends on the interaction of biologically based sex characteristics, the parents' approaches to gender role socialization, the child's personal capacities and preferences, and the cultural and familial values that create gender-linked expectations for behavior.

A child's gender identity becomes a basic cognitive scheme that influences the interpretation of experiences. Children learn that people are grouped into two sexes—male and female. In our society, this dichotomy imposes itself on a wide array of social situations, including work, play, and politics—arenas where one's genital sex is not especially relevant. Once children have this powerful category, they go about the business of figuring out how to apply it. They recognize people as men and women, boys and girls, and they identify themselves as members of one of these two groups. They form expectations based on this categorization—that certain toys, interests, and behaviors are appropriate for boys and others are appropriate for girls; that certain activities, dispositions, and occupations are appropriate for men and others for women. These expectations are generally reinforced by the beliefs of the older children and adults with whom children interact. Thus, the gender schemes that are conceived during childhood play a significant role in guiding a child's daily activities and in shaping a preliminary vision of oneself in the future. Gender-based beliefs may become integrated into moral development, so that children begin to believe that it is morally right to adhere to certain gender role standards and morally wrong to violate these standards.

## EARLY MORAL DEVELOPMENT

The moral dilemmas facing young children are not about plagiarism or cloning or abortion. Rather, they are about understanding that lying, cheating, stealing, hurting others, or making fun of other children's differences are morally wrong, and that telling the truth, playing fairly, sharing, being helpful, and respecting people's differences are morally right. The following analysis of moral development focuses on how children learn moral standards and apply them to their own behavior as well as the behavior of others.

For early-school-age children, achievements in moral development include changes in three interrelated domains:

1. *Emotions.* (a) Experiencing the array of emotions that foster caring about others and that produce anxiety, guilt, and remorse when a moral standard has been violated; and (b) recognizing these emotions in others.
2. *Knowledge.* Learning the moral code of one's community and making judgments about whether something is good or bad, right or wrong.
3. *Action.* Taking appropriate actions to inhibit negative impulses or to act in a caring, helpful manner, depending on the situation.

Early moral development involves a process called **internalization**, which means taking parental standards and values as one's own. During toddlerhood, a child's attention is focused on limits of and standards for behavior. Toddlers typically feel that demands for proper behavior do not come from within themselves but emanate from the external world. During early school age, standards and limits become part of a child's self-concept. Specific values are acquired from parents, but they become integrated elements of the child's worldview. Morality includes inhibiting harmful or socially unacceptable impulses and striving to do what is right.

For example, a 3-year-old boy may take great delight in hitting his dog with a stick. In the midst of one of these attacks, his mother scolds him. She insists that he stop and explains that it is cruel to hurt the dog. She may have to remind the boy on several other occasions that hitting the dog is not permitted. As the boy internalizes this standard, he begins to experience internal control over his own behavior. He may see the dog lying calmly in the sun and, with a gleam in his eye, begin to pick up a stick. At that moment, his behavior is interrupted by a feeling of tension, which is accompanied by the thought that it is wrong to hit the dog. If the standard has been successfully internalized, the emotional tension and the thought will be sufficient to inhibit the boy from hitting the dog.

A variety of theories explain how the domains of emotion, knowledge, and action converge to produce the internalized moral behavior considered appropriate for the early-school-age child. The three theoretical approaches presented here—learning theory, cognitive developmental theory, and psychoanalytic theory—each offer distinct views about the way morality becomes internalized. You may find it helpful to refer back to Chapter 4 (Major Theories for Understanding Human Development) to review the basic orientation of these theories.

These theories focus on the *process* of moral development, not the content. Each culture or subcultural group has its own set of moral standards. For example, in many Asian cultures, children are taught that teachers are highly revered. Children learn to show respect to a teacher and to view their teachers as important role models. Children who are disrespectful of a teacher would be shamed. In the United States,

the role of teacher does not have especially high status in comparison to many other occupations. Parents may express criticism of teachers openly in front of their children. They may write excuses for children's absences or failure to complete their homework, even though both the children and parents know these excuses are fabrications. Children may learn that some teachers are fair and helpful, but others are not. They may not believe that it is immoral to ignore a teacher's request or to make fun of a teacher with the other children. The theories that follow suggest how children internalize moral standards; they do not explain what the standards are or suggest what they should be.

## ■ LEARNING THEORY

From the behavioral learning theory perspective, moral behavior and the process of internalization are viewed as a response to environmental reinforcements and punishments (Aronfreed, 1969). Moral behaviors, like other operant responses, can be shaped by the *consequences* that follow them. A positive, prosocial behavior, like offering to help put the toys away or comforting another child who is distressed, is likely to be repeated if it is rewarded. In contrast, if a behavior is ignored or punished, it is less likely to occur again. If a child performs a misdeed or defies an authority and suffers negative consequences, these consequences ought to reduce the likelihood that such behavior will recur. If a child is in an unpleasant or painful environment and performs a behavior that reduces or eliminates the unpleasantness, he or she is more likely to perform this same behavior again in similar situations. For example, if a child says, "I'm sorry. I'll try to do better next time," and this apology reduces the parent's anger or irritability, this behavior is likely to be repeated at other times when the parent is angry at the child. According to learning theory, internalization results as the behaviors that lead to a more comfortable, less threatening environment become more common and the behaviors that produce parental anger or conflict disappear.

The special case of **avoidance conditioning** is viewed as a paradigm for understanding how internalization is sustained. Having been disciplined in the past for wrongdoings, a child contemplating a misdeed should feel tension. Avoiding or inhibiting the impulse to misbehave reduces the tension and is therefore reinforcing. This process may occur even when the person who was involved in administering the discipline is absent. In other words, the scenario of thinking about a wrong or naughty action, feeling the anxiety that is associated with past discipline, and reducing that anxiety by exercising restraint may take place mentally, without any observable behavior. Over time, the reinforcement of tension reduction that is linked to controlling a wrongful impulse strengthens the tendency to inhibit it, and the child's behavior becomes less impulsive. This theory suggests that a child learns to control his or her impulses to do wrong by having been punished for wrongdoing in the past.

Social learning theory adds another avenue for moral learning: the *observation of models*. By observing and imitating helpful models, children can learn prosocial behavior. By observing the negative consequences that follow the misdeeds of models, they can also learn to inhibit their own misbehavior. Their moral behavior is not limited to the actions they have performed—it may be based on expectations formulated from observations of how the conduct of relevant models has been rewarded or punished (Bandura, 1977). For example, early-school-age children are more likely to judge an act of televised violence as *right* if the act goes unpunished. Having viewed such unpunished acts, children formulate abstract rules, concepts, and sets of propositions about when aggressive behavior is justified (Kremar & Cooke, 2001). Children form a mental representation by selecting and organizing observed responses and use this mental model to guide, compare, and modify their own moral behavior (Bandura, 1991).

Cognitive learning theory describes how moral behavior is influenced by *situational factors* and by the child's *expectations, values, and goals* (Mischel, 1973). For example, some people place great value on success in athletics and may be more tempted to lie or cheat in order to succeed in an athletic competition than in an academic setting. Another situational factor is the presence or absence of monitoring. The expectation that a misdeed will be observed and punished leads to greater resistance to temptation than does the expectation that a misdeed will go unnoticed. Similarly, the belief that positive, prosocial behaviors are expected and will be noticed influences a child's generosity and helpfulness (Froming, Allen, & Jensen, 1985). According to this theoretical perspective, the specific situation will influence the extent to which moral behavior is displayed (Carroll & Rest, 1982). The formation of moral character is built on the accumulation of many experiences across different situations day after day where children learn which behaviors are acceptable and which are not.

## ■ COGNITIVE DEVELOPMENTAL THEORY

Cognitive developmental theorists have focused on the orderly sequence of development of the child's thoughts about moral issues. In comparison to the learning theories, cognitive developmental theorists focus more on *moral reasoning* than on moral behavior. They place emphasis on the child's active construction of moral meaning, rather than on environmental factors such as rewards, punishments, models, or situational factors. Piaget (1932/1948) described the major transition in moral judgment as a shift from *heteronomous* to *autonomous* morality. In **heteronomous morality**, rules are understood as fixed, unchangeable aspects of social reality. Children's moral judgments reflect a sense of subordination to authority figures. An act is judged as right or wrong depending on the letter of the law, the amount of damage that was done, and whether or not the act was punished.

In **autonomous morality**, children see rules as products of cooperative agreements. Moral judgments reflect a child's

participation in a variety of social roles and in egalitarian relationships with friends. Give-and-take with peers highlights mutual respect and mutual benefit as rewards for holding to the terms of agreement or abiding by the law. Piaget posed situations like the following to young children in order to help clarify the difference between heteronomous and autonomous morality:

> Mark rushes into the kitchen, pushing open the door. Although he did not realize it, his mother had left a set of 10 cups and saucers on a stool behind the door. When he pushed the door open, the cups and saucers fell off the stool and broke.
>
> Matt was climbing up on the kitchen counter to reach some cookies that his mother told him he was not supposed to eat. While climbing on the counter, he broke one cup and saucer.
>
> Who committed the more serious moral transgression?
>
> Which boy should be more severely punished?

Children operating with a heteronomous morality believe that the child who breaks 10 cups by accident has committed a much more serious transgression than the child who broke only one. Children who have achieved an autonomous morality believe that the child who disobeyed and violated his

*When Camilla gets a scolding for breaking a plate, she learns that intentions are not as important as consequences. She reasons that she was naughty because the plate got broken and her mother got angry.*

© Michael Siluk/The Image Works

**Table 8.2** Stages in the Development of Moral Judgment

**LEVEL I: PRECONVENTIONAL**

| | |
|---|---|
| Stage 1 | Judgments are based on whether behavior is rewarded or punished. |
| Stage 2 | Judgments are based on whether the consequences result in benefits for self or loved ones. |

**LEVEL II: CONVENTIONAL**

| | |
|---|---|
| Stage 3 | Judgments are based on whether authorities approve or disapprove. |
| Stage 4 | Judgments are based on whether the behavior upholds or violates the laws of society. |

**LEVEL III: POSTCONVENTIONAL**

| | |
|---|---|
| Stage 5 | Judgments are based on preserving social contracts based on cooperative collaboration. |
| Stage 6 | Judgments are based on ethical principles that apply across time and cultures. |

Source: Based on Kohlberg, 1969, 1976.

mother's trust committed the more serious transgression. In general, younger children are likely to judge the moral seriousness of an action based on the magnitude and nature of the consequences. If an action, no matter what the intent, produced harm, it should be punished. Older children are able to consider both the intention and the consequences in making a moral judgment. If an action was intended to harm and produced harm, it should definitely be punished (Helwig, Zelazo, & Wilson, 2001).

Expanding on the distinction between heteronomous and autonomous morality, cognitive developmental theorists have described a sequence of stages of moral thought (Kohlberg, 1976; Gibbs, 1979; Damon, 1980). As children become increasingly skillful in evaluating the abstract and logical components of a moral dilemma, their moral judgments change. At the core of this change is the mechanism called equilibration—efforts to reconcile new perspectives and ideas about basic moral concepts, such as justice, intentionality, and social responsibility, with existing views about what is right and wrong. Children's reasoning may be thrown into disequilibrium by external sources, such as their parents' use of explanations and inductions regarding a moral dilemma or encounters with friends who reason differently about a moral conflict. Children's own cognitive maturation, especially the ability to think abstractly and hypothetically about interrelated variables, determines how their reasoning about moral dilemmas will be structured (Piaget, 1978/1985; Walker, Gustafson, & Hennig, 2001).

Kohlberg (1969, 1976) described three levels of moral thought, each characterized by two stages of moral judgment (see Table 8.2). At Level I, preconventional morality, Stage 1 judgments of justice are based on whether a behavior is rewarded or punished. Stage 2 judgments are based on an instrumental view of whether the consequences will be good for "me and my family." The first and, to some degree, the second stages of Level I characterize children of early school age. Level II, conventional morality, is concerned with maintaining the approval of authorities at Stage 3 and with up-

holding the social order at Stage 4. Level III, postconventional morality, brings an acceptance of moral principles that are viewed as part of a person's own ideology rather than simply being imposed by the social order. At Stage 5, justice and morality are determined by a democratically derived social contract. At Stage 6, a person develops a sense of universal ethical principles that apply across history and cultural contexts.

According to this theory, the stages form a logical hierarchy. At each new stage, individuals reorganize their view of morality, realizing the inadequacy of the preceding stage. For example, once a person sees morality in terms of a system that upholds and protects the social order (Stage 4), then the reasoning that argues for an act as moral because it was rewarded or immoral because it was punished is seen as inadequate. The stages form an invariant sequence, moving from a very idiosyncratic, personal view of morality to a view in which rules and laws are obeyed because they have been established by an authority or a society, and finally to an understanding of rules and laws as created to uphold basic principles of fairness, justice, and humanity (Boom, Brugman, & van der Heijden, 2001).

This view of moral development leads one to expect the moral reasoning of early-school-age children to be at Level I, preconventional morality, which is dominated by concerns about the consequences of their behavior. At Stage 1, children's judgments of good and bad, right and wrong, are based on whether a behavior has been rewarded or punished or is expected to be rewarded or punished. At Stage 2, children's moral judgments are based on whether the behavior will bring about benefits for them or for other people they care about. Thus, young children's moral outlook has a *utilitarian* orientation (Kohlberg, 1976). Research with first-graders confirms that this preconventional outlook is quite common, whether children are discussing hypothetical or real-life moral dilemmas (Walker, 1989).

However, children understand that not all misbehavior involves a moral transgression (see the box on Moral

APPLYING THEORY AND RESEARCH TO LIFE

# Moral Transgressions, Social Convention, and Personal Choice

NOT ALL SOCIAL rules or prohibitions have to do with moral concerns. There is a difference between **morality**, which usually involves the rights, dignity, and welfare of others, and **social convention**, which involves socially accepted norms and regulations (Smetana, 1985; Turiel, 1983). For example, in the preschool context, stealing another child's toy would be a moral transgression; a transgression of social convention would be getting up and wandering away during circle time. Preschool-age children are consistently able to differentiate between moral and social convention transgressions. They understand that moral transgressions are wrong because they affect the welfare of others and that social convention transgressions are wrong because they are disruptive or create disorder (Turiel, 2002).

Social convention transgressions depend on the situation. At home, it may be permissible to get up from the table during dinnertime before everyone has finished and go somewhere to play, whereas it is not permissible to get up from the snack table at preschool until the teacher says everyone may leave. Moral transgressions apply more consistently across settings: It is morally wrong to steal at home, at preschool, or at a friend's house. Children as young as 3

and 4 make this distinction when they evaluate transgressions. In contrast to social convention transgressions, young children tend to judge moral transgressions to be more serious, deserving of greater punishment, and independent of the rules or authority in a situation (Smetana, Schlagman, & Adams, 1993).

In addition to moral and social convention, some behaviors fall within the domain of **personal choice**. Within the boundaries of fairness and social reciprocity, children recognize a domain of personal freedom. Where moral and social decisions are often guided by adult authority and regulations, personal choices are typically guided by a child's own preferences (Nucci & Turiel, 2000). These choices might include preferences for certain toys or play activities, foods, or choice of friends. Children perceive that they have more latitude for expressing their personal preferences at home than at school, where social convention and teachers' authority may restrict some of their choices (Weber, 1999). Studies of Colombian and Chinese preschool-age children suggest that even in cultures that are considered strongly hierarchical or collectivist, young children perceive that they have a legitimate role in certain personal decisions, such as which

© David Young-Wolff/Photo Edit

*Personal choice is exercised when children reject food.*

foods or toys they prefer, so long as these decisions are coordinated with consideration for others (Ardila-Rey & Killen, 2001; Yau & Smetana, 2003).

Transgressions, Social Convention, and Personal Choice). What is more, the nature of a child's moral reasoning can be altered by exposure to a consistent sociomoral environment. For example, in the preschool and early primary grades, children can function at a more flexible, autonomous level when the moral atmosphere consistently emphasizes mutual respect. Classrooms where children are involved in rule making and conflict resolution give children an opportunity to appreciate each other's perspectives and to construct a social order that is largely regulated by the children themselves (De-Vries, Hildebrandt, & Zan, 2000).

The notion that people move through a hierarchical sequence of stages of moral reasoning prompted by a process of cognitive disequilibrium has been challenged on a number of fronts. The direction of development over the stages has been viewed as too linear, valuing justice over social cooper-

ation. It has been criticized as embodying a Western cultural orientation, and a male-oriented value system, which places the individual good and individual freedoms above the good of the group or community (Arnold, 2000). However, cross-cultural comparisons have found support for the idea that as people mature, they find increasingly sophisticated ways of approaching moral situations. A study of more than 500 high school and university students in Taiwan found that the students showed evidence of high levels of postconventional reasoning, even though they adopted a culturally collectivist Chinese moral ethic (Gielen & Miao, 2000). Longitudinal studies in a variety of countries have observed an evolution of moral thought much like that proposed by Kohlberg, in which the reasoning shifts from an idiosyncratic to a more principled approach to evaluating moral conflicts (Gielen & Markoulis, 2001).

# ■ PSYCHOANALYTIC THEORY

The psychoanalytic theorists focus on morality as the ability of children to control their impulses and resist temptation, rather than on their cognitive understanding of what constitutes a moral transgression. This perspective suggests that a moral sense develops as a result of strong parental identification. Classical psychoanalytic theory views a child's conscience, or **superego**, as an internalization of parental values and moral standards. It holds that the superego is formed during the phallic stage, between the ages of about 4 and 7, as a result of the conflict between internal sexual and aggressive impulses and the ways in which the parents deal with the behavioral manifestations of those impulses.

According to psychoanalytic theory, the more severely a parent forces a child to inhibit her or his impulses, the stronger the child's superego will be. Freud (1925/1961) assumed that boys would develop more highly differentiated and punitive superegos than girls because he believed that boys' impulses are more intense. He also believed that because of the greater impulsive energy demonstrated by boys, boys are treated more harshly by their parents than are girls. Finally, Freud suggested that boys identify with their fathers for two reasons: fear of losing the father's love and fear of the father as an aggressor. This identification with the father is intense and typically leads to a fully incorporated set of moral standards. According to Freud, a girl identifies with her mother for a single reason: fear of losing her love. As Freud considered this motivation for identification less intense than that of the boy, he believed that the girl's superego would be correspondingly weaker.

Research on the development of conscience has failed to support Freud's hypotheses. Studies that have investigated the ability to resist temptation or to confess after wrongdoing have found that young girls are *better* able to resist temptation than boys and show a pattern of decreasing moral transgressions over the toddlerhood and early school years (Mischel et al., 1989). Studies that have attempted to assess the relative contributions of mothers and fathers to their children's moral behavior have found that mothers' values and attitudes are strongly related to the moral behavior of their children, whereas the values and attitudes of fathers have little relationship to such behavior (Hoffman, 1970). Finally, research has found that the children of parents who use harsh physical punishment do not have higher levels of internalization. These children are likely to inhibit impulsive behaviors in the presence of their parents, but when they are observed with their peers away from home, they tend to be physically aggressive and do not control their behavior well (Hart, Ladd, & Burleson, 1990; Pettit, Dodge, & Brown, 1988). Parental warmth, limited use of power assertion, involving children in decision making, and modeling resistance to temptation contribute to high levels of prosocial behavior and social responsibility (Maccoby, 1992).

**NEOPSYCHOANALYTIC THEORY.** In contrast to Freud's views on the formation of conscience, contemporary psychoanalytic theory, sometimes referred to as **object relations theory**, views the critical time for moral development as infancy rather than the early-school-age years (Klein, 1932/1975; Kohut, 1971; Winnicut, 1958; Mahler, 1963). Infants develop an awareness of three domains: the body and its

*According to the psychoanalytic view, young children act on their impulses. As the superego develops, they are more successful at resisting temptation.*

physical experiences and needs; the existence of others; and the relations between the self and others (Beit-Hallahmi, 1987). All subsequent psychological growth must be assimilated into these three domains. According to this view, the origins of moral reasoning and behavior have links to early feelings about the self and its needs, especially the feelings of pleasure and pain, and the way these feelings are mirrored or accepted by the loving caregiver.

Morality has a basis in a young child's awareness of valued others and in behaviors that strengthen or threaten the bonds between the self and these others. Drawing on the psychoanalytic tradition, all humans are seen as confronted by a dynamic tension between positive and negative emotions—love and hate, kindness and cruelty. One basis of early morality lies in the child's own sense of self-love, a wish to enhance and not harm or violate the self. Another basis is the extension of this self-love to the other and the wish to preserve feelings of connection, trust, and security that have been established in the early parent–infant relationship. Through experiences with sensitive caregiving, infants becomes increasingly aware of the loved object as an integrated whole with feelings, motives, and goals as well as a physical reality. At the same time, this realization about the other fosters the child's own awareness of his or her inner mental life. When a child is distressed, for example, a calm, reassuring caregiver will use a certain tone of voice, facial expressions, and comforting strategies to help the child cope with the difficulty. This gives the child a chance to feel safe about experiencing the inner world of painful emotions. The loving caregiver allows the child an intimate context in which to encounter his or her own impulses, emotions, and fears. As a result, the child does not have to split off from his or her angry, vengeful self or project it onto others. By seeing the loved other as both good and bad, and the self as both good and bad, the child's capacity for caring and empathy expands (Fonagy, 1999).

# CASE STUDY

## EARLY LEARNING ABOUT OBEDIENCE

*Jung Chang describes the moral environment to which she was exposed in her early childhood years through interactions with her grandmother.*

For my grandmother, all flowers and trees, the clouds and the rain were living beings with a heart and tears and a moral sense. We would be safe if we followed the old Chinese rule for children, *ting-hua* ("heeding the words," being obedient). Otherwise all sorts of things would happen to us. When we ate oranges my grandmother would warn us against swallowing the seeds. "If you don't listen to me, one day you won't be able to get into the house. Every little seed is a baby orange tree, and he wants to grow up, just like you. He'll grow quietly inside your tummy, up and up, and then one day, Ai-ya! There he is, out from the top of your head! He'll grow leaves, and bear more oranges, and he'll become taller than our door. . . ."

The thought of carrying an orange tree on my head fascinated me so much that one day I deliberately swallowed a seed—one, no more. I did not want an orchard on my head; that would be too heavy. For the whole day, I anxiously felt my skull every other minute to see whether it was still in one piece. Several times I almost asked my grandmother whether I would be allowed to eat the oranges on my head, but I checked myself so that she would not know I had been disobedient. I decided to pretend it was an accident when she saw the tree. I slept very badly that night. I felt something was pushing up against my skull. (Chang, 1991, p. 208–209)

## ■ CRITICAL THINKING AND CASE ANALYSIS

1. What is the moral lesson of this case?
2. How does the case illustrate the themes of moral emotion, knowledge, and action?
3. How does each of the theoretical perspectives discussed earlier contribute to an understanding of this case?
4. How does this case illustrate the particular orientation of early-school-age children to moral dilemmas?
5. How generalizable is this case? Can you imagine similar moral conflicts among non-Chinese children?

## ■ EMPATHY AND PERSPECTIVE TAKING

The theoretical views about moral development have been expanded through research in several directions. The following sections focus on empathy and perspective taking. They consider how the child understands the emotional state and the intention or motivation of others. These are both factors that contribute to a child's ability to care about another person's distress and to consider the other person's needs and intentions when judging a moral act (Eisenberg, 2000).

**EMPATHY.** **Empathy** has been defined as sharing the perceived emotion of another—"feeling with another" (Eisenberg & Strayer, 1987, p. 5). This definition emphasizes one's emotional reaction to the observation of another person's emotional condition. By merely observing the facial expressions, body attitudes, and vocalizations of another person, a child can identify that person's emotion and feel it personally. The range of emotions with which one can empathize depends on the clarity of the cues the other person sends and on one's own prior experiences.

The capacity for empathy changes with development. Hoffman (1987) described four levels of empathy, especially in reference to the perception of another person's distress:

1. **Global empathy**: You experience and express distress as a result of witnessing someone else in distress. Example: A baby cries upon hearing the cries of other infants.
2. **Egocentric empathy**: You recognize distress in another person and respond to it in the same way you would respond if the distress were your own. Example: A toddler offers his own cuddle blanket to another child who is crying.

3. **Empathy for another's feelings**: You show empathy for a wide range of feelings and anticipate the kinds of reactions that might really comfort someone else. Example: A child sees another child crying because his favorite toy is broken. She offers to help fix the toy.

4. **Empathy for another's life conditions**: You experience empathy when you understand the life conditions or personal circumstances of a person or group. Example: A child learns of children in another town who have become homeless after a flood. The child asks his mother if he can send some of his clothes to those children.

The capacity for empathy begins in infancy. Infant imitation, observed in the first months of life, provides an initial link between the observation of emotional expressions in another person and the expression of that emotion (Meltzoff, 2002). Infants appear to be able to recognize and interpret auditory and facial cues that suggest emotional expressions in others. In the newborn nursery, when one infant starts to wail, the other infants begin to cry (Martin & Clark, 1982; Sagi & Hoffman, 1976). Following from object relations theory, the intimate infant–caregiver relationship forms an early framework for empathy. The coordination of rhythmic interactions, the creation of joint attention, and the achievement of intersubjectivity through early gestures and words provide infants with an understanding of their caregiver's state. In a study of 125 first-born girls, empathic concern for their mothers' distress was observed to increase from 16 months to 22 months of age. In contrast, empathic concern for a stranger was observed to decrease. In infancy, empathy for others appears to be situational, requiring an ability to overcome wariness or fearfulness in order to offer comfort to another person (van der Mark, van IJzendoorn, & Bakermans-Kranenburg, 2002).

Three- and 4-year-olds can recognize the emotional reactions of other children to specific problems. Both American and Chinese children were able to recognize "happy" and "unhappy" reactions by age 3. The differentiation among "afraid," "sad," and "angry" developed slightly later. The specific cues for these feelings were linked to cultural patterns of expressing emotions. Nevertheless, it was clear that the youngest children in both cultural groups could recognize emotional states in another person (Borke, 1973).

In addition to being able to correctly recognize another's emotions, early-school-age children can usually identify the circumstances that may have produced another child's emotional response, especially anger and distress, and they can understand and empathize with another child's feelings. Children are most likely to think that external events produce emotional reactions: "The teacher made her put her toys away," or "He tripped over the blocks." But they can also think about internal states that may produce strong emotions: "He's mad because he didn't get a turn," or "She's sad because her stomach hurts" (Dunn, Cutting, & Demetriou, 2000; Fabes, Eisenberg, McCormick, & Wilson, 1988; Fabes, Eisenberg, Nyman, & Michealieu, 1991). The ability to understand the emotions and mental state of another person allows children to justify someone's moral behavior and perhaps to forgive a transgression:

*Young children can be very caring and supportive in comforting others, especially if they understand the reason behind another child's distress.*

"The dad just spilled juice on his paper, so he yelled at his daughter. He was upset; he didn't really mean it."

The ability to identify pleasurable and unpleasurable emotions in others and to empathize with them makes the child receptive to moral teachings. Experiences of empathy can result in *sympathy*, a concern for the other person that may motivate the child to help relieve the other person's distress. It can also serve a reactive function, where the child experiences personal distress by recognizing the distress of the other (Eisenberg et al., 1999). In the case of social attitude formation, empathy has been engaged in efforts to help children develop more compassion and acceptance of stigmatized groups (Batson et al., 1997).

**PERSPECTIVE TAKING.** The terms *empathy* and *perspective taking* are sometimes confused. **Empathy** typically refers to the ability to identify and experience the *emotional* state of another person. **Perspective taking** refers to the *cognitive* capacity to consider a situation from the point of view of another person. This requires a recognition that someone else's point of view may differ from one's own. It also requires the ability to analyze the factors that may account for these differences (Flavell, 1974; Piaget, 1932/1948; Selman, 1971).

Imagine a child who wants to play with another child's toy. If the first child thinks, "If I had that toy, I would be happy, and if I am happy, everyone is happy," then she or he may take the toy without anticipating that the other child will be upset. Although empathy provides an emotional bridge that enables children to discover the similarities between self and others, it does not teach them about differences. Recognizing these differences requires perspective taking. The capacity to take another person's perspective is achieved gradually through parental inductions, peer interaction, social pretend play, conflict, and role playing.

Children at ages 4 and 5 frequently exhibit prosocial behaviors that evidence an understanding of others' needs. The most common of these behaviors are sharing, cooperating, and helping. Two examples illustrate the nature of this kind of social perspective taking:

> The path of a child with an armload of play dough was blocked by two chairs. Another child stopped her ongoing activity and moved the chair before the approaching child reached it.

> A boy saw another child spill a puzzle on the floor and assisted him in picking it up. (Iannotti, 1985, p. 53)

Robert Selman (1980) studied the process of social perspective taking by analyzing children's responses to a structured interview. Children watched audiovisual filmstrips that depicted interpersonal conflicts. They were then asked to describe the motivation of each actor and the relationships among the various performers. Four levels of social perspective taking were described. At Level 1, the youngest children (4–6 years old) recognized different emotions in the various actors, but they assumed that all the actors viewed the situation much as they did. The children at Level 4 (about 10–12 years old) realized that two people were able to take each other's perspective into account before deciding how to act. Furthermore, they realized that each of those people may have viewed the situation differently from the way they did.

Many moral dilemmas require that children subordinate their personal needs for someone else's sake. To resolve such situations, children must be able to separate their personal wants from the other person's. Selman's research suggests that children under 10 can rarely approach interpersonal conflicts with this kind of objectivity (Selman, 1994).

One longitudinal study followed children from the ages of 4 and 5 into early adulthood. Those children who showed spontaneous sharing, helping, and other prosocial behaviors in the early childhood years continued to exhibit prosocial behavior, sympathy, and perspective taking over the course of adolescence and early adulthood (Eisenberg et al., 1999). Some combination of a genetically based social orientation, an ability to regulate or inhibit one's impulses, and a consistent socialization environment contribute to a young child's sympathetic response toward others' distress. Over time, this outlook combines with a more mature capacity for moral reasoning and deepening social ties that help sustain a prosocial orientation.

## ■ PARENTAL DISCIPLINE

Another contribution to an understanding of moral development comes from the research on parental discipline, which was introduced in Chapter 6 in relation to self-control. Par-

ents are the child's first teachers about the content of the moral code the child will be expected to internalize. Parents must make a stand for certain values, beliefs, and behaviors that embody the foundation of a moral way of life. When disciplining a child, the parent emphasizes that certain behaviors are wrong and should be inhibited; other behaviors are right and should be repeated. This distinction between good and bad behaviors and the accompanying parental approval or disapproval forms the content of the child's moral code.

Parents use specific discipline techniques to bring about compliance with the moral code. Four elements are important in determining the impact of these techniques on the child's future behavior:

1. The discipline should help the child interrupt or inhibit the forbidden action.
2. The discipline should point out a more acceptable form of behavior, so that the child will know what is right in a future instance.
3. The discipline should provide some reason, understandable to the child, why one action is inappropriate and the other more desirable.
4. The discipline should stimulate the child's ability to empathize with the victim of his or her misdeeds. In other words, children are asked to put themselves in their victim's place and to see how much they dislike the feelings they caused in the other person.

In considering discipline as a mechanism for teaching morality, one becomes aware of the many interacting and interrelated components of a moral act. The discipline techniques that are most effective in teaching morality to children are those that help them control their own behavior, understand the meaning of their behavior for others, and expand their feelings of empathy. Discipline techniques that do not include these characteristics, such as power assertion, may succeed in inhibiting undesired behavior but may fail to achieve the long-term goal of incorporating moral values into future behavior.

The child's temperament is often overlooked in determining the likely effectiveness of certain disciplinary techniques (Kochanska, 1997). In particular, children who are temperamentally fearful and inhibited in response to novel stimuli, and who choose to stay close to their mothers during toddlerhood, are especially sensitive to messages of disapproval. For these children, a small dose of parental criticism is adequate to promote moral internalization, and too much power assertion appears to be counterproductive. In contrast, children who are highly active and who are insensitive to messages of disapproval require more focused and directive discipline, especially a consistent program of recognizing and rewarding good behaviors and minimizing the situations and stimuli that may provoke impulsive or aggressive actions.

In addition to the use of discipline, parents guide moral development by modeling positive, prosocial behaviors and by talking with their children about moral issues. In Chapter 6, we discussed the use of scaffolding to promote more effective communicative competence. In the same way, parents can scaffold their child's moral reasoning by talking with their children, raising questions about moral decisions their children are facing, and introducing new arguments or alternative views as their children think about moral conflicts (Walker & Taylor, 1991).

For example, Beth's mother asks her to help pick up the toys and put them away. Beth says that her brother made the mess, and he should pick up the toys. Beth's mother might acknowledge Beth's frustration about picking up after her little brother. But then she could point out that Beth would be helping her by picking up the toys, and that at some time in the future, she will want her brother to help clean up a mess that Beth made. Meanwhile, it is important to pick up the toys so they do not get broken and so no one trips or falls over them. The idea that helping in a family is not just about what each person does, but about what is good for the family as a whole, challenges Beth's moral reasoning and encourages her to move to a new level of moral reasoning.

Security in the child–caregiver attachment, the expression of warmth and affection in the relationship, and a parent's willingness to talk about feelings and moral concerns all contribute to a child's early moral development (Laible & Thompson, 2000). Children and parents encounter many examples when children behave well and show signs of kindness, caring, and truthfulness. They also encounter many examples when children misbehave, exhibiting selfishness, anger, or cruelty. Especially at times when children are experiencing emotional distress, parents teach and model positive moral behavior through their tone of voice, their willingness to hear a child's explanations, their willingness to provide explanations for their rules, and their ability to maintain a line of open communication, even during conflict. They convey a sense that we are all imperfect, that we continue to strive toward a moral ideal, and that we can forgive and try again.

## ■ THE IMPACT OF TELEVISION ON MORAL DEVELOPMENT

Moral influences extend beyond the family to include schools, religious institutions, and the community. One of the societal influences that is of great concern is the impact of the media, especially television, on children's attitudes and behavior. Some people suggest that the television has become a part of the family system. In about 80% of homes, the television is often on even when no one is watching. Family interactions are different in the presence of the television, involving less talking and more touching. Images, information, and dramatic situations portrayed on television influence family members, resulting in new kinds of behaviors, shared experiences, points of discussion, and exposure to distressing images that may require comforting or interpretation (Gentile & Walsh, 2002).

A primary focus of research has been on the role of televised *violence* on the beliefs and behaviors of young children (Huesmann & Skoric, 2003). Concern about television violence is particularly meaningful in the context of the child's growing moral consciousness. More than 30 years of laboratory experiments, field experiments, and analyses of naturally

occurring behaviors have led to the conclusion that televised violence has definite negative consequences for young children's behaviors and beliefs.

Those who monitor contemporary television estimate that a typical child, watching an average of 27 hours of TV a week, will view "8,000 murders and 100,000 acts of violence from age 3 to age 12" (Silver, 1995, p. 62). An analysis of music television videos found that almost one fourth of the videos included images of violence and carrying weapons. Video games are especially permeated with violent themes. Many video games require children to become increasingly adept at killing off characters with the use of special weapons or superpowers. Studies suggest that engaging in violent video game play is associated with lower empathy for others, increased aggressive behavior, and desensitization to real-life violence (Carnagey & Anderson, 2004; Funk, Baldacci, Pasold, & Baumgardner, 2004).

The American Academy of Pediatrics has issued a policy statement on television viewing in which they make the

© Bill Aron/Photo Edit

*Exposure to many hours of televised violence increases young children's repertoire of violent behavior and increases the prevalence of angry feelings, thoughts, and actions. These children are caught up in the violent fantasy, taking part in the televised situation while they watch.*

**Table 8.3** Three Processes That May Increase the Level of Aggression in Children Who Watch Televised Violence

| PROCESS | POSSIBLE CONSEQUENCE |
|---|---|
| Observing role models who engage in aggressive actions. | Imitation of violent action is likely when: 1. Hero is provoked and retaliates with aggression. 2. Hero is rewarded for violent actions. New violent behaviors added to repertoire. |
| Viewing aggressive actions leads to heightened level of arousal. | Brings network of aggressive thoughts, feelings, memories, and action tendencies into consciousness. Repeated stimulation strengthens this network. Stimulation interacts with aggressive temperament to increase the likelihood of aggressive action. |
| Viewing aggression affects beliefs and values. | Aggressive behavior is seen as an acceptable way to resolve conflicts. Viewers are hardened to use of aggression in peer interactions. Aggression is used as a response to frustration. Viewers expect others to be aggressive toward them. Viewers worry about being victims of aggression. Viewers see the world as a dangerous place. |

following recommendations (American Academy of Pediatrics, 2001):

1. Discourage television viewing for all children under age 2.
2. Remove televisions from children's bedrooms.
3. Limit children's total entertainment media time (television, video games, computer games) to no more than 1 to 2 hours per day.
4. Focus on programs that are informational, educational, and nonviolent.

These recommendations are based on research evidence suggesting that about two thirds of current television programming contains a great amount of violence, children's television contains the most violence, and portrayals of violence are often glamorized and go unpunished. As a result, watching television has a strong impact on a child's willingness to engage in real-life violence or to be frightened by these violent images (Federman, 1998; Wilson et al., 2002).

Studies of children in the United States and in other countries have provided evidence that at least three processes are at work that may increase the level of aggressiveness in children who watch televised violence (Comstock & Paik, 1991; Huesmann & Eron, 1986; Huesmann & Malamuth, 1986; Huston et al., 1992; Josephson, 1987; Liebert & Sprafkin, 1988; see Table 8.3). First, children observe televised role models who perform aggressive actions. Especially when the hero is provoked and retaliates with aggression that goes unpunished, the child is likely to imitate the aggressive actions. Thus, viewing televised violence adds new violent behaviors to the child's repertoire. Moreover, when the hero is rewarded or viewed as successful because of his or her violent actions,

children's tendencies to express aggression are increased (Bandura, 1973).

Second, viewing televised violence produces a heightening of arousal (Simons et al., 2003). The fast action that usually accompanies televised violence captures the viewer's attention. The violent incident raises the child's level of emotionality, bringing to the fore other aggressive feelings, thoughts, memories, and action tendencies. The more frequently this network of elements is activated, the stronger will be their association. Thus, children who have seen a lot of televised violence and are temperamentally aggressive are likely to engage in overt acts of aggression because of the strength of arousal prompted by the televised stimulus (Berkowitz, 1984, 1986).

Finally, exposure to televised violence affects a young child's beliefs and values. Children who are exposed to frequent episodes of televised violence are more likely to believe that aggressive behavior is an acceptable way to resolve conflicts, and they become hardened to the use of aggression in peer interactions. They are also more accepting of the use of aggression as a response to frustration. Children (and adults) who are exposed to televised violence are more likely to expect that others will be aggressive toward them, to worry about being victims of aggression, and to see the world as a dangerous place (Huesmann & Skoric, 2003).

Exposure to television violence has long-lasting effects. In a longitudinal study, TV viewing habits in childhood (ages 6 to 10) were related to adult aggressive behavior 15 years later. The study found a significant relationship between extensive exposure to televised violence in childhood and later aggressive behavior for both men and women, even after controlling for mitigating factors such as intelligence, parenting characteristics, and family's socioeconomic status. The more children identified with aggressive TV characters, the stronger this relationship to adult aggressive behavior (Huesmann, Moise-Titus, Podolski, & Eron, 2003).

Researchers have barely begun to scratch the surface of television's uses to promote prosocial development. There is clear evidence that children who are exposed to prosocial programming are influenced toward more positive social behavior. One study recontacted more than 500 adolescents whose television viewing had been studied when they were in early childhood. Watching educational programming in the early years was associated with many positive characteristics in adolescence, including higher grades, reading more books, greater creativity, and less aggression (Anderson, Huston, Schmitt, Linebarger, & Wright, 2001).

Many programs—some developed for children and others intended for a broader viewing audience—convey positive ethical messages about the value of family life, the need to work hard and sacrifice in order to achieve important goals, the value of friendship, the importance of loyalty and commitment in relationships, and many other cultural values. A number of contemporary programs include characters of many races and ethnic backgrounds. Many feature women in positions of authority or performing acts of heroism. Increasingly, programs include characters with physical disabilities who play important roles. Through exposure to these programs, children learn to challenge social stereotypes and develop positive images of people from many ethnic groups. In one study, children were shown episodes of television sitcoms like *The Cosby Show* and then interviewed to see if they could understand the moral messages embedded in the program. The majority of first- and third-graders understood the moral of the program. This study also found a positive correlation between those who understood the prosocial message of the television programs and the frequency of their own prosocial behavior (Rosenkoetter, 1999).

## ■ REVIEW OF INFLUENCES ON MORAL DEVELOPMENT

In early school age, children are developing an initial moral code. The approaches to this issue are summarized in Table 8.4. Each contribution highlights an essential element of the larger, more complex phenomenon. *Learning theory*

**Table 8.4** Contributions to the Study of Moral Development

| CONCEPTUAL SOURCE | SIGNIFICANT CONTRIBUTIONS | CONSEQUENCES FOR A PARTICULAR ASPECT OF MORAL DEVELOPMENT |
|---|---|---|
| Learning theory | Relevance of an external system of rewards and punishments<br>Imitation of models<br>Formation of expectations about the reward structure | Moral behavior<br>Internalization of a moral code |
| Cognitive theory | Conceptual development of notions of intentionality, rules, justice, and authority<br>Stages of moral judgment | Moral judgments<br>Distinction between moral transgressions and social convention transgressions |
| Psychoanalytic theory | Parental identification<br>Formation of the superego | Internalization of parental values<br>Experience of guilt |
| Research on empathy and perspective taking | Ability to experience another's feelings begins very early and changes with age<br>Ability to recognize differences in point of view emerges slowly during early-school-age and middle childhood years<br>Peer conflict, peer interactions, and specific role-taking training all increase perspective-taking skills | Empathy heightens concern for others and helps inhibit actions that might cause distress<br>Perspective taking can foster helping and altruism |
| Research on parental discipline | Parents define moral content<br>Parents point out the implications of a child's behavior for others<br>Creation of a reward structure<br>Differential impact of power, love withdrawal, warmth, and inductions | Moral behavior<br>Moral reasoning<br>Internalization of moral values<br>Empathy and guilt |
| Research on watching televised violence | Observing aggressive role models<br>Arousal of aggressive emotions, memories, and action tendencies<br>Formation of beliefs and values | New repertoire of aggressive behavior<br>Lower threshold for aggressive action<br>Expectation of aggression from others<br>Desensitization to acts of violence |

# Media Use by Infants, Toddlers, and Preschoolers

FROM A PSYCHOSOCIAL perspective, development is a product of the ongoing interaction of the changing person in a changing environment. The media environment is an excellent example of this idea, with children being exposed at younger and younger ages to electronic media, including television programs and videos designed specifically for infants, video games and handheld game players, computer software for toddlers and preschoolers, and Internet sites for the very young. Relatively little is known about the scope and extent of use of these electronic media by very young children. How much time do children spend with electronic media? How much autonomy do they have in the use of these media? How much do these media activities replace traditional childhood activities, such as playing outside or reading and being read to?

A national survey sponsored by the Kaiser Family Foundation was designed to provide descriptive information to address some of these questions (Rideout, Vandewater, & Wartella, 2003). The study was a random, national telephone survey of families with children ages 6 months to 6 years old. The parent who spent the most time with the child was asked to complete the survey. When both parents spent equal amounts of time, one parent was chosen at random to reply.

Almost all the children (99%) had TVs in their homes, with 50% having 3 or more TVs. Children spent on average 2 hours a day with some type of screen media, about the same amount of time playing outside, and about 39 minutes reading or being read to. About two thirds of the children lived in homes where the TV is on at least half the time, even if no one is watching. Children are not just passive consumers of TV; they are making choices and affecting their media environment: 77% turn on the TV by themselves; 67% ask to watch specific shows; 62% can use a remote to change the channel; and 71% ask for their favorite DVDs or videos. By the time they are 4 to 6 years old, 70% have used a computer, and of those who use a computer, 64% can point and

click with a mouse, and 40% can load a CD-ROM.

Some homes were characterized as "heavy TV households" where the TV was on always or most of the time. When children grow up in homes where TV is on most of the time, they begin watching at a younger age (before the age of 1), they watch TV longer, and they read less often and for shorter amounts of time. Among 4- to 6-year-olds, 34% of those in heavy TV viewing households can read, compared to 56% in households where TV is on less often; 30% of children under 3 and 43% of those ages 4 to 6 have a TV in their rooms. Many of these children have their own VCR or DVD player and video game console as well. DVDs and videos are a common part of many children's lives, with 25% watching at least one video daily. Parents appear to have confidence in the educational value of these resources, seeing them as very important for their child's cognitive development. Even when children have TVs in their rooms, parents say that their children are not alone while they are watching TV, but that someone else is usually in the room.

When parents were asked about the role of media in their child's intellectual development, they consistently mentioned reading books as very important (96%). Activities such as building with blocks or doing puzzles were viewed as very important by a large majority (77%). About half the parents considered watching educational television or watching educational videos and DVDs as very important (58% and 49%, respectively).

The relationship of early television viewing and school readiness illustrates the bidirectional influence of children and television. Children of ages 2½ and 4½ were studied over 3 years. Those children who watched child-oriented educational programs when they were 2 and 3 scored higher on measures of academic skills, including reading, math, vocabulary, and school readiness than children who watched more "general audience" and cartoon programming. Children who had better academic skills

*Even toddlers have an idea about the power of the remote control. Will he be able to change the channel?*

at age 5 chose more child-oriented educational programs and less general audience television programming in later elementary grades. Those children with lower academic skills at age 3 were doing more general audience viewing by ages 4 and 5 (Wright, Huston, Murphy, St. Peters, Pinon, Scantlin, & Kotler, 2001).

Given the extensive exposure to electronic media at young ages, additional research is needed to help clarify the impact of these media. Concerns about the relationship of extensive TV viewing to childhood obesity, possible interference with social communication and language development, and exposure to non-educational content deserve empirical study. The media environment may also contribute to the emergence of self-directed goal attainment, new capacities for managing multiple stimuli at once (multitasking), and new appreciation for music, art, poetry, and the natural environment through early exposure.

points out that an external reward structure inhibits or reinforces behavior. Children also learn about how to behave morally by observing the behaviors of others and noting whether those behaviors are rewarded or punished. *Cognitive theory* suggests that in early childhood, children are most likely to take a pragmatic view about whether something is right or wrong, based largely on the consequences. However, children can distinguish between moral transgressions and social convention transgressions and do not regard them with the same degree of seriousness. *Psychoanalytic theory* is especially concerned with the relationship between parental identification and the development of conscience. Drawing on object relations theory, the importance of early, loving relationships with a sensitive caregiver is emphasized as the path through which a child comes to value himself or herself and to care about others.

The work on *empathy* and *perspective taking* shows that moral behavior requires an emotional and cognitive understanding of the needs of others. These prosocial skills help children appreciate how other children or adults may be experiencing reality. With this insight, children can modify their own actions to benefit others. Theory and research on *parental discipline* suggest that parents promote moral development when they establish clear standards, involve their children in dialogue, and try to increase children's understanding of the effects of their behavior on others. Research on *television violence* shows that children who are exposed to many hours of violent programming are more likely to act aggressively, accept violence as a method for resolving conflicts, and interpret the behavior of others as having an aggressive intention. Early exposure to high doses of television violence have long-term consequences for a person's tendency toward aggressive behavior.

## SELF-THEORY

Both gender identification and moral development are components of the child's self-concept. They are fundamental to the way a child conceives of the self in relation to the social world. Who are you? I am a boy. I have brown hair and brown eyes. I am a member of a family. I live at a certain address in a certain town. I know the difference between right and wrong. I know how my family, my teachers, and my friends expect me to behave. These are basic elements of a sense of self.

The development of the self-concept is at the heart of psychosocial development. Psychosocial theory provides a framework for understanding how the ego is transformed through ongoing interaction with society over the life span. It describes the creative process through which very rudimentary experiences of the physical self in infancy are transformed into self-consciousness, self-control, a sense of self–other relationships, a personal identity, a style of life, and finally a sense of integrity about the life one has lived.

The self-concept can be viewed as a theory that links the child's understanding of the nature of the world, the nature of the self, and the meaning of interactions between the two (Epstein, 1973, 1991, 1998). The function of the **self-theory** is to make transactions between the self and the world turn out as positively and beneficially as possible. One's theory about oneself draws on such inner phenomena as dreams, emotions, thoughts, fantasies, and feelings of pleasure or pain. It is also based on the consequences of interactions with the environment. When I tell my mother that I had a dream about monsters, does she tell me not to be ridiculous—that there are no monsters? Or does she ask me to tell her all about the monsters—what they looked like, how they smelled, what they ate? As I share my inner world with others, do they confirm or disconfirm my reality? Do they validate or invalidate my inner experiences?

As with any concept, the complexity and logic of the self-theory depend on the maturation of cognitive functions. Furthermore, because the self-theory is based on personal experiences and observations, one would expect it to be modified over the life course by changing physical, cognitive, and socioemotional competencies as well as by participation in new roles.

In the sections that follow, the self-theory is discussed in relation to the distinction between the *me* and the *I*, a general description of how the self-theory changes from infancy through middle childhood, and the nature of self-esteem—the evaluative aspect of a child's sense of self.

## ■ THE ME AND THE I

One of the earliest psychological analyses of self-theory was provided by William James (1892/1961). He described two elements of the self, the *me* and the *I*. The *me* is the self as object—the self one can describe—including physical characteristics, personality traits, social roles and relationships, thoughts, and feelings. The *I* is more subjective. It is the self as one who is aware of one's own actions. It can be characterized by four fundamental features: (1) a sense of agency or initiation of behaviors, (2) a sense of uniqueness, (3) a sense of continuity from moment to moment and from day to day, and (4) an awareness of one's own awareness (i.e., metacognition; [Damon & Hart, 1988]).

Building on these ideas, Damon and Hart (1988) devised a model of self-understanding that includes both the *me* (*self as object*) and the *I* (*self as subject*; see Figure 8.2). Along the front face of the cube—the self as object—Damon and Hart identified four domains of the *me*: *physical self* (my physical appearance and observable characteristics), *active self* (my behaviors and actions), *social self* (my social bonds and social skills), and *psychological self* (my personality, emotions, and thoughts). Along the side of the cube—the self as subject—they identified three domains of the *I*: *continuity* (experiences that allow me to know that I am the same person from day to day), *distinctiveness* (experiences that illustrate how I differ from others and perceive myself to be a unique individual), and *agency* (experiences that allow me to believe that I have an impact, that I am a causal agent).

| Developmental Level | General organizing principle | The self-as-object | | | | The self-as-subject | | |
| --- | --- | --- | --- | --- | --- | --- | --- | --- |
| | | Physical self | Active self | Social self | Psychological self | Continuity | Distinctiveness | Agency |
| 4. Later adolescence | Systematic beliefs and plans | Physical attributes reflecting volitional choices or personal and moral standards | Active attributes that reflect choices, personal or moral standards | Moral or personal choices concerning social relations or social-personality characteristics | Belief systems, personal philosophy, self's own thought processes | Relations between past, present, and future selves | Unique subjective and experiences interpretations of events | Personal and moral evaluations self influence |
| 3. Early adolescence | Interpersonal implications | Physical attributes that influence social appeal and social interactions | Active attributes that influence social appeal and social interactions | Social-personality characteristics | Social sensitivity, communicative competence, and other psychologically related social skills | Ongoing of recognition self by others | Comparisons between self and other along isolated dimensions | Communication and reciprocal interaction self influence |
| 2. Middle childhood | Comparative assessments | Capability-related physical attributes | Abilities relative to others, self, or normative standards | Abilities or acts considered in light of others' reactions | Knowledge, cognitive abilities, or ability-related emotions | Permanent, and cognitive capabilities active and immutable self-characteristics | Categorical identifications | Efforts, wishes, and talents self influence |
| 1. Early school age | Categorical identifications | Bodily properties or material possessions | Typical behavior | Fact of membership in particular social relations or groups | Momentary moods, feelings, preferences, and aversions | Categorical identifications | Categorical identifications | External, uncontrollable factors determine self |

Domains of the "me"

Domains of the "I"

**FIGURE 8.2**

A Developmental Model of Self-Understanding

Source: From *Self-Understanding in Childhood and Adolescence*, W. Damon & D. Hart, p. 56. Copyright © 1988 by Cambridge University Press. Reprinted by permission.

Characteristics of the self as *me* and *I* at a particular stage of life can be understood by following along one row around the cube. Development over time, shown by the vertical changes in each of the seven domains, is traced from early childhood through late adolescence. According to Damon and Hart, one can recognize evidence of self-understanding in each domain even in early childhood. Development of the self is not viewed as a shift in awareness of the physical self in childhood to an awareness of the social self at a later age. Rather, each domain of the self changes according to the general organizing principle around which all aspects of the *me* and the *I* are synthesized. Self-understanding is transformed from a categorical and concrete assessment of the self in early childhood to a comparative assessment of self and others in middle childhood. This is followed by a shift to an understanding of the social implications of one's self-characteristics in early adolescence. In later adolescence and early adulthood, the organizing principle becomes the formulation of a personal and social identity, which integrates the characteristics of the self into a set of beliefs and plans that guide future actions. By later adolescence, a dynamic relationship is formed, which links aspects of the self-theory, including personal values, experiences, and interpretations of life events, to interpersonal relationships and moral choices.

## ■ DEVELOPMENTAL CHANGES IN THE SELF-THEORY

At each stage, the self-theory is the result of a person's cognitive capacities and dominant motives as he or she comes into contact with the stage-related expectations of the culture (Stipek, Recchia, & McClintic, 1992). In infancy, the self consists of a gradual awareness of one's independent existence. The infant discovers body boundaries, learns to identify recurring need states, and feels the comfort of loving contact with caregivers. Basic needs to maximize pleasure and avoid pain and to preserve closeness to the loving caregiver serve as organizing principles for the infant's behavior. Many theorists emphasize the close connection of the infant's internal working model of the self with the responsiveness of the other (Bretherton & Munholland, 1999). The infant relies on the other to be accessible, to permit exploration, and to comfort and reassure. During the second year of life, self-recognition and the sense of the self as a causal agent add new dimensions to the self-theory. Gradually, these experiences are integrated into a sense of the self as a permanent being who has an impact on the environment, existing in the context of a group of other permanent beings who either do or do not respond adequately to the infant's internal states.

In toddlerhood, the self-theory grows through an active process of self-differentiation. Children explore the limits of their capacities and the nature of their impact on others. Because of toddlers' limited ability to entertain abstract concepts and their tendency toward egocentrism (the perception of oneself as the center of the world), their self-theories are based largely on the accumulation of daily experiences of competence, self-directed goal attainment, and praise or dis-

© Lawrence Migdale/Getty Images

*As Rundine reacts to the class, she demonstrates her ability to take her audience into account.*

approval. There is little recognition of social comparisons (being better or worse than someone else), but an increasing sensitivity to the positive and negative reactions of others.

During early school age, the self-theory becomes more differentiated. Children can distinguish between the real self (how one actually is) and the ideal self (how one would like to be). They recognize some discrepancies between how they describe themselves and how their parents or friends may describe them (Oosterwegel & Oppenheimer, 1993). They can differentiate among various areas of activities like math, reading, and music, indicating perceptions of strength in certain areas and weakness in others (Eccles, Wigfield, Harold, & Blumenfeld, 1993).

According to Damon and Hart (1988), in early childhood, the self is understood as an accumulation of **categorical identifications**. No additional linkage or significance is taken from these categorical statements—simply a recognition that they exist.

EXAMPLES: What kind of person are you? *I have blue eyes.*

Why is that important? *It just is.*

What kind of a person are you? *I'm Catholic.*

*What does that say about you?* I'm Catholic, and my mother is, and my father is, and my grandmother, and my grandfather, and I'm Catholic too. (pp. 59–60)

In middle childhood, the organizing principle shifts to **comparative assessments**. Self-understanding relies on comparisons of oneself with social norms and standards or with specific other people.

EXAMPLES: *What are you like?* I'm bigger than most kids.

*Why is that important?* I can run faster than everybody.

*What are you like?* I'm not as smart as most kids.

*Why is that important?* It takes me longer to do my homework. (pp. 62–63)

One might point to the period of early childhood as the beginning of self-consciousness. Through conversations, stories, photographs, and rituals, early-school-age children begin to understand that their experiences have a uniqueness. They realize that they exist in a specific time, not in the long ago of dinosaurs or pioneers, nor in near past of their grandmother's or their mother's childhood (Nelson, 2000). Their culture shapes the content and the context of their sense of self. For example, one study reported on U.S. and Chinese college students' earliest childhood memories (Wang, 2001). The following is a U.S. college student's response to a request to think of her earliest memory and to describe it as precisely as possible. Students were asked to produce something that they actually remembered, not something someone had told them. This memory comes from a time when the student was about 3.

> I remember standing in my aunt's spacious blue bedroom and looking up at the ceiling. Then something caught my eye—it was the white wainscoting that bordered the top of the wall with the ceiling. I remember staring, fixated with its intricate design. And while I was doing this, all of sudden, I had an epiphany, a sort [of] realization. It was almost my first realization of a sense of "self." Because, as I was staring at the ceiling, I realized that no one else was around. I remember being taken aback by the ability to amuse myself without any toys. (Wang, 2001, p. 220)

The average age for these first memories was 3½ years for U.S. students, and 4 years for the Chinese students. The U.S. students' memories tended to be discreet events where they had the lead role in a drama of some emotional event or moment. The Chinese students' memories tended to be more routine events involving family and neighborhood. The cultural difference in the way self is construed is preserved in each society's view of the self. In the United States, the self is valued as a unique, bounded, autonomous being. Self-memories and narratives are told to preserve a sense of the self that guides the life history through choices and action. In China and in other Asian cultures, the self is an interdependent, relational being. Remembering about the self supports the sense of one's ongoing relationships and the interdependence of self and others (Wang, 2001; Wang, Leichtman, & Davies, 2000).

## ■ THEORY OF MIND

From ages 4 to 6, children become more aware that people have different points of view. Work on the **theory of mind** focuses on the natural way children understand each other's behavior. In day-to-day functioning, the theory of mind suggests that beliefs, desires, and actions are logically linked. A person engages in some action because he or she believes that this action will satisfy a specific desire. For example, Jakob *wants* his father to take him to the toy store because he *wants* a new toy train, and he *believes* that he can get one at the toy store. In trying to understand a person's actions, it is important to consider the interaction of beliefs and desires as they operate together to guide action (Wellman, 1991).

Research on the theory of mind typically poses situations to children to see what they understand about someone else's beliefs and desires. For example, in the early research, children watched a character named Maxi put a chocolate candy in one location. Then, when Maxi leaves, children watched while another character moved the chocolate to a new place. Children were asked what Maxi thinks or what Maxi will do when he comes back into the room. Where will Maxi *think* the chocolate is located? Where will Maxi *look* (action) for the chocolate? Three-year-olds typically said that Maxi will look for the chocolate where *they* know it is—in the new location. Older children, ages 4 and 5, realized that Maxi has an incorrect belief and predicted that Maxi will look for the chocolate in its old location (Wimmer & Perner, 1983; Wellman, Cross, & Watson, 2001).

Subsequent research using similar scenarios has found that children as young as 3 are very good at considering what a character *wants*, even if it is different from what they might want. However, they have trouble thinking about what someone else might *believe*, especially disconnecting their own knowledge of the situation from the point of view of another. By the time children are 5, however, they are quite facile at detecting the possibility of false or incorrect beliefs. They can separate what they know about a situation from what someone else may know, and they expect that a character's actions will be based on the character's beliefs, even when those beliefs are incorrect (Ziv & Frye, 2003).

The ability to appreciate that what you know or believe to be true is different from what others know and believe to be true is a salient feature of self-awareness. It allows children to begin to speculate about what others may think about them, and how their behavior may be understood or misunderstood. Gender role standards are especially important in this regard. Children are very sensitive to any implication that they are not living up to the expectations of how a boy or girl ought to act. Children are also aware of moral imperatives that define good and evil. These cognitive gains make a child more sensitive to social pressure, more likely to experience feelings of guilt or failure, and more preoccupied with issues of social comparison, self-criticism, and self-evaluation. For these reasons, the issue of self-esteem becomes especially salient during early and middle childhood.

## SELF-ESTEEM

For every component of the self—the physical, active, social, and psychological self—a person makes an evaluation of worthiness. This self-evaluation, or **self-esteem**, is based on three sources: (1) messages of love, support, and approval from others; (2) specific attributes and competencies; and (3) the way one regards these specific aspects of the self in comparison with others and in relation to one's ideal self (Pelham & Swann, 1989). The need to protect and enhance one's self-esteem is considered a basic psychological motive that drives behavior. Views of the self as being loved, valued, admired, and successful contribute to a sense of worth. Views of the self as being ignored, rejected, scorned, and inadequate contribute to a sense of worthlessness. These early affective experiences contribute to a general sense of pride or shame, worthiness or worthlessness, that is captured in the global statements children make about themselves even as early as age 3 or 4 (Eder, 1989; Eder, Gerlach, & Perlmutter, 1987).

Information about specific aspects of the self is accumulated through experiences of success and failure in daily tasks or when particular aspects of one's competence are challenged. A young child may develop a positive sense of self in athletics, problem solving, or social skills through the encouraging reactions of others as well as through the pleasure associated with succeeding in each of these areas (Harter, 1985, 1998).

With experience in a variety of roles and settings, each specific ability takes on a certain level of importance for a person. Not all abilities are equally valued at home, at school, and by friends. People may believe they have abilities in some areas but not in those they consider highly important. Others may believe they have only one or two areas of strength, but they may highly value those areas and believe them to be critically important to their overall success. Self-esteem is influenced by the value one assigns to specific competencies in relation to one's overall life goals and personal ideals. Thus, it is possible to be a success in the eyes of others and still feel a nagging sense of worthlessness. Similarly, it is possible to feel proud and confident even when others do not value the activities and traits in which one takes satisfaction.

Feelings of positive self-worth provide a protective shield. If a person has a positive, optimistic self-evaluation, then messages that are negative and incongruent with it will be deflected. People with high self-esteem will explain a failure by examining the task, the amount of time needed for its completion, the other people involved, or the criteria for evaluating success and failure. They use a variety of strategies to minimize the importance of negative feedback. They do not permit a failure to increase doubt about their basic worth. Rather, their high self-esteem functions to protect their positive self-evaluation by coping effectively with negative feedback and reclaiming their view of the self as someone who has socially valued qualities (Brown, Dutton, & Cook, 2001).

Experiences of success build confidence and contribute to positive self-esteem. Abby is thrilled to be able to ride her big two-wheeler without the training wheels. She feels competent, proud of her accomplishment, and happy to be riding so well. What other kinds of accomplishments are likely to contribute to self-esteem at this age?

By contrast, people with low self-esteem feel worse after a failure, tend to view failure as new evidence of their lack of worth, and are less likely to cope effectively with the negative feelings that accompany failure (Heimpel, Wood, Marshall, & Brown, 2002). People with low self-esteem appear to accept negative moods that follow a failure experience and are less likely to take action to try to improve their mood. Because negative feedback is so painful for those with low self-esteem, they avoid unfavorable comparisons with others, leading them to be more cautious in situations that might expose them to criticism (Bernichon, Cook, & Brown, 2003).

Despite the many positive correlates of high self-esteem, some scholars have questioned whether high self-esteem is necessarily a universally positive quality. Some researchers have suggested that there is such a thing as unrealistic or fragile high self-esteem (Kernis, 2003). For example, people with high self-esteem seem to deflect failure messages in one area by emphasizing their abilities in another area (Brown & Smart, 1991). When employed consistently, this strategy can be perceived as a defensive reaction that allows the individual to preserve a sense of self-worth rather than to address underlying feelings of inferiority or shame (Jordan et al., 2003).

A different criticism about self-esteem is that the emphasis on high self-esteem is a value that reflects the individualist nature of Western culture. In contrast, Eastern cultures are less concerned with affirming the positive qualities of the indi-

*By the age of 5 or 6, children are trying hard to gain acceptance from adults and peers. Even mild criticism from a teacher is often enough to arouse feelings of guilt or remorse. What kind of teacher criticism do you imagine might be taking place in this photo?*

© Elena Rooraid/Photo Edit

vidual, valuing instead self-discipline and self-improvement (Marku, Mullally, & Kitayama, 1997). A pancultural or universalist perspective suggests that it is a universal tendency for humans to strive for and protect their self-regard. However, the norms for what one considers evidence of self-worth and the strategies that human beings use to advance their self-regard are shaped by culture. In the West, individual success and social status are valued. In the East, the expectation of respect based on seniority is valued. Both cultural traditions sanction self-enhancement, but the dimensions that count as worthy differ (Sedikides, Gaertner, & Toguchi, 2003; Brown, 2003).

**SELF-ESTEEM AND THE EARLY-SCHOOL-AGE CHILD.** At each life stage, as individuals set new goals for themselves or as discrepancies in competence become apparent, temporary periods of lowered self-esteem may be anticipated. Although we tend to think of self-esteem as a stable trait that characterizes individuals across settings, there appear to be periods of life when self-esteem is more vulnerable to fluctuation, especially as individuals encounter dramatic changes in roles, environments, and normative expectations for behavior (Trzesniewski, Donnellan, & Robins, 2003). Early childhood appears to be one of those periods.

Early-school-age children are increasingly aware of the discrepancy between their own competencies and what they recognize as the skills expected of them by their teachers and parents or exhibited by older children. They are able to view themselves as objects of evaluation by others. They are also aware of the importance of acceptance by adults and peers outside the family, especially their teachers and classmates (Weinstein, Marshall, Sharp, & Botkin, 1987). These newly valued others may not be as proud of their skills or as understanding about their limitations as are their family members. In peer competition, they begin to feel anxious about their performance and about how their abilities will be evaluated in comparison with those of others (Butler, 1989). At school,

for example, young children often make critical comments about one another's work. Criticisms tend to outnumber compliments, and boys tend to be more critical than girls of their peers' work (Frey & Ruble, 1987). The combination of open peer criticism and a heightened emphasis on peer competition may make the school an environment in which one's self-esteem is frequently challenged.

For all these reasons, early-school-age children are likely to experience feelings of depression and worthlessness. This decrease in self-esteem may be seen as a temporary fluctuation. However, it may endure. In research with kindergartners, children were faced with a challenging task. The way they approached the task, their hopefulness about succeeding, and their general expression of positive or negative attributes were combined to reflect a measure of helplessness. Five years later, the expressions of helplessness assessed in kindergarten proved to be a good predictor of depression and a low sense of self-worth. The implication is that a scheme for low self-esteem and helplessness may begin to be crystallized in the early childhood period and, unless challenged through positive intervention, may color one's sense of mastery and competence in the years ahead (Davis-Kean & Sandler, 2001; Kistner, Ziegert, Castro, & Robertson, 2001). Young children need frequent reassurance from adults that they are competent and loved. They need numerous opportunities to discover that their unique talents and abilities are useful and important, and that they can have a positive impact on others. As competencies increase, as thought becomes more flexible, and as the child makes meaningful friendships, self-esteem is expected to increase.

## PEER PLAY

Although experiences in the family provide the primary information that guides a young child's construction of the social world, interactions with peers contribute important

## HUMAN DEVELOPMENT AND DIVERSITY

## Hopscotch

AN ANCIENT GAME played around the world, hopscotch takes children from earth to heaven and back again. A hopscotch diagram is inscribed into the floor of the Forum in Rome. As the Roman empire expanded, soldiers copied this or similar diagrams on the cobblestone roads in Europe. Children have improvised on the Roman diagrams, but they usually have some type of fantasy theme. Across the continents, hopscotch has been described in 16 countries, including the United States, Britain, Russia, India, Aruba, and Nepal, each with their own regional variations. Children toss their markers, hop over boxes, avoid danger areas like hell, moon, water, or boxes marked by other players, and return to home base (Grunfeld, 1975; Lankford, 1996; see Figure 8.3). The widespread appeal of the game reflects many of the competencies and challenges of the early-school-age period.

The game symbolizes the perils of early childhood, as children try to move ahead in their lives without stepping on lines, going outside the boxes, or stepping into forbidden areas. Children in all cultures must balance carefully in order to stay within the parameters of their socialization.

At the same time, the game provides an opportunity to exercise mas-

*Hopscotch combines fantasy, mastery, and a bit of strategy as children hop from earth to heaven and back again.*

tery. Children are the creators of their hopscotch world, and they have the skills to conquer it by being careful, agile, and having a bit of luck. Erikson (1982) would emphasize the link in language and thought between hopping and hoping. Children take a leap

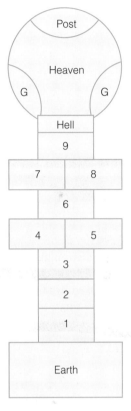

**FIGURE 8.3**

Hopscotch

of faith as they hop from box to box, facing perils, overcoming some, failing sometimes, and starting over.

---

opportunities for physical, cognitive, social, and emotional development. The quality of play expands during the early school-age period, introducing more complex games with larger numbers of participants. Children form friendship groups that allow them to sustain more elaborate fantasy play, experience group conflict, participate in group problem solving, and encounter varying ideas about the topics discussed previously: gender, morality, and the self.

### ■ GROUP GAMES

The early-school-age child continues to use vivid fantasies in play. During this period, a new form of play emerges. Children show interest in group games that are more structured and somewhat more oriented to reality than play that is based primarily on imagination. Duck-Duck-Goose, London Bridges, and Farmer-in-the-Dell are examples of early group play. Hide-and-Seek and Statue-Maker are more complex games of early school age. They involve more cognitive complexity, physical skill, and ritual. These games combine fantasy with an emphasis on peer cooperation. Group play is a transitional form between the fantasy play of the toddler and the team sports and other games with rules of middle childhood (Erikson, 1977).

Group games usually include a few rules that are simple enough so that a child can use them effectively to begin a game and determine a winner without the help of an adult. Usually, no team concept is involved. A game is played repeatedly, so that many children have an opportunity to win. The particular pleasure that children derive from these games seems to result more from peer cooperation and interaction than from being a winner (Garvey, 1977).

Many of these games permit children to shift roles. A child is the hider and then the seeker, the catcher and then the thrower, the statue maker and then the statue. Through group play, children experience the reciprocal nature of role relationships. Whereas many of their social roles are fixed—son or daughter, sibling, student—in play with peers, children have opportunities to experience a variety of perspectives (Lee, 1975; Sutton-Smith, 1972).

## ■ FRIENDSHIP GROUPS

In early school age, friendships are based on the exchange of concrete goods and the mutual enjoyment of activities. Friendships are maintained through acts of affection, sharing, or collaboration in fantasy or constructive play. By the age of 4 or 5, children who have stable friendships become skilled at coordinating their interactions with their friends, creating elaborate pretend games, and being willing to modify their play preferences so that both members in the friendship have a chance to enjoy the kinds of play they like best (Park, Lay, & Ramsay, 1993; Vaughn, Colvin, Azria, Caya, & Krzysik, 2001). Children may build snow forts together, play dolls or space adventure, or sleep over at one another's homes. Friendships may be broken by taking away a toy, hitting, or name-calling. The opportunity to form friendships benefits young children by enhancing their interpersonal sensitivity, social reasoning skills, and conflict resolution skills (Volling, Youngblade, & Belsky, 1997).

**CONFLICTS AMONG FRIENDS.** Young children tend to evaluate situations on the basis of outcomes rather than intentions. Therefore, they are often harsh in assigning blame in the case of negative outcomes. For example, children were asked how much they should be blamed for another child's getting hurt. The "injury" took place in six different hypothetical situations. In the case of the lowest level of responsibility, the child was accidentally hurt by someone's toy, but the owner did not actually cause the injury. At this level, 6-year-olds were more likely than older children or adults to blame themselves for the outcome (Fincham & Jaspars, 1979). Because of this rigid approach to social responsibility, peer play is frequently disrupted by quarrels, "tattling" on others, and hard feelings about injustices.

Even though children appear to be drawn into the active world of peer friendships, it is an uneven, difficult, and often extremely frustrating terrain for many early-school-age children. For example, many 5- and 6-year-olds participate in play fighting. In a study of children's perceptions of play fighting, Italian and British children of ages 5, 8, and 11 were surveyed about the differences between real fighting and play fighting (Smith, Hunter, Carvalho, & Costabile, 1992). About half the children liked play fighting—a somewhat larger number of boys than girls. But about 80% thought there was a risk that play fighting could lead to a serious, "real" fight. This might happen if there was an accidental injury, if the play fighting got carried away into mean name-

calling, or if, when one child accidentally hurt the other, the second child mistook the injury as purposeful and hurt the first child back. Five-year-olds said that if play fighting turned into real fighting, they would tell an adult. No matter whether the other child was a friend or not, they believed that such a transgression had to be handled with a serious intervention by a grown-up. The older children were more likely to forget about it, especially if the other person was a friend.

**SEX SEGREGATION AMONG FRIENDS.** One of the most noticeable characteristics of young children's friendship groups is that they are likely to be segregated by sex. When boys and girls are free to choose play companions, they tend to choose others of their own sex. This pattern of same-sex social groupings among children is found not only in the United States but also in most other cultures (Edwards & Whiting, 1988). In one longitudinal study, children at age 4½ were found playing with same-sex friends about three times more often than with opposite-sex friends. By age 6½, they were *eleven* times more likely to be playing with same-sex friends (Maccoby & Jacklin, 1987).

Sex segregation is promoted by both cognitive and behavioral factors (Barbu, Le Maner-Idrissi, & Jouanjean, 2000). Based on the earlier discussion of gender identification, it is clear that children expect others of the same sex to like similar activities, toys, and forms of play. Children form internal representations of what boys and girls are like as friends and playmates. These internal models guide the inferences they make as they engage in peer interaction (Markovits, Benenson, & Dolenszky, 2001). Thus, children are likely to seek others of the same sex because they believe these other children will have the same play preferences they have.

At the same time, boys and girls do appear to play differently, especially when in same-sex and mixed-sex groups. Thus, a preference for same-sex play groups may be fostered by feelings of comfort or discomfort as children accumulate play experiences. Finally, some cultures discourage girls and boys from participating in the same types of play. For example, when children in a Brazilian tribal culture play "family," the boys ("husbands") go off to pretend to be hunting and fishing, returning with leaves that are then given to the girls ("wives"), who pretend to cook them and pass them out to the boys to eat (Gregor, 1977).

The significance of the formation of same-sex social groups is that boys and girls grow up in distinct peer environments (Maccoby, 1988, 1990). They tend to use different strategies to achieve dominance or leadership in their groups. Boys are more likely to use physical assertiveness and direct demands; girls are more likely to use verbal persuasiveness and polite suggestions. The verbal exchanges in all-boy groups are apt to include frequent boasts, commands, interruptions, heckling, and generally playful teasing. Boys try to top one another's stories and to establish dominance through verbal threats. The interactions in all-girl groups, on the other hand, tend to include agreeing with and acknowledging the others' comments, listening carefully to one another's statements, and

*At this age, boys and girls tend to prefer same-sex play companions. Boys enjoy rough and tumble play; girls enjoy fantasy-based, relational play.*

talking about things that bind the group together in a shared sentiment or experience (Leaper, Tenenbaum, & Shaffer, 1999). In mixed-sex groups, boys may do less controlling and dominating than they would in all-boy groups, but this may still be more than girls find acceptable or comfortable. As a result, girls' negative views of boys are reinforced and their tendency to seek all-girl peer interactions increases.

Of course, many young children do form friendships with children of the opposite sex. These friendships may begin as early as infancy or toddlerhood between children who live in the same neighborhood or attend the same child care center. They are sustained by a compatibility of interests and play preferences and may survive the trend toward seeking same-sex friendships, even during early and middle childhood (Howes & Phillipsen, 1992). However, the general preference for same-sex friendship groups is an important aspect of social development that is established during the early childhood years and continues into adolescence (Bukowski, Gauze, Hoza, & Newcomb, 1993). Although a boy and a girl grow up in the same culture, the same neighborhood, and even the same family, the tendency to establish separate play and friendship groups fosters the development of distinctive gender-linked communication strategies and makes the achievement of mutual understanding between boys and girls difficult.

**GROUPS AND DYADS.** In addition to the preference for same-sex friends, boys and girls tend to prefer to interact in groups of different size. Early-school-age girls seem to enjoy *dyadic* (two-person) interactions over larger groups, whereas boys seem to enjoy larger groups (Benenson, 1993; Markovits, Benenson, & Dolenszky, 2001). This is not to say that boys and girls cannot function effectively in both dyadic and larger peer group situations, but when given the choice, boys prefer the group and girls the dyad. These two configurations, the group and the dyad, provide different opportunities for intimacy, different needs to exercise dominance and control, and different problems in the coordination of action. They pro-

vide models for different forms of adult social relationships—the dyad being associated with intimacy between partners or in parent–child relationships, and the peer group being associated with sports teams, work groups, and families.

# THE PSYCHOSOCIAL CRISIS: INITIATIVE VERSUS GUILT

As children positively resolve the toddlerhood crisis of autonomy versus shame and doubt, they emerge from that stage with a strong sense of themselves as unique individuals. During early school age, children shift their attention toward investigation of the external environment. They attempt to discover the same kind of stability, strength, and regularity in the external world that they have discovered within themselves.

## INITIATIVE

**Initiative** is an expression of agency—an outgrowth of early experiences of the self as a causal agent that continues to be demonstrated as children impose themselves and their ideas and questions onto their social world. It is a manifestation of the *I*, the executive branch of the self that was discussed earlier in the section on self-concept (Damon & Hart, 1988). Initiative is the active, conceptual investigation of the world, in much the same sense that autonomy is the active, physical manipulation of it (Erikson, 1963). It can be recognized in a child's curiosity, exploratory behavior, and active coping strategies in the face of obstacles (Frese, 2001).

The child's motivation for and skill in investigation depend on the successful development of a strong sense of autonomy in toddlerhood. Having acquired self-control and confidence in themselves, children can perform a variety of actions and observe the consequences. They discover, for example, what makes parents or teachers angry and what pleases them. They may deliberately perform a hostile act in order to evoke a hostile response. Children's curiosity about the order of the universe ranges from the physical to the metaphysical. They may ask questions about the color of the sky, the purpose of hair, the nature of God, the origin of babies, or the speed at which fingernails grow. They take things apart, explore the alleys and dark corners of their neighborhood, and invent toys and games out of odds and ends.

One expression of initiative is children's playful exploration of their own bodies and sometimes of their friends' bodies. It is not uncommon to find 5- and 6-year-olds intently involved in a game of "doctor" in which both "doctor" and "patient" have their pants off. Boys of this age may occasionally be observed in a game that is won by the individual who can achieve the longest urine trajectory. Girls report occasions on which they have attempted to urinate from a standing position "in the same way a boy does." Both boys and girls engage in some form of masturbation. These behaviors are evidence of children's growing curiosity about and pleasure in their bodies and their physical functioning.

Children may express initiative while they are alone, by attempting to discover how things work and by building or inventing novel devices:

> Donald kicked and knocked over an endless variety of things at hand. He put a block on top of a toy car, a leaf on top of that, then knocked the leaf off. Then he turned a truck over on its side, put a block on top of it, moved over to the car, stacked three blocks on top of it, and knocked the whole structure over. He took the car again, spanked it as if it were a doll, knocked it upside down, placed a leaf on top of it, then swept the leaf off. He played a little longer in this way, then ran out of the garage. (Murphy, 1962, p. 102)

Children may also express initiative in social situations by asking questions, asserting their presence, and taking leadership. In one study of social competence, children described the strategies they used to enter a peer play group (Dodge, Pettit, McClaskey, & Brown, 1986). Two children were playing a game (they were referred to as the *hosts*), and a third child was asked to enter the room and try to initiate play with the others. The entry episode was videotaped and coded. Both the child who tried to initiate play and the two hosts were interviewed about the episode and asked to evaluate how successful the entry child had been. Three strategies for initiating interaction were judged to be effective and were associated with other evidence of social competence:

1. Children established common ground by giving meaningful information in response to questions.
2. Children engaged in a positive, friendly interchange with the others.
3. Children did not show evidence of negative, irritable behaviors. The children who were least successful in initiating entry into the play "were disruptive, . . . made

nagging, weak demands, . . . engaged in incoherent behaviors, or . . . disagreed with hosts without citing a rule or reason" (Dodge et al., 1986, p. 25).

Children who experience a positive sense of initiative can apply this orientation to investigation of the physical as well as the social world. They innovate through the creation of "magic potions" mixed together with soap, perfume, pine cones, leaves, and other powerful ingredients. They create plays, stories, puppet shows, dances, and ceremonies. They dress up in costumes, entertain company by standing on their heads, engage in daring acts by hanging from tree limbs or walking on the tops of high ledges, and impose themselves in any and all curious and private discussions. They spend time trying to figure out ways to catch a glimpse of Santa Claus on Christmas Eve or the Tooth Fairy when she comes at night to collect her treasures. These are the "Little Rascal" years, when a sense of initiative is associated with a naive, exuberant, entrepreneurial spirit and a desire to discover, direct, and dominate. All manner of investigation and inquiry is fair game.

## GUILT

**Guilt** is an emotion that accompanies the sense that one has been responsible for an unacceptable thought, fantasy, or action (Izard, 1977). It is recognized as a fundamental negative emotion that is usually accompanied by remorse and a desire to make reparation for real or imagined wrongdoing. It has the adaptive function of promoting social harmony, because it disrupts or inhibits aggressive actions and leads people to ask for forgiveness or to try to compensate for wrongs they may have done. In comparison to *shame*, which often is accompanied by strong feelings of anger or resentment, guilt is typically tied to constructive efforts to repair the harm done to others (Tangney, 2001).

Three theories offer different explanations for the dynamics that underlie feelings of guilt (Zahn-Waxler & Kochanska, 1990). The psychoanalytic perspective views guilt as an emotional reaction to one's unacceptable sexual and aggressive impulses. These impulses are especially threatening during the phallic stage, when hostility and feelings of sexuality toward one's parents become a focus of the child's wishes and must be repressed.

Second, research on empathy suggests that guilt may be awakened at a very early age through emotional arousal and sensitivity to another person's emotional distress. This view of guilt based on empathy is not defensive; it is closely linked to prosocial feelings and the basic emotional ties between infants and their caregivers (Hoffman, 1982).

The third, cognitive perspective suggests that guilt occurs when one fails to act in accord with one's own personal standards and beliefs. This view supposes a more advanced level of self-reflection and the ability to compare one's behaviors against personal standards. In this theory, guilt begins to be experienced in early and middle childhood as children begin

*Saniosa made her sister cry by calling her a bad name. Now she is in her room, thinking things over. For most children, occasional feelings of guilt lead to wanting to set things right and regain positive feelings with their family or friends.*

to be more comparative in their organization and evaluation of self.

Every culture imposes some limits on legitimate experimentation and investigation. Some questions may not be asked; some acts may not be performed. Adults' reactions determine whether the child will learn to view specific behaviors, such as aggressiveness, sexual play, or masturbation, as wrong or acceptable. Children gradually internalize cultural prohibitions and learn to inhibit their curiosity in the taboo areas. One taboo shared by most cultures is the prohibition of incest. Most children learn that any behavior that suggests sexual intimacy between family members is absolutely forbidden. Even the thought of such a relationship comes to generate feelings of anxiety and guilt.

The child's curiosity in other domains is limited to the extent that the family and the school impose restrictions on certain areas of inquiry or action. The psychosocial crisis of initiative versus guilt is resolved positively when children develop the sense that an active, questioning investigation of the environment is informative and pleasurable. Inquiry is tempered by a respect for personal privacy and cultural values. However, the dominant state of mind is curiosity and experimentation. The child learns that, even though certain areas are off limits, efforts to understand most aspects of the world are appropriate.

Guilt, like other negative poles of the psychosocial crises, can have an adaptive function. As children grow in their sense of empathy and ability to take responsibility for their actions, they are able to acknowledge when their actions or words may have caused harm to someone else. Normal levels of guilt have been associated with positive levels of prosocial behavior and high levels of empathy (Tangney, 1991). Feelings of guilt generally lead to remorse and some attempt to set things right again, to restore the positive feelings in a relationship.

Girls and boys may show different patterns in the experience of guilt, based on different patterns of socialization and relationships (Maccoby, 1990). Girls tend to have higher levels of empathy and boys higher levels of aggression. Girls are socialized to be concerned about others and to pay attention to preserving connections with them. Thus, they are more likely to experience guilt when they have lied or been inconsiderate to others. They are also more likely to experience guilt when they blame themselves for unhappiness or conflict among others. In contrast, boys are socialized to be assertive and control the expression of their emotions. They are more likely to experience guilt over overt actions like fighting, victimizing other children or animals, or damaging property (Williams & Bybee, 1994).

Some children suffer from overwhelming guilt. They feel that each of their questions or doubts about the world is inappropriate. They may experience guilt about their own impulses and fantasies, even when they have taken no actions and no negative consequences have resulted. Moreover, these children begin to believe that their thoughts and actions are responsible for the misfortune or unhappiness of others. For example, young children of depressed mothers express unusually high levels of distress, concern, and feelings of responsibility for others' unhappiness. Mothers who are consistently sad set an example of blaming themselves for most of the bad things that happen. Depressed mothers are likely to withdraw love when the child has misbehaved—a discipline technique associated with high levels of guilt and anxiety (Zahn-Waxler, Kochanska, Krupnick, & McKnew, 1990). In this environment, children learn to restrict new behaviors out of fear that they may cause harm or unhappiness to someone else. Children who resolve the crisis of initiative versus guilt in the direction of guilt are left to rely almost totally on their parents or other authorities for directions on how to operate in the world.

The psychosocial crisis of initiative versus guilt highlights the close tie between intellectual curiosity and emotional development. During this stage, parents and the school transmit the cultural attitudes toward experimentation, curiosity, and investigation. They also make demands that direct the child's curiosity away from familial, subgroup, and cultural areas of taboo. Children are expected to develop the ability to control their own questions and behavior. Whereas violations may bring disapproval and punishment, successful self-control may attract no notice whatsoever. Children must develop a strong internal moral code that will help them avoid discipline. They must also develop the ability to reward themselves for correct behavior. The more areas of restriction that are imposed on children's thinking, the more difficult it is for children to distinguish between legitimate and inappropriate areas of investigation. The only way that children have of coping with this problem is to develop a rigid moral code that restricts many aspects of thought and action.

# THE CENTRAL PROCESS: IDENTIFICATION

The discussion of the developmental tasks during early school age points directly to **identification** as the central process in the resolution of the conflict between initiative and guilt. The self-theory and self-esteem develop in the context of social interactions. Children at this age actively strive to enhance their self-concepts by incorporating into their own behavior some of the valued characteristics of their parents. Through a variety of processes, including watching the behavior of others, imitating others, engaging in activity where others are watching, and participating in play, conversation, and problem solving with others, children form an internal representation of the self that is coordinated with the representation of the other (Decety & Chaminade 2003; Sherkow, 2001).

There appear to be four substantially different theories about the motives for identification (see Table 8.5). The *fear of loss of love* is founded on a child's initial realization of dependence on the parents. A child behaves like a parent in order to ensure a continued positive relationship. Eventually, the child incorporates aspects of the loved one's personality into his or her own self-concept. The child can then feel close to the loved person even when they are not physically together (Jacobson, 1964). If a child can be like a loved parent, the parent's continuous presence is not required to reassure the child about that parent's love.

*Identification with the aggressor* is aroused when children experience some fear of their parents. In order to protect themselves from harm, they perform behaviors that are similar to those they fear. Children identify even with parents who are extremely brutal. Because most of the behaviors that these children incorporate are aggressive, they often tend to be aggressive toward others. This kind of identification may give children a magical feeling of power and decrease the parents' tendency to mistreat them. Parents who see great similarity between themselves and their children are less likely to threaten or harm them (Freud, 1936).

A third motive for identification is the *need for status and power* (Bandura, 1977, 1986). Studies of modeling show that children are more likely to imitate the behavior of a model who controls resources than they are the behavior of a model who is rewarded. The imitative behavior is motivated by a vicarious feeling of power experienced when they behave in the same way as the powerful model. Within a family, children are likely to have personality characteristics similar to those of the more dominant parent (Hetherington, 1967).

A fourth motive for identification results from the *children's need to increase the perceived similarity with their parents* (Kagan, 1958). Children attribute a number of valued characteristics to their parents, including physical size, good looks, special competencies, power, success, and respect. Children more readily share these positive attributes when they perceive a similarity between themselves and their parents. They experience this sense of similarity in three principal ways: (1) by perceiving actual physical and psychological similarities, (2) by adopting parental behaviors, and (3) by being told about similarities by others. Increasing perceptions of similarity promote stronger identifications.

These four motives apply to the process of identification at all ages and regardless of the sex of the identifier or the model. For a particular child, one of these motives may dominate,

**Table 8.5** Four Motives for Parental Identification

| MOTIVE | DEFINITION |
|---|---|
| Fear of loss of love | A child behaves like a parent in order to ensure a continued positive love relationship. |
| Identification with the aggressor | A child behaves like a parent in order to protect himself or herself from the parent's anger. |
| Identification to satisfy needs for power | A child behaves like a parent in order to achieve a vicarious sense of the power associated with the parent. |
| Identification to increase perceived similarity | A child behaves like a parent to increase his or her perceived similarity to the parent and thereby to share in the parent's positive attributes. |

but all four motives are involved in the process. Parental identification allows children to feel that their parents are with them even when they are not physically present. This feeling of connection with parents provides an underlying sense of security for children in a wide variety of situations.

Viewed from another perspective, identification allows children a growing sense of independence from their parents (Jacobson, 1964). Children who know how their parents would respond in a given situation no longer need the parents' physical presence to direct their behavior. Children who can praise or punish themselves for their actions are less dependent on their parents to perform these functions.

Parental identification affects children's development in two different ways. On the one hand, the closeness with parents provides the basis for the incorporation of parental sanctions and prohibitions. Once children have integrated these guidelines for behavior, they are bound to feel guilty whenever they anticipate abandoning them. On the other hand, the security that results from strong parental identification allows children increased freedom when they are away from their parents. The child whose parental identification is strong is more likely to engage the environment, take risks, and initiate action.

Identification with parents results in a strengthening of the child's personality. An important outcome of early-school-age identification is the formation of an ideal self-image, which psychoanalytic theorists sometimes refer to as the **ego ideal** (Freud, 1909/1955; Sandler, Holder, & Meers, 1963). The conscience not only punishes misdeeds but also rewards actions that bring children closer to some aspect of their ideal self-image. The ideal self is a complex view of the self as it may be in the future, including skills, profession, values, and personal relationships. It is a fantasy, a goal that is unlikely to be attained even in adulthood. Nonetheless, the discrepancy between the real self and the ideal self is a strong motivator. As children strive to achieve their ideal, they attempt new activities, set goals that strain the limits of their abilities, take risks, and resist temptations that might interfere with their desired goals.

The ego ideal is more unrealistic during early school age than at later stages. Young children fantasize anything they wish about themselves in the future. They take their parents' values literally and use them to project an ideal person of mythic proportions. The ideal self may include the strength of Hercules, the wealth of Queen Elizabeth II, the wisdom of Confucius, and the compassion of Jesus. The lack of realistic constraints on the ego ideal allows children to investigate and vicariously experience certain human qualities that may always be beyond their reach. As people grow older, it is important that the fantasy of the ideal self-image becomes increasingly attainable, although still beyond what has been attained. People who find it difficult to modify their ideal self-images become vulnerable to personal frustration and psychological despair because they are unable to be what they wish. Many 6-year-old children may wish to become President of the United States. This largely unrealistic fantasy is

Identification is the central process through which children develop an ego ideal.

exciting and, for some, ennobling. However, few people actually achieve this position. By the time one reaches early adulthood, it is important to have developed an occupational ideal that is closer to what is actually attainable.

Identification with parents is the process by which the ideal self-image and moral prescriptions are blended into the child's personality. When children are unable to control their behavior so that it corresponds to the sanctions and ideals that they have internalized, they will experience guilt. In contrast, when children's behavior approaches their ideals and conforms to internalized sanctions, they will experience feelings of self-confidence that allow them to take initiative. The balance between guilt and self-confidence determines the eventual resolution of the psychosocial crisis of initiative versus guilt.

The crisis of initiative versus guilt captures the child's need to question existing norms and the emerging feelings of moral concern when these norms are violated. This crisis does not focus specifically on intellectual development; however, one may assume that the level of questioning that takes place during this stage is possible only because of an increase in cognitive complexity. The process of positive parental identification promotes the incorporation of cultural norms and strengthens the child's sense of competence. Socialization during this stage may either foster a creative openness or an anxious dread of novelty.

# THE PRIME ADAPTIVE EGO QUALITY AND THE CORE PATHOLOGY

As a result of efforts to resolve the crisis of initiative versus guilt, children emerge from the period of early school age with the benefit of the prime adaptive ego quality of purpose or the core pathology of inhibition. These predispositions suggest an orientation that leaves a child with coping resources that will support directed, action-oriented problem solving or a more passive, self-protective approach to stress, in which the child is more likely to allow others to guide the course of his or her behavior.

## PURPOSE

**Purpose** is thought or behavior with direction, and therefore, with meaning. "Purposefulness is the courage playfully to imagine and energetically to pursue valued goals" (Erikson, 1978, p. 29). It is a cognitively more complex extension of the will gained in toddlerhood, in that it combines a sense of agency with a plan. In contrast to the toddler, who exercises his or her will through the mere delight in action, the early school-age child imposes intention and goals on action. This is the difference, for example, between running around the yard, laughing and shouting—typical behavior for toddlers—and saying to a friend, "Let's play tag," which is more likely for early-school-age children. Toddlers may enjoy stacking blocks or splashing in water, whereas early-school-age children want to turn materials and toys into a story or a project. Their actions are going in a direction; their play has a plan. Behind the process of planning is a complex sense of the situation, the creation of a goal, strategies to achieve it, and monitoring success in realizing the goal (Scholnick, 1995). The sense of purpose, expressed in planning and enacting plans, reflects a significant expansion of the ego into the realm of the present and the future.

A sense of purpose suggests not only that the action does have meaning, but also that the person initiating it has meaning. Ricky enters a play situation and says, "I have an idea. Let's play trains." This kind of suggestion reflects Ricky's sense of a goal-directed plan, and a sense of confidence about introducing his idea into the ongoing activities of the group.

## INHIBITION

**Inhibition** refers to the restraint or suppression of behavior. In a psychological context, one might define inhibition as a conscious or unconscious blocking of unacceptable wishes

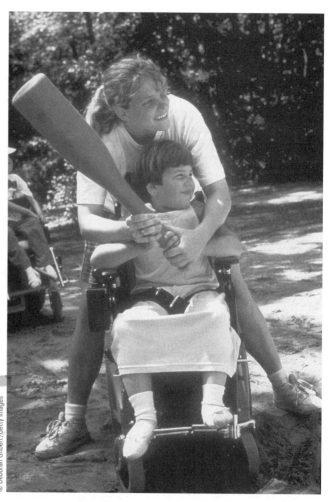

*Katie is supported by her counselor to become more purposeful and goal directed in her play.*

and behaviors. Inhibition is assumed to emerge when parents or caregivers use high levels of love withdrawal and guilt-inducing interactions with their children. These kinds of interactions suggest to the child that the parent's love, affection, and approval are conditional on the child matching certain specific parental standards. In order to adapt in this kind of environment and avoid risking loss of love, the child becomes self-conscious and restrained in action. In contrast to the sense of confidence and agency implied in the notion of purpose, a child who is inhibited does not want to take the risks associated with imposing a plan or suggesting a direction, for fear that his or her suggestions will result in parental disapproval.

Lois Murphy (1972) proposed that inhibition has even earlier origins in the mother–infant relationship. She suggested that in "healthy" mother–infant interactions, mothers take care to provide meaningful feedback and consequences for their babies' actions. When mothers are very depressed or psychologically unavailable, they may be unable to engage in the kinds of consistent, rhythmic behaviors that produce early experiences of cause and effect. Babies who have never internalized the schemes for these kinds of behaviors cannot impose them on external circumstances. As a result of the lack of early, structured cause–effect interactions in the mothering relationship, some early-school-age children have a very passive orientation toward play and social interactions. According to Murphy, their inhibition is not so much a product of guilt but a lack of basic early structures or schemes for the positive process of initiation. These children do not impose organization on toys or integrate sensory and motor play into a more complex scenario. They remain focused on the sensory activity itself, like digging in the sand, or on the imitation of basic behaviors, like feeding the baby.

Inhibited children are likely to emerge as shy, withdrawn, and often lonely during the subsequent period of middle childhood. Without some form of social intervention, they become increasingly withdrawn, not knowing how to impose their ideas into the ongoing activities of the group, and not experiencing the confidence-building effects of making suggestions and having them accepted. Consequently, by the end of the early-school-age period, their inhibition produces new deficits in social skill development.

## APPLIED TOPIC
# SCHOOL READINESS

IN 1989, PRESIDENT George H. W. Bush and the state governors created an educational agenda for the United States. The first goal was that by the year 2000, all children in the United States would start school *ready to learn*. This goal identified the importance of the first years of schooling in setting the long-term course for school achievement and entry into adulthood as an educated person ready to undertake the roles and responsibilities of adult life. This goal, which seems positive and appropriate on the face of it, has resulted in important dialogue about what is meant by readiness, how to measure it, what obstacles stand in its way, and who should be responsible for achieving it (Wesley & Buysse, 2003).

## DEFINING READINESS

The concept of **readiness** is a familiar idea in the study of development. Typically, the term is used to refer to a time when the child's physical, cognitive, social, and emotional maturation are at a level to undertake new learning or to engage in a more complex, demanding type of activity or relationship. It is sometimes referred to as a critical or sensitive period or a teachable moment. The idea of a *sensitive period* was identified in Chapter 6 in relation to attachment relationships, in Chapter 7 in relation to language use and toilet training, and in this chapter in relation to gender role identification. Vygotsky's concept of a *zone of proximal development* is another way of conceptualizing readiness; it is the next higher level of performance one can achieve with the help of more competent teachers.

When thinking about the goal that all children should come to school ready to learn, the concept of readiness becomes somewhat more complicated. Does it refer to readiness to learn or readiness to start school? One might argue that all children—except perhaps those with severe neurological damage—are both ready and eager to learn. However, not all children have the combined physical, cognitive, emotional, and social skills that allow them to adapt to the demands of the kindergarten environment or to succeed at the academic challenges of its curriculum without support (Early, Pianta, Taylor, & Cox, 2001).

## MEASURING KINDERGARTEN READINESS

In the past, kindergarten readiness was established largely by chronological age. School districts typically established a birthday cutoff. For example, if a child was 5 by December 1 of a given year, he or she could start kindergarten in September of that year. Those who missed the December 1 date had to wait until the following year. In the 1980s, concern about the quality of education in the United States led to an upgrading of the elementary school curriculum. As part of this school reform, academic demands for school performance were raised, and children were exposed to a more challenging curriculum in earlier grades. Many skills that had been introduced in first grade are now part of the kindergarten curriculum, and more children are having trouble meeting the expectations for school performance. In efforts to prevent early school failure, some states began to administer school readiness tests. However, there is no agreement or universal acceptance of a measure of kindergarten readiness, and some educators dispute whether any test given to 5-year-olds can accurately predict a child's ability to learn in the school environment (American Academy of Pediatrics, 1995; Pyle, 2002).

Most 5-year-olds do not read or write, so mass testing is not feasible. Any approach to measuring kindergarten readiness must involve one-on-one evaluation. Many early childhood educators emphasize that cognitive skills in reading, mathematics, and general knowledge are not enough to understand the child's readiness for school. Physical development and motor coordination, social skills, communication skills, and a child's enthusiasm for learning all play a part in how well a child will adapt to the school environment.

To address the question of what kindergartners are able to do at the start of school, the U.S. Department of Education initiated the Early Childhood Longitudinal Study, Kindergarten Class of 1998–1999 (Zill & West, 2000). A national sample of more than 19,000 kindergartners who were attending their first year of regular school were evaluated in one-on-one assessments. Information about the children was also gathered from parents and teachers. Children were evaluated in reading, mathematics, and general knowledge as well as physical health, motor development, social skills, problem behaviors, and the child's approach to learning. The hope is that these assessments will provide some norms for

*These children are learning a funda-mental skill for success in school: walking in line.*

© Bill Aron/Photo Edit

what most children can do when they come to kindergarten, and a look to the future for how these early abilities may predict subsequent school success. A report of how kindergartners performed on each of the areas assessed can be found in *America's Kindergartners* (West, Denton, & Germino-Hausken, 2000). Table 8.6 provides information on children's performance on four concrete tasks that are part of a national assessment of children's emerging literacy and school readiness (U. S. Census Bureau, 2003).

Given the lack of an objective, accepted measure or screening test, what do parents and teachers think are essential markers of school readiness? How can a parent judge if a child is ready or should wait a year before beginning kindergarten? In two separate national surveys, parents and teachers were asked what characteristics a child needs to be ready to start school. Teachers emphasized that children need to be

physically healthy, well rested, and well nourished as the most important aspects of readiness. Beyond that, they emphasized the ability to communicate effectively, demonstrate enthusiasm and curiosity, follow directions, not be disruptive, and show sensitivity to the feelings of other children as important indicators (Lewit & Baker, 1995). From the teachers' perspective, many of the components of readiness focus on social aspects of learning and cognitive skills that support self-regulation. Parents tended to emphasize the importance of specific skills—such as using a pencil or scissors, knowing the alphabet, or counting to 20—more frequently than the teachers (Lewit & Baker, 1995). Typically, the teachers' opinions about kindergarten readiness placed greater emphasis on social and emotional competence than on skills and knowledge, although these expectations differed by geographic region and by teachers' years of experience. Children need to be

**Table 8.6** Children's School Readiness Skills: 2001
(Percentages of Children Ages 3–5 Not Yet in School)

| CHARACTERISTICS | RECOGNIZES ALL LETTERS | COUNTS TO 20 OR HIGHER | WRITES NAME | READS OR PRETENDS TO READ | HAS 3–4 SKILLS |
|---|---|---|---|---|---|
| **Total** (%) | 23 | 57 | 53 | 71 | 39 |
| SEX | | | | | |
| Male | 19 | 52 | 47 | 68 | 34 |
| Female | 27 | 61 | 58 | 74 | 43 |
| POVERTY STATUS | | | | | |
| Above poverty threshold | 25 | 61 | 55 | 75 | 44 |
| Below poverty threshold | 14 | 43 | 45 | 57 | 23 |

Source: U.S. Census Bureau, (2003). *Statistical Abstract of the United States: 2003*, Table No. 238.

ready to separate comfortably from their parents, interact in a positive way with other children, and engage in the "appropriate" behaviors associated with the student role: following directions, being quiet when asked, and asking and answering questions. School success relies more on being able to focus one's attention, express one's needs and thoughts, and exercise what has been described as effortful control than it does on being able to count to 20 or name the colors (Blair, 2002; Lin, Lawrence, & Gorrell, 2003).

## OBSTACLES TO SCHOOL READINESS

Success in kindergarten is based on a combination of intellectual and social skills, enthusiasm for learning, and the motivation to succeed. Most children are excited about going to kindergarten and doing well. However, certain demographic characteristics are associated with the likelihood of poor school adjustment, even in kindergarten. According to the national study of America's kindergartners, four family risk factors are (1) parents who have not graduated from high school, (2) low income or welfare dependence, (3) single-parent families, and (4) families where a language other than English is the primary language spoken at home (Zill & West, 2000).

Forty-six percent of U.S. kindergartners have one or more of these risk factors. Figure 8.4 shows the percentage of children from each of six types of communities who have none, one, or multiple risk factors. Having one or more of these risk factors was associated with lower scores in reading and mathematics and poorer health. Children with multiple risk factors were more likely to show aggressive behavior in school and were judged as having somewhat more difficulty making friends, listening to other children's ideas, and comforting other children than those with no risk factors. Children with multiple risk factors were more likely to be described by teachers as having difficulty paying attention or persisting in the completion of a task and were more likely to be described as sometimes or never eager to learn, in contrast to children with no risk factors.

## WHO IS RESPONSIBLE FOR MEETING THE GOAL FOR SCHOOL READINESS?

In establishing a national goal for children to start school ready to learn, we are faced with the question, "Whose responsibility is it to meet this goal?" Do we need to place more responsibility on families to provide the early experiences that will foster health, confidence, motivation, and cognitive and social development during the first 4 years of life? Do we need to place more responsibility on schools to work with children where they are by providing the environment, services, curriculum, and methods of instruction that will facilitate learning for an increasingly diverse group of students? Do we need to place more responsibility on local, state, and federal government to sustain and expand programs such as Head Start, so that more children can participate in early ed-

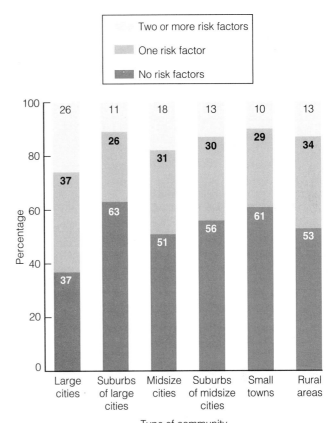

**FIGURE 8.4**

Percentage Distribution of First-Time Kindergartners by Number of Risk Factors and Type of Community: Fall, 1998

Source: U.S. Department of Education, NCES Early Childhood Longitudinal Study. Kindergarten Class of 1998–1999, Fall 1998.

ucational experiences that help offset the negative effects of poverty?

A psychosocial perspective suggests action on all three fronts. The child's chances of success in school can be improved if *all* interacting systems support one another and keep the goal of academic success for the widest range of students in focus. Schools need to be attuned to the characteristics of their incoming kindergartners and become "ready schools." Professionals need to identify the cognitive, social, and motivational factors that support school success and find ways to support development in those domains during the infancy and early childhood years. Educators and parents must become partners for the optimal development of children, identifying those children who are at risk for school failure and making plans for integrated, multiyear, multiservice programs to support their success.

One such model, described as the *CoZi schools*, integrates the philosophies of James Comer, a psychiatrist, and Edward Zigler, a developmental psychologist (Hornblower, 1996; Zigler, Kagan, & Hall, 1996). In these schools, the staff reach out to families as early as the last trimester of pregnancy. They

## Supporting School Readiness for Young Children with Disabilities

A SIGNIFICANT NUMBER of young children enter the early-school-age period with moderate to severe disabilities. For the 2000–2001 school year, close to 600,000 children of ages 3 to 5 were being served under the Individuals with Disabilities Education Act—an increase of 32% from 1992–1993 (U.S. Department of Education, 2002). By definition, these children are performing at or below the 50th percentile of their age-mates in one or more domains, including motor skills, speech and language, social and emotional competence, and learning and memory (Siegel, 1996).

The term *disability* can refer to a wide variety of possible functional challenges. The two most common impairments are speech and language delays (55% of those receiving services) and developmental delays (25% of those receiving services). In the study of American kindergartners, parents reported that "substantial minorities of children are already experiencing risks for developmental difficulties, with one in five being described as overly active, one in six having prob-

lems concentrating for sustained periods, and one in nine not articulating words clearly or fluently" (Zill & West, 2000).

Preschool and kindergarten programs that include children with disabilities face a significant task—to ensure that the inclusion benefits the child both socially and academically. Many children with disabilities are mainstreamed in a classroom without any provision for encouraging social interaction with the other children. One of the major concerns facing teachers is the ability to promote positive social skills, including appropriate levels of assertiveness, self-control, and cooperation among students of varying abilities (U.S. Department of Education, 2002). The school setting makes specific demands on children to function in more constrained, regulated ways than might be required at home. Some children benefit from the routine and predictability of the school setting, whereas others have difficulty regulating their behavior to comply with teacher and peer expectations.

Effective inclusion requires strategies for promoting contact between students with and without disabilities and creating an accepting social climate among students. The interventions must be tailored to address the unique areas of deficit. A child with autism, for example, may need to be taught how to imitate a model and may have difficulty cooperating with peers, but might be able to play successfully with puzzles or to listen to the teacher read a story. A child with moderate mental retardation may have difficulty with tasks that require fast reaction time, such as competitive games among students, but could perform well if speed of response is not a concern. Children with speech and language difficulties may find it difficult to express themselves or to engage in conversation with peers. As a result, they may withdraw from social interactions. Teachers need to find ways to build on each child's level of performance so that the child is not stigmatized for his or her disability and continues to make progress toward an appropriate academic standard.

visit the homes of families, encourage interest in books and educational activities, and talk with parents about child development and childrearing. The schools involve parents in school-based activities that meet their own needs (e.g., exercise classes, adult education classes) as well as the needs of their children. The schools are sites for child care, before- and after-school care, and summer programming. Staff members take the responsibility of mentoring specific children who suffer from neglect or are going through unusual family disorganization. These schools have redefined their role to be a community resource. The goal of each child's educational success is reached by addressing the child's and the family's broader social, emotional, and physical needs at the earliest possible moment (Dryfoos, 1994).

## Chapter Summary

Early school age marks the beginning of work on developmental tasks that will persist well into adulthood. The four tasks of early school age are closely interrelated. The complex process of gender identification has cognitive, affective, physical, and interpersonal elements. As young children clarify the content of their gender identity, they create a set of beliefs about the self, including their self-worth, relationships with other children, and the kinds of activities and interests that are appropriate for them, not only in the present but also in the future. The gender identity of the early-school-age child will be revised and reintegrated as it becomes a core element of personal identity in adolescence.

The development of conscience, with its capacity to reward and punish, brings an internalization of moral standards. Moral development is accompanied by a heightened sensitivity to violating basic cultural standards, many of which relate to interpersonal behavior, especially toward adults and peers. The child's experiences with transgressions, guilt, or praise for prosocial behavior have implications for the elaboration of the self-theory and particularly for the establishment of self-esteem.

Although the self-theory is continuously revised with entry into new roles and cognitive capacities, the establishment of a positive sense of worth in early school age brings an important tone of optimism as the child faces new challenges. Competence and social acceptance are the essential antecedents of self-esteem. Increased involvement with peers during play brings about an appreciation of others' perspectives, social acceptance, and delight in the intimacy of friends.

The psychosocial crisis of initiative versus guilt has direct implications for such essential personality characteristics as self-esteem, creativity, curiosity, and risk taking. The child who resolves this crisis positively will be fortified with an active, exploratory approach to the environment. Guilt plays an important role in orienting children toward the implications of their actions for others. In moderation, guilt is an essential ingredient in preserving social bonds. In the extreme, however, guilt restricts creative thought and limits action.

The applied topic of school readiness illustrates the potential conflict between development and socialization. The society has determined that 5-year-old children will attend school. At the same time, 5-year-olds are at a wide array of developmental levels, bringing them to the door of the school with substantial differences in physical, cognitive, social, and emotional competence. Factors such as disabilities, poverty, and a non-English-speaking home environment may all complicate the child's ability to adapt to the school environment.

## Further Reflection

1. What are some examples of the interconnections among the developmental tasks of this stage? Think about how gender identification, moral development, and peer play influence a child's self-theory, and how the self-theory might influence these other areas?
2. How might the biological system, including physical appearance, disabilities, motor development, and health, affect a child's ability to master the developmental tasks of this age?
3. What are your earliest recollections about your own moral development? What factors were most important

in shaping what you believed to be right and wrong? Did you develop a sense of yourself as a "good" or a "naughty" child? What difficulties did you face in trying to comply with the standards for good behavior?

4. Think about the crisis of initiative versus guilt. What does it mean to you? What would you look for in a child's behavior or conversation that would indicate a strong sense of initiative or guilt? How do you distinguish initiative from autonomy? How is the concept of initiative related to challenges for coping and adaptation that are required in adulthood?
5. Consider the role of the media as part of the child's family environment. What is the bidirectional nature of influence between children and the media? What role did the media play in structuring your own childhood? How did you make use of the media to meet your own needs?
6. What would you do to foster a child's sense of initiative and purpose in the transition to kindergarten? How does a caring community promote early school achievement for diverse learners? How can you conceptualize the biological, psychological, and societal factors that interact to shape the transition to kindergarten?

## On the Web

**VISIT OUR WEBSITE**

Go to http://www.wadsworth.com/psychology to find online resources directly linked to your book.

## Casebook

For additional case material related to this chapter, see the case entitled "Delaney Goes to Kindergarten" in *Life Span Development: A Case Book*, by Barbara and Philip Newman, Laura Landry-Meyer, and Brenda J. Lohman, pp. 87–94. This case illustrates some of the challenges that children face in the transition to kindergarten and how home, preschool, and kindergarten systems can work together to foster a child's continuing school success.

# CHAPTER 9

# MIDDLE CHILDHOOD (6–12 YEARS)

*Study for "War & Peace" Dancers, 1952./Pablo Picasso/© 2005 Estate of Pablo Picasso/Artists Rights Society (ARS), New York*

*Children move into a dynamic social world where the self concept is shaped by new experiences of peer acceptance or peer rejection and the formation of close friendships. New levels of cognitive complexity allow children to engage in more stimulating activities and to experience the satisfaction of accomplishment.*

■ **DEVELOPMENTAL TASKS**

Friendship
Concrete Operations
Skill Learning
Self-Evaluation

CASE STUDY: BECCA

Team Play

■ **THE PSYCHOSOCIAL CRISIS: INDUSTRY VERSUS INFERIORITY**

Industry
Inferiority

■ **THE CENTRAL PROCESS: EDUCATION**

■ **THE PRIME ADAPTIVE EGO QUALITY AND THE CORE PATHOLOGY**

Competence
Inertia

■ **APPLIED TOPIC: VIOLENCE IN THE LIVES OF CHILDREN**

Consequences of Exposure to Violence
Prevention Strategies

■ **CHAPTER SUMMARY**

■ **FURTHER REFLECTION**

## CHAPTER OBJECTIVES

▶ *To clarify the role of friendship in helping children to learn to take the point of view of others, be sensitive to the norms and pressures of the peer group, and experience closeness in relationships, and to clarify the negative consequences that result from social rejection and loneliness.*

▶ *To describe the development of concrete operational thought, including conservation, classification skills, combinatorial skills, and the child's ability to understand and monitor his or her own knowledge and understanding.*

▶ *To explore skill learning, including the presentation of a model for the process of acquisition of complex skills such as reading and the examination of societal factors that provide the context in which skill learning occurs.*

▶ *To analyze the development of self-evaluation skills, including self-efficacy, and ways that social expectations of parents, teachers, and peers contribute to a child's self-evaluation.*

▶ *To describe a new level of complexity in play as children become involved in team sports and athletic competition.*

▶ *To explain the psychosocial crisis of industry versus inferiority; the central process through which the crisis is resolved, education; the prime adaptive ego quality of competence; and the core pathology of inertia.*

▶ *To explore the impact of exposure to violence on development during middle childhood.*

THE THEORIES OF Jean Piaget and Erik Erikson stimulated developmental research focusing on children between the ages of 6 and 12. These theories emphasize intellectual growth and a growing investment in mastery and competence. During this time, children are learning the fundamental skills that are valued in their culture, whether those are reading, writing, and arithmetic or hunting, fishing, and weaving. As children gain confidence in their abilities, they begin to have more realistic images of their potential contributions to the larger community.

For many children, this is a joyful, vigorous time. The fears and vulnerabilities of their early school days are behind them. Energized by ego qualities of hope, will, and purpose, most children are able to enjoy many of the resources and opportunities of their communities. Even as the presence of their family members continues to be a comfort to them, they begin to explore more complex social relationships with their peers and other significant adults.

In some parts of the world, however, the lives of children between ages 6 and 12 are marked by extreme disorganization and exploitation. Children are vulnerable to the violence of war as victims of terrorist attacks, civil wars, injury from explosions of abandoned land mines, and forced enlistment as soldiers among warring tribes (Pearn, 2003). Slavers travel through impoverished areas, kidnapping, buy-

ing, or luring children into forms of slave-like labor where they are often beaten, sexually abused, and degraded. Children as young as 6 are being sold or given away by poor families as slaves or bonded laborers. An estimated 60 million children worldwide are involved in the harshest forms of slave labor and bondage, used in armed conflicts and in the service of drug trafficking, as well as in all forms of hazardous work (Human Rights Watch, 2004). Tens of thousands of young children in West Africa have been kidnapped and sold into slavery to work in cocoa farms, where their labor contributes to the production of the chocolates that children worldwide love (Bess, 2001). As many as 300,000 children across 80 countries are forced to participate in armed conflict in which they not only witness bloodshed, but may be forced into combat or used as soldiers'"wives" (Smith, 2001).

In such circumstances, the opportunity for children to work on the developmental tasks of friendship formation, concrete operational reasoning, skill learning, self-evaluation, and team play may be viewed as a great luxury. Having the time, resources, and security to promote areas of cognitive, social, and emotional development is only possible in the context of communities that are economically and politically stable and ideologically committed to the intellectual and interpersonal future of their children. ■

# DEVELOPMENTAL TASKS

New developmental tasks are highlighted as children become focused on friendship formation, concrete mental operations, skill learning, self-evaluation, and team play. This mix of tasks coupled with new capacities for complex social, emotional, and intellectual activity produce a remarkable synergy. Whereas play dominates the behavior of early-school-age children, middle childhood is characterized by more purposeful, industrious behavior. This is not to say that play is lost. New thrills and excitement accompany the capacity to engage in more complex forms of play and the desire to take new risks—riding one's bike farther from home, jumping and then diving from the high board, or riding on the big, fast roller-coasters without a parent.

## FRIENDSHIP

Can you remember some things about a friend you had when you were 10 years old? Friendships of middle childhood may not be as enduring as the attachment relationships of infancy. Yet some of these friendships are quite memorable; they have many of the elements of a close affectionate bond. At this age, children describe close friends as people who play together, like the same activities, share common interests, enjoy each other's company, and count on each other for help. Peer relationships include forming meaningful dyadic and group relationships, participating in larger peer networks, and experiencing peer acceptance or rejection (Gifford-Smith & Brownell, 2003).

Friendships may not be as essential to survival as attachment relations, but they clearly provide social and developmental advantages (Berndt & Murphy, 2002). As highlighted in psychosocial theory, human beings are social animals whose development is intricately dependent on a network of close, supportive social relationships. In middle childhood, the radius of significant relationships expands to include classmates, team mates, and close friends. According to ethological theory, being a member of a group has protective advantages. Group cooperation gives a selective advantage to many social species, especially in tracking and hunting for food. Therefore, the skills of cooperation and sociability may advance the species as a whole as well as the individual. On an individual level, children who are able to participate in positive peer friendships are embedded in an intellectually and socially stimulating environment.

### FAMILY INFLUENCES ON SOCIAL COMPETENCE

Not all children enter middle childhood with the same capacity to make friends and enjoy the benefits of close peer relations. Early family experiences contribute to a child's sociability and social competence; the process of becoming ready for friendship may begin in infancy. Children who have secure attachments in infancy are more popular in preschool and engage more freely in social interactions. They are perceived as more helpful and better able to consider the needs of others (Sroufe & Fleeson, 1986; Park & Waters, 1989).

By figuring out the rules to informal games, friends exchange points of view and learn to work out their differences. What might these boys have to decide in order to play an informal game of basketball?

© Philip Newman

Children who had secure attachments in infancy have more friends by age 10 than those with insecure attachments. Various studies have suggested that when two children with histories of secure attachments are friends with one another, those friendships are likely to be more responsive, less critical, and offer more companionship than friendships between children whose attachment history is mismatched (e.g., secure-insecure [Berlin & Cassidy, 1999]).

A mother's discipline techniques, the way she speaks to her child, and her parenting values are all linked to a child's social competence and popularity. Children whose mothers interact with them in positive, agreeable ways and openly express their feelings are likely to have more positive friendship relations than children whose mothers are harsh or neglectful. These patterns are observable as early as preschool and continue to be found in the elementary grades (Youngblade & Belsky, 1992). In contrast, mothers who use power-assertive discipline techniques and who believe that aggression is an acceptable way of resolving conflicts have children who expect to get their way by asserting power in peer conflicts (Dishion, Patterson, Stoolmiller, & Skinner, 1991; Haskett & Kistner, 1991; McCloskey & Stuewig, 2001). In observations of the social relationships of 8- to 12-year-old children who had been physically abused, these children had lower ratings of social status among their peers, were described by their peers as being aggressive and uncooperative, and by their teachers as showing noticeable behavior problems (Salzinger, Feldman, Hammer, & Rosario, 1993).

The family environment influences a child's social competence in at least three ways. First, children may directly imitate their parents' interpersonal communication styles or positive or aggressive behaviors. If parents ask a lot of questions and invite their child's opinions, for example, the child may be more likely to show interest in others' ideas and opinions. One study asked children and parents to describe characteristics of parental conflict, and related this to the child's friendship quality (Kitzmann & Cohen, 2003). Children who perceived their parents' conflicts as poorly resolved (e.g., "Even after my parents stop arguing, they stay mad at each other") also had difficulty resolving conflicts in their own close friendships. Children's perceptions of poor parental conflict resolution were correlated with lower friendship quality, including seeing their friends as less of a source of companionship, help, or intimacy.

Second, a parent's disciplinary technique may influence what a child expects in a social interaction. Children who have been exposed to aggressive parental techniques or to violence between their parents believe that these same strategies will work with their peers. As a result, these children are more likely to have conflicts with their friends and experience social rejection.

Third, parents who are highly restrictive and who try to control their children's behavior are less likely to permit their young children to have many peer social interactions. Thus, these children arrive at the middle childhood years with less experience in peer play (Hart, Ladd, & Burleson, 1990; McCloskey & Stuewig, 2001).

## THREE CONTRIBUTIONS OF FRIENDSHIP TO SOCIAL DEVELOPMENT

Children learn at least three lessons from daily interactions with their peers. The first lesson is an increasing appreciation of the many points of view represented in the peer group. As children play together, they discover that there may be several versions of the same song, different rules for the same game, and different customs for the same holiday. In learning about others through the friendly exchange of ideas, children also learn about themselves. The second lesson teaches children to be sensitive to the social norms and pressures of their peer group. The third lesson is closeness to a same-sex peer (Bukowski, 2001). The passion and vitality of middle childhood friendships are captured in the following scene from Mark Twain's *The Adventures of Huckleberry Finn*:

> We went down the hill and found Joe Harper and Ben Rogers, and two or three more of the boys, hid in the old tanyard. So we unhitched a skiff and pulled down the river two mile and a half, to the big scar on the hillside, and went ashore.
>
> We went to a clump of bushes, and Tom made everybody swear to keep the secret, and then showed them a hole in the hill, right in the thickest part of the bushes. Then we lit the candles, and crawled in on our hands and knees. We went about two hundred yards, and then the cave opened up. Tom poked about amongst the passages, and pretty soon ducked under a wall where you wouldn't 'a' noticed that there was a hole. We went along a narrow place and got into a kind of room, all damp and sweaty and cold, and there we stopped. Tom says: "Now, we'll start this band of robbers and call it Tom Sawyer's Gang. Everybody that wants to join has got to take an oath, and write his name in blood.". . .
>
> And if anybody that belonged to the band told the secrets, he must have his throat cut, and then have his carcass burnt up and the ashes scattered all around, and his name blotted off the list with blood and never mentioned again by the gang, but have a curse put on it and be forgot forever. (Twain, 1962, pp. 9–10)

**PERSPECTIVE TAKING AND COGNITIVE FLEXIBILITY.** As children interact with peers who see the world differently than they do, they begin to understand the limits of their own points of view. Piaget (1932/1948) suggested that peers have an important influence in diminishing one another's self-centered outlook precisely because they interact as equals. Children are not forced to accept one another's ideas in quite the same way as they are with adults. They argue, bargain, and eventually compromise in order to maintain friendships. The opportunity to function in peer groups for problem solving and for play leads children away from the egocentrism of early childhood and closer to the eventual flexibility of adult thought. The benefit of these interactions is most likely to occur when peers have differences in perspective that result in conflicts that must be resolved. The benefits are especially positive for children who interact with slightly more competent peers who can introduce more advanced or flexible approaches to problem solving (Tudge, 1992).

The behavior of well-adjusted, competent children is maintained in part by a number of social cognitive abilities, including social perspective taking, interpersonal problem solving, information processing, and communicative competence. These cognitive abilities foster a child's entry into successful peer interactions. At the same time, active participation with peers promotes the development of these social cognitive abilities. In a longitudinal study of the influence of friendship on motivation and school adjustment, students who had a reciprocated friendship in sixth grade showed greater prosocial behavior, higher academic achievement, and less emotional distress than those who had no reciprocated friendship. The children whose friends had high levels of prosocial behavior in sixth grade were more likely to express prosocial goals for themselves in eighth grade (Wentzel, Barry, & Caldwell, 2004).

Perspective-taking ability relates to other social skills that contribute to the quality of a child's social relationships. Such skills include the ability to analyze social problems, empathize with the emotional state of another person, understand that others may construe a situation differently because of their own information or beliefs, and accept individual differences in personality or abilities (Chalmers & Townsend, 1990; Wellman, 1990; Pillow, 1991; Montgomery, 1993). Children who are sensitive to the variety of perspectives that coexist in a social situation are also likely to be more positively evaluated and trusted by their peers. Those who are perceived as more trustworthy and attuned to the concerns of others are likely to form more friendships (Rotenberg, McDougall, Boulton, Vaillancourt, Fox, & Hymel, 2004). An interactive process is thus set in motion. Children who have opportunities to participate in peer friendships make progress in achieving new levels of interpersonal understanding. As interpersonal understanding grows, children acquire the skills and sensitivity with which to be more effective with—and usually more valued by—their peers.

**SOCIAL NORMS AND PEER GROUP PRESSURE.** The peer group evolves norms for acceptance and rejection. As children become aware of these norms, they begin to experience pressures to conform to the peer group. Adults, particularly teachers, then lose some of their power to influence children's behavior. In the classroom, the early-school-age child focuses primarily on the teacher as a source of approval and acceptance. By age 9 or 10, children perceive the peer group as an equally significant audience. Children often play to the class instead of responding to the teacher. The roles of class joker, class snob, and class hero or heroine emerge during

middle childhood and serve as ways of gaining approval from the peer group.

The need for peer approval becomes a powerful force toward conformity. Children learn to dress, talk, and joke in ways that are acceptable to their peers. They learn to inhibit the expression of certain emotional reactions—especially sadness, vulnerability, and anger—in order to present a cool, competent public image to their peers (Salisch, 2001). Heterosexual antagonism, which is common at this stage, is perpetuated by pressures toward conformity. If all the fifth-grade boys hate girls, Johnny is not very likely to admit openly that he likes to play with Mary. There are indications that perceived pressures to conform are stronger in the fifth and sixth grades than at later times, even though the importance of specific peer groups has not yet peaked (Gavin & Furman, 1989).

**CLOSE FRIENDS.** Peer acceptance is not the same thing as close friendship (Gifford-Smith & Brownell, 2003). To gain peer acceptance, children may need to conform to group norms for dress, action, and attitude; they may have to conceal certain strong feelings (Salisch, 2001; Lansford & Parker, 1999). With close friends, there is a more intimate level of disclosure, trust, and supportiveness. Close friendships are often measured through a *mutual nomination strategy*. Children are given a roster of the names of their classmates and asked to circle the names of children who are their friends. When two children circle each other's names, they are identified as friends. Close friendships are then identified by the children as those characterized by high levels of shared activity, companionship, help or guidance, and ease of conflict resolution (Asher & Paquette, 2003). In the context of these friendships, children share private jokes, develop secret codes, tell family secrets, set out on "dangerous" adventures, and help each other in times of trouble. They also fight, threaten, break up, and reunite.

Sullivan (1949) pointed out the significance of these early friendships as building blocks for adult relationships. Intimacy in best friend relationships provides a degree of understanding and openness that is often not possible with parents or family members. Within these friendships, private thoughts and fantasies are shared without worrying about being judged as silly, gross, or impractical. It is significant that the child experiences love for and closeness to a peer rather than an adult. The relationship is more likely to allow for mutuality of power, status, and access to resources (Youniss, 1980). Conflicts in a relationship may be worked out in terms that the children control, rather than escalating into dimensions having adult significance. One child cannot take away another child's allowance or send the other child out of the room when a conflict arises. The children must resolve their differences within the framework of their commitment to each other.

The stability of close friendships is quite variable, with some children remaining friends over several years, despite

*Carly and Michelle have been best friends since first grade. They love to spend time together whether they're washing the dog, going for bike rides, or listening to music. They depend on each other for fun, support, and problem solving.*

© Nancy Sheehan/Photo Edit

changes in classrooms and schools, whereas other children seem to be in different friendship relationships every few months (Kindermann, 1996). The structure of a school or classroom influences friendship formation and stability. Close friends often see each other during the school day in classes and extracurricular activities. In schools that promote stable classroom groupings, where children remain in the same homeroom or class group from one grade to the next, friendship groups also remain more stable (Neckerman, 1996).

Close friendships are influenced by attractiveness, intelligence, classroom social status, and satisfaction with and commitment to the best friend (Clark & Ayers, 1988). In a study of more than 800 children in Grades 3 to 5, 78% had at least one reciprocating best friend (i.e., one child named another as one of his or her three best friends, and that other child named the first child on his or her list as well), and 55% had a *very* best friend. More girls than boys had best friends, and the quality of their best friendships was somewhat different. Girls and boys described their best friend relationships quite similarly with respect to having low levels of conflict or betrayal and high levels of companionship and shared recreational activities. However, girls described their best friend relationships as having higher levels of caring and personal validation ("makes me feel good about my ideas"), intimacy ("we always tell each other our problems"), help and guidance ("help each other with schoolwork a lot"), and conflict resolution ("we make up easily when we have a fight"; Parker & Asher, 1993).

## ■ LONELINESS

With the increased emphasis on friendship and peer acceptance comes the risk of peer rejection and feelings of loneliness. In the period from preschool to middle childhood, issues of shyness, social anxiety, and peer victimization become increasingly salient. Experiences of social rejection or dissatisfaction in friendship quality become linked to a more general sense of anxiety in the school environment and a decline in self-worth (Asher & Gazelle, 1999; Asher, Parkhurst, Hymel, & Williams, 1999; Fordham & Stevenson-Hinde, 1999).

Four social characteristics combine to increase a child's experiences of loneliness. First, peer rejection is especially powerful in producing feelings of loneliness. Children who experience a generally positive level of peer acceptance feel less alone than those who are rejected by their peers. This relationship between peer rejection and loneliness has been found across countries and grades from kindergarten through middle school (Asher & Paquette, 2003; Crick & Ladd, 1993). Second, children who have trouble forming close friendships that provide emotional closeness and companionship are more likely to feel lonely. It is not necessarily important to have many friends. However, children who have at least one enduring, high-quality friendship are less likely to experience loneliness (Nangle, Erdley, Newan, Mason, & Carpenter, 2003). Third, among the children who are unpopular or rejected by peers, those who are withdrawn, victimized, or bullied report higher levels of loneliness than other unpopular children (Kochenderfer-Ladd & Wardrop, 2001). Finally, children who tend to blame themselves for their lack of social acceptance feel more lonely and are possibly less likely to believe that they can do anything to improve their situation (Cassidy & Asher, 1992; Renshaw & Brown, 1993; Rubin, LeMare, & Lollis, 1990).

**REJECTION.** Research has identified three paths to peer rejection. Some children who are rejected are disruptive and aggressive with their peers; others are socially withdrawn but do not exhibit aggressive tendencies; a third group has been

## APPLYING THEORY AND RESEARCH TO LIFE

# Bullying

BULLYING IS A common and long-standing problem for children in many cultures. A child is considered to be bullied when he or she is repeatedly exposed to negative actions by peers, including physical contact, harsh and degrading words and gestures, exploitation, and exclusion. Dan Olweus (1995), who has been studying aggression and bullying since the 1970s, has estimated that roughly 9% of children ages 7 through 16 have been victims of bullying, and 7% of school-age children have bullied others. This suggests that as many as five million children in the United States are involved in problems of bullying or peer intimidation each year.

What are the characteristics of bullies and their victims? Bullies typically are physically stronger than their peers. They have strong needs for power and enjoy being in control. They have been reared in a family environment characterized by indifference, low involvement, and lack of warmth. This context results in little sense of personal empathy and a high degree of hostility toward others. Bullies are often aggressive toward teachers and other authority figures as well as toward peers. It is not uncommon for aggressive boys to have best friends who are also aggressive. Within these relationships, the boys encourage each other toward rule breaking (Bagwell & Coie, 2004). Finally, bullies often find some reward or reinforcement for their behavior, especially when they coerce their victims into giving them money, taking things of value, and being treated with respect by other peers.

Victims of bullying, on the other hand, commonly have low self-esteem. They are anxious, cautious, and fit into the withdrawn category of rejected children. In comparison to the bullies, the victims, especially boys, are physically weaker. When attacked, they do not retaliate. As a result, the abuse continues and often escalates.

Olweus has designed a school-based intervention program to reduce bullying and prevent children from feeling harassed and degraded at school (Olweus, Limber, & Mihalic, 1999). The program, which has been implemented in Norway, the southeastern United States, England, and Germany, calls for intervention at three levels: the school, the classroom, and the individual. Intervention begins with awareness of the extent of bullying and victimization within the school through the use of an assessment survey. Once the nature of the problem and the seriousness of its impact on students have been identified, interventions are implemented that focus on five basic principles:

1. Create an environment in which children experience warmth, interest, and frequent involvement with adults.
2. Set clear, firm limits about unacceptable behavior that are endorsed at school and home.
3. When rules and limits are violated, sanctions should be nonhostile and nonviolent, but consistently enforced.
4. Student activities during and after school must be monitored through the presence of adult supervision.

*Bullies often use their size to intimidate their victims.*

The topic of monitoring and appropriate adult supervision must be discussed with parents during PTA meetings and parent conferences.
5. Students need to meet regularly with teachers to discuss problems associated with the social environment of the school and to work on ways of improving the school climate.

For more information about this bullying prevention approach, visit the website for the Center for the Study and Prevention of Violence, where the Bullying Prevention Program is described in greater detail.

---

described as both aggressive and withdrawn (French, 1988, 1990; Hymel, Bowker, & Woody, 1993). All these groups tend to have multiple problems. **Aggressive-rejected** children, often referred to as *bullies*, are more likely than nonaggressive children to attribute hostile intentions to others. They see peer interactions as threatening and say they would be likely to use aggressive strategies in response to negative peer behaviors (Quiggle, Garber, Panak, & Dodge, 1992; Waldman, 1996). The aggressive-rejected children tend to have an exaggerated idea of their competence and social status. They are less accurate in reading their own social status among their classmates, although they are just as accurate as other children in reading the social status of others (Zakriski & Coie, 1996).

However, not all aggressive children are rejected. One study looked at the relationship of antisocial and prosocial characteristics of young children and their social standing in the classroom (Farmer & Rodkin, 1996). Children in four different types of classroom groups were compared: academic giftedness, emotional and behavioral disorders, general education, and learning disabilities. Across all four types of classrooms, the most popular and socially central children were more athletic, cooperative, and studious and were rated as having more leadership skills than the less popular children. Aggressive, disruptive characteristics were strongly associated with peer rejection or isolation for girls. For boys in the general education classes, however, aggressive behavior was positively associated with popularity. Thus, one is led to consider person–environment fit in evaluating the relationship between aggressiveness and peer rejection. In some classroom contexts, aggressiveness, particularly among boys, may be a viable path toward bonding with other boys and asserting one's leadership, especially for boys who cannot achieve notice through their academic performance (Poulin & Boivin, 2000).

Children in the **withdrawn** group tend to be inhibited, anxious, and interpersonally reserved. They have a negative self-concept and tend to interpret negative peer reactions as resulting from their own personal failings (Hymel et al., 1993). They have difficulty dealing with stress. These children may exhibit inappropriate emotions and display various unusual behavioral mannerisms that are likely to draw ridicule from their peers (French, 1988). Studies of children with developmental disabilities and language disorders suggest that these children begin to have more relationship problems in the upper elementary school grades. Their social status among classmates is likely to decline, they may become targets of bullying, and they are less likely to be involved in reciprocal friendships. Over time, children who experience a combination of anxiety, lack of a close friend, and peer victimization are likely to be continued targets of victimization (Asher & Gazelle, 1999; Goldbaum, Craig, Pepler, & Connolly, 2003; Hall & McGregor, 2000).

Children in the **aggressive-withdrawn** group tend to be the least well liked of all three types of rejected children. They exhibit anxiety, poor self-control, and social withdrawal in addition to aggressive behavior. They are rated by other children as incompetent in school ability; unattractive; showing the poorest skills in leadership, cooperation, or sense of humor; and the most likely to behave inappropriately in school. Despite high levels of peer rejection, however, they do not have the same low self-concept and negative view of their abilities as the withdrawn children. They are likely to have future adjustment problems and often require psychiatric treatment in adolescence or adulthood (Coie & Krehbiel, 1984; Hymel et al., 1990).

## CONCRETE OPERATIONS

Children's abilities to analyze and manage social relationships, including friendships, are linked to their ability to solve other kinds of problems. Advances in reasoning about the physical world may stimulate new ways of handling complex social situations; similarly, engaging in complex social

situations may enhance the child's ability to bring flexibility and perspective to problems of the physical world.

Thinking back to the period of infancy, the discussion of infant intelligence focused on the establishment of sensory and motor patterns used to explore the environment, manipulate means–end relationships, clarify the nature of physical objects, and begin to form simple categories. During toddlerhood, cognition moves beyond the experiential domain as children develop a variety of representational skills that free them from complete reliance on their immediate physical environment. Toddlers create novel situations and solve problems by using thought, fantasy, and language. Piaget (Piaget & Inhelder, 1969) suggested that at about age 6 or 7, a qualitatively new form of thinking develops, which he referred to as **concrete operational thought**. This type of reasoning guides thought by imposing certain logical rules on one's judgments, leading to the acceptance of certain inferences that adhere to the logic as more compelling or convincing than others (Moshman, 2004).

The word *operation* refers to an action that is performed on an object or a set of objects. A mental operation is a transformation that is carried out in thought rather than in action. Piaget argued that such transformations are built on some physical relationship that the younger child can perform but cannot articulate. For example, a toddler can arrange a graduated set of circles on a stick so that the largest circle is at the bottom of the stick and the smallest circle is at the top. The child does not have a verbal label for the ordering operation but can perform it. With the emergence of concrete operations, children begin to consider a variety of actions that can be performed on objects and can do so mentally without having to do them physically. Thus, a mental operation is an internal representation of an alteration in the relationships among objects. For example, one of the most powerful mental operations is *reversibility*. One can imagine an action, such as filling a glass with water, and then undoing the action by emptying the glass. One can even imagine adding salt to water and then removing the salt, even though this would be difficult in practice. In contrast to sensorimotor schemes, which unfold in a sequence, operations can be done and undone in the mind (Lerner, 2002).

Piaget (1972a) used the term *concrete* to contrast this quality of thinking to the more hypothetical reasoning of adolescents and adults. The child reasons about objects and the relations among them but has difficulty entertaining hypothetical statements or propositions. Thinking is typically focused on real objects that exist in the world, even if the child is not seeing or manipulating these objects at the moment. For example, children can reason about problems involving the grouping of trees into different categories and identifying the features of these categories. However, if you pose a problem involving trees that migrate from North to South with the seasons, a child in the concrete stage of thinking will have difficulty even entertaining the problem, because trees do not migrate.

During the stage of concrete operations, the three conceptual skills that have received the most attention are (1) con-

Mental operations are critical to the game of chess. In order to play well, you have to be able to manipulate relationships in your mind, coordinate related pieces, and anticipate your opponent's responses to your moves. These third-graders are just beginning to show some finesse in their play.

servation, (2) classification, and (3) combinatorial skills. Over the period of middle childhood, children apply these skills to achieve a clearer understanding of the logic, order, and predictability of the physical world. As children take a new approach to problem solving through the use of the logical principles associated with concrete operational thought, they generalize these principles to their thinking about friendships, team play and other games with rules, and their own self-evaluation.

As the order of the physical world becomes more apparent, children begin to seek logic and order in social and personal domains as well. Sometimes, this search for order is frustrated by the unpredictability of the social world. At other times, children use their enhanced capacities for reasoning to solve interpersonal problems and to arrange their daily life so that it better meets their interests and needs. A hallmark of this period is an increase in logical, focused problem solving. Children are able to consider two competing explanations, look at a problem from another person's point of view as well as their own, and, using this information, plan a strategy to reach a goal.

### ■ CONSERVATION

The basic meaning of **conservation** is that physical matter does not magically appear or disappear despite changes in form, shape, or container. The concept of conservation can be applied to a variety of dimensions, including mass, weight, number, length, and volume. A child who "conserves" is able to resist perceptual cues that alter the form of an object, insisting that the quantity remains the same despite the change in form. One of the most common problems of this type that Piaget investigated involves *conservation of mass*. The child is presented with two clay balls and asked to tell whether or not

they are equal. Once the child is satisfied that the balls are equal, one of them is flattened out into a pancake. The child is then asked, "Which has more—this one [the pancake] or this one [the ball]?" Sometimes, the child is also asked whether the clay pieces are still the same. The child who does not conserve might say that the pancake has more clay because it is a lot wider than the ball. This child is still in the preoperational stage of thought: He or she is using personal perceptions to make judgments. In contrast, the child who conserves knows that the two pieces of clay are still identical in mass and can explain why.

Children eventually use the three concepts illustrated in Figure 9.1 to ascertain that equality in any physical dimension has not been altered. First, the child may explain that the pancake has the same amount of clay as the ball; no clay has been added or taken away. This is an example of the concept

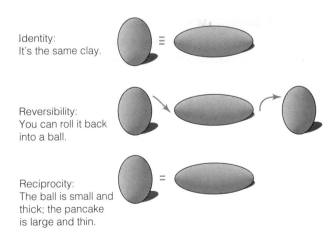

Identity:
It's the same clay.

Reversibility:
You can roll it back into a ball.

Reciprocity:
The ball is small and thick; the pancake is large and thin.

**FIGURE 9.1**

Three Concepts That Contribute to Conservation

of **identity**. The pancake is still the *same* clay, and nothing has been changed except its shape. Second, the child may point out that the experimenter can turn the pancake back into a ball. This is an example of the concept of **reversibility**. The child becomes aware that operations can be reversed, so that their effects are nullified. Third, the child may notice that, although the pancake has a larger circumference, the ball is much thicker. When the child can simultaneously manipulate two dimensions, such as circumference and thickness, we observe the concept of **reciprocity**. In the clay ball example, change in one dimension is compensated for by change in another; the total mass remains the same. With consolidation of the concepts of identity, reversibility, and reciprocity, the child is able to conserve in any physical dimension. There appears to be a developmental sequence in the capacity to conserve. Children generally conserve mass and number earliest, weight later, and volume last.

Conservation may not generalize across all of the physical modes. For example, children who are unable to conserve quantity in an unfamiliar object, such as poker chips, can do so with a more familiar one, such as M & M's (Gulko, Doyle, Serbin, & White, 1988). In one study, girls were able to perform a conservation of liquid task when it was presented in the standard manner of comparing the experimenter's glass and their own. However, when the task was embedded in a story where juice had to be divided between two dolls, their performance declined. Evidence of a lack of generalizability of knowledge from in-school to out-of-school contexts is found in other areas of reasoning, especially mathematical codes and scientific principles (Perret-Clermont, Perret, & Bell, 1991).

**EXTENSIONS OF PIAGET'S IDEAS ABOUT CONSERVATION.** Researchers have raised questions about the meaning of conservation tasks, the timing of the emergence of conservation, and the possibility of teaching children to conserve. The way the task is presented and the kinds of questions asked may influence a child's responses. For example, the task may emphasize identity or equivalence. In an *identity* task, the child is asked to judge whether a single clay ball has the same amount of clay after it has been rolled into a sausage. In an *equivalence* task, there are two balls of clay. The child is asked to judge whether the ball that is rolled into a sausage has the same amount of clay as the standard, comparison ball. Some studies have shown that children can perform the identity task earlier than the equivalence task; others have shown the opposite; and still others have argued that identity and equivalence are achieved at the same time (Silverstein et al., 1982). In a study of 5- to 7-year-olds, children were asked to tell how the materials looked, and then to tell how they really were. Giving the child this distinction between appearance and reality resulted in more correct answers than the standard procedure, in which this distinction was not made (Bijstra, Van Geert, & Jackson, 1989).

In a study of fifth-graders, half the students were identified as being in the preoperational stage, even at age 10. This finding in itself suggests that Piaget's view that children will enter the stage of concrete operational reasoning through active construction and experimentation around the age of 6 or 7 is not universally true. The study examined strategies for enhancing concrete operational reasoning through guided intervention. Half the children received training involving special activities intended to promote logical problem solving and abstract thinking. Children received the training in English or Spanish depending on their language competence. This intervention was found to be successful in promoting concrete operational thought (Bakken, Thompson, Clark, Johnson, & Dwyer, 2001).

Theoretically, Piaget's view of development suggests that there is a period of maturational readiness for the application of logical operations to physical objects. Left to their own process of exploration and experimentation, Piaget argued that children would discover the regularities and operations that underlie conservation. Showing a child a conservation problem and then explaining and reinforcing the correct answer should not be very effective if the child is not ready to assimilate this information. However, research has shown that it is possible to train young children of preschool age to conserve (Brainerd, 1977). These early training studies have both theoretical and practical implications. The training studies suggest that it is possible to introduce such concepts as identity and reversibility so that children as young as 4 can achieve conservation. They also transfer conservation from the tasks involved in training to other materials and dimensions (Field, 1981; May & Norton, 1981).

An important element in modifying a child's approach to conservation is being confronted by someone else's reasoning that contradicts one's own. For this contradiction to be effective, however, the child must be approaching a level of readiness to reorganize his or her thinking, and the gap between the child's current level of reasoning and the new ideas must not be too great. This reminds us of Vygotsky's concept of the zone of proximal development. The implication here is that entry into a new stage of thought may emerge earlier and may be more readily influenced by the social environment than Piaget's cognitive developmental theory predicts. However, Piaget himself was not especially impressed by faster and sooner. He believed in the enduring benefits of personal discovery.

Practically speaking, research has demonstrated that preschool- and kindergarten-age children can integrate and apply more abstract concepts than educators once believed they could. For example, studies of children as young as 3 and 4 have shown that they understand the idea that materials are made of tiny particles that retain their properties even when they are invisible. They can use this notion of particles to explain how a substance, such as sugar, continues to exist in a solution and retains its sweetness even when it is invisible (Au, Sidle, & Rollins, 1993; Rosen & Rozin, 1993). Early childhood educators have found that, through a planned program of exploring, experimenting, and describing the transformation of materials, young children can be guided to conceptualize the physical world in a systematic, logical manner.

# ■ CLASSIFICATION SKILLS

Classification was first discussed in Chapter 6, describing infants' basic categorization skills. **Classification** is the ability to identify the properties of categories, to relate categories or classes to one another, and to use categorical information to solve problems. Two components of classification provide the essential ability to apply knowledge from a known or familiar instance to a new instance: categorization and induction. **Categorization** simply means that if one apple belongs to the category of fruit, then *all* apples are fruit. You do not need to learn this categorization label for each type of apple. **Induction** refers to the realization that whatever holds true for one member of a category is likely to hold true for other members as well. For example, water and juice are both liquids. If you can pour water, you can pour juice. Other substances classified as liquids should also have this property—even substances one has never seen. The value of classification skills is not merely to organize objects or experiences into classes, but to take advantage of what is known about these categories to make inferences about the characteristics and dynamics of members of the same categories, members of hierarchically related categories, and objects that are not members of a specific category (Kalish & Gelman, 1992; Lopez, Gelman, Gutheil, & Smith, 1992; Farrar, Raney, & Boyer, 1992).

One component of classification skills is the ability to group objects according to some dimension that they share. The other component is the ability to order subgroups hierarchically, so that each new grouping will include all previous subgroups. Vygotsky (1962) suggested a method for studying classification in young children. Children are presented with a variety of wooden blocks that differ in shape, size, and color. Under each block is a nonsense syllable. The children are instructed to select, one at a time, all the blocks that have the same syllable. The youngest children, who would be char-

acterized as preoperational in Piaget's stage theory, tend to select blocks by their color. Their technique for grouping is highly associative. They choose each new block to match some characteristic of the previous selection, but they do not hold in mind a single concept that guides their choices.

Children who have entered the stage of concrete operations tend to focus on one dimension at first, perhaps shape, and continue to select blocks until they discover that they have made an incorrect choice. They use this discovery to change their hypothesis about which characteristics of the blocks are associated with the nonsense syllable. This classification task demonstrates the child's ability to hold a concept in mind and to make a series of decisions based on it. It also demonstrates that during the stage of concrete operations, children can use information from their mistakes to revise their problem-solving strategy.

Piaget studied reasoning about class hierarchies or inclusion by asking questions about whether a group of objects included more members of one subtype than of the group as a whole (Piaget, 1941/1952; see also Chapman & McBride, 1992). Thus, when a set of pictures shows three ducks, six sparrows, and two robins, one might ask, "Are there more sparrows or more birds in these pictures?" This is an unusual kind of question, one that children are probably rarely asked. By the age of 8 or 9, however, many children can respond correctly because they recognize the distinction between classes and subclasses. In order to handle such problems, children have to inhibit their tendency to reinterpret the question in line with a more common comparison, such as, "Are there more sparrows than ducks?"

In one study of class inclusion reasoning, an intriguing pattern was found. Children of ages 3 and 4, who could not repeat the question and who clearly had not learned any rules about classes, were more likely to answer correctly than children of ages 5 and 6. Children of ages 7 and 8 performed better than any of the younger children. The 5- and 6-year-olds, who answered quickly and confidently, were consistently incorrect. They seemed unable to inhibit the more obvious comparison in order to consider the actual question (McCabe, Siegel, Spence, & Wilkinson, 1982).

Two processes appear to contribute to classification judgments among young children. First, perceived similarities among target objects guide judgments about whether the objects belong to the same category. Second, verbal labels play an important role in cuing children into the similarities among objects. When there are no verbal labels available, children judge whether two objects are members of the same category based on the number of similar features. In comparison to adults, who rely less on verbal labels than on similarity of features, young children expect the labels to provide important information about objects, but they do not rely solely on these labels to guide their judgment (Sloutsky & Fisher, 2004).

From age 6 to 12, children's knowledge of categories and of the information associated with them expands dramatically. What is more, children have a broad range of categories

After many family trips to the beach, Randy has accumulated quite a collection of shells. Now he is learning to categorize them and group them by species.

available into which to incorporate a novel observation. The capacity for classifying and categorizing has been explored in relation to specific domains, such as health and illness or concepts of the family. For example, children were told about 21 different human groupings and asked to say whether these groupings were a family: "Here are Mr. Mead and his son, Tom. They live together, just the two of them. Are they a family?" The youngest participants (4- to 6-year-olds) had trouble accepting examples involving single parents or biologically related people who did not live in the same home as instances of a family. Principles of biological relatedness and shared physical residence were both important to these children's view of a family. By middle childhood, the children were able to accept a wider variety of groups as meeting certain essential criteria of a family, usually biological relatedness and emotional closeness. Emotional closeness was endorsed by 80% of the participants as a defining feature of a family and was used repeatedly as a basis for judging whether a specific instance of a grouping could be considered a family or not (Newman, Roberts, & Syre, 1993).

## ◼ COMBINATORIAL SKILLS

A third characteristic of concrete operational thought is the development of **combinatorial skills**. The number symbols (1, 2, etc.) can provide three types of information: nominal, cardinal, and ordinal. *Nominal numbers* are used like names, such as the number on a football player's jersey or a home address. They do not refer to an amount. *Cardinal numbers* refer to a quantity (e.g., two siblings or 5 minutes). *Ordinal numbers* refer to the position or progression of things in a set (e.g., first, second, third) rather than to a specific amount. In the transition from preoperational to concrete operational thought, children shift from using numbers in a nominal way (knowing and reciting the names of numbers, or reciting their street address) to the ordinal and cardinal nature of numbers.

Conservation of number is achieved around age 6 or 7 (Halford & Boyle, 1985). Once they have acquired the operations underlying conservation of number, children understand that certain physical transformations will not alter the number of units in a set. If 10 poker chips are lined up in a row, the number remains constant whether they are spread out, squeezed tightly together, or stacked. Children can use counting to answer a "how many" question sometime between the ages of 3 and 4. For example, they can assign one number to each item in a set of four poker chips and tell you that there are four chips in all. However, young children have more difficulty selecting a set of 6 chips from a larger pile, or establishing that 2 sets of chips are equal in number. They also have trouble solving verbal story problems when no concrete objects are present (Jordan et al., 1992; Sophian, 1988).

Young children differ widely in their mathematical knowledge and problem-solving skills. Success in doing addition and subtraction requires counting knowledge; working memory; understanding of part–whole relationships; familiarity

with the language and features of specific problems; and experience with a variety of strategies for estimating answers, solving problems, and checking one's answers (Canobi, Reeve, & Pattison, 2003; Ginsburg & Pappas, 2004). The ability to solve addition problems begins with an understanding that cardinal numbers refer to quantities and that there is a relationship between counting objects and adding or subtracting them as part of a larger set or whole (Canobi, 2004; Zur & Gelman, 2004). Over the first few elementary grades, most children acquire the complementary operations of addition, subtraction, multiplication, and division and learn to apply these operations no matter what specific objects or quantities are involved.

There appears to be a distinction between a cognitive understanding of combinatorial operations, such as addition and subtraction, and computational abilities. As the problems become more complex, involving larger numbers, more numbers, or numbers embedded in story problems, same-grade children demonstrate notable differences in the speed and accuracy of their solutions. The explanation for these differences may lie in part in the confidence of teachers in their own mathematical abilities, the ability to identify children's understanding of mathematics and to select appropriate approaches to mathematics instruction, and the confidence that children bring regarding their ability to succeed in mathematics. More research is needed to distinguish between factors that support the cognitive basis of combinatorial problem solving and factors that support the skills required for advanced computational ability. In a longitudinal study of cognitive development, children who were especially competent in number manipulation tasks during the period of concrete operational thought were more likely to achieve formal operational reasoning as young adolescents (Bradmetz, 1999).

The stage we identified as early school age (4 to 6) marks the beginnings of concrete operational thought. At this age, children's performance on tests of cognitive maturity is inconsistent. For example, children can conserve mass (using the clay balls task) but may make errors in conservation of weight, volume, or space. They may be able to perform a classification task correctly when they sort by one dimension, such as color, but they may make errors when asked to sort objects that have more than one dimension in common. Combinatorial operations involving addition and subtraction are applied to simple, one-digit problems at first, and are gradually extended to larger, more complex problems. The variety of concrete operations that emerge during this age period may not be fully integrated and available for purposeful problem analysis until adolescence or adulthood (Flavell, 1982).

As concrete operational intelligence develops, the child gains insight into the regularities of the physical world and the principles that govern relationships among objects. Perceptions of reality become less convincing than a logical understanding of how the world is organized. For example, even though it looks as if the sun sinks into the water, we know that what we see is a result of the earth's rotation on its axis.

**Table 9.1** Components of Concrete Operational Thought

| COMPONENT | NEW ABILITIES |
|---|---|
| Conservation | Ability to apply the identity operation |
| | Ability to apply the reversibility operation |
| | Ability to apply the reciprocity operation |
| Classification | Ability to categorize objects according to some common dimensions |
| | Ability to induce that properties of one member of a class apply to others |
| | Ability to order subclasses in a hierarchy |
| Combinatorial Skills | Ability to understand that numbers represent quantities |
| | Ability to manipulate quantities using the operations of addition, subtraction, multiplication, and division |

Table 9.1 summarizes the components of concrete operational thought.

## ■ METACOGNITION

As Piaget began his method of inquiry into concrete operational thought, he pointed the way to the study of metacognition. Rather than being concerned with the exact answers that children gave to the questions he asked, he was concerned about how they explained their answers. How do children know what they know? What reasons do they give to justify or support their answers? **Metacognition** refers to a range of processes and strategies used to assess and monitor knowledge. It includes the "feeling of knowing" that accompanies problem solving—the ability to distinguish those answers about which we are confident from those we doubt (Butterfield, Nelson, & Peck, 1988). One element of this "feeling of knowing" is understanding the source of one's beliefs. For example, we can be told about sand, we can see it for ourselves, or we can feel and touch it. All three of these sources of information may coincide to create a single belief, or we may discover that there are inconsistencies between what someone says is true and what we perceive through sight or touch. By the ages of 4 and 5, children are able to understand how all three sources of information have contributed to their understanding of an experience (O'Neill & Gopnik, 1991).

Metacognition includes the ability to review various strategies for approaching a problem in order to choose the one that is most likely to result in a solution. It includes the ability to monitor one's comprehension of the material one has just read and to select strategies for increasing one's comprehension (Currie, 1999): "I need to reread this section." "I need to underline and take notes to focus my attention on new information." "I need to talk about this with someone in order to understand it better." Recent research has considered "psychological mindedness" as an aspect of metacognition. This refers to the ability to think about what might be accounting for one's own or another person's behavior. It requires building a link between experiences, emotions, and behaviors. For example, a child who is feeling sad may think about what happened in the recent past that is producing this feeling. This would be a type of reflection on one's psychological state (Lagattuta & Wellman, 2001).

Metacognition develops in parallel with other cognitive capacities. As children develop their ability to attend to more variables in their approach to problems, they simultaneously increase their capacity to take an "executive" posture in relation to cognitive tasks. They can detect uncertainty and introduce strategies to reduce it. They can learn study techniques that will enhance their ability to organize and recall information. These capacities continue to develop as the child becomes a more sophisticated learner (Veenman, Wilhelm, & Beishuizen, 2004). They are also quite amenable to training, both at home and at school. Metacognition appears to be a natural component of cognitive development. However, just like first-level cognitive capacities, it is constructed in a social context. Interactions between children and adults or peers may nurture and stimulate metacognition by helping children to identify sources of information, talk about and recognize the differences between feelings of certainty and uncertainty in their knowledge, and devise effective strategies for increasing their "feelings of knowing" (Stright, Neitzel, Sears, & Hoke-Sinex, 2001; Teong, 2003).

## ▍SKILL LEARNING

Concrete operational thought refers to an approach to reasoning about the physical world that is guided by the compelling logic of certain mental operations. In addition to this general cognitive achievement, middle childhood brings impressive growth in the acquisition of skills. Skills are the basis of intellectual competence. They combine knowledge (knowing *about*) and practice (knowing *how*) directed toward identifying and solving significant, meaningful problems (Gardner, 1983; Kuhn, Garcia-Mila, Zohar, & Andersen, 1995). Typically, a person moves through a developmental progression within a skill area, starting off as a novice, becoming more proficient, and then, depending on a combination of aptitude, training, and practice, becoming an expert.

Cultures differ in the kinds of abilities that are valued as evidence of intelligence. In some societies, like ours, symbolic skills focusing on reading, mathematics, and abstract reasoning are highly valued. In other cultures, reading and mathematics are of less use and value than agricultural skills, hunting, or food preparation. In some subgroups, parents consider social skills (knowing how to behave appropriately with peers and teachers), practical skills necessary for adjustment to school (completing one's homework), and motivation (working hard to understand a problem) as more important

## HUMAN DEVELOPMENT AND DIVERSITY

# What Is Intelligence?

THE TERM *INTELLIGENCE* is used in many contexts, with a variety of meanings. Informally, it may refer to the ability to solve difficult problems, to draw on scholarly research or literature in defending an argument, or to adapt to environmental conditions. At a psychometric level, it may refer to the score on a standardized test composed of one type of item (such as *Peabody's Picture Vocabulary Test*) or many kinds of items (such as the *Stanford-Binet Intelligence Test*). Some theorists emphasize a general underlying factor, *g*, that reflects what many different types of test items have in common (Spearman, 1927). Other models suggest multiple intelligences with distinct areas of specialization. The remarkable adaptive and inventive capacities that human beings exhibit suggest a diversity of intellectual abilities, which are captured in the three theories of intelligence described here.

Jean Piaget (1972b) analyzed intelligence from a developmental perspective. He described four types of intelligence, each emerging at a different period of life: (1) *sensorimotor intelligence* (the ability to know through direct observation and manipulation of objects); (2) *representational intelligence* (the ability to distinguish between the real and the pretend; to think about and represent objects and events that are not present); (3) *concrete operational intelligence* (the ability to detect the logical relationships among objects; to place objects in sequences; and to comprehend and manipulate numbers); and (4) *formal operational intelligence* (the ability to use experimental techniques and hypothetical reasoning to solve problems, to generalize observations from one situation to another, and to relate cause and effect in complex, multidimensional problems). These approaches to problem solving are not lost as one moves from stage to stage. Rather, each is integrated into the next level, with lower levels of reasoning being viewed as inadequate as the person achieves new capacities.

Howard Gardner's (1983) theory of multiple intelligences identifies at least eight distinct intelligences, each with its own content and unique contribution to solving important, meaningful problems. These include *linguistic*, *musical*, *logical-mathematical*, *spatial*, *naturalist*, *bodily-kinesthetic*, and two forms of personal intelligence—one directed toward understanding one's own internal feelings (*intrapersonal*) and the other directed toward identifying and differentiating among the characteristics of others (*interpersonal*). This theory recognizes domains of human functioning that show evidence of high levels of achievement that are not necessarily related to scientific, mathematical, or verbal reasoning. They cover a broader range of skills than are normally included in tests of intelligence, validating the variety of individual differences in competence typically observed among school-age children (Gardner, Kornhaber, & Wake, 1996).

A third view, devised by Robert Sternberg (1985; Sternberg, Castejon, Prieto, Hautamäki, & Grigorenko, 2001), describes three kinds of intelligence—analytic, creative, and practical. According to Sternberg, only the first is systematically measured by tests of intelligence, but the latter two are often required in job performance or adaptation to the demands of daily life. In two studies involving children in third and eighth grades, a classroom approach that focused on analytic skills was contrasted to an approach that included activities that called on analytic, creative, and practical intelligence. Children in the latter groups showed higher levels of performance, reflecting the effectiveness of drawing on the three kinds of intelligence for more fully embedded learning (Sternberg, Torff, & Grigorenko, 1998).

*Toys designed to foster spatial intelligence have become increasingly diverse, allowing new areas of creativity and problem solving to be explored.*

© Nancy Sheehan/Photo Edit

indications of intelligence than cognitive accomplishments (Neisser et al., 1996; Okagaki & Sternberg, 1993).

In the United States, one observes the emergence of a wide range of valued skills during middle childhood, including mathematics, science, writing, computer operation, sports, mechanics, music, dance, theater, art, cooking, sewing, crafts, and reading. The nature and diversity of these skills and the fact that individual children can function at high levels in some but not in others raises the question of exactly what is meant by *intelligence*. The debate about intelligence is especially relevant in middle childhood, because this is when intelligence tests are administered and school placement decisions are made. As children discover the results of these tests, they make personal attributions about their ability or potential. Thus, IQ tests have a direct impact on the kind of educational experiences that children encounter and on their

sense of academic self-efficacy. Three approaches to the definition of intelligence are discussed in the box on Human Development and Diversity: What Is Intelligence?

## ■ FEATURES OF SKILLED LEARNING

Four principles have been identified for understanding how
complex behavioral skills are achieved. First, the development of a skill depends on a combination of sensory, motor,
perceptual, cognitive, linguistic, emotional, and social processes. In sports, for example, a child must learn to coordinate specific sensory information and motor activities, understand the rules of the game, be able to communicate with
the coach and the other players, gain control over emotions
such as fear or anger that might interfere with performance,
and sustain motivation to keep trying despite errors or defeat.

Second, skills are attained through the simultaneous integration of many levels of the component behaviors. They are
not acquired in strict sequence from simple to complex. Instead, children work on the simple and more complex components of the skill at the same time. For example, in art, children may experiment with mixing paints to achieve new
colors at the same time as they are experimenting with line
drawing, perspective, and shading.

Third, the limits of the human system place constraints on
an individual's capacity to perform skilled behavior. With
practice, lower level processes begin to function automatically, so a person can attend to higher order processes. In
writing, for example, young children struggle with the physical act of printing and writing, concentrating largely on the
motor skills necessary to make each letter, word, and sentence. A skilled writer can write with little effort, focusing attention on the meaning of the writing, the plot, or the character development rather than on the physical aspects of
the task.

Fourth, skilled behavior requires the use of strategies.
Skillful people operate with purpose and continuously monitor their performance. They perceive breakdowns in performance, are selective in focusing attention on various aspects
of what they are working on, and refine higher order processes as they perform the skill. This model of skill development focuses on the elements that are necessary in order to
move from what might be considered a novice level to a more
advanced level in skill performance.

One must keep in mind that children vary widely in their
rate of intellectual development and in their capacities to perform skills. For example, by Grade 1 or 2, children have been
identified as mathematically gifted, normal, or mathematically "disabled" (Geary & Brown, 1991; Geary, Hoard, Byrd-
Craven, & DeSoto, 2004). These designations relate to children's abilities to perform relatively simple mathematical
operations, such as addition. Differences in early mathematical ability relate to children's capacity for using a variety of
counting strategies as well as to their ability to retain and recall math facts from memory. In each distinct area of skill
development, a combination of maturational factors, aptitude

or talent, opportunities for exposure and training, and the
value placed on the skill by the family, school, or larger society all play a role in how rapidly and how well a skill will be
developed.

In the sections that follow, we look at reading as a specific
case of skill development, and at the social and cultural contexts within which skill learning occurs.

## ■ READING

Reading may be the most significant skill that develops for
children in the United States, because it opens the door to all
the others. Literacy transforms children, just as the advent of
the written alphabet transformed civilization. Reading provides access to new information, new uses of language, and
new forms of thinking. Children are limited in their ability to
learn mathematics, social studies, and science if they cannot
read. However, once they can read fluently, the possibilities
for independent inquiry expand significantly.

© Jose Luis Pelaez, Inc. /CORBIS

*Children who enjoy reading books outside of school show the
greatest gains in reading achievement between second and
fifth grades. Reading opens up limitless sources of information,
new experiences, and fun.*

Children begin to read in a variety of ways. As David and his mother drove from home to preschool every day, they used a game with street signs along the road to build the bridge from language to literacy. At first, David would ask his mother to tell him what every sign said. After a while, David began to "read" the signs by memorizing words and phrases that were linked to certain shapes and patterns in the signs. Other children begin to read by learning letters and the sounds linked to them, and by experimenting with sounding out the letters when they are strung together. At first, most children are bewildered and confused by these experiences. This is a time when they require a good deal of support and encouragement for their efforts. Gradually, through a process of trial, feedback, and repetition, children learn to read simple words and sentences (Knight & Fischer, 1992). At some point, a child begins to articulate the concept "I can read" or "I am a reader." Once this idea is part of the self-concept, efforts to read increase and are energized by a confidence in one's potential for success.

Reading is a complex skill that involves the acquisition and integration of many new techniques (Hall, 1989). Children do not have to score extremely high in intelligence tests to make substantial progress in learning to read (Share, McGee, & Silva, 1989). Most children, unfortunately, spend little or no time reading books outside school; over time, those who do some book reading show the greatest gains in reading achievement between the second and fifth grades (Anderson, Wilson, & Fielding, 1988).

**PARENTS INFLUENCE THEIR CHILD'S READING ABILITY.** Parents affect their children's reading in at least six ways (Tudge, Putnam, & Valsiner, 1996):

1. the value they place on literacy
2. the emphasis they place on academic achievement
3. the reading materials they make available at home
4. the time they spend reading with their children and listening to their children read
5. the way they read with their children
6. the opportunities they provide for verbal interaction in the home

There are many different ways to approach the social occasion of reading. Some parents ask their children about the story as they read along to make sure the child understands. Some try to expand on the story, talking with their children about other things they notice in the pictures or experiences related to the story. Some parents point out words and specifically teach about the sounds of letters as they read (Justice & Ezell, 2000; Reese & Cox, 1999).

In a study of parents' contributions to their children's literacy development in the United States and Japan, family members in both countries were found to employ a wide range of strategies both at home and away from home to encourage their children's ability to read. These included reading and telling stories, discussing stories, teaching vocabulary, writing about their experiences, playing board games, and watching certain types of television programs (Saracho & Shirakawa, 2004). Parents who value the ability to read do some direct teaching to promote reading, urge their children to do well in school, provide resources for reading, take turns reading and listening to their children read, and talk with them about what they are reading. All these strategies produce children who are more skilled readers (Bus, van IJzendoorn, & Pellegrini, 1995; Haney & Hill, 2004).

Parents also have an indirect effect on how well a child will learn to read by influencing the child's placement in a school reading group. Ability grouping for reading instruction is practically universal in elementary schools (Slavin, 1987). Teachers depend on their perceptions of a child's ability, work habits, and behavior when they assign students to reading groups (Haller & Waterman, 1985). The higher the level of the children's reading group, the better they learn how to read. Parents need to understand the school's approach to ability grouping and discourage arrangements that use classroom or whole-class ability tracking (National Association of School Psychologists, 2002). Parents may help a child understand his or her school's reading curriculum (schools differ in their approaches to teaching reading) and encourage good work habits and appropriate classroom behavior. Parents who do these things influence a teacher's perception of their child and, as a result, the child's assignment to a reading-level group.

**THE SOCIAL AND CULTURAL CONTEXTS OF READING.** Recent attention has been given to the social and cultural contexts in which many skills, especially school-related abilities such as reading, emerge (Eccles, 1993). Progress in skill development is influenced by parental and school expectations regarding levels of performance in a specific culture (see Human Development and Diversity: Cross-National Comparisons of Mathematics Ability). The analysis of reading provides many good examples of the importance of context.

First, societies differ in their level of literacy. For example, in Afghanistan, 51% of men and 21% of women are literate (Central Intelligence Agency, 2004). In Finland, a country with a population of more than five million, compulsory public schooling does not begin until age 7, and 100% of the population is literate. Expectations that children should be read to, should be able to read, and the level of skill development they are expected to reach at a certain age depends on cultural norms for literacy. The Progress in International Reading Literacy Study (PIRLS) assessed reading comprehension among fourth-graders in 35 countries. In the United States, 35% reported reading daily or almost every day; this was lower than the average of 40% across all the countries. In the United States, 32% of children said they never or almost never read just for fun outside of school. This was a much higher percentage than the international average of 18% (National Center for Education Statistics, 2004a).

Second, the purpose of literacy varies from one culture to the next. For example, missionaries introduced literacy to the Kaluli of New Guinea primarily as a way to teach the Bible.

## HUMAN DEVELOPMENT AND DIVERSITY

## Cross-National Comparisons of Mathematics Ability

IN 1980, COMPARATIVE studies showed that first- and fifth-grade children in Minneapolis, Minnesota, were substantially behind their age-mates in Sendai, Japan, and Taipei, Taiwan, in tests of mathematics achievement. In a 10-year follow-up, U.S. children still lagged behind, and by the 11th grade, the gap in achievement had widened (Stevenson, 1992; Stevenson, Chen, & Lee, 1993). Even the top 10% of the Minneapolis students scored at about the average level of the Taipei and Sendai students.

Beginning in 1995, and then again in 1999 and 2003, the U.S. National Center for Education Statistics sponsored the Trends in International Mathematics and Science Study (TIMSS), which examined mathematics and science teaching practices and student accomplishment for eighth-graders in 38 countries. Analysis of the 1999 data confirmed the earlier international comparisons. Students in 14 countries, including Taiwan and Japan, had mathematics scores that were significantly higher than those for children in the United States (Trends in International Mathematics and Science Study, 2004).

It is difficult to account for these cross-national comparisons on the basis of ability. All three countries have practically universal enrollment of school-age children. What is more,

when children were compared in their knowledge of general information of the type not included in the school curriculum, the U.S. children in first and fifth grades scored higher than the Japanese and Chinese children.

At least four sociocultural factors interact to contribute to the advantage that Japanese and Chinese children show in mathematical skill development. First, there is a difference in parents' views about what they should expect of their children. U.S. parents appear to be satisfied with their children's level of mathematics performance and do not expect their children to do better. In contrast, Japanese and Chinese parents have high expectations for their children's performance.

Second, parents differ in how they evaluate their children's schools. U.S. parents are generally satisfied with the school curriculum and think that the schools are doing a good job. Far fewer Japanese and Chinese parents view the schools as good or excellent. The public pressure in these cultures is for greater improvement in the quality of education. They are more critical of their schools. Even though Japanese and Chinese children spend more time on homework than do U.S. children, their parents are more likely to encourage them to spend even more time on homework.

Third, there are cultural differences

in the emphasis given to ability as compared to effort. U.S. parents and teachers highlight the importance of natural ability as a major factor in accounting for individual differences in mathematical ability. Japanese and Chinese parents and teachers are more likely to see outstanding performance as being a result of studying hard. On the one hand, if you believe that skill depends on natural ability, you might conclude that not much can be done to improve performance. On the other hand, if you believe that skill depends on effort, you may be more inclined to devote additional time and focused application to reach a new level of performance.

Finally, there are notable differences in the approach to mathematics instruction across countries. In Japan, for example, the classroom teaching approach is quite distinct from that in the United States. Based on videotapes of U.S. and Japanese classrooms, one can observe Japanese teachers spending more time introducing new concepts and less time on reviewing previous content, focusing more on complex problems that require four or more steps to reach a solution, and spending more time on problems that are mathematically related but not simply a repetition of the previous problem (National Center for Education Statistics, 2004b).

---

Among the Kaluli, reading is viewed as having limited purpose for daily life, and as too difficult for children (Schieffelin & Cochran-Smith, 1984). In many societies, the ability to read the Bible, the Koran, or the Torah is the principal reason for literacy, and that one book has been the primary written resource.

Third, the mark of a literate person varies by context. In the United States, we have age-graded expectations for reading and tests to measure reading ability. By the time they are applying to college, students are expected to be able to analyze a complex text for meaning, to know advanced principles of grammar, and to write a well-organized essay under time constraints. In other cultures, a good reader might be someone who can read a letter for someone else, someone

who can keep track of business accounts, or someone who can accurately make a copy of a text. The point is that the achievement of literacy is a product of cultural expectations, individual capacity, and opportunities to learn (Tudge, Putnam, & Valsiner, 1996).

The emphasis on skill building and the energy that children ages 6 to 12 bring to the acquisition of new skills suggest a strong parallel to toddlerhood. At both stages, children's motives for competence and mastery are directed outward to the environment. At both stages, children appear to be delighted by the potential for learning that almost every new encounter offers. However, as a result of children's cognitive capacities and their awareness of social expectations, skill learning during middle childhood is embedded in a much more complex framework of continuous monitoring and self-assessment. Children's beliefs and attitudes about which skills are important, what they should expect of themselves, what others expect of them, and what kinds of competing demands should influence their dedication to skill development all contribute to the levels of performance they are likely to achieve.

## SELF-EVALUATION

During middle childhood, the emphasis on skill building is accompanied by a new focus on self-evaluation. Children strive to match their achievements to internalized goals and external standards. Simultaneously, they receive feedback from others about the quality of their performance. Some children may be asked to sit at one table to receive "special" help; others may be told to go down the hall for tutoring. Some children are designated as peer tutors who assist their classmates. These and many other signs are sources of social evaluation that children incorporate into their own self-evaluations.

During middle childhood, the process of self-evaluation is further complicated because the peer group joins the adult world as a source of social comparison, criticism, and approval. Toddlers and early school-age children are likely to observe and imitate their peers in order to learn new strategies for approaching a task, or out of curiosity to see how their peers are doing a particular project. But in middle childhood, pressures toward conformity, competition, and the need for approval feed into the self-evaluation process. At this age, children begin to pay attention to the work of others in order to assess their own abilities (Butler & Ruzany, 1993). Their athletic skills, intellectual abilities, and artistic talents are no longer matters to which only teachers and parents respond. Peers also identify others' skills and begin to generate profiles of one another: "Oh, Rafael is good in math, but he runs like a girl"; "Jane is kind of fat, but she writes great stories"; "I like Rashidah best, because she's good at everything." Depending on their resolution of the crises of toddlerhood and early school age, children approach the process of self-evaluation from a framework of either self-confidence or self-doubt. They may expect to find tasks easy to accomplish and approach them vigorously, or they may anticipate failure and approach tasks with hesitation.

In research involving children in the 8–13 age range, Susan Harter (1985, 1993) devised a method for assessing children's perceptions of competence in five specific domains: scholastic competence, athletic competence, likability by peers, physical appearance, and behavioral conduct. She also measured general or global self-esteem. Her research was guided by the idea that by the age of 8, children not only differentiate specific areas of competence, but view certain areas as more important than others. She found that self-esteem is highest in those children who view themselves as competent in domains that they judge to be important. Competence

in relatively unimportant domains is not strongly related to overall self-esteem.

Thus, self-evaluation takes place in two contexts: **internal frames of reference**, as a child compares how well he or she can perform in one domain versus another; and **external frames of reference**, as a child evaluates his or her own performance in light of parent, teacher, or peer feedback and observations of the performance of other children in the class (Skaalvik & Skaalvik, 2004). In the sections that follow, we focus on two different paths toward self-evaluation: *self-efficacy*, which reflects a child's personal judgment of ability, and *social expectations*, which reflect the impact of the expectations of others on a child's performance.

## SELF-EFFICACY

How do children assess their competence in a specific ability area? Albert Bandura (1982) theorized that judgments of self-efficacy are crucial to understanding this process. **Self-efficacy** is defined as the person's sense of confidence that he or she can perform the behaviors demanded in a specific situation. Expectations of efficacy vary with the specific ability. In other words, a child may view efficacy in one way in a situation requiring mathematical ability and in another way when the situation requires physical strength.

Bandura theorized that four sources of information contribute to judgments of self-efficacy (see Figure 9.2). The first source is **enactive attainments**, or prior experiences of mastery in the kinds of tasks that are being confronted. Children's general assessment of their ability in any area (e.g., mathematics, writing, or gymnastics) is based on their past accomplishments in that area (Skaalvik & Hagtvet, 1990). Successful experiences increase their perceived self-efficacy, whereas repeated failures diminish it. Failure experiences are especially detrimental when they occur early in the process of trying to master a task. Many boys and girls are diverted from mastering such sports as tennis and baseball because they have made mistakes early in their participation. They develop doubts about their abilities, which then prevent them from persisting in the task.

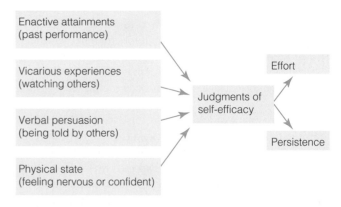

**FIGURE 9.2**

Four Components of Self-Efficacy

The second source of information is **vicarious experience**. Seeing a person similar to oneself perform a task successfully may raise one's sense of self-efficacy; seeing a person similar to oneself fail at a task may lower it.

**Verbal persuasion** is the third source. Children can be encouraged to believe in themselves and try a new task. Persuasion is likely to be most effective with children who already have confidence in their abilities, and it helps boost their performance level.

The fourth source is **physical state**. People monitor their body states in making judgments about whether they can do well or not. When children feel too anxious or frightened, they are likely to anticipate failure. In contrast, children who are excited and interested but not overly tense are more likely to perceive themselves as capable of succeeding.

Self-efficacy judgments are related to children's perceptions of their likelihood of success. These judgments also determine the factors to which children attribute their success or failure (McAuley, Duncan, & McElroy, 1989; Pajares, 1996). In the face of difficulty or failure, children who have confidence in their abilities and high self-efficacy will work harder to master challenges. They will attribute their difficulties to a failure to try hard enough, and they will redouble their efforts. Children who have a low sense of self-efficacy tend to give up in the face of difficulty because they attribute their failure to a basic lack of ability (Bandura & Schunck, 1981). The level of self-efficacy also affects how children prepare to handle new challenges. In their thoughts, emotions, and preparation for action, those who are preoccupied by self-doubts differ from those who believe in themselves.

Children with high levels of self-efficacy related to academic achievement are likely to set challenging goals for themselves. They are also likely to regulate their learning behaviors by deliberately enlisting a number of strategies including concentrating, organizing their work, finding a good place to study, taking notes in class, and completing their homework assignments so that they have the best chances of reaching their goals (Bandura, Barbaranelli, Caprara, & Pastorelli, 1996; Zimmerman, Bandura, & Martinez-Pons, 1992). The case study of Becca illustrates the behaviors and thoughts of a middle school student whose sense of self-efficacy has been declining.

# CASE STUDY

## BECCA

*Becca, an eighth-grader, is disengaging from school.*

Under the weight of her family burdens, Becca's academic confidence has begun to falter. . . . In sixth grade, Becca was an A student; at the end of seventh grade, she asked to be removed from the advanced math class; and by the middle of eighth grade, her grades in all of her classes were drifting to low C's.

As a quiet girl, Becca says she has never spoken much in class ("unless I'm really, really sure of an answer, and sometimes not even then"), but with her self-esteem flagging, she stops volunteering entirely. She even begins to see her silence as an advantage: As long as she's perceived as shy, her teachers won't notice that she has, in truth, disengaged from school. . . .

In a sense, Becca is invisible. Her teachers don't see her as someone in need of counseling or special help because, although her grades have dropped, she is never combustible: She never, for instance, yells in class, pounds desks, fights with other children, conspicuously challenges authority. Becca's is a passive resistance—a typically feminine resistance. By opting out rather than acting out, Becca still conforms to the image of the ideal female student—quiet, compliant, obedient; as such she is easily overlooked, or seen as "making choices" rather than expressing psychological distress. "Becca is so quiet," her math teacher admits, "she gets lost in the crowd. I don't like that to happen, but it has happened with her. She doesn't disrupt. She always looks like she's paying attention, but maybe she's not, I don't know."

"Maybe she thinks she'll be more cool as a C student," her history teacher says. "But she doesn't even get it together after she gets the bad grade. I'll say, 'Becca, you have a D, you may fail,' but then she doesn't turn in the next homework assignment, which is really easy. But I think of her as someone who's responsible for her own grade, and I let her be responsible for that."

Source: Orenstein, 1994, pp. 80–81.

## ■ CRITICAL THINKING AND CASE ANALYSIS

1. How would you describe Becca's level of academic self-efficacy?
2. Using Bandura's model, how are the four factors of enactive attainments, vicarious experiences, verbal persuasion, and physical states contributing to her self-efficacy?
3. What would you say is missing from Bandura's theory of self-efficacy that is illustrated in the case of Becca?
4. What are some gender issues that may underlie this case? In what ways is Becca's situation made possible because of gender stereotypes?
5. How might teachers intervene to reverse this decline in self-efficacy?
6. What might be the likely outcome for Becca if this pattern of disengagement continues?

## ■ SOCIAL EXPECTATIONS

Several theories of the self suggest that the appraisals and expectations of others become incorporated into one's own self-evaluation. Self-esteem is based on the general positive regard and approval of others and on the specific expectations they have for one's ability and achievement in certain areas of performance (Harter, 1993; Jussim, 1990a). In attempting to assess their own abilities, children rely on many external sources of evaluation, including grades, teachers' comments, and parental and peer approval (Hergovich, Sirsch, & Felinger, 2002). If feedback from important adults suggests to children that they are cooperative, intelligent, and creative, these attributes are likely to be incorporated into their self-evaluations. Children who see themselves as cooperative and intelligent are likely to approach social and intellectual tasks with optimistic expectations about their performance. Conversely, feedback suggesting lack of competitiveness, intelligence, or creativity can produce a pessimistic or antagonistic approach to the challenges of skill development.

Social expectations also contribute to children's expectations about their own abilities and behavior (Harris & Rosenthal, 1985). Evaluative feedback about intellectual ability or skill feeds into children's conceptualization of their own competence. Repeated failure information or remarks that imply lack of ability tend to make children less confident of success in subsequent tasks. The pattern of expectations appears to crystallize during Grades 2 and 3. Preschoolers do not make systematic use of success or failure feedback in predicting their next success (Parsons & Ruble, 1977). Even in the first grade, children's expectations about the grades they will receive on their first report cards are not clearly related to their IQs or to parents' or teachers' expectations, nor are they closely related to the children's later estimates of their grades. By the end of the first grade, however, children begin to be more accurate predictors of their performance (Alexander & Entwisle, 1988; Entwisle, Alexander, Pallas, & Cadigan, 1987). By middle school, children are more aware of their teachers' expectations for their performance and are likely to mirror those expectations in their own attitudes about school, academic achievement, and school behaviors (Alexander, Entwisle, & Kabbani, 2001; Weinstein et al., 1987).

**TEACHERS' EXPECTATIONS: THE SELF-FULFILLING PROPHECY.** The feedback that students receive from their teachers is not wholly objective. Teachers' expectations about their students' abilities may be based on objective assessments, but they may also be derived from stereotypes about certain types of children or from biases based on prior experiences, like having a child's older siblings in class in prior years or hearing unfavorable comments from other teachers. Merton (1948) suggested that problems may arise through a process that he called the **self-fulfilling prophecy**. This concept refers to the idea that false or inaccurate beliefs can produce a personal reality that corresponds with them.

In the original study on the effect of teacher expectations on student performance, teachers were led to believe that certain students were "late bloomers" who would show major gains in IQ later on in the school year. These children, chosen at random from among first- and second-graders, actually did show increases in IQ of 10 to 15 points in comparison to the control group (Rosenthal & Jacobson, 1968). The effect did not continue into the third and fourth grades, and over-

all, the correlation between teachers' expectations and students' measured IQ was modest.

Subsequent studies of the self-fulfilling prophecy in classroom settings have shown that it has a consistent but comparatively small effect on student performance (Rosenthal, 1994, 1995). In one longitudinal study, students' math achievement and mathematics self-concept data were collected at the end of fifth grade, early in sixth grade, and at the beginning of seventh grade. Teachers' expectations about student performance were assessed early in sixth grade as well. Both student achievement at the end of fifth grade and teachers' expectations in sixth grade were predictive of students' achievement at the beginning of seventh grade. In the analysis of these data, the researchers found that the self-fulfilling prophecy (the impact of teacher expectations separate from prior student achievement scores) was observable only for those students who were in the low achievement group. Both overestimates and underestimates of these students' abilities in sixth grade were predictive of the students' achievement in seventh grade. There was some tendency for overestimates to have a greater impact in boosting these students' performance than for underestimates to depress the students' performance (Madon, Jussim, & Eccles, 1997).

Teachers' expectations for a student's performance are influenced by their assessments of both the student's ability and his or her effort. In a study of elementary school teachers, a relationship was found between the teachers' explanations for students' success and failure and the emotions that teachers felt under the various conditions. These emotional reactions were assumed to be the major cues that teachers sent to students about their performances. When teachers believed that students' poor performances were due to a lack of effort, they were likely to feel angry toward the students, particularly if they believed the students were capable of good work. When children of low ability suddenly began putting forth a great deal of effort, teachers were likely to take pride in their own accomplishments, believing they had really helped these children become more motivated. If low-ability students who were trying hard failed, teachers felt a sense of guilt. Teachers were more willing to accept personal responsibility for certain configurations of student success and failure than for others. The students who made teachers the angriest were the bright ones who did not try hard (Prawat, Byers, & Anderson, 1983).

Research on teacher expectations illustrates how social expectations influence both perceptions of others and the quality of interpersonal communication. Intervention programs to improve the reading performance of first-graders in low-income minority schools have built on this line of research. Specific strategies were designed to help teachers recognize their assumptions about student ability and effort and to convey encouragement and positive attainment messages to students (Good & Nichols, 2001).

Certain conditions make children more or less vulnerable to internalizing false expectations. Children who are unsure about their abilities and children who are learning something

*Students react to teachers' interactions with their classmates. While Ms. White is correcting Lin's work, Eric, Stephanie, and Amy are watching or listening. What do you think they may be feeling in this situation?*

for the first time may be more likely to rely on the information they receive from others to assess their abilities. Being in a new situation, like moving to a new school or changing from elementary to middle school, may increase a child's dependence on social expectations for performance. In middle childhood, when many new domains of skill development are first being introduced, children may be more vulnerable to the effects of biased perceptions and erroneous expectations than are older children (Jussim, 1990b).

Some children appear to monitor their social environment more self-consciously than others (Musser & Browne, 1991). High **self-monitoring** children are more aware of the emotional and nonverbal behavior of others and make more use of social information to evaluate and regulate their own behavior. These children are more responsive to subtle forms of feedback about their performance, taking in more information about social expectations for their performance than do the children who are comparatively oblivious to the intricacies of the social environment.

**PARENTS' EXPECTATIONS.** Parents' as well as teachers' expectations influence children's perceptions of their abilities. This process was demonstrated in a study of parents' and children's attitudes toward mathematical aptitude (Parsons, Adler, & Kaczala, 1982). Children in Grades 5–11 and their parents were asked about their attitudes toward the children's mathematics achievement. Parents had lower expectations for their daughters' math achievement than for their sons'. They believed that mathematics is more difficult and requires more effort for girls than for boys. Their expectations about their children's aptitude were better predictors of the children's self-assessments than were the children's own past performances in mathematics.

Expanding on the relationship between gender role bias and the socialization of children's competencies and interests, Eccles (1993) proposed the following model (see Figure 9.3):

> The evidence suggests that general (parental) gender role beliefs influence perceptions of individual children's competencies and interests, which in turn affect the kinds of experiences parents provide. . . . Essentially, we believe that parents' gender role stereotypes, in interaction with their children's sex, affect the following mediators: (1) parents' causal attributions for the children's performance; (2) parents' emotional reaction to their children's performance in various activities; (3) the importance parents attach to their children's acquiring various skills; (4) the advice parents provide their children regarding involvement in various skills; and (5) the activities and toys parents provide. In turn, we predict that these subtle and explicit mediators influence the development of the following child outcomes across the various gender role stereotyped activity domains: (1) children's confidence in their ability; (2) children's interest in mastering various skills; (3) children's affective reaction to participating in various activities; and as a consequence of these self and task perceptions, (4) the amount of time and type of effort the children end up devoting to mastering and demonstrating various skills. (p. 170)

A number of studies support the underlying dynamics of this model. Independent of actual gender differences in specific domains, including math, sports, and English, parents' stereotypes about which gender is more talented in a particular area influence their perceptions of their own child's competence in that area. Parents' perceptions of competence are directly related to their children's perception of competence (Eccles, Jacobs, & Harold, 1990).

A longitudinal study followed a cohort of children, starting when they were in first grade, in 1982, through to the end of high school. Data were collected from these children, who

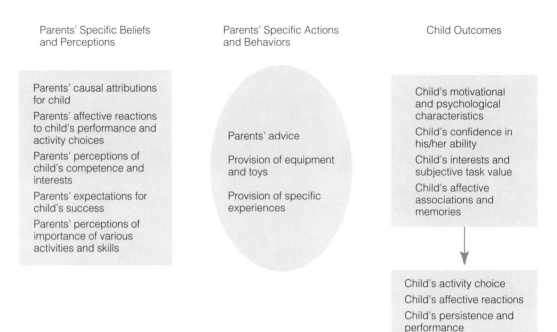

**FIGURE 9.3**

The Relationship of Parents' Gender Role Stereotype Beliefs and Perceptions to Parental Actions and Behaviors and Child Outcomes

Source: Data from I. Bretherton, "Open Communication and Internal Working Models: Roles in the Development of Attachment Relationships," R. Dienstbier & R. A. Thompson (eds.), *Nebraska Symposium on Motivation, 1988; Socioemotional Development, 36,* 60–61.

were from various socioeconomic and family backgrounds; from their parents; and from school records. In a recent report, the study examined factors that placed children from this group at risk for dropping out of school. Parental attitudes about their children's school success and school completion were significant predictors of children's school achievement starting in first grade and continuing through middle school and high school. Although socioeconomic status was a powerful predictor of dropping out of school, parental attitudes about their child's ability and promise moderated the impact of social class for students in low, middle, and high resource groups, but especially in the higher resource groups (Alexander, Entwisle, & Kabbani, 2001).

**ILLUSIONS OF INCOMPETENCE AND COMPETENCE.** In a phenomenon described as the **illusion of incompetence**, some children who perform well on tests of academic achievement (at the 90th percentile or above) perceive themselves as below average in academic ability. These children expect lower levels of success, are less confident, attempt less challenging tasks, and say that their schoolwork is more demanding than peers of similarly high ability who have more positive self-evaluations. It appears that parents play a central role in establishing these children's low assessments of themselves. Children who have an illusion of incompetence think that their parents have a low opinion of their abilities and expect little of them. They see their fathers, in particular, as having rigorous standards that they are not expected to meet (Phillips, 1984, 1987).

The parent–child dynamics that underlie this negative assessment were observed in a study involving children with high academic ability who had varying levels of perceived academic competence. Children worked with their mothers and fathers on solvable and unsolvable tasks. The fathers of children who had low perceptions of their own academic competence were found to interact with their children in more critical or unsupportive ways than did the fathers of children who had high perceptions of their academic competence. The children who had illusions of incompetence were more emotionally upset and dependent when they approached the unsolvable tasks (Wagner & Phillips, 1992).

Cross-sectional research suggests that children may infer messages of incompetence from parental control. In a comparison of children in Grades 2 through 5, the older children interpreted parental helping, monitoring, and decision making as evidence that the parents thought they were incompetent. As children get older and their desire for autonomy, initiative, and industry increases, they may interpret parental monitoring as evidence of a lack of confidence in their ability to make good decisions or to function competently (Pomerantz & Eaton, 2000).

In contrast to illusions of incompetence, some people have **illusions of competence.** In four separate studies, researchers found that those participants who scored in the lowest 12% of test takers on measures of grammar, logic, and humor substantially overestimated their own abilities. The extreme lack of ability in an area is accompanied by the inability to distinguish accurate from inaccurate responses, thus leading to a misconception of competence. In contrast to illusions of incompetence, where children underestimate their abilities, illusions of competence occur when people have such deficiencies that they do not even realize the extent of their limitations (Kruger & Dunning, 1999).

The discussion of self-evaluation highlights children's sensitivity to their social environment. They become aware of existing roles and norms and of the sanctions for norm violation. Direct experiences with success and failure are important, but they are embedded in the context of social expectations. Messages of reassurance and encouragement from parents and teachers can play a key role in establishing a positive sense of competence and in motivating children to persist in the face of difficult challenges. Parents also can advise children that some teachers have prejudiced attitudes and help them identify the signs that such attitudes are operating in the classroom.

By the end of middle childhood, children have had enough school experience that they can detect favoritism, bias, and unfair treatment and can devise strategies to protect themselves from the impact of negative biases. They are able to judge their abilities by considering their mastery level and the amount of effort they have to exert in order to do well. They are also able to decide when someone else might be a better judge of their abilities than they are (Burton & Mitchell, 2003). The more children are embedded in strong, supportive social relationships, the more confidence they will have in their general worth, and the more likely they will be to arrive at accurate assessments of their own abilities.

## ■ TEAM PLAY

During middle childhood, a new dimension is added to the quality of a child's play. Children begin to participate in team sports and, as a result, gain a sense of team success as well as personal success. Team sports are generally more complicated than the kinds of games described as group play in Chapter 8. The rules are so complex that they may require a referee or an umpire if they are to be followed accurately. In these sports, children join together into teams that remain together for the duration of the game. Some children join teams that play together for an entire season, such as Little League. A growing interest in physical activity and fitness in adulthood has shed new light on the importance of involvement in team sports in childhood and early adolescence. In a study of adult men ages 32 to 60, researchers found a strong link between voluntary participation in team sports in the middle childhood period and continued physical activity in adulthood (Taylor, Blair, Cummings, Wun, & Malina, 1999).

In addition to its contribution to fitness and enthusiasm for physical activity, participation in team play provides a context for "preworking" the skills and orientations that will apply to the world of work and to functioning in the family group (Van der Vegt, Emans, & Van De Vliert, 2001). Three significant characteristics of the experience of team member-

ship are relevant to development during this stage: (1) interdependence, (2) the division of labor, and (3) competition.

## ■ INTERDEPENDENCE

Team membership carries with it an awareness that one's acts may affect the success or failure of the entire group. There is a definite emphasis on winning and losing, and children may be ostracized or ridiculed if they contribute to a team loss. Although team sports do provide opportunities for individual recognition, it is quite clear that team success casts a halo over even the poorest players and team failure a shadow over even the best. In this sense, participation in team sports is an early lesson in **interdependence**. All of the team members rely on one another, and ideally, it is to everyone's advantage to assist the weaker members in improving the quality of their play. The best coaches are noted for inspiring this sense of interdependence and mutual support among team members. They urge team members to work together to improve their skills. Often, when teams are closely matched, it is the unexpected success of the weaker players that contributes to a victory.

## ■ DIVISION OF LABOR

Through participation with peers on teams, children discover that **division of labor** is an effective strategy for attaining a goal. Children learn that each position on a team has a unique function and that the team has the best chance of winning if each player performs his or her specific function rather than trying to do the work of all the other players. The concept of the team encompasses the variety of activities in which each of the team members actually engages. A complementary concept is **cooperation**: Team members learn that if the team as a whole is to do its best, the team members must help one another. Rather than playing all the roles, a team member tries to help every other member play his or her role as well as possible. Cooperation takes many forms: Members share resources, take time to help other team members improve their skills, plan strategies together, work together on the field, encourage each other, bring out the equipment, or clean up after the game. In many sports, there is a dynamic tension between competition and cooperation. Team members may compete with each other for a more desirable position or for the status of being the top player. At the same time, the team members know that they have to support each other, especially when they play against another team.

The team may become an experiential model for approaching other complex organizations. Once children learn that certain goals can best be attained when tasks are divided among a group of people, they begin to conceptualize the principles behind the organization of social communities. They recognize that some children are better suited to handling one aspect of the task and others to handling another. Some children enjoy the skill development associated with team play; others enjoy learning the rules and devising strategies; others especially value peer companionship; and still

All the players on this baseball team share the joy of victory. The fact that team members rely on each other and assist each other provides an important lesson about interdependence. This lesson can transfer to work and family situations as the players mature.

© Patrik Giardino/CORBIS

others have a strong inner motive to compete and win (Klint & Weiss, 1987). The distribution of roles to fit the children's individual skills and preferences is a subtle element of the learning that is acquired through team play.

## COMPETITION

Finally, team play teaches children about **competition**. In team sports, both sides cannot win; success for one side must result in failure for the other. If the team experience is a laboratory for learning lessons about the larger social community, this characteristic promotes a view of social situations in competitive terms. Some adults think of business, politics, popularity, and even interpersonal conflicts as win–lose situations, in which the primary goal is to beat one's opponents. The idea of a win–win strategy to resolve conflict is very foreign in this context.

Winning is a great high. Many young adults have fond memories associated with winning an important game or a big match. They hope to re-experience the energy that occurs as a result of winning as they approach their adult activities. The metaphor of playing on a winning team is deeply interwoven into the world of work, helping to give focus and drive to day-to-day work-related obligations and tasks. When adults look back on their childhood play experiences, many recall the excitement associated with competition and con-

tinue to long for this excitement in their daily life. In one study of women in traditional and nontraditional professions, for example, more professional businesswomen and other women in nontraditional fields remembered experiences playing in competitive sports and being on teams with both boys and girls during their childhood (Coats & Overman, 1992).

In contrast to those who are energized by the challenges of competition, some children are especially sensitive to the pain of failure. The public embarrassment and private shame that accompany failure are powerful emotions. Some children will go to remarkable extremes to avoid failing. In team sports, each game ends with a winning and a losing side. Children who have a low sense of self-esteem are more likely to experience intense anxiety about losing in a competitive situation (Brustad, 1988). Involvement in team sports is guaranteed to bring with it the bitterness of losing and the commitment to avoid it at all costs—experiences that drive some children away from sports and into other domains of competence.

Team play has implications for both social and intellectual development. Children who play team sports see themselves as contributors to a larger effort and learn to anticipate the consequences of their behavior for the group. Team play creates a valuable context for the formation of interpersonal relationships. Inclusion in a positive team experience often results in a child's identification with the coach and other team members. These new emotional investments can expand the child's sense of well-being and social support (Blanchard, Perreault, & Vallerand, 1998; Wylleman, 2000).

Games that involve teams are generally so complex that children are called on to learn many rules, make judgments about those rules, plan strategies, and assess the strengths and weaknesses of the other players. All of these characteristics of participation in team sports can stimulate cognitive growth (Smith, 1986). In one study, for example, children were divided into soccer "experts" and soccer "novices" (Schneider & Bjorklund, 1992). The experts had an impressive depth of knowledge about the game of soccer and, when given a memory task involving soccer-related items, were able to use their expertise to perform at a high level.

Interest in sports and competitive team play has been used as a motivational hook to promote other areas of school ability. For example, in Columbus, Ohio, a former Ohio State University football player who also played professional football organized a summer camp for fifth- through 12th-graders. The focus of the camp was to combine sports with math and science education. The curriculum was developed to teach math and science for 2½ hours each day and to spend the remainder of the time in practical sports applications. For example, the students might learn the principles of physics that account for why a baseball travels faster than a football and then experiment with these principles on the ball field (Beaulieu, 1992).

In another example, children diagnosed with attention-deficit/hyperactivity disorder (ADHD) were recruited for a basketball camp. Many of these children had difficulties regulating their impulses and showed poor social skills. The camp focused on athletic competence and sportsmanship. The combined efforts resulted in improved communication skills, reduced aggressiveness, increased interest in basketball as an activity, and some improvement in sports ability (Hupp & Reitman, 1999). These two examples illustrate how a well-designed sports program can have a broad impact on intellectual and social development by combining increased competence in physical activity with related emphasis on the cognitive and social components of team play.

## ■ INGROUP AND OUTGROUP ATTITUDES

Team membership provides a microsystem for the formation of ingroup and outgroup attitudes and behaviors. All human societies observe distinctions between ingroup and outgroup attitudes and behaviors. The **ingroup** members share common norms, goals, and values. They also share a common fate—in sports, for example, the team wins or loses as a team. Feelings of cohesiveness with and similarity to members of an ingroup prompt behaviors that are supportive of that group's survival. Typically, individuals distribute resources so that members of their ingroup receive more and members of the outgroup receive less. However, when ingroup norms emphasize fairness and reject discrimination, members are more

likely to treat members of the outgroup with fairness. Thus, ingroup norms can influence the degree to which outgroup hostilities are encouraged and expressed or suppressed (Jetten, Spears, & Manstead, 1996).

The **outgroup** is any group whose goals are either in opposition to or inconsistent with the goals of the ingroup. Any group may be perceived as an outgroup, even though it does not actually pose any physical threat to members of the ingroup. Students at one university may perceive students at another university as an outgroup (e.g., the long-standing football rivalry between Ohio State University and the University of Michigan). Students enrolled in one program or major may view students in a similar but competing major as an outgroup (e.g., chemical engineers vs. electrical engineers). In experimental studies, ingroups and outgroups have been formed based simply on wearing a blue or yellow badge, or based on those with blue eyes and those with brown eyes (Bigler, Spears, & Christia, 2001). Children as young as age 5 are aware of the status of their group. If they believe that their group has positive qualities and is valued, they are more likely to want to remain in the group and to see themselves as similar to other group members (Nesdale & Flesser, 2001).

Children learn to see the outcome of competition as a win–lose situation. For sports teams, the outgroup's goal of winning is in direct competition with the ingroup's similar goal. The other team is seen as the enemy, and there is no alternative to trying one's hardest to defeat it. Antagonism toward the outgroup is valued in team sports, and any attempt to assist the other team is seen as unethical. Moving to the level of interethnic or intertribal conflict, children may learn that moral principles that apply to members of the ingroup do not necessarily apply to members of the outgroup (Triandis, 1990). In the extreme, adults may justify killing a member of an outgroup under conditions of terrorism or war.

Children may belong to more than one team, and those who are categorized as members of an outgroup may change according to the situation. For example, Ryan and his friend Tom were on the school soccer team together, but they belonged to different summer baseball leagues. During the summer, they had to compete against each other, so it usually turned out that they spent more time together and were closer friends during the school year than they were during the summers.

Participation in team sports provides socialization experiences that have both positive and negative consequences. Table 9.2 shows the ingroup and outgroup attitudes that may result from experiences in team play. For most children, belonging to a team, making friends, learning new skills, and enjoying the sense of success associated with a collaborative effort are positive experiences of middle childhood. For example, in a study of what young people value about their sports experiences, most children placed the greatest emphasis on enjoyment and personal achievement, and the least emphasis on winning (Lee, Whitehead, & Balchin, 2000). However, we all know of instances where rivalries escalate into peer hatreds, children from neighboring schools turn against

**Table 9.2** Ingroup and Outgroup Attitudes That Develop Through Team Play Experiences

| INGROUP ATTITUDES | OUTGROUP ATTITUDES |
|---|---|
| The child learns: | The child learns: |
| 1. To value and contribute to team goals | 1. To view the goals of the opponent as inconsistent with the goals of the ingroup |
| 2. To subordinate personal goals to team goals | 2. To view the outcome of competition as a zero-sum game, in which only one team can win |
| 3. To receive and use feedback and help from team members | 3. To recognize that helping the other team is unethical |
| 4. To value one's role as an element in a larger system and the interdependence of the team members | 4. To accept the necessity for antagonism between members of opposing teams |
| 5. To recognize that team members share a common fate | 5. To devise strategies that will exploit the weaknesses of the opponent |

each other, and coaches humiliate and degrade children in order to instill a commitment to the team and a determination to win. Perhaps the question is whether—particularly in team sports—the focal point of the activity is to enhance children's natural impulses for competence and skill elaboration, or whether the team activity becomes a way for adults to vent their own frustrated needs for domination and power.

# THE PSYCHOSOCIAL CRISIS: INDUSTRY VERSUS INFERIORITY

According to psychosocial theory (Erikson, 1963), a person's fundamental attitude toward work is established during middle childhood. As children develop skills and acquire personal standards of evaluation, they make an initial assessment of whether or not they will be able to make a contribution to the social community. They also make an inner commitment to strive for success. Some children are keenly motivated to compete against a standard of excellence and achieve success. Other children have low expectations about the possibility of success and are not motivated by achievement situations. The strength of a child's need to achieve success is well established by the end of this stage (Atkinson & Birch, 1978). Supporting the psychosocial perspective, researchers found that many of the factors that predict youth unemployment could be traced to experiences of middle childhood. A longitudinal study followed children born in 1972–1973 for 21 years. Predictors of unemployment were taking shape in the middle childhood and preteen years as a result of limited family resources and a high level of family conflict, poor reading skills and poor school grades, early evidence of antisocial behavior, and a lack of attachment to school. The picture emerges of children who are not only doing poorly in school, but are failing to find the social and emotional support of family or school that helps children invest in their community (Caspi, Wright, Moffitt, & Silva, 1998).

## INDUSTRY

**Industry** is an eagerness to acquire skills and perform meaningful work. During middle childhood, many aspects of work are intrinsically motivating. The skills are new. They bring the child closer to the capacities of adults. Each new skill allows the child some degree of independence and may even bring new responsibilities that heighten his or her sense of worth. In addition to these self-motivating factors associated with increased competence, external sources of reward promote skill development. Parents and teachers may encourage children to get better grades by giving them material rewards, additional privileges, and praise. Peers also encourage the acquisition of some skills, although they may have some negative input with regard to others. Certain youth organizations, such as scouting and 4-H, make the acquisition of skills a very specific route to success and higher status.

Every culture has expectations for skill learning during middle childhood. Here, a boy is learning to polish semi-precious stones that will be used for inlay work. At age 10, he is considered old enough for this work and is proud of what he can accomplish.

Kowaz and Marcia (1991) described the construct of industry as comprising three dimensions:

1. The *cognitive* component of industry was defined as the acquisition of the basic skills and knowledge that are valued by the culture.
2. The *behavioral* component of industry was defined as the ability to apply the skills and knowledge effectively through characteristics such as concentration, perseverance, work habits, and goal directedness.
3. The *affective* component of industry was defined as the positive emotional orientation toward the acquisition and application of skills and knowledge, such as a general curiosity and desire to know, a pride in one's efforts, and an ability to handle the distresses of failure as well as the joys of success.

## INFERIORITY

Given the internal thrust toward skill building that is generated by motives for competence and external rewards for mastery, it may appear that there should be no real conflict at this stage. One might think that everyone is united in a commitment to the joy and fulfillment that accrue from experiences of competence.

What experiences of middle childhood might generate a sense of **inferiority**? Feelings of worthlessness and inadequacy come from two sources: the self and the social environment. Alfred Adler (1935) directed attention to the central role that organ inferiority may play in shaping a person's perceptions of his or her abilities. **Organ inferiority** is any physical or mental limitation that prevents the acquisition of certain skills. Children who cannot master certain skills experience some feelings of inferiority. Individual differences in aptitude, physical development, and prior experience result in experiences of inadequacy in some domain. No one can do everything well. Children discover that they cannot master every skill they attempt. Even a child who feels quite positive toward work and finds new challenges invigorating will experience some degree of inferiority in a specific skill that he or she cannot master. For example, students who are born just before the age cutoff date for a particular sports competition may find that they have a hard time competing with the slightly older children in their age group. Especially at younger ages, children who are matched with others who are 10 to 12 months older may experience disappointment when they cannot compete successfully (Musch & Grondin, 2001). For many children who have developmental delays or motor impairments, the challenge of experiencing mastery in school-based skills can be very frustrating.

If success in one area could compensate for failure in another, we would be safe in minimizing the effect of individual areas of inadequacy on the overall resolution of the psychosocial conflict of industry versus inferiority. However, the social environment does not reinforce success in all areas equally. During middle childhood, success in reading is much more highly rewarded than success in tinkering with broken automobile engines. Likewise, success in team sports is more highly valued than success in operating a ham radio. It is difficult for a child who does not excel in culturally valued skills to compensate through the mastery of others.

The social environment also generates feelings of inferiority through the process of *social comparison*. Particularly in the school setting, but even in the home, children are confronted by statements suggesting that they are not as good as some peer, sibling, or cultural subgroup. Children may be grouped, tracked, graded, or publicly criticized on the basis of how their efforts compare with someone else's. The intrinsic pleasure of engaging in a task for the challenge it presents conflicts with messages that stimulate feelings of self-consciousness, competitiveness, and doubt: "I like playing ball, but I'm not as good as Ted, so I don't think I'll play." As children become increasingly sensitive to peer acceptance and peer rejection, they may refuse to try a new activity because they fear the possibility of being bettered or embarrassed by their peers.

Finally, the social environment stimulates feelings of inferiority through the negative value it places on any kind of failure. Two types of failure messages that may contribute to feelings of inferiority have been described. One type consists of criticisms of the child's motivation or effort. Such criticisms imply that, if the child had "really tried," she or he could have avoided failure. The other type refers more specifically to a lack of ability. Here, the implication is that the child does not have the basic aptitude to succeed. This type of failure message is associated with a pattern of attitudes about the self that has been described as learned helplessness.

**Learned helplessness** is a belief that success or failure have little to do with one's effort and are largely outside one's control (Seligman, 1975; Nelson, 1987). In a study of fourth-, fifth-, and sixth-graders, children were asked to verbalize their thoughts as they worked on various tasks. The children's verbalizations following failure showed a clear difference between the mastery-oriented children and the helpless ones. The mastery-oriented children were able to keep a positive attitude, increase their problem-solving efforts, and use their past mistakes to correct their approach. The helpless children began to blame themselves ("I never did have a good memory"). They emphasized the negative aspects of the task or criticized their own abilities and tried to find ways to escape from the situation (Diener & Dweck, 1980).

Helpless children tend to discount their successes and, in response to even a few remarks about their lack of ability, generate a self-definition that leads them to take a pessimistic view of their future success. When faced with a difficult or challenging situation, children described as helpless experience a negative mood while working on the task, give up quickly, blame their failures on a lack of ability, and expect to fail in the future (Cain & Dweck, 1995). Messages about failure usually suggest that there is an external standard of perfection—an ideal that the child did not meet. A few failures may generate such strong negative feelings that the child will

# Disorders of Childhood That Interfere with School Success

WHAT HAPPENS WHEN children have real difficulty accomplishing the tasks associated with basic areas of school achievement? The centrality of success in school-based learning for a positive resolution of the psychosocial crisis of industry versus inferiority brings the problem of childhood disorders to our attention. Three groups of disorders are described here, each one posing significant challenges for academic and social success during middle childhood and beyond (American Psychiatric Association, 1994). Typically, these disorders become more disruptive as children encounter the increasingly complex demands of the school curriculum.

## LEARNING DISORDERS

*Learning disorders* are diagnosed when a child's skills and measured abilities in reading, mathematics, or written communication are well below the child's grade level and the level expected from the child's measured IQ. Learning disorders have been identified in approximately 5% of public school children in the United States. These children are differentiated from others who show low performance because of mental retardation, poor teaching, or cultural factors that interfere with school performance. Typically, learning disorders are linked with deficits in the primary processing system, including speed and accuracy of information processing, attention, and memory. These deficits may be a result of genetic disorders, neurological damage during the prenatal period, or lead poisoning during childhood, but not all children with learning disorders have a history of these conditions. Children who have learning

disorders commonly also suffer from low self-esteem and are more likely than other children to drop out of school.

## MOTOR SKILLS DISORDERS

Approximately 6% of children in the 5–11 age range have a developmental problem in the area of motor skills. They are clumsy and delayed in the typical acquisition of early motor skills such as walking, running, tying their shoes, or using a scissors or knife. In later school years, they have trouble writing with a pencil or pen, are slow to develop skills in putting together puzzles or models, and their athletic skills, such as throwing and catching a ball, are delayed. These children are distinguished from others who have some broader medical diagnosis such as cerebral palsy. Their delay in motor skills interferes with academic achievement to the extent that these children struggle with any kind of written assignment and have difficulty completing projects that require manual dexterity. They lack the satisfaction of excelling in physical activities because even simple motor skills such as running or playing catch are sources of frustration.

## COMMUNICATION DISORDERS

Some children experience a developmental delay in effective social communication. Difficulties may include delays in acquiring new vocabulary; oversimplified grammatical expressions; limited variation in sentence types and structures; problems in sound production, such as lisping, omitting certain sounds in spoken speech, or stuttering; and problems in understanding certain types of words, expres-

sions, and grammatical constructions. About 3 to 5% of children have some type of developmental communication disorder that is distinct from mental retardation or a hearing impairment that influences speech. These difficulties interfere with academic performance especially because school learning involves the ongoing communication of information and ideas. Children who have communication disorders are also likely to be the target of peer teasing and social ridicule, leading to a pattern of social withdrawal or inappropriate social participation.

Learning disorders, motor skills disorders, and communication disorders are three of the more common childhood disorders among a variety of mental, emotional, and physical disabilities that young children may face as they struggle to resolve the crisis of industry versus inferiority. Each of these conditions makes it more difficult for children to succeed in the daily tasks of schooling. Children who experience these disorders may find it difficult to carry out projects or to complete assignments that others view as simple. They may also become targets of peer teasing, bullying, or rejection. As a result, they may define themselves as incompetent, inferior, or unable to learn (Valas, 2001). With appropriate diagnosis and effective intervention, however, children can learn strategies to overcome or compensate for their disabilities. Success in coping with a disability may, in fact, strengthen a child's self-confidence and provide a basis for beliefs of self-efficacy. Many children use the experience of coping with a disability as evidence that they can face and overcome other difficult challenges in their lives.

avoid engaging in new tasks in order to avoid future failure. Longitudinal research suggests that children who are identified as helpless in their approach to tasks in kindergarten continue to show evidence of these same behaviors, expectations, and emotions as first-graders and as fifth-graders (Ziegert, Kistner, Castro, & Robertson, 2001).

Extreme cases of inferiority result in reluctance, self-doubt, and withdrawal. The resolution of the psychosocial crisis in the direction of inferiority suggests that these children cannot conceive of themselves as having the potential to contribute to the welfare of the larger community. This is a serious consequence. It makes the gradual incorporation of the individual into a meaningful social group difficult to achieve. The irony of the psychosocial crisis at this stage is that the social community, which depends on the individual's motives for mastery for its survival, is itself such a powerful force in negating those motives by communicating messages of inferiority.

# THE CENTRAL PROCESS: EDUCATION

Every culture must devise ways of passing on the wisdom and skills of past generations to its young. This is the meaning of *education* in its broadest sense. Education is different from schooling. The practice of separating formal educational experiences from the direct, intimate, hands-on activities of home and community is only about 200 years old. Before the industrial revolution, most children were educated by partic-

ipating with their parents in the tasks of home life, farming, commerce with neighbors, and participation in religious life (Coleman, 1987). In the case of the nobility, children often had tutors who supervised their education at home.

Today, however, schools bear the primary responsibility for education. Teaching, which began as an extension of the parental role, has become a distinct profession. In our culture, education is not the kind of continuous interplay between the skilled and the unskilled that it is in more traditional cultures. Formal learning takes place in a special building during certain hours of the day. To be sure, the success of that experience in promoting a child's skills and a sense of the self as a learner depends heavily on the ongoing involvement and commitment of family members (Hill & Taylor, 2004). However, schools play a key role in providing opportunities for skill development and mastery, contexts for assessment, social comparison, and self-evaluation, and socialization for the behavioral characteristics—including focus, persistence, and organization—that contribute to the formation of a personal sense of industry.

© Richard Hutchings/Photo Edit

*In the modern classroom, children are encouraged to bring their skills in reading, math, science, and communication to the solution of complex problems. Teachers provide resources, encourage persistence, and give ongoing feedback.*

During the elementary school years, the goal of education is to help children develop the basic tools of learning. Central to this process is an introduction to the language of concepts, theories, and relationships that will allow them to organize their experiences (Cole & D'Andrade, 1982). Schools strive to develop verbal and analytic problem solving. Instruction focuses on rules, descriptions, and abstract concepts (Tharp, 1989). Children are exposed to a range of disciplines and methods of inquiry for dealing with complex problems. Throughout the educational process, children are presented with problems of increasing difficulty. They are given many opportunities to practice their newly developing skills, receiving continuous feedback about their level of competence.

In addition to the acquisition of skills and knowledge, schools emphasize an approach to behavior that can be described as a combination of *citizenship, social competence*, and *study habits*. Schools impart a code of conduct that is intended to facilitate the teacher's ability to guide students' attention, help children organize and focus on the tasks at hand, and foster a respectful, cooperative attitude toward adults and peers.

In general, the students' experiences of academic success are a product of the interaction between the teachers' background and ability to relate to students of various cultural backgrounds and the students' cognitive and behavioral resources, especially their citizenship and study habit behaviors. As part of the school-based educational process, children are exposed to a combined agenda, focusing both on the elaboration of skills and on the acquisition of behaviors that are associated with success within the school culture. Teachers judge children's academic ability and achievement levels based in part on the children's work habits, daily attendance and participation in classroom activities, and compliance with school rules. Low school engagement behaviors in the early elementary grades are as strong predictors of dropping out of school as are grades and test scores (Alexander, Entwisle, & Kabbani, 2001).

Going to school results in exposure to adults who provide models for commitment to learning (Rutter, 1983). These adults have skills of their own that give children some sense of how much more there is to learn. Schooling, therefore, provides opportunities not only to gain mastery but also to acquire goals and standards for the development of more advanced skills.

Children are at a stage of cognitive development that permits them to grasp the fundamental principles of the problems that the school poses for them. The art of teaching lies in presenting these problems at a level of complexity that is meaningful to each child but a step beyond his or her present ability level. As a result, learning becomes a tantalizing process, in which the problems themselves lure the children into expending effort to solve them. The sense of this process is captured in an adult's reminiscences about his music teacher from high school:

Beyond anything else, Griff wanted you to love and be as deeply affected by music as he was. His daughter, Ann, recently reminded me that when he was sometimes criticized for the problems students experienced with the difficult music he assigned, Griff would respond: "I don't care what a kid does to music. I care what the music does to the kid." Ever since he first convinced me to take voice lessons and seriously consider a career in music, Griff's visions have been a daily realization, as my life's work has, happily, been devoted to the arts. (Mosel, 1992, p. 12)

Not all children approach schooling with the same expectations of success or the same trust in adults or in the formal education process. Some groups view education as the means to economic security, intellectual development, and political empowerment. Others are skeptical of teachers, schools, and education. In some cases, parents find that they have no access to or voice in decisions affecting their children. They and their children have experienced barriers to achieving success in the skills that schooling values. For example, in a study of Latino immigrant families, parents experienced language barriers, an inability of teachers to explain their children's school difficulties, and constraints in making contact with teachers. Even though parents expressed a desire to support their children's school success, they felt helpless and dismissed as they tried to make contact with the school (Ramirez, 2003).

Failure in school and the public ridicule that it brings have been shown to play a central role in the establishment of a negative self-image. School represents the voice of the larger society. Children who continually fail to meet the standards set by school adults are likely to incorporate a view of themselves as failures. Sometimes, children defend themselves against the threat of failure messages by blaming others for their failures or by bragging that they can succeed in other ways. Much as it may appear that these children do not care about school or scorn school goals, the school remains a symbol of cultural authority. Children in these groups may conclude that the only way to retain a basic sense of self-confidence is to withdraw from school and try to establish their competence among their peers by accelerating their transition to adulthood through more risky paths (Alexander, Entwisle, & Kabbani, 2001; Clark, 1991; Gregory, 1995; Ogbu, 1987).

An integral approach to providing a successful educational environment for all children is to **contextualize** learning. To contextualize instruction is to carry it out in ways that first draw on a child's existing experiences, previous knowledge, and concepts, and then expand that understanding in new directions. For example, to contextualize math concepts, students were asked to use their computational and problem-solving math skills to plan and build two skateboard ramps (Bottge, 1999). Contextualizing calls for a recognition that classroom activities should make meaningful connections with students' lives outside of school and, at the same time, promote increasingly more complex ways of talking, writing, and thinking about these experiences. The classroom may be organized in a variety of ways: Children may engage in private study and small-group problem solving, for instance, as well as form a large group that listens and responds to the teacher. Teachers may include the heroes and heroines, stories, songs, and myths of a cultural group in order to help children feel comfortable with more abstract concepts. Contextualizing involves acknowledging different modes of expression, patterns of social conversation, and language. Finally, contextualizing draws parents and other important community figures into the learning process, so that children are not isolated from their social community (Dalton & Tharp, 2002).

All these efforts may be particularly beneficial to groups who have been alienated from schooling or who approach schooling with mistrust (Ladson-Billings, 2002). When the educational process is contextualized, children are strengthened in their own cultural identity. When their strivings for personal and cultural achievement are validated, the conflict that often develops between school professionals and members of ethnic groups need not arise. Initiatives to integrate technology in the classroom pose new opportunities for contextualizing learning in the classroom. Both teacher and student attitudes and values about learning may be challenged by computer technology (Parr, 1999).

# THE PRIME ADAPTIVE EGO QUALITY AND THE CORE PATHOLOGY

## COMPETENCE

The term **competence** has been used broadly and with diverse meanings in the human development literature. Ford (1985) offered a summary of five distinct uses of this concept:

1. Competence as an *outcome measure* reflecting one's effectiveness in a specific situation. For example, one might say that a child was competent at solving a specific problem or finding the necessary resources to meet his or her needs.
2. Competence as a *personality type*. This use of the concept is similar to *resilience*, a term used to discuss children who successfully overcome stressful life circumstances and continue to perform well in school (Garmezy & Masten, 1991). Some individuals are described as competent, and others are described as vulnerable or incompetent.
3. Competence as a *motivational system*. Competence has been used in this sense by Robert White (1959) to describe what he believed is a universal tendency to strive

toward higher and higher levels of mastery. According to White, once a child becomes competent at a certain level of functioning, there is an intrinsic push to move to a new, more challenging level. This notion is readily captured in children's fascination with computer games. These games are designed to take the player from one level or domain to the next, each time introducing new dangers, faster speed of play, or a new complexity of movements.

4. Competence as a *composite of knowledge, skills, and abilities* that permit successful adaptation. For example, one can refer to language competence as a global term encompassing the many different kinds of abilities that come into play in understanding the language of others, expressing one's own thoughts, and adapting to the language demands of specific situations. Each of the developmental tasks might be considered a domain for the development of age-related competence as defined by specific cultural expectations (Masten et al., 1995).
5. Competence as a *belief in one's effectiveness*. This definition refers to a general belief in one's ability to "get the job done." It is closely related to Bandura's concept of *self-efficacy*.

This last definition is closest to Erikson's (1982) notion of competence as the prime adaptive ego quality—a belief in one's ability to make sense of and master the demands of a situation: "Competence, in turn, is the free exercise of dexterity and intelligence in the completion of tasks, unimpaired by infantile inferiority. It is the basis for cooperative participation in technologies, and it relies, in turn, on the logic of tools and skills" (Erikson, 1978, p. 30).

Competence provides the child with a deep confidence in his or her ability to engage new situations and do well. This idea is illustrated by a study that monitored children's perceptions of competence during school transitions from Grade 5 to 6 and from Grade 6 to 7. The children who had the highest levels of perceived competence also had the strongest positive feelings about how they were doing in school and showed the highest scores on a measure of intrinsic motivation. They wanted to be challenged by their schoolwork and they liked working independently and figuring things out for themselves. They expressed curiosity about the tasks, saying they would work hard because of their own interest rather than to please the teacher or to get good grades (Harter, Whitesell, & Kowalski, 1992).

As she conceptualized the relationship of competence and self-esteem, Harter (1993) described two distinct paths of development that emerge during middle childhood: daily monitoring of self-esteem and stable self-esteem. For one group, day-to-day self-esteem is based on current experiences of competence and social approval. For these children, feelings of self-worth vary depending on how people who are important to them treat them that day and on whether the child is comparing his or her accomplishments with someone who is

*Erika is an excellent student who enjoys teaching others. Here she is demonstrating her reading and spelling competence as she guides the class in a word-recognition activity.*

quite a bit better, about the same, or not really as competent. The second group of children tends to have had many positive experiences of approval and competence in the past, which lead to a stable, positive sense of self-worth. As a result, these children are not as dependent on changing day-to-day conditions to sustain a positive feeling of worth. They tend to feel good about themselves, and thus enter new situations with a more positive, optimistic expectation of being liked and doing well. Sensing that they are competent, they leave this stage capable of using mastery and the resulting coping strategies to add to their repertoire of adaptive ego qualities—hope, will, and purpose—as they begin to encounter the new demands of early adolescence.

Children who have internalized a sense of competence love to learn and work. They are excited about developing new skills and optimistic about being able to achieve success. These children are the ones who sign up for new activities or start neighborhood clubs, want to be on two or three sports teams, look forward to field trips and school projects, and take pleasure in being asked to help with difficult tasks like planting trees along the highway, building a new playground, or raising money for earthquake victims. In contrast, some children feel a powerful sense of apathy or disinterest, which Erikson referred to as *inertia*.

## INERTIA

**Inertia** is the core pathology of middle childhood: "The antipathic counterpart of industry, the sense of competent mastery to be experienced in the school age, is that inertia that constantly threatens to paralyze an individual's productive life and is, of course, fatefully related to the inhibition of the preceding age, that of play" (Erikson, 1982, pp. 76–77).

Children who leave early school age with a sense of inhibition fail to participate and engage much during middle childhood. These are not the students who try and fail repeatedly, nor are they the ones whose sense of competence must be reconfirmed daily. Instead, they are students who tend to be passive and withdrawn, never engaging psychologically with the demands of their schools or their communities. Children who leave middle childhood with a sense of inertia continue to be withdrawn and passive. They will have trouble instigating actions or changing the course of events in their lives. As a result, they will not be likely to address challenges or problems by formulating plans of action, evaluating them, and then executing them. Children with a sense of inertia will not believe that they can master the challenges they face, and thus, they are likely to be swept along by the tide of events.

We all experience periods of inertia—times when we cannot muster the energy, enthusiasm, or confidence to take action. We may become besieged by doubts about our competence and worth—doubts that can produce work blocks, writer's block, waves of fatigue, boredom, procrastination, or aimlessness. Typically, one can survive a few days or even weeks on "automatic pilot," doing the bare minimum to survive. And children may be able to get by for quite a while without exercising much energy or direction, especially if they are being sustained by parents and teachers. Eventually, however, life brings demands for change and expectations to meet new challenges that have never been faced before. At those times, children who are burdened with a pervasive sense of inertia will be unable to cope.

# Technology and Schooling

One day we were supposed to go on a field trip, but I was worried about the weather. I stood at the window looking at the sky. The kids got online and called up the National Weather Service. (Malanowski, 1997, p. 43)

IN THE ONGOING debate about how to improve schooling in the United States, almost everyone agrees that all children should have access to computers at school, that schools need to be wired for the Internet, and that teachers need to be able to integrate computer technology into their teaching (Wulf, 1997). About 85% of children ages 6 to 9 use computers at school, and 62% use computers at home (U.S. Department of Commerce, 2003).

There is a widely shared expectation that the full incorporation of computers in the educational process will dramatically revise the climate and culture of schooling. Computer experiences are quite different from reading books or watching television. Computer use, especially participation in the Internet, is interactive, flexible, and responsive to the surfer's interests and abilities. It provides access to a wide variety of information, giving children a chance to question and evaluate as well as to support their beliefs. Through e-mail, chat groups, and bulletin boards, computers can support collaborations among children with shared interests. websites offer homework help, hands-on projects, and virtual field trips. Students are designing personalized websites where they can experiment with visual representations of their self-concept, express their opinions, share their enthusiasm for art, music, or science, and link their friends to other websites.

The CEO Forum on Education and Technology issued a report on recommendations for improving the integration of computer use into all aspects of education (CEO Forum, 2001). They emphasized the use of computer technology to promote "inventive thinking, effective communication, teamwork, and the ability to create high-quality products." Evidence suggests that computer technology can have a positive impact on children's learning as well as on their motivation and self-esteem. These bene-

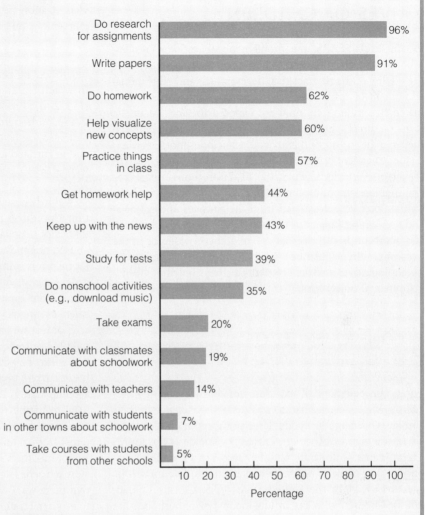

**FIGURE 9.4**

Students' Use of Computers at School

Source: Education Week, Harris Interactive Poll of Students and Technology, *Technology Counts, 2001.*

fits occur when the technology is applied to the achievement of important learning objectives and when teachers have opportunities for professional development to identify appropriate computer technologies for their classroom.

Figure 9.4 shows the percentage of students who use the computer at school for a variety of purposes (Education Week, 2001). The possibilities for collaboration with teachers, other students, and experts beyond the school are not yet being fully realized. The use of computer technology allows students to proceed at their own pace, administer self-evaluations in order to get immediate feedback about their progress, and cre-

ate personalized databases to monitor their progress. Students' knowledge deepens as they explore a variety of sources of information, extend the scope of their inquiry, and work in groups to exchange ideas. Because of the diversity of ideas and opinions as well as data sources available on the Internet, students can learn to evaluate information and seek out expert opinion as they solve problems (CEO Forum, 2001).

For examples of school-related resources on the Internet for middle school-age children, visit http://www.homework.org or Kids Web at http://www.npac.syr.edu/textbook/kidsweb/index.html

# VIOLENCE IN THE LIVES OF CHILDREN

IN RECENT YEARS, the problem of violence in families, schools, and neighborhoods has threatened to undermine the quality of the psychosocial development and educational attainment of many American children. Each year, an estimated five million children are exposed to violence in the form of direct physical abuse, domestic violence between their parents or other members of their household, and exposure to violent crimes in their neighborhood or school. In the terrorist attacks of September 11, 2001, thousands of U.S. children lost one or both parents in an act of violence; thousands more were evacuated from their homes and schools; and continuing threats of violence have raised new levels of fear about unpredictable harm. The topic of violence in the lives of children illustrates the interaction of the biological, psychological, and societal systems as they contribute to developmental trajectories.

## CONSEQUENCES OF EXPOSURE TO VIOLENCE

Three consequences of exposure to violence are of especially grave concern. First, as a result of the violence in their families and neighborhoods, large numbers of children and youth are victims of violent crimes. Homicide is the fourth leading cause of death for children ages 5 to 14, and the second leading cause of death for adolescents and young adults ages 15 to 24 in the United States (U.S. Census Bureau, 2003). Children who live in low-income neighborhoods are especially vulnerable to exposure to violence. In a survey of youth ages 9 to 15 living in public housing communities, one third of the children reported both being a victim of violence and witnessing violence (Feigelman, Howard, Li, & Cross, 2000). Neighborhoods that are centers of illegal drug trade are also often the sites of violence, including stabbings, shootings, and gang raids. In these communities, the loss of a legitimate economic base, with few people in stable or high-status occupations, leads to takeovers by gangs and other organized criminal activities. Children are lured into dangerous forms of drug-related transactions, which make them targets of violence on the streets as well as victims of abuse by drug-addicted family members and youth (National Research Council, 1993; Okundaye, 2004). According to a report issued by the National Center for Educational Statistics, in 1999 more than three million children ages 12 through 18 (about 12% of U.S. children) reported exposure to theft or violent crimes at their schools (National Center for Educational Statistics, 2003).

A second consequence of exposure to violence is the number of children who are themselves aggressive and violent. Many studies report a significant relationship between victimization or witnessing violence and carrying out violent actions on others. The accumulation of exposure to violence across several settings, including community, school, and home, coupled with low parental monitoring and the likelihood of being a victim of violence, create a context in which children exhibit serious violent behaviors (Garbarino, 2001; Preski & Shelton, 2001; Weist & Cooley-Quille, 2001). Although the number of arrests for cases of juvenile violent offenses (criminal homicide, forcible rape, robbery, and aggravated assault) has been declining since 1994, there were 78,443 such arrests in 2001 (U.S. Census Bureau, 2003).

A third consequence of exposure to violence is the disruption it produces in children's cognitive functioning and mental health (Osofsky, 1995). Children who have been severely abused or exposed to intense violence are now viewed as suffering from symptoms similar to post-traumatic stress disorder (Hamblen, 2003). **Post-traumatic stress disorder** can result from direct experience of a grave threat to personal safety or injury, witnessing the injury or death of another person, or learning about the violent death or injury of a family member or someone close. The response usually includes "intense fear, helplessness, or horror," and the person typically has recurrent vivid recollections or dreams of the event with accompanying strong emotional reactions. Children may have recurring nightmares, repeat the same play sequences that reenact some part of the traumatic event, withdraw interest from activities they used to enjoy, and show physical symptoms that they did not have before the event, such as stomach aches or headaches. School-age children may believe that there were warning signs that would have allowed them to avoid the trauma if they had been alert enough to recognize them. As a result, these children maintain a type of *hypervigilance* or increased arousal, directing their attention to threat-related stimuli (Dalgleish, Moradi, Taghavi, Neshat-Doost, & Yule, 2001). These symptoms last for more than 1 month and often interfere with sleep, schoolwork, concentration, and normal social life (American Psychiatric Association, 1994).

Symptoms of post-traumatic stress disorder can be long lasting and, in some cases, can emerge long after the event has passed. For example, one study focused on 69 children who had lived within 100 miles of Oklahoma City in 1995 when the federal building was bombed. These children, studied in 1997, did not see the explosion, they did not live near the explosion, and no one they knew personally was injured or killed in the explosion. Yet 2 years after the event, many of these children showed evidence of post-traumatic stress disorder symptoms and related difficulties in functioning. Their symptoms were attributed to experiences of the event through the media and indirect loss through friends or fam-

*Incidents of violence in or near schools have led to new preventive steps. A teacher gives instructions as children participate in a playground drill to protect themselves in case of random shooting.*

ily members who know someone who was killed (Pfefferbaum et al., 2000).

Evidence suggests that children preserve sensory and motor memories of the conditions associated with their trauma, which are then released under contemporary conditions of fear. In boys, these symptoms commonly reflect hyperarousal, including startle response, increases in heart rate, sleep disturbance, anxiety, and motor hyperactivity. In girls, the symptoms are more likely to be dissociation, gastrointestinal symptoms, and pain. Under threatening conditions, children who have been traumatized in the past automatically return to these disruptive states, making it difficult to access higher order problem-solving and reasoning skills.

According to the neurobiology of aggression, simple regulatory and impulsive functions are governed by the more primitive, reactive areas, including the brainstem and the midbrain. More complex functions of language and abstract reasoning develop later and are located largely in the subcortical and cortical areas. The capacity to modify and regulate impulses is a combination of the intensity of the signals emerging from the brainstem and the maturation of the expressive and coping strategies governed by the cortex (Perry, 1994). An overreactive brainstem that produces intense and frequent impulses may result from any one or a combination of factors, including fetal exposure to alcohol and drugs, environmental exposure to lead, hormonal abnormalities, head injuries, or exposure to child abuse. Children reared in a socialization environment of chaos, violence, parental aggression, and harsh and abusive discipline lack the opportunity to develop empathy, self-control, and higher order problem-solving skills that might allow them to modulate their strong impulses (American Psychological Association, 1996).

## PREVENTION STRATEGIES

The prevention of violence in society and the reduction in exposure to violence among children have become significant public health issues (Dorfman, Woodruff, Chavez, & Wallack, 1997). Rather than focusing solely on the criminal justice definitions and strategies for deterrence, a public health perspective emphasizes the understanding of the contexts of violence from which strategies for prevention can be devised and evaluated, and invites collaboration in identifying many layers of prevention. We must learn more about what predisposes young children to respond to events in their lives with violence. We must try to determine what kinds of socialization environments can help children control their aggressiveness. Furthermore, we must discover strategies to reduce violence in neighborhoods, schools, and in the media (Sampson, Raudenbush, & Earls, 1997; Henrich, Brown, & Aber, 1999). Several directions for prevention have been identified and require coordination:

1. Prevent prenatal and perinatal conditions that cause neurological damage and increase the biological vulnerability for violent behaviors.
2. Develop effective techniques for educating parents and teachers about socialization practices that help develop self-control, empathy, and perspective taking.
3. Develop effective techniques for teaching children alternative, non-aggressive strategies to handle and respond to insults, threats, and frustration.
4. Devise educational experiences that help children to reframe cognitions and beliefs that lead them to interpret the behaviors of others as threatening.

5. Reduce exposure to violence at home, in the neighborhood, and on television.
6. Decrease children's access to guns.
7. Increase the sense of social control and cohesion in neighborhoods, so that mutual trust is higher, people help one another more, and people are more willing to take steps to intervene when children are acting destructively.

To learn more about strategies that are designed to reduce violence in schools and support a positive school climate, visit the website of the Center for the Prevention of School Violence at http://www.ncdjjdp.org/cpsv

# Chapter Summary

During middle childhood, cognitive and social skills develop that are crucial to later life stages. Remarkable synergies occur across the cognitive domains, bringing new levels of skill development, expanded access to information, and elaborate strategies for approaching and solving problems. Children apply their cognitive abilities not only in academic, school-related domains, but also in an increased capacity for social cooperation, self-evaluation, and peer group participation. As a result of the combination of cognitive and social skill development, children are able to make significant contributions to the social groups to which they belong. They are also likely to seek approval and acceptance from these groups.

Industry focuses primarily on building competence. The family, peer group, and school all play their part in the support of feelings of mastery or failure. However, in our society, school is the environment in which continuous attention is given to the child's success or failure in basic skill areas. The child's emerging sense of industry is closely interwoven with the quality of the school environment and the extent to which the child encounters experiences that both foster enthusiasm for new learning and provide objective feedback about levels of mastery. An understanding of skill development must combine an appreciation of the child's intellectual maturity with a sense of the significant motives that may influence his or her willingness to learn.

The achievements of middle childhood contribute in key ways to coping and adaptation in adulthood. Issues of industry, mastery, achievement, social expectations, social skills, cooperativeness, and interpersonal sensitivity are all salient themes during this stage. A person's orientation to friendship and work—two essential aspects of adult life—begin to take shape.

The applied topic illustrates the biological, psychological, and societal contexts of violence. Children can be exposed to prenatal and perinatal risks that disrupt their neurological development. They may be embedded in a family system in which abusive or disorganized parenting reduces their ability to cope with threats or stress. Violence in the neighborhood, media, and school strengthens impulsive, reactive responses and makes it increasingly difficult for children to draw on their higher order reasoning skills to reinterpret or interrupt their sense of anger and threat. Access to weapons, especially guns, leads to new heights of destructive expression for these children.

# Further Reflection

1. Think back on your middle childhood years, between the ages of 6 and 12. What are some examples of experiences that made you feel competent and self-assured? What are examples of experiences that led to feelings of inferiority or self-doubt?
2. Consider the role of friendship during this period of life. How might friends contribute to skill development? Self-evaluation? Cognitive problem solving?
3. How does the environment of school change from age 6 (Grade 1) through age 12 (Grade 7)? How well do changes in the school environment match the developmental changes that take place during this period of life?
4. Think about school success and failure in middle childhood. What personal, family, cultural, and environmental factors might contribute to school success? To school failure? Suppose that you were asked to provide guidance to a local school board about improving their middle schools. What ideas from this chapter might inform your recommendations?
5. The psychosocial crisis of industry versus inferiority is closely linked to one's attitude about work in later stages of life. What is your view about how young adults view entry into the world of work? What contribution might events from middle childhood make to this outlook?
6. What are the primary factors that promote violence among children in middle childhood? What steps are needed to buffer children from the negative impact of violence and to promote a cooperative, peaceful resolution of conflicts?

## On the Web

### VISIT OUR WEBSITE

Go to http://www.wadsworth.com/psychology to find on-line resources directly linked to your book.

## Casebook

For additional case material related to this chapter, see the case entitled "Ayesha and the Dinosaurs" in *Life Span Development: A Case Book*, by Barbara and Philip Newman, Laura Landry-Meyer, and Brenda J. Lohman, pp. 100–104. The case suggests how new cognitive skills, skill learning, and a sense of competence come together to promote new levels of leadership and problem solving in middle childhood. The case also illustrates some of the challenges that children face in the transition to kindergarten and how home, preschool, and kindergarten systems can work together to foster a child's continuing school success.

# CHAPTER 10

# EARLY ADOLESCENCE
# (12–18 YEARS)

Boy with a Pipe, 1905,/Pablo Picasso/© 2005 Estate of Pablo Picasso/Artists Rights Society (ARS), New York,/Bridgeman Art Library, London,/SuperStock

*Rapid physical changes, self-consciousness, and a need for peer approval are all characteristics of early adolescence. Here, Picasso shows us the delicacy of youth, the boy taking on a contemplative pose and emerging, almost as a work of art, into young manhood.*

■ DEVELOPMENTAL TASKS

Physical Maturation

CASE STUDY: CARLY PATTERSON, OLYMPIC GYMNAST

Formal Operations
Emotional Development
Membership in the Peer Group
Romantic and Sexual Relationships

■ THE PSYCHOSOCIAL CRISIS: GROUP
IDENTITY VERSUS ALIENATION

Group Identity
Alienation

■ THE CENTRAL PROCESS: PEER PRESSURE

Affiliating with a Peer Group
Peer Pressure in Specific Areas
Conflicts Between Belonging and Personal Autonomy
Ethnic Group Identity

■ THE PRIME ADAPTIVE EGO QUALITY
AND THE CORE PATHOLOGY

Fidelity to Others
Dissociation

■ APPLIED TOPIC: ADOLESCENT ALCOHOL
AND DRUG USE

Factors Associated with Alcohol Use
Early Entry into Alcohol and Drug Use

■ CHAPTER SUMMARY

■ FURTHER REFLECTION

## CHAPTER OBJECTIVES

▶ *To describe the patterns of physical maturation during puberty for female and male adolescents, including an analysis of the impact of early and late maturing on self-concept and social relationships.*

▶ *To introduce the basic features of formal operational thought, highlighting the new conceptual skills that emerge and the factors that promote the development of formal operational thought.*

▶ *To examine patterns of emotional development in early adolescence, including three examples of emotional disorders: eating disorders, delinquency, and depression.*

▶ *To describe the further evolution of peer relations in early adolescence, especially the formation of cliques and crowds, and to contrast the impact of parents and peers during this stage.*

▶ *To characterize the development of sexuality, with a special focus on the transition to coitus, the formation of a sexual orientation, and a detailed review of the factors associated with pregnancy and parenthood in adolescence.*

▶ *To describe the psychosocial crisis of group identity versus alienation; the central process through which the crisis is resolved, peer pressure; the prime adaptive ego quality of fidelity to others; and the core pathology of isolation.*

▶ *To review the patterns of adolescent alcohol and drug use and the factors associated with their use and abuse within a psychosocial framework.*

AT THIS POINT in our discussion of life stages, we depart again from Erikson's conceptualization. His psychosocial theory viewed adolescence as a single stage, unified by the resolution of the central conflict of identity versus identity confusion. Erikson's approach attempted to address the tasks and needs of children and youth ranging in age from about 11 to 21 within one developmental stage. Based on our own research on adolescence and on our assessment of the research literature, we have come to the conclusion that two distinct periods of psychosocial development occur during these years—early adolescence (12–18 years) and later adolescence (18–24 years). This chapter discusses the stage of early adolescence, and Chapter 11 discusses later adolescence.

**Early adolescence** begins with the onset of puberty and ends with graduation from high school (or roughly at age 18). This stage is characterized by rapid physical changes, significant cognitive and emotional maturation, newly energized sexual interests, and a heightened sensitivity to peer relations. We have called the psychosocial crisis of this stage **group identity** versus **alienation**. **Later adolescence** begins at approximately age 18 and continues for about 6 years. This stage is characterized by new advances in the establishment of autonomy from the family and the development of a personal identity. The psychosocial crisis of this period is **individual identity** versus **identity confusion**.

The elaboration of adolescence into two stages is closely tied to social and historical changes. At the turn of the 20th century in the United States, few youths in the 12–18 age range were in school; at the turn of the 21st century, almost all of them are. The time between entry into puberty and entry into the self-sustaining roles of adulthood has expanded. In contrast to life 100 years ago, we have a longer period of required education and training, fewer opportunities to enter the full-time labor force without a high school education, laws restricting the employment of children under the age of 16, and a workplace that requires more advanced technical, representational, and interpersonal skills for success. At the same time, occupational choices are much more diverse, and the process of selecting a career path has become increasingly difficult. Thus, adolescence has stretched out as a period of life. Young people reach the biological capacity to reproduce and the physical stature of an adult at an earlier age, but they do not yet have the education, skills, training, or sense of purpose to create a sustainable lifestyle independent of their family of origin.

Many people think of early adolescence as a difficult time, filled with turmoil, risks, parent–child conflict, and indifference to societal norms. But these views say as much about the adult generation and its developmental preoccupations as about adolescents. We all traverse the rapid transformations of puberty on the path from childhood to adulthood. For adolescents, the challenge and even the joy of the period is to construct a sense of self that is at once connected to meaningful individuals and groups and, at the same time, authentic and autonomous. Adolescence is a thrilling time of life, a time of lasting memories about first experiences. Young people emerge into a wider, more varied social environment. Their social relationships take on a new intensity and complexity. New and more intricate thoughts are possible, accompanied by new insights about the self as well as the physical, social, and political environment. Many adolescents experience new levels of emotional intensity, including positive feelings such as romantic sentiments, sexual desires, tenderness, and spirituality, as well as the negative emotions of jealousy, hatred, and rage. Although the media and the research literature tend to focus on the difficulties of the period, most young people make important new strides toward maturity during this time. They reach new levels of mastery and a new appreciation of their interdependence with family, friends, community, and culture. ■

# DEVELOPMENTAL TASKS

## PHYSICAL MATURATION

Coming on the heels of a period of gradual but steady physical development in middle childhood, early adolescence is marked by rapid physical changes, including a height spurt, maturation of the reproductive system, appearance of **secondary sex characteristics**, increased muscle strength, and the redistribution of body weight. At the same time, the brain continues to develop, with changes that increase emotionality, modify memory, and gradually improve connections among areas of the brain that regulate emotion, impulse control, and judgment (Brownlee, 1999; Spear, 2000). Variability in the rate and sequence of development is well documented (Brooks-Gunn & Reiter, 1990; Tanner, 1990). The time from the appearance of breast buds to full maturity may range from 1 to 6 years for girls; the male genitalia may take from 2 to 5 years to reach adult size. These individual differences in maturation suggest that during early adolescence, the chronological peer group is biologically far more diverse than it was during early and middle childhood.

Adaptation at puberty requires an integration of biological, psychological, and social changes. A young person may be responding to noticeable physical changes, such as a height spurt or the growth of pubic hair. Some changes in behavior may be due to less readily observable biological changes in hormone production associated with new levels of arousal and emotionality. Psychological changes may be due to age as well as pubertal status and the changes that are as-

sociated with age. For example, some children make a school transition into seventh grade at age 12, leading to new status, a new sense of responsibilities, and new expectations for school performance. Some responses to puberty are cued by the way other people, including parents, teachers, siblings, and peers, respond to a child whose physical appearance has changed. In many cultures, *rites of passage* occur with entry into puberty, giving the young person new roles and new status within the community. Finally, some responses to puberty have to do with the timing of these changes—whether pubertal changes are perceived to be early, on time, or late in relation to their peers. Thus, puberty is not one event, but a *biopsychosocial* transition that takes on meaning in the context of a child's culture and community.

The degree to which one's body matches the desired or socially valued body build of the culture influences social acceptance by peers and adults. This match between body shape and cultural values also influences the future course of psychosocial development. The European American culture gives self-esteem advantages to muscular, well-developed boys and petite, shapely girls. In contrast, it detracts from the self-esteem of thin, gangling boys, underdeveloped girls, and overweight boys and girls. Changes in body size and shape at puberty can bring advantages or disadvantages, depending on the context (see case study on Carly Patterson).

# CASE STUDY

## CARLY PATTERSON, OLYMPIC GYMNAST

*At age 16, Carly Patterson was an all-around gold medal Olympic champion in gymnastics.*

Carly was born February 4, 1988, in Baton Rouge, Louisiana, the first of two children to Ricky and Natalie Patterson. A straight-A high school student, Carly enjoys things almost all sixteen-year olds do: shopping, movies, the beach. But Carly is far from normal. Patterson works with coaches Yevgeny Marchenko and Natasha Boyarskaya at the World Olympic Gymnastics Academy in Plano, Texas. Marchenko calls her "Harley Davidson" because of her power. She trains twice a day, six days a week, for about 32 hours a week. She balances her training and competition schedule with a regular high school workload. On a typical day, she's at the gym from 8 to 11:30 a.m., then at school in the middle of the day, and then at the gym again from 4 to 7:30 p.m.

Carly began gymnastics in 1994, after attending a cousin's birthday party at Elite Gymnastics in Baton Rouge. Less than a decade later, she made her debut at the senior international elite level, winning back-to-back American Cup titles in 2003 and 2004, as well as the title of 2004 U.S. Co-National Champion. Carly was also a part of the 2003 World Championship team where she won a silver medal in the all-around and helped lead the U.S. to their first ever World Championship team gold medal! It was also at this competition that Carly's signature beam dismount (an Arabian double front) was officially named the Patterson. A year later, Carly achieved her ultimate goal in gymnastics by earning a trip to the 2004 Olympic Games in Athens, Greece.

Carly came home from Athens with three Olympic medals. The U.S. women won silver in the team competition—the first medal for the U.S. women in eight years, as well as the second highest finish for the Americans in a fully attended Olympic Games. Carly also earned a silver medal on her specialty, the beam. However, it was on August 19th that all of Carly's hard work, dedication, and love for gymnastics paid off. She won the most prestigious title in gymnastics, the title of 2004 Olympic All-Around Champion. Carly is the U.S.A.'s first Olympic all-around champion in twenty years, as well as the first American woman to win an Olympic all-around title in a fully attended Olympic Games!

Source: Retrieved November 28, 2004, from http://www.acepeople.com/c/Carly-Patterson.asp

We cannot fully predict how puberty will transform a child's body into that of an adult. Often, adults focus on the challenges and difficulties that youth face, such as eating disorders or high-risk behaviors. For many young people, however, puberty opens up expanded opportunities for athletic achievement. As a gymnast, Carly's small stature (4′9″) and slight build were accompanied by a significant increase in musculature that allowed her to perform explosive jumps with unusual athletic ability. We do not know what might have happened to Carly's gymnastic career if her puberty had been accompanied with a greater height spurt or more breast development. There is concern that competitive events in which athletes are punished for weight gain or encouraged to manipulate their weight in order to compete may contribute to serious health risks, especially during adolescence (Brown University, 2004).

## ■ CRITICAL THINKING AND CASE ANALYSIS

1. Thinking about the world of competitive athletics, what are some examples of how the physical changes of puberty might open up new opportunities for adolescents? How might the physical changes of puberty reduce such opportunities?
2. How does Carly's case illustrate the interaction of biological, psychological, and societal systems?
3. How might a training program interact with the changes of puberty to promote athletic ability? What might be the risks of too much training or poor training at this age?
4. What personal, emotional, and intellectual attributes do you think are necessary in order to function as a world-class athlete? How likely is it that a person in early adolescence has these attributes?
5. What messages might someone like Carly be able to convey to other adolescents about health and physical development in early adolescence?

## ■ PHYSICAL CHANGES IN GIRLS

The window for the transition into puberty appears to be expanding for girls in the United States. When European American, African American, and Latina girls of the same socioeconomic background were compared, the average age at menarche was about age 12 for European American and African American girls. Latina girls reached menarche slightly earlier than the African American girls (Obeidallah, Brennan, Brooks-Gunn, Kindlon, & Earls, 2000). However, menarche is not one of the first events in the transitions of puberty. A study of more than 17,000 girls ages 3 to 12 found that roughly 15% of European American girls and 50% of African American girls were showing evidence of secondary sex characteristics, including breast buds and pubic hair, by age 8 (Herman-Giddens et al., 1997; Lemonick, 2000). There are speculations about the cause of this early onset of puberty. Some consider obesity in children as a stimulus for early puberty; others point to the breakdown of insecticides in the soil, or hormones given to cattle that eventually make their way into a child's diet. Finally, some argue that the exposure to sexual stimulation in television, movies, advertisements, and overt behavior plays a role in promoting the production of hormones that stimulate puberty. None of these speculations has been accepted as the determining factor (Lemonick, 2000).

For girls, the earliest evidence of puberty is usually breast bud development and the beginning of the height spurt, which occur on average between ages 10 and 11—almost 2 years sooner than the parallel experiences for boys (see Table 10.1). Initially, the increase in height may be embarrassing when a girl finds herself towering above her male classmates. To compensate, girls often slouch or wear baggy clothes.

Generally, girls are more dissatisfied than boys with their physical appearance and their overall body image. For girls, self-consciousness and dissatisfaction with their appearance reach their peak between the ages of 13 and 15. The cultural, family, or community emphasis on a thin ideal, combined with the view that thinness can be achieved through effort, lead many girls to experience dissatisfaction with their body. In studies carried out in the United States, Korea, and Australia, body dissatisfaction is associated with lower levels of self-esteem and increased likelihood of depression among early adolescent girls (Dunkley, Wertheim, & Paxton, 2001; Kim & Kim, 2001).

**CONCERNS ABOUT OBESITY.** The greatest concern that adolescent girls express about their bodies is the perception that they are too fat. This concern is not so much that being overweight is unhealthy, but that it results in peer rejection from both boys and girls.

Lisa is a seventh-grader who attends a White, upper middle class, middle school. She is clearly overweight. As a newcomer to her school, she found that her weight was the major factor in determining her social and academic experiences.

**Table 10.1** The Development of Primary and Secondary Sex Characteristics for Boys and Girls

| GIRLS | AVERAGE AGE OF OCCURRENCE | BOYS |
|---|---|---|
| Onset of height spurt | 10–11 | **Growth of testes** |
| Initial breast development | 11 | Development of pubic hair |
| Increased activity of oil and sweat glands (acne can result from clogged glands) | 11–12 | Increased activity of oil and sweat glands (acne can result from clogged glands) |
| Development of pubic hair | 12 | **Growth of penis** |
| **Onset of menarche** (age range is 9–17) | 12–13 | Onset of height spurt |
| Development of underarm hair | | |
| **Earliest normal pregnancy** | 14 | Deepening of the voice |
| Completion of breast development (age range is 13–18) | 15–16 | **Production of mature spermatozoa** |
| | | **Nocturnal emissions** |
| | | Development of underarm and facial hair |
| Maturation of skeletal system | 17–18 | Maturation of skeletal system |
| | | Development of chest hair |

Note: Primary sex characteristics are boldface type.
The primary sex characteristics relate to the development of genitalia and reproductive organs.
Secondary sex characteristics are other physical changes associated with puberty, such as body hair or breast development.

Source: Adapted from Turner and Rubinson, 1993.

**FIGURE 10.1**

The Relationship of Body Image to Eating Disturbances

Source: Based on Stice and Shaw, 2002.

"At first I thought if I got good grades and tried to fit in it wouldn't matter how I looked. But I still got teased, it didn't make a difference. All the good things about me—like that I was smart—it was just, 'You don't fit. You don't look good. You're fat.' I felt like I was doing all the good things for no reason. So I just said, 'Fine, if it's going to be that way, then I don't care.' And I don't try at all anymore. I don't care about school." (Orenstein, 2000, pp. 100–101)

In a national survey of adolescents' health concerns, 85% of adolescents said they thought that girls cared a lot about controlling their weight. In contrast, only 30% thought that boys cared a lot about controlling their weight. Despite the strong interest expressed in controlling weight, less than 10% of adolescents thought that their peers cared a lot about eating healthy foods. In a review of research on body dissatisfaction and eating pathologies, Stice and Shaw (2002) found support for a relationship between body image disturbances and eating disorders (see Figure 10.1).

Three factors appear to contribute to body dissatisfaction among adolescent girls: social pressures to be thin; an internalized thin ideal body type; and higher than average body mass. Those girls who have higher body dissatisfaction are likely to start dieting and also to experience negative emotional states, especially depression. The combination of these factors can lead to future eating pathologies. In an attempt to attain a thin ideal and to reduce negative feelings about themselves, many early adolescent girls begin a process of strict and often faddish dieting. This strategy is ill-timed, because their bodies require well-balanced diets and increased caloric intake during the period of rapid growth (Stice & Shaw, 2004).

Concern about being overweight is culturally linked. For example, studies have found that girls who have strong religious backgrounds have a heavier real and ideal weight than less religious girls. Black girls view a slightly heavier body image as ideal in comparison to White girls. With Black youth, one does not see the relationship of obesity and low self-esteem that is often observed in studies of White adolescents (Flynn & Fitzgibbon, 1996; Abell & Richards, 1996; Martin et al., 1988).

Obesity is related to activity level. For girls, one of the compounding factors in obesity is that they tend to reduce their activity level with age. One longitudinal study monitored common physical activities for children from Grades 3 through 10. During Grades 6 through 8, those girls who were more advanced in their pubertal status were less active than the girls who were less physically mature. Pubertal status was not a factor that predicted activity level for boys in those same grades (Bradley, McMurray, Harrell, & Deng, 2000). In an ethnically diverse sample of more than 550 girls in Grades 5 to 12, only 36% met the national goal for strenuous activity (15 minutes of strenuous activity at least three times per week; Wolf et al., 1993). The amount of overall activity and strenuous activity decreased with age, and obesity was negatively correlated with activity. The study also revealed differences in exercise patterns across ethnic groups. Hispanic and Asian American girls had significantly lower scores on activity level than African American and European American girls. Two cultural hypotheses were formulated to explain this pattern, but neither one has been tested: First, strenuous physical activity may be viewed as especially unfeminine by Asian Americans and Hispanics. Second, it is possible that the slender body type is not seen as desirable by these ethnic groups; thus, there is less motivation to do strenuous exercise.

**REACTIONS TO BREAST DEVELOPMENT AND MENARCHE.**    For girls, two of the most noticeable events of puberty are the development of breast buds and the onset of the menstrual cycle (**menarche**). To the average girl, the development of breast buds is a welcome sign of her growing maturity and femininity (Brooks-Gunn & Warren, 1988). Some

girls begin to wear brassieres early in puberty in anticipation of the onset of breast development. However, the trend toward earlier breast development has parents and mental health experts concerned about the compression of childhood. Eight-year-old girls with breasts are still emotionally and cognitively like their undeveloped 8-year-old peers. Their physical development may result in new expectations for more mature behavior and new sexualized attention from older boys (Lemonick, 2000).

Although most girls are prepared by their mothers for menstruation, the topic is often handled as a matter of hygiene rather than as a sexual transition (Logan, 1980). Many girls do not understand the relation of menstruation to reproduction. They simply accept their monthly periods as another sign of their femininity. The process of learning about menarche may be somewhat more anxiety producing for girls who are not living with their mothers or with a female caregiver. In a qualitative study of girls who were living without their mothers, the girls were often embarrassed to ask questions of their fathers and experienced more distress around this issue if they did not have access to a woman who could answer their questions (Kalman, 2003). This has special implications for the health of girls who may be separated from their mothers due to maternal death, war, or imprisonment.

At the age when most girls begin to menstruate (approximately age 12 to 12½, or seventh grade), their male peers may be unaware of these changes. As a result, girls may try to hide the facts of their growth. Girls rarely tell their male peers or their fathers about the onset of menarche, but they do discuss it with their female friends and their mothers. The discrepancy in the onset of puberty in boys and girls and the uneven dissemination of information about it may make it difficult for a girl to fully accept the changes she is experiencing.

Most girls seem to react to menstruation with a mix of positive and negative feelings. The positive feelings reflect their

*Selecting the first bra is a sign of a girl's transition from childhood to adolescence.*

© Michael Newman/Photo Edit

pride in maturing and the confirmation of their womanliness. The negative feelings reflect the inconvenience, some unpleasant symptoms, and the possible embarrassment of menstruation (Brooks-Gunn & Reiter, 1990). Negative feelings are especially likely if a girl matures early, at age 9 or 10. In a retrospective study involving more than 1,500 Chinese junior high school girls, students were asked about their knowledge and attitudes about menarche and their emotional responses to their first menstruation. Although 85% reported feeling annoyed and embarrassed by their first menstruation, about 66% also reported positive feelings, especially feeling more grown up. The more adequate their preparation for menarche and the more they saw menarche as a natural, healthy event, the more positive were their emotional responses (Tang, Yeung, & Lee, 2003).

## ■ PHYSICAL CHANGES IN BOYS

Boys generally welcome the changes involving increased height and muscle mass that bring them one step closer to adult maturity. Nonetheless, some ambivalence is likely as boys experience the transitions of puberty. On the one hand, a mature physique usually brings well-developed physical skills that are highly valued by peers and adults alike. On the other hand, the period of rapid growth may leave a boy feeling awkward and uncoordinated for a time. This awkwardness results because growth does not take place at the same rate in all parts of the body. One particular discrepancy is the time lag between the height spurt and the increase in muscle strength. For boys, the increase in the rate of growth in height starts at about 12.5 years and reaches a peak around age 14. The peak increase in muscle strength, however, usually occurs about 12 to 14 months after the peak height spurt (Brierley, 1993). This time lag results in a temporary period during which a boy simply cannot accomplish what he might expect given his height. Psychologically, this awkward period poses challenges to a boy's self-esteem. For boys, body image dissatisfaction is typically associated with frustration about not looking muscular or strong—a concern that is magnified by the lag between the height spurt and the increase in muscle mass (Cohane & Pope, 2001).

The onset of the growth of the testes and the penis also poses important challenges for early adolescent boys. Testicular growth is one of the first signs of puberty in boys. A somewhat controversial study of U.S. boys reported that genital growth was observed to begin sometime between ages 9 and 10—more than 2 years before the estimate given by prior studies (Associated Press, 2001). Boys are generally not well prepared by their parents with information on the maturation of their reproductive organs (Bolton & MacEachron, 1988). Specifically, they are not taught about spontaneous ejaculation and may be surprised, scared, or embarrassed by it. The sexual connotation of the event may make it difficult for boys to seek an explanation from their parents. They are left to gain information from friends and reading material or to worry in private about its meaning. For many boys, spon-

© Michael Newman/Photo Edit

*Shaving is a symbol of a boy's transition into adolescence and continues to be an element of a young man's masculine identity throughout young adulthood.*

taneous ejaculation provides an important clue to the way in which physical adult sexuality and reproduction are accomplished. The pleasure of the ejaculation and the positive value of the new information that it provides are counterbalanced by a mild anxiety (Gaddis & Brooks-Gunn, 1985; Marsiglio, 1988; Adegoke, 1993). This is only one of the developments that arouse ambivalence in many boys during early adolescence.

A third area of physical development that has psychological and social meaning for boys is the development of secondary sex characteristics, particularly the growth of facial and body hair. In many societies, the equipment and ritual behaviors associated with shaving are closely linked to the masculine gender role. Most boys are eager to express their identification with this role, and they use the slightest evidence of facial hair as an excuse to take razor in hand. The ritual of shaving not only provides some affirmation of the boy's masculinity, but it also allows him an acceptable outlet for his narcissism. As he shaves, it is legitimate for him to gaze at and admire his changing image. In some societies, the ability to grow a mustache or a beard is a sign of one's masculinity. In these cultures, boys cultivate and admire their mustaches or beards as evidence of their enhanced male status.

## ■ CULTURAL CONTEXTS OF PUBERTY

The way adolescents react to the physical changes of puberty may depend in part on the cultural context. For example, studies of Mexican youth find that girls become somewhat more depressed as they go through puberty, whereas boys experience an improved sense of body image and well-being (Benjet & Hernandez-Guzman, 2002). These gender differences may reflect the greater status and new responsibilities given to male children in Mexican culture, and the new restrictions that apply to female children as they enter puberty in order to protect their chastity. In another cultural comparison, several studies comparing African American and European American adolescent girls were summarized. In general, African American adolescent girls are more satisfied with their body image and less inclined toward eating disorders than European American girls. Furthermore, early pubertal onset and weight increases were not particularly strong predictors of negative body image and depression among African American girls, as they are for European American girls (Franko & Streigel-Moore, 2002).

## ■ THE SECULAR GROWTH TREND

Along with the genetic influence that guides the timing of pubertal growth and sexual maturation, the environment plays an important role in the eventual attainment of one's growth potential. A **secular growth trend** is a decrease over time in the average age at which physical maturation takes place (Van Wieringen, 1978). Changes in hygiene, nutrition, and health care have contributed to an earlier growth spurt over the past century. Children ages 10 to 14 increased in height by an average of 2 to 3 centimeters every decade from 1900 to 1960. Adult height is not necessarily greater due to this increase; it is simply attained at an earlier age.

Other evidence of a secular trend is the shift in age at menarche. There is some controversy about the extent of this shift. Data reported by Tanner (1990) showed a decrease in the average age at menarche from the 1950s (13.5 to 14 years) to the 1970s (12.5 to 13 years). At present, the mean age at menarche is 12.3, but the range is from 9 to 17. Age at menarche varies among countries and even among socioeconomic groups within a country. Historical records based on Roman, Islamic, and medieval writings suggest that girls have matured in the age range of 12 to 14 for many centuries (Bullough, 1981). Lack of precise records and the confounding of health and social class with age at menarche make it difficult to confirm these long-term historical trends.

What is the relevance of the secular trend for understanding the development of contemporary adolescents in postindustrialized societies? Reproductive capacity and physical adult stature occur at a younger age than at the turn of the 20th century, but full engagement in the adult society requires more training, education, and complex preparation than in the past. Thus, adolescence is prolonged, with more

time to experience the risks of unwanted pregnancy, the sense of being in a marginal social status, and disruptions in the transition from childhood to adulthood.

The concept of the secular trend alerts us to the importance of the psychosocial context of physical development. Not only are peers experiencing diverse patterns of growth, but parents and grandparents may also be reacting to a discrepancy between their children's development and their own timetable for growth. What is more, because the period of reproductive capacity starts earlier than it did 50 years ago, young people must cope with special challenges in the expression and regulation of their sexual impulses. One consequence of the earlier onset of puberty is that adolescents may find themselves in potentially high-risk situations at a relatively young age. Given the risks inherent in a technological society, it is no wonder that adolescent exposure to risk behaviors is a major contemporary health concern.

## ■ INDIVIDUAL DIFFERENCES
## IN MATURATION RATE

The age at onset of puberty and the rate of change in physical maturation vary. Early and late maturing have psychological and social consequences for both boys and girls. Recent research about the effects of pubertal timing has challenged the view that was established by researchers in the 1950s and 1960s. In those studies, boys who matured early experienced positive consequences, including greater opportunities for leadership and social status, and as a result, they had higher self-esteem (Clausen, 1975; Mussen & Jones, 1957). A similar advantage for early maturation for fifth- and sixth-grade boys was reported in the early 1990s. The boys who were more physically mature described more positive daily emotions, better attention, and feelings of being strong (Richards & Larson, 1993). The explanation for these advantages was that early-maturing boys are likely to be given increased responsibility by their parents and teachers. They are generally more satisfied with their bodies, feel more positive about being boys, and are likely to be more involved in school activities by the 10th grade than are late-maturing boys (Blyth, Bulcroft, & Simmons, 1981). In contrast, boys who mature later than their age-mates may experience psychological stress and develop a negative self-image. Late-maturing boys are treated as if they were younger than they really are. They may become isolated from their peers or behave in a silly, childish manner to gain attention.

Recent research has painted a somewhat different picture of the consequences of early maturing for boys, especially those who mature in Grade 7 or before. These studies show that early-maturing boys have more hostile feelings, greater levels of anxiety and depression, more problems with drug and alcohol use, and more deviant activities and problems in school than boys who mature "on time" (Alasker, 1995; Ge, Conger, & Elder, 2001; Wichstrom, 2001). The associa-

By Grade 8, the physical diversity of the peer group is quite noticeable. Differences in height, weight, and body shape have implications for popularity, leadership, and self-confidence.

tion of early maturation and heightened rates of violent and nonviolent delinquent behavior has been observed for African American, Mexican American, and European American youth (Cota-Robles, Neiss, & Rowe, 2002)

How can we account for these differences? Is early maturing a benefit or a risk for boys? Explanations for this new view of the impact of early maturation for boys vary. One explanation is that we are looking at a cohort effect. Maturing early in the 1950s may have been a more positive experience, whereas maturing early in the 1990s may expose adolescent boys to more stressors. Another explanation is that in today's society, physical maturation at age 12 and earlier converges with other stressful life events, especially school transitions, disruption of the peer network, more challenging expectations for school performance, and the related risk of failure. More stressful life events coupled with the pubertal transition increase uncertainty and may leave boys feeling out of control. A third explanation is that boys who mature early have not had time to fully master the tasks of the middle childhood period. With an early height spurt and a more mature physical appearance, they may be accelerated into situations where they are faced with expectations for a level of self-control, decision making, and leadership for which they are not prepared. Too much, too soon produces overload (Ge, Conger, & Elder, 2001).

The different views of the impact of early maturing may *both* be correct. For example, it may be true that early-maturing boys do experience greater opportunities for leadership and social status, and at the same time, because they look older, they may begin to engage in some of the high-risk behaviors of slightly older boys.

Several studies suggest that early pubertal onset is also a source of stress for girls (Kornfield, 1990; Caspi & Moffitt, 1991). Because pubertal changes occur about 2 years earlier for girls than for boys, the early-maturing girl stands out among all her male and female age-mates. Early onset of menstruation is especially stressful, resulting in heightened self-consciousness and anxiety (Hill, 1988). Early maturers are less likely to have been prepared for the onset of menstruation, and they are less likely to have close friends with whom they can discuss it. Early pubertal maturation may result in feelings of social isolation for girls.

Early-maturing girls experience higher levels of conflict with their parents and are more likely to report depression and anxiety (Wierson, Long, & Forehand, 1993). Early-maturing girls who are dissatisfied with their physical appearance are especially vulnerable to low self-esteem (Williams & Currie, 2000). There is some evidence that early-maturing girls earn lower grades and lower scores on academic achievement tests. They are also more likely to be identified as having behavior problems in school (Blyth et al., 1981). Early-maturing girls start dating earlier and perceive themselves as more popular with boys than do late-maturing girls. Some studies report that early-maturing girls are more likely to engage in high-risk, promiscuous sexual behavior. In general, however, the timing of the transition to puberty in and of itself is not a strong predictor of a girl's emotional well-being. Rather, this timing interacts with other events, including school transition, family conflict, or peer acceptance, to influence how girls construct the meaning of this physical transition (Booth, Johnson, Granger, Crouter, & McHale, 2003).

## FORMAL OPERATIONS

As the body undergoes significant changes during puberty, so too does mental activity. Early adolescents begin to think about themselves and their world in new ways that reflect a broadening of consciousness. This includes greater introspection or monitoring of their thoughts, greater integration of information from various sources, and more focused planning and control of behaviors guided by goals and strategies. Young people are able to think about several dimensions at once rather than focusing on just one domain or issue at a time. They are able to generate hypotheses about events that they have never perceived and to use logical reasoning to evaluate evidence to support or disconfirm these hypotheses (Keating, 2004).

It should come as no surprise that the major transformations in conscious thought, reasoning, and problem solving

**APPLYING THEORY AND RESEARCH TO LIFE**

## Sleep Loss in Adolescence

ALONG WITH MANY changes in physical stature and appearance, puberty brings changes in sleep patterns. Research carried out in sleep labs suggests that when allowed to sleep as long as they wished, adolescents would sleep about 9 hours. However, as they get older, the quality of the sleep changes, with less time spent in deep sleep, leaving adolescents more tired during the day even when they get the same amount of sleep as younger children (Dahl & Caskadon, 1995). In actuality, as adolescents make the transition to high school, they get less sleep than younger children, leaving them more tired and more likely to fall asleep during the day.

The study of sleep and its relation to psychosocial outcomes is a growing field (Johnson, 2004). Questions of interest include how the biological changes of puberty contribute to changes in sleep quality; sociocultural factors that contribute to sleep deprivation; and the impact of sleep habits on moddiness, self-esteem, depression, substance abuse, and school achievement. A combination of factors contributes to sleep deprivation in adolescence. Middle school tends to start earlier than elementary school, and high school starts earlier still. Many adolescents are in activities that involve before-school preparation. Adolescents are likely to stay up late on school nights doing homework, talking with friends, using the computer, or watching television. Some adolescents have jobs at restaurants and stores where they stay until closing time. In addition to these contextual factors, there is some evidence that the natural biorhythm for adolescents shifts toward a preference for a later sleep phase. In comparison with younger children, who sleep about the same amount during the weekdays as on weekends, adolescents tend to sleep much later on the weekends (Gaina, Sekine, Chen, Hamanishi, & Kagamimori, 2004). When they have a choice, as on the weekends, older adolescents stay up later at night, when they feel alert and energized, and sleep later in the morning. This shift is tied to pubertal status; those teens who are in a more advanced pubertal status show a greater tendency toward this delay and a greater difference between weekend and weekday sleep (Laberge, Petit, Simard, Vitaro, Tremblay, & Montplaisir, 2001).

In a longitudinal study of more than 2,000 children, the amount of sleep that children said they got on a typical school night was tracked for 3 years, in sixth, seventh, and eighth grades (Fredriksen, Rhodes, Reddy, & Way, 2004). The amount of sleep for both boys and girls declined from sixth to eighth grade. In the sixth grade, children who got fewer hours of sleep also had lower self-esteem, lower grades, and more depressive symptoms. Those students who experienced the greatest decline in hours of sleep over the 3 years also showed greater increases in depressive symptoms and lower self-esteem by eighth grade. Given the strong associations of depression and self-esteem with risky health behaviors, the role of sleep deprivation clearly deserves greater attention in family and school contexts.

---

that are evidenced in adolescence are accompanied by important changes in the brain. Three changes are of special note:

1. New developments in the prefrontal cortex, which are implicated in a variety of coordinating and executive functions, such as self-evaluation, long-term planning, and the synthesis of emotion, attention, and behavior.
2. Continuing myelination of nerve fibers, leading to faster connectivity and communication among different areas of the brain; and
3. Focused "synaptic pruning," or reduction of synapses, which reflects the use of certain pathways over others (Diamond, 2002; Johnson, 2001).

Figure 10.2 highlights the peaks in cortical development during childhood and adolescence, pointing out the new mental abilities that are associated with each new phase of development. The continued maturation of the frontal lobes well into later adolescence is associated with several cognitive capacities, including the ability to reject irrelevant information, formulate complex hypothetical arguments, organize an approach to a complex task, and follow a sequence of steps to task completion (Davies & Rose, 1999; Spear, 2000).

### ■ PIAGET'S THEORY OF FORMAL OPERATIONAL THOUGHT

Without the benefit of brain scans, Jean Piaget proposed a qualitative shift in thinking during adolescence from concrete to formal operational thought (Inhelder & Piaget, 1958; Piaget, 1970, 1972). In the period of **concrete operational thought**, children use mental operations to explain changes in tangible objects and events. In the period of **formal operational thought**, young people use operations to manipulate and modify thoughts and other mental operations (Piaget, 1972). A central feature of formal operational reasoning is the ability to separate and distinguish between *reality* and *possibility*. For example, in thinking about trying to get a part-time job, adolescents may consider the number of hours they want to work, their access to transportation, the kind of work they want to do, and the kind of work they think they are qualified

**Peak 1. Ages 1–6.** Rapid brain growth across several areas. Associated with ability to form images, use words, place things in serial order, development of problem-solving tactics.
**Peak 2. Ages 6–10.** Peak growth in the sensory-motor regions. Associated with operational functions such as determining weight and reasoning about mathematical problems.
**Peak 3. Ages 10$\frac{1}{2}$–13.** New growth in the visual and auditory regions of the brain. New abilities to perform calculations and to perceive new meanings and functions for familiar objects.
**Peak 4. Ages 13–17.** New growth in the visuoauditory, visuospatial, and somatic systems of the brain. New ability to review mental operations, find flaws in their reasoning, and use information to revise their problem-solving strategies.
**Peak 5. Ages 17–21.** New growth in the frontal executive region. New capacities to question and evaluate information, form new and original hypotheses integrating their own experiences with information taken from other sources.

**FIGURE 10.2**

Peak Periods of Cerebral Maturation

Source: From "The Effects of Neurologic Injury on the Maturing Brain," by M. Allison, *Headlines*, October/November, pp. 2–4.

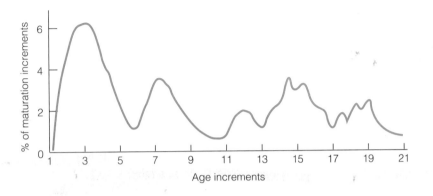

for before they start filling out applications. They are able to create different scenarios about working, based partly on what they want and partly on what they know, and then modify their plan based on new information they get about available jobs.

An important characteristic of formal operational thought is the ability to raise *hypotheses* to explain an event, and then to follow the logic that a particular hypothesis implies. One of the classic experiments that Piaget and Inhelder designed to demonstrate the development of hypothetical deductive reasoning involves the explanation of the swing of a pendulum.

The task is to find out what variable or combination of variables controls the speed of the swing. Four factors can be varied: the mass of the object, the height from which the pendulum is pushed, the force with which it is pushed, and the length of the string. To investigate this problem, it is necessary to begin by isolating the separate factors and then varying only one factor at a time while keeping the others constant. As it happens, only the length of the string influences the speed of the pendulum. The challenge, then, is to demonstrate that the length of the string accounts for the speed of the pendulum and that the other factors do not. Children at

*The opportunity to manipulate variables in an experimental situation stimulates formal operational thought. At the same time, the capacity for hypothesis testing makes it possible for students to evaluate the results of their experiments. How might you design chemistry experiments so that they are most likely to foster formal operational reasoning?*

the stage of concrete operational thought have difficulty co-ordinating the interaction among four separate variables and may lose track of what is being varied and what is held constant. After trying one or two strategies, they may simply give up. In contrast, being able to use formal operational thought, a child can create a matrix of variables and test each factor separately to evaluate its contribution (Inhelder & Piaget, 1958; Flavell, 1963).

## SIX CHARACTERISTICS OF FORMAL OPERATIONAL THOUGHT

Formal operational thought is not a specific skill or expertise; rather, it is a way of approaching and solving problems. Six conceptual skills emerge during the stage of formal operations that have implications for how adolescents approach interpersonal relationships and the formulation of personal plans and goals and for how they analyze scientific and mathematical information (see Table 10.2; Demetriou & Efklides, 1985; Gray, 1990; Neimark, 1982). First, adolescents are able to mentally manipulate more than two categories of variables at the same time; for example, they can consider the relationship of speed, distance, and time in planning a trip (Acredolo, Adams, & Schmid, 1984). They can draw on many variables to explain their behavior as well as that of others. Second, they are able to think about things changing in the future. They can realize, for instance, that their current friendships may not remain the same in the years ahead.

Third, adolescents are able to hypothesize about a logical sequence of possible events. For example, they are able to predict college and occupational options that may be open to them, depending on how well they do in certain academic coursework in high school. Fourth, they are able to anticipate the consequences of their actions. For instance, they realize that if they drop out of school, certain career possibilities will be closed to them.

Fifth, they have the capacity to detect the logical consistency or inconsistency of a set of statements. They can test

the truth of a statement by finding evidence that supports or disproves it. They are troubled, for example, by the apparent contradiction between statements such as "all people are equal before the law" and the reality that people who have more money can afford better legal representation and are likely to have different experiences with the legal system than those who live in poverty.

Sixth, adolescents are able to think in a relativistic way about themselves, other individuals, and their world. They know that they are expected to act in a particular way because of the norms of their community and their culture. Adolescents also know that in other families, communities, and cultures, different norms may govern the same behavior. As a result, the decision to behave in a culturally accepted manner becomes a more conscious commitment to their cultural group. At the same time, it is easier for them to accept members of other cultures, because they realize that these people are the products of societies with different sets of rules and norms.

These qualities of thought reflect what is *possible* for adolescents rather than what is typical. Most adolescents and older adults approach problem solving in a practical, concrete way in their common, daily functioning. However, under the most supportive conditions, more abstract, systematic, and self-reflective qualities of thought can be observed and bring a new perspective to the way adolescents approach the analysis of information and the acquisition of knowledge (Lee & Freire, 2003).

## EGOCENTRISM AND DECENTERING

The term *egocentrism* refers to the child's limited perspective at the beginning of each new phase of cognitive development (Piaget, 1926; Inhelder & Piaget, 1958). In the sensorimotor phase, egocentrism appears as an inability to separate one's actions from their effects on specific objects or people. As the scheme for causality is developed, the first process of decentering occurs. Infants recognize that certain actions have predictable consequences and that novel situations call for new, relevant behaviors. For example, one cannot turn the light on by turning the knob on the radio. At each developmental stage, decentering allows the person to approach situations from a more objective, analytic point of view.

In the phase of preoperational thought, egocentrism is manifested in an inability to separate one's own perspective from that of the listener. When a 4-year-old girl tells you about something that happened to her at the zoo, she may explain events as if you had seen them too. When a 3-year-old boy is explaining something to his grandmother over the phone, he may point to objects in the room, unaware that his grandmother cannot *see* over the phone lines.

The third phase of heightened egocentrism occurs in the transition from concrete to formal operational thought. As children develop the capacity to formulate hypothetical sys-

---

**Table 10.2**  New Conceptual Skills That Emerge During the Stage of Formal Operational Thought

1. Ability to mentally manipulate more than two categories of variables simultaneously.
2. Ability to think about the changes that come with time.
3. Ability to hypothesize logical sequences of events.
4. Ability to foresee consequences of actions.
5. Ability to detect logical consistency or inconsistency in a set of statements.
6. Ability to think in relativistic ways about self, others, and the world.

tems, they begin to generate assumptions about their own and others' behavior that will fit into these systems. For example, an early adolescent boy may insist that cooperation is a more desirable mode of interaction than competition. He argues that cooperation ought to benefit each participant and provide more resources for the group as a whole. This boy may become angry or disillusioned to discover that teachers, parents, and even peers seek competitive experiences and appear to enjoy them. He may think, "If the cooperative system is so superior, why do people persist in their illogical joy in triumphing over an opponent?" This kind of egocentrism reflects an inability to recognize that others may not share one's own hypothetical system.

In early adolescence, decentering requires an ability to realize that one's ideals are not shared by all others. We live in a pluralistic society, in which each person is likely to have distinct goals and aspirations. Adolescents gradually discover that their neat, logical life plans must be constantly adapted to the expectations and needs of others. As they develop the flexibility of thought that accompanies formal operational perspective taking, their egocentrism usually declines.

Early adolescent egocentrism has two characteristics that may affect adolescents' social interactions as well as their problem solving: (1) preoccupation with their own thoughts and (2) a belief that others are also preoccupied with their thoughts. First, adolescents may become withdrawn and isolated as the domain of their consciousness expands. Thoughts about the possible and the probable, the near and the distant future, and the logical extension of contemporary events to future consequences all flood their minds. David Elkind (1967) described one aspect of this process as the formation of a **personal fable**—an intense investment in one's own thoughts and feelings, and a belief that these thoughts are unique. Adolescents may conclude that they alone are having certain insights or difficulties and that no one else could understand or sympathize with their thoughts. This tendency to withdraw into their own speculations may cut off access to new information or ideas and inhibit social interaction.

Second, early adolescents may assume that they are the center of interest of others' thoughts and attentions. Elkind (1967) referred to this as an **imaginary audience**. Instead of considering that everyone is equally wrapped up in his or her own concerns and plans, early adolescents may envision their own thoughts as being the focus of other people's attention. This subjectivity generates an uncomfortable self-consciousness that makes interaction awkward. There is some question about the outcome of this heightened self-consciousness. On the one hand, a preoccupation with the idea that others are watching your every move may be an important element in decentering, directing attention to others and how you may be viewed in their eyes. Thus, self-consciousness may stimulate cognitive perspective taking. On the other hand, an increased ability to consider the point of view of others and their expectations for your behavior may increase self-consciousness.

Egocentrism is a problem not only during the adolescent years. At each new phase of expanding awareness, people rely heavily on their own experiences and perceptions in order to minimize the anxiety associated with uncertainty. Part of the progress of formal thought implies a reliance on reason over experience, placing greater confidence in what is known to be true than in what is seen or heard. This can lead to becoming confined to the world of one's familiar beliefs. We may interpret new experiences as examples of familiar concepts rather than as novel events. We may reject evidence for an argument because it does not support an already carefully developed explanation. The business of casting around for new evidence and explanations is a lifelong challenge. It is much easier to rely on earlier assumptions than to continually question one's perspective.

## ■ FACTORS THAT PROMOTE FORMAL OPERATIONAL THOUGHT

Neurological development alone is not enough to foster formal operational thought. Healthy brain development must be coupled with a social environment that encourages hypothetical, abstract reasoning; opportunities to investigate and explore alternative solutions; and a well-developed symbolic capacity for carrying out mental representations and operations. The affective components of interest, motivation, and self-efficacy are also involved in sustaining engagement with complex problems and the emotional regulation that allows one to stay focused despite frustrations and failures.

Several environmental conditions facilitate the development of formal operational thought and reduce egocentrism. First, early adolescents begin to function in a variety of role relationships that place both compatible and conflicting demands on them. Among these role relationships are son or daughter, worker, student, friend, dating partner, religious believer, and citizen. Early adolescents experience firsthand the pressures of multiple expectations for behavior. Participating in a variety of roles also facilitates relativistic thinking by demonstrating that what is acceptable and valued in one situation may not be in another (Chandler & Boyes, 1982).

A second environmental factor is the adolescent's participation in a more heterogeneous peer group (Looft, 1971). When children move from their community elementary school to a more centralized junior high and high school, they are likely to meet other students whose family backgrounds and social class are different from their own. In working and playing with these friends, they realize the extent to which their expectations for the future differ from those of their new acquaintances because their values are shaped by the families and neighborhood from which they come.

The use of formal operational skills can be observed in adolescent discussions of peer-related issues and in the formation of intimate or romantic relationships—domains that

*Conversations with parents often force adolescents to rethink their assumptions or come up with support for their decisions. Although this is not always pleasant, these kinds of interactions are an important stimulus for more advanced reasoning.*

© Robert Brenner/Photo Edit

require a wide range of hypothesis raising and testing. An example of a conversation between a 15-year-old girl and her best friend follows:

CINDY: I'm so frustrated I can't stand it. Before Sean and I started to date, he was nice to me. I enjoyed being with him. He said hello to me in the halls; we'd walk along together. We talked about all kinds of things. Now that we're going out, he seems rude and uncaring. When we're with other people, he jumps in when I start to talk, and his eyes say "be quiet." He breezes by me in the halls sometimes, and when we talk about things (if we talk), he acts as if he is always right. I don't think he cares about me anymore. What's going on?

DONNA: I know he likes you because he tells me. Maybe you should talk to him and tell him what he does and how it makes you feel.

CINDY: No, if I do that he'll get mad and he won't like me anymore. Why don't you talk to him?

DONNA: No, that wouldn't do any good, because then he would know you talked to me about this and he would not like it, or he would just say what he thinks would make him look good.

As this conversation continues, many possible scenarios are proposed about why this behavior is occurring, and many hypotheses are raised about what could be done. The girls propose likely outcomes of each set of possible actions and attempt to evaluate the results of each. Finally, a tentative conclusion is reached: Boys treat girls differently when they are involved in a boyfriend–girlfriend relationship than when they are not. In the "just friends" situation, there is a tendency to treat the girl as an equal, but in the boyfriend–girlfriend situation, there is a tendency for the boy to expect that he

should dominate the girl. A solution is derived: Cindy must shape up Sean. Because she still likes him and wants to go out with him, she must try to tell him how she feels and hope he will change his behavior so that it is supportive and comfortable for her.

The context of friendship between Cindy and Donna allows Cindy to trust discussing her problem with Donna so that they can examine it fully. It also allows Donna to disagree with Cindy without terminating the conversation. Thus, Cindy can get a somewhat different point of view on her situation and the two friends together can explore a personal problem on a more objective, rational basis than Cindy probably could have done on her own.

The third condition that fosters the development of the cognitive skills of early adolescence is the content of the high school curriculum. Courses in science, mathematics, and language formally expose the students to the logical relationships inherent in the world and introduce them to the hypothetical deductive style of reasoning. The fine arts and the humanities foster conceptions of ways in which the world has been or might be. They expand the repertoire of representational thought. According to Gardner's model of multiple intelligences (discussed in Chapter 9), the visual arts provide a means of integrating and innovating spatial intelligence with interpersonal intelligence. The more complex, differentiated academic environment of the high school can bring substantial gains in conceptual skills for those students who become actively engaged in its academic programs (Kuhn, Amsel, & O'Loughlin, 1988; Linn, Clement, Pulos, & Sullivan, 1989; Adey & Shayer, 1993).

Although schooling can be a vehicle that promotes formal operational reasoning, not all school experiences are equally effective in promoting abstract, hypothetical reasoning. Keating (1990) described the following characteristics that are important in creating a cognitively stimulating school experience:

> Students need to be engaged with meaningful material; training of thinking skills must be embedded in a knowledge of subject matter, for acquisition of isolated content knowledge is likely to be unproductive; serious engagement with real problems has to occur in depth and over time; students need experiences that lead to placing a high value on critical thinking, to acquiring it as a disposition, not just as a skill; and many of these factors occur most readily, and perhaps exclusively, when students have the opportunity for real, ongoing discourse with teachers who have reasonably expert command of the material to be taught. (p. 77)

One does not expect to see a mature scientist or a profound philosopher by the end of early adolescence. A young person's formal operational reasoning awaits further encounters with a specific discipline and its full range of significant problems. However, the opportunity for cognitive growth during this period is extensive. Adolescents are able to generate novel solutions and apply them to current life challenges. They also are able to be increasingly objective about the problem-solving process and to gain insight into their own mental activity.

## ■ CRITICISMS OF THE CONCEPT OF FORMAL OPERATIONAL THOUGHT

In Piaget's theory, formal operational reasoning is viewed as the final stage in the development of logical thought. A number of scholars have pointed to limitations in this construction. Three criticisms are discussed here. First, some scholars question whether there really is a qualitative, stage-like consolidation in the use of formal reasoning. Although most researchers agree that formal operational thinking exists and does characterize the nature of mature, scientific reasoning, many studies show that adolescents and adults typically do not function at the formal operational level, and that their use of formal reasoning is inconsistent across problem areas (Bradmetz, 1999). For example, Neimark (1975) followed changes in the problem-solving strategies of adolescents over a 3½-year period. Even the oldest participants in her study, who were 15, did not apply formal operational strategies across all problems. Research has not been able to confirm Piaget's claims that thinking becomes consistently more propositional across problem areas or that formal operational reasoning is a universal characteristic of adolescent reasoning in a variety of cultures. At the same time, the evidence does suggest that adolescents become more aware of the need to coordinate logic and evidence as they evaluate propositions (Keating, 2004). Even Piaget speculated that people were most likely to use formal operational reasoning primarily in the area of their greatest expertise.

A second criticism of formal operational reasoning is that it is not broad enough to encompass the many dimensions along which cognitive functioning matures in adolescence.

Increases in speed, efficiency, and capacity of information storage and retrieval have been documented during the period from ages 11 to 16 (Kwon & Lawson, 2000; Thatcher, Walker, & Giudice, 1987). Improvements in logical reasoning are in part a result of being able to handle greater quantities of information more quickly and efficiently. In addition to development in basic processing, there are gains in knowledge, both as a result of schooling and experience. Knowledge in each specialized subject, such as mathematics, language, or science, expands, bringing not only increases in logic but increases in understanding the procedures or strategies that are most likely to work for a given problem. Complementing changes in specialized knowledge, adolescents demonstrate increases in self-monitoring and conscious control of mental activity, such as the ability to hold conclusions in abeyance while they examine alternative solutions or gather new information. These capacities for cognitive flexibility contribute to the potential for more mature solutions (Donald, 2001).

Finally, some scholars claim that formal operational thought does not represent the apex or endpoint of adult thought and reasoning. As adults mature, they face many problems in which abstract, logical-mathematical reasoning must be integrated with the special emotional and social demands of the circumstances. The problem may need to be reframed to suit the situation. The solution may need to be evaluated for its impact on many interrelated parties. The cognitive processes associated with psychotherapy, diplomacy, and spiritual leadership are all examples of what might be considered *postformal* reasoning (Torbert, 1994; Richards & Commons, 1990).

## ■ EMOTIONAL DEVELOPMENT

Descriptions of adolescence often refer to new levels of emotional variability, moodiness, and emotional outbursts. However, evidence suggests that this is also a time of increased emotional complexity, with new capacities to identify, understand, and express a wider range of emotions (Kang & Shaver, 2004). These capacities illustrate the close interdependence of cognition and emotion, especially as reasoning about the consequences of expressing emotions may result in the control or management of emotional expression (Hoeksma, Oosterlaan, & Schipper, 2004). Given the likelihood of a more differentiated range of emotions during adolescence, a major task during this time is to gain insight into one's emotionality, and to expand one's capacity for empathy with the emotional state of others (Weissberg & O'Brien, 2004). This means accepting one's feelings and not interpreting them as a sign of "going crazy" or "being strange." Adolescents who are highly sensitive to social expectations or overly controlled about expressing or accepting their feelings probably experience a sense of shame about their emotional states. Attempts to rigidly control or defend oneself against feelings are likely to result in social alienation or maladaptive

*Adolescents become aware of a new variety of emotions. Girls are likely to turn inward, experiencing feelings of self-doubt, guilt, or depression. Boys are more likely to experience irritability and anger. What might account for these differences?*

© David Kelly Crow/Photo Edit

behaviors. In contrast, those who experience a diverse and well-differentiated range of emotions are also more likely to be characterized by greater openness to experience, empathy, and interpersonal adaptability (Kang & Shaver, 2004).

Clearly, adolescents are more aware than younger children of gradations in their emotional states and are able to attribute them to a wider range of causes. However, some researchers have questioned whether adolescence really brings the peaks and valleys of emotional intensity that are stereotypically linked to this time of life. In an attempt to assess this question, researchers gave an electronic paging device to children and adolescents ages 9 to 15 and asked them to describe their emotional state every time they were paged (Larson & Lampman-Petraitis, 1989). Over one week, each participant responded about 37 times. The variability of emotions was not found to increase with age. However, both the boys and the girls in the older group expressed fewer extremely positive emotions and more mildly negative emotions than did the children in the younger group. In a subsequent study using similar methods, daily emotions were monitored in relation to children's pubertal status (Richards & Larson, 1993). Boys and girls with a more mature body shape at each age reported more frequent thoughts and feelings about love. Pubertal development was slightly related to heightened feelings of anger in girls, but in general, physical maturation was not closely linked to patterns of specific emotions in girls. In boys, the relationships between pubertal development and emotions were much stronger. Those boys who were more physically mature reported more experiences of feeling frustrated, tense, and "hyper." They also reported a more positive mood, a greater ability to focus their attention, and more feelings of strength. Thus, in boys, pubertal changes were associated with both positive moods and a restless irritability.

After puberty, boys and girls show noticeably different levels of aggression and depression, with girls showing more problems coping with depression and boys showing more problems managing and controlling their aggressive impulses (Leadbeater, Kuperminc, Blatt, & Hertzog, 1999). These differences are often expressed in terms of *internalizing* problems, such as feelings of hopelessness or worthlessness, in which the adolescent's conflicts are directed inward on the self; and *externalizing* problems, such as aggression or delinquency, in which the adolescent's conflicts are directed outward toward property or other people (Achenbach, 1991). Three topics considered are examples of internalizing and externalizing problems: eating disorders, delinquency, and depression.

## ■ EATING DISORDERS

Eating disorders are an example of *internalizing* problems—turning one's frustration, anger, or fear inward on the self. Eating disorders are typically diagnosed in adolescence, and primarily but not exclusively among girls. Roughly 3% of young women have one of three eating disorders: anorexia, bulimia, or binge eating (U.S. Department of Health and Human Services, 1999). **Anorexia** is characterized by a fear of gaining weight, refusal to maintain a minimally normal body weight, and perceptions of one's body as overweight in general or in specific areas (Herzog et al. 1999). Weight loss is viewed as an important accomplishment and is accompanied by increased self-esteem. Anorexia is found primarily in girls, with symptoms beginning either shortly after the weight spurt that accompanies puberty or at about age 18. Adolescents with this condition focus their behavior on weight loss. They take an obsessive, determined position in rejecting most foods, accompanied by dieting, fasting, or excessive exercise. They also tend to have a distorted perception of their body image, seeing themselves as much fatter than they really are. The outcome of this condition is a potentially life-threatening loss of key body functions as a result of starvation (Millstein & Litt, 1990).

**Bulimia** involves spurts of binging and overeating, followed by the use of different strategies to prevent the absorption of food, such as induced vomiting, the use of laxatives, or strenuous exercise. Bulimia has an incidence of between 1 and 3% in the female adolescent population and is experienced somewhat more commonly by male adolescents than is anorexia. Individuals who suffer from bulimia are usually ashamed of their eating and often eat in secret. Their eating is often experienced as a frenzy or an intense loss of control, followed by self-criticism and depression (American Psychiatric Association, 1994).

The origins of eating disorders are not fully understood. Many authors implicate the cultural infatuation with thinness as a stimulus of this condition. A combination of parent, peer, and media idealization of thinness, coupled with a tendency for girls to experience body dissatisfaction during puberty, leads teens to restrict their food intake and engage in faddish diets (Dunkley, Wertheim, & Paxton, 2001; McCabe & Ricciardelli, 2001; Stice & Shaw, 2004).

> Evie tells me that she learned how to throw up in school, in fact in health class, from a one-day lesson designed to discourage eating disorders. . . . Evie says she vomited after dinner three to five times a week off and on for almost a year. She didn't do it over the summer, she says, just when school was in session; and never during lunch—only after dinner, especially when her mother's boyfriend, a frequent guest at the table, urged her on to extra helpings of Tater Tots or dessert. On those nights, she'd wait until the dishes were done, then, a little while later, she'd mosey into the kitchen and pilfer a spoon. (Orenstein, 2000, p. 91)

A preoccupation with body appearance may be provoked by the relatively rapid physical changes associated with puberty. The psychoanalytic view is that eating disorders link back to fear of sexual maturity and are an unconscious strategy to delay entry into adulthood. The family system perspective emphasizes the child's control or overcontrol by parents. Eating disorders, in this view, are a way for the child to exert control or power over one key area in a context where little power is permitted. In addition to these theories, some clinicians describe the adolescents who suffer from anorexia as having difficulty accepting and expressing their emotions. Compared with adolescents who have other types of emotional disorders, adolescents with anorexia show less emotional expressivity, greater timidity, and more submissiveness. Adolescents with anorexia have been described as "duty bound, rigidly disciplined, and moralistic with underlying doubts and anxious hesitancy" (Strober, 1981, pp. 289–290). Studies of long-term outcomes following the diagnosis of anorexia find that appropriate treatment can restore normal body weight. However, a large number of young people who suffered from anorexia as adolescents continue to have social and emotional difficulties, especially problems in empathy, difficulty recognizing and identifying their emotions, obsessive-compulsive disorders, and anxiety (Herpertz-Dahlmann, Wewetzer, Hennighausen, & Remschmidt, 1996; Hsu, 1996). Over a 10-year period, an estimated 5.6% of people with anorexia die from the disorder (DeAngelis, 1997).

Because of the seriousness and widespread nature of eating disorders, public health experts are working to create a more positive acceptance of people of various body types and shapes, with less focus on thinness. Advertisers are being urged to regulate ads promoting weight loss programs and products to children and adolescents and to disclose more accurately the amount of weight that can be lost. Physicians are being encouraged to rely less on height–weight tables as they discuss health with adolescents, as those tables do not take into account body type and the range of individual differences in healthy weight (DeAngelis, 1997).

## ■ DELINQUENCY

Delinquency is an example of *externalizing* problems, related to difficulties in controlling or regulating one's impulses. Delinquent offenses are actions for which an adult could be prosecuted. Then there are offenses such as truancy, running away, or underage drinking that are known as **status offenses**, which are illegal for adolescents. Many adolescents commit some type of delinquent act that goes undetected. For most young people, the fear and guilt that follow a delinquent act are usually enough punishment to prevent further violations.

For some adolescents, however, committing several delinquent acts weakens the ability to impose social constraints on such behavior, and their involvement in delinquency intensifies. In 1999, roughly 17% of the total number of arrests in the United States involved youth under the age of 18, but this age group accounted for 27.5% of the serious crimes, such as motor vehicle thefts, arson, burglary, and murder (U.S. Census Bureau, 2001). One national survey categorized about 30% of teenage boys and 10% of teenage girls as serious violent offenders. These adolescents had committed three or more violent crimes in a 1-year period sometime before their 18th birthday. The boys committed more crimes than the girls, and their crimes tended to be more serious (Elliott, Huizinga, & Menard, 1989; McCord, 1990).

In a longitudinal study of more than 4,500 high school seniors and high school dropouts in California and Oregon, more than half the sample reported being involved in violent behavior—65% of the boys and 41% of the girls. Those youths who were persistently involved in violent acts were also significantly more likely to be involved in other high-risk delinquent behaviors such as selling drugs; committing felonies; and using alcohol, marijuana, or other drugs. These extremely violent youths were also more likely to drop out of school and to have other mental health problems. The find-

*In an effort to protect students and staff, many schools have installed metal detectors or security guards at the entrance to the school. What might be some positive and some negative consequences of this kind of monitoring?*

© Hussein Akhtar/Corbis Sygma

ings of this study suggest that efforts to curb youth violence must pursue a differentiated approach. In addition to focusing on the serious offenders who have multiple problems and are likely to come to the attention of school and law enforcement authorities, communities need to find ways to reach the large number of youth who express periodic violence in family and peer contexts (Ellickson, Saner, & McGuigan, 1997).

Weapon carrying has also increased dramatically over the past 20 years. As part of the National Longitudinal Study of Adolescent Health, students in Grades 7 through 12 were asked about their involvement in weapon-related violence. Among seventh- and eighth-graders, 22% of European American teens, 30% of Hispanic teens, and 39% of African American teens responded that they had some type of involvement (Blum et al., 2000). Because many young people carry some type of weapon with them—especially knives and guns— questions are raised about the emotional correlates of this type of behavior. Are children who carry weapons primarily preoccupied with fear and motivated by self-defense, or are the weapons an extension of their aggressive motives? In one analysis, teens who carried guns were found to differ from those who carried knives (Webster, Gainer, & Champion, 1993). For girls, the more people they knew who had been victims of violence, the more likely they were to carry a knife. For boys, the two strong predictors of carrying a knife were having been threatened with a knife and having been frequently involved in fights, although not usually as the one who started them. Carrying a knife is linked to self-protective motives.

Too few girls carried guns for the researchers to identify predictors for that group. For the boys, however, the correlates of carrying a gun included having been arrested before, having been involved in many fights and being one of the people who started them, and believing that shooting people was justifiable in certain circumstances. Gun carrying was linked to a much more violent, aggressive orientation, and could not really be construed as a strategy for self-protection. Subsequent studies support the picture of boys who carry guns as being motivated by the desire to gain respect or to frighten others. These boys are likely to be bullies, whose friends also engage in high-risk activities. Some authors suggest that many boys who commit violent crimes are suffering from a form of post-traumatic stress disorder, which leaves them angry, disconnected from their feelings, and unable to anticipate or control overwhelming images of violence that surge up with minimal provocation (Cunningham, Henggeler, Limber, Melton, & Nation, 2000; Slovak & Singer, 2001).

## ■ DEPRESSION

One of the emotions that has received considerable attention in the literature is depression (Graber, 2004). **Depression** is used in at least three different contexts (Petersen et al., 1993). First, one can speak of **depressed mood**, which refers to feelings of sadness, a loss of hope, a sense of being overwhelmed by the demands of the world, and general unhappiness. Almost everyone experiences this kind of depression at some time or another, describing it as the "blues," feeling "down in the dumps," or feeling "low." Related symptoms include worrying, moodiness, crying, loss of appetite, difficulty sleeping, tiredness, loss of interest in or enjoyment of activities, and difficulty concentrating. Depression may range from mild, short-lived periods of feeling sad and discouraged to severe feelings of guilt and worthlessness. A depressed mood may be predictive of more serious emotional disorders, but it is not in itself a clinical diagnosis. Depression appears to increase

## Adolescent Suicide

"I thought how easily you could kill yourself when you were drunk. Take a bath, fall asleep, drown. No turtle would come floating by to rescue you, no spotter plane would find you. I took my mother's knife and played johnny johnny johnny on the playhouse floor. I was drunk, stabbed myself every few throws. I held my hand up and there was satisfaction at seeing my blood, the way there was when I saw the red gouges on my face that people stared at and turned away" (Fitch, 1999, pp. 184–185).

SUICIDE AT ANY age is deeply troubling, but adolescent suicide is cause for special anguish and soul searching. Why would a young person, with all of his or her adult life ahead with its endless possibilities and opportunities, choose death? Is it possible that the prospect of becoming an adult is so threatening and terrifying that some young people would rather die than grow up?

Public concern over adolescent suicide has been increasing in response to the rise in the suicide rate among adolescents since the early 1960s. Suicide, which is the third leading cause of death among adolescents ages 15 to 24, rose from 5.2 per 100,000 in 1960 to 13.3 per 100,000 in 1995. By 2001, the rate had declined for 6 straight years to 9.6. In the age range from 15 to 24, there were approximately 4,000 suicides—one death by suicide every 2 hours and 15 minutes (U.S. Census Bureau, 2003). Some claim that these suicide rates are underestimated, as there is a social stigma to reporting a death as suicide, and there are financial consequences to identifying a death as a suicide rather than as an accident. It is suspected that a sig-

nificant number of adolescent deaths involving automobile accidents were actually suicides. According to the Youth Risk Behavior Surveillance System reports, 19% of high school students had seriously considered suicide in the preceding 12 months, and 8.8% actually attempted suicide (Grunbaum, Kann, Kinchen, et al., 2002). Girls are twice as likely as boys to attempt suicide, but boys are five to six times as likely as girls to die in a suicide attempt (Irwin, Burg, & Cart, 2002).

Instances of suicides prompted by widely publicized suicides, copycat suicides, and clusters of friends who commit suicide as part of a pact suggest that suicidal ideation can be triggered by a variety of external events as well as by internal depression or as a reaction to humiliation or loss. In attempting to understand the causes of suicide, primary risk factors have been identified (Garland & Zigler, 1993; King et al., 2001; Russell & Joyner, 2001). These factors were reconstructed by studying the lives of adolescents who committed or attempted suicide. However, they may not be very useful in predicting whether a particular individual will commit or attempt suicide. Although depression and low self-esteem are often included in the profile of those who attempt suicide, they are usually coupled with other issues. The risk factors include

- drug and alcohol abuse
- mood disorders, especially depression
- a prior suicide attempt
- a history of psychiatric illness
- a history of antisocial, aggressive behavior
- a family history of suicidal behavior

- low parental monitoring
- a high number of stressful life events
- a minority sexual orientation
- the availability of a firearm

In addition to these factors, there is usually some precipitating event. A shameful or humiliating experience, a notable failure, and rejection by a parent or a romantic partner are all examples. Use of drugs that alter cognitive functioning and decrease inhibitions, coupled with easy access to a gun, suggest one likely path from suicidal ideation to suicidal action.

The national Substance Abuse and Mental Health Services Administration (SAMHSA; 2001) has issued a monograph, the *National Strategy for Suicide Prevention: Goals and Objectives for Action*. A key premise of this monograph is that suicide is a public health problem that is preventable. Two action components of prevention include broadening community support for mental health education and reducing the stigma associated with seeking mental health services. A study of the impact of the Signs of Suicide (SOS) program in 92 schools demonstrated the potential impact of effective intervention. Students who participated in the program showed an increase in help seeking of 60% in the month following the introduction of the curriculum. School coordinators found no negative reactions among students who were exposed to information about suicide and suicide prevention, and some improvement in student and teacher communication following this intervention (Aseltine, 2003). To learn more about suicide prevention, visit http://www.mentalhealth.samhsa.gov/suicideprevention/

for both boys and girls during adolescence, with a peak at about ages 17 or 18 (Petersen et al., 1993). One estimate is that about 35% of adolescents—a higher percentage for girls than for boys—have experienced a depressed mood in the previous 6 months.

The second use of the concept of depression is the notion of a **depressive syndrome**. This term refers to a constellation

of behaviors and emotions that occur together. The syndrome usually includes complaints about feeling depressed, anxious, fearful, worried, guilty, and worthless. Roughly 5% of the normal population experiences this syndrome.

The third use of the concept of depression is its central role in clinical diagnosis. For a diagnosis of **major depressive disorder**, the adolescent must have experienced five or more of the following symptoms for at least 2 weeks: "Depressed mood or irritable mood most of the day; decreased interest in pleasurable activities; changes in weight or perhaps failure to make necessary weight gains in adolescence; sleep problems; psychomotor agitation or retardation; fatigue or loss of energy; feelings of worthlessness or abnormal amounts of guilt; reduced concentration and decision-making ability; and repeated suicidal ideation, attempts, or plans of suicide" (Petersen et al., 1993, p. 156).

**FACTORS ASSOCIATED WITH ADOLESCENT DEPRESSION.** Adolescents face a number of challenges that make them vulnerable to depression. At present, no single theory is accepted as the explanation for depression. Some research points to genetic factors associated with the clinical diagnosis of depression. However, in recalling the research on the interaction between depressed mothers and their infants discussed in Chapter 6 (Infancy), it is hard to separate genetic and environmental factors in the etiology of clinical depression. Having a depressed mother increases the risk of depression during adolescence. Teens whose mothers are depressed are characterized by more anxious attachments, more suicidal thoughts, and more frequent episodes of depression than teens whose mothers are not depressed (Essau, 2004).

Parental loss or rejection has been found to increase an adolescent's vulnerability to depression (Robertson & Simons, 1989). In one longitudinal study of the consequences of economic pressures on families, a connection was shown between the family's economic stresses and increased parental depression. Economic strain is associated with heightened marital conflict, increased hostility, and less nurturance toward the children, resulting in subsequent adjustment problems in adolescent daughters, especially problems with hostility and depression (Conger et al., 1993; Tomarken, Dichter, Garber, & Simien, 2004).

Even though scholars no longer view adolescence as a unique period of emotional turmoil, they recognize that adolescents are often exposed to more negative events than are younger children. Adolescents are more aware of what other people are experiencing, and because more is expected of them, there is more to worry about. School is more demanding, and there are more instances of "high stakes" testing, selection or rejection in teams, clubs, and activities, and new performance standards (Locker & Cropley, 2004). Teens have a wider circle of relationships than younger children, through which they are exposed to more problems, expectations, and disappointments.

Adolescents report experiencing hassles in the following domains: social alienation (disagreements with teachers, disliking other students); excessive demands (not enough time to meet responsibilities, not enough time for sleep); romantic concerns (dissatisfaction in a romantic relationship); decisions about one's personal future (important decisions about a future career); loneliness and unpopularity (being ignored); assorted annoyances and concerns (money problems, disagreement with a boyfriend or girlfriend); social mistreatment

(being taken advantage of, having one's trust betrayed); and academic challenge (struggling to meet other people's standards of performance at school; Kohn & Milrose, 1993). In this list, peer relations, including boyfriend–girlfriend relations and the elements of interpersonal experience that are part of being a member of a friendship group, play a central role. Depression is linked to experiencing negative peer comparisons in areas that are considered to be important to others, such as good looks, athletic ability, having money, or having good social skills (Thwaites & Dagnan, 2004).

Adolescents are relatively inexperienced in coping with these kinds of stressors. They may not have developed strategies for interrupting or reducing the feelings of grief or discouragement that accompany stressful life events. The combination of pressures on parents, especially marital conflicts and economic pressures that affect youth, plus exposure to their own failures, disappointments, and loss of relationships with peers and in school, are clearly linked to a negative mood in adolescents, especially sadness and depression (Larson & Ham, 1993). Feelings of depression may be intensified by accompanying hormonal changes (Hartlage, Brandenburg, & Kravitz, 2004). Young people may become convinced of their worthlessness, and this distortion of thought may lead them toward social withdrawal or self-destructive actions.

**GENDER DIFFERENCES IN DEPRESSION.** Most studies find no differences in depression between prepubescent boys and girls; however, during the period from about age 11 to 15, gender differences are systematically noted and continue to be evident into adulthood (Crawford, Cohen, Midlarsky, & Brook, 2001; Jones-Webb & Snowden, 1993). Experiences of depression appear to be more common in adolescent girls than in boys. This gender difference has been found in comparisons of the depression scores of European American, African American, Mexican American, and other Hispanic adolescents (Roberts & Sobhan, 1992).

Several ideas have been offered to explain this gender difference. First, the estrogen cycle has been linked to changes in mood, with periods of low estrogen production linked to negative feelings and low self-esteem. Second, at puberty, girls become critical of their bodies and especially have concerns about being overweight and unattractive. This attitude may lead to prolonged feelings of dissatisfaction with the self and a consequent depression. When coupled with restricted dietary intake, girls may feel listless and drained of energy. Third, girls tend to look within for explanations of their failures and problems, blaming them on their own lack of ability; in contrast, boys tend to focus on factors outside the self, blaming other people or unfair conditions for their failures.

Fourth, even when girls receive strong social support from their parents and friends, they are also somewhat more sensitive to the problems that people in their support network are having. Girls who have higher levels of caring and are involved in the problems of their close friends are more vulnerable to depression (Gore, Aseltine, & Colten, 1993). Any negative experiences that a girl's best friend or members of her

*Ironically, the fact that girls are likely to try to comfort and support their friends during periods of emotional turmoil makes them more vulnerable to negative moods and depression. How might adolescent girls protect themselves from this negative consequence of close friendships?*

family are going through tend to add to her own negative mood. For example, one study found a significant link between mothers' emotional distress and their daughters' internalizing symptoms over the period from age 11 to 22. The same association was not found for adolescent boys and their mothers (Crawford et al., 2001).

Finally, adolescent girls may begin to experience numerous micro-aggressions spawned by the sexist views of teachers, male peers, and even their parents. These negative messages create a picture of a world in which the adolescent girl is viewed as less important, less competent, and less entitled to her own independent views than her male peers. The result is increased feelings of insecurity, lack of confidence, and new feelings of worthlessness.

Depressed mood is of special concern during early adolescence for several reasons. First, it is associated with adolescent suicide. Although depression is not always a precursor to suicide, there is a link between depression and suicidal thoughts. Second, depression is linked to alcohol and drug abuse. Adolescents who are struggling with strong feelings of depression may turn to alcohol or other drugs to try to alleviate or escape from these feelings. Third, adolescents who are depressed may be unable to participate effectively in the classroom, so that their academic performance deteriorates. Finally, depression during adolescence may be a forerunner of severe depression later in adulthood.

## MEMBERSHIP IN THE PEER GROUP

The importance of peer interaction for psychosocial development is a continuous theme across the life span. During early adolescence, the peer group becomes more structured and organized than it was previously (Newman, 1982). The implications of the individual's relation to the peer group become more clearly defined. Before the adolescent period, it is important to have friends but not so important to be a member of a definable group. The child's friends are often found in the neighborhood, local clubs and sports teams, community centers, or classrooms. In early adolescence, young people spend more time away from home. In middle school and high school, students are more likely to interact with each other across classroom boundaries, leading to the formation of larger, more loosely affiliated friendship groups. Dyadic friendships become an increasingly important source of social support, and the quality of these friendships changes. In addition to dyadic friendships, adolescents form small groups of friends, sometimes referred to as *cliques*, and in most communities they also become identified with a larger constellation of teens who have a common social identity, usually referred to as a *crowd* (Brown, 2004).

### ■ CLIQUES AND CROWDS

**Cliques** are small friendship groups of 5 to 10 friends (Ennett & Bauman, 1996). Usually, these groups provide the framework for frequent interactions both within the school and in the neighborhood. Adolescents usually do not refer to their group of friends as a clique, but the term is used to connote a certain closeness among the members. They hang out together, know about each others' families, plan activities together, and stay in touch with each other from day to day. Within cliques, intimate information is exchanged and, therefore, a high degree of loyalty is expected. In the transition from middle school or junior high school to the larger, more heterogeneous environment of the high school, there is a reordering of students according to a variety of abilities and a corresponding reordering of friendship groups. It may take some time for adolescents to find their clique, the members of which may change from time to time over the first year or two of high school. There is quite a lot of variability in the stability of the cliques; some dissolve over the course of a school year, and others remain intact throughout high school.

**Crowd** refers to a large group that is usually recognized by a few predominant characteristics, such as their orientation toward academics, involvement in athletics, use of drugs, or involvement in deviant behavior. Crowds are more reputational than cliques, reflecting students' values and attitudes, preferred activities, and school and nonschool engagement. Students can typically name the crowds at their school, but when asked, not all students clearly fit with a specific crowd, and some students are in more than one.

Membership in a crowd at the high school may be based on one or more of the following characteristics: good looks; athletic ability; social class; academic performance; future goals; affiliation with a religious, racial, or ethnic group; special talents; involvement with drugs or deviant behavior; or general alienation from school. Although the criteria for group membership may not be publicly articulated, the groups tend to include or exclude members according to consistent standards. In a racially diverse sample of more than 600 middle school and high school students, some of the most common crowds mentioned were floaters (belonging to more than

*This group of high school students is clearly identifiable by their style of dress and the place where they hang out. Would you say they are a clique or a crowd?*

© Scott Houston/Corbis

one group), nice or regulars, populars, middles (related to income), jocks, nerds/unpopulars, preps, skateboarders, and misfits/alternatives. Roughly 20% of the students said they did not belong to any group (Lohman, 2000).

In racially diverse schools, it is not uncommon for students to identify crowds based specifically on ethnic categories, such as the Asian American group, the Mexican Americans, and the African Americans. The crowds can be identified in a school setting by their dress, their language, the activities in which they participate, and the school settings in which they are most likely to congregate. For example, in one school, the peer groups take their names from the place in the school where they hang out: "The fashionable 'wall people' who favor a bench along the wall outside the cafeteria, and the punkish 'trophy-case' kids who sit on the floor under a display of memorabilia" (Adler, 1999, p. 57). The peer culture in any high school is determined largely by the nature of the peer groups that exist and their characteristic patterns of interaction (Youniss, McLellan, & Strouse, 1994). These large, visible groups provide an array of prototypical identities. Although many adolescents resist being labeled as part of one crowd or another, they usually recognize that these categories of students exist in their school.

In one analysis of more than 3,000 students in Grades 9 to 12 in nine different high schools, nine crowd types were identified with a high degree of regularity across the schools. The crowds were labeled by the students as jocks, populars, popular nice, average-normal, brains, partyers, druggies, loners, and nerds (Durbin, Darling, Steinberg, & Brown, 1993). These crowds had distinct profiles with respect to their school grades, use of alcohol and drugs, involvement in delinquent acts, involvement in fights and carrying weapons to school, and perceptions of how involved they were in the social life at the school. Thus, the youth culture, as it is some-

times called, actually comprises a number of subcultures, each endorsing somewhat different attitudes toward adults and other authority figures, school and academic goals, and drugs and deviant behavior, and expressing different orientations toward partying and social life (Brown, Mounts, Lamborn, & Steinberg, 1993).

## ■ BOUNDARIES AND NORMS

Membership in cliques is relatively stable but always vulnerable to change. One description suggests that these groups have some central members who serve as leaders, others who are regularly included in clique activities, and still others who are on the periphery. At the same time, there are the "wannabes," who would like to be part of the clique but for one reason or another are never fully included (Hansell, 1985). Some students try to push their way into a certain group; others may fall out of a group. Dating someone who is a member of a clique or getting involved in a school activity (such as athletics or cheerleading) may be a way of moving into a new peer group. A more likely scenario is that through gossip, refusal to adhere to group norms, or failure in heterosexual relationships, individuals may slip outside the boundaries of their clique. Even when the specific members of a clique change, new members tend to have some common characteristics. Cliques of druggies find new friends who do drugs; cliques of jocks find new friends who excel in sports.

Changing one's crowd identity may be more difficult than changing from one clique to another. When the school population is relatively stable, it is more difficult to lose the reputational identity one has already established. In some schools, specific crowds have strong animosity toward each other. Members of the opposing crowds may occupy different areas of the school, participate in different activities, mock or ridicule each other, or articulate their differences in symbolic ways through dress, art, and music. When these differences are widely known, it becomes even more difficult to shift crowd identities. More research is needed about the contexts that permit changes in crowd membership and the motives that students might have for wanting a new crowd affiliation (Brown, 2004).

Important skills that are learned by becoming a member of a peer group are the assessment of group structure and the selection of the particular group or groups with which one would like to affiliate. As one begins to develop a focused peer group affiliation, one becomes aware of that group's internal structure and norms. In adolescence, the structure may include patterns of dominance, dating, and relationships with others outside the group. Associated with each of these dimensions of social structure are sets of norms or expectations for the behavior of the peer group members. As adolescents discover their positions in the dominance hierarchy of the group, they learn how they may advance within it and what behaviors are expected at various levels. On the basis of all this information, they must decide whether their personal growth is compatible with the peer group affiliation they have made.

Membership in an adolescent peer group is a forerunner of membership in an adult social group. Adolescent peer groups are somewhat less organized than their adult counterparts, but they are considerably more structured than childhood friendship groups. Through peer group membership, adolescents begin to learn techniques for assessing the organization of social groups and their own position within them. They develop aspirations for advancing their own social standing. Also, adolescents gain some insight into the rewards and costs of extensive group identification. Although the actual friends made during adolescence may change as one grows older, the social skills learned at this time provide a long-lasting basis for functioning in a mature social group.

## ■ PARENTS AND PEERS

How does involvement with peers during early adolescence relate to one's closeness to family members? Do adolescents abandon family interactions and values for peer interactions and values? Can closeness to peers compensate for a lack of closeness to parents, or does the intimacy achieved with parents extend outward to a circle of friends? To what extent do parents continue to have an influence on adolescent peer relationships?

In the transition from childhood to adolescence, the child's radius of significant relationships changes. One study looked at the structure and function of social support among African American, European American, and Hispanic children in three age groups: 7-, 10-, and 14-year-olds (Levitt, Weber, & Guacci, 1993). In the transition from age 7 to 10, extended family members became increasingly important to children as a source of support. This pattern was found in all three ethnic groups, but the African American and Hispanic

children were more likely to identify extended family members as sources of support than were the European American children. From age 10 to 14, friends become an increasingly important source of support. The number of people mentioned as friends increased notably from age 7 to 14. However, at all three ages and in all three ethnic groups, family members were mentioned as the most central in these children's lives—"the people who are the most close and important to you—people you love the most and who love you the most" (Levitt et al., 1993). What is more, at each age, support from this close, inner circle made up largely of family members was an important correlate of well-being and sociability.

Under optimal conditions, the increasingly important role of peer relationships in early adolescence takes place against a background of continuing close, supportive relationships with family members. Adolescents describe a variety of overt signs of independence from their families: They may make decisions about clothes, dating, and so on; they may drive cars; they may stay out late; and they may earn their own money. However, they continue to maintain an emotional attachment to their families and to family values.

What is the nature of parent–adolescent interaction? How do differences in its quality influence the adolescent's well-being? Using the attachment paradigm as a frame of reference, one can think of adolescence as a time when young people strive to expand their range of exploration with reduced needs to return to the "secure base." Adolescents try to decrease their dependence on their parents for setting goals, establishing patterns of tastes and preferences, and making decisions. This does not mean that the sense of closeness and connection with parents is less important. For example, adolescents may not want to seek help from parents when they are experiencing difficulty in their social relationships, but at the same time, if a serious problem arises, they want to know that their parent is available to be supportive and understanding. Adolescents can take the point of view of their parents. They realize when their behavior has been a source of distress to their parent, of if they have tested the limits of previously agreed-upon rules or boundaries. Within the context of a secure attachment, these times lead to a goal-corrected revision in the balance of autonomy and closeness. In many ways, the parent's desire to foster a child's self-reliance and a child's goal to reduce the parent's authority over day-to-day behaviors are compatible. In the process of achieving these goals, some loss of emotional closeness is likely (Allen & Land, 1999).

As adolescents go through puberty, conflicts with their parents increase. Conversations are marked by new levels of assertiveness on both sides (Papini, Datan, & McCluskey-Fawcett, 1988; Papini & Sebby, 1988). These conflicts tend to be about rather mundane issues, like household chores, how money will be spent, whether the child is spending enough time on schoolwork, or curfews, rather than on basic value issues like political ideology or religious beliefs (Montemayor, 1983; Steinberg, 1990). Mild, periodic conflicts reflect a changing balance of power or control within the fam-

| Parenting Practices | Adolescent Behaviors | Crowd Membership |
|---|---|---|
| Parental emphasis on achievement | Grade point average | Popular |
| | | Jock |
| Parent monitoring | Drug use | Brain |
| | | Normal |
| Joint decision making | Self-reliance | Druggie |
| | | Outcast |

**FIGURE 10.3**

A Model of the Relationships Among Parenting Practices, Adolescent Behaviors, and Peer Group Memberships

Source: "Parenting Practices and Peer Group Affiliation in Adolescence," by Brown et al., 1993, *Child Development, 64*, p. 476. Copyright © 1993 The Society for Research in Child Development, Inc. Reprinted by permission.

ily, as adolescents give voice to their own opinions and defend their choices and parents periodically concede to their children's positions (Collins, 1995; Smetana, Yau, & Hanson, 1991). This process appears to be negotiated somewhat differently by boys and girls.

The quality of the home environment, especially the nature of parenting practices, has implications for the adolescent's peer relationships as well as for the quality of parent–child interactions. Recall from the discussion in Chapter 8 that high levels of power assertion by parents are associated with a greater likelihood of peer rejection during middle childhood. Studies of the relationship of parenting practices to adolescent peer group membership are extending this analysis. A model was proposed to examine the relationship of parenting practices to adolescent behaviors and ultimately to crowd affiliation (see Figure 10.3; Brown et al., 1993; Durbin et al., 1993). Parenting practices, listed in the left-hand column of Figure 10.3, were operationally defined as the extent to which parents emphasized academic achievement, parental monitoring of adolescent behaviors, and the degree to which parents involved adolescents in decision making. Three adolescent behaviors, listed in the center column, were measured: the students' grade point averages, drug use, and self-reliance. Finally, the students were identified as members of one of six crowds: popular, jocks, brains, normals, druggies, or outcasts.

Parenting practices were significantly linked to the children's behavior, which in turn was a strong predictor of their crowd affiliation. Parenting practices had both direct and indirect impacts on adolescents' crowd memberships. For ex-

ample, parents who emphasized academic achievement were more likely to have children who were members of the popular or jock crowds and less likely to be druggies. Parents who emphasized academic achievement were likely to have adolescents who had high grades and who were self-reliant, factors that also predicted being popular and not being members of the druggie or outcast groups. Low parental monitoring and little joint decision making were associated with drug use, low self-reliance, and membership in the druggie crowd. Even though adolescents may perceive their involvement with their peers as a domain that is separate and distinct from their family life, this research suggests that parental socialization practices influence peer relations.

# ROMANTIC AND SEXUAL RELATIONSHIPS

During adolescence, romantic relationships, sexual fantasies, and sexual behaviors increase, partly as a result of biological changes and partly as a result of social, cultural, and historical contexts. The adrenal gland produces a sex hormone (DHEA) that is the same in male and female adolescents. The amount of this hormone that is absorbed in the blood reaches a peak between the ages of 10 and 12—a time when both boys and girls begin to be aware of sexual feelings toward others (Herdt & McClintock, 2000; La Freniere, 2000). The way these sexual feelings are expressed depends largely on cultural factors.

## THE TRANSITION INTO SEXUALIZED RELATIONSHIPS

Most young people are involved in a variety of romantic relationships during adolescence, including dating, feelings of tenderness and love, and deepening commitments (Levesque, 1993). Components of both gender identity and sexual orientation are formulated during this period of life. Some adolescents are reticent about sexual behavior. Others are sexually permissive and regularly active in sex play, from petting to intercourse. Roughly 75% of U.S. teens have engaged in what they describe as "heavy petting" by the age of 18 (Haffner, 1998). The manner in which early adolescents think about sexual relationships varies. Some are preoccupied by thoughts of very romantic, idealized relationships. They can become infatuated with rock stars, athletes, movie stars, or other sex symbols. Some have crushes on boys or girls in their school or neighborhood, and still others manifest perverse obsessions with sexual material. Early adolescents' sexual awakenings represent a system that is just being started up and tested out. As a result of these sexual experiences, adolescents begin to think of themselves as sexual, develop scripts and schemes for how to act sexually with others, and begin to formulate ideas about the kinds of people they find sexually attractive.

**DATING.**  Dating relationships provide the initial context for most sexual activity. Pubertal changes may increase a young person's interest in sexual ideation, but the timing and rituals or *script* of dating depends heavily on the norms of the peer group and the community (Garguilo, Attie, Brooks-Gunn, & Warren, 1987). Young people learn the art of flirtation, practice the "dance" of how to approach and how to coyly refuse, and learn the rules of engagement between the sexes, which vary from culture to culture and from cohort to cohort. The following description of dating in the United States in the 1920s reflects the values regarding gender, sexuality, and economics of the time:

> Boys or young men asked for the company of a girl or young woman to some public amusement—dance, movie, party, or other social event. They went without adult supervision or interference. The male member of the couple paid and frequently in the 1920s provided transportation. After the main event, the couple often went out to eat and frequently would try to find some private place for necking. Whereas physical intimacy became an expected element of dating, the limits of sexual experience depended on the girl and to a large extent on her [social] class. (Spurlock & Magistro, 1998, p. 26)

Involvement in romantic relationships increases over the middle school and high school years, and the quality of these relationships becomes increasingly intimate. Furman and Wehner (1997) suggested that four types of needs are met in these romantic relationships: *affiliation, attachment, caregiving,* and *sexual gratification.* As suggested by Sullivan's (1953) interpersonal theory, the ability to engage in close and confiding friendships during middle childhood lays the groundwork for the capacity to have romantic relationships. Those children who have close friendships in middle childhood are

more likely to have romantic relationships in adolescence (Neeman, Hubbard, & Master, 1995).Participation in mixed-sex friendship groups is also likely to provide the context for the formation of romantic pairing, which becomes more exclusive and less group oriented over time (Connolly, Furman, & Konarski, 2000; Dunphy, 1969).

**FIRST INTERCOURSE.**  The sexual transition may take place in very different contexts for adolescents. It may be a planned event or an unplanned impulse, often combined with alcohol use or a drug high. The sexual encounter may be viewed as a marker of independence or as an act of rebellion against and defiance of the family. It may take place in the context of an ongoing close relationship or as part of a casual encounter. Usually, the earlier the transition into sexual activity and intercourse, the more likely the act is to be part of a profile of high-risk behaviors, including alcohol use, drug use, and delinquent activity. For girls 14 years old and younger who reported being sexually active, about 40% said their first sexual experience was a result of being sexually assaulted (Haffner, 1998). The later the transition, the more likely it is to be seen as a marker of the transition into adulthood or as a planned aspect of the deepening commitment to an ongoing relationship (Flannery, Rowe, & Gulley, 1993; Ketterlinus, Lamb, Nitz, & Elster, 1992).

In the United States, the historical trend has been toward earlier involvement in sexual intercourse for both boys and girls, and greater sexual activity for girls. Figure 10.4 shows the percentage of U.S. girls and boys who have had sexual intercourse in Grades 9 through 12 by grade, race, and ethnic origin in 1999 (Centers for Disease Control and Prevention, 2000). The figure also indicates the percentage of teens at each grade who report having multiple sex partners (i.e., four or more). Eleventh grade (roughly age 16) appears to be the

*As adolescents mature, their sexual activity is more likely to take place in the context of deepening emotional commitment.*

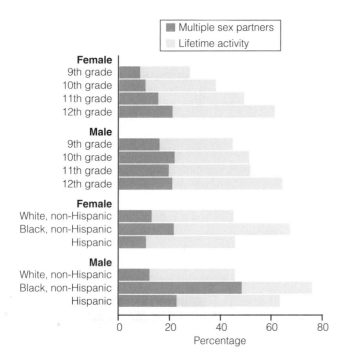

**FIGURE 10.4**

Lifetime Sexual Activity Among Students in Grades 9–12 by Sex, Grade Level, Race, and Ethnic Origin: United States, 1999

Note: Multiple sex partners defined as four or more sex partners in the student's lifetime.

Centers for Disease Control and Prevention, National Center for Chronic Disease Prevention and Health Promotion, Youth Risk Behavior Survey (YRBS).

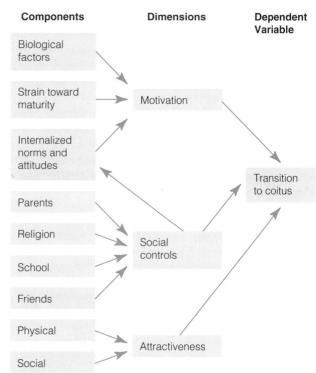

**FIGURE 10.5**

A Model of Transition to First Coitus in Early Adolescence

normative turning point—the age at which more than 50% of both boys and girls report having had intercourse. The data show that although boys are more likely to report being sexually active than girls at the younger ages, by Grade 12, boys and girls are equally likely to be sexually active and report about the same likelihood of having multiple partners. These data also show that a significant percentage of U.S. adolescents (roughly one third) have not had sexual intercourse by 12th grade. This does not mean that they have had no experience with genital sexual arousal and orgasm.

Data regarding entry into sexual activity and age at first intercourse must be interpreted with caution (Savin-Williams & Diamond, 2004). First, teens who are uncomfortable or whose parents are uncomfortable participating in research on this topic will not be included. Second, studies rarely include questions about same-sex sexual activity that might be comparable to first intercourse. Third, the reporting is retrospective (i.e., asking adolescents to think back to when they first engaged in sexual activities) and thus is vulnerable to inconsistencies and memory errors. Cultural and social contexts may influence reporting. It may be socially desirable to exaggerate one's sexual experiences in some communities, and socially responsible to conceal one's sexual experience in others. Finally, most studies focus on individual reports and do not gather data to confirm reported sexual experiences by participating partners.

**FACTORS AFFECTING THE INITIATION OF SEXUAL INTERCOURSE.** Udry and Billy (1987) devised a model that is very useful for conceptualizing the transition to coitus in early adolescence (see Figure 10.5). In that model, three basic dimensions account for the adolescent's initiation of sexual activity: motivation, social controls, and attractiveness. *Motivation* can be accounted for by biological factors, especially new levels of hormone production; a new level of desire to achieve independence and engage in adult behaviors; and certain internalized norms and attitudes that may either encourage or reduce the motivation for sexual activity. The *social controls* provide the normative environment in which sexual activity is embedded. According to the model, these controls are a product of parental socialization and practices, school achievement and educational aspirations, and the attitudes and sexual experiences of friends. We have added the important influence of religious beliefs and values to the model's list of social controls. The third dimension, *attractiveness*, influences the availability of partners. Attractiveness is defined in part by pubertal maturation, social acceptance or popularity, and also by whether one is judged to be pretty or handsome.

In an effort to assess this model, researchers found that the transition to sexual intercourse for White boys was most strongly predicted by hormonal levels and by popularity with the opposite sex. In contrast, there was no clear relationship between hormone levels and girls' sexual activity (Katchadourian, 1990; Udry, Billy, Morris, Groff, & Raj, 1985). For girls, various social controls—including parents, school achievement, friends' attitudes and behaviors, and religious values—all play an important part in predicting sexual intercourse. Girls must reach some level of pubertal maturation before the decision about voluntary entry into sexual activity becomes an issue. Beyond that point, however, a girl's decision to become sexually active is influenced by her own self-esteem, her personal aspirations, her parents' values, her educational expectations, the capacity of her parents to exercise appropriate control over her social and school activities, and the norms of her peer group (Crockett, Bingham, Chopak, & Vicary, 1996; Meschke, Zweig, Barber, & Eccles, 2000; O'Sullivan, Meyer-Bahlburg, & Watkins, 2000).

**THE EFFECTS OF RELIGIOUS BELIEFS ON SEXUAL BE-HAVIOR.** One of the clearest cultural influences on adolescent sexual behavior is religious participation. Adolescents who frequently attend religious services and church-related activities and who value religion as an important aspect of their lives have less permissive attitudes toward premarital sex. This finding applies equally to Catholic, Protestant, and Jewish young people. The relationship is accentuated in adolescents who describe themselves as Fundamentalist Protestant or Baptist. However, an adolescent's attitudes toward premarital sex are shaped by many factors in addition to religious beliefs. By the time young people are making independent decisions about religious participation, they also have opinions on premarital sex. Thus, those young people who have more permissive views on sex may be less likely to attend religious services and may find less satisfaction in religious participation (Thornton & Camburn, 1989).

As an example of how religious beliefs can affect sexual behavior, the Southern Baptist Church initiated a program that encouraged teens to make a public virginity pledge. Since 1993, more than 2.5 million youth have taken this pledge, in which they vow to abstain from sex until marriage. In a study of those who participated in the program, the pledge was found to be most effective in delaying the age of first intercourse when taken by younger teens. It is also more effective for pledge takers who are a minority among their peers. Taking the pledge is then viewed as an act of independent decision making and identity commitment rather than as compliance to peer norms (Bearman & Brueckner, 2001). Findings based on the national longitudinal study of adolescent health suggest that one of the hazards of taking the pledge is that when it is broken, youth are less well prepared to engage in protected sex and are therefore at risk for sexually transmitted diseases (USA Today, 2004).

## ■ SEXUAL ORIENTATION

Although one might assume that sexual orientation—heterosexual, homosexual, or bisexual—begins to take shape in early adolescence, the research on this point is limited and suggests a more differentiated path. Although 6 to 8% of youth responding to the National Adolescent Health Survey said that they had experienced same-sex attractions or same-sex relationships, only a small number acknowledged same-

sex behaviors, and even fewer identified themselves as gay, lesbian, or bisexual. Many teens who have self-identified as gay or lesbian have also had cross-sex experiences. In studies of adults, many people who consider themselves heterosexual have had same-sex attractions and experiences (Savin-Williams & Diamond, 2004). For sexual minority youth, two aspects of a sexual orientation have been identified: self-labeling and disclosure (Savin-Williams, 1996). **Self-labeling** refers to applying a label such as gay, lesbian, or bisexual to oneself. **Disclosure** refers to sharing this information with others.

**SELF-LABELING.** In one study of 77 gay men, most recalled having an awareness of gay feelings as early as middle school or early adolescence, but they did not label themselves gay until later adolescence (D'Augelli, 1991). The majority (75%) knew they were gay *before* their first sexual experience. However, once they had labeled themselves gay, they waited an average of 8 years to disclose their homosexuality to someone else.

Self-labeling may begin with experiences in early childhood when boys or girls recall "feeling different" from their peers. These feelings, typically captured in retrospective studies of gay or lesbian young adults, may include a general sense that they did not share the same interests as others of their same sex. Boys may recall being more sensitive than their peers or being drawn to more artistic and aesthetic interests. Girls may remember passionate, mysterious friendships in the prepubertal and early adolescent period (Diamond, 2000). In many instances, these feelings of being different are associated with confusion and a sense of isolation or lack of belonging.

Often, at puberty, the implications of these earlier childhood experiences become more evident. A growing awareness of one's own sexual interests and fantasies, coupled with new information about the variety of sexual orientations that may exist in the peer group or in the community, leads to new insights about one's own sexual preferences. In some ways, this may be a shocking realization. In other ways, it may help focus and clarify feelings of uncertainty and dissociation that had been difficult for the child to understand at an earlier age. Not all young people who eventually recognize their same-sex sexual orientation reach the point of self-labeling in adolescence. However, with the greater visibility, openness, and acceptance of differences in sexual orientation and the presence of homosexual role models, it is increasingly likely that this will happen.

**DISCLOSURE.** Disclosure may be a prolonged process in which young people carefully decide which individuals can be trusted with this information, or it can be a very open, obvious statement of personal identity. Reports of adolescents who are openly gay suggest that disclosure is a very stressful situation—one that is commonly accompanied by negative reactions from parents and friends and by acts of open hostility from school peers (Remafedi, 1987). Anticipating the strong social censure attached to an unconventional sexual

*A group of several hundred people demonstrate in support of a new high school for lesbian and gay students in New York City. The Harvey Milk High School opened for the first day of school with 100 students. What might be some developmental outcomes of attending a gay high school?*

© Jeff Christensen/Reuters/Corbis

orientation, adolescents may deny it or mask it by functioning as heterosexuals during this period of life:

> I feared not being liked and being alienated. I was president of various school clubs, and once I beat up a guy for being a faggot. I was adamant that fags should be booted out of the Boy Scouts. Other kids asked me why I was so rough on them. I did not say. No one suspected me because I did sports and had several girlfriends (Savin-Williams, 1996, p. 169).

Disclosure typically occurs first with close friends, and later, if at all, with family members. Studies of gay, lesbian, and bisexual youth suggest that parental acceptance and the ability to maintain closeness and autonomy with parents after disclosure are very important to their continued identity development and well-being (Floyd, Stein, Harter, Allison, & Nye, 1999). Most mental health professionals suggest that even when disclosure is accompanied by negative reactions, it has many emotional and social advantages. By disclosing, the young person has a greater sense of authenticity and freedom. Once adolescents disclose to their friends and family, they can be more readily integrated into the gay community and find others who will help support their emerging identity. They can direct more of their effort to the task of integrating their gender identity, sexual identity, and social relationships and figuring out how to cope with the challenges that their minority sexual orientation poses. Despite increas-

ing societal awareness of the diversity of sexual orientations, sexual minority youth continue to face negative attitudes from teachers, peers, and community members; possible social rejection; and difficulty finding age-appropriate, nonexploitive sexual partners.

## ◼ PROBLEMS AND CONFLICTS ASSOCIATED WITH SEXUALITY

The sexual system is one of the most problematic components of psychosocial development for young people in the United States. Most parents do not feel comfortable discussing sexuality with their children. In addition to private thoughts, impulses, and fantasies, which may result in feelings of guilt or confusion, young people confront conflicting messages about sexual behavior from their peers, the mass media, and the religious community. For example, in the late 1990s, the U.S. Congress authorized funding to support programs that taught abstinence as the primary approach to sex education. These programs were required to teach about the social, psychological, and health benefits of abstinence; the risks of sex outside of marriage; and the importance of monogamy. At the same time, adolescents recognize that nonmarital abstinence is not being practiced now and was not practiced by their parents' generation. National studies show that the vast majority of both men and women are not virgins when they marry (Laumann, Ganon, Michael, & Michaels, 1994). In a congressional review of 13 government-funded abstinence-only curricula, 11 presented information that included "unproved claims, subjective conclusions, or outright falsehoods regarding reproductive health, gender traits, and when life begins" (Connolly, 2004, p. AO1).

**SEXUALLY TRANSMITTED DISEASES.** About 25% of sexually active teens contract a sexually transmitted disease each year. Teens are especially at risk for chlamydia, genital herpes, and gonorrhea. In the year 2000, of those cases of chlamydia where the age of the person was reported, 75% were between the ages of 15 and 24 (Weinstock, Berman, & Cates, 2004). Untreated, chlamydia and gonorrhea can produce pelvic inflammatory disease, leading to infertility and abnormal pregnancies (Alan Guttmacher Institute, 1999).

A major focus of AIDS and HIV education has been directed toward adolescents. The number of AIDS cases among U.S. adolescents increased from 53 in 1986 to 3,313 in 1997. Most of these cases are a result of sexual transmission (Meschke, Bartholomae, & Zentall, 2002). Although adolescents believe that they have a strong understanding of AIDS as a disease, including its transmission and prevention, studies have shown that their knowledge is often confused or incorrect. At the same time, adolescents express little interest in learning more about AIDS. Many young people overestimate how well they understand this health problem. Others are cynical about getting the specific information they need from typical school-based sex education courses. These courses are often unable to provide the practical information that is needed to resolve questions about contraception, sexual intimacy, and specific patterns of physical contact that might lead to transmission of the disease. For example, many state and federal policies *prohibit* teaching about correct condom use as part of their sex education program, even in programs intended to focus on HIV/AIDS prevention (Alan Guttmacher Institute, 2002).

**UNWANTED SEXUAL ATTENTION.** Young people see numerous examples of sexual intimacy on television and in films, suggesting that sexual gratification ought to be more immediate and more satisfying than it is likely to be in real life. Often, they do not find the emotional closeness and understanding they may seek in a sexually intimate relationship. What is more, many adolescents, especially girls, are exposed to unwanted sexual activity. In a sample of seventh-, ninth-, and 11th-grade girls, 21% reported unwanted sexual contact, ranging from unwanted touching and fondling to unwanted or forced intercourse (Small & Kerns, 1993). In many of these instances, unwanted sexual intercourse occurred on the first date or in a dating relationship. This pattern illustrates the problematic nature of sexual contact in early adolescence. The boundaries for acceptable sexual contact are unclear; the sexual agenda for boys and girls is likely to be very different; and other risk-taking behaviors, including alcohol and drug use, may create an unwanted sexual encounter.

In an effort to learn more about adolescents' reactions following their involvement in sexual intercourse, Australian researchers surveyed students in secondary schools in seven of the eight Australian states and territories (Donald, Lucke, Dunne, & Raphael, 1995). Students were asked about the context of their most recent sexual experience and how they felt about it. The majority of boys and girls said they felt good about their most recent sexual experience, with older students (ages 16 and 17) more likely to be positive about it than the younger students (15 and under). For girls, five factors were significantly associated with feeling good about their most recent sexual experience: believing that there was a low risk for contracting a sexually transmitted disease; having a "steady" relationship with the partner; having talked with their partner about avoiding pregnancy; having talked with their partner about ways of having sexual pleasure without having intercourse; and not being drunk or high. For boys, two factors were significantly associated with feeling good about their most recent sexual experience: having sex with a "steady" partner and not being drunk or high. Larger percentages of girls than boys were likely to say they felt used or bad after their most recent sexual experience, and the younger girls were more likely than older girls to say they felt bad or used. About equal percentages of girls and boys said they felt guilty after their most recent sexual experience.

The lack of supervision and monitoring by adults, as well as the lack of opportunity to talk about sexuality with them, can place adolescents at risk for early sexual experiences that are abusive or associated with negative feelings. The sex-linked problems that many people encounter—unintended pregnancy, marital infidelity, rape and other forms of unwanted sexual contact, child sexual abuse, pornography, sexually transmitted diseases—are evidence that the socialization process—including efforts by parents, teachers, and religious leaders—is failing to promote mature sexuality in significant numbers of adolescents and adults in the United States.

**CONTRACEPTION.** In spite of the fact that many parents and teachers do not provide information about the use of contraceptives as part of their education about sex and sexual behavior, the use of contraceptives by U.S. teens has increased. By 1995, 78% of teens used a contraceptive at the time of their first intercourse (Alan Guttmacher Institute, 1999). Unfortunately, teens do not use contraceptives consistently, and in some cases, not correctly. The use of contraceptives is associated with religious beliefs, family attitudes and behaviors, and peer norms.

In one national survey of adolescent boys ages 15 to 19, 30% reported using condoms all the time, including with their recent partners and with their last partner, and 57% reported using a condom in their last intercourse. These rates are higher than those observed in the early 1980s (Pleck, Sonenstein, & Ku, 1991). However, this still leaves 70% of adolescent boys who are inconsistent in their use of condoms or who do not use them at all. The view that boys have a responsibility to prevent pregnancy, concern about the partner's wishes, and concern about AIDS were all positively related to adolescent boys' consistent condom use. On the other hand, concerns about reduced sexual pleasure and the embarrassment of using a condom, coupled with the pattern of having multiple sexual partners, were related to inconsistent condom use. Variations in attitudes about the costs and benefits, religious beliefs, and lack of concrete knowledge about how to use contraceptives help explain why the technology of contraception is not as successful among sexually active American youth as it could be.

### ■ PARENTHOOD IN EARLY ADOLESCENCE

One of the consequences of early entry into sexual activity is adolescent pregnancy. In 2000, 469,000 infants were born to women age 19 or younger. From 1990 to 2001, the pregnancy rate for adolescent girls ages 15 to 17 declined by 33% to 53.5 per 1,000 girls in 2001. Putting this rate into an international context, the birthrate for children born to 15- to 17-year-olds in the United States was found to be one of the top 2 highest among 46 developed countries (Alan Guttmacher Institute, 2002).

In efforts to explain the decline in birthrates during the 1990s, data were collected that focused on sexual activity and contraceptive use. Both delays in the initiation of sexual activity and more effective contraceptive use were important factors that contributed to the decline in teen pregnancy (Santelli et al., 2004). Social policies advocating the prevention of early pregnancy and public programs for family planning and abortion tend to emphasize the negative consequences of pregnancy for adolescent girls and their babies. However, studies of pregnant adolescents generally find that these girls do not differ much in attitudes, mental health, or cognitive abilities from those who are sexually active but did not become pregnant. Society must be careful not to label a group of adolescent girls as deviant simply because they are pregnant.

**CONSEQUENCES OF TEENAGE PREGNANCY.** The phenomenon of teenage parenthood is complex, touching the lives of the adolescent mother and father, the child or children born to them, their parents, and the schools, counseling services, and family planning services that have been created to help young parents cope with parenthood. The consequences of teenage pregnancy and parenthood for the young mother and her infant depend on the psychosocial context of the pregnancy. Within the time period of early adolescence, there is a big difference between becoming a mother at 14 or at 18. For the younger teens (i.e., those younger than 14), the pregnancies are typically unplanned and often a result of involuntary or forced sexual encounters. For the older teens, the girl's partner is usually within 2 years of her age, and even if the pregnancy was unplanned, the majority of girls go ahead with the birth (Alan Guttmacher Institute, 1999). Two common consequences of early pregnancy are its association with poverty, and the increased risk of birth complications associated with a lack of prenatal care.

The most significant measurable impact of early pregnancy is its association with subsequent poverty. Teens growing up in high-poverty neighborhoods are at greater risk for teenage pregnancy and dropping out of school, both of which contribute to their continuing in poverty in adulthood (Harding, 2003; Hao & Cherlin, 2004). The relation between age at first pregnancy and family income by age 27 was studied in a sample of African American, Hispanic, and European American women (Moore et al., 1993). This effect is mediated through a number of other personal and family factors that unfold following the first birth, such as continuing in school, the chances of getting married, the kind of work one does and one's personal earnings, and the earning capacity of other family members. For African American women, the poverty

*In this classroom the teacher is showing students wrapped condoms as part of her instruction about safe sex. This is not always permitted as part of sex education, especially in programs that promote abstinence only.*

© Mary Kate Denny/Photo Edit

level is high regardless of age at first birth. However, the earlier African American women begin childbearing, the more children they are likely to have—a factor that increases their level of poverty. For Hispanic women, delaying childbearing resulted in higher educational attainment, a factor that predicts higher personal income by age 27. For European American women, delaying the age of childbearing was associated with older age at first marriage, fewer children, and higher personal earnings. For all three ethnic groups, but especially for European Americans and Hispanics, each year of delayed childbearing had a substantial impact on reducing the chances of ending up in poverty by age 27.

Complications during labor and delivery may be devastating to the newborn's health. Are young mothers more likely than older ones to experience such complications? Mothers under 19 are less likely than older mothers to initiate prenatal care during the first trimester of pregnancy. Infants born to mothers under 17 are at greater risk than those born to women in their 20s and 30s. They have a higher risk of dying during the first year, of being born prematurely or with a low birthweight, and of suffering neurological damage as a result of complications associated with delivery (McCarthy & Hardy, 1993; U.S. Census Bureau, 2003). Thus, young parents are more likely to have to cope with the special needs of a child with developmental disabilities. However, these risks arise from converging socioeconomic factors rather than from any biological inadequacies of being young. Studies involving large numbers of births at urban hospitals have found that younger mothers (i.e., those under 20) are actually *less likely* to experience complications of pregnancy and negative birth outcomes than older mothers, particularly when factors associated with poverty are taken into account (Roosa, 1984; McCarthy & Hardy, 1993).

Complications of pregnancy and negative birth outcomes for adolescent mothers are linked to the contexts of pregnancy. One study found that in a sample of 170 African American teens, the pregnancy was unplanned or unwanted in about half the cases (Crosby, DiClemente, Wingood, Rose, & Lang, 2003). Other studies have linked sexual abuse in childhood with earlier sexual activity and teen pregnancy (Brown, Cohen, Chen, Smailes, & Johnson, 2004; Cinq-Mars, Wright, Cyr, & McDuff, 2003). When pregnancy occurs in these abusive or exploitive contexts, it is likely to be accompanied by alcohol or drug use, cigarette smoking, and heightened anxiety, all of which may contribute to low birthweight and neurological impairments for the infants. Teens who become pregnant under these circumstances are more likely to be socially isolated and to become psychologically disengaged from their infants. In contrast, when teen pregnancy occurs in the context of family, peer, and partner support, teen mothers are likely to receive encouragement for their caregiving, greater financial support, and opportunities to engage in appropriate social and educational activities that contribute to their own psychosocial maturity (Bunting & McAuley, 2004).

For some teens, the experience of motherhood has an enhancing or "self-righting" impact. In a comparison of adoles-

cent mothers who ended their pregnancies through abortion and those who kept their babies, the latter group demonstrated some important changes in their behavior. Rates of delinquency declined in this group, and they reduced their cigarette smoking and marijuana use (Hope, Wilder, & Watt, 2003). Young mothers may be inspired by their infant to make a better future for themselves and their baby. This often means completing their education, creating a more stable home environment, and taking better care of their own health.

**ADOLESCENT FATHERS.** Although the focus of studies on adolescent pregnancy has been on girls, there is growing concern about adolescent fathers. It is difficult, however, to determine the number of teenage fathers. Many young mothers will not reveal the name of their baby's father. Although most fathers of babies born to teen mothers are within 2 years of the mother's age, about 20% are 5 or more years older than the mother (Alan Guttmacher Institute, 1999).

*Not much is known about the impact of teen fathering on a boy's psychological development. What factors might influence whether the boy becomes committed to nurturing and supporting his child or leaves the parenting entirely to the mother and her family?*

© Nancy Sheehan/Photo Edit

## HUMAN DEVELOPMENT AND DIVERSITY

## Teen Fathers

THE CULTURAL CONTEXT shapes the way adolescents conceptualize their role as fathers. William Marsiglio (1989) compared African American and European American male adolescents' preferences about pregnancy resolution and family formation. These data were gathered from responses to this hypothetical statement: "Please imagine that you have been dating the same girl who is about your age for the past year and that she told you last week that she was 2 months pregnant with your child. For the purpose of this survey, assume that your girlfriend wants you to live with her and your child." Beginning with this premise, the boys were asked how likely they would be to live with the child, their attitudes about the situation, their evaluation of what might be the positive and negative consequences of their decision, and their overall preference on how they would like to see the pregnancy resolved if it were entirely their decision.

African American adolescents were significantly less likely to endorse abortion as the solution to this situation. African American boys were more likely than European American boys to see an advantage to living with the baby as providing a chance to care for the baby's daily physical needs and to enable them to assume greater financial responsibility. In other respects, African American and European American boys viewed the positive consequences of the situation similarly. European American boys were more likely than African American boys to see the situation as reducing their chances of pursuing further education and limiting their chances to spend time with their friends. In other respects, African American and European American boys evaluated the negative consequences of the situation similarly.

The study illustrated that African American male adolescents have a positive attitude toward continuing their relationship with the baby and the baby's mother. However, this intention is typically not realized, perhaps because African American men are younger when they father their first child, and are therefore less likely to be able to leave their own homes. It may be that African American adolescents have less chance to find a steady job, so they do not have the resources to support their baby. Another explanation may be that in the African American community, the mother's family is more willing to have her and the baby live with them, so there is no real place for or urgent need of the unwed father.

Most studies of adolescent pregnancy find that—contrary to the stereotype—many fathers remain in contact with the mother and the child in the first months after the child is born. However, by the time the children are in school, contact drops off. In one study, half of the new adolescent fathers had weekly contact with their child, but by the time the children were in school, only 25% were still seeing the child weekly (Lerman, 1993). Some adolescent fathers marry the mothers; others live with them for a while. Often, the couple continues to date. In some instances, they actually marry several years after the child is born. In many cases, the father contributes financial support to the mother and child, even when the couples do not marry. Many adolescent fathers, however, have little education and are minimally employed, so the material support they can provide is limited (Bunting & McAuley, 2004).

Fathering a child is bound to stimulate conflicting feelings of pride, guilt, and anxiety in the adolescent boy. He must struggle with the fact that he contributed to a pregnancy that may bring conflict and pain to someone for whom he cares. Also, he must confront the choices that he and his girlfriend have in coping with an unplanned pregnancy. Furthermore, he may feel excluded from the birth of a child he has fathered. Feeling obligated to provide financial support for his girlfriend and child may lead him to drop out of school and enter the labor market, even though he can only hope to be minimally employed (Hendricks & Fullilove, 1983).

Little systematic research has been done on the attitudes, knowledge, or behaviors of adolescent fathers or the impact of fatherhood on a teenage boy's subsequent development. One study followed a large sample of adolescent boys through their teen years. Those who became fathers were characterized as having lower self-esteem and a lower sense of internal control than their age-mates who did not become fathers. Shortly after fatherhood, these boys experienced a boost in self-esteem, but in the next several years, their self-esteem declined to its prefatherhood level (Pirog-Good, 1995).

Researchers who have studied the problem of unwed fathers argue that much stronger emphasis should be placed on the father's responsibility, not only for financial support of the mother and child, but also for his continued interaction with his child. School counselors, for example, tend to have a much clearer idea about how to support the continuing psychosocial development of teen mothers and their children than about how to support the continuing development of teen fathers (Kiselica, Gorcynski, & Capps, 1998). Efforts to include young fathers in family planning programs, parent education, and employment training initiatives would help strengthen the social context for the young mother and her child and would contribute to the young father's psychosocial development (Armstrong et al., 1999).

For both girls and boys, a key to the prevention of early pregnancy requires the building of greater confidence in and commitment to the consistent use of contraception as part of any sexual relationship and comfortable, "user-friendly" access to reproductive health care (Cicatelli, 2004). For girls, fostering a sense of self-efficacy and investment in academic goals leading to postsecondary education or professional training is an especially important area for intervention. For boys, building greater social expectations and commitment to assuming the financial and social responsibilities associated with fatherhood—including sending clearer messages from family and community that boys have responsibilities in these areas and devising specific opportunities for them to enact these responsibilities—seem promising directions for future intervention. For more information on pregnancy prevention programs, visit the website of Cicatelli Associates, where a thorough review of best practices can be found.

# THE PSYCHOSOCIAL CRISIS: GROUP IDENTITY VERSUS ALIENATION

Throughout life, tensions arise between the desires for individuality and for connection. Certain cultures emphasize connection over individuality, whereas others put individuality ahead of connection. However, all societies must deal with both aspects of the ego, the *I* as agent, originator, and executive of one's individual thoughts and actions, and the *we* as agent, originator, and executive of collective, cooperative enterprises that preserve and further the survival of the group (Triandis, 1990). During the early years of adolescence, one confronts a new psychosocial conflict, in which pressures to ally oneself with specific groups and to learn to be comfortable functioning as a member of a group are major preoccupations. This conflict is called *group identity versus alienation* (Newman & Newman, 2001).

## GROUP IDENTITY

In early adolescence, young people form a *scheme*—an orchestrated, integrated set of ideas about the norms, expectations, and status hierarchy of the salient groups in their social world, building these representations from groups of which they are members or in which they aspire to hold membership (*reference groups* [Gurin & Markus, 1988]). Associated with these schemes are strong emotional investments, cognitions, and possibly behavioral patterns. As a young person prepares to engage in the larger social world, a positive sense of group identity provides confidence that he or she is meaningfully connected to society, has a cognitive map of the characteristics of the social landscape, and the skills or tools to navigate the terrain. Perceiving oneself as a competent member of a group or groups is fundamental to one's self-concept as well as to one's willingness to participate in and contribute to society.

Early adolescents experience a search for membership—an internal questioning about the groups of which they are most naturally a part. They ask themselves, "Who am I, and with whom do I belong?" Although membership in a peer group may be the most pressing concern, questions about other group identifications also arise. Adolescents evaluate the nature of their ties to immediate and extended family members, and they begin to understand the unique characteristics of their racial, ethnic, cultural, and sexual identities. They may become identified with various organizations (e.g., religious, political, civic). Research confirms that in the most positive pattern, peer group membership does not replace attachment to parents or closeness with family. Rather, the adolescent's network of supportive relations is anchored in the family and expands into the domain of meaningful peer relationships. Adolescents who show strong signs of mental health and adaptive coping strategies have positive communication and trusting relationships with parents or other close family members as well as strong feelings of trust and security among their friends (Levitt et al., 1993; Raja, McGee, & Stanton, 1992).

In the process of seeking group affiliation, adolescents are confronted by the fit—or lack of fit—between their personal needs and the norms and values of relevant social groups in the environment. The process of self-evaluation takes place within the context of the meaningful groups whose members are available for comparison and identification. Individual needs for social approval, affiliation, leadership, power, and status are expressed in the kinds of group identifications that are made and rejected during the period from age 12 to 18. In a positive resolution of the conflict of group identity versus alienation, adolescents discover one or more groups that provide them with a sense of group belonging, meet their social needs, and allow them to express their social selves. They become psychologically connected to social life.

## ■ COGNITIVE PROCESSES THAT SUPPORT FORMATION OF GROUP IDENTITY

Adolescence is not the first time that children are aware of being a group member or claiming an affiliation with a group. Young children tend to define groups on the basis of common activities. In comparison, older children are likely to understand the ways that groups affect attitudes and values, shape interests, and influence one's self-concept through acceptance and rejection. Older children begin to be able to map the groups in their world (Bettencourt & Hume, 1999). Three cognitive capacities necessary for the formation of group identity are representations, operations, and reflective thinking.

**GROUP REPRESENTATIONS.** Group representations provide the earliest forms of group identity, reflecting the ability to use words and symbols to signify membership in a group. Infants and young children have a wide variety of group experiences and are able to represent their group membership using verbal labels and drawings. The capacity for representing groups and the relationships among groups expands in early adolescence, so that youth are able to map more groups simultaneously, including those in their immediate family, school, and peer environments. The expansion of this representational ability may be stimulated by exposure to a greater variety of groups, by increases in representational skills, and by new social demands to establish one's place within the range of existing groups. It may also be a product of neurological changes that accompany puberty.

**GROUP OPERATIONS.** Group operations include such diverse processes as joining a group, forming ingroup and outgroup attitudes, stereotyping, quitting or rejecting a group, and exercising leadership in a group. Some of these operations can be observed among toddlers and early-school-age children. They recognize the common members of a group, use fantasy play to coordinate roles with other members of a group, and talk about themselves as part of a family, school, or friendship relationship. Group operations can be observed in neighborhoods, with some children experiencing exclusion and others experiencing acceptance and support. Children as young as 5 or 6 may join sports teams and learn lessons of team spirit, teamwork, and team pride. Research has shown that by the fourth and fifth grades, some children have already begun to experience social isolation and social rejection (Farmer & Rodkin, 1996; Hymel, Bowker, & Woody, 1993).

In early adolescence, teens develop more advanced skills and strategies for connecting to their groups, experiencing bonding and acceptance, participating in leadership and team building, and becoming more concerned about the possibility of rejection by their significant groups. These skills are refined and extended as teens confront a wider array of groups with varying degrees of associational closeness.

**REFLECTIVE THINKING ABOUT GROUPS.** The level of conceptualization necessary for the formation of group identity involves reflective and comparative thinking. It requires decentering from one's own groups to consider how these groups may be perceived by others, evaluating the strengths and weaknesses of a group, and considering the implications of group membership for how one is treated in the community. Early adolescence is characterized by a new consciousness about one's membership in groups, the boundaries and barriers that separate groups or limit membership in groups, and the social implications of being in one group or another. The emergence of formal operational reasoning may help produce new capacities for reflection and speculation about social relationships and complex social systems.

## ■ FOUR DIMENSIONS OF GROUP IDENTITY

Given the three capacities that permit the formation of a sense of group identity, we hypothesize that the actual formation of a group identity requires four interconnected elements: (1) a capacity to categorize people into groups and to recognize distinguishing features that define members, (2) experiencing a sense of history as a member of a group, (3) an emotional

investment in the group, and (4) a social evaluation of one's group and its relation to other groups.

**CATEGORIZING PEOPLE AND RECOGNIZING DISTINGUISHING FEATURES OF GROUP MEMBERS.** Beginning in toddlerhood, young children use social categories related to gender and age to group people (Hirschfeld, 1994; Leinbach & Fagot, 1986; Lobel & Menashri, 1993; Martin et al., 1990). Toddlers have a sense of the family group and understand that some people are in the family, whereas others are not (Newman, Roberts, & Syre, 1993). With a broadening of exposure to social settings, children learn to recognize a wider variety of groups. By middle childhood, they can appreciate their simultaneous membership in a variety of groups such as family, sports team, and friendship groups (O'Brien & Bierman, 1988).

Groups typically have *boundaries* that limit membership and *shared markers* that bind the members together. In early adolescence, young people learn to read, categorize, and relate to informal peer networks where clique structures provide a comparatively egalitarian learning environment, determine social status, and help define a person's feelings of belonging and worth. Language use, nonverbal gestures, style of dress, use of certain spaces, behaviors such as cigarette smoking or drug use, and participation in specific activities may become markers that delineate group membership and provide a sense of group identification. Friends may invent expressions or unique ways of speaking that help define a group and strengthen members' commitment. Over time, the similarities among members of a peer group are strengthened, thereby clarifying their commitment to certain values and behaviors. Although much of the literature that explores this process has focused on deviant or risky behaviors, such as cigarette smoking, alcohol use, or truancy, the process can support prosocial commitments as well (Dielman, 1994; Berndt & Keefe, 1995).

**EXPERIENCING A SENSE OF HISTORY AS A GROUP MEMBER.** In a gym class, one may be assigned to the red team one day and to the gray team another. These assignments do not foster a meaningful sense of group identity. However, if one joins the band and practices every day, goes to games, travels on the bus, and parties with the band members, the sense of being a "bandie" begins to take shape. Group identity emerges out of continuous interactions, through which one becomes visible and known to other group members while they become visible and known to you (Reicher, Levine, & Gordijn, 1998). What was done in fun last year may become next year's tradition as a group selects rituals to symbolize how important they all are to each other.

Of course, memberships in groups change. One may transfer to a new school, join a new team or club, or become part of a group that only gets together in the summers. In each case, the formation of a sense of group identity requires the accumulation of interactions and the sense of having a history of shared experiences (Worchel, 1998). Here one sees the interconnection of the *I* and the *we*. One may think of

*In posing for the camera, these high school students demonstrate their group cohesiveness and their positive feelings for their group.*

© Ed Kashi /CORBIS

the *I* as the agent that seeks out group membership, choosing to join one group or avoid another. At the same time, as one participates in a group and experiences a sense of shared history, one begins to internalize values, beliefs, and practices held in common by the group, thus leading to a revision of the *I* and strengthening of the *we*.

**EMOTIONAL INVESTMENT IN THE GROUP.** The intensification of emotions that occurs with puberty and early adolescence is often evidenced in a deepening dedication and commitment to one's groups, including family and kinship groups (Bettencourt & Hume, 1999). One sees here the seeds of nationalism and patriotism—a redirection of narcissism to the group and a binding of energy to the group as an extension of oneself (Markovsky & Chaffee, 1995). As evidence of this emotional investment, one finds the expression of pride about one's group, a tendency to idealize the members of the group in comparison to others outside the group, and a willingness to make personal sacrifices in order to support or advance the group's goals (Reicher et al., 1998). The emotional investment can be expressed as positive feelings of attraction to other members of the group and negative feelings of depression or jealousy associated with betrayal. New levels of intimacy are possible, as are new levels of hurt. Emotional investment in a group is a binding process that helps explain an adolescent's unwillingness to leave a group, even when the group no longer appears to meet the young person's needs. This binding process indicates the depth of commitment—in this stage to groups, in the next stage to individual components of group roles.

**SOCIAL EVALUATION OF ONE'S GROUP AND ITS RELATION TO OTHER GROUPS.** As a result of new ego capacities, adolescents are able to assess the diverse landscape

of groups and to recognize the harmonies as well as the inconsistencies between groups of common identity (e.g., race, religion, gender, region, social class) and groups of common bond (any collection of friends, soul mates, family members, band members, team mates) for which there is a shared concern about each other's fate (Prentice, Miller, & Lightdale, 1994). Adolescents become aware of the status hierarchy of the groups in their neighborhood and school. They recognize how their groups are viewed by others, and they form their own views of each group's value and importance to them (Dunbar, 1997). Adolescents spend a good deal of time analyzing and evaluating the groups in their lives. Studies of racial and ethnic identity clearly show that adolescents are able to differentiate between being viewed negatively by others or being a target of discrimination, and expressing personal pride in their racial group (Valk, 2000; Williams & Thornton, 1998). In some contexts, when one's group is a target of threat or debasement, this serves to strengthen the cohesiveness of the group members (Dietz-Uhler & Morrell, 1998). The important point is that the group identity established during early adolescence occurs in the context of a social reality in which one's own group can be located in a status hierarchy leading to judgments about the merits of the group and about oneself as a member of the group (Luhtanen & Crocker, 1992).

## ALIENATION

**Alienation** refers to a sense of social estrangement, an absence of social support or meaningful social connection (Mau, 1992). Alienation can be viewed as deriving from dilemmas associated with issues of common identity, common bond, or both. Alienation associated with issues of

**common identity** may occur when young people are forced to take on roles or are expected to comply with group expectations to which they do not subscribe. This might occur as a result of stereotyping, racism, or elitism within a school or community. Under these conditions, adolescents perceive that their opinions, beliefs, and values differ substantially from those of the groups they are viewed as belonging to. In many schools, some subset of students are marginalized due to some marker such as minority status, physical abnormalities, or developmental delays, or as a result of poor social skills and low academic motivation. These students are often typed as "nobodies," "loners," "disengaged," or "outcasts" (Brown et al., 1993; Clark, 1962; Rigsby & McDill, 1975). In a longitudinal study of crowd identity, Strouse (1999) found that not all students in the uninvolved crowd remained so over the 4 years of high school. Many changed to the "average" crowd orientation, usually by finding new friends, engaging in social activities, and placing more emphasis on getting good grades.

Alienation associated with issues of **common bond** occur when adolescents are unable to form interpersonal ties that provide feelings of acceptance and emotional support. This type of alienation may arise from several different sources. Under conditions of parental coldness, distancing, neglect, or rejection, children find that they cannot count on the family to serve as a source of emotional or instrumental support (Dishion, Poulin, & Medici-Skaggs, 2000). They lack a template for experiencing the foundational benefits of belonging that are associated with group identity. As a result of harsh parenting, some adolescents have poor social skills—they are either overly aggressive and domineering, or overly withdrawn and socially inept (Poulin, Dishion, & Haas, 1999). Over time, children with poor social skills are less likely to form satisfying social relationships with friends and are more likely to engage in delinquent behaviors that reflect their sense of alienation from family and peers.

Alienation may result from personality characteristics, such as shyness, introversion, or lack of sociability. Some young people experience social anxiety, mistrust in others, or cautiousness in interactions that prevent them from forming interpersonal connections. Others are overly self-conscious, becoming so preoccupied with their own feelings and thoughts that they withdraw from social interactions (Kochanska, Murray, & Coy, 1997). Feelings of shame over an illness, disability, or perceived inadequacy may lead to perceptions of peer rejection or an unwillingness to form social bonds (Fife & Wright, 2000).

Finally, alienation may result from a combination of problems with common identity and common bond. For example, friendships across racial groups may be very difficult to preserve in a neighborhood but supported in the school environment. If an African American and a European American adolescent become close friends at school, both may feel alienated from the same-race peers in their community. Youth who are recent immigrants may experience this conflict as they become acculturated. They may become increasingly distant from their families as they take on U.S. language and practices, but they may still be unable to form close, supportive relationships with U.S. adolescents who view them as outsiders.

■ THE CONTRIBUTION OF ALIENATION TO GROUP IDENTITY AND INDIVIDUAL IDENTITY

To some degree, experiences of alienation are important for the continued formulation of both group and individual identity. A period of feeling alone and lonely may help teens to appreciate how good social acceptance feels and how important it is for their well-being. What is more, experiences of alienation within a group may help a young person see the *I* against the backdrop of the *we*. The discomfort of not fitting in helps one recognize the distinctiveness of one's point of view. In the extreme, however, the lack of social integration that may result from a negative resolution of this crisis can have significant implications for adjustment to school, self-esteem, and subsequent psychosocial development. Chronic conflict about one's integration into a meaningful reference group can lead to lifelong difficulties in areas of personal health, work, controlling anger, and the formation of intimate family bonds (East, Hess, & Lerner, 1987; Spencer, 1982, 1988; Weigel, Devereux, Leigh, & Ballard-Reisch, 1998).

# THE CENTRAL PROCESS: PEER PRESSURE

Adolescents' family backgrounds, their interests, and styles of dress quickly link them to subgroups of peers who lend continuity and meaning to life within the context of their neighborhoods or schools. The peer group social structure is usually well established in most high schools, and members of that structure exert pressure on newcomers to join one peer group or another. **Peer pressure** refers to demands for conformity to group norms and a demonstration of commitment and loyalty to group members. At the same time, young people outside the groups form expectations that reinforce adolescents' connections to specific peer groups and prohibit their movement to others. Likewise, an individual who becomes a member of a group is more acceptable to the social system than one who tries to remain unaffiliated and aloof.

The term *peer pressure* is often used with a negative connotation, suggesting that young people behave in ways that go against their beliefs or values because of a fear of peer rejection. However, we suggest an alternative meaning that highlights the emerging role of the peer group in the radius of significant others. The pressure from those close by—those with whom a young person interacts each day—is not necessarily perceived as oppressive or coercive. It is, more often, the subtle co-adaptation of those who interact in the same social space, shaping and guiding one another toward inter-subjectivity, much as an infant and a caregiver achieve mutual regulation.

Brown (2004) suggested four modes of peer influence, all of which may serve to encourage some behaviors and discourage others. The most overt mode is the direct suggestion that a teen should perform a behavior (e.g., smoke marijuana) or risk group rejection. This is the usual connotation of peer pressure, and parents or educators are often focused on helping teens resist this type of influence. A second type of peer influence occurs through modeling. Teens who spend time with one another watch each others' style of dress, gestures, and use of language, and imitate those behaviors in an effort to consolidate their sense of group membership. A third type of influence is more subtle "normative regulation," where peers use teasing, gossiping, or sarcasm to influence each others' attitudes and behavior. Finally, peer influence occurs when friends create opportunities for unsupervised activities—having parties where beer is served, cruising in cars, or arranging to meet at a park or mall when adults are not likely to be present.

## AFFILIATING WITH A PEER GROUP

The process of affiliating with a peer group requires an adolescent to accept the pressure and social influence imposed by it. This process provides the context in which the crisis of group identity versus alienation is resolved. Adolescents are at the point in their intellectual development when they are able to conceptualize themselves as objects of expectations. They may perceive these expectations as forces urging them to be more than they think they are—braver, more outgoing, more confident, and so forth. These expectations help define the zone of proximal development for group skills and social competencies. Peer pressure may have a positive effect on the adolescent's self-image and self-esteem, serving as a motive for group identification. Those dimensions of the self that are valued by one's own peer group become especially salient in each young person's self-assessment (Hoge & McCarthy, 1984).

As members of peer groups, adolescents have more influence than they would have as single individuals; they begin to understand the value of *collective enterprise*. In offering membership, peer groups expand adolescents' feelings of connection and protect them from loneliness. When family conflicts develop, adolescents can seek comfort and intimacy among peers. For adolescents to benefit in these ways from their affiliation with a peer group, they must be willing to suppress some of their individuality and find pleasure in focusing on the attributes they share with those peers.

## PEER INFLUENCE IN SPECIFIC AREAS

Peer influence may be exercised in a variety of areas including time spent with peers, school, and family; academic achievement; drug use; engaging in misconduct; sexual activity; religious participation; community service; or preference in dress, music, or entertainment. Within a particular group, pressures may be strong in one or two areas but not in others. For example, in a comparison of three crowds—the jock-populars, the druggie-toughs, and the loners—the druggie-toughs perceived the strongest peer pressure toward misconduct. Jock-populars perceived greater pressure toward school involvement than the druggie-toughs. However, pressure toward peer involvement (i.e., spending free time with peers) was equally high in all three groups (Clasen & Brown, 1985).

Norms for cigarette smoking have been studied as an example of a voluntary behavior that may be influenced through peer pressure. For example, in one study of sources of peer influence on cigarette smoking, the crowd identified as the "burnouts" (a combination of druggies, radicals, and punks) smoked four times as many cigarettes per week as the average student and 10 times as many cigarettes as the jock/preps (Urberg, 1992). One might expect that the pressure to conform to this behavior would be exceedingly strong within the burnouts crowd, whereas there might be much more variability in the norms related to smoking among the other groups.

## CONFLICTS BETWEEN BELONGING AND PERSONAL AUTONOMY

Peer groups do not command total conformity. In fact, most peer groups depend on the unique characteristics of their members to lend definition and vigor to the roles that emerge within them. However, the peer group places importance on some level of conformity in order to bolster its structure and strengthen its effectiveness in satisfying members' needs. Indeed, most adolescents find some security in peer group demands to conform. The few well-defined characteristics of the group lend stability and substance to adolescents' views of themselves. In complying with group pressure, adolescents have an opportunity to state unambiguously that they are someone and that they belong somewhere.

Adolescents may also find that some peer expectations conflict with their personal values or needs. For example, they may feel that intellectual skills are devalued by the peer group, that they are expected to participate in social functions they do not enjoy, or that they are encouraged to be more independent from their families than they prefer to be. In most cases, adolescents' personal values are altered and shaped by peer group pressure to increase their similarity with the other group members. If, however, the peer group's expectations are too distant from the adolescents' own values, establishing

# Gangs

IN THE LATE 1920s and 1930s, the study of delinquency included an analysis of the role of gangs. Early on, it was understood that delinquent behavior was typically group behavior, involving two or more boys in some type of criminal activity. Gangs were viewed as social groups, not unlike the kinds of groups that boys in more stable, prosperous neighborhoods create. The motives for joining a gang—"desires for recognition, approbation, and esteem of his fellows, for stimulation, thrill, and excitement, for intimate companionship, and for security and protection" (Burgess & Bogue, 1967, p.300)—do not differ much from the motives that adolescents have for joining any number of social groups and clubs. However, the focus of these gangs developed a delinquent emphasis and tradition that was passed from one generation of gang members to the next in a neighborhood. The ethical standards and values of these groups were often contrary to conventional values. In fact, actions that might bring a nondelinquent boy dishonor or shame—such as being arrested, appearing in juvenile court, or being sent to a correctional institution—would be viewed as a source of pride and distinction to a gang member (Burgess & Bogue, 1967).

This analysis of the nature of gangs has not changed much over the years. Gangs continue to thrive in communities all across the United States. According to a survey carried out by the National Youth Gang Center, youth gangs were active in 2,300 cities that had populations higher than 2,500. Although the number of people involved in gangs seemed to be declining, about 42% of respondents (members of police and sheriff's departments) said that they thought the problems involving gang members had gotten worse over the past year. In Chicago and Los Angeles, half the homicides committed over the preceding year were gang related (Egley & Major, 2004).

*Four Cambodian gang members are flashing hand signals. These signs can be used to identify their gang membership, send messages to each other, and taunt rival gangs. To learn more about gangs and gang behavior you may want to go the knowgangs.com website.*

Gangs actively recruit new members, engage in violent acts of initiation, and are becoming increasingly associated with drug trafficking and violent crime. Experts say that what drives young people to gangs are poverty, the desire to belong, and the desire to be loved and recognized (Howell, 1994). One teenager said that his mother was hooked on crack cocaine. He joined the gang looking for love. Another one had an eye that was a little crossed. He said that some people at school made fun of him, but that members of his gang did not make fun of him.

Young people seek love, money, protection, and prestige from gang membership. Adolescents who join gangs are often unsuccessful in school and may have been suspended or expelled. School failure leads to periods of unsupervised time in the community and an inability to find work. Modern gang activities are supported by a growing and spreading drug trade; easy access to guns; and the communication technology of beepers, cell phones, and voice

mail, which allow gang members to coordinate their activities and preserve control over a wider area with increased mobility.

The concept of gangs is closely linked to the theme of *group identity*. Although gangs have a violent, criminal, and antisocial value system, they provide a highly organized social group for identification. Gangs have clothing, colors, symbols, and signs that provide recognition across settings. Young people are recruited into gangs, making them feel valued and protected by the older gang members. Despite the great risks associated with gang activities, the pervasive presence of gangs in cities and larger towns suggests that gangs address a number of needs of today's youth—needs that are not being met by communities, schools, and families.

To learn more about gangs and ideas about preventing adolescent involvement in gangs, visit the website sponsored by the U.S. Office of Juvenile Justice and Delinquency Prevention or the National Youth Gang Center.

a satisfying group identification will become much more difficult. As a result, adolescents experience tension and conflict as they try to balance the allure of peer group membership with the cost of abandoning personal beliefs.

Susceptibility to coercive peer pressure seems to peak about age 13 or 14, when adolescents are most sensitive to peer approval and make the initial transition toward new levels of behavioral autonomy and emotional independence from parents (Urberg, Shyu, & Liang, 1990; Lamborn & Steinberg, 1993). During the years from 14 to 16, adolescents become more adept at resisting peer pressure. Through encounters with peer pressure and opportunities to see how it feels to conform or resist, they develop a growing appreciation for the content of their personal values against the backdrop of peer expectations. However, if the emotional costs of identifying with the peer group become too great, adolescents may not open themselves up to group pressures. Therefore, they will be unable to establish the sense of group identity that is so central to psychosocial growth. An inability to reduce the tension and conflict between group pressure and personal values produces a state of alienation, in which the individual is unable either to identify with social groups or to develop personal friendships.

## ETHNIC GROUP IDENTITY

One of the most challenging aspects of establishing group identity facing minority adolescents is the formation of an **ethnic group identity** (Spencer & Markstrom-Adams,

1990). Ethnic identity is not merely knowing that one is a member of a certain ethnic group, but recognizing that some aspects of one's thoughts, feelings, and actions are influenced by one's ethnic identity. One's ethnic group becomes a significant reference group, whose values, outlook, and goals are taken into account as one makes important life choices. Ethnic identity varies across ethnic groups and among individuals within groups. For example, some young people have had more exposure to the cultural norms and values of their ethnic group than others. Some have had more guided parental socialization about the existence of prejudice and ways of coping with discrimination. Thus, ethnic identity is more aptly viewed as a psychosocial rather than a demographic variable (Phinney, 1996).

In the United States, a history of negative imagery, violence, discrimination, and invisibility has been linked to African Americans, Native Americans, Asian Americans, and Hispanics. Young people in each of these groups encounter conflicting values as they consider the larger society and their own ethnic identity. They must struggle with the negative or ambivalent feelings that are linked with their own ethnic group because of the cultural stereotypes that have been conveyed to them through the media and the schools and because of the absence of role models from their own group who are in positions of leadership and authority.

Issues of ethnic group identity may not become salient until early adolescence. As minority children grow up, they tend to incorporate many of the ideals and values of European American culture. Suddenly in adolescence, however, they may find themselves excluded from it. At that time, peer groups become more structured. Sanctions against cross-race

*These Hispanic girls have learned the traditional dance and costume of their Mexican heritage. By becoming engaged in the celebration of their ethnic heritage, they will be better prepared to negotiate the challenges of identity formation that lie ahead.*

© A. Ramey/Photo Edit

friendships and dating relationships become more intense. Minority adolescents may encounter more overt rejection and failure in academic achievement, employment, and school leadership. They may find that their family and ethnic group values conflict with the values of the majority culture. These minority adolescents may also feel that they have to choose between their ethnic group identity and membership in a nonminority group. In some cases, commitment to an ethnic group identity takes the place of membership in some other peer group. In other instances, minority youth are rejected by their European American peers. They may then flounder, not having established a clear ethnic identity, and may struggle through a period of bitter rejection.

In the wake of the terrorist attack on the World Trade Center in New York on September 11, 2001, Muslim adolescents became a focus of some attention. The nature of their ethnic identity and their divided allegiances were highlighted. Students at a Muslim high school in Brooklyn, New York, were interviewed about their feelings and their conflicts:

> "We have a burden on us," said Andira Abudayeh, who is 16 and attends Al Noor. "We're Muslims, and we feel like other Muslims around the world do. And we're Americans." . . . The students also said the Koran, which Muslims consider the literal word of God, provides a perfect blueprint for their lives. Their ideal society would follow Islamic law and make no separation between religion and state. In the meantime, they said, they want to become doctors and lawyers and teachers in the United States. (Sachs, 2001, p. B1)

Peer group membership may not be as salient for ethnic minority youth as it has been described for European American adolescents. In one study of family and peer relations, after controlling for social class, African American adolescents reported both higher levels of parental control and higher levels of family intimacy than did European American adolescents (Giordano, Cernkovich, & DeMaris, 1993). African American adolescents reported that they perceived less peer pressure, less need for peer approval, and somewhat lower levels of intimacy in their friendships. One ought not to interpret this pattern as an indication that friendship relationships are unimportant for African American adolescents. Rather, African American adolescents may be socialized to function more independently, to be more flexible in accepting their friends, but to be less dependent on them than on their family for feelings of self-worth and emotional security.

In the transition from early to late adolescence, most minority youth experience some critical evaluation of the values and beliefs of the dominant culture and how they conflict with the values and beliefs of their own ethnic group. The more fully immersed young children are in the values and traditions of their ethnic heritage, the more likely it is that they will experience a *dual* or *multiple identity*—for example, seeing themselves as both American and African American or American and Chinese (Phinney, 1997). Over time, and with

the benefit of exposure to reading, conversations, and interactions with people from other subgroups, young people begin to synthesize a sense of how their ethnic identity fits into their overall personal identity and how it will influence the quality of their relationships with members of their own and other ethnic groups (Cross, 1991; Phinney, 1996).

# THE PRIME ADAPTIVE EGO QUALITY AND THE CORE PATHOLOGY

## FIDELITY TO OTHERS

A positive resolution of the psychosocial crisis of group identity versus alienation results in the achievement of the prime adaptive ego quality referred to as **fidelity to others**—a capacity to freely pledge one's loyalty to a group and to sustain one's faithfulness to the promises and commitments one makes to others. Fidelity to others produces the sentiments that are necessary to preserve small groups and larger communities alike: dedication to family, civic pride, and patriotism. One of the by-products of fidelity to others is *mattering*, a "feeling that others depend upon us, are interested in us, are concerned with our fate" (Rosenberg & McCullogh, 1981, p. 163). When we pledge ourselves to others, we also become salient for them. We make a difference in their lives, and that, in return, contributes to our sense of well-being (Taylor & Turner, 2001).

Looking ahead to subsequent life stages, one can anticipate the significant role that this ego quality plays in pledging long-term faithfulness to friends, marital partners, children, one's aging parents, and other groups. Research on factors that buffer the effects of stress often cite the contribution of social support to the long-term abilities of individuals to cope with change and to adapt positively to life challenges. Social support implies a capacity for fidelity. People who function as sources of support have the ability to remain compassionately connected to others during periods of hardship and loss as well as during periods of success and prosperity. When one thinks of a true friend, one pictures someone who stands by you even when it is not especially advantageous to do so. A true friend is someone who cares about you and supports you during moments of adversity as well as in times of joy.

Fidelity to others becomes a source of family solidarity as family members age and adults are called on to meet the needs of their own aging parents—a topic we will cover in Chapter 13 (Middle Adulthood). The role one plays in caring for one's aging parents is largely voluntary. It is based on one's own definition of **filial obligation**, a sense of duty and responsibility for one's parents. Surely the way adults enact this role reflects their capacity for fidelity to others.

## DISSOCIATION

**Dissociation** refers to a sense of separateness, withdrawal from others, and an inability to experience the bond of mutual commitment. It does not mean a preference for being by oneself, but rather a tendency toward social distancing and a reluctance to make the kinds of commitments to others that are required for the establishment and maintenance of enduring friendships:

> What can I tell you about that time in my life? Hunger dominated every moment, hunger and its silent twin, the constant urge to sleep. School passed in a dream. I couldn't think. Logic fled, and memory drained away like motor oil. My stomach ached, my period stopped. I rose above the sidewalks, I was smoke. The rains came and I was sick and after school I had nowhere to go. (Fitch, 1999, p. 201)

Dissociation may occur as a result of rejection, abuse, or neglect. It may be a symptom of a more serious mental disorder, such as schizophrenia or depression. Adolescents who experience dissociation are likely to mistrust their peers and may even develop an attitude of hostile resentment toward the amiability and companionship they observe in others. Over time, dissociation results in the formulation of a mental world that is not well coordinated with social reality. A young person who experiences dissociation is likely to feel misunderstood and to lack confidence in his or her ability to communicate with or connect to others.

At a basic level, any sense of "we-ness" requires a shared understanding between at least two people and a recognition that they experience some bond of investment in or identification with a common reality. This common reality could involve facing a common enemy, encountering a common crisis, or embracing a common goal. The core pathology of dissociation occurs when the young person is unable to experience the level of mutual understanding or symbolic connection that creates such bonds of "we-ness."

### APPLIED TOPIC
## ADOLESCENT ALCOHOL AND DRUG USE

AMERICAN HIGH SCHOOL-AGE youth show a higher level of illicit drug use than those of any other industrialized nation. By their senior year in high school (typically age 17–18),

51% of American high school students have tried an illegal drug—whether marijuana, amphetamines, heroin or other opiates, cocaine, or barbiturates (Johnston, O'Malley, Bachman, & Schulenberg, 2004).

Figure 10.6 provides a historical overview of the lifetime prevalence of illicit drug use for 12th-graders from 1975 to 2000. Following a period of decline in drug use from 1981 through 1992, drug use among adolescents increased over the 1990s and is now beginning to decline again, though not to its 1992 low. Alcohol use has remained at a stable and relatively high level since 1975. In 2003, 37% of eighth-graders had tried alcohol, and 14% said that they have been drunk at least once in their lives. By the 12th grade, 70% had tried alcohol and 48% had gotten drunk. About 28% of 12th-graders had experienced binge drinking (5 or more drinks in a row) in the past month (Johnston et al., 2004).

## FACTORS ASSOCIATED WITH ALCOHOL USE

Let us look at some of the factors associated with the use of alcohol and the part it plays in the adolescent's life. We are especially concerned about understanding the relationship between alcohol use and the major themes of early adolescence—physical development, cognitive development, peer relations, and parent–child relationships.

### PHYSICAL EFFECTS OF ALCOHOL

Alcohol depresses the central nervous system. Although many people think that alcohol makes one high, at its highest levels of concentration in the body it can cause death by suppressing breathing. Although this outcome is extremely rare, it may occur after chugging large quantities of alcohol, a practice that is sometimes included in certain adolescent initiation rites and demonstrations of manliness. Deaths associated with fraternity initiation activities on college campuses have brought the practice of *chugging* to heightened attention ("Parents Should Talk to College Students," 1997). There are two other situations in which alcohol use has potentially lethal consequences. One is the use of alcohol in combination with other drugs, especially barbiturates. The other is its use in combination with driving.

The physical development accompanying puberty leads to a heightened awareness of body sensations. In small quantities, alcohol has a relaxing effect that may accentuate pleasurable bodily sensations. Adolescents may use alcohol in an attempt to increase their sense of physical arousal, reduce sexual inhibitions, and minimize the self-consciousness that is a barrier to social interactions. In larger quantities, alcohol may alter reality in such a way that adolescents are willing to

**FIGURE 10.6**

Trends in Lifetime Prevalence of an Illicit Drug Use Index for Twelfth-Graders

Source: Johnston, O'Malley, Bachman, & Schulenberg, 2004.

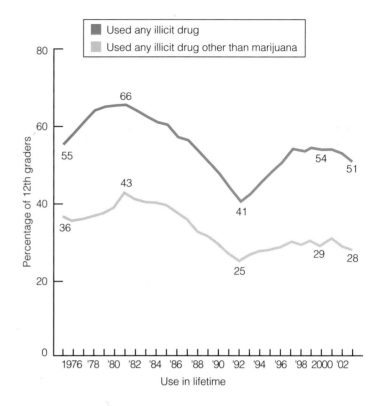

take risks or ignore certain physical limitations. When adolescents are intoxicated, the barriers of physical appearance, height, weight, or sexual immaturity may be minimized. Thus, dissatisfaction with one's body image may contribute to an inclination to drink heavily in social situations.

### ■ ASSESSMENT OF RISK

Many adolescents do not view alcohol consumption as especially risky. In a national survey, only 25% of high school seniors saw daily drinking as involving great risk, and 43% of high school seniors saw binge drinking (five or more drinks once or twice over a weekend) as involving great risk (Johnston et al., 1999). Students who drink alcohol frequently are less likely to view drinking as risky, whereas those who drink little or not at all are more likely to see drinking as involving risk (Small, Silverberg, & Kerns, 1993). This pattern suggests cognitive consistency—in other words, adolescents who view a certain level of drinking behavior as highly risky are less likely to engage in it.

In addition to the assessment of risk, some adolescents can be characterized by high levels of *sensation seeking* including thrill seeking, adventure seeking, disinhibition, and susceptibility to boredom. Youth who have a great need for novel, complex sensory experiences may be willing to take physical risks in order to satisfy this need (Tang, Wong, & Schwarzer, 1996). Teens who have difficulty conceptualizing the future

impact of their behaviors and who have a strong need for thrill seeking are more likely to become involved in frequent and heavy alcohol use (Robbins & Bryan, 2004).

### ■ REFERENCE GROUPS

The two **reference groups** that influence the acceptability of drinking and the manner in which alcohol is consumed are the family and the peer group. There appear to be many similarities between the ways in which students and adults in a community think about and use alcohol. For both adults and adolescents, drinking is viewed primarily as a social activity. Barnes (1981) surveyed students and adults in the same community to assess the similarity in their respective patterns of alcohol use. The survey results showed similar patterns of use of beer, wine, and other liquors. The adults and students described similar patterns of alcohol use in the home on special occasions or at mealtimes. Three basic reasons for drinking were described by the two groups: social, festive functions ("It's a good way to celebrate"); conforming functions ("So I won't be different from my friends"); and personal effects ("It helps relieve pressure"). The first reason was most important to both groups; the second and third reasons were somewhat more important to adolescents than to adults. Barnes concluded that the adult members of a community set the attitudinal and behavioral tone for alcohol use, and that adolescents are socialized to internalize that position.

A somewhat different view is discovered if one asks adolescents about parental approval of drinking patterns. Adolescents perceive their parents as disapproving of almost any drug use. With respect to alcohol use, more than 90% perceive their parents to be disapproving of having one or two drinks a day; however, they said their parents had a somewhat more flexible view of binge drinking, with 85% of high school seniors saying their parents would disapprove (Johnston, O'Malley, & Bachman, 1996). Alcohol is a part of the life experience of most adolescents. Drinking is something they can do that symbolizes celebration, adult status, and a degree of behavioral independence from parents. Because most adults drink alcohol, young people may perceive their disapproval of adolescent drinking as hypocritical. In this way, drinking may become an avenue for testing the limits of adult authority or for expressing behavioral autonomy from parental control.

The impact of parental sanctions against alcohol use depends heavily on the quality of the parent–child relationship. Nonusers are more likely to describe their parents as creating an environment of strict rules coupled with praise, encouragement, and closeness. In these relationships, the way parents exercise their guidance does not alienate adolescents, but establishes a bond of trust and respect. Nonusers do not want to disappoint their parents or to humiliate themselves by becoming drunk (Coombs & Landsverk, 1988).

The peer group also contributes to the patterns of alcohol and drug use in adolescence, which helps explain potential inconsistencies in alcohol use. The majority of high school seniors say that they are around peers who use alcohol to get high, and 32% say they are around friends who get drunk at least once a week (Johnston et al., 1999). Even among eighth-graders, about 75% say they are around friends who drink.

Given the central role of the peer group during this stage of life, we must assume that alcohol and drug use are influenced largely by peer pressure to conform to a group norm coupled with an adolescent's vulnerability to this pressure (Webster, Hunter, & Keats, 1994). Two related processes are at work: socialization forces and selection forces.

*Socialization forces* refer to the enthusiasm and encouragement coming from the peer group about trying drugs and getting high. Peer group leaders who experiment with alcohol and drugs at a young age or who approve of binge drinking, alcohol, and marijuana use at parties, or driving while intoxicated are highly influential in encouraging other group members to share these experiences. Peer expectations for drug use may become one criterion for peer group acceptance. On the other hand, if peer norms reject drug use, the peer group may serve to shield its members from drugs and deny membership to those who use or abuse them. The social reference group's support of drug use during adolescence has long-term effects.

*Selection forces* suggest that some adolescents seek out friends who will support their involvement with drugs as part of a more general pattern of deviance or thrill seeking. Both factors—increased socialization pressures toward alcohol and drug use, and increased willingness to seek out peers who misuse drugs and alcohol—increase over the high school years, with a consequent increase in the likelihood that adolescents will become involved in the misuse of alcohol and drugs themselves (Schulenberg & Maggs, 2001).

## EARLY ENTRY INTO ALCOHOL AND DRUG USE

A growing concern is focused on those children who begin to be involved in alcohol and other drug use at young ages. In one study of fourth- and fifth-graders, 15% reported alcohol use without their parents' knowledge (Iannotti & Bush, 1992). Both peer and family variables were significant predictors of the use of alcohol without the parents' knowledge. Children who perceived that many of their friends had been drinking and experienced peer pressure to drink were more likely to drink. Children who were in classrooms where a larger number of children reported drinking were also at greater risk of drinking. Perceptions of the amount of drinking that occurred in the family were another important predictor of early alcohol use. Another study of alcohol and drug use among seventh-graders confirmed the importance of peer and family influences (Farrell, Danish, & Howard, 1992).

Significant predictors of alcohol use included several peer factors: friends' approving of alcohol and drugs; feeling pressure to use alcohol and drugs; and knowing friends who had an alcohol and drug problem. There were also two family-related factors: being home alone after school 20 or more times in the past 30 days, and reporting that half or more of the adults the adolescents knew had an alcohol or drug problem.

The risk factors associated with early alcohol and drug use are linked to social class and culture. Control over the sale of alcohol to minors, its cost, and the efforts of parents and other adults—including school officials and the police—to monitor its use among adolescents are all community factors that influence the use of alcohol in early adolescence. Alcohol plays a somewhat different role in various ethnic, cultural, and religious groups. For example, a comparative analysis of African American, Cuban, non-Cuban Hispanic, and European American sixth- and seventh-grade boys in Dade County, Florida, found different rates of alcohol use and different patterns of risk factors that predicted early use in the four groups (Vega, Zimmerman, Warheit, Apospori, & Gil, 1993). In this study, European Americans had the highest percentage of early alcohol users (48%), Cubans the next highest (41%), non-Cuban Hispanics the next highest (31%), and African Americans the lowest (25%). In all groups, low family pride and the adolescent's willingness to participate in delinquent behavior or to break the law were significant predictors of early alcohol use.

A combination of biological, psychological, and societal factors converge to make alcohol and drug use a part of the life of normal adolescents during the high school years. Experimentation with alcohol is relatively easy to understand in the context of the adolescent's psychosocial needs and the modeling of alcohol use in the family, peer group, and community. Although alcohol and drug use may be considered a normative rite of passage for most adolescents, it appears that children who begin to drink or use drugs early in adolescence—that is, before ninth grade—are especially vulnerable to more serious involvement with alcohol and drug use later (Murray, 1997). They experience some combination of family, peer, and psychosocial pressures that increase their willingness to engage in deviant behavior and to ignore or minimize the risks.

# Chapter Summary

Early adolescence provides vivid evidence of the interaction of the biological, psychological, and societal systems during a period of rapid growth and development. The period is characterized by biological changes of puberty, new cognitive capacities, and a new range and intensity of emotional life. For most adolescents, the physical and psychological changes are taking place in a context of new and more demanding expectations for self-reliance, more challenging academic tasks, new expectations for social participation, and new pressures from parents and peers about how to behave. For some, these expectations and demands are overwhelming. Depression and eating disorders reflect two of the maladaptive consequences of heightened uncertainty and loss of control. For others, the new expectations are exhilarating. Leadership; mastery of complex knowledge; success in social relationships; and new respect from parents, teachers, and peers reflect some of the positive consequences of effective coping.

The radius of significant relationships expands as adolescents enter new roles and new settings. Parents continue to be an important source of reassurance and support. However, the period is characterized by strong desires to find membership and acceptance among peers. Within this context, adolescents seek like-minded peers and are open to peer influence. Relationships also take on a sexual tone as adolescents find ways to express sexual impulses in the context of socially acceptable practices. The majority of adolescents engage in forms of sexual behavior, including intercourse, with its accompanying risks and rewards, by the end of high school.

The crisis of group identity versus alienation involves a potential tension between the *I* and the *we*, the desire to feel meaningfully connected to a valued group and, at the same time, to have an authentic, autonomous sense of self. In the process of resolving this conflict, most adolescents experience moments of alienation, a sense of separateness and disconnection, out of which can grow a new personal confidence or a deep well of resentment and rage. The threat of peer rejection may push those adolescents who lack confidence in their own worth to violate essential values in the pursuit of acceptance. Teenage pregnancy, drug addiction, drunkenness, and serious delinquent behavior all reflect adolescents' capacity to engage in high-risk behaviors that have a great potential for modifying the life course and exposing them to new and serious physical and emotional hazards.

# Further Reflection

1. Think back on your early adolescence, from the age of about 12 to the end of high school. How would you characterize that time of your life? What are some examples of experiences that made you feel competent and self-assured? What are examples of experiences that led to feelings of inferiority or self-doubt?

2. Consider the role of friendship during this period of life. How did your friendships change from middle childhood to adolescence? Can you recall being part of a clique? A crowd? How would you describe those groups in terms of attitudes, values, dress, orientation toward school, or involvement in high-risk behaviors? What are some lessons learned from high school peer relations that continue to be meaningful to you today?

3. What happens in the context of schooling that supports the development of formal operational reasoning? How well does the high school environment match the cognitive developmental changes that take place during early adolescence?

4. Think about the impact of physical development, including the emergence of sexuality and sexual interests, on adaptation during early adolescence. What personal, family, cultural, and environmental factors help adolescents cope effectively with these changes? What factors lead to dissatisfaction with body image, risk taking, and harmful or unhealthy behaviors?

5. Suppose that you were asked to provide guidance to a parents' group about how to improve health among adolescents. What ideas from this chapter might inform your recommendations?

6. The psychosocial crisis of group identity versus alienation is closely linked to the issue of intergroup relations. What factors in school or community foster positive intergroup relations among adolescents? What factors promote intergroup hostilities? What is your view about how to promote positive intergroup relations at the middle school and high school levels?

# On the Web

**VISIT OUR WEBSITE**

Go to http://www.wadsworth.com/psychology to find online resources directly linked to your book.

# Casebook

For additional case material related to this chapter, see the case entitled "The Early Bloomer" in *Life Span Development: A Case Book*, by Barbara and Philip Newman, Laura Landry-Meyer, and Brenda J. Lohman, pp. 120–123. The case focuses on the challenges of early maturing for girls and how pubertal timing influences social relationships.

# CHAPTER 11

# Later adolescence
# (18–24 years)

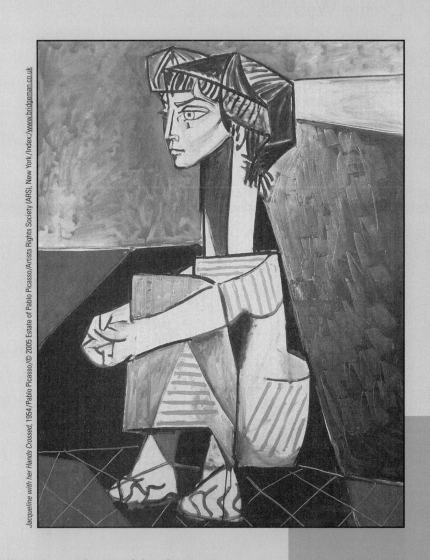

Jacqueline with her Hands Crossed, 1954/Pablo Picasso/© 2005 Estate of Pablo Picasso/Artists Rights Society (ARS), New York /Index./www.bridgeman.co.uk

*Engaged in the active resolution of the identity crisis,
young people make commitments that will shape the
structure of their adult lives. In this portrait, Picasso
suggests the balance, focus, and purposefulness of
a young woman who is striving to achieve a sense
of personal identity.*

■ DEVELOPMENTAL TASKS

Autonomy from Parents
Gender Identity
Internalized Morality
Career Choice

■ THE PSYCHOSOCIAL CRISIS: INDIVIDUAL
IDENTITY VERSUS IDENTITY CONFUSION

Individual Identity
CASE STUDY: HOUSTON A. BAKER, JR.
Identity Confusion
Identity Formation for Men and Women

■ THE CENTRAL PROCESS: ROLE EXPERIMENTATION

Psychosocial Moratorium
CASE STUDY: TURNING POINTS
IN THE IDENTITY PROCESS
Role Experimentation and Ethnic Identity

■ THE PRIME ADAPTIVE EGO QUALITY
AND THE CORE PATHOLOGY

Fidelity to Values and Ideologies
Repudiation

■ APPLIED TOPIC: THE CHALLENGES OF SOCIAL LIFE

Unwanted Sexual Attention
Binge Drinking
Sexually Transmitted Diseases

■ CHAPTER SUMMARY

■ FURTHER REFLECTION

▶ *To examine the concept of autonomy from parents and the conditions under which that autonomy is likely to be achieved.*

▶ *To trace the development of gender identity in later adolescence, including a discussion of how the components of gender role identification that were relevant during the early-school-age period are revised and expanded.*

▶ *To describe the maturation of morality in later adolescence, with special focus on the role of new cognitive capacities that influence moral judgments and the various value orientations that underlie moral reasoning.*

▶ *To analyze the process of career choice, with attention to education and gender role socialization as two major influential factors.*

▶ *To define and describe the psychosocial crisis of later adolescence, individual identity versus identity confusion; the central process through which this crisis is resolved, role experimentation; the prime adaptive ego quality of fidelity to values and ideals; and the core pathology of repudiation.*

▶ *To examine some of the challenges of social life in later adolescence that may result in high-risk behaviors.*

THE YEARS FROM 18 to 24 are characterized by a heightened sensitivity to the process of identity development. Personal identity is developed as an individual struggles to answer the questions, "What is the meaning of my life? Who am I? Where am I headed?" Most young people are cognitively complex enough to conjure up alternative scenarios about their own future, including possible kinds of work and various meaningful relationships. They struggle with the uncertainty of having to choose many of their own life's directions. This period is often characterized by a high level of anxiety. Even though most young people are energetic and capable, they are also troubled by the lack of certainty about their future. Some worry whether they will be able to succeed in a chosen direction; others may be anxious because they do not even know what direction they wish to take.

Identity development is a cornerstone of the unique individuality that becomes more fully expressed in adulthood. With the increase in life choices and life roles in contemporary society, it is probably more important today than it was in the past for young people to embrace particular values, goals, and life commitments as central to their identity. What is more, they must recognize that the process of clarifying and evaluating their values and goals will continue to be a challenge. Identity is not firm or fixed for life. Rather, identity is an orienting framework, a blueprint that helps shape decision making.

Throughout adulthood, there are many opportunities to revisit the identity commitments of later adolescence. Still, the vision of selfhood created during this period remains salient later in life. People can recall these images as they evaluate their life in middle and later adulthood. They think back to what they may have hoped for or what they may have predicted for their future when they were 18 to 24 years old. Adults may be surprised by how much more they have actually accomplished or how much more pleasure they have experienced in certain roles than they thought they might at that age. Or they may be disappointed to realize that some of the hopes, dreams, and goals they had for themselves turned out to be unattainable. Across the span of adulthood, the identity formulations of later adolescence must be reworked and extended.

Although the theme of identity development is often conceptualized within the framework of the college experience, this process is critical for all those in the 18- to 24-year-old range who are making the transition from adolescence into adulthood. In the United States in 2001, 62% of adolescents who graduated from high school in the previous year were enrolled in college either part time or full time (U.S. Census Bureau, 2003). This compares to about 45% who went to college after graduating from high school in 1960. Thus, over the past 40 years, it has become normative to continue some form of postsecondary schooling. However, more than one third of later adolescents do not go to college after high school graduation. Many go directly to work, join the military, or enter technical training programs.

Unfortunately, most research on later adolescence has focused on college students, who are a captive target for scholars of human development. Thus, less is known about the identity process or the developmental trajectory for later adolescents who do not go on to college; including those who join the military. In this chapter, we will find ways to illustrate how the construct of personal identity and the related themes of one's relationship with parents, the formulation of a moral ideology, a gender identity, and a set of behaviors and goals related to work are subjects of psychological activity for later adolescents whether they do or do not attend college. ■

# DEVELOPMENTAL TASKS

## AUTONOMY FROM PARENTS

Achieving a psychological sense of autonomy from one's parents must be understood as a multidimensional task that is accomplished gradually over the course of later adolescence and early adulthood. **Autonomy** is the ability to regulate one's own behavior and to select and guide one's own decisions and actions without undue control from or dependence on one's parents (Steinberg, 1990). It is not the same as rejection, alienation, or physical separation from parents. Rather, it is an independent psychological status in which parents and children accept each others' individuality. Many areas of similarity between parents and children may provide bonds for a continued close, supportive relationship into adulthood. However, those bonds are re-created in later adolescence and early adulthood through a process of self-definition. Adolescents who achieve autonomy can recognize and accept both the similarities and the differences between themselves and their parents, while still feeling a sense of love, understanding, and connection with them.

Autonomy requires independence of thoughts, emotions, and actions (Steinberg, 2005). Much of the psychosocial development that has occurred before this stage can be understood as preparing the individual for behavioral independence from his or her parents. Such skills as dressing oneself, handling money, cooking, driving a car, reading, and writing have been mastered. Although it is easy to take these skills for granted, they are essential for someone who is living independently. The physical maturation that has taken place also contributes to the possibility of autonomy. Daily survival requires a certain amount of physical strength, coordination, and endurance—qualities that arrive with the physical maturity of adolescence.

Beyond these physical requirements, autonomy involves a psychological sense of confidence about one's unique point

of view and an ability to express opinions and beliefs that may differ from those of one's parents (Herman, Dornbusch, Herron, & Herting, 1997). In early school age, the process of identification and the accompanying internalization of parental values allow the young child to function with a sense of what is appropriate behavior. In early adolescence, the child's ability to emerge from the intimacy of the family may also be promoted by a growing involvement with the peer group. As peer relations become more reciprocal, they satisfy many of the needs for closeness and support that were initially satisfied only within the boundaries of the family. Gradually, a young person's cognitive maturity provides a fund of information, problem-solving ability, and capacity to plan for the future that help sustain independent living.

The concept of differentiation, which emerged from family systems theory, has been associated with psychosocial maturity and a healthy emergence of individuality in adolescence. **Differentiation** is the extent to which a social system encourages intimacy while supporting the expression of differences (Bomar & Sabatelli, 1996). Within the family context, identity exploration is facilitated by an open exchange of ideas and a certain level of challenge. Adolescents must have opportunities to express their separateness within the boundaries of the family. They must feel that their parents accept and understand their need to have distinct opinions and views. This takes place as parents encourage their children to express new ideas and differing points of view without making them feel guilty when they disagree (Best, Hauser, & Allen, 1997). Adolescents who experience high levels of parental control and frequent exposure to parental conflict are likely to have difficulties in achieving a comfortable sense of autonomy (Taylor & Oskay, 1995). Ideally, individuality is achieved in a context of mutual caring and emotional support. A secure attachment to parents, based on a perception of them as committed to their child's well-being, is essential for growth toward independence (Palladino-Schultheiss & Blustein, 1994; Perosa, Perosa, & Tam, 1996).

The meaning a young person gives to achieving autonomy from parents varies depending on personal, family, and cultural values, such as commitment to education, financial independence, and marriage. For example, some cultural groups are more accustomed to living in multigenerational families and place great value on the filial bond between children and their parents. Parents in these cultures may be more comfortable with the idea of having their later adolescent children living in their home without paying rent, and the children may perceive it as part of their obligation to stay near their parents and grandparents in order to provide them with social and instrumental support. In contrast, in some cultures, families expect their later adolescent children to achieve residential separateness. They may expect that children age 18 to 24 who are living at home will contribute to the cost of housing. Paths toward autonomy are also influenced by the young person's family context. For example, children living with their two biological parents are likely to leave home later than are children living in a stepfamily.

Three components of achieving autonomy from parents are discussed in the following sections: leaving home, attending college, and self-sufficiency.

## ■ AUTONOMY AND LEAVING HOME

Living away from one's parents' household may be a symbol of independence; however, it is not as readily achievable in the age range from 18 to 24 as it was in the past. Before about 1960, marriage was the most traditional reason for moving to a new residence, other than leaving temporarily for college or the military. Since that time, however, the median age at marriage has increased, so that close to 80% of those in the age range from 20 to 24 have never been married. Roughly 56% of men and 43% of women in this age range live at home with one or both parents. Few later adolescents live alone, but a large group—30% of young men and 35% of young women—live with roommates, close friends, or intimate partners (Fields & Casper, 2001).

Parents and adolescent children have different views about the age at which children are expected to leave home. Parents tend to expect children to leave home at an older age—more closely tied to the expected age of marriage—than do adolescent children. Also, parents expect daughters to live at home longer than sons. However, these differences are not reflected in the expectations of the adolescents themselves. Thus, this issue is a potential source of family conflict. Family structure is also associated with the age of leaving home. Children in single-parent families and girls in stepfamilies leave at an earlier age (Cooney & Mortimer, 1999; Goldscheider & Goldscheider, 1998).

Economic factors and social norms play a significant role in the timing of leaving home. A child's ability to live away from home may depend on whether the family is willing to provide financial support during this period. This, in turn, depends on the family's values and the later adolescent's values. For example, many families are strongly committed to having their children complete college and are willing to provide financial support while the child is away at school. However, if the child gets married while still in college, some families may feel that their financial obligation to support the child is over. Some parents are willing to support their children who are away from home if the child is in college, but not willing to provide support if the child wants to live away from home but not attend school (Goldscheider, Thornton, & Yang, 2001). Imagine that, after 1 or 2 years of college, a child wants to move to a new city, live with a same-sex partner, and seek opportunities in the entertainment industry. Some parents might encourage this path toward self-discovery; others might consider it risky, immoral, or frivolous. When children and parents disagree about the appropriate path toward self-reliance and adulthood, parents may be unwilling to provide the financial resources that would make this level of autonomy possible.

## ■ AUTONOMY AND THE COLLEGE EXPERIENCE

Going away to college is an intermediate step between living at home and establishing a permanent residence in early adulthood. The mere act of going to college does not in itself bring a sense of leaving home or of psychological autonomy from one's parents. In fact, most students do not go far from home when they enter college as freshmen; roughly 80% attend college in their home state ("Attitudes and Characteristics of Freshmen," 2001). Many students continue to live at home while they attend college, and most still request and receive both emotional and instrumental support from their parents (Valery, O'Connor, & Jennings, 1997).

*Students who go away to college use their group identity skills to form new relationships while creating a physical environment that preserves a connection to family, friends, and home.*

© Mark Richards/PhotoEdit

College freshmen express a variety of attitudes that suggest different views about their desire to be independent from their family. Of students entering college in the fall of 2000, 21% said that an important reason for deciding to go to college was to get away from home, and 36% were going to college because their parents wanted them to go. When asked about reasons that were important in selecting the college that they ended up attending, 17% said they wanted to live near home ("Attitudes and Characteristics of Freshmen," 2001). In fact, as they enter college, students differ markedly in how much work they have already done toward achieving autonomy from their parents, how much they desire autonomy, and what evidence they use to determine whether they have achieved autonomy.

**REVISION OF ATTACHMENT TO PARENTS.** The experience of entering college focuses new attention on one's attachment relationships. An area of special interest has been the changing quality of the attachment relationship between college students and their parents as the students leave home (Bloom, 1987). Students who live at college are more likely to rely on the mental representations of their attachment figures, whereas students who live with their parents continue to be involved daily with concrete interactions. Issues of autonomy and control, establishing new guidelines and limits related to participation in family life, involvement in relationships with peers, and management of time and money are resolved in the absence of direct input from parents for most students who live at college, but these decisions continue to involve parental input for students who live at home.

For students who live on campus, preoccupation with thoughts and concerns about their parents tends to diminish over the course of the first semester, while new relationships form and a new confidence in their independent decision making builds. The attachment scheme or representation, rather than the actual interactions with parents, is what becomes modified. Many students who attend college away from home begin to have more positive thoughts and feelings about their parents. At the same time, they begin to detect a new level of confidence and respect from their parents, who appreciate that their children are managing to take on new responsibilities and to make good decisions on their own:

> Over the past year I have become very close with my dad. Before college there was a definite parent–child relationship with my father. Now he is more like a mentor or friend. Overall, the relationship between my parents and I has been a growing mutual respect. (Arnett, 2004, p. 215)

In other cases, going to college represents a move toward upward mobility and a decision to seek a life path quite different from one's parents. Even when parents are supportive of a child's college attendance, the experiences of college may introduce their child to new ideas, values, and interests that create conflict. Parents who have not attended college may not understand what their child is doing, why it is important

or valued, or how their child's involvement in certain classes or campus activities will lead to economic betterment. For some, this distance is gradually bridged as parents become familiar with their children's lives, and children become more skilled at giving parents ways of understanding what they are doing. For others, as in the case of Mary, the distance widens over time:

> I go home, we talk about the weather, talk about people in the family, people in the neighborhood. . . . The stuff I would like to talk about, [my mother] can't. She doesn't understand it. Stuff she'd like to talk about I think would be incredibly boring. . . . I learned very early on that they couldn't discuss [school]. To try to discuss it with them would be very frustrating to me, and embarrassing for them. . . . I realized I had far educated myself past my parents. (Roberts & Rosenwald, 2001, p. 102)

Students who live at home while attending college tend to continue to be preoccupied by concerns and thoughts about their parents based on their actual daily interactions, and the quality of their relationships is viewed as more conflictual (Berman & Sperling, 1991; Sullivan & Sullivan, 1980). Based on many observations of college-age students, it is clear that some are much less ready than others to embrace the demands for new levels of independence and responsibility. The relationship between emotional closeness and living at home appears to be culturally based. For example, in the United States, later adolescents who live at home and have frequent daily interactions with their parents tend to be *least* close to them. In comparison, studies of European later adolescents find that young people who live at home are quite happy with their living arrangements, find their parents to be an important source of emotional support, and experience considerable autonomy in the context of their parents' household (Arnett, 2000). The box on Attachment and Identity Formation (p. 352) provides more detail on the relationship of parental attachment to identity formation in later adolescence.

The delay in age at marriage also has implications for the revision of the parental attachment relationship. When the majority of young people in the 20–24 age range were married, it was normal to expect that some of the emotional investment in one's family of origin would shift to the new intimate marital bond. Thus, emotional distancing from one's parents made sense in the context of forming a culturally approved marital commitment. Today, many young people have deeply valued love relationships, but they are not married and are not ready to make lifelong commitments to these relationships. This results in lengthening the period when both children and parents feel that their primary emotional attachment is to the family of origin.

## ■ AUTONOMY AND SELF-SUFFICIENCY

Despite the variety of life paths and demographic characteristics of those in the period of later adolescence, most young people can recognize when they have achieved a sense of

## Attachment and Identity Formation

IDENTITY FORMATION IS usually viewed as a process that requires young people to distance themselves from the strong expectations and definitions imposed by parents and other family members. To achieve an individual identity, one must create a vision of the self that is authentic—a sense of having taken hold of one's destiny in an effort to reach goals that are personally meaningful. Yet research has demonstrated that the quality of family relationships contributes significantly to a young person's ability to achieve a personal identity (Allen & Land, 1999).

The relationship can be compared with the contribution of a secure attachment in infancy to a subsequent willingness to explore the environment. Securely attached infants will move away physically from their caregiver, confident that the caregiver will be available when they are in need of help. For later adolescents, autonomy-seeking behaviors can be interpreted as a more advanced form of the exploratory activities observed in infancy. Later adolescents who have a secure relationship with their parents and who are comfortable in loosening these ties can begin to explore the ideological, occupational, and interpersonal alternatives that will become the content for their own identities.

Attachment to parents has been measured in later adolescence and adulthood using the *Adult Attachment Interview* (AAI), which asks participants to describe their relationship with their parents when they were younger, including specific memories of that relationship; recall incidences of distress in the relationship; and discuss factors that have influenced their relationship (George, Kaplan, & Main, 1996). The interview

is then coded to characterize the attachment state of mind as (1) *autonomous*, which is reflective of an open, coherent narrative about the parent–child relationship; (2) *dismissive*, which is reflective of minimizing the importance of the parent–child relationship, inability to recall many details, and a tendency to idealize one's parents; or (3) *preoccupied*, which is reflective of continuing anger toward one's parents and a confused, vague, or passive narrative (Bernier et al., 2004). Interviews with students at the beginning and end of the first year of college found that the preoccupied students had the most difficulty adapting to college and actually did worse with respect to adjustment and grades as the year went along. These students had the greatest difficulty transferring their emotional investment from parents to peers, even if that investment was negative (Bernier et al., 2004).

Male and female college students who have a positive attachment to their mothers are more likely to have an achieved identity and are less likely to be in a moratorium or identity-confused status than are students who have insecure, mistrustful relationships with their mothers. On the other hand, those who are still emotionally dependent on their parents and require constant reassurance of their affection show a greater tendency to experience identity confusion (Benson, Harris, & Rogers, 1992).

By the time young people reach later adolescence, those who are securely attached to their parents are confident about parental affection and support. At the same time, they trust in their own worth and in their ability to make decisions (Blain, Thompson, & Whiffen,

1993). In a study comparing university students who lived with their parents with those who lived away from home, those who lived away from their parents experienced more daily life challenges, but they also used more effective problem-solving strategies to address those challenges. In comparison to students who lived at home, those who lived away from their parents had made more progress in the formation of their personal identity, suggesting that the pressures toward self-reliance may contribute to the clarification of values and commitments (Jordyn & Byrd, 2003). Later adolescents may make a point of *not* seeking parental support, but in a secure relationship, they know that help is available if needed. By imposing emotional distance and achieving greater self-reliance, later adolescents are able to reach a more objective evaluation of their parents as figures for identification and, thereby, to create the needed space for the emergence of their own identity (Kobak, 1999).

A secure parental attachment fosters identity formation in the following ways:

- It fosters confidence in the exploration of social relationships, ideologies, and settings.
- It establishes positive expectations in regard to interpersonal experiences outside the family.
- It fosters the formation of group identities apart from the family, thus providing a transitional context for work on individual identity.
- It provides a basic layer of self-acceptance, permitting the young person to approach the process of identity formation with optimism.

autonomy from their parents. One important underlying theme is a sense of self-sufficiency, which is expressed by making independent decisions, taking responsibility for one's actions, and achieving a degree of financial independence (Arnett, 1998; Greene, Wheatley, & Alvada, 1992). With respect to financial independence, roughly 16% of those in the

18–24 age range fall below the poverty level ($9,044 annual income for a single person in 2001). This rate varies by race/ethnicity: 14% of White adolescents; 27% of Black adolescents; 19% of Asian and Pacific Islanders; and 21% of Hispanics (U.S. Census Bureau, 2003).

A sense of self-sufficiency goes beyond personal income.

It is a subjective experience that is distinct from a person's living arrangement, student status, having a steady job, or being in a serious love relationship. A subjective sense of self-sufficiency is achieved gradually as young people face and meet important challenges of school, work, and family life and build a degree of confidence in their capacity to make good decisions.

The process of achieving autonomy from parents opens the door to new considerations of basic ego structures, including gender identity, morality, and career aspirations. In each of these areas, a young person has the opportunity to *decenter*—to step back from the close socialization pressures of family and neighborhood—and construct his or her own point of view. After a period of **role experimentation and introspection**, some may choose to adopt the framework that was in place at the end of the high school years. Others may invent novel and nontraditional perspectives. The growth that takes place during the period of later adolescence in each of these areas reflects a willingness to evaluate multiple perspectives and to integrate personal commitments with societal expectations and resources.

## GENDER IDENTITY

In later adolescence, new and important revisions and elaborations of the child's earlier work on gender role identification are taking place (see Chapter 8, Early School Age). The developmental task of forming one's gender identity reflects the need to integrate and synthesize the three basic components of gender—its biological, psychological, and social meanings—into a view of oneself as a man or a woman entering into the complex social world of adult life. The formulation of **gender identity** refers to the acquisition of a set of beliefs, attitudes, and values about oneself as a man or a woman in many areas of social life, including intimate relations, family, work, community, and religion (Giele, 1988).

### THE ROLE OF CULTURE

As discussed in Chapter 4, according to social role theory, *roles* are basic building blocks of social organizations. Every organization, including a family, a workplace, a community, and a culture, can be described by its roles. Individuals learn the roles of their social system throughout their lives. Through the socialization process, people internalize the expectations associated with many life roles and apply the socially shared norms and standards linked to these roles to their own behaviors. This process occurs with respect to gender-related roles as well as to kinship, age, occupation, and other socially constructed roles. For example, when a person becomes a parent, a man is called a *father* and a woman is called a *mother*. Both are parenting roles, but gender is identified, and each role is associated with somewhat different expectations.

© Philip Newman

*Cultures construct gender-differentiated roles. In the United States, the traditional attire of the bride and groom create an ideal image of feminine beauty and masculine respectability to which many young people aspire.*

All cultures construct gender-differentiated roles, and people expect one another to behave in certain ways because they are male or female. Perhaps more important, they form expectations of how men and women ought to act when they are together, so that the distinctions between the genders are demarcated (Freud, 1994). These expectations are taught and learned, beginning early in life. For later adolescents, the gendered nature of the family is an especially important factor in shaping gender identity. Family experiences from the past provide the gender script with which they are most familiar. The family life they envision for themselves in the future creates many of the priorities that shape their current commitments and goals (Valsiner, 2000).

In the United States, many people argue that gender-based role distinctions are inappropriate, at least as a part of public life. They believe that men and women should be considered equal and treated identically in all public matters. But in many cultures, there are distinct, agreed-upon norms prescribing differences in how men and women are treated, which tasks they are expected to perform, and what status they hold in their family and community. Often, these norms establish specific power differences as part of the gender

HUMAN DEVELOPMENT AND DIVERSITY

## Gender Roles in the Hindu Joint Family

Hindu joint family involves the sharing of the same household territory by the parallel kin and their offspring (brothers or sisters, their spouses, and their children). Two lines of dominance—male and female—are mutually intertwined, both honoring the age of the participants. . . . Under the traditional pattern of authority, the eldest male member of the joint family was considered the head of the whole family. He had authority over others—yet not unlimited authority. He could not use the power arbitrarily, without collectively coordinating his decisions. In the second generation, the eldest son used to hold a superior position among the other male members of the family, yet had a position subordinate to the head and the elder women. Thus, decisions within a joint family relied on making of coalitions between less and more powerful members of the family. The age-respecting dominance system allowed the older members of the family—particularly the older women—remarkable power. . . .

The particular system of social relations within Hindu joint family created a collective cultural meaning system of attributing high value to becoming mother-in-law. . . . Becoming mother-in-law meant takeover of the running of the whole joint family system in the sphere of home life. Becoming mother-in-law obviously required passing through the phase of being daughter-in-law in the joint family of one's husband. Despite the heavy workload involved in the phase, women in the daughter-in-law phase of their lives internalize the value and positive expectations for the "promotion" to the upcoming role of mother-in-law which is the state of "mature adulthood" in the Hindu life course. (Valsiner, 2000, p. 89)

The organization of the joint family, including the special role of the man as head of the whole family and the woman as head of the household, is internalized as children grow up and is transformed into a commitment to daily life activities in the transition to adulthood. As the female elders in a joint household, women are expected to supervise their daughters-in-law, and daughters-in-law subject themselves to the power and guidance of their mothers-in-law. Daughters-in-law make all the meals, sweep the house, make the bread, serve each person as he or she arrives at the home for each meal, and wash the dishes. In response to real and symbolic acts of service, the mother-in-law makes sure her daughter-in-law's needs are met, allows her time to visit her own family, buffers her from any jealousy or bickering from other family members, and gives her blessings. A daughter-in-law's status increases when she gives birth to a son (Gardiner & Kosmitzki, 2005).

---

distinctions. Typically, men have more power than women, but this is not always the case. The box on Human Development and Diversity: Gender Roles in the Hindu Joint Family illustrates a way in which male and female dominance work together.

Others argue that men and women should be considered equal, but that they should be treated in ways that take into account the differences in their needs and capacities. For example, a bill introduced in the U.S. Congress required that all public places, such as auditoriums, stadiums, and theaters, have twice as many public bathroom facilities for women as for men to take into account the physiological and social differences in women's toileting practices.

In the United States, and in many other industrialized nations, people are engaged in a wide-ranging dialogue about the scientific, legal, and sociohistorical bases of gender roles that is leading to a revision—perhaps even a revolution—in how gender serves as an organizing social structure. Although this dialogue takes place across many groups and in many contexts, there is still powerful pressure on young people to achieve their own personal gender identity. They may be influenced by voices and views in the larger society; however, later adolescents must decide for themselves about the meaning they will make of their own designation as male or female.

### ■ REEVALUATING GENDER CONSTANCY

Each of the components of gender identification discussed in Chapter 8 (Early School Age) undergoes some transformation as work on gender identity continues. Later adolescents can appreciate that the use of gender labels is a social convention and that, apart from the genital basis of this label, there are wide individual differences *within* gender groups in most traits and abilities. What is more, information about genetic anomalies and medical technologies may lead later adolescents to realize that it is possible to have a conflict between one's genetic sex and one's external genitalia. *Transsexuals* develop a gender identity that is opposite to their biological sex. They feel certain of their gender and are at odds with their genital features. In these cases, the possibility of a sex-change operation provides an alternative to the notion of gender constancy (Crooks & Bauer, 2005). One study followed the adjustment of 20 adolescent transsexuals who had experienced sex-reassignment surgery. In the 1 to 4 years following treatment, these young people were functioning well, and none of them expressed regrets about their decision (Smith, van Goozen, & Cohen-Kettenis, 2001). Later adolescents may realize that gender is not quite as fixed and constant as they may have believed. Furthermore, those who experience psychological conflict about their gender may learn that a new designation is not only possible but desirable.

# ■ REEVALUATING EARLIER GENDER ROLE STANDARDS AND LEARNING NEW ONES

Gender role expectations exist at the cultural, institutional, interpersonal, and individual levels. As later adolescents learn about these expectations, they must integrate and synthesize them with their assessments of their personal needs and goals. The content of gender role standards—that is, the cultural and subcultural expectations concerning the appropriate behavior of male and female individuals—is different for later adolescents than for young children. This content changes as a result of changing age-related expectations and social change. For a 6- or 7-year-old boy, it may have been important to learn to be tough and not to cry or whimper, to stand up for himself, and not to hit girls. For a young man in later adolescence, the gender role expectations may include holding a steady job, demonstrating sexual prowess, or being competitive. For a 6- or 7-year-old girl, on the other hand, the emphasis may have been on taking turns, not being too bossy, and staying clean. For a young woman in later adolescence, gender role expectations may focus on being a caring, supportive friend; expressing maternal, nurturant behavior; or having an attractive figure and knowing how to dress well.

In later adolescence, young men and women begin to develop an analysis of what it takes to "get ahead" in their social world, whether success is defined as finding a mate, getting a good job, being a good parent, or being popular. They may learn to be more flexible in their interpersonal behavior, modifying their strategy to suit their goals. They discover that such traits as assertiveness, goal-directed behavior, competitiveness, being a good communication partner, personal disclosure, and negotiation are all required in social situations, and they learn to develop and apply them as required. In previous generations, some of the aforementioned traits were considered "masculine" and some "feminine." Today, however, they are perceived as helpful to both men and women to be able to succeed in work and family life.

The knowledge base regarding the implications and consequences of gender for each individual broadens as new understanding about adult roles is acquired. The person's specific social system or social convoy operates to engage the individual by making demands for various degrees and amounts of gender-linked behavior. For example, in a national survey of college freshmen, students were asked to respond to a number of statements about attitudes and values. One of those statements was, "Activities of married women are best confined to home and family." In 1970, 48% of freshmen agreed with that statement; in 2000, only 22% of freshmen agreed ("Attitudes and Characteristics of Freshmen," 2001; U.S. Bureau of the Census, 1996). Historical trends modify the outlook of both men and women on their appropriate and "normative" roles.

Gender role standards may change within one's lifetime, even over the 10-year period from a person's early-school-age years to later adolescence. For example, mothers of daughters who were born in the 1970s may have emphasized early autonomy training and encouraged self-reliance, believing that their daughters were more likely to remain single longer and to enter nontraditional careers in which they would need to compete effectively with men. However, these girls entered adulthood in the 1990s, a period when many of the "traditionally feminine" qualities, such as good interpersonal skills, the capacity for empathy, and the ability to build bonds of connection with others, are making a fashionable comeback—not just at home but in industry and global affairs, and not just for women but for men as well.

As one considers the contemporary context of gender role expectations, it appears that the main U.S. culture is moving toward more flexible standards. Today, it is recognized that it benefits both men and women to be appropriately assertive and to be sensitive communicators. With the delay in age of marriage and the greater social acceptance of those who choose to be childless, former rigid expectations have been relaxed and replaced by a greater diversity of behavior that is considered acceptable for both men and women in our society. The greatest impact of this revision is on the later adolescent population as they formulate their gender identities. There are more options, choices, and goals, and fewer obstacles to expressing personal preferences.

Within this context of greater freedom from gender role stereotypes, however, certain ethnic groups face new conflicts between adhering to traditional cultural expectations and embracing gender roles that are less scripted. For example, Hispanic women experience a strong cultural emphasis on the role of women as mothers who are nurturant, virtuous, and devoted to their husbands and children. This gender role standard places pressure on them to restrict their occupational aspirations and to remain close to their family of origin, particularly when it comes to thinking about going to college or planning for a career (Chilman, 1993). In later adolescence, Hispanic women must review these expectations, weighing the benefits they have had from this kind of close, attentive mothering with their own changing desire for higher levels of educational and occupational attainment. As economic demands and educational opportunities have expanded, Hispanic women have found ways to satisfy their community's traditional expectations while still claiming some space for their own personal goals (Denner & Dunbar, 2004).

# ■ REVISING ONE'S CHILDHOOD IDENTIFICATION

The component of parental identification that contributes to gender identity is also reviewed and revised in later adolescence. During this time, young people begin to encounter a wide range of possible targets for identification. In the college environment, students meet teachers, residence hall counselors, and older students whose views and values may differ widely from those of their parents. Outside the college environment, workers meet supervisors, other workers, and social companions whose views and values may differ widely from those of their parents. Later adolescents may admire public figures, such as religious leaders, political leaders, artists, or scholars whose work and ideas are especially inspiring. In the process, later adolescents revisit the content of their parental identifications. They analyze those beliefs, attitudes, and values that they may have "swallowed whole" as children, evaluating which of them are still relevant to their own personal vision of themselves functioning as a man or a woman in their current situation. They try to determine whether the lessons they learned as children about how husbands and wives, fathers and mothers, men and women treat each other and think about each other remain applicable.

## ADDING A SEXUAL DIMENSION TO GENDER IDENTITY

In addition to revisions in parental identifications, later adolescents add a sexual dimension to their gender identity that did not play much of a role in their childhood gender role identifications. The biological changes of puberty must be incorporated into one's gender identity; adolescents must integrate an adult body into their self-concept. They become aware of their bodies as they experience changes in body shape, height, weight, and strength.

The changes associated with physical maturity for women—especially the development of breasts and the onset of menstruation—introduce new and compelling thoughts about the childbearing role and its place in the young woman's sense of self. These changes do not necessarily compel a young woman to accept the role of mother. However, they are a concrete reminder of her maternal potential and force her to confront her intentions about pregnancy and mothering as she integrates her physical self into a gender identity (Zilbach, 1993).

Notions of physical attractiveness become more salient during this time. Adolescents are aware that first impressions are based on physical appearance. Satisfaction with one's physical appearance provides an important basis for approaching social relations with a positive, optimistic outlook (Abell & Richards, 1996). Furthermore, it may influence one's attractiveness or initial desirability as a sexual partner. In contrast, dissatisfaction with one's physical appearance as integrated into the self-concept may interfere with the formation of positive social relationships, causing the person to approach interpersonal contacts with self-consciousness and a pessimistic expectation that he or she will be rejected.

Maturation of the hormonal system, which influences emotional arousal as well as sexual urges, contributes to the development of one's gender identity. The hormonal changes of puberty bring new sexual impulses as well as the capacity for reproduction. Hormonal changes may also contribute to changes in the basis of relationships. These changes call attention to new emotions, such as jealousy, love, depression over loss of love, sexual arousal, and passion. Individual differences in hormone levels are linked to gender role characteristics.

The general term for male sex hormones is **androgens**, the most prevalent of which is *testosterone*. Androgens, especially testosterone, are associated with sexual arousal, interest, and behavior. This relationship is observed in both men and women. For men, higher levels of androgens are associated with both increased sexual motivation and increased involvement in sexual activity. For women, higher levels of androgens are associated with increased sexual motivation, but estrogens appear to be implicated in their willingness to engage in sexual activity. This may be a result of the fact that estrogens contribute to the maturation of primary and secondary sex characteristics that make women more sexually attractive. In general, hormone levels are not as good a predictor of sexual activity for women as are the social contexts of family and peer group and the woman's own internalized standards about sexual behavior (Savin-Williams & Diamond, 2004).

## SEXUAL ORIENTATION

Sex, sexual orientation, and gender identity are three different constructs. **Sex** is biologically based and refers primarily to genetically guided genital and reproductive characteristics. **Sexual orientation** refers to erotic, romantic, and affectional attraction to people of the same sex, the opposite sex, or both sexes (Sexuality Information and Education Council of the United States, 2001). Sexual orientation can be understood along a continuum from completely heterosexual to bisexual to completely homosexual preferences. **Gender identity** refers to the meaning a person makes of being male or female and to the internalization of attitudes, beliefs, and values associated with male and female behaviors. Three terms that are often used in discussing gender identity are masculinity, femininity, and androgyny. Masculinity and femininity are separate dimensions, and people can have both masculine and feminine characteristics in varying degrees. In other words, some people can be highly masculine and only minimally feminine; others can be minimally masculine and feminine. **Masculinity** is typically associated with being instrumental and agentic (i.e., having leadership abilities, being assertive, taking control); **femininity** is typically associated with being expressive and communal (i.e., valuing interpersonal and spiritual development, being tender, sympathetic, and concerned about the well-being of others). **Androgyny** refers to the capacity to express both masculine and feminine characteristics as the situation demands. Androgynous men score high in both masculine and feminine characteristics in comparison to other men; androgynous women score high in both masculine and feminine characteristics in comparison to other women (Bem, 1993). When thinking of sexual orientation, it is important to realize that knowing a person's sex and sexual orientation does not allow one to predict that person's gender identity. Lesbians and gay men may be feminine, masculine, or androgynous.

Research on sexual orientation suggests that later adolescence is a common time for the emergence of a homosexual identity. During this time, young people begin a more active

*Girl Before a Mirror*, 1932/Pablo Picasso/© 2005 Estate of Pablo Picasso/Artists Rights Society (ARS), New York/Superstock

*The crystallization of gender identity requires the integration of one's sexuality, including physical appearance, primary and secondary sex characteristics, sexual drives, and fantasies. One's sexual identity is as much a mental representation as a physical reality.*

process of integrating their sexual fantasies, experiences of sexual arousal, and understanding about sexual behavior into a sexual identity (Herold & Marshall, 1996). Later adolescents who may have struggled with acknowledging and accepting their homosexual orientation during the high school period are likely to resolve these inner conflicts and disclose their sexual orientation to others. This process is fostered by support from at least one close person and by increasing involvement in the gay community. Although disclosure has its risks, failure to disclose or trying to continue to pass as heterosexual is typically associated with strong feelings of isolation and self-repudiation (Troiden, 1993).

Much of the progress on identifying one's sexual orientation takes place in the context of romantic relationships. In many early writings about the nature of homosexual couples, the concepts of gender identity and sexual orientation were blurred. One stereotype about homosexual relationships is that they are gendered like traditional heterosexual relationships—one partner playing the dominant or "male" role and the other partner playing the submissive or "female" role. Studies of same-sex couples reject this view. Lesbian and gay couples tend to have more equality in their relationships and greater flexibility than comparable heterosexual couples. Because the partners are of the same sex, they cannot rely on traditional gender role stereotypes to define their functions in the household. Rather, they have to find

solutions that meet their personal preferences and competencies and try to adapt to the constraints of other work or school commitments (Kurdek, 1995). In one study comparing gay and lesbian couples with cross-sex cohabiting couples, same-sex and mixed-sex couples who lived together appeared to be quite similar with respect to their "satisfaction as a couple." One noted difference was that the lesbian couples and the heterosexual men were more satisfied with the emotional expressiveness in their relationships and the amount of leisure time they spent together than were the gay men or the heterosexual women (Means-Christensen, Snyder, & Negy, 2003).

When viewed through a gendered lens, men tend to be more instrumental, achievement oriented, autonomous, and assertive than women; women tend to be more expressive, interpersonally oriented, and caring than men. Based on these gender differences, another misconception is that lesbian relationships are more likely to be *fused*, suffering from too great a need for connection, and gay relationships are more likely to suffer from *disengagement* and disruption (Krestan & Bepko, 1980). Research suggests that this description is overly simplistic. Just like heterosexual men and women, lesbians and gay men differ in their gender identities. As later adolescents engage in intimate relationships, the nature of their gender identity is clarified. Within the context of lesbian or gay relationships, the interaction between the partners helps each person clarify his or her gender identity. The conflicts that gay and lesbian partners experience with respect to power, decision making, sharing of responsibilities, disclosure, and closeness are not unlike the conflicts that heterosexual couples face as they take on roles and responsibilities in their relationship (Green, Bettinger, & Zachs, 1996).

## ■ INTEGRATING ONE'S GENDER IDENTITY

During later adolescence, young men and women formulate their gender identities as they encounter diverse and sometimes competing social messages, role relationships, sexual motives and activities, and dyadic interactions. These gender identities are situated in interpersonal, institutional, and cultural contexts. One of the salient factors contributing to the emergence of gender identity is *gender role preference*. This preference is based on an assessment of two factors: how well one can meet the cultural and social expectations associated with one's gender, and how positively one views the status associated with it. If later adolescents become aware that their gender prevents them from having access to resources, influence, and decision-making authority, they are likely to experience a decline in their gender role preference. This could happen to men as well as women, depending on the paths they choose to pursue and the gender biases they encounter. For example, in general, we tend to think of career aspirations as being stifled for women as a result of attitudes on the part of men who think that women are not suited to certain types of work. However, the reverse situation may apply to men who are interested in fields such as early childhood education or nursing.

If later adolescents perceive that, apart from real differences in ability, one gender group is treated with greater respect, given more opportunities, and responded to with more attention or greater rewards, then their gender role preferences are likely to be recalibrated. During the high school years, adolescent girls are likely to encounter stereotyped expectations that restrict their behavior, judge their appearance, or label them as "sluts" or "hos." Sometimes, these stereotypes intersect with race and social class, especially as they encounter negative expectations from teachers or suspiciousness from shopkeepers (Abrams, 2003). Strict cultural norms regarding femininity, especially about body type and sexual behavior, can result in negative affect and alienation. Although some young women give in to these pressures, others resist, refusing to give up their voice or their autonomy in the face of adult judgments:

> Well, a lot of adults—they look at me kinda like, "ooh, she's like really crazy looking," or something like that. And my mom always says "oh, people are gonna think you're a bad girl." And I'm like "Whatever. I don't care." (Abrams, 2003, p. 71)

It appears that college students do not see much of this type of gender discrimination or preference. They tend to view the college environment as providing many opportunities and equal access to resources for both male and female students. What is more, both male and female students feel equally oppressed by the stressors of college life and the uncertainties associated with the decisions they are trying to make. Typically, it is not until they enter the world of adult employment that they begin to experience the power differential that continues to operate to the benefit of White men in U.S. society (Heilman, 2001).

Later adolescents who enter the world of work at the end of high school are confronted by the power differential immediately and may experience intimidation that forces them to accept it. For example, a woman who makes two dollars per hour less than a male counterpart may be afraid to say anything because she needs the job. She will have to integrate the reality of what she experiences into the formulation of her gender identity. One strategy is to accept that this is the way things should be according to gender role norms—that women should defer to men, and their contributions should be treated as less worthwhile. Another strategy may be to look for a different kind of work, in a setting where women and men are paid equally.

The college population tends to set social trends by according more variety and less rigidity to gender-linked role expectations. Most studies find that during the college years, students become more flexible in their gender role attitudes and more egalitarian in their views about how men and women ought to function in school, work, family, and community life (Pascarella & Terenzini, 1991). On the other hand, the non-college population tends to set employment trends by breaking down barriers in many male-dominated areas of work, such as construction, trucking, and public safety. Individuals can shape and strengthen the nature of their gender identity by spending time with other people who support their views and values about how men and women ought to behave toward one another and what life paths are most desirable for them (Levitt, Guacci- Franco, & Levitt, 1993).

## ▌ INTERNALIZED MORALITY

The development of morality was introduced in Chapter 8. At early school age, morality consists primarily of internalizing parental standards and values, recognizing the difference between right and wrong, and learning to control one's behavior in anticipation of its moral consequences. As young people achieve new levels of autonomy from their parents and encounter new situations, they discover that some of the moral principles they learned as 6- or 7-year-olds neither apply to the new situation nor provide much of a rationale for why they should behave one way and not another. Later adolescents explore the distinction between *social conventions* and *moral issues*. Behaviors that may have been viewed as moral issues during childhood may be reevaluated as social conventions. Some aspects of one's childhood morality must be dissolved and restructured to meet the impending demands of adulthood.

Within the overall process of formulating a personal identity, later adolescents begin to see themselves as moral beings whose actions have implications for the well-being of others. They make moral commitments and judge their behavior and the behavior of others according to new moral standards (Damon, 1996). In the framework of forming a moral identity, the three elements of moral knowledge or judgment, caring, and action come together in an increasingly complex political, social, and interpersonal environment. Morality may be expressed in a variety of behaviors, including acts of consideration and kindness; resistance to temptation; opposition to unfair laws, rules, or practices; and contributions of time, money, or other resources to enhance the well-being of others. The following sections examine Kohlberg's analysis regarding advances in moral reasoning, experiences that promote moral reasoning, and the expansion of research on moral development, which includes prosocial behavior and the ethics of care.

## ■ NEW COGNITIVE CAPACITIES

Later adolescents bring new cognitive capacities to the arena of moral decision making. They are able to use abstract reasoning to consider the logical consequences of their actions, both for themselves and for others. They can project alternative paths in a probabilistic future. They are also able to consider the multiple perspectives that are possible in a moral situation. They are increasingly aware of the rights and needs of others, and they are able to step outside the situation in order to examine how an action may satisfy their own needs but harm others. Later adolescents can reflect about how principles of social responsibility, human rights, and justice can be preserved in a moral decision.

## ■ STAGES OF MORAL REASONING

Building on Piaget's theory of cognitive development, Lawrence Kohlberg (Colby & Kohlberg, 1987; Kohlberg, 1964, 1969) suggested that a qualitative change in a person's ability to reason about moral issues is expected from early school age to later adolescence. With age and exposure to moral conflicts, moral reasoning advances in much the same way that other domains of logical reasoning mature, from an early reliance on direct perceptions and immediate consequences to more complex, abstract, and relativistic judgments. Kohlberg's theory includes three levels of moral reasoning divided into six substages (see Chapter 8, Table 8.2).

At Stage I, the **preconventional level**, from about age 4 to 10, children judge an action as morally justifiable based on the immediate consequences of the behavior and the approval of powerful authority figures. Stage II, the **conventional level**, from about age 10 to 18, reflects a concern about the maintenance of the existing rules and laws, and a respect for legitimate authority. Stage III, the **postconventional** level of

moral reasoning, from about age 18 into adulthood, brings an awareness of social, cultural, and political processes that result in the formulation of rules and laws. Morality is viewed as a system of rules that are agreed upon in order to preserve human rights and social order. These rules are understood as having been created in cultural and historical contexts, and can be altered as the norms of the community change. Beyond this appreciation for the cultural relativism of moral principles, there may emerge a commitment to overarching universal moral principles, including greater concern for the value of human life, human dignity, and justice for all members of society. The proportion of people who reach this final level of moral reasoning is small, but it increases during early and middle adulthood.

Longitudinal data provide evidence of the sequential nature of these stages during childhood and adolescence (Colby & Kohlberg, 1987; Colby, Kohlberg, Gibbs, & Lieberman, 1983; Nisan & Kohlberg, 1982; Snarey, Reimer, & Kohlberg, 1985). The sequence of stages proposed by Kohlberg is noted in a variety of cultures outside the United States. Research confirming this has been done in Israel, Turkey, the Bahamas, Honduras, Mexico, India, Kenya, Nigeria, and Taiwan. Participants in these studies used forms of reasoning similar to those used by U.S. samples. The adults and adolescents in every culture used levels of reasoning that were higher than those used by the children (Colby & Kohlberg, 1987; Dawson, 2002; Nisan & Kohlberg, 1982; Rest, 1983; Snarey et al., 1985). The stages reflect qualitatively distinct ways of reasoning about moral dilemmas that are supported by increasingly complex cognitive capacities (Dawson, 2003).

## ■ EXPERIENCES THAT PROMOTE MORAL REASONING

Later adolescents must formulate an integrated value system with which to guide their behavior, particularly in the face of strong pressures to violate their moral beliefs. Young people encounter situations that they have never faced before—situations that require moral evaluation, judgment, and decisions about action. College students may be asked to lend a paper that they have written so that another student can turn it in as his or her own work. Dilemmas about using illegal drugs, stealing books and journals from the library, or maintaining religious traditions and practices may confront a young person who is away from home for the first time. In these situations, the young person has the opportunity to envision the self as a moral actor and take a course of action most congruent with other facets of her or his personal identity.

Although the *sequence* of moral stages appears to be well established, the *level* of moral reasoning that an individual actually attains depends on the kinds of moral challenges and situations encountered. For college students, like the one in the following example, the academic curriculum itself often creates a degree of cognitive disequilibrium that promotes a revision in moral reasoning:

I was taking a theology class as a freshman in college and was presented with "bold" alternatives to understand and interpret the creation story—primarily to understand it as a myth. My life up to that point was characterized by asking many questions but arriving at few answers. To those in my fundamentalist background, those questions were annoyances but not insurmountable problems. In my shift to some answers to those questions, I moved away from fundamentalism to a more broadly based and responsible manner of critical thinking. [What happened?] The professor was very bright and responsible, yet in a sophisticated way he was somewhat irreverent. I was troubled by the dilemmas that this posed for me in terms of my belief structures, but something about the information and the self-assurance of the professor encouraged me to embrace this new way of thinking. (Chickering & Reisser, 1993, p. 240)

Through participation in thought-provoking discussions or challenging life experiences, moral reasoning can advance to the next higher level. Social and educational experiences tend to promote moral reasoning when they draw on existing constructs, but they also challenge those constructs by making their inadequacies clear (Gfellner, 1986). During later adolescence, young people are exposed to a broader social context at work, in their college courses, or through greater involvement in community and national affairs. Many young people participate in community service, such as volunteering at a soup kitchen or tutoring younger children in reading or math. These experiences can stimulate discussions about differing points of view and a more complex analysis of the many interdependent factors that contribute to the social order. In fact, some communities have established youth development programs that involve adolescents in community service. As a result, a growing number of young people are likely to have new insights into moral situations (Mason & Gibbs, 1993; Yates & Youniss, 1996; Nasir & Kirshner, 2003).

Exposure to a diversity of information, relationships, and worldviews stimulates moral reasoning. The change from conventional to postconventional morality that begins during adolescence involves a rethinking of traditional moral principles. During this period, there may be a loosening of ties to the family of origin and an increase in encounters with an expanding network of friends, students, and coworkers. Through interactions with diverse reference groups, there is an increasing recognition of the subcultural relativity of one's moral code. There may also be a degree of conflict over which moral values have personal meaning.

## ■ EXPANSIONS OF KOHLBERG'S VIEW OF MORAL DEVELOPMENT

Kohlberg's view of moral development focuses on reasoning or moral knowledge, not on the emotional or behavioral aspects of morality. One criticism of the theory is that studies do not find a consistent relationship between a person's level of moral reasoning and that person's willingness to behave in a morally caring way. For example, several studies have taken

the approach of identifying *moral exemplars*—people who have dedicated themselves to improving the lives of others—and comparing them to others who are not especially exemplary (Hart & Fegley, 1995). The moral exemplars are not more complex or advanced in their *reasoning* than the comparison group. What the exemplars demonstrate is a **moral identity**—a sense in which they define themselves in moral terms and evaluate their behavior against moral standards. Moral identity reflects an integration of parental socialization about caring for others, an appreciation for the cultural and social contexts of moral actions, and experiences that have required moral action (Blasi, 1984; Reimer, 2003).

A second criticism of Kohlberg's approach to understanding moral development is that his theory is based on a specific method that emphasizes **prohibitive** moral judgments, in which a person is asked to reach a decision about violating a law or breaking a promise in order to achieve some other goal. A typical example is the case of Heinz, a man who is faced with the dilemma of having to steal a drug from a pharmacist if he is to save his wife's life. These dilemmas place justice—usually framed in terms of the legitimate needs or rights of the individual—in conflict with rules, laws, authority figures, and the obligations associated with adhering to these rules or laws.

Not all moral dilemmas are of this type, however. Some moral judgments involve a conflict between doing something helpful for someone else and meeting one's own needs. An example would be stopping to help a person whose car has stalled on the highway at the risk of being late for a very important job interview. These dilemmas are described as **prosocial judgments**. The prosocial aspect of morality includes a concern for the welfare and rights of others and a willingness to act in order to benefit or enhance the lives of others. Just as society depends on people adhering to rules and laws in order to preserve order, it also depends on a commitment to caring. People seem to be able to think more flexibly about a prosocial moral dilemma than about a prohibitive one. Moral decisions that draw on empathy and concern for the well-being of another person tend to evoke a higher level of moral reasoning than those that would require breaking a law (Eisenberg & Fabes, 1998; Eisenberg & Strayer, 1987; Kurdek, 1981).

Expanding on the theme of prosocial morality, Carol Gilligan (1977, 1982/1993, 1988) challenged Kohlberg's perspective, arguing that his description of the developmental course of reasoning about moral dilemmas is incomplete because it is based largely on the reasoning of male respondents about hypothetical rather than real-life situations. She claimed that men and women have distinct orientations toward moral dilemmas. According to Gilligan, women approach moral decisions with greater sensitivity to the context of the problem and a strong sense of **caring**, focusing on one's responsibility for others and feelings of connection to them. Gilligan asserted that men, in contrast, emphasize abstract principles, rules and laws, and the conflicts between the rights of the parties involved in the conflict. A woman, for example, might ask

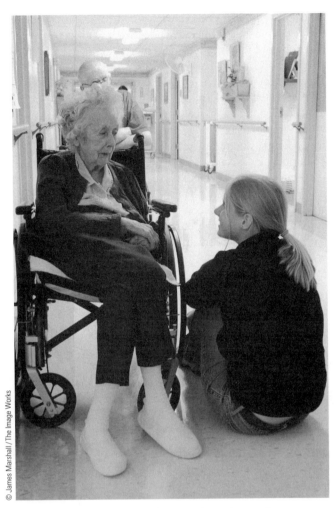

The caring orientation is evidenced when Alison volunteers to spend time visiting with older adults in a nursing home in her university community.

which outcome of a moral dilemma would result in the least harm for all concerned; whereas a man might ask whether one person has the right to infringe on the rights of others (Friedman, Robinson, & Friedman, 1987). These differences, according to Gilligan, are the product of different socialization patterns and result in different orientations to values, family life, and the basis of self-worth.

Several investigators have examined the claims of consistent differences between men and women in moral orientation. The literature is inconclusive regarding the strength and consistency with which men and women differ in their use of what have come to be called the *justice orientation* and the *caring orientation*. It appears that experiential and situational issues as well as concerns about interpersonal obligations and caring are more dominant in open-ended responses from both men and women than are issues of justice and individual rights. However, with age, both men and women add more autonomous, justice-oriented reasoning to their repertoire (Colby & Damon, 1994; Galotti, 1989; Galotti, Kozberg, & Farmer, 1991; Walker, de Vries, & Trevethan, 1987). The

tendency of men and women to approach a moral dilemma using a justice-based or a care-based form of reasoning is dependent on the social distance between the self and the other person involved. Regardless of gender, a caring orientation is more likely when the other person is viewed as a close friend or a member of one's relevant social group; a justice orientation is more likely when the other person is viewed as a member of an outgroup, a stranger, or when the nature of the relationship to the other person is not specified (Ryan, David, & Reynolds, 2004)

In studies of prosocial behavior and empathic response to others, gender differences are commonly observed. Women report more caring behaviors, are rated as being more kind and considerate than men, emphasize the importance of helping others as a value, and exhibit more personal distress when faced with the distress of others (Eisenberg & Morris, 2004). In many cultures, family socialization practices emphasize the importance of prosocial behavior and social responsibility for female children. As a result of this focus, perhaps women are more likely than men to integrate a prosocial orientation into their gender identity (Froming, Nasby, & McManus, 1998).

The process of achieving a moral identity is made more difficult in a pluralistic society, where one's moral concerns may be at odds with others' social concerns. This is especially evident in situations where individualist values clash with a collectivist perspective. Certain groups are consistently wronged by deeply ingrained inequalities in the social structure. Acts of resistance or subversion by groups in positions of less power may be labeled as immoral by those in higher positions and as heroic by those in the disenfranchised groups (Turiel, 2003). In later adolescence, young people begin to appreciate the moral ambiguities of their communities and may take action to express their commitments to justice and care through individual or group efforts. Whereas some young people appear to be characterized by self-indulgence and social indifference, others are intensely engaged in actions fueled by the passion of moral indignation.

## CAREER CHOICE

The choice of occupation sets the tone for one's early adult lifestyle. The world of work determines one's daily routine, including the time one wakes up, daily activities, expenditures of physical and mental energy, and conditions for both immediate and long-term rewards. Because one's occupation has implications for income and earning potential, one's career choice will influence one's personal financial resources and opportunities. Occupation confers social status and provides varying opportunities for advancement. Finally, it represents a direct or indirect expression of one's value system. In subsequent chapters, we will discuss socialization in the work setting and the management of a career. Here, we focus on the process of career choice and its impact on development during later adolescence.

## ■ WORK EXPERIENCES
## IN EARLY ADOLESCENCE

Many adolescents hold part-time jobs while they attend high school. In 2002, 47% of 16- to 19-year-olds were in the labor force, and 16% were unemployed—meaning that they were recently fired or had been unsuccessful in looking for work during the preceding 4 weeks (U.S. Census Bureau, 2003). There is some controversy about the benefits of working during high school and the extent to which these work experiences actually make a positive contribution to the occupational component of identity development. Some have found that adolescents who work long hours in stressful jobs are more likely to evidence increased cigarette smoking, marijuana and alcohol use, truancy, and poor academic performance in school (Manning, 1990; Steinberg & Dornbusch, 1991). Students who work long hours have less time for school activities, socialization with friends, or the development of other areas of interest. The kinds of work opportunities that are available to adolescents are usually minimally skilled jobs with high turnover, low pay, little decision-making responsibility, and little stimulation of skill development. These kinds of jobs are likely to produce depression and low self-esteem and may contribute to feelings of alienation from the school environment. For some adolescents, the time spent in these kinds of work settings is associated with the development of cynical attitudes toward work and greater acceptance of unethical practices by workers.

Other researchers have emphasized the diversity of work experiences and the potential benefits of certain kinds of work. Students who are able to find and keep a good job may feel more confident about themselves and their promise for future employment. When the work does not involve too many hours, and when it involves skill development that young people see as related to their future career direction, the experience is likely to be associated with higher levels of well-being and less involvement in problem behaviors. For girls, the perception of continuity between school and work and the feeling that work improves one's school performance had an especially positive relationship with mental health and well-being (Mortimer, Finch, Shanahan, & Ryu, 1992; Mortimer & Johnson, 1999).

## ■ FACTORS INFLUENCING CAREER CHOICE

As Figure 11.1 suggests, career choice is influenced by six major factors: individual, psychosocial-emotional, socioeconomic, societal, familial, and situational (O'Neil et al., 1980). These same factors contribute to gender role socialization. It is important to see the interrelationship of these two domains

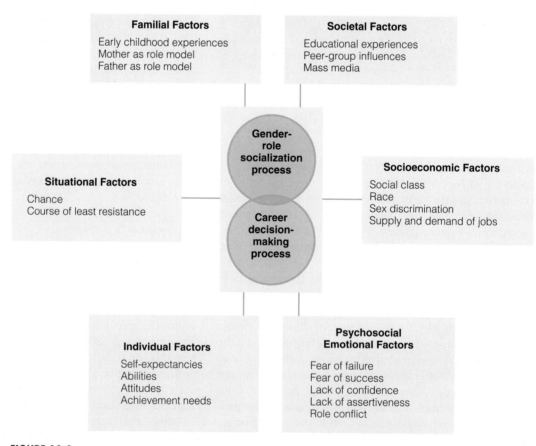

**FIGURE 11.1**

Factors Affecting the Gender Role Socialization and Career Decision-Making Process

Source: O'Neil, Ohlde, Barke, Prosser-Gelwick, and Garfield, 1980.

for young people in our culture. Gender role socialization creates a powerful filter through which choices related to career development are made (Eccles, 1987). Gender role stereotyping may apply to certain occupational fields, thereby limiting their desirability to those with traditional gender role expectations. Over time, as the process of identity formation unfolds, involvement in careers and exposure to nontraditional role models can also modify one's gender identity.

Of the six types of factors described in Figure 11.1, high school and college students reported that the individual factors, such as abilities, achievement needs, attitudes, and self-expectancies, most strongly affected their career decision making. They perceived familial, societal, and socioeconomic factors as having little or no impact (O'Neil et al., 1980). This is contrary to social science research evidence. Family factors play a key role in shaping educational aspirations and occupational goals. Societal and socioeconomic conditions are major factors influencing the job market and the chances of both employment and advancement.

**FAMILY BACKGROUND AND CAREER OPPORTUNITIES.** Family background characteristics, including parents' occupation, educational background, income, culture, and community, are associated with educational opportunities, aspirations, and academic achievement from early school age through the high school and college years. In the period of early adolescence, children from low-income families and from families in which the parents did not graduate from high school are more likely to drop out of high school and less likely to be enrolled in postsecondary education. Of the seniors graduating from high school in 1999, 66% of European-American, non-Hispanic students went on to college, compared to 55% of African Americans and 53% of Hispanic students (National Center for Education Statistics, 2003). Children whose parents are in the top 25% of family income are 10 times more likely to graduate from college than children from families in the lowest 25% of family income (Halperin, 1998). Differences in families' ability to support occupational exploration, the parents' own occupational attainments, and their ideas about ideal career paths influence their children's career decision-making process. For example, in a comparison of Chinese American and European American youth, the Chinese Americans emphasized the importance of entrepreneurial opportunities in their career interests, and the European Americans emphasized the importance of social features (Leong, Kao, & Lee, 2004; Marjoribanks, 1997–1998).

**EDUCATION AND CAREER CHOICE.** Differences in family resources result in diverging educational backgrounds, which have direct implications for the kinds of careers one is prepared to enter. In 2000, 66% of public high school graduates went on to college; 90% of private high school graduates went on to college (National Center for Educational Statistics, 2003). It is well documented that career advancement and the associated earnings are closely linked to levels of educational attainment. Table 11.1 shows the median earned income on the basis of educational level for men and women who were

**Table 11.1** Median Annual Income of Men and Women 25 Years and Older, 2001, by Level of School Completed and Sex

| EDUCATION | Median Annual Income ($) | |
|---|---|---|
| | MEN | WOMEN |
| 9th to 12th grade, no diploma | 28,890 | 24,318 |
| High school graduate | 37,362 | 26,660 |
| Some college, no degree | 44,377 | 31,698 |
| Bachelor's degree or more | 80,170 | 50,220 |

Source: U.S. Census Bureau, 2003.

25 years or older in 2001. Educational attainment has a significant relationship to annual income. As the data indicate, however, educational achievement does not result in the same economic advantages for men and women. Women with 1 to 3 years of college earned less than men who were high school graduates (U.S. Census Bureau, 2003).

For youth who leave high school or who graduate but do not go on to college, the job market has several unattractive features:

> Most of the jobs available at this level of educational attainment are routine, menial, temporary, more likely to be part time and to provide reduced monetary and nonmaterial rewards compared with jobs held by older workers. . . . Moreover, jobs within this sector are unusually unstable and may be supervised by rigid, autocratic employers, many of whom, particularly in the fast food industry, are not much older than the novice worker (Borman & Hopkins, 1987, p. 136).

The impact of school experiences on subsequent career development goes beyond whether one plans to attend college or not. Vocational coursework of a specific nature, such as agricultural training; an emphasis on math and science courses; and frequent conversations with teachers about one's work-related decisions are all associated with higher income and more stable work records after high school. Identity formation, self-insight, and active clarification of work values are all related to greater career confidence and more mature career decision making (Schulenberg, Vondracek, & Kim, 1993; Vondracek, Schulenberg, Skorikov, & Gillespie, 1995).

For those who do not go on to college, career development is a bumpy path. In a 10-year follow-up to a report on 18- to 24-year-olds who do not go on to college, full- and part-time employment rates were lower in 1997 than they were in 1989, inflation-adjusted earnings were significantly lower, and more than 25% of those working full-time were making less than $16,000 per year (Halperin, 1998).

Given the kinds of jobs that are available and the outlook on work that is developed during high school, many young people start out with a rather cavalier approach to work. They take whatever job is available, work without much intention of long-term commitment, and exhibit erratic work behavior.

After high school, Rick decided to work in a local fish market. He will probably quit when he has earned enough money to buy the truck he has been wanting. Then he'll travel for a while and get a job in another town.

© Paul A. Souders/CORBIS

For example, in a survey carried out by the Junior Achievement Program, employers found that most high school graduates working for their companies were unprepared to meet their high-priority workplace skills, including punctuality, dependability, and completing work assignments on time ("Students, Employers Disagree," 1998). Because most of these jobs do not require much training, one might infer that young workers are simply not motivated to approach them with high levels of conscientiousness. They are likely to quit these jobs when they have earned enough money to pay for the things they want, and then remain unemployed for a while until they need more money.

When they reach their 20s, a second phase of career development begins, as young adults become more serious about their work. They try to find a good job, become more conscientious about their work performance, and stay with the job for a longer period. This new seriousness about work is likely to be associated with other commitments, especially marriage, and is usually seen as a positive step in the transition to adulthood.

In modern, postindustrialized societies, the path toward occupational attainment is intimately linked to the educational aspirations and achievements expressed in high school. In a longitudinal study of students who were high school seniors in 1980, 36% of those who said they hoped to earn a bachelor's degree had done so by 1986. In comparison, only 7% of those who expected to attend less than 4 years of college had earned a bachelor's degree by 1986 (National Center for Education Statistics, 1995).

**GENDER ROLE SOCIALIZATION AND CAREER CHOICE.**
Gender role socialization shapes career decisions through two significant psychological factors: (1) perceptions of ability, and (2) career-related values and goals. First, as a result of

socialization, men and women are likely to form different expectations about their ability to succeed at various career-related skills. Self-expectancies about the ability to fulfill the educational requirements and the job duties of specific careers are a major factor in determining career choices. Recall from Chapter 9 (Middle Childhood) the discussion of parents' expectations about their children's competence in certain skill areas and its relation to the child's own perceptions of competence. In a longitudinal study, mothers' gender-stereotyped beliefs about their young child's math and science abilities predicted their child's self-perceptions of math and science self-efficacy 2 years after high school. Mothers' predictions of their child's ability to succeed in a math-oriented career was a significant predictor of their college-age child's career choice (Bleeker & Jacobs, 2004). In the process of career decision making, strong gender-typed conceptualizations of the job demands of specific careers intervene to screen out some alternatives and highlight others (Gati, Osipow, & Givon, 1995; Stromquist, 1991). For example, there is a clear path from belief in one's competence in math to aspirations about careers in math, science, and engineering (Correll, 2001). Gendered beliefs about mathematics competence, influenced in part by parental expectations, may contribute to the persistent gender divide with respect to women enrolling in university and graduate programs in mathematics, physics, and engineering. Studies of career choice or career aspirations find that women with a strong sense of their own goals, an awareness of their personal needs, and an ability to cope realistically with stress have been more likely to adopt a nontraditional career choice.

Second, as a result of socialization, women and men are likely to establish different value hierarchies, reflecting different long-range life goals. For example, one study compared college students' work goals, the goals viewed as likely to be

**Table 11.2** Life Objectives Considered Essential or Very Important by College Freshmen, 2000

| OBJECTIVE | MEN (%) | WOMEN (%) |
|---|---|---|
| Becoming accomplished in a performing art | 13.3 | 15.5 |
| Becoming an authority in my field | 61.6 | 58.1 |
| Obtaining recognition from colleagues for contributions to field | 51.7 | 50.8 |
| Influencing the political structure | 20.4 | 15.3 |
| Influencing social values | 33.5 | 40.9 |
| Raising a family | 72.7 | 73.4 |
| Having administrative responsibility for the work of others | 39.4 | 34.8 |
| Being very well off financially | 76.1 | 71.1 |
| Helping others who are in difficulty | 52.8 | 68.8 |
| Making a theoretical contribution to science | 18.9 | 13.7 |
| Writing original works | 15.2 | 14.4 |
| Creating artistic work | 13.7 | 15.7 |
| Becoming successful in own business | 45.1 | 34.6 |
| Becoming involved in programs to clean up environment | 17.4 | 17.5 |
| Developing a meaningful philosophy of life | 43.1 | 41.8 |
| Participating in a community-action program | 18.5 | 26.1 |
| Helping to promote racial understanding | 28.1 | 32.9 |
| Keeping up to date with political affairs | 31.8 | 25.1 |
| Being a community leader | 31.4 | 30.4 |
| Integrating spirituality into my life | 41.3 | 48.1 |

Source: Adapted from *Chronicle of Higher Education, 2001*, p. 23.

achieved in certain careers (called *goal affordances*), and the link between goal affordances and how interesting the career was to the students (Morgan, Isaac, & Sansone, 2001). Women rated interpersonal goals as more important and high pay and high status goals as less important than men. Both men and women viewed careers in physical and mathematical science as offering less in the way of interpersonal goals and more in the way of salary and status. As a result, women were less interested in careers in physical and mathematical science and less likely to identify those fields as career choices.

The consequences of gender role socialization for career choice can be seen in the objectives that freshmen entering college in 2000 said were essential or very important in their lives (see Table 11.2). Although men and women shared many common objectives, about 7% more women than men endorsed social values, 16% more women than men emphasized helping others who were in difficulty, and 7% more women than men expressed a desire to integrate spirituality into their lives. About 10% more men than women valued becoming successful in their own business ("Attitudes and Characteristics of Freshmen," 2001). Values are likely to direct students toward majors and future careers that will help them experience a sense of personal integrity and achieve a balance between what they say is important and what they do.

Gender identity is shaped by cultural values that may determine one's career goals and related choices. In a study of the educational and occupational attainment of low-income, rural Appalachian women, the importance of family socialization influences was highlighted (Wilson, Peterson, & Wilson, 1993). These families tend to have strong kinship ties and high levels of consensus about norms for appropriate behaviors. They endorse traditional gender roles in which the men are the dominant decision makers and the women are expected to be homemakers and also hold low-paying jobs to help support the family. Educational and occupational aspirations are generally higher for male than for female children in these families, but both are encouraged to restrict their aspirations to career options that will keep them close to their childhood homes.

## ■ CAREER DECISION MAKING

The idea of career decision making must be evaluated in light of rapid changes in the nature of work, the pervasiveness of the two-earner family lifestyle, the increased likelihood of multiple job and career changes over the life course, and the constant reconfiguration of the job market—especially the current trends toward "downsizing," "workforce reductions," and "retraining" (Church, 1993). The idea of occupational choice should not be confused with choice about labor mar-

*Many women enter professions that emphasize helping others. What might account for this trend?*

© L.W.A.-Dann Tardif/corbisstockmarket.com

ket participation. Although they may have a wide choice in the kind of work they will do, most people in the United States do not have a choice about whether to work or not. In fact, 5.5% of young people in the 20–24 age range have more than one job (U.S. Census Bureau, 2003).

Career choice reflects a central component of a person's emerging identity. For some young people, occupational choice is a reflection of continued identification with their parents. They may select the same job or career as that of one of their parents, or they may select a career because it reflects their parents' aspirations for them. Little personal choice is involved. For some young people, primarily women, there continues to be a path of primary identification with the roles of wife and mother, with only secondary investment in the labor market. Many of these women, especially those who marry and have children after high school, return to school or to technical training in their 30s and 40s in order to pick up the thread of career development, either as a result of divorce or when their children get older. Increasing numbers of men and women realize that their occupational career will need to be coordinated and integrated with that of their spouse. In anticipation of a dual-earner lifestyle, young people begin to screen their career aspirations through the lens of the compatibility of job demands with family commitments and personal aspirations.

Concerns about future educational and career decisions constitute a major source of worry for college students. Of the students entering college as freshmen in 2000, 72% said that an important reason for going to college was to be able to get a better job ("Attitudes and Characteristics of Freshmen," 2001). Many people assume that the younger a person is when he or she makes a career choice, the better. Most career development professionals, however, advise that a decision about a career be delayed until later adolescence or early

adulthood. The concept of **career maturity** suggests that with increased cognitive and affective development, a person develops decision-making strategies, gains access to information, and achieves a degree of self-insight that permit a realistic and consistent choice (Schmitt-Rodermund & Silbereisen, 1998). A person who delays the decision has a clearer sense of his or her adult interests and goals. By delaying the career decision, one also has more opportunities to explore alternative work scenarios and to understand more about the labor market.

Nonetheless, high schools, colleges, and various industries urge young people to make career choice decisions as early as possible. Thus, some of the tension that later adolescents experience in connection with a choice of career is a product of the lack of fit between socialization pressures and their own developmental timetable. With the increased likelihood of living to be 80 years old, there is no great rush to decide on a career by age 20. In the United States, the average person with a bachelor's degree has 10 jobs between the ages of 18 and 36 (U.S. Census Bureau, 2003). In this context, selecting the first career ought to be viewed as an extension of one's occupational education, not a decision that has to last a lifetime.

**PHASES OF CAREER DECISION MAKING.** Once a person begins to accept certain elements of her or his self-concept as they relate to the occupational aspect of identity, the process of career decision making begins. Tiedeman (Tiedeman & O'Hara, 1963; Tiedeman & Miller-Tiedeman, 1985) developed a model of the phases of career decision making. This model illustrates how making career-related decisions helps to clarify one's occupational identity and, at the same time, uses the context of work to promote new learning about other aspects of the self (see Figure 11.2). A career decision depends on the outcomes of several tasks during adolescence and early

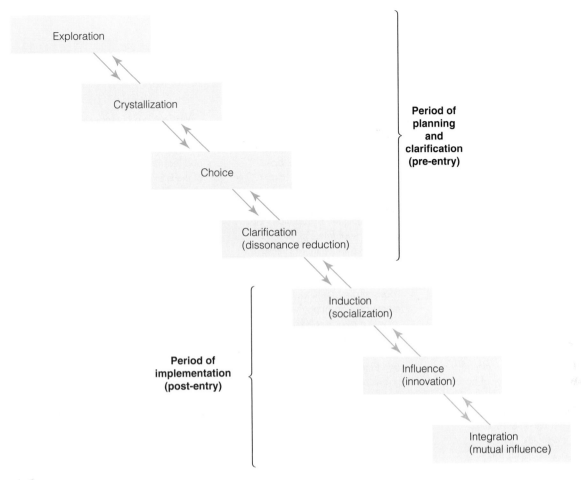

**FIGURE 11.2**

Seven Phases of Career Decision Making

Source: Based on Tiedeman and O'Hara, 1963.

adulthood. With effective problem solving, the person gains increased control over life events and is better prepared to meet the challenges of the next phase of decision making. Tiedeman identified seven phases; the first four emphasize planning and clarification; the last three emphasize implementation. The model reflects an individual's capacity for ongoing adaptation and change. At each phase in the process, people can redefine the self and transcend the conditions of the work environment to change their minds (Miller-Tiedeman, 1999).

In the **exploration phase**, the person realizes that a career decision must be made and therefore begins to learn more about those aspects of the self and the occupational world that are relevant to the impending decision. The person begins to generate alternatives for action. Uncertainty about the future and the many possible alternatives is accompanied by feelings of anxiety.

In the **crystallization phase**, the person becomes more aware of the alternatives for action and their consequences. Conflicts among alternatives are recognized, and some are discarded. The person develops a strategy for making the decision, in part by weighing the costs and benefits of each alternative.

In the **choice phase**, the person decides which action alternative to follow. The decision is solidified in the person's mind as he or she elaborates the reasons why the decision is beneficial. There is a sense of relief and optimism as the person develops a commitment to executing the decision.

In the **clarification phase**, the person more fully understands the consequences of the commitment to the decision that has been made. He or she plans definite steps to take and may actually take them or may delay them until a more appropriate time. The self-image is prepared to be modified by the decision.

During the **induction phase**, the person encounters the new career environment for the first time. He or she wants to be accepted and looks to others for cues about how to behave. The person identifies with the new group and seeks recognition for his or her unique characteristics. Gradually, the self-image is modified as the person begins to believe in the values and goals of the new group.

In the **influence phase**, the person is very much involved with the new group. He or she becomes more assertive in asking that the group perform better. The person also tries to influence the group to accommodate some of his or her

## TECHNOLOGY AND HUMAN DEVELOPMENT

## Career Exploration on the Web

THE CAREER EXPLORATION process is an active, creative effort to link your interests, talents, skills, values, and goals with possible occupations. The Internet provides a vast world of resources that can support this process. The following phases of career exploration can be enhanced through online resources:

1. *Exploration.* Know enough about your own personality, interests, abilities, and values to select several appropriate occupations. A number of occupational inventories are available, such as the *Campbell Interest and Skill Survey*, which shows how your interests compare to those of people who are already employed in a wide variety of occupations. You can read more about this inventory by visiting http://www.pearsonassessments.com/tests/ciss.htm#scales

    Sometimes inventories are available online. The *Self-Directed Search*, developed by John Holland, can be taken online for a small fee. His method links personality types with families of careers. The inventory helps you create a profile of your personality along six dimensions and provides you with a list of occupations in which workers share this personality profile. If you want to consider this approach, go to the website http://www.self-directedsearch.com

2. *Crystallization.* Find out as much as possible about the occupations that best match your interests and personality. Two excellent resources that can support this process are
   - The America's Career Infonet, sponsored by the U.S. Department of Labor: http://www.acinet.org/acinet/explore.asp
   - JobWeb, a site developed by the National Association of Colleges and Employers: http://www.jobweb.com

    Both sites give information about career paths, links to job opportunities by location, information about how to prepare for these careers, and resources that can be helpful in funding your training.

3. *Choice.* Learn by doing. Many career counselors suggest volunteering or doing an internship as an excellent way to discover the realities of the career you have chosen.

WetFeet is a career exploration website that provides excellent resources for identifying internships and learning how to make the most of these experiences. It also includes first-person accounts from students who report about their internship experiences. To learn more about internships at WetFeet, visit http://www.wetfeet.com/advice/internships.asp

   If you want even more information, go to Google (http://www.google.com) and search for specific internships in your chosen field.

4. *Clarification.* Investigate the future job market, career ladder, and wage trends in the occupations you are considering. The Bureau of Labor Statistics has this information, published in the *Occupational Outlook Handbook*. Revised every 2 years, the handbook describes what workers do on the job, working conditions, the training and education needed, earnings, and expected job prospects in a wide range of occupations. You can access the fields you are interested in by visiting http://www.bls.gov/oco/

---

values. The self is strongly committed to group goals. During this phase, the group's values and goals may be modified to include the orientation of the new member.

Finally, in the **integration phase**, group members react against the new member's attempts to influence them. The new member then compromises. In the process, he or she attains a more objective understanding of the self and the group. A true collaboration between the new member and the group is achieved. The new member feels satisfied and is evaluated as successful by the self and others.

This model emphasizes continuous interaction between the individual and the work context. At first, interaction is necessary to clarify the person's talents and choice of career. Later, it is necessary to achieve a satisfactory level of adaptation to the work environment. At each juncture, whether the decision relates to college major, occupation, job change, or career redirection, effective decision making involves all seven phases.

**THE IMPACT OF THE LABOR MARKET ON CAREER DECISION MAKING.** Each birth cohort faces unique labor market conditions as they enter the career search process in later adolescence and early adulthood. Characteristics of the contemporary labor market may be contributing to new difficulties that later adolescents encounter as they attempt to move through the first four phases of Tiedeman's model:

- The increasing number of jobs and careers available make the exploration phase more difficult.
- As a result of changes in technology and in organizational structure, some skills become obsolete and some job markets dry up. A career may become obsolete in the time it takes a young person to prepare for it.
- As established firms lose their identities in corporate mergers, identification with a particular company ceases to be appropriate.

© Bob Daemmrich / The Image Works

*With changing technologies, new careers are constantly emerging. Victoria is a controller at Johnson Space Center. The ongoing exploration of space will open up careers that are not yet imagined.*

- As most large companies go through restructuring and downsizing, the people who are left are asked to do more tasks of a greater variety. In addition to one's special area of training, it is important to develop support skills, such as word processing, data management, literature search skills, and verbal and written communication skills.
- New careers emerge at a rapid pace. From the time one enters the choice phase to the time one enters the influence phase, new kinds of work roles may become available.
- Career paths are less clear than they once were. Young people are being advised to expect three or four career changes in their lifetime. They may end up moving from the private to the nonprofit sector, from business to education, from service provider to entrepreneur.
- The cost of living—especially the costs of housing, health care, and education—introduces concerns about the amount of money that will be needed to live comfortably. Worries about making money may interfere with effective career decision making.

As a result of the anxiety and complexity that attends career decision making, career counseling has become a significant new career.

Ideally, one's choice of occupation is the result of personal experimentation, introspection, self-evaluation, fact finding, and intuition. This process becomes intimately interwoven with one's psychological development. In order to make a career choice, people may first choose to pose difficult questions to themselves about their skills, temperament, values, and goals. When they make a decision based on this kind of personal evaluation, they are likely to see their careers as a well-integrated part of their personal identities rather than as activities from which they are alienated or by which they are dominated.

# THE PSYCHOSOCIAL CRISIS: INDIVIDUAL IDENTITY VERSUS IDENTITY CONFUSION

## INDIVIDUAL IDENTITY

Erik Erikson provided a comprehensive treatment of the meaning and functions of individual identity, from his inclusion of this concept in the theory of psychosocial development in 1950 to his analysis of American identity in 1974. His notion of identity involves the merging of past identifications, future aspirations, and contemporary cultural issues. The major works in which he discussed identity are the article "The Problem of Ego Identity" (Erikson, 1959) and the book *Identity: Youth and Crisis* (Erikson, 1968). Our discussion, which is grounded in these works, is broadened to include the ideas of others who have begun to extend and operationalize the concept of identity (Schwartz, 2001).

Later adolescents are preoccupied with questions about their essential character in much the same way that early school-age children are preoccupied with questions about their origins. In their efforts to define themselves, later adolescents must take into account the bonds that have been built between them and others in the past as well as the direction they hope to take in the future. Identity serves as an anchor point, providing the person with an essential experience of continuity in social relationships:

> The young individual must learn to be most himself where he means the most to others—those others, to be sure, who have come to mean most to him. The term identity expresses

such a mutual relation in that it connotes both a persistent sameness within oneself (self-sameness) and a persistent sharing of some kind of essential character with others. (Erikson, 1959, p. 102)

## ■ THE PRIVATE AND THE PUBLIC FACES OF IDENTITY

As the preceding quotation suggests, identity achievement is associated with an internal sense of individual uniqueness and direction accompanied by a social or community validation about the direction one has chosen. Thus identity includes both a private and a public self. The **private self**, often described as a *sense of self*, refers to one's inner uniqueness and unity, the subjective experience of being the originator of one's thoughts and actions and of being self-reflective. Through the private self, one recognizes the range of values and beliefs to which one is committed, and one can assess the extent to which certain thoughts and actions are consistent with those beliefs. The private, subjective sense of self, which develops over the course of the life span, includes four basic elements (Blasi, 1991; Glodis & Blasi, 1993):

A sense of *agency*—being the originator of thoughts and actions.

A sense of *unity*—sensing that one is the same basic self from one moment or one situation to the next.

A sense of *otherness*—recognizing the boundaries between the self and others.

A sense of *decentering* or *distancing*—reflecting on oneself so that one can recognize and own one's thoughts and actions.

The elements of the **public self** include the many roles one plays and the expectations of others. As young people move through the stage of later adolescence, they find that social reference groups—including family members, neighbors, teachers, friends, religious groups, ethnic groups, and even national leaders—have expectations of their behavior. A young person may be expected to work, attend college, marry, serve the country in the military, attend religious services, vote, and provide economic support for family members. Persistent demands by meaningful others result in decisions that might have been made differently, or not made at all, if the individual were surrounded by a different configuration of social reference groups. In the process of achieving personal identity, one must synthesize the private sense of self with the public self derived from the many roles and relationships in which one is embedded.

## ■ THE CONTENT AND EVALUATION COMPONENTS OF IDENTITY

The structure of identity has two components: content and evaluation (Breakwell, 1986; Whitbourne, 1986). The *content* includes what one thinks about, values, and believes in, and the traits or characteristics by which one is recognized and

*Woman with a Hat, 1962/Pablo Picasso/© 2005 Estate of Pablo Picasso/Artists Rights Society (ARS), New York/Private Collection, Bonhams, London, UK/www.bridgeman.co.uk*

*This image captures a contemporary sense of the search for individual identity: a young woman with a broad-rimmed hat, hair flowing, one eye looking outward to the world, and one turned inward on the self.*

known by others. Erikson suggested that identity was achieved by finding one's sense of direction with respect to salient roles and values, especially vocational decisions, political and religious ideologies, sexual expression, and gender role or interpersonal values. In many measures of identity formation, these domains comprise the foundational content areas (Kroger, 2003). The second structural component of identity, *evaluation*, refers to the significance one places on various aspects of the identity content. Even though most people play many of the same roles, their identities differ in part because they place different values on some of these roles. Some people are single-minded, placing great value on success in one domain, such as their vocational goals, and little value on the others. Other people strive to maintain a balance in the roles they play; they consider themselves successful if they can find enjoyment in a variety of relationships and activities.

A person's assessment of the importance of certain content areas in relation to others influences the use of resources, the direction of certain decisions, and the kinds of experiences that may be perceived as most personally rewarding or threatening. College students, for example, may differ in whether academic success and professional preparation or interpersonal success is most central to their sense of identity. Students who are more concerned about academic success take a different approach to the college environment, become involved in different kinds of activities, and have a different reaction to academic feedback than do students who are more concerned about making friends and having new kinds of social and interpersonal success (Green & Hill, 2003).

Both the content and evaluation components of identity may change over the life course. In later adolescence, the focus is on integrating the various sources of content and determining which elements have the greatest salience. This is a major accomplishment that requires self-awareness, introspection, and the active exploration of a variety of roles and relationships. Insight into this process is provided in the case study of Houston A. Baker, Jr. However, the identity that is formed at the end of this period is often very abstract, because later adolescents have not yet encountered many of the responsibilities, pressures, and conflicts of adult life. The ideological framework of identity has not yet been forged in the flames of reality.

# Case study

## HOUSTON A. BAKER, JR.

*A poet and literary scholar tells of the impact of one of his college professors on his personal identity.*

He intrigued us. Slowly puffing on the obligatory pipe, he would chide us for the routineness of our analyses of revered works in the British and American literary canons. He wore—always—a tie and tweed of Ivy provenance, and at the end of the first session of his "World Literature" course at Howard University in the fall of 1963, I had but one response—I wanted to be exactly like him.

The task was to prove myself worthy. I labored furiously at the beginning assignment—an effort devoted to Marvellian coy mistresses and pounding parodies thereof. The result was a D and the comment: "This is a perfunctory effort. You have refused to be creative. There are worlds on worlds rolling ever. Try to make contact with them." I was more than annoyed; I was livid. Who did he think he was? I'd show him. My next essay would reveal (cleverly, of course) that I didn't give a tinker's dam for his grade or his comments. "Creative"—indeed!

My second essay might properly have been entitled: Love's labor loosed on William Blake. I strained to see every nuance of the "Songs of Innocence." I combed the poems for every mad hint that would help forward my own mad argument. I never turned my eyes from the text as I sought to construct the most infuriating (yet plausible) analysis imaginable. I felt my feet dancing to Muhammad Ali rhythms as I slaved away, darting logical jabs at Professor C. Watkins who would (I was certain) be utterly undone when I threw my irreverent straight right. The paper came back with the comment: "This is a maverick argument,

but stubbornly logical—A–." Bingo! The grade in itself gave me almost enough courage to seek him out during office hours—but not quite. I corralled a friend to make the pilgrimage with me.

He was extraordinarily gracious on the mid-autumn afternoon when we had our first long talk. "Come in, Mr. Baker—Miss Pierce. How are you?" His tie was loose; he was reared back in his desk chair. There was a clutter of papers and blue books, and they provided a friendly setting for a two-hour conversation. . . . We were thrilled that he considered us (potentially) enough like him to invite us to visit him and his wife two weeks hence—for dessert.

The evening surprisingly took on (in my youthful imagination) the cast of Greenwich Village "Beats" and verboten revelations. The greatest stimulation, however, came when he played the Library of Congress recording of T. S. Eliot reading "The Wasteland." In that moment, I became, willy-nilly, a party to "modernism" in its prototypical form. I was surprised and delighted. I had heard nothing like it before. The Eliotian reading initiated my habit of "listening" for poems rather than "looking" for them. . . . I stepped into a late fall evening with an entirely new sense of myself and of "worlds on worlds rolling ever."

Source: From "An Apple for My Teacher: Twelve Writers Tell About Teachers Who Made All the Difference," by H. A. Baker, Jr., pp. 317–319. In H. L. Gates, Jr. (Ed.), *Bearing Witness: Selections from African-American Autobiography in the Twentieth Century.* Copyright © 1991 Pantheon Books.

### ■ CRITICAL THINKING AND CASE ANALYSIS

1. What elements of the identity process are evident in this case?
2. What are some of the characteristics of Professor Watkins that may have made him a target for identification for Houston Baker?
3. What aspects of the college environment are likely to stimulate the identity process?
4. Have you ever had an intellectual experience that gave you a "new sense of yourself"? What combination of factors come together to permit that to happen?

### ■ IDENTITY STATUS

The basic conflict of the psychosocial crisis of later adolescence is individual identity formation versus identity confusion. It results from the enormous difficulty of pulling together the many components of the self—including changing perspectives on one's inner sense of beliefs and values as well as new and changing social demands—into a unified image that can propel the person toward positive, meaningful action. As part of this process, a young person struggles to formulate a worldview, an outlook on those goals and values that are personally important and to which the person is willing to make a commitment. Over the period of later adolescence, whether in the context of college or in other work and community settings, young people begin to examine the beliefs and goals they may have internalized from childhood. Through self-reflection, role experimentation, and feedback

*As part of the identity process, young people often challenge themselves to take on new levels of achievement and test their resolve.*

© Robert Ginn/Photo Edit

from significant others, later adolescents make decisions about whether these beliefs and goals are still meaningful as they look ahead to the future (Arnett, 2000).

The identity process takes place in a historical and cultural context. During early and later adolescence, young people are aware of the age-graded expectations that exist in their families and communities, typically structured around specific tasks and roles, including educational attainment, occupation, intimacy, marriage, and childrearing. In most modern societies, each of these areas presents a variety of opportunities or possible paths as well as some constraints about which paths are possible given certain personal, financial, and cultural resources. In later adolescence, the identity work includes selecting goals in these domains and preparing for the achievement of these goals (Nurmi, 2004).

Identity formation is a dynamic process that unfolds as young people assess their competencies and aspirations within a changing social context of expectations, demands, and resources. The idea that this identity has to be meaningful as the young person anticipates an uncertain future adds some anxiety to the process. A variety of potential resolutions of the psychosocial crisis of individual identity versus identity confusion have been described. At the negative pole of the crisis, identity confusion or diffusion, the person is not able or possibly not willing to make any commitments to adult roles and values. At the positive pole, identity achievement, the person has made meaningful commitments to a defined set of values and goals. In between these two outcomes, other identity resolutions have been described, including premature resolution, identity foreclosure, postponement of resolution, psychosocial moratorium, and negative identity (Kroger, 1993, 2003).

One of the most widely used conceptual frameworks for assessing identity status was devised by James Marcia (1980; Waterman, 1982). Using Erikson's concepts, Marcia assessed

identity status on the basis of two criteria: *crisis* and *commitment*. **Crisis** consists of a period of role experimentation and active decision making among alternative choices. **Commitment** consists of a demonstration of personal involvement in the areas of occupational choice, religion, political ideology, and interpersonal relationships. On the basis of Marcia's interview, the status of respondents' identity development is assessed as identity achievement, foreclosure, moratorium, and diffusion (see Table 11.3). People who are classified as **identity achieved** have already experienced a crisis time and have made occupational and ideological commitments. People who are classified as **foreclosed** have not experienced a crisis but demonstrate strong occupational and ideological commitments. Their occupational and ideological beliefs appear to be close to those of their parents. The foreclosed identity is deceptive. A young person of 18 or 19 who can say exactly what he or she wants in life and who has selected an occupational goal may appear to be mature. This kind of clarity of vision may impress peers and adults as evidence of a high level of self-insight. However, if this solution has been formulated through the wholesale adoption of a script that was devised by the young person's family, it may not actually reflect much depth of self-understanding.

**Table 11.3**  Relationship of Crisis and Commitment to Identity Status

| STATUS | CRISIS | COMMITMENT |
|---|---|---|
| Identity achievement | + | + |
| Foreclosure | − | + |
| Moratorium | + | − |
| Identity confusion | +/− | − |

People who are classified as being in a state of **psychosocial moratorium** are involved in an ongoing crisis. Their commitments are diffuse. Finally, people who are classified as **identity confused** may or may not have experienced a crisis, and they demonstrate a complete lack of commitment. Marcia described the identity-confused group as having a rather cavalier, "party" attitude that allows members to cope with the college environment. He suggested that the more seriously confused persons (such as those described by Erikson, 1959) may not appear in his sample because they are unable to cope with college.

Sometimes, cultural expectations and demands provide the young person with a clearly defined self-image that is completely contrary to the cultural values of the community. This is called a **negative identity** (Erikson, 1959). *Failure, good-for-nothing, juvenile delinquent, hood, gangster,* and *loser* are some of the labels that the adult society commonly applies to certain adolescents. In the absence of any indication of the possibilities of success or contribution to society, the young person accepts such negative labels as a self-definition and proceeds to validate this identity by continuing to behave in ways that will strengthen it. Some young people grow up admiring people who have become very successful by following antisocial or criminal paths. Drug lords; gang leaders; leaders of groups that advocate hate, violence, and vengeance; and people who use elected political positions for personal gain are all examples of possible role models around which a negative identity may be formed.

A negative identity may also emerge as the result of a strong identification with someone who is devalued by the family or the community. A loving uncle who is an alcoholic or a clever, creative parent who commits suicide may stimulate a crystallization within the adolescent as one who may share these undesirable characteristics. Linda, for example, established the negative identity of a person going crazy:

> Her father was an alcoholic, physically abusive man, who terrified her when she was a child. . . . Linda, herself a bright child, became by turns the standard bearer for her father's proud aspirations and the target of his jealousy. Midway through grade school she began flunking all her courses and retreating to a private world of daydreams. . . . "I always expected hallucinations, being locked up, down the road coming toward me. . . . I always resisted seeing myself as an adult. I was afraid that at the point I stopped the tape [the years of wild experimentation] I'd become my parents. . . . My father was the closest person I knew to crazy." (Ochberg, 1986, pp. 296–297)

## IDENTITY CONFUSION

The foreclosed identity and the negative identity both resolve the identity crisis in ways that fall short of the goal of identity achievement. Yet both still provide the person with a concrete identity. The more maladaptive resolution of the crisis is **identity confusion**. Young people in this state are unable to make a commitment to any single view of themselves. They may be unable to integrate the various roles they play. They may be confronted by opposing value systems or by a lack of confidence in their ability to make meaningful decisions. Within the private, subjective self, some young people may reach later adolescence having difficulty accepting or establishing clear ego boundaries, or they may not experience feelings of agency. Individuals with identity confusion have been shown to have low self-esteem; they are more likely than individuals with other identity statuses to be influenced by peer pressures toward conformity, and they approach problem solving with tendencies toward procrastination and avoidance, which contribute to difficulties in adjusting to the college environment (Berzonsky & Kuk, 2000; Kroger, 2004). At an unconscious level, they may have incorporated two or more conflicting ideas about the self—for example, an abusive, harsh, rejecting powerful father and a wise, loving, nurturant, powerful grandmother—that stand in opposition to each other. Under any of these conditions, the demands for integration and synthesis of a personal identity arouse anxiety, apathy, and hostility toward the existing roles, none of which they can successfully adopt.

In comparison to the moratorium group, young people with a confused identity status are less conscientious, more likely to experience negative emotions, and more disagreeable (Clancy & Dollinger, 1993). They are generally not outgoing; rather, they describe themselves as self-conscious and likely to feel depressed. Their relationship with their parents is described as distant or rejecting. Several studies have found that young people who are characterized as identity confused have had a history of early and frequent involvement with drug use and abuse (Jones, 1992). Difficulties in resolving earlier psychosocial crises—especially conflicts related to autonomy versus shame and doubt and initiative versus guilt—leave some young people with deficits in ego formation that interfere with the kind of energy and playful self-assertiveness that are necessary in the process of identity achievement.

Dolores, an unemployed college dropout, describes the feeling of meaningless drifting that is associated with identity confusion:

> I have two sisters, and my father always told me I was the smartest of all, that I was smarter than he was, and that I could do anything I wanted to do . . . but somehow, I don't really know why, everything I turned to came to nothing. . . . I had every opportunity to find out what I really wanted to do. But . . . nothing I did satisfied me, and I would just stop. . . . Or turn away. . . . Or go on a trip. I worked for a big company for a while. . . . Then my parents went to Paris and I just went with them. . . . I came back . . . went to school . . . was a researcher at Time-Life . . . drifted . . . got married . . . divorced . . . drifted. [Her voice grew more halting.] I feel my life is such a waste. I'd like to write, I really would; but I don't know. I just can't get going. (Gornick, 1971)

The theoretical construct of identity status assumes a developmental progression. Identity confusion reflects the least defined status. Movement from confusion to foreclosure, moratorium, and finally identity achievement reflects a developmental progression. Movement from any other status to confusion suggests regression. A person who has achieved identity at one period may conceivably return to a crisis period of moratorium. However, those who are in a moratorium or achieved status can never be accurately described as foreclosed, because by definition they have already experienced some degree of crisis (Meeus, 1996; Waterman, 1982). A number of studies, both cross-sectional and longitudinal, have shown that over time, more young people are characterized as having the mature identity statuses of moratorium and achievement, and fewer are in foreclosure or identity confusion. However, many of these studies also find that as many as half the participants studied retain their foreclosed or identity-confused status from the beginning to the end of college; and some studies find regression from the achieved to the foreclosed status (Meeus et al, 1999). One implication is that both the confused and the foreclosed identity status may be more stable and adaptive during later adolescence than has been theoretically conceptualized. Another implication is that identity statuses are better thought of as self-theories or ways of linking information about the self and the world, rather than formal stages that evolve in a strict sequence from one level to the next (Berzonsky, 2003).

In the process of evolving an individual identity, everyone experiences temporary periods of confusion and depression. The task of bringing together the many elements of one's experience into a coordinated, clear self-definition is difficult and time consuming. Adolescents are likely to experience moments of self-preoccupation, isolation, and discouragement as the diverse pieces of the puzzle are shifted and reordered into the total picture. Thus, even the eventual positive identity formation will be the result of some degree of identity confusion. The negative outcome of identity confusion, however, suggests that the person is never able to formulate a satisfying identity that will provide for the convergence of multiple identifications, aspirations, and roles. Such individuals have the persistent fear that they are losing their hold on themselves and on their future.

## IDENTITY FORMATION FOR MEN AND WOMEN

Questions have been raised about the process of identity formation and its outcome for young men and women in our society. Some investigators have argued that the concept of identity as it has been formulated is a reflection of a male-oriented culture that focuses heavily on occupation and ideology rather than on interpersonal commitments. These criticisms also suggest that the construct of personal identity places greater value on self-sufficiency and autonomy, to the exclusion of relationships and connection to the group. From this point of view, identity development ignores the fact that many women tend to be socialized to look to others to define

their identity rather than to assume a proactive stance with respect to identity formation. All of these ideas reflect the impact of traditional distinctions in the male and female gender roles on identity formation (Archer, 1992).

Other researchers have pointed out that Erikson's construct of personal identity is embedded in a relational context. The process of identity formation requires a reexamination of earlier identifications and a selective internalization of the views and voices of significant others. The interpersonal and ideological commitments around which identity is forged result in a closer bond between the young person and the society (Marcia, 1993; Horst, 1995).

What is more, the kinds of ego strengths associated with identity achievement are equally important to the adaptive functioning of men and women (Ginsburg & Orlofsky, 1981). From this point of view, one might expect to find differences between men and women in the content of identity-related commitments and in the value placed on these content areas, but not in the process of crisis and commitment that leads to achieved identity. However, few sex differences in identity status have been discovered (Kroger, 1997). Men and women are equally likely to be distributed across the four identity statuses; they show the same pattern of increasing frequencies in the moratorium and achievement categories and decreasing frequencies in the foreclosed and confused categories. For both sexes, identity achievement is associated with positive ego qualities: "Identity achieved youths generally exhibit higher levels of self-esteem, greater cognitive and ego complexity, post-conventional levels of moral reasoning, and a strong capacity for inner-directed behavior" (Craig-Bray, Adams, & Dobson, 1988, p. 175).

Men and women appear to handle the *process* of role experimentation and identity achievement somewhat differently. The uncertainty of the identity crisis is often accompanied by greater anxiety in women than in men (Ollech & McCarthy, 1997). This anxiety may be linked to concerns about achievement strivings. Many women experience conflict between their image of femininity and their desire to set ambitious personal goals (Ginsburg & Orlofsky, 1981). Anxiety may also be a product of the general distress that women feel when they focus on their own agendas rather than on facilitating the agendas of others, as society seems to expect them to do. The family context is especially important for young women who need to experience continued attachment with parents in the process of individuation (Schultheiss & Blustein, 1994). In this context, the moratorium status, which is considered a positive interlude on the path toward achievement, has been found to be linked to higher levels of self-doubt in women than in men. This finding may result from the strong feelings of guilt that women experience when they attempt to assert their self-sufficiency or when they try to disconnect from demanding relationships in order to focus on their own ideas and needs.

Some evidence of gender differences has been found in the *content* of identity. Erikson's (1968, 1982) work suggests that ideological and vocational commitments are central to identity formation. Gilligan (1982/1993) criticized this orientation, arguing that interpersonal commitment may be more central for women, and that its clarification opens the way for more advanced exploration of vocations and ideology. Research findings lend some support to this concept, but gender identity rather than gender itself may be the more important predictor of domain salience (Kroger, 2003). The quality of interpersonal relations and the establishment of satisfying social commitments are more relevant to those women who endorse more traditional gender role expectations.

## THE CENTRAL PROCESS: ROLE EXPERIMENTATION

Later adolescents experiment with roles that represent the many possibilities for their future identities. They may think of themselves in a variety of careers in an effort to anticipate what it would be like to be members of specific occupational groups. They may take a variety of summer jobs, change their college major, read extensively, and daydream about success in several occupations. They consider whether or not to marry, and they begin to define the ideal qualities they are looking for in a long-term intimate partner. Dating is one form of role experimentation; it allows for a different self-presentation with each new date. Friendship is another important context within which young people begin to clarify their interpersonal commitments. Later adolescents may also evaluate their commitment to their religion, consider religious conversion, or experiment with different rationales for moral behavior. They may examine a variety of political theories, join groups that work for political causes, or campaign

for candidates. During later adolescence, people have few social obligations that require long-term role commitments. They are free to start and stop or to join and quit without serious repercussions to their reputations. As long as no laws are broken in the process of experimenting, young people have the opportunity to play as many roles as they wish in order to prepare themselves for the resolution of the identity crisis without risking serious social censure.

## PSYCHOSOCIAL MORATORIUM

The process of role experimentation takes many forms. Erikson (1959) used the term **psychosocial moratorium** to describe a period of free experimentation before a final identity is achieved. Ideally, the moratorium allows individuals freedom from the daily expectations for role performance. Their experimentation with new roles, values, and belief systems results in a personal conception of how they can fit into society so as to maximize their personal strengths and gain positive recognition from the community. The idea of being able to disconnect from daily demands and experiment with new roles may be more difficult for some later adolescents than for others. For example, young people who marry early and who go into the labor force right after high school may not have the luxury of a moratorium.

The concept of the psychosocial moratorium has been partially incorporated into some college programs that permit students to enroll in pass-fail courses before they select a major. The concern is to eliminate the problems of external evaluation during the decision-making process. Some high-school students take a year off for work, travel, or volunteer service before deciding about college or a career. College students often express a need for a moratorium by leaving school

*The study abroad program in Trier, Germany, brings students together from many countries. Their informal interactions are a rich source of ideas for role experimentation.*

for a while, disrupting the expected path of educational and career development. They assert their autonomy by imposing their own timetable and agenda on a socially prescribed sequence. Travel abroad is another strategy for experiencing moratorium. The time spent in another culture can give students an opportunity to demonstrate their self-sufficiency, examine many of their assumptions about values and goals, express their individuality, and break out of whatever social environment they may feel is constraining or overshadowing their sense of self. The moratorium offers temporary relief from external demands and an opportunity to establish their identity.

As parents observe the process of role experimentation, they may become concerned because their adolescent son or daughter appears to be abandoning the traditional family value orientation or lifestyle. The adolescent talks of changing religions, remaining single, or selecting a low-status career. The more vehemently the family responds to these propositions, the more likely the young person is to become locked into a position in order to demonstrate autonomy rather than being allowed to continue the experimentation until a more suitable personal alternative is discovered. Many adolescents seem to want to take a "shocking" stand or to question the "unquestionable" so that they have a feeling of control—a feeling that they have chosen their own path rather than simply followed the one carved out for them by their family, culture, and time in history. Parents are well advised to understand role experimentation as the expression of an appropriate developmental process in which a young person is trying on various roles, beliefs, and philosophies to see how they fit. If at all possible, parents need to trust in this process, giving their opinions and reactions when appropriate, but encouraging the young person to find the combination of roles, values, goals, and commitments that bring him or her the greatest feelings of enthusiasm and optimism about his or her own future.

Not all young people approach the process of role experimentation with the same degree of openness to new experiences and new information. Michael Berzonsky (1989, 1993,

2003; Berzonsky & Sullivan, 1992) hypothesized that in later adolescence, individuals differ in how they select, process, and apply self-relevant information. Three types of approaches to identity-related information processing were described, each with a somewhat different implication for the place of role experimentation in the resolution of the identity search. The *informational types* "actively seek out and evaluate self-diagnostic information when negotiating identity issues and making decisions" (Berzonsky, 1993, p. 289). The *normative types* are "relatively more defensive and closed to feedback that may threaten hard core areas of the self" (Berzonsky, 1993, p. 290). The *diffuse-avoidant types* "procrastinate and delay dealing with self-relevant issues as long as possible. When push comes to shove, they tend to be influenced by immediate rewards and operate in a situation- sensitive fashion" (Berzonsky, 1993, p. 290).

The implication of this way of viewing styles of identity-related information processing is that the informational types are most likely to initiate role experimentation as a means of clarifying existing beliefs and values. The normative types have to process contradictions among the demands and expectations of the varying roles they play, but if possible, they will probably avoid novel experiences that would challenge their views. The diffuse-avoidant types may engage in role experimentation if it is viewed as "cool" or is positively regarded among others in their peer group, but they probably would not take the initiative to seek out new experiences as a conscious, proactive strategy. Figure 11.3 shows the relationship between the three information-seeking styles and the four identity statuses described earlier. In this model, exploration

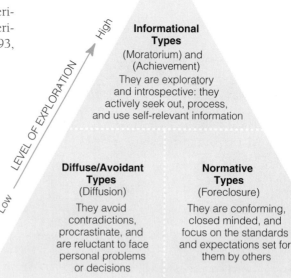

**FIGURE 11.3**

Relations Among Identity Status, Level of Exploration, and Level of Commitment

*White, Wampler, and Winn, 1998, p. 226.*

or seeking information is associated with both the moratorium and the achieved statuses (White, Wampler, & Winn, 1998).

Role experimentation implies an active process by which later adolescents sort through various identifications, scripts, and social pressures in order to find their niche. For some young people, however, a turning point or critical incident marks the point of commitment. Often, a dramatic loss, an unexpected victory, or an experience of victimization can help crystallize a young person's vision of how the self can fit in with the community or transcend the community. Two examples of turning points are illustrated in the case study on Turning Points in the Identity Process.

# CASE STUDY

## TURNING POINTS IN THE IDENTITY PROCESS

*The following two examples illustrate how a critical life event can refocus personal identity toward a new consolidation of energy, purpose, and commitment. In the first example, Sullivan experiences personal losses that lead to a new occupational and value commitment. In the second example, Rachel experiences a national tragedy that reorients her political ideology.*

### ■ SULLIVAN

With her mother, Sullivan was living in a housing project. In high school, when life got very hard, she began drinking and using drugs. She often stayed out late "to all hours" without her mother knowing or caring. Her father stepped in, put his foot down, and tried to teach her better habits. Soon after high school, she eloped with a young man who tried to control her and keep her from going to college. . . . The marriage ended after two years, then tragedy followed. An old boyfriend of Sullivan's committed suicide, and shortly thereafter her sister was hospitalized because of a suicide attempt.

The near-death of her sister changed Sullivan. She did not want to be a "loser"—someone who could not pull her weight—so she enrolled in a local community college. She went on to earn a bachelor's degree and then a master's degree, and she became a licensed social worker. Now Sullivan's work is aimed at helping people who are like she was. (Levine & Nidiffer, 1996, pp. 122–123)

### ■ RACHEL

When I was 19, I moved to New York City to be a musician. The first thing I did was get a tattoo on each hand: One was a treble clef, the other was the insignia for Silvertone guitars. . . . If you asked me to describe myself then, I would have told you I was a musician, a poet, an artist and, on a somewhat political level, a woman, a lesbian, and a Jew. Being an American wouldn't have made my list.

I'm a junior at a Manhattan college. In my Gender and Economics class earlier this semester we discussed the benefits of socialism, which provides for all members of society, versus capitalism, which values the self-interests of business people. My girlfriend and I were so frustrated by inequality in America that we discussed moving to another country. On Sept. 11, all that changed. I realized that I had been taking the freedoms I have here for granted. Now I have an American flag on my backpack, I cheer at the fighter jets as they pass overhead, and I am calling myself a patriot.

I had just stepped out of the shower when the first plane crashed into the North Tower of the World Trade Center. I stood looking out the window of my Brooklyn apartment, dumbfounded, as the second plane barreled into the South Tower. In that moment, the world as I had known it was redefined. (Newman, 2001, p. 9)

### ■ CRITICAL THINKING AND CASE ANALYSIS

1. How are turning points different from role experimentation?
2. What might determine whether a turning point leads to identity achievement or identity confusion?
3. What is the difference between the events that Sullivan experienced and those that Rachel experienced? How might the differences in these two kinds of events relate to subsequent identity work?
4. What factors might be necessary to preserve the focus and sense of purpose that are evoked in these critical life events? For example, how might family support, the response of close friends, or opportunities for enacting new roles influence whether these changes are sustained?

## ROLE EXPERIMENTATION AND ETHNIC IDENTITY

In Chapter 10 (Early Adolescence), we introduced the idea that group identity precedes individual identity. One component of group identity is an orientation toward one's ethnic group. Efforts to understand one's ethnic identity and to clarify one's commitment to a particular ethnic subculture lead to self-definition that facilitates work on personal identity as well. Part of forming a clear sense of personal identity requires an understanding of one's ancestry, especially one's cultural and ethnic heritage and the values, beliefs, and traditions that may have shaped one's childrearing environment as well as one's vision of the future. Ethnic group identity typically involves the incorporation of certain ideals, values, and beliefs that are specific to that ethnic group; a sense of how this ethnic group is regarded by outsiders; and the way in which one orients oneself with respect to this group—that is, whether one seeks out other members of the group, feels proud of one's membership in it, and has positive attitudes about it (Cross, 1991).

As you might imagine, young people make the transition from early to later adolescence having done different amounts

*The college environment provides an opportunity to learn about the cultural traditions and history of one's ethnic group, as well as the traditions of other groups. UCLA dance majors are performing traditional African dances for the freshman student convocation.*

of work in exploring their ethnic group identity. One theory of ethnic minority identity development offers a five-stage model (Atkinson, Morten, & Sue, 1983):

1.  *Conformity*. Identification with the values, beliefs, and practices of the dominant culture.
2.  *Dissonance*. Recognition and confusion about areas of conflict between the values, beliefs, and practices of the dominant culture and those of one's own ethnic group.
3.  *Resistance and immersion*. Rejection of many elements of the dominant culture; education about and involvement in one's own ethnic group and its beliefs, values, and practices.
4.  *Introspection*. Critical examination of the values, beliefs, and practices of both the dominant culture and one's own ethnic group's views.
5.  *Articulation and awareness*. Identification of those values, beliefs, and practices from the dominant culture and from one's own ethnic group that are combined into a unique synthesis that forms a personal, cultural identity.

In this model, one senses the interaction between ethnic identity and personal identity (Rotheram-Borus & Wyche, 1994). Not all young people experience all of these stages. Some children are raised in families where ethnic socialization begins at a young age, and they never experience a sense of accepting the dominant culture. In fact, if they are raised in a racially segregated community, they may not encounter members of the dominant culture as significant figures during their early childhood years.

For many people, the stage of articulation and awareness may not occur until sometime later in adulthood. But for many later adolescents, the transitions from Stage 1 (conformity) to Stages 2 and 3 are commonly stimulated by the college experience. The student body is usually much more diverse than one's high school. Young people of many racial, ethnic, social-class, regional, and religious backgrounds come together in college and are expected to live together in the residence halls, learn together in the classrooms, and collaborate in college organizations, social activities, sports, and cultural events. Exposure to this diversity may be accompanied by experiences of racial and ethnic prejudice, cultural ethnocentrism, and intergroup conflict. At the same time, racial diversity often contributes to more divergent thinking, introduces new perspectives, and, as a result, promotes more complex thinking about social issues (Antonio, Chang, et al., 2004). Exposure to the college curriculum offers an intellectual framework for understanding the historical, psychological, and sociological foundations of racism, prejudice, and cultural conflict (Phinney, 1996).

For young people who remain in low-income, urban communities and do not attend college, the interaction of ethnic identity and personal identity can serve as an adaptive process for coping with high-risk environments. Identification with the history, struggles, and heroism of one's people serves

## HUMAN DEVELOPMENT AND DIVERSITY

### Ethnic Identity and Adjustment

ETHNIC IDENTITY HAS been studied for individual ethnic groups as a component of the self-concept, usually focusing on how important people's ethnicity is to them, how often they think about themselves as members of their ethnic group, and how close they feel to other members of their ethnic group (Sears, Fu, Henry, & Bui, 2003). Ethnic identity has also been measured as a general concept, allowing one to compare the strength of ethnic identity across groups. The *Multigroup Ethnic Identity Measure* (MEIM) is one such measure, which consists of three subscales:

1. *Affirmation and belonging*, which assesses one's feelings of connection and pride.

2. *Ethnic identity achievement*, which assesses a person's understanding and acceptance of their group membership in the face of existing societal discrimination. It reflects a positive but realistic identification with one's group.
3. *Ethnic behaviors* (Phinney, 1992).

The ethnic identity subscale allows one to characterize individuals along a continuum from an unexamined ethnic identity acquired with little exploration or commitment (*low ethnic identity*) to a well-developed, achieved ethnic identity (Yasui, Dorham, & Dishion, 2004). The parallels with personal identity status are striking.

Ethnic identity, as measured by the MEIM, has been positively associated with self-esteem across middle childhood, early adolescence, and later adolescence. Individuals with positive ethnic identity have been found to deal more effectively with threatening social situations involving discrimination and stereotyping (Roberts et al., 1999). A sense of belonging to one's ethnic group may be important as part of one's social identity for all groups. However, the *salience* of ethnic identity is not the same for all groups. The establishment of a clear acceptance of their ethnic identity may be especially relevant for those who face discrimination or oppression on the basis of their ethnic membership.

---

as an anchor of dignity and hope in communities that are disrupted by unemployment and violence (Spencer, Cunningham, & Swanson, 1995). Through interaction with other members of their ethnic group, young people build competence and a set of strategies for managing the poverty and hostility that they face.

## THE PRIME ADAPTIVE EGO QUALITY AND THE CORE PATHOLOGY

### FIDELITY TO VALUES AND IDEOLOGIES

Fidelity is closely linked with the notion of *commitment*. In later adolescence, the ego strength of **fidelity** refers to "the ability to sustain loyalties freely pledged in spite of the inevitable contradictions and confusions of value systems" (Erikson, 1978, p. 28). Fidelity incorporates the trust and hope of infancy and directs it toward a belief in values and ideologies. Fidelity may be fostered by identification with inspirational role models or by participation in meaningful institutions. It is also achieved as a result of the new cognitive capacities of adolescence that permit self-reflection, relativistic thinking, and insight. Fidelity to values and ideals provides evidence of a reflective person who has taken time to

struggle with opposing views and to select those that best reflect his or her personal convictions (Waterman, 1992).

The emergence of fidelity provides a channel for strong passions and drives, guiding this energy toward the preservation of values and ideals. It strengthens one's ethical resolve, especially in the face of the many pressures and temptations of adult life. It also creates a bond of belonging with others who share the same loyalties. At the same time, fidelity in the individual strengthens the society by drawing on the commitments of those who share a common set of values to sustain and support basic institutions, such as religious organizations, political parties, educational institutions, and social service agencies (Markstrom-Adams, Hofstra, & Dougher, 1994).

### REPUDIATION

**Repudiation** refers to a rejection of certain values, beliefs, and roles. In the diverse and pluralistic society of the United States, some degree of repudiation may be necessary in order to forge an integrated identity. One cannot embrace all ideologies and roles; each commitment brings some boundaries to one's values and limits one's investment to a certain vision of the self continuing into the future. Repudiation can serve as a mechanism for intergenerational change. For example, a young person may decide that he or she will reject the characteristics of an unloving or abusive parent. In this context, the young person will form his or her identity around suppressing certain negative qualities and learning to enact and endorse opposing positive qualities.

In the extreme case, repudiation results in a hostile rejection of all the ideas, values, and groups that do not adhere to one's own beliefs (Erikson, 1982). It fosters a rigid worldview that does not admit to the contributions of others' ideas. The roots of militancy, prejudice, and terrorism lie in the formation of the core pathology of repudiation. Imagine young people who, on the threshold of adulthood, see their future as grim or hopeless. They may perceive themselves as subjugated victims, rejected by the mainstream. They may believe that their culture, their ethnic identity, or their religion is mocked or berated. They may transform the mistrust and shame of childhood into fury against the "other." The energy of youth that can mobilize noble, courageous acts of fidelity can also crystallize around hate, turning against one or more groups in acts of violence.

## APPLIED TOPIC

# THE CHALLENGES OF SOCIAL LIFE

DURING LATER ADOLESCENCE, most young people find ways to loosen themselves from the moorings of family, tradition, and convention. We have referred to this process as *role experimentation* and have treated it as a positive, healthy dynamic through which young people begin to know themselves more authentically. In the process of forming a personal identity, young people are likely to be surrounded by others like themselves who have not yet settled on a clear set of values and beliefs to which they are willing to commit. In this social context, some young people become greedily self-absorbed; others become avidly ideological; yet others become depressed and confused. As our students have discussed the issues of this period of life and reflected on its challenges, they have pointed out some of the risks that accompany this period of uncertainty and experimentation. The following discussion identifies three of these risks: unwanted sexual attention, binge drinking, and sexually transmitted diseases.

## ▌ UNWANTED SEXUAL ATTENTION

Unwanted sexual attention can range from unwanted teasing, joking, and suggestive gestures to rape. At the University of Michigan, the Sexual Awareness and Prevention Center focuses on four major issues: sexual assault, dating or domestic violence, sexual harassment, and stalking. To find out more about their prevention and education efforts, visit their website. The center defines *sexual assault* as "any form of unwanted sexual contact obtained without consent and/or obtained through the use of force, threat of force, intimidation, or coercion."

*Sexual harassment* is defined as "unwelcome sexual advances, requests for sexual favors, and other verbal or physical conduct of a sexual nature when either: (a) The conduct is made as a term or condition of an individual's employment, education, living environment, or participation in a University Community; (b) The acceptance or refusal of such conduct is used as the basis or a factor in decisions affecting an individual's employment, education, living environment, or participation in a University Community; or (c) The conduct unreasonably impacts an individual's employment or academic performance or creates an intimidating, hostile, or offensive environment for that individual's employment, education, living environment, or participation in a University Community."

Sexual harassment is a form of sex discrimination. Sexual harassment can create such a hostile environment that the student cannot participate fully in activities or benefit from the educational resources of the university. To learn more about sexual harassment in educational settings, visit the U.S. Department of Education's Office for Civil Rights website.

*Stalking* is defined as a willful course of conduct involving repeated or continuing harassment made against the expressed wishes of another individual, which causes that individual to feel emotional distress, including fear, harassment, intimidation, or apprehension.

A large number of college-age students experience some type of unwanted sexual attention. In one study of more than 4,000 students, faculty, and staff at a large university, more than 40% indicated that they had experienced at least one type of unwanted sexual attention at least once (Cochran, Frazier, & Olson, 1997). A relatively new form of sexual harassment is sexually harassing and offensive e-mail including sexist jokes, sexually explicit materials, and sexual propositions. These unsolicited messages, much like obscene phone calls, have an especially negative impact on women who see them as uncontrollable and potentially threatening (Khoo & Senn, 2004).

Within the workplace, there is also growing concern about sexual harassment, with abuses occurring between supervisors and employees and among employees themselves. This kind of experience can have negative consequences for young people, especially if the attention goes on for a long time and there is no way to avoid it. Young people typically try to ignore this kind of attention, but this is more difficult when the person involved is a faculty member or someone in a position of authority. The second most common strategy is to avoid the person by changing classes, avoiding places where the person is known to go, or, in extreme cases, dropping out of school or quitting the job temporarily.

Some young people will confront the person, especially if they view the behavior as severe, but generally they avoid confrontation if the person is in a position of authority. Few will report the unwanted sexual attention or make a formal complaint. For many young people, the unwanted sexual attention comes from other members of their social group. The ambiguity of the situation and the lack of clear rules about this kind of behavior leave the burden on the targets of unwanted sexual attention to alter or modify their own behavior, even if that means disrupting their daily life.

## BINGE DRINKING

Reports of deaths on college campuses have raised new concerns about binge drinking (Thompson, 1998). In comparison to high school seniors or non-college-bound youth, students who are enrolled full time in college are more likely to engage in binge drinking (i.e., five or more drinks in a row). National surveys have found that 40% of college students report this kind of heavy "weekend" drinking, with male students participating at a somewhat higher rate (52%) than female students (31%; Johnston, O'Malley, & Bachman, 1999).

Binge drinking is part of college social life. More than 80% of college students say that they have some friends who get drunk at least once a week, and 45% say that their friends would not disapprove if they had five or more drinks once or twice each weekend (Johnston, O'Malley, & Bachman, 1997). Binge drinking is often part of the initiation into special clubs or a rite of passage at the 21st birthday.

Binge drinking is an expression of autonomy gone awry. The highest rates of binge drinking are among college students who are not living with their parents. Rates are higher among residential colleges than among commuter colleges, and among members of fraternities and sororities (Gfroerer, Greenblatt, & Wright, 1997). Young people get together and begin partying and drinking routinely each weekend. They drink if the football team wins or loses; if exams are over or before they begin; to celebrate birthdays, Halloween, or winning a bet; to recover from breaking up; to welcome new friends or to say goodbye; to forget the week past and to cheer

Binge drinking has become a socially acceptable activity on many college campuses. Many celebrations and rituals are centered around the performance of unique feats of consumption.

on the week ahead. Every so often, the drinking turns into chaos. Fires are started, fights break out, cars are overturned, and furniture and windows are smashed. At this point, young people have trouble asserting control over one another.

Colleges and universities have taken a variety of stands regarding the prevention or reduction of heavy drinking. Some prohibit alcohol use on campus for anyone under age 21. Others include alcohol policies and penalties in their recruitment materials, hoping to discourage students who want to do a lot of heavy drinking from enrolling. Still other schools have active alcohol prevention programs, including on-campus, alcohol-free forms of entertainment and activities well into the early morning hours. Colleges and universities have begun to form stronger allegiances with local bars and restaurants, encouraging them to monitor student IDs more stringently and to limit the amount of alcohol they serve (Thompson, 1998).

## SEXUALLY TRANSMITTED DISEASES

**Sexually transmitted diseases** (STDs) include a wide range of bacterial, viral, and yeast infections that are transmitted through different forms of sexual contact. Approximately 15 million people contract one or more STDs each year, with the early and later adolescent age groups showing the greatest risk. Although much of the recent attention about STDs has focused on HIV and AIDS, in fact, trichomoniasis, chlamydia, herpes, and human papillomavirus infections are thought to be the most prevalent of the STDs in the United States (Centers for Disease Control, 2000). Although cases of syphilis and gonorrhea have declined over recent years, women ages 15–19 have the highest rates of gonorrhea of all age groups of women; and men ages 20–24 have the highest rates of all age groups of men (Centers for Disease Control and Prevention, 2004). A full report of the current status of STD infections in the United States can be found at the website of the Centers for Disease Control and Prevention, http://www.cdc.gov/nchstp/dstd/disease_info.htm

Some basic practices are relevant for preventing all STDs. These include limiting the number of sexual partners, consistent use of condoms during sexual intercourse, avoiding unprotected contact during any type of genital sexual activity, and refraining from sexual intercourse when either you or your partner is infected. Some young people who have not experienced vaginal intercourse engage in other types of sexual experiences through which STDs can also be spread (Schuster, Bell, & Kanouse, 1996).

What factors have been identified as placing later adolescents, and college students in particular, at risk for STDs? The following list suggests some of the key issues:

1. College students do not perceive themselves to be a high-risk group. This may be due in part to the sense of egocentrism and personal fable discussed in Chapter 10 (Early Adolescence). Students may think of themselves as

invincible and underestimate their risk. Even if they understand the principles related to the transmission of STDs, they do not define themselves as personally at risk (Serovich & Greene, 1997).

2. Young people in the United States are inconsistent in their use of contraceptives. In one short-term longitudinal study, female college students were asked about their use of contraceptives over a 6-month period. Many who were using oral contraceptives did not continue to use them 6 months later. Others who were using condoms consistently at the first interview were no longer using them 6 months later (Kusseling, Wenger, & Shapiro, 1995).

3. Inconsistent condom use is associated with other health-related factors. Young people who are more likely to use and abuse alcohol and drugs are also likely to be inconsistent in their condom use. Those who follow a more health-promoting lifestyle, including getting regular exercise and eating a balanced diet, are more likely to be consistent in their condom use (Fortenberry, Costa, Jessor, & Donovan, 1997).

4. Unprotected sexual activity is often associated with drunkenness, an activity that is frequent on college campuses. When young people get drunk several times a month, they are more likely to have sexual relations with multiple partners.

5. The consistent use of condoms requires open communication between the partners. Adolescents are often reluctant to discuss the use of a condom and lack the assertive communication skills to insist. In cases where young women are less sexually experienced than their male partners, they may lack the confidence to make this a condition of sexual activity (Crooks & Bauer, 1996).

The three examples of unwanted sexual attention, binge drinking, and sexually transmitted diseases illustrate common challenges associated with entry into the expanded social world of later adolescence. These problems are linked to the difficulties that later adolescents have in imposing structure and norms on the behavior of their peers and in acknowledging their own vulnerability. In a period of life characterized by openness to new experiences and experimentation with the limits and boundaries of life's roles, some young people place themselves and others at risk by pushing those boundaries too far.

# Chapter Summary

At the close of later adolescence, most young people are making the transition from childhood to adulthood. However, the process is gradual for most and increasingly prolonged into the decades of the 20s and 30s. Later adolescents are striving for self-sufficiency in a complex culture. Many have achieved a new degree of independence from their parents, so that ties of love, trust, and support are expressed within a framework of mutual respect and autonomous decision making. The process of achieving autonomy from parents opens the door to new considerations of basic ego structures, including gender identity, morality, and career aspirations. In each of these areas, a young person has the cognitive ability to reflect on the earlier socialization pressures of family and neighborhood and to construct his or her own point of view.

The formulation of gender identity requires an integration of the biological, psychological, and societal meanings associated with being a man or a woman. It is a powerful lens through which many other aspects of personal identity are interpreted, including the content of values, commitment to family relationships, preferences and expectations for career choice, and beliefs about one's role in an intimate relationship.

Exposure to a diversity of information, relationships, and worldviews stimulates moral reasoning. The change from conventional to postconventional morality that often occurs during later adolescence involves a rethinking of traditional moral principles. During this period, there may be a loosening of ties to the family of origin and an increase in encounters with an expanding network of friends, students, and coworkers. Through interactions with diverse reference groups, there is an increasing recognition of the subcultural relativity of one's moral code. There may also be a degree of conflict over which moral values have personal meaning.

The process of career choice, often accompanied by periods of uncertainty and confusion, is influenced by interacting factors, including personal abilities and attributes, emotional and motivational factors, family and societal factors, educational background, gender identity and gender role socialization, and the situational realities of the current labor market. Ideally, one's choice of occupation is the result of personal experimentation, introspection, self-evaluation, fact finding, and intuition. As such, this choice becomes intimately interwoven with one's psychological development.

Those who have resolved the psychosocial crisis of individual identity versus identity confusion have an integrated identity that includes a definition of themselves as sexual, moral, political, and career participants. Identity achievement represents a private sense of unity and confidence in one's beliefs as well as a more public integration of roles and commitments to specific values.

The strain of this stage is felt in the tension between the person's need to question and experiment and the society's expectations for closure on significant themes, particularly occupation, gender identity, and political ideology. The expansion of roles and relationships exposes many young people to new views that require evaluation. The crisis of individual identity versus identity confusion suggests a new synthesis of earlier identifications, present values, and future goals into a consistent self-concept. This unity of self is achieved only after a period of uncertainty and open questioning. Role experimentation during this time is an essential strategy for coping with new information and new value orientations. Once young people know what they stand for, they can commit themselves more deeply to others.

The prime adaptive ego quality of fidelity reflects the capacity to commit oneself to an ideology or belief system. The core pathology of repudiation suggests an intense rejection of certain values and beliefs. Although most later adolescents are forming a positive vision of the self that is connected to a shared community, some are defining themselves in opposition, as rebels, terrorists, or avengers.

## Further Reflection

1. What distinguishes the stage of later adolescence from early adolescence and early adulthood?
2. How is the process of achieving autonomy from parents related to identity development?
3. What changes would you expect to see in gender identity over the college years? Do you think men and women become more traditional or more nontraditional in their views about gender roles during college? Why?
4. What aspects of the college experience influence moral development? What is the direction of that influence?

5. Consider the bidirectional influence of career decision making and identity development. How do the two influence each other?
6. What are some contemporary factors that may make it difficult to resolve the conflict of individual identity versus identity confusion during the period from age 18 to 24?
7. What is ethnic identity? How does it contribute to adjustment and identity achievement in later adolescence?

## On the Web

**VISIT OUR WEBSITE**

Go to http://www.wadsworth.com/psychology to find online resources directly linked to your book.

## Casebook

For additional case material related to this chapter, see the case entitled "Life Turning Points and Career Choice" in *Life Span Development: A Case Book*, by Barbara and Philip Newman, Laura Landry-Meyer, and Brenda J. Lohman, pp. 153–156. The case illustrates how a young person's encounter with a difficult personal situation leads to a revised sense of self and a new focus on meaningful goals for the future.

# CHAPTER 12

# EARLY ADULTHOOD (24–34 YEARS)

*Family of Acrobats with Monkey, 1905/Pablo Picasso (1881-1973)/© 2005 Estate of Pablo Picasso/Artists Rights Society (ARS), New York; Scala/Art Resource, NY*

*The major themes of early adulthood—work, intimacy, marriage, and parenting—are all captured in this image of the Young Harlequin Family. The challenges of adulthood often emerge in efforts to balance and integrate diverse life roles.*

■ MAJOR CONCEPTS IN THE STUDY OF ADULTHOOD

Social Roles
Life Course
Fulfillment Theories

■ DEVELOPMENTAL TASKS

Exploring Intimate Relationships
CASE STUDY: HOW LOVE MAKES
ITS WAY INTO A RELATIONSHIP
Childbearing
Work
CASE STUDY: JAY CROWE
Lifestyle

■ THE PSYCHOSOCIAL CRISIS:
INTIMACY VERSUS ISOLATION

Intimacy
Isolation

■ THE CENTRAL PROCESS: MUTUALITY AMONG PEERS

■ THE PRIME ADAPTIVE EGO QUALITY
AND THE CORE PATHOLOGY

Love
Exclusivity

■ APPLIED TOPIC: DIVORCE

Factors Contributing to Divorce
Coping with Divorce

■ CHAPTER SUMMARY

■ FURTHER REFLECTION

▶ *To identify and define selected concepts that are especially relevant for understanding development during adulthood, including social roles, the life course, and fulfillment theories.*

▶ *To analyze the process of forming intimate relationships, including initial attractions, mate selection, and commitment to a long-term relationship; the role of cohabitation in forming close relationships; and the challenges that one faces in adjusting to the early years of marriage.*

▶ *To describe the factors associated with the decision to have children, the impact of childbearing on the intimate relationship, the developing parental relationship, and the contribution of childbearing to growth in adulthood.*

▶ *To explore the concept of work as a stimulus for psychosocial development in early adulthood, with special focus on the technical skills, authority relations, demands and hazards, and interpersonal relations in the work environment.*

▶ *To examine the concept of lifestyle as the expression of individual identity, with consideration for the pace of life, balancing competing role demands, building a supportive social network, and adopting practices to promote health and fitness.*

▶ *To define and describe the psychosocial crisis of intimacy versus isolation; the central process through which the crisis is resolved, mutuality among peers; the prime adaptive ego quality of love; and the core pathology of exclusivity.*

▶ *To analyze divorce as a life stressor in early adulthood, including the factors contributing to it and the process of coping with it.*

WELCOME TO THE study of adulthood. All that has gone before can be seen as preparation; all that follows can be viewed as actualization. We have considered psychosocial development through seven preparatory stages of life, encompassing approximately 24 years. During these stages, an individual undergoes rapid physical, cognitive, social, and emotional development. In the United States, life expectancy at birth is currently about 77 years. Thus, more than 50 years remain after the seven preparatory stages. In our conceptual scheme, four stages of psychosocial development unfold during these 50 years. In this chapter, we discuss a few new theoretical concepts about development in adulthood, and then we address the period of early adulthood. ∎

# MAJOR CONCEPTS IN THE STUDY OF ADULTHOOD

In Chapters 3 (Psychosocial Theory) and 4 (Major Theories for Understanding Human Development), we introduced psychosocial theory and a number of other theories that ex-

plain the processes of continuity and change over the life span. In this chapter, we expand the arsenal of theoretical constructs that help account for the directions of growth in adult life. Biological factors associated with maturity and aging play an ongoing role in shaping the life story. The biological, psychological, and societal systems continue to interact, but the nature of lives becomes increasingly diverse and more difficult to characterize as "stagelike" over time. Life stories are guided by historical events, unexpected crises and opportunities, and personal choices. The focus and aim of life becomes increasingly contextualized, based on societal expectations, the nature of interpersonal relationships, work, and family. The roles and experiences of earlier life stages serve as a unique personal context in which new roles and activities are assumed. At the same time, new levels of mastery and autonomy allow individuals to make decisions and choices about the kinds of environments in which they participate. The bidirectional nature of development is increasingly obvious in adulthood as interests, beliefs, and goals guide the direction and focus of actions, and these actions and their consequences in turn create the context for the revision of interests, beliefs, and goals. In the following section, we review the concepts of social roles, the life course, and personal fulfillment, ideas that help us understand the psychosocial dynamics of adulthood.

## SOCIAL ROLES

**Social role** is one of the concepts most frequently used for understanding adulthood (Brim, 1966, 1968; Parsons, 1955). The major concepts of social role theory, which were introduced in Chapter 4, are summarized in Table 12.1. We considered this concept in Chapter 8 (Early School Age) when we discussed gender role identification, and again in Chapter 11 (Later Adolescence) when we examined individual identity versus identity confusion. Clearly, many roles are learned and enacted during childhood. In adulthood, however, people assume multiple roles that expand their opportunities for self-expression and bring them into contact with new social demands. Adulthood can be seen as a series of increasingly differentiated and complex roles that the individual plays for substantial lengths of time. The salient roles of adulthood, such as worker, spouse, friend, parent, teacher, mentor, volunteer, or community leader, give structure to adult identity and meaning to life.

Social roles link individuals to their social environments. The roles that an individual plays exist as socially shared patterns of expectations for behavior. All roles can be characterized by costs and benefits that accumulate over time. For example, by assuming the role of worker, one has access to the benefits associated with the role, such as social status, social support, or financial resources. One also becomes responsible for meeting the expectations of the role, such as working for a certain number of hours each week or completing one's work to a certain standard of quality. Over one's life, the costs and benefits of the roles accumulate, influencing the ease or difficulty with which new roles and role transitions can be managed (Jackson, 2004). For example, if a person's worker role involves many short-term jobs with no retirement benefits, the transition to retirement may be more difficult financially, but the person may have less identification with a specific worker role and find the transition into retirement psychologically easier.

© Paul Barton / The Stock Market

*The social roles of loving partner, parent, and worker are coming together in a comfortable balance that allows time for playfulness and personal fulfillment.*

Roles are reciprocal, requiring complementary role identities such as teacher–student, mother–child in order to be enacted and sustained. Thus, participation in multiple roles brings with it a form of social integration and social support (Thoits, 1999; Wethington, Moen, Glasgow, & Pillemer,

**Table 12.1** Major Concepts of Social Role Theory

| CONCEPT | EXPLANATION |
|---|---|
| Social role | Parts or identities a person assumes that are also social positions: kinship roles, age roles, gender roles, occupational roles |
| Role enactment | Patterned characteristics of social behavior generated by a social role |
| Role expectations | Scripts or shared expectations for behavior that are linked to each role |
| Role gain | Addition of roles |
| Role strain | Stress caused by too many expectations within a role |
| Role conflict | Conflict caused by competing demands of different roles |
| Role loss | Ending of a role; may result in stress and disorientation |
| Dimensions of life roles that vary from person to person | Number of roles |
| | Intensity of involvement in roles |
| | Time demands of each role |
| | Structure or flexibility of the role |

2000). Involvement in multiple roles allows adults to help socialize younger generations. Only in adulthood do individuals experience the behavioral requirements of many of their roles, which in turn provide a basis on which to train their children for the demands of adulthood (Kite, 1996).

The expectations associated with adult roles provide a frame of reference within which individuals make their own personal decisions. For example, a man may know what is expected of him in the worker role, but he may choose to ignore those expectations and strive for greater responsibilities, more power, or more autonomy. People can conform to role expectations, revise them, or reject them altogether. In addition to the tensions produced by role conflicts and role strain, some of the stresses of adulthood result from the need to redefine certain role expectations in order to preserve an authentic sense of self.

## LIFE COURSE

**Life course** refers to the integration and sequencing of phases of work and family life over time. Glen Elder (1985, 1996), who has been a leader in the elaboration of the life course perspective, described the two central themes of *trajectories* and *transitions*. A **trajectory** is the path of one's life experiences in a specific domain, particularly work and family. The family trajectory might include marriage, parenthood, grandparenthood, and widowhood. A **transition** is the beginning or ending of an event or role relationship. In the work trajectory, for example, transitions might be getting one's first job, being laid off, and going back to school for an advanced degree. Transitions are the events that make up a lifelong trajectory. A person's work and family trajectories are embedded in a sociohistorical context. For example, for people born in the early 1920s, the events of World War II, occurring during their 20s, influenced their work and family formation. For many young men, the planned work trajectory was interrupted by military service, and many young women entered the labor market unexpectedly. At the close of the war, in the late 1940s and early 1950s, many couples who had delayed parenting started their families, which gave rise to the baby boom generation.

The life course concept can be applied to the content of individual life histories as they are expressed in a social and historical time period. Each person's life course can be thought of as a pattern of the adaptations to the configuration of cultural expectations, resources, and barriers experienced during a particular time period. One form of cultural expectations is what Bernice Neugarten and her colleagues (Neugarten, Moore, & Lowe, 1965) termed the **social clock**. This term refers to "age norms and age expectations [that] operate as prods and brakes upon behavior, in some instances hastening behavior and in some instances delaying it" (p. 710). Neugarten and her associates suggested that social class groups tend to agree on the appropriate age for significant life events, such as marriage, childrearing, and retirement. This consensus exerts social pressure on individuals in the group, pushing them to assume a particular role at an expected age. Age norms may also suppress behaviors that are considered inappropriate for one's age. Adults are aware of existing norms regarding the timing of certain behaviors and evaluate their own behaviors as being "on time," "too soon," or "too late."

Implied in the notion of the social clock are expectations about the sequencing of entry into new roles and age-related role transitions. For example, European-American adults in the United States tend to view an ideal sequence as work, marriage, and parenting, in that order. Research indicates that for women, following this sequence is associated with better mental health, including less depression and greater happiness in adulthood. Among African Americans, however, the sequence of work, parenting, and then marriage is associated with less depression and greater happiness. This suggests that different social norms for **role sequencing** may be operating in the respective ethnic communities (Jackson, 2004).

The social clock is constantly being reset as people confront the challenges, demands, and new structures of modern society. In contemporary society, with the lengthening of the life expectancy and the increasing vitality of older adults, there are fewer and fewer domains in which a person is considered "too old" to participate (Neugarten 1990).

Figure 12.1 provides a view of the age-linked changes in occupational and family careers. The figure maps the convergence of transitions across the occupational and family trajectories, illustrating periods of potential harmony and conflict between the demands in the two trajectories. The bottom line shows a model of transitions in a family career. The line above shows a model of transitions in an occupational career. Sometimes these transitions occur around the same time in life. For example, in Figure 12.1, marriage occurs during a period of job experimentation when a person may be changing jobs. This could create tension in the marriage if it results in economic insecurity. Occupational experimentation might be cut short in order to establish financial stability for the marriage. The conflicts that arise in coordinating these family and occupational careers may contribute to the high divorce rate in the first year following marriage. Looking at Figure 12.1, you could consider many other examples where the demands of the family and occupational careers influence each other.

In considering adult lives in contemporary society, one can see that this is only one possible map of the interconnections between work and family in the course of a life. The occupational and family careers look quite different for the following people: a woman who extends her educational preparation to include a professional degree, works before marriage, and delays childbearing into her middle to late 30s; a woman who remains single and dedicates her energy to excellence in a career; and a woman who marries right after high school, begins having children at 18, works during her childbearing years, and then retires at 55 to enjoy her grandchildren and her personal freedom.

The pattern of the life course is influenced by the historical era. The life course of a person who was born in 1900 and died in 1975, including the ages of completion of educational

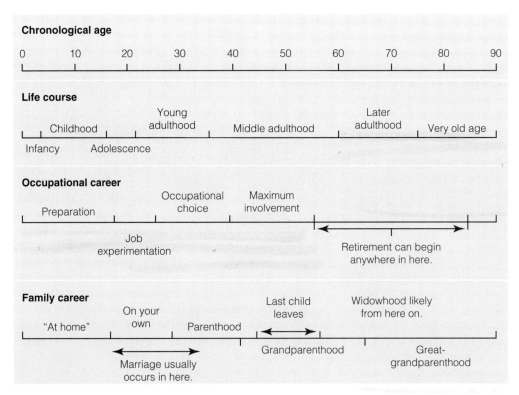

**Chronological age**

| 0 | 10 | 20 | 30 | 40 | 50 | 60 | 70 | 80 | 90 |

**Life course**

Childhood | Young adulthood | Middle adulthood | Later adulthood | Very old age

Infancy    Adolescence

**Occupational career**

Preparation | Occupational choice | Maximum involvement | Retirement can begin anywhere in here.

Job experimentation

**Family career**

"At home" | On your own | Parenthood | Last child leaves | Widowhood likely from here on.

Marriage usually occurs in here.

Grandparenthood | Great-grandparenthood

**FIGURE 12.1**

A Hypothetical Life Course

Source: Adapted from Atchley, 1975.

attainment, entry into the labor market, marriage, and retirement, would look quite different from that of a person born in 1925 and reaching age 75 in 2000. The two people would have gone through the same chronological ages, but during different periods of history, with different opportunities, expectations, and challenges. The first person would have been 30 at the time of the great depression. Her family could have been seriously influenced by loss of employment, difficulty in finding work, and loss of savings for retirement. The second person would have been 30 in the 1950s. Having served in the military during World War II, he would have been eligible for the GI Bill benefits to go to college, resulting in new occupational opportunities that contribute to occupational advancement during a booming economy. There are many other possibilities of historical impact, but these example illustrates how historical factors might affect the life course.

All the people who are roughly the same age during a particular historical period are referred to as a **cohort**. Differences in medical advances, occupational opportunities, educational resources, and the number of people in the cohort are four factors that may affect the pattern of life events for cohort members. Moreover, major crises, such as war, famine, and political unrest, may alter a trajectory by introducing unanticipated transitions—for example, closing off certain activities, as when young men interrupt their education to go to war, or opening up new opportunities, as when women enter the labor market because many of the men are in the mil-

itary (Elder, 1986; Elder, Caspi, & van Nguyen, 1986; Elder, Shanahan, & Clipp, 1997).

The study of the life course focuses not only on the sequencing of events but on the psychological growth that occurs as adults strive to adjust to changing and sometimes conflicting role demands. At different ages, people bring a distinct perspective to these events. For example, a crisis such as widespread unemployment may have a direct impact on the work trajectory of an adult, and also on the family environment or educational opportunities of a child. The person's developmental level and the particular developmental tasks and psychosocial crises that are most salient at the time will determine how a specific event will influence the life course.

## FULFILLMENT THEORIES

As the norms and cultural expectations of modern life become more flexible, there is a renewed interest in personal fulfillment and self-actualization as concepts that guide individual choices and directions for growth. The humanistic or fulfillment theorists emphasize the purposive, goal-oriented strivings that characterize adult life. People do not always act to reduce tension, achieve equilibrium, or avoid risk. Over the course of adult life, people seek out new challenges, impose new and difficult standards on their behavior, and put themselves in unfamiliar situations in order to seek fulfillment.

Charlotte Buhler was one of the earliest and most continuously productive of the humanistic or fulfillment theorists. Her work emphasized the centrality of life goals and intentionality through the life course (Buhler & Massarik, 1968). In her view, each person experiences life within a complex orientation to past, present, and future time. It is the hope for meeting future goals and for achieving a sense of fulfillment that prompts psychological growth. Buhler saw the years of early and middle adulthood as a time of setting definite goals and striving to achieve them. Toward the end of middle adulthood, there is focused preoccupation with the assessment of goals and the analysis of successes and failures. This process ends with a sense of fulfillment, partial fulfillment, or despair.

The last phase of life is seen as a reaction to this assessment. People may resign themselves to their successes and failures (as Erikson suggests in the concept of integrity). However, some people may be motivated to return to an earlier phase of striving to achieve unfulfilled goals or to undo past failures. Some people end their lives in a despondent state of unfulfillment, concluding that their existence has not been meaningful (as we suggest in the concept of immortality versus extinction). Three concepts from fulfillment theory are especially relevant for understanding the directions of growth in adulthood: competence, self-acceptance, and self-actualization.

## ■ COMPETENCE

Robert White (1960, 1966), introduced the term **competence motivation** to explain behaviors that are motivated by a desire for new levels of mastery. People strive to increase their competence through repetition and practice of skills, by gaining new information, through education and training, and through feedback from earlier efforts at mastery. The competence motive can be seen in an infant's efforts at self-feeding even when those efforts result in less food making its way from dish to mouth. The competence motive can be seen in the determination of an adult to learn to ski despite the cold, the expense, and the sore muscles. It can be seen when retired persons enroll in adult education courses to expand their knowledge. Over the course of adulthood, competence is expanded through a deepening of interests, by pursuing information and experiences that contribute to what we often term "expert" knowledge.

## ■ SELF-ACCEPTANCE

According to Carl Rogers's theory of personality development, an essential component of continued growth is to experience and accept the authentic self (Rogers, 1959, 1961). This means achieving a sense of trust in one's ideas and impulses rather than denying or constantly disapproving of them. It means fostering acceptance and trust in relationships with others, so that people bring their most authentic selves into interactions. Self-acceptance is a product of the positive feelings that come from being direct and from the acceptance one receives from others.

In Rogers's view, barriers to self-acceptance come largely from conditions that others place on their love or approval. If significant others only give approval based on meeting certain conditions, then the person learns to modify his or her behavior so that it conforms to those conditions. However, these modifications are made at the price of self-acceptance. They lead a person into a pattern of inhibiting or rejecting new thoughts and relying more and more on the opinions of others. The greater the discrepancy between the authentic self as one perceives it and daily experience, the more one is likely to experience life as threatening and stressful. The greater the harmony between the authentic self and experience, the more likely one is to experience a sense of trust, freedom, and creativity in daily functioning. An implication of this theory is that well-being is a product of person–environment co-adaptation. In the search for self-acceptance, the person seeks social settings where his or her thoughts, beliefs, and actions are highly valued and where the social setting can be modified to value and endorse the talents of those who participate in it.

## ■ SELF-ACTUALIZATION

According to Abraham Maslow's theory, human beings are always in a state of striving (Maslow, 1968). **Self-actualization** is a powerful, growth-oriented motive that sits atop a pyramid of needs (see Figure 12.2). In Maslow's view, the primary human motives concern physiological needs, such as hunger, thirst, and a need for sleep. The second level focuses on safety and security—the need to find protection from dangers and threats. As those needs are satisfied and maintained at a relatively stable level, people direct their energy to satisfying needs for belongingness, love, and self-esteem. Finally, if those needs can be met and sustained, the person directs energy to self-actualization, a motive that urges the person to make optimal use of his or her full potential, to become a more effective, creative participant in daily life. The need for self-actualization, like White's idea of competence, becomes a driving force, urging the person to seek new levels of insight and personal fulfillment.

The fulfillment theories suggest that growth and maturation in adulthood are characterized by successful encounters with life challenges that result in a sense of purpose, meaning, and mastery. Questions have been raised about the possible negative impact of prejudice and discrimination on the mental health and sense of personal self-worth of members of minority groups. A study of a national sample called "Midlife in the U.S." examined this issue (Ryff, Keyes, & Hughes, 2003). Psychological well-being was defined in terms of constructs basic to fulfillment theory, including a sense of autonomy, environmental mastery, personal growth, positive relations with others, purpose in life, and self-acceptance. The results showed that individuals who were members of minority

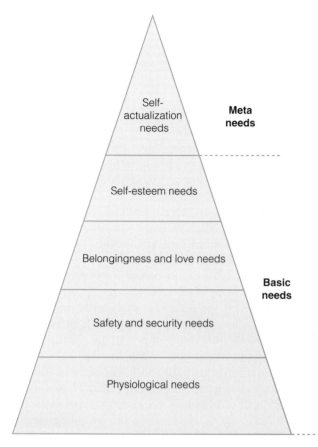

**FIGURE 12.2**

Maslow's Hierarchy of Needs

© Jeff Janowski/Getty Images

*Maya Angelou exemplifies Maslow's theory of self-actualization. She transcended the challenges of her early childhood and found a powerful poetic voice. She is able to connect to the passions and fears of others and offers a sense of personal dignity.*

groups, including African Americans and Hispanics, had higher levels of well-being than comparable European American participants, even after perceived discrimination was taken into account. With regard to the sense of purpose of life, this advantage was especially noteworthy among the more highly educated participants, where the more highly educated African Americans had a greater sense of purpose in life than the highly educated European American participants. The study found that perceived discrimination was negatively associated with psychological well-being for women but not for men. Thus, two processes seem to be at work at once: (1) perceived discrimination undermines psychological well-being for women, and (2) minority status is associated with many indicators of psychological strength for both women and men.

The research did not examine the processes through which psychological growth might be enhanced for members of minority groups. One explanation is that minority group parents help their children make meaning of discrimination and identify the emotions associated with it so that it does not harm their sense of personal worth. Thus when they grow up, children who experience this positive racial/ethnic socialization are inoculated against the negative impact of discrimination. Another explanation is that individuals who are more

closely identified with their ethnic group experience a sense of purpose, pride, and social support that helps to buffer them from the stressful impact of discrimination. Finally, it may be that encounters with adversity bring forth new strengths that enhance a person's sense of mastery. All these explanations suggest that under conditions of adversity, many members of minority groups emerge into adulthood with ego strengths that provide critical resources for coping with the challenges of life.

In summary, the concepts of life roles, the life course, and fulfillment theories extend an understanding of psychological development in adulthood. Childhood is over. One addresses life with great expectations and exhilaration. After the initial excitement of the period subsides, one comes to realize that there is serious work to be done. Young adults engage in intense and meaningful relationships in marriage or with intimate partners, friends, and coworkers. They attempt to cope with the complex challenges of daily life by balancing multiple roles. At the same time, they put into action the practices that express the values and beliefs to which they became committed at the close of later adolescence. They establish and revise goals, setting new standards for competence and self-acceptance. Over the course of adulthood, people return periodically to reflect on the meaning of their life and the value of their accomplishments. The expanding period of later adulthood and very old age provide new opportunities to seek self-actualization and moments of joy through intense dedication to personal and interpersonal achievements.

# DEVELOPMENTAL TASKS

We have identified age 24 as the beginning of the psychosocial stage of early adulthood. This is merely an approximation. From a psychosocial perspective, the time of entry into a new stage is based on a convergence of experiences—including the accomplishments of the previous stage, the resolution of the prior psychosocial crisis, and the beginning efforts to achieve the tasks of the new stage—rather than on chronological age. In contemporary society, one begins to experience adulthood as several roles emerge, typically those of worker, committed partner, and parent. The average age of entry into marriage has advanced over the past 20 years to the point where the majority of young adults in the 20–24 age range in the United States are unmarried. Later age at marriage is associated with an older age for first childbearing. Students take an average of 5 to 6 years to complete college, and young people seem to be involved in a longer period of job experimentation before settling into their occupational career. All of these factors argue for advancing the approximate age of entry into adulthood.

At the same time, one must keep in mind the diversity of life stories. Some young adults assume significant role responsibilities, autonomy from their family, and self-sufficiency at relatively early ages. Others delay the typical commitments of adulthood well into their 30s. The subjective sense of being an adult is not highly correlated with chronological age nor with passing through specific transitions such as voting, graduating from college, getting married, or starting out in a career. Rather, the psychological sense of being an adult is associated with perceptions of making one's own decisions, taking responsibility for oneself, and becoming financially independent of one's parents (Arnett, 2000). In today's world, adulthood is a psychosocial transition during which commitments, priorities, and preferences are translated into action.

The most important social factors contributing to the creation of a lifestyle are whether one establishes a permanent, intimate relationship with a partner; the characteristics of one's partner; whether one has children; the characteristics of those children; and one's work. The extent to which one has a choice about each of these factors depends on cultural values and restrictions, societal norms and barriers, and socioeconomic factors, especially educational attainment. Each factor interacts with personality, interests, and life goals to shape a lifestyle.

## EXPLORING INTIMATE RELATIONSHIPS

The period of early adulthood is a time when men and women explore the possibility of forming relationships that combine emotional closeness, shared interests, a shared vision of the future, and sexual intimacy. The nature of these relationships differs for various couples. Some young adults engage in a form of "serial monogamy"—a sequence of dyadic pairings with no commitment to marriage. Others find a same-sex partner with whom they make a long-term commitment even though formal marriage is not possible. Most young people become involved in dating relationships that involve both sexual and emotional intimacy. In this section, we emphasize marriage as the context in which intimate relationships develop. This is due in part to the great tendency for U.S. adults to marry, and in part because much of the research literature focuses on satisfaction among married couples. However, it is important to recognize that many forms of intimate relationships in addition to marriage are being established during early adulthood, including serious dating, cohabitation with or without the intention of marriage, and commitments between gay and lesbian couples.

Marriage is one context in which work on intimate social relationships takes place. In 2003, 89% of men and 91% of women had been married at least once by the ages of 45 to 54. Among those between 65 and 74 years old in 2003, 95% of men and 97% of women had been married (U.S. Census Bureau, 2004). The main change in the marriage pattern in the United States over the past 50 years is that more young adults postpone marriage until the end of their 20s. The percentage of single, never-married women between the ages of 20 and 24 rose from 28% in 1960 to 75% in 2003. The comparable increase for single men was from 53% in 1960 to 86% in 2003 (U.S. Bureau of the Census, 1976, 2004). In the United States, it is now normative for men to be single throughout their 20s and for women to be single in the first half of their 20s.

Delaying the age at marriage is related to several other social trends, including having children at a later age, smaller projected family size, and, therefore, fewer years devoted to childrearing. Delaying age at marriage is also related to changing norms regarding sexual experimentation as a single person. The 1980s brought the uncoupling of sexual activity, marriage, and childbearing. Younger age at entry into sexual activity and increases in rates of affairs and cohabitation suggest that even though many young adults do not marry, they become involved in intimate relationships during their 20s.

Roughly 100 years of social science research has established that satisfaction in the relationship of marriage contributes significantly to psychological well-being, including a greater sense of social integration and protection from other life stressors. For most adults, happiness in life depends more on having a satisfying marriage than on any other domain of adult life, including work, friendships, hobbies, and community activities. Longitudinal studies of adults who either remained single or got married and remained married over a 7-year period found that those who were married had higher levels of well-being and fewer mental health problems (Horwitz, White, & Howell-White, 1996; Williams, 2003). The research suggests that the benefits of being married for mental health and life satisfaction accrue primarily in the context of happy marriages, where the partners describe their relationship as one in which their spouse makes them feel valued and cared for (Williams, 2003).

## ■ READINESS TO MARRY

What determines whether a dating relationship will end in matrimony? A basic factor is the person's underlying desire to marry. In a national sample of unmarried people ages 19 to 25, the mean score on a 5-point scale (where 1 = *strongly disagree* and 5 = *strongly agree*) to the statement "I would like to get married some day" was 4.3 (South, 1993). Only 12.6% of the respondents indicated that they did not want to marry.

Beyond the desire to marry, an important factor is the readiness of the two people for a long-term commitment. Work on identity must be far enough along so that the possibility of a deep, emotional involvement with another person will be regarded as exciting rather than frightening. In studies of college students, a relationship was found between identity status and the quality of intimacy. Those students who had achieved identity reported the most genuine intimate relationships. In contrast, those who were characterized as identity confused were the least intimate and the most isolated (Craig-Bray et al., 1988; Dyk & Adams, 1990).

Early and later adolescents are likely to be thinking about intimacy issues long before their work on identity is completed. Thus, intimacy does not come after identity but emerges alongside identity work (Adams & Archer, 1994). However, when faced with dilemmas in which needs for identity and intimacy conflict, both men and women tend to give identity issues higher priority. The following example and others like it were presented to adolescents to determine whether identity or intimacy would be the primary developmental issue guiding an important decision:

Allison has been accepted to a very prestigious college with a reputation for a high quality English department. She knows she wants to major in English. The main drawback to this college is that it is a six hour driving distance from her boyfriend. She also has been accepted to a college located within an hour away from her boyfriend, which has an average English department. She is unsure of which one to choose. How much consideration should be given to each of the following issues in resolving this dilemma?

a. the quality of the program
b. the distance from her boyfriend

Why? (Lacombe & Gay, 1998, p. 801)

In this study, young people placed greater emphasis on the identity-oriented solutions than on the intimacy-oriented solutions. However, women were more likely to try to balance the two, seeking ways to meet identity and intimacy needs in the same solution (Lacombe & Gay, 1998).

School enrollment as well as educational attainment have important links to relationship commitment. Young adults who are still in school are less likely to make a serious long-term commitment to an intimate partner, either through marriage or through cohabitation, than those who have completed school (Thornton, Axinn, & Teachman, 1995). The combination of educational and occupational goals and cultural views about the value of marriage create community expectations about the ideal age at marriage. The ideal age for marriage is likely to be younger in a working class community than in a middle class community, because expectations for continued education are not as great (Teachman, Polonko, & Scanzoni, 1987). In contrast, young people who attend college tend to have a later timetable for marriage. Advanced education delays marriage more frequently for women than for men, perhaps because young women who have had more years of education have alternative means to secure economic resources (Qian & Preston, 1993).

In addition to educational goals, readiness for a long-term intimate relationship may be determined by other aspects of one's personal agenda, such as reaching a certain level of achievement in one's career, completing military service, or earning a certain income. In each case, a person with this kind of ambition is less likely to seek a long-term partner or to be receptive to expressions of love from someone than he or she may be once the goal is achieved.

In the United States, most individuals have a great deal of freedom to choose their time of marriage and their marriage partner. Cultural values of individualism and autonomy provide support and justification for addressing personal goals prior to making a commitment to an intimate relationship. Although expectations that one will marry are strong, young adults have the freedom to follow their own timetables. However, in some ethnic groups, such as Asian Indians and Arab Americans, there is still a strong expectation that parents will guide the selection of a marriage partner. In other groups, such as the Mormons, the high value placed on sexual abstinence prior to marriage results in an earlier age at marriage than for other groups (DeGenova, 1997).

## ■ SELECTION OF A PARTNER

In the United States and other individualist cultures, most people believe that romantic love is the central reason for choosing a marriage partner. In societies with a more collectivist orientation, however, love is not necessarily relevant to

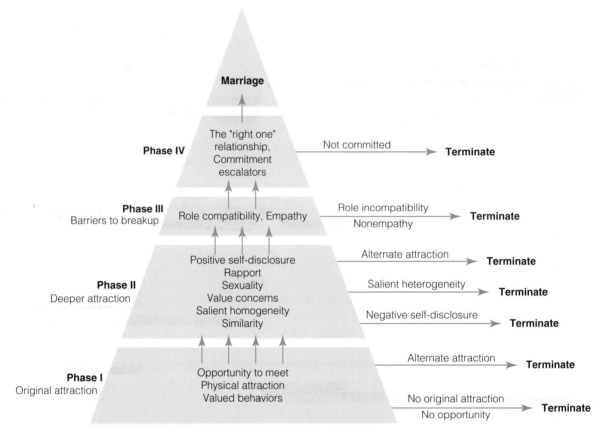

**FIGURE 12.3**

The Mate Selection Process in the United States

Source: Based on Adams, 1986.

the selection of a partner. In these cultures, the choice may be made by family members, based on religious, financial, or family background factors believed to contribute to a good match, not only for the person but also for the extended family system (Dion & Dion, 1993). In these cultural groups, the principle of **endogamy**, or marriage within one's well-defined group, is encouraged. An Asian Indian college student of Muslim faith describes her orientation toward marriage:

> A few years ago I fell in love with a Hindu guy, but after a while I realized I had to end the relationship. My mom, it would have broken her heart. I care too much about my family. People would look down on my parents if I married outside of our religion. . . . Muslims are good people. We are very focused. We have morals. I want to give my children that sense of identity. So I'm comfortable waiting until I meet an acceptable Muslim man. (Belsky, 1997, p. 279)

Figure 12.3 provides a theoretical model including four phases of increasing involvement in the mate selection process (Adams, 1986). At each phase, the relationship may be terminated if the key issues produce undesirable information or evaluation results. Also, the relationship may end if an alternative attraction becomes so strong that it reduces invest-

ment in the first relationship. The alternative attraction may be another person, a job, school, or the desire to achieve a personal goal. In contrast, investment in the relationship may increase if no attractive or acceptable alternatives are available (Bui, Peplau, & Hill, 1996).

Phase I, *original attraction*, captures the early process of partner identification. The principle of **homogamy** suggests that people are attracted to others who share important areas of similarity. Two of the salient similarities that have been studied are race and educational level. Using data from the 1990 census, researchers found that both married and cohabiting couples are quite homogamous with respect to race and educational level (Blackwell & Lichter, 2000). However, similarity extends beyond these basic demographic characteristics. For example, in a study of dating and mating preferences among college students, women preferred to date men who were similar to them in education and occupational level, and preferred to marry someone who was also similar in religious values and desire for children (Knox, Zusman, & Nieves, 1997). Other studies show that couples are similar in their preferences for leisure, their political orientation, and whether their parents had been divorced or not (Wolfinger, 2003).

Partners are selected from among those who are available for interaction. Many of the choices one makes during adolescence and young adulthood—such as where to go to college, where to work, which activities and social functions to attend, and where to take a vacation—determine whom one meets. People who occupy similar settings such as neighborhoods, college environments, work settings, or religious institutions are likely to be similar in certain characteristics that contribute to the observed homogamy in couples (Kalmijn & Flap, 2001).

Demographic realities influence the possibility of meeting suitable partners. In each community, for each age group of women, for example, the number of suitable, available partners may differ, depending on such characteristics as the educational level, employment opportunities, and racial composition of the men in that community (South & Lloyd, 1992). The number and characteristics of potential marriage partners differ if one lives in a metropolitan or in a more rural community. In one analysis, the sex ratio was 119 unmarried men for every 100 unmarried women in rural communities, and 106 unmarried men for every 100 unmarried women in metropolitan communities. Later age at marriage for women in urban communities may be explained in part by a lower availability of male partners (McLaughlin, Lichter, & Johnston, 1993).

Declines in the marriage rates for African Americans appear to be closely linked to the decline in the availability of appropriate African American male partners. Single, never-married African American women increased from 17% of the total female African American population in 1970 to 37% in 2004 (U.S. Census Bureau, 2004). This pattern is related in part to the high rates of mortality and imprisonment of African American men and in part to their economic marginality. The decline in employment opportunities from 1970 to 1990 in the manufacturing industries, where African American men had made earlier gains, coupled with increased crime and drug use in the urban communities contribute to the decline in the pool of "marriageable" African American men (Raley, 1996; Taylor, Chatters, Tucker, & Lewis, 1990).

Once two people meet, the question arises about what factors support their continued involvement. One's style of interaction—for example, whether one is shy and withdrawn or expressive and outgoing—influences the number and kinds of interactions one has with others. In the most general sense, the choice of a partner depends on the network of interactions in which one is involved. Among the people one encounters, some attract attention and others do not. For many young adults, online dating has become a way to expand one's contacts and reach a wider network of potential partners (see the box on Computer-Mediated Relationships, p. 396).

In contrast to the principle of homogamy, which emphasizes the role of similarity in the attraction process, **social evolutionary theory** suggests that men and women differ in the features they emphasize in evaluating someone as a desirable partner. The evolutionary perspective highlights the reproductive potential and the reproductive investment of one's partner. *Reproductive potential* refers to the physical, material, and social resources that a partner may be able to contribute to one's fertility and childrearing. *Reproductive investment* refers to the willingness of a potential partner to commit these resources to one's children. Men tend to emphasize the biological or physical resources of a potential partner, valuing youth and physical appearance in a partner more than do women. Women tend to emphasize the social status and economic resources of a potential partner, valuing earning potential and job stability in a partner more than do men (Geary, Vigil, & Byrd-Craven, 2004). In a cross-national study of heterosexual mate preferences in samples collected in Africa, Asia, Australia, Europe, New Zealand, and North and South America, David Buss (1994) found that men placed more emphasis on a partner's youth and physical appearance, whereas women placed more emphasis on a partner's financial prospects, dependability, and industriousness. In addition to physical appearance and social status, people who behave in an admirable, effective manner may be viewed as attractive or desirable. People seek others who will support their goals, who can be encouraging and positive, and who appear to be able to collaborate effectively in shared experiences (Sanders, 1997).

Phase I, *original attraction*, moves on to Phase II, *deeper attraction*, as the partners begin to disclose information about themselves, interact in ways that deepen the relationship, and discover areas of important similarity. In Phase II, the discovery of basic similarities and a feeling of rapport are central to continuing the relationship. Each person has key values and background characteristics that serve as a filter for assessing whether the other person is an eligible partner. Of course, eligibility is defined differently by different people. For some, any person who is conscious is eligible. Others have criteria that limit the choice of a marriage partner to someone of a certain age range, religion, race, educational background, and family history. For example, some adults would not consider marriage to someone who does not share their religious faith. For these people, only members of their own religious group are perceived as eligible partners. Looking at trends in the United States from the 1920s to the 1980s, religion appeared to play a lesser role and educational level played a greater role in limiting one's choice of a potential marriage partner. Young adults who were raised as Protestants and Catholics are more likely to marry one another today than in the past, whereas those whose highest educational level is a high school diploma and those who have attended college are less likely to intermarry (Kalmijn, 1991).

Many individuals may not even be aware of their own criteria for the eligibility of potential partners. For example, most men expect to marry women who are a few years younger than they are. Although they do not deliberately state this as a criterion for marriage, they simply do not interact with or feel drawn to a partner who is "too old" (Buunk et al., 2001).

TECHNOLOGY AND HUMAN DEVELOPMENT

# Computer-Mediated Relationships (Online Dating)

THESE TWO PERSONALS were posted on Lovecity.com and retrieved from the Internet on December 23, 2001:

Name: Mary. Age: 39. Sex: Female. Sexual Preference: Straight. Location: Rhode Island, US.

I'm a SWF 39 5'5" 125" blonde hair w/blue eyes. I'm in great shape and love to workout. I'm a fun loving, teddy bear type, love to be cuddled. Love to be outdoors, I love animals, children, camping, mountainbiking, hiking, waterfalls, romantic walks on the beach, traveling, very much into nature. I go to school full-time and I'm graduating in December of this year with a Associate in Computer Science, Micro-computing Networking Tech. I'm going for my CCNA at the end of August. I'm very honest, open, respectful, family and marriage minded. My dream would be to find someone who is spiritual, has principals, who is just high on life. I am an extremely positive person who cares about people and I don't play head games. I'm living and loving life and would love to grow old with that special man! Let's spend the rest of our lives building on a relationship that is one of a kind.

Name: Matthew. Age: 39. Sex: Male. Sexual Preference: Straight. Location: Rhode Island, US.

hello, im 6ft tall 190lbs short dirty blond hair brown eyes, i keep my self in shape, i enjoy mountain bike riding hiking or just spending time with some one intresting, i like a good movie or a day on the beach. i am looking for some one with same interest, not a couch potato. some one who cares about them self as well as other people i guess just a real person so if you like to enjoy life and have some fun with it then email me hope to here from ya matt ps im told i dont look my age.

In the short time from its beginnings in the mid-1990s, online dating has become a 1.5 billion-dollar business.

There are hundreds of online dating services that allow people to meet one another without the constraints of physical proximity, the emphasis on physical appearance, or the investment in time and money of a first date. By going to an online dating service, people can sort personals by gender, age, race, religion, sexual orientation, location, and other personal characteristics in order to narrow their search. People can begin to contact each other through e-mail as soon as they see a description they want to follow up on.

Online dating is so popular that there are books and websites about how to date online. There is a website that provides a categorized guide to other dating sites, helping the surfer find specialized dating services. Another site gives guidance about how to start up your own online dating service. Sites vary in what they offer, including finding pen pals, participating in chat rooms, listing your own personal, creating your own Web page, reviewing personals by category, and finding partners who will participate in online sex.

We know relatively little about what has been termed "computer-mediated relationships" (Merkle & Richardson, 2000). One study, commissioned by Microsoft of Canada, carried out phone interviews with 1,200 people and an Internet survey of more than 6,500 subscribers to webpersonals.com (Habib, 2001). They found that the majority of subscribers (about 68%) were men. About 63% said they had sex with someone they met online; about 60% had formed at least one long-term relationship through online dating; 3% said they eventually married someone they met online. Of those surveyed, 25% admitted to giving inaccurate information about themselves, and 26% complained that they were pestered after the first date by the person they met online. The results of this type of survey are difficult

to interpret. We do not have information about the ages and life stages of the respondents, nor do we know about their motives for using the Internet for relationship formation. If 25% say they give inaccurate information about themselves, then their responses to the survey may also be questionable.

The characteristics of computer-mediated relationships are just beginning to be studied. Referring to the model of mate selection in Figure 12.3, some of the most obvious distinctions of this kind of interpersonal experience are as follows (Merkle & Richardson, 2000):

1. Lack of physical proximity is not a barrier to forming a relationship. In the world of face-to-face relationships, people are limited to the people they meet, often at work, in their community, or through friends. The Internet permits people to overcome geographic boundaries and meet people literally all over the globe.
2. The e-mail and chat room contexts reduce the emphasis on physical attraction in the formation of relationships.
3. The Internet permits greater anonymity than face-to-face interactions. This may lead to greater dishonesty and "image experimentation." It may also result in higher levels of disclosure early on in a relationship. This can produce very intense intimacies between people who are uniquely open with one another in the Internet environment.
4. It is much easier to disengage from an Internet relationship than from a face-to-face relationship, especially if the participants have not shared contact information such as telephone, address, or true e-mail addresses. If conflicts or disagreements arise, participants can simply withdraw from the interaction rather than try to resolve it.

Most people seek marriage partners who will understand them and provide a sense of emotional support. They do not find attractive those who hold opposing views, come from quite different family backgrounds, or have temperamental qualities unlike their own. People of similar age and economic, religious, racial, and educational backgrounds marry each other in far greater proportions than would be expected by chance alone (Eshelman, 1985; Schoen & Wooldredge, 1989). For example, in 2003, only $^7/_{10}$ of 1% (.007) of all married couples were made up of one African American and one European American partner (U.S. Census Bureau, 2004).

There are many dimensions along which two people may recognize similarities or differences. They may seem quite different on some dimensions, such as religion and social class, yet discover that they are quite similar on others, such as life goals and political ideology. For example, partners who have similar ideas about gender roles and how men and women ought to function in a marriage are likely to be drawn to one another. The more aware individuals are of the themes that are central to their own sense of personal identity, the better they can recognize the dimensions of similarity and difference in other people that will contribute to intimate relationships.

In addition to the preferences that individuals express about potential partners and the availability of those partners in a particular community, "third parties" can play a role in the progression or termination of a relationship during Phase II (Kalmijn, 1998). Parent and family support can help enhance a partner's attractiveness if family members are enthusiastic about the partner and encourage the relationship. As the earlier example of the Muslim college student illustrated, parent and family reactions can also interfere with a deepening attraction if the potential partner meets with family disapproval. Research on interethnic dating has identified the role of social network diversity as a factor that contributes to the likelihood of college students dating across ethnic boundaries (Clark-Ibanez & Felmlee, 2004). Students who had an ethnically diverse group of friends were significantly more likely to have had one or more experiences with interethnic dating relationships. Students of color and male students were more likely than White or female students to have had experiences of interethnic dating. Those students whose parents had a diverse group of friends were most likely to respond that they had experienced interethnic dating more than once or twice. In the open-ended responses, students were asked how easy or how difficult it might be to date someone of a different ethnic group. The majority mentioned social pressures and social networks in their responses. For most of the students, the social network exercised pressures against interethnic dating. As one Korean student wrote, "My parents, just as most Korean parents that I have contact with, banish the idea of interracial dating." However, those who say it would be easy to date across ethnic lines often mention the role of friends and associates: "[It is] easy [to date interethnically]. I see people of different ethnicities every day. I'm used to them" (male Latino).

© Philip Newman

*As role compatibility and empathy grow, the relationship takes on a new degree of intimacy and the couple begins to conceptualize a future together.*

The relationship is likely to proceed from Phase II to Phase III, *barriers to breakup*, if the partners extend the domains in which self-disclosure occurs, including sexual needs, personal fears, and fantasies. With each new risk taken, the discovery of a positive, supportive reaction in the partner deepens the level of trust in the relationship. Negative reactions following disclosures or the revelation of information that is viewed as undesirable may lead to the termination of the relationship. For instance, premarital conflict about sex and problems in achieving sexual satisfaction in a relationship are likely to be associated with subsequent problems in the relationship, including higher levels of conflict in general and lower levels of relationship satisfaction (Long, Cate, Fehsenfeld, & Williams, 1996).

In Phase III, the discovery of role compatibility and empathy begins to give the relationship a life of its own. **Role compatibility** is a sense that the two partners approach a situation in ways that work well together. Whether it is a visit to a relative's home, an office party, a casual evening with friends, or running out of gas on the highway, the two people discover that they like the way each behaves and that their combined behavior is effective. Empathy builds through these observations, enabling each partner to know how the other responds and how to anticipate the other's needs.

One aspect of this new level of intimacy is the special way in which romantic partners interact with one another. In affectionate and playful exchanges, partners often use "baby talk," a type of gentle, high-pitched register, in which features of words are altered and new vocabulary may be created. Partners may give one another affectionate nicknames and create unique signals for communication. The establishment of this intimate communication system acts as another bond between the couple, creating a personal environment that is not shared with and often not even known to others (Bombar & Littig, 1996). At some point in Phase III, partners may begin to think that they are in love. They may even tell each other, "I love you." As described in the case study on How Love Makes Its Way into a Relationship, this is more difficult for some couples than for others.

The intensity of romantic love has been documented in studies that contrast romantic love and friendship (Davis, 1985; Hatfield, 1988). Lovers describe their relationships as characterized by *fascination*, *exclusiveness*, and *sexual desire*: "I would go to bed thinking about what we would do together, dream about it, and wake up ready to be with him again" (Davis, 1985, p. 24). They also express more intense caring for their loved ones than for friends. This caring includes giving their utmost, even to the point of self-sacrifice. The intensity of these characteristics accounts for some of the specialness and unsettling euphoria associated with being in love. It may also explain the relative instability of love relationships. Intense emotion is difficult to sustain. In contrast, friendship or companionate relationships reflect a high level of disclosure and a sense of having shared many life experiences. This leads to a sense of truly knowing the person, experiencing mutual understanding, and being concerned about each other's welfare.

# CASE STUDY

## HOW LOVE MAKES ITS WAY INTO A RELATIONSHIP

*Gail and Dick talk about how love entered into their relationship as they made the transition from living together to deciding to get married.*

**Dick:** We never mentioned love in our relationship. And that's for at least three years. We never committed ourselves to loving each other until well into the fourth year, although I don't know *why*. We'd ask each other if we like each other and placed a great deal of significance on that, but just as significantly we avoided the word "love," and all I remember about the first time we did mention love was that it was kind of a trauma.

**Gail:** I can remember everything. I think we were arguing about us. And Dick was trying to tell me, without telling me, that he was leaving me. You know, saying there's this problem and that it's stale and it's . . . and so on. And I'm all ready to change and work it out and then he just got frustrated and he said, "But I love you and I really care for you," and then he walked out. That I really couldn't understand. You told me you loved me and walked out and left me! I thought, "Well, that's crazy." I thought that was just the nuttiest thing I ever heard. I thought, "Well, does he feel guilty about hurting me and is that why he's saying it? And if he is all that crazy about me, he wouldn't have been walking out to somebody else!" And he didn't tell me, you know, he never told me he had another girlfriend, which bugged me a lot because I thought he could at least do that. And I had to go through this whole painful thing of finding out, when somebody said they saw Dick with this little blonde. And I thought, "Well, if that's true, he's probably at her house," and so I went over there and there they were and Dick was mortified. I was bitchy and I wouldn't go away. I just sat there making small talk—and I know now that I loved every minute of it. And so I really didn't believe it.

**Dick:** You mean you didn't believe it when I said I loved you. . . .

**Gail:** Yeah. But I guess I sort of had it in the back of my mind that we would get back together.

**Dick:** I was very dissatisfied with this other girl after a very short period of time, and it was interesting, because she outwardly seemed to have everything. I could, you know, I could list off consciously what I wanted and she had it, but it wasn't enough. I think one thing that I was very impressed about was that in comparing the two girls, this girl seemed not to have an independent life of her own. She seemed to be tied to whoever she was with. When we'd be talking with somebody else, she'd voice *my* opinions, and Gail doesn't do that hardly at all. She forms her own opinions and sticks to them. And I found that this really takes a great burden off me in a relationship. And I don't have to be carrying the emotional stability, or the opinions, for two people. It's really like having a burden lifted off yourself when you're not living with a mirror image of yourself but actually another person. At that point I realized that for me Gail was another individual whom I did care for.

Source: From *Becoming Partners: Marriage and Its Alternatives*, by C. R. Rogers. Copyright © 1972 by Delacorte Press. Reprinted by permission.

## ■ CRITICAL THINKING AND CASE ANALYSIS

1. What does love mean for Dick and Gail; in what ways might love be different from liking?
2. How is the relationship between Dick and Gail transformed when love is mentioned?
3. What are the qualities of an intimate relationship that you see illustrated in the case of Dick and Gail? What elements of an intimate relationship appear to be missing in this relationship?
4. How does the case illustrate the concept of homogamy? How does the case illustrate the concepts from social evolutionary theory?

5. What challenges do you imagine Dick and Gail might face in the first few years of marriage? What resources might help them cope with these challenges?

Once the partners enjoy role compatibility and empathy, they move on to Phase IV, *the "right one" relationship*. More than likely, the relationship is characterized by both romantic love and friendship to reach this point. In this phase, barriers to breaking up help consolidate the relationship. First, the partners have disclosed and taken risks with each other that they probably have not taken with others. Second, they have achieved comfortable feelings of predictability and empathy that make them more certain about each other than about possible alternative attractions. Third, they have been identified by others in their social network, including family and friends, as a couple. Subsequently, there is usually social support for them to remain together. At this point, the costs of breaking up begin to be quite high, including loss of a confidant, a companion, and disruption or even disapproval in their social network.

Even with the help of this model, the final step of commitment to marriage is not easy to understand. In today's society, many young couples agree to live together and make a commitment to their partnership without marriage. The step from cohabitation to marriage is still not well understood.

### ■ COHABITATION

In contemporary society, cohabitation rather than marriage has become a common expression of a committed relationship. In 2000, there were 5.5 million unmarried-couple households, an increase from 1.6 million such households in 1980 (U.S. Census Bureau, 2004). The increase in the number of couples who live together but do not marry has been accompanied by a significant increase in the number of children born in the context of cohabiting relationships (Heuveline & Timberlake, 2004). These two trends raise new questions about the nature and meaning of cohabitation. Is it an informal alternative to marriage, or is it more like singlehood, except that it involves a bond of connection with a partner? In a cross-national comparison, six types of cohabiting relationships were described that reflect a couple's decisions to live together, have children, and stay together (Heuveline & Timberlake, 2004, pp. 1216–1218):

1. *Marginal.* Cohabiting is infrequent, its duration short, and few children are born within this relationship, because the cultural norms strongly discourage this kind of union.

2. *Prelude to marriage.* In the face of high divorce rates, cohabiting may be viewed as a way for couples to test the relationship prior to marriage. The duration of cohabitation should be relatively brief, frequently transition into marriage, with few children born to cohabiting couples.

3. *Stage in the marriage process.* Couples in this type of relationship may see some disadvantages to marrying immediately, but they do intend to marry. Childbearing in the context of this relationship is more common, because the partners expect to marry. The relationships are of longer duration than in Type 2, more often involve childbearing, and end in transition to marriage.

4. *Alternative to being single.* Couples want to postpone marriage and family formation, perhaps because they think they are too young to marry. These couples are more like single, dating couples than like married couples. These relationships should be relatively short in duration, end in separation, and few children are born in these relationships.

*Andy and Jennifer take a moment to celebrate their decision to move in together. What factors will influence the future of this cohabiting relationship?*

5. *Alternative to marriage.* Couples view cohabiting as an alternative to marriage. These relationships are often established in the context of cultural support for children born outside the bonds of marriage. These relationships are of long duration, less likely to transition into marriage, and more likely to involve children.

6. *Indistinguishable from marriage.* Because of the cultural acceptability of unmarried couples and institutional support for all parents, couples consider cohabitation versus marriage on pragmatic grounds. These relationships are not a conscious alternative to marriage based on attitudes or values. The relationships are likely to involve children, but they may be of shorter duration than in the alternative to marriage, if only because many of them do transition into marriage.

The cross-national comparison was based on data from 14 European countries plus Canada, New Zealand, and the United States. Cohabitation among never-married women is comparatively rare in Spain, Italy, and Poland (less than 15%) and quite common in France, Finland, New Zealand, and Sweden (more than 60%). The median duration of cohabiting relationships is 3 years or longer in France, Sweden, and Canada; and comparatively short in the United States, where the median duration is 1.2 years. Across 11 countries where there are substantial numbers of cohabiting relationships, 61% of these relationships end in marriage. In comparison, 64% of Canadian cohabitation relationships end in separation, as do 52% of cohabitation relationships in the United States.

Using the indicators of incidence of cohabitation, proportion ending in marriage, and incidence of children born to mothers in a cohabiting relationship, the researchers tried to match countries with the six types of cohabitation most characteristic of their population. In Italy, Poland, and Spain, cohabitation was considered marginal. In Belgium, the Czech Republic, Hungary, and Switzerland, cohabitation was most likely a prelude to marriage. In Austria, Finland, Germany, Latvia, and Slovenia, cohabitation was a stage in the marriage process. In New Zealand and the United States, cohabitation was an alternative to being single. In Canada and France, cohabitation was an alternative to being married. In Sweden, cohabitation was indistinguishable from being married. The authors warned, however, that these national patterns may not reflect all the differences that are present within a culturally diverse society such as the United States. These comparisons do provide a frame of reference for interpreting the meaning of cohabitation in national contexts. They illustrate differences in cultural support for varying patterns of family formation by highlighting the frequency, duration, and path of cohabiting relationships.

**Consensual union** without a civil or religious marriage has been practiced in Latin America for centuries and is regarded as a form of marital union. The practice is becoming less common on the island of Puerto Rico itself, but it is regarded as legitimate among mainland Puerto Rican women.

Women who had a child within such a relationship were more likely to describe it as informal marriage than as cohabitation. Women who had been married before were also more likely to describe their current relationship as informal marriage rather than cohabitation. It appears that consensual unions were perceived by women to be more like marriage than like singlehood.

## ■ PARTNERS OF THE SAME SEX

Gay men and lesbians are a diverse group with respect to their interests, talents, educational backgrounds, family backgrounds, careers, and other important aspects of adult roles. The description of gay and lesbian relationships that can be derived from the existing research misses much of the diversity that one would expect to uncover as this form of intimate relationship is studied in greater detail (Macklin, 1987).

One of the common themes in the literature is the impact on the relationship of coming out to parents and other family members. In comparison to heterosexual couples, this is a specific challenge that may place strain on the relationship. In one study of 20 gay couples, all those who had come out to their parents had experienced ongoing disapproval from their own parents and their partner's parents (LaSala, 2000). The following reflections from the mother of a gay man suggest some of the strains that are likely to arise as gay couples disclose to family members:

> Annette E. Brenner remembers joking when her oldest son was 4 that she'd approve his marrying outside the family's faith as long as he married a woman. When he "came out" to her and her husband at 17, one of her first reactions was to try to "negotiate" him out of his gayness. She offered him a car, a house, if only he would wait and try marriage. He was at boarding school in Connecticut at the time, and she was convinced it was "just a stage." She remembers thinking, "Sure, this week you're a homosexual. Enjoy the experiment, have fun. Next week you'll be a Hare Krishna." Then she became enraged. "What is this kid doing to me?" she'd ask herself. "What was he doing to his grandparents, his brother and sister?" (From "Born or Bred: The Origins of Homosexuality," by D. Gelman, *Newsweek*, February 24, 1992, pp. 46–53. © 1992 Newsweek, Inc. All rights reserved. Reprinted by permission.)

Homosexual relationships are often established in a climate of secrecy and social stigma, especially fears about parental rejection. Gay and lesbian couples often perceive less social support from family members and seek out other members of the gay or lesbian community to validate and encourage their relationship (Kurdek, 2004). Even when they are in committed relationships, gay and lesbian young adults are likely to manage the negative impact of family rejection by keeping the nature of their homosexual relationship a secret from family members.

In a national study of lesbians, 19% reported being "out" to no family members, and only 27% reported being "out" to

*The decision to adopt a child emerged as a result of the stability and intimacy of this lesbian couple's committed relationship.*

© Deborah Davis./Photo Edit

all family members (Bradford, Ryan, & Rothblum, 1994). Although this image management might seem to place a strain on intimate relationships, research shows no significant relationship between the couples' satisfaction in their relationship and the extent to which they are "out" to family members (Green et al., 1995; LaSala, 2000).

Lesbian and gay relationships are similar in many respects and distinct in others (Patterson, 1994). Lesbian and gay couples who are in a committed relationship tend to give great priority to maintaining and enhancing their relationship for several reasons. First, they share the conflicts around coming out and the complications that this poses in family and work settings. This provides a common bond and a need to protect the relationship from detractors. Second, they have to invent many of the details of their relationship, thus making it more salient and less scripted than heterosexual relationships. Finally, they face ongoing challenges, such as the complexities associated with the decision about whether and how to have children and how to ritualize their commitment to one another (Metz, Rosser, & Strapko, 1994). In a comparison of gay and lesbian couples, the two types of couples were similar in many respects (Kurdek, 2003). They had similar approaches to conflict resolution, similar experiences with support from their social networks, and similar rates of dissolution or instability in their relationships. The same variables predicted relationship dissolution for gay and lesbian couples. Lesbian couples were more alike than gay couples at the start of their relationship and scored higher on measures of liking their partners, trusting their partners, and perceiving equality in their relationship. Overall, lesbian couples had higher rates of relationship satisfaction. This finding is puzzling given that lesbian and gay couples had the same degree of stability.

Lesbian relationships often emerge out of close, same-sex friendships. Lesbians are somewhat more likely to be able to establish long-term relationships than gay men. Most lesbians describe their relationships as stable, sexually exclusive, and extremely close. They also describe their relationships as closer and more flexible than do gay men or heterosexual couples (Green et al., 1995). Greater levels of satisfaction in the relationship are associated with greater levels of equality and shared decision making. Equality in the relationship depends on equal resources and commitment to the relationship (Eldridge & Gilbert, 1990). In comparison with heterosexual wives, women in lesbian relationships are more likely to describe greater satisfaction in their sexual activity and greater dissatisfaction with inequalities in the relationship. These women place a strong value on companionship and on confiding in one another, but they also expect to experience high levels of autonomy within their relationships.

Gay men are also interested in long-term relationships. However, they are less likely than lesbians to be sexually exclusive, and there is less consensus among them about the importance of sexual exclusiveness (Deenen, Gijs, & van Naerssen, 1994; Kitzinger & Coyle, 1995). In comparison to lesbian relationships, gay men often find partners in the context of a more active, competitive social scene that involves multiple short-term relationships. In comparison to men in heterosexual couples, gay men are likely to be emotionally intimate. In the practical matters of household work, gay couples are more likely than heterosexual couples to divide tasks so that each partner does an equal number (Kurdek, 1993). Gay couples report higher levels of closeness and flexibility than do heterosexual couples. What is more, the combination of flexibility and closeness is strongly associated with couple satisfaction (Green et al., 1995).

Many of the same factors are associated with relationship quality across all types of couples: valuing security, permanence, and closeness; expressiveness; perceived rewards for being in the relationship; trust in the partner; good problem-solving and conflict resolution skills; egalitarian decision making; openness to the expression of differences; and perceived social support (Huston, 2000; Kurdek, 1995). At the same time, factors that are likely to lead to the dissolution of a gay or lesbian couple are a lack of investment in the relationship, a decline in expressions of positive affect and emotional support, an increase in conflicts, and an increased desire for personal autonomy. Interdependence sustains the relationships, and power inequalities disrupt them (Kurdek, 1996).

## ■ ADJUSTMENT DURING THE EARLY YEARS OF MARRIAGE

Once the choice has been made and the thrill of courtship has passed, the first few years of a committed relationship involve a process of mutual adaptation. They can be extremely difficult, particularly because the couple does not anticipate the strains. The partners may be quite distressed to find their "love nest" riddled with the tensions that are a normal part of carving out a life together. In fact, data suggest that the probability of divorce is highest during the first years of marriage, peaking between 2 and 4 years. Among marriages that end in divorce, the median time to separation is 6.6 years; the median time to divorce is about 8 years (Kreider & Fields, 2002).

There are many sources of tension in a new marriage. If the partners do not have similar religious, educational, or social class backgrounds, they will have to compromise on many value decisions. Assuming a shared value orientation, certain lifestyle decisions can generate tension. The couple must establish a mutually satisfying sexual relationship. They must work out an agreement about spending and saving money. They must also respond to each other's sleep patterns, food preferences, work patterns, and toilet habits. The couple may find the demands of their parents and in-laws to be an additional source of conflict. Usually, it is the number of demands rather than any single one that makes the adjustment process so difficult.

As part of the adjustment to marriage, the partners must achieve a sense of psychological commitment to each other. The marriage ceremony is intended to make that commitment public and binding. It is safe to say that most people probably do not fully accept the reality of their marriage vows until they have tested the relationship later. There is a period of testing in every marriage, during which each partner is likely to put strain on the relationship to see how strong it really is. The question of trust may be posed as, "Will you still love me even if I do . . . ?" or, "Am I still free to do what I did before we were married?" Every marriage relationship is different. The partners must discover the limits that their particular relationship can tolerate. But both partners must feel that they still have a degree of freedom within the marriage parameters. They must also believe that the limits on their freedom are balanced by the love, respect, and support they gain in return. As each test is successfully passed, the partners grow closer. They trust each other more and become increasingly sensitive to each other's feelings. Eventually, the tests diminish in number as the question of trust is resolved.

**COMMUNICATION AND MARITAL ADJUSTMENT.** Intimacy and a high level of relationship satisfaction require effective communication and the capacity to cope effectively with conflict. Conflict can be a product of the interaction of two well-developed identities, each with a distinct temperament, values, and goals. It can also be a product of the uneven distribution of power or resources. Conflict can result from the simple day-to-day need to make decisions that the couple has never made before. It can be a reflection of one or both partners' personalities, a tendency toward irritability, mistrust, or an aggressive temperament. Finally, it can be a product of disillusionment, as one or both partners perceive that the relationship fails to meet critical expectations. Whatever the source, marital stability and satisfaction are closely tied to how couples manage conflict (Huston, Niehuis, & Smith, 2001).

Three dimensions of conflict seem especially important in differentiating happy and distressed marital relationships. First, instances of negative communication—especially nonverbal negative expressions and hostile put-downs—are more frequent in distressed than in happy couples, even in the first few years of married life.

Second, distressed couples show a pattern of **coercive escalation**—a style of interaction in which the probability that a negative remark will be followed by another negative remark increases as the chain of communication gets longer and longer (Gottman & Levenson, 1986). This pattern has been observed at the behavioral level by coding the verbal and nonverbal characteristics of an interaction and at the physiological level by monitoring heart rate, blood pressure, and release of stress hormones during communication (Markman & Notarius, 1987; Schrof, 1994). As the communication becomes increasingly negative, the partners become so physiologically disorganized that they lose access to their more rational ego functions. Over repeated instances, they become sensitive to this physiological state, reaching it sooner. In comparison, happy couples become more effective in soothing each other and in finding ways of preventing conflicts.

Third, distressed couples have different perceptions of the approach that their partners are taking to resolve a conflict. For example, one partner may think that he or she is acting in a constructive way to find a solution, but the other partner may view the behavior as patronizing or minimizing the importance of the issue. Congruence between the partners in how they think they and their partners are approaching the resolution of conflict is significantly related to marital satisfaction (Acitelli, Douvan, & Veroff, 1997).

*The Two Saltimbanques, 1901/Pablo Picasso/© 2005 Estate of Pablo Picasso/Artists Rights Society (ARS), New York/© Superstock*

*To sustain a marriage, the partners must be able to interact even during periods of conflict. Withdrawal, rejection, and distancing are common reactions to conflict. These strategies may be effective during a brief cooling-off period, but they do not replace direct communication for exploring or resolving differences.*

In an analysis of effective problem solving among newly married couples, partners were asked to identify the areas where they had their most significant disagreements (Tallman & Hsiao, 2004). The four most common issues were money, who does what around the house, communication, and time spent with the spouse (p. 177). The premise of the study was that couples who were able to resolve problems so that both partners were satisfied with the outcome would experience greater levels of marital satisfaction. Another assumption was that both trust in one another and cooperative approaches to problem solving were needed in order to come to mutually satisfying solutions. Over time, the couples who were able to use cooperative problem-solving strategies had greater marital satisfaction, which in turn contributed to improved cooperative behavior in subsequent problem-solving efforts. What is more, those couples who exhibited cooperative, mutually respectful problem solving were able to maintain their relationship quality in the face of economic distress.

Apart from how they perceive and handle conflict, happy couples enjoy being together. They start out their marriages being very much in love, and they also view one another as responsive. They value the companionship aspects of their marriage, such as spending time together with friends or having dinner together (Kamo, 1993). In a comparison of American and Japanese couples, the latter were significantly less likely to share time together in these ways. However, for both the American and the Japanese couples, those who spent more leisure time together had higher levels of marital satisfaction. The causal nature of this relationship is not fully understood. One might assume that happy couples choose to spend more time together, but it may also be that couples who have opportunities to spend more time together come to feel more positive about their marriage as a result.

Partners who have a high level of marital satisfaction report frequent, pleasurable interaction and a high degree of disclosure (Lippert & Prager, 2001). High levels of disclosure and disclosure reciprocity (i.e., you tell the other person what you are thinking about, and they tell you what they are thinking about) are associated with greater relationship satisfaction among marital partners (Finkenaure, Engles, Branje, & Meeus, 2004). Emotional expressiveness, especially by husbands, and a lack of ambivalence about expressing one's feelings are important elements in this communication process, particularly among White, middle class U.S. families (King, 1993). In contrast, declines in affectionate and pleasurable interactions and increases in ambivalence about the union predict a high probability of divorce (Huston et al., 2001).

**COMMUNICATION STYLES OF MEN AND WOMEN.** A growing body of literature suggests that men and women communicate differently and have different perceptions of the process. This idea has mixed empirical support. In many ways, men and women are alike. For example, both perceive the value of affective or emotional skills in promoting and sustaining friendships and romantic relationships. They both expect close friends—and especially romantic partners—to have the ability to encourage, soothe, reassure, and validate one another (Burleson, Kunkel, Samter, & Werking, 1996). When faced with upsetting problems, both women and men are most likely to try to offer suggestions for how to solve the problem or to take some action, rather than to simply empathize and identify with the person's problem (Goldsmith & Dun, 1997). When asked about their preferred mode or style of interaction as a couple, husbands and wives both prefer interactions that are **contactful**—that is, open to the other person's point of view—and that also clearly express the speaker's own position. They least prefer **controlling** interactions, in which one person expresses his or her point of view and does not take the other person's point of view into consideration (Hawkins, Weisberg, & Ray, 1980). These similarities suggest that men and women approach the process of establishing intimate relationships with many common skills and values.

Despite these similarities, some differences in the ways men and women approach communication have implications for the quality of an intimate relationship. The socialization of both sexes in U.S. culture is still sufficiently distinct to result in differences in expectations and competencies. For example, when faced with a problem, men are more likely to want to deny it or to spend time analyzing and defining it in comparison with women (Goldsmith & Dun, 1997). Similarly, men tend to value the skills of being a good conversationalist or storyteller and being able to laugh and joke as well as to argue and defend a position somewhat more than do women (Burleson et al., 1996). They tend to be more ambivalent than women about expressing emotions and withdraw to avoid escalating conflict. Women, on the other hand, tend to want to talk things out so that everyone feels comfortable with the situation. In conflicts, these styles can become incompatible, especially if the woman is trying to reach consensus and the man withdraws. In general, women expect and desire a degree of closeness that is often not reciprocated. Men, on the other hand, are more likely to be satisfied with the degree of intimacy that they find in marriage and have fewer expectations of or less desire for greater closeness (Dindia & Allen, 1992).

## ADJUSTMENT IN DUAL-EARNER MARRIAGES

One of the greatest changes in U.S. families in the second half of the 20th century was the increase in the number of married women who were employed. It is now normative for married women, including those with young children, to be in the labor market. The percentage of employed, married women whose husbands are present rose from 32% in 1960 to 61% in 2003. The number of women with young children who work outside the home has also grown substantially. In 2003, 57% of married women with children under 3 years old were in the labor force, compared with 33% in 1975 (U.S. Census Bureau, 2004). Rather than drop out of the labor force and return to work after their children are grown, the majority of women now remain in the labor force throughout the early years of parenthood.

There is no question that the involvement of both husband and wife in the labor market requires a departure from traditional family roles and a dialogue about the division of labor. Uncertainty about the expectations and behaviors of the spousal roles must be worked out between the partners. Sometimes, this uncertainty helps to produce greater intimacy by generating interactions that lead to greater self-disclosure by each partner. Personal preferences and habits must be examined if the partners are to arrive at an effective division of labor that is mutually satisfying. Sometimes, however, this process is threatening. The partners may not really be aware of their expectations of themselves or of the other person until they are married.

One analysis of the potential conflicts for dual-earner couples focused on the relative balance of power and demands for household labor for the two partners (Rosenfeld, 1992). In the traditional male breadwinner, female homemaker family model, the husband has more power as a result of his access to financial resources and participates little in the low-status household tasks. The wife, in contrast, has little power and carries the majority of responsibility for the

As they walk to work, Ken is getting Lily's ideas about a proposal he is developing. In their busy lives, they have to make use of every minute of time together.

household tasks. As women have entered the labor market, their access to financial resources has increased. To the extent that their husbands also help in sharing the household tasks, their well-being and mental health improve.

For men, especially in families where there is a relatively high family income, as their wives' income matches or surpasses their own and they have to take on a greater role in domestic tasks, their well-being declines and their mental health suffers. This is true primarily for men who have traditional views about the importance of men as breadwinners (Brennan, Barnett, & Gareis, 2001). Men who feel demeaned or threatened by demands to participate in household labor are likely to experience depressive symptoms that are similar to the reactions that women have when they try to carry the full responsibility of household tasks while also participating in the labor market. Finding the balance of power and of household responsibilities that preserves mutual respect and support is a major challenge in the early years of the marriage and has to be fine-tuned and renegotiated throughout the marriage.

Evidence from a variety of sources suggests that in contemporary U.S. society, there are a number of benefits for couples when husbands and wives have multiple roles that include marriage, career, and parenting (Barnett & Hyde, 2001). Four benefits are summarized here:

1. Involvement in multiple roles means that both partners are likely to be more fully integrated into meaningful social support systems.
2. Participation of both partners in the labor force increases financial resources and buffers the couple against fluctuations in each person's job situation.
3. Success in one role can buffer each person against negative experiences in other roles. For example, negative work experiences can be offset by marital happiness and the centrality of parenting.
4. Involvement in similar roles provides husbands and wives with a shared frame of reference. Thus, partners are more likely to appreciate one another's point of view and to empathize with each other's struggles and accomplishments.

There are limits to the benefits of the dual-earner arrangement. The advantages of the dual-earner, multiple-role lifestyle can be offset when one or both partners experience role overload—for example, if the care of an ill parent is added to an already full basket of responsibilities. The quality of the roles can undermine the benefits, as when a person is in a terrible job with inadequate wages and oppressive work conditions. Chronic stressors at home that create feelings of overload or lack of control can make the daily hassles of home or work life seem even worse. These ongoing stressors, which result in frequent but unpredictable demands, can cause psychological distress in the individual and disrupt relationship satisfaction (Serido, Almeida, & Wetherington, 2004). Multiple roles can be disruptive if a partner holds traditional gender role values that are in conflict with the enactment of multiple roles. Finally, couples may find that their actual work schedules do not fit well together, leaving too little time to be together or too little control over their non-work life (Barnett, Brennan, & Gareis, 1999).

## CHILDBEARING

One of the central commitments of early adulthood revolves around the decision whether to have children or not. During early adulthood, the issue of reproduction is confronted many times. Young adults make choices to delay parenting, have an abortion, have a child, wait before having another child, or stop having children altogether. As discussed in Chapter 5 (Pregnancy and Prenatal Development), many couples undergo difficult and expensive procedures to conceive a child. Others who are unable to conceive decide to adopt children. Some adults become foster parents, whether or not they have children of their own. Even unplanned pregnancies are products of some kind of decision making—

whether to have sexual relations knowing that pregnancy is possible, to avoid using effective means of birth control, to abort the pregnancy, or to carry the child to term (Lydon, Dunkel-Schetter, Cohan, & Pierce, 1996). In all of these decisions, many powerful themes are reflected: one's sense of fulfilling a masculine or feminine life purpose by having children; one's childhood socialization and identification with parental figures; religious beliefs about sexuality, contraception, or abortion; and ideas about carrying on a family's ancestry and traditions. Reproduction is the means by which the species perpetuates itself. Regardless of the decisions one reaches, this issue cannot help but heighten one's sense that the decisions of adulthood make a difference.

## ■ FERTILITY RATE

The average number of births required for the natural replacement of a population is estimated at 2.1 births per adult woman. This number is calculated by assuming that for every adult woman in a population, a female child must be born who will reach reproductive maturity and have children. Because slightly more male than female children are born, and because not all children reach childbearing age, the estimate for a replacement reproductive rate is 2.1 children (Bachu & O'Connell, 2001).

The fertility rate in the United States has fluctuated from the late 1950s, when the rate was 3.5 births per woman, to a low of 1.8 in the 1970s. In 2002, the rate was 2.0, slightly less than the replacement estimate. Fertility rates in the United States vary by race/ethnicity and socioeconomic status. Hispanic women have the highest fertility rate; Asian or Pacific Islanders and American Indians have the lowest (Hamilton, 2004). Women who have graduated from high school have a higher fertility rate than women who graduated from college or have a graduate degree. Women who are not in the labor force have a higher fertility rate than those in the labor force. Women whose family income is below $25,000 have a higher fertility rate than those above $25,000 (Bachu & O'Connell, 2001).

## ■ DECISIONS ABOUT CHILDBEARING

In contemporary society, decisions about childbearing are made in the context of other personal and family goals and commitments. Factors such as religious beliefs, career aspirations, ideals about family life, and social expectations in the family and culture all contribute to a couple's commitment to bearing children and the timing of first and subsequent pregnancies. Cultures differ in the norms and expectations they convey about the value of having children and the appropriate timing and frequency of pregnancies.

In a study of 4 decades of trends in attitudes toward marriage, divorce, cohabitation, and childbearing, Thornton and Young-DeMarco (2001) compared responses from men and women as well as adolescents from five different national U.S. samples. Data were collected in the 1960s, 1970s, 1980s, and 1990s, with the most recent data coming from adolescents

## The Reproductive Career of the Gusii

ROBERT LEVINE (1980) described the patterns of adulthood among the Gusii, a tribe living in the highlands of western Kenya, about 50 miles south of the equator. The Gusii live in a well-protected, fertile area where they were able to expand their communities and grow their crops. LeVine characterized their adult life course as being composed of three interdependent spheres: reproductive, economic, and spiritual. His description of the reproductive career illustrates how personal and societal expectations influence the childbearing decisions of young adults:

The reproductive career seems to be the most salient for both sexes. Its goal is to become the ancestor of a maximally expanding genealogy. For women, this means to have children as frequently between marriage and menopause as is consistent with child health, which the Gusii believe to be every two years. A man who fails to impregnate his wife that often will be publicly accused by her of neglect. The woman must have at least one son to take care of her in her old age and whose wives work with her; to have nothing but daughters (who move away at marriage) is second only to barrenness as a disaster. If her husband dies, it is her right as well as her obligation to have a leviratic husband to impregnate her regularly so she will continue to bear children "for the dead man." For men, the goal means not only maximizing his wife's offspring but taking additional wives as he can afford them and so appending their reproductive careers to his. If a man has been a monogamist, he might take a younger second wife when his first wife reaches menopause, for that would extend his reproductive career by a decade or more. The reproductive career as I see it, however, is not limited to the individual's own procreation but includes that of his or her offspring. Grandchildren are as fervently desired as one's own children and, not incidentally, play an essential role in the burial of the grandparents. (LeVine, 1980, p. 94)

surveyed in 1997–1998. Over time, two themes emerged. First, in the 1980s and 1990s, people viewed childbearing within marriage as more of an option than an obligation. Over that time, respondents increasingly disagreed with the idea that "all married couples who can ought to have children." This concept was positively endorsed by 84% of mothers in 1962, but by only 41% of mothers and 22% of their adult daughters in 1993. Similarly, in the 1980s and 1990s, the majority of people disagreed with the idea that having children is the main reason for getting married, or that people who did not have children led meaningless lives.

In light of this changing sense of social obligation to have children, one might think that people would be less enthusiastic about the meaning of parenting and less likely to want to become parents, but this did not happen: The second trend was a steady endorsement of the value of parenting. The majority of high school seniors who were surveyed from the mid-1970s through the late 1990s agreed that fatherhood and motherhood are among the most fulfilling experiences of adulthood; roughly 60% of these students (both male and female) said they were likely to want to have children.

Although the great majority of married couples intend to have children, the timing of their entry into parenthood varies. Between 1980 and 2000, the number of births per 1,000 women between the ages of 15 and 29 decreased (from 104/1,000 to 86/1,000), and the total number of births per 1,000 women between the ages of 30 and 44 increased (from 35/1,000 to 46/1,000; U.S. Census Bureau, 2003). Both the social and the biological clocks come into play in this deci-

sion. The social clock refers to expectations from family and friends that it is time to start a family. Children who grew up in large families where their own mothers began parenting at a young age may experience both social pressure and social support from their families to have children early (Barber, 2000). Couples who wait to begin their families may be pressured by parents who are eager to become grandparents or by friends who have already experienced the lifestyle changes that accompany the birth of their first child.

In recent years, many couples have begun to resist these social pressures, postponing childbearing until after the first years of their marriage. This decision is related to several other aspects of adult life and needs to be understood in the context of competing goals, including education, career aspirations, and a desire to experience the intimacy of the marriage. Couples who have a dual-earner marriage have to consider the effect of children on their family income. They may try to anticipate the best timing for childbearing in relation to job security or career advancement. Some couples set certain material goals for themselves as a prerequisite to having children. For example, they may decide to wait until they can buy a home, purchase some furniture, or travel together before they have children. Given the high divorce rate, couples are likely to want to feel confident that their relationship is strong before deciding to have children.

Delayed entry into parenthood has typically been studied in relation to the characteristics of the woman. It has been found to be related to a woman's level of education, her career commitment, and the family's income.

*This couple's affection for and commitment to each other is expanding to include love for their unborn child. How might the quality of the parent's relationship influence the experience of pregnancy?*

Zine Magubane (age 32) and her husband, Patrick McCabe, married in June. She's got a tenure-track university teaching job; he's a sports agent who travels constantly. They want to wait at least a year before beginning a family "to get a little more stability," says Magubane, whose mother delivered her at 36. Today she works hard to stay healthy, knowing she'll be an older mom. (Kalb, 2001, p. 43)

In a study of the timing of entry into fatherhood, men who were characterized as late-entry fathers (30 years old or older) were more involved with their children and had more positive feelings about them than did the on-time or early fathers (Cooney, Pedersen, Indelicato, & Palkovitz, 1993). Older fathers may feel that they have less conflict between their commitments to work and to family. They may feel that they have already demonstrated their ability to succeed in the breadwinner role and, therefore, can approach parenthood with more confidence and a greater sense of self-efficacy. Older fa-

thers may have more emotional resources to bring to their marriage and their parenting relationship.

Decisions to postpone childbearing are also constrained by the biological clock. Despite the number of highly publicized late pregnancies, the biological limits on age of childbearing are still significant. After age 30, women's fertility rates decline, and by age 40, miscarriages increase. Reproductive technologies that involve fertilizing a woman's own eggs decrease from 40% effectiveness for women in their late 20s to less than 10% for women in their 40s. However, new ideas are being introduced that may push back these constraints, such as transferring the cell nucleus from an older woman's egg, transplanting it into the cytoplasm of a younger woman's egg, and implanting the new, improved egg into the older mother so that she can experience pregnancy and childbirth (Kalb, 2001).

## ■ THE DUAL ROLES OF INTIMATE PARTNER AND PARENT

In contrast to the elation that usually accompanies the anticipation of and preparation for the newborn, the arrival of the first child often brings a period of stress to the relationship (Newman, 2000). Belsky and Rovine (1990) found clear evidence of individual differences in how couples adapted to the transition to parenthood. In their longitudinal study of 128 families, they observed four patterns of change in the assessment of marital quality: (1) Some couples showed a rapid decline in marital quality after the first baby was born. (2) Others showed a slow, steady decline. (3) A third group showed no significant change. (4) A fourth group showed slight increases in marital quality. These findings caution us not to overgeneralize group trends to individual cases.

The quality of marital adjustment over the transition to parenthood is closely related to marital quality before the child was born (Heinicke, 1995). Couples who are in close, confiding, satisfying marriages before their children are born tend to show higher levels of marital adjustment 3 months after childbirth than do couples in conflictual marriages. However, many studies find that couples experience increased conflict after the birth of their first child. If the relationship was negative and the partners had high levels of conflict prior to the baby's birth, these difficulties are likely to increase (Crohan, 1996).

In an attempt to clarify the effects of many factors on marital satisfaction during the transition to parenthood, researchers compared marital activities and evaluations of the marriage by parents and nonparents who had been married the same number of years (MacDermid, Huston, & McHale, 1990). They found that over the first 3 years of marriage, couples' ratings of love and satisfaction declined somewhat. There were no differences in the magnitude of the decline for parents and nonparents. Having children did not account for a greater drop in love or satisfaction than appeared to occur as a result of adjusting to marriage in general. This is an im-

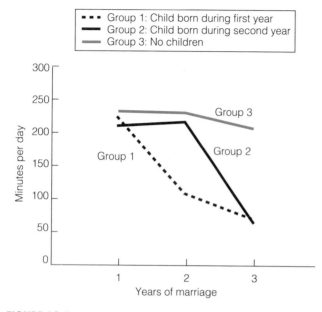

**FIGURE 12.4**

Duration of Joint Husband–Wife Leisure Without Child for Parents and Nonparents

Source: Based on MacDermid, Huston, and McHale, 1990.

portant observation that provides new insight into much of the earlier research on marital satisfaction and the transition to parenthood.

Having children did have an impact on marital companionship. The percentage of leisure activities shared by the husband and wife dropped sharply after the baby was born, but it declined only slightly for the couples without children. During the third year of marriage, parents had a greater number of shared activities per day than nonparents, but few when the child was not present. Figure 12.4 shows the number of minutes of joint leisure time per day without the child for two groups of parents in comparison with joint leisure time for nonparents in the first, second, and third years of marriage. After the birth of their child, couples have only about one third as many minutes together alone as they had when they were childless. The nature of companionship in marriage changes to incorporate a baby and therefore may become less intimate.

Coping with the early months of childrearing may strengthen the bond between the man and the woman. The partners begin to respect each other's competence in caring for their child. They also begin to conceptualize their roles as parents and to view the increasing complexity of their family structure as a challenge rather than a burden. The new baby adds a degree of energy to the family through expressions of satisfaction, pleasure, and affection.

As the roles of mother and father are added to the adults' repertoire of role relationships, their own expectations (and those of others) concerning the raising of a child are aroused. The daily demands of the child help the parents define their own roles more realistically. Instead of wondering what par-

ents should do, they are occupied with the actual demands of parenting. Through this experiential learning, young adults formulate their own definitions of parental roles. Assuming that the early experiences are successful and the parents are able to meet their child's needs, they gradually achieve a new level of self-efficacy in the parenting role, gaining new confidence in their ability to provide a nurturing environment for their child.

The process of social attachment and its impact on the infant were discussed in Chapter 6 (Infancy). The theme of mutuality as the central process for the establishment of trust was stressed. Mutuality also has an impact on parents. Infants actively engage their parents, evoke unique responses, and, through their differential behaviors, begin to shape parenting behaviors. Infants respond to their parents with shrieks of delight, elaborate smiles, and the active pursuit of them. They are unrestrained in their loving. They mouth, bite, grab, laugh, smile, squeal, and coo in response to pleasure. Through their open demonstrations of affection, infants teach adults about the expression of love and increase their parents' ability to demonstrate it. As parents and children begin to engage in playful interactions, the capacity to establish and maintain reciprocal interactions expands. Children learn how to initiate a play sequence by bringing a toy or making a playful gesture. Parents then learn how to respond by complying to the request for play, sitting down on the floor, bringing out the box of favorite play materials, or tickling and tumbling. As children and parents experience mutual, congruent playful interactions, the bond of affection is strengthened and communication is enhanced (Lindsey, Mize, & Pettit, 1997).

### ■ THE DECISION NOT TO HAVE CHILDREN

Not all couples choose to have children. In 2000, 19% of women age 40 to 44 had never had a child (Bachu & O'Connell, 2001). The percentage was lower for Hispanic women (11%) than for White non-Hispanic women and Black women. Much like attitudes toward remaining single, attitudes toward a lifestyle in which a couple chooses not to have children are becoming more accepting. As discussed earlier, childbearing is increasingly viewed as a choice rather than an obligation. This shift is evidenced in part by a change in the sociological jargon from the term "childless" to the newer term "voluntarily child-free." The decision not to have children is becoming increasingly common, not only in the United States but also in other industrialized nations, especially as women's educational attainment and occupational commitments reach new levels.

Nonetheless, the U.S. culture continues to be *pronatalist*, placing a high value on the meaning of parenthood in adult life. In some ethnic and religious groups, having children is considered a sacred trust. For example, within the Mormon Church, children are highly valued. "Mormon doctrine states that children are the spirit sons and daughters of heavenly parents, and that G-d holds parents responsible for their

*Couples with children find new ways to spend time together that includes their child. Rather than a romantic ski weekend for two, this family goes sledding together.*

stewardship in raising them in righteousness" (Lambert & Thomasson, 1997, p. 90).

Through a pronatalist lens, motherhood is viewed as the symbol of a woman's ultimate identity, regardless of her other talents or accomplishments. Mary Blair-Loy (2001) describes a powerful "family devotion" schema among women—a view that the ideal mother should be committed full-time to her children and the well-being of her family. This view is contrasted to the "work devotion" schema, which suggests that an ideal employee should devote all of his or her time to the work setting. In comparison to people in many European countries, workers in the United States work longer days, take less vacation, have no paid maternity leave, and have limited access to quality infant care. The tensions between pronatalist cultural values, the devotion to the work ideal, and the lack of policies that support parenting result in many women leaving the labor market during their childbearing years or reducing their labor participation to part-time employment (Williams & Cooper, 2004). Resisting social expectations that married couples ought to bear children requires a high level of personal autonomy and less need for social support from a wide range of reference groups. It may also require a competing positive identity, such as commitment to one's career goals, or a redefinition of gender roles to sustain and validate this decision (Wager, 1998; Somers, 1993).

## WORK

Within the life course framework, the occupational career is a major structural factor in each person's life story. In combination with intimate relationships and parenting, efforts to balance and coordinate work and family life produce some of the greatest challenges of adult life. Work is the primary means of accumulating financial resources. It is the focus of attention for much of the waking day. One's work determines in large part the activities, social relationships, challenges, satisfactions, and hassles or frustrations of daily life. Finally, work is the context in which many adults express their personal identity and experience a sense of personal value and social status.

In Chapter 11 (Later Adolescence), we discussed the developmental task of career choice, emphasizing the link between career decision making and other aspects of individual identity. Here we focus on adaptation to the world of work, where the demands of work present new challenges and opportunities for development.

The concept of work is complex. The following discussion considers very general characteristics of work and their potential impact on one's cognitive, social, and emotional development and on one's sense of self in adulthood. This type of analysis is necessary because occupational roles in U.S. society are so varied. Each job role places the individual in a somewhat different psychosocial context, with a unique combination of expectations, resources, and strains.

## ■ THE WORLD OF WORK

To gain an appreciation for the variety of career paths and their associated impact on daily life, you may want to visit WetFeet.com and go to their list of Real People by Industry. In this website, people from various industries are interviewed and their typical day is described. The case study of Jay Crowe, which was retrieved from this website, provides an excerpt from an interview with an elementary school social worker in Albuquerque, New Mexico. He describes what he does, what it takes to do well in his type of work, and how a person can get a job like the one he has. Then he describes his daily schedule.

# CASE STUDY

## JAY CROWE

*Jay Crowe is an elementary school social worker. This interview provides a glimpse of the demands, rewards, and daily requirements of that occupation.*

### What do you do?

As a school social worker, my formal caseload consists of special-needs children who are in the special education program. They have psychiatric diagnoses ranging from clinical depression to thought disorders to character disorders. My job is to work with the children on an individual and/or group basis during regular school hours. I have a classroom, and in that classroom I've got therapeutic games, as well as basic kid games, and I also do a lot of outdoor activities, such as baseball, football, soccer, tag, and chasing games. In an individual situation, I use one-on-one play therapy. We use a play environment to build trust and acceptance. Then the therapist can open up important topics.

### What kinds of people do well in this business?

Empathetic types with the understanding that the generations who are coming after them make a difference in the long run do well. People who generally care about other people do well. You can't see the shady side of life and internalize it and take it home every day and become self-destructive. That's an easy trap to fall into. People who do well have a lot of self-awareness and understand their own needs.

### What do you really like about your job?

Something new comes up every day because people are not machines. You can't make absolute predictions, and that's what I like.

### What do you dislike?

I dislike the paperwork and the administrative double standards. Our school is defined as being site-based, meaning that the principal and the staff have autonomy. That's fine, until the site decides to do something that the district wants to do. Then the district will pull it away from the site. But it could be a lot worse. For the most part, we're able to implement programs as we see fit.

### How can someone get a job like yours?

After you get the education, there are a couple of things you can do. You can write queries to the heads of Human Resources at school districts and ask them if they have social work positions. State governments also often have listings for educational jobs on the Internet. You can also look at the classified ads in the newspaper. I've been able to get the vast majority of my jobs by talking to people who are already in the positions. As tempting as it may be at the time, don't burn any bridges. Keep all your options open, personally and professionally.

### Describe a typical day.

**8:30** I've already arrived and I'm typically in the bus parking lot waiting to supervise the first busloads of students coming to school. The duty teachers are not supposed to be out there until 8:40, but the first buses come in around 8:30, so the principal asked me to supervise the bus embarking and debarking in the morning and afternoon. I stay until the duty teachers arrive.

**8:40** I'm in my classroom, looking at messages that came in the day before. I follow up on urgent calls. I often get messages from parents wanting to discuss the events of the day before. Maybe their child came home with a complaint about something that happened on the bus and the parents want to make me aware of it. For children in my caseload who get write-ups, the parents and the principal might ask me to intervene and help determine consequences. If there's any information I need to pass on to teachers, I do it before 8:55, because that's when classes start.

**9:00** I might have a group meeting. For instance, this past year, I met with a group of third-grade boys every Tuesday at nine. First we sit down together and do what we call the round-table. We go around the table and check in with each other. That includes me checking in with the boys, because I work from an equality model. The groups have basic rules, which are all phrased in a positive way. Instead of "Don't interrupt," the rule is "One will wait one's turn." Other rules are "One will raise one's hand," "Use polite phrases like 'excuse me,'" and "All conversation is to be respectful." Once we do our check-in, we talk about old business that was unfinished from the week before. We review what game we decided to play for this week. If we didn't pick an activity, we have a vote to choose one. Then we play the game, focusing on social skills and problem solving.

**9:45** We end the group session by reviewing the game and how everybody did, not in terms of winning or losing, but in terms of their ability to get along and share.

**10:00** I have sessions for much of the day, and each lasts between 45 and 55 minutes. In an individual session, we use one-on-one play therapy. For instance, I might play chess with a child, or the child might teach me a new game. After we build up trust and acceptance, I can bring up topics such as the child's family situation.

**11:00** This year, the school counselor and I started something we call "lunch bunch." Each grade level has a 45-minute lunch, with 15 minutes to eat and 30 minutes on the playground, where there are two teachers on duty at the most. Some children do not do well with such limited supervision, and they're able to come to my classroom at lunch. The school counselor and I are there to engage them in games, discussion, and arts and crafts. We have, at the most, 15 children at one time, and a total of 50 kids signed up for lunch bunch.

**1:30** The school counselor and I go into classrooms and do 30 to 35 minutes of class meetings. There are classrooms that the principal has targeted as being almost leaderless—the teachers are just not competent at maintaining balanced discipline. We team up and work with the children so that, by the end of the school year, they give more respect both to each other and to the teacher. Also, the teacher learns new ways to manage the classroom.

**2:00** I take care of emergencies or do some follow-up calls. This is my case-management work.

**2:30** I start up with direct services again. The afternoon is mostly taken up with group sessions.

**3:30** I take 10 minutes to put chairs on the tables and get ready for the custodian. When the bell rings at 3:40, I'm out there helping maintain discipline in the bus lines.

**3:55** The buses are gone, and I have five minutes to go in and check for any messages that might have come in and make sure everything's in order. I leave at four o'clock, but most of the time, there's more work to be done and more calls to be made. There are some parents whom I call every week, no matter what. I make those calls from my classroom or from home in the evenings.

Source: Jay Crowe, *Jay Crowe—Elementary School Social Worker.* Retrieved December 18, 2001, from www.wetfeet.com. Reprinted with permission.

The nature of the workplace is changing rapidly. Many factors have introduced new levels of uncertainty into the process of choosing a career, finding work, and staying employed. These factors include the transformation from agricultural to manufacturing to service and information industries; the increasingly global nature of business; the higher educational standards required for entry into many careers; the expectation that workers will be able to perform across a variety of tasks; and the rapid evolution and extinction of specific types of work brought on by new technologies.

In many fields, there are now a few huge global organiza-

tions and a large number of small innovative companies that do the exciting, creative work of the industry (Handy, 2001). Neither type offers what used to be known as job security, but the work environment of these two kinds of settings is likely to be vastly different. Because economic, technical, and social conditions are changing so rapidly, young adults face two related challenges as they navigate the world of work. First, they cannot expect that strategies or patterns that led to success in the past will necessarily lead to success in the future. Second, they need to be more proactive in designing or inventing an occupational identity (Handy, 1996).

The early phases of career decision making, presented in Tiedeman's model in Chapter 11, focus on self-understanding; career exploration; identifying a good match between personal interests, skills, and values and particular careers; and learning as much as possible about the specific job opportunities in a career domain. However, because of the wide variety of possible occupational choices and associated work settings, one can make only limited progress in preparing to enact a specific occupational role. Even though many employers consider educational attainment a selection criterion, they often use it more as an element in determining one's eligibility for the job rather than as a detailed assessment of whether one has the background and skills to perform it. Most jobs require a period of training for the novice employee, which varies from a few weeks in the case of an assembly-line worker to 10 years in the case of a physician. This is the induction phase in Tiedeman's model.

Most people do not stay at their first job. A national longitudinal study followed the work experiences of people who were 18 years old in 1978 through their 36th birthday. During this period, the average number of jobs they held was 9.6,

*During the training period, new workers learn technical skills as well as strategies for fitting into the social environment with coworkers.*

© Rhonda Sidney/Stock Boston

with less than 20% of the sample having 3 jobs or fewer in these years. Between the ages of 25 and 34, half the sample had been at their current job 2.7 years or less. This figure disguises a great deal of variability, with 30% having been at their current job 1 year or less, and 30% having been at their current job more than 6 years (U.S. Census Bureau, 2004). These data suggest that job mobility is to be expected in early adulthood, and the formation of what has been called an attachment to one's job takes most young adults a while to establish. Therefore, the training phase is not only about acquiring the specific knowledge and skills necessary to carry out the work, but also about developing the personal, interpersonal, and transferable skills that will be important as one moves around the labor market (Posner, 2001).

The training period involves a process of socialization of the new worker. During this time, the individual must evaluate the match between his or her personal characteristics and goals and four central components of the work situation: (1) technical skills, (2) authority relations, (3) unique demands and hazards, and (4) interpersonal relations with coworkers. These are the major arenas for new learning in early adulthood.

**TECHNICAL SKILLS.** Most jobs require a certain degree of technical expertise, which varies greatly from one occupation to another. The job training phase involves learning new skills. Roughly 70% of employees have received formal training, with the most hours of training reported by those with a college degree, performing professional and technical work (U.S. Bureau of the Census, 1999). In addition to specific training, half of all workers are expected to use a computer at their work, with greater percentages in some fields than others (U.S. Census Bureau, 2004). Thus, specific skill training and general technical competence are part of the job demands. Individuals must evaluate whether the particular skills required are within their range of competence. They must also determine whether they have the potential to improve their skills, and evaluate whether they derive pleasure and satisfaction from demonstrating these abilities. The success of individuals in learning and applying new skills determines to some extent whether they will become attached to the occupation. At the same time, the opportunity to learn new skills is part of what permits new workers to advance and seek new employment.

**AUTHORITY RELATIONS.** Each job role specifies status and decision-making relationships among people. One aspect of job training is learning which people evaluate one's work, the criteria they use, and the limits of one's autonomy in the job. In today's organizational environment, career ladders are less obvious, and the authority hierarchy may be difficult to identify. Young workers may be assigned to a number of projects with different leadership; they may be asked to take on significant leadership roles early in their careers; and they may need to form interdependent, collaborative teams (Collin & Young, 2000). New workers must attend to both the authority structure and the people who occupy positions in it. They must also assess the channels for decision making and the

ways in which they can influence decisions. With respect to the people who occupy positions of authority, new workers must be able to deal with a variety of personalities in positions of higher and lower status. Having a good relationship with one's supervisor is a key element in job satisfaction.

**DEMANDS AND HAZARDS.** Each job has unique occupational demands, including norms for self-preservation, productivity, and availability. In some work settings, there are expectations for a high level of personal commitment. A licensed vocational nurse described the tensions that come with being berated by a patient's family members:

> If you are working in an office and someone comes in and they're having words with you and maybe they're rude and you can say "Listen, you've gone too far and you need to leave," whereas we have family members who come up to us and say, "HOW COME YOU . . . ? HOW DARE YOU . . . ?" And they can just be rude and say terrible things and we cannot, we really cannot, we really are not expected to, nor are we really allowed to answer back. (Bullock & Morales Waugh, 2004, p. 775)

Leisure time, family activities, and political or community roles are all influenced by one's participation in the work role. In some work settings, workers may become alienated, feeling little sense of personal contribution to their employers' overall objectives. The norms vary greatly from one occupation to another. It is the task of individuals to assess how well they fit and how strongly they wish to do so with the unique characteristics of a particular occupational role.

Occupational hazards include a broad range of potential physical and psychological risks associated with the workplace, including exposure to toxins, work-related injuries, and exposure to diseases, reproductive hazards, and working conditions that have negative psychological consequences, such as noise or shift work. The rate of work-related deaths and disabling injuries has decreased substantially since the 1960s. Nonetheless, each year since 1995, there are about 5,000 deaths and 3.8 million disabling injuries on the job (U.S. Census Bureau, 2004).

Settings differ in the kinds of pressures or hazards they impose on workers. Similarly, individuals differ in their vulnerability to these pressures and hazards, their willingness to risk certain potential dangers, and their evaluation of the payoff for enduring some degree of stress. The individual must ultimately decide whether the particular vulnerabilities are tolerable in light of the rewards.

**INTERPERSONAL RELATIONSHIPS WITH COWORKERS.** Although the potential for friendships in the work setting is usually not advertised as a central component of job satisfaction, it is clearly a dominant feature in the decision to be committed to a particular work setting. The need for friends with whom one can share the anxieties of learning the new job provides a strong motive for seeking comradeship on the job. The presence of congenial coworkers who can relax together and share feelings of accomplishment greatly enhances any

*Opportunities for congenial relationships with coworkers is a valued feature of the work setting.*

© Tony Freeman/Photo Edit

work setting. In fact, the spirit of friendship on the job may compensate for many stressful situational demands.

Some work settings stress competition among coworkers; incentives are arranged to stimulate competition rather than cooperation. In such settings, new workers must shoulder the strains of their new learning independently. They must learn the game of one-upmanship, taking credit for successes and blaming others for failures. A competitive orientation is more likely to be fostered when workers are organized into teams or units. Intergroup relations tend to be more distrustful and more supportive of the group's self-interest, whereas individual relations tend to be more trusting and cooperative (Pemberton, Insko, & Schopler, 1996).

## ■ POVERTY AND CAREER OPPORTUNITIES

A number of factors limit the range of occupations open to a given person during the work search phase. Among the most obvious limiting factors are educational attainment, ability, and location. Discrimination on the basis of race and gender also continues to thwart the full participation of women and minorities in the workforce. Recent policy changes in the U.S. welfare system have led to a renewed interest in the process of supporting the transition from welfare to work. Analyses of programs that try to prepare individuals and families for self-sufficiency show that they typically emphasize some combination of basic education, job skills training, and adaptive work orientation with supports such as child care subsidies and medical benefits. Some programs put more time and resources into improving the conditions of the jobs and fostering employee skills (Friedlander & Burtless, 1994; Kirby, 1996).

The biggest challenge facing individuals in this transition is the lack of jobs that will provide the salary and benefits necessary to raise workers above the poverty level. Since the 1970s, manufacturing jobs have been replaced by service

jobs. Although there are high-level management positions in the service sector, many of the new jobs are characterized by low wages, limited benefits, and little opportunity for career advancement. These positions may provide a short-term reduction in welfare participation, but for many—especially single mothers who have to cover the costs of child care arrangements and medical coverage for their children—they do not hold the promise of moving the family out of poverty (Bowen, Desimone, & McKay, 1995).

In a study of low-income, single mothers, Edin and Lein (1997) found that cash from welfare, food stamps, and social security supplements covered only about three fifths of their expenses. Those in paid jobs were earning about $8.00 per hour and could not meet their expenses with these earnings. Jobs in the "secondary labor market" involve working in "factories producing cartons, lightbulbs, dog bones, sneakers, turkey parts, doorstops, and manhole covers. [Women] worked as waitresses or caregivers, in 'basement jobs' leading nowhere, in which they hit the 'cellar ceiling' and were vulnerable and powerless. In such jobs, a worker is expendable, can be easily replaced, receives the lowest possible wages, typically works part-time, receives no benefits, has no upward mobility, and has no job security" (Lott & Bullock, 2001, pp. 200–201).

Experts predict that it will be hard to sustain motivation if people who work cannot cover their basic needs, including child care, and do not feel the enhanced sense of personal worth that is typically associated with working.

## ■ CAREER PHASES AND INDIVIDUAL DEVELOPMENT

In an attempt to synthesize career and individual development, Kathy Kram (1985) proposed a developmental model of career issues (see Table 12.2). In this model, careers are

**Table 12.2** Characteristic Developmental Tasks at Successive Career Stages

| | EARLY CAREER | MIDDLE CAREER | LATE CAREER |
|---|---|---|---|
| Concerns about self | *Competence*: Can I be effective in the managerial/professional role? Can I be effective in the role of spouse and/or parent? | *Competence*: How do I compare with my peers, with my subordinates, and with my own standards and expectations? | *Competence*: Can I be effective in a more consultative and less central role, still having influence as the time to leave the organization gets closer? |
| | *Identity*: Who am I as a manager/ professional? What are my skills and aspirations? | *Identity*: Who am I now that I am no longer a novice? What does it mean to be a "senior" adult? | *Identity*: What will I leave behind of value that will symbolize my contributions during my career? Who am I apart from a manager/ professional, and how will it feel to be without the role? |
| Concerns about career | *Commitment*: How involved and committed to the organization do I want to become? Do I want to seriously explore other options? | *Commitment*: Do I still want to invest as heavily in my career as I did in previous years? What can I commit myself to if the goal of advancement no longer exists? | *Commitment*: What can I commit myself to outside of my career that will provide meaning and a sense of involvement? How can I let go of my involvement in my work role after so many years? |
| | *Advancement*: Do I want to advance? Can I advance without compromising important values? | *Advancement*: Will I have the opportunity to advance? How can I feel productive if I am not going to advance further? | *Advancement*: Given that my next move is likely to be out of the organization, how do I feel about my final level of advancement? Am I satisfied with what I have achieved? |
| | *Relationships*: How can I establish effective relationships with peers and supervisors? As I advance, how can I prove my competence and worth to others? | *Relationships*: How can I work effectively with peers with whom I am in direct competition? How can I work effectively with subordinates who may surpass me? | *Relationships*: How can I maintain positive relationships with my boss, peers, and subordinates as I get ready to disengage from this setting? Can I continue to mentor and sponsor as my career comes to an end? What will happen to significant work relationships when I leave? |
| Concerns about family | *Family role definition*: How can I establish a satisfying personal life? What kind of lifestyle do I want to establish? | *Family role definition*: What is my role in the family now that my children are grown? | *Family role definition*: What will my role in the family be when I am no longer involved in a career? How will my significant relationships with spouse and/or children change? |
| | *Work/family conflict*: How can I effectively balance work and family commitments? How can I spend time with my family without jeopardizing my career advancement? | *Work/family conflict*: How can I make up for the time away from my family when I was launching my career as a novice? | *Work/family conflict*: Will family and leisure activities suffice, or will I want to begin a new career? |

Source: From *Mentoring at Work: Developmental Relationships in Organizational Life*, by K. E. Kram. Copyright © 1985 Scott Foresman.

delineated in three phases—early career, middle career, and late career—which correspond roughly to the phases of career exploration, career establishment and advancement, and career maintenance and disengagement (McAuliffe, 1997; Osipow, 1986). In each phase, career development reflects *concerns about self*, including questions of competence and identity; *concerns about career*, including questions of occupational commitment, advancement, and the quality of relationships in the work setting; and *concerns about family*, especially family role definition and possible conflicts between work and family life. Typical issues facing the person at each phase are suggested in Table 12.2.

Issues of greatest concern during the early career phase reflect the need to demonstrate competence and also to establish a satisfying lifestyle. Career development is never a completely rational process. As organizational loyalty gives way to a "free agent" orientation to career development, individuals have to take a more assertive, risk-taking approach to their career development. In this process, one confronts many myths and uncertainties about the meaning of work, worries about financial self-sufficiency, and conflicts between work and other spheres of life, especially intimate relations and family responsibilities. Fears of the unknown—of taking on new responsibilities, of discovering the limits to one's abilities, and of disappointing important people in one's life— must all be faced and reframed if one is to achieve the adaptive flexibility necessary in today's world of work (Patterson, 1997; Stroh & Reilly, 1997).

## LIFESTYLE

**Lifestyle** is a social psychological construct that integrates personality characteristics, goals, convictions, and inner conflicts with social opportunities and resources into an organizing pattern of actions and choices (Lombardi, Melchior, Murphy, & Brinkerhoff, 1996; Slavick, 1995). Simply put, a lifestyle is the "self in action" (Richman, 2001). Central components of the lifestyle include the tempo or pace of activities, the balance between work and leisure, the focus of time and energy in specific arenas, and the establishment of social relationships at varying degrees of intimacy. One's lifestyle guides decisions about how to organize time and prioritize the use of resources (Englis & Solomon, 1997). One can think of lifestyle as the first translation of the values and commitments of individual identity into action through the devotion of time and energy to certain tasks and relationships and the development of domains of competence. The following discussion illustrates some ways in which the overlapping systems of early adulthood—intimate relationships, parenting, and career—interact to organize characteristics of the lifestyle.

### PACE OF LIFE

Some counselors use the metaphor of a three-dimensional space to describe the lifestyle (Amundson, 2001). *Length* is the length of life, or where one is along a developmental continuum. *Width* is the "busyness" of life, including multiple role demands and how much activity one tries to jam into each day. *Depth* is the sense of purpose and meaning in life and the experiences of satisfaction or fulfillment that come with it. This three-dimensional configuration changes over the course of life, both as a result of personal changes in goals or developmental needs and as a result of situational changes in demands or resources.

The pace of life, or the busyness of life, is shaped by work, family, personality, and environmental context. For most young adults, the work setting largely determines the structure of time, including when one goes to work and returns, what one feels energetic enough to do after work, how much time is free for leisure or vacations, and the amount of preparation required during nonworking hours to prepare for the next day (Small & Riley, 1990). People who are trying to combine parenting with a long work day experience the greatest time bind. Schedule control, rather than reducing the number of hours of work, seems to be especially important for helping people maintain a sense of lifestyle balance (Tausig & Fenwick, 2001).

Activity level, or the pace of life, is influenced in part by one's temperament, health, and fitness. This is a circular issue. Adults whose lives are very sedentary are likely to have lower levels of endurance and to feel the strain of daily exertion. Those who are more active and who include physical activity in their lifestyle are likely to have more energy and to be able to handle the demands of an active life.

The pace of life is also influenced by the climate and community. In northern climates, for example, there may be fewer social events away from home during the winter, and life may therefore revolve primarily around the home. In spring and summer, neighborhood activities become a more important stimulus for social life as people emerge and renew their friendships. Rural communities often provide a calmer pace of life than urban communities. People often choose to live in rural or rural-like communities, even when they work in the city, to escape from the hectic pace of urban life.

### SOCIAL NETWORK

As a result of participation in multiple roles, most people expand their social network during early adulthood. They form friendships in the neighborhood and at work. In some work settings, coworkers help each other balance their work and family life by taking shifts for one another, covering special family holidays, or carpooling to help save on expenses. Young adults may become involved in the social life of their religious community or civic associations. They may engage in community volunteer projects with friends and become more invested in the social needs of their neighborhood. If they have young children, the parents of other young children at the child care center or preschool may become important sources of social support. When options are possible, individuals often look for housing in neighborhoods where there are others in their same life stage and lifestyle orientation. For example, when couples with young children live in a community with other young families, they tend to rate the community more favorably than couples living in the community who do not have children (Swisher, Sweet, & Moen, 2004). The contribution of friendships to personal satisfaction and lifestyle differs widely during this time, with single adults and couples without children typically having more time for adult friendships than do parents.

### COMPETING ROLE DEMANDS

A challenge that must be faced in early adulthood is the competition of role demands. One part of role learning involves a widening circle of competencies and relationships. Another part involves balancing the conflicting expectations of simultaneous role responsibilities. Adults struggle with the conflict between the demands of the work setting and the demands of building an intimate relationship; with the tension between the desire to have children and the desire to achieve in the workplace (Gilbert, 1993; Parcel & Menaghan, 1994). For both men and women, the world of work is likely to provide

*The social network for young mothers often includes other young mothers.*

© Michelle Salmieri/Getty Images

the most rigorous test of commitment and the greatest pressures for productivity during the early adult years. Pressure in the work setting competes directly with needs for intimacy and also with the time and energy needed for parenting.

In an analysis of the role demands of dual-earner families, Crouter and Manke (1997) identified three distinct dual-earner lifestyles—high status, low stress, and main-secondary—each with its own pattern of role relationships, costs, and benefits. In the *high-status* couples, both partners had high-prestige careers, earned comparatively high salaries, and were involved in their work. In these couples, the division of household work was more equal than in the other two types. They experienced the greatest amount of role overload, had lower levels of love and marital satisfaction, and more marital conflict than the other two groups.

The *low-stress* couples worked about the same amount of hours as the high-status couples, but their jobs were in less prestigious categories. Examples were a mechanic and a secretary, and a salesman and a substitute teacher. Although the couples had levels of involvement similar to the high-status group, they had the lowest amount of role overload. This group had the highest scores in marital satisfaction and love for their spouse, and the lowest scores in marital conflict. These couples monitored their children more closely and seemed to be more accurate in describing their children's daily activities.

The *main-secondary* couples reflected a lifestyle in which husbands were the primary workers, with higher occupational prestige, more hours worked, and more work involve-

ment than their wives, who typically worked part time. Women in these relationships had less education and tended to have more household responsibilities. A gender-typed division of labor was reflected in the pattern for female children, who performed more household tasks than girls in the other family types, whereas male children in these families performed fewer household tasks than boys in the other family types.

The more involved one is in the competitive demands of work, the less likely one is to feel comfortable about spending time away from it. Conversely, the more engrossed one is in a variety of activities away from work, including hobbies and family events, the more time one will find for leisure. In some occupations, the time schedule leaves little room for personal choice. In others, the income from a single job may not suffice to support the family. Time that might otherwise be spent in leisure must be spent in earning additional income through extra work.

The balance of work and leisure is a result of one's disposition toward them and the demands of the work setting. For some people, time with the family is more important than time at work. They highly value the time they have at home with their families and make it a priority when they choose a career. For other people, advancement in work through the expenditure of large amounts of time supersedes commitments to home and leisure. For them, the lifestyles of partners may evolve somewhat separately, because the amount of leisure time they share may be limited. Couples who are able to enjoy leisure activities together that provide opportunities

*Communities can contribute to a healthy lifestyle by providing walking paths, bike trails, and fitness areas in attractive locations.*

for relaxed, open conversation find that these contribute substantially to the strength of and satisfaction in their intimate relationship (Kalmijn & Bernasco, 2001).

### ■ HEALTH AND FITNESS

The contemporary emphasis on health and fitness indicates the importance of lifestyle decisions for illness prevention and longevity. Research on health and health-related risks has begun to identify characteristics of a healthy lifestyle, including factors that operate at an individual level and those that reflect community commitment (Healthy People 2010, 2001; Hofer & Katz, 1996). Leading health indicators include such practices as the use of preventive health services, regular exercise, eating a well-balanced diet high in fruits and vegetables and low in fat, avoiding smoking, limiting the number of sexual partners, and using contraceptives. The concept of encouraging young adults to adopt a lifestyle that promotes health is becoming a focus for preventive health care. (Studies of people who have lived to an old age are discussed in detail in Chapters 14, Later Adulthood, and 15, Very Old Age.) Much of this research suggests that lifestyle patterns established in early and middle adulthood, including one's diet, activity level, exercise, encounters with challenging and intellectually stimulating tasks, and involvement with cigarette smoking and alcohol, all influence health and vitality in later life.

At the same time, healthy communities are shaped by adults who share a common vision about the lifestyle they want for themselves and their families (U.S. Department of Health and Human Services, 2001). Adults may commit themselves to creating resources and programs to increase the involvement of children and adults in regular physical activity. They may form a coalition of parents, health care professionals, business leaders, and law enforcement agencies to devise a plan to decrease incidents of violence in their community. Commitment to a healthy lifestyle may be enacted through efforts to improve air and water quality, reduce exposure to secondhand smoke, or improve availability and access to health care services and health education.

Lifestyle is an umbrella concept for the variety of patterns of activities, commitments, and satisfactions that make up adult experience. The cultural expectations and personal aspirations for establishing committed relationships, childbearing, and work are confronted, evaluated, and accepted or rejected during these early adult years. In the process of deciding about each of these life tasks, the person begins to crystallize a life pattern that reflects his or her personal vision of a meaningful path toward maturity.

# THE PSYCHOSOCIAL CRISIS: INTIMACY VERSUS ISOLATION

## INTIMACY

**Intimacy** is defined as the ability to experience an open, supportive, tender relationship with another person without fear of losing one's own identity in the process. An intimate relationship has both cognitive and affective components. The partners are able to understand each other's point of view. They usually experience a sense of confidence and mutual regard that reflects their respect as well as their affection for each other. Intimacy in a relationship supports independent judgments by each partner. It also permits the disclosure of

APPLYING THEORY AND RESEARCH TO LIFE

## Attachment Styles and Relationship Formation

ATTACHMENT THEORY HAS become an important construct in understanding the process of relationship formation. One's attachment style, established in infancy, provides a template for orienting toward intimate relationships in adulthood. Anxiety over abandonment, comfort or discomfort with closeness or emotional disclosure, and the level of self-esteem associated with a secure or insecure attachment can all contribute to the type of partner one seeks and one's ability to sustain an intimate relationship (Brennan & Morris, 1997; Brennan & Shaver, 1995; Jones & Cunningham, 1996).

Bartholomew (1990) developed an attachment typology based on one's attachment experiences in infancy and toddlerhood. One can have a positive or negative assessment of the self, and a positive or negative assessment of others (see Table 12.3).

**Secure individuals** have a positive model of themselves and of others: "It is easy for me to become emotionally close to others. I am comfortable depending on them and having them depend on me."

**Preoccupied individuals** have a positive model of others, but a negative model of the self: "I want to be completely emotionally intimate with others, but I often find that others are reluctant to get as close as I would like. I am uncomfortable being without close relation-

**Table 12.3** The Attachment Typology

|  |  | WORKING MODEL OF OTHERS | |
|---|---|---|---|
|  |  | POSITIVE | NEGATIVE |
| **Working Model of the Self** | POSITIVE | Secure | Dismissing Avoidant |
|  | NEGATIVE | Preoccupied | Fearful Avoidant |

Source: Based on Bartholomew, 1990.

ships, but I sometimes worry that others don't value me as much as I value them."

**Dismissing avoidant individuals** have a positive model of self, but a negative model of others: "I am comfortable without close emotional relationships. It is very important to me to feel independent and self-sufficient, and I prefer not to depend on others or have others depend on me."

**Fearful avoidant individuals** have a negative model of both self and others: "I am uncomfortable getting close to others. I want emotionally close relationships, but I find it difficult to trust others completely, or to depend on them." (Crowell, Fraley, & Shaver, 1999, p. 451)

The secure and the dismissing individuals have high self-esteem; however, they differ markedly in the value they place on intimacy and in their interpersonal style. Secure individuals value re-

lationships and are viewed as warm and nurturing. In contrast, dismissing individuals minimize relationships in favor of self-reliance and are viewed as cold or competitive. The fearful avoidant and the preoccupied individuals lack the self-esteem of the secure or dismissing groups. However, the fearful individuals avoid social contact, whereas the preoccupied individuals try hard to engage in relationships.

Interestingly, individuals seek out partners with similar attachment styles. Not everyone is looking for a partner with a secure attachment. Fearful avoidant individuals, for example, prefer other anxious partners over dismissing or secure ones—perhaps because they are better able to interpret and predict the relationship behaviors of those who have a similar attachment orientation (Frazier, Byer, Fischer, Wright, & DeBord, 1996).

personal feelings, as well as the sharing and developing of ideas and plans.

There is a sense of mutual enrichment in intimate interactions. Each person perceives enhancement of his or her well-being through affectionate or intellectually stimulating interactions with the other (Erikson, 1963, 1980). Coming as it does after the establishment of personal identity, the possibility of establishing intimacy depends on individuals' perceptions of themselves as valuable, competent, and meaningful people.

It is not difficult to understand that a person would be on intimate terms with parents and siblings. The family is a central context for sharing confidences, expressing love, and re-

vealing weaknesses and areas of dependence. In fact, there is growing evidence that the nature of one's parental attachment orientation influences the ability to form new intimate relationships (see the box on Attachment Styles and Relationship Formation). The unique task of young adulthood is to establish an intimate relationship with someone outside of one's family. Two people who eventually establish intimacy may begin as complete strangers who have very few, if any, common cultural bonds. Although an extreme degree of difference is unusual, it represents the greatest challenge that may confront two people.

Whether they are established in the context of marriage, friendship, or work, intimate relationships are often characterized by an atmosphere of romantic illusions, such as, "Together we can conquer the world." The romance of an intimate relationship is a reflection of the energy and sense of well-being that come from the support and understanding that are shared within it (Murray, Homes, & Griffin, 1996). There is a deep sense that intimate relationships are not replaceable. There may also be a degree of jealousy in the relationship. The devotion and commitment of intimate partners are vulnerable to threats of competing alliances (Sharpsteen & Kirkpatrick, 1997).

## ■ INTERACTION STYLES OF MEN AND WOMEN

Men interact less intimately than women. They generally demonstrate more competitiveness, less agreement, and lower levels of self-disclosure than women. However, levels of self-disclosure are not related to loneliness for men as they are for women. It appears that men have the same capacity for intimate interaction as women, but they do not choose to exercise it with other men. Whereas women consider intimacy appropriate for both same-sex and opposite-sex relationships, men tend to restrict their intimate interactions to women (Bank & Hansford, 2000).

In a national sample of more than 2,500 adults, men's and women's relationships were compared (Umberson, Chen, House, Hopkins, & Slaten, 1996). Women were shown to have more support from friends; they experienced higher levels of social integration (involvement in personally meaningful relationships), and they were more likely to report having a confidant than were men. Married women received more support from their adult children than did men, whereas men received more support from their spouses than did women. In fact, almost 50% of men said that their confidant was their wife, whereas only 20% of women said their confidant was their husband.

## ■ INTIMACY IN THE WORK SETTING

A common context for the establishment of intimacy is the work setting. Affiliation and close friendship are likely to develop among coworkers. Workers may express devotion to an older leader or teacher. Through conversations, correspondence, conferences, or informal interaction on the golf course or at the bowling alley, coworkers can achieve an affectionate, playful, and enriching relationship. This kind of intimacy is demonstrated in a conversation reported by Kram (1985):

> Alan was very influential. I respected him as being pretty sharp and pretty astute. He had a lot of guts to tackle the problems that existed in the area and that was the union-management business. I was really identifying with him in terms of what and how you run something, how you manage something. You would sit down and talk about or debate how you do certain things, what should we do in this kind of situation. We would be right in line. I think it was

the way I came at a problem; it might be similar to the way he would come at a problem. (p. 33)

The increased presence of men and women as coworkers in the work setting has introduced new difficulties in the establishment of intimacy among coworkers. Problems with sex discrimination and sexual harassment at work are evidence that many men and women have not developed mature strategies for forming mutually respectful, close relationships with adults of the opposite sex. Often, men and women find it difficult to establish an egalitarian relationship at work. They have a hard time engaging in the kinds of informal interactions that bring a sense of closeness to same-sex coworkers, like going to lunch together, stopping for a drink at the end of the day, or going to the gym to work out. Many men find it difficult to establish a style of interaction with women that is forthright but not sexual in tone. Many women find it difficult to be adequately assertive with men so that their ideas are taken seriously and their views are given full consideration.

## ■ ISOLATION

The negative pole of the psychosocial crisis of early adulthood is **isolation**. As social beings, people have a deep need for a sense of connection and belonging. Isolation, and the accompanying feeling of being unable to experience intersubjectivity or shared meaning, is a major source of psychological distress (Jordan, 1997). As with the negative poles of other psychosocial crises, most people experience some periods of this extreme. The more fully developed the ego becomes, the more it is characterized by clear boundaries. One by-product of individuality and independence is a heightened sense of separateness from others. During a period of intense personal growth and discovery, a person may experience a sense of interpersonal isolation, feeling preoccupied by thoughts and emotions that cannot be easily shared with others (Rokach & Neto, 2001).

The obstacles to attainment of an intimate relationship are many. Some arise from childhood experiences of shame, guilt, inferiority, or alienation, which undermine the achievement of personal identity. Others result from incompatibility between partners. The number of adjustments that intimacy requires may overwhelm some young adults. Obstacles to intimacy derive from environmental circumstances that may erode the person's feelings of self-worth or interfere with the evolution of a sense of mutuality. Finally, these obstacles may be embedded in the socialization process, as children learn distinct gender roles that introduce antagonism between men and women and foster interpersonal styles that stand in the way of forming open, caring interpersonal relationships. Seven themes discussed in the next sections illustrate experiences of isolation: loneliness, depression, fragile identity, sexual disorders, situational factors, divergent spheres of interest, and enmeshment.

*Even though most people desire intimacy, there are many obstacles to its attainment. Organization of the work environment often contributes to a sense of isolation.*

© Amy Etra/Photo Edit

## ■ LONELINESS

Feelings of loneliness can be separated into three categories: transient, situational, and chronic (Meer, 1985). *Transient loneliness* lasts a short time and passes, as when you hear a song or an expression that reminds you of someone you love who is far away. *Situational loneliness* accompanies a sudden loss or a move to a new city. *Chronic loneliness* lasts a long time and cannot be linked to a specific stressor. Chronically lonely people may have an average number of social contacts, but they do not achieve the desired level of intimacy in these interactions (Berg & Peplau, 1982). Many chronically lonely people are highly anxious about all types of social activities. They believe that success in social relationships is important, but expect social encounters to be difficult and to end poorly. People who have high levels of social anxiety tend to use interpersonal strategies that place barriers in the way of intimacy. They are likely to be self-deprecating and obsessed by the possibilities of negative outcomes of social interactions. These people tend to let others establish the direction and purpose of interpersonal activities (Langston & Cantor, 1989). Thus, there appears to be a strong relationship between social skills and loneliness. People who have higher levels of social skills, including friendliness, communication skills, appropriate nonverbal behavior, and appropriate responses to others, have more adequate social support systems and lower levels of loneliness (Rokach, Bacanli, & Ramberan, 2000).

## ■ DEPRESSION

Isolation may be a cause as well as a consequence of depression. For some women, clinical depression appears to be linked to an orientation toward intimacy in which the self is systematically inhibited and devalued (Jack & Dill, 1992). They have a rigid view of how they should act in an intimate relationship, which is characterized by four major themes:

1. They judge themselves by external standards, feeling that they never quite measure up to what other people expect of them.
2. They believe that they should build a close relationship with a man by putting his needs ahead of their own, and that to do otherwise is selfish.
3. They try to maintain a relationship by avoiding conflict and repressing their own views, if they think those views may lead to disagreement.
4. They perceive themselves as presenting a false front, in which they appear happy and satisfied on the outside although they are angry or resentful inside.

Over time, women who endorse this outlook lose contact with their authentic self, and even if the relationship remains stable, they become increasingly depressed.

For some, the roots of depression may begin in adolescence. Those young people who tend to internalize their feelings under conditions of stress are likely to experience feelings of loneliness, lack of self-worth, anxiety, and depression. People who develop internalizing disorders in adolescence are at greater risk of continuing to experience depression as adults (Pine, Cohen, Gurley, Brook, & Ma, 1998). One of the most common stressors that may set off a bout of depression in adolescence is the breakup of a romantic relationship (Monroe, Rohde, Seeley, & Lewinsohn, 1999). As adolescents move into early adulthood, they may be more inclined to isolation as a way of protecting themselves from the depression that they have learned to associate with risks of rejection in romantic relationships.

## ■ FRAGILE IDENTITY

For some people, the possibility of closeness with another person seriously threatens the sense of self. They imagine intimate relationships to be a blurring of the boundaries of their own identities and thus cannot let themselves engage in them. People who experience isolation must continually erect barriers between themselves and others in order to keep their sense of self intact. Their fragile sense of self results from accumulated experiences of childhood that have fostered the development of personal identities that are either rigid and brittle or else totally confused. Such a tenuous sense of identity requires that individuals constantly remind themselves who they are. They may not allow their identities to stand on their own strength while they lose themselves, even momentarily, in others. They are so busy maintaining their identities or struggling to make sense out of confusion that they cannot attain intimacy.

## ■ SEXUAL DISORDERS

Isolation may be linked to sexual disorders. Two widely cited "desire disorders" are **hypoactive sexual desire**, a decrease or absence of interest in sexual activity, and **compulsive sexual behavior**, a compulsive need to relieve anxiety through sex (Coleman, 2003). A loss of sexual desire is usually accompanied by physical withdrawal from the partner and by feelings of guilt and dread about losing intimacy. At the same time, the unafflicted partner often feels angry and guilty about imposing his or her sexual needs on an unresponsive and uninterested partner, as in the following example:

> At first it was fun: feverish kisses in his red Chevy, giggly nights of passion in the apartment. But then came marriage, two kids, and suddenly her husband's hands on her flesh felt like tentacles, and the sight of him approaching made her body stiffen with revulsion. Then the disagreements began, hurtful scenes ending with each of them lying wedged against opposite sides of the bed, praying for sleep. (From L. Rosellini, 1992, "Sexual Desire," *U.S. News & World Report,* 113(1), p. 62. Reprinted by permission.)

In the case of compulsive sexual behavior, as in the following anecdote, sex is disconnected from pleasure or intimacy. Satisfaction of sexual drives is often accompanied by shame and disgust:

> Gary's pattern was always the same: First, the unbearable anxiety, never feeling good enough to handle the latest stress at his architect's job. Then, the familiar response—a furtive scanning of newspaper ads, a drive to a strip show, two straight Scotches to catch a buzz, and finally a massage parlor. . . . Afterward, he'd sit naked on the edge of the bed, his thought roiling in disgust: "I must be sick . . . I can't change." But a few days later, the anxiety would begin again and he'd pore over the ads. (From L. Rosellini, 1992, "Sexual Desire," *U.S. News & World Report,* 113(1), p. 64. Reprinted by permission.)

Some psychologists view compulsive sexual behavior as an anxiety-based disorder, like other compulsions. Others argue that it is an addiction, like alcoholism. All agree that those who suffer from this disorder are not able to integrate sexual behavior as a meaningful component of an intimate relationship.

## ■ SITUATIONAL FACTORS

Isolation can also result from situational factors. A young man goes off to war and returns to find that the previously eligible women in his town are married. A young woman rejects marriage in order to attend medical school and finds little time for the formation of intimate relationships. Under these circumstances, desires for intimacy cannot be met. Although it is logical to suggest that the lonely person should try harder to meet new people or develop new social skills, it is possible that the sense of isolation interferes with more active coping strategies.

## ■ DIVERGENT SPHERES OF INTEREST

Isolation can also be a product of diverging spheres of interest and activity. In a traditional marriage, for example, the husband and wife may participate in distinct roles and activities. Marriages characterized by such a division of life spheres are sometimes referred to as *his-and-her* marriages (Bernard, 1972). The wife stays home most of the day, interacting with the children and the other wives in the neighborhood. The husband is away from home all day, interacting with his coworkers. When the partners have leisure time, they pursue different interests: for instance, the woman likes to play cards and the man likes to hunt. Over the years, the partners have less and less in common. Isolation is reflected in their lack of mutual understanding and lack of support for each other's life goals and needs.

## ■ ENMESHMENT

Although Erikson tended to cast the construct of intimacy in tension with the construct of isolation, some family therapists offer another tension: between healthy intimacy and enmeshment (Minuchin, 1978). Within this framework, a family is viewed as a structured system that contains individuals grouped into subsystems linked by patterns of communication, boundaries, alliances, and rules. As individual family members change and grow, the adaptive family experiences transitions that alter the structure. Families are characterized along a continuum from disengaged to enmeshed. The **disengaged** relationships are characterized by infrequent contact and a sense that the members of the family do not really seem to care about one another. This pattern may be viewed as similar to Erikson's concept of isolation within a family group. The **enmeshed** relationships, in contrast, are characterized by overinvolvement in one another's lives, to the extent that any change in one family member is met by strong resistance by the others; individuality is viewed as a threat to the relationship. Individuals in an enmeshed relationship may fear isolation to such a degree that they prevent one another from any movement toward autonomy.

# THE CENTRAL PROCESS: MUTUALITY AMONG PEERS

The central process through which intimacy is acquired is **mutuality** among peers. Mutuality refers to empathic awareness of one another, understanding of self and other, and the ability and willingness to regulate one's needs in order to respond to the needs of one's partner (Skerrett, 1996). One must be able to give and receive pleasure within the intimate context (Jeffries, 1993). The two young adults must bring equal strengths and resources to the relationship. Their intimacy is built on their ability to meet each other's needs and accept each other's weaknesses. When one partner needs to be dependent, the other is strong and supportive; at other times, the roles may be reversed. Each partner understands that the other is capable of many kinds of relationships. Mutuality facilitates the couple's ability to meet each other's needs in different ways over time rather than producing a static, unitary relationship. In fact, mutuality should enhance both individual and couple development. In the process of supporting each other, both partners perform in ways that they might not have adopted had they been alone.

The concept of mutuality has been used in previous chapters to describe the development of a sense of basic trust during infancy. In that context, the distribution of resources, experience, and strength is quite uneven. Mutuality is possible only because the caregiver is committed to the infant's well-being. Through caregivers' consistent efforts, children eventually learn to regulate their needs to fit the family pattern.

*You can see in their expressions, the happiness and mutual regard that form the basis for this couple's love.*

However, children at this stage are not expected to be sophisticated enough to assess and meet their caregivers' needs. In young adulthood, the partners are responsible for fulfilling each other's needs. In most cases, there is no benevolent, superordinate caregiver. Just as the infant learns to trust the caregiver's ability to meet personal needs, each adult partner learns to trust the other's ability to anticipate and satisfy his or her needs. By expressing trust and commitment to one another, each partner strengthens the other partner's ability to believe in and invest in the relationship (Avery, 1989). The partners may also realize that they depend on each other to solve the problems that they face as a couple.

Mutuality in relationships has been studied by asking participants to read brief descriptions of relationship styles and to say which style characterizes their relationship with their mother, father, best friend, and romantic partner (Neff & Harter, 2003). Three relationship styles were described: one that emphasized autonomy and one's personal needs; one that emphasized connection and the needs and feelings of the other person; and one that described an effort to balance autonomy and connection by reflecting on what would be an effective response to the other person as well as meeting one's own needs. This last style was considered evidence of mutuality. Mutuality in a romantic relationship was associated with the most ideal outcomes, including relationship satisfaction, relational self-worth, and lack of relational depression.

Mutuality is strengthened as the two partners learn to rely on each other and as they discover that their combined efforts are more effective than their individual efforts would be. Mutuality, like attachment, is a characteristic of the dyadic relationship rather than of the individual members in it (Rusbult & Arriaga, 1997). It is formed as two individuals, each of whom has a well-defined identity, discover that they can have open, direct communication, hold each other in high regard, and respond effectively to each other.

# THE PRIME ADAPTIVE EGO QUALITY AND THE CORE PATHOLOGY

## LOVE

For thousands of years, the nature of love and the qualities of a loving relationship have been described in songs and stories. In the resolution of the crisis of intimacy versus isolation in early adulthood, the ego quality of love emerges as the capacity for mutuality and devotion that transcends the secure attachment of infancy. Robert Sternberg (1988) has described love as a set of feelings, thoughts, and motives that contribute to communication, sharing, and support. According to his theory, almost all types of love may be viewed as a combination of three dimensions: *intimacy*, the emotional investment in a relationship that promotes closeness and connection;

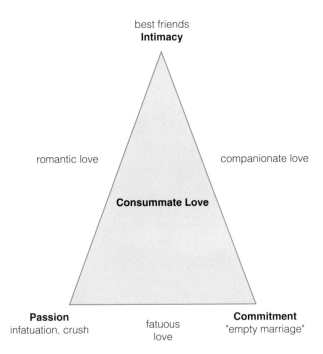

best friends
**Intimacy**

romantic love                    companionate love

**Consummate Love**

**Passion**                                    **Commitment**
infatuation, crush          fatuous          "empty marriage"
                            love

By combining the different types of love,
we get the relationships seen in life.

**FIGURE 12.5**

Sternberg's Triangle of Types of Love

4. Being able to count on the loved one in time of need
5. Mutual understanding of the loved one
6. Sharing oneself and one's possessions with the loved one
7. Receiving emotional support from the loved one
8. Giving emotional support to the loved one
9. Intimate communication with the loved one
10. Valuing the loved one in one's own life

These 10 dimensions are present in relationships with parents, siblings, friends, and lovers. The weighting of the 10 components, however, may vary. Also, some love relationships include a dimension of sexual attraction, and others do not.

## EXCLUSIVITY

The core pathology of this period is **exclusivity**—a shutting out of others. To some extent, exclusivity is a natural element in intimate relations. For example, sexual exclusivity tends to be valued in monogamous, sexual relationships. As a characteristic of a close personal relationship, sexual exclusivity tends to be valued somewhat more by women than by men, and somewhat more by heterosexual men than by homosexual men (Hickson et al., 1992; Masuda, 1994; Perusse, 1994). At some level, however, exclusivity can become destructive to one's ability to have relationships. Exclusivity of this type is characterized by intense jealousy, a rivalrous orientation toward anyone who shows an interest in one's friend or loved one, and preoccupation with intense feelings of anger and resentment, both toward the loved one and toward others (de Silva & Marks, 1994). The person has to expend tremendous energy monitoring the activities of the loved one. As a result, the person is cut off from relationships and ends up excluding himself or herself. Ideally, the experiences of intimacy and love should broaden one's sense of connection and social integration. Through exclusivity, however, one's social support network is limited.

Exclusivity may be extended to the overestimation of one's family, religious group, and national group. As the result of a belief about one's superiority, individuals become unwilling to seek out new people or new experiences. Exclusivity may limit one's willingness to entertain new ideas. In order to preserve the belief in the value of one's exclusive world, one has to distort reality, limit access to new information, and restrict movement in the social environment. Thus, exclusivity becomes a substantial impediment to coping.

**APPLIED TOPIC**
## DIVORCE

AMERICANS HAVE ONE of the highest rates of marriage among modern industrial societies. Almost everyone in the United States wants to get married, and does. However, the

---

*passion*, the expression of physical and psychological needs and desires in the relationship; and *commitment*, the cognitive decision to remain in the relationship. These dimensions form a triangle that helps characterize the different types of love (see Figure 12.5). Each of these dimensions changes over time. Passion is the most fleeting and, without commitment, is likely to result in a short-lived love. Intimacy and commitment can grow stronger over time. However, if passion and intimacy both decline, commitment may dwindle as well (Belsky, 1997). An important aspect of this theory is that it helps account for loving relationships that do not follow the "romantic" ideal of U.S. culture. The factor of commitment, which may originate from valued kinship obligations or economic practicalities, can sustain a relationship and foster an enduring love with or without intimacy or passion.

Conceptions of love usually include four aspects: ideas about the beloved, feelings that are associated with love, thoughts associated with love, and actions that are likely to occur between the lover and the beloved (Beall & Sternberg, 1995). The exact content of these feelings, beliefs, and actions differs from culture to culture, based on the culture's ideals about human nature, relationships, and cultural roles, especially courtship, marriage, childrearing, and religion.

In Western cultures, 10 components of a loving relationship have been identified:

1. Promoting the welfare of the loved one
2. Experiencing happiness with the loved one
3. High regard for the loved one

For couples in a distressed marriage, hostility and resentment that have been characteristic of their relationship in the past are likely to escalate in the divorce process. Despite the presence of attorneys, the divorce negotiations are often riddled with angry exchanges.

© Michael Newman/Photo Edit

divorce rate is also extremely high. For example, in 1998, there were 2,244,000 marriages and 1,136,000 divorces (U.S. Bureau of the Census, 2000). A recent analysis of the marriage history of a nationally representative sample of women ages 15 to 44 in the United States provided an estimate of the duration of first marriages and the probability that they will end in separation or divorce in 6-month intervals from 6 months to 20 years (Bramlett & Mosher, 2001). This study found that 20% of all first marriages have dissolved through separation or divorce at the end of 5 years; 33% have dissolved after 10 years; and 43% have dissolved after 15 years. These data are especially accurate for understanding the marital trajectory for women who married at younger ages, because a woman who married at age 30, for example, would be 50 after 20 years of marriage, and she would not have been included in the study. This study does not include information about the rate of dissolution of cohabiting couples, which would add another dimension to our understanding of relationship instability.

The focus of the following section is on the experiences of adults who are going through divorce rather than on the impact of divorce on children. The median age at first marriage is about 24 for women and 26 for men, and the median length of marriage is 7 years; therefore, one can expect that many individuals experience the divorce process during their early adulthood.

## FACTORS CONTRIBUTING TO DIVORCE

How can we explain the high divorce rate? Here are some of the many hypotheses offered to account for the high divorce rate in the United States:

- We have an overly romantic idea about marriage; the reality of married life cannot live up to our expectations.

- We are overly individualistic and unprepared to make the commitment to achieve a collective goal.
- Men and women are socialized to fear and mistrust or devalue one another.
- We are an overly secular culture with too little commitment to religious values.
- The need for both partners to be involved in the world of work interferes with the establishment and nurturing of intimate relationships.
- Marriage is an outmoded institution, perpetuated by a patriarchal power structure.
- Women who work do not need to remain in unsupportive marriages.
- Men whose wives work do not feel obligated to remain in a marriage to support their wives.
- Smaller family size means less time devoted to child-rearing, and more opportunity for nonparental, adult exploration.
- The longer life span makes it unrealistic that marriages can endure throughout adulthood.
- Children who experience insecure attachments and marital instability grow up to be young adults who are unable to sustain intimate relationships.
- Marriage is a status that requires access to financial resources; lack of equitable employment opportunities and high risks of unemployment threaten the stability of marriage among low-income populations.

A large number of variables have been examined as correlates or predictors of divorce. The scope of these analyses encompasses cross-national studies, historical cohort analyses, multi-county comparisons, and cross-sectional comparisons of couples (White, 1990). At the societal level, countries where there are fewer women than men and where women marry at a later age have lower divorce rates. In traditional patrilineal societies, such as many Arab cultures, the social order is organized around families linked through ties of blood and marriage. Relationships are organized in a hierarchy of obligations and privileges that are maintained through an interdependence of family ties. Divorce rates are low in traditional Arab cultures, where the stigma of disrupting a marriage is not only felt at the individual level but results in harming important kinship bonds that are critical to the larger social structure (Savaya & Cohen, 2003). Two other societal factors show a curvilinear relationship: the socioeconomic development of the country, and women's participation in the labor force. With respect to both of these variables, the divorce rate is lower in the mid-range than at either extreme (Trent & South, 1989).

In a comparison of divorce rates across more than 3,000 counties in the United States, another important construct was identified—**social integration**, or the degree to which "people are tied or connected to one another, shared values being an important element in such integration" (Breault & Kposowa, 1987, p. 556). The characteristics of a community influence this sense of connectedness. Among the most significant of these characteristics are *population change*, the number of people who move in or out of a community each year; *religious integration*, the percentage of the population that belongs to a religious organization; and *urbanity*, the percentage of people in each county who live in an urban area. Divorce rates are significantly linked to each of these characteristics: They are higher in counties with high population change, low religious integration, and high urbanity. These findings suggest that the difficulties that individual couples experience in their marriages may be aggravated by the community context. On the positive side, marriages may be buffered and supported by a critical sense of community identity and shared destiny.

At the level of couple-to-couple comparisons, four variables have been associated with the likelihood of divorce: age at marriage, socioeconomic level, differences in socioemotional development, and the family's history of divorce.

### ■ AGE AT MARRIAGE

In the United States, the incidence of divorce is especially high for couples who marry before the age of 20 (see Figure 12.6). For women who marry younger than age 18, 48% have experienced marital disruption within 10 years following the marriage. In contrast, for women marrying at age 25 and older, only 24% have experienced marital disruption within 10 years (Bramlett & Mosher, 2001).

Both for couples who marry young and for those who marry at an older age, dissatisfaction with role performance is a significant factor in marital instability. For young couples, dissatisfaction centers on sexual infidelity and jealousy. For older couples, it focuses on interpersonal conflict, a domineering style, and lack of companionship. Age at marriage is associated with different developmental needs and varying threats to marital stability. Of course, age at marriage is not a single explanatory dimension. For those who marry young, there is also a greater incidence of premarital pregnancy,

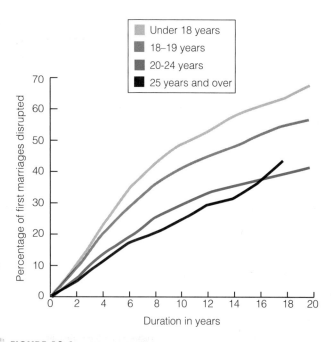

**FIGURE 12.6**

Probability of First-Marriage Disruption by Duration of Marriage and Wife's Age at Marriage: United States, 1995

dropping out of school, and lower paying employment—all of which contribute to the likelihood of divorce.

### ■ SOCIOECONOMIC LEVEL

The concept of **socioeconomic level** is complex. It may be thought of as a combination of education, occupation, and income. Each of these components is uniquely related to the divorce rate (White & Rogers, 2000). Men with more education have lower divorce rates. Women with more education also have lower divorce rates, except that those with 5 or more years of college are somewhat more likely to divorce than those who have had only 4 years (that is, have graduated from college). Within this overall pattern, there is also evidence of the **Glick effect:** Men and women who have dropped out of high school or college have higher divorce rates than those who have completed high school or college. Furthermore, those who have graduated from high school have a lower divorce rate than those who have had 1 to 3 years of college. Glick (1957) explained this pattern as evidence of lack of persistence. Those who are not committed to completing a unit of schooling may also lack the commitment to work at resolving the problems they encounter in marriage.

Many people believe that divorce is a privilege of the rich, but the evidence suggests that the opposite is true. The divorce and separation rates are generally higher among couples with minimal education and low incomes. Total family income is related to marital stability in some distinct ways. First, an erratic income and a high level of debt are more strongly associated with marital disruption than a low, steady income. Second, the relationship between income and marital instability is different for men and women. For men, higher income is associated with low divorce rates. For women, when wives contribute 50 to 60% of the total family income, and when they express low to moderate marital happiness, divorce is more likely. This explanation suggests that when both partners bring about equal economic resources to the marriage, there is less of a sense of obligation to remain in an unhappy relationship (Rogers, 2004).

### ■ SOCIOEMOTIONAL DEVELOPMENT OF THE PARTNERS

Socioemotional development is reflected in such dimensions as the partners' self-acceptance, autonomy, and expressiveness. Personality factors associated with emotionality and constraint have been linked with the risk of divorce. Both positive and negative emotionality increase the risk of divorce, whereas constraint decreases it. The genetic basis of these personality factors and the study of the link between personality factors and marital history among twins has led some researchers to argue that genetic factors play a role in the risk of divorce (Jockin, McGue, & Lykken, 1996).

Problems in communication are frequently cited by men and women as a major cause of divorce. Couples who are characterized as conflicted in their relationship during the premarital period, who have frequent disagreements, and who have different perceptions of how to resolve arguments are more likely to be separated or divorced 3 years after marriage (Fowers, Montel, & Olson, 1996). Generally, women experienced more stress and reported more problems in adjusting to marriage than men (Cotten, 1999). They tend to be more dissatisfied with the level of intimacy in their marriage than are men. These factors were examined earlier in the discussion of adjustment to marriage. Mutual satisfaction in marriage depends heavily on the husband's qualities. The stability of the husband's masculine identity, the happiness of his parents' marriage, his educational level, his social status, and his ability to be comfortable with the expression of emotions all affect marital happiness. Many husbands, however, enter marriage with a deep need to be nurtured and to continue the pattern of care that they received in childhood. The stability of a marriage depends on both partners' achieving a sense of their own identity. This achievement helps to establish the balance of power and mutual respect that is so central to emotional and intellectual intimacy.

### ■ FAMILY HISTORY OF DIVORCE

The family's history of divorce is yet another factor that contributes to marital instability. Children of divorced parents are more likely to get divorced themselves than are children of intact marriages. A number of large national studies find that parental divorce markedly increases the chances that an adult child's marriage will end in divorce. For example, Amato (1996) reported that "the odds of divorce increased by 69% if the wife's parents had been divorced and by 189% if

both the wife's and the husband's parents had been divorced" (cited in Amato & DeBoer, 2001, p. 1038).

There are many interpretations of this intergenerational transmission of divorce (Amato & DeBoer, 2001). One interpretation is that, having seen their parents voluntarily end their marriage, children of divorce do not view marriage as a lifelong commitment and hold more favorable attitudes toward divorce as a reasonable strategy for resolving marital conflict (Greenberg & Nay, 1982). Another explanation is that children in single-parent and remarried families are likely to marry at an earlier age than children in intact marriages, thus increasing the probability of divorce. A third explanation is that children whose parents are in low-quality, high-conflict marriages are exposed to high levels of negative affect and parental hostility. This may create insecure attachment relations and result in poor relationship skills, which in turn make it difficult to form and sustain intimate adult relationships (Amato & Booth, 1996).

In a 17-year longitudinal study of marital stability, Amato and DeBoer (2001) were able to link the quality of the parents' marriage to the probability that their children's marriage would end in divorce. Of 335 married children, 20% had experienced a divorce or separation. Discord in the parents' marriage was not a strong predictor of divorce among the children. Rather, the study found that children who divorced were in families in which there was relatively little conflict, but which nonetheless ended in divorce. This lends support to the explanation that these children are not as committed to a lifelong view of marriage. When marital unhappiness occurs, these children have less inhibition about ending the relationship, especially if a more attractive alternative is likely.

## ■ COPING WITH DIVORCE

Divorce is not a single event, but a relatively long process starting with thoughts about the possibility of divorce through possible steps of marital counseling, reconciliation, mediation, trial separation, and legal action. It is an understatement to say that divorce is stressful. Divorce is associated with numerous losses, including the loss of financial resources, emotional support, one's marital and parental role, and social support (Demo, Fine, & Ganong, 2000). Loss of income may result in other kinds of material loss. For example, a divorced woman and her children may have to move to less expensive housing, sell many of their possessions, and leave the community where they have established a network of friends and social support.

Divorce can also bring role loss and social isolation. Even when a divorce is viewed as a desirable solution, the period from the suggestion of divorce to its conclusion involves a variety of decisions and conflicts that may be painful. Divorced partners may lose contact with family and friends as each person's social support system takes sides in the split (Kunz & Kunz, 1995). Many people who experience divorce go through a time of intense self-analysis. They try to integrate the failure of their marriage with their personal definition of masculinity or femininity, competence as loving people, and long-held aspirations to enact the role of husband or wife, father or mother. The stress-related correlates of divorce include increased health problems, a higher incidence of suicide, and the overrepresentation of divorced adults in all forms of psychiatric settings (Stack, 1990).

The process of leaving a marriage is different for the partner who initiates the divorce than for the partner who is being left. The initiators view the process as more voluntary and tend to be more aware of support services and feel more in control, even if they experience some sentiments of self-doubt and redefinition. On the other hand, those who do not initiate the divorce are more likely to experience a period of shock and disbelief. They, too, must go through a process of identity redefinition, which often takes longer and may be associated with stronger feelings of emotional turmoil (Duran-Aydintug, 1995; Vannoy, 1995).

Evidence of the impact of divorce on adjustment is provided in a comparison of divorced adults with those who are remarried and those who are in first marriages and have never experienced divorce (Weingarten, 1985). Divorced people had lower morale than those who had remarried. They recalled the past as having been much happier than the present and were more likely to say they were not happy at present. However, they did not have lower self-esteem, more anxiety, or more physical symptoms of stress than did remarried adults. In comparison with married people who have never divorced, the divorced people had lower feelings of satisfaction, less zest for life, and greater anxiety.

Even after remarriage, the experience of divorce had a lingering influence on adjustment. Remarried people said they had experienced a lot of difficult life events, were more likely to have used professional help in dealing with personal problems, and were more likely to suffer from stress-related physical symptoms than married people who had never divorced. The remarried were no different from the never-divorced in personal happiness, self-esteem, or optimism about the future. Reentering the marital state appears to boost morale, but it does not remove the strain of having encountered divorce.

## ■ ATTACHMENT TO A FORMER SPOUSE

One challenge in coping with divorce is that many divorced people retain a strong attachment to their former spouse. Grief in divorce has been compared to bereavement in widowhood. In both cases, there is a loss and a need to adjust to it. Although the loss due to death may be more intense, especially if it was sudden, the loss due to divorce may be more bitter. If an affectionate bond has been established, there is certain to be ambivalence about losing it even when the divorce is desired. Attachment to a former spouse may be positive or negative (one may wish for a reconciliation or blame the spouse, respectively) or both.

In a study of more than 200 divorced people, 42% expressed moderate or strong attachment to their former spouse. Some people wondered what their former spouse was doing, spent a lot of time thinking about her or him, expressed disbelief that the divorce had really taken place, and felt that they would never get over it. The attachment was stronger for those who had not initiated the divorce. The lingering feelings of attachment were associated with greater difficulties in adjustment to divorce, especially problems of loneliness and doubt about being able to cope with single life (Kitson, 1982). The stronger the positive or negative postdivorce attachment, the more difficult the adjustment in the years following the divorce (Tschann, Johnston, & Wallerstein, 1989).

The fact that divorce is stressful and that people have lingering attachments to their former spouse does not mean that they consider the divorce undesirable. Studies that ask divorcing people what went wrong in the relationship suggest that for many, the conditions of the marriage were demeaning, exploitive, or oppressive:

> Common complaints by wives include their husband's authoritarianism, mental cruelty, verbal and physical abuse, excessive drinking, lack of love, neglect of children, emotional and personality problems, and extramarital sex. . . . More men than women describe themselves as having problems with alcohol, drugs, or physical abuse that contributed to the divorce. (Demo, Fine, & Ganong, 2000, pp. 283–284)

Many divorced parents report that, despite the difficulties of single parenting, life is more manageable than it was in the midst of the arguments and hostility that preceded the divorce.

## ■ COPING STRATEGIES

Most people who experience divorce are determined to cope with the stresses it brings. Unfortunately, many adults do not anticipate the specific kinds of stressors that they will encounter. Of course, they have different coping strategies, some of which may not be effective for the special demands of divorce. In a longitudinal study that focused on how people adjusted to divorce, the researchers emphasized (1) the *kinds of stressors* that the individuals encountered, (2) the *resources* they had to help them cope, and (3) the *meaning* they gave to the divorce situation (Wang & Amato, 2000). The major stressors were large losses in income, losing friends, and having to move. Those whose postdivorce adjustment was judged most positive had higher income levels, were dating someone steadily or remarried, were most favorable about the marital dissolution before the divorce, or actually initiated the divorce. The magnitude of the stressors was not as important in predicting adjustment as were the coping strategies (resources and meaning).

In another study of widowed and divorced women, the contribution of social support to coping was examined in more detail. Those women who were most stressed by their loss received increased social support from friends and rela-

*For many adults, the experience of divorce creates a new willingness to confront their fears and frustrations about intimacy. Group therapy offers a safe context where recently divorced adults can learn new communication skills and find support from others who have gone through similar experiences.*

tives in the following year. For the two groups, the most beneficial type of support differed. For widows, practical support, such as transportation or help with household chores, was positive; for those who had been divorced, having someone who would listen to their personal problems was especially helpful. For both groups, receiving monetary support was associated with an increase in distress. Thus, some types of social support appear to foster recovery, whereas others may serve to highlight the extent of one's loss (Miller, Smerglia, Gaudet, & Kitson, 1998).

The process of coping with divorce requires strategies devised to deal with the aspects of it that are perceived as most troublesome. Further, many coping strategies, including becoming involved in new activities, spending more time with family and friends, gaining new skills, or taking a new job, may promote new levels of functioning. Human service professionals can be effective in helping adults develop coping skills for resolving some of the stresses of divorce and transforming a difficult life event into an opportunity for personal growth.

## Chapter Summary

Three theoretical concepts were introduced to help consider the challenges and directions of growth in adulthood: social roles, the life course, and fulfillment theories. Adulthood comprises a series of increasingly complex and demanding roles, role gain and role loss, and the challenges of balancing multiple roles. The life course perspective is a framework for examining adulthood as the interface of family and occupational careers against the backdrop of chronological age, historical period, and societal norms and expectations. Through the life course lens, one gains appreciation for the

developing person and the changing historical context. Fulfillment theories emphasize the ability of adults to go beyond meeting daily needs and achieving equilibrium to make plans, strive toward goals, and seek personal meaning in life.

The developmental tasks of early adulthood require that individuals apply the many competencies they have acquired in childhood and adolescence to solving new and complex challenges. They may marry or make a commitment to an intimate partner, have children or decide to delay or forgo childbearing, and choose work roles. Gradually, they evolve a style of life. In this process, their commitment to social institutions and to significant others expands. Their worldview becomes more diverse, and their appreciation of the interdependence of systems increases. One of the major sources of stress at this life stage is the need to balance and integrate multiple roles.

In the period of occupational training, many new areas of intellectual awareness are stimulated. Self-understanding is integrated with social expectations and historical opportunities as men and women embark on their career paths. Four components of the work environment must be mastered: technical skills, authority relations, interpersonal relations with coworkers, and ways of coping with the hazards and risks of the workplace. One of the most challenging aspects of career development in this early phase is the coordination of work with the establishment of meaningful intimate relationships.

The psychosocial crisis of intimacy versus isolation emphasizes the evolution of adult sexuality into an interpersonal commitment. This crisis requires that needs for personal gratification be subordinated to needs for mutual satisfaction. Success is comparatively difficult to achieve in our culture because of the basic tension between the norm of independence and the desire for closeness. The research on marriage suggests that willingness to make a personal commitment to another adult is one of the key aspects of success. The elaboration of communication skills, the ability to engage in and resolve conflict, and the ability to find time for companionate, leisurely interaction are emphasized as central to marital stability.

Coping with the challenges of early adulthood requires the integration of cognitive capacities, emotional openness, and effective interpersonal relationships. The high rate of divorce suggests that many societal, community, and interpersonal factors work against the support of stable intimate relationships. In the process of coping with divorce, there is a clear need for daily problem solving and emotional expression to manage the grief, loss, and role transitions that accompany this crisis.

3. What characteristics are important to you in a romantic, long-term partner? What characteristics are important to people in your family who might influence your choice? On what dimensions is homogamy important to you in the choice of a mate?
4. What are your own views about the importance of having children? Where does childbearing fit into your view of yourself as an adult?
5. Describe your current lifestyle. How do you use your time? What are your priorities for work/school, intimate relationships, parenting or other family roles, leisure activities, involvement in religious, political, and charitable organizations? As you think about yourself in the period of life from 24 to 34, what do you envision as the pillars (the essential structure) of your lifestyle?
6. How does culture contribute to the way adulthood is defined? What are the cultural markers of the transition into adulthood? What cultural expectations shape your decisions about marriage, childbearing, and work? Imagine a society in which commitment to family and intimate relationships would be valued ahead of work. What policies and practices would provide evidence of this priority?
7. How do you account for the high divorce rate in the United States? Give five different answers to that question, focusing on different levels of analysis: societal, historical, cultural, developmental, and interpersonal.

## On the Web

**VISIT OUR WEBSITE**

Go to http://www.wadsworth.com/psychology to find online resources directly linked to your book.

## Further Reflection

1. What are some of the developmental tasks of infancy, toddlerhood, early and middle childhood, and early adolescence that contribute to the capacity to form intimate relationships in adulthood?
2. What are some of the ways that success in the world of work competes with success in an intimate relationship? How might success in the world of work enhance one's success in an intimate relationship?

## Casebook

For additional cases related to this chapter, see the case entitled "To Marry or Not" in *Life Span Development: A Case Book,* by Barbara and Philip Newman, Laura Landry-Meyer, and Brenda J. Lohman, pp. 163–170. The case focuses on the development of Jonah's and Abby's dating relationship, their decision to marry, and the early years of their married life as they are influenced by work and extended family relationships.

# CHAPTER 13

# MIDDLE ADULTHOOD
# (34–60 YEARS)

*Portrait of Gertrude, 1906./Pablo Picasso./© 2005 Estate of Pablo Picasso/Artists Rights Society (ARS), New York./© Francis G. Mayer/Corbis*

*Gertrude Stein was Picasso's friend and mentor. She provided an environment where creative people could get together and share ideas. This portrait was the only one that Stein felt represented her true sense of self. Middle adulthood is the period when one's energy and talent are directed toward building and maintaining the structures upon which future generations depend. It is the stage when self-fulfillment is integrated with caring for others.*

■ DEVELOPMENTAL TASKS

Managing a Career
Nurturing an Intimate Relationship
CASE STUDY: THE STRUGGLE FOR COMMITMENT
TO GROWTH IN A VITAL MARRIAGE
Expanding Caring Relationships
CASE STUDY: A DAUGHTER CARES
FOR HER AILING MOTHER
Managing the Household

■ THE PSYCHOSOCIAL CRISIS:
GENERATIVITY VERSUS STAGNATION

Generativity
CASE STUDY: MY LEADERSHIP JOURNEY
Stagnation

■ THE CENTRAL PROCESS: PERSON–ENVIRONMENT
INTERACTION AND CREATIVITY

Person–Environment Interaction
Creativity

■ THE PRIME ADAPTIVE EGO QUALITY
AND THE CORE PATHOLOGY

Care
Rejectivity

■ APPLIED TOPIC: DISCRIMINATION IN THE WORKPLACE

Disparities in Income and the Occupational Structure
How Discrimination Perpetuates Itself
Psychosocial Analysis: Discrimination and Coping

■ CHAPTER SUMMARY

■ FURTHER REFLECTION

▶  *To examine the world of work as a context for development, focusing on interpersonal demands, authority relations, and demands for the acquisition of new skills; considering midlife career changes; examining the interaction of work and family life; and examining the impact of joblessness in middle adulthood.*

▶  *To examine the process of maintaining a vital, intimate relationship in middle adulthood, especially a commitment to growth, effective communication, creative use of conflict, and preserving passion.*

▶  *To describe the expansion of caring in middle adulthood as it applies to two specific roles— that of a parent and that of an adult child caring for one's aging parents.*

▶  *To analyze the tasks required for effective management of the household and their impact on the cognitive, social, and emotional development of family members.*

▶  *To explain the psychosocial crisis of generativity versus stagnation and the central processes through which the crisis is resolved: person–environment interaction and creativity. To define the primary adaptive ego strength of care and the core pathology of rejectivity.*

▶  *To apply a psychosocial analysis to the issue of discrimination in the workplace, with special focus on the cost to society and to the individual when discrimination operates to restrict career access and advancement.*

MIDDLE ADULTHOOD LASTS from about age 34 to 60. According to psychosocial theory, a new reorganization of personality occurs during middle adulthood that focuses on the achievement of a sense of generativity—a concern about the well-being of future generations. This new stage integrates the skills and perspectives of the preceding life stages with a commitment of energy to the future. During this period, individual and societal development are intimately interwoven. In order for societies to thrive and grow, adults must dedicate their energy and resources to preserving the quality of life for future generations. In order for individuals to continue to thrive and grow, societies must provide opportunities for adults to express and fulfill their generative strivings.

Because middle adulthood covers a relatively long period, there are opportunities to review and revise one's commitments and goals along the way. Over the course of adulthood, many situations call for decisions that have no single correct answer. Several alternatives may be possible, and adults must rely on their ability to gather and evaluate information to determine which choice is best for them and their loved ones. Flexibility coupled with a good sense of humor and creative problem solving emerge in this stage as key coping strategies. ■

# DEVELOPMENTAL TASKS

Each adult typically engages in all of the following developmental tasks: managing a career, nurturing an intimate relationship, expanding caring relationships, and managing the household. Through their roles in the family, at work, and in the community, middle adults have broad responsibilities for the nurturance, education, and care of children, adolescents, young adults, and older adults (Lachman & James, 1997). The strains of middle adulthood result largely from difficulties in balancing many roles and striving to navigate through predictable as well as sudden role transitions (Elder, George, & Shanahan, 1996). The emotional well-being of the society as a whole rests largely on the capacity of middle adults to succeed in the developmental tasks of their life stage.

## MANAGING A CAREER

Work is a major context for adult development. Every person who enters the labor market has an occupational career. However, this career may not appear to be orderly or progressive. It may involve changes in the kind of work performed over time, short- or long-term exit from the labor market due to unemployment or family responsibilities, and periodic return to school for new training. One can argue that as long as a person is involved in an effort to make use of her or his skills and talents, there will be significant interactions between the world of work and the person's individual development.

Using the framework of systems theory, one can appreciate that the microsystem of work is embedded in a larger societal macrosystem. Each society has an economic orientation that influences policies and practices related to work. The United States is a **capitalist economy**, where the profits of a company are reinvested into the company and shared with the owners and stockholders. Owners exert pressure on workers to increase productivity and reduce costs. In comparison to European countries, the labor union structure is less powerful in the United States and often cannot protect workers from these new demands. U.S. workers are working longer hours today than in the past. A third of the labor force works 49 hours a week or more. In comparison to Western Europeans, workers in the United States work 9 weeks longer per year (Tiedje, 2004). The buying power of wages has declined, so that most families find it necessary for both partners to work in order to meet a reasonable standard of living. The costs of housing, education, and health care have increased dramatically; and the projection of a longer life expectancy has placed new pressures on workers to save for a more diverse set of needs in retirement. The lack of universal health insurance adds to the financial worries of many middle adults, both out of concern for their ability to pay for their own immediate family's medical expenses and for their ability to support their aging parents, whose health care costs are often not fully covered by insurance. All these features of the macrosystem in the United States have implications for the way individuals orient to the world of work and for the potential conflicts between work and family life.

There is reciprocity between work experiences and individual growth. We expect that people with certain kinds of experiences, abilities, and values will enter certain kinds of work roles (Holland, 1997). Once those roles have been entered, the work environment and the kinds of activities that the person performs also influence his or her intellectual, social, and value orientation. One's lifelong occupational career is a fluid structure of changing activities, ambitions, and sources of satisfaction. As people move through middle adulthood, the management of their occupational career becomes a task of central importance to their sense of personal effectiveness, identity, and social integration. Four themes in the management of a career are discussed for their contribution to adaptation and individual development: achieving new levels of competence; midlife career changes; balancing work and family life; and the impact of joblessness.

## ■ ACHIEVING NEW LEVELS OF COMPETENCE IN THE WORLD OF WORK

Middle adulthood brings new challenges, a reformulation of ambitions and goals, and new levels of competence in the workplace. Three areas are emphasized here as they relate to the interpersonal and cognitive components of career development: understanding and managing leadership and authority relationships; expanding interpersonal skills; and meeting new skill demands by achieving new levels of mastery in critical skill areas.

In middle adulthood, new workplace expectations focus on decision-making skills, effective leadership, and the ability to recognize when change is needed.

© Myrleen Ferguson Cate/Photo Edit

**UNDERSTANDING AND MANAGING LEADERSHIP AND AUTHORITY.**  **Authority relations** encompass all the hierarchical relationships that give people decision-making power and supervisory responsibility for others. Returning to Tiedeman's model, which was introduced in Chapter 11 (Later Adolescence), in the *induction* phase of career development one must identify the authority structure operating in the work setting and begin to establish one's position in it. In the *reformation* phase, which typically occurs in middle adulthood, advancement in a career inevitably involves taking on positions of increased responsibility and power to make decisions. Career advancement means assuming leadership in some areas, while recognizing and cooperating with the leadership of others.

What is leadership? Most people can recognize leadership, but cannot define it accurately. Current views suggest that leadership is not a quality of personality as much as it is a relationship among people. Woyach (1991) defined *leadership* as "the process of helping a group shape a vision of its purpose and goals and of getting people, both inside and outside the group, to commit and recommit themselves to accomplishing that vision" (p. 7).

This definition embodies three basic assumptions: (1) leadership is a relationship among people; (2) leaders provide a sense of vision or direction; and (3) leaders have an impact on getting the group to work toward achieving its vision.

Building on this view of leadership, Woyach (1991) argued that leaders try to balance the good of the group with their own self-interest. They try to take into account the best interests of individuals, groups, and communities while they also participate and lead. Groups may benefit from having many members who have leadership qualities. This should not result in constant competition for authority and recognition, but in tremendous energy produced as a result of combining the contributions and positive spirit of each participant.

The requirements of leadership may change as the group develops and members become more aware of others' abilities (Clark & Clark, 1994). As levels of trust and confidence among members increase, a group may take on more complex tasks and, therefore, draw on the leadership skills of various group members. Groups may go through phases when everyone is overloaded and distracted. During those times, leaders help the group return to its mission and recommit to working together. At other times, the group members may understand their roles and tasks so clearly that the primary acts of leadership involve delegating responsibilities and removing obstacles to the group's success. Thus, understanding leadership and authority relations typically involves the ability to assume authority, respond to higher authorities, and collaborate as a member of a team.

With the reorganization of many large companies, the focus has been on having fewer employees who are asked to be more productive. Leaders need to develop adaptive expertise to accompany their technical expertise (Smith, Ford, & Kozlowski, 1997). This involves mobilizing and guiding the direction of innovation, coordinating people and projects, communicating, and managing one's own time and effort (Evers & Rush, 1996). Leaders need to be able to understand the underlying dynamics of their work situation and motivate others to respond to new and changing conditions.

The idea that leaders are able to motivate others is explored in detail by Rosabeth Moss Kanter (2004) in her analysis of how organizations are able to turn a losing streak around. Kanter (2004) highlights the role of leaders in inspiring confidence. Based on hundreds of interviews and a national survey of more than 1,000 companies, Kanter identified strategies that successful leaders use to encourage members of their organization to reach new, higher levels of performance. When leaders believe in the goals of the organization and in the ability of people to achieve those goals, people will rise to meet those expectations. In inspiring confidence, leaders set high standards and are role models for these standards. They establish systems for individual and system accountability. They foster collaboration though mutual respect and effective communication. They recognize and encourage initiative, imagination, and innovation. They are able to convince others outside the organization to invest in the goals of the organization, which makes their success more attainable. Thus, it falls to the leader of a group to embrace a vision of success and to build commitment to that vision rather than to be caught up in all the many obstacles that prevent success.

**EXPANDING INTERPERSONAL RELATIONSHIPS.** Most occupations place a great deal of emphasis on the development and use of interpersonal skills—especially the ability to interact well with customers and coworkers and the ability to communicate effectively—as underlying criteria in the selection and promotion process (Moss & Tilly, 1996). Even though these skills are not mentioned explicitly in the job description, success in career management requires the ability to influence others, appear credible, develop a fluent conversational style, and learn to work effectively in groups or teams. Problems in interpersonal relationships can have a negative impact on employees, on the image of the organization, and on overall productivity.

The interpersonal values held by the leaders in a work group influence the work environment. In one analysis of professional expertise, coworkers were asked to nominate individuals who they thought were excellent computer software professionals. The nominees had high technical knowledge, broad-based experience, and a high level of social skills (Sonnentag, 1995). Thus, even in a field that might be described as technical, product oriented, and highly competitive, the most admired professionals were more frequently involved in a review and feedback process, consultation with others, and the facilitation of group problem solving.

When individuals work in teams, especially when there is frequent interaction, there is a tendency toward social comparison. One may learn that a colleague has made a lot of sales, received recognition for an accomplishment, or solved an important work-related problem. This might be viewed as an *upward* comparison—a person believes that the colleague performed better than he or she did. In contrast, one may learn that a colleague made a lot of errors, worked too slowly, or failed to make a sales quota. This might be viewed as a *downward* comparison—a person believes that the colleague performed worse than he or she did. This type of social comparison is an ongoing aspect of the interpersonal environment at work, with some people being more likely to base their self-evaluation on comparisons with others.

In a study of social comparison among general physicians in community health centers in Spain, researchers asked whether the cooperative social climate of the work setting would influence how people reacted to social comparisons (Buunk et al., 2005). A *cooperative* social climate at work was characterized as one where people helped each other, there was a sense of team unity, satisfaction with team functioning, and participation in team decision making. Thinking about reactions to social comparisons, one could observe that others are doing better than oneself and be happy for them; or one could be jealous or envious of their success. One could observe that others are doing worse than oneself and be relieved or proud that one is doing so well; or one could feel bad about their failures. In general, respondents made more upward than downward comparisons, and their overall emotional reactions were more positive to upward comparisons than to downward comparisons. However, there was more negative reaction to upward comparisons than positive reaction to downward comparisons.

The kind of reaction that people had to these social comparisons was influenced by the nature of the work climate. In settings described as cooperative, there was a stronger negative response to downward comparisons and a stronger positive response to upward comparisons. The implication is that in a cooperative work environment, people view the fate of their colleagues as directly affecting them. In such a setting, one can imagine a positive interpersonal dynamic, where people feel proud of those who are doing better than they are and are encouraged to seek out these high performers to exchange ideas in order to learn. People who feel bad when others are not doing as well as they are may be willing to help them raise their skills or improve their performance. Given the very specific group of participants in this study, one must be cautious about generalizing these results to other cultures and other categories of workers.

**MEETING NEW SKILL DEMANDS.** The characteristics of the occupation and the work setting determine what kinds of work-related skills will dominate the adult's energies. It makes sense to expect that the actual tasks a person performs from day to day will influence his or her intellectual development. The *Dictionary of Occupational Titles* (U.S. Department of Labor, Employment and Training Administration, 1993) was recently updated and converted to a Web-based resource called *O\*NET* (http://www.doleta.gov/programs/onet/), which is maintained by the U.S. Department of Labor, Employment and Training Administration. O\*NET describes

950 occupational titles and describes each occupation with regard to skills, abilities, knowledge, tasks, work activities, work context, experience levels required, job interests, and work values and needs. Each of these dimensions has implications for workers' adaptation to their work setting. It is likely that in the process of adapting to these dimensions, the adult will carry over aspects of work-related competence to family and community roles.

The idea that social structure influences personality through occupational demands was developed in some detail by Melvin Kohn (1980; Miller, Slomczynski, & Kohn, 1988). One of the strongest relationships he identified was between the substantive complexity of the job and intellectual flexibility. **Substantive complexity** is the degree to which the work requires thought, independent judgment, and frequent decision making. Those whose work is characterized by substantive complexity also tend to have relatively low levels of supervision, and their work is not overly routinized. As a result of these work conditions, they tend to value self-direction, encourage self-direction in others—including their children—and show evidence of **intellectual flexibility**, the ability to handle conflicting information, grasp several perspectives on a problem, and reflect on one's own values and solutions.

This relationship between substantive complexity at work and personal intellectual flexibility was found among workers in the United States, Poland, and Japan (Kohn, 1999). In the cross-national comparison, U.S. workers whose jobs were characterized as substantively complex also had greater personal satisfaction and a sense of well-being, whereas those whose work was highly routinized and supervised had a lower sense of well-being. In Poland, when these data were collected in 1978, the workers who had the more substantively complex work were also more distressed. The workers at the more routinized jobs were more confident of job security and less threatened by instability. Thus, although the Polish workers at the routinized jobs had the least self-direction of all the three countries, they felt a high sense of satisfaction about their current and future employment. In contrast, the managers, whose jobs were more substantively complex, were also at greater risk. They were held accountable for productivity with little opportunity to influence rewards or working conditions.

One of the most frequently cited areas of skill development in the contemporary labor market is *creative problem solving* (Hunt, 1995). The combination of increasingly complex technology, instant international communication, and continuing reorganization of the network of interrelated businesses results in the emergence of a new and changing array of problems. These problems may relate to the need to recruit and train the workforce, bring together changing teams of workers depending on the task, find new strategies for the manufacture and delivery of products, or integrate technologies. The concept of **managerial resourcefulness** is sometimes used to capture the nature of this problem solving (Kanungo & Misra, 1992). It exemplifies what we referred to in Chapter 10 (Early Adolescence) as *postformal reasoning*. By middle adulthood, individuals have accumulated a deep knowledge of the specific tasks and routines associated with their work. At the same time, they have either tried or observed a variety of problem-solving strategies. Thus, the challenge for the middle-adult worker is to synthesize these two bodies of knowledge to create a flexible approach to emerging problems. Successful development in this area requires recognizing when conditions have changed such that past solutions will not be adequate. At the same time, it requires confidence in one's ability to find new solutions and remain creative under stressful conditions.

## ■ MIDLIFE CAREER CHANGES

Management of a career does not necessarily mean remaining within the same occupational structure throughout adult life. Recall from the discussion of work in Chapter 12 (Early Adulthood) that between the ages of 18 and 36, the average number of jobs held was 9.6. Although the rate of job turnover slows down after age 30, people still need to remain flex-

© Justin Sullivan/Getty Images

*Arnold Schwarzenegger made a dramatic midlife career change. He left his role as a movie star and was elected governor of California.*

ible about their attachment to a specific job. Descriptions of the changing nature of organizations suggest that the segment of workers employed full-time by corporations is a shrinking percentage of working-age adults. As today's working-age labor force moves through middle adulthood, from 34 to 60, the nature of the labor market is also predicted to change to a more decentralized, fee-for-services model. This requires individuals to create what Charles Handy (1996) described as a "portfolio" approach to their career—developing a resume that highlights one's products, skills, talents, and experiences, and taking a proactive stance to market these assets to others.

Work activities or work-related goals may change for at least five reasons during middle adulthood. First, some careers end during middle adulthood. One example is the career of the professional athlete, whose strength, speed of reaction time, and endurance decline to the point where he or she can no longer compete.

Second, some adults cannot resolve conflicts between job demands and personal goals. Some workers recognize that the kinds of contributions they thought they could make are simply not possible within their chosen work structure. Others feel like outsiders within their corporations:

> Trish Millines Dziko didn't discover her affinity for computers until she attended college on a basketball scholarship. Later, while she was rising through the mostly White, male ranks at Microsoft, she felt uncomfortable being one of the few African Americans in Redmond. At age 39, she retired as one of many Microsoft millionaires and used $100,000 of her kitty to establish the Technology Access Foundation, designed to bring more kids of color into the game. . . . "I want to change the dynamics of the [corporation] club," says Dziko, "by changing the demographics" (Schultz, 2001, pp. 68–69).

A third explanation for midlife career change is the realization that one has succeeded as much as possible in a given career. Adults may realize that they will not be promoted further or that changing technology has made their expertise obsolete. Consequently, they may decide to retrain for new kinds of work or return to school to move in new career directions. In 1996, the U.S. Department of Commerce conducted a study of reasons people gave for why they were not working in the prior 4 months. Among those ages 25 to 44, roughly one million adults said they were going to school (Weismantle, 2001).

Fourth, some women decide to make a greater commitment to career once their children are in school all day; others wait until their children are in high school or college. Many have chosen to withdraw from the labor market, work part-time, or work from home for a time in order to fulfill parenting roles. As they redirect more energy to their careers in midlife, women continue to expect to combine responsibilities as homemakers with career goals. However, their life course has an anticipated midlife career change built in as they shift their primary involvement from the home to the labor market. Other women who have never worked before marriage face the labor market as novices. These women—sometimes referred to as **displaced homemakers**—may enter the job market as a consequence of divorce or early widowhood, facing extreme economic pressures and competing with younger workers for entry-level positions.

Fifth, with the restructuring of the workforce, some workers are laid off and cannot be rehired in the same field. They have to retrain for a new line of work or for similar work in a new industry. One must be cautious not to idealize midlife career change. Patterson (1997) outlined some of the fears that may be associated with making a career transition: fear of making an unfavorable discovery about one's abilities as a result of the change; fear of failing to satisfy the expectations of important others; fear of taking on new responsibilities; and fear of giving up a known present for an unknown future. Although this type of change is increasingly common as a result of the changing characteristics of the labor market, the ease or difficulty of making such a change depends in part on the extent to which workers perceive that they have control over the conditions of the change. For example, executives of large corporations are likely to become disillusioned or displaced as a result of reorganization. In a study of executives who started up their own businesses after working for a Fortune 500 company, those who were successful in their next endeavor were able to see the change as an opportunity for the achievement of new goals; they had significant expertise to bring to the new career, and they drew on important environmental support in the transition (Eggers, 1995).

## ■ BALANCING WORK AND FAMILY LIFE

Almost everyone manages a career while juggling commitments to spouse, children, parents, other household members, and friends. A decision to assume more authority, work longer hours, accept an offer with another company, quit a job, accept a transfer to a new location, or start up one's own business will touch the lives of other household and family members.

In thinking about balancing work and family life, it is useful to consider three interrelated concepts: role overload, role conflict, and role spillover (Nickols, 1994). **Role overload** occurs as a result of too many demands and expectations to handle in the time allowed. For example, a parent with three children ages 8, 11, and 15 may find that the demands of getting the children ready for school, attending functions at three different schools, picking children up and dropping them off at various places, and trying to be emotionally available for the "problem of the day" are exhausting. Role overload can be experienced in one or more adult roles.

**Role conflict** refers to ways that the demands and expectations of various roles conflict with each other. For example, role conflict occurs when a worker is expected to stay late at the job to finish a project, but that same night is a spouse's birthday or a child's performance.

**Role spillover** occurs when the demands or preoccupations about one role interfere with the ability to carry out another role. For example, a person may be disrupted at work by worries about an ill parent or distracted at home by a work assignment that is due the next day.

The combination of role overload, role conflict, and role spillover can lead to reduced satisfaction at work and in family roles, and in a decline in the person's sense of well-being (Beale, 1997). In contrast, multiple role involvement has been shown to contribute to well-being. Spousal support for the partner's involvement in work can increase work satisfaction, and feelings of success and pride in one's accomplishments at work can contribute to marital satisfaction (Dreman, 1997).

The domains of work and family, both central to adult lives across cultures, are likely to conflict under certain circumstances. In order to understand the nature of this conflict, researchers have identified the elements of work and the elements of family life that appear to be most central to this conflict. The basic assumption is that there are role pressures from work and family that are mutually incompatible, so that meeting the expectations in one domain makes it very difficult to meet expectations in the other. Moreover, there may be interactions such that conflicts from work make it difficult to meet role expectations in the family; but then the disruptions in the family make it difficult to meet role expectations at work (Frone, 2003). Despite these tensions between work and family obligations, people strive to find ways for the two roles to work together (work–family fit), which leads to greater job satisfaction. Job flexibility is viewed as a factor that can contribute to this successful adaptation. This model is presented in Figure 13.1.

In a study of the interface between work and family roles, the model just described was tested in 48 countries (Hill, Yang, Hawkins, & Ferris, 2004). The characteristics of a job that were identified as producing work–family conflict were job responsibility, job workload, and job travel. The characteristics of the family that were identified as producing family–work conflict were responsibility for children, responsibility for elders, and being married. The model was tested by analyzing survey responses of more than 25,000 IBM workers, whose average age was 39. The countries were divided into 11 Eastern countries with a collectivist orientation, and three groups of countries with a more individualist orientation: Western developing countries, Western affluent countries, and the United States.

The results of this study showed that the model was a good fit for all four groups of countries. The three job characteristics were significantly related to work–family conflict across all 48 countries, although the strength of the relationship was greater in the three individualist groups of countries. Responsibility for children and elders were related to family–work conflict across all the countries, but this relationship was stronger for women than for men. Contrary to expectations, marriage was related to less family–work conflict across all the countries. Job flexibility was associated with less

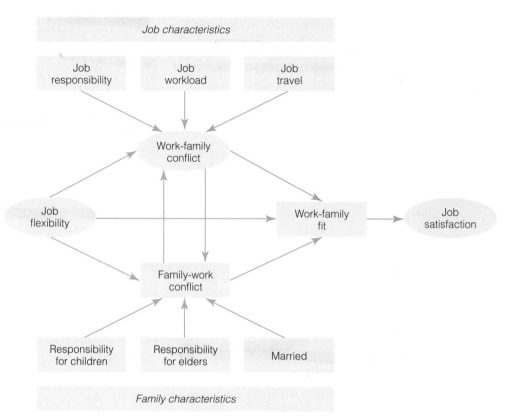

**FIGURE 13.1**

A Model of the Work–Family Interface

Source: Hill, Yang, Hawkins, and Ferris, 2004, fig. 1, p. 1302.

work–family conflict in the Eastern countries and the Western developing countries, but not in the Western affluent countries or the United States. Across all the countries, work was much more likely to create conflict in family life than family life was to be disruptive for work. The general model was a good predictor of job satisfaction across these very different work environments. One might ask whether the global corporate environment of IBM might have smoothed out some of the cultural variations that would have been observed had workers been drawn from a greater diversity of businesses. However, this research is a very exciting beginning in trying to understand the dynamics of work–family interactions at a global level.

This cross-national study adds to a growing literature documenting that women are more distressed by family–work conflict, possibly because responsibilities for household and child care continue to rest more on the shoulders of employed women than on those of employed men (Voydanoff, 2004). Nonetheless, trends in the United States are moving toward a more egalitarian model. Men and women increasingly agree about the value of having women in the labor market and the importance of family-friendly workplace policies. Employed men are spending an increasing amount of time on household and child care tasks, both on workdays and non-workdays.

Between 1977 and 2002, the gap between the amount of time women and men spent on household tasks decreased from 3 hours to 1 hour on non-workdays and from 2.5 hours to 1 hour on workdays. As men spend more time on child care tasks, the result is that children actually have more time with a parent than they did in 1977 (Barnett, 2004).

Women use a variety of strategies to cope with the strains of balancing work and family life (Denmark, Novick, & Pinto, 1996). Some women resolve the conflict between career aspirations and family commitment by limiting their competitive, achievement-oriented strivings. For them, the dual-earner relationship is a matter of negotiation with their spouse, who is regarded as giving them permission to go to work and who sets the limits on their involvement in work. In contrast, other women find that their workplace sets limits on their achievement through gender-stereotyped assumptions about the woman's commitment to her family role (Ridgeway & Correll, 2004). In these settings, women do not tend to be promoted to high-level administrative or managerial positions in which work demands would begin to invade family commitments. As an example, some companies are reluctant to put women in positions in which they may have to be transferred, for fear that their husbands will refuse to make the move. Sometimes, women who request flexible or part-time work schedules

*After the birth of her twins, Karen decided to try working from home. She balances work and family life by having a babysitter 3 half days and trying to work on small projects for a half hour here and there while the twins are awake. The twins love their mom's computer and are eager to help.*

© LWA-JDC/corbisstockmarket.com

are labeled as not serious enough about their career. Finally, other women create a salient professional identity and look for a partner who will support their ambitions.

What is the impact of the dual-career arrangement on men? Studies have consistently found that men's happiness in their family roles is a stronger predictor of psychological well-being than their adjustment at work (Pleck, 1985). Most men find personal meaning and emotional support in their roles as husband and father. For many men, the positive quality of their marital and parental roles helps them cope more effectively with the stresses of work (Barnett, Marshall, & Pleck, 1992). In many instances, specific lessons from home—including the patience and communication necessary to be an effective parent, the willingness to plan and work out alternative strategies for managing daily tasks with his wife, and the admiration he has for his wife in her paid labor force activities—actually help a man function more effectively at work.

Perhaps because of the centrality of the quality of home life to men's well-being, many men are sensitive to the possibility that their wife's involvement in the labor force may interfere with the emotional comfort and stability they seek at home. A wife's success in the world of work may reduce a husband's sense of power or importance in the marital relationship. Many men are especially uncomfortable if their wives earn more money than they do. Some men find themselves ill prepared to assume the more direct responsibilities of childrearing in order to support their wives' involvement in the labor market. However, among dual-career couples, marital harmony is sustained when husbands support their wives' involvement in the world of work and do not feel competitive with them (Wright, Nelson, & Georgen, 1994).

Adaptations to balancing work and family life are not simple. We are looking at the interface of multiple, interacting systems—each partner's work environment, each partner's role demands within the family, and the partners' relationships with one another and with their children. An interesting example of this dynamic interaction was highlighted in research about the link between work-related stress and its impact on children's adjustment. When mothers worked long hours and felt overloaded, they were less warm and accepting toward their adolescent children. When fathers worked long hours and felt overloaded, they experienced more conflict with their adolescent children. Husbands' negative work-related stressors also increased their wives' sense of overload beyond what the wives were experiencing because of their own work situation (Crouter & Bumpus, 2001). Thus, for wives, balancing work and family life required coping with their husband's experiences of work-related strain as well as their own.

The ability to bring positive energy from work to family is a product of individual and workplace characteristics. Voydanoff (2004) referred to this as *work-family facilitation*. Although people experience many types of work–family conflict, they may also find that experiences in the workplace increase their sense of self-worth, competence, and fulfillment, resulting in a more positive outlook on their interpersonal relationships at home. Voydanoff (2004) suggested that work-family facilitation is supported by resources in the workplace that make it easier for employees to address pressing family demands within the scope of their daily work. For example, policies that allow workers to take family-related leaves without risking their job security, or to take time off during the day to take a child to the doctor or meet with a

**Table 13.1** Unemployment Rates by Ethnicity and Educational Attainment, 2003

| RACE | Educational Level | | | |
| --- | --- | --- | --- | --- |
| | LESS THAN HIGH SCHOOL | HIGH SCHOOL GRADUATE | LESS THAN BACHELOR'S DEGREE | COLLEGE GRADUATE |
| European American | 7.8 | 4.8 | 4.2 | 2.8 |
| African American | 13.9 | 9.3 | 7.9 | 4.5 |
| Asian American | 9.5 | 5.6 | 5.9 | 4.4 |
| Hispanic | 8.2 | 5.9 | 5.7 | 4.1 |

teacher, reduce work–family conflict. A supportive work climate in which supervisors help workers feel comfortable about using these family-flexible policies and accommodating significant family obligations contribute to work-family facilitation. The implication of this research is that the responsibility for success in achieving an effective balance between work and family demands should fall not only on the coping strategies of individuals but on the policies and climate of the work setting.

### THE IMPACT OF JOBLESSNESS

Even though the workplace can be a major source of stress, joblessness can be even more disruptive to personal mental health and family functioning. Some people are alienated from work—they find little satisfaction in the work setting and few opportunities for meaningful labor. Others are "downsized" out of work. In 2003, the U.S. unemployment rate was 6%, slightly higher for men than for women. The modal period of unemployment was less than 5 weeks, but about 14% were unemployed for 27 weeks or more. Table 13.1 summarizes the unemployment rates in 2003 by race and educational attainment for individuals from 25 to 64 years old. African Americans, Asian Americans, and Hispanics were more likely to be unemployed than were European Americans at every educational level (U.S. Census Bureau, 2004b).

There is a difference in how people cope with seasonal or short-term (less than 5 weeks) unemployment and chronic unemployment. Chronically unemployed men have few opportunities to develop competence within the context of work. Because of the cultural emphasis on productive work, they are likely to experience guilt about being unemployed. Moreover, unemployment disrupts the self-concept of the traditional definition of the adult male role as breadwinner for the family. As a result of guilt, shame, and anger, these men may find it hard to direct their energy toward creative solutions to life problems. Thus, the inability to work can be expected to become a serious hurdle to the resolution of the psychosocial conflict of generativity versus stagnation for

*Economic recessions bring plant closings, downsizing, and the replacement of full-time with part-time employees. Job loss and underemployment are significant sources of individual and family stress.*

© Cindy Charles/Photo Edit

TECHNOLOGY AND HUMAN DEVELOPMENT

## Workplace Aggression

A WORKER LEAVES the building in tears after being humiliated by her boss. Another slams down the phone and begins to swear. Another throws his keyboard on the floor when the computer freezes up. A fourth discovers that ugly rumors are being spread about her among her coworkers.

The workplace itself is an expression of modern technology. The space, equipment, lighting, air quality, and opportunities for interaction or for privacy can enhance productivity or foster sentiments of frustration. Also, the social environment of the workplace may create a productive or a disruptive climate. Within the United States, workplace aggression, sometimes dubbed "desk rage," appears to be on the rise. Workers experience rudeness, hostility, ridicule, or dirty looks from their superiors or coworkers. In one study of more than 1,500 workers, about half said that they worried about being the target of hostil-

ity at work, and many said that they were less committed to their job because of the hostile environment in which they had to function (Daw, 2001).

It is hard to pin down the nature of the workplace that leads to this kind of hostility, but a combination of job overload, lack of shared norms about civility, poor management skills, and unfavorable workplace conditions appear to play a role. The following aspects of the workplace environment have been identified as contributing to workplace aggression (InteliHealth.com, 2002):

1. overcrowded working conditions
2. exposure to uncontrollable noise and interruptions
3. downsizing, with an increase in workload on those remaining
4. worry about job security
5. bullying, by a boss or coworker
6. unwillingness by a supervisor to deal with an aggressive worker

Some researchers suggest that there are personality characteristics that predispose people to aggressive or threatening behavior toward others (Lee & Allen, 2002; Lee, Ashton, & Shin, 2005). These people are likely to view themselves as victims and to be suspicious that others "are out to get them." These characteristics are very similar to the qualities of the aggressive-withdrawn children we described in Chapter 9 (Middle Childhood). However, at present there is no accepted profile for identifying or screening out potentially problematic employees (Beck & Schouten, 2000). The idea that workplace violence is a product of the interaction between a vulnerable worker and a nonsupportive physical or social work environment needs further investigation in the psychosocial perspective.

---

men (Hopper, 1990). The impact of chronic unemployment on women has not yet been studied.

As a result of the restructuring of the labor market, plant closings, downturns in the "e-conomy," and workforce reorganizations, many middle adults who had a history of steady employment, including increased responsibility and advancement, have recently faced job loss. Unemployment in middle adulthood has a major psychological impact on an individual's sense of self-worth and hope for the future. Among middle-adult workers, job loss is associated with material deprivation, disruption in family life, and increases in marital conflict. Children and spouses are commonly acutely involved in the effects of job loss on a middle-adult parent, and often the entire family experiences new feelings of alienation from social institutions as a result of the experience (Lobo & Watkins, 1995; Perrucci, Perrucci, & Targ, 1997).

Job loss has been associated with both physical and psychological consequences, such as self-doubt, passivity, and social withdrawal. Depression is a common consequence, and the associated family strains may also lead to new levels of conflict and family violence. In some instances, adjustments that families make to a husband's unemployment result in a further reduction of his sense of importance and accentuate the decline in his self-respect (Piotrkowski, Rapoport, &

Rapoport, 1987). Social support—especially family strengths and marital satisfaction—are important buffers for the negative effects of unemployment (Vosler & Page-Adams, 1996).

In a study of 300 unemployed men, social support from among the person's close relationships played two distinct roles (Vinokur, Caplan, & Williams, 1987). First, when a significant person reaffirmed the unemployed man's beliefs that looking for a new job was worthwhile and gave him hopeful encouragement, he was more likely to engage in active job-seeking efforts. In addition to this specific support for job seeking, social support provided an important sense of worth and caring that was especially important when job-seeking efforts were not successful. The authors warned that efforts to encourage intensive job seeking may backfire when a highly motivated person meets with repeated failure. Under these conditions, it is especially important for the person to be embedded in social relationships that provide global, unconditional acceptance in order to prevent a process of demoralization and self-destructive behavior.

The threats of job loss can create stress for those who remain employed as well as for those who become unemployed. For example, in a study of employment conditions on job-related distress, workers in industries that were experiencing high levels of unemployment had a higher incidence of depression than did workers in industries where unemployment was low. Similarly, studies have shown that workers who are "spared" during downsizing and mergers show signs of anxiety and depression. These observations highlight the salience that work has in middle adulthood, especially for those involved in professions that are personally as well as financially rewarding (Locker, 1997; Reynolds, 1997).

# NURTURING AN INTIMATE RELATIONSHIP

Although people derive a significant sense of personal identity from their jobs and may worry a lot about them, happiness in an intimate relationship is a stronger predictor of overall well-being in adulthood than is satisfaction with work. Marriage and other long-term intimate bonds are salient, dynamic relationships. They change as the partners mature, as the family constellation changes, and in response to changing events, including family crises and historical events. Focus and effort are required to keep these relationships healthy and vital.

What is a vital marriage? Drawing on a variety of studies of long-lasting marriages, Crooks and Bauer (2005) described it as follows:

> Couples liked and respected one another. Respect was based on the integrity of the partner's honesty, compassion, decency, fairness, and loyalty to the family. Happy couples found pleasure and comfort in each other's company and treated their marriages as needing continued attention. They understood that a good marriage is a process of ongoing change, dealing with each individual's needs and wishes pertaining to work, sex, parenting, friends, and health as they evolve during the life cycle. They believe that their marriages enhance them as individuals and that the fit between their own needs and their partner's responses was unique and irreplaceable. They felt lucky to be with their spouse and did not take each other for granted. (p. 410)

Three themes have been identified as contributing to long-lasting, happy marriages: the strengths of the individual partners; the nature of the partners' interpersonal interactions; and the partners' commitment to nurturing the future of the relationship.

## ■ CHARACTERISTICS OF THE PARTNERS

Happy marriages are built on love and affection between two people who are basically even tempered and warm hearted (Huston & Melz, 2004). They are not overly anxious, depressed, or impulsive. They are nurturant, expressive, gentle, understanding, and conscientious. They care about each other, rather than being self-absorbed or indifferent to one another's fate. These individuals also contribute other types of social capital that help sustain the relationship. For example, they may have a supportive network of family members and friends; they may contribute financial resources to the family;

they are cooperative rather than domineering in the way they participate in decision making; or they bring unique competencies to the tasks of household maintenance (Edin, 2000).

## ■ PARTNERS' INTERPERSONAL INTERACTIONS

The couple must develop an effective communication system. This requires adequate opportunities for interaction. If competing life roles, including work and parenting, dramatically reduce opportunities for interaction, the couple will risk drifting apart. They will have increasingly fewer shared experiences and be less readily influenced by each other's observations and reactions. Studies of the correlates of marital happiness find that there is a reciprocal relationship between interaction and happiness. In a longitudinal study, couples who were happier early in their marriage showed higher levels of interaction in later years (Zuo, 1992). After a number of years of marriage, the two variables were strong predictors of each other: Those who were happy were involved in more frequent interactions, and similarly, those who were involved in frequent interactions were happier.

John Gottman and his colleagues have conducted a number of studies to examine the nature of interactions among heterosexual married couples. Their technique involves videotaping couples as they discuss a difficult issue in their marriage. At the same time, they gather physiological data, including changes in heart rate and blood pressure. The couples are followed in later years of their marriage using surveys and interviews. Based on their research, they have been able to predict with a high degree of accuracy whether couples will separate in the first few years of their marriage or stay together (Gottman, Coan, Carrere, & Swanson, 1998; Gottman & Silver, 2000).

Gottman found that enduring relationships are characterized by a high ratio of positive to negative interactions. Couples in satisfied marriages did argue, but the balance of 5 positive statements to 1 negative statement was an important constant in predicting relationship stability. In stable, satisfied couples, the woman tends to use a gentle, diplomatic beginning when she introduces a problem or concern, and the man accepts his wife's influence. When the woman expresses contempt, is overly negative, or aggressive, and the man is overly domineering or defensive in the face of conflict, the relationship is less likely to endure.

For couples who do not have an effective communication system, resentments tend to accumulate with no opportunity to resolve them. A common experience is that the wife wants to talk things over, but the husband does not see what good this will do. Harmonious, satisfied couples listen to and consider each other's problems. They validate each other's concerns by expressing understanding, even if they cannot offer solutions. Dissatisfied couples, on the other hand, avoid problems or counterattack. Instead of validating the spouse's concern, the partner raises his or her own complaints and criticisms, or withdraws. Over the years, expressions of affection, enjoyment, laughter, and support decline. Even if negative or critical interactions do not increase, they are embed-

*Vern and Linda treasure the time they have together. Their marriage is energized by their diverse interests coupled with the enjoyment they take in each other's company.*

ded in a less positive overall context. The ideal 5 to 1 ratio may drop to 3 or 2 to 1, making the negative interactions more salient. This takes the couple along the path to marital disruption.

### PARTNERS' COMMITMENT TO NURTURING THE FUTURE OF THE RELATIONSHIP

In order for a marriage to last over the long period of middle and later adulthood, couples must learn to work toward change in areas where it is possible, and to accept one another and the characteristics of the relationship in areas where change cannot be accomplished. By expanding their tolerance for differences and admiration for their strengths, new levels of intimacy can be achieved (Jacobson & Christensen, 1996). Research by Wallerstein and Blakeslee (1995) on long-lasting, satisfying marriages identified a set of psychosocial tasks that couples have to master. Salient in this list are the following challenges:

- Preserving a balance between intimacy in the couple and autonomy for the individuals
- Expanding the bonds of affection to include children while preserving and nurturing the couple relationship
- Shifting the focus of energy from the family of origin to the newly formed family while preserving relationships with the extended kinship network
- Managing the adversities in life, such as serious illness, death, or disaster, in ways that strengthen the relationship
- Sharing laughter and delight in daily life

The partners must be committed to growth both as individuals and as a couple. This means that they accept the idea that they will change in important ways and that the relationship, too, will change. Within any enduring relationship, each person experiences a dynamic tension between pres-

sures and desires for personal growth on the one hand and the pressures and desires to preserve the relationship on the other hand. Both of these forces have the potential to overwhelm or dominate the sense of mutuality, as is illustrated in the case study on the struggle for commitment to growth in a vital marriage. A vital marriage requires both partners to be open to the need to be themselves (as they continue to discover new dimensions of self) and an energizing, interpersonal chemistry that is resilient even in the face of the harshest challenges.

# CASE STUDY

## THE STRUGGLE FOR COMMITMENT TO GROWTH IN A VITAL MARRIAGE

*One common example of the need to permit individual growth within a marriage occurs when a woman who has been primarily responsible for child care and household management expresses an interest in entering or returning to the paid labor force.*

Annette, who had worked as a nurse before she married, decided that it was time to go back to work. Her three children were in elementary and middle school, and her husband had a full-time job, so that she was by herself for long hours during the day. She began to feel depressed and jealous of everyone else's active lives, so she took a position at a local hospital, working three afternoons and on Saturday each week.

At first, her husband, Gary, fussed and resisted. "Why did she need to go to work?" he asked. They didn't really need the money, and Gary liked to know that she would be at home when he came back from work. He wasn't used to having to take the kids to their activities after school. Plus, Saturday used to be his day to hang out with his friends from work. The kids fussed at being asked to get dinner ready. But Annette insisted that she had to get back to work—her mental health and happiness depended on it.

The first months were terrible. Annette wondered if she were doing the right thing, and Gary used every trick in the book to lure her back to the house. But there was no denying the value of this new job for Annette's self-confidence, her renewed feeling of personal identity, and her ability to return to the home with new energy and enthusiasm for her husband, children, and family life. Gary began to get more involved in the children's lives and actually looked forward to the Saturdays they spent together. Soon the children began to see their mother in a new light, as a professional who took care of other people as well as them. They also felt a new surge of independence in being able to handle the dinner meal on their own. Gary and Annette felt closer to each other as a result of Annette's self-confidence and Gary's new level of involvement in the lives of the children.

## ■ CRITICAL THINKING AND CASE ANALYSIS

1. What are the obstacles to continued growth for Annette in this case?
2. How might childrearing responsibilities prevent new growth for women or men in middle adulthood?
3. How does Annette's decision lead to new opportunities for growth for Gary and her children?
4. What are some alternatives that Annette might have considered that could have satisfied her needs for continued growth and perhaps been less disruptive for her family?
5. Imagine that Gary had been the one looking for a new structure—perhaps going into business for himself or going back to school for a new profession. What types of changes might this have caused in the family system? On the marital relationship?

## ■ PRESERVING PASSION IN A LONG-TERM RELATIONSHIP

According to Sternberg's three-dimensional model of love, passion is the first thing to go. However, preserving an erotic and sexual aspect to intimacy continues to play a role in fostering vital relationships. Relationship satisfaction is associated with openness about sexual needs, satisfaction with sexual frequency, and experiencing a playful enjoyment of sexual pleasure (Crooks & Bauer, 2005). This means coping with the physiological changes in sexual responsiveness that accompany aging, and finding new ways to enjoy sexual contact in the context of parenting demands, chronic illness or disability, or other stressful life events that interfere with one's sexual interest.

Changes in sexual responsiveness over the middle adult years have been well documented (Crooks & Bauer, 2005;

Masters & Johnson, 1966). For men, erections take longer to develop, orgasm is less intense, and the erection fades more quickly in midlife than in early adulthood. With age, it may take a longer period, from several hours to days, to experience a new erection. Even though the sexual response changes, orgasm continues to be a source of pleasure. Although there is a reduction in sperm production, most men remain fertile well into very old age. Most men are able to enjoy sexual activity throughout their life, provided that they continue to have a partner.

For some men, periods of illness, certain medications, heart disease, or high blood pressure can interfere with the ability to have an erection. Anxiety about being able to have an erection or a preoccupation with the quality of sexual performance may interfere with the ability to become aroused. The introduction of a variety of new drugs to treat erectile disorders has increased openness and awareness of this problem and provided new avenues for couples to discuss changes in their sexual vitality. One study estimated that 30 million men in the United States have erectile disorder (Levine, 2003). Although the incidence increases with age, usually it is not age itself but the chronic illnesses that are associated with aging and the accompanying medications that account for this relationship.

One of the common changes experienced by men in midlife is inflammation or increased size of the prostate gland. This gland produces fluids that are released during ejaculation. When the prostate becomes enlarged, it may put pressure on the urethra and restrict the flow of urine. A significant number of men experience prostate cancer. Although treatments for prostate cancer vary, they can interfere with sexual functioning (Litwin et al., 1995).

Physical changes that affect the sexual response also occur for women. At some time during their late 40s or 50s, women experience the **climacteric**, or the involution and atrophy of the reproductive organs. Many physiological changes accompany the close of fertility, including the cessation of menstruation (*menopause*), gradual reduction in the production of estrogen, atrophy of the breasts and genital tissues, and shrinkage of the uterus (Crooks & Bauer, 2005). The most commonly reported symptom is a frequent "hot flash," a sudden onset of warmth in the face and neck that lasts several minutes. Sometimes it is accompanied by dizziness, nausea, sweating, or headaches. About 75% to 85% of women going through natural menopause report this symptom. Other physiological symptoms are related to the reduction of vaginal fluid and loss of elasticity, sleeplessness, and increased anxiety (Huerta, Mena, Malacara, & Diaz, 1995). The symptoms appear to be closely related to a drastic drop in the production of estrogen. Postmenopausal women produce only one sixth as much estrogen as do women who regularly menstruate. Several studies on the use of estrogen treatment have found that the administration of this hormone to menopausal women alleviates or even prevents menopausal symptoms. Hormone replacement therapy is associated with other health benefits as well as risks.

## HUMAN DEVELOPMENT AND DIVERSITY

### Menopause

IT IS WELL established that menopause causes recognizable physical changes that an adult woman may view as unpleasant. The severity of symptoms is determined by both the biological changes related to decreases in estrogen production and by the attitude of the culture toward the infertile, older woman. In cultures that reward women for reaching the end of the fertile period, menopause is associated with fewer physiological symptoms. In a study describing the reaction of women in India, menopause was associated with increased social status: "The absence of menstrual flow signaled an incredible elevation of stature for these women. Women were released from a veiled, secluded life in a compound to talk and socialize (even drink) with menfolk. They then became revered as models of wisdom and experience by the younger generation" (Gillespie, 1989, p. 46).

A woman's attitudes toward aging and her involvement in adult roles influence the ease or difficulty with which she experiences menopause. In U.S. society, for example, a woman who is going through menopause at age 50 may also be experiencing the severe illness or death of her parents and the marriage of her youngest child. Menopausal status is not a good predictor of a woman's health or her psychological well-being; role strain and prior health are more accurate predictors (McKinlay, McKinlay, & Brambilla, 1987).

The majority of publications dealing with menopause focus on issues such as the treatment of symptoms and the pros and cons of hormone replacement therapy (Utian, 2003). Comparatively few studies have focused on the social and psychological correlates of menopause. The tendency in the U.S. medical culture is to treat menopause as an illness or a deficit leading to the loss of reproductive capacity rather than as a normative transition into a new phase of adult life (Rostosky & Travis, 1996).

Women differ in how they interpret the meaning of menopause. Some are embarrassed by the hot flashes when they occur in a public setting. Others see the symptoms of menopause as a reminder that they are aging in a culture that values youth and physical attractiveness in women above other characteristics. An emerging group has recast hot flashes as "power surges," suggesting the beginning of a new, competent period of life. In 1997, the North American Menopause Association sponsored a Gallup poll of postmenopausal women in the United States. The respondents were divided about equally, with half seeing menopause as a medical condition that required treatment and half seeing it as a natural transition that could be weathered without medical intervention (Kaufert, Boggs, Ettinger, Woods, & Utian, 1998).

This conflict between the medical and the developmental perspectives was illustrated in a study that compared the concerns regarding menopause and related health care needs of Uruguayan women and the perceptions that gynecologists had of these concerns. Gynecologists thought that women were more concerned about hormone replacement therapy, surgery, physical symptoms, and sexual functioning than the women actually were. The women were more concerned about future opportunities for self-development and opportunities for increased independence and a changed lifestyle than the physicians realized (Defey, Storch, Cardozo, & Diaz, 1996). Other studies have supported the view that women see menopause as both a limited physiological experience and a more general marker of entry into a new period of life (Jones, 1997).

For more information about menopause, see the North American Menopause Society website (http://www.menopause.org).

The reduction in estrogen is associated with changes in the sexual response cycle. The most noticeable change is decreased lubrication and less expansion of the vagina during the excitement phase. This can cause pain during intercourse and reduced sensitivity, which interfere with sexual pleasure. Although the number of orgasmic contractions may be fewer, orgasm remains a very important and pleasurable experience for postmenopausal women. Without the risk of pregnancy, many women are more enthusiastic about sexual relations after menopause than they were before. The impact of menopause for women is determined in part by its cultural meaning. As with other aspects of an intimate relationship, preserving the sexual dimension requires good communication and a sense of humor.

Nurturing vitality in an intimate relationship is a long-term task. The challenge is for the partners to create continued interest, nurturance, and appreciation for each other even after they have achieved high levels of security, trust, and empathy, so that the components of a loving relationship operate continuously in the relationship. The significance of this task is relevant for the ongoing nature of the relationship and the social support it provides as the couple enters later life. The quality of the parents' marital relationship during middle adulthood provides the context for the children's emerging understanding of intimacy and marital roles. As children mature into middle childhood and early adolescence, they pay attention to and try to make sense of the quality of their parents' interactions with each other. As children observe their parents, they acquire a sense of how they function as husband and wife. Of course, children do not perfectly replicate their parents' marriages. However, the degree of egalitarianism, conflict style, and expression of affection that children observe can influence their ideas about the kind of partner they seek and how they will enact the marital role (VanLear, 1992).

## EXPANDING CARING RELATIONSHIPS

Middle adults have opportunities to express caring in many roles. This section focuses on two of those: parenting and the care of one's own aging parents. Both domains offer numerous challenges to the intellectual, emotional, and physical resources of the adult caregiver.

### PARENTING

In parenting, we see the critical intersection of adult development and child development. As parents, adults bring a psychosocial history of ego strengths and core pathologies, coping skills and defenses, and adequate or inadequate resolutions of previous psychosocial crises to the task of nurturing a child. They have scripts from their own childhood, modified by information from friends, relatives, and experts about how to approach the task. With all this, they have to adapt to the unique temperament, developmental level, and strengths or vulnerabilities of each of their children and to the work, family, cultural, and community contexts in which childrearing is taking place.

Parenting takes place over a long period of time. In a two-parent family, the partners have many opportunities to observe and appreciate each other's approaches to the care, nurturing, and guidance of their children. The concept of a *parenting alliance* has been introduced into the family literature as a way to capture the importance of the working relationship between the partners as they engage in parenting behaviors. The **parenting alliance** is defined as "the capacity of a spouse to acknowledge, respect, and value the parenting roles and tasks of the partner" (Cohen & Weissman, 1984, p. 35). As adults establish their parenting alliance, they benefit from knowing that their partner values, trusts, and respects the way they enact their parenting role. The confidence and sense of appreciation that come with this knowledge help adults to engage more joyfully in their parenting and to weather periods of stress. It also provides a context of reassurance for children who observe the way their parents encourage and sustain each other (Hughes, Gordon, & Gaertner, 2004).

Being a parent is a difficult, demanding task that requires a great deal of learning. Because children are constantly changing and are often unpredictable, adults must be sensitive and flexible in new situations in order to cope successfully with their demands. Each period of the child's development calls for new and innovative parenting strategies.

Childrearing experiences are different with each child, and the changing family constellation brings new demands for flexibility and learning. With each successive child, however, there seems to be less anxiety about parenting skills. Children help adults learn about parenting through their responses to their parents' efforts and their own persistence in following the path of development.

### DEVELOPMENTAL STAGES OF THE FAMILY

At each stage of a child's life, the demands on parents change. Infants require constant care and attention. Preschoolers require educational toys and interaction with peers. They can spend a great deal of time in independent play, but they require mindful supervision. Early and middle school-age children require parental reassurance about their skills, talents, and fears. The early adolescent requires less in the way of physical care but needs continuing emotional support and guidance, faces new financial demands, and needs help in facilitating participation in athletics, after-school activities, and social life.

Several models of family development have been proposed by family researchers. These schemes—especially the ones described by Duvall (1977), Hill (1965), and Spanier, Sauer, and Larzelere (1979)—emphasized changes in the family that are tied to changes in the developmental levels of children. The implication is that the changing needs, competence, and social interactions of the children stimulate changing interactions, activities, and values among family members.

There are criticisms of this view of family development. First, the length of the marriage and the ages of the parents are confounded with the ages or life stages of the children. It is possible that the parents' ages, the children's ages, or some combination of the two account for changes in family emphasis. Second, this view does not explain development in families that do not have children or that are a product of remarriage, in which the marital relationship has a shorter history than the parental one. Third, this view assumes a similar set of experiences with children for both parents. However, in the case of remarried couples, for example, the parenting histories of the partners may be quite different if one partner has never had children and the other is a parent from a former relationship. Fourth, the developmental stage of the family may be difficult to characterize when the children are spread out across a wide age range. Especially in blended families, parents may be trying to meet the needs of adolescent children from an earlier marriage while caring for a newborn that is a product of their new marital bond. From a systems perspective, each family member can prompt conflict, change, or growth in every other member. The affectional bonds that family members share, as well as the need to protect one another from external threats, contribute to a dynamic interdependence. To some degree, each family member is vulnerable to the influence of every other member.

For the purposes of this discussion of parenting, we have chosen to consider the potential influences of the phases of family development on adult development. This approach has the advantage of showing the reciprocity of psychosocial themes across the generations. It highlights the processes through which family development may prompt new growth among parents. Although middle adults might be parenting children at any age, we will focus on the following four periods, which correspond to the most likely transitions that take place as parents age from 34 to 60:

1. The years when children are in early and middle childhood.
2. The years when children are adolescents.
3. The years when children are adults.
4. Grandparenthood.

**THE YEARS WHEN CHILDREN ARE IN EARLY AND MIDDLE CHILDHOOD.** School-age children tap parents' resources for ideas about things to do, places to go, and friends to meet. They seek new experiences in order to expand their competence and investigate the larger world outside the home. The role that parents play in exposing their children to cultural resources such as music, art, travel, theater, and science contributes positively to the children's school achievement, even beyond the impact of the parents' own educational background, beliefs, and expectations (Roscigno & Ainsworth-Darnell, 1999). Parents become active as chauffeurs, secretaries, and sometimes as buffers between their children and the rest of the community. During this time, parents have many opportunities to function as educators for their children. They actively contribute to their children's academic success through such activities as reading with them, helping them with homework, praising them for school success, and talking with teachers, visiting the school, and participating in school projects. Research on academic success makes it clear that parents' aspirations for their children, their overall parenting skills, and their involvement in their children's education make a substantial contribution to their children's progress (Gutman & Midgley, 2000). Parents who combine appropriate challenges with warmth and support typically have children who are highly motivated, think of themselves as academically capable, and want to do well in school (Bronstein et al., 1998).

Parenting during this period has the potential for boosting an adult's sense of pride in the skills and knowledge already accumulated. Parents are gatekeepers to the resources of the community. They come to see themselves through their children's eyes, as people who know about the world—its rewards, treasures, secrets, and dangers.

**THE YEARS WHEN CHILDREN ARE ADOLESCENTS.** Parents tend to view the years of their children's adolescence as extremely trying. Adolescents are likely to seek new levels of behavioral independence. They spend most of the day away from home and apart from adult supervision. As adolescents gain in physical stature and cognitive skills, they are likely to challenge parental authority. During this time, the principles that parents have emphasized as important for responsible, moral behavior are frequently tested. Children are exposed to many voices—including the media, popular heroes and heroines, peers, and school adults—that suggest there may be more than one ideal way to behave and more than one definition of success. Successful parents of adolescents attempt to balance autonomy granting (opportunities for their children to make their own decisions), responsiveness, warmth and support, communication about high standards, and limit setting in the needed proportions so that their children can grow increasingly independent while still being able to rely on an atmosphere of family guidance and reassurance (Steinberg, 2001).

The Carlsons have taken lots of trips. Now that the boys are adolescents, they enjoy reminiscing about past adventures and planning new ones. It's getting harder to reach agreement, however, because the boys push harder for their own preferences and Mom and Dad have less power over the final decision.

© Elizabeth Crews / The Image Works

Adolescent children are the front line of each new generation. The questions they raise and the choices they make reflect not only what they have learned, but also what they are experiencing in the present and what they anticipate in the future. Parents of adolescents are likely to feel persistent pressure to reevaluate their own socialization and their effectiveness as parents. Questions are raised about their preparation for their own future as well as their children's. The ego boost parents experienced from being viewed as wise and resourceful is likely to be replaced by doubt as they and their children face an uncertain future. Parents who can respond to their adolescents in an open, supportive way can benefit by finding opportunities to clarify their own values. They can begin building new parent–child relationships that will carry them and their emerging adult children into later adulthood.

**THE YEARS WHEN CHILDREN ARE ADULTS.**   The period during which children make their own transitions into adulthood results in new patterns of interaction between parents and children and in new opportunities for the middle adult parents. Alternative patterns are clearly evident in current U.S. families, as children take a variety of paths toward self-sufficiency and entry into adult roles. In 2003, 55% of men and 46% of women ages 18 to 24 were living at home with one or more parents; 14% of men and 7% of women ages 25 to 34 were living at home with one or more parent (Field, 2004). By the time adult children marry, they are almost always ready to leave the parental home.

Family roles change during this time. Most women enter menopause during this period, bringing a close to the couple's natural childbearing years. The relationship between the husband and the wife also changes as parenting activities diminish. Some couples become closer—closer than they have been since they first fell in love. However, divorces also occur after the children leave home. Parents are likely to begin a review and evaluation of their performance as parents as they see the kinds of lives that their children have established for themselves. Erikson (Erikson et al., 1986) found that during this period, many parents continue to build their identities on the accomplishments of their children. Parents also begin to find new targets for the energy and commitment that they had previously directed toward the care of their children.

The transitional period during which children leave home does not seem to be a negative time for adults. A woman who was anticipating her children leaving home described her feelings this way:

> From the day the kids are born, if it's not one thing, it's another. After all these years of being responsible for them, you finally get to the point where you want to scream, "Fall out of the nest already, you guys, will you? It's time." It's as if I want to take myself back after all these years—to give me back to me, if you know what I mean. Of course, that's providing there's any "me" left. (Rubin, 1980, p. 313)

Parents are usually pleased as they follow their children's accomplishments. Furthermore, children's independence may permit parents to use their financial resources to enhance their own lifestyle.

Of course, adults maintain certain parental functions during this stage. Many children remain fully or partly financially dependent on their parents during their 20s. If the children are in college or in postgraduate study, the parents may experience greater financial demands than at any earlier period in their parenting history. In many families, parents take on additional labor market activities and additional loans to meet the financial requirements of their children's college and professional education. Children who have left home may not have resolved decisions about occupation and marriage. For them, their parents may remain a source of advice and support as they go through periods of identity and intimacy formation and consolidation. Parents begin to feel the pressure of challenges to their value orientation as their children experiment with new roles and lifestyles. During this stage, parents may serve as sounding boards, as sources of stability, or as jousting partners in young people's attempts to conceptualize their own lifestyle.

As less time is taken up with direct parenting responsibilities, parents may begin to alter their roles and redirect their energies. However, some parents experience resistance from their children, who expect their parents to remain the same as they themselves change and grow. In many cases, young adult children return home for intervals when they look for a new job, find a new roommate, recover from a love relationship that has ended, return from military service, or drop out of college (Thornton, Young-DeMarco, & Goldscheider, 1993). Throughout these transitions, young adults look to their parents as a source of stability and to their home as a "safe harbor" while they try to establish their own life structure.

One of the major events that occurs during this period is the child's decision to marry. Parents are expected to accept a new person into their family—their child's intimate partner. Along with this new relationship comes a connection to an entirely new—and often totally unknown—group of in-laws. In the United States, parents are usually at the mercy of their child's decision in this matter. They may find themselves associated through marriage with a family that differs significantly from their own or with one that shares many of their own family's beliefs and values.

The first few years of marriage (as discussed in Chapter 12, Early Adulthood) are somewhat precarious. Parents may have to reintegrate an adult child into the family at this stage if his or her marriage is not successful. It can be assumed that a child who leaves a marriage needs some temporary parental reassurance and support in order to regain confidence in his or her ability to form an intimate relationship. Thus, at times of crisis, middle adults may need to practice parenting skills they have not used for a while and develop new skills in helping their children deal with new challenges.

**GRANDPARENTHOOD.**   Grandparenthood—the time when an adult witnesses the birth of a new generation— might be considered the beginning of an additional stage in

*Grandparents often take the role of teaching their grandchildren new skills. These Japanese grandparents, who are avid baseball fans, are very proud of what their grandson can accomplish.*

family development. However, the transition to grandparenthood is outside one's own control. Whenever one's children have children of their own, the grandparent becomes alerted to a new sense of ancestry, lineage, and membership in an expanding kinship network. With grandparenthood, adults begin to observe their children as parents. As people reflect on their own roles 20 to 30 years earlier, they may attribute some of their children's successes to their own parenting techniques and may take responsibility for some of the failures, too (Erikson et al., 1986). In Chapter 14 (Later Adulthood), we consider in greater detail the role of grandparenthood and its significance to the adult. Suffice it to say that as grandparents, adults have the opportunity to relate to small children as an expression of the continuity of their lives into the future. Of course, not all grandparents relate to their grandchildren from this philosophical point of view. However, the attainment of the grandparent role has the potential for bringing with it a new perspective on time, purpose, and the meaning of life that may serve as a source of reassurance during later adulthood.

Adults differ in how they define the role of grandparent. They may see themselves as carriers of the family traditions and dispensers of wisdom, as needed experts in child care, as convenient and trusted baby-sitters, or as admirers from afar. As grandparents, adults are asked to reinvest energy in small children. The quality of the relationship that develops between grandparents and their grandchildren depends not so much on the fact that they are relatives as on the kinds of experiences that the two generations share. Grandparents may also find that the quality of their relationship with their grandchildren is mediated by the child's parents. Especially when the grandchildren are little, the amount of time they spend with their grandparents and the way the grandparents view them are filtered through the quality of the adult rela-

tionship that their parents have with their own parents, the grandparents (Brubaker, 1990; Erber, 2005).

Parenting can be stressful. It is full of conflicts and challenges, demanding time that the partners might otherwise spend with each other or in pursuit of their own interests and ambitions. We argue, however, that parenting generates the kind of conflict that promises an enormous potential for personal growth. By providing a meaningful, responsive context for children, parents have the opportunity to articulate their own value systems and to observe the consequences of their efforts in the continuous development of their children. Psychosocial growth requires a willingness to engage in tasks that may temporarily increase stress, uncertainty, and complexity. Thus, it does not mean turning away from or minimizing tension. It frequently means choosing the challenge that is noticeably difficult or intriguingly complex in hopes of growing while struggling to meet it.

## ■ CARING FOR ONE'S AGING PARENTS

People tend to regard middle adulthood as a time devoted to future generations. However, another test of one's capacity for generativity comes in the form of commitment to one's aging parents. One of the significant challenges of middle adulthood is the struggle to respond effectively to one's parents as well as one's children and grandchildren. That is why middle adults are sometimes referred to as the "sandwich" generation, tucked in the middle between caring for one's children and caring for one's aging parents. As one ages from 30 to 50, one's parents may age from 60 to 80. The number of adults over the age of 65 increased from more than 25 million in 1980 to 36 million in 2003. The number of adults over the age of 85 was more than 4.5 million, an increase of more than 100% since 1980 (U.S. Census Bureau, 2004b). It is becom-

*It is quite common for an adult daughter to have responsibility for her aging mother. The closer the two women were during the daughter's childhood, the easier it is for the two to preserve a positive relationship as the aging mother becomes more dependent on the daughter's help.*

*Femme au Miroir, 1905/Pablo Picasso/© 2005 Estate of Pablo Picasso/Artists Rights Society (ARS), New York*

ing increasingly likely that most middle adults will confront the challenge of meeting the needs of their own aging parents and grandparents. It is also increasingly probable that their aging parents will survive through a period of vigorous and independent later adulthood into a period of frail and vulnerable old age.

What is the nature of filial obligation as it is viewed from the perspectives of adult children and their aging parents? Who provides what kinds of help? What characterizes optimal parent–child relationships during this phase of life?

**WHAT IS FILIAL OBLIGATION?**   **Filial obligation** is a feeling of responsibility to care for one's parents. Although filial obligation begins long before middle adulthood, it may become more salient as aging parents require more support and assistance to carry out the tasks of daily living. What can aging parents expect of their adult children? How do adult children define their responsibilities for their parents? In one study of filial obligation, elderly parents and their adult children were asked to respond to 16 items that could be viewed as elements of filial obligation (Hamon & Blieszner, 1990). The items included such things as helping parents to identify and understand resources, giving emotional support, and writing once a week. Parents and adult children clearly agreed on the top three items: (1) helping to understand resources, (2) giving emotional support, and (3) talking over matters of importance. They also agreed that children should not be expected to live near the parent, or to write or visit weekly. However, the study found that children had a greater sense of obligation than their parents expected of them. Parents were less likely to expect certain forms of help, such as accepting financial assistance, having their children revise their work schedules in order to provide help, and living in a child's home. In fact, studies of intergenerational economic transfers find that, on average, older adults (i.e., those 65 and older) give more in cash and gifts than they receive from younger generations and that it is more likely that an adult child will

live in the household of an older parent than the reverse (Aquilino, 1990).

**WHO PROVIDES HELP?**   The evidence suggests that daughters assume much more of the responsibility for their aging parents than do sons—including care for their spouse's parents as well as their own (Allen, Blieszner, & Roberto, 2001). This involvement is one element of the basic "kinkeeping" tasks that have traditionally been incorporated into women's socialization. Daughters are more likely than sons to provide care for their aging parents even when the daughters are employed. However, several structural aspects of an adult child's employment may influence this gender difference (Sarkisian & Gerstel, 2004). Women typically earn less than men; and more men than women are self-employed. Both of these factors predict how much time an adult child will spend helping their aging parents. Adult children who earn lower wages are more likely to take time off to help their aging parent; and children who are self-employed are less likely to take time off to help their aging parent. Thus, some of the gender difference in caregiving is interdependent with the nature of workplace commitments and demands.

In addition to the amount of time that adult children spend helping their parents, daughters also provide somewhat different kinds of help. Daughters provide more direct care, such as bathing or dressing a parent, as well as emotional support, such as listening to a parent's concerns or helping her or him feel important and loved. However, both sons and daughters are about equally likely to assist in some of the tasks involving relations with health and human service organizations, scheduling medical checkups, and reviewing insurance and other financial matters. Research shows that aging adults who have three or more children—whether they are sons or daughters—are more likely to end up living with one of them than are adults with fewer than three children. However, for other forms of support, such as receiving telephone calls, visiting, and helping in daily tasks, older adults who have one daughter receive more support than those who have only sons (Spitze & Logan, 1990).

## WHAT FACTORS PROMOTE AN OPTIMAL RELATIONSHIP BETWEEN ADULTS AND THEIR AGING PARENTS?

The nature of the continuing relationship between adult children and their aging parents is not focused solely on caregiving. The norms of independence and self-sufficiency are strong among the current aging population, many of whom state that they do not need assistance from their adult children. However, when asked whom they view as their preferred source of assistance should they need it, aging parents mention their children first, before their friends, siblings, or other relatives. Likewise, adult children view themselves as being primarily responsible for meeting their parents' needs; however, most do not expect to have to meet a variety of such needs (Hogan, Eggebeen, & Clogg, 1993).

In adulthood, the ongoing parent–child relationship is one of choice. Most families continue to live relatively close to one another, with 80% of adults reporting that at least one child is less than an hour's drive away. Also, more than 75% of older adults talk to their children at least once a week. Even under conditions of geographic distance, many children say they feel close to their parents and share a positive sense of connection (Hooyman & Kiyak, 1993).

Adult children are sometimes in a position of trying to supplement the care and support they provide their parents by coordinating social services and interacting with various public agencies. Many feel unprepared for this aspect of the caring relationship (Zarit & Eggebeen, 1995). They are not comfortable dealing with hospitals, insurance agencies, social service agencies, or residential treatment facilities. However, when older adults require the services of these organizations, their adult children typically know their parents' unique needs and are among the best people to interpret them for service providers. Through such contacts, middle adults have the opportunity to modify and improve the services offered by these agencies, making them more effective for future generations of aging adults.

Research on caregiving within the family has begun to examine the rewards as well as the costs in this relationship. Although quite a bit of attention has been given to caregiver strain, caregivers experience both positive and negative aspects of this role. The costs may include feelings of exhaustion, never having time for oneself, feeling overwhelmed by the demands of multiple roles, or experiencing the physical strain of caregiving. Rewards of the caregiving role may include feelings of being appreciated, putting life's demands into a new perspective, or feeling closer to the care recipient. In some cases, the care recipient is able to exchange resources with the caregiver, for example by providing baby-sitting time for help with the grocery shopping. In a study of the costs and rewards experienced by children and spouses who were caring for an aging parent or partner, adult children experienced more rewards in their caregiving role than did spouses, and women experienced more caregiving costs than

did men. An unexpected finding was that for women, companionship from their spouse was an especially rewarding response from the care recipients (i.e., their husbands). Thus, the research underscores the reciprocal nature of caregiving, with rewards and costs flowing in both directions (Raschick & Ingersoll-Dayton, 2004). These ideas are reflected in the case study of a daughter caring for her ailing mother.

# ❚ CASE STUDY

## A DAUGHTER CARES FOR HER AILING MOTHER

*Lois Lyles reflects on what she learns from her mother as she provides care during her mother's last days of life.*

Mama is down, I am up. Up, and up, and up. She wants Vaseline for her char-dry lips, her St. Francis church bulletin, her rosary. The vase on the dresser must be moved out of the way of the black-faced digital clock. Two twenty-five, New Year's afternoon. She stares at the red numerals each like an imp or an infernal flame, as the five becomes a six; the six, a seven.

"Water the plants, Lois."

Nervously, I dribble water into the flower pots. I work fast. She has approximately one request every three minutes.

"Thank you, darling. I feel so worthless and useless. Why can't I do anything?"

"Mama, you are not worthless. You are a beautiful person. You still look beautiful to me," I say, and mean it. She was my childhood idol. Her soulful-eyed, smooth-haired beauty was my first acquaintance with romance.

"No, I'm not," she whimpers; then says, "Thank you, darling."

"Mama, whatever happens, I'm with you, and I'm for you."

She cries. Her misery makes me recall how my fear of death had once made me, to my mortal shame, abandon a sick woman I loved. I am the namesake of Mama's sister Florence, who died of cancer four summers ago. Florence is my middle name. Mama must be thinking of Aunt Flo, too, for she says, "I took care of Sister when she went up to her bedroom three days before she died and never came downstairs again. I remember she was amazed that I would wash her down there, you know, her private parts. She didn't want me to have to do that." After pausing, my mother adds, "I thought, Lois, it would help you after this is over, to be with me now when I need you, and do things for me."

I am astonished at her, the good mother. She has called me to her sickbed, not so much as to help her as to help *me.* I, in childhood, was never hungry, never homeless, never seriously ill; and was never exposed to the sight of physical suffering. My parents had made sure of all that. But an easy ride of a life is only a half-truth. Now, Mama's gift is to let me know her pain. She is letting me see if I am strong enough to grapple, by proxy, with Death. (Lyles, 1991, p. 242)

## ■ CRITICAL THINKING AND CASE ANALYSIS

1. How would you describe the costs of caregiving in this case?
2. How would you describe the rewards of caregiving in this case?
3. From what you can gather, what is the quality of the mother–daughter relationship in this case?
4. What role might caring for her dying mother play in Lois's development as an adult?

## MANAGING THE HOUSEHOLD

People tend to live in groups. According to the U.S. Census Bureau (2004b), all the people who live in a house or other "housing unit," such as an apartment, a single room, or any space designated as separate living quarters, are part of a **household**. In the United States, the Census Bureau records all individuals as living either in households or in group quarters (e.g., emergency shelters, juvenile detention centers, mental hospitals, prisons, military barracks, college dormitories). In 2003, there were 118,278,000 households in the United States. The average household size was 2.57 people, and 68% were defined as **family households** involving two or more individuals related by birth, marriage, or adoption.

### ■ MANAGING RESOURCES AND MEETING NEEDS

Households are much more than a convenient way of counting people. *Household* is a term that describes an entity that is created by people for a particular style of living. Households are bounded units that pool their resources, earn and spend money, interact with the labor market, and engage in social interaction with their neighbors (Wallerstein & Smith, 1991). Management of the household refers to all the planning, problem solving, and activities in which adults must engage in order to take care of themselves and others who are entrusted to their care.

The value of the many tasks required to establish and maintain a supportive household environment is difficult to assess. However, in recent, high-profile divorce cases, corporate spouses expected to share equally in the assets that their partners had accumulated during the years of their marriage. In one case, Lorna Wendt wanted half the $100 million in assets she said her husband, Gary Wendt, the CEO of a major corporation, was worth. The court agreed to a $20 million settlement—half of Gary Wendt's "hard assets." The rationale for this type of settlement is based on the following ideas:

A lot of work that's done in the home is invisible: cooking, cleaning, marketing, clerical work. Plus there's emotional work, which is particularly invisible—whether it's child-rearing, dealing with problems at school, providing support to your spouse. . . . These corporate [spouses] perform other kinds of work which is more business-related. They move frequently, so there's the challenge of finding houses, buying new houses, fixing them up, settling children into new schools. They're also directly involved in the business in terms of entertaining, meeting clients, being a confidante, helping their [partners] make hiring decisions, knowing the business. (Cohn, 1998, p. 14)

At present, society's ability to recognize and value the accomplishments linked to the management of the household is poorly developed. At the same time, more emphasis is being placed on the centrality of the home environment in fostering intellectual development, social competence, health, and emotional well-being.

The household system has the potential for providing an environment that facilitates human growth and mental health. Learning to create such an environment is a developmental task of the middle adult years. Households have the potential for much greater variety and flexibility than most work settings. However, many of the tasks required for household maintenance are tedious, physically demanding, repetitive, and time consuming. Over the past 40 years, as women have become more intensively involved in the labor market, research has focused on how much time people spend at the tasks of household maintenance and who is performing those tasks.

Data gathered through time diaries over the period from 1965 through 1995 provide a picture of historical changes in the amount of time devoted to household tasks and the changing contribution of men and women to those tasks (Bianchi, Milkie, Sayer, & Robinson, 2000). Household tasks were divided into two categories: *core tasks* that need to be accomplished frequently, including cooking, cleaning, and laundry; and *other tasks* that are more intermittent, including yard work, household repairs, and financial management. As illustrated in Table 13.2, women spend more time in total housework than men, but the difference in the amount of time spent by men and women has been decreasing over the years. Women still spend more time in the core tasks than men, but men's contributions in those areas increased from 1965 to 1985, and then leveled out. As times have changed, fewer hours are devoted to household tasks overall, and more time is devoted to child care by both men and women. Dual-career couples are more likely to purchase services for household tasks, and are especially likely to order in meals or to eat out as a way of saving time. The drop in the number of hours dedicated to household tasks among women is not solely due to women's participation in the labor market; the decline in hours of household work was greater over time for those who were not employed than for those who were (Casper & Bianchi, 2002).

The challenge of household management is to create an environment that will enhance the potential of each household member and thereby benefit the entire unit. The significance of the household can be appreciated by thinking about the consequences of its absence, especially in the case of homeless individuals and families. Management of the household, much like the workplace, requires leadership in order

**Table 13.2** Trends in Weekly Housework by Gender for Men and Women Ages 25 to 64: 1965–1995

| | All Women | | | | All Men | | | | Ratio of Women's Time to Men's | | | |
|---|---|---|---|---|---|---|---|---|---|---|---|---|
| | 1965 | 1975 | 1985 | 1995 | 1965 | 1975 | 1985 | 1995 | 1965 | 1975 | 1985 | 1995 |
| Total housework (hours) | 30 | 23.7 | 19.7 | 17.5 | 4.9 | 7.2 | 9.8 | 10 | 6.1 | 3.3 | 2 | 1.8 |
| Core housework (total) | 26.9 | 21 | 16.3 | 13.9 | 2.3 | 2.5 | 4 | 3.8 | 11.9 | 8.3 | 4 | 3.7 |
| Cooking meals | 9.3 | 8.1 | 7 | 4.6 | 1.1 | 1.5 | 2 | 1.6 | 8.8 | 5.3 | 3.4 | 2.8 |
| Meal cleanup | 4.5 | 2.4 | 1.9 | 0.7 | 0.5 | 0.3 | 0.4 | 0.1 | 9.9 | 9.4 | 4.9 | 5.4 |
| Housecleaning | 7.2 | 7.3 | 5 | 6.7 | 0.5 | 0.5 | 1.3 | 1.7 | 15.5 | 14 | 3.9 | 3.8 |
| Laundry, ironing | 5.8 | 3.2 | 2.4 | 1.9 | 0.3 | 0.2 | 0.3 | 0.3 | 22.1 | 13.5 | 7.5 | 6.9 |
| Other housework (total) | 3.1 | 2.7 | 3.4 | 3.6 | 2.6 | 4.7 | 5.7 | 6.2 | 1.2 | 0.6 | 0.6 | 0.6 |
| Outdoor chores | 0.3 | 0.7 | 0.5 | 0.8 | 0.4 | 1 | 1.3 | 1.9 | 0.7 | 0.7 | 0.4 | 0.4 |
| Repairs | 0.4 | 0.6 | 0.5 | 0.7 | 1 | 2 | 1.8 | 1.9 | 0.4 | 0.3 | 0.3 | 0.4 |
| Garden, animal care | 0.6 | 0.8 | 0.8 | 0.8 | 0.2 | 0.7 | 0.9 | 1 | 2.4 | 1.1 | 0.9 | 0.8 |
| Bills, other financial | 1.8 | 0.7 | 1.6 | 1.3 | 0.9 | 1 | 1.6 | 1.5 | 2 | 0.7 | 1 | 0.9 |
| N | 579 | 927 | 1,725 | 493 | 469 | 783 | 1,405 | 359 | | | | |

Source: Reprinted from *Social Forces* vol. 79, no. 1, 2000. "Is Anyone Doing the Housework? Trends in the Gender Division of Household Labor" by Suzanne M. Bianchi, Melissa A. Milkie, Liana C. Sayer, and John P. Robinson. Copyright © The University of North Carolina Press.

to set priorities and goals, manage resources, and operationalize plans. The scarcer the resources, the greater the pressure on the adult to make careful decisions and to find creative solutions to the daily challenges of meeting the household's physical and psychological needs. Leadership begins as adults model the process of shared decision making and children (if there are any) learn to participate in problem solving. Household members discover ways to work together to achieve a shared vision of the future (Blanchard, 1996; Woyach, 1991). The home environment is the first place where many children discover that they can have a voice. Parents can create a family atmosphere in which the spirit of democracy comes alive through a careful balance of freedom and responsibility, respect for individuality, and commitment to the welfare of others.

## ■ BUILDING NETWORKS AND COALITIONS

One of the most difficult and subtle kinds of new learning that occurs during middle adulthood is the development of an understanding of how the structures of other organizations affect one's life and the lives of family members. These other organizations may include (1) members of the extended family (e.g., one's in-laws), (2) other families, (3) business or work-related associations, (4) religious groups, (5) educational groups, and (6) community groups. This concept was introduced briefly in Chapter 4 (Theories for Understanding Human Development) in describing Bronfenbrenner's (1979) model of the *mesosystem*. The family is interconnected with other social systems that can expand its resources. Its contact with social groups must include the maintenance of goodwill and some evidence of group identification and commitment.

Social groups also generate norms that may make demands on the family. Hence, adults must be able to protect the family from excessive external demands, while retaining valuable and satisfying external relationships.

Families differ in their investment in relationships outside the family unit. In some households, the nuclear family is more important than any other group. Such households expend little energy outside the family boundaries. At the other extreme are families who are involved in a number of community groups and who incorporate their extended families into frequent group activities. In some families, each person is encouraged to establish a group of close friends. In others, each person's friends are screened or evaluated by the other family members. The adult's task is to define the family's preferred stance toward other social groups and to create opportunities to build desired relationships.

Preserving relationships within the **extended family** is a delicate matter. This is the realm of family politics. In close family relations, it is likely that positive feelings of warmth and affection are coupled with negative feelings of irritation and aggravation (Fingerman, Hay, & Birditt, 2004). Failed expectations about courtesies and obligations or thoughtless insults and slights from family members are typical stressors that occur within the family network. Family members may have opposing political, religious, or childrearing views; they may have competing motivations; or they may try to form alliances among family subgroups. When children decide to marry, they bring two family networks together that may or may not get along. Parents may or may not convey support to their child's partner or spouse; sisters and brothers have partners who may or may not support each other. Likewise, parents may divorce and remarry, bringing one family system into contact with another. All these transitions introduce challenges to sustaining valued coalitions within the extended family and protecting the family from disruptive forces (Whitbeck, Hoyt, & Huck, 1994).

## ■ REMARRIAGE AND BLENDED FAMILIES

About 40% of all marriages involve a remarriage for the bride, the groom, or both. Although the U.S. Census Bureau does not distinguish between those married couples who are in first and in subsequent marriages, the psychosocial reality of *remarriage* is unique. Partners come to the remarriage with different marital histories. One or both have a former spouse and in-laws from a previous marriage. In some cases, the relationships with the former spouse or the in-laws may involve unresolved conflicts. In other cases, relationships with the former spouse or in-laws from a previous marriage may continue to be close. If either partner has children, the remarriage involves not only a family formation between the adult partners, but may involve the establishment of new parental roles and the negotiation of ties with noncustodial parents and grandparents. Custody arrangements may require that the parents remain in the same state or community in order to facilitate visitation. As a result, the remarried couple's life choices are constrained. As the new, blended family approaches traditional holidays, celebrations, and transitions, the complexities of considering these extended family bonds can become difficult.

One of the significant sources of ambiguity in a blended family is the relationship of stepparents to their nonbiological stepchildren. The most common blended family is one in which a man marries a woman who has custody of her children, thereby entering into the role of stepfather. What determines whether a man will embrace this role, investing in another man's children as his own? William Marsiglio (2004) has provided a glimpse into the complexity of this process as men approach the social, personal, and interpersonal nature of becoming invested in their stepfather role. For some men, like Monty, the role is continuously ambiguous: "I never really understood what I was to her; I still don't. I felt, I've always felt, like I should have been her father, but I never was, and I never will. . . . I was always there for her, in positive ways, and he never was; I mean, never" (p. 28).

For others, like Terry, there is an openness to the possibility of sharing the role with the biological father: "Look, it's OK to have two dads. You have a couple sets of grandparents and whatever. It's OK to have two different fathers. I'm the one that's here with you all the time and he's the one up there. If he gets more involved in your life, then great! If he doesn't, nothing changes. I'm still here. I'm the one that's going to be here every day" (p. 30).

For still others, like Doug, there is no room for ambiguity: "I told her, I'll marry you, but that's my son legally. No step involved, nothing like that. That's my son. She said, 'fine; I don't see anything wrong with that.' So that's when she went

In this loving family, Tony is Berta's stepfather and Andrew's biological father. The children mean everything to Tony, and they both adore him.

back to him [biological father] and said she don't want any alimony, child support, nothing. Just want you out of the picture. He signed the papers; he said no problem. I won't cause any trouble. So when the papers came back, they just simply read my name, didn't say stepfather or nothing else" (p. 33).

In remarriage, partners must find ways to create boundaries around the blended family, so that children can benefit from the love and support of their parents, grandparents, and other relatives, while protecting the new family from unwanted intrusions and pressures for competing loyalties. Blended families have to find new traditions and rituals to mark their distinctiveness while preserving links to valued relationships from the past.

## ■ ONE-PARENT FAMILIES

In 2003, about 32% of all families with children under the age of 18 were one-parent families; 26% were headed by women, and 6% were headed by men (U.S. Census Bureau, 2004b). This compares to 22% of all U.S. families in 1980.

Among African American families, the proportion of female-headed families with children under 18 rose from 49% in 1980 to 65% in 2003. Among European American families, the proportion rose from 17% in 1980 to 27% in 2003. Among Hispanic families, the increase was from 24% in 1980 to 35% in 2003.

The greatest stressor for single mothers is the lack of financial resources. In 2003, 35% of all families comprising single mothers and children had a family income below the poverty level (U.S. Census Bureau, 2004a). To put this figure in context, 5% of all married-couple families with children were in poverty that year. Thus, single mothers with children are about seven times more likely to live in poverty than two-parent families. Poverty in these families is the result of a number of factors: single mothers tend to have a lower earning capacity; they work fewer hours; and even when they receive some support from the child's father, they bear a substantial portion of their children's expenses.

In addition to stresses associated with poverty, single parents may suffer from social isolation, continuous pressure to meet the needs of their children, and experiencing overload in trying to combine work, parenting, and household decision making without a partner. How well can single mothers manage their parenting role in the face of their many role demands? Some studies emphasize a deficit perspective—for example, identifying factors that place children or adolescents from single-parent families at risk for antisocial behavior and delinquency (Bank, Forgatch, Patterson, & Fetrow, 1993). Other studies focus on adaptation and coping within the single-parent structure. They consider factors that help sustain a positive parent–child relationship, such as sharing a strong emotional connection with other family members, being able to help one another in concrete ways, talking with one another and listening to what your child is saying, and

spending time together with your child and other family members (McCreary & Dancy, 2004; Simons, Beaman, Conger, & Chao, 1993). Retrospective studies show that many children who are identified as having psychological problems, especially temper tantrums, bullying, cheating, stealing, and fighting, are from divorced, single-mother families. However, prospective studies—those that look at childrearing practices and subsequent child outcomes—show that poor parenting practices, especially emotional unavailability, ineffective discipline, minimal supervision, and a dominating, hostile style of interaction, produce these negative child outcomes in both single-parent and two-parent families (G. R. Patterson, 1992). Although single-parent families face many additional problems, it is clearly inaccurate to label all of them "problem families."

Among single-mother families, one of the fastest growing subgroups is low-income women who have never been married (Casper & Bianchi, 2002). These women may be in cohabiting or serious romantic relationships, but for a variety of reasons they have rejected the idea of getting married. It is not that marriage is devalued; in fact, some argue that it is the high standards that these women have for marriage that makes them decide to stay single (Edin, Kefalas, & Reed, 2004). Women want to be able to find a partner whom they can trust to be faithful—someone who is not addicted to drugs or alcohol, who will treat them and their child with kindness, and who will be able to contribute financially to their family. In many communities, this type of partner is difficult to find. Rushing into a marriage with someone who does not have these qualities just because one has a child seems foolhardy. These women know of too many instances of couples who start out with great expectations and then run into job loss, infidelity, abuse, drunkenness, or criminal behavior. Thus, for many women, being an unmarried, single

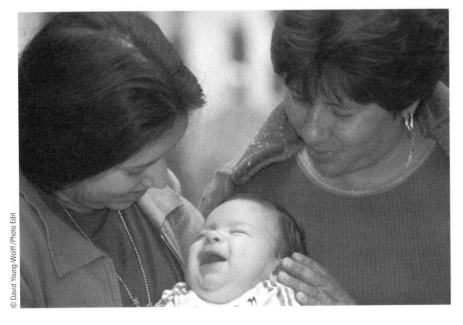

© David Young-Wolff / Photo Edit

*Kin support is an important resource that buffers many single-parent families from the negative impact of poverty and role overload. Cecilia's mother Maria is willing to provide housing and child care for her and her new grandchild so that Cecilia can continue working.*

APPLYING THEORY AND RESEARCH TO LIFE

## Homelessness

THE HOUSEHOLD PROVIDES a basic life structure for most people in all cultures. The demands and tasks of household management call forth responses that stimulate cognitive, social, and personal development during adulthood. The household is not only a physical setting, but also a shared psychological context for a group of people. In nomadic tribal groups, for example, the continuity of the household is preserved by the group of people and their shared belongings even though the location of the household changes. The capacities to maintain a household and to nurture household members reflect the leadership skills, creativity, and self-reliance that are characteristics of maturity in middle adulthood.

The term *homeless* refers to people who live on the streets or in public shelters. They have no permanent resting place and no private space (Nunez, 2004). It is very difficult to assess the exact number of people who experience homelessness; the numbers often reflect a specific point in time rather than a lifetime estimate. In 2000, the U.S. Census Bureau identified 171,000 people who were counted on a single day living in emergency and transitional shelters

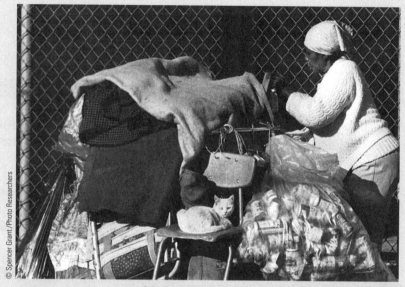

Louise earns a bit of money by redeeming aluminum cans. Because of her cat, she cannot be admitted to a shelter, so she keeps her belongings close by in her cart and sleeps outdoors.

(Smith & Smith, 2001). This count did not include people who were in shelters for abused women, people who were living in outdoor areas typically inhabited by the homeless, people who may have avoided the shelter on that day in order to prevent being counted, and people who were housed in some other form of temporary housing with family and friends. In some locations, many people who seek shelter cannot be accommodated. A survey by the Urban

---

parent is a deliberate strategy for avoiding a difficult and potentially costly divorce.

### ■ PEOPLE WHO LIVE ALONE

In the discussion of household management, we have assumed that the household consists of two or more people whose lives are intertwined. Questions about decision making, consensus, and shared responsibilities are all raised in the context of a group of people living together. However, in 2003, about 29 million people in the United States lived alone. These one-person households most frequently consist of men in the younger age groups (under 44) and women in the older age groups (45 and older; U.S. Census Bureau, 2004b). Single-person households include people who have never married, are divorced or separated, and are widowed. The reasons for living alone and the backgrounds for this life pattern vary considerably.

Little is known about the differences in psychosocial development between adults who live alone and those who live together with others. Some of the aspects of household management, including organizing time, planning for the future, making decisions, and establishing relationships with other social groups, pose challenges to the person living alone. On the other hand, assigning responsibility and establishing a pattern for group decision making clearly are not required. People who live alone may not feel the need to engage in elaborate planning and evaluation when they are the only ones who will be immediately affected by their choices. Therefore, they may be freer to decide spontaneously as each opportunity presents itself.

In summary, the developmental task of household management draws on many leadership skills in order to build a home environment that is comfortable, adaptive to changing demands, and responsive to the needs and goals of those who live together. The realm of the household is unique because it

Institute (2000) estimated that each year, about 2.5 million people are homeless in October and 3.5 million in February. Roughly 38% of those who are included in this count are children. The National Coalition for the Homeless provides information about this and other aspects of homelessness on its website (http://www.nationalhomeless.org).

The fastest growing segment of the homeless population—families with children—constitutes approximately 40% of people who become homeless (Shinn & Weitzman, 1996). A survey of 30 U.S. cities in 1998 found that families represented 38% of the homeless, and children under the age of 18 accounted for 25% of the homeless population (U.S. Conference of Mayors, 1998). These proportions are likely to be higher in rural areas.

A combination of three major factors contributes to the continued risk of homelessness for families with children in the United States: (1) the decline in the value of the minimum wage, coupled with the prevalence of insecure jobs with few or no benefits (an estimated 22% of homeless people are employed); (2) the decline in the availability and value of social welfare benefits; and (3) shortages in low-income housing and public-assistance housing (National Coalition for the Homeless, 2002).

Paths toward homelessness for families are diverse. Some of the most common precursors are job loss, domestic violence, substance abuse, mental illness, and divorce. Although some homeless individuals are in a sudden crisis, many have stumbled from one temporary living situation to the next, and others have never been able to establish a permanent home. Some of these people are singularly alone and unable to develop minimal social relationships. This is an unusual phenomenon, because most people have some ability to have meaningful social relationships. Among homeless mothers, for example, many have friends or family, but cannot count on them for housing support. For some, the nature of their housing crisis may disrupt their social network, making it impossible to ask for help from family or friends. Following an episode of homelessness, some families are relocated far from their social network, making it likely that they will become vulnerable to homelessness in the future (Toohey, Shinn, & Weitzman, 2004). As a result

of victimization earlier in their lives, some women suffer from a degree of emotional dysfunction, exacerbated by the use of alcohol and drugs. An estimated 10% to 15% of homeless parents have a problem with drug addiction, making it difficult for them to hold a job, sustain a relationship, or be approved for low-cost housing (Nunez, 2004).

In homelessness, society confronts a painful example of psychosocial stagnation—the inability of mature adults to meet their basic needs for shelter, food, and clothing—combined with its own failure to prevent their condition from reaching this degree of vulnerability. In the face of the cultural value placed on independence, self-sufficiency, and hard work, U.S. society has difficulty making effective public responses. Policies and programs to assist homeless families have typically focused on short-term emergency intervention. A coordinated effort is required to address the complex needs of homeless people, including living arrangements, employment, mental health services, drug or alcohol treatment, creation of a network of support, and gradual integration into a sense of community (National Coalition for the Homeless, 2002).

allows adults to perform with maximum flexibility, creativity, and adaptability in response to the daily needs and long-term goals of the household members.

# THE PSYCHOSOCIAL CRISIS: GENERATIVITY VERSUS STAGNATION

## GENERATIVITY

The psychosocial crisis of *generativity* versus *stagnation* can be understood as a pressure on the adult to be committed to improving the life conditions of future generations (Erikson, 1963). **Generativity** "encompasses procreativity, productivity, and creativity, and thus the generation of new beings, as

well as of new products and new ideas, including a kind of self-generation concerned with further identity development" (Erikson, 1982, p. 67). According to Erikson's observations (Erikson et al., 1986), generativity is formed as a result of experiences of maintaining the world, nurturing and being concerned, and caring.

It is worth pausing to consider what it means to *generate*. A basic dictionary definition is "to bring into existence." Through generativity, adults may change the world by introducing new things, ideas, beings, or bonds of relationship—all of which had not existed before. Although Erikson directed us to the heightened importance of generativity to development in middle adulthood, it makes sense to view this critical capacity as emerging over the life course. Stewart and Vandewater (1998) suggested that generativity arises through three phases: (1) generative desire or motivation, (2) a belief in one's capacity for generative action, and (3) a subjective sense of generative accomplishment.

*Volunteering one's time to share knowledge and skills with young children is clearly an expression of caring. How might generativity and volunteering be related?*

In later adolescence and early adulthood, many individuals experience a desire to be generative—to have an impact on the world. This motive might be expressed in a person's goals. For example, young people who want to promote better interracial understanding or to improve the educational experiences of young children might be said to have generative motives. One may then begin to realize opportunities for generative action and a growing confidence in one's capacity to have an impact on the world. Generativity may be expressed through a wide variety of actions, including procreation, parenting, invention, teaching, expanding the knowledge base, improving the physical or social environment, and artistic creation (Kotre, 1995).

Generativity may be expressed by making a success of a remarriage involving children who have been neglected in their early childhood. It may also mean innovating in the workplace; in the scientist's lab; in poetry, art, music, or literature; or in creating some splendid form of recreation, like a theme park, or a refreshing new food like frozen yogurt. Finally, in looking back on one's life, one can assess these actions and make a judgment about whether one's generative aspirations or motives have been realized.

Generativity is critical to the survival of any society. At some point, adult members of the society must begin to feel an obligation to contribute their resources, skills, and creativity to improving the quality of life for the young (de St. Aubin, McAdams, & Kim, 2004). To some degree, this motive is aroused as one recognizes the inevitability of mortality—that one will not be around forever to direct the course of events. Therefore, one must make contributions to the society, on both personal and public levels, that will stand some chance of continuing after one's death.

There is an old story about three men who were observed laying bricks for the wall of a church. When asked what they were doing, the first man said he was laying bricks, the second said he was building a wall, and the third said he was building a church. During middle adulthood, one must arrive at a philosophy of life that will impart significance to daily activities. One part of generativity lies in the actual attainment of creative goals. The other part lies in the perspective one brings to one's lifework.

Erikson suggested that the outcome of the crisis of generativity versus stagnation has implications for adults at the next life stage in the form of *grand-generativity*:

> The reconciling of generativity and stagnation involves the elder in expressing a "grand-generativity" that is somehow beyond middle age's direct responsibility for maintaining the world. The roles of aging parent, grandparent, old friend, consultant, adviser, and mentor all provide the aging adult with essential social opportunities to experience grand-generativity in current relationships with people of all ages. In these relationships, the individual seeks to integrate outward-looking care for others with inward-looking concern for self. As a complement to caring for others, the elder is also challenged to accept from others that caring which is required, and to do so in a way that is itself caring. In the context of the generational cycle, it is incumbent upon the aged to enhance feelings of generativity in their caregivers from the younger generations. (Erikson et al., 1986, pp. 74–75)

## ■ MEASURING GENERATIVITY

The meaning of generativity is being clarified and elaborated through attempts to operationalize it (Hawkins & Dollahite, 1997; McAdams & de St. Aubin, 1998; Peterson & Stewart, 1993). One line of research provided a cross-sectional comparison of dimensions of generativity among participants in early (22–27), middle (37–42), and later (67–72) adulthood (McAdams, de St. Aubin, & Logan, 1993). Four aspects of generativity were measured:

- generative concern—a sense that one is making a difference in the lives of others;
- generative commitment—personal strivings or goals that have a generative nature;
- generative action—a checklist of actions that the person has performed in the past 2 months that involved creating, maintaining, or offering; and
- generative narrative—autobiographical recollections coded for generative meaning.

Based on these measures, the results suggest the following trends:

1. Across all age groups, generative concern was significantly correlated with happiness and life satisfaction.
2. When all four measures of generativity were combined, the middle adults scored higher than the young or older age groups.
3. The measures of generative commitment and generative narration were higher for the middle adult group.
4. The pattern of responses showed significant differences between the middle adult and the younger adult groups, but the middle adults and the older adults were not significantly different.

The implication of these results is that once the generative orientation emerges, it appears to endure in the life goals and activities of a person into later adulthood. A similar example is found in the psychosocial crisis of identity. Once the identity orientation emerges, it, too, appears to endure as a recurring theme to be revised and reworked in later stages.

The theme of generativity versus stagnation permeates the psychological dynamics of adult life. In the following section, we discuss the negative pole, stagnation, and its expression in narcissistic self-preoccupation and depression. Since the mid-1980s, the severity of problems related to depression in adulthood have been documented, and several different patterns have been described. Although much has been written about the negative side of adult life, including people who commit crimes or betray their families, it is important to recognize that the positive forces of generativity are equally dominant in guiding the lives of most adults and that they produce acts of creative leadership and caring.

# ▌CASE STUDY

## MY LEADERSHIP JOURNEY

*Lourie Campos describes how a leadership training experience transformed her generative strivings into action.*

In the fall of 1999, I was encouraged to apply to the Women's Health Leadership program by my former boss. At that time,

my job was a hodgepodge of responsibilities, although I was beginning to focus more and more on policy work. I felt that I lacked direction and the tools to make changes in my job. I didn't consider myself a "leader" even though my colleagues saw me as one. I wanted to be proactive in making positive changes in my job, so I decided to apply to WHL. What I didn't expect was to learn as much about myself as I did about women's health issues.

In 1997, I was diagnosed with metastatic cancer. Years earlier, I saw my father lose his battle with colon cancer, which he courageously fought for 12 years, and in 1999 my brother was diagnosed with the same cancer. It has changed the way I think about my future. While work was important to me, I needed to set limits. While it may seem that participating in the WHL program would have added more stress to my life, it was just the opposite. Through WHL, I worked on an individual leadership development program that not only allowed me to be effective at my job by sharpening my skills and learning new ones but [also included] activities that I wanted to concentrate on outside of work. I spent more time having fun, learning new things, and spending quality time with my family and friends. WHL encourages personal and professional growth as well as teaching women to be advocates for themselves and other women in their community.

My major accomplishment was the creation of the *Women's Health Advocacy Guidebook*. The guidebook is specific to Santa Clara County and is full of information on the gaps and barriers low-income, medically underserved women face in Santa Clara County. It is a tool to help women's health advocates understand the legislative process and how they can participate in the process. I distributed 40 guidebooks to women in my community and I have had such a positive response from them. The guidebook is something I wish I had when I began doing policy work.

Prior to WHL, I had never spoken about my experience with cancer. I did not fully understand or recognize the positive impact my story could have. I was always afraid that if I spoke about my cancer and my family's experience with cancer people would just feel sorry for me, and that is the last thing I wanted. But WHL has taught me to take risks and to find my voice. This past year, I have been a featured speaker in a "Living with Cancer" series in Santa Cruz; I submitted my cancer story to the *San Jose Mercury News* and it was printed with a picture of me and my dog on the front page; I was a panelist on assembly member Elaine Alquist's "Women's Health Forum"; and I was selected as one of 8 people to represent California and to provide testimony to the President's Cancer Panel. Many people, especially women, have shared their experiences with me and I have felt so honored to listen to their stories.

Source: Littlefield, Robison, Engelbrecht, Gonzalez, & Hutcheson, 2002, p. 579.

## ■ CRITICAL THINKING AND CASE ANALYSIS

1. What kinds of changes did Lourie Campos experience as a result of the Women's Health Leadership training experience?

2. What evidence does the case provide about generative concern? Generative commitment? Generative action? Generative narrative?

3. How did the experience of expanding her social network of professionals outside of her job contribute to Lourie's psychosocial development?

4. What lessons can be learned from this case about how to support and nurture a sense of generativity in middle adulthood and how to overcome feelings of stagnation?

5. What role does the environment play in promoting generativity? Can you think of some examples of community programs or workplace initiatives that may foster psychosocial development in adulthood?

## STAGNATION

**Stagnation** suggests a lack of psychological movement or growth. Those unable to cope with managing a household, raising children, or managing their career are likely to feel psychological stagnation at the end of middle adulthood.

The experience of stagnation may differ for the narcissistic adult and the depressed adult. **Narcissistic** people—adults who devote their energy and skills to the sole end of self-aggrandizement and personal satisfaction—are likely to have difficulty looking beyond their own needs or experiencing satisfaction in taking care of others. They expend energy accumulating wealth and material possessions. They relate to others in terms of how people can serve them. Narcissistic people can exist quite happily until the physical and psychological consequences of aging begin to make an impact. At that point, and continuing toward old age, self-satisfaction is easily undermined by anxieties related to death. It is not uncommon for such people to undergo some form of religious or humanitarian "conversion" after a serious illness or an emotional crisis forces them to acknowledge the limitations of a totally self-involved lifestyle.

**Chronically depressed** people do not feel a sense of accomplishment during middle adulthood—they think of themselves as worthless. They are unable to perceive themselves as having sufficient resources to make any contribution to their society. These people are likely to have low self-esteem, doubt their opportunities for future improvement, and are therefore unwilling to invest energy in conceptualizing future progress.

One of the most commonly noted sources of stagnation in middle adulthood is *role stagnation* associated with employment. People who have been in their job a long time may be threatened by younger workers, stuck in a routine, or passed over for recognition and leadership. Rather than taking up the challenge to mentor new employees or to invent new approaches to their work, they become resentful, avoidant, and withdrawn, and they may develop physical or emotional symptoms associated with the stress of their frustration (Raskas & Hambrick, 1992; Yerushalmi, 1993). The case of Lourie Campos illustrates how important the encouragement

of professional development can be in forestalling stagnation and promoting continued generative growth in the workplace.

Middle adulthood extends over many years. During this stage, people encounter many complex challenges for which they may not be fully prepared. Promotion to an administrative position, the need to care for an aging parent, and the negotiation of a divorce are examples. Brim (1992) argued that both success and failure bring people face to face with redefining and reexamining their goals. At many points, adults doubt their ability to move ahead, achieve their goals, or make meaningful contributions. Feelings of stagnation surge temporarily.

People may recognize that unless they redefine their situation or take some new risks, the quality of their lives will deteriorate. They face the possibility of feeling outdated by new technology, outmoded by new lifestyles, overburdened by role demands, or alienated from meaningful social contacts. At these moments of crisis, adults may become entangled in a process of self-protection and withdrawal that results in permanent stagnation. However, they may also be able to muster new resources and see things from a new perspective that will permit continuing growth and the expansion of generativity.

## THE CENTRAL PROCESS: PERSON–ENVIRONMENT INTERACTION AND CREATIVITY

Two aspects of the central process that lead to the development of generativity in middle adulthood are person–environment interaction and creativity. The first is a facilitative interaction between the individual and the social environment, which includes the family, work setting, neighborhood, and larger political community. To a large extent, this environment provides a person's basis of experience. Day-to-day interactions, the expectations for behavior, the available resources, and the social supports that are necessary for the growth of self-confidence are elements of the social environment. The second part of the central process in the establishment of generativity is personal creativity. Although **creativity** has been defined in many ways, for our purposes we will define it as the willingness to abandon old forms or patterns of doing things in favor of new ways. This requires the generation, evaluation, and implementation of new ideas.

## PERSON–ENVIRONMENT INTERACTION

Successful personality growth depends on the interaction between a person's needs, skills, and interpersonal style and the demands of the environment in which he or she is embedded. The concept of interaction suggests a potential for reciprocal influence between individuals and settings. Consequently, the structure and demands of settings may alter a person's behavior, values, goals, and sense of self-worth. People also have an impact on the settings in which they participate.

People have multiple identities and, as a result, participate in a variety of settings within their community. Adults do more than maintain or respond to their environments; they shape them. Those with higher status—that is, more resources and power—are more able to influence the quality of interactions they have with others in their environment. In turn, they are more likely to create conditions in which their identities are verified because they receive greater respect and recognition from others for the roles that they play (Stets & Harrod, 2004).

In creating their environments, adults decide whom they will marry, whether or not to have children, which occupation they will follow, and where they will live. To the degree that they have a choice in these matters, they are able to influence the kinds of transactions that occur between their personality and their social milieu. They build families with lifestyles that suit the members. Making good decisions about social settings requires that they understand themselves, the nature of other people, and the social institutions that are part of their social environment. The degree of fit between family needs and community characteristics helps support the essential functions of middle adulthood, including caring for children or aging parents, coordinating work and family life, and sustaining a vital marriage. When the community consists of other families facing similar tasks, the resources, mutual support, and validation for one's life choices are likely to be greater (Swisher, Sweet, & Moen, 2004).

Although participation in some settings is a matter of choice, many others are the result of chance. Some settings can be abandoned or altered if they do not meet the individual's need; other settings are permanent and difficult to alter. If one is in an unsuitable setting, one must be willing to leave it if possible or discover a way to influence it so that it meets one's needs more adequately. Some people, however, find themselves in social settings that can be neither abandoned nor altered. For example, a group of workers in Michigan were trained for employment in an automotive plant. When the economy slumped, they were laid off. These workers did not have enough money saved to move to another town, there were no new jobs, and they did not have the resources or the incentive to retrain for other types of employment.

When one is forced to remain in social settings that are contrary to one's needs, the possibility of developing generativity is seriously diminished. If one is unable to experience a personal sense of effectiveness at home, at work, or in the community, then one is unlikely to feel capable of contributing to future growth in these spheres. Fortunately, the social environment is so multifaceted that individuals are likely to experience satisfaction in their participation in at least one setting, even if they are dissatisfied in others. For example, people are likely to experience a sense of validation in their relationships with friends and close family members even

© Vicki Silbert/Photo Edit

*Some Chinese Americans choose to live and work in a Chinese ethnic community. They experience a sense of acceptance and support while contributing to the continuity of their cultural heritage.*

when they have difficulty experiencing recognition at work. Under these conditions, individuals can compensate for their inability to be generative in some settings by placing increased effort and investment in those in which they can more easily attain satisfaction. This may require that individuals reorder their priorities. If there is little opportunity to find satisfaction in work, for example, one might begin to reinvest in contributions to one's family, religion, or community. Creativity is required in order to find a new balance among competing role demands while retaining a sense of joy and optimism.

## CREATIVITY

The importance of a creative response, no matter how small, is that it redefines the world and opens the door to new possibilities. Although the idea of creativity tends to be associated with the arts, we are using the term in a broader sense to suggest a novel transformation in any of a variety of domains from the practical to the theoretical—from creating a new

*Picasso, who never fit in to traditional society, created a vibrant world of his own. Here in his studio, he has even created companions who entertain him while he works.*

© Hulton Archive/Getty Images

recipe to creating a painting, a dance, or a theory of human behavior. Through creative effort, adults impose a new perspective on the organization, expression, or formulation of ideas.

Creative adults are not dominated by social forces but are able to direct the course of events themselves. They are at a point in their development at which their own creative responses can become a source of influence on others. Think about the menopausal woman who referred to her first hot flash as a "power surge." Imagine the person who invented wheelchair basketball, or the person who invented "Post-Its." Consider the influence of parents who, by creating a flexible, open, and loosely structured home environment, nurture the self-expression of their children. Through the process of creative problem solving, adults help reshape the social and physical environments in order to meet both personal and social needs more satisfactorily.

Throughout middle adulthood, adults are faced with situations in family, childrearing, and work settings that provide stimuli for creative problem solving. In their efforts to take into account the requirements of the social setting and to be productive in it, people must develop creative plans. They must also attempt to carry out those plans—a task that itself may require further creativity. The essence of creative problem solving is the ability to think "outside the box"—to resist defining the situation as it has been defined for you by others; then to formulate a new plan and translate the plan into action.

The roots of creativity can be found in childhood, in the semiotic, representational, playful thinking of toddlerhood.

"As if" thinking—the ability to imagine a situation in some different configuration, to use objects to stand for something else, to give new names to familiar objects, to devise private symbols for common experiences, to take on imagined roles—all these capacities of symbolic play are the foundational building blocks of creativity. In our view, all humans are creative in the sense that they can pretend. All humans are creative when they cope effectively in a changing, unpredictable environment. All humans are creative in that they can invent games, songs, tools, artifacts, or messages that are new to them. It is not so important that the creative act is new to the world, but that it is new to the person who is inventing it (Sternberg, Grigorenko, & Singer, 2004).

From the outset, the creative process involves frustrations and risk. Typically, a creative solution is required because the standard way—the scripted way—is not working. In order to try new things, people must give up some old, reliable ways of thinking or behaving. In this process, people must anticipate the possibility that their efforts will fail. They may flounder for a seemingly long period, unable to identify the solution that will allow forward movement. They may worry about public embarrassment or humiliation. Given one's embeddedness in many demanding social roles, it is often difficult to step aside and view one's situation from a fresh perspective. For some, the anxiety and self-consciousness associated with prolonged uncertainty and possible failure may be so great that creative solutions are never realized (Sapp, 1992). Their creativity is blocked by a fear of the unknown, or by an inability to violate conventional norms of behavior.

For those who are not inhibited by the fear of failure,

the achievement of a creative solution is invigorating. For the great creative geniuses—such as Freud, Einstein, or Picasso—a breakthrough or a profound creative insight fueled their commitment to pursue the creative path with increased energy (Gardner, 1993). Personal talent combined with an appreciation of the inadequacies of the current situation can lead to a significant creative act, which then promotes future efforts. Creativity provides an outlet for caring for something that has not yet been defined or experienced. Repeated efforts to generate creative solutions eventually result in the formulation of a transforming philosophy of life. Through risk taking, occasional failure, and a predominance of successful creative efforts, adults achieve a sense of what they believe in and what gives meaning to life. With this remarkable integration of experience and information, people enter later adulthood.

# THE PRIME ADAPTIVE EGO QUALITY AND THE CORE PATHOLOGY

## CARE

The ego strength associated with the achievement of generativity is care. Care "is a widening commitment to take care of the persons, the products, and the ideas one has learned to care for. All the strengths arising from earlier developments in the ascending order from infancy to young adulthood (hope and will, purpose and skill, fidelity and love) now prove, on closer study, to be essential to the generative task of cultivating strength in the next generation, for this is indeed the 'store' of human life" (Erikson, 1982, p. 67).

Parenting contributes to the expansion of caring. Seven aspects of emotional development can be identified as potential consequences of parenting. First, parenting brings a depth of commitment that is tied to the responsibility for the survival of a child. This depth of commitment is strengthened through the reinforcing nature of the child's responses to attempts to meet his or her needs. Second, parenting brings adults into contact with new channels for expressing affection. Third, it requires that adults achieve a balance between meeting their own needs and those of others. Fourth, parenting enhances adults' feelings of value and well-being through the significant role they play in the child's life. Fifth, parents achieve a degree of empathy for their child that widens the array of their emotional experiences. Sixth, parents may experience new levels of emotional intensity in reaction to their child's behavior. Finally, many parents learn to help their children express and understand emotions. By playing a therapeutic role for their children, parents may become more effective in accepting and expressing their own emotions.

Not all adults experience the expansion of caring through parenting. The psychosocial achievement of middle adult-

hood is to identify the domains in which one has opportunities to influence the quality of the social environment, so that it becomes more hospitable, humane, nurturant, or supportive of one's own visions for the future. Caring expands in different domains for different people, but it always leads to having the welfare of people and enduring things (including ideas) deeply at heart. There is an action component to caring, in that people work to care for what they can. As the crisis of generativity versus stagnation is resolved in a positive direction, adults find new energy and innovative ways to express their capacity for care.

## REJECTIVITY

Caring strongly for certain people, products, and ideas can cause people to reject any person or group that appears to threaten them. **Rejectivity** refers to an unwillingness to embrace certain individuals, groups, or ideas in one's circle of care and, at an extreme level, to view these threats as appropriate targets for hostility, even annihilation. Ironically, one may exhibit great courage and dedication to protect the objects of one's care by directing intense aggression toward the objects that one rejects.

Erikson (1982) referred to this process as "pseudospeciation," in which one defines another group as different, dangerous, and potentially less human than one's own. Under the rubric of pseudospeciation, family members can become scapegoats, neighboring communities can establish intense rivalries, racial or religious groups can terrorize others, and regions or countries can go to war. Thus, rejectivity goes beyond an intellectual selectivity of certain ideas and groups as more central to one's identity than others, taking on an aggressive energy, drawn from the power and authority of one's status in middle adulthood. The risk of rejectivity for the society is that certain groups will become so powerful that they can cause the extermination or domination of other groups. As each subgroup falls out of the circle of caring, the society as a whole reaches a new level of stagnation.

## APPLIED TOPIC
# DISCRIMINATION IN THE WORKPLACE

The U.S.A. is just a horrible place to try to raise a family and have a career. . . . When I was working in the U.S.A., it was a struggle to find decent day care . . . and if I missed a half-day of work [because] my kid had a temperature of 104, I was lectured on how this let down the [department]. In Israel there is 3 months paid maternity leave, day-care centers on every block, and if you don't take off from work for your kid's birthday party the department chairman will lecture you on how important these things are to kids and how he never missed one while his kids were little (Astrophysicist Sara Beck, currently a tenured professor at Tel Aviv University; quoted in Barinaga, 1994, p. 1472).

A big-city police officer once shared with me his frustration at waiting nineteen years to make detective. In those days before affirmative action, he had watched, one year after another, as less qualified Whites were promoted over him. Each year he had swallowed his disappointment, twisted his face into a smile, and congratulated his White friends as he hid his rage—so determined was he to avoid being categorized as a race-obsessed troublemaker. . . . Even though he made detective years ago, and even though, on the side (and on his own time), he managed to become a successful businessman and an exemplary member of the upwardly striving middle class, he says the anger still simmers within him. He worries that someday it will come pouring out, that some luckless White person will tick him off and he will explode, with tragic results (quoted in Cose, 1993, p. 61).

THE UNITED STATES has been characterized as an "achieving society." As a cultural group, we value individual achievement, usually expressed through accomplishments in the world of work. Thus, in the United States, for men and increasingly for women, the mark of successful adulthood is frequently equated with success in the labor market, which is typically attributed to personal characteristics of ability, intelligence, and motivation. Conversely, a lack of success in the labor market is attributed to deficiencies in personal characteristics—lack of ability, low intelligence, and poor motivation. Individuals are unlikely to attribute their successes to conditions of the workplace, vagaries in the economy, luck, or conditions of society that give them a special advantage and others an unfair disadvantage. Yet many Americans face serious and persistent disadvantages in the workplace that are linked to being different from the White, male, Protestant, middle-class norm (Jones, 1988).

In the past, women and minority workers in the United States have been restricted to low-paying jobs in the agricultural, service, or factory sectors. In 1964, the Civil Rights Act made it illegal to refuse to hire a person or discriminate in compensation, firing practices, or any other employment benefits based on race, color, religion, sex, or national origin. This act made the practice of restricting access to employment opportunities illegal and opened up many arenas for professional development that had previously been denied to minorities (Hodson & Sullivan, 1995). Nonetheless, barriers to full involvement of women and minorities in the labor market continue to exist.

Discrimination in the workplace is an exceedingly costly problem for the society as a whole. Discriminatory practices that lead to the disaffection of individuals from the world of work is costly in economic terms—in lower levels of productivity, high turnover, high levels of irritability and conflict among workers, lawsuits, and less identification with the company and its goals. It is costly in personal terms as well: Feelings of frustration about not being recognized for one's competence or being passed over for promotion by less competent workers interfere with the development of a generative

orientation. These experiences may lead to a more self-serving orientation, focusing exclusively on "protecting me and mine," or to a pervasive sense of futility about the future.

## DISPARITIES IN INCOME AND THE OCCUPATIONAL STRUCTURE

In 2001, the median income of people with income in constant 2001 dollars was $16,652 for White women and $30,240 for White men; $16,282 for Black women and $21,466 for Black men; $12,583 for Hispanic women and $20,189 for Hispanic men. Women with bachelor's degrees had median salaries that were 63% of those of men with the same degrees (U.S. Census Bureau, 2003). In 2003, 21.5% of Blacks, 21% of Hispanics, and 7.8% of Whites had incomes below the poverty level. Unemployment patterns showed that African Americans were twice as likely as European Americans to be unemployed (U.S. Census Bureau, 2004a).

One explanation for the racial, ethnic, and gender differences in salary, rates of poverty, and rates of unemployment is that workers from different groups are distributed unevenly in the occupational structure. Jobs continue to be gender stereotyped, with women being socialized and encouraged to work in vocations that involve helping and serving others. For example, women were 46% of those employed in 2003. However, they made up 64% of those working in sales, office work, and administrative support, and 57% of those in service occupations such as child care, food preparation, and service. On the other hand, women made up only 23% of chief executives, 14% of architects and engineers, and a small segment of the skilled trades where strong unions can protect salary scale and benefits.

Group differences in occupational position that result in different salary structures and risks of layoffs are not necessarily evidence of discrimination. Discrimination exists when two people doing the same job are paid substantially different wages. It occurs when factors other than merit prevent a person from being hired, promoted, or rewarded through various forms of compensation or increase a person's risk of being fired. Specifically, discrimination occurs when a person is evaluated on the basis of group membership rather than individual performance. In the workplace, this process operates as an ingroup–outgroup dynamic, in which members of the ingroup view members of the outgroup as deficient and, at some level, possibly threatening to their own continued success and well-being.

## HOW DISCRIMINATION PERPETUATES ITSELF

Employers, supervisors, and others in positions of power typically establish a normative profile for their employees and judge each new employee against it. In some work settings, the judgment about competence is equated with a willingness to dedicate long hours to the job, to be available at a moment's

*To prevent discrimination and improve the corporate environment, many companies create diversity councils or committees that plan training, advise on policies, and anticipate solutions to emerging problems.*

notice, and to keep one's Blackberry on at all times, including evenings and weekends. Against this norm, women who are mothers are expected to direct their time and energy toward their parenting role and, thus, are often judged to be less committed and less competent workers than women who are not mothers or than men who are fathers (Ridgeway & Correll, 2004). For example, in one study, participants rated women who were mothers as less competent—and thus less worthy of investing in hiring them, training them, or promoting them—than women who did not have children. Participants also rated women as less competent after they had children than before they became mothers (Cuddy, Fiske, & Glick, 2004).

These highly internalized norms about the ideal worker may include deeply held beliefs and values on the part of men about women. Men may wonder whether women can perform the same kinds of jobs as men and can effectively assume responsibility to supervise men; whether clients will place their trust in female executives; or whether women will be dedicated to their work when conflicts between work and family arise. In the same vein, these norms may include deeply held beliefs and values on the part of Whites about people of color—especially beliefs that they are superior to people of color in ability, that the cultural characteristics of people of color will be disruptive or damaging to productivity in the workplace, or that people of color are better suited to some types of jobs than others (Feagin & McKinney, 2003). In many organizations, one can observe what has been called "racial segmentation"—the creation of specific kinds of administrative positions that were created to carry out affirmative action agendas, community relations with specific racial or ethnic communities, or to promote the recruitment of minority employees (Forman, 2003). Because of the historical and continuing separation of neighborhoods, schools, and churches on the basis of race, few White adults have firsthand, personal relationships with people of color. Decisions about promotions or assignments to positions of increased responsibility are often made in situations where senior employees, mostly White, make decisions that do not take into account the values, beliefs, and practices of non-White groups.

Consider the following situation: "FedEx's prohibition against individuals involved in customer contact from wearing dreadlocks, beards, ponytails or braids had been company policy for years but it was not enforced until 1999 when the Memphis, Tenn.-based company gave at least seven couriers who wore dreadlocks and worked in New York an ultimatum to cut them off or lose their jobs" (Cukan, 2001).

The employees were Rastafarians, who wear dreadlocks for religious reasons. They all offered to cover their hair with a hat or some other businesslike attire. However, FedEx refused this arrangement. The men were placed on a 90-day unpaid leave and then fired because no non-customer contact positions could be found. These men had worked for FedEx for 5 years and had excellent service records with the company. The state of New York sued FedEx for violation of antidiscrimination laws, arguing that they fired the employees based on their religious observances. In response, FedEx changed its policy, allowing individuals to request an exception to the company's policy regarding hairstyles in order to respect their religious beliefs. This example illustrates the continuing need for examination of workplace practices that create hostile or disrespectful environments for workers.

## PSYCHOSOCIAL ANALYSIS: DISCRIMINATION AND COPING

In general, in discussing psychosocial development, one examines the outcome for the individual in achieving a positive resolution of the psychosocial crisis. But when considering discrimination in the workplace, one must also look at the

© Mark Richards/Photo Edit

consequences for a society. Discrimination in the workplace is one expression of *societal stagnation*. It is a defensive posture, in which those in power try to protect their own status and profits by preventing members of less powerful groups from gaining a foothold. Rather than treating diversity as a factor that can improve productivity in the work setting, discrimination operates to reduce it.

Over time, the fate of individuals who have been discriminated against becomes a great cost to the society at large. Perceived discrimination in the workplace has been associated with lower job satisfaction, reduced life satisfaction, health problems, depression, and general anxiety (Feagin & McKinney, 2003). Some targets of discrimination give up and become chronically unemployed or underemployed, resulting in a loss of human capital. Others remain in a discriminatory workplace, trying to get by, not making trouble, and yet operating behind a veil of caution. African American middle-class adults tell the same stories repeatedly about how much effort and energy they spend trying to help European American people feel comfortable with them (Whitaker, 1993). Over time, this expenditure is both exhausting and deeply frustrating. One outcome of the various forms of discrimination is the development within a person of an unspoken resentment of work that may be communicated in some form to his or her children, thus transmitting a cross-generational, cynical outlook on work.

However, the history of the United States is also filled with many cases of individuals who succeed against the odds. These adults recognize the risks of staying in a setting that does not fit well with their healthy desire to create, produce, and care. They may strike out on their own by setting up their own companies, they may challenge unfair practices through the courts, and they may mentor younger workers to help them cope with the conflicts they face in the workplace. The responsibility for coping with discrimination does not rest entirely on its victims. There are also examples of work settings that have taken active steps to challenge their own practices. Companies have been cited for their policies to support the hiring and promotion of women into senior positions, and for their innovations in weaving new levels of understanding about diversity into all aspects of employee development (Gleckman, Smart, Dwyer, Segal, & Weber, 1991; Konrad, 1990).

The American workforce of the 21st century is becoming increasingly diverse. Women and ethnic minorities are the fastest growing groups of new employees. An estimated 13% of the workforce is composed of legal and illegal immigrants. In the year 2003, 24% of U.S. resident children under the age of 5 were children of color (U.S. Census Bureau, 2004b). Their preparation for and participation in the labor market will be a determining factor in the quality and productivity of the U.S. economy in the 21st century. The psychosocial approach, which highlights the interdependence of the individual and the society, is dramatically illustrated in the connection between contemporary workplace policies and practices and their implications for the maturation of a sense of initiative and industry during childhood. Children who believe that their parents and other adult members of the community are thriving in work environments that respect and value them are more likely to make the commitment to schooling that is needed to participate fully when it is their turn to enter the labor market.

# Chapter Summary

During the middle adult years, people have an opportunity to make significant contributions to their culture. Through work, home, childrearing and other caring relationships, people express their own value orientations, moral codes, personalities, and talents. They grow more sensitive to the multiple needs of those around them and more skillful in influencing the social environment.

The developmental tasks of middle adulthood are extremely complex and require long-term persistence. During middle adulthood, people gauge their self-worth largely in relation to their contributions to complex social units, especially work, family, and community. Each task calls for a new level of conceptualization of the interaction of the self with immediate and more remote social systems and an increased ability to balance one's individual needs with system goals.

Nurturing, managing, caring, and the attainment of new levels of skill are fostered as one engages in the primary tasks of middle adulthood. These competencies provide a foundation for establishing the emotional and social support for oneself and others that is central to collaborative efforts in the workplace, mentoring younger workers, maintaining and expanding intimate relationships, and preserving optimal functioning for older adults. The well-being of the community as a whole rests largely on the effectiveness of people in middle adulthood in reaching new levels of psychosocial maturity.

The psychosocial crisis of the middle adult years—generativity versus stagnation—is really a moral crisis of commitment to a better way of life. The society must encourage adults to care for others beside themselves. The egocentrism of toddlerhood, early school age, and adolescence must eventually come to an end if the social group is to survive. In the same way that intimacy (giving oneself to another) requires identity, generativity (giving oneself to the next generation) requires love of specific others. Interpersonal sources of satisfaction are the primary forces propelling people toward a generative approach to society as a whole.

The applied topic of discrimination in the workplace provides evidence of societal stagnation. Often, it is middle adults in leadership positions who, by deliberate practice or informal example, set a tone that promotes the exclusion of certain workers on the basis of age, gender, racial or ethnic group, or other group characteristics. At the same time, others in middle adulthood suffer from discriminatory policies and are unable to reach the levels of achievement and contribution that their talents merit. Social policies and practices that interfere with individuals' abilities to perform meaningful work or to achieve recognition and respect for their work pose a hazard to individual psychosocial development and to the future of the social group. These practices, born from the core pathology of rejectivity, act in opposition to the fundamental needs of a society to care about its members and foster the most optimistic ambitions and goals possible in younger generations.

## Further Reflection

1. How do the demands of managing a career change from early to middle adulthood?
2. What are some examples of historical changes over the past 50 years that have increased strain on adults in their middle adult years?
3. How might the challenges of balancing work and family roles contribute to new directions for development and growth in middle adulthood?
4. How might generativity be expressed among people with limited education and few financial resources?

5. Why is creativity an especially important process for the resolution of the psychosocial crisis of middle adulthood?
6. What evidence do you see of workplace discrimination in the settings where you work? Where you go to school? Where you shop or do business? What are the psychosocial resources of earlier stages of life that might help a person cope with workplace discrimination?

## On the Web

**VISIT OUR WEBSITE**

Go to http://www.wadsworth.com/psychology to find online resources directly linked to your book.

## Casebook

For additional case material related to this chapter, see the case of "Annie and Career Contemplation," in *Life Span Development: A Case Book*, by Barbara and Philip Newman, Laura Landry-Meyer, and Brenda J. Lohman, pp. 176–179. In this case, Annie evaluates her current work situation in light of health concerns and a desire for greater personal satisfaction.

# CHAPTER 14

# LATER ADULTHOOD
# (60–75 YEARS)

*Clovis Sagot, 1909/Pablo Picasso/© 2005 Estate of Pablo Picasso/Artists Right Society (ARS), New York/Superstock*

*The integrating theme of later adulthood is a search for personal meaning. When older adults achieve a sense of integrity, it leads to inner peace and serves as a source of reassurance to the next generation.*

■ DEVELOPMENTAL TASKS

Accepting One's Life

CASE STUDY: GOAL ADJUSTMENT
IN LATER ADULTHOOD

Promoting Intellectual Vigor
Redirecting Energy to New Roles and Activities
Developing a Point of View about Death

CASE STUDY: MORRIE SCHWARTZ REFLECTS
ON HIS VIEWS ABOUT DEATH

■ THE PSYCHOSOCIAL CRISIS:
INTEGRITY VERSUS DESPAIR

Integrity
Despair

■ THE CENTRAL PROCESS: INTROSPECTION

■ THE PRIME ADAPTIVE EGO QUALITY
AND THE CORE PATHOLOGY

Wisdom
Disdain

■ APPLIED TOPIC: RETIREMENT

Adjustment to Retirement
Difficulties with Retirement

CASE STUDY: RETIREMENT AS
A RELEASE FROM TEDIOUS WORK

The Future of Retirement

■ CHAPTER SUMMARY

■ FURTHER REFLECTION

## CHAPTER OBJECTIVES

▶  *To explore the construct of life satisfaction in later adulthood and the factors associated with subjective well-being.*

▶  *To describe factors that promote intellectual vigor, with a focus on memory, postformal operational thought, crystallized and fluid intelligence; and to consider the interaction of heredity and environment on intelligence in later life.*

▶  *To examine the process of redirecting energy to new roles and activities, with special focus on role gain, such as grandparenthood; role loss, such as widowhood; and new opportunities for leisure.*

▶  *To describe the development of a point of view about death.*

▶  *To explain the psychosocial crisis of integrity versus despair, the central process of introspection, the prime adaptive ego quality of wisdom, and the core pathology of disdain.*

▶  *To apply theory and research to understanding the process of adjustment to retirement in later adulthood.*

IN THIS CHAPTER and the next, we consider the challenges, changes, and new avenues for development in later life. The French refer to the years from 60 onward as the "troisième age," the third stage of life (Rubenstein, 2002). One can think of the first 30 years of life as a period of construction and learning, when many avenues are open and the person is building the skills and knowledge to engage in the roles of adulthood. The second 30 years, from 30 to 60, are a period of enactment, when commitments established during identity formation are translated into roles and relationships. In this period, life is shaped by the interaction of work, family, and community demands and expectations. The individual strives to achieve personal ambitions and goals while coping with planned and unexpected changes in adjoining systems. The final 30 years are a period of reinvention. For many, this stage of life brings a gradual release from the daily demands of work and family and, depending on one's health and resources, provides the opportunity to invent a new life structure. This is a time when one faces both significant adversity and great joy.

Psychosocial theory assumes that new opportunities for growth emerge at each life stage. In strong contrast to the stereotype of aging as an undesirable process associated with accumulated deficits and decline, these chapters highlight continuous coping and adaptation. Like each of the preceding stages, later adulthood is marked by stressors, risks, and forces that can disrupt growth.

However, the epigenetic principle implies that one cannot understand the full unfolding of human life without appreci-

ating the beliefs, practices, and social relationships of those in later adulthood and old age. What is more, the interdependence of the stages in a human life story suggests that the ways in which older adults function and are treated will have immediate impact on the psychosocial development of individuals in all the earlier periods of life. The courage and vitality of older adults are sources of inspiration that motivate children and younger adults to continue facing the challenges of their daily lives with optimism.

The integrating theme of later adulthood is a search for personal meaning. On entering this stage, adults draw on the competence and creativity attained during middle adulthood to invent solutions to their changing conditions. As life progresses, motivation for achievement and power may give way to a desire for understanding and experimentation. The toddler's need to know why and the later adolescent's need to challenge and experiment with life roles provide earlier fields for learning the coping skills required in later life. The individual continues to be confronted with essential problems of definition and explanation during later adulthood. At this stage, adults apply the wealth of their life experiences, their perspective on time, and their adaptation to life crises to construct personally satisfying answers to the questions of life's meaning.

Physical, social, emotional, and intellectual development are intricately interrelated during later life. The more research is carried out on aspects of aging, the greater the appreciation for the fact that patterns of aging are neither universal nor irreversible. For example, although many older adults become more sedentary and lose aerobic capacity, others continue to perform strenuous labor and remain free from heart disease and respiratory difficulties. Many life conditions, especially poverty, malnutrition, poor sanitation, and limited health care, can accelerate the aging process. Other life conditions, such as access to a stimulating social environment, participation in a program of physical activity, and a well-balanced diet, can increase physical and intellectual functioning (Rowe & Kahn, 1998). It is essential to keep in mind individual differences in physical and mental health when thinking about patterns of growth in later adulthood.

For people in the United States who were 65 years old in 2001, the average life expectancy was an additional 16.4 years for men, and an additional 19.4 years for women (U.S. Census Bureau, 2003, Table No. 106); 78% of men and 86% of women in the birth cohort from 1935 lived to reach age 65 in the year 2000. Major improvements in hygiene, nutrition, preventive medicine, and medical treatments and technologies have allowed more people to experience a vigorous later adulthood today than was true 70 years ago. As a result, more and more people are facing the developmental tasks of later adulthood. ■

# DEVELOPMENTAL TASKS

The tasks discussed here reflect major themes that are likely to be confronted in the later years of life: accepting one's life and achieving a sense of life satisfaction; promoting intellectual vigor; redirecting energy to new roles and activities; and developing a point of view about death. These themes suggest new barriers to adaptation as well as new opportunities. Changes in memory and speed of neural processing may make the accomplishment of daily tasks more difficult. Role loss and the death of loved ones stimulate needs for new kinds of support and changes in daily lifestyle. They also convey a concrete message that a new period of life is under way. Success in these tasks requires considerable psychological effort. As the more structured roles of parent and worker become less demanding, a person has to find new sources of personal meaning and a new pattern to daily life. In some cultures, aging takes place in a context of reverence and high regard, which makes the loss of certain instrumental activities less significant. In other cultures, emphasis on autonomy, instrumentality, and achievement form a challenging context for the preservation of dignity in late life.

## ACCEPTING ONE'S LIFE

One of the significant challenges of aging is learning to accept the reality of one's life and formulate a vision of this new phase of later adulthood:

"Weren't you ever afraid to grow old?" I asked.

"Mitch, I *embrace* aging."

"Embrace it?"

"It's very simple. As you grow, you learn more. If you stayed at twenty-two, you'd always be as ignorant as you were at twenty-two. Aging is not just decay, you know. It's growth. It's more than the negative that you're going to die, it's also the positive that you *understand* you're going to die, and that you live a better life because of it." (Albom, 1997, p. 118)

By later adulthood, evidence about one's successes and failures in the major tasks of middle adulthood—marriage, childrearing, and work—has begun to accumulate. Data by which to judge one's adequacy in these areas are abundant. The process of accepting one's past life as it has been may be a difficult personal challenge. One must be able to incorporate certain areas of failure, crisis, or disappointment into one's self-image without being overburdened by a sense of inadequacy. Individuals also must be able to take pride in areas of achievement, even when those accomplishments fall short of personal expectations. At the same time, older adults face the work of defining new goals for the future.

Robert Peck (1968) explored the paths toward life satisfaction in later adulthood. His ideas emphasized the ability of the ego to transcend the role loss and physical disabilities associated with aging and to find satisfaction in new activities, new pleasures, and a sense of one's contribution to the lives of others. Peck highlighted three areas where adults have to reinvent their lives: work and family roles, physical activity, and committing to the lives of others. In each of these areas, the person in later adulthood needs to identify new goals and sources of satisfaction. Preoccupation with loss and incapacity are risks that stand in the way of life satisfaction.

## ■ LIFE GOALS AND SATISFACTION

The majority of older adults express a generally high level of life satisfaction. Nonetheless, they continue to aspire to new goals and strive for new levels of optimal functioning. A person's life goals and needs may change over the course of later adulthood, depending on life circumstances. Rather than viewing satisfaction in later adulthood solely in terms of wrapping things up and facing a roleless, undifferentiated future, older adults continue to formulate personal goals and assess their current life satisfaction in light of how well they are able to achieve those goals.

Brandtstadter (2002) considered the paradox that many older adults have high levels of life satisfaction even though they face serious stressors and physical limitations. He proposed a dual process model of coping that uses Piaget's ideas of assimilation and accommodation. In this view, a positive perspective on self and personal development in later life requires a balance between active goal pursuit and appropriate goal adjustment.

*Ray and Carla have more time for each other now that they are getting closer to retirement. Their happiness as a couple is an important source of life satisfaction.*

© Chuck Savage/The Stock Market

# CASE STUDY

## GOAL ADJUSTMENT IN LATER ADULTHOOD

*Orville Gilbert Brim, who contributed to the field of human development through his work on social role theory (see Chapter 4), became increasingly interested in ambition and self-directed goal attainment in adulthood. He describes his father's successful adaptations in later life as an example of this process (Brim, 1992):*

Brim's father, also named Orville, lived to be 103. He was born in a small farming community in a rural area of Ohio in 1883. After receiving his bachelor's degree in education at Valparaiso University, he taught school in a one-room school house for 2 years and then became principal of a high school in Indiana. Eventually he left the rural Midwest to attend Harvard and then Columbia to get his PhD. He was a professor at Ohio State University until he retired at age 60. Then Orville and his wife, Helen, bought an abandoned farm of several hundred acres in Connecticut, remodeled the farmhouse, and settled into farming. In the early years of retirement, he cleared and thinned the trees on the hills and mountains of his farm. After a while, he stopped working the hillsides and planted a large vegetable and flower garden. Orville tilled the garden with a power tiller. When he was 90, he bought a riding tractor. When he could no longer manage the large garden, he focused on a small border garden and four large window boxes that he planted with flowers. As his eyesight became more impaired, he shifted from reading to listening to "talking books," and when he had to give up actually planting the window boxes, he enjoyed watering them and looking at the flowers. Orville approached each

new challenge of physical decline by correctly assessing his abilities, investing in a new project, and taking pride in his achievements within that domain.

### ■ CRITICAL THINKING AND CASE ANALYSIS

1. How does this case reflect Brandtstadter's ideas about assimilation and accommodation of goals in later adulthood?
2. In this case, Brim's father drew on early life experiences growing up on a farm to guide his goals in later adulthood. What are some other examples of how earlier life roles might be integrated into a satisfying lifestyle in later adulthood?
3. What are some of the resources Brim's father had that allowed him to achieve new goals for mastery?
4. Based on Peck's views about the challenges for ego development in later adulthood, what might be missing in Brim's father's approach to adaptation?

In a study of older adult volunteers, participants were asked to describe the personal goals that were most important to their life satisfaction (Rapkin & Fischer, 1992a, 1992b). The 10 groups of life goals listed in Table 14.1 all relate to daily life concerns. These goals were used to create five clusters of older adults:

1. a *high-demand* group of people, who had many goals that were seen as important or vital to their life satisfaction;
2. an *age-prescribed* group that was concerned with safety, security, and increased dependence on services, and that showed a preference for disengagement from activities and social relationships;
3. a *self-focused* group that was especially concerned about having an easy life with little regard for safety, security, or independence;

**Table 14.1** Personal Goals of Older Adults

| GOAL | DEFINITION |
|---|---|
| Active improvement | To actively improve or increase involvement in many domains of life |
| Maintenance of social values and relationships | To maintain reciprocal social relationships and community ties, to uphold religious beliefs, and to be financially self-sufficient |
| Disengagement | To reduce social and community obligations, to increase religious involvement, and to remain independent from social services |
| Energetic lifestyle | To be romantically involved and physically attractive, to be energetic and healthy, to get around independently, and to improve one's living situation |
| Safety and security | To worry about safety and security in the neighborhood and in getting around, avoiding health hazards and financial problems |
| Stability | To worry about stability in the neighborhood and predictability in the health-care system |
| Increased reliance on services | Not to be troubled with having to solve problems and wanting to be able to rely on services to meet one's needs |
| Easy life | To be able to be impulsive, do what one wants, stay independent from family, live in comfort, and have plenty of leisure time |
| Reduced activity | To reduce volunteer activities because of poor health |
| Independence in living | To live independently and to have privacy |

Source: Based on Rapkin and Fischer, 1992a.

4. a *socially engaged* group that had strong concerns about independence and maintaining their social roles and relationships; and

5. a *low-demand* group that had few goals except for reducing activity and disengaging.

In a comparison of these five groups, the socially engaged group had significantly lower scores in depression than the other four. They had the highest score in self-esteem, whereas the self-focused group had the lowest self-esteem. An implication of this research is that life satisfaction must be understood in the context of how each person frames his or her contemporary situation and his or her view of the future. Individual differences in satisfaction are due in part to how well people are able to achieve what they perceive as most possible and desirable as they face the challenges of aging.

In a longitudinal study, men who had participated in the Terman Study of Gifted Children when they were in early childhood were interviewed about their life satisfaction at ages 58–72. Four styles of adaptation emerged: (1) poorly adjusted, (2) career focused but socially disengaged, (3) family focused, and (4) well rounded. Health and socioeconomic resources were generally predictive of life satisfaction for the group as a whole. Goals related to family life and religious life provided a greater sense of meaning, social benefits, and emotional support than occupational goals, especially for the family-focused and well-rounded groups (Crosnoe & Elder, 2002). The family-focused and well-rounded groups had many areas of similarity, as did the career-focused and the poorly adjusted groups. There is some suggestion that people who place too great a priority on occupational attainment during middle adulthood may find it difficult to reorient toward satisfying life goals in later adulthood.

## ■ PERSONALITY AND WELL-BEING

We all know people who have lived difficult lives yet appear to be full of zest and enthusiasm. We also know people who appear to have had the benefits of many of life's resources yet are continually complaining about problems. Whether specific events will contribute to feelings of satisfaction or dismay depends on how they are interpreted. Some people are more likely to be grumblers; others are more likely to be celebrants of life. In response to this reality, some researchers have looked to personality factors to predict subjective life satisfaction in later adulthood (Ryff, Kwan, & Singer, 2001). The construct of *personality*, which is typically viewed as stable across situations, provides ways of understanding individual differences in coping, goal orientation, and self-evaluative processes. Personality dimensions interact with changing life tasks to produce individual differences in the ways these tasks are interpreted.

Five personality characteristics have been linked with life satisfaction in later life: extroversion, lack of neuroticism, usefulness/competence, optimism, and a sense of control (Costa, Metter, & McCrae, 1994). **Extroversion** includes such qualities as sociability, vigor, sensation seeking, and positive emotions. People who are outgoing and who enjoy social interaction tend also to report high levels of life satisfaction. A personality dimension described as **neuroticism** is characterized by anxiety, hostility, and impulsiveness. People who are neurotic experience discouragement, unhappiness, and hopelessness. For them, real-life events are screened and interpreted through a negative filter, resulting in low levels of satisfaction. Another personality factor associated with well-being and high self-esteem in older adults is **usefulness/ competence**. This quality is associated with informal volunteer work, higher levels of involvement with others, and a greater sense of purpose and structure in the use of time (Ranzijn, Keeves, Luszcz, & Feather, 1998).

**Optimism** is also a predictor of life satisfaction. Optimism is a belief that one's decisions will lead to positive consequences and that uncertain situations will turn out well. Under conditions of uncertainty and stress, adults who are optimistic have less depression, greater hopefulness, and, as a result, a greater sense of well-being (Chang & Sanna, 2001).

A sense of control is systematically associated with life satisfaction (McConatha, McConatha, Jackson, & Bergen, 1998). Life experiences such as engaging in physical activity, the opportunity to select one's leisure activities, or the ability to decide when to retire are all examples of factors that can improve an older adult's sense of control. Loss of financial resources and social support or reduced physical resilience can diminish this sense.

### ▪ ILLNESS AND HEALTH

The ability to experience a sense of well-being and acceptance of one's life is associated with physical health. In addition to an increase in vulnerability to acute illnesses, such as influenza, more than 80% of people over the age of 65 have at least one chronic condition such as arthritis. Chronic illnesses are long-lasting and can be characterized by periods of intense illness followed by periods of remission or by progressive decline. The most common chronic conditions in the 65–74 age range are arthritis, hearing impairments, heart conditions, and high blood pressure (U.S. Bureau of the Census, 2000).

Heart disease is the leading cause of death for men and women in the United States. However, it begins about 10 years earlier for men than for women. After menopause, the risk of heart disease for women increases. What is more, women are less likely than men to be accurately diagnosed as suffering from a heart attack, are less likely to recover from it, and are more likely to suffer the complications of stroke. The lifestyle factors associated with heart disease are about the same for men and women. However, men are more likely to be at risk because they do not get the physical activity they need; they eat more meat and fat and less fruit and fiber than women; they are less likely to go to the doctor for regular check-ups; and they are generally more likely to deny being sick (Guttman, 1998).

Longitudinal studies of men consistently find that current health status and functional autonomy are significant predictors of life satisfaction (Crosnoe & Elder, 2002; Vaillant & Western, 2001). However, the relationship of health to life satisfaction is likely to be mediated by personality, resources, and personal goals. A chronic illness, such as arthritis, may result in a significant loss of control and reduced opportuni-

*In his later life, Renoir suffered from severe arthritis. To compensate, he tied paint brushes to his hands so that he could continue to function in this highly valued domain.*

ties for physical activity or social interaction. A person who is characterized by a neurotic personality may be more discouraged and embittered by these losses than one who is less neurotic. A person whose leisure activities have focused on physical activities, such as skiing or running, may find the restrictions of arthritis more frustrating than someone whose hobbies and lifestyle are more sedentary.

### ▪ THE SOC MODEL

Over the life span, people confront the challenges of balancing and matching a variety of opportunities with fluctuations in resources (Freund & Baltes, 1998). At every period of life, there are limited resources—whether time, energy, or money—to address all the opportunities that present themselves. For example, in later adulthood, a person may want to continue to work (an opportunity) but find that a chronic heart condition makes it difficult to bring the required energy and resilience to the task (loss of a resource). According to the *SOC model*, adaptation requires the integration of three processes:

Selection: Identifying the opportunities or domains of activity that are of the greatest value or importance.
Optimization: Allocating and refining resources in order to achieve higher levels of functioning in the selected domains.

Compensation: Under conditions of reduced resources, identifying strategies to counteract the loss and minimize the negative impact on functioning in the selected domains.

In later life, adults are inevitably faced with changes in resources. They may have more time but less physical stamina and fewer financial resources. Life satisfaction and a sense of well-being are linked to selecting specific goals as important areas of functioning and then effectively directing both internal (e.g., energy, thought, planning) and external (e.g., hiring help, taking classes, technical assistance) resources in order to maximize their level of functioning. As this model implies, demographic factors alone—such as gender, race, age, and income—are not adequate predictors of life satisfaction. Instead, well-being rests on an ability to manage or reduce the impact of stressful life events by directing resources in order to continue engaging in valued roles and activities (Hamarat et al., 2001; Salvatore & Sastre, 2001).

## ERIKSON ON ACCEPTING ONE'S LIFE

Erikson et al. (1986) highlighted the importance of trust in the acceptance of one's life:

> The life cycle, however, does more than extend itself into the next generation. It curves back on the life of the individual, allowing, as we have indicated, a reexperiencing of earlier stages in a new form. This retracing might be described as a growth toward death, if that did not ring false as a metaphor. Maples and aspens every October bear flamboyant witness to this possibility of a final spurt of growth. Nature unfortunately has not ordained that mortals put on such a fine show.
>
> As aging continues, in fact, human bodies begin to deteriorate and physical and psychosocial capacities diminish in a seeming reversal of the course their development takes. When physical frailty demands assistance, one must accept again an appropriate dependence without the loss of trust and hope. The old, of course, are not endowed with the endearing survival skills of the infant. Old bodies are more difficult to care for, and the task itself is less satisfying to the caretaker than that of caring for infants. Such skills as elders possess have been hard won and are maintained only with determined grace. Only a lifetime of slowly developing trust is adequate to meet this situation, which so naturally elicits despair and disgust at one's own helplessness. Of how many elders could one say, "He surrendered every vestige of his old life with a sort of courteous, half humorous gentleness"? (p. 327)

## PROMOTING INTELLECTUAL VIGOR

Memory, reasoning, information processing, problem-solving abilities, and mental rigidity or fluidity all influence an adult's capacity to introspect, select meaningful goals, manage changing resources, and plan for the future. These intellectual capacities also influence the adult's ability to remain involved in productive work, advise and guide others, and invent new solutions to the problems of daily life. The person's capacity to cope with the challenges of later adulthood depend on the ability to promote and sustain intellectual vigor.

How can one understand cognitive functioning and change in later life? The study of intelligence and cognition in later adulthood is plagued by practical and theoretical challenges that make it difficult to make broad generalizations. In the following section, we review four problems associated with the study of intelligence and aging. Specific topics are then discussed, including memory, postformal operational reasoning, and an overview of age-related changes in various mental abilities. The focus then shifts to an analysis of the impact of heredity and environment on intelligence, and factors that help to sustain high levels of intellectual functioning in later life.

## PROBLEMS IN DEFINING AND STUDYING INTELLIGENCE IN LATER ADULTHOOD

The primary goals in the study of development are to describe and explain patterns of change and continuity over time. Four problems arise in evaluating the research on intelligence in later life (Stuart-Hamilton, 1996). First, one must differentiate between *age differences* and *age changes*. Suppose that in a cross-sectional study conducted in 2000, 70-year-olds performed less well on tests of flexible problem solving than 40-year-olds. The difference may be clear, but it may not be a result of age alone. The 70-year-olds would have been born in 1930, and the 40-year-olds in 1960. Differences in performance may be a product of different educational opportunities, varying experiences with standardized tests, or other cohort-related factors. Educational opportunities increased markedly during the 20th century, so that younger cohorts are much more likely to have benefited from formal schooling at both the high school and college levels (U.S. Bureau of the Census, 2000). For example, only 10% of people ages 65–74 in 2000 had completed a bachelor's degree; whereas 18% of adults ages 35–44 had attained that level of education. In the older cohort, 26% had not graduated from high school, compared to 11% in the younger cohort. Advanced education is associated with greater reflectiveness, flexibility, and relativistic thinking. People who have attended college have been exposed to the scientific process as a way of gaining knowledge and, as a result, are more likely to consider that their understanding of the world is tentative pending new information or new technologies (King & Kitchener, 1994; Labouvie-Vief & Diehl, 2000).

In cross-sectional studies of cognitive functioning, historical factors may be confounded with developmental or aging factors that may contribute to observed differences in performance. In longitudinal studies that follow change over time, if only one cohort is sampled, it is impossible to tell whether changes from one period to the next are products of age and development or of particular resources and deficits characterizing that particular generation.

A second problem is the *definition of abilities*. **Cognitive functioning** is a broad term that encompasses such varied abilities as vocabulary, problem solving, and short-term memory. It is possible that the pattern of change in abilities with age depends on which abilities are tested. Some abilities are frequently used and have been developed to a high level of efficiency. For example, an architect is more likely to retain abilities in spatial relations and reasoning than is someone whose lifework is not intimately connected with the construction and organization of spatial dimensions.

A third related problem is the *relevance of the tasks* used to measure adult cognitive functioning. The definition of intelligence that is used in the design and application of most intelligence tests refers to capacities that are predictive of school-related success. The criteria for assessing adult intelligence are necessarily more varied than the ability to succeed in a school curriculum. Furthermore, motivational factors come into play in the measurement of intelligence. This raises the distinction between *ability* and *performance*. If a test is perceived as irrelevant or unimportant, an adult may not give much effort to performing well (Dixon, 1992).

Finally, *factors associated with health* are intertwined with the functioning of older adults, although they are often not directly measured. A number of age-related diseases have an impact on an individual's ability to learn and retain new information. However, the boundaries between what might be considered normal cognitive changes associated with age and disease-related changes are not easy to detect, especially in the early stages of an illness (Albert, 2002). In a longitudinal study of intelligence, Riegel and Riegel (1972) found clear declines in performance among participants who died before the next testing period. Vocabulary skills, which normally remain high or continue to show increases with age, are especially likely to decline in older individuals who will die within the coming few years (White & Cunningham, 1988). Adults who are in the early stages of dementia but who have not yet been diagnosed as suffering from the disease are often included in samples described as "normal" or "normative." This inclusion lowers the mean of the total group and overestimates the negative association of age and intelligence (Sliwinski, Hofer, Hall, Buschke, & Lipton, 2003). At each older age, the inclusion of adults who are in an early phase of a progressive illness lowers the average performance of the group as a whole.

### ■ MEMORY

Several aspects of cognitive functioning, including reaction time, visual-motor flexibility (the translation of visual information into new motor responses), and memory show evidence of decline with age. The exact nature of changes in memory with age are a topic of active and ongoing research (Giambra, Arenberg, Zonderman, & Kawas, 1995; Johnson, 2003). A common model of memory functions breaks memory into three forms: the sensory register, short-term memory, and long-term memory. In this model, the **sensory register** is the neurological processing activity that is required to take in visual, auditory, tactile, and olfactory information. Speed of processing, which is most closely linked to the sensory register, can be slowed as a result of illness. Illness does not seem to affect higher order aspects of memory, particularly the recall of past life events (Rosnick et al., 2004). **Short-term memory** is the working capacity to encode and retrieve five to nine bits of information in the span of a minute or two. This is the "scratch pad" of memory that is used when someone tells you a telephone number or gives you his or her address. **Long-term memory** is a complex network of information, concepts, and schemes related by associations, knowledge, and use. It is the storehouse of a lifetime of information. Remembering something for more than a few minutes involves moving the information from short-term to long-term memory, storing it in relation to other associated knowledge, and being able to recognize, retrieve, or reconstruct it at a later time (Hultsch & Dixon, 1990).

The memory functions most relevant to an understanding of cognitive ability in aging have to do with the ability to transfer information from short-term to long-term memory and then retrieve it. Studies that compare the short-term memory abilities of older and younger adults find that age is not associated directly with the capacity of short-term memory but with the ability to transfer newly learned information to long-term memory and then retrieve it on demand. Older adults are just as effective as younger adults in recognizing information that was learned in the past, but they have difficulty summoning up a specific name or number when they want to find it (Rowe & Kahn, 1998).

Furthermore, older adults find that their memory functions are especially likely to be disrupted under conditions in which information is presented rapidly and contextual cues are absent. Older adults rely on meaning to store and retrieve new information. For example, in a memory task involving the recall of five- and eight-word strings, older adults (ages 65–73) retained fewer words than younger adults (ages 18–22) when the word strings were presented at high speed and were not arranged in a meaningful sentence. However, the speed of presentation did not significantly reduce recall when the words were arranged in a normal semantic order (Wingfield, Poon, Lombardi, & Lowe, 1985).

With each passing year of life, there is more to remember. We do not really know the limits of the storage capacity of long-term memory. Studies of memory focus on different kinds of tasks, each with its own trajectory of growth and decline. **Semantic memory** focuses on basic knowledge, such as recalling the meaning of words like *vegetable*, *democracy*, or *insect*. Once learned, semantic memory seems very resistant to loss. People continue to grow in the accumulation of new ideas and information over adulthood.

**Episodic memory** focuses on specific situations and data. Measures of episodic memory may ask people to recall words from a list or remember what they had for breakfast 3 days ago. With age, so many daily events and bits of information are encountered that unless the events have some particular importance, they may not be encoded, or they may become difficult to retrieve in the accumulated network of memories.

A third type of memory task is called **prospective memory**. This is memory about events or actions taking place in the future. An example would be remembering to take your pills at 4 p.m. or to call your husband when you arrive at the hotel after traveling on a business trip. This type of memory task requires recalling that something needs to happen at a future time or under some future condition, and also remembering specifically what needs to be done. Older adults do not do as well as young adults on prospective memory tasks in laboratory conditions. However, in naturalistic studies, the older adults do better than the young adults (Henry, MacLeod, Phillips, & Crawford, 2004). Prospective memory is a critical component of adaptive coping, and older adults use a variety of strategies to help stay attuned to their functional future.

Research using the narrative method suggests that people *construct* memories that make sense of their past. They tell a story about the past that puts events in a chronological sequence, highlighting events that, in retrospect, are important achievements or turning points. For example, in one study, participants were asked to provide a narrative about a time when they said, thought, or did something "wise." Adolescents, young and old adults were all able to retell experiences where wisdom helped them to turn a negative experience into something positive. Adults were also able to describe how the wisdom experience helped shape their outlook or life philosophy (Bluck & Gluck, 2004). Memory may be used in a new way in later adulthood in order to resolve the conflict of integrity versus despair. Memory is used to recall and evaluate certain life events that may preoccupy one's attention until the role of these events can be integrated into a meaningful sense of one's purpose. This process may interfere with an adult's ability to attend to current minutiae or to rehearse and recall new information.

There is wide variability in people's memory skills. Measurement of changes in memory across different types of tasks suggests more stability than change over much of adulthood (Zelinski & Lewis, 2003). Some people pay great attention to details and are more able to recall them. Others ignore many details and are not able to retrieve them. A salesman or a politician may have a knack for remembering the names of friends, acquaintances, and their family members. A historian may have a memory for historical events and personalities. A police detective may pay great attention to the details of the physical environment from specific cases. As the demands of work and family life accumulate, people adapt by focusing attention on the details and events that are most salient for their success. Over time, the differences in people's approaches to what they have learned, recalled, and found useful in coping with life shape the context for whether and how new information is encoded and retrieved.

In addition to actual declines in some kinds of memory performance, older adults complain of memory problems. It is interesting that even after participating in programs de-

signed to improve memory performance, these complaints persist (Scogin, Storandt, & Lott, 1985). Anxiety and frustration over memory loss nag many older adults, even those whose memory performance has not dramatically declined. However, memory complaints may reflect the person's accurate subjective assessment of a slowing in the retrieval process (Jonker, Launer, Hooijer, & Lindeboom, 1996). The seriousness of the memory complaints and people's assessment of whether they can do anything to improve their memory combine to influence older adults' worries about memory loss and their general sense of well-being (Verhaeghen, Geraerts, & Marcoen, 2000).

## ■ POSTFORMAL OPERATIONAL THINKING

Research based on the standard Piagetian tasks has been criticized for its lack of relevance and familiarity to older participants. The traditional tasks are dominated by the role of pure logic, disconnected from the situation. They emphasize problems that have a scientific rather than a pragmatic focus. Although the solution to most formal operational problems requires the manipulation of multiple variables, there is typically only one correct solution. For example, in the pendulum problem described in Chapter 10 (Early Adolescence), four factors can be varied: the mass of the object, the height from which the pendulum is pushed, the force with which it is pushed, and the length of the string. However, only the length of the string influences the speed of the pendulum. In adult life, most problems involve multiple dimensions with changing or poorly defined variables and more than one solution. For example, given my limited resources, should I buy more life insurance, put cash in a certificate of deposit, or invest in the stock and bond market to best protect my family's financial future?

As a result of these limitations or criticisms of formal operational reasoning, scholars have formulated a view of **postformal thought**, which has been characterized in the following ways:

- A greater reliance on reflection on self, emotions, values, and the specific situation in addressing a problem.
- A willingness to shift gears or take a different approach depending on the specific problem.
- An ability to draw on personal knowledge to find pragmatic solutions.
- An awareness of the contradictions in life and a willingness to try to include conflicting or contradictory thoughts, emotions, and experiences in finding a solution.
- A flexible integration of cognition and emotion so that solutions are adaptive, reality oriented, and emotionally satisfying.
- An enthusiasm for seeking new questions, finding new problems, and new frameworks for understanding experience.

People who operate with postformal thought do not do so in every situation. When a problem has clear parameters

*People with academic backgrounds in science and engineering continue to use their formal operational problem-solving skills well into later life.*

© Cindy Charles/Photo Edit

and needs a single solution, concrete or formal operations will work. However, when a problem is value laden, ambiguous, or involves many interpersonal implications, postformal thinking comes into play (Labouvie-Vief, 1992; Sinnott & Cavanaugh, 1991).

Given the complexity of adult life, adaptive problem solving requires flexibility, differentiation of positive and negative aspects of a single alternative, and the ability to consider the implications of a course of action. Increasingly, problem solving becomes a social task, where several people or groups of people work together to arrive at solutions. A component of postformal reasoning includes the ability to collaborate with others, balancing the interpersonal and the analytical aspects of the work. Because members of groups are vulnerable to pressures toward conformity or groupthink, it is important for individuals to retain their capacity to differentiate or distance themselves from the group in order to examine the group's product in a more objective light.

## ■ PATTERNS OF CHANGE IN DIFFERENT MENTAL ABILITIES

Cognitive functioning involves the coordination of a variety of mental abilities that change as a result of experience and aging. John Horn (1979) proposed that the course of mental abilities across the life span is not uniform. Some areas are strengthened, and others decline. Horn suggested differentiating **crystallized intelligence** ($G_c$) and **fluid intelligence** ($G_f$). $G_c$ is the ability to bring knowledge accumulated through past learning into play in appropriate situations. $G_f$ is the ability to impose organization on information and generate new hypotheses. Both kinds of intelligence are required for optimal human functioning.

$G_c$ and $G_f$ can be identified as integrated structures in both early and later adulthood (Hayslip & Brookshire, 1985;

McArdle, Ferrer-Caja, Hamagami, & Woodcock, 2002). However, Horn argued that the two kinds of thinking draw on somewhat different neurological and experiential sources. $G_c$ reflects the consequences of life experiences within a society. Socialization in the family; exposure to the media; and participation in school, work, and community settings all emphasize the use and improvement of $G_c$. $G_c$ increases with age, experience, and physical maturation, and remains at a high level of functioning throughout adulthood.

$G_f$ is characteristic of what is meant by the expression that someone has a "good head on his or her shoulders." Finding a general relationship and applying it without having been schooled in that problem-solving area is an example of $G_f$, as is being able to approach new problems logically, systematically, and quickly. Horn hypothesized that $G_f$ depends more on the specific number of neurons available for its functioning than does $G_c$. Thus, neurological loss would be more damaging to $G_f$ than to $G_c$. Subsequent research has supported the notion that neural efficiency, often recognized through changes in sensory functioning and speed of response, is closely related to fluid intelligence and shows an age-related decline, independent of disease (Baltes & Lindenberger, 1997). However, the extent of this decline may be related to the domain in which it is studied. For example, one study focused on men who had different levels of expertise in playing the game of Go. Measures of reasoning, memory, and cognitive speed were developed to apply specifically to that game. Older players generally showed the expected decline in deductive reasoning and cognitive speed. However, for those older men who were very expert players, no decline was observed (Masunaga & Horn, 2000). The implication is that in areas where there is highly developed expertise, aging is not necessarily accompanied by declines in either $G_f$ or $G_c$.

K. Warner Schaie (Hertzog & Schaie, 1988; Schaie, 1994; Schaie & Hertzog, 1983) reported on the results of a 35-year

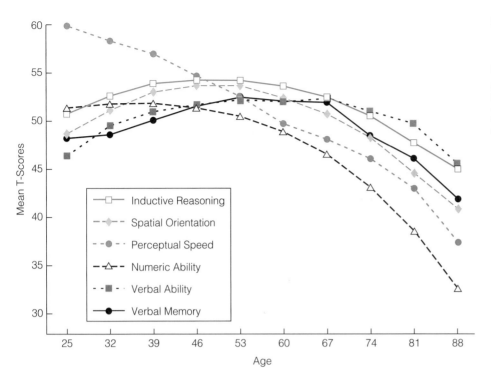

**FIGURE 14.1**

Longitudinal Estimates of Mean Factor Scores for the Six Ability Constructs

Source: From "The Course of Adult Intellectual Development," by K. W. Schaie, 1994, *American Psychologist, 49*, pp. 304–313. Copyright © 1994 American Psychological Association. Reprinted by permission.

cohort sequential study of adult intellectual development. The youngest participants had an average age of 25, the oldest an average age of 88. Six mental abilities were measured: inductive reasoning, spatial orientation, perceptual speed, numeric ability, verbal ability, and verbal memory. In general, the longitudinal data showed less decrement with age than did the cross-sectional data (see Figure 14.1). Verbal ability showed no decline between age 25 and 88. Perceptual speed and numeric ability showed the greatest declines. The rate of decline in performance was modest but consistent when participants were in their late 60s, and more substantial in their 80s. Once factors associated with the slowing of processing and response time were taken into account, however, the degree of decline with advanced age was notably smaller. The variation within age groups in the sample remained stable over time. In other words, even though measured intelligence changed over time, the position of one person in relation to another in the same age group remained about the same. People who were high functioning in one ability area remained high functioning in comparison to their age group over time.

## ■ THE INTERACTION OF HEREDITY AND ENVIRONMENT ON MENTAL FUNCTIONING

For years, it was assumed that the environment played an increasingly major role in intellectual functioning over time. The accumulation of life experiences, education, and socialization were expected to introduce new bases of knowledge and problem-solving structures. Recent work suggests that the construct of the **reaction range**, introduced in Chapter 5 (Pregnancy and Prenatal Development), provides a more appropriate framework for understanding intelligence in adulthood. Genetic factors, early childhood family environment, and contemporary work and family environments all contribute to adult cognitive functioning (DeFrias & Schaie, 2001; Schaie & Zuo, 2001). Research on identical and fraternal twins who were 80 years or older found that the heritability of general cognitive ability was about 60% (McClearn et al., 1997). In other words, genetic factors substantially contribute to the stability of cognitive capacities over the life span.

Given the strong contribution of heredity to cognitive ability, its expression in observable behavior depends on the nature of the environment. Roughly 30% of the variability between twins was accounted for by their environment—both the shared environment reflected in growing up in the same family and community and the unshared environment, including the different interactions they had with their parents, other siblings and friends, and their participation in different types of educational and social settings. The stimulating or stifling nature of the environment—including access to social support, the quality of health care, exposure to disease, and opportunities for continuing involvement in challenging work—transforms the genotype into an observed phenotype (Gottesman, 1997).

The noted learning theorist B. F. Skinner (1983) described some possible environmental qualities that fail to reinforce systematic thinking or new ideas in aging people. Many people who live alone, for example, lack the diversity of social interaction that produces cognitive discrepancy and new concepts. Older people may be reinforced for talking about the past. Their recollections of early memories are interesting to students and younger colleagues. However, preoccupation with these reminiscences does not encourage thinking in new directions.

APPLYING THEORY AND RESEARCH TO LIFE

## Age and Workplace Productivity

HOW ARE CHANGES in cognitive functioning related to productivity in the workplace? The relationship of creative productivity to age has been studied since the early 1800s, and a common picture has emerged. The number of a person's creative products, such as articles, paintings, musical compositions, or scientific papers, increases steadily into the late 30s and 40s, and then the rate gradually declines. The age at the peak of productivity depends in part on the field. For mathematicians and physicists, the peak is often earlier than in the humanities and social sciences (Simonton, 1990).

Although the pattern of decline in productivity in the later years is well documented, several points color the interpretation of this pattern (Simonton, 1991, 1997):

1. Although the rate of productivity declines, it does not necessarily fall to zero. Even if a person's productive output is less at age 65 than at age 40, this does not mean that there is no output at all. The average rate of productivity in the 60s is about half what it was during the 30s and 40s. So if scholars are writing four articles a year for scientific journals at their peak, they may be writing one or two articles a year toward the end of their academic careers.

In his later adulthood, actor Paul Newman continues to be creative in films and theater. He also owns a company, Newman's Own, which donates its profits for the relief of refugees and war victims, among other causes.

2. The productivity curve differs by discipline, perhaps due to the different demands for information processing and reliance on $G_c$ versus $G_f$ aspects of intelligence. In some fields, there is almost no documented decline at all into the 50s and 60s; in other fields, such as pure mathematics, the peak is early and dramatic. This suggests that there is no systematic age-related

decline in cognitive functioning that interferes with productive work.

3. The quality of the work is related to the quantity. The period when one is most active tends to be the period when one produces work of the greatest quality as well. So the number of quality contributions may go down in later life as a result of the overall decline in output, but the ratio of quality to quantity remains about the same.

4. There are impressive differences in productivity across individuals. Some older artists or scholars are producing more at their 50% rate than younger artists or scholars who simply do not produce as much, even at their peak.

5. Evidence of a "renaissance" of creative energy often observed during the decade of the 60s and 70s suggests that the capacity for career achievement is not undermined by normal aging. As adults perceive that they may be approaching the end of their career, they may be especially inspired to make a distinctive statement through their art or discipline. Late works or career "swan songs" are often marked by a profound simplicity and originality that set them apart from earlier work and illustrate a special facet of the person's creative potential.

Skinner claimed that one is more likely to repeat oneself as one ages. He suggested that it may be important for older adults to move into new areas of work in order to prevent repetition of old ideas. Skinner believed that it is possible to analyze how the quality of one's thinking is influenced by the circumstances of aging and also to identify interventions that will prevent the deterioration of cognitive abilities. These interventions include attempts to be sensitive to the signs of fatigue, planning for regular opportunities for stimulating verbal interactions with others, making careful outlines of written work to avoid distraction, and acting on ideas as they come to one's mind rather than counting on remembering them later.

Cognitive functioning in later adulthood is multidimensional, with substantial differences among individuals as well as differences among cognitive domains within the same per-

son (McArdle et al., 2002). Adults experience tremendous growth in domain-specific areas of knowledge. Within these domains, many complex networks of information, strategies, and frameworks of meaning are elaborated that result in high-level, flexible functioning. The overall level of functioning is subject to environmental influences that promote particular specialization and cognitive organization based on the demands of the situation, the stresses and challenges of daily life, and the opportunities for mastery in particular areas of competence. At the same time, certain aspects of the processing base that are dependent on neural functioning may decline with age. This decline, however, is not always great, and studies have shown that capacities described as elements of fluid intelligence, such as speed of response, inductive reasoning, and spatial orientation, can benefit from targeted interventions (Saczynski, Willis, & Schaie, 2002; Van Boxtel, Paas, Houx, & Adam, 1997). The implications of age-related changes in cognitive functioning are discussed in the box about Age and Workplace Productivity.

On the basis of extensive longitudinal research, Schaie (1994) identified seven factors that are associated with retaining a high level of cognitive functioning in later adulthood:

1. Absence of cardiovascular and other chronic diseases
2. Favorable environment linked to high socioeconomic status
3. Involvement in a complex and intellectually stimulating environment
4. Flexible personality style at midlife
5. High cognitive functioning of spouse
6. Maintenance of a high level of perceptual processing speed
7. Rating oneself as being satisfied with life accomplishments in midlife

This list illustrates the interplay of the biological, psychological, and social systems that contribute to cognitive functioning in the later years. Retaining one's intellectual complexity and creative problem-solving skills are closely linked to the ability to cope with the inevitable role transitions that occur in later life.

## REDIRECTING ENERGY TO NEW ROLES AND ACTIVITIES

Role transition, role gain, and role loss occur in every period of the life span. In later adulthood, however, a convergence of role transitions is likely to lead to a revision of major life functions and a reformulation of one's lifestyle. Roles are lost through widowhood, retirement, and the death of friends. At the same time, new roles, such as grandparent, senior adviser, or community leader, require the formation of new patterns of behavior and relationships.

### ■ GRANDPARENTHOOD

The role of *grandparent* may require a renewal of parenting skills that have been stored away along with the bottle sterilizer and potty chair. Grandparents begin to renew their acquaintance with the delights of childhood, including diapering the baby; telling fairy tales; taking trips to the zoo; and having the pleasure of small helping hands with baking, gardening, or carpentry. A person's parenting skills, patience, and knowledge come into play in a new configuration and may be more in demand in the grandparent role than they were in the parent role.

**GRANDPARENTING STYLES.** Grandparenthood involves a three-generational family system. The average age for becoming a grandparent is in the decade of the 50s, resulting in the potential of a 20- to 30-year relationship with one's grandchildren (Giarrusso, Silverstein, & Bengston, 1996). The enactment of the grandparent role depends on the timing of

entry into this role and on the outlook or interest of each generation in having interactions and access to one another. The quality of the grandparent–grandchild relationship is negotiated through the adult child and is likely to change as the grandchildren mature (Smith & Drew, 2002).

People differ in the way they enact the grandparent role. In one of the first empirical studies of grandparenthood, Neugarten and Weinstein (1964) interviewed the grandparents in 70 middle class families. The following five grandparenting styles were identified, each expressing a distinct interpretation of the role:

1. *Formal.* This type of grandparent was interested in the grandchildren but careful not to become involved in parenting them other than by occasional baby-sitting.
2. *Funseeker.* This type of grandparent had informal, playful interactions with the grandchildren, enjoying mutually self-indulgent fun with them.
3. *Surrogate parent.* This style was especially likely for grandmothers who assumed major child care responsibilities when the mother worked outside the home.
4. *Reservoir of family wisdom.* This style was an authoritarian relationship in which a grandparent, usually the grandfather, dispensed skills and resources. Parents as well as grandchildren were subordinate to this older authority figure.
5. *Distant figure.* This type of grandparent appeared on birthdays and holidays but generally had little contact with the grandchildren.

More than 35 years later, Bengston (2001) offered a revised picture of the nature of multigenerational family bonds. His research was based on the Longitudinal Study of Generations (LSOG), begun in 1971, and continuing with data collection every 3 years to the present. The study is based on more than 2,000 members of three-generational families, allowing the assessment of relationship characteristics between parents and their adult children, adult children and their children, and grandparents and grandchildren. The study highlights that the way a person enacts the grandparent role is not only a product of his or her personal definition of the role, but also a result of how the interconnected family members permit and support intergenerational interactions.

The LSOG identified five aspects of **intergenerational solidarity**—a construct that reflects closeness and commitment within the parent–child and grandparent–grandchild relationships. These dimensions were as follows:

1. *Affectional solidarity*: feelings of affection and emotional closeness
2. *Associational solidarity*: type and frequency of contact
3. *Consensual solidarity*: agreement in opinions and expectations
4. *Functional solidarity*: giving and receiving emotional and instrumental support
5. *Structural solidarity*: geographic proximity that would allow for interaction

Based on these measured dimensions, five intergenerational family types were identified, which closely resemble

## Intergenerational Relationships in Various Ethnic Groups

MUCH OF THE research about the grandparent role has been carried out by European American investigators with European American families. As a result, the work tends to begin from an individualist perspective, in which the nuclear family and the autonomy of the generations are highly valued. The results of this research suggest that grandparents play a variety of roles in U.S. families, and that these roles can vary from remote and minimally involved to actively engaged. This picture misses the qualitatively different ways that grandparents are viewed in ethnic groups that emerge from a more collectivist orientation, and the central role that grandparents play in the socialization process and family support systems. Although the majority of U.S. families do not have three generations living together in one household, the presence of grandparents living with their grandchildren is more than twice as likely in African American, Asian American, and Hispanic families than in European American families. This may, in part, be a result of the financial pressures on ethnic families, but it is also a result of a more collectivist outlook, in which family and kinship relationships are more central to the value system and priorities of many ethnic groups.

In an interview study of African Americans, Latin Americans, Filipino Americans, and Cambodian Americans, older adults (ages 50 and up) described the importance of mutual assistance and its critical role in fostering a sense of continuity across the generations. This can be especially important for immigrant families. Older adults provide care, guidance, and instrumental assistance for families, especially when there are young children in the home and the parents have to work (Becker, et al, 2003).

Even when grandparents and their adult children are not living together in the same home, there is an intensity and frequency of involvement that is not as obvious in European American families. In many ethnic groups, the grandparent generation is highly revered. In others, the intimacy of the family's daily concerns extends to grandparents, aunts and uncles, and other kin (Burnett, 1999; Lockery, 1991).

The following brief descriptions suggest the outlook of five U.S. ethnic groups on intergenerational relations. Each has a slightly different flavor, but each suggests a more integrated role for the grandparent generation than is characteristic of European American families (Contreras et al., 1999; DeGenova, 1997).

*African Americans* value strong kinship bonds and a supportive extended family system. Caregiving responsibilities are shared among kin as needed. Grandparents tend to support working parents by providing care to young children, and are cared for in return. Their active role in the family often contributes a strong moral and religious strength and provides emotional support to the parent generation, which reduces stress in the household.

*Arab American* families have elaborate and intensive networks of family members with a strong value for reciprocity, mutual protection, and care. Intimate family relationships extend to commitment to care for older family members.

*Chinese Americans* place a strong value on bringing honor to the family. Filial piety is one of the highest values, evidenced in a great sense of obligation, respect, and responsibility for parents.

*Japanese Americans* demonstrate strong feelings of respect and commitment to parents. They have a deep sense of obligation for the care of aging parents. Retired parents may live with their adult child who takes on the leadership role for the family.

*Puerto Rican* and many other Latino cultures embrace the value of familialism, a sense of closeness and interdependence among members of the nuclear and extended family, which includes a deep respect for elders. Family members serve many functions, including socialization, protection, companionship, social and business contacts, and economic support. Puerto Rican families create a formal intergenerational link through the role of the *compadrazgo*, or godparent, who has a responsibility for the child's well-being through life.

the grandparenting roles characterized by Neugarten. The *tight-knit* families were emotionally close, lived near one another, interacted often, and both gave and received help. The *sociable* families were emotionally close and had frequent contact, but they did not offer much functional help. The *intimate but distant* families had high levels of agreement and felt emotionally close but did not interact often, lived far apart, and offered little functional help. The *obligatory* families lived near one another and had frequent contact, but they were not emotionally close and did not share much in the way of common opinions or expectations. Finally, the *detached* families had low levels of all measures of solidarity.

Looking at the adult children's views of their parents, the sample was divided rather evenly across the five groups. Tight-knit and sociable families were each about 25% of the sample; obligatory and intimate but distant families were each about 16%; detached families were about 17%. When ethnic groups were compared, European Americans were more likely than African Americans or Hispanics to describe their relationship with their mother as obligatory or detached. Cultural dimensions including the emphasis on filial obligation, immigration or acculturation status, and the symbolic meaning of linkages to one's ancestry all influence the emphasis that various cultures place on the grandparent role (Ikels, 1998).

Two important ideas emerge from these descriptions. First, contemporary U.S. families are characterized by a variety of intergenerational relationships. No single type is normative. Second, about two thirds of these relationships can be characterized as showing high levels of affectional and consensual solidarity. This has been observed in repeated measurements between 1971 and 1997. Thus, despite many changes in family characteristics, including decreased family size, increased involvement of mothers in the labor force, parental divorce, and increasing educational attainment of the parent generation, sentiments of intergenerational closeness are strong. This implies an important stabilizing role for the grandparent generation—a role that may become increasingly important for the large number of children growing up in single-parent and dual-earner parent families.

**THE MEANING OF THE GRANDPARENT ROLE.** Grandparenthood has a variety of personal meanings that contribute to the grandparent's overall sense of purpose and worth (Gattai & Musatti, 1999; Kivnick, 1988). Grandchildren symbolize an extension of personal influence that will most assuredly persist well beyond the grandparent's death. To this extent, grandchildren help older adults feel more comfortable about their own death. Grandchildren offer concrete evidence that some thread of their lives will persist into the future, giving a dimension of immortality to themselves and to the family ancestry that they represent. Active grandparenting can also promote a process of life review, stimulating a revisitation of one's own parenting role and possibly supporting the achievement of a psychosocial sense of integrity.

In an analysis of the sources of vitality in later life, Erikson, Erikson, and Kivnick (1986) found that relationships with grandchildren played the following critical role:

The major involvement that uniformly makes life worth living is the thought of and participation in their relationships with children and grandchildren. Their pride in their own achievement in having brought up their young, through thick and thin, and their satisfaction in the way these young have developed gives them, for the most part, deep gratification. With the arrival of grandchildren, they may identify themselves as ancestors, graduated to venerability. Listen to their voices as they trace their own ancestry and that of their children's traits: "She has her mother's fire, that first girl of ours. She has more energy and more projects than anyone. Come to think of it, my mother had that fire, too. And my wife's two grandmothers." "My son is a perfectionist, like me." "The kids are innately smart, like their father." (p. 326)

Grandchildren also stimulate older adults' thoughts about time, the changing of cultural norms across generations, and the patterning of history. In relating to their grandchildren as they grow up, grandparents discover elements of the culture that remain stable. Some familiar stories and songs retain their appeal from generation to generation. Certain toys, games, and preoccupations of children of the current generation are remembered by grandparents from their own childhood. Grandparents may become aware of changes in the culture that are reflected in new childrearing practices; new equipment, toys, games, and forms of entertainment; and new expectations for children's behavior at each life stage. By maintaining communication with their grandchildren, older adults keep abreast of the continuities and changes in their culture that are reflected in the experiences of childhood. Through their grandchildren, adults avoid a sense of alienation from the contemporary world (Gutmann, 1985). The more involved grandparents are in the daily care and routines of their grandchildren, the more central they become to a

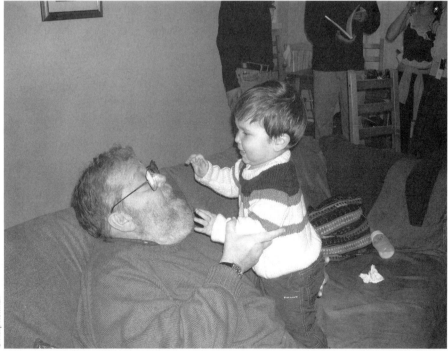

*Grandpa and Max share a mirth-filled moment as Max tries to pull Grandpa's beard and grab his glasses.*

© Philip Newman

*Increasingly, more grandparents fall into the "involved" category, taking on parenting responsibilties for their grandchildren on a daily basis.*

© Michael Newman/Photo Edit

young child's sense of security and well-being. This kind of importance is a benefit not only to the child but also to the older adult's assessment of his or her personal worth (Tomlin & Passman, 1989).

Some adults interpret the role of grandparent as an opportunity to pass on to their grandchildren the wisdom and cultural heritage of their ancestry. In the process of fulfilling this role, older adults must try to find meaning in their experiences and communicate it in meaningful ways to their grandchildren. Grandparents select many avenues to educate their grandchildren, influencing their thoughts and fantasies. Storytelling, special trips, long walks, attending religious services, and working on special projects are all activities that allow grandparents some moments of intimacy with their grandchildren. Educating one's grandchildren involves a deep sense of investment in experiences and ideals that one believes to be central to a fruitful life.

The many ways in which grandchildren can contribute to an adult's feelings of well-being have been replicated in studies conducted in European countries (Smith, 1991). A German grandmother addressed the meaning that her grandson gave to her life, stating,

> Yes, he is the most important thing in my life, because I have nothing else at the moment. They all say I spoil him. I don't know. Mama is a little bit strict, and so I always am careful not to spoil him too much. And it is actually Carsten this and Carsten that; he means so much to me. Since I am a pensioner, I have time for him (Sticker, 1991, p. 39).

**GRANDPARENT CAREGIVERS.** Roughly 5.6 million children under the age of 18, or 8% of all U.S. children, live in households with at least one grandparent present. For about ⅓ of these children, their parents are the primary householders and one or more grandparents lives at home with them.

These grandparents are likely benefiting from some types of support or care from their adult children. They may also provide direct and indirect support for their grandchildren, including being home when the children return from school, taking care of the children when they are ill and the parents have to work, and taking over household tasks so that parents and children can have time together. In comparison to other ethnic groups, Hispanic children are especially likely to be living in this type of extended family arrangement, where both their grandmother and grandfather are living with them in their parents' household.

In the other ⅔ of this group, the grandparents are the householders, suggesting that many grandparents are using their resources to help support their adult children and grandchildren. About 1.3 million children live with their grandparents with no parents in the household. These children are more likely to be living in poverty, to be without health insurance, and to be receiving some type of public assistance than are children who live in their grandparents' household with their own parents present (Fields, 2003). In a national survey of families and households, 1 in 10 grandparents was found to have a custodial or primary role in the care of their grandchild for a minimum of 6 months. In most cases, the care was far longer (Fuller-Thomson, Minkler, & Driver, 1997; Triffon, 1997).

Many grandparents play an especially important role in supporting the development of their grandchildren during times of family stress (Goodman, 2003; Landry-Meyer, 1999). In contemporary American society, one can view grandparents as a potential resource that is called into active duty when certain difficulties arise for parents. In cases of parental divorce, grandparents often assume a central role in the lives of young children. Some custodial mothers move back home with their parents. Grandparents often assume more child care responsibilities during this time.

Following divorces in which the mother has primary custody of the children, the grandchild's relationship with his or her maternal grandparents is more likely to be enhanced, whereas the relationship with the paternal grandparents is likely to decline. Several studies have shown that having positive ongoing relationships with grandparents during the years following the parents' divorce is associated with a child's ability to manage school demands, maintain positive relationships with peers and teachers, and have fewer behavior problems (Heatherington, Cox, & Cox, 1985; Heatherington, Stanley-Hagan, & Anderson, 1989).

Grandparents also play a key role when their young, unmarried daughters become pregnant. The pattern of unmarried teen mothers living with parents is especially common in African American families (Tolson & Wilson, 1990). African American grandmothers are likely to perceive themselves and to be perceived by their daughters as actively involved in childrearing (Werner, 1991). Among young adult, African American parents, the grandmother is most often viewed as the person to count on for child care assistance, advice, and emotional support (Hunter, 1997). These grandmothers may be young themselves, just entering middle adulthood, when they assume the grandparent role.

The presence of grandmothers appears to affect the family atmosphere as well as the childrearing environment in African American families. In one study of 64 African American families, the presence of a grandmother was associated with a high level of moral and religious orientation in the family (Tolson & Wilson, 1990). Having a grandmother in the home allows the mother to be more flexible in managing daily demands, thereby reducing much of the stress that characterizes single-parent families.

Maternal employment is another condition in which grandparents are likely to give direct support. Increasingly, parents of young children call on grandparents to provide all or part of daily child care (Brandon, 2000; Goodfellow & Laverty, 2003). In a national sample of 796 mothers who had children under age 5 and who were employed, 24% said that their mother, or the child's grandmother, was the principal child care provider (Presser, 1989). These grandmothers provided an average of 27 hours per week of child care, and almost 40 hours per week if the mothers were employed full time. Clearly, these grandmothers were intimately involved in the lives of their grandchildren and were directing significant energy, talent, and time to this role. For more information on model programs for grandparents who are raising their grandchildren, visit the website on grandparenting developed by the AARP.

**LOSS OF GRANDPARENT–GRANDCHILD CONTACT.** In contrast to the picture of an increasing role for grandparents in caring for their grandchildren, a growing number of grandparents are losing contact with their grandchildren as a result of parental divorce, conflict between the parents, death of an adult child, or adoption of a grandchild after remarriage. Disruption in the grandparent–grandchild relationship is especially great when the grandparent's adult child is not named as the custodial parent after a divorce. In the 1980s, most states created statutes allowing grandparents to file for a legal right to enforced visitation with their grandchildren, even over parental objections. The laws differ from state to state, establishing different conditions under which grandparents may be granted visitation. In 1998, a law was passed to ensure that grandparents who have visitation rights in one state may visit their grandchildren in any state. However, in some states, earlier visitation laws have been overturned, finding that they interfere with parental rights regarding the rearing of their children. Legal recourse is not very effective given that it tends to increase the hostilities between grandparents and their adult children, making "normalized" visitation even less likely (Drew & Smith, 1999). For more information about grandparent visitation rights, visit the website of the Foundation for Grandparenting (Kornhaber, 2004).

## ■ WIDOWHOOD

Among those 65 years and older, 14% of men and 45% of women describe their marital status as widowed (U.S. Bureau of the Census, 2000). For many adults, the psychosocial consequences of widowhood include intense emotional grief, loss of social and emotional support, and loss of material and instrumental support. Emotions of depression, anger, shock, and overall grief as well as yearning for the deceased partner are observed 6 and 18 months after the loss (Carr, House, Wortman, Neese, & Kessler, 2001). Most older widowers remarry, whereas the majority of widows remain unmarried and live alone.

**WIDOWS.** Widows must learn to function socially and in their own households without the presence of a marriage partner. Adaptation to this role requires resilience, creative problem solving, and a strong belief in one's personal worth. A woman who is widowed at age 60 can expect more than 20 years of life in which to create a new, single head-of-household lifestyle.

In addition to the bereavement itself, a number of stressors challenge the coping resources of widows. Studies of economic changes among widows show that many continue to experience marked fluctuations in their financial resources for years following widowhood (Bound, Duncan, Laren, & Oleinick, 1991; Zick & Smith, 1991). Women who have never participated in the labor market during their married years may have no marketable skills and feel insecure about entering the labor force. They may be uninformed or uneasy about using social service agencies to meet their needs. For most women, the loss of their husband is most keenly felt as a loss of emotional support, as expressed in the following example: "He is most apt to be mentioned as the person the widow most enjoyed being with, who made her feel important and secure" (Lopata, 1978, p. 221). The transition to widowhood may be especially difficult for those who have been caring for an ill partner, hoping for recovery yet observing constant decline (Bass & Bowman, 1990).

Despite the extreme pain and prolonged grief that accompany widowhood, most women cope with it successfully. In a study of women ages 60 through 98 who had recently become widows, there was a high degree of self-sufficiency (O'Bryant & Morgan, 1990). The majority of respondents said they performed a variety of daily tasks, including transportation, housekeeping, shopping, preparing meals, personal care and hygiene, financial and other decisions, and providing financial support without help from others. More than 30% said they managed their own home repairs, yard work, and legal questions without help. From this study, a picture emerges of older, widowed women functioning at a high level of independence and autonomy and benefiting from assistance from others, especially their children, in specific domains, depending on where help is needed. Research on a large sample of Australian women confirmed this picture. These women reported that widowhood was a very difficult negative life event, but that after a period of bereavement they found themselves making a shift to a new, positive phase of adult life (Feldman, Byles, & Beaumont, 2000).

Widows are likely to find support from their siblings, children, and friends. Over time, a widow's siblings, especially her sisters, may become a key source of emotional support and direct, instrumental assistance with home repairs and shopping (O'Bryant, 1988). In an exploratory analysis of the responses of widows in a support-group discussion, comments about the positive and negative contributions of their social support network were analyzed (Morgan, 1989). The widows described their nonfamily, reciprocal friendship relationships as somewhat more positive than their family relationships. In many cases, widows found that as a result of their own sense of family obligation, they were drawn into negative events occurring in their families, especially divorce, illness, and the death of other family members. These negative events added to their distress and prevented them from receiving the support they felt they needed at the time of their own loss.

The analysis also concluded that the most positive form of immediate support from family, especially children, was a willingness to accept the widow's feelings of grief and to talk openly about their father. Social support from friends included a similar willingness to allow the widow to take her time in finding a new identity. These women did not want to be forced to "get over it" too quickly or to be told how strong they were and how well they were handling their grief: "'The fact that you're using the strength that you have, just to cope, and to stay alive (another voice: 'to survive') is a big job and they don't recognize that, you know it makes you angry'" (Morgan, 1989, p. 105). The widows wanted to have their anger, grief, and the disruption in their lives acknowledged and accepted by their friends. In this way, they felt they could begin to come to terms with their loss and build a new life.

**WIDOWERS.** Widowers suffer greater increases in depression following the loss of their spouses than do widows (Lee, DeMaris, Bavin, & Sullivan, 2001; Umberson, Wortman, & Kessler, 1992). Perhaps because men in traditional marriages rely heavily on their wives for both the instrumental support

of managing daily household tasks and the emotional and social support of companionship and social activity, their lives are more intensely disrupted when their wives die. This may result in an immediate search for a new marriage partner. In a 2-year follow-up study of dating and remarriage after widowhood, 61% of men and 19% of women had remarried or were in a new romantic relationship by 25 months after the death of their spouses. For men, a higher monthly income and level of education were the best predictors of being remarried. For both men and women, involvement in a new relationship was positively associated with psychological well-being and was interpreted as a positive coping strategy (Schneider, Sledge, Shuchter, & Zisook, 1996).

Widowhood also results in increased death rates among surviving spouses. In a longitudinal study of more than 1.5 million married Finnish adults, the rates of mortality after the death of a spouse were calculated. For all causes of death that were monitored in this study, mortality rates were higher for widowed persons than for those persons still married. Higher mortality rates were especially notable for the men in the study, particularly in the first 6 months after the death of their spouses. The process of bereavement seems to accelerate the course of preexisting diseases, and leads to increased rates of suicides, accidents, and alcohol-related deaths (Martikainen & Valkonen, 1996). Thus, many adults cope successfully with widowhood, either by forming a new, intimate relationship or establishing a new, independent lifestyle; however, others find it difficult to recover from the impact of their loss.

**PATTERNS OF ADAPTATION DURING WIDOWHOOD.** In a prospective, longitudinal study of widowhood, married couples where the husband was 65 years old or older were surveyed. Following the death of one partner, the surviving spouse was surveyed again at 6 and 18 months following the loss (Bonanno, Wortman, & Nesse, 2004). Five paths following the death of a spouse were described:

1. common grief
2. chronic grief
3. chronic depression
4. depression followed by improvement
5. resilience

The most common patterns, for 56% of the sample, were common grief and resilience. These two groups had no signs of depression before the loss. The common grief group had evidence of depression at 6 months, but returned to pre-loss levels at 18 months. The resilient group had low levels of depression even at 6 months following loss. Although these groups experienced fond memories and moments of yearning for their partners, they did not experience long-term grief at 18 months. A second, unexpected pattern, characteristic of about 10% of the sample, was a group that showed a change for the better following widowhood. The participants in this group had high levels of depression before the loss, and lower levels at 6 and 18 months following the loss. Participants in this group were in unhappy marriages, and many of them had

Table 14.2 Participation in Various Leisure Activities by Age, 2002

| AGE | Activity* (% Participation) | | | | |
| | EXERCISE | PLAY SPORTS | CHARITY WORK | HOME IMPROVEMENT | GARDENING |
|---|---|---|---|---|---|
| 55 to 64 | 48 | 16 | 28 | 45 | 57 |
| 65 to 74 | 47 | 14 | 29 | 38 | 57 |
| 75 and older | 31 | 6 | 21 | 22 | 48 |

*Respondent has participated in the activity at least once in the past 12 months.

Source: U.S. Census Bureau, *Statistical Abstract of the United States, 2003.* Table No. 1239.

been caring for chronically ill partners. They reported being more confident and having found a new sense of personal strength in coping with the events of widowhood.

Two other groups were described as chronically grieving and chronically depressed. The chronically grieving group was not depressed before the death of their spouse, but continued to show high levels of depression at 6 and 18 months following the death. These widows and widowers were often coping with the sudden loss of a healthy spouse and had trouble finding meaning in the death of their partners. The chronically depressed were already depressed prior to the death of their spouse. The death added a new stressor that increased their levels of depression at 6 and 18 months after the loss.

The study suggests that the majority of adults are able to cope effectively with the loss of a spouse. An understanding of the context of the loss and the emotional well-being of the surviving spouse before the loss are important factors that influence the bereavement process. Those striving to support widows and widowers need to be mindful of these differences in order to offer appropriate interventions.

### ■ LEISURE ACTIVITIES

Whereas widowhood brings role loss, one way of coping with it is to become more involved in new kinds of activities and interests. As the role responsibilities of parenthood and employment decrease, older adults have more time and resources to devote to leisure activities. Involvement in leisure activities is associated with higher levels of well-being and lower stress. In a study of adaptation to widowhood, such activities were most commonly social activities with family and friends. Recent widows and widowers who were more involved in leisure activities had lower levels of stress than those who did not participate. This does not mean that they were less bereaved, but perhaps social activities helped them to feel less isolated and gave them a sense of continuing social value (Patterson, 1996).

Different types of leisure activities are available that meet a variety of psychosocial needs. Table 14.2 shows the percentage of older adults, ages 55 to 64, 65 to 74, and 75 and older, who participated in five types of leisure activities at least once in the prior year: exercise programs, playing sports, charity work, home improvement and repair, and gardening (U.S.

*© Macduff Everton / The Image Works*

*Grace and Bert, a widow and widower, met at a cross-country ski weekend sponsored by their senior center. Involvement in this physical activity helps reduce stress and widens their social support network.*

TECHNOLOGY AND HUMAN DEVELOPMENT

## The Use of the Internet Among Older Adults

THE U.S. CENSUS Bureau, in cooperation with the National Telecommunications and Information Administration,
published a study showing changes in
electronic access over a 15-year period
from 1984 to 1998 (National Telecommunications and Information Administration, 2002). The study provides a
picture of how much involvement adults
have with computers, including whether
they have a computer in their home, a
modem, and e-mail.

In 1984, 2.5% of adults age 55 and
older had computers in their home. In
1998, this figure was 25%. The groups
least likely to have computers in 1998
were those with the least education and
the lowest family income, especially
those living in rural areas.

One indication of Internet access
used to be ownership of a modem. This
indicator was useful until 1997; after
that, virtually all PCs were equipped with
built-in modems. Those 55 and older
were less likely than other age groups
to have a modem (13.2% in 1997).
However, this group showed the greatest growth rate over the period, suggesting that the idea was catching on.

Another indication of Internet use
is having an e-mail account. This was

*Having e-mail helps Lillian stay in touch with her daughter, who has taken a job far from home. Two years ago Lillian never would have guessed how important her Internet access would become in maintaining family ties.*

tracked from 1994 to 1998. E-mail use
increased 4.5 times over this 4-year period. Figure 14.2 shows the percentage
of households with e-mail for 1994 and
1998 by age of the householder. Older
adults are least likely to have e-mail,

even though growth in this group is
substantial.

In a study of people age 45 and
older who had computers in their homes,
the challenges facing older adults were
highlighted (AARP, 2002). Even though

---

Census Bureau, 2003). Gardening tops the list in each of
these age groups, with relatively little difference between
those 55 to 64 and those 65 to 74.

In a study of the benefits of leisure activities, men and
women ages 56 and older were asked to describe the sources
of satisfaction found in their primary leisure activities (Tinsley, Teaff, Colbs, & Kaufman, 1985). In this study, six clusters
of leisure activities and their primary benefits were described.
The six benefits suggest the range of needs that may be met
through leisure pursuits: companionship; experiencing something new and unusual; escaping from the pressures of dealing with others; finding solitude and security; having opportunities for expressiveness; and finding opportunities for
intellectual stimulation, self-expression, and service.

**VOLUNTEERISM.**  **Volunteerism** is a salient area for activity
among older adults. In the United States, about 28% of 55- to

64-year-olds volunteer, giving a median of 60 hours annually
of unpaid time. Among those 65 and older, about 23% volunteer, giving a median of 90 hours annually of unpaid time
(U.S. Census Bureau, 2003). Especially in the year or two following retirement, individuals who are not already involved
in volunteer service are especially open to considering it
(Caro & Bass, 1997). Volunteering provides a meaningful
structure to daily life, especially when other significant work
and family roles are becoming less demanding. High rates of
volunteering are associated with increases in life satisfaction
and improved perceptions of physical health (Van Willigen,
2000). At the same time, certain types of volunteer work have
been shown to have a positive impact on cognitive complexity and memory functions. The opportunity to assume new
responsibilities and learn new skills are two of the rewards
of volunteering in later adulthood (Newman, Karip, &
Faux, 1995).

they had computers, those over age 65 were more likely to consider themselves novices and to express low levels of confidence in their ability to use computers to carry out financial transactions. Older adults spent only a small amount of money on software and hardware upgrades.

Older adults are moving cautiously into the world of the Internet. They are also a group ripe for computer education and training. The prospects of increasing social contact and intellectual stimulation, plus the convenience of managing one's financial activities and purchases, promise to draw more older adults into the fold. On the other hand, for those older adults who are mobile, face-to-face interaction may be more important than convenience in carrying out the tasks of daily life. The Administration on Aging (http://www.aoa.gov) has provided a website, *Aging Internet Information Notes*, that focuses specifically on these issues, including data about Internet use by older adults, suggested websites for additional training, websites that are likely to be useful to seniors, and ideas about how to develop user-friendly websites for older adults.

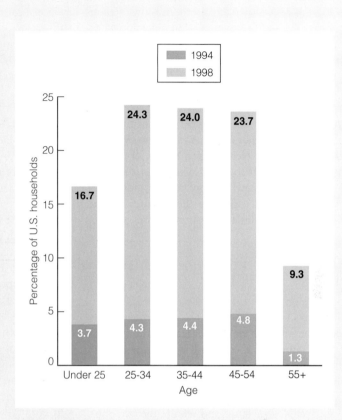

**FIGURE 14.2**

Percentage of U.S. Households with E-Mail by Age in 1994 and 1998

**EXERCISE.** Physical exercise is becoming a focus of leisure activity for increasing numbers of older adults, as benefits are linked to better health, positive self-esteem, and a new zest for life. Almost 50% of adults ages 65 to 74 report being involved in an exercise program during the prior 12 months. Research suggests a relationship between physical fitness—especially a regular pattern of aerobic exercise—and the improvement of certain visual-spatial cognitive abilities that typically decline with age (Shay & Roth, 1992). In the past, professionals were reluctant to encourage vigorous activity for older adults. They believed that a person who was unaccustomed to active physical exercise might be harmed by it. However, research on exercise in adulthood suggests that adults profit from a program of exercise, and that through systematic exercise, some of the negative consequences of a sedentary lifestyle can be reversed (Riebe, Burbank, & Garber, 2002). For example, Hopkins and her associates de-

scribed a program in which women ages 57 to 77 participated in a low-impact aerobic dance class three times a week for 12 weeks. The program included stretching, walking, dance movements, large arm movements, and major leg muscle movement. After 12 weeks, the group showed improvement in cardiorespiratory endurance (walking half a mile as fast as possible), flexibility, muscle strength, body agility, and balance. A comparison group of women who did not participate showed stability or decline in all of these areas (Hopkins, Murrah, Hoeger, & Rhodes, 1990).

Physical exercise has been identified as a component of optimal aging. Regular participation in moderate activity, such as walking, biking, or gardening ½ hour a day, may provide protection from certain chronic diseases and ease the discomfort of arthritis (DiPietro, 2001). Exercise is associated with increased muscle tone, strength, and endurance, which build confidence about one's body movement, coordination, and stamina. Exercise also increases perceptions of self-control and self-efficacy in meeting one's own needs. As a result, people who exercise tend to have a generally more positive self-evaluation and higher levels of self-confidence than their inactive peers (Clark, Long, & Schiffman, 1999; Fontane, 1996). Fitness training has also been shown to contribute to improved cognitive functioning in older adults, especially in the area of executive control processes such as decision making, problem solving, and emotional regulation (Kramer & Willis, 2002).

Redirection of energy to new roles in later adulthood requires a degree of flexibility and resilience that often goes unnoticed in observations of older adults. Try to imagine what life might be like for you 30 or 40 years from now. Will you be prepared to embrace the technology, lifestyle, or age role expectations that you will encounter during your own later adulthood? We are impressed by how readily most older adults adapt to new roles, especially those of retiree and widow, for which there is little early preparation or social reward.

## DEVELOPING A POINT OF VIEW ABOUT DEATH

During later adulthood, it is inevitable that serious, possibly frightening, preoccupations about death will fill the individual's thoughts. In middle adulthood, most people experience the death of their parents. During later adulthood, one's peers, including siblings and spouses, may die. These deaths are sources of psychological stress and require the emotional process of grief and mourning and the cognitive strain of trying to accept or understand them. At the same time, these deaths stimulate a more immediate recognition of one's own mortality.

### ■ CHANGING PERSPECTIVES ABOUT DEATH

The development of a perspective on death is a continuous process that begins in childhood and is not fully resolved until later adulthood. The earliest concern with death, which occurs during toddlerhood, reflects an inability to conceive of an irreversible state of lifelessness. Toddlers are likely to think that a person may be dead at one moment and "undeaded" the next. By middle school age, children have a rather realistic concept of death, but they are unlikely to relate that concept to themselves or to others close to them (Kastenbaum, 1992). Thoughts about one's death and the formulation of a conceptualization of death become increasingly well articulated from early through later adolescence (Noppe & Noppe, 1997). In the process of forming a personal identity, young people ask new questions about mortality, the meaning of life, and the possibility of life after death.

During middle adulthood, people recognize that they have already lived more than half of their lives. There is more time in the past than in the future. The issue of death becomes increasingly concrete as parents and older relatives die. At the same time, adults begin to have a larger impact on their families and communities. Increased feelings of effectiveness and vitality lessen the threat of death. The degree to which individuals gain satisfaction from their own contributions to future generations determines the extent of their anxiety about death during this stage. The achievement of a sense of generativity usually allows adults to accept that their impact will continue to be felt even after death.

Ideally, during later adulthood, ego concerns about death decrease. Individuals come to accept their own lives as they have lived them and begin to see death as a natural part of the life span. Death no longer poses a threat to personal value, the potential for accomplishment, or the desire to influence the lives of others. As a result of having accepted one's life, one can accept its end without discouragement. As the case of Morrie Schwartz suggests, coming to terms with death does not imply a desire for but an acceptance of the fact of death. Along with this acceptance may come a greater appreciation for life itself. It takes great courage to face the fact of one's own death and, at the same time, to live out the days of one's life with optimism and enthusiasm. Older adults who achieve this degree of acceptance of their death appreciate that the usefulness of their contributions does not necessarily depend on their physical presence (Kübler-Ross, 1969, 1972).

The notion that one's understanding of the concept of death changes with development is complemented by the idea that people go through a process in coming to terms with their own death. In the 1960s, Elisabeth Kübler-Ross engaged in ground-breaking work to understand the thoughts, feelings, and needs of patients who were dying. Through her interviews with more than 400 patients, she began to clarify a process of coping with one's death. She identified five stages that are likely to occur between the awareness of a terminal illness and ultimate acceptance of one's death: denial; anger and resentment; bargaining for a reprieve; depression and mourning one's death; and acceptance or a willingness to face the reality of one's death. She also discovered how eager most people were to have someone who would listen to their thoughts and how grateful they were to interact with someone about their death rather than have it treated as a taboo or unmentionable topic (Kübler-Ross, 1969, 1981).

Subsequent research has suggested that there is no single, typical path in the dying process. Some people alternate between accepting and denying their death. They understand their situation, yet they fall into periods of disbelief. Some people are able to bring what they view as an acceptable close to their life, saying goodbye to family and friends, finding comfort in the support of others. Others die while still in a state of fear or denial (Kastenbaum, 1981, 1985). Kübler-Ross's stages are not a fixed sequence but a useful model for considering the dynamic ego processes that are engaged as one faces death. The capacity to confront the reality of death can be seen as a profound occasion for new insight.

# CASE STUDY

## MORRIE SCHWARTZ REFLECTS ON HIS VIEWS ABOUT DEATH

*Mitch Albom, in his 40s, rediscovered his former college professor, Morrie Schwartz, who was dying from amyotrophic lateral sclerosis (ALS), a progressive neurological disease that attacks body muscles and leaves one increasingly paralyzed. Mitch and Morrie met every Tuesday for the last 4 months of Morrie's life.*

"Everyone knows they're going to die," he said again, "but nobody believes it. If we did, we would do things differently."

"So we kid ourselves about death," I said.

"Yes. But there's a better approach. To know you're going to die, and to be *prepared* for it at any time. That's better. That way you can actually be *more* involved in your life while you're living."

"How can you ever be prepared to die?"

"Do what the Buddhists do. Every day, have a little bird on your shoulder that asks, 'Is today the day? Am I ready? Am I doing all I need to do? Am I being the person I want to be?'" He turned his head to his shoulder as if the bird were there now.

"Is today the day I die?" he said. . . .

"The truth is, Mitch," he said, "once you learn how to die, you learn how to live." I nodded.

"I'm going to say it again," he said. "Once you learn how to die, you learn how to live." He smiled, and I realized what he was doing. He was making sure I absorbed this point, without embarrassing me by asking. It was part of what made him a good teacher.

"Did you think much about death before you got sick?" I asked.

"No." Morrie smiled. "I was like everyone else. I once told a friend of mine, in a moment of exuberance, 'I'm gonna be the healthiest old man you ever met!'"

"How old were you?"

"In my sixties."

"So you were optimistic."

"Why not? Like I said, no one really believes they're going to die."

"But everyone knows someone who has died," I said. "Why is it so hard to think about dying?"

"Because," Morrie continued, "most of us all walk around as if we're sleepwalking. We really don't experience the world fully, because we're half-asleep, doing things we automatically think we have to do." . . .

"Mitch. Can I tell you something?"

"Of course," I said.

"You might not like it."

"Why not?"

"Well, the truth is, if you really listen to that bird on your shoulder, *if you accept that you can die at any time*—then you might not be as ambitious as you are." I forced a small grin.

"The things you spend so much time on—all the work you do—might not seem as important. You might have to make room for some more spiritual things."

"Spiritual things?"

"You hate that word, don't you? 'Spiritual.' You think it's touchy-feely stuff."

"Well," I said.

He tried to wink, a bad try, and I broke down and laughed.

"Mitch," he said, laughing along, "even I don't know what 'spiritual development' really means. But I do know we're deficient in some way. We are too involved in materialistic things, and they don't satisfy us. The loving relationships we have, the universe around us, we take these things for granted."

He nodded toward the window with the sunshine streaming in. "You see that? You can go out there, outside, anytime. You can run up and down the block and go crazy. I can't do that. I can't go out. I can't run. I can't be out there without fear of getting sick. But you know what? I *appreciate* that window more than you do."

Source: From *Tuesdays with Morrie: An Old Man, a Young Man, and Life's Greatest Lessons* by Mitch Albom, pp. 81–84. Copyright © 1997 Doubleday.

## ■ CRITICAL THINKING AND CASE ANALYSIS

1. What is the point of view about life and death that Morrie is developing?
2. Why is it difficult for most people to listen to a dying person express his or her thoughts about death?
3. What does this conversation suggest about Morrie's psychosocial development? To what extent are issues of intimacy, generativity, and integrity reflected in this dialogue?
4. How might the conditions of Morrie's illness influence his outlook on death?
5. What issues would you want to discuss if you had a mentor like Morrie who was willing to help you learn about living and dying?

The evolution of a point of view about death requires the capacity to absorb the loss of one's close relatives and friends and to accept one's own death. The former task may be even more difficult than the latter, in that the death of peers begins to destroy one's social group. Losing one's friends and relatives means losing daily companionship, a shared world of memories and plans, and a source of support for values and social norms. The circumstances surrounding the deaths of others may also be very frightening. Older adults observe their peers suffering through long illnesses, dying abruptly in the midst of a thriving and vigorous life, or dying in absurd, meaningless accidents. After each death, the surviving adults must ask themselves about the value of these lives and subsequently about the value of their own life.

*Many elements of a traditional U.S. funeral are depicted here: the casket, religious leader, flowers, and mourners gathered at a pleasant, wooded gravesite.*

© Spencer Grant/Photo Edit

## ◼ DEATH ANXIETY

Several researchers have considered the sources of personal anxiety about death and the changes in preoccupation with death at various ages. Although older adults seem to think about death more frequently than do young adults, they do not appear to feel more threatened by it. In a survey of more than 400 adults in early, middle, and later adulthood, death was a more salient issue for the oldest (60 and older) age group (Kalish & Reynolds, 1976). They felt that they were more likely to die in the near future. They knew more people who had died and were more likely than younger respondents to have visited a cemetery or attended a funeral. The oldest adults were more likely to have made some specific arrangements related to their death, including purchasing cemetery space, writing a will, and making funeral arrangements. Yet the fear of death was lowest in this age group, and the percentage who said that they were unafraid of death or even eager for it was highest.

Fear of personal death is natural and normal. Death may be feared for a variety of reasons, some of which relate to the actual process of dying and others to the consequences of it. Concerns about the process of dying include fears of being alone, being in pain, having others see one suffering, or losing control of one's mind and body. Concerns about the consequences of dying include fears of the unknown, loss of identity ("People will forget about me"), the grief that others will feel, the decomposition of the body, and punishment or pain in the hereafter (Tomer & Eliason, 2000).

Death does not seem to be as frightening to older adults as it is to younger people. Table 14.3 shows the responses of three age groups of adults to the question, "Some people say they are afraid to die and others say they are not. How do you feel?" Admission of fear decreased with age, and lack of fear

or even eagerness to die increased. Recent research comparing younger adults (ages 20 to 29) and older adults (ages 70 to 97) replicated these findings; the younger adults had the greater fear of death (Cicirelli, 2001).

What are the factors that help older people cope with fears about death? Several resources have been identified. People who describe themselves as religious, those who have a strong social support system, and those who have a strong sense of self-worth are less likely to be preoccupied with fear of death (Tomer & Eliason, 2000). Frey (2003) extended this perspective by focusing on the relationship of self-beliefs to death anxiety. Older adults who have a positive sense of self-efficacy have less fear of the unknown following one's death and less fear of the pain and suffering associated with dying. In particular, the sense of spiritual self-efficacy—one's perceived ability to generate spiritually based faith and inner strength—was strongly associated with low levels of death anxiety.

**Table 14.3** Fear of Death by Age (percentage of respondents)

|  | Age | | |
| RESPONSE | 20–39 | 40–59 | 60+ |
| --- | --- | --- | --- |
| Afraid/terrified | 40 | 26 | 10 |
| Neither afraid nor unafraid | 21 | 20 | 17 |
| Unafraid/eager | 36 | 52 | 71 |
| Depends | 3 | 3 | 2 |

Source: Based on Kalish and Reynolds, 1976.

# THE PSYCHOSOCIAL CRISIS: INTEGRITY VERSUS DESPAIR

The conflict of integrity versus despair is resolved through a dynamic process of life review and self-evaluation. Contemporary factors, such as health, family relationships, and role loss or role transition, are integrated with an assessment of one's past aspirations and accomplishments. Thoughts of the past may be fleeting or a constant obsession. Memories may be altered to fit contemporary events, or contemporary events may be reinterpreted to fit memories. The achievement of integrity is the culmination of a life of psychosocial growth. Psychologically speaking, it is the peak of the pyramid, in that it addresses the ultimate question, "How do I find meaning in life given the ultimate reality of death?" Achievement of integrity in later adulthood inspires younger age groups to continue to struggle with the challenges of their own life stages.

## INTEGRITY

The term **integrity**, as used in Erikson's theory, refers to the ability to accept the facts of one's life and face death without great fear. The attainment of it is ultimately a result of the balance of all the psychosocial crises that have come earlier, accompanied by all the ego strengths and core pathologies that have accumulated along the way. Integrity comes only after some considerable thought about the meaning of one's life. Older adults who have achieved a sense of integrity view their past in an existential light. They appreciate that their lives and individuality are due to an accumulation of personal satisfactions and crises. Integrity is not so much a quality of honesty and trustworthiness—as the term is used in daily speech—as it is an ability to integrate one's past history with one's present circumstances and to feel content with the outcome.

Most people have some regrets. One may look back and wish that one had taken advantage of certain opportunities, been smarter about saving or investing money, or spent more time with one's children while they were young (Baum, 1999). The challenge in achieving integrity is to face the decisions and experiences of the past with acceptance. In this process, a person seeks to find an integrative thread that makes sense of the life one has led without belaboring past mistakes.

Ryff and Heincke (1983) used a psychosocial model to test the possible changes in personality configurations in later adulthood. Early, middle, and later adults were asked to respond to a variety of statements from three time perspectives: in the present, in the past during an earlier life stage, and in the future in a later life stage. Generativity was perceived by all age groups as being highest during middle adulthood, regardless of the respondents' ages. Similarly, integrity was perceived as being highest in later adulthood. Older adults rated themselves as being higher in integrity at present than in the

past. Young and middle-aged adults expected to be higher in integrity in the future than they were at present. This research suggests that people not only experience changes in the directions that psychosocial theory predicts, but that they also anticipate changes in those directions at various life stages. These expectations influence how one prepares for future life stages and evaluates them once they arrive.

## DESPAIR

The opposite pole of integrity is **despair**. It is much more likely that adults will resolve the crisis of integrity versus despair in the negative direction than that infants will resolve the crisis of trust versus mistrust in the negative direction. For infants to experience trust, they must depend on the benevolence of a responsible caregiver who will meet their essential needs. In most cases, this caregiver is present, and the infant learns to rely on him or her. In order to experience integrity, however, older adults must incorporate into their self-image a lifelong record of conflicts, failures, and disappointments, along with accomplishments. They must confront what is sometimes referred to as the "death of dreams"—a realization that some of their most cherished hopes for themselves or their children cannot be accomplished in their lifetime (Oates, 1997).

Older adults may also face some degree of **ageism**—devaluation and even hostility from the social community. The negative attitudes expressed by family members, colleagues, and younger people toward the perceived lack of competence, dependence, or old-fashioned ways of older people may lead many of them to feel discouraged about their self-worth. The gradual deterioration or loss of certain physical capacities—particularly hearing, vision, and motor agility—contribute to an older person's frustration and discouragement. Older adults recognize that they cannot perform certain tasks as well as they did in the past or that their domains of independent functioning and mastery have diminished.

Furthermore, there is a general cultural sentiment that the death of an older person—in contrast, for example, with the death of a child or youth—though sad, is not a great loss to society, because that person had already contributed what she or he was likely to contribute. Thus, older adults may perceive that society is already letting go of them, even before they are ready to let go of life (Jecker & Schneiderman, 1994).

All of these factors are likely to create a feeling of regret about one's past and a continuous, haunting desire to be able to do things differently, or of bitterness over how one's life has turned out. People who resolve the crisis of later adulthood in the direction of despair cannot resist speculating about how things might have been or about what actions might have been taken if conditions had only been different. They are preoccupied with the "if only's" of their past, disrupting a calm acceptance of death. Despairing individuals either seek death as a way of ending a miserable existence or desperately fear death because it makes impossible any hope of compensating for past failures.

## ▪ DEPRESSION

The theme of depression has been treated in several sections of this text. Given the close link between the concepts of depression and despair, it should come as no surprise that depression has been a topic of research in the study of adulthood and aging. Contrary to stereotypes, the population with depression is composed largely (61%) of younger adults between 18 and 44 years old (National Academy on an Aging Society, 2000). About 5% of older adults living independently are experiencing depression at any one time; about 15% experience depression sometime in later life (Castleman, 2001).

Many of the same factors that are associated with depression in younger age groups are also associated with depression in older age groups: poverty; poor physical health; lack of social involvement; and being single, divorced, or widowed. The risk of depression in later life cannot be attributed to the aging process itself. The negative physiological changes associated with aging—such as high blood pressure, reduced breathing capacity, reduced muscle strength, slower reaction time, memory loss, and loss of visual or auditory acuity—are not associated with depression in and of themselves (Lewinsohn, Rohde, & Crozier, 1991). However, among older adults, those who rate their own health as fair to poor and those who have a chronic condition are more likely to be depressed than those who say their health is good to excellent. Whether the illness contributes to the depression or the depression leads people to be more discouraged by their physical limitations is difficult to say. Thus, depression as a complex affective and cognitive syndrome does not automatically come with the territory of aging, but it occurs in a subset of older adults. It is especially likely among those who have experienced a decreased activity level, have reduced access to a significant, close, confiding relationship, and have accumulated physical health problems that limit their independence and dampen the sense of enthusiasm for pleasant activities (Lewinsohn et al., 1991).

## THE CENTRAL PROCESS: INTROSPECTION

In order to achieve a sense of integrity, the individual must engage in deliberate self-evaluation and private thought. The final achievement of a sense of integrity requires the ability to **introspect** about the gradual evolution of life events and to appreciate their significance in the formation of the adult personality (Walasky, Whitbourne, & Nehrke, 1983–1984). This state can be reached only through individual effort. It

may even require temporary isolation, shutting out the influences of potentially competitive or resentful associates. One mode for engaging in self-evaluation is reminiscence.

**Reminiscence** has been defined as the recollection of "long-term memories of events in which the reminiscer is either a participant or an observer" (Ross, 1989, p. 341). This process of nostalgic remembering allows adults to recapture some of the memorable events in their life histories. Reminiscence may be a playful recalling of a life adventure or a painful review of some personal or family crisis. The process of simple reminiscence has been described as comprising four elements: the *selection* of an event or story to retell or review; *immersion* in the details of the story, including the strong emotions linked to the event; *withdrawal* from the past by distancing oneself from the event or comparing past and present; and bringing *closure* to the memory by summing up, finding some lesson, or making a general observation. Through this kind of process, a person builds a mental and emotional bridge between the past and the present (Meacham, 1995).

Reminiscence is linked to positive adjustment in later life, especially better health, a more positive outlook, and a better ability to cope with the challenges of daily life. However, not all forms of reminiscence are of equal benefit. In particular,

© Michael Newman /Photo Edit

*The process of nostalgic remembering allows adults to recapture some of the memorable people and events in their life histories.*

reminiscences of the integrative or instrumental type tend to be associated with high levels of well-being, whereas obsessive reminiscences are not. **Integrative reminiscence** involves reviewing one's past in order to find meaning or to reconcile one's current and prior feelings about certain life events. **Instrumental reminiscence** focuses on the past, on accomplishments, efforts to overcome difficulties, and experiences to help cope with current difficulties. **Obsessive reminiscence** suggests an inability to resolve or accept certain past events and a persistent guilt or despair about them (Wong & Watt, 1991). Contrast the following two narratives:

- When I was a teenager, my parents broke up and both remarried. I was very resentful because they did not seem to care about my feelings or needs. But as I grow older and look back, I understand that they were really not compatible with each other. They had suffered for many years before their divorce. [Integrative reminiscence]

- My husband died when I was away for two days visiting my friends in the West. He fell in the bathtub and eventually died because there was no one there to help him. It has been years now, but I still cannot forgive myself for leaving him home alone for two days. [Obsessive reminiscence] (Wong & Watt, 1991, p. 276)

Reminiscence appears to lend continuity to older adults' self-concepts. They can trace the path of their own development through time and identify moments that were of central importance in the crystallization of their personal philosophies. Through reminiscence, older adults can revise the meaning of past events by using current wisdom to understand or accept what took place in the past. For example, reminiscence was encouraged in a group of veterans who had been involved in the Normandy invasion at the end of World War II. The veterans retold their experiences of loss, grief, and shock, and how those experiences influenced their lives over the subsequent 50-year period. Formulating their experiences in a storylike format and retelling their stories to others provided a means of coping with the stressors of this past experience (Harvey, Stein, & Scott, 1995).

Reminiscence serves as an integrating process that has positive value in an eventual attainment of integrity. In a review of 20 studies with older adults who suffered from depression, guided reminiscence was found to be as effective as drug treatment or psychotherapy for alleviating depressive symptoms (Bohlmeijer, Smit, & Cuijpers, 2003). In excess, however, reminiscence can dominate reality, taking over the time and energy that might be directed toward more appropriate active social involvement. Some adults tend to dwell on sad events and allow earlier disappointments to preoccupy their current thoughts. In that case, their past lives take precedence over their current circumstances. No new events can compete successfully with past memories for their attention. The focus of reminiscence depends on personality, the specific nature of stressful life events, and the degree to which the older person is searching for new levels of self-understanding (Cappeliez & O'Rourke, 2002).

# THE PRIME ADAPTIVE EGO QUALITY AND THE CORE PATHOLOGY

## WISDOM

When people are asked about the positive goals of later life, they frequently mention wisdom, which they expect to emerge in later adulthood and to grow with increasing age. **Wisdom** is defined as the "fundamental pragmatics of life"— a type of expert knowledge that reflects sound judgment and good advice about "planning, managing, and understanding a good life" in the face of typically high levels of uncertainty (Baltes & Staudinger, 2000). Erikson identified wisdom as the prime adaptive ego quality of later adulthood, in that it reflects a detached concern for life and a desire to learn and communicate essential lessons from experience in the face of impending death (Erikson et al., 1986).

Wisdom has been characterized by five basic features (Baltes, Smith, & Staudinger, 1992, p. 272):

1. *Factual knowledge* about fundamental life matters, such as general knowledge about the human condition and specific knowledge about life events, their age-related occurrence, and their expected and unexpected course.

2. *Procedural knowledge*, composed of strategies for approaching the management and interpretation of life matters, including linking past, present, and future.

3. *Life-span contextualism*, approaching problems with the realization that events are embedded in a multidimensional context—including age-related, culturally defined, role-related, and sociohistorical frameworks—and that events take their meaning from certain distinct domains, especially family, work, and leisure.

4. *Relativism of values and life goals*, allowing the person to appreciate differences among individuals and societies with respect to the priorities they place on certain values, as well as the ability to preserve a certain core of universal values.

5. *Recognition and management of uncertainty*, incorporating the realization that the future cannot be totally predicted and that many aspects of the past and present are not fully known, plus an ability to manage and cope with this uncertainty.

One of the concepts that helps link the idea of intelligence in adulthood with the ego strength of wisdom is **expertise**. With age, individuals who focus their intelligence in intensive study, training, and repeated opportunities for problem solving within a domain become *experts*. A variety of intellectual processes support expertise, including deductive reasoning, a rich and complex working memory, and the ability to organize large amounts of information for storage and subsequent recall. We rely on experts to help inform important and diffi-

*Joseph looks forward to these quiet talks with his father. He knows he will always come away with new insight about planning, managing, or understanding the challenges he is facing in his own life.*

© Jose Galvez/Photo Edit

cult decisions. In that sense, we come to see experts as having wisdom in their particular specialization. Although we may be inclined to look to experts in one field to help us solve a wide range of problems, the assumption behind expertise is that it is discipline specific. In that sense, expertise and wisdom are not identical (Horn & Masunaga, 2000; Masunaga & Horn, 2001).

Not all people who live to old age function at a high level of wisdom. However, when older people are asked to focus their responses on excellence and virtue, they appear to be able to generate solutions that are characterized by higher levels of wisdom. What is more, people interacting together or even reflecting on the inner voice of those whom they consider wise are better able to produce rich, contextualized, and subtle responses (Baltes & Staudinger, 2000).

Three dimensions that have been hypothesized to promote wisdom are (1) opportunities to experience a wide variety of life situations and circumstances; (2) encouragement by a mentor or guide to expand one's capacity for thinking about problems from a multidimensional, psychohistorical perspective; and (3) a strong generative orientation or a desire to continue to gain insight into how people meet the challenges of life (Baltes & Smith, 1990).

## DISDAIN

Wisdom reflects flexibility of thought, openness to new interpretations, and a willingness to accept the complexity of life. In contrast, **disdain** conveys a rejection of ideas and persons and an arrogance that implies that one's own opinions and views are superior. It can be understood as a defensive response to the repulsion that one feels for one's physical self and failed past. Rather than becoming more patient, more compassionate, and less critical in their later life, older adults who develop disdain are more likely to express contempt for others and detach from the world around them (Erikson et al., 1986).

**APPLIED TOPIC**
## RETIREMENT

RETIREMENT IS A social concept that has a variety of definitions. One definition of retirement is that the person works less than full-time year round and receives income from a retirement pension earned during earlier periods of employment (Atchley, 1977, 1993). Some people define retirement as the time at which people begin to receive social security or other pension benefits, regardless of their employment status. However, retirement also refers to a psychosocial transition— a predictable, normative change that involves preparation, redefinition of roles and role behaviors, and ongoing psychological adjustment as the structure and significance of paid employment are replaced by other activities (Floyd et al., 1992).

Of course, some people never retire; some die before they reach retirement age, and others continue to work on a part-time schedule. Some people of retirement age leave their primary job and take another full-time or part-time job in a related field or in a totally different one. Many adults who are self-employed or whose work involves creative skills, such as acting, music, painting, or writing, simply continue to work into their late adulthood (Herzog, House, & Morgan, 1991). In fact, from a historical perspective, retirement is a relatively new concept. At the turn of the 20th century, almost 70% of men over the age of 65 were in the paid labor force, compared to 17% at the turn of the 21st century (U.S. Senate, Special Committee on Aging, 1986; U.S. Bureau of the Census, 2000).

## ADJUSTMENT TO RETIREMENT

Adjustment during the retirement transition is an individual process. Most older adults cope effectively with the changes associated with retirement, viewing it as a desired transition. In retrospect, however, they often realize that preparation for retirement should have included more emphasis on the psychosocial aspects of this change rather than focusing so exclusively on its financial impact. Retirement is a major life change; those who cope successfully with it tend to be more optimistic, actively confronting new challenges and remaining physically active in the transition (Rosenkoetter & Garris, 2001; Sharpley & Yardley, 1999).

Weiss (1997) described a longitudinal study of men and women who were over age 63 and intended to retire in the coming year or had recently retired. Most anticipated that retirement would bring a reduction in stress, especially in coping with the challenges and crises of the workplace. Workplace conditions such as lack of challenge, reorganization, and downsizing (with its accompanying increased demands on the remaining employees) are stressors that workers are glad to leave behind when they retire (Henkens & Tazelaar, 1997). In a study of young retirees ages 51 to 59, the most commonly mentioned positive aspects of retirement were the lack of pressure, more time with their spouse, and the ability to relax. In contrast, their greatest concerns were financial (not being able to keep up with inflation) and health concerns (National Academy on an Aging Society, 2001). In contrast

to those who are adjusting easily, approximately one third of adults report significant difficulty during this process (Fletcher & Hansson, 1991).

From a systems perspective, it makes sense to think about adaptation to retirement in the context of the other life roles one is playing. One of the most relevant is the marital relationship. With the large number of married women in the labor market, it is important to consider the impact of retirement for a couple as well as for the individual. Retirement transitions can involve one partner remaining in the labor market when the other retires; both partners retiring at about the same time; and one or both partners retiring from their primary work and becoming involved in secondary work after retirement. These configurations can have consequences for the couple's marital satisfaction as the change in work status affects their relationship.

The Cornell Retirement and Well-Being Study focused on workers and retirees ages 50 to 72. Participants were interviewed once in 1994–1995 and again in 1996–1997. Among the people in this sample, 25% were not yet retired and their spouses were also not yet retired. For another 36%, both the respondent and his or her spouse were retired. In the remainder, one spouse was working and the other spouse was retired. Several observations were made about marital quality during this transition. First, both men and women reported decreases in marital quality when they moved from work to retirement. The role transition from work to retirement appears to have a short-term negative impact on the marriage. Second, if one spouse remains in the labor market and the other retires, the retired partner reports more marital conflict. In this case, the stress of the role transition from work to retirement seems to be compounded by the lack of synchrony between the partners in the structure of their daily lives (Moen, Kim, & Hofmeister, 2001).

*Sophie decided to take up painting when she retired. This new direction provides intellectual stimulation, an avenue for creative expression, and the fun of being a beginner after 35 years of teaching others.*

© Jeff Greenberg/The Image Works

## DIFFICULTIES WITH RETIREMENT

Perceptions of retirement involve a person's enthusiasm, positive anticipation, or resentment about it. This is linked to the important ways in which work structures one's lifestyle throughout early and middle adulthood. In addition to the obvious functions of paid employment—especially income and social status—there are a number of latent functions that provide important psychological benefits (Jahoda, 1982; Lo & Brown, 1999). Work provides a structure for the use of time; a context for social contact; a content for self-identity; regular, predictable activities into which one can channel intellectual, physical, and emotional energy; and a sense of participation in a collective effort. Retirement may be perceived as resulting in deprivation in each of these areas and therefore present a threat to psychological well-being.

Several measures have been devised to assess the stresses associated with retirement and the anxiety that people feel as they anticipate it. Sharpley (1997) found that when retirees reflected on factors that caused them stress in everyday living, three areas emerged: missing work, problems with personal health, and relationship issues. Fletcher and Hansson (1991) constructed a measure of retirement anxiety that captures some of the apprehensions that adults have as they anticipate retirement. It illustrates how people come to rely on work as a primary social structure and highlights the difficulties they face as they confront the transition to retirement. For those who suffered from **retirement anxiety**, two factors were especially troubling. First, people who had high levels of retirement anxiety worried about the loss of structured social involvement and connection. This concern was linked to worry about losing friendships, being lonely, and having little in common with former coworkers after retirement. Second, people worried about having to be assertive or proactive in finding new relationships and activities that would meet their needs. This concern was linked to a general difficulty in handling life transitions, a high level of uncertainty about the future, and a general feeling of loss of identity. Although one might think that people who have high levels of retirement anxiety would use services that help people plan for retirement, this was not the case. They may try to deny this transition by avoiding planning and counseling sessions.

In addition to worries about being unable to meet one's social needs following retirement, some adults find the transition difficult because they feel a lack of control. When people perceive that they are working or not working by their own choice and that they determine how much work to do, they have higher levels of health and well-being. However, when they perceive that their level of involvement in work is being decided by someone else and they have little say in it, they are likely to have more difficulty adjusting to retirement, more health problems, and a greater incidence of depression (Gall, Evans, & Howard, 1997; Schultz, Morton, & Weckerle, 1998).

People whose work has brought them little satisfaction and those who are ready to become involved in new activities may feel more effective and independent after they retire (Floyd et al., 1992). They are likely to find new sources of enjoyment, new opportunities to spend time with family and friends, a sense of relief at not having to deal with the stressors of their job, and a new feeling of freedom to develop their interests or to exert more control over their daily life.

# CASE STUDY

## RETIREMENT AS A RELEASE FROM TEDIOUS WORK

This widowed man lives alone in a cabin in a sparsely populated, rural area. Throughout his working career, he held a variety of low-paying jobs that, in retrospect, neither required nor permitted real discipline or enterprise. He did not particularly like his jobs, and he was never viewed as performing them with particular success. For this man, retirement seems to signify not the loss of valuable structure, but his release from a series of rigid, repetitive demands that in and of themselves precluded inventiveness and enthusiasm. Retirement presents him with a new opportunity to re-experience the initiative that he now recalls as having characterized him until his mid-teens.

This man has always enjoyed music. He has always loved listening to the radio and playing records. As an adolescent, he tinkered with radio equipment until the advent of transistors and integrated circuits. Over the years he has accumulated a collection of some two to three thousand 78 rpm records. Recognizing that plastic record disks are likely to warp or break, he has recently begun to copy them onto cassettes. He has removed his tape deck and large loudspeakers from their cabinet and strapped them to a mover's dolly, onto which he has built appropriate shelves. Each day, when he goes to the senior center for lunch, he wheels his movable entertainment center out from his pickup truck and brings his friends their favorite songs.

This man has also begun to make his own TV dinners, using the partitioned trays on which his "meals on wheels" are delivered. He cooks large quantities of meat and vegetables and freezes them in these single-meal trays for easy access. The quality of this man's products is far from professional. In fact, his entertainment center looks rather slapdash, and the contents of his frozen meals do not always retain their flavor or texture when reheated. What is striking, instead, is the enthusiasm, the delight, and the pride with which he has devised his various projects. In each case, he perceived a problem, combined his own ingenuity with the resources at hand to devise a solution that is satisfactory for his own needs, and created something that is usable, gives him pleasure, and remains a real source of personal pride.

Source: From *Vital Involvement in Old Age*, E. Erikson, J. Erikson, & H. Kivnick, pp. 181–182. Copyright © 1986 W. W. Norton & Co.

■ CRITICAL THINKING AND CASE ANALYSIS

1. How are the developmental tasks of later adulthood reflected in this case?
2. Erikson mentioned the theme of initiative as reemerging for this man in later adulthood. What other psychosocial themes do you detect in this case?
3. How are the themes of person–environment fit and creativity, the central processes of middle adulthood, related to this case?
4. What challenges do older adults face in trying to make a successful adjustment to retirement? How might communities help to support adults in this transition?
5. What stereotypes about retirement and later adulthood are challenged in this case?

Adjustment to retirement is expected to change with time. Atchley (2001) proposed phases of anticipation, transition, and eventual adaptation. Four markers in this process include (1) a *honeymoon* period, which is busy and positive; (2) a *disenchantment* or letdown phase, in which the meaning and structure of work are missed; (3) a *reorientation* phase, in which a more realistic lifestyle is created; and (4) a *stable* period, which may last 10 or 15 years until changes in health, financial resources, or one's social support system require a significant revision.

In an attempt to assess this model, one study grouped retired men into six 6-month intervals from the date of retirement. In the period 13 to 18 months after retirement, men were significantly more dissatisfied with life and had lower levels of physical activity than did those in the first 6 months after retirement. Later periods showed lower levels of satisfaction than the first 6 months but not the marked depression of the 13- to 18-month period (Ekerdt, Bosse, & Levkoff, 1985). These findings support the idea of an early euphoric phase followed by a later letdown phase and reorientation. The pattern and degree of recovery are not as clearly described in this research.

■ INCOME LOSS

Adjustment to retirement is especially difficult when it is associated with a dramatic reduction in income. There is about a 25–30% reduction in income after retirement, which is somewhat greater for those who retire before age 65. Although work-related expenses, taxes, and child care expenses may decrease, health and recreational expenses may increase. In addition to reduced income, not all the sources of income are adjusted to keep pace with inflation. Thus, the value of retirees' fixed income declines over time.

Older householders' annual income is derived from five primary sources: social security, property and other assets, pensions, earnings, and supplemental security income (see Table 14.4; Social Security Administration, 2000). Access to these various resources varies by race and ethnicity, with older Whites having greater access to personal assets and pen-

**Table 14.4** Percentage Receiving Income by Source for Black, White, and Hispanic Adults Age 65 and Older

| SOURCE OF INCOME | WHITE | BLACK | HISPANIC |
|---|---|---|---|
| Social security | 91 | 88 | 77 |
| Asset income | 63 | 29 | 28 |
| Pensions | 43 | 33 | 22 |
| Earnings | 23 | 19 | 19 |
| Supplemental security income | 3 | 10 | 16 |

Source: Social Security Administration, 2000, *Income of the Aged Chartbook, 2000.* Retrieved July 28, 2004, from http://www.ssa.gov/policy/docs/chartbooks/income_aged/2000/text_c6.html

sions, and Blacks and Hispanics drawing more on supplemental security income due to their poverty status. In 2001, the median income for families headed by someone 65 years or older was $33,816. This can be compared to a median family income of $68,114 for families headed by someone age 45 to 54. About 10% of individuals 65 years and older had incomes below the poverty level. Poverty is greater for older minorities and for those older adults who live alone (U.S. Census Bureau, 2003).

■ THE FUTURE OF RETIREMENT

The ongoing dialogue among older workers, retirees, and industry is creating more varied, flexible alternatives to full retirement. Certain social forces are influencing continuing involvement in the labor market after age 65. An increasing number of businesses are eliminating a mandatory retirement age. In 2000, the earnings limit for receiving full social security benefits after age 65 was lifted. Finally, the age for full eligibility for social security retirement benefits will be rising to 67 for those born in 1960 or later. At the same time, movements toward reducing labor force participation for older workers include the development of early retirement plans, phased retirement, part-time work, and reduced or redefined job expectations. Innovation in retirement options seems to be taking two directions at the same time: how to retain older workers in meaningful work roles, and how to permit more flexible earlier retirement programs (AARP, 2000).

Several long-range concerns suggest a need to reexamine the "right to retirement" concept. First, prospects for a longer, healthier adulthood mean that a large proportion of the population will be out of the labor force for nearly one third of their adult lives if people continue to retire fully at age 65. With a reduced fertility rate, there may not be enough younger workers available to support this large nonworking population. Furthermore, it is becoming increasingly difficult to earn and save enough during the 40 or so years of employment to pay for 20 or more years of retirement.

Second, many older adults who are well educated and have enjoyed working want to continue some of their positive experiences through constructive work. They do not want to retire, and with the lifting of the mandatory retirement age, they do not have to. It is not uncommon for men and women to take new jobs, perhaps with fewer or more flexible hours, after they retire from their primary work. In the year 2002, 18% of men and 10% of women 65 years and older were in the labor market. The great majority of these older workers remain in the labor market by choice. A developing resistance to retirement is evident in the attitudes of professionals in their 50s and 60s. In-depth interviews with university professors, physicians, lawyers, business professionals, and social service professionals revealed that more than 35% were negative about retiring, and another 20% were ambivalent. One of those who was quite negative expressed it this way: "I'd probably try to get part-time teaching jobs, writing or editing, or research somewhere until I fall over. I mean really, I just can't imagine [retirement]. . . . This teaching is a rewarding activity. I don't hanker to retire to the sun belt and sit around and contemplate my navel. I just couldn't do that." (Karp, 1989, p. 752).

Third, people who reenter the labor force during midlife or make major career changes then want to persist in these new activities in order to fulfill both personal and societal expectations of achievement. Many women who delayed their entry into the labor market or achieved a professional degree after their spouse had completed his degree want to extend their work life into their late 60s and 70s (Carp, 1997). The current cohort of workers who are now in their 50s and 60s have become used to a more fluctuating work history, moving from one company or employer to another. They are more accustomed to taking charge of their occupational career rather than relying on the built-in career ladder of a single occupation or employer. Thus, just as the past few generations have begun to grow accustomed to retirement, new generations of older adults are finding ways to prolong their productive work lives, negotiating new and innovative ways of making transitions in and out of the paid labor force.

## Chapter Summary

Variability in the patterns of adjustment during later adulthood results from the interaction among biological, psychological, and societal factors, including the individual's personality characteristics, health, coping strategies, and ego strengths, and the range of circumstances that may befall him or her. Certain regularities can be anticipated in the termination of old roles and the establishment of new ones. Consolidation of attitudes toward one's life and the reality of one's death bring about a new perspective on life and lead to a more universal moral orientation.

The tasks of later adulthood—accepting one's life, promoting intellectual vigor, redirecting energy to new roles and activities, and developing a point of view about death—require a balance among investments in past, present, and future. There is an expectation that energy will be spent in the evaluative process of reviewing and accepting one's past achievements. However, this focus on the past must be complemented by the enactment of new roles, the resolution of new problems, and efforts to find new, engaging challenges in the present.

The psychosocial crisis of integrity versus despair captures the courage and creative synthesis required in later adulthood. In the face of an increasingly evident mortality, experiences in physical changes, role loss, and the death of peers, most older adults are able to define and articulate the thread of meaning in their lives. They are able to look back with satisfaction at past achievements and with acceptance of past failures. In this process, they find a certain practical wisdom that is shared with others and becomes their legacy for the future.

The role transitions that accompany retirement illustrate the challenge of later adulthood. Retirement usually results in leaving a major life structure—one that provided social status, focus, purpose, and economic resources. The potential loss of daily stimulation poses threats to both cognitive and social functioning. Because so much of one's social status is linked to one's occupational attainment, leaving one's work role is almost like giving up one's social identity. Older adults face numerous adjustments after retirement, including role loss. They must restructure their lives so that they continue to feel pride in past achievements without dwelling in the past, and so that they seek new and realistic opportunities for making use of their talents in the present.

It is critical to be sensitive to the image that children, adolescents, young and middle-aged adults, and older adults themselves have of later adulthood. One should not underestimate the impact that one's perceptions of later life have on one's well-being and optimism at every earlier life stage. If the later years hold no promise, all earlier stages will be tainted with a sense of desperation. On the other hand, if the later years can be anticipated with optimism, people will be free at each earlier stage to experience life in a more confident, accepting manner.

## Further Reflection

1. What are some of the new directions for growth in later adulthood? How are they reflected in the developmental tasks of this stage?

2. What are some strategies that older adults might use to preserve and extend intellectual vigor during this period?

3. What might be some barriers to achieving a sense of integrity in later adulthood? How do the primary adaptive ego qualities of earlier stages contribute to the successful resolution of this crisis?

4. What is the relationship between developing a point of view about death and achieving a sense of integrity?

5. How do ethnic and cultural factors influence the grandparent role? What have you observed in your own family and community about cultural differences in how this role is enacted?

6. What are your own thoughts about retirement? If you were promised a full pension that would allow you to stop working, would you continue to work? Is age a relevant factor in deciding about when a person should retire? If not, what factors should be considered?

## On the Web

### VISIT OUR WEBSITE

Go to http://www.wadsworth.com/psychology to find online resources directly linked to your book.

## Casebook

For additional case material related to this chapter, see the case of "Lola" in *Life Span Development: A Case Book*, by Barbara and Philip Newman, Laura Landry-Meyer, and Brenda J. Lohman, pp. 209–212. This case focuses on the role of reminiscence in resolving the psychosocial crisis of integrity versus despair and the opportunity for earlier expertise to be used in redirecting energy to new roles.

# CHAPTER 15

# VERY OLD AGE (75 UNTIL DEATH)

*Self Portrait, 1972/Pablo Picasso/© 2005 Estate of Pablo Picasso/Artists Rights Society (ARS), New York*

At the age of 91, a year before his death, Picasso painted this remarkable self-portrait. He faces his death with eyes wide open—no pretenses, some fear, some wonder.

■ THE LONGEVITY REVOLUTION

A New Psychosocial Stage: Very Old Age
The Gender Gap Among the Very Old

■ DEVELOPMENTAL TASKS

Coping with the Physical Changes of Aging
Developing a Psychohistorical Perspective
Traveling Uncharted Territory: Life Structures of the Very Old
CASE STUDY: MR. Z

■ THE PSYCHOSOCIAL CRISIS:
IMMORTALITY VERSUS EXTINCTION

Immortality
Extinction

■ THE CENTRAL PROCESS: SOCIAL SUPPORT

The Benefits of Social Support
The Dynamics of Social Support
The Social Support Network

■ THE PRIME ADAPTIVE EGO QUALITY
AND THE CORE PATHOLOGY

Confidence
Diffidence

■ APPLIED TOPIC: MEETING THE
NEEDS OF THE FRAIL ELDERLY

Defining Frailty
Supporting Optimal Functioning
The Role of the Community
The Role of Creative Action

■ CHAPTER SUMMARY

■ FURTHER REFLECTION

▶  *To identify very old age as a unique developmental period for those of unusual longevity—a stage with its own developmental tasks and psychosocial crisis.*

▶  *To describe some of the physical changes associated with aging, including changes in fitness, behavioral slowing, sensory changes, and vulnerability to illness, and the challenges that these changes pose for continued psychosocial well-being.*

▶  *To develop the concept of an altered perspective on time and history that emerges among the long-lived.*

▶  *To explore elements of the lifestyle structure for the very old, especially living arrangements and gender role behaviors.*

▶  *To identify and describe the psychosocial crisis of immortality versus extinction, the central process of social support, the prime adaptive ego quality of confidence, and the core pathology of diffidence.*

▶  *To apply research and theory to concerns about meeting the needs of the frail elderly.*

PABLO PICASSO, WHOSE works illustrate this book, lived to be 91 years old. When he was 79, he married Jacqueline Roque, with whom he enjoyed 12 years of married life. During the last 20 years of his life, he remained productive and energetic, persistently experimenting with new art forms and ideas.

Here are some other examples of people who achieved major accomplishments after the age of 80 (Wallechinsky & Wallace, 1993; Wallechinsky, Wallace, & Wallace, 1977):

At 100, Grandma Moses was still painting.

At 99, twin sisters Kin Narita and Gin Kanie recorded a hit CD single in Japan and starred in a television commercial.

At 94, George Burns, who won an Oscar at age 80 for his role in *The Sunshine Boys*, performed at Proctor's Theater in Schenectady, New York, 63 years after he had first played there.

At 93, George Bernard Shaw wrote the play *Farfetched Fables*.

At 91, Eamon de Valera served as president of Ireland.

At 91, Hulda Crooks climbed Mount Whitney, the highest mountain in the continental United States.

At 89, Arthur Rubenstein gave one of his greatest piano recitals in New York's Carnegie Hall.

At 88, Konrad Adenauer was chancellor of Germany.

At 87, Mary Baker Eddy founded the *Christian Science Monitor*.

At 81, Benjamin Franklin effected the compromise that led to the adoption of the U.S. Constitution. ∎

# THE LONGEVITY REVOLUTION

In 1997, Jeanne Calment, the world's officially longest living person, died at the age of 122. In an interview the year before her death, Calment was quoted as saying, "I've never had but one wrinkle and I'm sitting on it." In 1996, she recorded a rap CD as a document of her love of life (*Time*, August 18, 1997).

We are entering a period of human experience in which increasing numbers of people are living into old age. In 2005, 6% of the U.S. population was 75 and older, and this age group is expected to make up 11.6% of the population in 2050. In 1980, more than 2 million people were 85 and older; by 2005, this group had grown to 5.1 million. Of these, 65,000 were 100 years and older. The 85-and-older population, which is the fastest growing age group in the United States, is expected to reach 7.2 million in 2020 (U.S. Census Bureau, 2004b).

The 20th century was unique in human history in the large percentage of people who lived well beyond their reproductive and childrearing years into later adulthood and very old age. This new facet of life raises questions about the pattern of mortality after achieving reproductive success and about what, if any, limit there might be to the human life span. Current demographic extrapolations suggest that the average life expectancy at birth will be 85 by the year 2050 (Wilmoth, 1998). Genetically based diseases that emerge only in the second half of life, such as breast and colon cancer or adult-onset diabetes, become more common as larger numbers of people reach advanced age. At the same time, the mapping of the human genome and medical and technologi-

Jeanne Calment, who died in 1997 at the age of 122, was the world's longest living person whose birth date could be verified. Mme. Calment liked chocolates, smoked cigarettes, and had a wonderful sense of humor. Here she displays her Guinness certificate acknowledging her record-winning longevity.

cal interventions hold the promise of preventing some of the diseases now associated with later life. Life expectancy is most influenced by interventions that prevent infants and children from dying, ensuring that more people will reach advanced ages of 70 or older. Interventions that influence the life expectancy at ages 70 and older, however, will only increase overall life expectancy by a few years. Nonetheless, significant discoveries that might prevent death from cancers or cardiovascular diseases could affect large populations and continue to extend human longevity.

From an evolutionary perspective, the human species is a highly complex organism, designed to survive over a relatively long period in order to find a mate, reproduce, and rear and nurture the young until they are old enough to reproduce. The adaptive value of life after this sequence is not well understood. One hypothesis is that the extended family—composed of grandparents as well as parents—provides more resources for the support of the young, and forms an added protective layer against crises that might leave the younger generation vulnerable. It is clear that there is a genetic basis to longevity, suggesting that for some subgroups, being long-lived has proven adaptive (Olshansky, Carnes, & Grahn, 1998).

Each new cohort of the very old will benefit from the information and technology that have been developed. The more knowledge is gained about the biological processes of aging and the genetic basis of diseases that emerge in later life, the more likely it is that human longevity can be extended.

Those adults in the current baby boom generation (born between 1943 and 1954) are quite likely to be high school graduates, to have benefited from many of the health-related innovations of the late 20th century, and to be even more vigorous than our current older population. The projections of increased numbers of people reaching advanced age are due to increases in longevity due to improvements in health care and fitness and to the size of the baby boom cohort.

In an attempt to learn the secrets of longevity, Jim Heynen (1990) interviewed 100 people who were 100 years or older. He found wide variations in their lifestyles and philosophical perspectives. Some of the advice they offered on how to live a long life follows:

> "Mind your own business, have a good cigar, and take a shot of brandy." *Brother Adelard Beaudet, Harrisville, Rhode Island*
> "I've lived long because I was so mean." *Pearl Rombach, Melbourne, Florida*
> "I always walked several miles a day. I'd talk to the flowers." *Mary Frances Annand, Pasadena, California*
> "Don't smoke before noon. Don't drink or smoke after midnight. The body needs 12 hours of the day to clear itself." *Harry Wander, Boise, Idaho*
> "I've been a tofu eater all my life; a mild, gentle man, never a worrier." *Frank Morimitsu, Chicago, Illinois*
> "I picked my ancestors carefully." *Stella H. Harris, Manhattan, Kansas*
> "Regular hours, taking it easy, smiling, whistling at the women when they walk by." *John Hilton, Fort Lauderdale, Florida*

## A NEW PSYCHOSOCIAL STAGE: VERY OLD AGE

The fact that an increasing number of people are reaching advanced years and that they share several characteristics leads us to hypothesize a new stage of psychosocial development that emerges at the upper end of the life span, after one has exceeded the life expectancy for one's birth cohort. We call this stage **very old age**. Although it was not specifically identified in Erikson's original formulation of life stages, in the book *Vital Involvement in Old Age* (Erikson et al., 1986), Erikson began to characterize the dynamics of psychosocial adaptation in this period of life. Throughout this chapter, we have drawn on Erikson's insights to enrich our appreciation of the courage, vitality, and transformations that accompany this period.

We have formulated a psychosocial analysis of development for the very old, based on research literature, first-hand reports, and personal observations to describe the developmental tasks, psychosocial crisis, central process, prime adaptive ego quality, and core pathology of this stage. We approach this formulation of a new stage realizing that in

© Mark Peterson /Corbis

*In his very old age, Jimmy Carter is an inspirational humanitarian. He is an active spokesperson for Habitat for Humanity and an advocate for peaceful resolution of international conflicts.*

in relation to one's potential and to greater vulnerability to the restrictive impact of illness in later life. In contrast, adequate finances, social integration, social support, and access to appropriate services are likely to be linked to higher levels of functioning in relation to one's potential and to greater resilience in the face of illness.

Twelve Cuban men and women reported to be more than 100 years old were interviewed by nutritionists, psychologists, physicians, and gerontologists about their daily diets and lifestyles. The one theme they all agreed upon was the importance of an optimistic outlook on life. The coordinator of the meeting, Dr. Eugenio Selman, said that the six basic elements to longevity are (1) motivation to live, (2) appropriate diet, (3) medical attention, (4) intense physical activity, (5) cultural activities, and (6) a healthy environment. In this formula, one sees the interaction of the biological, the psychological, and societal systems (CNN.com, 2005).

The variations in life experiences and outlook among the very old are great. As a result, chronological age becomes less useful as an indicator of aging. Neugarten (1981) found it useful to distinguish between two groups of the very old: the *old-old* and the *young-old*. The **old-old** have "suffered major physical or mental decrements," which increase their dependence on health and social services. This group will grow as the number of adults over 75 increases. Currently, it forms a minority of the very old. The majority of people over 75 can be described as **young-old**. They are competent, vigorous, and relatively healthy. They live in their own households and participate in activities in their communities.

Our intention is to discuss some of the most salient characteristics of life after age 75 and to articulate what appears to be a psychosocial crisis specific to this period. We report evidence of common challenges and successful strategies for coping amid the great diversity of individual experiences.

## THE GENDER GAP AMONG THE VERY OLD

A discussion of aging in the United States must acknowledge the shifting sex composition of the population at older ages. In 2000, 54% of those between 65 and 69 years old were women, 56% of those between 70 and 74 years old were women, and 70% of those 85 years and older were women. This gender difference in longevity is observed in virtually all countries of the world, but the differences are accentuated in the developed countries (U.S. Bureau of the Census, 2000). The imbalance in the sex composition is much more noticeable today than it was 50 years ago, when there were about as many men as women in the older-than-65 category (U.S. Bureau of the Census, 1983). Because those currently at the stage of very old age are predominantly women, many of the social issues of aging—especially poverty, health care, the future of social security, and housing—are also viewed as "women's issues."

many domains—especially physical functioning, reaction time, memory, and fluid intelligence—variability increases significantly with age (Morse, 1993). The following are some of the many reasons why an increasing number of individual differences can be noted during later life: "The combined effects of individuals' unique experiences over more years would produce increasing differences among them; genetically based differences would have more time to be expressed and to cause individuals to diverge; and older people, somewhat freer of societal constraints, would be more likely to choose their own courses of action" (Morse, 1993, p. 156).

The concept of *reaction range* introduced in Chapter 5 (Pregnancy and Prenatal Development) offers a framework for understanding the enormous variability in vitality and functioning during very old age. Genetic factors influence longevity, vulnerability to illnesses, intelligence, and personality factors that contribute to coping (Pollack, 2001). Conditions of poverty, discrimination, social alienation, and lack of social support are likely to be linked to lower levels of functioning

# DEVELOPMENTAL TASKS

Despite the wide variability in capacities, lifestyles, and worldviews in later life, three themes characterize the challenges that face individuals in very old age. First, they must adapt to *physical changes*, monitoring their health and modifying their lifestyles to accommodate these changes. Second, they must conceptualize their lives within a new *time frame*, realigning their thoughts about past, present, and future in order to stay connected to the present in a meaningful way. Third, they must develop new *life structures*—especially living arrangements and social relationships—that provide comfort, interest, and appropriate levels of care.

## COPING WITH THE PHYSICAL CHANGES OF AGING

There is no way to avoid the realization that one's body is not what it used to be. Erikson described it as follows:

> With aging, as the overall tonus of the body begins to sag and innumerable inner parts call attention to themselves through their malfunction, the aging body is forced into a new sense of invalidness. Some problems may be fairly petty, like the almost inevitable appearance of wrinkles. Others are painful, debilitating, and shaming. Whatever the severity of these ailments, the elder is obliged to turn attention from more interesting aspects of life to the demanding requirements of the body. This can be frustrating and depressing. (Erikson et al., 1986, p. 309)

The theme of the physical changes of aging can be approached much like its counterpart in early adolescence. Although the rate of change may be slower, older adults notice changes in a wide range of areas, including appearance, body shape, strength and stamina, and the accumulation of chronic illnesses. Just as in adolescence, the rate and sequence of changes varies from person to person. This section will identify major areas of physical change. The patterns of change described here are average trends. Not all adults experience all of these changes, nor to the same degree. The important issues are the meaning that adults attribute to their physical condition and the coping strategies they invent to adapt to these changes.

Most of us know older adults who are vigorous and zestful. On the other hand, we also know older adults who are painfully limited in their ability to function because of physical disabilities. Many factors influence the progression of physical changes associated with aging, not the least of which is the level of fitness that was established and maintained during early and middle adulthood. The topics of fitness, behavioral slowing, sensory changes, health, illness, and functional independence combine to provide a picture of the physical changes of aging.

## ■ FITNESS

There is a great deal of variation in fitness among people after age 70 as patterns of activity or inactivity, endurance or frailty, and illness or health take their toll. What is described here might be thought of as the usual patterns of aging. However, these changes are not inevitable and, in many instances, are reversible or modifiable with appropriate intervention (Rowe & Kahn, 1998). Most people begin to notice declines in their physical health and fitness in their late 20s and early 30s. As those who love baseball are likely to claim, "the legs are the first to go." On a more positive note, most people's strength and capacity for moderate effort are about the same at age 70 as they were at age 40 (Stevens-Long & Commons, 1992). However, older people are less resilient after a period of prolonged exertion. The respiratory and circulatory systems usually degenerate to some extent and are less capable of providing the heart and muscle tissue with oxygenated blood as quickly as they once could. One result is that sudden changes in posture can cause an older person to feel lightheaded. In order to adapt successfully to this kind of bodily change, an older person may find it necessary to move more slowly and to change positions more deliberately. This observable change in the tempo of movement may be incorrectly interpreted as fatigue or weakness when, in fact, it is often a purposeful strategy for preventing dizziness.

Slowed metabolism reduces the need for calories, but there is a new risk. Reduction in food intake—particularly the elimination of foods such as milk—may result in the lack of essential vitamins and minerals in an older person's diet. The resulting malnutrition may then contribute to osteoporosis and iron deficiencies, which produce feelings of weakness, fatigue, and a lack of resilience (Klesges et al., 2001). Many health concerns of later adulthood that may have been attributed to the aging process itself are in fact a direct or indirect result of malnutrition. In order to cope successfully with a diminished appetite, a very old person must become more conscientious in selecting foods that will provide the nutritional elements necessary for healthy functioning.

An increasing number of factors make it difficult to maintain a high level of physical fitness in later life. Figure 15.1 illustrates the patterns of loss of bodily functions associated with age in six areas. For each body area, the level of functioning at age 30 is taken as 100%, and the losses are plotted in comparison with this level. Most of the bodily changes begin in middle adulthood, but the rate of change appears to increase after age 60. As you can see, maximum breathing capacity decreases the most, and brain weight changes the least. The consequences of an inactive life—especially obesity and degeneration in muscle strength—contribute to an even greater decline in physical capacity, particularly after age 60.

Commitment to physical fitness is important for adults in

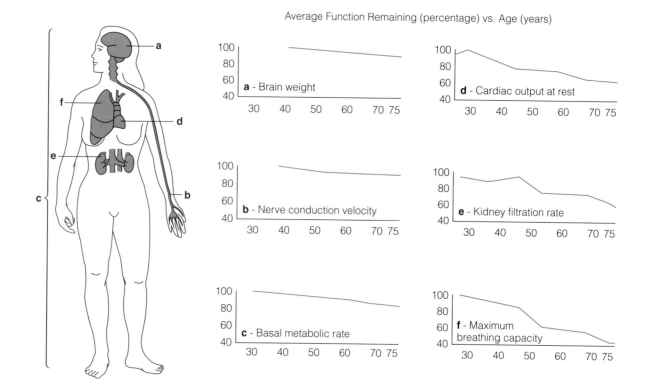

**FIGURE 15.1**

Loss of Bodily Functions with Increasing Age

Source: Adapted from "Growing Old," by A. Leaf, 1973, *Scientific American*, p. 229.

order to face their later years in the best possible physical condition. Maintenance of optimal physical condition in very old age depends on being active in earlier periods of adulthood. Overweight adults—and those of average or below-average weight—need to commit themselves to a program of moderate physical activity that can be continued throughout life.

In its report *Healthy People 2010*, the U.S. government placed regular physical activity at the top of the list of health concerns. A primary goal is to promote regular, daily physical activity for at least 30 minutes per day. Regular physical activity is associated with decreased rates of death from heart disease, lower risk of diabetes and colon cancer, and prevention of high blood pressure. Physical activity also improves muscle and bone strength, contributes to weight control, and improves strength, flexibility, and balance. Despite these advantages, by age 75, one third of men and one half of women are not at all involved in physical activity (U.S. Department of Health and Human Services, 2001).

With advancing age, some people tend to become more sedentary and lose interest in physical activity. In order to maintain optimal functioning and to retard the degenerative effects of aging, very old adults must continue to have frequent and regular opportunities for physical exercise. A regular program of walking or other aerobic exercise can enhance cardiovascular functioning and reverse some of the effects of a sedentary adult lifestyle. Research on weight, or resistance, training shows that even among the very old, a

steady program of exercise builds muscle strength, which contributes to agility and an overall sense of well-being (Ades, Ballor, Ashikaga, Utton, & Nair, 1996). Experimental studies of the effects of exercise on cognitive functioning show that it also leads to improvements in various central nervous system functions. These benefits of exercise are attributed to higher levels of oxygen, which improve the metabolism of glucose and neurotransmitters in the brain, as well as to increased levels of arousal, which increase response speed (Dustman et al., 1989; Birren & Fisher, 1992).

■ **BEHAVIORAL SLOWING**

One of the most commonly noted markers of aging is a gradual slowing in response to stimuli. Such **behavioral slowing** is observed in motor responses, reaction time, problem-solving abilities, memory skills, and information processing (Salthouse, 1996). The speed of behavior is a composite outcome of the time it takes to perceive a stimulus, retrieve related information from memory, integrate it with other relevant stored information, reason as necessary about the required action, and then take action—whether that means simply pressing a button or performing a surgical procedure. Age-related slowing is more readily observable in complex tasks requiring mental processing than in routine tasks (Lemaire, Arnaud, & Lecacheur, 2004). The more complex the task, the greater the **processing load**—that is, the more domains of information are called into play and the more time it takes to select response strategies (Cerella, 1994).

The number of tasks presented in a sequence and the complexity or choice required to make a response are all factors that influence response time. Under conditions where a choice of response is required, older adults do not show evidence of slowing in the early phase of processing the stimuli but in the executive functions associated with enacting the appropriate response (Yordanova, Kolev, Hohnsbein, & Falkenstein, 2004). In many studies, older adults show improvements in response time when given opportunity for practice. However, when older and younger adults are both given opportunities for practice, the older adults do not improve as much as the younger, and the performance gap may actually increase (Hein & Schubert, 2004).

Biological, learned, and motivational factors have been identified to account for behavioral slowing. At the biological level, there is evidence of the slowing of neural firing in certain brain areas, which may result in a slower speed of information processing. The extent of this slowing depends on the kinds of tasks and the specific cognitive processes involved (Bashore, van der Molen, Ridderinkhof, & Wylie, 1997).

As a result of behavioral slowing, it takes longer for older adults to perform daily tasks. When Ben takes his trip to the grocery, it takes him more time than it did 10 years ago to walk through the aisles, read the labels, decide on his purchases, and count his change.

The slowing of responses may also be a product of learned cautiousness. With experience, people learn to respond slowly in order to avoid making mistakes. When confronted with new, experimental problem-solving tasks, older adults may take longer because they are not confident in using a new strategy. They may revert to a more familiar if more time-consuming approach in order to solve the problem correctly. Thus, a conservative orientation to the selection of problem-solving strategies may result in slower responses but not be strictly due to neurological causes (Touron & Hertzog, 2004). Finally, response slowing may be a product of a low level of motivation to perform a task. In experiments in which reaction time is being tested, adult participants may be uninterested in the task and thus unwilling to try to achieve a high level of functioning.

The implications of the consequences of behavioral slowing are currently being examined. Some researchers have argued that even the slightest reduction in the speed of neural firing may result in reduced sensory and information-processing capacities. Furthermore, response slowing may reduce a person's chances of survival if a situation arises in which a sudden evasive action or an immediate response is required. Others have suggested that if a moment of thought is required before an action is taken, slowness may increase a person's chances of survival.

A common consequence of slowing is its impact on cognitive functioning. If the nervous system functions at a slower rate, it takes more time to scan and perceive information, to search long-term memory, to integrate information from various knowledge domains, and to make a response (Madden, 2001). With increased input each year, it is possible that the time needed for processing information increases. In the face of complex cognitive tasks, information may be lost, or distractions may intervene if the process takes too long (Birren & Fisher, 1992). For example, Hertzog (1989) examined the relationship of age and speed of performance in a variety of mental abilities among people ranging in age from 43 to 89. He found that the speed of performance measure was a better predictor of mental abilities than was age. Other research looked at crystallized and fluid intelligence. Recall from Chapter 14 (Later Adulthood) that crystallized intelligence tends to increase with age, whereas fluid intelligence declines. When the factor of speed of responding was removed from the tests of fluid intelligence, the decline with age was significantly less. These studies support the claim that changes in speed of responding account for much—though probably not all—of the documented evidence of decline in intellectual performance with age. The debate continues, however, about whether this slowing is general—influencing all types of cognitive activity—or specific to certain domains. There is considerable evidence that contemporary circumstances—especially physical fitness and health, as well as the kinds of medications one is taking and the presence of immediate stressors in one's life—influence speed of responding (Willis, Diehl, Gruber-Baldini, Marsiske, & Haessler, 1990).

As slowing occurs gradually, most adults compensate for it

by making their environments more convenient or by changing their lifestyles. However, slowing becomes more hazardous in situations that require the older adult to keep pace with a tempo that cannot be modified, such as highway driving or crossing the street with the light. For instance, some older people encounter problems because the amount of time the light stays green at a pedestrian crosswalk is insufficient to permit them to get to the other side of the street safely.

As older people recognize some situations in which they have trouble responding quickly, they must review the tempo of their day. Very old people need to become more selective in their choice of activities, so that they can allocate enough time for the tasks most important to them and perform them satisfactorily. This means exercising greater control over their time and being less concerned about whether they are in harmony with the tempo of others.

### ■ SENSORY CHANGES

Every sense modality—vision, hearing, taste, touch, and smell—is vulnerable to age-related changes. With age, greater intensity of stimulation is required to make the same impact on the sensory system that was once achieved with lower levels of stimulation. Some of the changes in vision, hearing, taste, and smell are given in Table 15.1. These changes begin in early adulthood, and their effects increase throughout the remainder of life (Erber, 2005).

**VISION.** **Visual adaptation** involves the ability to adjust to changes in the level of illumination. Pupil size decreases with age, so that less light reaches the retina. Thus, older adults need higher levels of illumination to see clearly, and it takes them longer to adjust from dark to light and from light to dark. Many older adults are increasingly sensitive to glare and may draw the shades in their rooms to prevent bright light

from striking their eyes. Slower adaptation time and sensitivity to glare interfere with night driving. Some of the visual problems of people older than 75 are difficulties with tasks that require speed of visual performance, such as reading signs in a moving vehicle; a decline in near vision, which interferes with reading and daily tasks; and difficulties in searching for or tracking visual information (Kline, 1994; Kosnik, Winslow, Kline, Rasinski, & Sekuler, 1988).

Several physiological conditions seriously impair vision and can result in partial or total blindness in old age. These conditions include cataracts, which are a clouding of the lenses, making them less penetrable by light; deterioration or detachment of the retina; and glaucoma, which is an increase in pressure from the fluid in the eyeball. The incidence of visual impairments, especially cataracts, increases dramatically from later adulthood (65 to 74) to very old age (beyond 75).

By very old age, 19% of men and 20% of women experience problems with cataracts. According to vision experts, recent medical innovations have made cataract surgery much less complicated than it was in the past. Cataracts are typically removed on an outpatient basis. The surgeon removes the clouded lens and, in most cases, replaces it with a clear, plastic intraocular lens (IOL). Nine out of 10 people who have cataract surgery regain very good vision, somewhere between 20/40 and 20/20 (Lee, 2002).

Loss of vision poses serious challenges to adaptation—it has the effect of separating people from contact with the world. Such impairment is especially linked with feelings of helplessness. Most older adults are not ready to cope with the challenge of learning to function in their daily world without being able to see. For them, the loss of vision reduces their activity level, autonomy, and willingness to leave a familiar setting. For many older adults, impaired vision results in the decision to give up driving altogether, or at least night driving, causing a significant loss of independence. However, this loss

**Table 15.1** Changes in Sensory Systems After Age 20

| AGE GROUP | VISION | HEARING | TASTE AND SMELL |
|---|---|---|---|
| 20–35 | Constant decline in accommodation as lenses begin to harden at about age 20 | Pitch discrimination for high-frequency tones begins to decline | No documented changes |
| 35–65 | Sharp decline in acuity after 40; delayed adjustment to shifts in light and dark | Continued gradual loss in pitch discrimination to age 50 | Loss of taste buds begins |
| 65+ | Sensitivity to glare; increased problems with daily visual tasks; increases in diseases of the eye that produce partial or total blindness | Sharp loss in pitch discrimination after 70; sound must be more intense to be heard | Higher thresholds for detecting sour, salt, and bitter tastes; higher threshold for detecting smells, and errors in identifying odors |

Source: Based on Newman and Newman, 1983.

*Irene still relies on her sense of smell to select the ripest fruit and the juiciest tomatoes.*

© Carl Glassman / The Image Works

can be minimized by the availability of inexpensive, flexible public transportation.

**HEARING.** Hearing loss increases with age. About 46% of men and 32% of women age 75 and older have some hearing impairment (U.S. Bureau of the Census, 2000). The most common effects of hearing loss are a reduced sensitivity to both high-frequency (high-pitched) and low-intensity (quiet) sounds and a somewhat decreased ability to understand spoken messages. Certain environmental factors—including exposure to loud, unpredictable noise and injuries, such as damage to the bones in the middle ear—influence the extent of hearing loss.

Loss of hearing interferes with a basic mode of human connectedness—the ability to participate in conversation. Hearing impairment may be linked to feelings of isolation or suspiciousness. A person may hear things imperfectly, miss parts of conversations, or perceive conversations as occurring in whispers rather than in ordinary tones (Wallace, Hayes, & Jerger, 1994).

The very old adult who is aware of these facts may be able to compensate intellectually for diminished auditory sensitivity. Knowing the people one is with and believing that one is valued by them can help reassure a person about the nature of conversations and allay suspicions. Self-esteem plays an important part in this process. The older person with high self-esteem is likely to be able to make the intellectual adjustment needed to interpret interactions and to request clarification when necessary. Such requests may even serve to stimulate greater interaction and produce greater clarity in communication. Older people with a hearing loss and high self-esteem tend to insist that people who want to communicate with them should face them when they speak.

In contrast, older people who have low self-esteem are likely to be more vulnerable to suspicions about the behavior of others because they doubt their own worth. They are more likely to perceive inaudible comments as attempts to ridicule or exclude them. These experiences contribute to feelings of rejection and can produce irritability and social withdrawal.

**TASTE AND SMELL.** There are wide variations in the density of taste receptors among adult humans. With age, the number of taste buds decreases. Older adults have a higher threshold than young adults for detecting sweet, sour, bitter, and salty tastes. Some of this reduced sensitivity may be related to the impact of certain medications or to poor oral hygiene (Receputo, Mazzoleni, DiFazio, & Alessandria, 1996). An especially important implication of insensitivity to salt is that older adults may add more salt to their food and thereby aggravate hypertension. Older adults also require greater intensity to detect odors and are more likely to misidentify them (Receputo, Mazzoleni, Rapisarda, & Di Fazio, 1996). Changes in the senses of smell and taste may result in a loss of appetite or a disruption of normal eating habits. Loss of appetite (which may accompany illness and new medications), pain due to dental problems, and changes in the digestive system all contribute to malnutrition among the elderly.

**COPING WITH SENSORY CHANGES.** As a result of the various patterns of aging among the very old, it is impossible to prescribe an ideal pattern of coping. The SOC model (introduced in Chapter 14, Later Adulthood) becomes increasingly relevant as sensory and motor functions are impaired. According to this model, in order to cope effectively, older adults must select the areas where they are most invested in sustaining optimal functioning and direct their resources to enhancing those areas, while compensating for the areas

APPLYING THEORY AND RESEARCH TO LIFE

## Organic Brain Syndromes: Dementia

IN ACUTE BRAIN syndromes, the onset of confusion is relatively sudden. Often, this pattern is associated with a severe illness, such as heart failure, alcoholism, or extreme malnutrition. In these cases, the symptoms of the brain syndrome can often be reversed if the accompanying illness can be treated. Supportive counseling, attention to diet, and skill training to reestablish control of daily functions may restore the person's previous level of adaptive behavior.

*Chronic brain syndrome,* on the other hand, produces a more gradual loss of memory, reduced intellectual functioning, and an increase of mood disturbances—especially hostility and depression. Whereas a large number of conditions can cause acute brain syndrome, a smaller number of diseases are linked to chronic brain syndrome. *Alzheimer's disease* is the most common form of this syndrome, accounting for about 50% of the dementias among the elderly. The incidence of this disease increases with age, with fewer than 2% of people below the age of 60 affected by it, whereas an estimated 30% to 50% of those ages 85 to 100 experience some

symptoms (Hooyman & Kiyak, 1993; Rowe & Kahn, 1998).

A person with Alzheimer's disease experiences gradual brain failure over a period of 7 to 10 years. Symptoms include severe problems in cognitive functioning, especially increased memory impairment and a rapid decline in the complexity of written and spoken language; problems with self-care; and behavioral problems, such as wandering, asking the same questions repeatedly, and becoming suddenly angry or stubborn (Kemper, Thompson, & Marquis, 2001; O'Leary, Haley, & Paul, 1993). Currently, there is no treatment that will reverse Alzheimer's disease. Treatments address specific symptoms—especially mood and memory problems—and attempt to slow its progress.

As the number of older adults with Alzheimer's disease and related disorders has grown, the plight of their caregivers has aroused increasing concern (Roth et al., 2001). Most Alzheimer's patients are cared for at home, often by their adult children. The caregiving process is ongoing, with an accumulation of stressors and periodic transitions in

the patient's condition that require a restructuring of personal, work, and family life for the caregiver. Caregivers often experience high levels of stress and depression as they attempt to cope with their responsibilities and as they assess the effectiveness or ineffectiveness of their efforts. Over time, they are likely to experience physical symptoms of their own, associated with the physical and emotional strains of this role.

The care of an older person with some form of dementia is fraught with problems and frustrations, but it also provides some opportunities for satisfaction and feelings of encouragement (Aneshensel, Pearlin, Mullan, Zarit, & Whitlatch, 1995). The "uplifts" and "hassles" frequently reported by caregivers give some insight into the typical day-to-day experience of caring for a person who is suffering from Alzheimer's disease (Kinney & Stephens, 1989).

The uplifts include the following:

- seeing care recipient calm;
- pleasant interactions between care recipient and family;

in which functioning is more limited. What one hopes to achieve is a balance between self-sufficiency and willingness to accept help, preserving one's dignity as much as possible and optimizing day-to-day mobility. This is described in the following excerpt from Erikson's study of the very old:

> Appropriate dependence can be accommodated and accepted by elders when they realistically appraise their own physical capacities. One of our more practical elders simply states, "Of course, you're still interested in everything. But you don't expect yourself to do everything, the way you used to. Some things you just have to let go." However, inappropriate restriction can be, in its way, insulting and belittling. In describing his current life, one widowed man expresses both his refusal to accept restriction and his willingness to rely on appropriate assistance: "I can stay up here in the woods because I know if I really need help, my son will be here inside of three hours. Now, this deal with fixing my own water pipes, I'd have never tried that without my son so nearby, and I didn't even need him." (Erikson et al., 1986, pp. 309–310)

### ■ HEALTH, ILLNESS, AND FUNCTIONAL INDEPENDENCE

How can we characterize the level of health, illness, and functional independence in later life? A mild but persistent decline in the immune system is observed as a correlate of aging. As a result, older adults are more susceptible to infections and take a longer time to heal. Substantial numbers of older adults are afflicted with one or more chronic conditions, such as arthritis, diabetes, or high blood pressure, which may require medication and interfere with daily functioning.

Data from the National Health Interview Study provided a look at trends in chronic diseases and their impact on limitations in functioning (Freedman & Martin, 2000). People who were age 70 and older in 1984 and 1995 were asked about several chronic diseases and conditions. They were also asked about whether they had certain upper-body and lower-body limitations. Upper-body limitations included such things as reaching up over one's head or using one's fingers to grasp a handle. Lower-body limitations included walking for a quar-

- seeing care recipient responsive;
- care recipient showing affection;
- friends and family showing understanding about caregiving;
- care recipient recognizing familiar people;
- care recipient being cooperative;
- leaving care recipients with others at home;
- care recipient smiling or winking;
- receiving caregiving help from family.

Some of the hassles include:

- care recipient being confused or not making sense;
- care recipient's forgetfulness;
- care recipient's agitation;
- care recipient not cooperating;
- care recipient's bowel or bladder accidents;
- seeing care recipient withdrawn or unresponsive;
- dressing and bathing care recipient;
- assisting with care recipient's toileting;
- care recipient declining physically;

- care recipient not sleeping through the night;
- care recipient asking repetitive questions.

Two of the symptoms that are most difficult to manage are sleep disturbances and wandering. As cognitive functioning declines, the pattern of sleep deteriorates. A person with Alzheimer's disease sleeps for only short periods, napping on and off during the day and night. Often, the napping is accompanied by wakeful periods at night, during which the person is confused, upset, and likely to wander. Caregivers must therefore be continuously alert, night and day. Their own sleep is disturbed as they try to remain alert to the person's whereabouts. When the disease reaches this level, family caregivers are most likely to find it necessary to institutionalize the family member (Aneshensel et al., 1995).

A woman who remembers her mother as independent, with strong views and a deep commitment to social justice, describes some of the ups and

downs as she witnesses her mother's condition:

> My mother also had strong views on quality of life issues for the elderly. We had often spoken about the importance of being able to die in a dignified way. She has a living will and opposes heroic measures to prolong life. I am convinced that Mom wouldn't want the quality of life she now has. She can't express herself, is unable to hold a knife or fork, has no control over her bodily functions and can't walk.

However, on a recent visit to her mother, who is living in a group home, she describes the following scene:

> I worried . . . that Mom wouldn't recognize me this time. But when I got there, she looked up at me and broke into a huge smile. She was truly excited to see me. She laughed and as I hugged her, we both cried. Then she began to speak nonstop gibberish. Although she can't tell us otherwise, my mother appears to be happy. . . . I honestly don't know if she has any thoughts about quality of life. (Simon, 2002, p. B7)

ter mile or stooping, crouching, or kneeling. Although the presence of the chronic diseases increased over the period, the percentage of respondents who had upper- and lower-body limitations decreased. Arthritis, in particular, was less disruptive to daily functioning in 1995 than it had been in 1984. The implication is that although the diseases are not being prevented, they may be diagnosed earlier and treated more effectively than in the past.

One of the most difficult health challenges of very old age is a group of disorders referred to as *organic brain syndromes*. These conditions, which result in confusion, disorientation, and loss of control over basic daily functions, present obstacles for adaptation to the person with the disease as well as to the caregivers who are responsible for the older person's well-being (see the box on organic brain syndromes: dementia).

Do people generally experience a rapid, general decline in health after age 65 or 70? Not according to self-ratings. In a national survey of older adults, people were asked to rate their health from *poor* to *excellent*. In the 75–84 age range, 71% of non-Hispanic Whites, 54% of non-Hispanic Blacks,

and 50% of Hispanics rated their health as good, very good, or excellent. Among those 85 and older, the percentage who rated their health as good, very good, or excellent declined somewhat for the three groups, to 67%, 52%, and 53%, respectively (Federal Interagency Forum on Aging Related Statistics, 2004).

Among those in their 80s and early 90s, one health-related crisis may result in marked decline in other areas. For example, the loss of a spouse may result in social withdrawal, loss of appetite, sleep disturbance, loss of energy, unwillingness to take medication, and decline in physical activity. All of these changes can produce a rapid deterioration of the respiratory, circulatory, and metabolic systems.

Studies of people in their later 90s and older find that these survivors demonstrate unexpected good health. They appear to be more disease free than those who are 10 or 15 years younger. Perls (2004) suggested that a combination of genetic factors protect some people from the diseases of aging through two complementary processes. First, they are less vulnerable to some of the damaging effects of *oxygen radicals*

*Those who survive into their 90s demonstrate surprising good health. Solly has been bowling since he was 10; now, at age 96, he still enjoys the sport and carries a 123 average in the 80 and older league.*

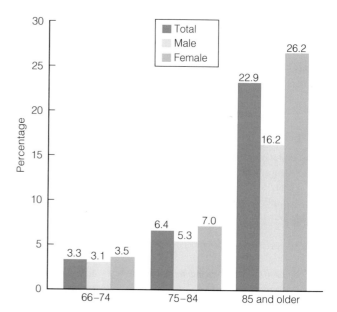

**FIGURE 15.2**

Percentage of Adults 65 and Older Who Need Help with Personal Care Needs: January–September, 2003.

Source: *National Health Interview Survey,* January–September 2003.

that destroy DNA and cells. Thus, during their 70s and 80s, they do not suffer from the major diseases such as heart disease, cancer, stroke, or Alzheimer's disease. Second, they have a greater *functional reserve,* meaning that they require less of their organs to perform basic adaptive functions, so that they can tolerate a degree of damage without losing basic capacities. Studies of centenarians confirm this view of aging; they typically have a short period of poor health before death rather than suffering from prolonged disease-torn illness and disability.

In contrast to negative stereotypes about later life, the level of independent functioning among adults 80 years and older is high. Although roughly 70% of those 80 and older have one or more disabilities, only 34% require personal assistance with tasks required for instrumental daily life, such as shopping, light housecleaning, or fixing themselves a meal (U.S. Bureau of the Census, 1999). Figure 15.2 shows the percentages of men and women in a national sample of adults ages 65 and older who needed help with personal care needs, such as eating, bathing, dressing or getting around inside the home (*activities of daily living;* ADLs). The percentage of adults needing assistance is small (around 3%) for those ages 65–74; increases to slightly more than 6% for those 75–84; and in-

creases markedly to 23% for those 85 and older. However, even among this oldest group, only about one fourth require help with personal care. Over the past decade, the proportion of elderly people reporting such needs has declined. Many factors may account for this improvement in daily functioning for recent cohorts of the very old, including improved design of interior space in senior housing, new devices that make it easier for older adults to compensate for physical limitations, and medications that help alleviate the symptoms of chronic illness (National Center for Health Statistics, 2004).

## DEVELOPING A PSYCHOHISTORICAL PERSPECTIVE

Development in very old age includes gains as well as losses. Through encounters with diverse experiences, decision making, parenting and other forms of tutoring or mentoring of younger generations, and efforts to formulate a personal philosophy, adults reach new levels of conscious thought. Very old adults are more aware of alternatives; they can look deeply into both the past and the future, and they can recognize that opposing forces can exist side by side (Riegel, 1973). Through a process of creative coping, very old adults in each generation blend the salient events of their past histories with the demands of current reality. The product of this integration of past, present, and future is the formation of a **psychohistorical perspective**.

Think about what it means to have lived for 75 or more years. Those adults who were 80 years old in 2005 have lived through the Great Depression; World War II; the Korean war; the Vietnam war; the Gulf war; the assassination of President Kennedy; Watergate; the Clinton impeachment trials; the terrorist attacks of September 11, 2001; and the war on Iraq. They have experienced the political leadership of 18 presidents. During their lives, they have adapted to dramatic technological innovations in communication, transportation, manufacturing, economics, food production, leisure activities, and health care. They have also experienced striking changes in cultural and political values.

One consequence of a long life is the accumulation of experiences. Another is the realization that change is a basic element of all life at the individual and social levels (Clayton & Birren, 1980). Sometimes, these changes appear cyclical; at other times, they appear to bring real transformations. For example, people who are now age 80 lived through a period during World War II, when women were involved in the labor market while men served in the military; a period during the 1950s, when many women withdrew from the labor market and committed themselves to working at home; and a period beginning in the 1970s up to the present, when it has become normative for women to be employed outside the home, even when they have very young children. The patterns of behavior that a younger age group might view as normative and necessary, the very old may recognize as part of a social or historical condition. Within the framework of an extended life, very old adults have opportunities to gain a special perspective on conditions of continuity and change within their culture. In the process of developing such a psychohistorical perspective, they develop a personal understanding of the effects of history on individual lives and of one's place in the chain of events.

As society becomes more accustomed to having a significant group of very old adults functioning in the community, some scholars anticipate that a *culture of aging* will emerge in technological societies. This culture is likely to provide more opportunities for the expression of the pragmatic wisdom accumulated over a long lifetime through theater, music, the arts, and critical commentary. At the same time, new roles will evolve for "successful agers" as mentors and advisors to the young (Baltes & Staudinger, 1993; Keith, 1994).

In this context, a psychohistorical perspective contributes to the wisdom that the very old bring to their understanding of the meaning of life. As a result of living a long time, a person becomes aware of life's lessons as well as its uncertainties. The integration of a long-term past, present, and future combined with an appreciation for the relativistic nature of human experience allows these adults to bring an acceptance of alternative solutions and a commitment to essential positive values (Baltes & Staudinger, 2000).

We are all part of the process of psychosocial evolution. Each generation adds to the existing knowledge base and reinterprets the norms of society for succeeding generations. The very old are likely to be parents, grandparents, and great-grandparents. Many are seeing their lines of descent continue into the fourth generation, which will dominate the 21st century. The opportunity to see several generations of offspring brings a new degree of continuity to life, linking memories of one's own grandparents to observations of one's great-grandchildren (Wentowski, 1985). We can expect the value of the oral tradition of history and storytelling to take on new meaning as the very old help their great-grandchildren feel connected to the distant past. We can also expect a greater investment in the future, as the very old see in their great-grandchildren the concrete extension of their ancestry three generations into the future.

Erikson (Erikson et al., 1986) identified the emergence of these tendencies in the very old in the following excerpt:

> The elder has a reservoir of strength in the wellsprings of history and storytelling. As collectors of time and preservers

*Ben tells his young listeners what it was like to be a soldier in World War II. Through his stories, this period of American history comes alive for a new generation.*

© Bill Aron/Photo Edit

of memory, those healthy elders who have survived into a reasonably fit old age have time on their side—time that is to be dispensed wisely and creatively, usually in the form of stories, to those younger ones who will one day follow in their footsteps. Telling these stories, and telling them well, marks a certain capacity for one generation to entrust itself to the next, by passing on a certain shared and collective identity to the survivors of the next generation: the future. (p. 331)

## TRAVELING UNCHARTED TERRITORY: LIFE STRUCTURES OF THE VERY OLD

How should very old people behave? What norms exist to guide their social relationships or the structure of their daily lives? What does a healthy 85-year-old woman consider appropriate behavior, and what expectations do others have of her? When we talk about traveling uncharted territory, we are assuming that very old age is a time of life for which there are few age-specific social norms. The very old are creating their own definitions of this life stage. You may have heard the expression "life begins at 80." One interpretation of this adage is that because there are so few norms for behavior and so few responsibilities when one reaches very old age, one can do whatever one wants.

Changes in role relationships—especially role loss in later adulthood—present significant challenges to the preservation of a coherent self-concept. In early adulthood, there is an opportunity to engage in many new roles and to establish a lifestyle that expresses the priorities of one's personal identity. In middle adulthood, the press of life roles and their competing demands may be at its peak. During later adulthood, the challenge is to establish an integrated sense of self that helps to compensate for the loss of salient life roles and to protect the person from a sense of despair. By very old age, those who cope most effectively have been able to focus on certain valued characteristics of the self and to optimize them despite difficult changes in their social and physical resources (Diehl, Hastings, & Stanton, 2001).

The MacArthur Foundation Research Network on Successful Aging (Rowe & Kahn, 1998) has offered a new, interdisciplinary perspective on the distinction between usual and successful aging. Those characterized by *usual aging* may be functioning well but are at high risk for disease, disability, and reduced capacity for functional independence. In contrast, the *successful agers* are characterized by three interdependent features (see Figure 15.3). They have a "low risk of disease and disease-related disabilities; high mental and physical function; and active engagement with life" (p. 38). This last feature, *active engagement*, is a frequently repeated theme in the field of gerontology.

In an effort to describe the norms that older adults use to guide their conduct, researchers asked older adults from New York City and Savannah, Georgia, to respond to six pictures

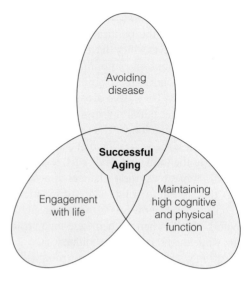

**FIGURE 15.3**

Components of Successful Aging

Source: "I Feel More Like 17," by B. K. Stone, *Bryn Mawr Alumnae Bulletin*, 1998, Summer, p. 4.

similar to the two drawings in Figure 15.4 (Offenbacher & Poster, 1985). The responses to the following two questions were used to construct a code of conduct: "How do you think that people who know this person, such as family or friends, feel about him or her?" and "How do you feel about this person?" Four normative principles were found in the responses:

1. Don't be sorry for yourself.
2. Try to be independent.
3. Don't just sit there; do something.
4. Above all, be sociable.

This code of conduct suggests that older people believe that being sociable, active, and independent constitute successful living in later life. Of course, older adults are not alone in valuing these qualities. However, these norms are important as sources of self-esteem for this age group. They promote a sense of vigor and a shield against depression or discouragement.

The themes "Don't be sorry for yourself" and "Don't just sit there" suggest that the very old continue to see their lives as precious resources that are not to be wasted in self-pity and passivity. The emphasis on activity as opposed to meditation reflects the Western cultural value of a *sense of agency*—thinking is not as highly valued as action. In contrast, doing things, having an impact, and receiving the feedback that action stimulates provide the keys to successful living. Although the results of this research cannot be taken as the final word on the norms that govern the behavior of all very old adults, they are an important step in understanding the importance of the structure that very old people impose on their lives. Subsequent studies have supported the idea that finding meaning in one's existence, continuing to experience a

**FIGURE 15.4**

Typical Drawings that Researchers Might Use to Establish the Social Norms of Very Old People

Source: Drawings based on Offenbacher and Poster, 1985.

sense of social competence, and perceptions of self-efficacy help older adults maintain a sense of well-being (Baltes & Baltes, 1990; Coleman, 1992; Ryff, 1995). For example, by continuing to participate in intellectually complex and challenging leisure activities—such as reading stimulating books and magazines; going to museums, concerts, and plays; or participating in hobbies that require decision making and problem solving—older adults contribute to preserving their intellectual flexibility (Schooler & Mulatu, 2001). The fact that older adults must carve out new patterns of adapting to later life is illustrated in the following sections in two specific areas of functioning: living arrangements and gender role definitions.

## ■ LIVING ARRANGEMENTS

Approximately 78% of U.S. adults age 75 and older own their own homes. However, the pattern of living arrangements changes after age 75, especially for women (see Figure 15.5). Before that age, the majority of older adults live in family households, mostly as married couples. Among adults age 75 and older, however, only 44% live with a spouse; the others

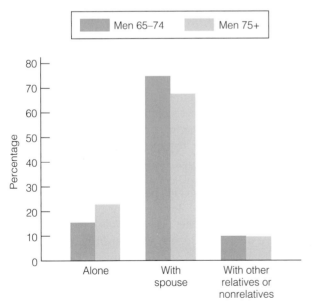
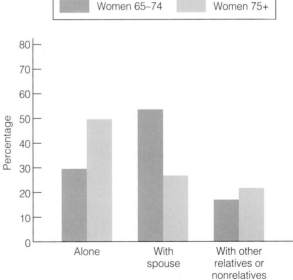

**FIGURE 15.5**

Living Arrangements for Older Adults by Age and Sex: 2003

Source: U.S. Census Bureau, 2004b.

either live alone or with family or nonrelatives. The pattern differs by gender. Among women age 75 and older, 50% live alone; among men age 75 and older, only 23% live alone (Fields, 2003). Older women are less likely than men to remarry after the death of their spouse, and older women are less likely to live with other family members than they were in the past.

**LIVING ALONE.** One implication of these trends in living arrangements is that increasing numbers of very old women are establishing a new single lifestyle, in which they function as heads of households, at age 75 and older. Though still in need of social interaction and support services, they are often relieved of the responsibilities of caring for spouses who were ill. Depending on their own health, these women may be freer to direct their time and interests toward their friends, grandchildren, hobbies, and activities than they have been at any other time in their lives. In a qualitative study of older widows' experiences, four themes emerged: (1) making aloneness acceptable, (2) going my own way, (3) reducing my risks, and (4) sustaining myself (Porter, 1994). One aspect of this process of adaptation, often linked to "going my own way" and "reducing my risks," is a decision to move from one's residence. In a longitudinal study of residential mobility, individuals were interviewed over a 20-year period. Widowhood was found to be a significant event that triggered a decision to move, often within the first year after becoming widowed (Chevan, 1995).

The pattern of elderly women living alone is similar in Canada, the United Kingdom, and many other European countries, but it is not common in developing countries, where both older men and women, whether married or widowed, live in multigenerational families. For example, data gathered in four Asian countries—Thailand, Singapore, Philippines, and Vietnam—in the mid-1990s found that from 60% to 90% of older adults lived with their children and grandchildren. The case of Japan illustrates the possible impact of modernization on the living arrangements of the elderly. In 1960, about 90% of older adults lived with their children (or one might say that the children lived with them in their households). By 1990, this type of living arrangement had declined to 50%. Both the increasing longevity and the improved financial resources of older adults contribute to this trend toward independent housing, which is coupled with a continued desire for close kinship ties (Kinsella & Velkoff, 2001).

In the United States, living arrangements for older women differ by race and ethnic group (Choi, 1991). Older unmarried Asian American women, for example, are much more likely to live with other family members than to live alone in comparison to European American women of similar economic and educational backgrounds. Within the Asian American ethnic groups, acculturation appears to increase the likelihood of choosing to live alone. Those who immigrated to the United States before 1965 or who were born in the United

Most older women who live alone tend to adapt well to this independent life style. Ruth lives in her home in the country, but she keeps in touch with her friends and family by phone. The grocery and pharmacy deliver, and Ruth can always get a ride into town with a neighbor. What factors might force Ruth to give up her independence?

States are more likely to live alone than the more recent immigrants. In a comparison among the Asian American cultures, older Japanese women were more likely to live alone than the Chinese, Filipino, and Korean women. Consistent with patterns for European American women, the more children these Asian American women had, the less likely they were to be institutionalized (Burr & Mutchler, 1993).

The majority of very old men—about 70%—are married and live with their spouses; only 21% are widowed. In contrast, 30% of very old women are married, and 60% are widowed (U.S. Census Bureau, 2004b). Widowed men are much more likely to remarry, which they tend to do quickly. However, remarriage among the very old is still a new frontier. Sexual and social stereotypes inhibit some older people from considering remarriage. Also, potential financial consequences may make remarriage undesirable. For instance, a widow may lose her husband's pension or her social security benefits if she remarries. However, some older couples cope with this problem by living together instead of marrying. In 2003, there were 280,000 men and women age 65 and older living as unmarried heterosexual couples (Fields, 2003). Those who do remarry usually view the new relationship quite positively. One older woman described her new marriage as follows: "We're like a couple of kids. We fool around—have fun. We go to dances and socialize a lot with our families. We enjoy life together. When you're with someone, you're happy" (Rosenfeld, 1978, p. 56).

## The Impact of Gentrification on the Very Old

**GENTRIFICATION** IS A process of urban renewal or renovation in which middle and upper income residents move into areas that have been deteriorating, often displacing poorer residents who have lived in that area for some time. Several consequences of gentrification have a negative impact on the housing options of older adults (Singelakis, 1990). First, rental apartments are converted to condominiums, which older adults cannot afford. Second, in areas where there is no rent control, the rent rises above the rate that the older person is able to pay. Where there is rent regulation, some landlords use harassment to force out the original residents. Third, properties that have been used as single-room-occupancy hotels are demolished, and new structures are built. Single-room-occupancy hotels provide low-cost housing and social support to many older adults who live alone. From 1970 to 1982, more than half the single-room-occupancy units in

the United States were lost to various urban gentrification projects (Hopper & Hamberg, 1986). A similar study of gentrification in London found a significant displacement of the elderly, with the hidden costs of overcrowding in family, friends', or relatives' homes; homelessness; and expanded unmet housing needs (Atkinson, 2000).

As an illustration of this problem, older adults living on the Upper West Side of Manhattan were surveyed. The mean age of the group was 75; 79% had incomes of less than $10,000 in 1989 (Singelakis, 1990). Of this group, 99% rented, 68% lived alone, and 74% paid less than $300 per month for rent. In this community, 52% of the single-room units had become unavailable over the past 7 years. These older adults reported that gentrification had resulted in having to walk farther to find affordable shopping. They knew that if they were forced to leave their current apartment because of increased rent, they

could not afford to live in the same neighborhood. And if they were forced to leave, 64% did not know where they could live. Fewer than 8% of the sample felt that they could live with a friend or a family member if their apartment was no longer available.

Although gentrification poses threats to housing for the elderly, the alternative of ongoing neglect and decay brings its own risks—especially increased crime, health and safety hazards, and lack of services. Over time, people with more resources leave these neighborhoods, making them vulnerable to continued deterioration. More positive approaches suggest a gradual rehabilitation or redevelopment of urban communities that preserves the identity of the neighborhood but encourages new building and new businesses at a slower rate of growth (West, 1999). At the same time, deliberate efforts must be made to find appropriate housing for long-term community residents.

**INTERSTATE MIGRATION.** The great majority of older adults (more than 90%) remain in their home communities as they age, many preferring to stay in their own home, even after their children move out and their spouse dies. Yet the trend toward interstate migration has increased since the mid-1960s (Flynn, Longino, Wiseman, & Biggar, 1985). Each year, roughly 1% to 2% of those 75 and older move to a new residence across state lines (U.S. Census Bureau, 2004b). Many of these older interstate migrants will live out their lives in communities in which they did not grow up, work, or raise their children. They are pioneers, establishing new friendships, community involvements, and lifestyles. Another significantly large group of older adults return to their birth state, especially after one spouse dies or, in the case of serious disability, in order to be close to family caregivers (Stoller & Longino, 2001). In the face of some new physical limitations, older adults may want to be able to remain independent but require more help. By moving back to their home community, they are more confident about being able to draw on needed support from family and friends (Rowles & Ravdal, 2002). In addition to these permanent moves, many older adults participate in seasonal migration—residents from southern states go north for the summer, and residents

of northern states go south for the winter. Over time, some of these seasonal migrants decide to establish a permanent residence in the state they visit. This is especially likely for northern residents who establish permanent residence in the South (Hogan & Steinnes, 1998).

**HOUSING OPTIONS.** Differences in lifestyle, health, interest, ability to perform daily activities, marital status, and income enter into the very old person's preference for housing arrangements. Housing for the elderly—sometimes referred to as *retirement housing*—has expanded dramatically, and developers have experimented with a great variety of housing configurations that are intended to meet the special needs of particular aging populations (Shapiro, 2001). These options range from inner-city hotels for those with minimal incomes to sprawling luxury villages with apartments, medical clinics, and sponsored activities. Retirement communities are typically age-restricted residences. They may be apartments in a high-rise, townhouses, or homes with shared recreational resources, like a fitness center, pool, or golf course, and social and cultural programming. Often, they provide the option for prepared meals or a communal eating center. Life satisfaction in a retirement community may depend on the fit between one's marital status and the demographics of the community. For example, one study assessed the life satisfaction of widows who were living alone in retirement communities. When widows outnumbered married couples in the community, the widows had a high frequency of seeing friends and participating in activities. However, when married couples outnumbered widows, the widows experienced less satisfaction and were more socially isolated (Hong & Duff, 1994).

The majority of older adults live in urban areas, and 31% of them live in inner-city neighborhoods. As a result, any economic factors that affect the housing options in urban communities have a significant impact on the living arrangements of older adults (see the box on the impact of gentrification on the very old). Because older adults tend to have a limited income and depend on the quality of community resources and social support for their well-being, moving can be an especially difficult life event, adversely affecting their overall well-being (Ryff & Essex, 1992; Singelakis, 1990).

**INSTITUTIONAL CARE.** About 1.6 million adults older than 65 live in nursing homes. This includes any arrangement with three or more beds that provides nursing and personal care services (U.S. Census Bureau, 2004b). The likelihood of institutionalization increases with age and limitations in family support. About 75% of people in nursing homes do not have spouses. The likelihood of a person living in a nursing home increases when there is no family member who can help to manage his or her daily living needs. Among nursing home residents, about 13% are 65 to 74 years old, 35% are 75 to 84, and 51% are 85 and older (U.S. Census Bureau, 2004b). People tend to think that once older adults are admitted to a nursing home, they stay there until they die. In fact, there is a high annual turnover among nursing home residents. Often, a person enters a nursing home for a period of convalescence after hospitalization and then returns home or to a setting that provides less intensive care.

Many nursing homes are part of a **continuing care retirement community**—a residential setting offering housing and medical, preventive health, and social services to residents who are well at the time they enter the community. Once admitted, they are guaranteed nursing care if they become ill or disabled (Shapiro, 2001). In an analysis of nursing home use among residents in continuing care retirement communities, the risk of being transferred to the nursing home facility appeared to be greater than the rate for older adults in the local community, but the length of stay per admission was shorter (Cohen, Tell, Bishop, Wallack, & Branch, 1989). The nursing home may be used for recuperative purposes rather than having patients stay in the hospital for a longer period. This practice may reduce overall medical costs and provide a better recovery environment than being discharged to one's home before one can fully manage all the demands of self-care.

The advantages of a continuing care community are described by Glenn Smith:

"We'd seen a lot of people our age struggle when one went into a skilled nursing facility 6 miles away," says 76-year-old Glenn Smith. "Then someone has to drive Momma over to see Daddy every day." So Smith and his wife, Kathleen, moved to a CCRC (continuing care retirement community) atop a hill overlooking Oregon's Rogue River Valley. A nursing home is just a short walk from their spacious three-bedroom cottage. Smith, who is a retired college administrator, has one bit of advice: Move in while you are younger and healthy in order to take full advantage of the activities—and pay a lower entry fee. (Shapiro, 2001, p. 60)

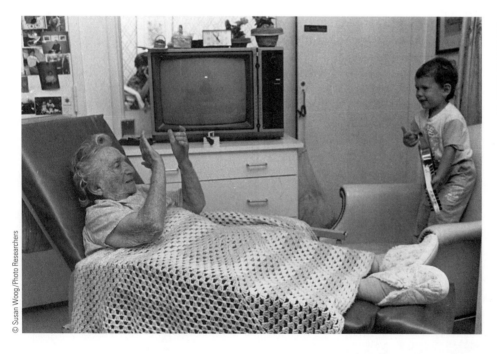

At 97 years of age, Stella has had to move into a nursing home because she can no longer walk. Periodic visits from her great-grandson keep her in good spirits. He plays, and she is a most appreciative audience.

© Susan Woog/Photo Researchers

**ASSISTED LIVING.** The fastest growing component of the Medicare program is *community-based long-term health care*, which provides medical and social services to those who are chronically ill and are eligible for institutionalization but who, nevertheless, live in the community. At their best, these programs are designed to complement and support informal caregiving, supplementing and providing relief for family members and friends who are trying to care for the very old. They bring comfort to the very old clients who prefer to remain in their homes.

These programs also offer flexibility by providing needed services and modifying them as a person's condition changes. For example, a home health service may provide a case manager who can identify the required services and coordinate a program of home care providers, services, and adult day care to meet the needs of the client and his or her support system. Long-term home health care programs evolve in response to the pattern of need that emerges in a community and the quality of the services available. As the programs develop, their emphasis tends to shift from providing services to those who would otherwise be institutionalized to preventing institutionalization among a high-risk population (Kasper, 1997; Kaye, 1995).

The benefits of remaining in one's home, despite serious limitations in functional independence, are (1) preserving one's sense of autonomy and dignity, (2) reducing expenses, and (3) sustaining relationships with family and friends. In contrast, the move to a nursing home tends to be associated with higher levels of dependence and greater emphasis on "going along with the program" rather than on initiating one's own plans and projects. In a comparison of older women living in their homes and those living in a nursing care facility, researchers were interested in how the living arrangements might influence cognitive problem solving. The home-based group became more engaged in the hypothetical problems, their solutions suggested a greater sense of perceived control over the solutions, and they approached the problems in a more abstract, relativistic manner (Collins, Luszcz, Lawson, & Keeves, 1997). The results of this work suggest that the nursing home environment may operate to undermine cognitive functioning by reducing the need for independent problem-solving activity. However, as the case study about Mr. Z suggests, there are nursing home residents who retain their positive spirit and are able to help others while receiving the level of support they require given their serious physical disabilities.

# CASE STUDY

## MR. Z

*The following case illustrates the importance of psychological attitudes in allowing a person with serious physical problems to play a meaningful role in a social setting for the frail elderly.*

*Mr. Z.'s outlook helps him maintain his vitality and express his love of life.*

Mr. M. L. Z. is an 89-year-old White male of Eastern European origin. He lives in a midsized nursing home in the Midwest. Many of his daily activities revolve around his circulating among the facility's residents, chatting, playing cards, reading to them, and "fetching things." Most important, Mr. Z. carries his old battered violin about with him and at the drop of a hat will play a tune or break into song in a surprisingly strong, clear, melodic voice. He claims to be able to sing songs in any one of seven languages, and with the least encouragement will try out several for anyone who will listen.

Mr. Z. is small (5'3"), frail-looking, and completely bald. He has facial scars and wears extremely thick-lensed glasses. He seems to be known and well liked by practically all residents and staff of the facility in which he resides, and by many visitors there as well.

He recalls a colorful history. He "escaped" his homeland at the tender age of 15½ to avoid compulsory military service and fled to Russia. There he was inducted into the army, and was subsequently sent off to duty in Siberia, where he lived for about six years. After another tour of duty in a border patrol he deserted, made his way across Europe, and eventually came to the United States. Here he took odd jobs, educated himself, and in time "got into show business"; he became a vaudeville prompter. In time his contacts in entertainment took him around the world. Yet time took its toll.

He tells of marrying a woman with whom he lived for "almost 40 years." They had no children and she died some 15 years ago. Following her death, he began to experience a series of physical difficulties. An operation for cataracts left him with the need for very thick glasses. At one time he had a toupee made, which he has not worn for some time. One leg was amputated because of a diabetic condition, and he now wears a prosthetic leg. In addition, he wears a hearing aid, false teeth, and, for the last year, a heart pacer. Several years ago he experienced what he calls a "small stroke," which left him "mixed up" for a few days. But he "worked this out," he reports, by "walking a lot," an activity in which he engages frequently.

Mr. Z. says he has never smoked and drinks only on "occasions" or holidays, and then only to a limited degree. He scorns food fads, and eats "mostly" fresh fruits and "lots of vegetables"; he loves fish and drinks lots of tea.

Despite all his troubles, Mr. Z. maintains what is apparently a cheerful, optimistic view of life and circumstances, while he pursues his "hobby" of energetically helping his fellow residents keep their spirits up and their interests high. He is very highly regarded and seen as filling a very important role in his nursing home as a storyteller and entertainer.

Source: Excerpt from *Aging and Life: An Introduction to Gerontology*, second edition, A. N. Schwartz, C. L. Snyder, and J. A. Peterson, pp. 33–34. Copyright © 1984 Holt, Rinehart & Winston, Inc. Reprinted by permission of the publisher.

## ■ CRITICAL THINKING AND CASE ANALYSIS

1. Imagine that you were having lunch with Mr. Z. What questions would you want to ask him?

2. What are the physical challenges of aging with which Mr. Z. must cope?

3. Why might Mr. Z. be living in a nursing home?

4. How would you describe Mr. Z.'s psychohistorical perspective?

5. What are the unique, creative adaptations that characterize Mr. Z.'s story?

6. In what sense is the nursing home optimizing Mr. Z.'s functioning?

## ■ GENDER ROLE DEFINITIONS

The way in which very old adults view masculinity and femininity is yet another aspect of traveling uncharted territory. How do the very old define gender roles? How does gender influence behavior? Do very old adults make the same distinctions as college-age individuals about the behaviors that are appropriate or desirable for men and women? These questions remain to be answered.

**EVALUATING THE CONCEPT OF GENDER ROLE CONVERGENCE.** The idea of **gender role convergence** suggests a transformation of gender role orientation during midlife. According to this theoretical perspective, men become more nurturant and more concerned with social relationships. Women become more assertive and concerned with independence and achievement. As a result, men and women become more androgynous and, in that sense, more similar in gender orientation during later life (Gutmann, 1987).

The extent to which men and women become more similar in outlook and behavior in later adulthood and very old age is a subject of controversy. Unfortunately, few data from longitudinal or cohort sequential studies are available to address this topic. Cross-sectional data collected from men and women across a wide age span from early adulthood to very old age have focused on men's and women's endorsement of affiliative and instrumental values. Men and women appear to be similar in their **affiliative values**—that is, the values placed on helping or pleasing others, reflected in the amount of time they spend and the degree of satisfaction they achieve in such actions. At each age, men are more invested than women in **instrumental values**—that is, the values placed on doing things that are challenging, reflected in the amount of time they spend and the degree of satisfaction they achieve in such actions. However, the youngest age groups value instrumentality more highly and devote more time to it than the oldest age group. Thus, gender differences in instrumentality persist, but instrumentality becomes somewhat less important for older men and women. Affiliative behavior is equally important for men and women at both ages (Fultz & Herzog, 1991).

The stereotypes that are applied to aging men and women reflect similar patterns. College students and older adults (with a mean age of 70) were asked to generate characteristics in response to one of four target stimuli: a 35-year-old man, a 35-year-old woman, a 65-year-old man, and a 65-year-old woman (Kite, Deaux, & Miele, 1991). Age stereotypes were more prevalent than gender stereotypes. The attributes that were used to characterize older men and women were similar and distinct from the attributes used to characterize younger men and women.

In general, the older target people were evaluated more negatively by the younger participants, but not as negatively by the older participants. These negative judgments included unattractive physical qualities as well as irritable and depressed personality qualities. What is more, younger partici-

Gardening has become a shared activity for William and Sue. It has both affiliative and instrumental features. Because of their arthritis, neither William nor Sue could do this much work alone, but together they can enjoy planning and caring for their garden.

© Paul Barton/Corbis

*After 55 years of marriage, Alma and Frank still find the joy of romance in an evening of dining and dancing.*

pants were more likely to characterize both male and female older target people as lacking in instrumental traits, such as achievement orientation and self-confidence. However, they did not view older target people as lacking in affiliative traits, such as caring about others or being kind or generous. Thus, the gender role convergence that has been hypothesized as taking place with advanced age is reflected in the stereotypes that younger people apply to older adults.

Gender role convergence, where it is observed, may be due to changing circumstances rather than to a normative pattern of development in later life. For example, many older women experience a transition from living with their husbands to living alone after age 75. This change is linked to new demands for independence, self-reliance, and agency. Women who are able to meet these challenges by developing independent living skills, making effective use of social supports and community resources, and initiating new relationships are likely to experience a heightened sense of well-being.

For many older married couples, the physical effects of aging bring new needs for assistance in some of the tasks of daily living. Because men usually marry younger women, they are more likely to require the assistance of their wives in the later years of marriage, thus shifting the balance of power and increasing their sense of dependency. This may be especially true when husbands retire while their wives continue to work; when husbands can no longer drive and must depend on their wives for transportation; or when, due to health constraints, husbands are restricted from performing the types of household tasks that once were their domain, such as mowing the grass, shoveling snow, repairing the home, or other tasks requiring muscle strength and endurance. On the other hand, among adults of 75 years and older, more women than

men have difficulties with mobility and require assistance in the tasks of independent living. Thus, health and fitness more than gender may guide the nature of dyadic interactions among older couples. As men and women become more equal with respect to power and resources in their marital relationship, there may be fewer clear-cut gender expectations. Still, to the extent that gender role distinctions help stabilize a relationship, older adults may be reluctant to make dramatic changes to the way their relationships have been structured (Silver, 2003).

**ROMANCE AND SEXUALITY.** Romance, intimacy, and sexuality remain important among older married couples. The majority of couples who have enjoyed a close, sexually active relationship report little change in satisfaction from age 60 to 85. Some couples explore different ways of experiencing sexual pleasure in later life, and others report a more relaxed, sexually satisfying quality in their lovemaking. Using Sternberg's (1988) model of the three dimensions of love relationships (see Chapter 12, Early Adulthood), long-lasting marriages tend to be more companionate in nature, emphasizing intimacy and commitment over passion. In this model, lovemaking may take on a different intensity and quality over time. Current research on sexuality in later life confirms that older adults have sexual needs, benefit from sexual expression, and are able to be sexually active. A national survey of adults ages 60 and older found that more than half were sexually active, meaning that they had intercourse, oral sex, anal intercourse, or masturbated at least once a month (Dunn & Cutler, 2000). This study found that sexual activity declined with age, but that 20 to 25% of those in their 80s were still sexually active. Older couples may find greater satisfaction in intimate physical contact, such as kissing and caressing, and experimentation with new ways of experiencing sexual stimulation as genital intercourse becomes less frequent. Following along with the idea of gender role convergence, men and women become more similar in their sexual behavior and more harmonious in their lovemaking (Crooks & Bauer, 2005).

Today's cohort of older men and women, born in the 1930s, tend to be tied to many of the traditional gender role standards of their historical era. For example, older women are likely to believe that the only kinds of relationships that are possible between men and women are romantic or courtship relationships. Few very old women have friendships with very old men, partly because few older men are available, but also because most older women have no models for independent friendship relationships with men. During their early and middle adult years, their friendships with men either were formed while they were part of a couple or were mediated by some other situation, such as a work setting. Many men in the current very old age cohort also behave in accordance with the gender role standards of their young adulthood. Although women far outnumber men at advanced ages, men still seem to prefer to remarry rather than play the field, although they have become a scarce and valuable commodity. The norm of serial monogamy guides these men's behavior. They are probably motivated to remarry by a desire to continue to be taken care of as well as to satisfy their sexual needs.

One of the greatest challenges to continued romantic and sexual intimacy in later life is widowhood. Despite the fact that older men are much more likely to remarry than older women, remarriage is relatively uncommon in later adulthood and very old age. One estimate found that among 1,000 widowed men and women older than 65, 3 women and 17 men remarried (Clarke, 1995). These data do not address the question whether older men and women would like to have a romantic relationship after widowhood. This question was addressed in a study of older couples that followed men and women 6 and 18 months after widowhood (Carr, 2004). Participants were asked two questions about their romantic interests: "At this point do you have any interest in dating?" which was answered *yes* or *no*, and "Some day I would like to remarry," answered on a scale from *not true at all* to *very true*. They were also asked if they were dating. At 6 months after widowhood, men were more likely to want to be dating than women (17% vs. 6%), more likely to want to remarry (30% vs. 16%), and more likely to be dating (15% vs. less than 1%). At 18 months after widowhood, men were still more likely to want to be dating (37% vs. 15%) and more likely to be dating (23% vs. 9%), but about equally likely to want to remarry (26% vs. 19%). The most important predictor of whether men or women wanted to date or remarry was the quality of their social support system. In general, women had more supportive relationships with friends than did men prior to widowhood. The more social support men had, the less likely they were to express interest in remarriage. Those men and

women who had comparable levels of social support from friends were equally disinterested in remarriage.

This research suggests that the picture we have about gender differences in motivations to find a new partner after widowhood need to be revised. First, although men are clearly more interested in new romantic relationships than women, the majority of men do not express this interest. Second, when social support systems are comparable, men and women are about equally likely to reject the idea of a new romantic relationship. One limitation of this research was the way in which interest in a new partner was defined, limiting the alternatives for romantic relationships to dating and marriage. Given the potential costs of remarriage in later life, older adults may be looking for a different kind of intimacy that does not require the responsibilities of coresidence and the legal commitments of marriage (Davidson, 2002; Ghazanfareeon Karlsson & Borrell, 2002).

**AGEISM AND SEXUALITY.**  Older adults continue to face negative, ageist social attitudes about sexual activity that may inhibit their sexual behavior. These social attitudes include assumptions that very old adults do not have sexual desires, that they cannot have intercourse because of sexual dysfunction, that sex may be dangerous to their health, that they are physically and sexually unattractive, and that it is morally wrong or "sick" for older adults to be sexually active (Crooks & Bauer, 2005). Current cohorts of very old adults have limited knowledge about sexuality and aging. A number of studies have demonstrated that increasing knowledge through various types of sex education programs can increase permissive attitudes about sexuality among older adults (Hillman & Stricker, 1994). These interventions have involved the elderly people themselves, nursing students, college students, nursing home staff, and adult children of aging parents. However, increased knowledge does not always result in more permissive attitudes. Especially among health care staff in institutional settings, the institutional regulations, personal moral values, and the practical problems of permitting sexual activity among residents may combine to promote a more negative attitude even with advanced information about sexuality and aging.

Cohort factors may change the current societal attitudes toward sexuality among the very old. Because so many more adult women are in the workplace, they have more experience with male colleagues. Also, changing sexual norms have already led many more adults to experience nonmarital sexual relationships. A growing openness about homosexual relationships may reduce some of the stigma against forming same-sex bonds in later life. Acceptance of new sexual relationships in later life is more likely because many adults will have experienced a larger number of sexual relationships in their earlier years of adulthood. The high divorce rate since the mid-1970s means that in the future, more women will have had the experience of developing a single lifestyle that includes a network of both male and female friends. As the value of intimacy for health and well-being is more fully recognized, we may expect future groups of older adults to be more comfortable about forming homosexual as well as heterosexual intimate relationships.

# THE PSYCHOSOCIAL CRISIS: IMMORTALITY VERSUS EXTINCTION

By the end of later adulthood, most people have developed a point of view about death. Although they may continue to experience anxiety about their impending death, they have found the courage to confront their fears and overcome them. If older adults have achieved integrity, they believe that their life has made sense. This amplifies their confidence about the choices they have made and the goals they have achieved without despair over the failures, missed opportunities, or misfortunes that may have occurred. Thus armed, the very old can accept the end of life and view it as a natural part of the life span. They are capable of distilling wisdom from the events of their lives, including their successes and mistakes.

However, the very old are faced with a new challenge—a conflict between the acceptance of death and the intensifying hope for immortality. Having lived longer than their cohort of friends, family members, and even, in some cases, their children, the very old struggle to find meaning in their survival. All of us face a certain disbelief about our own mortality. Although we know that death is a certainty, an element of human thought prevents us from facing the full realization of death; we continue to hope for immortality. This quality may be adaptive, in that people who have a sense of hope cope with the reality of death better than those who do not.

© David Hiser/Photographers/Aspen/Picturequest

*Immortality can be achieved by preserving the link between the living and the dead. This Mexican woman celebrates the Day of the Dead by making a cross from flower petals on the floor in front of an altar. She is honoring her dead ancestors and showing her appreciation for their role in her life.*

## IMMORTALITY

We have argued that the very old have a unique appreciation of change. They begin to see themselves as links in a long, fluid chain of historical and biological growth and change. The positive pole of this crisis is a confidence in the continuity of life, a transcendence of death through the development of a symbolic sense of immortality.

A psychosocial sense of **immortality** may be achieved and expressed in many ways (Lifton, 1973). Here, we explore five possible paths toward immortality. First, one may live on through one's children, sensing a connection and attachment to the future through one's life and the lives of one's offspring. This type of immortality can be extended to include devotion to one's country, social organizations or groups, or humankind.

Second, one may believe in an afterlife or in a spiritual plane of existence that extends beyond one's biological life. Most religions espouse the concept of a state of harmony with natural forces, so that after death, one endures beyond this earthly life. Among many indigenous peoples, there is a sacred link between the living and the dead—a responsibility on the part of the living to protect and respect the sacred burial grounds, and a responsibility on the part of the dead ancestors to look after the spiritual well-being of the living. This belief is illustrated in the box on the responsibility of Native Hawaiians for their ancestors' remains.

Third, one may achieve a sense of immortality through creative achievements and their impact on others. Many people find comfort in believing that they are part of a chain of positive influences on the lives of others. This sense of immortality is linked to the achievement of generativity in middle adulthood. Adults who have made a commitment to

## The Responsibility of Native Hawaiians for their Ancestors' Remains

THE FOLLOWING NARRATIVE describes the crisis of immortality versus extinction in the context of the desecration of a Native Hawaiian burial site. In fighting to stop the destruction, those involved were reminded of the commitment that the living have for the care and protection of the burial grounds of their ancestors:

> Hawai'i Nei was born December 1988 from the *kaumaha* (heaviness) and *aokanaka* (enlightenment) caused by the archaeological disinterment of over 1,100 ancestral Native Hawaiians from Honokahua, Maui. The ancestral remains were removed over the protests of the Native Hawaiian community in order to build the Ritz Carlton Hotel. The desecration was stopped following a 24-hour vigil at the State Capital. Governor John Waihe'e, a Native Hawaiian, approved of a settlement that returned the ancestral remains to their *one hanau* (birth sands), set aside the reburial site in perpetuity, and moved

the hotel inland and away from the ancestral resting place. . . .

> In one sense Honokahua represents balance, for from this tragedy came enlightenment: the realization by living Native Hawaiians that we were ultimately responsible for the care and protection of our ancestors and that cultural protocols needed to be relearned and laws effectively changed to create the empowerment necessary to carry out this important and time-honored responsibility to *malama* (take care) and *kupale* (protect) our ancestors.

> Hui Malama I Na Kupuna O Hawai'i Nei members have trained under the direction of Edward and Pualani Kanahele of Hilo in traditional protocols relating to care of *na iwi kupuna* (ancestral remains). These commitments were undertaken as a form of *aloha* and respect for our own families, our ancestors, our parents, and our children.

> Hui Malama I Na Kupuna O Hawai'i Nei has been taught by the

Kanahele family about the importance of *pule* (prayer) necessary to *ho'olohe* (listen) to the calling of our ancestors. Through *pule* we request the assistance of *ke akua* and our ancestors to provide us the tools necessary to conduct our work:

> E homai ka ike, e homai ka ikaika, e homai ka akamai, e homai ka maopopo pono, e homai ka 'ike papalua, e homai ka mana.

> (Grant us knowledge, grant us strength, grant us intelligence, grant us righteous understanding, grant us visions and avenues of communication, grant us mana.)

> Moreover, we have been taught that the relationship between our ancestors and ourselves is one of interdependence—as the living, we have a *kuleana* (responsibility) to care for our *kupuna* (ancestors). In turn, our ancestors respond by protecting us on the spiritual side. Hence, one side cannot completely exist without the other.

Source: Pell (2002)

---

improving the quality of life for others during middle adulthood are likely to see evidence of this effort by the time they reach very old age. The bond between an individual and his or her community makes death less final. An African proverb advises that you live as long as someone knows your name. The more embedded you are in your community, and the more lives you have touched, the greater the sense of continuity or transcendence.

Fourth, one may develop the notion of participation in the chain of nature. In death, one's body returns to the earth, and one's energy is brought forth in a new form.

Fifth, one may achieve a sense of immortality through what Lifton (1973) described as **experiential transcendence**:

> This state is characterized by extraordinary psychic unity and perceptual intensity. But there also occurs . . . a process of symbolic reordering. . . . Experiential transcendence includes a feeling of . . . "continuous present" that can be equated with eternity or with "mythical time." This continuous present is perceived as not only "here and now" but as inseparable from past and future. (p. 10)

This concept of immortality is independent of religion, offspring, or creative achievement. It is an insight derived from moments of rapture or ecstasy in which all that one senses is the power of the moment. In these experiences, life and death dissolve, and what remains is continuous being.

## EXTINCTION

The negative pole of this psychosocial crisis is a sense of being bound by the limits of one's own life history. In place of a belief in continuous existence and transformation, one views the end of life as an end to motion, attachment, and change. Instead of faith in the ideas of connection and continuity, one experiences a great fear of **extinction**—a fear that one's life and its end amount to nothing.

The following quotations from a study of very old men suggest the range in sentiment about immortality and extinction (Rosenfeld, 1978, p. 10). About 28% of the adults in the study were described as having low morale and made state-

## Erikson on Coping with Aging

THE ERIKSONS' ADVICE (Erikson et al., 1986, pp. 332–333) suggests the achievement of experiential transcendence:

With aging, there are inevitably constant losses—losses of those very close, and friends near and far. Those who have been rich in intimacy also have the most to lose. Recollection is one form of adaptation, but the effort skillfully to form new relationships is adaptive and more rewarding. Old age is necessarily a time of relinquishing—of giving up old friends, old roles, earlier work that was once meaningful, and even possessions that belong to a pre-

vious stage of life and are now an impediment to the resiliency and freedom that seem to be requisite for adapting to the unknown challenges that determine the final stage of life.

Trust in interdependence. Give and accept help when it is needed. Old Oedipus well knew that the aged sometimes need three legs; pride can be an asset but not a cane. When frailty takes over, dependence is appropriate, and one has no choice but to trust in the compassion of others and be consistently surprised at how faithful some caretakers can be.

Much living, however, can teach us only how little is known. Accept that es-

sential "not-knowingness" of childhood and with it also that playful curiosity. Growing old can be an interesting adventure and is certainly full of surprises.

One is reminded here of the image Hindu philosophy uses to describe the final letting go—that of merely being. The mother cat picks up in her mouth the kitten, which completely collapses every tension and hangs limp and infinitely trusting in the maternal benevolence. The kitten responds instinctively. We human beings require at least a whole lifetime of practice to do this.

Source: From *Vital Involvement in Old Age*, E. H. Erikson, J. M. Erikson, & H. Q. Kivnick (1986), pp. 332–333.

ments such as "I feel I'm a forgotten man. I don't exist anymore. . . . I don't feel old. . . . I'm just living out my life." About 25% were stoic but not very positive about their condition: "You know you're getting old. You have to put your mind to it and take it as it comes. You can't get out of it. Take it gracefully." Almost half found their lives full and rewarding: "I go home with my cup overflowing. There are so many opportunities to do things for people. These are the happiest days of my life."

The possibility of ending one's life with a sense of extinction is reflected in the public health concern about suicide among the elderly. Data from the *World Health Statistical Annual* provide a basis for describing the incidence of suicide for men and women in the age groups from 65 to 74 and 75 years and older (Kennedy & Tanenbaum, 2000). Men commit suicide at higher rates than women at all ages, but the discrepancy increases with age. Suicide rates are much higher among those 75 years and older than in the younger group. Finally, national and geographic differences are substantial. For example, in Germany more than half the suicides are committed by people age 65 and older.

In the analysis of factors associated with suicide in Germany, severe physical disease, loneliness and isolation, and feelings of meaninglessness were identified as forming a biopsychosocial context for late-life suicide (Schmitz-Scherzer, 1995). In Japan, suicide rates among older adults are greater in rural than in urban communities. The authors of this research suggested that changes in Japanese society have led to a reduced valuing of older family members and less extended

family support. The rural elderly are less able to accept these changes, which undercut their sense of purpose and meaning (Watanabe, Hasegawa, & Yoshinaga, 1996). Without appropriate social support, and in the face of substantially reduced physical or psychological resources, a significant number of the very old end their own lives.

## THE CENTRAL PROCESS: SOCIAL SUPPORT

**Social support** has been defined as the social experiences that lead people to believe that they are cared for and loved, esteemed and valued, and belong to a network of communication and mutual obligation (Cobb, 1979). Social support is a broad term that includes the quantity and interconnectedness or web of social relationships in which a person is embedded, the strength of those ties, the frequency of contact, and the extent to which the support system is perceived as helpful and caring (Bergeman, Plomin, Pedersen, McClearn, & Nesselroade, 1990). It is commonly divided into two different but complementary categories: socioemotional support, which refers to expressions of affection, respect, and esteem, and instrumental support, which refers to direct assistance, including help with chores, medical care, or transportation. Both types of social support—but especially emotional support—contribute to maintaining well-being and fostering the possibility of transcending the physical limitations that accompany aging (Rowe & Kahn, 1998).

## THE BENEFITS OF SOCIAL SUPPORT

Social support plays a direct role in promoting health and well-being, even when a person is not facing a specific stressful situation. First, because social support involves meaningful social relationships, it reduces isolation. People who have intimate companions in later life have higher levels of life satisfaction. They feel valued and valuable. This kind of social support is likely to be most appreciated when it comes from friends and neighbors—members of the community who are not bound by familial obligation to care about the person, but who do so anyway.

Second, the presence of caring, familiar people provides a flow of affection, information, advice, transportation, and assistance with meals and daily activities, finances, and health care—all critical resources. The presence of a support system tends to reduce the impact of stressors and protect people from some of their negative consequences, especially serious

These four women have been playing bridge together almost every week for 20 years. Movement of one of them to a retirement community has not disrupted the game. The continuity of social support is a mainstay of their emotional and physical well-being.

illnesses and depression (Murrell & Norris, 1991). The health benefits of social support are especially notable for older men (Seeman, Berkman, Blazer, & Rowe, 1994).

Third, social integration and membership in a meaningful social support network are associated with increased longevity. Five different longitudinal studies have demonstrated that a high level of social integration is associated with lower mortality rates (Rowe & Kahn, 1997). The support system often serves to encourage an older person to maintain health care practices and to seek medical attention when it is needed. Members of the immediate family, close relatives, and friends provide direct care during times of grave illness or loss and encourage the older person to cope with difficulties and to remain hopeful (Russell & Cutrona, 1991).

Very old people are likely to experience declines in physical stamina. They may also have limited financial resources. In order for the very old to transcend the limitations of their daily living situations, they must be convinced that they are embedded in a network of social relationships in which they are valued. But their value cannot be based solely on a physical exchange of goods and services. Rather, it must be founded on an appreciation of the person's dignity and a history of reciprocal caring.

## THE DYNAMICS OF SOCIAL SUPPORT

The benefits of receiving social support can be diminished if the recipients adhere to a strong cultural norm for reciprocity. The **norm of reciprocity** implies that you are obligated to return in full value what you receive: "One good turn deserves another." People want and expect to be able to give about the same as or more than they receive. What is given does not have to be identical to what was received, but it has to be perceived as having equal worth. Being in someone's debt may be considered stressful and shameful. In a study of Japanese American elderly people, receiving material support from their family was associated with higher levels of depression and less satisfaction in life, especially for those who had very traditional values about reciprocity. The general principle of trying to mobilize social support to enhance the functioning of the very old has to be modified to include sensitivity to the context and meaning of that support (Nemoto, 1998).

Most older adults continue to see themselves as involved in a reciprocal, supportive relationship with their friends. Feelings of usefulness and competence continue to be important correlates of well-being in later life. Older adults are especially likely to experience positive feelings of life satisfaction when they are able to provide assistance to others at times of significant life transition or need, such as the unemployment or divorce of a child (Davey & Eggebeen, 1998). Even though they are comforted by knowing that support would be available when needed, older adults are likely to experience negative feelings when the support received is more than was needed or when there is no opportunity for them to reciprocate (Liang, Krause, & Bennett, 2001).

Older adults may expect to receive more care from their children when they are ill than they can provide in exchange. By shifting to a life-span perspective, however, they can retain a sense of balance by seeing the help they receive now as comparable to the help they gave their children at earlier life stages (Ingersoll-Dayton & Antonucci, 1988). When very old people are highly valued, it is not as important that they reciprocate in the exchange of tangible resources. Wisdom, affection, joie de vivre, and a positive model of surviving into old age are intangible resources that are highly valued by members of the very old person's social support network. Being valued may also mean that the person's advice and conversation are adequate exchange for some of the services and assistance provided by family and friends.

Social relationships can include both positive and negative interactions. Within one's social network, positive interactions might include enjoying shared activities, confiding about one's worries, or asking for help when one is ill. Negative interactions might include being taken advantage of, having one's privacy invaded, or being insulted. Sometimes, the same people can be sources of both positive and negative interactions. Not surprisingly, the overall frequency of positive exchanges is related to lower levels of depression. When older adults experience the effects of negative social interactions in one relationship—for example, when they have an argument with their adult child—they can buffer these emotions by having positive interactions with another member of their social network—for example, a friend or spouse (Okun & Keith,1998).

Many older adults are selective about the people in their social network, striving to interact primarily with people who engage in harmonious interactions. They also take steps to prevent conflict in the relationships they value. For example, they impose certain constraints on their interactions—not criticizing someone in public, respecting others' privacy, and keeping a confidence. These strategies help to avoid negative interactions and to maximize the satisfaction and stability of their relationships. These strategies are not a sign of weakness or passivity, but a deliberate attempt to protect meaningful relationships and avoid the negative affect associated with interpersonal conflict (Sorkin & Rook, 2004).

## THE SOCIAL SUPPORT NETWORK

Of course, being an integral part of a social system does not begin in later life. It has its origins in infancy, with the formation of a mutual relationship with a caregiver. Social support systems are extended in childhood and early adolescence through identification with a peer group, and in early and middle adulthood through marriage, childrearing, and relationships with coworkers and adult friends. In later life, family members are usually the primary sources of social support, especially one's spouse, children, and siblings. The quality of the relationship between an adult child and an aging parent has a long history. Clearly, the nature of the support that an aging parent is able to receive or that an adult child is willing to provide is influenced by the feelings of closeness and connection that were fashioned during the childrearing process and also by the child's relationship to the parents during early adulthood years.

In the United States, age is a predictor of the size of the social support network. Younger people have larger social support networks than do older people. This may be true for a variety of reasons. For very old people, especially women, the likelihood of living alone is high. After the death of a spouse, men and women must realign their social support systems from among relationships that include their adult children, friends, relatives, neighbors, and new acquaintances in order to satisfy their needs for interaction and companionship. In a study of social relationships following widowhood, women clearly benefited from the social network that existed prior to their husband's death. However, contrary to expectations, efforts to modify this network by renewing old acquaintances or forming new friendships did not help to reduce feelings of depression or loneliness, even 2 years after the loss (Zettel & Rook, 2004). Very old adults who are childless or who have no surviving children or siblings are especially vulnerable to ending their lives in isolation. In contrast, those who are able to preserve a diverse social network are more likely to be the healthiest, to make the most use of appropriate community services, and to experience the highest levels of well-being (Antonucci et al., 2001; Bosworth & Schaie, 1997; Litwin, 1997).

For many older adults, religious participation provides an additional source of social support. Older adults are more likely than younger adults to describe themselves as religious in their beliefs and their behavior. Mary, who at age 80 has experienced the deaths of three brothers, her husband, and her daughter-in-law, gives and receives emotional support through her faith:

> I always have a lot of faith. The good Lord has always given me the strength to go on. I was raised to believe and pray when I have problems. I go to Mass every Sunday, and we have other special days when we go to Mass. I'm a eucharistic minister. God makes me do things to feel better—I serve people and God. I go to buildings to give communion to people who can't get out. (Rowe & Kahn, 1998, p. 164)

The place of religion in the lives of the very old is especially significant for African Americans, who are more likely than European Americans to attend religious services regularly, even at advanced ages. They are also more likely to describe themselves as very religious—a characterization that reflects the frequency of their private prayer, of their strong emotional commitment, and of their reading of religious material. Religious involvement among elderly African Americans is not predicted by income or education, however (Taylor, 1986). In one study of older African American residents in an urban area, church membership was significantly related to well-being, particularly as a result of the perceived support they received from other church members (Walls & Zarit, 1991).

Ethnic identity itself may also become an important vehicle for social support in later life (Cool, 1987). It can provide a variety of sources of nonfamilial support, from a loose network of associations to membership in formal clubs and organizations. Members of an ethnic group may feel a strong sense of community as a result of their shared exposure to past discrimination, a realization of common concerns, and a sense of responsibility to preserve some of the authenticity of their ethnic identity for future generations. Participation in such a support network may be another vehicle for contributing wisdom gained through life experiences to those who will follow. Insofar as members of ethnic groups have felt somewhat marginal in the larger society in the past, their mutual support in later life may protect them from some of the negative stereotypes that the society imposes on the very old.

Involvement in a social support system can be viewed as an essential ingredient in the achievement of a sense of immortality. The social support system confirms the value of very old people, providing direct evidence of their positive impact on others and a sense of embeddedness in their social communities. The social support system of the very old usually includes adult children. Positive interactions with them contribute to the sense of living on through one's offspring and their descendants. Interactions with members of the social support system—especially those marked by feelings of warmth, caring, and celebration—may be moments of experiential transcendence for very old people. They feel the fullness and joy of existence that transcend physical and material barriers.

# THE PRIME ADAPTIVE EGO QUALITY AND THE CORE PATHOLOGY

## CONFIDENCE

In this discussion, **confidence** refers to a conscious trust in oneself and an assurance about the meaningfulness of life. In this definition, one finds the earliest psychosocial crisis of trust versus mistrust integrated with the crisis of integrity versus despair. In very old age, after a lifetime of facing challenges and experiencing losses and gains, one has a new belief in the validity of one's intuition, a trust in one's worldview, and a continued belief in one's capacity to participate in the world on one's own terms. Confidence is sustained by a stable, supportive social network (Lang, Featherman, & Nesselroade, 1997). Older adults who feel they are able to engage

in the activities they enjoy and to interact with people they value are also more likely to believe that they can adapt to the challenges they face. As a result of their confidence, they are less disrupted by stressful events and more hopeful about being able to find successful solutions in the face of negative events (Pushkar, Arbuckle, Conway, Chaikelson, & Maag, 1997).

Physical health and age, per se, are not the best predictors of confidence. One's perceptions of physical health problems and how one sees oneself in comparison to others may be more important predictors of confidence than any objective measure of health status. Some people view themselves as more impaired and dependent than they actually are; others, who may be suffering from serious illnesses, continue to view their situation with optimism (Ryff, 1995). Similarly, one's perception of the adequacy of social support and its appropriateness in response to one's needs is more important to one's sense of confidence than the financial value of the resources exchanged (Davey & Eggebeen, 1998).

Over the course of the life span, psychosocial theory predicts that each individual will confront issues related to the negative poles of the psychosocial crisis of each stage. We argue that finding ways to integrate the negative pole of each stage into an overall positive worldview strengthens and humanizes one's character. Encounters with each negative pole provide a deeper sense of empathy for the suffering of others and a more profound appreciation for the courage that it takes to live out one's life with an open, generous, hopeful outlook. Confidence emerges not because of a life of one success after the next, but out of a sequence of struggles in which creative energy is required to find a positive balance between positive and negative forces (J. M. Erikson, 1988).

## DIFFIDENCE

**Diffidence** refers to an inability to act because of overwhelming self-doubt. It is considered one of the basic factors underlying personality disorders (Livesley, Jackson, & Schroeder, 1992). Diffidence is evidenced by an unusual amount of difficulty in making daily decisions without advice and reassurance from others; great reluctance in undertaking projects or becoming involved in activities because of lack of confidence; and fears of being unable to care for oneself, which result in the fear of being alone (American Psychiatric Association, 1994).

Diffidence is likely to be associated with hopelessness. Among the elderly, hopelessness is experienced as a negative expectancy about the future and a sense of futility about having an impact on impending events. The combination of hopelessness and depression are strongly associated with suicidal ideation among the elderly (Uncapher, Gallagher-Thompson, Osgood, & Bongar, 1998). Feelings of diffidence can result from increased dependency and loss of control due to physical illness, loss of social support, or marked reduction in the quality of life; or they can be a product of a continuous process of ego pathology, building on the negative resolutions of earlier psychosocial crises. It is clear that in later life, the courage and energy required to remain flexible and adaptive to change must be derived from the well of ego resources established over the life course. For some of the very old, this precious resource is missing, and they face the end of life in a state of passivity and doubt.

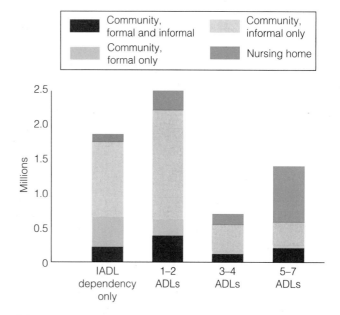

**FIGURE 15.6**

Levels of Dependency and Types of Care. Number of persons who receive nursing home care and informal and formal care in the community according to level of disability. Community-dwelling persons in this figure actually receive help for one or more basic activities of daily living (ADLs) or instrumental activities of daily living (IADLs). ADLs include bathing, dressing, eating, transferring, using the toilet, and continence. IADLs include preparing meals, shopping, managing money, doing light housework, doing heavy housework, and getting outside.

Source: Based on Hing and Bloom, 1990.

## APPLIED TOPIC
## MEETING THE NEEDS OF THE FRAIL ELDERLY

THE GOAL OF providing services or community resources to the frail elderly should be to enhance a realistic level of performance. On the one hand, one should not try to encourage 80-year-olds to live the lives of teenagers or people in their 50s. On the other hand, one should not hold such minimal expectations for the elderly that they are robbed of their autonomy and ability to meet challenges or to strive toward achievable goals. One of the current issues that has become a focus of research and policy debate is the extent to which physical frailty in very old age is treatable or preventable, and how to reduce dependency, especially in long-term nursing care (Hadley, Ory, Suzman, & Weindruch, 1993). In 2004, the U.S. Administration on Aging announced a new initiative focused on supporting "Seniors Aging in Place" (SeniorJournal .com, 2004) in response to the strong preference among the very old to remain independent. Innovative projects were funded that provided new resources or access to services in the community, so that older adults with a wide range of needs and abilities could retain an optimal level of independent functioning.

## DEFINING FRAILTY

*Frailty* has typically been operationalized in terms of **dependency**. One common approach is to list difficulties in the **activities of daily living** (ADLs), including bathing, dressing, transferring from the bed to a chair, using the toilet, and eating. Sometimes, these assessments include walking a short distance, as this degree of motor ability is usually required to function independently. Beyond these basic types of self-care, an expanded notion of dependency refers to difficulties in managing **instrumental activities of daily living** (IADLs), such as shopping, preparing meals, doing light housework, using transportation, or using the telephone. These tasks, though clearly more complex than the basic ADLs, are essential to maintaining one's daily life without dependence on informal or formal community support services (Guralnik & Simonsick, 1993). Figure 15.6 shows the numbers of adults who receive different types of care in relation to the extent of

their dependency—that is, the number of activities of daily living with which they need assistance. The largest group requires help with one or two ADLs, the vast majority of assistance coming from informal community resources, especially family and friends.

Dependency or difficulty in managing activities of daily living increases markedly after age 85. Many factors combine to produce this dependency. In most postindustrial societies, later adulthood is characterized by a sedentary lifestyle. Estimates suggest that only about 10% of older adults are active enough to sustain appropriate levels of muscle strength and cardiovascular capacity (Fiatarone & Evans, 1993). Weakness resulting from disuse combines with certain biological changes, diseases, medications, and malnutrition to produce muscle atrophy, risk of falling, reduced arousal and cognitive capacity, and a gradual decline in confidence in being able to cope with even moderate types of physical exertion.

Measures of functional limitations often fail to differentiate between what people say they might be able to do in a hypothetical context (when completing a survey) and what they actually do in their day-to-day lives. For example, some people may respond to a questionnaire saying that they are able to walk half a mile without help, but they do not actually

*Because of his problems walking, Caleb was practically homebound. But once his children got him this motorized chair he was able to enjoy going outdoors, interacting with neighbors, and taking Pebbles for a walk. What other technological inventions help support optimal functioning in very old age?*

ever walk that much. Others may respond that they cannot walk half a mile without help, but in fact they walk several blocks on most days to go to the store near their home. When observed in their natural setting, many older adults use compensatory strategies to overcome some physical impairment or integrate the support of others so that they can enact certain functions even though they have serious disabilities. For example, in a sample of women who needed assistance in more than three areas of daily living, more than one fourth still managed to get to church services once a week or more. They did not allow their physical limitations to restrict their role involvement (Glass, 1998; Idler, 1987).

For many older adults, problems with remaining independent change from time to time. In the winter, when streets are icy and the weather is cold, a person may need more help because it is difficult to walk outside or to wait for the bus. In the event of an acute illness requiring a period of hospitalization, the person may temporarily need support during the post-hospital recovery but does not require long-term institutionalization. Full recovery from a week or two of being bedridden may require additional physical therapy, rebuilding muscle tone and endurance, and rebuilding confidence in being able to manage daily tasks. The outcome for the older person depends on the patient, caregiver, and health care system—all sharing expectations for recovery and rehabilitation rather than viewing the person as permanently weakened and destined for prolonged dependency (Schulz & Williamson, 1993).

## ▌ SUPPORTING OPTIMAL FUNCTIONING

**Optimal functioning** is what a person is capable of doing when he or she is motivated and well prepared. To support optimal functioning of elderly people, one must accurately

assess their limitations. One does not want to take away the supports that help very old adults sustain their independence or overreact to their physical or intellectual limitations. This tendency, however, is observed in the responses of some adult children to their aging parents. Once the children realize that their parents are not functioning at the same high level of competence that they enjoyed previously, the children move toward a **role reversal**. The children may infantilize or dominate their parents, insisting on taking over all financial matters or attempting to relocate their parents to a more protective housing arrangement. Gradually, some children take away all their parents' decision-making responsibilities.

Although children may view such actions as being in their parents' best interests, they may fail to take their parents' preferences into account. For example, adult children tend to overemphasize the importance of health and financial considerations for their parents and to overlook the significance of familiar housing in preserving the companionship and daily support that are critical to their parents' sense of well-being (Kahana, 1982). Adult children may also fail to realize how important decision-making tasks and responsibility for personal care are to the maintenance of their parents' personality structure. In mutually satisfying relationships between adult daughters and their aging mothers, the daughters made sure that their mothers were consistently involved in decisions that affected their lives, even when the mothers were heavily dependent on their daughters for daily care (Pratt, Jones, Shin, & Walker, 1989).

In many nursing homes, there is a similar tendency to reduce or eliminate expectations of autonomy by failing to give residents responsibilities for planning or performing the activities of daily life. Routine chores such as cooking, cleaning, shopping for groceries, doing laundry, planning meals, answering the phone, paying bills, and writing letters all give older adults the sense that life is going along as usual. Replacing these responsibilities with unstructured time may subject very old people to more stress than continuing to expect some forms of regular contribution to daily life. Thus, paid work assignments and structured daily responsibilities are activities that an institutional setting can provide to help maintain a high level of social and intellectual functioning among the residents. The "Eden Alternative" is an emerging concept in nursing home care that gives residents responsibilities for some aspect of their environment depending on their level of functioning. These responsibilities—such as watering plants, volunteering in a nearby child care center, or reading to other residents—help overcome the negative impact of dependency and institutionalization (Hooyman & Kiyak, 2002).

Supporting the optimal functioning of frail elderly people requires an individualized approach. Each person has a unique profile of competencies and limitations. For some, the physical environment presents the greatest barriers to optimal functioning. For example, older adults who are in a wheelchair are likely to experience a fall every so often. However, those who have installed modifications in their home—including widened doorways and halls, railings, and easy-open doors—are less likely to fall than those whose homes have not been modified (Berg, Hines, & Allen, 2002). A person who cannot walk without fear of falling, cannot see well, or cannot grasp objects because of arthritis may need to have modifications in the home that will compensate for these limitations. Many creative strategies have been introduced that permit people with serious physical disabilities to retain an optimal level of autonomy in their homes.

## THE ROLE OF THE COMMUNITY

Interventions at the community level may be necessary to meet the safety, health, and social needs of some older adults who want to remain in their communities. It is important for resources to be accessible. In promoting optimal functioning in urban settings, for example, it is important to provide health care settings that are more easily accessible for elderly people with limited mobility. Andrulis (2000) has taken this point of view one step further by arguing that as the number of elderly people in the urban centers of the United States increases, health care organizations and providers supported by local, state, and federal governments must be prepared to reach out to the growing population of elderly people. Many of these people are poor, have physical limitations, and experience psychological barriers such as perceived threat of violence, confusion, fear, and embarrassment over lack of financial resources. As a result, they may be unable or unwilling to leave their immediate environment. Community outreach would have to provide a wide variety of services to a culturally diverse population with special attention to poverty-related concerns.

In one community intervention service in New Haven, Connecticut, called LIFE (Learning Informally From the Elderly), community professionals charged with providing services to the frail elderly organized interviews and community meetings with them to learn what challenges they were facing in trying to remain as independent as possible in their neighborhood (Pallett-Hehn & Lucas, 1994). The professionals were surprised to find that the older adults brought safety concerns to the fore as a primary issue and that health and service concerns were secondary. In order to preserve and continue the dialogue, the professionals fostered the creation of Elder Forums—neighborhood groups where older adults discuss their mutual concerns and possible solutions. Each month, representatives from the Elder Forums come together in an assembly with professionals and policymakers to raise concerns that have been discussed in the Elder Forums and to identify community resources or changes in policy and procedures for addressing these concerns.

For some very old adults, the absence of meaningful interpersonal relationships is the greatest barrier to optimal functioning. The role of the informal social support system in meeting the needs of the frail elderly cannot be underestimated. Children, spouses, other relatives, and neighbors are all important sources of help. Within communities, very old people are themselves likely to provide significant help to age-mates who may be ill, bereaved, or impaired in some way. Most older adults prefer not to have to ask for help. However, they are much better off if they have someone to turn to than if they have no one.

Beyond personal networks of social support, communities have been characterized by different levels of **collective efficacy**, which combines a strong sense of social cohesion with a high level of informal social control (Sampson, Raudenbush, & Earls, 1997). People who live in communities characterized by high collective efficacy are willing to take on important community concerns and to intervene on each other's behalf even if they do not know one another on a personal level. Examples of the impact of collective efficacy include reducing violent victimization, child or elder abuse, and illicit drug trafficking in a neighborhood. Communities that are high in collective efficacy will act to draw on the required resources to attract health care services, create new recreational settings, and improve transportation resources. In all these ways, communities characterized by collective efficacy can enhance the health and optimal functioning of the frail elderly (Browning & Cagney, 2003).

## THE ROLE OF CREATIVE ACTION

People can do a lot for themselves to promote a fulfilling later life. Very old adults can alter the structure of their environment to enhance their sense of well-being. They may move to a warmer climate, to homogeneous-age communi-

At age 85, George preserves his playful outlook by spending time with his great granddaughter. They take turns surprising each other with new costumes, songs, and games.

ties, or to more modest homes or apartments that entail fewer maintenance responsibilities. They may participate in exercise classes or other guided physical activity to improve their strength, endurance, and flexibility. Very old adults may select some family and friendship relationships that they sustain through frequent interaction, mutual help giving, and shared activities. They may participate in activities in community settings, including churches, senior centers, libraries, and volunteer organizations, through which they retain a sense of purpose and social connection. For example, 40% of people age 75 and older participate in some form of charity work (U.S. Bureau of the Census, 1999). They may decide to focus their interest on a single remaining role that is most important to them. One study has found that older people may live longer if they are able to maintain a sense of control over the role that is most important to them (Krause & Shaw, 2000). As at earlier ages, very old people make certain choices that direct the course of their lives, provide a sense of meaning, and influence their overall level of adjustment.

Consider the following life plan written by an older woman for her college alumnae magazine:

I feel more like 17, but I am 85½, the aged parent of four loving, busy children in four distant states, children I hope will stay loving by my being as little nuisance to them as possible.

To reduce my nuisance to the earth also, I have tried to limit my travel, pets and housing. I do, though, like having more than one room, so that when one space becomes fouled with work, escape to another is possible.

Soon I expect to move to a Quaker retirement place, one chosen because from it I can walk to an open stacks college library, college swimming pool, and to a Quaker meeting. One chosen, also, because in its possibly ultimate nursing wing, the patients look bright-eyed, not as if they were doped, as in so many such places.

Because bit by bit I see my memory disappearing, I have asked the child who is my successor trustee and executor to record the final names and numbers of my life. I have also been gradually unloading property I don't need, but keeping a few beautiful objects. Finally, I have arranged for a medical school to get my body, and then, at last, to have my ashes cremated and thrown into the sea. No need for a memorial service.

With all these necessary details seen to, despite a certain bodily unsteadiness and a right knee that seems to lock up on me, I am looking forward to, indeed I expect—or anyway hope for a decade or more of interest, possibly a little usefulness, and, if all goes well—a reasonable amount of plain, good fun. (Stone, 1998, p. 4)

In summary, the quality of life for the frail elderly depends on four factors: (1) the specific nature and timing of the health-related limitations that accompany aging; (2) the availability of appropriate resources within the home, family, and community to help compensate for or minimize those limitations; (3) the selective emphasis that the person gives to some life experiences over others as being central to his or her well-being; and (4) the person's motivational orientation to continue to find creative strategies to adapt to change.

# Chapter Summary

The stage of very old age is a period of new challenges and opportunities that will be faced by an increasing number of people in the years ahead. Those who are 80 years and older are the fastest growing segment of the U.S. population. Having reached a sense of acceptance of one's death, the task is to find meaning and enjoyment in the "bonus" years of life. This requires ongoing adaptation to changing physical and cognitive capacities, a deepening sense of time and the place of one's life in the history of one's people, and a willingness to find new and flexible solutions to the demands of daily life. Coping with very old age requires courage.

In attempting to describe the psychosocial development of the very old, we are drawn to concepts that have a strong non-Western philosophical flavor. We have introduced such concepts as psychohistorical perspective, experiential transcendence, immortality, and social support—themes that reflect the need to assume a long-range perspective on life and its meaning. The concept of time changes with advanced age, so that the continuity of past, present, and future becomes clearer. With the attainment of a deep confidence in being meaningfully integrated into an effective social system, the very old can find pleasure in the natural flow of events without concern about the accumulation of material goods or the need to exercise power.

The quality of daily life for the very old is influenced to a great extent by their physical health. For some, daily activities are restricted by one or more chronic diseases. Nevertheless, the majority of very old people continue to live in their own households and perform tasks of daily living independently. A key to their independence lies in whether or not they are integrated into effective social support networks. Social support provides help, resources, meaningful social interaction, and a psychological sense of being valued. The very old who survive within a support system can transcend the real limitations of their health, finding comfort and continuity in their participation in a chain of loving relationships. Those who are isolated, however, are more likely to face the end of their lives bound to the tedium of struggling with their physical limitations and resenting their survival.

The topic of the care of the frail elderly illustrates the relevance of a psychosocial framework. The resources and services available in the community can support optimal functioning. Children and other family members need to be able to interpret the needs of their parents without underestimating their capacity or resilience. Finally, older adults can guide the direction of their care by the decisions they make, both in earlier periods of life and as they detect new signs of frailty.

# Further Reflection

1. Imagine that you are now 85 years old. What kind of life do you hope to be living? What kinds of changes or modifications do you envision having to make from the period of your 50s and 60s in order to adapt in very old age?
2. What is a psychohistorical perspective? What insights might come along with living a very long time?
3. The majority of the very old are women. What are some implications of this for social policy and community development?
4. How would you describe the difference in the major challenges and areas for new growth between later adulthood and very old age?
5. In what ways may the experiences of those who are very old today differ from those who will be very old 50 years from now (those who are 25–30 today)?
6. Reflecting on your study of human development, what are the salient factors that promote optimal functioning at each stage of life?

# On the Web

**VISIT OUR WEBSITE**

Go to http://www.wadsworth.com/psychology to find online resources directly linked to your book.

# Casebook

For additional cases related to this chapter, see "Still Going Strong," in *Life Span Development: A Case Book*, by Barbara and Philip Newman, Laura Landry-Meyer, and Brenda J. Lohman, pages 215–218. This case highlights the importance of living arrangements for the health and well-being of an active 93-year-old woman.

# CHAPTER 16

# UNDERSTANDING DEATH, DYING, AND BEREAVEMENT

*Colombe aux fleurs*, 1957/Pablo Picasso/© 2005 Estate of Pablo Picasso/ Artists Rights Society (ARS), New York/Bridgeman Art Library, London/New York

*When the dove returned to the ark with an olive branch in its beak, Noah and his family perceived the sign that the period of turmoil was at an end and that life could begin anew. The dove has become a symbol of peace and hope—an image of comfort in a time of grief—providing the sense that rebirth accompanies death.*

■ MORTALITY AND PSYCHOSOCIAL DEVELOPMENT

■ DEFINITIONS OF DEATH

■ THE PROCESS OF DYING
   CASE STUDY: TOO LATE TO DIE YOUNG
   The Good Death
   Ethical Issues at the End of Life

■ DEATH-RELATED RITUALS
   Care of the Body
   Care of the Spirit
   Care of the Surviving Family, Friends, and Community

■ GRIEF AND BEREAVEMENT
   Definitions
   Grief Work
   Five Patterns of Bereavement Among Widows
   Factors That Affect the Stress of Survivors

■ PSYCHOSOCIAL GROWTH THROUGH BEREAVEMENT

■ CHAPTER SUMMARY

■ FURTHER REFLECTION

### CHAPTER OBJECTIVES

▶  *To understand the role of mortality in shaping psychosocial development*

▶  *To define the biological state of death*

▶  *To describe factors associated with the process of dying and the modern ideal of a good death*

▶  *To describe death-related rituals and their functions*

▶  *To analyze factors that affect grief and bereavement*

LIKE BOOKENDS, BIRTH and death bracket the story of development. Birth is preceded by a long chain of biological transformations, in which the biochemical thread of DNA is passed from generation to generation. Pregnancy and birth occur in a psychosocial context of relationships, resources, and cultural beliefs and practices (see Chapter 5, Pregnancy and Prenatal Development). So, too, it is with death: The biological process of dying takes place in a psychosocial context of relationships, resources, and cultural beliefs and practices. As the psychosocial concept of immortality implies, death is accompanied by a series of transformations at the biological, psychological, and societal levels. It is the role of culture and religion to provide a narrative or explanation for the transformations of energy that occur in death. Because we cannot empirically test many of these explanations, it is the role of the ego to cope with the unknown aspects of death, to give it personal meaning.

Death is at once a certainty, in that all living things die, and a random event, in that the timing of death is unknown. We know for sure that we will die, but when and how are not known. What is more, whereas through observation, systematic study, and the transmission of knowledge from generation to generation, we have a good idea about the trajectory of development beginning with the prenatal period until death, we have only speculations and belief systems to guide our understanding of what occurs at death and beyond. Thus, death is both inevitable and unknowable.

**Thanatology** is the field of science that addresses dying, death, and the psychological mechanisms of coping with them. This field includes an analysis of the attitudes toward dying, the meaning of death for individuals and societies, the rituals and practices associated with death, the bereavement process, and the expressions of bereavement across situations and cultures. ■

# MORTALITY AND PSYCHOSOCIAL DEVELOPMENT

Psychosocial development focuses on the ongoing interaction between the person and the environment. The person's ability to understand the self and others matures and changes with each psychosocial crisis. At each stage of life, the ego is shaped by the perplexing nature of mortality. In infancy, as one achieves a balance between trust and mistrust, an outlook of hopefulness emerges. This outlook shapes one's orientation toward risk, toward transitions, and ultimately toward death. If one has lived a life of hopefulness about the future, this same orientation is likely to extend toward one's beliefs about death—a sense that whatever follows the death of the physical body is going to be good.

In the resolution of the crisis of identity versus role confusion, one confronts the need to impose a sense of meaning on one's life: Where am I going? What do I want out of life? What is my path? Even though one may believe that death is far off in the distant future, the creation of a personal identity reflects an understanding that one's life is finite; one's choices should count for something.

The crisis of generativity versus stagnation brings the issue of mortality even more to center stage. Here, one begins to consider the impact of one's life on future generations: What can I do to contribute to the quality of life for others, even after my death? How can I use my resources, talents, and creative abilities to ensure a good future for those who come after me? While still in the throes of caring for children, aging parents, colleagues, and communities, the generative action of middle adults suggests a concern for a time when the ego is not present to nurture and maintain.

Developing a point of view about death is a major developmental task during later adulthood. The resolution of the crisis of integrity versus despair requires recognition that death is increasingly imminent. Integrity is achieved on the

*In older communities it is common to find small family cemeteries where people are buried near their home or farmland. These cemeteries suggest a time when there was a greater intimacy between the living and their ancestors.*

© William K. Daby/Getty Images

shoulders of earlier ego strengths that allow the person to celebrate his or her achievements, cherish meaningful relationships, and look with satisfaction at the life he or she has lived. The integrity expressed by those in later adulthood—an ability to celebrate life in the face of impending death—is a model for younger generations.

Finally, the crisis of immortality versus extinction brings the confidence of continuity. One is ready—though not necessarily eager—to close one door, confident that another will open. In this period, the possibility of death cannot dampen the joy of being and the certainty that one's life is intimately connected with all life.

Over time, direct personal experiences with dying and death have changed. One hundred years ago, most people died in their homes. Many women and infants died in childbirth. As a result, death was experienced by family members, who cared for the dying and were present at the death. As you travel through New England, it is common to find small cemeteries near churches and homes, where you sense the intimate gathering of families who buried their dead nearby.

With the growth of modern medicine, people who were very ill were taken to hospitals. Those who were dying were removed from the home, and death occurred more in hospitals or nursing homes. Death was sanitized through embalming practices. A culture of "death as medical failure" emerged, leaving people increasingly alienated from the realities of dying. The discussion of topics related to death and dying became taboo. Children were shielded from experiences with death. Doctors often tried to protect people from the knowledge that they were dying. Once people became terminally ill, they were deprived of the right to have a voice in decisions re-

lated to their treatment and the conditions surrounding the end of life.

Beginning with the works of Elizabeth Kübler-Ross (1969, 1983), the needs of the dying person were given a voice again. Concern about allowing people to talk about their fears, to plan for their funeral, and to bring closure to their personal affairs led people to face death more openly and directly. This approach also led to new ways of thinking about the care of the dying. Currently, we have new technologies that allow for the prolongation of life, but we are still caught in conflicts about whether we should let a person live or die.

## DEFINITIONS OF DEATH

The definition of death has changed. Historically, the criteria for death were lack of a heartbeat and lack of respiration, called **cardiopulmonary death**. This definition was used for hundreds of years. In 1981, the President's Commission for the Ethical Study of Problems in Medicine and Biomedical and Behavioral Research identified eight criteria for the determination of **whole-brain death**:

1. No spontaneous movement in response to any stimuli
2. No spontaneous respirations for at least one hour
3. Total lack of responsiveness to even the most painful stimuli
4. No eye movements, blinking, or pupil responses
5. No postural activity, swallowing, yawning, or vocalizing
6. No motor reflexes

7. A flat electroencephalogram (EEG) for at least 10 minutes
8. No change in any of these criteria when they are tested again 24 hours later

In addition to these eight criteria, certain other conditions, such as deep coma, have to be ruled out. There are two areas in the brain that control different types of life functions: the *brainstem* controls heartbeat and respiration, and the *cortex* controls sensory integration and cognitive function. It is possible for a person's brainstem functions to continue even when there is no cortical functioning. This condition is called **persistent vegetative state**. If you refer back to the list of eight criteria, you can see that the person in this state is not technically dead. When this state occurs, family members, doctors, and sometimes the courts are faced with the difficult decision about whether to let the person die.

In response to the report of the President's Commission, Congress passed the Uniform Determination of Death Act (UDDA). All 50 states and the District of Columbia recognize whole-brain death as the one legal standard. However, the UDDA allows physicians or hospitals to apply the cardio-pulmonary definition or the whole-brain death definition, whichever applies first. On the one hand, because of the great need for transplantable organs, there is urgency in deciding whether or not a person has died. On the other hand, it is not legal to remove an organ when that removal would cause a person's death. Therefore, the decision whether to harvest organs from people who are experiencing whole-brain death poses a difficult ethical question (DeGrazia, 1998).

Because there are a variety of technologies that can extend life when a person is no longer able to communicate his or her preferences, it is recommended that adults prepare some form of **advance directive**, such as a *durable power of attorney* or a *living will*. These documents can inform a physician or a hospital about a person's wishes about life-sustaining procedures in the face of terminal illness or imminent death and designate someone to act on their behalf. Through a **living will**, a person can direct physicians or a hospital to withhold life-sustaining procedures and prevent the use of unwanted medical measures when that person is unable to convey his or her wishes. Some older people wear bracelets that say, "living will—do not resuscitate (DNR)." The **durable power of attorney** authorizes someone to act on behalf of the person about financial and property matters and health care decisions. This directive can go into effect when the agreement is signed or when the disability occurs (Hooyman & Kiyak, 1993). It is possible to register a living will online at http://www.uslivingwillregistry.com.

One of the more troubling health conditions is Alzheimer's disease, in which there is a gradual loss of mental competence, so that a decision must be made about when the person is no longer competent and the living will or durable power of attorney will go into effect. The preparation of advance directives requires that people think about the kind of care they want to receive and the conditions under which they want treatment to be withheld. Currently, most Americans do not complete advance directives (Kersting, 2004). Even though it is recommended that people consider these issues while they are flourishing, the fact remains that it seems to be difficult for people to face these issues and make decisions about their death.

# THE PROCESS OF DYING

People can experience death in many different ways. Their psychological coping strategies differ depending on the conditions of the experience. In Chapter 14 (Later Adulthood), we described Kübler-Ross' concept of stages in coming to terms with one's death: denial, anger and resentment, bargaining, depression and mourning one's death, and acceptance. Although these emotional reactions are all important aspects of understanding how people may cope with the reality of their death, the differences in the conditions of death mean that this stage process is not likely to be experienced universally.

In contrast to the notion of stages, some people write about the **dying trajectory** (Lawton, 2001)—that is, the time during which the person's health goes from good to death. Certain illnesses such as some cancers or AIDS result in a gradual decline. Under these conditions, people have more time to acknowledge their death and to plan for it. They may be asked to make a number of decisions about their treatment, in each case weighing the risks or side effects of treatment against the chances of prolonging life. Some people experience unpredictable, sudden death in the midst of a healthy life, as in an automobile accident, by homicide, or by a heart attack. This trajectory does not allow the person to confront the reality of death. For some, death involves an ambiguous decline, in which periods of illness may alternate with periods of remission, as in the case of leukemia or muscular dystrophy. For these people, there is a complex process of learning to live with a terminal disease, in which there may be periods of health as well as periods of decline. In this scenario, the person may wrestle with the question whether they are dying from the illness or living with the illness. The case study of Harriet McBryde Johnson illustrates the complex process of making meaning in the face of an ambiguous trajectory.

# CASE STUDY

## TOO LATE TO DIE YOUNG

*Harriet McBryde Johnson was diagnosed with muscular dystrophy as a little girl. She has faced a life of surviving the expectation that she would die young.*

I'm three or four years old. I'm sitting on the living room floor, playing with dolls. I look up at the TV and see a little boy. He's sitting on the floor, playing with toy soldiers. Then he's in Little League; he stumbles on his way to first base. He visits a doctor. His parents are sad. He's in a wheelchair. Then a bed. Then I see the toy soldiers. No boy. An unseen narrator says, "Little Billy's toy soldiers have lost their general." It's a commercial for the Muscular Dystrophy Association. As the narrator makes the pitch, a realization comes to me: I will die.

Is it really one of my earliest memories? Or was it manufactured by my imagination? I don't suppose it matters. Either way, it was my truth. I'm a little girl who knows she will die, but I don't say anything. Somehow my mother guesses. "That boy," she says, "has a different kind of muscular dystrophy. Girls don't get it." Maybe, I think, but he looks a lot like me. And pretty soon I see little girls on the telethon and hear that girls too have "killer diseases." I don't know the word, but I figure my mother is in denial.

By the time I am five, I think of myself as a dying child. I've been sick a lot. There is some discussion before my parents decide to send me to kindergarten. I am glad they do. When I die, I think, I might as well die a kindergartner.

**\*\*\*\***

I've just turned 30. I've been lolling in bed for nearly three weeks; I say I've strained my neck, but really it's major depression. Just before my birthday my mother had brain surgery. She's come through it beautifully, but I'm terrified to think I could actually outlive my parents. I am further set adrift by the sudden death of the crazy German doctor who nursed me with pea soup and sausages when I refused to go to the hospital with pneumonia. My thoughts race by, but I manage to grab them and take a look. I find that I'm bonkers but rational. I know what's bothering me; my plan to die young hasn't worked out. What do I do now? My thoughts take on the structure of a song with a repeated chorus; it's too late to die young.

**\*\*\*\***

I decide to embrace the death sentence. No need to fear it; no need to hasten it. Mortality is something all people share, a unifying force. Every life, whether long or short, is a treasure of infinite value. These things are true, I figure, and it's my job to say so. When I die, I might as well die honest. (Johnson, 2005, pp. 44–46)

## ■ CRITICAL THINKING AND CASE ANALYSIS

1. What are the challenges of facing an ambiguous dying trajectory? For the dying person? For close relatives?
2. What are some of the possible reasons for Harriet's depression at age 30?
3. According to psychosocial theory, what are some of the life themes that Harriet is facing at age 4? At age 30?
4. How might her psychosocial development be affected by her illness at age 4 and age 30? By her sense of herself as someone who is dying?
5. What are some of Harriet's' coping strengths? Weaknesses?

6. If you were Harriet's parents, what would you do to try to prepare Harriet for her life? For her death?

The dying process may bring a high **degree of suffering**, including shortness of breath, inability to eat, limited mobility, and pain. In some instances, this suffering can be alleviated with medications, but in some cases it grows worse. Health care providers and family members often express great dissatisfaction with these end-of-life conditions for the dying person and for the surviving loved ones.

Finally, the dying process may be conceptualized in different ways depending on the *age* of the dying person. The primary cause of death differs for people of various age groups, thus creating different contexts for dying. Children and adolescents are most likely to die of injuries due to fires, auto accidents, or abuse. In middle adulthood, cancer, heart disease, and AIDS are common causes of death, along with accidents and homicide. Older adults are most likely to die of the complications from chronic diseases, such as heart disease, diabetes, pneumonia, or cancer (U. S. Census Bureau, 2004b).

People of different ages have differing cognitive abilities, psychological coping mechanisms, and views of the future that they bring to the tasks of preparing for death. Kübler-Ross reported the following poem that was written by Mike, a teenage boy, to his parents on the day of his death:

> The time has come,
> My job is done.
> Now it's time for another one
> The gates will open, open soon
> I now will go.
> See you soon.
> Time, time will never stop
> Everlasting time
> Love is eternal
> Forevermore love
> I will always love you. (cited in Kübler-Ross, 1983, p. 189)

Because of the nature of his illness, Mike had time to prepare for his death. His mother reports that he taped messages to his family and friends, helped plan his funeral, and gave a few things away before he died. At this age, Mike appears to have a hopeful view about an everlasting life. He is able to conceptualize dying as a transition that allowed some continuity between the life he had and the life he is going to have. He also sees a future in which he will be reunited with the other loved ones in his life before too long. Another teenager, John, who was terminally ill, stated that before he died he wanted two things: to own a van and to make love to a woman (Kübler-Ross, 1983, p. 184). Here we see a youthful approach to the dying process. John's goals are more fun loving and pragmatic, whereas Mike's approach is more spiritual and interpersonal.

Ray Bradbury provided a portrait of a great-grandmother's approach to her own death. At 90, Great Grandma told her children and grandchildren:

*For many people, the concept of a good death includes dying peacefully at home in the company of those you love and who love you.*

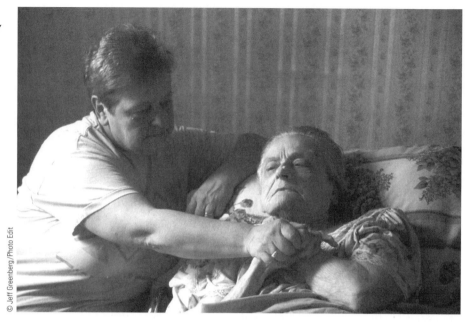

© Jeff Greenberg/Photo Edit

I don't want any Halloween parties here tomorrow. Don't want anyone saying anything sweet about me; I said it all in my time and my pride. I've tasted every victual and danced every dance; now there's one last tart I haven't bit on, one tune I haven't whistled. But I'm not afraid. I'm truly curious. Death won't get a crumb by my mouth I won't keep and savor. So don't you worry over me. Now, all of you go, and let me find my sleep. (Bradbury, 1957/1964, pp. 140–141)

In this case, Great Grandma reassures her children that she is ready—that she has experienced a full life and sees death as the next dance.

In addition to the way death is perceived by the dying, the death will be perceived and conceptualized differently by caregivers. The death of a child or adolescent may be seen as quite tragic in the minds and hearts of parents and friends; the death of an older person may be seen as the natural close to a full life. In some cultures, the death of an elder is especially painful, as it results in the loss of wisdom and guidance for younger generations. In other cultures, the death of a child is especially tragic, because it results in the loss of promise and potential for the future.

## THE GOOD DEATH

The professionals who are responsible for the care of the dying have begun to define the characteristics of "a good death" or "dying well" (Emanuel & Emanuel, 1998; Webb, 1997). The Hospice Education Institute (2001) offers the following goals for high quality end-of-life care:

1. Promote relief from pain
2. Integrate the psychological and spiritual aspects of patient care
3. Offer a support system to help patients live as actively as possible until death
4. Help the family cope during the patient's illness and their own bereavement

In a research project (Carr, 2003), the ideals of a good death were studied by asking recent widows and widowers to rate their spouses' end-of-life experiences along the following dimensions:

1. Spouse was at peace with the idea of dying
2. Spouse was aware of impending death
3. Respondent and spouse discussed the death
4. Respondent was with spouse at the moment of death
5. Spouse led a full life
6. Spouse was not in pain
7. Spouse did not receive negligent care

These dimensions represent concrete evidence of what people perceive to be a good death. Of all these features, the greatest psychological distress for the survivor was associated with seeing the spouse in great pain at the end of life. Although roughly 70% of Americans say they would prefer to die at home, about 75% actually die in a hospital, many undergoing painful medical interventions in attempts to prolong life (Cloud, 2000).

In a study of what patients, family members, and their health care professionals were concerned about in preparing for the end of life, the following issues were highlighted: naming someone to make decisions, knowing what to expect about one's physical condition, having one's financial affairs in order, having one's treatment preferences in writing, and knowing that one's physician is comfortable talking about death. Dying patients were also concerned about planning their funeral (Steinhauser et al., 2001).

There appear to be two different paths to achieving a good death among people who are in a slow, painful death trajectory. One is *hospice care*. The other is *euthanasia*.

## ■ HOSPICE CARE

**Hospice care** is an integrated system of medicine, nursing, counseling, and spiritual care for the dying person and his or her family. Its goal is to achieve the highest possible quality of life for the dying person and the family, alleviating physical and emotional pain to the highest degree possible, while supporting family strengths to cope with the process of dying, loss of the loved one, and long-term bereavement (Smith, 1997).

Hospice care differs from traditional hospital care in that the focus is on enhancing the quality of life for the dying person and his or her loved ones rather than on treating the disease or intervening to delay the end of life. The first role of hospice care is to relieve the person's pain and suffering through a variety of medical, physical, psychological, and spiritual means. Dying patients are encouraged to take an active role in as many aspects of their end-of-life care as their cognitive functioning and health permit. They are supported in talking about their death and interacting with their family. Hospice care has many advantages for those with a terminal illness. It prevents the experience of dying alone for those who do not have family and friends nearby. It allows the person to die in a more natural, familiar setting rather than in a hospital or nursing home. It offers emotional, spiritual, and physical comfort, helping more people experience a good death.

The story of the hospice movement illustrates how many factors converge to create a new set of policies and practices. The concept of the hospice as a setting for the care of terminally ill patients is attributed to Dr. Cicely Saunders, who founded St. Christopher's Hospice in London in 1967. In 1963, she gave a talk at Yale University about her work with terminally ill cancer patients and their families, illustrating the many ways in which patients benefited from an integrated approach to care. Following her talk, Florence Wald, the Dean of the Yale School of Nursing, invited Dr. Saunders to be a visiting faculty member for a semester. Subsequently, in 1968, Dr. Wald took a sabbatical and spent time with Dr. Saunders at St. Christopher's. These two health care leaders were supported in their efforts to create hospice settings in the United States by the publication of Dr. Kübler-Ross' book, *On Death and Dying*, in 1969. In 1972, the U.S. Senate Special Committee on Aging heard testimony from Dr. Kübler-Ross about the negative impact of institutionalizing and isolating the dying. Between 1978 and 1982, several demonstration programs to explore the benefits of hospice care were funded by federal agencies and private foundations. As a result, the U.S. Congress included hospice care as a reimbursable Medicare benefit in 1982—a provision that became permanent in 1986.

Since that time, Congress has increased the level of reimbursement for hospice care, included hospice care as part of veterans' benefits, and included hospice care in the review of efforts to reduce waste and abuse in the Medicare and Medicaid systems. Clear guidelines have been established for the range and quality of services that hospices must offer in order to receive Medicare reimbursements, and an increasing range of educational and training programs have emerged to provide professional interdisciplinary training for those working in hospice and end-of-life care settings. In 1999, the U.S. Postal Service issued the Hospice Care Commemorative Stamp, marking the recognition of this successful model as part of the continuum of health care (National Hospice and Palliative Care Organization, 2005).

To take advantage of hospice through Medicare, one must make a decision to forgo any further life-saving or life-prolonging treatments. A physician must also submit certification that the person is terminally ill, with 6 months or less to live. This provision is one of the current limitations in the use of hospice care within the Medicare system. In advanced stages of Alzheimer's disease and other forms of dementia, the demands on caregivers can be intense, but survival can be prolonged beyond 6 months. As a result, only a small percentage of those with Medicare hospice coverage are patients with Alzheimer's disease (Kersting, 2004). To learn more about hospice care, you can visit the website of the National Hospice Foundation (http://www.hospiceinfo.org).

## ■ EUTHANASIA

*Euthanasia* is the practice of ending someone's life for reasons of mercy. In comparison to hospice care, euthanasia is considered when pain medication is ineffective in reducing suffering; when a person is in a persistent vegetative state, being kept alive by mechanical equipment; or when a person is in the final stages of a terminal illness. Euthanasia generally involves hastening the end of life by allowing people to have control over their death.

**PASSIVE EUTHANASIA.** Imagine that a person in the late stages of Alzheimer's disease is diagnosed as having cancer. Should treatments including surgery, chemotherapy, and radiation be administered to prolong the life of someone who is already near death? **Passive euthanasia** refers to withholding treatment or removing life-sustaining nourishment and breathing aids. The result is that death occurs more quickly than if these procedures were continued. Through a living will, a person can make his or her wishes known to others, including the hospital or care center, the physicians, and family members or legal representatives. Through the durable power of attorney, a person assigns life-prolonging or -ending decision making to his or her representative. Thus, by refusing treatment or by granting discretion to others to end heroic or extraordinary treatment, individuals may hasten their own death. In the preceding example, if the person had a living

*Many technical innovations allow physicians to save a person in hopes of recovery; in other situations life is sustained with no chance of recovery. These advances present many ethical questions about conditions under which lives should be sustained and treatment continued.*

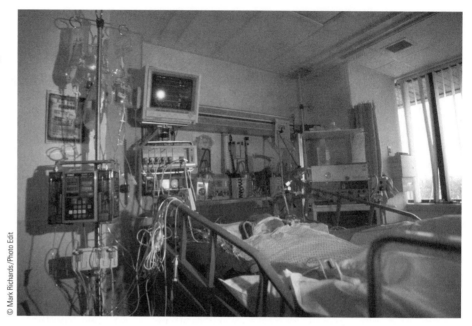

© Mark Richards/Photo Edit

will or a durable power of attorney, a decision could be made by someone else to withhold treatment for the cancer, even though the person is no longer capable of decision making on his or her own behalf.

**ACTIVE EUTHANASIA.** Activities designed to end a person's life are referred to as **active euthanasia.** There are several ways in which this may happen. **Mercy killing** involves actively taking a person's life. This is sometimes done in order to end a person's suffering. In our society, this is considered to be murder. States vary widely on whether the killer will be prosecuted for this act and whether juries will be willing to convict. In a Michigan case of a nurse who ended the lives of more than 20 patients at the Ann Arbor VA hospital, the jury found the nurse to be guilty of murder and sentenced her to life imprisonment. In a California case of a spouse who strangled her husband to end his suffering because she could not help him any longer, the state decided not to prosecute.

Physician-assisted suicide involves either the administration of a lethal dose of some medication by a physician or arranging for a terminally ill patient to administer his or her own lethal dose of medication using a suicide machine. This is an extremely controversial procedure. In 1994, Oregon passed a Death With Dignity Act allowing individuals who are terminally ill to request a prescription from their physician for a lethal dose of medication. According to that act, doctors would be allowed to help patients commit suicide by prescribing a lethal dose of medication under the following conditions:

1. Patients would have less than 6 months to live
2. The patient requests it three times
3. There is a second opinion from another doctor

4. There is a 15-day waiting period for the patient to change his or her mind.

In 1997, The U.S. Supreme Court ruled that there is no constitutional right to physician-assisted suicide, leaving the issue up to the states. They did not overturn the Oregon law. In 1997, Oregon voters affirmed the decision to allow physician-assisted suicide by passing the measure again.

How common are these measures? In the United States, assisted suicide and active euthanasia are illegal, which makes it difficult to know how often these strategies are used. In The Netherlands, however, there are guidelines for these procedures, and records are accurate. In a study in The Netherlands, Wolf (1996) found that 38% of all deaths involved some kind of medical decision. Of these, 18% were the result of passive euthanasia where treatment was not provided, and 18% involved hastening death by providing pain medication or other care that led to death occurring more quickly than it might have by not using these treatments. Only about 2% of all cases involved the administration of a lethal drug or physician-assisted suicide. Thus, even in a country where assisted suicide is permitted, it is approached cautiously and used sparingly.

## ETHICAL ISSUES AT THE END OF LIFE

Ethical issues surrounding end-of-life decisions bring to mind the applied topic of abortion that was discussed in Chapter 5. One might view abortion as a special case of decisions about ending life. End-of-life decisions are not only relevant for elderly people; they may be addressed when parents decide to limit treatment for a terminally ill child, when family members decide to remove life support for an adult who is in a vegetative state, or when a person seeks assisted suicide in order to avoid a decline into an immobile or help-less state. The matter is made even more complex because de-cisions about ending life conflict with the commitment of the medical profession to prolong life. As a result of many new technologies, medications, and genetic interventions, there are ongoing innovations that may be effective in slowing the progression of a disease or sustaining life even if the condition cannot be cured.

Decisions about ending one's life are not made lightly. Most people agree that when a dying person who is in ex-treme pain asks a doctor to end his or her life, that request should be honored. In a Harris Poll conducted in 2001, re-spondents were read a description of the Oregon Death with Dignity Act. A majority (61%) of respondents said that they would favor such a law in their state; 63% disagreed with the Supreme Court ruling that individuals did not have a consti-tutional right to doctor-assisted suicide (Taylor, 2002). These results reflect a public sentiment that people have a right to make their own health decisions, including decisions about their own death.

Despite public opinion supporting measures to actively end life, these measures are illegal in the United States—with the exception of Oregon—and continue to be a topic of eth-ical controversy. Some opponents argue that legalizing as-sisted suicide might put undue pressure on elderly people to end their lives rather than be a burden to their families or to use precious financial resources for end-of-life care. There is already some sense that health care professionals in hospitals and nursing homes are less aggressive in using advanced technologies to prolong the life of elderly patients. Especially for those who have struggled to have access to quality health care during their adult lives, there is great mistrust about giv-ing someone the right to withhold care or accelerate their death (Belsky, 1997). Other opponents suggest that permit-ting those who are terminally ill to choose death would be one step toward a process of killing people who have mental disabilities or are born with serious defects that affect their quality of life. Some argue that the dying person who is in a great deal of pain may be depressed and lose sight of the pos-sibilities for medical treatments that could improve his or her condition. With effective counseling, the person might be less desperate about his or her suffering and find ways to achieve a new sense of closeness with loved ones. Finally, there are those who feel that allowing someone to decide to end their own life is a violation of their religious or political views.

# DEATH-RELATED RITUALS

Death is a powerful change of state that has mysterious qual-ities. Typically, it is accompanied by a range of symbolic rituals. These rituals address at least three critical aspects of

the meaning of death. The first is how to treat the physical body—the corpse—in an appropriate way. The second is how to address the fate of the spiritual aspect of the person—the soul. The third is how to meet the emotional needs of the survivors and the needs of the society as a whole. Across cul-tures, people feel a strong need to carry out funeral rituals for the burial or cremation of the dead. Rituals have the advan-tage of offering a prescribed set of practices at a time when people may be too distressed to make complex decisions. Over one's life span, prior attendance and participation in fu-neral rituals provides some comfort and familiarity, which may help reduce the distress when a loved one dies.

Funeral rituals allow survivors to say goodbye to their loved one, to honor the dead person, and, in the process, to begin to detach themselves from the dead person. The con-crete evidence of the body proves beyond a doubt to sur-vivors that the person is dead. This helps break down natural tendencies to want to deny the loss. When there is no body, as sometimes happens in natural disasters, mass killings, and war, survivors may be overcome by distress and anxiety caused by uncertainty. Under these conditions, communities sometimes create memorial services or monuments to sym-bolically bury their dead (Boss, 2002a). The specific practices described in the following section are examples of traditional customs, which are often modified depending on the ortho-doxy of the mourners, community practices, and the context of the death.

## CARE OF THE BODY

Most funeral preparations include specific practices for car-ing for the corpse. Often, the corpse is washed and wrapped in a funeral shroud or cloth. Muslims wash the body in warm water and soap and, finally, with a scented water. Among American Indians, a powdery substance made of corn is used to cover the dead person's face. Among Protestants and Catholics in Europe and the United States, the body is usually washed, embalmed, and dressed in clothes selected by the family. Often, cosmetics are applied to make the person look as if he or she is sleeping. The corpse is placed in a casket and laid out for viewing. In some cultures, the body is cremated; in others, the body is buried. Cremation is typically associ-ated with a belief in the liberation of the spirit. Burial is often tied to beliefs about the afterlife. For example, ancient Egyp-tians believed that in order for the person's soul to move on to the next life, the body needed to remain intact. As a result, they developed techniques for embalming and mummifica-tion to preserve the body as long as possible (Encarta, 2005).

Cultures have different practices concerning how quickly the body is to be disposed of after death. In most Protestant and Catholic families, there is a 1- to 3-day viewing period after death, when family and friends come to the funeral home to see the body and pay respects to family members. This precedes the actual funeral service and burial. In contrast, among Islamic families, the body is prepared by family members when possible, men caring for the body of men and women for the body of women. The burial is expected to take place as soon as possible after the death, preferably within 24 hours (IslamOnline, 2003). Viewing of the dead body after it has been prepared for burial is forbidden. In Japan, Buddhists allow 3 days to pass before the body is burned. On the first day, a priest comes to the home and recites a prayer called a *sutra*. On the second day, the family members burn incense sticks before the family altar. On the third day, the body is burned at a funeral hall, and the ashes are brought back to the house and then taken to the cemetery.

## CARE OF THE SPIRIT

Most cultures believe that there is a spiritual component of a person's being that is not destroyed as the body decomposes or burns. Certain funeral practices are designed to help the spirit make a transition to whatever existence the culture believes takes place after death. This preparation may be in the form of specific prayers that are recited, or burying the person with possessions that may be useful in the afterlife. Singing, dancing, and playing musical instruments are sometimes used to speed the departed spirit on its way to the next life. Hindus believe that at death, the spirit leaves the body and enters a small flame that is lit next to the body. The spirit remains in the home because of attachments to family and possessions. The body is cremated, and there is a period of prayers in the person's home that lasts for 12 days. On the tenth day, the flame with the spirit is taken to the sea. Placing the flame in the sea is a signal to the spirit to leave the attachments of the earthly life and begin the transition to the afterlife.

In New Mexico, the Navajo believe that the dead person will need certain resources in the afterlife. The dead are often buried with an extra set of clothes, food, water, and other items that may be of value in the afterworld. The Navajo believe that everything a person creates has some part of the person's spirit in it. As a result, at death, many of the artifacts a person made, such as pottery or blankets, are cracked or torn in order to release the person's spirit (Santillanes, 1997).

Many societies also observe rituals in years following the death to nurture and respect the spirit of the ancestor and to establish a link between the living and the departed. In Estonia, it is thought that there is a day each year when the dead return to their home for a visit. Rooms are cleaned, and food is laid out for a banquet. This is to preserve and strengthen relationships between the living and the souls of the dead. Many Japanese families visit the cemetery four times each year. They have small altars in their homes, where they pray to their ancestors. They believe that the ancestors are always with them, guiding their lives and providing protection. In America, many people of different cultures visit the cemetery for periods of reflection, solitude, and discussion with dead relatives. Practices of leaving flowers and wreaths at the grave site are expressions of respect.

## CARE OF THE SURVIVING FAMILY, FRIENDS, AND COMMUNITY

In addition to addressing the treatment of the body and the soul, death rituals are important for helping the people who remain to cope with their grief and to reorient their lives in a world without the person who died. These rituals also allow the society to elaborate the meaning of death and to decrease the ambiguity surrounding death. Most cultures have funer-

*Every culture has rituals associated with death. In this Balinese cremation ceremony, people gather to prepare the ashes so the spirit can be released.*

© Paul A. Souders/Corbis

HUMAN DEVELOPMENT AND DIVERSITY

## The Amish Way of Death

THE IMPORTANCE THAT the Amish place on their funeral ceremonies is reflected not only in familiarity with death but also in an intensified awareness of community. As an Amish man reported in a family interview, "The funeral is not for the one who dies, you know; it is for the family."

The Amish community takes care of all aspects of the funeral occasion, with the exception of the embalming procedure, the coffin, and the horse-drawn wagon. These matters are taken care of by a non-Amish funeral director who provides the type of service that the Amish desire.

The embalmed body is returned to the home within a day of the death. Family members dress the body in white garments in accordance with the biblical injunction found in Revelation 3:5. For a man, this consists of white trousers, a white shirt, and a white vest. For a woman, the usual clothing is a white cape and apron that she wore at both her baptism and her marriage. At baptism, a black dress is worn with the white cape and apron; at marriage, a purple or blue dress is worn with the white cape and apron. It is only at her death that an Amish woman wears a white dress with the cape and apron that she put away for the occasion of her death. This is an example of the lifelong preparation for death as sanctioned by Amish society. The wearing of white clothes signifies the high ceremonial emphasis on the death event as the final rite of passage into a new and better life.

Several Amish women stated that making their parents', husbands', or children's funeral garments was a labor of love that represented the last thing they could do for their loved ones. One Amish woman related that

© AP/Wide World Photos

At the time of death, the whole Amish community comes together to support the mourners and say farewell to their cherished friend.

each month, her aged grandmother carefully washed, starched, and ironed her own funeral clothing so that it would be in readiness for her death. This act appears to have reinforced for herself and her family her lifelong acceptance of death and to have contributed to laying the foundation for effective grief work for herself and her family. This can be seen as an example of the technique of preventive intervention called *anticipatory guidance* (Caplan, 1964), which focuses on helping individuals to cope with impending loss through open discussion and problem solving before the actual death.

After the body is dressed, it is placed in a plain wooden coffin that is made to specifications handed down through the centuries. The coffin is placed in a room that has been emptied of all furnishings, in order to

accommodate the several hundred relatives, friends, and neighbors who will begin arriving as soon as the body is prepared for viewing. The coffin is placed in a central position in the house, both for practical considerations of seating and to underscore the importance of the death ceremonial.

The funeral service is held in the barn in the warmer months and in the house during the colder seasons. The service is conducted in German and lasts 12 hours, with the same order of service for every funeral. The guests view the body when they arrive and again when they leave to take their places in the single-file procession of the carriages to the burial place.

Source: From "The Amish Way of Death: A Study of Family Support Systems," by K. B. Bryer, *American Psychologist, 34,* 255–261. Copyright © 1979 American Psychological Association. Reprinted by permission.

als for the dead. These funerals involve a gathering of family, friends, and spiritual leaders to carry out the rites for the dead person, to provide a social context for expressions of grief, to celebrate the life of the person who died, and to begin the process of social support for those who remain. Depending on cultural custom, these social gatherings may occur before or after the burial or cremation. Funerals or memorial services provide a transition period surrounding death when people often have difficulty believing that the loved one has really died.

Among Africans who have migrated to the United States in recent years, a complex set of funeral rituals are observed that help mark the status of the deceased and to reaffirm traditional customs of the African community. The wake may last many days, as mourners gather from distant locations. The entire community contributes money to cover the costs of food, burial expenses, and the family's support during the period of mourning. The funeral begins with drumming, singing, and dancing, which continue when the funeral procession moves to the burial site or to the airport if the person is returned to Africa to be buried with his or her ancestors. The more important the social position of the deceased, the more elaborate the funeral (Hazell, 1997).

In the Jewish tradition, the period of mourning is prescribed in some detail, taking the bereaved from the days immediately following the funeral through the first year, and annually thereafter. Special focus is given to the practices expected of children on the death of their parents. This may be related to the importance placed on the fifth commandment, to honor thy father and thy mother. Upon returning to the home after the burial, the family members light a *shiva* (shiva means 7) candle, which represents the everlasting soul of the deceased. They then begin 7 days of mourning. This is a time when family members stay at home and focus their attention on their grief and their recollections of the deceased. Friends usually come by to visit, but no business is transacted. It is a solemn time, when luxuries and recreation are set aside. The Kaddish, a prayer which affirms life and faith in G-d, is recited daily. On the seventh day, the *shiva* candle is blown out, and the family members take a walk outside, symbolically escorting the loved one's soul out of the house and indicating that the family is strong enough to carry on their lives. The period of mourning typically lasts 12 months for those who have lost a parent and is marked by the unveiling of the tombstone or grave marker. After that time, children note the anniversary of their parents' death by lighting a *yahrzeit* (year's time) candle and attending services where the Kaddish is said (Louchheim, 1997).

Other rituals help to address the impact of the death on the larger social system. In the United States, people typically have a will, which is read to the heirs. This ritual provides for the distribution of resources and assets according to the deceased person's wishes. The reading of the will and distribution of the assets helps to realign the social system following a death. Obituaries, which are published in local newspapers, are another custom that notifies the larger community of a death. These statements often acknowledge the person's accomplishments and recognize their family members. This public statement can provide an opportunity for community members to offer support and condolences to the bereaved family members. There are a variety of other ways that the lives of people are memorialized, including contributions to charities in the name of the dead person, the creation of monuments, naming of buildings or programs, listing of names on a wall or plaque, and the establishment of scholarships, grants, or other types of endowments. In the face of widespread catastrophes, such as the terrorist attacks of September 11, 2001, public memorial services are televised to permit international mourning.

The box on the Amish Way of Death illustrates how one culture openly incorporates death into every aspect of life. The service and ritual are expressions of the belief in a spiritual immortality and a simultaneous recognition of separation. Families customarily care for their aging parents in their own homes. Dying persons are surrounded by their families, who provide reassurance of generational continuity. The bereaved family members receive help and care from community members for at least the first year after a family death. In one study, Amish families found six conditions especially helpful for coping with death (Bryer, 1979, p. 260):

1. The continued presence of the family, both during the course of the illness and at the moment of death.
2. Open communication about the process of dying and its impact on the family.
3. Maintenance of a normal lifestyle by the family during the course of the illness.
4. Commitment to as much independence of the dying person as possible.
5. The opportunity to plan and organize one's own death.
6. Continued support for the bereaved for at least a year following the funeral, with long-term support given to those who do not remarry.

Religiosity leads to lower levels of anxiety and anger for the survivors and may provide them with an analysis of the meaning of the death of their loved one (Carr, 2003). The social support and dignity provided by religious rituals may also help survivors and decrease feelings of loneliness.

# GRIEF AND BEREAVEMENT

## DEFINITIONS

**Grief** refers to the cognitive and emotional reactions that follow the death of a loved one. It can vary in duration and intensity, and it can fade and reappear at unexpected moments. In a study of family members who were responsible for caring for a person suffering from later-life dementia, five aspects of grief were identified: (1) preoccupation with thoughts of the deceased person, (2) longing for the person, (3) painful emotions, (4) feelings of dissociation—feeling disconnected from reality—and, (5) sensory illusions that led to the impression that the deceased person was still present. Of these five aspects of grief, preoccupation was the most common and lasted the longest after the person's death (Aneshensel et al., 1995).

There is no timetable for grief. One study followed the grief reactions of family members whose loved one died from cancer (Ringdal, Jordhov, Ringdal, & Kaasa, 2001). The intensity of grief response showed significant declines by the end of the first year after the death. In monitoring the grief response, however, one often finds conflicting evidence of devastation and impressive coping. A widow may be handling daily tasks at a high level of competence and still find herself in tears at seeing her husband's hat in the closet. Over time, one expects to see gradual improvement in the intense, disruptive feelings of grief, but it is hard to say if there is a time when mourning is completed. Perhaps the most important sign is that the person is able to reinvest in new activities and relationships, even while preserving affection for the deceased loved one.

**Bereavement** is the long-term process of adjustment to the death of a loved one and is more all-encompassing than grief. It is commonly accompanied by physical symptoms, role loss, and a variety of intense emotions, including anger, sorrow, anxiety, and depression. The stress of bereavement increases the likelihood of illness and even death among survivors.

## GRIEF WORK

In the face of bereavement, there is a need to work through the reality of the loss as well as the feelings that accompany it. The experience of the bereaved person is not that different from the experience of the person who is coping with his or her own death. Psychiatrist Erich Lindemann (1944) worked with many of the people whose relatives had died in the Coconut Grove fire in Boston. His writings continue to provide a basis for understanding the bereavement process. Lindemann described the normal grief reaction as involving three phases. First, the person must achieve "emancipation from bondage to the deceased." This bondage may include feelings of guilt about ways in which he or she had criticized or even harmed the person who had died; feelings of regret for things left unsaid or undone. Second, the person must make an adjustment to all the aspects of the environment from which the deceased is missing. The more closely linked the lives of the living and the dead, the more difficult this may be. Third, the person must begin to form new relationships—what we have called redirecting energy to new roles. Lindemann found that one major obstacle to working through this loss is a desire to avoid the accompanying emotions and intense physical distress. According to his analysis, the strategy of avoiding grief only prolongs the survivor's physical, mental, and emotional preoccupation with the dead person.

Questions have been raised about how universally applicable Lindemann's idea of **grief work** really is. In some cultures, intense emotional expressions of grief are considered inappropriate. Under conditions of grave trauma, some counselors suggest that an early period of denial helps the person cope with immediate demands. For some, the loss of a loved one comes after a long period of painful illness. Death may be viewed as a relief from suffering and, as such, brings a form of comfort to those who are still living. Thus, the context of death and its meaning for those who mourn suggests a more individualized view of the adaptive process of bereavement (Stroebe, 1993).

The depression and confusion that accompany grieving may decrease the survivors' sensitivity to their own physical health and pose risks to their mental health as well. People in deep mourning may have feelings of uselessness or emptiness that prevent them from seeking help for their own physical or emotional health problems. Some people try to cope with their grief by increasing their use of medication, alcohol, or tranquilizers, which may threaten their physical health. Loss of appetite and lack of sleep are other symptoms of grief that

*Bernice comes each month to "visit" with her husband at the cemetery. She never remarried and still thinks of herself as Bill's wife. She finds comfort knowing that her husband died bravely in the service of his country.*

© Joseph Sohm, ChromoSohm Inc./Corbis

contribute to the pattern of increased vulnerability during this time.

Among people who have lost a spouse, intense depression is more likely to be experienced by those who described their marriage as positive and vital. It is clear that this loss strikes at the core of an older adult's sense of attachment, social integration, and personal worth (Futterman, Gallagher, Thompson, Lovett, & Gilewski, 1990). In a comparison of older widows and widowers with adults who were not experiencing bereavement, the widowed adults showed greater signs of depression, psychopathology, and grief at 2 months after the loss (Thompson, Gallagher-Thompson, Futterman, Gilewski, & Peterson, 1991). At 12 and 30 months after the loss, the two groups were comparable in levels of depression and psychopathology, but the bereaved group continued to experience higher levels of grief than the nonbereaved group. This research, confirmed by other observations, suggests that among older adults, one may not expect a full resolution of the grief work associated with the death of a spouse. Rather, older adults come to accept a certain empty place in their hearts for their deceased partner and learn to find appropriate times to experience their profound sense of loss.

## FIVE PATTERNS OF BEREAVEMENT AMONG WIDOWS

A study that followed older couples from before the death of a spouse until 18 months after the death identified five patterns of bereavement-related adjustment (Bonanno, Wortman, & Nesse, 2004). These patterns, shown in Figure 16.1, were:

1. *Common grief pattern.* These people had low levels of depression before the spouse died. They experienced an increase in depression 6 months after the loss. After 18 months, they returned to the same low level of depression that characterized them before the loss.
2. *Resilient pattern.* People in this group had low levels of depression before the death of the spouse and continued to have low levels after the death of the spouse.
3. *Chronic grief pattern.* These people had low depression before the loss but showed increased grief responses at both 6 months and 18 months after the loss.
4. *Chronic depression pattern.* These people had high levels of depression before the loss, and depression continued at high levels at both 6 and 18 months.
5. *Depressed-improved pattern.* These people had elevated levels of depression before the loss, but lower depression scores at 6 and 18 months after the loss.

The results of this research help to clarify the importance of the context of loss as it affects the bereavement process. The context of the loss can include the nature of the relationship between the deceased person and the survivor, the sudden or gradual trajectory of death, the causes of death, the psycho-

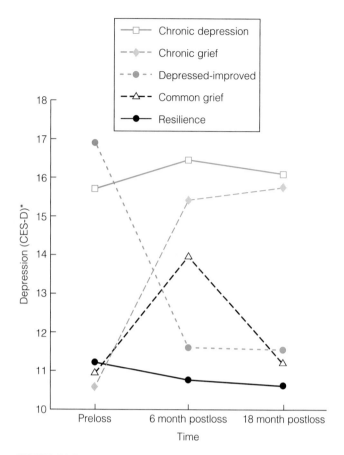

**FIGURE 16.1**

Five Patterns of Bereavement

Note: Depression measured by the Center for Epidemiologic Studies of Depression (CES-D).

Bonanno, Wortman, and Nesse, 2004, fig. 1, p. 263. Copyright 2004 by the American Psychological Association. Reprinted with permission.

logical health of the surviving spouse before the death of the partner, and the extent to which a spouse believes that his or her partner led a full life. The depressed-improved group, for example, was composed of people who were in unhappy or unsatisfying marriages; many had a substantial caregiving burden for an ailing spouse. Although people in this group did show evidence of grief responses at 6 months, they also reported benefits of widowhood and pride in the ability to cope with their new status.

In contrast, the chronic grievers comprised people whose lives were suddenly disrupted by the death of a healthy spouse. This group was especially preoccupied with a search for meaning as they tried to make sense of their spouse's death. They had sustained experiences of yearning for their spouse, thinking about their spouse, and talking with others about their spouse at 6 months, with some evidence of improvement in these aspects of grief by 18 months. The results of the study suggest that for some groups, especially the resilient and the depressed-improved groups, the relative lack of expression of grief-related symptoms may not be due to denial of their loss, but to evidence of appropriate coping.

## FACTORS THAT AFFECT THE DISTRESS OF SURVIVORS

Bereavement may be more difficult for those who lose a loved one in a sudden death. Under these conditions, there is no opportunity to discuss end-of-life decisions, no opportunity for final expressions of caring and love, and no opportunity for the bereaved to begin to anticipate life without the loved one. Bereavement may be difficult if the dying person is unable to receive effective pain control in their last days of life. Survivors who feel that the death of their loved one was brought about by physicians' negligence feel greater distress and anger than survivors who feel that the loved one received high-quality medical care. An aspect of the dying process that is seen as negative for the dying person but is protective for the survivor is nursing home usage. It leads to reduced anxiety for the survivor and may prepare them for the separation that death finalizes, while sparing them from the burden and strain of direct caregiving.

**Ambiguous loss** is another especially difficult challenge for loved ones. Two types of ambiguous loss have been described (Boss, 1999). In the first instance, the person is missing and may be dead, as in soldiers who are missing in action or people who may have died in a disaster, but there are no physical remains. In the second instance, the person is physically present but unable to participate in any meaningful way in family interactions, as when a person is in a coma or in the late stages of Alzheimer's disease. As a result of the 9-11 tragedy, some children experienced both types of loss: One parent died in the destruction of the towers, but no remains

were recovered, and the other parent was so distraught by the spouse's death that they became unable to enact their parent role. These children experienced the ambiguous loss of both parents (Boss, 2004). The box on ambiguous loss describes some of the issues surrounding this unique context of bereavement.

Finally, bereavement may be difficult if the survivor has experienced many positive benefits of caregiving, including feelings of being needed, important, and effective, as they addressed the needs of an ailing spouse (Boerner, Schulz, & Horowitz, 2004). Although family caregiving is often viewed as a source of stress, some people find that they gain comfort and even a personal sense of worth through caregiving. In this context, the death of the ailing spouse or parent brings a double loss—loss of the loved one and loss of the meaningful caregiving role.

## ■ UNACKNOWLEDGED AND STIGMATIZED LOSS

The bereavement process is influenced by a society's interpretation of who the legitimate mourners are and who has experienced a legitimate death. There are some people who grieve but who may not be recognized as legitimate mourners. These might include former spouses, foster children, partners in a gay relationship, professional caregivers, extramarital lovers, families of addicts and criminals, and people who have had abortions. When communities do not sanction or support their grief, it may be difficult for these people to acknowledge that they have suffered a loss or to experience

© Prakash Singh /AFP /Getty Images

*In the terrible aftermath of the tsunami of December 2004, many families experienced ambiguous loss. In one town, several families claimed Baby 81 as their own. Here, the baby's parents are shown in crisis, having to give the baby back to the nurse until DNA testing could establish their parental claim.*

## Ambiguous Loss

IN 2005, THE Chief Medical Examiner's Office of the City of New York announced that it would stop efforts to identify body parts that were recovered from the destruction of the World Trade Center on September 11, 2001. Of the 2,749 people who were reported missing, 1,161 have not been identified from the remains. Despite the use of a variety of approaches to identification, more than 9,000 body fragments were not identified. These fragments have been stored for future analysis, in case new technologies are developed that allow for their identification (Chen, 2005). At some point after the tragedy, the Mayor of New York offered "presumed death" certificates to families when there was no body that could be identified. Some families accepted those certificates, whereas others continued to wait for DNA testing results. Thousands of families suffered ambiguous loss— some for days not knowing if their loved one was in the buildings, many for months as they waited for the remains to be excavated from Ground Zero, and some are still suffering because there is no physical evidence of their loved one's body.

Pauline Boss (2002b, 2004) has developed an understanding of ambiguous loss through clinical observation, theory, and research. She has worked with many families who have experienced this type of loss, including merchant marine families, soldiers' families, 9-11 families, and families in Kosovo. Much of this discussion is based on her observation and methods. Ambiguous loss is a problem for the structural and functional characteristics of a family. Families may try to hold a place for the person in daily life. Confusion about

whether a loved one is dead or alive may lead some families to ignore parental roles, put off decisions, neglect daily tasks, and isolate living family members. Many families stop carrying out rituals and celebrations, which leads to further disconnection among family members.

Psychologically, the chronic uncertainty and lack of new information produce feelings of hopelessness, passivity, and immobilization. Because they do not have proof of death, family members may become confused—they do not know what to think or how to act. They may become stagnant by denying the loss and continuing to hope. The result is that family members are not grieving, and they are not coping with their loss.

Questions arise such as, "Should you have a funeral if you do not have a body?" Families would get into protracted arguments about this. Some parents did not want to tell their children that their father or mother was dead. Many children got the impression that they were not supposed to talk about the missing parent. People in these families are trying to hold two opposing ideas in their minds: (1) The loved one is still alive; (2) The loved one is dead. As a result, their grief process is blocked. It takes a very long time to create a family life that includes acceptance and integration of this ambiguity.

In working with the 9-11 families, Boss cited several techniques that helped people to cope with their loss. First, she created family storytelling meetings, where adults and children were encouraged to tell something they remembered about the missing person. Second, she arranged for groups of families who lived in the same community to meet together and tell stories

about their missing family members. These meetings helped foster community connections. People were able to identify others who had the same needs, and they began to find ways to meet those needs. Third, she explained the idea of ambiguous loss and helped people to see why it was causing them so much distress. This helped to reduce self-blame and family discord. Fourth, she encouraged families to revise family rituals and celebrations but to continue having them, because they are so important to preserving the unity of a family. Fifth, she told them not to become agitated and distressed by pushing for closure. She believes that closure is a myth and that death always produces ambiguity and uncertainty. Being done with grief, putting an end to mourning, and moving on are unrealistic expectations. People will always feel somewhat sad about the death of someone they love.

Some families were less distressed than others. The characteristics of these families included a belief that the loss of the loved one was predestined and perhaps a product of the will of G-d; some had a deep faith that G-d would care for their loved one and guide them; some had prior experience in coping with ambiguous loss; some were cognitively or temperamentally better able to hold the two opposing ideas in their minds and still retain the ability to function. Boss (2004) reported some comments that were made to her by people who were less distressed: "My son has been missing so long now—he's probably dead, but I feel he's here with me, and always will be" (p. 559). "I must move on and organize life without my son, but at the same time I can hope and remember" (p. 559).

closure after the death. These unacknowledged mourners may be confused about their status and feel guilty or embarrassed by their attachment to the dead person (Murray, 2000).

There are also situations in which a person survives a loved one who had a stigmatized death. **Stigmatized deaths** are those in which people attribute the death to an immoral,

illegal, or evil cause. Some survivors may feel conflict in their grief and anger toward the dead person because they believe that person was involved in immoral or unclean behavior. These feelings may lead the griever to secrecy and misrepresentations about the death. Social networks may shun people who are grieving for someone who died a stigmatized death.

*An aerial view of the AIDS Memorial Quilt displayed on the Mall in Washington, D.C.*

Negative stereotypes surround these deaths and are often extended to include survivors (Murray, 2000).

Death by suicide is an example of a stigmatized death, in which survivors may feel guilty about not having been able to prevent the death and anger at that person for killing him- or herself. They may experience great conflict because of their love for the person who died and their belief that death by suicide is immoral. Communities look down on death by suicide and may not provide the customary rituals that help support the grieving persons. Many religions consider suicide to be a sin and will not provide religious services or burial rights for the deceased.

AIDS is another example of a stigmatized loss. In the 1980s, as the AIDS epidemic was taking hold, many survivors found that there was little support for their grief. The devastating effects of AIDS and the associated end-of-life conditions, compounded by fear of contamination, left many survivors isolated and traumatized by their stigmatized loss. In 1985, gay rights activist Cleve Jones discovered that more

than 1,000 people had died of AIDS in San Francisco alone. He and other activists conceived of the NAMES Project AIDS Memorial Quilt as a way of honoring and memorializing this loss. The first national display of the AIDS Quilt took place on the National Mall in Washington, D.C. at a lesbian and gay rights march in 1987. At the time, the quilt had 1,920 panels and was seen by more than half a million people. By 1988, the quilt was taken on a 20-city tour and had grown to 6,000 panels. Today, there are 21 NAMES chapters in the United States and 40 affiliates around the world. The quilt has 44,000 panels commemorating people who have died from AIDS (The Names Project Foundation, 2005). As a result of this and other initiatives, the focus shifted from shunning the ill to investing in new medical research for causes and cures. Resources were invested in research about AIDS, AIDS education, and the discovery of treatments to slow the course of the illness and prolong life.

## PSYCHOSOCIAL GROWTH THROUGH BEREAVEMENT

Bereavement brings new opportunities for psychosocial growth. The intense experiences of sadness and emptiness are universal human emotions. Just as happiness and joy are innate, so is sadness. Having these feelings is part of the human experience. Even though they are unpleasant, the emotions associated with grief connect people to their essential human nature. The expressions of grief have a social consequence. An infant's cries have the effect of bringing the caregiver into contact with the infant; the tears of grief communicate to others a person's needs for comfort and reassurance. Without experiences of grief, the moments of treasured happiness would mean less. These experiences help people understand the essence and limits of their existence. They provide a bridge for understanding the grief and unhappiness of others. Grief stimuli lead to greater levels of understanding of oneself and others.

When a person who is close dies, it stimulates reflection about that relationship. There may be a new appreciation of the qualities of the relationship and its importance. One may consider what the other person did to make the relationship especially valued. The bereaved person may begin to examine his or her own behavior, thinking of ways to bring some of the valued qualities of the relationship with the dead person to ongoing friendships and family ties. People may make resolutions to do a better job of supporting valued relationships by "staying in touch," "writing more often," or "calling home." In the process of experiencing your loss, you realize that you ought not take these important relationships for granted because they will not last forever. It is important to give them the appropriate care and nurturance. This leads to a growth in commitment to one's radius of significant relationships and to maintaining excellent quality in them.

The death of a loved one may stimulate the process of life review by causing you to think about the meaning of your own life. This process of taking stock may be reflected in questions that you ask yourself. Because time is finite, are you spending time in ways that are meaningful? Is your work an expression of your real values? Are your relationships satisfying and meaningful? Are you making any contribution to your community and to the well-being of others? This kind of examination may lead you to revise and change your lifestyle. Life review may also lead you to increase the valuation of some of your experiences and to take new meaning from them.

The loss of someone whose presence serves to help you define your identity will require a redefinition of your identity. Social roles are typically reciprocal—children have parents, husbands have wives. If you lose someone in a reciprocal role, then the whole role concept has to be reorganized. When a parent dies, children may have to assume some elements of the parental role. These elements are often concerned with greater levels of responsibility and caregiving. When a spouse dies, the remaining spouse has a new identity as a widow or widower. This brings with it new social meaning and, sometimes, a change in social status. When a person dies, the links to their social identity and social network may no longer exist for the person who remains. As a result, the survivors have to redefine themselves and establish new personal identities. For example, when Carl died, his wife Lois was no longer invited to social events that were hosted by Carl's coworkers. Lois no longer maintained her membership at Carl's golf club. She found that it was awkward to introduce herself to new people without being able to say that she was Carl's wife. She recognized that her social status was based on Carl's work and leisure activities. Being Carl's widow did not carry the high level of social status and value that she was used to. Lois had to begin to create a new identity in her community. This work is not easy, but it is very important and necessary.

The death of a loved one may stimulate a revisitation of psychosocial crises. For example, upon the death of a parent, one may reflect on earlier issues of autonomy versus shame and doubt, realizing a new sense of responsibility for one's actions. When parents are alive, even as they get older, an adult child is somehow buffered from the full weight of autonomous self-determination. When parents die, one may reflect on the many ways in which their values and beliefs have guided one's attitudes and behavior. In bereavement, there is a revisitation of the crisis of autonomy versus shame and doubt and an opportunity for a new resolution of this crisis within the context of adulthood.

When a spouse dies, in addition to the need to reconfigure

one's identity, issues of intimacy versus isolation may be revisited. A person may reflect on the quality of his or her intimate relationship, thinking about the nature of trust, levels of disclosure, sense of mutual respect, and openness to change. One may reexamine some of the ways in which intimacy was expressed and some of the ways in which isolation was experienced in the relationship. If the opportunity arises for the formation of a new intimate relationship, this revisitation could lead the person to approach that new relationship with different strategies, assumptions, or expectations for self and other.

When a person you admire dies, it often promotes new levels of identification with the deceased. This process sometimes begins with the eulogy, where the community is reminded of the strengths and accomplishments of the person who died. In reflecting on the person's life, a survivor may take on a valued characteristic, such as integrity, fairness, sense of humor, or patience. Survivors may find themselves using expressions or participating in activities that were associated with the person who died. In this way, they expand their repertoire of behaviors, activities, and ego strengths. In addition to identification, the survivor may *introject* the lost person (i.e., take the person's essence inside themselves in thought and feelings). **Introjection** is different from identification, in that the person feels that the lost person is in them. They may carry on meaningful conversations with this person and sense their guiding presence. This is similar to having an imaginary companion. Introjection allows the bereaved person to keep the dead person alive and to preserve their relationship. While still carrying on a mature and sensible existence, the bereaved add a psychological dimension to their abilities by preserving the characteristics of the revered and adored loved one.

In bereavement, thoughts are likely to turn to your own death. The manner of the loved ones' demise and the way they faced their death may help survivors prepare for the possibilities involved in their own death. The dead person's courage may lead the living person to work to develop courage. The creation of a living will by the deceased may be seen as beneficial by surviving people, who proceed to establish their own living wills. The depth of emotion created by the death of someone close helps persons to understand the value of their own life and the emotions that significant others will experience when they die. In bereavement, a person can find comfort in the faith, confidence, and hopefulness of the person who died, and be inspired to achieve that sense of integrity with regard to his or her own death.

## Chapter Summary

In the study of the life span, we have come to a new openness about the role of death and dying. There is an increasing sense that people can make decisions about the quality of

their death and that these decisions can and should be discussed with family members. In addition to experiences with death and the anticipation of one's own mortality, dialogues about death are taking place in families to a greater degree than they did in the past.

The psychosocial perspective helps to direct our attention

to how people determine the meaning of the events of their lives as they interact with the environment over time. Death presents one of the greatest challenges to meaning-making. At each stage of life, our understanding of death changes because of the different cognitive and emotional resources we have available and as a result of the salience and proximity to death. The way people conceptualize their own death and the death of others is influenced by the cultural context.

The definition of the biological state of death has changed as a result of the development of new technologies. In addition to the lack of a heartbeat and the lack of respiration, death may not be determined until a combination of eight criteria confirms the end of brain functioning. As a result of this greater ambiguity surrounding death, there are new procedures or advance directives that allow people to convey their preferences about end-of-life treatment and to appoint people to make decisions for them if they are incapacitated.

The process of dying can follow different trajectories, involve different degrees of suffering, and occur at different ages. Professionals have begun to define characteristics of a good death, and dying patients are having a greater voice in determining the nature of their death. Hospice care and euthanasia are two paths that people may choose when they are experiencing a slow, painful death trajectory. These end-of-life decisions are a focus of ongoing ethical controversies and debate.

Death-related rituals are found in all cultures. They tend to focus on three aspects of the meaning of death: (1) care of the body, (2) care of the spirit, and (3) care of the surviving family, friends, and community. These rituals provide a context for acknowledging the death, preparing the spirit for its transition, and legitimizing the grief of the bereaved survivors.

Bereavement is the long-term process of adjustment to the death of a loved one. Grief is the cognitive and emotional reaction to loss. The concept of grief work refers to the emotional expression, cognitive reorganization, and social adjustments that take place as a result of the death of a loved one. There are many patterns of bereavement, depending on the context of the death, the relationship of the survivor to the dead person, the religious orientation of the survivor, and the finality or ambiguity surrounding the death. Communities play a role in supporting the bereavement process by the way they respect or stigmatize the death and the way they memorialize and honor the dead.

# Further Reflection

1. How does the inevitability of death affect your own approach to life?
2. What is the meaning of a good death? How is this concept influenced by U.S. culture?
3. What are the functions of funerals?
4. What are the most important issues facing the survivors?
5. How does the community influence the process of bereavement?
6. What are likely outcomes for a person who denies a loved one's death and does not engage in grief work? As a professional, how would you help such a person?

# On the Web

**VISIT OUR WEBSITE**

Go to http://www.wadsworth.com/psychology to find online resources directly linked to your book.

# Casebook

For additional case material related to this chapter, see the case entitled "Till Death Do Us Part" in *Life Span Development: A Case Book*, by Barbara and Philip Newman, Laura Landry-Meyer, and Brenda J. Lohman, pp. 195–199. The case focuses on the role of a sudden illness in opening up communication about end-of-life issues for an older couple.

# Glossary

**abortion**   Termination of a pregnancy before the fetus is capable of surviving outside the uterus.

**accommodation**   (1) In Piaget's theory of cognitive development, the process of changing existing schemes in order to account for novel elements in the object or the event. (2) In vision, changes in the curvature of the lens in response to the distance of the stimulus.

**active euthanasia**   Activities—such as mercy killing or physician-assisted suicide—that are designed to end a person's life, often to end a person's suffering.

**activities of daily living**   Basic types of self-care that are required to function independently.

**adaptation**   (1) In evolutionary theory, the total process of change in response to environmental conditions. (2) In Piaget's theory of cognitive development, a process of gradually modifying existing schemes and operations in order to take into account changes or discrepancies between what is known and what is being experienced.

**adaptive self-organization**   The process by which an open system retains its essential identity when confronted with new and constant environmental conditions. It creates new substructures, revises the relationships among components, and establishes new, higher levels of organization that coordinate existing substructures.

**adaptive self-regulation**   Adjustments made by an operating system in which feedback mechanisms identify and respond to environmental changes in order to maintain and enhance the functioning of the system.

**advance directive**   A document that allows people to say what type of care they want to receive in case they cannot speak for themselves.

**advocate**   A person who pleads another's cause.

**affect**   Emotion, feeling, or mood.

**affiliative values**   The values placed on helping or pleasing others, reflected in the amount of time spent in and the degree of satisfaction achieved from such actions.

**age-graded expectations**   Views held within societies about what would be appropriate behavior at a given time in life.

**ageism**   A devaluation of older adults by the social community.

**agency**   Viewing the self as the originator of action.

**aggressive-rejected**   A path to peer rejection in which children are aggressive and attribute hostile intentions to others.

**aggressive-withdrawn**   A path to peer rejection in which children are both aggressive and self-conscious.

**alienation**   Withdrawal or separation of people or their affections from an object or position of former attachment.

**allele**   The alternate state of a gene at a given locus.

**Alzheimer's disease**   The most common form of chronic organic brain syndrome, involving gradual brain failure over a period of 7 to 10 years.

**ambiguous loss**   A condition in which death is uncertain because there is no verification of death, as when a soldier is missing in action and there is no body, or when a person is physically present but unable to participate in any meaningful way in interactions with others.

**amniocentesis**   The surgical insertion of a hollow needle through the abdominal wall and into the uterus of a pregnant woman to obtain fluid for the determination of sex or chromosomal abnormality of the fetus.

**amniotic sac**   A thin membrane forming a closed sac around the embryo and containing a fluid in which the embryo is immersed.

**androgens**   General term for male sex hormones, the most prevalent of which is testosterone.

**androgyny**   The capacity to express both masculine and feminine characteristics as the situation demands.

**anomaly**   Irregularity, something that is inconsistent with the normal condition; abnormality.

**anorexia nervosa**   An emotional disorder in which the person loses the ability to regulate eating behavior; the person is obsessed with a fear of being overweight and avoids food or becomes nauseated after eating.

**anxious-avoidant attachment**   Infants avoid contact with their mothers after separation or ignore their efforts to interact. They show less distress at being alone than other babies.

**anxious-resistant attachment**   Infants are very cautious in the presence of a stranger. Their exploratory behavior is noticeably disrupted by the caregiver's departure. When the caregiver returns, the infants appear to want to be close to the caregiver, but they are also angry, so that they are very hard to soothe or comfort.

**Apgar scoring method**   Assessment method of the newborn based on heart rate, respiration, muscle tone, response to stimulation, and skin color.

**appraisal of the situation**   In coping, an estimate of the nature, quality, and importance of the stressors in a situation.

**artificial insemination**   Injection of donor sperm into a woman's vagina to promote conception.

**assimilation**   In Piaget's theory of cognitive development, the process of incorporating objects or events into existing schemes.

**assumption**   A fact, statement, or premise that is considered true and that guides the underlying logic of a theory.

**attachment**    The tendency to remain close to a familiar individual who is ready and willing to give care, comfort, and aid in time of need.

**attachment behavior system**    A complex set of reflexes and signaling behaviors that inspire caregiving and protective responses in adults; these responses shape a baby's expectations and help create an image of the parent in the child's mind.

**attachment scheme**    A set of internal mental representations that an infant has of the anticipated responses of a caregiver.

**auditory acuity**    The ability to recognize sounds of varying pitch and loudness.

**authority relations**    All the hierarchical relationships that give one person decision-making authority and supervisory control over another.

**autonomous morality**    A relatively mature moral perspective, in which rules are viewed as a product of cooperative agreements.

**autonomy**    The ability to behave independently, to do things on one's own.

**autosomal**    Being or pertaining to a chromosome other than a sex chromosome.

**avoidance conditioning**    A kind of learning in which specific stimuli are identified as painful or unpleasant and are therefore avoided.

**babbling**    The vocal sounds of infants after about the sixth week that are initially characterized by sounds used in many languages and then begin to reflect the sounds and intonation infants are most likely to hear in their caregivers' speech.

**behavioral slowing**    Age-related delay in the speed of response to stimuli.

**bereavement**    The long-term process of adjustment to the death of a loved one that is more all encompassing than grief and is commonly accompanied by physical symptoms, role loss, and a variety of intense emotions, including anger, sorrow, anxiety, and depression.

**bilingualism**    The ability to speak two languages fluently.

**binge drinking**    Quickly consuming five or more drinks in a row.

**biological system**    Includes all those processes necessary for the physical functioning of the organism. Sensory capacities, motor responses, and the workings of the respiratory, endocrine, and circulatory systems are all biological processes.

**birth culture**    A culture's beliefs, values, and guidelines for behavior regarding pregnancy and childbirth.

**boundaries**    In family systems theory, what determines who is considered to be a family member and who is an outsider. They influence the way information, support, and validation of the family unit are sought and the way new members are admitted into the family.

**bulimia**    A habitual disturbance in eating behavior, mostly affecting young women of normal weight, which is characterized by frequent episodes of grossly excessive food intake followed by self-induced vomiting to prevent weight gain.

**capitalist economy**    An economic system in which companies are privately owned and the profits of companies are reinvested in the companies and shared with the owners and stockholders.

**cardiopulmonary death**    A set of criteria for death that includes lack of a heartbeat and lack of respiration.

**care**    The commitment to be concerned.

**career maturity**    The stage at which a person has developed decision-making strategies and the self-insight that permit a realistic career choice.

**caregiving**    The nurturing responses of the caregiver that form a corresponding behavioral system we often refer to as *parenting*.

**categorical identifications**    Self-understanding that relies on the categories one fits into, such as physical characteristics and religion.

**categorization**    The process of arranging, classifying, or describing by labeling or naming.

**causality**    The relation between a cause and an effect.

**cell differentiation**    A process whereby cells take on specialized structures related to their function.

**cell nucleus**    The part of the cell that contains the genetic material essential to reproduction and protein synthesis.

**central process**    The dominant context or mechanism through which the psychosocial crisis is resolved.

**cervix**    The narrow lower end of the uterus, which forms the beginning of the birth canal.

**choice phase**    In Tiedeman's career decision model, the phase when the person decides which action alternative to follow. The decision is solidified in the person's mind as he or she elaborates the reasons why the decision is beneficial. There is a sense of relief and optimism as the person develops a commitment to executing the decision.

**chromosome**    One of the rodlike bodies in a cell nucleus that contains genetic material and that divides when the cell divides. In humans, there are 23 pairs of chromosomes.

**chronically depressed**    Experiencing depression over a long period of time.

**chronosystem**    In Bronfenbrenner's theory, this is the temporal dimension: Individdividuals, the systems in which they are embedded, and resources all may change over time.

**clarification phase**    In Tiedeman's career decision model, the phase when the person more fully understands the consequences of his or her commitment to the decision that has been made. He or she plans definite steps to take and may actually take them or may delay them until a more appropriate time. The self-image is prepared to be modified by the decision.

**classical conditioning**    A form of learning in which a formerly neutral stimulus is repeatedly presented together with a stimulus that evokes a specific reflexive response. After repeated pairings, the neutral stimulus elicits a response similar to the reflexive response.

**classification**    The action of grouping objects according to some specific characteristics they have in common, including all objects that show the characteristic and none that do not.

**climacteric**   The period of menopause for women and a parallel period of reduced reproductive competence for men.

**clinical samples**   Populations who are or have been treated for a problem, or who are waiting to be treated.

**clique**   A small friendship group of 5 to 10 people.

**codominance**   A condition in which both alleles of a specific gene contribute to the characteristic that is expressed, as in AB blood type.

**coercive escalation**   A style of interaction in which the probability that a negative remark will be followed by another negative remark increases as the chain of communication gets longer and longer.

**cognition**   The capacity for knowing, organizing perceptions, and problem solving.

**cognitive competencies**   A person's knowledge, skills, and abilities.

**cognitive functioning**   A very broad term that encompasses the range of cognitive abilities.

**cognitive map**   An internal mental representation of the environment.

**cognitive unconscious**   The range of mental structures and processes that operate outside awareness but play a significant role in conscious thought and action.

**cohort**   In research design, a group of individuals who are studied during the same time period. In life course analysis, a group of people who are roughly the same age during a particular historical period.

**cohort sequential study**   A research design that combines cross-sectional and longitudinal methods. Cohorts consist of participants in a certain age group. Different cohorts are studied at different times. New cohorts of younger groups are added in successive data collections to replace those who have grown older. This design allows the analysis of age differences, changes over time, and the effects of social and historical factors.

**collective efficacy**   A strong sense of social cohesion with a high level of informal social control in a community.

**collectivism**   Worldview in which social behavior is guided largely by the shared goals of a family, tribe, work group, or other collective.

**combinatorial skills**   The ability to perform mathematical operations, including addition, subtraction, and multiplication. These skills are acquired during the stage of concrete operational thought.

**commitment**   Consists of a demonstration of personal involvement in the areas of occupational choice, religion, and political ideology.

**common bond**   Interpersonal ties that provide feelings of acceptance and emotional support.

**common identity**   Shared roles involving pressure to comply with group expectations.

**communication repairs**   Periods of recovery in normal mother–infant interactions that follow periods of mismatch, so that infants and mothers cycle again through points of coordination in their interactions.

**communicative competence**   The ability to use all the aspects of language in one's culture, such as systems of meaning, rules of sentence formation, and adjustments for the social setting.

**communion**   The commitment to and consideration for the well-being of others.

**comparative assessments**   Self-understanding that relies on comparisons of oneself with social norms and standards or of oneself with specific other people.

**competence**   The exercise of skill and intelligence in the completion of tasks; the sense that one is capable of exercising mastery over one's environment.

**competence motivation**   The desire to exercise mastery by effectively manipulating objects or social interactions.

**competition**   A contest between rivals.

**compulsions**   Repetitive ritualized actions that serve as mechanisms for controlling anxiety.

**compulsive sexual behavior**   A compulsive need to relieve anxiety through sex.

**concrete operational thought**   In Piaget's theory, a stage of cognitive development in which rules of logic can be applied to observable or manipulable physical relations.

**confidence**   A conscious trust in oneself and in the meaningfulness of life.

**consensual union**   A relation between two people without civil or religious marriage ceremonies but regarded as a form of marital union.

**conservation**   The concept that physical changes do not alter the mass, weight, number, or volume of matter. This concept is acquired during the concrete operational stage of cognitive development.

**constructivist perspective**   The view that gender differences are a product of particular interactions that have a socially agreed-upon, gender-related meaning. In this view, the specific behaviors that are described as masculine or feminine depend largely on the situation, including expectations that people will behave in gender-appropriate ways.

**contactful interactions**   Interactions that are open to the other's point of view and clearly express the speaker's point of view.

**contextual dissonance**   The difference between the characteristics of the primary childrearing and home environment and other environments in which the child participates.

**contextualization of learning**   Offering instruction in ways that first draw on a child's existing experiences, knowledge, and concepts and then expand them in new directions.

**continuing care retirement community**   A residential setting offering housing and medical, preventive health, and social services to residents who are well at the time they enter the community.

**continuity**   A condition that characterizes a culture when a child is given information and responsibilities that apply directly to his or her adult behavior.

**continuous reinforcement**  In operant conditioning, the schedule in which reinforcement is given on every learning trial.

**control group**  The participants in an experiment who do not experience the manipulation or treatment and whose responses or reactions are compared with those of participants who are treated actively to determine the effects of the manipulation.

**controlling interactions**  Interactions in which one person expresses his or her point of view and does not take the other person's point of view into consideration.

**conventional morality**  A stage of moral reasoning described by Kohlberg, in which right and wrong are closely associated with the rules created by legitimate authorities, including parents, teachers, or political leaders.

**cooperation**  Working or acting together for a common purpose or benefit.

**coordination**  Refers to two related characteristics of interaction—matching and synchrony.

**coping behavior**  Active efforts to respond to stress. Coping includes gathering new information, maintaining control over one's emotions, and preserving freedom of movement.

**core pathologies**  Destructive forces that result from severe, negative resolutions of the psychosocial crises.

**correlation**  A measure of the strength and direction of the relationship among variables.

**couvade**  A ritual in which an expectant father takes to his bed and observes specific taboos during the period shortly before birth.

**creativity**  The ability to abandon old forms or patterns of doing things and to think in new ways.

**crisis**  A dramatic emotional or circumstantial upheaval in a person's life. In psychosocial theory, this often refers to a normal set of stresses and strains rather than to an extraordinary set of

events, and it consists of a period of role experimentation and active decision making among alternative choices.

**critical period**  A time of maximum sensitivity to or readiness for the development of a particular skill or behavior pattern.

**cross-sectional study**  A research design in which the behavior of individuals of different ages, social backgrounds, or environmental settings is measured once to acquire information about the effects of these differences.

**crowd**  A large group that is usually recognized by a few predominant characteristics, such as the "preppies," the "jocks," or the "druggies."

**crystallization phase**  In Tiedeman's career decision model, the phase when the person becomes more aware of the alternatives for action and their consequences. Conflicts among alternatives are recognized, and some alternatives are discarded. The person develops a strategy for making the decision, in part by weighing the costs and benefits of each alternative.

**crystallized intelligence (*G*c)**  Skills and information that are acquired through education and socialization.

**cultural determinism**  The theoretical concept that culture shapes individual experience.

**culture**  Refers to the socially standardized ways of thinking, feeling, and acting that are shared by members of a society

**cumulative relation**  In heredity, when the allelic states of a gene in a single pair of chromosomes combine to influence a trait.

**decentering**  Gaining some objectivity over one's own point of view; reducing the dominance of one's subjective perspective in the interpretation of events.

**defense mechanism**  A technique, usually unconscious, that attempts to alleviate the anxiety caused by the conflicting desires of the id and the superego in relation to impulses (e.g., repression, denial, projection).

**degree of suffering**  Amount or intensity of pain and other symptoms, including shortness of breath, inability

to eat, and limited mobility, that a person experiences at the end of life.

**delay of gratification**  The exertion of willpower in order to resist the strong immediate pull or temptation of something desirable.

**dependency**  In the study of aging, an assessment of difficulties in the activities of daily living usually required to function independently. Beyond very basic types of self-care, an expanded notion of dependency refers to difficulties in managing instrumental activities of daily living.

**dependent variable**  A factor that is defined by a participant's responses or reactions and that may or may not be affected by the experimenter's manipulation of the independent variable.

**depressed mood**  Refers to feelings of sadness, a loss of hope, a sense of being overwhelmed by the demands of the world, and general unhappiness.

**depression**  A state of feeling sad, often accompanied by feelings of low personal worth and withdrawal from relations with others.

**depressive syndrome**  This term refers to a constellation of behaviors and emotions that occur together. The syndrome usually includes complaints about feeling depressed, anxious, fearful, worried, guilty, and worthless.

**despair**  Feeling a loss of all hope and confidence.

**developmental stage**  A period of life dominated by a particular quality of thinking or a particular mode of social relationships. The notion of stages suggests qualitative changes in competence at each phase of development.

**developmental tasks**  Skills and competencies that are acquired at each stage of development.

**differentiation**  The extent to which a social system encourages intimacy while supporting the expression of differences.

**diffidence**  The inability to act, due to overwhelming self-doubt.

**dilation**  The condition of being stretched open beyond normal limits.

**disclosure**  Sharing information with others about whether one is gay, lesbian, or bisexual.

**discontinuity**    A condition that characterizes a culture when a child is either barred from activities that are open only to adults or forced to unlearn information or behaviors that are accepted in children but considered inappropriate for adults.

**disdain**    A feeling of scorn for the weakness and frailty of oneself or others.

**disengaged relationships**    Infrequent contact and a sense that the members of the family do not really seem to care about one another.

**dismissing avoidant attachment**    An attachment outcome in which people have a positive model of the self and a negative model of others.

**disorganized attachment**    Babies' responses are particularly notable in the reunion sequence. In the other three attachment patterns, infants appear to use a coherent strategy for managing the stress of the situation. The disorganized babies have no consistent strategy: They behave in contradictory, unpredictable ways that seem to convey feelings of extreme fear or utter confusion.

**displaced homemakers**    Women in middle adulthood who enter the labor market for the first time. Many of these women enter the job market as a consequence of divorce or early widowhood, face extreme economic pressures, and must compete with much younger workers for entry-level positions.

**dissociation**    A sense of separateness or withdrawal from others; an inability to experience the bond of mutual commitment.

**division of labor**    Splitting the activities needed to accomplish a task between participants.

**dizygotic twins**    Twins developed from two separate fertilized ova; also called *fraternal twins.*

**DNA**    Deoxyribonucleic acid. DNA molecules are the chemical building blocks of the chromosomes found in the cell nucleus.

**dominance**    If one allele is present, its characteristic is always observed, whether the other allele of the allelic pair is the same or not.

**doubt**    A sense of uncertainty about one's abilities and one's worth.

**Down syndrome**    A chromosomal irregularity in which the child has an extra chromosome 21. The condition results in mental retardation.

**durable power of attorney**    A document that authorizes someone to act on behalf of a person in financial and property matters and health care decisions that can go into effect either when the agreement is signed or when a disability occurs

**dying trajectory**    The time during which a person goes from good health to death.

**early adolescence**    The period of psychosocial development that begins with the onset of puberty and ends around 18 years of age, usually with graduation from high school.

**ecological niche**    The position or function of an organism in a community of plants and animals.

**ecological validity**    The applicability of a controlled laboratory situation in the real world.

**effacement**    The shortening of the cervical canal preceding childbirth.

**efficacy**    The capacity for producing a desired result, including planning intentional actions, guiding and directing one's own behaviors toward a goal, and reflecting on one's actions to assess their quality, impact, and purpose.

**effortful control**    A child's ability to suppress a dominant response and perform a subdominant response instead.

**ego**    In psychosexual theory, the mental structure that experiences and interprets reality. The ego includes most cognitive capacities, including perception, memory, reasoning, and problem solving.

**egocentric empathy**    When one recognizes distress in another person and responds to it in the same way one would respond if the distress were one's own.

**egocentric speech**    In Piaget's observation, toddlers use this to control and direct their behavior. The speech is considered egocentric because it is not intended to communicate with anyone else and often doesn't make sense to anyone else. Vygotsky suggested that

egocentric speech is a component of the problem-solving function.

**egocentrism**    The perception of oneself at the center of the world; the view that others and events base their behavior on or occur as a result of one's own perceptions.

**ego ideal**    A set of positive standards, ideals, and ambitions that represent the way a person would like to be.

**electronic fetal heart rate monitoring**    The continuous monitoring of fetal heart rate using an electronic amplification device.

**embryo**    The developing human individual from the time of implantation to the end of the eighth week after conception.

**emotional regulation**    Strategies for coping with intense emotions, both positive and negative. Caregiver behavior and observation are important factors in the development of emotional regulation.

**empathy**    The capacity to recognize and experience the emotional state of another person.

**empathy for another's feelings**    When one shows empathy for a wide range of feelings and anticipates the kinds of reactions that might really comfort someone else.

**empathy for another's life conditions**    When one experiences empathy in understanding the life conditions or personal circumstances of a person or group.

**enactive attainments**    Personal experiences of mastery.

**encodings**    In cognitive behaviorism, the constructs that a person has about the self, the situation, and others in the situation.

**enculturation**    The process by which culture carriers teach, model, reward, punish, and use other symbolic strategies to transmit critical practices and values.

**endogamy**    Marriage within one's well-defined group, such as one's ethnic or religious group.

**enmeshed relationships**    Characterized by overinvolvement in one another to the extent that any change in one family member is met by strong resistance by the others; individuality is viewed as a threat to the relationship.

**enzymes**   Complex proteins produced by living cells that act as catalysts for biochemical reactions.

**epigenetic principle**   A biological plan for growth such that each function emerges in a systematic sequence until the fully functioning organism has developed.

**episodic memory**   Recall of situations and data.

**equilibration**   Efforts to reconcile new perspectives and ideas about basic moral concepts, such as justice, intentionality, and social responsibility, with one's existing views about what is right and wrong when a stage change occurs.

**equilibrium**   In Piaget's theory, the balance that every organism strives to attain in which organized structures (sensory, motor, or cognitive) provide effective ways of interacting with the environment.

**estrogen**   The major female sex hormone.

**ethics**   Principles of conduct founded on a society's moral code.

**ethnic group**   A group of people who share a common cultural ancestry, language, or religion within a larger cultural context.

**ethnic-group identity**   Knowing that one is a member of a certain ethnic group; recognizing that aspects of one's thoughts, feelings, and actions are influenced by one's ethnic membership; and taking the ethnic group's values, outlook, and goals into account when making life choices.

**ethnic subculture**   The cultural values and behavioral patterns characteristic of a particular group in a society that shares a common ancestry; memories of a shared historical past; and a cultural focus on symbolic elements that distinguish the group from others.

**ethology**   The comparative investigation of the biological basis of behavior from an evolutionary perspective, to determine the proximal causes of behavioral acts, the relative contribution of inheritance and learning to these acts, and the adaptive significance and evolutionary history of different patterns of behavior within and across species.

**euthanasia**   The practice of ending someone's life for reasons of mercy.

**evolutionary psychology**   The study of the long-term, historical origins of behavior.

**exclusivity**   A shutting out of others for elitist reasons.

**exosystem**   One or more settings that do not involve the developing person as an active participant but in which events occur that affect or are affected by what happens in the setting containing the developing person.

**expansion**   Elaborating on a child's expression by adding more words.

**expectancies**   Expectations about one's ability to perform, the consequences of one's behavior, and the meaning of events in one's environment.

**expectations**   Views held by oneself or by others about what would be appropriate behavior in a given situation or at a given stage of development.

**experiential transcendence**   A way of experiencing immortality through achieving a sense of continuous presence.

**experiment**   A research method best suited for examining causal relationships, in which some variable or group of variables is systematically manipulated to examine its effect on an outcome.

**experimental group**   The participants who experience the manipulation or treatment in an experiment.

**expertise**   A quality of individuals who focus their intelligence on intensive study, training, and repeated opportunities for problem solving within a domain in which they become specialists.

**exploration phase**   In Tiedeman's career decision model, the phase when a person realizes that a career decision must be made and therefore begins to learn more about those aspects of the self and the occupational world that are relevant to the impending decision. The person begins to generate alternatives for action. Uncertainty about the future and the many alternatives is accompanied by feelings of anxiety.

**extended family**   The family group that includes family members other than the nucleus of parents and children.

**external frames of reference**   When a child evaluates his or her own performance in light of parent, teacher, or peer feedback and observations of the performance of other children in the class.

**external validity**   The degree to which the results of an experiment are applicable to situations beyond the experiment itself.

**extinction**   (1) In psychosocial theory, the negative pole of the psychosocial crisis of very old age, in which it is feared that the end of one's life is the end of all continuity. (2) In operant conditioning, a process in which an expected reinforcement no longer occurs following the behavior. Eventually, the behavior is no longer emitted.

**extroversion**   Personality dimension that includes such qualities as sociability, vigor, sensation seeking, and positive emotions.

**fallopian tube**   The tube, extending from the uterus to the ovary, in which fertilization takes place.

**family constellation**   The many variables that describe a family group, including the presence or absence of mother and father; the number, spacing, and sex of siblings; and the presence or absence of extended family members in the household.

**family household**   Two or more individuals living together who are related by birth, marriage, or adoption.

**family of origin**   The family into which one is born.

**family of procreation**   The family one begins as an adult.

**fast mapping**   Forming a rapid, initial, partial understanding of the meaning of a word by relating it to the known vocabulary and restructuring the known-word storage space and its related conceptual categories.

**fearful avoidant attachment**   An attachment outcome in which people have a negative model of both self and others.

**feedback mechanisms**   In systems theory, the operations in an open system that produce adaptive self-regulation by identifying and responding to changes in the environment.

**femininity**   Gender traits associated with being expressive and communal (e.g., valuing interpersonal and spiritual development, being tender, sympathetic, and concerned about the well-being of others).

**fertilization**   The penetration of an egg by a sperm.

**fetal alcohol syndrome**   A condition of the fetus involving central nervous system disorders, low birthweight, and malformations of the face; the condition is associated with heavy use of alcohol by mothers, especially during the last trimester of pregnancy.

**fetoscopy**   Examination of the fetus through the use of a fiber-optic lens.

**fetus**   The unborn infant. Usually, the term *fetus* refers to infants between 8 weeks of gestational age and birth. See *embryo*.

**fidelity**   The ability to freely pledge and sustain loyalties to others; the ability to freely pledge and sustain loyalties to values and ideologies.

**filial obligation**   The responsibilities of adult children for their aging parents.

**fitness**   (1) The genetic contribution of an individual to the next generation's gene pool relative to the average for the population, usually measured by the number of that individual's offspring or close kin that survive to reproductive age. (2) Patterns of activity or inactivity, endurance or frailty, and illness or health that influence the ability to manage tasks of independent daily living.

**fluid intelligence ($G_f$)**   The ability to impose organization on information and to generate new hypotheses.

**formal operations**   Complex cognitive capacities, such as reasoning, hypothesis generation, and hypothesis testing.

**formal operational thought**   In Piaget's theory, the final stage of cognitive development, characterized by reasoning, hypothesis generation, and hypothesis testing.

**foundational category**   In cognitive development, a fundamental mental classification, such as the distinction between human beings and inanimate objects.

**fraternal twins**   Children born at the same time who developed from two different ova.

**gamete**   A mature germ cell involved in reproduction; a sperm or an ovum.

**gender**   Refers to the integrated cognitive, social, and emotional schemes associated with being male or female.

**gender constancy**   When children learn the biological basis of gender and that one's gender does not change.

**gender identification**   Incorporation into one's self-concept of the valued characteristics of male or female that become integrated into an early scheme for thinking of oneself as either male or female.

**gender identity**   A set of beliefs, attitudes, and values about oneself as a man or woman in many areas of social life, including intimate relations, family, work, community, and religion.

**gender label**   The word *boy* or *girl*. First component of gender identity, in which children learn to refer to themselves as a boy or girl and to identify other children by applying the word correctly.

**gender preference**   The development of a personal preference for the kinds of activities and attitudes associated with the masculine or feminine gender role.

**gender role convergence**   A transformation in which men and women become more androgynous and more similar in gender orientation during later life.

**gender role standards**   Attributes held by the culture for males and females. These attributes can include both precepts and sanctions.

**gender scheme**   A personal theory about cultural expectations and stereotypes related to gender.

**gene**   The fundamental physical unit of heredity. A gene is a linear sequence of nucleotides along a segment of DNA that carries the coded instructions for the synthesis of RNA, which, when translated into protein, leads to hereditary characteristics.

**gene pool**   The genetic information contained in the genes of the population or culture that provides the ancestry for an individual.

**generalizability**   The extent to which we can say with confidence that the observations made for a sample would apply to other groups.

**generativity**   The capacity to contribute to the quality of life for future generations. A sense of generativity is attained toward the end of middle adulthood.

**genetic anomalies**   Neurological or physical abnormalities that have a genetic cause.

**genetic counseling**   Recent discoveries make it possible to identify the genes responsible for certain forms of disease and genetic anomalies. Couples who have reason to believe that they may carry genes for one of these disorders can be tested and advised about the probability of having children who may be afflicted.

**genome**   The full set of chromosomes that carries all the inheritable traits of an organism.

**genotype**   The hereditary information contained in the cells of an individual. Genotype may or may not be observable in the phenotype. See *phenotype*.

**gentrification**   A pattern of real-estate change in which a higher income group buys property and develops residential and commercial projects in an area that has previously been serving a lower income group.

**gestation**   The period from conception to birth.

**Glick effect**   Statistical evidence of a lack of persistence that relates dropping out of high school or college with a high probability of divorce.

**global empathy**   Distress experienced and expressed as a result of witnessing someone else in distress.

**goal**   The result or achievement toward which effort is directed.

**goal-corrected partnership**   In Bowlby's attachment theory, the capacity that emerges in toddlerhood and early school age in which children begin to find more flexible and adaptive ways to maintain proximity with the object of attachment and to seek reassurance under stressful situations. As a result, children are able to manage negotiated separations more easily.

**grammar**  Rules for the arrangement of words and phrases in a sentence and for the inflections that convey gender, tense, and number.

**grief**  The cognitive and emotional reactions that follow the death of a loved one.

**grief work**  A person's psychological efforts to work through the reality of loss of a loved one and the feelings in which the person must (1) achieve freedom from feelings of guilt about ways he or she had criticized or even harmed the person who died and feelings of regret for things left unsaid or undone; (2) make an adjustment to all the aspects of the environment from which the deceased is missing; and (3) begin to form new relationships.

**group identity**  The positive pole of the psychosocial crisis of early adolescence, in which the person finds membership in and value convergence with a peer group.

**guilt**  An emotion associated with doing something wrong or the anticipation of doing something wrong.

**habituation**  A form of adaptation in which the child no longer responds to a stimulus that has been repeatedly presented.

**heteronomous morality**  A child's moral perspective, in which rules are viewed as fixed and unchangeable.

**heterozygous**  Characterized by the presence of different alleles of a particular gene at the same locus.

**holophrase**  A single word functioning as a phrase or sentence.

**homeostasis**  A relatively stable state of equilibrium.

**homogamy**  When people are attracted to others who share important areas of similarity.

**homozygous**  Characterized by the presence of two matched alleles of a particular gene at the same locus.

**hope**  An enduring belief that one can attain one's essential wishes.

**hormones**  A group of chemicals, each of which is released into the bloodstream by a particular gland or

tissue and has a specific effect on tissues elsewhere in the body.

**hospice care**  An integrated system of medicine, nursing, counseling, and spiritual care for the terminally ill and their family that emphasizes pain control and emotional support and typically refrains from extraordinary measures to prolong life.

**household**  All persons who occupy a housing unit, including both related family members and all unrelated persons.

**hypoactive sexual desire**  A decrease or absence of interest in sexual activity.

**hypothesis**  A tentative proposition that can provide a basis for further inquiry.

**hypotheticodeductive reasoning**  A method of reasoning in which a hypothetical model based on observations is first proposed and then tested by deducing consequences from the model.

**id**  In psychoanalytic theory, the mental structure that expresses impulses and wishes. Much of the content of the id is unconscious.

**identical twins**  Children born at the same time who developed from the same ovum.

**identification**  The process through which one person incorporates the values and beliefs of a valued other such as a parent.

**identity**  In cognitive theory, the concept that an object is still the same object even though its shape or location has been changed.

**identity achievement**  Individual identity status in which, after a crisis, a sense of commitment to family, work, political, and religious values is established.

**identity confusion**  The negative pole of the psychosocial crisis of later adolescence, in which a person is unable to integrate various roles or make commitments.

**identity foreclosure**  Individual identity status in which a commitment to family, work, politics, and religious values is established prematurely, without crisis.

**illusion of incompetence**  Expressed by children who perform well in aca-

demic achievement tests yet perceive themselves as below average in academic ability and behave in accordance with this perception.

**imaginary audience**  The preoccupation with what you believe other people are thinking about you.

**imitation**  Repetition of another person's words, gestures, or behaviors.

**immortality**  The positive pole of the psychosocial crisis of very old age, in which the person transcends death through a sense of symbolic continuity.

**imprinting**  The process of forming a strong social attachment at some point after birth.

**inclusive fitness**  The fitness of an individual organism as measured by the survival and reproductive success of its kin, each relative being valued according to the probability of shared genetic information, an offspring or sibling having a value of 50% and a first cousin 25%.

**independent variable**  The factor that is manipulated in an experiment, and the measured effects of the manipulation.

**individual differences perspective**  The view that gender differences exist within the individual as persistent, internal attributes and that differences between boys and girls are stable characteristics that individuals bring to various situations.

**individual identity**  The commitment to a personal integration of values, goals, and abilities that occurs as personal choices are made in response to anticipated or actual environmental demands at the end of adolescence.

**individualism**  Worldview in which social behavior is guided largely by personal goals, ambitions, and pleasures.

**induction**  (1) A form of discipline that points out the consequences of a child's actions for others. (2) In cognitive development, the realization that whatever holds true for one member of a category is likely to hold true for other members as well.

**induction phase**  In Tiedeman's career decision model, the phase when a person encounters the new work environment for the first time. He or she wants to be accepted and looks to others for cues about how to behave. The person identifies with the new group and seeks recognition for his or her unique characteristics. Gradually, the self-image is modified as the person begins to believe in the values and goals of the work group.

**industry**    A sense of pride and pleasure in acquiring culturally valued competences. The sense of industry is usually acquired by the end of the middle childhood years.

**inertia**    A paralysis of thought and action that prevents productive work.

**inferiority**    A sense of incompetence and failure that is built on negative evaluation and lack of skill.

**infertility**    Inability to conceive or carry a fetus through the gestational period.

**influence phase**    In Tiedeman's career decision model, the phase when the person is very much involved with the new group. He or she becomes more assertive in asking that the group perform better. The person also tries to influence the group to accommodate some of his or her values. The self is strongly committed to group goals. During this phase, the group's values and goals may be modified to include the orientation of the new member.

**ingroup**    A group of which one is a member; contrasted with *outgroup*.

**inhibition**    A psychological restraint that prevents freedom of thought, expression, and activity.

**initiative**    The ability to offer new solutions, to begin new projects, or to seek new social encounters; active investigation of the environment.

**instrumental activities of daily living**    Basic tasks that are essential to maintaining one's daily life without dependence on informal or formal community support services

**instrumental reminiscence**    Reminiscence that emphasizes past accomplishments, past efforts to overcome difficulties, and the use of past experiences to approach current difficulties.

**instrumental values**    The values placed on doing things that are challenging, reflected in the amount of

time spent on and the degree of satisfaction achieved in such actions.

**integration phase**    In Tiedeman's career decision model, the phase when group members react against the new member's attempts to influence them. The new member then compromises. In the process, he or she attains a more objective understanding of the self and the group. A true collaboration between the new member and the group is achieved. The new member feels satisfied and is evaluated as successful by the self and others.

**integrative reminiscence**    Reminiscence that involves reviewing one's past in order to find meaning or to reconcile one's current and prior feelings about certain life events.

**integrity**    The ability to accept the facts of one's life and to face death without great fear. The sense of integrity is usually acquired toward the end of later adulthood.

**intellectual flexibility**    A person's ability to handle conflicting information, to take several perspectives on a problem, and to reflect on personal values in solving ethical problems.

**interdependence**    A condition in which systems depend on each other, or in which all the elements in a system rely on one another for their continued growth.

**intergenerational solidarity**    The closeness and commitment within parent–child and grandparent–grandchild relationships.

**intermittent reinforcement**    A schedule of reinforcement that varies the amount of time or the number of trials between reinforcements.

**internal frames of reference**    When a child compares how well he or she can perform in one domain versus another.

**internalization**    A process in which the values, beliefs, and norms of the culture become the values, beliefs, and norms of the individual.

**internal validity**    The meaningfulness of an experiment.

**interobserver reliability**    Two or more observers' codings of the same situation are compared to determine

whether different observers rated the same event in the same way.

**intersubjectivity**    A shared repertoire of emotions that enables infants and their caregivers to understand each other and create shared meanings. They can engage in reciprocal, rhythmic interactions, appreciate state changes in one another, and modify their actions in response to emotional information about one another.

**intimacy**    The ability to experience an open, supportive, tender relationship with another person without fear of losing one's own identity in the process of growing close. The sense of intimacy is usually acquired toward the end of early adulthood.

**introjection**    An unconscious psychic process by which a person incorporates the characteristics of another person into his or her own psychic apparatus.

**introspection**    Deliberate self-evaluation and examination of private thoughts and feelings.

**isolation**    A crisis resolution in which situational factors or a fragile sense of self lead a person to remain psychologically distant from others; the state of being alone.

**labor**    The period of involuntary contractions of the uterine muscles that occurs prior to giving birth.

**language perception**    The ability to recognize sounds and differentiate among sound combinations before the meanings of these sounds are understood.

**language production**    The generation of language material by an individual. One of the first significant events is the naming of objects.

**latency stage**    In Freud's psychosexual theory, the fourth life stage, during which no significant conflicts or impulses are assumed to arise. Superego development proceeds during this period.

**later adolescence**    The period of psychosocial development that begins around the time of graduation from high school and ends in the early 20s.

**launching period**    The time in family life during which children leave home.

**learned helplessness**   A belief that one's efforts have little to do with success or failure and that the outcome of task situations is largely outside one's control.

**learning**   Any relatively permanent change in thought or behavior that is the consequence of experience.

**life course**   Refers to the integration and sequencing of phases of work and family life.

**life expectancy**   The average number of years from birth to death, as based on statistical analyses of the length of life for people born in a particular period.

**lifestyle**   A relatively permanent structure of activity and experience, including the tempo of activity, the balance between work and leisure, and patterns of family and social relationships.

**living will**   A document instructing physicians, relatives, or others to refrain from the use of extraordinary measures, such as life support equipment, to prolong one's life in the event of a terminal illness.

**longevity**   The length or duration of life.

**longitudinal study**   A research design in which repeated observations of the same participants are made at different times, in order to examine change over time.

**long-term memory**   A complex network of information, concepts, and schemes related by associations, knowledge, and use. It is the storehouse of a lifetime of information.

**love**   An emotion characterized by a capacity for mutuality that transcends childhood dependency.

**love withdrawal**   A form of discipline in which parents express disappointment or disapproval and become emotionally cold or distant.

**low-birthweight babies**   Infants who weigh less than 2,500 grams (about 5 pounds 8 ounces) at birth. This may be a result of being born before the full period of gestation, or it may result from the mother's inadequate diet, smoking, or use of drugs.

**macrosystem**   Refers to consistencies in the form and content of lower order systems (micro-, meso-, and exosystems) that exist or could exist at the level of the subculture or the culture as a whole, along with any belief systems of ideology underlying such consistencies.

**major depressive disorder**   A disorder in which a person will have experienced five or more of the following symptoms for at least 2 weeks: depressed mood or irritable mood most of the day; decreased interest in pleasurable activities; changes in weight, or perhaps failure to make necessary weight gains in adolescence; sleep problems; psychomotor agitation or retardation; fatigue or loss of energy; feelings of worthlessness or abnormal amounts of guilt; reduced concentration and decision-making ability; and repeated suicidal ideation, attempts, or plans of suicide.

**managerial resourcefulness**   Flexible, creative problem solving in the workplace, particularly when facing new problems and changing conditions.

**masculinity**   Gender traits associated with being instrumental and agentic (e.g., having leadership abilities, being assertive, taking control).

**matched groups sampling**   Two or more groups of participants who are similar on many dimensions are selected as the sample for an experiment. The effects of different treatments or manipulations are determined by comparing the behavior of these groups.

**matching**   The infant and the caregiver are involved in similar behaviors or states at the same time.

**menarche**   The beginning of regular menstrual periods.

**mental image**   A form of representational thought that involves the ability to hold the picture of a person, object, or event in one's mind even in the absence of the stimulus itself.

**mental operations**   A transformation—carried out in thought rather than action—that modifies an object, event, or idea.

**mercy killing**   Taking a person's life in order to end their suffering. In our society, this is considered to be murder.

**mesosystem**   The interrelations among two or more settings in which the developing person actively participates (e.g., for a child, the relations between home, school, and neighborhood peer groups; for an adult, between family, work, and social life).

**metabolism**   A collective term for all the chemical processes that take place in the body: In some (*catabolic*), a complex substance is broken down into simpler ones, usually with the release of energy; in others (*anabolic*), a complex substance is built up from simpler ones, usually with the consumption of energy.

**metacognition**   Thinking about one's own thinking, including what individuals understand about their reasoning capacities and about how information is organized, how knowledge develops, how reality is distinguished from belief or opinion, how to achieve a sense of certainty about what is known, and how to improve understanding.

**microsystem**   A pattern of activities, roles, and interpersonal relations experienced by the developing person in a given setting with specific physical and material characteristics.

**miscarriage**   Spontaneous termination of a pregnancy.

**mismatch**   The infant and caregiver are not involved in the same behaviors or states at the same time.

**mistrust**   A sense of unpredictability in the environment and suspicion about one's own worth. Experiences with mistrust are most critical during infancy.

**monozygotic twins**   Twins who develop from a single fertilized egg. These twins have identical genetic characteristics.

**moral development**   The acquisition of the principles or rules of right conduct and the distinction between right and wrong.

**moral identity**   The sense in which a person defines himself or herself in moral terms and evaluates his or her behavior against moral standards that represent an integration of parental socialization about caring for others, an appreciation for the cultural and social contexts of moral actions, and experiences that have required moral action.

**morality**    Conforming to rules of right or virtuous conduct that involves conceptions of the rights, dignity, and welfare of others.

**mutuality**    The ability of two people to meet each other's needs and to share each other's concerns and feelings.

**myelination**    The formation of a soft, white, fatty material called *myelin* around certain nerve axons to serve as an electrical insulator that speeds nerve impulses to muscles and other effectors.

**narcissistic**    Extremely self-absorbed and self-loving.

**natural selection**    A process whereby those individuals best suited to the characteristics of the immediate environment are most likely to survive and reproduce.

**negative identity**    A clearly defined self-image that is completely contrary to the cultural values of the community.

**negative reinforcer**    In operant conditioning, a stimulus—such as an electric shock—that increases the rate of response when removed.

**neural tube**    The tube formed during the early embryonic period that later develops into the brain, spinal cord, nerves, and ganglia.

**neuron**    A nerve cell with specialized processes; the fundamental functional unit of nervous tissue.

**neuroticism**    A personality dimension consistently associated with discouragement, unhappiness, and hopelessness. Neuroticism includes such qualities as anxiety, hostility, and impulsiveness.

**nonparental care**    Child care arrangements in which infants and toddlers are taken care of by persons who are not their parents. Center-based care includes day care centers, Head Start programs, preschool, prekindergarten, and other early childhood programs

**norm of reciprocity**    The cultural norm that you are obligated to return in full value what you receive.

**norms**    Collective expectations or rules for behavior held by members of a group or society.

**nuclear family**    A household grouping that includes the mother, father, and their children.

**nuclear transplantation**    A procedure in which the nucleus of an egg cell, which contains its DNA, is removed and replaced with the DNA from an adult cell.

**object permanence**    A scheme acquired during the sensorimotor stage of development, in which children become aware that an object continues to exist even when it is hidden or moved from place to place.

**object relations**    The component of ego development that is concerned with the self, self-understanding, and self–other relationships.

**objective**    Based on facts and not influenced by personal feelings, interpretations, or prejudices.

**observation**    A research method in which behavior is watched and recorded.

**obsessions**    Persistent repetitive thoughts that serve as mechanisms for controlling anxiety.

**obsessive reminiscence**    Reminiscence that suggests an inability to resolve or accept certain past events and a persistent guilt or despair over these events.

**old-old**    Among the very old, those who have suffered major physical or mental decrements.

**open system**    A structure that maintains its organization even though its parts constantly change.

**operant conditioning**    A form of learning in which new responses are strengthened by the presentation of reinforcements.

**operational definition**    In research, the way an abstract concept is defined in terms of how it will be measured.

**operationalize**    To translate an abstract concept into something that can be observed and measured.

**optimal functioning**    What a person is capable of doing when motivated and well prepared.

**optimism**    A belief that one's decisions will lead to positive conse-

quences and that situations will turn out well.

**organic brain syndromes**    Disorders involving memory loss, confusion, loss of ability to manage daily functions, and loss of ability to focus attention.

**organ inferiority**    In Adler's theory, a strong sense that some organ of one's body is weak and inferior. The person becomes preoccupied with thoughts of this weakness.

**outgroup**    A group that competes with one's own group; contrasted with *ingroup*.

**overregularization**    In language acquisition, the tendency to use a grammar rule for the formation of regular verbs or nouns when one cannot remember the irregular form. As a child's vocabulary grows, the need to apply the rule to unfamiliar words declines.

**ovum**    An egg; the female germ cell.

**parenting**    The rearing of children.

**parenting alliance**    The capacity of a spouse to acknowledge, respect, and value the parenting roles and tasks of the partner.

**participant observation**    Observation in which the researcher actively engages in interactions with other members of the setting.

**passive euthanasia**    Withholding treatment or removing life-sustaining nourishment and breathing aids for the dying person, with the result that death occurs more quickly than if these procedures were continued.

**peer play**    Play interactions with one's peers, which provide opportunities for physical, cognitive, social, and emotional development.

**peer pressure**    Expectations to conform and commit to the norms of one's peer group.

**peer review**    The process in which other professionals read and critically evaluate a researcher's materials before they are published.

**persistent vegetative state**    State in which a person's brainstem functions to continue to maintain heartbeat and respiration even when there is no cortical functioning.

**personal choice**    When children recognize a domain of personal freedom in decision making that is not guided by adult authority and regulations but by the child's own preferences.

**personal fable**  An intense investment in one's own thoughts and feelings and a belief that these thoughts are unique.

**perspective taking**  The ability to consider a situation from a point of view other than one's own.

**phenotype**  The observable characteristics that result from the interaction of a particular genotype and a particular environment.

**physical culture**  Encompasses the objects, technologies, structures, tools, and other artifacts of a culture.

**physical state**  In self-efficacy theory, the state of arousal or excitement that provides information as one makes a judgment whether one is likely to succeed or fail in a certain task.

**physician-assisted suicide**  The administration of a lethal dose of some medication by a physician or arranging for a terminally ill patient to administer his or her own lethal dose of medication using a suicide machine.

**placenta**  The vascular organ that connects the fetus to the maternal uterus and mediates metabolic exchanges.

**plasticity**  The capability of being molded.

**population**  All units for potential observation.

**positive reinforcer**  In operant conditioning, a stimulus—such as food or a smile—that increases the rate of response when present.

**positivism**  An approach to the study of human behavior that seeks causal relationships among factors, with the goal of trying to predict outcomes.

**postconventional morality**  In Kohlberg's stages of moral reasoning, the most mature form of moral judgment. Moral decisions are based on an appreciation of the social contract that binds members of a social system and on personal values.

**postformal thought**  A qualitatively new form of thinking that emerges after formal operational thought, which involves a higher use of reflection and the integration of contextual, relativistic, and subjective knowledge.

**postpartum depression**  A period of sadness that may be experienced by the mother after giving birth, which appears to be related to hormonal activity.

**post-traumatic stress disorder**  A mental disorder that occurs after a traumatic event outside the range of usual human experience, characterized by symptoms such as reliving the event, reduced involvement with others, and manifestations of autonomic arousal such as hyperalertness and exaggerated startle response.

**power assertion**  A discipline technique involving physical force, harsh language, or control of resources.

**preconventional morality**  In Kohlberg's stages of moral reasoning, the most immature form of moral judgment. Moral decisions are based on whether the act has positive or negative consequences, or whether it is rewarded or punished.

**prediction**  Declaration in advance, usually with precision of calculation.

**preoccupied attachment**  An outcome of attachment in which a person has a positive model of others and a negative model of the self.

**preoperational thought**  In Piaget's theory of cognitive development, the stage in which representational skills are acquired.

**prime adaptive ego qualities**  Mental states that form a basic orientation toward the interpretation of life experiences; new ego qualities emerge in the positive resolution of each psychosocial crisis.

**private self**  Refers to a person's inner uniqueness and unity and the subjective experience of being the originator of one's thoughts and actions and of being self-reflective.

**processing load**  In problem solving, the number of domains of information called into play and the amount of work necessary to select response strategies.

**prohibitive moral judgment**  A judgment involving a conflict between violating a law and breaking a promise in order to achieve some other goal.

**prompting**  Urging a child to say more about an incomplete expression.

**prosocial moral judgment**  A judgment involving a conflict between doing something helpful for someone else and meeting one's own needs.

**prospective memory**  Memory about events or actions taking place in the future.

**psychohistorical perspective**  An integration of past, present, and future time with respect to personal and societal continuity and change.

**psychological system**  Includes those mental processes central to the person's ability to make meaning of experiences and take action. Emotion, memory and perception, problem solving, language, symbolic abilities, and orientation to the future all require the use of psychological processes. The psychological system provides the resources for processing information and navigating reality.

**psychosocial**  Of or pertaining to the interaction between social and psychological factors.

**psychosocial crisis**  A predictable life tension that arises as people experience some conflict between their own competencies and the expectations of their society.

**psychosocial evolution**  The contribution of each generation to the knowledge and norms of society.

**psychosocial moratorium**  A period of free experimentation before a final identity is achieved.

**psychosocial theory**  A theory of psychological development that proposes that cognitive, emotional, and social growth are the result of the interaction between social expectations at each life stage and the competencies that people bring to each life challenge.

**puberty**  The period of physical development at the onset of adolescence when the reproductive system matures.

**public self**  The many roles that one plays and the expectations that social reference groups, including family members, neighbors, teachers, friends, religious groups, ethnic groups, and even national leaders, have for one's behavior.

**punishment**    (1) A penalty or negative experience imposed on a person for improper behavior. (2) In operant conditioning, a negative stimulus applied in order to decrease the expression of an undesirable response. Compare *negative reinforcer*.

**purpose**    The ability to imagine and pursue valued goals.

**qualitative inquiry**    An approach to the study of human behavior that tries to understand the meanings, motives, and beliefs underlying a person's actions.

**quasi-experimental study**    A study in which the assignment of participants to treatment was not controlled by the experimenter but was a result of some pattern of life events.

**quickening**    Sensations of fetal movement, usually beginning during the second trimester of fetal growth.

**radius of significant relationships**    The groups of important people in one's life. The breadth and complexity of these groups change over the life span.

**random sampling**    A method for choosing the sample for a study in which each member of the population under investigation has an equal chance of being included.

**range of applicability**    The nature of the concepts and principles that a theory is trying to explain.

**rapport**    Conveying a feeling of trustworthiness and acceptance in an interview or in a counseling setting.

**reaction range**    The range of possible responses to environmental conditions that is established through genetic influences.

**reactive attachment disorder**    Clinical diagnosis that is linked to serious disturbances in infant attachment. Two expressions of this disorder have been described: *inhibited type*, in which the person is very withdrawn, hypervigilant in social contacts, and resistant to comfort; and *uninhibited type*, in which the person shows a lack of discrimination, being overly friendly and attaching to any new person.

**reactive nature of surveys**    The ability of some surveys to create attitudes where none existed before.

**reactivity**    A child's threshold for arousal, which indicates the likelihood of becoming distressed.

**readiness**    A time when a child's physical, cognitive, social, and emotional maturation is at a level to undertake new learning or to engage in a more complex, demanding type of activity or relationship.

**receptive language**    The ability to understand words.

**reciprocity**    A scheme describing the interdependence of related dimensions, such as height and width or time and speed.

**reference group**    A group with which an individual identifies and whose values the individual accepts as guiding principles.

**reflex**    An involuntary motor response to a simple stimulus.

**reinforcement**    In operant conditioning, the application of any stimulus that makes the repetition of a response more likely.

**rejectivity**    The unwillingness to include certain others or groups of others in one's generative concerns.

**relational paradigm**    In contemporary psychoanalytic theory, the view that humans have basic needs for connection, contact, and meaningful interpersonal relationships, and that the self is formed in an interpersonal context and emerges through interactions with others. Maturity requires the achievement of a sense of vitality, stability, and inner cohesiveness formulated through interpersonal transactions. Psychopathology or dysfunction arise when a person internalizes rigid, rejecting, or neglectful relational experiences and then uses these internalizations to anticipate or respond to real-life social encounters.

**reliability**    The consistency of a test in measuring something.

**reminiscence**    The process of thinking or telling about past experiences.

**repeatable**    In research, it is important that others carry out a similar investigation and observe the same results as the original investigator. For this to occur, the original investigator must carefully define all the procedures and equipment used, describe all

the essential characteristics of the participants (such as age, sex, and social class background), and describe the setting or situation where the observations were made.

**representational skills**    Skills learned in the preoperational stage—including mental imagery, symbolic play, symbolic drawing, imitation, and language—that permit the child to represent experiences or feelings in a symbolic form.

**repudiation**    Rejection of roles and values that are viewed as alien to oneself.

**resilience**    The capacity to recover from stress, or the ability to withstand the effects of stressors that are typically associated with negative outcomes.

**retirement anxiety**    Apprehensions that adults have as they anticipate retirement.

**retrospective study**    Research that asks the participants to report on experiences from an earlier time in their lives.

**reversibility**    A scheme describing the ability to undo an action and return to the original state.

**ritual**    A formal and customarily repeated act or series of acts.

**role**    A set of behaviors that have some socially agreed-upon functions and for which there exists an accepted code of norms, such as the role of teacher, child, or minister.

**role compatibility**    When partners in a relationship approach situations in a manner that works well; their behaviors and responses complement one another.

**role conflict**    The state of tension that occurs when the demands and expectations of various roles conflict with each other.

**role enactment**    Patterned characteristics of social behavior that one performs as a result of being in a specific role.

**role expectations**    Shared expectations for behavior that are linked to a social role.

**role experimentation**    The central process for the resolution of the psychosocial crisis of later adolescence, which involves participation in a variety of roles before any final commitments are made.

**role overload**  The state of tension that occurs when there are too many role demands and expectations to handle in the time allowed.

**role reversal**  Assuming the behaviors of a person in a reciprocal role, as when a child acts toward his or her parent as a parent.

**role spillover**  The state of tension that occurs when the demands or preoccupations about one role interfere with the ability to carry out another role.

**role strain**  The conflict and competing demands made by several roles that the person holds simultaneously.

**rule**  Principle or regulation governing conduct, action, procedure, or ritual.

**sampling**  A method of choosing participants in a study.

**scaffolding**  A process through which a child and an adult attempt to arrive at a shared understanding about a communication, at which point the adult interacts so as to expand or enrich the child's communicative competence.

**schedules of reinforcement**  The frequency and regularity with which reinforcements are given.

**scheme**  In Piaget's theory, the organization of actions into a unified whole, a mental construct.

**secondary sex characteristics**  The physical characteristics other than genitals that indicate sexual maturity, such as body hair, breasts, and deepened voice.

**secular growth trend**  A tendency, observed since approximately 1900, for more rapid physical maturation from one generation to the next, probably as a result of favorable nutrition, increased mobility, and greater protection from childhood diseases.

**secure attachment**  Infants actively explore their environment and interact with strangers while their mothers are present. After separation, the babies actively greet their mothers or seek interaction. If the babies were distressed during separation, the mothers' return reduces their distress, and the babies

return to exploration of the environment. In adulthood, this is an attachment outcome in which a person has a positive model of the self and of others.

**self actualization**  A motive that urges the person to make optimal use of his or her full potential, to become a more effective, creative participant in daily life.

**self-efficacy**  A sense of confidence that one can perform the behaviors that are demanded in a specific situation.

**self-esteem**  The evaluative dimension of the self that includes feelings of worthiness, pride, and discouragement.

**self-fulfilling prophecy**  False or inaccurate beliefs can produce a reality that corresponds with these beliefs.

**self labeling**  Refers to applying a label such as gay, lesbian, or bisexual to oneself. Compare *disclosure*.

**self-monitoring children**  Some children appear to monitor their social environment more self-consciously than others. *High self-monitoring children* are more aware of the emotional and nonverbal behavior of others and make more use of social information to evaluate and regulate their own behavior than *low self-monitoring children*.

**self-presentation bias**  Research participants may present themselves in the way they want the interviewer to see them.

**self-regulation**  Behavior inhibition in response to stimuli.

**self-regulatory plan**  A strategy for achieving one's goals, including techniques for managing internal emotional states, creating a plan, and putting the plan into action.

**self-theory**  An organized set of ideas about the self, the world, and the meaning of interactions between the self and the environment.

**semantic memory**  Recall of basic knowledge, such as the meaning of words like "vegetable," "democracy," or "insect."

**semiotic thinking**  The understanding that one thing can stand for another.

**sensitive period**  A span of time during which a particular skill or behavior is most likely to develop.

**sensitivity (of caregiver)**  Attentiveness to an infant's state, accurate interpretation of the infant's signals, and well-timed responses that promote mutually rewarding interactions.

**sensorimotor adaptation**  Infants use their reflexes to explore their world, and they gradually alter their reflexive responses to take into account the unique properties of objects around them. This provides the basis for sensorimotor intelligence.

**sensorimotor intelligence**  In Piaget's theory of development, the first stage of cognitive growth, during which schemes are built on sensory and motor experiences.

**sensorimotor play**  Sensory exploration and motor manipulation that produce pleasure.

**sensory register**  The neurological processing activity that is required to take in visual, auditory, tactile, and olfactory information.

**separation anxiety**  Feelings of fear or sadness associated with the departure of the object of attachment.

**sex**  Refers to biological features or distinctions of men and women that are determined by chromosomal information.

**sex-linked characteristics**  Characteristics for which the allele is found on the sex chromosomes.

**sexual orientation**  Refers to one's preference for sexually intimate partners. The three common sexual orientations discussed in the literature are *heterosexual*, *homosexual*, and *bisexual*.

**sexually transmitted diseases (STDs)**  A wide range of bacterial, viral, and yeast infections that are transmitted through forms of sexual contact.

**shame**  An intense emotional reaction to being ridiculed or to a negative self-assessment.

**short-term memory**  The working capacity to encode and retrieve five to nine bits of information in the span of a minute or two. This is the scratch pad of memory that is used when someone tells you a telephone number or gives you his or her address.

**sign**  Something that represents something else, usually in an abstract, arbitrary way; for example, a word for an object.

**small for gestational age (SGA)** Fetus who does not weigh as much as a normal fetus of the same age. These fetuses are at greater risk for health problems than those who are born prematurely but are of average weight for their gestational age.

**social clock** Expectations for orderly and sequential changes that occur with the passage of time as individuals move through life.

**social cognition** Concepts related to understanding interpersonal behavior and the point of view of others.

**social conventions** Socially accepted norms and regulations that guide behavior.

**social culture** Encompasses the norms, roles, beliefs, values, rites, and customs of a culture.

**social evolutionary theory** A theory that men and women differ in the features they emphasize in evaluating someone as a desirable partner.

**social identity** The aspect of the self-concept that is based on membership in a group or groups and the importance and emotional salience of that membership.

**social integration** Being comfortably involved in meaningful interpersonal associations and friendship relations.

**socialization** The process of teaching and enforcing group norms and values to the new group members.

**social learning theory** A theory of learning that emphasizes the ability to learn new responses through observation and imitation of others.

**social play** Children joining with other children in some activity.

**social pretend play** Children who coordinate their pretense. They establish a fantasy structure, take roles, agree on the make-believe meaning of props, and solve pretend problems.

**social referencing** The process by which infants use facial features and verbal expressions as clues to the emotional responses of another person, often the mother, and as information about how to approach an unfamiliar, ambiguous situation.

**social role** A set of behaviors that have some socially agreed-upon functions and for which there exists an accepted code of norms, such as the role of teacher, child, or minister.

**social role theory** The theory that emphasizes participation in varied and more complex roles as a major factor in human development.

**social support** The social experiences leading people to believe that they are cared for and loved, that they are esteemed and valued, and that they belong to a network of communication and mutual obligation.

**societal system** Includes those processes through which a person becomes integrated into society. Societal influences include social roles, rituals, cultural myths, social expectations, leadership styles, communication patterns, family organization, ethnic and subcultural influences, political and religious ideologies, patterns of economic prosperity or poverty and war or peace, and exposure to racism, sexism, and other forms of discrimination, intolerance, or intergroup hostility. The impact of the societal system on psychosocial development results largely from interpersonal relationships, often relationships with close or significant others.

**sociobiology** The scientific study of the biological basis of social behavior that focuses on practices within populations that increase the likelihood of certain genes surviving in subsequent generations of offspring.

**socioeconomic level** One's ranking based on a number of social and financial indicators, including years of education, occupation, and income.

**solitary pretense** Children are involved in their own fantasy activities, such as pretending that they are driving a car or giving a baby a bath.

**solicitude** State of caring, attentiveness, and helpfulness.

**sperm** The male germ cell.

**stagnation** A lack of psychological movement or growth during middle adulthood that may result from self-aggrandizement or from the inability to cope with developmental tasks.

**statistically significant** Pertaining to observations that are unlikely to oc-

cur by chance and that therefore indicate a systematic cause.

**status offense** Behavior that is criminalized for minors, such as running away or truancy, which would not be against the law for adults.

**stigmatized death** People attributing someone's death to an immoral, illegal, or evil cause.

**strange situation** A standard laboratory procedure designed to study patterns of attachment behavior. A child is exposed during a 20-minute period to a series of events that are likely to stimulate the attachment system. Child and caregiver enter an unfamiliar laboratory setting; a stranger enters; the caregiver leaves briefly; and the caregiver and infant have opportunities for reunion while researchers observe child, caregiver, and their interactions.

**stranger anxiety** Feelings of fear or apprehension in the presence of unfamiliar people, especially during infancy.

**stratified sampling** A method for choosing the sample for a research study in which participants are selected from a variety of levels or types of people in the population.

**substantive complexity** The degree to which one's work requires thought, independent judgment, and frequent decision making.

**superego** In psychoanalytic theory, the mental function that embodies moral precepts and moral sanctions. The superego includes the ego ideal, or the goals toward which one strives, as well as the punishing conscience.

**swaddling** The practice of wrapping a baby snugly in a soft blanket, which is a common technique for soothing a newborn in many cultures.

**symbol** An object, image, or word that represents something. A symbol can be a word that represents an object, as *chair*, or an object that represents a concept, as a dove.

**symbolic play** Imaginative or pretend activities that express emotions, problems, or roles.

**synchrony** Infant and caregiver move from one state to the next in a fluid manner. Interactions of the infant and caregiver are rhythmic, well timed, and mutually rewarding.

**systematic** In a careful, orderly way. Scientists have a framework of questions that they strive to answer based on what is already known and what theories predict. They approach research by having clear objectives, carefully defining the purpose of their work, and describing the specific methods they will use.

**teachable moment** A time when a person is most ready to acquire a new ability.

**telegraphic speech** Two-word sentences used by children that omit many parts of speech but convey meaning.

**temperament** Innate characteristics that determine the person's sensitivity to various sense experiences and his or her responsiveness to patterns of social interaction.

**teratogens** Agents that produce malformations during the formation of organs and tissues.

**testis-determining factor (TDF)** The gene or genes on the Y chromosome that are responsible for setting into motion the differentiation of the testes during embryonic development.

**testosterone** A hormone that fosters the development of male sex characteristics and growth.

**thanatology** The field of science that addresses dying and death as well as the psychological mechanisms of coping with them.

**theory** A logically interrelated system of concepts and statements that provides a framework for organizing, interpreting, and understanding observations, with the goal of explaining and predicting behavior.

**theory of mind** The natural way in which children understand each other's behavior. In day-to-day functioning, the theory of mind suggests that beliefs, desires, and actions are logically linked.

**trajectory** In the life course, the path of one's life experiences in a specific domain, particularly work and family life.

**transition** In the life course, the beginning or close of an event or role relationship. For example, work transi-

tions might be getting one's first job, being laid off, and going back to school for an advanced degree.

**triangulation** Confirming a researcher's insights by looking at written documents about the setting, interviewing other informants, and sharing observations with other members of the research team.

**trust** An emotional sense that both the environment and oneself are reliable and capable of satisfying basic needs.

**ultrasound** A technique for producing visual images of the fetus in utero through a pattern of deflected sound waves.

**unconscious** Psychological processes that occur outside of awareness, including problem solving.

**usefulness/competence** Personality dimension associated with well-being and high self-esteem through volunteer work, involvement with others, and a sense of purpose and structure in the use of time.

**uterus** In the female reproductive system, the hollow muscular organ in which the fertilized ovum normally becomes embedded and in which the developing embryo and fetus is nourished and grows.

**validity** The extent to which a test measures what it is supposed to measure.

**value** A principle or quality that is intrinsically desirable.

**verbal persuasion** Encouragement from others.

**very old age** A stage of psychosocial development that emerges at the upper end of the life span, after one has exceeded the life expectancy for one's birth cohort.

**viability** Reaching the stage of development in which a fetus is capable of living outside the uterus.

**vicarious experience** An experience achieved through the imagined participation in events that happen to another person.

**vicarious reinforcement** Through observing others, a person can learn a behavior and also acquire the motivation to perform the behavior or resist performing that behavior depending

on what is observed about the consequences of that behavior.

**visual acuity** The ability to detect visual stimuli under various levels of illumination.

**visual adaptation** The ability to adapt to changes in the level of illumination.

**visual tracking** Following an object's movement with one's eyes.

**vocabulary** A list of the words a person uses and understands.

**volunteerism** Involvement in some form of volunteer service.

**volunteer sampling** Sampling in which participants for a study are selected from volunteers.

**whole-brain death** A technical definition of death with eight criteria that was developed in 1981 by the President's Commission for the Ethical Study of Problems in Medicine and Biomedical and Behavioral Research.

**will** The determination to exercise free choice and self-control.

**wisdom** A type of expert knowledge that reflects sound judgment and good advice in the face of high levels of uncertainty.

**withdrawal** General orientation of wariness toward people and objects.

**withdrawn** A path to peer rejection in which children are shy and self-conscious.

**word** A unit of language, consisting of one or more spoken sounds or their written representation, that functions as a principal carrier of meaning.

**working model of attachment** An infant's expectations of the behavior of their caregiver that is based on the quality of attachment.

**worldview** A way of making meaning of the relationships, situations, and objects encountered in daily life in a culture.

**young-old** Among the very old, those who remain healthy, vigorous, and competent.

**zone of proximal development** The emergent developmental capacity that is just ahead of the level at which the person is currently functioning.

**zygote** The first phase of fetal development, when a single cell is formed from two gametes.

# References

AARP. (2000). *Update on the older worker: 2000*. Retrieved January 30, 2002, from http://research.aarp.org/econ/dd62_worker.html

AARP. (2002). *AARP national survey on consumer preparedness and e-commerce: A survey of computer users age 45 and older*. Retrieved January 27, 2002, from http://research.aarp.org/consume/ecommerce_1.html

Abbey, A. (1995). Provision and receipt of social support and disregard: What is their impact on the marital life quality of infertile and fertile couples? *Journal of Personality and Social Psychology, 68*, 455–469.

Abel, E. L. (1984). *Fetal alcohol syndrome and fetal alcohol effects*. New York: Plenum.

Abell, S. C., & Richards, M. H. (1996). The relationship between body shape and satisfaction and self-esteem: An investigation of gender and class differences. *Journal of Youth and Adolescence, 25*, 691–703.

Aber, J. L. (1994). Poverty, violence, and child development: Untangling family and community level effects. In C. A. Nelson (Ed.), *Threats to optimal development: Integrating biological, psychological, and social risk factors* (pp. 229–272). Hillsdale, NJ: Erlbaum.

Aber, J. L., Belsky, J., Slade, A., & Crnic, K. (1999). Stability and change in mothers' representations of their relationship with their toddlers. *Developmental Psychology, 35*, 1038–1047.

Abrams, L. (2003). Contextual variations in young women's gender identity negotiations. *Psychology of Women Quarterly, 27*, 64–74.

Achenbach, T. M. (1991). *Manual for the youth self-report and 1991 profile*. Burlington: University of Vermont, Department of Psychiatry.

Acitelli, L. K., Douvan, E., & Veroff, J. (1997). The changing influence of interpersonal perceptions on marital well-being among Black and White couples. *Journal of Social and Personal Relationships, 14*, 291–304.

Ackerman, G. L. (1993). A congressional view of youth suicide. *American Psychologist, 48*, 183–184.

Acredolo, C., Adams, A., & Schmid, J. (1984). On the understanding of the relationships between speed, duration, and distance. *Child Development, 55*, 2151–2159.

ADAM. (2004). *Hemophilia A*. Retrieved August 4, 2004, from http://www.nlm.nih.gov/medlineplus/ency/article/000538.htm

Adams, B. N. (1986). *The family: A sociological interpretation* (4th ed.). San Diego: Harcourt Brace Jovanovich.

Adams, G. R., & Archer, S. L. (1994). Identity: A precursor to intimacy. In S. L. Archer (Ed.), *Interventions for adolescent identity development* (pp. 193–213). Thousand Oaks, CA: Sage.

Adegoke, A. A. (1993). The experience of spermarche (the age of onset of sperm emission) among selected boys in Nigeria. *Journal of Youth and Adolescence, 22*, 201–209.

Adelson, J., & Doehrman, M. J. (1980). The psychodynamic approach to adolescence. In J. Adelson (Ed.), *Handbook of adolescent psychology* (pp. 99–116). New York: Wiley.

Ades, P. A., Ballor, D. L., Ashikaga, T., Utton, J. L., & Nair, K. S. (1996). Weight training improves walking endurance in healthy elderly persons. *Annals of Internal Medicine, 124*, 568–572.

Adey, P., & Shayer, M. (1993). An exploration of long-term far-transfer effects following an extended intervention program in the high school science curriculum. *Cognition and Instruction, 11*, 1–29.

Adler, A. (1935). The fundamental views of individual psychology. *International Journal of Individual Psychology, 1*, 5–8.

Adler, J. (1999, May 10). The truth about high school. *Newsweek*, pp. 56–58.

Adler, N. E., David, H. P., Major, B. N., Roth, S. H., Russo, N. F., & Wyatt, G. (1990). Psychological responses after abortion. *Science, 248*, 41–44.

Adler, P. A., & Adler, P. (1998). Observational techniques. In N. K. Denzin & Y. S. Lincoln (Eds.), *Collecting and interpreting qualitative materials* (pp. 79–109). Thousand Oaks, CA: Sage.

Adolph, K. E., & Eppler, M. A. (2002). Flexibility and specificity in infant motor skill acquisition. In J. W. Fagen & H. Hayne (Eds.), *Progress in infancy research* (Vol. 2, pp. 121–167). Mahwah, NJ: Erlbaum.

Ainsworth, M. D. S. (1973). The development of infant–mother attachment. In B. M. Caldwell & H. N. Ricciuti (Eds.), *Review of child development research* (Vol. 3). Chicago: University of Chicago Press.

Ainsworth, M. D. S. (1979). Infant–mother attachment. *American Psychologist, 34*, 932–937.

Ainsworth, M. D. S. (1985). Patterns of infant–mother attachments: Antecedents and effects on development. *Bulletin of the New York Academy of Medicine, 61*, 771–791.

Ainsworth, M. D. S. (1989). Attachments beyond infancy. *American Psychologist, 44*, 709–716.

Ainsworth, M. D. S., Bell, S. M. V., & Stayton, D. J. (1971). Individual differences in strange situational behavior of one-year olds. In H. A. Schaffer (Ed.), *The origins of human social relations*. London: Academic Press.

Ainsworth, M. D. S., Blehar, M. C., Waters, E., & Wall, S. (1978). *Patterns of attachment: A psychological study of the strange situation*. Hillsdale, NJ: Erlbaum.

Alan Guttmacher Institute. (1999). *Teen sex and pregnancy*. Retrieved November 3, 2001, from http://www.agi-usa.org/pubs/fb_teen_sex.html

Alan Guttmacher Institute. (2002). Sexuality education. *Facts in Brief*. Retrieved December 4, 2004, from http://www.agi-usa.org/pubs/fb_sex_ed02.pdf

Alan Guttmacher Institute. (2002). Teenagers' sexual and reproductive health. *Facts in Brief*. Retrieved December 4, 2004, from http://www.agi-usa.org/pubs/fb_sex_ed02.pdf

Alasker, F. D. (1995). Timing of puberty and reactions to pubertal changes. In M. Rutter (Ed.), *Psychosocial disturbances in young people: Challenges for prevention* (pp. 37–82). Cambridge, UK: Cambridge University Press.

Albert, M. S. (2002). Memory decline: The boundary between aging and age-related disease. *Annals of Neurology, 51*, 282–284.

Albert, S., Amgott, T., Krakow, M., & Marcus, H. (1977, August 26–30). *Children's bedtime rituals as a prototype rite of safe passage*. Paper presented at the annual convention of the American Psychological Association, San Francisco, CA.

Albom, M. (1997). *Tuesdays with Morrie: An old man, a young man, and life's greatest lesson*. New York: Doubleday.

Alessandri, S. M. (1992). Mother–child interactional correlates of maltreated and non-maltreated children's play behavior. *Development and Psychopathology, 4*, 257–270.

Alexander, B. H., Checkoway, H., van Netten, C., Muller, C. H., Ewers, T. G., Kaufman, J. D., et al. (1996). Semen quality of men employed at a lead smelter. *Occupational and Environmental Medicine, 53*, 411–416.

Alexander, C. S., Somerfield, M. R., Ensminger, M. E., Johnson, K. E., & Kim, Y. J. (1993). Consistency of adolescents' self-report of sexual behavior in a longitudinal study. *Journal of Youth and Adolescence, 22*, 455–473.

Alexander, K. L., & Entwisle, D. R. (1988). Achievement in the first two years of school: Patterns of processes. *Monographs of the Society for Research in Child Development, 53* (2, Serial No. 218).

Alexander, K. L., Entwisle, D. R., & Kabbani, N. S. (2001). The dropout process in life course perspective: Early risk factors at home and school. *Teachers College Record, 103*, 760–822.

Alexander, K. L., Entwisle, D. R., & Thompson, M. S. (1987). School performance, status relations, and the structure of sentiment: Bringing the teacher back in. *American Sociological Review, 52,* 655–682.

Allen, J. P., & Land, D. (1999). Attachment in adolescence. In J. Cassidy & P. R. Shaver (Eds.), *Handbook of attachment: Theory, research, and clinical applications* (pp. 319–335). New York: Guilford Press.

Allen, K. R., Blieszner, R., & Roberto, K. (2001). Families in the middle and later years: A review and critique of the research in the 1990s. *Journal of Marriage and the Family, 62,* 911–926.

Alter, R. C. (1984). Abortion outcome as a function of sex-role identification. *Psychology of Women Quarterly, 8,* 211–233.

Amato, P. R. (1988). Parental divorce and attitudes toward marriage and family. *Journal of Marriage and the Family, 50,* 453–462.

Amato, P. R. (1996). Explaining the intergenerational transmission of divorce. *Journal of Marriage and the Family, 58,* 628–640.

Amato, P. R., & Booth, A. (1996). A prospective study of divorce and parent–child relationships. *Journal of Marriage and the Family, 58,* 356–365.

Amato, P. R., & De Boer, D. D. (2001). The transmission of marital instability across generations: Relationship skills or commitment to marriage? *Journal of Marriage and the Family, 63,* 1038–1051.

American Academy of Pediatrics. (1995). The inappropriate use of school "readiness" tests. *Pediatrics, 95,* 437–438.

American Association for the Advancement of Science. (2003). *AAAS policy brief: Human cloning.* Retrieved August 13, 2004, from http://www.aaas.org/spp/cstc/briefs/cloning/index/shtml

American Academy of Pediatrics. (1996). Use and abuse of the Apgar score. *Pediatrics, 98,* 141–142.

American Academy of Pediatrics. (1999). *Caring for your baby and young child.* New York: Bantam.

American Academy of Pediatrics. (2001). Children, adolescents, and television. *Pediatrics, 107,* 423–426.

American Civil Liberties Union. (1996). *Violence chip.* Retrieved August 18, 2001, from http://www.aclu.org/library/aavchip.html

American Psychiatric Association. (1994). *Diagnostic and statistical manual of mental disorders, DSM-IV* (4th ed.). Washington, DC: Author.

American Psychological Association. (1992). Ethical principles of psychologists and code of conduct. *American Psychologist, 47,* 1597–1611.

American Psychological Association. (1996). *Reducing violence: A research agenda.* Washington, DC: Author.

Amundson, N. E. (2001). Three-dimensional living. *Journal of Employment Counseling, 38,* 114–127.

Anderson, D. R., Huston, A. C., Schmitt, K., Linebarger, D. L., & Wright, J. C. (2001). Early childhood television viewing and adolescent behavior: The recontact study.

*Monographs of the Society for Research in Child Development, 66* (Serial No. 264).

Anderson, R. C., Wilson, P. T., & Fielding, L. G. (1988). Growth in reading and how children spend their time outside of school. *Reading Research Quarterly, 23,* 285–303.

Anderssen, N., Amlie, C., & Ytteroy, E. A. (2002). Outcomes for children with lesbian or gay parents: A review of studies from 1978 to 2000. *Scandinavian Journal of Psychology, 43,* 335–351.

Andrulis, D. P. (2000). Community, service, and policy strategies to improve health care access in the changing urban environment. *American Journal of Public Health, 90,* 858–862.

Aneshensel, C. S., Pearlin, L. I., Mullan, J. T., Zarit, S. H., & Whitlatch, C. J. (1995). *Profiles in caregiving: The unexpected career.* San Diego: Academic Press.

Anglin, J. M. (1993). Vocabulary development: A morphological analysis. *Monographs of the Society for Research in Child Development, 58.*

Annie E. Casey Foundation. (1999). *Kids count data book.* Baltimore: Author.

Anthony, S. (1972). *The discovery of death in childhood and after.* New York: Basic Books.

Antonio, A. L, Chang, M. J., Hakuta, K., Kenny, D. A., Levin, S., & Milem, J. F. (2004). Effects of racial diversity on complex thinking in college students. *Psychological Science, 15,* 507–510.

Antonucci, T. C., Lansford, J. E., Schaberg, L., Smith, J., Baltes, M., Akiyama, H., et al. (2001). Widowhood and illness: A comparison of social network characteristics in France, Germany, Japan, and the United States. *Psychology and Aging, 16,* 655–665.

Aoki, C., & Siekevitz, P. (1988). Plasticity in brain development. *Scientific American, 259,* 56–64.

Apgar, V. (1953). Proposal for a new method of evaluating the newborn infant. *Anesthesia and Analgesia, 32,* 260–267.

Aquilino, W. S. (1990). Likelihood of parent–adult child coresidence. *Journal of Marriage and the Family, 52,* 405–419.

Arbuckle, T. Y., Gold, D. P., Andres, D., Schwartzman, A., & Chaikelson, J. (1992). The role of psychosocial context, age, and intelligence in memory performance of older men. *Psychology and Aging, 7,* 25–36.

Archer, J. (1991). Human sociobiology: Basic concepts and limitations. *Journal of Social Issues, 47,* 11–26.

Archer, S. L. (1992). A feminist's approach to identity research. In G. R. Adams, T. P. Gullotta, & R. Montemayor (Eds.), *Adolescent identity formation: Advances in adolescent development* (pp. 25–49). Newbury Park, CA: Sage.

Ardila-Rey, A., & Killen, M. (2001). Middle class Colombian children's evaluations of personal, moral, and social-conventional interactions in the classroom. *International Journal of Behavioral Development, 25,* 246–255.

Arias, E. (2002). United States life tables, 2000. *National Vital Statistics Reports, 51,* 1–6.

Aries, E. (1998). Gender differences in interaction: A reexamination. In D. J. Canary & K. Dindia (Eds.), *Sex differences and similarities in communication: Critical essays and empirical investigations of sex and gender in interaction* (pp. 65–81). Mahwah, NJ: Erlbaum.

Armstrong, B., Cohall, A. T., Vaughan, R. D., Scott, M., Tiezzi, L., and McCarthy, J. F. (1999). Involving men in reproductive health: The young men's clinic. *American Journal of Public Health, 89,* 902–905.

Arnett, J. J. (1998). Learning to stand alone: The contemporary American transition to adulthood in cultural and historical context. *Human Development, 41,* 295–315.

Arnett, J. J. (2000). Emerging adulthood: A theory of development from the late teens through the twenties. *American Psychologist, 55,* 469–480.

Arnett, J. J. (2004). *Adolescence and emerging adulthood: A cultural approach* (2nd ed.). Upper Saddle River, NJ: Prentice Hall.

Arnold, M. L. (2000). Stage, sequence, and sequels: Changing conceptions of morality, post-Kohlberg. *Educational Psychology Review, 12,* 365–383.

Aronfreed, J. (1969). The concept of internalization. In D. A. Goslin (Ed.), *Handbook of socialization theory and research.* Chicago: Rand McNally.

Aseltine, R. H., Jr. (2003). Evaluation of a school based suicide prevention program. *Adolescent & Family Health, 3,* 81–88.

Asher, S. R., & Gazelle, H. (1999). Loneliness, peer relations, and language disorder in childhood. *Topics in Language Disorders, 19,* 16–33.

Asher, S. R., & Paquette, J. A. (2003). Loneliness and peer relations in childhood. *Current Directions in Psychological Science, 12,* 75–78.

Asher, S. R., Parkhurst J. T., Hymel, S., & Williams, G. A. (1999). Peer rejection and loneliness in childhood. In S. R. Asher & J. D. Coie (Eds.), *Peer rejection in childhood* (pp. 253–273). New York: Cambridge University Press.

Aslin, R. N. (1987). Visual and auditory development in infancy. In J. D. Osofsky (Ed.), *Handbook of infant development* (2nd ed., pp. 5–97). New York: Wiley.

Associated Press. (2001). *Boys, like girls, may be hitting puberty earlier, study suggests.* Retrieved October 20, 2001, from http://stacks.msnbc.com/news/628473.asp

Astone, N. M. (1993). Are adolescent mothers just single mothers? *Journal of Research on Adolescence, 3,* 353–372.

Atchley, R. C. (1975). The life course, age grading, and age-linked demands for decision making. In N. Datan & L. H. Ginsberg (Eds.), *Life-span developmental psychology: Normative life crises.* New York: Academic Press.

Atchley, R. C. (1977). *The social forces of later life.* Belmont, CA: Wadsworth.

Atchley, R. C. (1993). Critical perspectives on retirement. In T. R. Cole & W. A. Achenbaum (Eds.), *Voices and visions of aging: Toward a critical gerontology* (pp. 3–19). New York: Springer Verlag.

Atchley, R. C. (2001). *Continuity and adaptation in aging.* Baltimore: Johns Hopkins University Press.

Atkinson, D. R., Morten, G., & Sue, D. W. (1983). *Counseling American minorities: A cross-cultural perspective.* (2nd ed.). Dubuque, IA: William C. Brown.

Atkinson, J. W., & Birch, D. (1978). *Introduction to motivation* (2nd ed.). New York: Van Nostrand.

Atkinson, R. (2000). Measuring gentrification and displacement in Greater London. *Urban Studies, 37,* 149–166.

Atkinson, R. H. (2001). *Standardized tests and access to American universities.* Retrieved November 18, 2004, from http://www.ucop.edu/news/sat/speech.html

Attitudes and characteristics of freshmen at 4-year college: Fall, 2000. (2001, August 31). *Chronicle of Higher Education,* p. 23.

Au, T. K., Sidle, A. L., & Rollins, K. B. (1993). Developing an intuitive understanding of conservation: Invisible particles as a plausible mechanism. *Developmental Psychology, 29,* 286–299.

Avery, C. S. (1989). How do you build intimacy in an age of divorce? *Psychology Today, 23*(5), 21–31.

Azar, B. (1997). It may cause anxiety, but day care can benefit kids. *APA Monitor, 28,* 13.

Bachu, A., & O'Connell, M. (2001). Fertility of American women: June 2000. *Current Population Reports,* P20-543RV. Washington, DC: U.S. Bureau of the Census.

Bagwell, C. L., & Coie, J. D. (2004). The best friendships of aggressive boys: Relationship quality, conflict management, and rule-breaking behavior. *Journal of Experimental Child Psychology, 88,* 5–24.

Bailey, J. M., & Pillard, R. (1991). A genetic study of male sexual orientation. *Archives of General Psychiatry, 48,* 1089–1096.

Bailey, J. M., & Pillard, R. (1994). The innateness of homosexuality. *The Harvard Mental Health Letter, 10,* 4–6.

Bailey, J. M., Bobrow, D., Wolfe, M., & Mikach, S. (1995). Sexual orientation of adult sons of gay fathers. *Developmental Psychology, 31,* 124–129.

Baillargeon, R. (1987). Object permanence in 3½- and 4½-month-old infants. *Developmental Psychology, 23,* 655–664.

Baillargeon, R. (2004). Infants' physical world. *Current Directions in Psychological Science, 13,* 89–94.

Baillargeon, R., & DeVos, J. (1991). Object permanence in young infants: Further evidence. *Child Development, 62,* 1227–1246.

Baillargeon, R., & Graber, M. (1988). Evidence of location memory in 8-month-old infants in a nonsearch AB task. *Developmental Psychology, 24,* 502–511.

Bakeman, R. (2000). Behavioral observation and coding. In H. T. Reiss & C. M. Judd (Eds.), *Handbook of research methods in social and personality psychology* (pp. 138–159). New York: Cambridge University Press.

Baker, H. A., Jr. (1991). An apple for my teacher: Twelve writers tell about teachers who made all the difference. In H. L. Gates Jr. (Ed.), *Bearing witness: selections from African-American autobiography in the twentieth century* (pp. 317–319). New York: Pantheon Books.

Bakken, L., Thompson, J., Clark, F. L., Johnson, N., & Dwyer, K. (2001). Making conservationists and classifiers of preoperational fifth-grade children. *Journal of Educational Research, 95,* 56–61.

Balter, N. (2001). In search of the first Europeans. *Science, 291,* 1722–1725.

Baltes, P. B. (1997). On the incomplete architecture of human ontogeny: Selection, optimization, and compensation as foundation of developmental theory. *American Psychologist, 52,* 366–380.

Baltes, P. B., & Baltes, M. M. (1990). *Successful aging: Perspectives from the behavioral sciences.* Cambridge, UK: Cambridge University Press.

Baltes, P. B., & Lindenberger, U. (1997). Emergence of a powerful connection between sensory and cognitive functions across the adult life span. A new window to the study of cognitive aging? *Psychology and Aging, 12,* 12–21.

Baltes, P. B., & Smith, J. (1990). The psychology of wisdom and its ontogenesis. In R. J. Sternberg (Ed.), *Wisdom: Its nature, origins and development* (pp. 87–120). New York: Cambridge University Press.

Baltes, P. B., Smith, J., & Staudinger, U. M. (1992). Wisdom and successful aging. In T. B. Sonderegger (Ed.), *Psychology and aging* (pp. 123–168). Lincoln: University of Nebraska Press.

Baltes, P. B., & Staudinger, U. M. (1993). The search for a psychology of wisdom. *Current Directions in Psychological Science, 2,* 75–80.

Baltes, P. B., & Staudinger, U. M. (2000). Wisdom: A metaheuristic (pragmatic) to orchestrate mind and virtue toward excellence. *American Psychologist, 55,* 122–136.

Bandura, A. (Ed.). (1971). *Psychological modeling.* Chicago: Aldine-Atherton.

Bandura, A. (1973). *Aggression: A social learning analysis.* Englewood Cliffs, NJ: Prentice Hall.

Bandura, A. (1977). *Social learning theory.* Englewood Cliffs, NJ: Prentice Hall.

Bandura, A. (1982). Self-efficacy mechanism in human agency. *American Psychologist, 37,* 122–147.

Bandura, A. (1986). *Social foundations of thought and action: A social cognitive theory.* Englewood Cliffs, NJ: Prentice Hall.

Bandura, A. (1989). Regulation of cognitive processes through perceived self-efficacy. *Developmental Psychology, 25,* 729–735.

Bandura, A. (1989). Social cognitive theory. *Annals of Child Development, 6,* 1–60.

Bandura, A. (1991). Social cognitive theory of moral thought and action. In W. M. Kurtines & J. L. Gewirtz (Eds.), *Handbook of moral behavior and development: Vol. 1. Theory* (pp. 45–103). Hillsdale, NJ: Erlbaum.

Bandura, A. (2000a). Self efficacy: The foundation of agency. In W. J. Perrig & A. Grob (Eds.), *Control of human behavior, mental processes, and consciousness: Essays in honor of the 60th birthday of August Flammer* (pp. 17–33). Mahwah, NJ: Erlbaum.

Bandura, A. (2000b). Social cognitive theory: An agentic perspective. *Annual Review of Psychology, 52,* 1–26.

Bandura, A., & Schunck, D. H. (1981). Cultivating competence, self-efficacy, and intrinsic interest through proximal self-motivation. *Journal of Personality and Social Psychology, 41,* 586–598.

Bandura, A., & Walters, R. H. (1963). *Social learning and personality development.* New York: Holt, Rinehart & Winston.

Bandura, A., Barbaranelli, C., Caprara, G. V., & Pastorelli, C. (1996). Multifaceted impact of self-efficacy beliefs on academic functioning. *Child Development, 67,* 1206–1222.

Bank, B. J., & Hansford, S. L. (2000). Gender and friendship: Why are men's best same-sex friendships less intimate and supportive? *Personal Relationships, 7,* 63–78.

Bank, L., Forgatch, M. S., Patterson, G. R., & Fetrow, R. A. (1993). Parenting practices of single mothers: Mediators of negative contextual factors. *Journal of Marriage and the Family, 55,* 371–384.

Bankart, B. (1989). Japanese perceptions of motherhood. *Psychology of Women Quarterly, 13,* 59–76.

Barber, J. S. (2000). Intergenerational influences on the entry into parenthood: Mothers' preferences for family and nonfamily behavior. *Social Forces, 79,* 319–348.

Barbu, S., Le Maner-Idrissi, G., & Jouanjean, A. (2000). The emergence of gender segregation: Towards an integrative perspective. *Current Psychology Letters: Behavior, Brain, and Cognition, 3,* 7–18.

Bard, K. A., Coles, C. D., Platzman, K. A., & Lynch, M. E. (2000). The effects of prenatal drug exposure, term status and caregiving on arousal and arousal modulation in 8-week-old infants. *Psychobiology, 36,* 194–212.

Barinaga, M. (1991). How long is the human life-span? *Science, 254,* 936–938.

Barinaga, M. (1994). Surprise across the cultural divide. *Science, 263,* 1468–1472.

Barnard, K. E., & Morisset, C. E. (1995). Preventive health and developmental care for children: Relationships as a primary factor in service delivery with at risk populations. In H. E. Fitzgerald, B. M. Lester, et al. (Eds.), *Children of poverty: Research, health, and policy issues* (pp. 167–195). New York: Garland.

Barnes, G. M. (1981). Drinking among adolescents: A subcultural phenomenon or a model of adult behaviors? *Adolescence, 16,* 211–229.

Barnett, R. C. (2004). Preface: Women and work: Where are we, where did we come from, and where are we going? *Journal of Social Issues, 60,* 667–674.

Barnett, R. C., Brennan, R. T., & Gareis, K. C. (1999). A closer look at the measurement of burnout. *Journal of Applied Biobehavioral Research, 4,* 65–78.

Barnett, R. C., & Hyde, J. S. (2001). Women, men, work, and family. *American Psychologist, 56,* 781–796.

Barnett, R. C., Marshall, N. L., & Pleck, J. H. (1992). Men's multiple roles and their relationship to men's psychological distress. *Journal of Marriage and the Family, 54,* 358–367.

Bartholomew, K. (1990). Avoidance of intimacy: An attachment perspective. *Journal of Social and Personal Relationships, 7,* 147–178.

Bartz, K. W., & Levine, E. S. (1978, November). Child rearing by black parents: A description and comparison to Anglo and Chicano parents. *Journal of Marriage and the Family, 40,* 709–719.

Bar-Yam Hassan, A., & Bar-Yam, M. (1987). Interpersonal development across the lifespan: Communion and its interaction with agency in psychosocial development. *Contributions to Human Development, 18,* 102–128.

Bashore, T. R., Osman, A., & Heffley, E. F., III. (1989). Mental slowing in elderly persons: A cognitive psychophysiological analysis. *Psychology and Aging, 4,* 235–244.

Bashore, T. R., van der Molen, M. W., Ridderinkhof, K. R., & Wylie, S. A. (1997). Is the age-complexity effect mediated by reductions in a general processing resource? *Biological Psychology, 45,* 263–282.

Bass, D. M., & Bowman, K. (1990). The transition from caregiving to bereavement: The relationship of care-related strain and adjustment to death. *The Gerontologist, 30,* 35–42.

Bassett, M. T. (2001). Keeping the M in MTCT: Women, mothers, and HIV prevention. *American Journal of Public Health, 91,* 701–702.

Bates, E., & Goodman, J. C. (2001). On the inseparability of grammar and the lexicon: Evidence from acquisition. In M. Tomasello & E. Bates (Eds.), *Language development: The essential readings* (pp. 134–162). Malden, MA: Blackwell.

Bates, E., O'Connell, B., & Shore, C. (1987). Language and communication in infancy. In J. Osofsky (Ed.), *Handbook of infant development* (2nd ed., pp. 149–203). New York: Wiley.

Bates, E., Reilly, J., Wulgeck, B., Dronkers, N., Opei, M., Fenson, J., et al. (2001). Differential effects of unilateral lesions on language production in children and adults. *Brain & Language, 79,* 223–265.

Bates, J. E. (1987). Temperament in infancy. In J. D. Osofsky (Ed.), *Handbook of infant development* (2nd ed., pp. 1101–1149). New York: Wiley.

Batson, C. D., Polycarpou, M. P., Harmon-Jones, E., Imhoff, H. J., Mitchener, E. C., Bednar, L. L., et al. (1997). Empathy and attitudes: Can feeling for a member of a stigmatized group improve feelings toward the group? *Journal of Personality and Social Psychology, 72,* 105–118.

Bauer, P. J. (1993). Memory for gender-consistent and gender-inconsistent event sequences by twenty-five-month-old children. *Child Development, 64,* 285–297.

Baulieu, E. (1989). Contragestion and other clinical applications of RU486, an anti-progesterone at the receptor. *Science, 245,* 1351–1357.

Baum, S. K. (1999). Who has no regrets? *Psychological Reports, 85,* 257–260.

Baumgardner, A. H. (1990). To know oneself is to like oneself: Self-certainty and self-affect. *Journal of Personality and Social Psychology, 58,* 1062–1072.

Baumrind, D. (1995). Commentary on sexual orientation: Research and social policy implications. *Developmental Psychology, 31,* 130–136.

Beale, R. L. (1997). Multiple familial-worker role strain and psychological well-being: Moderating effects of coping resources among Black American parents. In R. J. Taylor, J. S. Jackson, & L. M. Chatters (Eds.), *Family life in Black America* (pp. 132–145). Thousand Oaks, CA: Sage.

Beall, A. E., & Sternberg, R. J. (1995). The social construction of love. *Journal of Social and Personal Relationships, 12,* 417–438.

Beard, A. J., & Bakeman, R. (2000). Boyhood gender nonconformity: Reported parental behavior and the development of narcissistic issues. *Journal of Gay and Lesbian Psychotherapy, 8,* 1–97.

Beardsley, T. (1996). Vital data. *Scientific American, 274,* 100–105.

Bearman, P. S., & Brueckner, H. (2001). Promising the future: Virginity pledges and first intercourse. *American Journal of Sociology, 106,* 859–912.

Beaulieu, L. (1992, June 28). Teaching more than just sports. *Columbus Dispatch,* p. 6D.

Beck, J. C., & Schouten, R. (2000). Workplace violence and psychiatric practice. *Bulletin of the Menninger Clinic, 64,* 36–48.

Becker, G., Beyene, Y., Newsom, E., & Mayen, N. (2003). Creating continuity through mutual assistance: Intergenerational reciprocity in four ethnic groups. *Journals of Gerontology: Series B: Psychological Sciences and Social Sciences, 58B,* S151–S159.

Beere, C. A. (1990). *Gender roles: A handbook of tests and measures.* New York: Greenwood.

Begley, S. (1995, September 2). The baby myth. *Newsweek,* pp. 38–41.

Beit-Hallahmi, B. (1987). Critical periods in psychoanalytic theories of personality development. In M. H. Bornstein (Ed.), *Sensitive periods in development: Interdisciplinary perspectives* (pp. 211–221). Hillsdale, NJ: Erlbaum.

Belanger, N. D., & Desrochers, S. (2001). Can 6-month-old infants process causality in different types of causal events? *British Journal of Developmental Psychology, 19,* 11–21.

Bell, S. M., & Ainsworth, M. D. S. (1972). Infant crying and maternal responsiveness. *Child Development, 43,* 1171–1190.

Belsky, J. (1996). Parent, infant, and social-contextual antecedents of father–son attachment security. *Development Psychology, 32,* 905–913.

Belsky, J. (1997). *The adult experience.* St. Paul, MN: West.

Belsky, J., & Rovine, M. (1990). Patterns of marital change across the transition to parenthood. *Journal of Marriage and the Family, 52,* 5–20.

Belsky, J., Campbell, S. B., Cohn, J. F., & Moore, G. (1996). Instability of infant–parent attachment security. *Developmental Psychology, 32,* 921–924.

Belsky, J., Fish, M., & Isabella, R. (1991). Continuity and discontinuity in infant negative and positive emotionality: Family antecedents and attachment consequences. *Developmental Psychology, 27,* 421–431.

Bem, S. (1993). *The lenses of gender.* New Haven, CT: Yale University Press.

Bem, S. L. (1981). Gender schema theory: A cognitive account of sex-typing. *Psychological Review, 88,* 354–364.

Bem, S. L. (1989). Genital knowledge and gender constancy in preschool children. *Child Development, 60,* 649–662.

Benasich, A. A., & Leevers, H. J. (2003). Processing of rapidly presented auditory cues in infancy: Implications for later language development. In H. Hayne & J. W. Fagen (Eds.), *Progress in infancy research* (Vol. 3, pp. 245–288). Mahwah, NJ: Lawrence Erlbaum.

Benedict, R. (1934/1950). *Patterns of culture.* New York: New American Library.

Benenson, J. F. (1993). Greater preference among females than males for dyadic interaction in early childhood. *Child Development, 64,* 544–555.

Bengston, V. L. (2001). Beyond the nuclear family: The increasing importance of multigenerational bonds. *Journal of Marriage and the Family, 63,* 1–16.

Benjet, C., & Hernández-Guzmán, L. (2002). A short-term longitudinal study of pubertal change, gender, and psychological well-being of Mexican early adolescents. *Journal of Youth and Adolescence, 31,* 429–442.

Benson, J. B., & Uzgiris, I. C. (1985). Effect of self-initiated locomotion on infant search activity. *Developmental Psychology, 21,* 923–931.

Benson, M. J., Harris, P. B., & Rogers, C. S. (1992). Identity consequences of attachment to mothers and fathers among late adolescents. *Journal of Research on Adolescence, 2,* 187–204.

Benson, P. L. (1992). *The troubled journey: A profile of American youth.* Minneapolis: RespecTeen/Lutheran Brotherhood.

Berg, J. H., & Peplau, L. A. (1982). Loneliness: The relationship of self-disclosure and androgyny. *Personality and Social Psychology Bulletin, 8,* 624–630.

Berg, K., Hines, M., & Allen, S. (2002). Wheelchair users at home: Few home modifications and many injurious falls. *American Journal of Public Health, 92,* 48.

Bergeman, C. S., Plomin, R., Pedersen, N. L., McClearn, G. E., & Nesselroade, J. R.

(1990). Genetic and environmental influences on social support: The Swedish adoption/twin study of aging. *Journal of Gerontology, 45*, P101–P106.

Berk, L. E. (2004). *Infants, children, and adolescents* (5th ed.). Needham Heights, MA: Allyn & Bacon.

Berkowitz, L. (1973). Control of aggression. In B. M. Caldwell & H. N. Ricciuti (Eds.), *Review of child development research* (Vol. 3). Chicago: University of Chicago Press.

Berkowitz, L. (1984). Some effects of thoughts on anti- and prosocial influences of media events: A cognitive-neoassociation analysis. *Psychological Bulletin, 95*, 419–427.

Berkowitz, L. (1986). Situational influences on reactions to observed violence. *Journal of Social Issues, 42*, 93–103.

Berlin, L. J., & Cassidy, J. (1999). Relations among relationships: Contributions from attachment theory and research. In J. Cassidy & P. R. Shaver (Eds.), *Handbook of attachment: Theory, research, and clinical applications* (pp. 688–712). New York: Guilford Press.

Berman, W. H., & Sperling, M. B. (1991). Parental attachment and emotional distress in the transition to college. *Journal of Youth and Adolescence, 20*, 427–440.

Bernard, J. (1972). *The future of marriage*. New York: World.

Berndt, T. J., & Keefe, K. (1995). Friends' influence on adolescents' adjustment to school. *Child Development, 66*, 1312–1329.

Berndt, T. J., & Murphy, L. M. (2002). Influences of friends and friendships: Myths, truths, and research recommendations. In R. V. Kail (Ed.), *Advances in child development and behavior* (Vol. 30, pp. 275–310). San Diego: Academic Press.

Bernichon, T., Cook, K. E., & Brown, J. D. (2003). Seeking self-evaluative feedback: The interactive role of global self-esteem and specific self-views. *Journal of Personality and Social Psychology, 84*, 194–204.

Bernier, A., Larose, S., Boivin, M., & Soucy, N. (2004). Attachment state of mind: Implications for adjustment to college. *Journal of Adolescent Research, 19*, 783–806.

Berrueta-Clement, J. R., Schweinhart, L. J., Barnett, W. S., Epstein, A. S., & Weikart, D. P. (1984). *Changed lives: The effects of the Perry Preschool Program on youths through age 19*. Ypsilanti, MI: High/Scope Press.

Bertalanffy, L. von (1950). The theory of open systems in physics and biology. *Science, 111*, 23–28.

Bertalanffy, L. von (1968). *General systems theory* (rev. ed.). New York: Braziller.

Berzonsky, M. D. (1989). Identity style: Conceptualization and measurement. *Journal of Adolescent Research, 4*, 267–281.

Berzonsky, M. D. (1993). Identity style, gender, and social-cognitive reasoning. *Journal of Adolescent Research, 8*, 289–296.

Berzonsky, M. D. (2003). The structure of identity: Commentary on Jane Kroger's view of identity status transition. *Identity, 3*, 231–245.

Berzonsky, M. D., & Kuk, L. S. (2000). Identity status, identity processing style, and the transition to university. *Journal of Adolescent Research, 15*, 81–98.

Berzonsky, M. D., & Sullivan, C. (1992). Social-cognitive aspects of identity style: Need for cognition, experiential openness, and introspection. *Journal of Adolescent Research, 7*, 140–155.

Bess, A. (2001, August 26). Chocolatiers face slavery minefield in Africa. *Reuters*. Retrieved September 8, 2001, from http://biz.yahoo.com/rf/010826/ n26310591.html

Best, K. M., Hauser, S. T., & Allen, J. P. (1997). Predicting young adult competencies: Adolescent era parent and individual influences. *Journal of Adolescent Research, 12*, 90–112.

Betancourt, H., & Lopez, S. R. (1993). The study of culture, ethnicity, and race in American psychology. *American Psychologist, 48*, 629–637.

Bettencourt, B. A., & Hume, D. (1999). The cognitive contents of social-group identity: Values, emotions, and relationships. *European Journal of Social Psychology, 29*, 113–121.

Bianchi, S. M., Milkie, M. A., Sayer, L. C., & Robinson, J. P. (2000). Is anyone doing the housework? Trends in the gender division of household labor. *Social Forces, 79*, 2–39.

Biddle, B. J. (1979). *Role theory: Expectations, identities, and behaviors*. New York: Academic Press.

Biddle, B. J. (1986). Recent developments in role theory. In R. H. Turner & S. F. Short, Jr. (Eds.), *Annual Review of Sociology, 12*, 67–92.

Biddle, B. J., & Thomas, E. J. (1966). *Role theory: Concepts and research*. New York: Wiley.

Bigler, R. S., & Liben, L. S. (1992). Cognitive mechanisms in children's gender stereotyping: Theoretical and educational implications of a cognitive based intervention. *Child Development, 63*, 1351–1363.

Bigler, R. S., Spears Brown, C., & Markell, M. (2001). When groups are not created equal: Effects of group status on the formation of intergroup attitudes in children. *Child Development, 72*, 1151–1162.

Bijstra, J., Van Geert, P., & Jackson, S. (1989). Conservation and the appearance–reality distinction: What do children really know and what do they answer? *British Journal of Developmental Psychology, 7*, 43–53.

Bilsker, D., Schiedel, D., & Marcia, J. (1988). Sex differences in identity status. *Sex Roles, 18*, 231–236.

Biringen, Z., Emde, R. N., Campos, J. J., & Appelbaum, M. I. (1995). Affective reorganization in the infant, the mother, and the dyad: The role of upright locomotion and its timing. *Child Development, 66*, 499–514.

Birren, J. E., & Fisher, L. M. (1992). Aging and slowing of behavior: Consequences for cognition and survival. In T. B. Sonderegger (Ed.), *Psychology and aging* (pp. 1–37). Lincoln: University of Nebraska Press.

Birsch, K. J., Munz, D., Bemmerer-Mayer, K., Terinde, R., Kreienberg, R., & Kachele, H. (2003). Coping styles of pregnant women after prenatal ultrasound screening for fetal malformation. *Journal of Psychosomatic Research, 55*, 91–97.

Blackwell, D. L., & Lichter, D. T. (2000). Mate selection among married and cohabiting couples. *Journal of Family Issues, 21*, 275–302.

Blain, M. D., Thompson, J. M., & Whiffen, V. E. (1993). Attachment and perceived social support in late adolescence: The interaction between working models of self and others. *Journal of Adolescent Research, 8*, 226–241.

Blair, C. (2002). Integrating cognition and emotion in a neurobiological conceptualization of children's functioning at school entry. *American Psychologist, 57*, 111–127.

Blair-Loy, M. (2001). Cultural constructions of family schemas: The case of women finance executives. *Gender & Society, 15*, 687–709.

Blanchard, C., Perreault, S., & Vallerand, R. J. (1998). Participation in team sport: A self-expansion perspective. *International Journal of Sport Psychology, 29*, 289–302.

Blanchard, K. H. (1996). *Empowerment takes more than a minute*. San Francisco: Berrett-Koehler.

Blasi, A. (1984). Moral identity: Its role in moral functioning. In W. Kurtines & J. Gewirtz (Eds.), *Morality, moral behavior, and moral development* (pp. 128–139). New York: Wiley.

Blasi, A. (1991). The self as subject in the study of personality. In D. Ozer, J. Healy, & A. Stewart (Eds.), *Perspectives in personality* (Vol. 3, Part A, pp. 19–37). London: Kingsley.

Blass, E. M., & Ciaramitaro, V. (1994). A new look at some old mechanisms in human newborns: Taste and tactile determinants of state, affect, and action. *Monographs of the Society for Research in Child Development, 59* (Serial No. 1).

Blass, E. M., & Hoffmeyer, L. B. (1991). Sucrose as an analgesic for newborn infants. *Pediatrics, 87*, 215–218.

Bleeker, M. M., & Jacobs, J. E. (2004). Achievement in math and science: Do mothers' beliefs matter 12 years later? *Journal of Educational Psychology, 96*, 97–109.

Bloom, L. (1993, Winter). World learning. *Society for Research in Child Development Newsletter*, pp. 1, 9, 13.

Bloom, M. V. (1987). Leaving home: A family transition. In J. Bloom-Feshbach & S. Bloom-Feshbach (Eds.), *The psychology of separation and loss* (pp. 232–266). San Francisco: Jossey-Bass.

Blos, P. (1979). *The adolescent passage*. New York: International Universities Press.

Bluck, S., & Gluck, J. (2004). Making things better and learning a lesson: Experiencing wisdom across the lifespan. *Journal of Personality, 72*, 543–572.

Blum, R. W., Beuhring, T., Shew, M. L., Bearinger, L. H., Sieving, R. E., & Resnick, M. D. (2000). The effects of race/ethnicity, income, and family structure on adolescent risk behaviors. *American Journal of Public Health, 90,* 1879–1884.

Blyth, D. A., Bulcroft, R., & Simmons, R. G. (1981). *The impact of puberty on adolescents: A longitudinal study.* Paper presented at the annual convention of the American Psychological Association, Los Angeles, CA.

Boerner, K., Schulz, R., & Horowitz, A. (2004). Positive aspects of caregiving and adaptation to bereavement. *Psychology and Aging, 19,* 668–675.

Bohan, J. S. (1993). Regarding gender. *Psychology of Women Quarterly, 17,* 5–21.

Bohlin, G., Bengtsgard, K., & Andersson, K. (2000). Social inhibition and overfriendliness as related to socioemotional functioning in 7- and 8-year-old children. *Journal of Clinical Child Psychology, 29,* 414–423.

Bohlmeijer, E., Smit, F., & Cuijpers, P. (2003). Effects of reminiscence and life review on late-life depression: A meta-analysis. *International Journal of Geriatric Psychiatry, 18,* 1088–1094.

Bolton, F. G., Jr., & MacEachron, A. E. (1988). Adolescent male sexuality: A developmental perspective. *Journal of Adolescent Research, 3,* 259–273.

Bomar, J. A., & Sabatelli, R. M. (1996). Family system dynamics, gender, and psychosocial maturity in late adolescence. *Journal of Adolescent Research, 11,* 421–439.

Bombar, M. L., & Littig, L. W. (1996). Babytalk as a communication of intimate attachment: An initial study in adult romances and friendships. *Personal Relationships, 3,* 137–158.

Bonanno, G. A., Wortman, C. B., & Nesse, R. M. (2004). Prospective patterns of resilience and maladjustment during widowhood. *Psychology and Aging, 19,* 260–271.

Boom, J., Brugman, D., & van der Heijden, P. G. M. (2001). Hierarchical structure of moral stages assessed by a sorting task. *Child Development, 72,* 535–548.

Booth, A., Johnson, D. R., Granger, D. A., Crouter, A. C., & McHale, S. (2003). Testosterone and child and adolescent adjustment: The moderating role of parent–child relationships. *Developmental Psychology, 39,* 85–98.

Borden, W. (2000). The relational paradigm in contemporary psychoanalysis: Toward a psychodynamically informed social work perspective. *Social Service Review, 74,* 352–380.

Borke, H. (1973). The development of empathy in Chinese and American children between 3 and 6 years of age: A cross-cultural study. *Developmental Psychology, 9,* 102–108.

Borkenau, P., Riemann, R., Angleitner, A., & Spinath, F. M. (2001). Genetic and environmental influences on observed personality: Evidence from the German Observational Study of Adult Twins. *Journal of Personality and Social Psychology, 80,* 655–668.

Borman, K. M., & Hopkins, M. (1987). Leaving school for work. *Research in the Sociology of Education and Socialization, 7,* 131–159.

Bornstein, M. H. (1985). How infant and mother jointly contribute to developing cognitive competence in the child. *Proceedings of the National Academy of Science, USA, 82,* 7470–7473.

Bornstein, M. H. (1992). Perception across the life cycle. In M. H. Bornstein & M. E. Lamb (Eds.), *Developmental psychology: An advanced textbook* (3rd ed., pp. 155–209), Hillsdale, NJ: Erlbaum.

Bornstein, M. H. (1995). Parenting infants. In M. H. Bornstein (Ed.), *Handbook of parenting: Vol. I. Children and parenting* (pp. 3–41). Mahwah, NJ: Erlbaum.

Bornstein, M. H. (2001). Mother–infant interaction. In G. Bremner & A. Fogel (Eds.), *Blackwell handbook of infant development* (pp. 269–295). Malden, MA: Blackwell.

Bornstein, M. H. (Ed.). (2002a). *Handbook of parenting* (5 volumes). Mahwah, NJ: Erlbaum.

Bornstein, M. H. (2002b). Parenting infants. In M. H. Bornstein (Ed.), *Handbook of Parenting: Vol. 1. Children and parenting* (2nd ed., pp. 3–43). Mahwah, NJ: Erlbaum.

Bornstein, M. H., Kessen, W., & Weiskopf, S. (1976). The categories of hue in infancy. *Science, 191,* 201–202.

Bornstein, M. H., & Tamis-LeMonda, C. S. (2001). Mother-infant interaction. In G. Bremner & A. Fogel (Eds.), *Blackwell handbook of infant development* (pp. 269–295). Malden, MA: Blackwell Publishers.

Boss, P. (1999). *Ambiguous loss.* Cambridge, MA: Harvard University Press.

Boss, P. (2002a). Ambiguous loss: Working with the families of the missing. *Family Process, 41,* 14–17.

Boss, P. (2002b). *Family stress management: A contextual approach* (2nd ed.). Thousand Oaks, CA: Sage.

Boss, P. (2004). Ambiguous loss research, theory, and practice: Reflections after 9/11. *Journal of Marriage and the Family, 66,* 551–566.

Bosworth, H. B., & Schaie, K. W. (1997). The relationship of social environment, social networks, and health outcomes in the Seattle longitudinal study: Two analytical approaches. *Journal of Gerontology, 52,* P197–P205.

Bottge, B. A. (1999). Effects of contextualized math instruction on problem solving in average and below-average achieving students. *The Journal of Special Education, 33,* 81–92.

Bouchard, T. J., Jr., & Pederson, N. (1999). Twins reared apart: Nature's double experiment. In M. C. LaBuda & E. L. Grigorenko (Eds.), *On the way to individuality: Current methodological issues in behavioral genetics* (pp. 71–93). Huntington, NY: Nova Science.

Bouldin, P., & Pratt, C. (1999). Characteristics of preschool and school-age children with imaginary companions. *Journal of Genetic Psychology, 160,* 397–410.

Bound, J., Duncan, G. J., Laren, D. S., & Oleinick, L. (1991). Poverty dynamics in widowhood. *Journal of Gerontology, 46,* S115–S124.

Bowen, G. L., Desimone, L. M., & McKay, J. K. (1995). Poverty and the single mother family: A macroeconomic perspective. *Marriage and Family Review, 20,* 115–142.

Bowen, M. (1978). *Family therapy and clinical practice.* New York: Aronson.

Bower, T. G. R. (1987). *Development in infancy* (2nd ed.). New York: W. H. Freeman.

Bowlby, J. (1960). Separation anxiety. *International Journal of Psychoanalysis, 41,* 69–113.

Bowlby, J. (1969/1982). *Attachment and loss: Vol. 1. Attachment.* New York: Basic Books.

Bowlby, J. (1980). *Attachment and loss: Vol. 3. Loss, sadness, and depression.* New York: Basic Books.

Bowlby, J. (1988). *A secure base: Parent–child attachment and healthy human development.* New York: Basic Books.

Boyatzis, C. J., & Watson, M. W. (1993). Preschool children's symbolic representation of objects through gestures. *Child Development, 64,* 729–735.

Boykin, A. W. (1994). Harvesting talent and culture. In R. J. Rossi (Ed.), *Schools and students at risk: Context and framework for positive change* (pp. 116–138). New York: Teachers College Press.

Bradbury, R. (1957/1964). *Dandelion Wine.* New York: Bantam Books.

Bradford, J., Ryan, C., & Rothblum, E. D. (1994). National lesbian health survey: Implications for mental health care. *Journal of Consulting and Clinical Psychology, 62,* 228–242.

Bradley, C. B., McMurray, R. G., Harrell, J. S., & Deng, S. (2000). Changes in common activities of 3rd through 10th graders: The CHIC study. *Medicine and Science in Sports and Exercise, 32,* 2071–2078.

Bradley, R. H., Caldwell, B. M., & Rock, S. L. (1988). Home environment and school performance. A ten-year followup and examination of three models of environmental action. *Child Development, 59,* 852–867.

Bradley, R. H., Whiteside, L., Mundfrom, D. J., Casey, P. H., Kelleher, K. J., & Pope, S. K. (1994). Early indications of resilience and their relation to experiences in the home environments of low birthweight, premature children living in poverty. *Child Development, 65,* 346–360.

Bradmetz, J. (1999). Precursors of formal thought: A longitudinal study. *British Journal of Developmental Psychology, 17,* 61–81.

Bradshaw, Z., & Slade, P. (2003). The effects of induced abortion on emotional experiences and relationships: A critical review of the literature. *Clinical Psychology Review, 23,* 929–948.

Braine, M. D. S. (1976). *Children's first word combinations. Monographs of the Society for Research in Child Development, 41*(1).

Brainerd, C. J. (1977). Cognitive development and concept learning: An interpretive review. *Psychological Bulletin, 84,* 919–939.

Braithwaite, V. (2004). The hope process and social inclusion. In V. Braithwaite (Ed.), *Hope, power, and governance. The Annals of the American Academy of Political and Social Science* (pp. 128–151). Thousand Oaks, CA: Sage.

Bramlett, M. D., & Mosher, W. D. (2001). First marriage dissolution, divorce, and remarriage: United States. *Advance Data,* No. 323, National Center for Health Statistics.

Brandon, P. E. (2000). An analysis of kin-provided child care in the context of intra-family exchanges: Linking components of family support for parents raising young children. *The American Journal of Economics and Sociology, 59,* 191.

Brandtstadter, J. (2002). Searching for paths to successful development and aging: Integrating developmental and action-theoretical perspectives. In L. Pulkkinen & A. Caspi (Eds.), *Paths to successful development: Personality in the life course* (pp. 380–408). New York: Cambridge University Press.

Braungart, J. M., Plomin, R., Defries, J. C., & Fulker, D. W. (1992). Genetic influence on tester-rated infant temperament as assessed by Bayley's Infant Behavior Record: Nonadoptive and adoptive siblings and twins. *Developmental Psychology, 28(1),* 40–47.

Braungart-Rieker, J. M., Garwood, M. M., Powers, B. P., & Wang, X. (2001). Parental sensitivity, infant affect, and affect regulation: Predictors of later attachment. *Child Development, 72,* 252–270.

Brazelton, T. B. (1974). *Toddlers and parents: A declaration of independence.* New York: Delacorte Press.

Brazelton, T. B. (1987a). Behavioral competence of the newborn infant. In G. B. Avery (Ed.), *Neonatology: Pathophysiology and management of the newborn* (pp. 379–399). Philadelphia: Lippincott.

Brazelton, T. B. (1987b). *What every baby knows* (pp. 11–13). Reading, MA: Addison Wesley.

Brazelton, T. B., Koslowski, B., & Main, M. (1974). The origins of reciprocity: The early mother–infant interaction. In M. Lewis & L. A. Rosenblum (Eds.), *The effect of the infant on its caregiver* (pp. 49–76). New York: Wiley-Interscience.

Brazelton, T. B., Nugent, J. K., & Lester, B. M. (1987). Neonatal behavioral assessment scale. In J. D. Osofsky (Ed.), *Handbook of infant development* (2nd ed., pp. 780–817). New York: Wiley.

Brazy, J. E. (2001). *Extreme prematurity.* Retrieved November 11, 2001, from http://www2.medsch.wisc.edu/childrenshosp/parents_of_preemies/index.html

Breakwell, G. M. (1986). *Coping with threatened identities.* London: Methuen.

Breault, K. D., & Kposowa, A. J. (1987). Explaining divorce in the United States, 1980. *Journal of Marriage and the Family, 49,* 549–558.

Brennan, K. A., & Morris, K. A. (1997). Attachment styles, self-esteem, and patterns of seeking feedback from romantic partners. *Personality and Social Psychology Bulletin, 23,* 23–31.

Brennan, K. A., & Shaver, P. R. (1995). Dimensions of adult attachment, affect regulation, and romantic relationship functioning. *Personality and Social Psychology Bulletin, 21,* 267–283.

Brennan, R. T., Barnett, R. C., & Gareis, K. C. (2001). When she earns more than he does: A longitudinal study of dual-earner couples. *Journal of Marriage and the Family, 63,* 168–182.

Bretherton, I. (1985). Attachment theory: Retrospect and prospect. In I. Bretherton & E. Everett (Eds.), *Growing points of attachment theory and research* (pp. 3–35). *Monographs of the Society for Research in Child Development, 50* (1–2, Serial No. 209).

Bretherton, I. (1990). Open communication and internal working models: Their role in the development of attachment relationships. In R. Dienstbier & R. A. Thompson (Eds.), *Nebraska Symposium on Motivation 1988: Vol. 36. Socioemotional Development* (pp. 57–113). Lincoln: University of Nebraska Press.

Bretherton, I., & Munholland, K. A. (1999). Internal working models in attachment relationships. In J. Cassidy & P. R. Shaver (Eds.), *Handbook of attachment: Theory, research, and clinical applications* (pp. 89–111). New York: Guilford Press.

Bretschneider, J. G., & McCoy, N. L. (1988). Sexual interest and behavior in healthy 80- to 102-year-olds. *Archives of Sexual Behavior, 17,* 109–129.

Brewster, A. L., Nelson, J. P., McCanne, T. R., Lucas, D. R., & Milner, J. S. (1998). Gender differences in physiological reactivity to infant cries and smiles in military families. *Child Abuse and Neglect, 22,* 775–788.

Bridges, L. J., Connell, J. P., & Belsky, J. (1988). Similarities and differences in infant–mother and infant–father interaction in the strange situation: A component process analysis. *Developmental Psychology, 24,* 92–100.

Brierley, J. (1993). *Growth in children.* London: Cassell.

Brim, G. (1992). *Ambition: How we manage success and failure throughout our lives.* New York: Basic Books.

Brim, O. G., Jr. (1966). Socialization through the life cycle. In O. G. Brim & S. Wheeler (Eds.), *Socialization after childhood: Two essays.* New York: Wiley.

Brim, O. G., Jr. (1968). Adult socialization. In J. Clausen (Ed.), *Socialization and society.* Boston: Little, Brown.

Brockner, J. (1984). Low self-esteem and behavioral plasticity. In L. Wheeler (Ed.), *Review of personality and social psychology* (Vol. 4, pp. 237–271). Beverly Hills, CA: Sage.

Broderick, C. B. (1993). *Understanding family process: Basics of family systems theory.* Newbury Park, CA: Sage.

Bronfenbrenner, U. (1979). *The ecology of human development.* Cambridge, MA: Harvard University Press.

Bronfenbrenner, U. (1995). Developmental ecology through space and time: A future perspective. In P. Moen, G. H. Elder, et al. (Eds.), *Examining lives in context: Perspectives on the ecology of human development* (pp. 619–647). Washington, DC: American Psychological Association.

Bronfenbrenner, U. (2004). *Making human beings human: Bioecological perspectives on human development.* Thousand Oaks, CA: Sage.

Bronson, G. (1979, February 9). Issue of fetal damage stirs women workers at chemical plants. *Wall Street Journal.*

Bronson, G. W. (1973). Infants' reactions to an unfamiliar person. In L. J. Stone, H. T. Smith, & L. B. Murphy (Eds.), *The competent infant.* New York: Basic Books.

Bronstein, P., Duncan, P., Clauson, J., Abrams, C., Yannett, N., Ginsburg, G., & Milne, M. (1998). Preventing middle school adjustment problems for children from lower-income families: A program for aware parenting. *Journal of Applied Developmental Psychology, 19,* 129–152.

Brookes, H., Slater, A., Quinn, P. C., Lewkowicz, D. J., Hayes, R., & Brown, E. (2001). Three-month-old infants learn arbitrary auditory-visual pairings between voices and faces. *Infant and Child Development, 10,* 75–82.

Brooks-Gunn, J., & Reiter, E. O. (1990). The role of pubertal processes. In S. S. Feldman & G. R. Elliott (Eds.), *At the threshold: The developing adolescent* (pp. 16–53). Cambridge, MA: Harvard University Press.

Brooks-Gunn, J., & Warren, M. P. (1988). The psychological significance of secondary sexual characteristics in 9- to 11- year-old girls. *Child Development, 59,* 161–169.

Brown, B. B. (1990). Peer groups and peer cultures. In S. S. Feldman & G. R. Elliott (Eds.), *At the threshold: The developing adolescent* (pp. 171–196). Cambridge, MA: Harvard University Press.

Brown, B. B. (2004). Adolescents' relationships with peers. In R. M. Lerner & L. Steinberg (Eds.), *Handbook of adolescent psychology* (2nd ed., pp. 363–394). New York: Wiley.

Brown, B. B., Mounts, N., Lamborn, S. D., & Steinberg, L. (1993). Parenting practices and peer group affiliation in adolescence. *Child Development, 64,* 467–482.

Brown, D. W., Balluz, L. S., Heath, G. W., Moriarty, D. G., Ford, E. S., Giles, W. H., & Mokdad, A. H. (2003). Associations between recommended levels of physical activity and health-related quality of life: Findings from the 2001 Behavioral Risk Factor Surveillance System (BRFSS) survey. *Preventive Medicine: An International Journal Devoted to Practice & Theory, 37,* 520–528.

Brown, I., Jr., & Inouye, D. K. (1978). Learned helplessness through modeling: The role of perceived similarity in competence. *Journal of Personality and Social Psychology, 36,* 900–908.

Brown, J., Cohen, P., Chen, H., Smailes, E., & Johnson, J. G. (2004). Sexual trajectories of abused and neglected youths. *Journal of Developmental and Behavioral Pediatrics, 25,* 77–82.

Brown, J. D. (2003). The self-enhancement motive in collectivistic cultures: The rumors of my death have been greatly exaggerated. *Journal of Cross-Cultural Psychology, 34,* 603–605.

Brown, J. D., Dutton, K. A., & Cook, K. E. (2001). From the top down: Self-esteem and self-evaluation. *Cognition and Emotion, 15,* 615–631.

Brown, J. D., & Gallagher, F. M. (1992). Coming to terms with failure: Private self-enhancement and public self-effacement. *Journal of Experimental Social Psychology, 28,* 3–22.

Brown, J. D., & Mankowski, T. A. (1993). Self-esteem, mood, and self-evaluation: Changes in mood and the way you see you. *Journal of Personality and Social Psychology, 64,* 421–430.

Brown, J. D., & Smart, S. A. (1991). The self and social conduct: Linking self-representation to prosocial behavior. *Journal of Personality and Social Psychology, 60,* 368–375.

Brown, J. L., & Pollitt, E. (1996). Malnutrition, poverty, and intellectual development. *Scientific American, 274,* 38–43.

Brown, J. R., & Dunn, J. (1992). Talk with your mother or your sibling? Developmental changes in early family conversations about feelings. *Child Development, 63,* 336–349.

Brown, J. V., Bakeman, R., Coles, C. D., Platzman, K. A., & Lynch, M. E. (2004). Prenatal cocaine exposure: A comparison of 2-year-old children in parental and non-parental care. *Child Development, 75,* 1282–1295.

Brown, R. (1965). *Social psychology.* New York: Free Press.

Brown, S. L., & Booth, A. (1996). Cohabitation versus marriage: A comparison of relationship quality. *Journal of Marriage and the Family, 58,* 668–678.

Brown University. (2004). The female athlete triad. *Health Education.* Retrieved November 28, 2004, from http://www.brown .edu/Student_Services/Health_Services/ Health_Education/nutrition/ec_fatriad .htm

Browning, C. R., & Cagney, K. A. (2003). Moving beyond poverty: Neighborhood structure, social processes, and health. *Journal of Health and Social Behavior, 44,* 552–571.

Brownlee, S. (1998, June 15). Baby talk. *U.S. News and World Report,* 48–55.

Brownlee, S. (1999). Inside the teen brain. *U.S. News and World Report, 127,* 44–54.

Brubaker, T. H. (1990). Families in later life: A burgeoning research area. *Journal of Marriage and the Family, 52,* 959–981.

Bruner, J. (2001). Human infancy and the beginnings of human competence. In J. A. Bargh & D. K Apsley (Eds.), *Unraveling the complexities of social life: A festschrift in honor of Robert B. Zajonc* (pp. 133–139). Washington, DC: American Psychological Association.

Brustad, R. J. (1988). Affective outcomes in competitive youth sport: The influence of intrapersonal and socialization factors. *Journal of Sport and Exercise Psychology, 10,* 307–321.

Bryant, J., Carveth, R. A., & Brown, D. (1981). Television viewing and anxiety: An experimental examination. *Journal of Communication, 31,* 106–119.

Bryer, K. B. (1979). The Amish way of death: A study of family support systems. *American Psychologist, 34,* 255–261.

Buckwalter, J. G., Stanczyk, F. A., McCleary, C. A., Bluestein, B. W., Buckwalter, D. K., Rankin, K. P., et al. (1999). Pregnancy, the postpartum, and steroid hormones: Effects on cognition and mood. *Psychoneuroendocrinology, 24,* 69–84.

Buescher, P. A., Roth, M. S., Williams, D., & Goforth, C. M. (1991). An evaluation of the impact of maternity care coordination on Medicaid birth outcomes in North Carolina. *American Journal of Public Health, 81,* 1625–1629.

Buhler, C., & Massarik, F. (1968). *The course of human life: A study of goals in the humanistic perspective.* New York: Springer Verlag.

Bui, K.-V. T., Peplau, L. A., & Hill, C. T. (1996). Testing the Rusbult model of relationship commitment and stability in a 15-year study of heterosexual couples. *Personality and Social Psychology Bulletin, 22,* 1244–1257.

Bukowski, W. M. (2001). Friendship and the worlds of childhood. In D. W. Nangle & C. A. Erdley (Eds.), *The role of friendship in psychological adjustment* (pp. 93–105). San Francisco: Jossey-Bass.

Bukowski, W. M., Gauze, C., Hoza, B., & Newcomb, A. F. (1993). Differences and consistency between same-sex and other-sex peer relationships during early adolescence. *Developmental Psychology, 29,* 255–263.

Bullock, H. E., & Morales Waugh, I. (2004). Caregiving around the clock: How women in nursing manage career and family demands. *Journal of Social Issues, 60,* 767–786.

Bullock, M., & Lutkenhaus, P. (1988). The development of volitional behavior in the toddler years. *Child Development, 59,* 664–674.

Bullough, V. L. (1981). Age at menarche: A misunderstanding. *Science, 213,* 365–366.

Bunting, L., & McAuley, C. (2004). Teenage pregnancy and motherhood: The contribution of support. *Child & Family Social Work, 9,* 201–215.

Burchinal, M. R., Roberts, J. E., Riggins, R., Jr., Zeisel, S. A., Neebe, E., & Bryant, D. (2000). Relating quality of center-based child care to early cognitive and language development longitudinally. *Child Development, 71,* 338–357.

Burgess, E. W., & Bogue, D. J. (1967). The delinquency research of Clifford R. Shaw and Henry D. McKay and associates. In E. W. Burgess & D. J. Bogue (Eds.), *Urban Sociology* (pp. 293–317). Chicago: University of Chicago Press.

Burke, B. (1987). The role of playfulness in developing thinking skills: A review with implementation strategies. In S. Moore & K. Kolb (Eds.), *Reviews of research for practitioners and parents* (No. 3, pp. 3–8). Minneapolis: Center for Early Education and Development.

Burleson, B. R., Kunkel, A. W., Samter, W., & Werking, K. J. (1996). Men's and women's evaluations of communication skills in personal relationships: When sex differences make a difference—and when they don't. *Journal of Social and Personal Relationships, 13,* 201–224.

Burnett, D. (1999). Social relationships of Latino grandparent caregivers: A role theory perspective. *The Gerontologist, 39,* 49–58.

Burr, J. A., & Mutchler, J. E. (1993). Nativity, acculturation, and economic statues: Explanation of Asian American living arrangements in later life. *Journal of Gerontology, 48,* S55–S63.

Burr, W. R., & Christensen, C. (1992). Undesirable side effects of enhancing self-esteem. *Family Relations, 41,* 480–484.

Burt, R. D., Vaughan, T. L., & Daling, J. R. (1988). Evaluating the risks of cesarean section: Low Apgar score in repeat C-section and vaginal deliveries. *American Journal of Public Health, 78,* 1312–1314.

Burton, S., & Mitchell, P. (2003). Judging who knows best about yourself: Developmental change in citing the self across middle childhood. *Child Development, 74,* 426–443.

Bus, A. G., van IJzendoorn, M. H., & Pellegrini, A. D. (1995). Joint book reading makes for success in learning to read: A meta-analysis on intergenerational transmission of literacy. *Review of Educational Research, 65,* 1–21.

Bushnell, E. W., & Boudreau, J. P. (1991). The development of haptic perception during infancy. In M. A. Heller & W. Schiff (Eds.), *The psychology of touch* (pp. 139–161). Hillsdale, NJ: Erlbaum.

Buss, A. H., & Plomin, R. (1984). *Temperament: Early developing personality traits.* Hillsdale, NJ: Erlbaum.

Buss, A. H., & Plomin, R. (1986). The EAS approach to temperament. In R. Plomin & J. Dunn (Eds.), *The study of temperament: Changes, continuities, and challenges.* Hillsdale, NJ: Erlbaum.

Buss, D. (1994). *The evolution of desire: Strategies of human mating.* New York: Basic Books.

Buss, D. M., Haselton, M. G., Shackelford, T. K., Bleske, A. L., & Wakefield, J. C. (1998). Adaptations, exaptations, and spandrels. *American Psychologist, 53,* 533–548.

Buss, F. L. (1985). *Dignity: Lower income women tell of their lives and struggles* (pp. 153–154). Ann Arbor: University of Michigan Press.

Butler, R. (1989). Mastery versus ability appraisal: A developmental study of children's observations of peers' work. *Child Development, 60,* 1350–1361.

Butler, R. (1990). The effects of mastery and competitive conditions on self-assessment at different ages. *Child Development, 61,* 201–210.

Butler, R., & Ruzany, N. (1993). Age and socialization effects on the development of social comparison motives and normative ability assessment in kibbutz and urban children. *Child Development, 64,* 532–543.

Butterfield, E. C., Nelson, T. O., & Peck, V. (1988). Developmental aspects of the feeling of knowing. *Developmental Psychology, 24,* 654–663.

Butterfield, N. (1994). Play as an assessment and intervention strategy for children with language and intellectual disabilities. In

K. Linfoot (Ed.), *Communication strategies for people with developmental disabilities: Issues from theory and practice* (pp. 12–44). Baltimore: Brookes.

Buunk, B. P., Kijkstra, P., Kenrick, D. T., & Warntjes, A. (2001). Age preferences for mates as related to gender, own age, and involvement level. *Evolution and Human Behavior, 22,* 241–250.

Buunk, B. P., Zurriaga, R., Peiro, J. M., Nauta, A., & Gosalvez, I. (2005). Social comparisons at work as related to cooperative social climate and to individual differences in social comparison orientation. *Applied Psychology: An International Review, 54,* 61–80.

Buysse, A. (1996). Adolescents, young adults, and AIDS: A study of actual knowledge vs. perceived need for additional information. *Journal of Youth and Adolescence, 25,* 259–271.

Cain, K. M., & Dweck, C. S. (1995). The relation between motivational patterns and achievement cognitions through the elementary school years. *Merrill-Palmer Quarterly, 41,* 25–52.

Cain, P. S., & Treiman, D. J. (1981). The DOT as a source of occupational data. *American Sociological Review, 46,* 253–278.

Caldas, S. J. (1993). Current theoretical perspectives on adolescent pregnancy and childbearing in the United States. *Journal of Adolescent Research, 8,* 4–20.

Caldera, Y. M., Huston, A. C., & O'Brien, M. (1989). Social interactions and play patterns of parents and toddlers with feminine, masculine, and neutral toys. *Child Development, 60,* 70–76.

Calkins, S. D. (2004). Early attachment processes and the development of emotional self-regulation. In R. F. Baumeister & K. D. Vohs (Eds.), *Handbook of self-regulation: Research, theory, and application* (pp. 324–339). New York: Guilford Press.

Calkins, S. D., & Fox, N. A. (1992). The relations among infant temperament, security of attachment, and behavioral inhibition at twenty-four months. *Child Development, 63,* 1456–1472.

Calkins, S. D., & Howse, R. B. (2004). Individual differences in self-regulation: Implications for childhood adjustment. In P. Philippot & R. S. Feldman (Eds.), *The regulation of emotion* (pp. 307–332). Mahwah, NJ: Erlbaum.

Calvert, G., Spence, C., & Stein, B. E. (2004). *The handbook of multisensory processes.* Cambridge, MA: MIT Press.

Campbell, J. (1990). Self-esteem and clarity of the self-concept. *Journal of Personality and Social Psychology, 59,* 538–549.

Campos, J. J., Campos, R. G., & Barrett, K. C. (1989). Emergent themes in the study of emotional development and emotion regulation. *Developmental Psychology, 25,* 394–402.

Campos, R. G. (1989). Soothing pain-elicited distress in infants with swaddling and pacifiers. *Child Development, 60,* 781–792.

Camras, L. A., Malatesta, C., & Izard, C. E. (1991). The development of facial expression in infancy. In R. Feldman & B. Rime (Eds.), *Fundamentals of nonverbal behavior*

(pp. 73–105). New York: Cambridge University Press.

Canfield, R. L., & Haith, M. M. (1991). Young infants' visual expectations for symmetric and asymmetric stimulus sequences. *Developmental Psychology, 27,* 198–208.

Canobi, K. H. (2004). Individual differences in children's addition and subtraction knowledge. *Cognitive Development, 19,* 81–93.

Canobi, K. H., Reeve, R. A., & Pattison, P. E. (2003). Patterns of knowledge in children's addition. *Developmental Psychology, 39,* 521–534.

Capaldi, D. M. (1996). The reliability of retrospective report for timing first intercourse for adolescent males. *Journal of Adolescent Research, 11,* 375–387.

Caplan, G. (1964). *Principles of preventive psychiatry.* New York: Basic Books.

Cappeliez, P., & O'Rourke, N. (2002). Profiles of reminiscence among older adults: Perceived stress, life attitudes, and personality variables. *International Journal of Aging and Human Development, 54,* 255–266.

Carlo, G., Knight, G. P., Eisenberg, N., & Rotenberg, K. J. (1991). Cognitive processes and prosocial behaviors among children: The role of affective attributions and reconciliations. *Developmental Psychology, 27,* 456–461.

Carlson, V., Cicchetti, D., Barnett, D., & Braunwold, K. (1989). Finding order in disorganization. Lessons from research on maltreated infants' attachment to their caregivers. In D. Cicchetti & V. Carlson (Eds.), *Child maltreatment: Theory and research on the causes and consequences of maltreatment* (pp. 494–528). New York: Cambridge University Press.

Carnagey, N. L., & Anderson, C. A. (2004). Violent video game exposure and aggression: A literature review. *Minerva Psichiatrica, 45,* 1–18.

Caro, F. G., & Bass, S. A. (1997). Receptivity to volunteering in the immediate post-retirement period. *Journal of Applied Gerontology, 16,* 427–441.

Caron, A. J., Caron, R. F., & MacLean, D. J. (1988). Infant discrimination of naturalistic emotional expressions: The role of face and voice. *Child Development, 59,* 604–616.

Carp, F. M. (1997). Retirement and women. In J. M. Coyle (Ed.), *Handbook of women and aging* (pp. 112–128). Westport, CT: Greenwood Press.

Carpendale, J. I. M., & Krebs, D. L. (1992). Situational variation in moral judgment: In a stage or on a stage? *Journal of Youth and Adolescence, 21,* 203–224.

Carper, J. (1995). *Stop aging now: the ultimate plan for staying young and reversing the aging process.* New York: HarperCollins.

Carr, D. (2003). A "good death" for whom? Quality of spouse's death and psychological distress among older widowed persons. *Journal of Health and Social Behavior, 44,* 215–232.

Carr, D. (2004). The desire to date and remarry among older widows and widowers. *Journal of Marriage and the Family, 66,* 1051–1068.

Carr, D., House, J. S., Wortman, C., Neese, R., & Kessler, R. C. (2001). Psychological adjustment to sudden and anticipated spousal loss among older widowed persons. *Journal of Gerontology, 56B,* S237–S248.

Carroll, J. L., & Rest, J. R. (1982). Moral development. In B. B. Wolman (Ed.), *Handbook of developmental psychology* (pp. 434–451). Englewood Cliffs, NJ: Prentice Hall.

Casper, L. M., & Bianchi, S. M. (2002). *Continuity and change in the American family.* Thousand Oaks, CA: Sage.

Caspi, A., & Moffitt, T. E. (1991). Individual differences are accentuated during periods of social change: The sample case of girls at puberty. *Journal of Personality and Social Psychology, 61,* 157–168.

Caspi, A., Wright, B. R. E., Moffitt, T. E., & Silva, P. A. (1998). Early failure in the labor market: Childhood and adolescent predictors of unemployment in the transition to adulthood. *American Sociological Review, 63,* 424–451.

Cassady, G., & Strange, M. (1987). The small-for-gestational-age (SGA) infant. In G. B. Avery (Ed.), *Neonatology: Pathophysiology and management of the newborn* (pp. 299–331). Philadelphia: Lippincott.

Cassia, V. M., Turati, C., & Simion, F. (2004). Can a nonspecific bias toward top-heavy patterns explain newborns' face preference? *Psychological Science, 15,* 379–383.

Cassidy, J. (1999). The nature of the child's ties. In J. Cassidy & P. R. Shaver (Eds.), *Handbook of attachment: Theory, research, and clinical applications* (pp. 3–20). New York: Guilford Press.

Cassidy, J., & Asher, S. R. (1992). Loneliness and peer relations in young children. *Child Development, 63,* 350–365.

Castleman, M. (2001). Depression. *SeniorNet's Healthy Aging Enrichment Center.* Retrieved January 29, 2002, from http://www.seniornet.org

Catalan, J., Sherr, L., & Hedge, B. (1997) *The impact of AIDS: Psychological and social aspects of HIV infection.* Amsterdam, The Netherlands: Harwood.

Catherwood, D., Freiberg, K., Green, V., & Holt, C. (2001). Intra-hemispheric dynamics in infant encoding of coloured facial patterns *Infant and Child Development, 10,* 47–57.

Ceballo, R., & McLoyd, V. C. (2002). Social support and parenting in poor, dangerous neighborhoods. *Child Development, 73,* 1320–1321.

Centers for Disease Control and Prevention. (2000). Adolescent health: Risk behaviors. *Health, United States, 2000.* Retrieved December 4, 2004, from http://www.cdc.gov/nchs/data/hus/hus00cht.pdf

Centers for Disease Control and Prevention. (2003). *2001 Assisted reproductive technology success rates: National summary and fertility clinic reports.* Washington, DC: U.S. Department of Health and Human Services.

Centers for Disease Control and Prevention. (2004). *Sexually transmitted disease surveillance, 2003.* Atlanta, GA: U.S. Department of Health and Human Services.

Central Intelligence Agency. (2004). Afghanistan. *The World Fact Book*. Retrieved November 18, 2004, from http://www.cia .gov/cia/publications/factbook/geos/ af.html#People

CEO Forum on Education and Technology. (2001). *The CEO Forum: School technology and readiness report. Key building blocks for student achievement in the 21st century*. Retrieved September 30, 2001, from http:// www.ceoforum.org/downloads/report4 .pdf

Cerella, J. (1990). Aging and information processing rate. In J. E. Birren & K. W. Schaie (Eds.), *Handbook of cognitive aging* (3rd ed., pp. 201–221). New York: Academic Press.

Cerella, J. (1994). Generalized slowing in Brinley plots. *Journal of Gerontology, 49*, P65–P71.

Cernoch, J. M., & Porter, R. H. (1985). Recognition of maternal axillary odors by infants. *Child Development, 56*, 1593–1598.

Cesarone, B. (1994). *Video games and children*. ERIC Digest EDO-PS-94-3. Retrieved August 18, 2001, from http://www .kidsource.com/kidsource/content2/video .games.html

Chalmers, J. B., & Townsend, M. A. R. (1990). The effects of training in social perspective taking on socially maladjusted girls. *Child Development, 61*, 178–190.

Chandler, M., & Boyes, M. (1982). Social cognitive development. In B. B. Wolman (Ed.), *Handbook of developmental psychology* (pp. 387–402). Englewood Cliffs, NJ: Prentice Hall.

Chang, E. C., & Sanna, L. J. (2001). Optimism, pessimism, and positive and negative affectivity in middle-aged adults: A test of a cognitive-affective model of psychological adjustment. *Psychology and Aging, 16*, 524–531.

Chang, J. (1991). *Wild swans: Three daughters of China*. New York: Random House.

Chapman, M. (1988). *Constructive evolution: Origin and development of Piaget's thought*. New York: Cambridge University Press.

Chapman, M., & McBride, M. L. (1992). Beyond competence and performance. Children's class inclusion strategies, superordinate class cues, and verbal justifications. *Developmental Psychology, 28*, 319–327.

Charlesworth, W. R. (1992). Darwin and developmental psychology: Past and present. *Developmental Psychology, 28*, 5–16.

Chase-Lansdale, P. L. (1993). The impact of poverty on family process. *Child, Youth, and Family Services Quarterly, 16*, 5–8.

Chavez, A., Martinez, C., & Soberanes, B. (1995). Effects of early malnutrition on late mental and behavioral performance. *Developmental Brain Dysfunction, 8*, 90–102.

Chazan, S. E. (1981). Development of object permanence as a correlate of dimensions of maternal care. *Developmental Psychology, 17*, 79–81.

Chen, D. W. (2005, February 24). As 9/11 remains go unnamed, families grieve anew. *New York Times*. Retrieved March 11, 2005, http://query.nytimes.com

Cheour-Luhtanen, M., Alho, K., Sainio, K., Rinne, T., & Reinikainen, K. (1996). The ontogenetically earliest discriminative response of the human brain. *Psychophysiology, 33*, 478–481.

Chevan, A. (1995). Holding on and letting go: Residential mobility during widowhood. *Research on Aging, 17*, 278–302.

Chickering, A. W., & Reisser, L. (1993). *Education and identity* (2nd ed.). San Francisco: Jossey-Bass.

Children's Defense Fund. (2003). *Key facts about America's children*. Retrieved September 15, 2004, from http://www .childrensdefense.org/data/default.aspx

Chilman, C. S. (1993). Hispanic families in the United States: Research perspective. In H. P. McAdoo (Ed.), *Family ethnicity: Strength in diversity* (pp. 141–163). Newbury Park, CA: Sage.

Choi, N. G. (1991). Racial differences in the determinants of living arrangements of widowed and divorced elderly women. *The Gerontologist, 4*, 496–504.

Christiansen, S. L., & Palkovitz, R. (1998). Exploring Erikson's psychosocial theory of development: Generativity and its relationship to paternal identity, intimacy, and involvement in childcare. *Journal of Men's Studies, 7*, 133–156.

Church, G. J. (1993, November 22). Jobs in an age of insecurity. *Time*, pp. 32–39.

Church, J. (1964). *Three babies: Biographies of cognitive development*. New York: Random House.

Church, J. (1966). *Three babies: Biographies of cognitive development*. New York: Random House.

Cicatelli Associates. (2004). *Best practices in adolescent pregnancy prevention*. Retrieved December 5, 2004, from http://www .cicatelli.org/BPAPP/default.htm

Cicchetti, D., & Schneider-Rosen, K. (1984). Theoretical and empirical considerations in the investigation of the relationship between affect and cognition in atypical populations of infants. In C. E. Izard, J. Kagan, & R. B. Zajonc (Eds.), *Emotions, cognition, and behavior* (pp. 366–408). Cambridge, UK: Cambridge University Press.

Cicirelli, V. G. (1999). Personality and demographic factors in older adults' fear of death. *The Gerontologist, 39*, 569–579.

Cicirelli, V. G. (2001). Personal meanings of death in older adults and young adults in relation to their fears of death. *Death Studies, 25*, 663–683.

Cincinnati Children's Hospital Medical Center. (1998). *Wellness: Infant safety tips*. Retrieved July 8, 2004, from http://www .cincinnatichildrens.org/health/info/ newborn/well/infant-tips.htm

Cincinnati Children's Hospital Medical Center. (2004). *Installing and using child safety seats and booster seats*. Retrieved July 8, 2004, from http://www.cincinnatichildrens.org/ health/info/safety/vehicle/harness.htm

Cinq-Mars, C., Wright, J., Cyr, M., & McDuff, P. (2003). Sexual at-risk behaviors of sexually abused adolescent girls. *Journal of Child Sexual Abuse, 12*, 2–18.

Clancy, S. M., & Dollinger, S. J. (1993). Identity, self, and personality: 1. Identity status and the five-factor model of personality. *Journal of Research on Adolescence, 3*, 227–246.

Clark, A. L., & Howland, R. I. (1978). The American Samoan. In A. L. Clark (Ed.), *Culture, childbearing, and the health professionals*, (pp. 154–172). Philadelphia: Davis.

Clark, B. (1962). *Educating the expert society*. Novato, CA: Chandler and Sharp.

Clark, J. E., & Phillips, S. J. (1993). A longitudinal study of intralimb coordination in the first year of independent walking: A dynamical systems analysis. *Child Development, 64*, 1143–1157.

Clark, J. E., Phillips, S. J., & Petersen, R. (1989). Developmental stability in jumping. *Developmental Psychology, 25*, 929–935.

Clark, K. E., & Clark, M. B. (1994). *Choosing to lead*. Charlotte, NC: Leadership Press.

Clark, M. L. (1991). Social identity, peer relations, and academic competence of African-American adolescents. *Education and Urban Society, 24*, 41–52.

Clark, M. L., & Ayers, M. (1988). The role of reciprocity and proximity in junior high school friendships. *Journal of Youth and Adolescence, 17*, 403–411.

Clarke, S. C. (1995, July 14). *Advance report of final marriage statistics, 1989 and 1990*. (Monthly Vital Statistics Report, Vol. 43, No. 12, Supplement Table 6). Hyattsville, MD: National Center for Health Statistics.

Clark, S. D., Long, M. M., & Schiffman, L. G. (1999). The mind–body connection: The relationship among physical activity level, life satisfaction, and cognitive age among mature females. *Journal of Social Behavior and Personality, 14*, 221–240.

Clarke-Stewart, K. A. (1989). Infant day care: Maligned or malignant? *American Psychologist, 44*, 266–273.

Clarke-Stewart, K. A., & Fein, G. G. (1983). Early childhood programs. In P. H. Mussen (Ed.), *Handbook of child psychology: Vol. 2. Infancy and developmental psychobiology* (pp. 917–1000). New York: Wiley.

Clark-Ibanez, M., & Felmlee, D. (2004). Interethnic relationship: The role of social network diversity. *Journal of Marriage and the Family, 66*, 293–305.

Clasen, D. R., & Brown, B. B. (1985). The multidimensionality of peer pressure in adolescence. *Journal of Youth and Adolescence, 14*, 451–468.

Clausen, J. A. (1975). The social meaning of differential physical and sexual maturation. In S. E. Dragastin & G. H. Elder (Eds.), *Adolescence in the life cycle: Psychological change and social context*. Washington, DC: Hemisphere.

Clayman, C. B. (1989). *The American Medical Association encyclopedia of medicine*. New York: Random House.

Clayton, V. P., & Birren, J. E. (1980). The development of wisdom across the life span: A reexamination of an ancient topic. In P. B. Baltes & O. G. Brim Jr. (Eds.), *Lifespan development and behavior* (Vol. 3, pp. 104–135). New York: Academic Press.

Clifton, R., Perris, E., & Bullinger, A. (1991). Infants' perception of auditory space. *Developmental Psychology, 27,* 187–197.

Cloud, J. (2000, September 18). A kinder, gentler death. *Time,* pp. 60–67.

Cloud, J. (2001). Should SATs matter? *Time, 157,* 62–76.

CNN.com (2005, February 10). Centenarians reveal longevity secrets. *World.* Retrieved February 21, 2005, from http://www.cnn.com/2005/WORLD/americas/02/09/cuban.centenarians.ap/

Coats, P. B., & Overman, S. J. (1992). Childhood play experiences of women in traditional and nontraditional professions. *Sex Roles, 26,* 261–271.

Cobb, S. (1979). Social support and health through the life course. In M. W. Riley (Ed.), *Aging from birth to death.* Boulder, CO: Westview.

Cochran, C. C., Frazier, P. A., & Olson, A. W. (1997). Predictors of responses to unwanted sexual attention. *Psychology of Women Quarterly, 21,* 207–226.

Cody, H., & Kamphaus, R. W. (1999). Down syndrome. In S. Goldstein & C. R. Reynolds (Eds.), *Handbook of neurodevelopmental and genetic disorders in children* (pp. 385–405). New York: Guilford Press.

Cohane, G. H., & Pope, H. G., Jr. (2000). Body image in boys: A review of the literature. *International Journal of Eating Disorders, 29,* 373–379.

Cohen, L. B., & Cashon, C. H. (2001). Do 7-month-old infants process independent features or facial configurations? *Infant and Child Development, 10,* 83–92.

Cohen, M. A., Tell, E. J., Bishop, C. E., Wallack, S. S., & Branch, L. G. (1989). Patterns of nursing home use in a prepaid managed care system: The continuing care retirement community. *The Gerontologist, 29,* 74–80.

Cohen, R. S., & Weissman, S. H. (1984). The parenting alliance. In R. S. Cohen, B. J. Cohler, & S. H. Weissman (Eds.), *Parenthood: A psychodynamic perspective* (pp. 33–49). New York: Guilford Press.

Cohn, B. (1998, March/April). What a wife's worth. *Stanford,* pp. 14–15.

Coie, J. D., & Krehbiel, G. (1984). Effects of academic tutoring on the social status of low achieving, socially rejected children. *Child Development, 55,* 1465–1478.

Colby, A., & Damon, W. (1994). Listening to a different voice: A review of Gilligan's "In a Different Voice." In B. Puka (Ed.), *Caring voices and women's moral frames: Gilligan's view. Moral development: A compendium,* Vol. 6 (pp. 275–283). New York: Garland.

Colby, A., & Kohlberg, L. (1987). *The measurement of moral judgment: Vol. 1. Theoretical foundations and research validation.* Cambridge, UK: Cambridge University Press.

Colby, A., Kohlberg, L., Gibbs, J., & Lieberman, M. (1983). A longitudinal study of moral judgment. *Monographs of the Society for Research in Child Development, 48* (1, Serial No. 200).

Cole, C. L., & Cole, A. L. (1985). Husbands and wives should have an equal share in making the marriage work. In H. Feldman & M. Feldman (Eds.), *Current controversies in marriage and family* (pp. 131–141). Newbury Park, CA: Sage.

Cole, D., & La Voie, J. C. (1985). Fantasy play and related cognitive development in 2 to 6 year olds. *Developmental Psychology, 21,* 233–240.

Cole, M., & D'Andrade, R. (1982). The influence of schooling on concept formation: Some preliminary conclusions. *Quarterly Newsletter of the Laboratory of Comparative Cognition, 4,* 19–26.

Coleman, E. (2003). Compulsive sexual behavior: What to call it, how to treat it? *SIECUS Report, 31,* 12–16.

Coleman, J. S. (1987). Families and schools. *Educational Researcher, 16,* 32–38.

Coleman, P. G. (1992). Personal adjustment in late life: Successful aging. *Reviews in Clinical Gerontology, 2,* 67–78.

Colin, V. (1996). *Human attachment.* New York: McGraw-Hill.

Coll, C. G. (2004). The interpenetration of culture and biology in human development. *Research in Human Development, 1,* 145–160.

Coll, C. T. G. (1990). Developmental outcome of minority infants: A process-oriented look into our beginnings. *Child Development, 61,* 270–289.

Collin, A., & Young, R. A. (2000). *The future of career.* New York: Cambridge University Press.

Collins, J. L., Leavy, M., & Kann, L. (1995). School health education. *Journal of School Health, 8,* 302–311.

Collins, K., Luszcz, M., Lawson, M., & Keeves, J. (1997). Everyday problem solving in elderly women: Contributions of residence, perceived control and age. *The Gerontologist, 37,* 293–302.

Collins, W. (1995). Relationship and development: Family adaptation to individual change. In S. Shulman (Ed.), *Close relationships and socioemotional development* (pp. 128–154). Norwood, NJ: Ablex.

Colombo, J., Mitchell, D. W., Coldren, J. T., & Freeseman, L. J. (1991). Individual differences in infant visual attention: Are short lookers faster processors or feature processors? *Child Development, 62,* 1247–1257.

Comstock, G. A. (with Haejung Paik). (1991). *Television and the American child.* San Diego: Academic Press.

Conger, R. D., Conger, K. J., Elder, G. H., Lorenz, F. O., Simons, R. L., & Whitbeck, L. B. (1993). Family economic stress and adjustment of early adolescent girls. *Developmental Psychology, 29,* 206–219.

Conger, R. D., Wallace, L. E., Sun, Y., Simons, R. L., McLoyd, V. C., & Brody, G. H. (2002). Economic pressure in African American families: A replication and extension of the family stress model. *Developmental Psychology, 38,* 179–193.

Congress and RU-486. (2001, April 26). *Washington Post,* p. A26.

Connolly, C. (2004, December 1). Some abstinence programs mislead teens, report says. *Washington Post,* p. AO1. Retrieved December 4, 2004, from http://www.washingtonpost.com/wp-dyn/articles/A26623-2004Dec1.html

Connolly, J., Furman, W., & Konarski, R. (2000). The role of peers in the emergence of heterosexual romantic relationship in adolescence. *Child Development, 71,* 1395–1408.

Connolly, K., & Dalgleish, M. (1989). The emergence of a tool-using skill in infancy. *Developmental Psychology, 25,* 894–912.

Constantinople, A. (1969). An Eriksonian measure of personality development in college students. *Developmental Psychology, 1,* 357–372.

Consumer Product Safety Commission. (1999). *Safety hazards in child care settings.* Washington, DC: Author. Retrieved December 21, 2001, from http://www.cpsc.gov/library/ccstudy.html

Conte, H. R., Weiner, M. B., & Plutchik, R. (1982). Measuring death anxiety: Conceptual, psychometric, and factor-analytic aspects. *Journal of Personality and Social Psychology, 43,* 775–785.

Contreras, J. M., Lopez, I. R., Rivera-Mosquera, E. T., Raymond-Smith, L., & Rothstein, K. (1999). Social support and adjustment in Puerto Rican adolescent mothers: The moderating effect of acculturation. *Journal of Family Psychology, 13,* 228–243.

Cool, L. E. (1987). The effects of social class and ethnicity on the aging process. In P. Silverman (Ed.), *The elderly as modern pioneers* (pp. 263–282). Bloomington: Indiana University Press.

Coombs, R. H., & Landsverk, J. (1988). Parenting styles and substance use in childhood and adolescence. *Journal of Marriage and the Family, 50,* 473–482.

Cooney, T. M., & Mortimer, J. T. (1999). Family structure differences in the timing of leaving home: Exploring mediating factors. *Journal of Research in Adolescence, 9,* 367–393.

Cooney, T. M., Pedersen, F. A., Indelicato, S., & Palkovitz, R. (1993). Timing of fatherhood: Is "on-time" optimal? *Journal of Marriage and the Family, 55,* 205–215.

Copple, C. (2003). Fostering young children's representation, planning and reflection: A focus in three current early childhood models. *Journal of Applied Developmental Psychology, 24,* 763–771.

Corcoran, M. E., & Chaudry, A. (1997). The dynamics of childhood poverty. *Future of Children, 7.*

Corijn, M., Liefbroer, A. C., & Gierveld, J. De J. (1996). It takes two to tango, doesn't it? The influence of couple characteristics on the timing of the birth of the first child. *Journal of Marriage and the Family, 58,* 117–126.

Corina, D. P., Vaid, J., & Bellugi, U. (1992). The linguistic basis of left hemisphere specialization, *Science, 255,* 1258–1260.

Cornelius, M. D. (1996). Adolescent pregnancy and the complications of prenatal substance use. In L. S. Chandler & S. J. Lane (Eds.), *Children with prenatal drug ex-*

posure (pp. 111–128). New York: Haworth Press.

Cornelius, M. D., Goldschmidt, L., Taylor, P. M., & Day, N. L. (1999). Prenatal alcohol use among teenagers: Effects on neonatal outcomes. *Alcoholism: Clinical and Experimental Research, 23,* 1238–1244.

Correll, S. J. (2001). Gender and the career choice process: The role of biased self-assessments. *American Journal of Sociology, 106,* 1691–1730.

Corter, C. M., & Fleming, A. S. (2002). Psychobiology of maternal behavior in human beings. In M. H. Bornstein (Ed.), *Handbook of parenting: Vol. 2. Biology and ecology of parenting* (pp. 141–181). Mahwah, NJ: Erlbaum.

Cosden, M., Peerson, S., & Elliott, K. (1997). Effects of prenatal drug exposure on birth outcomes and early child development. *Journal of Drug Issues, 27,* 525–539.

Cose, E. (1993, November 15). Rage of the privileged. *Newsweek,* pp. 56–63.

Cosmides, L., & Tooby, J. (1997). *Evolutionary psychology: A primer.* Retrieved November 6, 2002, from http://www.psych.ucsb.edu/research/cep/primer.html

Costa, P. T., Metter, E. J., & McCrae, R. R. (1994). Personality stability and its contribution to successful aging. *Journal of Geriatric Psychiatry, 27,* 41–59.

Cota-Robles, S., Neiss, M., & Rowe, D. C. (2002). The role of puberty in violent and nonviolent delinquency among Anglo American, Mexican American, and African American boys. *Journal of Adolescent Research, 17,* 364–376.

Cotten, S. R. (1999). Marital status and mental health revisited: Examining the importance of risk factors and resources. *Family Relations, 48,* 225–233.

Couzin, J. (2003, October). Is long life in the blood? *Science Now,* pp. 2–4.

Cowan, C. P., & Cowan, P. A. (1988). Who does what when partners become parents: Implications for men, women, and marriage. In R. Palkovitz & M. B. Sussman (Eds.), *Transitions to parenthood* (pp. 105–132). New York: Hawthorn Press.

Cowan, P. A., Cohn, D. A., Cowan, C. P., & Pearson, J. L. (1996). Parents' attachment histories and children's externalizing and internalizing behavior: Exploring family systems models of linkage. *Journal of Consulting and Clinical Psychology, 64,* 53–63.

Cowley, G. (1997, June 30). How to live to 100. *Newsweek,* pp. 56–67.

Cox, M. J., Owen, M. T., Henderson, V. K., & Margand, N. A. (1992). Prediction of infant–father and infant–mother attachment. *Developmental Psychology, 28,* 474–483.

Cox, M. J., Owen, M. T., Lewis, J. M., & Henderson, V. K. (1989). Marriage, adult adjustment, and early parenting. *Child Development, 60,* 1015–1024.

Crack-using woman admits guilt in the death of her fetus. (1997, December 3). *New York Times,* Sec. A., p. 33.

Craig-Bray, L., Adams, G. R., & Dobson, W. R. (1988). Identity formation and social relations during late adolescence. *Journal of Youth and Adolescence, 17,* 173–188.

Crain, W. C. (2000). *Theories of development: Concepts and applications* (4th ed.). Upper Saddle River, NJ: Prentice Hall.

Crain-Thoreson, C., & Dale, P. S. (1992). Do early talkers become early readers? Linguistic precocity, preschool language, and emergent literacy. *Developmental Psychology, 28,* 421–429.

Cramer, P. (2000). Defense mechanisms in psychology today. *American Psychologist, 55,* 637–646.

Crawford, T. N., Cohen, P., Midlarsky, E., & Brook, J. (2001). Internalizing symptoms in adolescents: Gender differences in vulnerability to parental distress and discord. *Journal of Research on Adolescence, 11,* 95–118.

Creswell, J. W. (1994). *Research design: Qualitative and quantitative approaches.* Thousand Oaks, CA: Sage.

Crick, N. R., & Ladd, G. W. (1993). Children's perceptions of their peer experiences: Attributions, loneliness, social anxiety, and social avoidance. *Developmental Psychology, 29,* 244–254.

Crockett, L. J., Bingham, C. R., Chopak, J. S., & Vicary, J. R. (1996). Timing of first sexual intercourse: The role of social control, social learning, and problem behavior. *Journal of Youth and Adolescence, 25,* 89–111.

Crohan, S. E. (1996). Marital quality and conflict across the transition to parenthood in African American and White couples. *Journal of Marriage and the Family, 58,* 933–944.

Crooks, R. & Bauer, K. (1996). *Our sexuality* (6th ed.). Pacific Grove, CA: Brooks/Cole.

Crooks, R. L., & Bauer, K. (2005). *Our sexuality* (9th ed.). Belmont, CA: Wadsworth.

Crooks, T. J. (1988). The impact of classroom evaluation practices on students. *Review of Educational Research, 58,* 438–481.

Crosby, R. A., DiClemente, R. J., Wingood, G. M., Rose, E., & Lang, D. (2003). Correlates of unplanned and unwanted pregnancy among African-American female teens. *American Journal of Preventive Medicine, 25,* 255–258.

Crosnoe, R., & Elder, G. H., Jr. (2002). Successful adaptation in the later years: A life course approach to aging. *Social Psychology Quarterly, 65,* 309–328.

Cross, W. E., Jr. (1991). *Shades of black: Diversity in African-American identity.* Philadelphia: Temple University Press.

Crouter, A. C., & Bumpus, M. F. (2001). Linking parents' work stress to children's and adolescents' psychological adjustment. *Current Directions in Psychological Science, 10,* 156–159.

Crouter, A. C., & Manke, B. (1997). Development of a typology of dual-earner families: A window into differences between and within families in relationships, roles, and activities. *Journal of Family Psychology, 11,* 62–75.

Crowell, J. A., Fraley, R. C., & Shaver, P. R. (1999). Measurement of individual differences in adolescent and adult attachment. In J. Cassidy & P. R. Shaver (Eds.), *Handbook of attachment: Theory, research, and clinical applications* (pp. 434–465). New York: Guilford Press.

Cuddy, A. J. C., Fiske, S. T., & Glick, P. (2004). When professionals become mothers, warmth doesn't cut the ice. *Journal of Social Issues, 60,* 701–718.

Cukan, A. (2001). FedEx sued for dreadlocks discrimination. *United Press International.* Retrieved January 7, 2002, from http://www.hirediversity.com/news/newsbyid.asp?id=4736

Cummings, E. M., Greene, A.-L., & Karraker, K. H. (Eds.). (1991). *Lifespan perspectives on stress and coping.* Hillsdale, NJ: Erlbaum.

Cummings, J. S., Pellegrini, D. S., Notarius, C. I., & Cummings, E. M. (1989). Children's responses to angry adult behavior as a function of marital distress and history of interparent hostility. *Child Development, 60,* 1035–1043.

Cunningham, F. G., Gant, N., Gilstrap, L., Leveno, G., Hauth, J., & Wenstrom, K. (2001). *Williams' obstetrics* (21st ed.). McGraw-Hill.

Cunningham, P. B., Henggeler, S. Q., Limber, S. P., Melton, G. B., & Nation, M. A. (2000). Pattern and correlates of gun ownership among nonmetropolitan and rural middle school students. *Journal of Clinical Child Psychology, 29,* 432–442.

Currie, L. A. (1999). "Mr. Homunculus the Reading Detective": A cognitive approach to improving reading comprehension. *Educational and Child Psychology, 16,* 37–42.

D'Augelli, A. R. (1991). Gay men in college: Identity processes and adaptation. *Journal of College Student Development, 32,* 140–146.

Dahl, R. E., & Carskadon, M. A. (1995). Sleep and its disorders in adolescence. In R. Ferber & M. H. Kryger (Eds.), *Principles and practice of sleep medicine in the child* (pp. 19–27). Philadelphia: Saunders.

Dalgleish, T., Moradi, A. R., Taghavi, M. R., Neshat-Doost, H. T., & Yule, W. (2001). An experimental investigation of hypervigilance for threat in children and adolescents with post-traumatic stress disorder. *Psychological Medicine, 31,* 541–547.

Dalton, S. S., & Tharp, R. G. (2002). Standards for pedagogy: Research, theory and practice. In G. Wells & G. Claxton (Eds.), *Learning for life in the 21st century: Sociocultural perspectives on the future of education* (pp. 181–194). Malden, MA: Blackwell.

Damon, W. (1980). Patterns of change in children's social reasoning: A two-year longitudinal study. *Child Development, 51,* 1010–1017.

Damon, W. (1996). The lifelong transformation of moral goals through social influence. In P. B. Baltes & V. M. Staudinger (Eds.), *Interactive minds: Life-span perspectives on the social foundation of cognition* (pp. 198–220). New York: Cambridge University Press.

Damon, W., & Hart, D. (1988). *Self-understanding in childhood and adolescence.* New York: Cambridge University Press.

Daniluk, J. C. (1999). When biology isn't destiny: Implications for the sexuality of women without children. *Canadian Journal of Counseling, 33,* 79–94.

Darling-Fisher, C. S., & Leidy, N. K. (1988). Measuring Eriksonian development in the adult: The Modified Erikson Psychosocial Stage Inventory. *Psychological Reports, 62,* 747–754.

Darwin, C. (1859/1979). *The illustrated "Origin of species."* (Abridged and introduced by Richard E. Leakey). New York: Hill & Wang.

Darwin, C. (1872/1965). *The expression of emotions in man and animals.* Chicago: University of Chicago Press.

Davey, A., & Eggebeen, D. J. (1998). Patterns of intergenerational exchange and mental health. *Journal of Gerontology, 53,* P86–P95.

Davey, G., & Cullen, C. (1988). *Human operant conditioning and behavior modification.* New York: Wiley.

Davidson, K. (2002). Gender differences in new partnership choices and constraints for older widows and widowers. *Ageing International, 27,* 43–60.

Davies, P. L., & Rose, J. D. (1999). Assessment of cognitive development in adolescents by means of neuropsychological tasks. *Developmental Neuropsychology, 15,* 227–248.

Davis, A. (1995). The experimental method in psychology. In G. Breakwell, S. Hammond, & C. Fyfe-Schaw (Eds.), *Research methods in psychology* (pp. 42–58). Thousand Oaks, CA: Sage.

Davis, K. E. (1985, February). Near and dear: Friendship and love compared. *Psychology Today, 19,* pp. 22–30.

Davis-Floyd, R. E. (1990). The role of obstetrical rituals in the resolution of cultural anomaly. *Social Science and Medicine, 31,* 175–189.

Davis-Kean, P. E., & Sandler, H. M (2001). A meta-analysis of measures of self-esteem for young children: A framework for future measures. *Child Development, 72,* 887–906.

Davison, M. L., King, P. M., Kitchener, K. S., & Parker, C. A. (1980). The stage sequence concept in cognitive and social development. *Developmental Psychology, 16,* 121–131.

Davydov, V. V. (1995). The influence of L. S. Vygotsky on education theory, research, and practice (S. T. Kerr, Trans.). *Educational Researcher, 24,* 12–21.

Daw, J. (2001). Road rage, air rage and now "desk rage." *Monitor on Psychology, 32,* 52–54.

Dawson, T. L. (2002). New tools, new insights: Kohlberg's moral judgement stages revisited. *International Journal of Behavioral Development, 26,* 154–166.

Dawson, T. L. (2003). A stage is a stage is a stage: A direct comparison of two scoring systems. *Journal of Genetic Psychology, 164,* 335–364.

De Frias, C. M., & Schaie, K. W. (2001). Perceived work environment and cognitive style. *Experimental Aging Research, 27,* 67–81.

De Magalhaes, J. P. (2003). Winning the war against aging. *Futurist, 37,* 48–51.

De St. Aubin, E., McAdams, D. P., & Kim, T. (2004). *The generative society: Caring for future generations.* Washington, DC: American Psychological Association.

de Silva, P., & Marks, M. (1994). Jealousy as a clinical problem: Practical issues of assessment and treatment. *Journal of Mental Health, 3,* 195–204.

DeAngelis, T. (1997a). APA co-sponsors briefing on anorexia. *APA Monitor, 28,* 51.

DeAngelis, T. (1997b). When children don't bond with parents. *APA Monitor, 28,* 10–12.

Deater-Deckard, K., & O'Connor, T. G. (2000). Parent–child mutuality in early childhood: Two behavioral genetic studies. *Developmental Psychology, 36,* 561–570.

Deater-Deckard, K., Pickering, K., Dunn, J. F., & Golding, J. (1998). Family structure and depressive symptoms in men preceding and following the birth of a child. *American Journal of Psychiatry, 155,* 818–823.

Deaux, K., Reid, A., Mizrahi, K., & Ethier, K. A. (1995). Parameters of social identity. *Journal of Personality and Social Psychology, 68,* 280–291.

DeCasper, A., & Fifer, W. (1980). Of human bonding: Newborns prefer their mothers' voices. *Science, 208,* 1174–1176.

DeCasper, A. J., Lecanuet, J. P., Busnel, M. C., Granier-Deferre, C., et al. (1994). Fetal reactions to recurrent maternal speech. *Infant Behavior and Development, 17,* 159–164.

DeCasper, A. J., & Spence, M. J. (1986). Prenatal maternal speech influences newborns' perceptions of speech sounds. *Infant Behavior and Development, 9,* 133–150.

Decety, J., & Chaminade, T. (2003). When the self represents the other: A new cognitive neuroscience view on psychological identification. *Consciousness and Cognition, 12,* 577–596.

Deeg, D. J. H., Kardaun, J. W. P. F., & Fozard, J. L. (1996). Health, behavior, and aging. In J. E. Birren, K. W. Schaie, R. P. Abeles, M. Gatz, & T. A. Salthouse (Eds.), *Handbook of the psychology of aging* (pp. 129–149). San Diego: Academic Press.

Deenen, A. A., Gijs, L., & van Naerssen, A. X. (1994). Intimacy and sexuality in gay male couples. *Archives of Sexual Behavior, 23,* 421–431.

Defey, D., Storch, E., Cardozo, S., & Diaz, O. (1996). The menopause: Women's psychology and health. *Critical Science and Medicine, 47,* 1447–1456.

DeGenova, M. K. (1997). *Families in cultural context: Strengths and challenges in diversity.* Mountain View, CA: Mayfield.

DeGrazia, D. (1998). *Biology, consciousness, and the definitions of death.* Report from the Institute for Philosophy & Public Policy. Retrieved March 4, 2005, from http://www.puaf.umd.edu/IPPP/winter98/biology_consciousness.htm

Dekeyser, M., Verfaillie, K., & Vanrie, J. (2002). Creating stimuli for the study of biological motion perception. *Behavior Research Methods, Instruments, & Computers, 34,* 375–382.

DeMaris, A., & Rao, K. V. (1992). Premarital cohabitation and subsequent marital stability in the United States: A reassessment. *Journal of Marriage and the Family, 54,* 178–190.

Demetriou, A., & Efklides, A. (1985). Structure and sequence of formal and postformal thought: General patterns and individual differences. *Child Development, 56,* 1062–1091.

Demo, D. H., Fine, M. A., & Ganong, L. H. (2000). Divorce as a family stressor. In P. C. McKenry & S. J. Price (Eds.), *Families and change: Coping with stressful events and transitions* (pp. 279–302). Thousand Oaks, CA: Sage.

Denmark, F. L., Novick, K., & Pinto, A. (1996). Women, work, and family: Mental health issues. In J. A. Sechzer, S. M. Pfafflin, F. L. Denmar, A. Griffin, & S. J. Blumenthal (Eds.), *Women and mental health. Annals of the New York Academy of Sciences* (Vol. 789, pp. 101–117).

Denner, J., & Dunbar, N. (2004). Negotiating femininity: Power and strategies of Mexican American girls. *Sex Roles, 50,* 301–314.

Denton, W. H., Burleson, B. R., & Sprenkle, D. H. (1994). Motivation in marital communication: Comparison of distressed and nondistressed husbands and wives. *American Journal of Family Therapy, 22,* 17–26.

Denzin, N. K., & Lincoln, Y. S. (1998). *Strategies of qualitative inquiry.* Thousand Oaks, CA: Sage.

DeVries, M. W., & DeVries, M. R. (1977). Cultural relativity of toilet training readiness: A perspective from East Africa. *Pediatrics, 60,* 170–177.

DeVries, R., Hildebrandt, C., & Zan, B. (2000). Constructivist early education for moral development. *Early Education and Development, 11,* 9–35.

Diamond, A. (2002). Normal development of the prefrontal cortex from birth to young adulthood: Cognitive functions, anatomy, and biochemistry. In D. T. Stuss & R. T. Knight (Eds.), *Principles of frontal lobe function* (pp. 466–503). London: Oxford University Press.

Diamond, L. M. (2000). Passionate friendships among adolescent sexual-minority women. *Journal of Research on Adolescence, 10,* 191–209.

Diaz, R. M. (1983). Thought and two languages: The impact of bilingualism on cognitive development. *Review of Research in Education, 10,* 23–54.

Dickinson, D. K., & Tabors, P. O. (2001). *Beginning literacy with language: Young children learning at home and school.* Baltimore: Brookes.

Dickstein, S., & Parke, R. D. (1988). Social referencing in infancy: A glance at fathers and marriage. *Child Development, 59,* 506–511.

Diehl, M., Hastings, C. T., & Stanton, J. M. (2001). Self-concept differentiation across the adult life span. *Psychology and Aging, 16,* 643–654.

Dielman, T. (1994). School-based research on the prevention of adolescent alcohol use and misuses: Methodological issues and advances. *Journal of Research on Adolescence, 4,* 271–293.

Diener, C. I., & Dweck, C. S. (1980). An analysis of learned helplessness: 2. The processing of success. *Journal of Personality and Social Psychology, 39,* 940–952.

Dietz-Uhler, B., & Murrell, A. (1998). Effects of social identity and threat on self-esteem and group attributions. *Group Dynamics, 2,* 24–35.

DiMatteo, M. R., Morton, S. C., Lepper, H. S., Damush, T. M., et al. (1996). Cesarean childbirth and psychosocial outcomes: A meta-analysis. *Health Psychology, 15,* 303–314.

Dindia, K., & Allen, M. (1992). Sex differences in self-disclosure: A meta-analysis. *Psychological Bulletin, 112,* 106–124.

Dion, K. K., & Dion, K. L. (1993). Individualistic and collectivistic perspectives on gender and the cultural context of love and intimacy. *Journal of Social Issues, 49,* 53–69.

DiPietro, J. A. (2004). The role of prenatal maternal stress in child development. *Current Directions in Psychological Science, 13,* 71–74.

DiPietro, J. A., Porges, S. W., & Uhly, B. (1992). Re-activity and developmental competence in preterm and full-term infants. *Developmental Psychology, 28,* 831–841.

DiPietro, L. (2001). Physical activity in aging: Changes in patterns and their relationship to health and function. *Journals of Gerontology: Series A: Biological Sciences and Medical Sciences, 56A,* 13–22.

Dishion, T. J., Patterson, G. R., Stoolmiller, M., & Skinner, M. L. (1991). Family, school, and behavioral antecedents to early adolescent involvement with antisocial peers. *Developmental Psychology, 27,* 172–180.

Dishion, T. J., Poulin, F., & Medici Skaggs, N. (2000). The ecology of premature autonomy in adolescence: Biological and social influences. In K. A. Kerns, A. M. Neal-Barnett, & J. M. Contreras (Eds.), *Family and peers: Linking two social worlds* (pp. 27–46). Westport, CT: Praeger.

Dixon, R. A. (1992). Contextual approaches to adult intellectual development. In R. J. Sternberg & C. A. Berg (Eds.), *Intellectual development* (pp. 350–380). New York: Cambridge University Press.

Dodge, K. A. (1989). Coordinating responses to aversive stimuli: Introduction to a special section on the development of emotion regulation. *Developmental Psychology, 25,* 339–342.

Dodge, K. A., Pettit, G. S., McClaskey, C. L., & Brown, M. M. (1986). Social competence in children. *Monographs of the Society for Research in Child Development, 51* (2, Serial No. 213).

Dole, N., Savitz, D. A., Siega-Riz, A. M., Hertz-Picciotto, I., McMahon, M. J., & Buekens, P. (2004). Psychosocial factors and preterm birth among African American and White women in central North Carolina. *American Journal of Public Health, 94,* 1358–1365.

Domar, A. D., Clapp, D., Slawsby, E., Kessel, B., Orav, J., & Freizinger, M. (2000). The impact of group psychological interventions on distress in infertile women. *Health Psychology, 19,* 568–575.

Domino, G., & Affonso, D. D. (1990). Erikson's life stages: The Inventory of Psychosocial Balance. *Journal of Personality Assessment, 54,* 576–588.

Donald, M. (2001). *A mind so rare: The evolution of human consciousness.* New York: Norton.

Donald, M., Lucke, J., Dunne, M., & Raphael, B. (1995). Gender differences associated with young people's emotional reactions to sexual intercourse. *Journal of Youth and Adolescence, 24,* 453–464.

Dorfman, L., Woodruff, K., Chavez, V., & Wallack, L. (1997). Youth and violence on local television news in California. *American Journal of Public Health, 87,* 1311–1316.

Doulas of North America. (1998). *The doula's contribution to modern maternity care.* Retrieved August 11, 2004, from http://www.dona.org

Downey, G., & Walker, E. (1989). Social cognition and adjustment in children at risk for psychopathology. *Developmental Psychology, 25,* 835–845.

Dowrick, P. W. (1991). *Practical guide to using video in the behavioral sciences.* New York: Wiley.

Dreman, S. (1997). *The family on the threshold of the 21st century: Trends and implications.* Mahwah, NJ: Erlbaum.

Drew, L. M., & Smith, P. K. (1999). The impact of parental separation/divorce on grandparent–grandchild relationships. *International Journal of Aging and Human Development, 48,* 191–215.

Dryfoos, J. G. (1994). *Full service schools: A revolution in health and social services for children, youth and families.* San Francisco: Jossey-Bass.

Dubler, N. N., & Sabatino, C. P. (1991). Age-based rationing and the law: An exploration. In R. H. Binstock & S. G. Post (Eds.), *Too old for health care? Controversies in medicine, law, economics, and ethics* (pp. 92–119). Baltimore: Johns Hopkins University.

Dunbar, E. (1997). The Personal Dimensions of Difference Scale: Measuring multigroup identity with four ethnic groups. *International Journal of Intercultural Relations, 21,* 1–28.

Duncan, G. J., Brooks-Gunn, J., & Klebanov, P. K. (1994). Economic deprivation and early childhood development. *Child Development, 65,* 296–318.

Dunkel-Schetter, C., Sagrestano, L. F., Feldman, P., & Killingsworth, C. (1996). Social support and pregnancy: A comprehensive review focusing on ethnicity and culture. In G. R. Pierce & B. R. Sarason (Eds.), *Handbook of social support and the family* (pp. 375–412). New York: Plenum.

Dunkley, T. L., Wertheim, E. H., & Paxton, S. J. (2001). Examination of a model of multiple sociocultural influences on adolescent girls' body dissatisfaction and dietary restraint. *Adolescence, 36,* 265–279.

Dunn, J., Brown, J., & Beardsall, L. (1991). Family talk about feeling states and children's later understanding of others' emotions. *Developmental Psychology, 27,* 448–455.

Dunn, J., Cutting, A. L., & Demetriou, H. (2000). Moral sensibility, understanding others, and children's friendship interactions in the preschool period. *British Journal of Developmental Psychology, 18,* 159–177.

Dunn, M., & Cutler, N. (2000). Sexual issues in older adults. *AIDS Patient Care and STDs, 14,* 67–69.

Dunphy, D. C. (1963). The social structure of urban adolescent peer groups. *Sociometry, 26,* 230–246.

Duran-Aydintug, C. (1995). Former spouses exiting role-identities. *Journal of Divorce and Remarriage, 24,* 23–40.

Durbin, D. L., Darling, N., Steinberg, L., & Brown, B. B. (1993). Parenting style and peer group membership among European-American adolescents. *Journal of Research on Adolescence, 3,* 87–100.

Durik, A. M., Hyde, J. S., & Clark, R. (2000). Sequelae of cesarean and vaginal deliveries: Psychosocial outcomes for mothers and infants. *Developmental Psychology, 36,* 251–260.

Dustman, R., Emmerson, R., Ruhling, R., Shearer, D., Steinhaus, L., Johnson, S., et al. (1989). Age and fitness effects on EEG, ERP's, visual sensitivity and cognition. *Neurobiology of Aging, 10,* 2–15.

Duvall, E. M. (1977). *Family development* (5th ed.). Philadelphia: Lippincott.

Dweck, C. S. (1992). The study of goals in psychology. *Psychological Science, 3,* 165–167.

Dyk, P. H., & Adams, G. R. (1990). Identity and intimacy: An initial investigation of three theoretical models using cross-lag panel correlations. *Journal of Youth and Adolescence, 19,* 91–110.

Early, D. M., Pianta, R. C., Taylor, L. C., & Cox, M. J. (2001). Transition practices: Findings from a national survey of kindergarten teachers. *Early Childhood Education Journal, 28,* 199–206.

East, P. L., Hess, L. E., & Lerner, R. M. (1987). Peer social support and adjustment of early adolescent peer groups. *Journal of Early Adolescence, 7,* 153–163.

East, P. L., & Rook, K. S. (1992). Compensatory patterns of support among children's peer relationships: A test using school friends, nonschool friends, and siblings. *Developmental Psychology, 28,* 163–172.

Easterbrook, M. A., Kisilevsky, B. S., Muir, D. W., & Laplante, D. P. (1999). Newborns discriminate normal faces from scrambled faces. *Canadian Journal of Experimental Psychology, 53,* 231–241.

Eccles, J. S. (1987). Gender roles and women's achievement-related decisions. *Psychology of Women Quarterly, 11,* 135–171.

Eccles, J. S. (1993). School and family effects on the ontogeny of children's interests, self perceptions, and activity choices. In J. E. Jacobs (Ed.), *Developmental perspectives on Motivation: Nebraska Symposium on Motivation, 1992* (pp. 145–208). Lincoln: University of Nebraska Press.

Eccles, J. S., Jacobs, J. E., & Harold, R. D. (1990). Gender-role stereotypes, expectancy effects, and parents' role in the socialization of gender differences in self perceptions and skill acquisition. *Journal of Social Issues, 46*, 182–201.

Eccles, J., Wigfield, A., Harold, R. D., & Blumenfeld, P. (1993). Age and gender differences in children's self- and task perceptions during elementary school. *Child Development, 64*, 830–847.

Eckerman, C. O., Davis, C. C., & Didow, S. M. (1989). Toddlers' emerging ways of achieving social coordinations with a peer. *Child Development, 60*, 440–453.

Eckerman, C. O., & Didow, S. M. (1989). Toddlers' social coordinations: Changing responses to another's invitation to play. *Developmental Psychology, 25*, 794–804.

Eckerman, C. O., & Didow, S. M. (1996). Nonverbal imitation and toddlers' mastery of verbal means of achieving coordinated action. *Developmental Psychology, 32*, 141–152.

Eckstein, S., & Shemesh, M. (1992). The rate of acquisition of formal operational schemata in adolescence: A secondary analysis. *Journal of Research in Science Teaching, 29*, 441–451.

Economic Policy Institute. (2004). *Minimum wage fact sheet.* Retrieved May 21, 2004, from http://www.epinet.org/content.cfm/issueguides_minwage_minwagefacts

Edelstein, R. S., Alexander, K. W., Shaver, P. R., Schaaf, J. M., Quas, J. A., Lovas, G. S., & Goodman, G. S. (2004). Adult attachment style and parental responsiveness during a stressful event. *Attachment and Human Development, 6*, 31–52.

Eder, R. A. (1989). The emergent personologist: The structure and content of 3½-, 5½-, and 7½-year-olds' concepts of themselves and other persons. *Child Development, 60*, 1218–1228.

Eder, R. A., Gerlach, S. G., & Perlmutter, M. (1987). In search of children's selves: Development of the specific and general components of the self-concept. *Child Development, 58*, 1044–1050.

Edhborg, M., Lundh, W., Seimyr, L., & Widstroem, A. (2001). The long-term impact of postnatal depressed mood on mother–child interaction: A preliminary study. *Journal of Reproductive and Infant Psychology, 19*, 61–71.

Edin, K. (2000). What do low-income single mothers say about marriage? *Social Problems, 47*, 112–133.

Edin, K., Kefalas, M. J., & Reed, J. M. (2004). A peek inside the black box: What marriage means for poor unmarried parents. *Journal of Marriage and the Family, 66*, 1007–1014.

Edin, K., & Lein, L. (1997). *Making ends meet: How single mothers survive welfare and low-wage work.* New York: Russell Sage Foundation.

Education Week. (2001). Harris interactive poll of students and technology. *Technology Counts, 2001*, pp. 7–8.

Edwards, C. P. (1995). Parenting toddlers. In M. H. Bornstein (Ed.), *Handbook of parenting: Vol. 1. Children and parenting* (pp. 41–63). Mahwah, NJ, Erlbaum.

Edwards, C. P., & Liu, W. (2002). Parenting toddlers. In M. H. Bornstein (Ed.), *Handbook of parenting: Vol. 1. Children and parenting* (pp. 45–71). Mahwah, NJ: Erlbaum.

Edwards, C. P., & Whiting, B. B. (1988). *Children of different worlds.* Cambridge, MA: Harvard University Press.

Egeland, B., Jacobvitz, D., & Sroufe, L. A. (1988). Breaking the cycle of abuse. *Child Development, 59*, 1080–1088.

Egeland, B., & Sroufe, L. A. (1981). Attachment and early maltreatment. *Child Development, 52*, 44–52.

Eggers, J. H. (1995). Developing entrepreneurs: Skills for the "wanna be," "gonna be," and "gotta be better" employees. In M. London (Ed.), *Employees, careers, and job creation* (pp. 31–42). San Francisco: Jossey-Bass.

Egley, A., Jr., & Major, A. K. (2004). Highlights of the 2002 National Youth Gang Survey. *Office of Juvenile Justice and Delinquency Prevention Fact Sheet.* Retrieved December 5, 2004, from http://www.ncjrs.org/pdffiles1/ojjdp/fs200401.pdf

Eisenberg, N. (2000). Emotion, regulation, and moral development. *Annual Review of Psychology, 51*, 665–697.

Eisenberg, N., & Fabes, R. A. (1998). Prosocial development. In W. Damon & N. Eisenberg (Eds.), *Handbook of child psychology: Vol. 3. Social, emotional, and personality development* (5th ed., pp. 701–778) New York: Wiley.

Eisenberg, N., Guthrie, I. K., Murphy, B. C., Shepard, S. A., Cumberland, A., & Carlo, G. (1999). Consistency and development of prosocial dispositions: A longitudinal study. *Child Development, 70*, 1360–1372.

Eisenberg, N., & Morris, A. S. (2004). Moral cognitions and prosocial responding in adolescence. In R. M. Lerner & L. Steinberg (Eds.), *Handbook of adolescent psychology* (2nd ed., pp. 155–188). New York: Wiley.

Eisenberg, N., & Strayer, J. (1987). Critical issues in the study of empathy. In N. Eisenberg & J. Strayer (Eds.), *Empathy and its development* (pp. 3–13). Cambridge, UK: Cambridge University Press.

Ekerdt, D. J., Bosse, R., & Levkoff, S. (1985). An empirical test for phases of retirement: Findings from the normative aging study. *Journal of Gerontology, 40*, 95–101.

Elder, G. H. (1985). *Life course dynamics: Trajectories and transitions, 1968–1980.* Ithaca, NY: Cornell University Press.

Elder, G. H. (1986). Military times and turning points in men's lives. *Developmental Psychology, 22*, 233–245.

Elder, G. H., Jr. (1995). The life course paradigm: Social change and individual development. In P. Moen, G. H. Elder, Jr., & K. Luscher (Eds.), *Examining lives in context: Perspectives on the ecology of human development* (pp. 101–139). Washington, DC: American Psychological Association.

Elder, G. H., Jr. (1996). Human lives in changing societies: Life course and developmental insights. In R. B. Cairns, G. H. Elder, Jr., & Costello, E. J. (Eds.), *Developmental science* (pp. 31–62). Cambridge, UK: Cambridge University Press.

Elder, G. H., Caspi, A., & van Nguyen, T. (1986). Resourceful and vulnerable children: Family influences in hard times. In R. K. Silbereisen et al. (Eds.), *Development as action in context* (pp. 167–186). Berlin: Springer Verlag.

Elder, G. H., Jr., George, L. K., & Shanahan, M. J. (1996). Psychosocial stress over the life course. In H. B. Kaplan (Ed.), *Psychosocial stress: Perspectives on structure, theory, life course, and methods* (pp. 247–291). Orlando, FL: Academic Press.

Elder, G. H., Jr., Shanahan, M. J., & Clipp, E. C. (1997). Linking combat and physical health: The legacy of World War II in men's lives. *American Journal of Psychiatry, 154*, 330–336.

Eldridge, N. S., & Gilbert, L. S. (1990). Correlates of relationship satisfaction in lesbian couples. *Psychology of Women Quarterly, 14*, 43–62.

Elias, M. (1998). Study: Most don't regret abortions. *USA Today: Health.* Retrieved November 18, 2001, from http//www.usatoday.com/life/health/women/abortion/1hwab009.htm

Elias, M. J., Beier, J. J., & Gara, M. A. (1989). Children's responses to interpersonal obstacles as a predictor of social competence. *Journal of Youth and Adolescence, 18*, 451–465.

Elkind, D. (1967). Egocentrism in adolescence. *Child Development, 38*, 1025–1034.

Ellickson, P., Saner, H., & McGuigan, K. A. (1997). Profiles of violent youth: Substance use and other concurrent problems. *American Journal of Public Health, 87*, 985–991.

Elliott, D. S., Huizinga, D., & Menard, S. (1989). *Multiple problem youth: Delinquency, substance use, and mental health problems.* New York: Springer Verlag.

Ellsworth, C. P., Muir, C. P., & Hains, S. M. J. (1993). Social competence and person–object differentiation: An analysis of the still-face effect. *Developmental Psychology, 29*, 63–73.

Elmer-Dewitt, P. (1991). Making babies. *Time, 138*, 56–63.

Emanuel, E. J., & Emanuel, L. (1998). The promise of a good death. *The Lancet, 251*, 21–29.

Emde, R. N., & Buchsbaum, H. K. (1990). "Didn't you hear my mommy?" Autonomy with connectedness in moral self-emergence. In D. Cicchetti & M. Beeghly (Eds.), *The self in transition: Infancy to childhood* (pp. 35–60). Chicago: University of Chicago Press.

Emery, A. E. H., & Mueller, R. F. (1992). *Elements of medical genetics* (8th ed.) Edinburgh, UK: Churchill Livingstone.

Encarta. (2004). *Finland*. Retrieved November 18, 2004, from http://encarta.msn.com/encyclopedia_761578960_5/Finland.html

Encarta Online Encyclopedia. (2005). *Funeral rites and customs*. Retrieved March 13, 2005, from http://au.encarta.msn.com/encyclopedia_761565630/Funeral_Rites_and_Customs.html

Englis, B. G., & Solomon, M. R. (1997). Where perception meets reality: The social construction of lifestyles. In L. R. Kahle & L. Chiagouris (Eds.), *Values, lifestyles, and psychographics: Advertising and consumer psychology* (pp. 25–44). Mahwah, NJ: Erlbaum.

Ennett, S. T., & Bauman, K. E. (1996). Adolescent social networks: School, demographic and longitudinal considerations. *Journal of Adolescent Research, 11*, 194–215.

Entwisle, D. R., & Alexander, K. L. (1987). Long-term effects of cesarean delivery on parents' beliefs and children's schooling. *Developmental Psychology, 23*, 676–682.

Entwisle, D. R., Alexander, K. L., Pallas, A. M., & Cadigan, D. (1987). The emergent academic self-image of first-graders: Its response to social structure. *Child Development, 58*, 1190–1206.

Epstein, S. (1973). The self-concept revisited; or, a theory of a theory. *American Psychologist, 28*, 404–416.

Epstein, S. (1991). Cognitive-experiential self-theory: An integrative theory of personality. In R. Cutis (Ed.), *The self with others: Convergences in psychoanalytic, social, and personality psychology* (pp. 111–137). New York: Guilford Press.

Epstein, S. (1998). Cognitive-experiential self-theory. In D. F. Barone & M. Hersen (Eds.), *Advanced personality* (pp. 211–238). New York: Plenum Press.

Epstein, S., Lipson, A., Holstein, C., & Huh, E. (1993). Irrational reactions to negative outcomes: Evidence for two conceptual systems. *Journal of Personality and Social Psychology, 62*, 328–339.

Erber, J. T. (2005). *Aging and older adulthood*. Belmont, CA: Wadsworth.

Erikson, E. H. (1959). The problem of ego identity. *Psychological Issues, 1*, 101–164.

Erikson, E. H. (1963). *Childhood and society* (2nd ed.). New York: Norton.

Erikson, E. H. (1968). *Identity: Youth and crisis*. New York: Norton.

Erikson, E. H. (1969). *Gandhi's truth: On the origins of militant nonviolence*. New York: Norton.

Erikson, E. H. (1972). Play and actuality. In M. W. Piers (Ed.), *Play and development* (pp. 127–167). New York: Norton.

Erikson, E. H. (1975). "Identity crisis" in autobiographic perspective. In E. H. Erikson (Ed.), *Life history and the historical moment* (pp. 17–47). New York: Norton.

Erikson, E. H. (1977). *Toys and reasons*. New York: Norton.

Erikson, E. H. (1978). Reflections on Dr. Borg's life cycle. In E. H. Erikson (Ed.), *Adulthood* (pp. 1–31). New York: Norton.

Erikson, E. H. (1980). Themes of adulthood in the Freud–Jung correspondence. In N. J. Smelser & E. H. Erikson (Eds.), *Themes of work and love in adulthood* (pp. 43–74). Cambridge, MA: Harvard University Press.

Erikson, E. H. (1982). *The life cycle completed: A review*. New York: Norton.

Erikson, E. H., Erikson, J. M., & Kivnick, H. Q. (1986). *Vital involvement in old age*. New York: Norton.

Erikson, J. M. (1988). *Wisdom and the senses: The way of creativity*. New York: Norton.

Escalona, S. K. (1968). *The roots of individuality*. Chicago: Aldine.

Eshelman, J. R. (1985). One should marry a person of the same religion, race, ethnicity, and social class. In H. Feldman & M. Feldman (Eds.), *Current controversies in marriage and family* (pp. 57–66). Newbury Park, CA: Sage.

Essau, C. A. (2004). Association between family factors and depressive disorders in adolescents. *Journal of Youth and Adolescence, 33*, 365–372.

Etzioni, A. (1976, November). The husband's rights in abortion. *Trial*.

Evans, D. W., Gray, F. L., & Leckman, J. F. (1999). The rituals, fears, and phobias of young children: Insights from development, psychopathology, and neurobiology. *Child Psychiatry and Human Development, 29*, 261–276.

Evans, N., Gilpin, E., Farkas, A. J., Shenassa, E., & Pierce, J. P. (1995). Adolescents' perceptions of their peers' health norms. *American Journal of Public Health, 85*, 1064–1069.

Evers, F. T., & Rush, J. C. (1996). The bases of competence: Skill development during the transition from university to work. *Management Learning, 27*, 275–299.

Fabes, R. A., Eisenberg, N., McCormick, S. E., & Wilson, M. S. (1988). Preschoolers' attributions of the situational determinants of others' naturally occurring emotions. *Developmental Psychology, 24*, 376–385.

Fabes, R. A., Eisenberg, N., Nyman, M., & Michealieu, Q. (1991). Young children's appraisals of others' spontaneous emotional reactions. *Developmental Psychology, 27*, 858–866.

Fagot, B. I. (1995). Parenting boys and girls. In M. H. Bornstein (Ed.), *Handbook of Parenting: Vol. 1. Children and parenting* (pp. 163–183). Mahwah, NJ: Erlbaum.

Fagot, B. I., & Leinbach, M. D. (1989). The young child's gender schema: Environmental input, internal organization. *Child Development, 60*, 663–672.

Farkas, G., Grobe, R. P., Sheehan, D., & Shuan, Y. (1990). Cultural resources and school success: Gender, ethnicity, and poverty groups. *American Sociological Review, 55*, 127–142.

Farmer, T. W., & Rodkin, P. C. (1996). Antisocial and prosocial correlates of classroom social positions: The social network centrality perspective. *Social Development, 5*, 174–188.

Farrar, M. J., Raney, G. E., & Boyer, M. E. (1992). Knowledge, concepts, and inferences in childhood. *Child Development, 63*, 673–691.

Farrell, A. D., Danish, S. J., & Howard, C. W. (1992). Risk factors for drug use in urban adolescents: Identification and cross-validation. *American Journal of Community Psychology, 20*, 263–286.

Farrell, M. P., & Rosenberg, S. D. (1981). *Men at midlife*. Boston: Auburn House.

Feagin, J. R., & McKinney, K. D. (2003). *The many costs of racism*. Lanham, MD: Rowman & Littlefield.

Federal Interagency Forum on Aging Related Statistics. (2004). *Older Americans 2004: Key indicators of well being*. Retrieved February 20, 2005, from http://www.agingstats.gov/chartbook2004/default.htm

Federman, J. (1998). *National television violence study* (Vol. 3). Thousand Oaks, CA: Sage.

Feeney, J. A. (1999). Adult romantic attachment and couple relationships. In J. Cassidy & P. R. Shaver (Eds.), *Handbook of attachment: Theory, research, and clinical applications* (pp. 355–377). New York: Guilford Press.

Feigelman, S., Howard, D. E., Li, P. H. X., & Cross, S. I. (2000). Psychosocial and environmental correlates of violence perpetration among African-American urban youth. *Journal of Adolescent Health, 27*, 202–209.

Feinman, C. F. (1992). *The criminalization of a woman's body*. Binghamton, NY: Hawthorn Press.

Feinman, S., & Lewis, M. (1983). Social referencing at ten months: A second-order effect on infants' responses to strangers. *Child Development, 54*, 878–887.

Feldman, R. (2003). Infant–mother and infant–father synchrony: The coregulation of positive arousal. *Infant Mental Health Journal, 24*, 1–23.

Feldman, S., Byles, J. E., & Beaumont, R. (2000). "Is anybody listening?" The experiences of widowhood for older Australian women. *Journal of Women and Aging, 12*, 155–176.

Fenson, L., Dale, P. S., Reznick, J. S., Bates, E., Thal, D. J., & Pethick, S. J. (1994). Variability in early communicative development. *Monographs of the Society for Research in Child Development, 59* (Serial No. 5).

Fenster, L., Eskenazi, B., Windham, G. C., & Swan, S. H. (1991). Caffeine consumption during pregnancy and fetal growth. *American Journal of Public Health, 81*, 458–461.

Fentress, J. C., & McLeod, P. J. (1986). Motor patterns in development. In E. M. Blass (Ed.), *Handbook of behavioral neurobiology: Vol. 8. Developmental psychobiology and developmental neurobiology*. New York: Plenum Press.

Fernald, A., Swingly, D., & Pinto, J. P. (2001). When half a word is enough: Infants can recognize spoken words using partial phonetic information. *Child Development, 72*, 1003–1015.

Ferster, C. B., & Culbertson, S. A. (1982). *Behavior principles* (3rd ed.). Englewood Cliffs, NJ: Prentice Hall.

Fiatarone, M. A., & Evans, W. J. (1993). The etiology and reversibility of muscle dysfunctions in the aged. *Journal of Gerontology, 48,* 77–83.

Field, D. (1981). Can preschool children really learn to conserve? *Child Development, 52,* 326–334.

Field, T., Diego, M., Hernandez-Reif, M., Schanberg, S., Kuhn, C., Yando, R., & Bendell, D. (2003). Pregnancy anxiety and comorbid depression and anger: Effects on the fetus and neonate. *Depression & Anxiety, 17,* 140–151.

Field, T., Healy, B., Goldstein, S., Perry, S., Bendell, D., Schanberg, S., et al. (1988). Infants of depressed mothers show "depressed" behavior even with nondepressed adults. *Child Development, 59,* 1569–1579.

Field, T. M. (1991). Young children's adaptations to repeated separations from their mothers. *Child Development, 62,* 539–547.

Field, T. M. (2002). Prenatal effects of maternal depression. In S. H. Goodman & I. H. Gotlib (Eds.), *Children of depressed parents: Mechanisms of risk and implications for treatment* (pp. 59–88). Washington, DC: American Psychological Association.

Field, T. M., Cohen, D., Garcia, R., & Greenberg, R. (1984). Mother–stranger face discrimination by the newborn. *Infant Behavior and Development, 7,* 19–25.

Field, T. M., Healy, B., Goldstein, S., & Guthertz, M. (1990). Behavior-state matching and synchrony in mother–infant interaction of nondepressed versus depressed dyads. *Developmental Psychology, 26,* 7–14.

Field, T. M., Sandberg, D., Garcia, R., Vega-Lahr, N., Goldstein, S., & Guy, L. (1985). Pregnancy problems, postpartum depression, and early mother–infant interactions. *Developmental Psychology, 21,* 1152–1156.

Field, T. M., Woodson, R. W., Greenberg, R., & Cohen, C. (1982). Discrimination and imitation of facial expressions by neonates. *Science, 218,* 179–181.

Fields, J. (2003). Children's living arrangements and characteristics: March 2002. *Current Population Reports,* P20-547. Washington, DC: U.S. Census Bureau.

Fields, J. (2004). America's families and living arrangements: 2003. *Current Population Reports,* P20-553. Washington, DC: U. S. Census Bureau.

Fields, J., & Casper, L. M. (2001). America's families and living arrangements: 2000. *Current Population Reports,* P20-537. Washington, DC: U.S. Census Bureau.

Fife, B. L., & Wright, E. R. (2000). The dimensionality of stigma: A comparison of its impact on the self of persons with HIV/AIDS and Cancer. *Journal of Health and Social Behavior, 41,* 50–67.

Fincham, F., & Jaspars, J. (1979). Attribution of responsibility to the self and other in children and adults. *Journal of Personality and Social Psychology, 37,* 1589–1602.

Finer, L. B., & Henshaw, S. K. (2003). Abortion incidence and services in the United States in 2000. *Perspectives on Sexual and Reproductive Health, 35*(1), 1–15.

Fingerman, K. L., Hay, E. L., & Birditt, K. S. (2004). The best of ties, the worst of ties: Close, problematic, and ambivalent social relationships. *Journal of Marriage and the Family, 66,* 792–808.

Finkenauer, C., Engels, R. C. M. E., Branje, S. J. T., & Meeus, W. (2004). Disclosure and relationship satisfaction in families. *Journal of Marriage and the Family, 66,* 195–209.

Finley, M. (1984). *Couvade and the cloud of unknowing.* Retrieved November 15, 2001, from http://www.mfinley.com/articles/couvade.htm

Finley, N. J. (1989). Gender differences in caregiving for elderly parents. *Journal of Marriage and the Family, 51,* 79–86.

Fischer, K. W. (1980). A theory of cognitive development: The control and construction of hierarchies of skills. *Psychological Review, 87,* 477–531.

Fischer, K. W., & Bidell, T. R. (1992, Winter). Ever younger ages: Constructive use of nativist findings about early development. *Newsletter of the Society for Research in Child Development,* pp. 1, 10, 11, 14.

Fischer, K. W., Bullock, D., Rotenberg, E. J., & Raya, P. (1993). The dynamics of competence: How context contributes directly to skill. In R. Wozniak & K. Fischer (Eds.), *Development in context: Acting and thinking in specific environments* (JPS Series on Knowledge and Development, Vol. 1, pp. 93–117). Hillsdale, NJ: Erlbaum.

Fischer, K. W., & Rose, S. P. (1994). Dynamic development of coordination of components of brain and behavior: A framework for theory and research. In G. Dawson & K. W. Fischer (Eds.), *Human behavior and the developing brain* (pp. 3–66). New York: Guilford Press.

Fischer, K. W., & Silvern, L. (1985). Stages and individual differences in cognitive development. *Annual Review of Psychology, 36,* 613–648.

Fitch, J. (1999). *White oleander.* Boston: Little, Brown.

Fitzgerald, B. (1999). Children of lesbian and gay parents: A review of the literature. *Marriage and Family Review, 29,* 57–75.

Flaks, D. K., Ficher, I., Masterpasqua, F., & Joseph, G. (1995). Lesbians choosing motherhood: A comparative study of lesbian and heterosexual parents and their children. *Developmental Psychology, 31,* 105–114.

Flannery, D. J., Rowe, D. C., & Gulley, B. L. (1993). Impact of pubertal status, timing, and age on adolescent sexual experience and delinquency. *Journal of Adolescent Research, 8,* 21–40.

Flavell, J. H. (1963). *The developmental psychology of Jean Piaget.* Princeton, NJ: Van Nostrand.

Flavell, J. H. (1974). The development of inferences about others. In W. Mischel (Ed.), *Understanding other persons.* Oxford: Blackwell, Basil & Mott.

Flavell, J. H. (1982). On cognitive development. *Child Development, 53,* 1–10.

Flavell, J. H. (1982). Structures, stages, and sequences in cognitive development. In W. A. Collins (Ed.), *The concept of development* (pp. 1–28). Hillsdale, NJ: Erlbaum.

Flavell, J. H., Flavell, E. R., & Green, F. L. (1987). Young children's knowledge about the apparent–real and pretend–real distinctions. *Developmental Psychology, 23,* 816–822.

Fleming, A. S., Ruble, D. N., Flett, G. L., & Shaul, D. L. (1988). Postpartum adjustment in first-time mothers: Relations between mood, maternal attitudes, and mother–infant interactions. *Developmental Psychology, 24,* 71–81.

Fletcher, W. L., & Hansson, R. O. (1991). Assessing the social components of retirement anxiety. *Psychology and Aging, 6,* 76–85.

Florian, V., & Kravetz, S. (1983). Fear of personal death: Attribution structure and relation to religious belief. *Journal of Personality and Social Psychology, 44,* 600–607.

Floyd, F. J., Haynes, S. N., Doll, E. R., Winemiller, D., Lemsky, C., Burgy, T. M., et al. (1992). Assessing retirement satisfaction and perceptions of retirement experiences. *Psychology and Aging, 7,* 609–621.

Floyd, F. J., Stein, T. S., Harter, K. S. M., Allison, A., & Nye, C. L. (1999). Gay, lesbian, and bisexual youths: Separation-individuation, parental attitudes, identity consolidation, and well-being. *Journal of Youth and Adolescence, 28,* 719–739.

Flynn, C. B, Longino, C. F., Jr., Wiseman, R. F., & Biggar, J. C. (1985). The redistribution of America's older population: Major national migration patterns for three census decades, 1960–1980. *The Gerontologist, 25,* 292–296.

Flynn, K., & Fitzgibbon, M. (1996). Body image ideals of low-income African American mothers and their preadolescent daughters. *Journal of Youth and Adolescence, 25,* 615–630.

Folkman, S., & Moskowitz, J. T. (2000). Positive affect and the other side of coping. *American Psychologist, 55,* 647–654.

Fonagy, P. (1999). Psychoanalytic theory from the viewpoint of attachment theory and research. In J. Cassidy & P. R. Shaver (Eds.), *Handbook of attachment: Theory, research, and clinical applications* (pp. 595–624). New York: Guilford Press.

Fonagy, P., Steele, H., & Steele, M. (1991). Maternal representations of attachment during pregnancy predict the organization of infant–mother attachment at one year of age. *Child Development, 62,* 891–905.

Fontane, P. E. (1996). Exercise, fitness, feeling well. *American Behavioral Scientist, 39,* 288–305.

Foote, D. (1998, February 2). And baby makes one. *Newsweek,* pp. 68, 70.

Ford, C. S. (1945). A comparative study of human reproduction. *Yale University Publications in Anthropology* (No. 32).

Ford, M. E. (1985). The concept of competence: Themes and variations. In H. A. Marlowe & R. A. Weinberg (Eds.), *Competence development: Theory and practice in special populations.* Springfield, IL: Thomas.

Fordham, K., & Stevenson-Hinde, J. (1999). Shyness, friendship quality, and adjustment during middle childhood. *Journal of Child Psychology and Psychiatry and Allied Disciplines, 40,* 757–768.

Forman, T. A. (2003). The social psychological costs of racial segmentation in the workplace: A study of African Americans' well-being. *Journal of Health and Social Behavior, 44*, 332–352.

Fortenberry, J. D., Costa, F. M., Jessor, R., & Donovan, J. E. (1997). Contraceptive behavior and adolescent lifestyles: A structural modeling approach. *Journal of Research on Adolescence, 7*, 307–329.

Fosburgh, L. (1977, August 7). The make-believe world of teen-age maturity. *New York Times Magazine*, pp. 29–34.

Fowers, B. J., Montel, K. H., & Olson, D. H. (1996). Predicting marital success for premarital couple types based on PREPARE. *Journal of Marital and Family Therapy, 22*, 103–119.

Fowler, F. L., Jr. (1993). *Survey research methods* (2nd ed.). Thousand Oaks, CA: Sage.

Fox, N. A., Kimmerly, N. L., & Schafer, W. D. (1991). Attachment to mother/attachment to father. *Child Development, 62*, 210–225.

Foxx, R. M. (2001). Lessons learned: Thirty years of applied behavior analysis in treating problem behaviors. In C. Maurice & G. Green (Eds.), *Making a difference: Behavioral intervention for autism* (pp. 183–194). Austin, TX: Pro-Ed.

Frankenberg, W. K., & Dodds, J. B. (1967). The Developmental Screening Test. *Journal of Pediatrics, 71*, 181–191

Franklin, D. L. (1988). Race, class, and adolescent pregnancy: An ecological analysis. *American Journal of Orthopsychiatry, 58*, 339–355.

Franko, D. L., & Striegel-Moore, R. H. (2002). The role of body dissatisfaction as a risk factor for depression in adolescent girls: Are the differences Black and White? *Journal of Psychosomatic Research, 53*, 975–983.

Frazier, P., Byer, A. L., Fischer, A. R., Wright, D. M., & DeBord, K. A. (1996). Adult attachment style and partner choice: Correlational and experimental findings. *Personal Relationships, 3*, 117–136.

Frea, W. D., & Vittimberga, G. L. (2000). Behavioral interventions for children with autism. In J. Austin & J. E. Carr (Eds.), *Handbook of applied behavior analysis* (pp. 247–273). Reno, NV: Context Press.

Fredriksen, K., Rhodes, J., Reddy, R., & Way, N. (2004). Sleepless in Chicago: Tracking the effects of adolescent sleep loss during the middle school years. *Child Development, 75*, 84–95.

Freedman, V. A., & Martin, L. G. (2000). Contribution of chronic conditions to aggregate changes in old-age functioning. *American Journal of Public Health, 90*, 1755–1760.

Freeman, R. B., & Wise, D. A. (1982). *The youth labor market: Problems in the United States*. Chicago: University of Chicago Press.

Freiberg, K., Tually, K., & Crassini, B. (2001). Use of an auditory looming task to test infants' sensitivity to sound pressure level as an auditory distance cue. *British Journal of Developmental Psychology, 19*, 1–10.

French, D. C. (1984). Children's knowledge of the social functions of younger, older and same-age peers. *Child Development, 55*, 1429–1433.

French, D. C. (1988). Heterogeneity of peer-rejected boys: Aggressive and nonaggressive subtypes. *Child Development, 59*, 976–985.

French, D. C. (1990). Heterogeneity of peer-rejected girls. *Child Development, 61*, 2028–2031.

Frese, M. (2001). Personal initiative: The theoretical concept and empirical findings. In M. Erez & U. Kleinbeck (Eds.), *Work motivation in the context of a globalizing economy* (pp. 99–110). Mahwah, NJ: Erlbaum.

Freud, A. (1936). *The ego and mechanisms of defense*. New York: International Universities Press.

Freud, A., & Dann, S. (1951). An experiment in group upbringing. In R. Eissler, A. Freud, H. Hartmann, & E. Kris (Eds.), *The psychoanalytic study of the child* (Vol. 6, pp. 127–168). New York: International Universities Press.

Freud, S. (1905/1953). Three essays on the theory of sexuality. In J. Strachey (Ed.), *The standard edition of the complete psychological works of Sigmund Freud* (Vol. 7, pp. 125–245). London: Hogarth Press.

Freud, S. (1909/1955). An analysis of a phobia in a 5-year-old boy. In J. Strachey (Ed.), *The standard edition of the complete psychological works of Sigmund Freud* (Vol. 10, 5–149). London: Hogarth Press.

Freud, S. (1925/1961). Some psychical consequences of the anatomical distinction between the sexes. In J. Strachey (Ed.), *The standard edition of the complete psychological works of Sigmund Freud* (Vol. 19, pp. 248–258). London: Hogarth Press.

Freud, S. (1933/1964). New introductory lectures on psychoanalysis. In J. Strachey (Ed.), *The standard edition of the complete psychological works of Sigmund Freud* (Vol. 22, pp. 3–182). London: Hogarth Press.

Freud, S. (1994). The social construction of gender. *Journal of Adult Development, 1*, 37–46.

Freund, A. M., & Baltes, P. B. (1998). Selection, optimization, and compensation as strategies of life management: Correlations with subjective indicators of successful aging. *Psychology and Aging, 13*, 531–543.

Frey, K. S., & Ruble, D. N. (1987). What children say about classroom performance: Sex and grade differences in perceived competence. *Child Development, 58*, 1066–1078.

Frey, P. S. (2003). Perceived self-efficacy domains as predictors of fear of the unknown and fear of dying among older adults. *Psychology and Aging, 18*, 474–486.

Fried, P. A., Watkinson, B., Dillon, R. F., & Dulberg, C. S. (1987). Neonatal neurological status in a low-risk population after prenatal exposure to cigarettes, marijuana, and alcohol. *Journal of Developmental and Behavioral Pediatrics, 8*, 318–326.

Friedlander, D., & Burtless, G. (1994). *Five years after: The long-term effects of welfare-to-work programs*. New York: Russell Sage Foundation.

Friedman, W. J., Robinson, A. B., & Friedman, B. L. (1987). Sex differences in moral judgments? A test of Gilligan's theory. *Psychology of Women Quarterly, 11*, 37–46.

Froming, W. J., Allen, L., & Jensen, R. (1985). Altruism, role-taking, and self-awareness: The acquisition of norms governing altruistic behavior. *Child Development, 56*, 1123–1228.

Froming, W. J., Nasby, W., & McManus, J. (1998). Prosocial self-schemas, self-awareness, and children's prosocial behavior. *Journal of Personality and Social Psychology, 75*, 766–777.

Frone, M. R. (2003). Work–family balance. In J. C. Quick & L. E. Tetrick (Eds.), *Handbook of occupational health psychology* (pp. 143–162). Washington, DC: American Psychological Association.

Fuller, B., Kagan, S. L., Caspary, G. L., & Gauthier, C. A. (2002). Welfare reform and childcare options for low-income families. *The Future of Children, 12*, 97–119.

Fuller-Thomson, E., Minkler, M., & Driver, D. (1997). A profile of grandparents raising grandchildren in the United States. *The Gerontologist, 37*, 406–411.

Fultz, N. H., & Herzog, A. R. (1991). Gender differences in affiliation and instrumentality across adulthood. *Psychology and Aging, 6*, 579–586.

Funk, J. B., Baldacci, H. B., Pasold, T., & Baumgardner, J. (2004). Violence exposure in real-life, video games, television, movies, and the Internet: Is there desensitization? *Journal of Adolescence, 27*, 23–39.

Furman, W., & Wehner, E. A. (1997). Adolescent romantic relationships: A developmental perspective. In S. Shulman & W. A. Collins (Eds.), *Romantic relationships in adolescence: Developmental perspectives* (pp. 21–36). San Francisco: Jossey-Bass.

Futterman, A., Gallagher, D., Thompson, L. W., Lovett, S., & Gilewski, M. (1990). Retrospective assessment of marital adjustment and depression during the first two years of spousal bereavement. *Psychology and Aging, 5*, 277–283.

Gaddis, A., & Brooks-Gunn, J. (1985). The male experience of pubertal change. *Journal of Youth and Adolescence, 14*, 61–69.

Gaina, A., Sekine, M., Chen, X., Hamanishi, S., & Kagamimori, S. (2004). Sleep parameters recorded by Actiwatch® in elementary school children and junior high school adolescents: Schooldays vs. weekends. *Sleep and Hypnosis, 6*, 66–77.

Gall, T. L., Evans, D. R., & Howard, J. (1997). The retirement adjustment process: Changes in the well-being of male retirees across time. *Journal of Gerontology, 52*, P110–P117.

Galler, J. R., & Tonkiss, J. (1998). The effects of prenatal protein malnutrition and cocaine on the development of the rat. In J. A. Harvey & B. E. Kosofsky (Eds.), *Cocaine: Effects on the developing brain* (pp. 29–39). New York: New York Academy of Sciences.

Galotti, K. M. (1989). Gender differences in self-reported moral reasoning: A review of new evidence. *Journal of Youth and Adolescence, 18*, 475–488.

Galotti, K. M., Kozberg, S. F., & Farmer, M. C. (1991). Gender and developmental differences in adolescents' conceptions of moral reasoning. *Journal of Youth and Adolescence, 20,* 13–30.

Galt, A. H. (1991). Magical misfortune in Locorotondo. *American Ethnologist, 18,* 735–750.

Galyer, K. T., & Evans, I. M. (2001). Pretend play and the development of emotion regulation in preschool children. *Early Child Development and Care, 166,* 93–108.

Ganea, P. A., Lillard, A. S., & Turkheimer, E. (2004). Preschoolers' understanding of the role of mental states and action in pretense. *Journal of Cognition and Development, 5,* 213–238.

Garbarino, J. (2001). An ecological perspective on the effects of violence on children. *Journal of Community Psychology, 29,* 361–378.

Gardiner, H. W., & Kosmitzki, C. (2005). *Lives across cultures: Cross-cultural human development* (3rd ed.). Boston: Pearson.

Gardner, H. (1983). *Frames of mind: The theory of multiple intelligences.* New York: Basic Books.

Gardner, H. (1993). *Creating minds.* New York: Basic Books.

Gardner, H., Kornhaber, M. L., & Wake, W. K. (1996). *Intelligence: Multiple perspectives.* Fort Worth, TX: Harcourt Brace.

Garguilo, J., Attie, I., Brooks-Gunn, J., & Warren, M. P. (1987). Dating in middle school girls: Effects of social context, maturation, and grade. *Developmental Psychology, 23,* 730–737.

Garland, A. F., & Zigler, E. (1993). Adolescent suicide prevention: Current research and social policy implications. *American Psychologist, 48,* 169–182.

Garmezy, N. (1991). Resilience in children's adaptation to negative life events and stressed environments. *Pediatric Annals, 20,* 459–466.

Garmezy, N., & Masten, A. S. (1991). The protective role of competence indicators in children at risk. In E. M. Cummings, A. L. Greene, & K. H. Karraker (Eds.), *Life-span developmental psychology: Perspectives on stress and coping* (pp. 151–174). Hillsdale, NJ: Erlbaum.

Garrison, C. Z., Schluchter, M. D., Schoenbach, V. J., & Kaplan, B. K. (1989). Epidemiology of depressive symptoms in young adolescents. *Journal of the American Academy of Child and Adolescent Psychiatry, 28,* 343–351.

Garton, A. F. (1992). *Social interaction and the development of language and cognition.* Hillsdale, NJ: Erlbaum.

Garvey, C. (1977). *Play.* Cambridge, MA: Harvard University Press.

Gati, I., Osipow, S. H., & Givon, M. (1995). Gender differences in career decision making: The content and structure of preference. *Journal of Counseling Psychology, 42,* 204–215.

Gattai, F. B., & Musatti, T. (1999). Grandmothers' involvement in grandchildren's care: Attitudes, feelings, and emotions. *Family Relations: Interdisciplinary Journal of Applied Family Studies, 48,* 35–42.

Gavin, L. A., & Furman, W. (1989). Age differences in adolescents' perceptions of their peer groups. *Developmental Psychology, 25,* 827–834.

Ge, X., Conger, R. D., & Elder, G. H., Jr. (2001). The relation between puberty and psychological distress in adolescent boys. *Journal of Research on Adolescence, 11,* 49–70.

Geary, D. C., & Brown, S. C. (1991). Cognitive addition: Strategy choice and speed of processing differences in gifted, normal, and mathematically disabled children. *Developmental Psychology, 27,* 398–406.

Geary, D. C., Brown, S. C., & Samaranayake, V. A. (1991). Cognitive addition: A short longitudinal study of strategy choice and speed-of-processing differences in normal and mathematically disabled children. *Developmental Psychology, 27,* 787–797.

Geary, D. C., Hoard, M. K., Byrd-Craven, J., & DeSoto, M. C. (2004). Strategy choices in simple and complex addition: Contributions of working memory and counting knowledge for children with mathematical disability. *Journal of Experimental Child Psychology, 88,* 121–151.

Geary, D. C., Vigil, J., & Byrd-Craven, J. (2004). Evolution of human mate choice. *Journal of Sex Research, 41,* 27–42.

Gelles, R. J. (1989). Child abuse and violence in single-parent families: Parent absence and economic deprivation. *American Journal of Orthopsychiatry, 59,* 492–501.

Gelman, D. (1992, February 24). Born or bred: The origins of homosexuality. *Newsweek,* pp. 46–53.

Gentile, D. A., & Walsh, D. A. (2002). A normative study of family media habits. *Applied Developmental Psychology, 23,* 157–178.

George, C., Kaplan, N., & Main, M. (1996). *Adult Attachment Interview protocol* (3rd ed.) Unpublished manuscript, Department of Psychology, University of California at Berkeley.

George, C., & Solomon, J. (1999). Attachment and caregiving: The caregiving behavioral system. In J. Cassidy & P. R. Shaver (Eds.), *Handbook of attachment: Theory, research, and clinical applications* (pp. 649–670). New York: Guilford Press.

Gerbner, G., Gross, L., Morgan, M., & Signorelli, N. (1980). The "mainstreaming" of America: Violence profile no. 11. *Journal of Communication, 30,* 10–29.

Gerhold, M., Laucht, M., Texdorf, C., Schmidt, M. H., & Esser, G. (2002). Early mother–infant interaction as a precursor to childhood social withdrawal. *Child Psychiatry & Human Development, 32,* 277–293.

Gernsbacher, M. A., & Kaschak, M. P. (2003). Neuroimaging studies of language production and comprehension. *Annual Review of Psychology, 54,* 91–114.

Getchell, N., & Robertson, M. A. (1989). Whole body stiffness as a function of developmental level in children's hopping. *Developmental Psychology, 25,* 920–928.

Geyman, J. P., Oliver, L. M., & Sullivan, S. D. (1999). Expectant, medical, or surgical treatment of spontaneous abortion in first trimester of pregnancy? A pooled quantitative literature evaluation. *Journal of the American Board of Family Practice, 12,* 55–64.

Gfellner, B. M. (1986). Ego development and moral development in relation to age and grade level during adolescence. *Journal of Youth and Adolescence, 15,* 147–163.

Gfroerer, J. C., Greenblatt, J. C., & Wright, D. A. (1997). Substance use in the U.S. college-age population: Differences according to educational status and living arrangement. *American Journal of Public Health, 87,* 62–65.

Ghazanfareeon Karlsson, S., & Borrell, K. (2002). Intimacy and autonomy, gender and ageing: Living apart together. *Ageing International, 27,* 11–26.

Giambra, L. M., Arenberg, D., Zonderman, A. B., & Kawas, C. (1995). Adult life span changes in immediate visual memory and verbal intelligence. *Psychology and Aging, 10,* 123–139.

Giarrusso, R., Silverstein, M., & Bengston, V. L. (1996). Family complexity and the grandparenting role. *Generations: Quarterly Journal of the American Society on Aging, 20,* 17–23.

Gibbs, J. C. (1979). Kohlberg's moral stage theory: A Piagetian revision. *Human Development, 22,* 89–112.

Gibson, E. J., & Pick, A. D. (2000). *An ecological approach to perceptual learning and development.* London: Oxford University Press.

Gibson, E. J., & Walker, A. S. (1984). Development of knowledge of visual-tactual affordances of substance. *Child Development, 55,* 453–460.

Gibson, F. L., Ungerer, J. A., McMahon, C. A., Leslie, G. I., & Saunders, D. M. (2000). The mother–child relationship following in vitro fertilisation (IVF): Infant attachment, responsivity, and maternal sensitivity. *Journal of Child Psychology and Psychiatry and Allied Disciplines, 41,* 1015–1023.

Giele, J. Z. (1988). Gender and sex roles. In N. J. Smelser (Ed.), *Handbook of sociology* (pp. 291–326). Newbury Park, CA: Sage.

Gielen, U. P., & Markoulis, D. C. (2001). Preference for principled moral reasoning: A developmental and cross-cultural perspective. In L. L Adler & U. P. Gielen (Eds.). *Cross-cultural topics in psychology* (2nd ed., pp. 81–101). Westport, CT: Praeger/Greenwood.

Gielen, U. P., & Miao, E. S. C. Y. (2000). Perceived parental behavior and the development of moral reasoning in students from Taiwan. In A. L. Comunian & U. P. Gielen (Eds.), *International perspectives on human development* (pp. 479–503). Lengerich, Germany: Pabst.

Gifford-Smith, M. E., & Brownell, C. A. (2003). Childhood peer relationships: Social acceptance, friendships, and peer networks. *Journal of School Psychology, 41,* 235–284.

Gilbert, L. A. (1993). *Two careers/one family.* Newbury Park, CA: Sage.

Gillespie, C. (1989). *Hormones, hot flashes, and mood swings.* New York: Harper & Row.

Gilligan, C. (1977). In a different voice: Women's conceptions of self and morality. *Harvard Educational Review, 47*, 481–517.

Gilligan, C. (1982/1993). *In a different voice: Psychological theory and women's development.* Cambridge, MA: Harvard University Press.

Gilligan, C. (1988). *Mapping the moral domain: A contribution of women's thinking to psychological theory and education.* Cambridge, MA: Harvard University Press.

Ginsburg, H. P., & Pappas, S. (2004). SES, ethnic, and gender differences in young children's informal addition and subtraction: A clinical interview investigation. *Journal of Applied Developmental Psychology, 25*, 171–192.

Ginsburg, S. D., & Orlofsky, J. L. (1981). Ego identity status, ego development, and focus of control in college women. *Journal of Youth and Adolescence, 10*, 297–307.

Giordano, P. C., Cernkovich, S. A., & DeMaris, A. (1993). The family and peer relations of black adolescents. *Journal of Marriage and the Family, 55*, 277–287.

Glass, T. A. (1998). Conjugating the "tenses" of function: Discordance among hypothetical, experimental, and enacted function in older adults. *The Gerontologist, 38*, 101–112.

Gleason, T. R. (2002). Social provisions of real and imaginary relationships in early childhood. *Developmental Psychology, 38*, 979–992.

Gleason, T. R., Sebanc, A. M., & Hartup, W. W. (2003). Imaginary companions of preschool children. In M. E. Hertzig & E. A. Farber (Eds.), *Annual progress in child psychiatry and child development: 2000–2001* (pp. 101–121). New York: Brunner-Routledge.

Gleckman H., Smart, T., Dwyer, P., Segal, T., & Weber, J. (1991, July 8). Race in the workplace. *Business Week*, pp. 50–62.

Glenn, N. D., & Kramer, K. B. (1987). Marriages and divorces of children of divorce. *Journal of Marriage and the Family, 49*, 811–826.

Glick, P. C. (1957). *American families.* New York: Wiley.

Gliner, J. A., & Morgan, G. A. (2000). *Research methods in applied settings: An integrated approach to design and analysis.* Mahwah, NJ: Erlbaum.

Glodis, K. A., & Blasi, A. (1993). The sense of self and identity among adolescents and adults. *Journal of Adolescent Research, 8*, 356–380.

Glover, V. (1997). Maternal stress or anxiety in pregnancy and emotional development of the child. *British Journal of Psychiatry, 171*, 105–106.

Godsil, B. P., Quinn, J. J., & Fanselow, M. S. (2000). Body temperature as a conditional response measure for Pavlovian fear conditioning. *Learning and Memory, 7*, 353–356.

Goldbaum, S., Craig, W. M., Pepler, D., & Connolly, J. (2003). Developmental trajectories of victimization: Identifying risk and protective factors. *Journal of Applied School Psychology, 19*, 139–156.

Goldberg, S. (1977). Infant development and mother–infant interaction in urban Zambia. In P. H. Leiderman, S. R. Tulkin, & A. Rosenfeld (Eds.), *Culture and infancy: Variations in the human experience* (pp. 211–244). New York: Academic Press.

Goldberg, S., & DiVitto, B. (1995). Parenting children born preterm. In M. H. Bornstein (Ed.), *Handbook of parenting, Vol. 1. Children and parenting.* (pp. 209–232). Mahwah, NJ: Erlbaum.

Goldberg, W. A., Clarke-Stewart, K. A., Rice, J. A., & Dellis, E. (2002). Emotional energy as an explanatory construct for fathers' engagement with their infants. *Parenting: Science & Practice, 2*, 379–408.

Goldenberg, C. N. (1989). Parents' effects on academic grouping for reading: Three case studies. *American Educational Research Journal, 26*, 329–352.

Goldfield, E. C. (1989). Transition from rocking to crawling: Postural constraints on infant movement. *Developmental Psychology, 25*, 913–919.

Goldman, H. I. (2001). Parental reports of 'MAMA' sounds in infants: An exploratory study. *Journal of Child Language, 28*, 497–506.

Goldscheider, F. K., & Goldscheider, C. (1998). The effects of childhood family structure on leaving and returning home. *Journal of Marriage and the Family, 60*, 745–756.

Goldscheider, F. K., Thornton, A., & Yang, L. (2001). Helping out the kids: Expectations about parental support in young adulthood. *Journal of Marriage and the Family, 63*, 727–740.

Goldsmith, D. J., & Dun, S. A. (1997). Sex differences and similarities in the communication of social support. *Journal of Social and Personal Relationships, 14*, 317–337.

Goldsmith, H. H., Buss, A. H., Plomin, R., Rothbart, M. K., Thomas, A., Chess, S., et al. (1987). Roundtable: What is temperament? Four approaches. *Child Development, 58*, 505–529.

Goldsmith, H. H., & Campos, J. J. (1986). Fundamental issues in the study of early development: The Denver twin temperament study. In M. E. Lamb & A. Brown (Eds.), *Advances in developmental psychology* (pp. 231–283). Hillsdale, NJ: Erlbaum.

Golinkoff, R. M., Hirsh-Pasek, K., Bailey, L. M., & Wenger, N. R. (1992). Young children and adults use lexical principles to learn new nouns. *Developmental Psychology, 28*, 99–108.

Golmand, M. B., Occhiuto, J. S., Peterson, L. E., Zapka, J. G., & Palmer, R. H. (2004). Physician assistants as providers of surgically induced abortion services. *American Journal of Public Health, 94*, 1352–1357.

Golombok, S., Cook, R., Bish, A., & Murray, C. (1995). Families created by the new reproductive technologies: Quality of parenting and social and emotional development of the children. *Child Development, 66*, 285–298.

Golombok, S., MacCallum, F., & Goodman, E. (2001). The "test-tube" generation: Parent–child relationships and the psychological well-being of in vitro fertilization children at adolescence. *Child Development, 72*, 599–608.

Good, T. L., & Nichols, S. L. (2001). Expectancy effects in the classroom: A special focus on improving the reading performance of minority students in first-grade classrooms. *Educational Psychologist, 36*, 113–126.

Goodfellow, J., & Laverty, J. (2003). Grandparents supporting working families: Satisfaction and choice in the provision of child care. *Family Matters, 66*, 14–19.

Goodman, C. C. (2003). Intergenerational triads in grandparent-headed families. *Journal of Gerontology: Series B: Psychological Sciences and Social Sciences, 58B*, S281–S289.

Gopnik, A., & Meltzoff, A. (1987). The development of categorization in the second year and its relation to other cognitive and linguistic developments. *Child Development, 58*, 1523–1531.

Gopnik, A., & Meltzoff, A. N. (1992). Categorization and naming: Basic-level sorting in eighteen-month-olds and its relation to language. *Child Development, 63*, 1091–1103.

Gopnik, A., & Meltzoff, A. N. (1997). *Words, thoughts, and theories.* Cambridge, MA: MIT Press.

Gore, S., Aseltine, R. H., & Colten, M. E. (1993). Gender, social-relational involvement, and depression. *Journal of Research on Adolescence, 3*, 101–126.

Gorer, G. (1938). *Himalayan village: An account of the Lepchas of Sikkim.* London: Michael Joseph.

Gornick, V. (1971, January 10). Consciousness. *New York Times Magazine.*

Gottesman, I. I. (1997). Twins: En route to QTLs for cognition. *Science, 276*, 1522–1523.

Gottman, J., Coan, J., Carrere, S., & Swanson, C. (1998). Predicting marital happiness and stability from newlywed interactions. *Journal of Marriage and the Family, 60*, 5–22.

Gottman, J., & Silver, N. (2000). *The seven principles for making marriage work.* New York: Crown.

Gottman, J. M., & Levenson, R. W. (1986). Assessing the role of emotion in marriage. *Behavioral Assessment, 8*, 31–48.

Graber, J. A. (2004). Internalizing problems during adolescence. In R. M. Lerner & L. Steinberg (Eds.), *Handbook of adolescent psychology* (2nd ed., pp. 587–626). New York: Wiley.

Grandquist, H. (1950). *Child problems among the Arabs.* Helsinki: Söderstrom.

Gratch, G., & Schatz, J. A. (1987). Cognitive development: The relevance of Piaget's infancy books. In J. D. Osofsky (Ed.), *Handbook of infant development* (2nd ed., pp. 204–237). New York: Wiley.

Gray, P. (1996). Incorporating evolutionary theory into the teaching of psychology. *Teaching of Psychology, 29*, 207–209.

Gray, W. M. (1990). Formal operational thought. In W. F. Overton (Ed.), *Reasoning, necessity, and logic: Developmental perspectives (pp. 227–253). Hillsdale, NJ: Erlbaum.

Green, L., Fein, D., Joy, S., & Waterhouse, L. (1995). Cognitive functioning in autism: An overview. In E. Schopler & G. B. Mesibov (Eds.). Learning and cognition in autism (pp. 13–31). New York: Plenum Press.

Green, R. J., & Hill, J. H. (2003). Sex and higher education: Do men and women attend college for different reasons? College Student Journal, 37, 557–563.

Green, R. J., Bettinger, M., & Zacks, E. (1996). Are lesbian couples fused and gay male couples disengaged? Questioning gender straightjackets. In J. Laird & R. J. Green (Eds.), Lesbians and gays in couples and families: A handbook for therapists (pp. 185–230). San Francisco: Jossey-Bass.

Greenberg, E. F., & Nay, W. R. (1982). The intergenerational transmission of marital instability reconsidered. Journal of Marriage and the Family, 44, 335–347.

Greene, A. L., Wheatley, S. M., & Alvada, J. F. (1992). Stages on life's way: Adolescents' implicit theories of the life course. Journal of Adolescent Research, 7, 364–381.

Greenfield, P. M., & Childs, C. P. (1991). Developmental continuity in biocultural context. In R. Cohen & A. W. Siegel (Eds.), Context and development (pp. 135–159). Hillsdale, NJ: Erlbaum.

Greenfield, P. M., & Suzuki, L. (1998). Culture and human development: Implications for parenting, education, pediatrics, and mental health. In I. Sigel & K. Renninger (Eds.), Handbook of child psychology, Vol. 4: Child psychology in practice (5th ed., pp. 1059–1109). New York: Wiley.

Gregg, T. R. (2004). Use of functional magnetic resonance imaging to investigate brain functioning. Retrieved August 24, 2004, from http://www.neuroguide.com/gregg.html

Gregor, T. (1977). Mehinaku: The drama of daily life in a Brazilian Indian village. Chicago: University of Chicago Press.

Gregory, K. M., Kim, A. S., & Whiren, A. (2003). The effect of verbal scaffolding on the complexity of preschool children's block constructions. In D. E. Lytle (Ed.), Play and educational theory and practice (pp. 117–133). Westport, CT: Praeger/Greenwood.

Gregory, L. W. (1995). The "turnaround" process: Factors influencing the school success of urban youth. Journal of Adolescent Research, 10, 136–154.

Grigsby, C., Baumann, D., Gregorich, S. E., & Roberts-Gray, C. (1990). Disaffiliation to entrenchment: A model for understanding homelessness. Journal of Social Issues, 46, 141–156.

Grolnick, W. S., Bridges, L. J., & Connell, J. P. (1996). Emotion regulation in two-year-olds: Strategies and emotional expression in four contexts. Child Development, 67, 928–941.

Groome, L. J., Mooney, D. M., Holland, S. B., Smith, Y. D., Atterbury, J. L., & Dykman, R. A. (2000). Temporal pattern and spectral complexity as stimulus parameters for eliciting a cardiac orienting reflex in hu-

man fetuses. Perception and Psychophysics, 62, 313–320.

Groome, L. J., Swiber, M. J., Bentz, L. S., Lynn, S., Holland, S. B., et al. (1995). Maternal anxiety during pregnancy: Effect on fetal behavior at 38 to 40 weeks of gestation. Journal of Developmental and Behavioral Pediatrics, 16, 391–396.

Grossman, F. K., Eichler, L. S., & Winickoff, S. A. (1980). Pregnancy, birth, and parenthood. San Francisco: Jossey-Bass.

Grunbaum, J. A., Kann, L., Kinchen, S. A., et al. (2002). Youth risk behavior surveillance: United States, 2001. Morbidity and Mortality Weekly Report, Center for Disease Control Surveillance Summary, 51, 1–62.

Grunfeld, F. V. (1975). Games of the world: How to make them, how to play them, how they came to be. New York: Holt, Rinehart & Winston.

Grusec, J. E. (1992). Social learning theory and developmental psychology: The legacies of Robert Sears and Albert Bandura. Developmental Psychology, 28, 776–786.

Grusec, J. E., & Abramovitch, R. (1982). Imitation of peers and adults in a natural setting: A functional analysis. Child Development, 53, 636–642.

Gulko, J., Doyle, A., Serbin, L. A., & White, D. R. (1988). Conservation skills: A replicated study of order of acquisition across tasks. Journal of Genetic Psychology, 149, 425–439.

Gunnar, M. R., Larson, M. C., Hertsgaard, L., Harris, M. L., & Brodersen, L. (1992). The stressfulness of separation among 9-month-old infants: Effects of social context variables and infant temperament. Child Development, 63, 290–303.

Gunnar, M. R., Mangelsdorf, S., Larson, M., & Hertsgaard, L. (1989). Attachment, temperament, and adrenocortical activity in infancy: A study of psychoendocrine regulation. Developmental Psychology, 25, 355–363.

Gur, R. C., Turetsky, B. I., Matsui, M., Yan, M., Bilker, W., Hughett, P., & Gur, R. E. (1999). Sex differences in brain gray and white matter in healthy young adults: Correlations with cognitive performance. The Journal of Neuroscience, 19, 4065–4072.

Guralnik, J. M., & Kaplan, G. A. (1989). Predictors of healthy aging: Prospective evidence from the Alameda County study. American Journal of Public Health, 79, 703–708.

Guralnik, J. M., & Simonsick, E. M. (1993). Physical disability in older Americans. Journal of Gerontology, 48, 3–10.

Gurin, P., & Markus, H. (1988). Group identity: The psychological mechanisms of durable salience. Revue Internationale de Psychologie Sociale, 1, 257–274.

Gutman, L., & Midgley, C. (2000). The role of protective factors in supporting the academic achievement of poor African American students during the middle school transition. Journal of Youth and Adolescence, 29, 223–248.

Gutmann, D. (1987). Reclaimed powers: Toward a new psychology of men and women in later life. New York: Basic Books.

Gutmann, D. L. (1985). Deculturation and the American grandparent. In V. L. Bengston & J. F. Robertson (Eds.), Grandparenthood (pp. 173–181). Newbury Park, CA: Sage.

Guttman, M. (1998, January 2–4). Who's healthier: Men or women? USA Weekend, p. 4–13.

Guttmann, B. (1932). Die Stammeslehvender des Chagga (Vol. 1). Munich: Beck.

Habib, M. (2001). Online dating becoming common. Canadian Press. Retrieved December 23, 2001, from http://www.canoe.ca/CNEWSTech- News0102/07 _dating-cp.html

Hack, M., & Fanaroff, A. A. (1999). Outcomes of children of extremely low birth weight and gestational age in the 1990s. Early Human Development, 53, 192–218.

Hadley, E. C., Ory, M. G., Suzman, R., & Weindruch, R. (1993). Foreword. Journal of Gerontology, 48, vii–viii.

Haffner, D. W. (1998). Facing facts: Sexual health for American adolescents. Journal of Adolescent Health, 22, 453–459.

Hahn, R. A., & Muecke, M. A. (1987). The anthropology of birth in five U.S. ethnic populations: Implications for obstetrical practice. Current Problems in Obstetrics, Gynecology, and Fertility, 10, 133–171.

Hahn-Smith, A. M., & Smith, J. E. (2001). The positive influence of maternal identification on body image, eating attitudes, and self-esteem in Hispanic and Anglo girls. International Journal of Eating Disorders, 29, 429–440.

Hakuta, K., & Garcia, E. E. (1989). Bilingualism and education. American Psychologist, 44, 374–379.

Halfon, N., Inkelas, M., & Hochstein, M. (2000). The health development organization: An organizational approach to achieving child health development. Milbank Quarterly, 78, 447–497.

Halford, G. S., & Boyle, F. M. (1985). Do young children understand conservation of number? Child Development, 56, 165–176.

Halford, W. K., Hahlweg, K., & Dunne, M. (1990). Cross-cultural study of marital communication and marital distress. Journal of Marriage and the Family, 52, 487–500.

Hall, L. J., & McGregor, J. A. (2000). A follow-up study of the peer relationships of children with disabilities in an inclusive school. The Journal of Special Education, 34, 114–126.

Hall, W. S. (1989). Reading comprehension. American Psychologist, 44, 157–161.

Haller, E., & Waterman, M. (1985). The criteria of reading group assignments. Reading Teacher, 38, 772–782.

Halperin, S. (1998). The forgotten half revisited: American youth and young families: 1988–2008. Washington, DC: American Youth Policy Forum.

Hamachek, D. (1985). The self's development and ego growth: Conceptual analysis and implications for counselors. Journal of Counseling and Development, 64, 136–142.

Hamachek, D. (1994). Changes in the self from a developmental/psychosocial perspective. In T. M. Brinthaupt & R. P. Lipka (Eds.), *Changing the self: Philosophies, techniques, and experiences* (pp. 21–68). Albany: State University of New York Press.

Hamarat, E., Thompson, D., Zabrucky, K. M., Steele, D., Matheny, K. B., & Aysan, F. (2001). Perceived stress and coping resource availability as predictors of life satisfaction in young, middle-aged, and older adults. *Experimental Aging Research, 27,* 181–196.

Hamblen, J. (2003). PTSD in children and adolescents. *National Center for Post-Traumatic Stress Disorder.* Retrieved November 25, 2004, from http://www.ncptsd.org/facts/specific/fs_children.html

Hamilton, B. E. (2004). Reproduction rates for 1990–2002 and intrinsic rates for 2000–2001: United States. *National Vital Statistics Reports, 52* (Whole No. 17).

Hamilton, W. D. (1964). The genetical evolution of social behavior. *Journal of Theoretical Biology, 7,* 1–52.

Hammer, C. S. (2001). Come and sit down and let Mama read: Book reading interactions between African American mothers and their infants. In J. L. Harris & A. G. Kamhi (Eds.), *Literacy in African American communities* (pp. 21–43). Mahwah, NJ: Erlbaum.

Hammill, D. D. (2004). What we know about correlates of reading. *Exceptional Children, 70,* 453–468.

Hamon, R. R., & Blieszner, R. (1990). Filial responsibility expectations among adult child–older parent pairs. *Journal of Gerontology, 45,* P110–P112.

Handy, C. (1996). *Beyond certainty: The changing worlds of organizations.* Cambridge, MA: Harvard Business School Press.

Handy, C. (2001). A world of fleas and elephants. In W. Bennis & G. M. Spreitzer (Eds.), *The future of leadership: Today's top leadership thinkers speak to tomorrow's leaders* (pp. 29–40). San Francisco: Jossey-Bass.

Haney, M., & Hill, J. (2004). Relationships between parent-teaching activities and emergent literacy in preschool children. *Early Child Development and Care, 174,* 215–228.

Hans, S. L. (1987). Maternal drug addiction and young children. *Division of Child, Youth, and Family Services Newsletter, 10,* 5, 15.

Hansell, S. (1985). Adolescent friendship networks and distress in school. *Social Forces, 63,* 698–715.

Hao, L., & Cherlin, A. J. (2004). Welfare reform and teenage pregnancy, childbirth, and school dropout. *Journal of Marriage and the Family, 66,* 179–194.

Harding, D. J. (2003). Counterfactual models of neighborhood effects: The effect of neighborhood poverty on dropping out and teenage pregnancy. *American Journal of Sociology, 109,* 676–719.

Hardy, J. B., & Duggan, A. K. (1988). Teenage fathers and the fathers of infants of urban teenage mothers. *American Journal of Public Health, 78,* 919–922.

Harel, J., & Scher, A. (2003). Insufficient responsiveness in ambivalent mother–infant relationships: Contextual and affective aspects. *Infant Behavior and Development, 26,* 371–383.

Harkness, S., & Super, C. H. (1995). Culture and parenting. In M. H. Bornstein (Ed.), *Handbook of parenting: Vol. 2. Biology and ecology of parenting* (pp. 211–234). Hillsdale, NJ: Erlbaum.

Harman, D., Holliday, R., & Meydani, M. (1998). *Towards the prolongation of the healthy life span: Practical approaches to intervention.* New York: New York Academy of Sciences.

Harrington, C. C., & Boardman, S. K. (2000). *Paths to success: Beating the odds in American society.* Cambridge, MA: Harvard University Press.

Harris, M. (1992). *Language experience and early language development: From input to uptake.* Hillsdale, NJ: Erlbaum.

Harris, M. J., & Rosenthal, R. (1985). Mediation of interpersonal expectancy effects: 31 meta-analyses. *Psychological Bulletin, 97,* 363–386.

Harris, P. L., & Kavanaugh, R. D. (1993). *Young children's understanding of pretense. Monographs of the Society for Research in Child Development, 58*(1).

Harris, T., Kovar, M. G., Suzman, R., Kleinman, J. C., & Feldman, J. J. (1989). Longitudinal study of physical ability in the oldest old. *American Journal of Public Health, 79,* 698–702.

Hart, B., & Risley, T. R. (1992). American parenting of language-learning children: Persisting differences in family–child interactions observed in natural home environments. *Developmental Psychology, 28,* 1096–1105.

Hart, C. H., Ladd, G. W., & Burleson, B. R. (1990). Children's expectations of the outcomes of social strategies: Relations with sociometric status and maternal disciplinary styles. *Child Development, 61,* 127–137.

Hart, C. H., Newell, L. D., & Olsen, S. F. (2003). Parenting skills and social-communicative competence in childhood. In J. O. Greene & B. R. Burleson (Eds.), *Handbook of communication and social interaction skills* (pp. 753–797). Mahwah, NJ: Erlbaum.

Hart, D., & Fegley, S. (1995). Prosocial behavior and caring in adolescence: Relations to self-understanding and social judgment. *Child Development, 66,* 1346–1359.

Harter, S. (1982). The perceived competence scale for children. *Child Development, 53,* 87–97.

Harter, S. (1985a). Competence as a dimension of self-evaluation: Towards a comprehensive model of self-worth. In R. Leahy (Ed.), *The development of the self* (pp. 55–121). New York: Academic Press.

Harter, S. (1985b). *The self-perception profile for children* (Manual). Denver, CO: University of Denver Press.

Harter, S. (1993). Visions of self: Beyond the me in the mirror. In J. E. Jacobs (Ed.), *Nebraska Symposium on Motivation: 1992* (Vol. 40, pp. 99–144). Lincoln: University of Nebraska Press.

Harter, S. (1998). The development of self-representations. In W. Damon & N. Eisenberg (Eds.), *Handbook of child psychology* (pp. 553–617). New York: Wiley.

Harter, S., Whitesell, N. R., & Kowalski, P. (1992). Individual differences in the effects of educational transitions on young adolescents' perceptions of competence and motivational orientation. *American Educational Research Journal, 29,* 777–807.

Hartlage, S. A., Brandenburg, D. L., & Kravitz, H. M. (2004). Premenstrual exacerbation of depressive disorders in a community-based sample in the United States. *Psychosomatic Medicine, 66,* 698–706.

Hartup, W. W. (1989). Social relationships and their developmental significance. *American Psychologist, 44,* 120–126.

Harvey, J. H., Stein, S. K., & Scott, P. K. (1995). Fifty years of grief: Accounts and reported psychological reactions of Normandy invasion veterans. *Journal of Narrative and Life History, 5,* 315–332.

Harwood, R. L. (1992). The influence of culturally derived values on Anglo and Puerto Rican mothers' perceptions of attachment behavior. *Child Development, 63,* 822–839.

Haskett, M. E., & Kistner, J. A. (1991). Social interactions and peer perceptions of young physically abused children. *Child Development, 62,* 979–990.

Haskins, R. (1989). Beyond metaphor: The efficacy of early childhood education. *American Psychologist, 44,* 274–282.

Hatfield, E. (1988). Passionate and companionate love. In R. J. Sternberg & M. L. Barnes (Eds.), *The psychology of love* (pp. 191–217). New Haven, CT: Yale University Press.

Hatfield, E., & Sprecher, S. (1995). Men's and women's preferences in marital partners in the United States, Russia, and Japan. *Journal of Cross-Cultural Psychology, 26,* 728–750.

Havighurst, R. J. (1972). *Developmental tasks and education* (3rd ed.). New York: David McKay.

Hawkins, A. J., & Dollahite, D. C. (1997). *Generative fathering: Beyond the deficit perspectives.* Thousand Oaks, CA: Sage.

Hawkins, J. L., Weisberg, C., & Ray, D. W. (1980). Spouse differences in communication style preference, perception, behavior. *Journal of Marriage and the Family, 42,* 585–593.

Hawley, G. A. (1988). *Measures of psychosocial development.* Odessa, FL: Psychological Assessment Resources.

Hayflick, L. (2000). The future of aging. *Nature, 408,* 267–269.

Haynes, J., & Miller, J. (2003). *Inconceivable conceptions: Psychological aspects of infertility and reproductive technology.* New York: Brunner-Routledge.

Hayslip, B., Jr., & Brookshire, R. G. (1985). Relationships among abilities in elderly adults: A time lag analysis. *Journal of Gerontology, 40,* 748–750.

Hayward, M. D., Crimmins, E. M., Miles, T. P., & Yang, Y. (2000). The significance of socioeconomic status in explaining the racial gap in chronic health conditions. *American Sociological Review, 65,* 910–930.

Hazan, C., & Shaver, P. R. (1987). Attachment as an organizational framework for research on close relationships. *Journal of Personality and Social Psychology, 52,* 511–524.

Hazell, L. V. (1997) Cross-cultural funeral rites. *The Director, 69,* 53–55.

*Healthy People 2000: National Health Promotion and Disease Prevention Objectives.* (1990). Washington, DC: U.S. Department of Health and Human Services, Public Health Service, DHHS publication PHS 91-50212.

*Healthy People 2010.* (2001). Retrieved October 3, 2001, from http://www.health.gov/healthypeople/LHI/lhiwhat.htm

Hearold, S. (1986). A synthesis of 1043 effects of television on social behavior. In G. Comstock (Ed.), *Public communications and behavior* (Vol. 1, pp. 65–133). New York: Academic Press.

Heath, S. B. (1989). Oral and literate traditions among black Americans living in poverty. *American Psychologist, 44,* 367–372.

Heatherington, E. M., Cox, M., & Cox, R. (1985). Long-term effects of divorce and remarriage on the adjustment of children. *Journal of the American Academy of Psychiatry, 24,* 518–530.

Heatherington, E. M., Stanley-Hagan, M., & Anderson, E. R. (1989). Marital transitions: A child's perspective. *American Psychologist, 44,* 303–312.

Heatherton, T. F. (2000). Having and losing control: Understanding self-regulation failure. *Psychological Science Agenda, 13,* 8–9.

Heckhausen, J. (1987). Balancing for weaknesses and challenging developmental potential: A longitudinal study of mother–infant dyads in apprenticeship interactions. *Developmental Psychology, 23,* 762–770.

Heckhausen, J., Dixon, R. A., & Baltes, P. B. (1989). Gains and losses in development throughout adulthood as perceived by different adult age groups. *Developmental Psychology, 25,* 109–121.

Heilman, M. E. (2001). Description and prescription: How gender stereotypes prevent women's ascent up the organizational ladder. *Journal of Social Issues, 57,* 657–674.

Heimpel, S. A., Wood, J. V., Marshall, M. A., & Brown, J. D. (2002). Do people with low self-esteem really want to feel better? Self-esteem differences in motivation to repair negative moods. *Journal of Personality and Social Psychology, 82,* 128–147.

Hein, G., & Schubert, T. (2004). Aging and input processing in dual-task situations. *Psychology and Aging, 19,* 416–432.

Heinicke, C. M. (1995). Determinants of the transition to parenting. In M. H. Bornstein (Ed.), *Handbook of parenting: Vol. 3. Status and social conditions of parenting* (pp. 277–303). Mahwah, NJ: Erlbaum.

Heinicke, C. M., & Guthrie, D. (1992). Stability and change in husband–wife adaptation and the development of positive parent–child relationships. *Infant and Behavior Development, 15,* 109–127.

Heinze, S. D., & Sleigh, M. J. (2003). Epidural or no epidural anaesthesia: Relationships between beliefs about childbirth and pain control. *Journal of Reproductive & Infant Psychology, 21,* 323–333.

Heitlinger, A. (1989). Current medical, legal, and demographic perspectives on artificial reproduction in Czechoslovakia. *American Journal of Public Health, 79,* 57–61.

Helman, C. G. (1990). *Culture, health, and illness* (2nd ed.). London: Wright.

Helwig, C. C., Zelazo, P. D., & Wilson, M. (2001). Children's judgments of psychological harm in normal and noncanonical situations. *Child Development, 72,* 66–81.

Hendricks, L. E., & Fullilove, R. E. (1983). Locus of control and use of contraception among unmarried Black adolescent fathers and their controls: A preliminary report. *Journal of Youth and Adolescence, 12,* 225–233.

Henkens, K., & Tazelaar, F. (1997). Explaining retirement decisions of civil servants in The Netherlands: Intentions, behavior, and the discrepancy between the two. *Research on Aging, 19,* 139–173.

Henrich, C. C., Brown, J. L., & Aber, J. L. (1999). Evaluating the effectiveness of school-based violence prevention: Developmental approaches. *Social Policy Report, 13,* 1–17.

Henry, G. T. (1998). Practical sampling. In L. Bickman & D. J. Rog (Eds.), *Handbook of applied social research methods* (pp. 101–126). Thousand Oaks, CA: Sage.

Henry, J. D., MacLeod, M. S., Phillips, L. H., & Crawford, J. R. (2004). A meta-analytic review of prospective memory and aging. *Psychology and Aging, 19,* 27–39.

Herbert, W. (1996). The moral child. *U.S. News and World Report, 120,* 52–59.

Herdt, G., & McClintock, M. (2000). The magical age of 10. *Archives of Sexual Behavior, 29,* 587–606.

Hergovich, A., Sirsch, U., & Felinger, M. (2002). Self-appraisals, actual appraisals, and reflected appraisals of preadolescent children. *Social Behavior and Personality, 30,* 603–612.

Herkovits, M. (1948). *Man and his works.* New York: Knopf.

Herman, M. R., Dornbusch, S. M., Herron, M. C., & Herting, J. R. (1997). The influence of family regulation, connection, and psychological autonomy on six measures of adolescent functioning. *Journal of Adolescent Research, 12,* 34–67.

Herman-Giddens, M. E., Slora, E. J., Wasserman, R. C., Bourdony, C. J., Bhapkar, M. V., Koch, G. G., & Hasemeier, C. M. (1997). Secondary sex characteristics and menses in young girls seen in office practice: A study from the pediatric research in office settings network. *Pediatrics, 99,* 505–512.

Hernandez, D. J. (1993). Childhood poverty: Trends, causes, and policies. *Child, Youth, and Family Services Quarterly, 16,* 3–4.

Herold, E. S., & Marshall, S. K. (1996). Adolescent sexual development. In G. R.

Adams, R. Montemayor, & T. P. Gullotta (Eds.), *Psychosocial development during adolescence: Advances in adolescent development* (Vol. 8, pp. 62–94). Thousand Oaks, CA: Sage.

Herpertz-Dahlmann, B., Wewetzer, C., Hennighausen, K., & Remschmidt, H. (1996). Outcome, psychosocial functioning, and prognostic factors in adolescent anorexia nervosa as determined by prospective follow-up assessment. *Journal of Youth and Adolescence, 25,* 455–472.

Herring, C., & Wilson-Sadberry, K. R. (1993). Preference or necessity? Changing work roles of Black and White women, 1973–1990. *Journal of Marriage and the Family, 55,* 315–325.

Hertzog, C. (1989). Influences of cognitive slowing on age differences in intelligence. *Developmental Psychology, 25,* 636–651.

Hertzog, D., & Schaie, K. W. (1988). Stability and change in adult intelligence: 2. Simultaneous analysis of longitudinal means and covariance structures. *Psychology and Aging, 3,* 122–130.

Herzog, A. R., House, J. S., & Morgan, J. N. (1991). Relation of work and retirement to health and well-being in older age. *Psychology and Aging, 6,* 202–211.

Herzog, D. B., Dorer, D. J., Keel, P. K., Selwyn, S. E., Ekeblad, E. R., Flores, A. T., et al. (1999). Recovery and relapse in anorexia and bulimia nervosa: A 7.5-year follow-up study. *Journal of the American Academy of Child and Adolescent Psychiatry, 38,* 829–837.

Hespos, S. J., & Baillargeon, R. (2001). Reasoning about containment events in very young infants. *Cognition, 78,* 207–245.

Hetherington, E. M. (1967). The effects of familial variables on sex typing, on parent–child similarity, and on imitation in children. In J. P. Hill (Ed.), *Minnesota Symposium on Child Psychology* (Vol. 1, pp. 82–107). Minneapolis: University of Minnesota Press.

Heuveline, P., & Timberlake, J. M. (2004). The role of cohabitation in family formation: The United States in comparative perspective. *Journal of Marriage and the Family, 66,* 1214–1230.

Heynen, J. (1990). *One hundred over 100: Moments with one hundred North American centenarians.* Golden, CO: Fulcrum.

Hickson, F. C., Davies, P. M., Hunt, A. J., & Weatherburn, P. (1992). Maintenance of open gay relationships: Some strategies for protection against HIV. *AIDS Care, 4,* 409–419.

High/Scope. (2003). *Perry Preschool Project: Significant benefits.* Retrieved August 29, 2004, from http://www.highscope.org/Research/PerryProject/perrymain.htm

Hill, E. J., Yang, C., Hawkins, A. J., & Ferris, M. (2004). A cross-cultural test of the work–family interface in 48 countries. *Journal of Marriage and the Family, 66,* 1300–1316.

Hill, J. P. (1988). Adapting to menarche: Familial control and conflict. In M. R. Gunnar & W. A. Collins (Eds.), *Development during the transition to adolescence. Minne-*

sota Symposium on Child Psychology (Vol. 21, pp. 43–77). Hillsdale, NJ: Erlbaum.

Hill, N. E., & Taylor, L. C. (2004). Parental school involvement and children's academic achievement: Pragmatics and issues. Current Directions in Psychological Science, 13, 161–164.

Hill, R. (1965). Decision making and the family life cycle. In E. Shanas & G. Streib (Eds.), Social structure and the family: Generational relations. Englewood Cliffs, NJ: Prentice Hall.

Hillman, J. L., & Stricker, G. (1994). A linkage of knowledge and attitudes toward elderly sexuality: Not necessarily a uniform relationship. The Gerontologist, 34, 256–260.

Hing, E., & Bloom, B. (1990). Long-term care for the functionally dependent elderly. Vital Health Statistics, 13, No. 104.

Hirschfeld, L. A. (1994). The child's representation of human groups. In D. L. Medin et al. (Eds.), The psychology of learning and motivation: Advances in research and theory (Vol. 31, pp. 133–185). San Diego: Academic Press.

Hodges, J., & Tizard, B. (1989). Social and family relationships of ex-institutional adolescents. Journal of Child Psychology and Psychiatry, 30, 77–97.

Hodnett, E. D. (2003). Caregiver support for women during childbirth. The Cochrane Library, 2, 1–72. Retrieved August 12, 2004, from http://www.maternitywise.org/pdfs/continuous_support.pdf

Hodson, D. S., & Skeen, P. (1994). Sexuality and aging: The hammerlock of myths. Journal of Applied Gerontology, 13, 219–235.

Hodson, R., & Sullivan, T. A. (1995) The Social Organization of Work (2nd ed.). Belmont, CA: Wadsworth.

Hoeksma, J. B., Oosterlaan, J., & Schipper, E. M. (2004). Emotion regulation and the dynamics of feelings: A conceptual and methodological framework. Child Development, 75, 354–360.

Hof, L., & Miller, W. R. (1981). Marriage enrichment: Philosophy, process, and program. Bowie, MD: Brady.

Hofer, T. P., & Katz, S. J. (1996). Healthy behaviors among women in the United States and Ontario: The effect on use of preventive care. American Journal of Public Health, 86, 1755–1759.

Hoffman, M. L. (1970). Moral development. In P. H. Mussen (Ed.), Carmichael's manual of child psychology (3rd ed., Vol. 2). New York: Wiley.

Hoffman, M. L. (1977). Moral internalization: Current theory and research. In L. Berkowitz (Ed.), Advances in experimental social psychology (Vol. 10). New York: Academic Press.

Hoffman, M. L. (1982). Development of prosocial motivation: Empathy and guilt. In N. Eisenberg (Ed.), The development of prosocial behavior (pp. 281–313). New York: Academic Press.

Hoffman, M. L. (1987). The contribution of empathy to justice and moral development. In N. Eisenberg & J. Strayer (Eds.),

Empathy and its development (pp. 47–80). Cambridge: Cambridge University Press.

Hoffman, S. J. (1985). Play and the acquisition of literacy. Quarterly Newsletter of the Laboratory of Comparative Human Cognition, 7, 89–95.

Hoffmann, M. L., & Powlishta, K. K. (2001). Gender segregation in childhood: A test of the interaction style theory. Journal of Genetic Psychology, 162, 298–313.

Hogan, D. P., Eggebeen, D. J., & Clogg, C. C. (1993). The structure of intergenerational exchanges in American families. American Journal of Sociology, 98, 1428–1458.

Hogan, T. D., & Steinnes, D. N. (1998). A logistic model of the seasonal migration decision for elderly households in Arizona and Minnesota. The Gerontologist, 38, 152–158.

Hoge, D. R., & McCarthy, J. D. (1984). Influence of individual and group identity salience in the global self-esteem of youth. Journal of Personality and Social Psychology, 47, 403–414.

Holahan, C. K., Sears, R. R., & Cronbach, L. J. (1995). The gifted group in later maturity. Stanford, CA: Stanford University Press.

Holden, C. (1989). Koop finds abortion evidence "inconclusive." Science, 243, 730–731.

Holland, J. L. (1997). Making vocational choices: A theory of vocational personalities and work environments (3rd ed.). Odessa, FL: Psychological Assessment Resources.

Holloway, S. D., & Fuller, B. (1992). The great child-care experiment: What are the lessons for school improvement? Educational Researcher, 21, 12–19.

Holmberg, L. I., & Wahlberg, V. (2000). The process of decision-making on abortion: A grounded theory study of young men in Sweden. Journal of Adolescent Health, 26, 230–234.

Holmes, T. H., & Rahe, R. H. (1967). The social readjustment rating scale. Journal of Psychosomatic Research, 11, 213–218.

Holstein, J. A., & Gubrium, J. F. (1995). The active interview. Thousand Oaks, CA: Sage.

Holzman, C., & Paneth, N. (1998). Preterm birth. From prediction to prevention. American Journal of Public Health, 88, 183–184.

Hong, L. K., & Duff, R. W. (1994). Widows in retirement communities: The social context of subjective well-being. The Gerontologist, 34, 347–352.

Honig, A. (1995). Choosing child care for young children. In M. H. Bornstein (Ed.), Handbook of parenting: Applied and practical parenting (Vol. 4, pp. 411–435). Mahwah, NJ: Erlbaum.

Honig, A. S. (2002). Choosing childcare for young children. In M. H. Bornstein (Ed.), Handbook of parenting: Vol. 5. Practical issues in parenting (pp. 375–405). Mahwah, NJ: Erlbaum.

Hooyman, N. R., & Kiyak, H. A. (1993). Social gerontology. Boston: Allyn & Bacon.

Hooyman, N., & Kiyak, H. A. (2002). Social gerontology: A multidisciplinary perspective (6th ed.). Boston: Allyn & Bacon.

Hope, T. L., Wilder, E. I., & Watt, T. T. (2003). The relationship among adoles-

cent pregnancy, pregnancy resolution, and juvenile delinquency. Sociological Inquiry, 44, 555–576.

Hopkins, B., & Westra, T. (1990). Motor development, maternal expectation, and the role of handling. Infant Behavior and Development, 13, 117–122.

Hopkins, D. R., Murrah, B., Hoeger, W. W. K., & Rhodes, R. C. (1990). Effect of low-impact aerobic dance on the functional fitness of elderly women. The Gerontologist, 30, 189–192.

Hopkins, J. R. (1995). Erik Homburger Erikson (1902–1994). American Psychologist, 50, 796–797.

Hopper, K. (1990). Public shelter as "a hybrid institution": Homeless men in historical perspective. Journal of Social Issues, 46, 13–29.

Hopper, K., & Hamberg, L. (1986). The making of America's homeless: From skid row to new poor, 1945–1984. In R. Bratt, C. Harman, & A. Meyerson (Eds.), Critical perspectives on housing. Philadelphia: Temple University Press.

Horn, J. L., & Masunaga, H. (2000). New directions for research into aging and intelligence: The development of expertise. In T. J. Perfect & E. A. Maylor (Eds.), Models of cognitive aging (pp. 125–159). London: Oxford University Press.

Horn, J. L. (1979). The rise and fall of human abilities. Journal of Research and Development in Education, 12, 59–78.

Hornblower, M. (1996). It takes a school. Time, 147, 36–38.

Hornik, R., & Gunnar, M. R. (1988). A descriptive analysis of infant social referencing. Child Development, 59, 626–634.

Hornik, R., Risenhoover, N., & Gunnar, M. (1987). The effects of maternal positive, neutral, and negative affective communications on infant responses to new toys. Child Development, 58, 937–944.

Horobin, K., & Acredolo, C. (1989). The impact of probability judgments on reasoning about multiple possibilities. Child Development, 60(1), 183–200.

Horowitz, M., Sundin, E., Zanko, A., & Lauer, R. (2001). Coping with grim news from genetic tests. Psychosomatics, 42, 100–105.

Horst, E. A. (1995). Reexamining gender issues in Erikson's stages of identity and intimacy. Journal of Counseling and Development, 73, 271–278.

Horwitz, A. V., White, H. R., & Howell-White, S. (1996). Becoming married and mental health: A longitudinal study of a cohort of young adults. Journal of Marriage and the Family, 58, 895–907.

Hospice Education Institute. (2001). A short history of hospice and palliative care. Essex, CT: Author.

How RU-486 works. (1997, March 3). U.S. News and World Report, pp. 66–69.

Howell, C. (1994, February 2). Coroner delivers primer to directors. Arkansas-Democrat Gazette.

Howell, E. M., Heiser, N., & Harrington, M. (1999). A review of recent findings on substance abuse treatment for pregnant women. *Journal of Substance Abuse Treatment, 16,* 195–219.

Howes, C. (1987). Peer interaction of young children. *Monographs of the Society for Research in Child Development, 53* (1, Serial No. 217).

Howes, C., & Phillipsen, L. (1992). Gender and friendship: Relationships within peer groups of young children. *Social Development, 1,* 230–242.

Howes, C., & Stewart, P. (1987). Child's play with adults, toys, and peers: An examination of family and child-care influences. *Developmental Psychology, 23,* 423–430.

Howes, C., Unger, O., & Seidner, L. B. (1989). Social pretend play in toddlers: Parallels with social play and with solitary pretend. *Child Development, 60,* 77–84.

Hoyer, W. J., & Rybash, J. M. (1994). Characterizing adult cognitive development. *Journal of Adult Development, 1,* 7–12.

Hsu, L. K. G. (1996). Outcome of early onset anorexia nervosa: What do we know? *Journal of Youth and Adolescence, 25,* 563–568.

Huber, J. (1990). Macro–micro links in gender stratification. *American Sociological Review, 55,* 1–10.

Hubert, N. C., Wachs, T. D., Peters-Martin, P., & Gandour, M. J. (1982). The study of early temperament: Measurement and conceptual issues. *Child Development, 53,* 571–600.

Huerta, R., Mena, A., Malacara, J., & Diaz, J. (1995). Symptoms at perimenopausal period: Its association with attitudes toward sexuality, life-style, family function, and FSH levels. *Psychoneuroendocrinology, 20,* 135–148.

Huesmann, L. R., & Eron, L. D. (1986). *Television and the aggressive child: A cross-national comparison.* Hillsdale, NJ: Erlbaum.

Huesmann, L. R., & Malamuth, N. M. (1986). Media violence and antisocial behavior: An overview. *Journal of Social Issues, 42,* 1–6.

Huesmann, L. R., Moise-Titus, J., Podolski, C. L., & Eron, L. D. (2003). Longitudinal relations between children's exposure to TV violence and their aggressive behavior in young adulthood: 1977–1992. *Developmental Psychology, 39,* 210–221.

Huesmann, L. R., & Skoric, M. M. (2003). Regulating media violence: Why, how, and by whom? In E. L. Palmer & B. M. Young (Eds.), *The faces of televisual media: Teaching, violence, selling to children* (2nd ed., pp. 219–240). Mahwah, NJ: Erlbaum.

Hughes, F. M., Gordon, K. C., & Gaertner, L. (2004). Predicting spouses' perceptions of their parenting alliance. *Journal of Marriage and the Family, 66,* 506–514.

Hultsch, D. P., & Dixon, R. A. (1990). Learning and memory in aging. In J. E. Birren & K. W. Schaie (Eds.), *Handbook of the psychology of aging* (pp. 258–274). San Diego: Academic Press.

Human Rights Watch. (2004). *Child labor.* Retrieved November 10, 2004, from http://www.hrw.org/children/labor.htm

Hunt, E. B. (1995). *Will we be smart enough? A cognitive analysis of the coming workforce.* New York: Russell Sage Foundation.

Hunter, A. G. (1997). Counting on grandmothers: Black mothers' and fathers' reliance on grandmothers for parenting support. *Journal of Family Issues, 18,* 251–269.

Hupp, S. D. A., & Reitman, D. (1999). Improving sports skills and sportsmanship in children diagnosed with attention-deficit/hyperactivity disorder. *Child and Family Behavior Therapy, 21,* 35–51.

Huston, A. C., Donnerstein, E., Fairchild, H., Feshbach, N. D., Katz, P. A., Murray, J. P., et al. (1992). *Big world, small screen: The role of television in American society.* Lincoln: University of Nebraska Press.

Huston, T. L. (2000). The social ecology of marriage and other intimate unions. *Journal of Marriage and the Family, 62,* 298–320.

Huston, T. L., & Melz, H. (2004). The case for (promoting) marriage: The devil is in the details. *Journal of Marriage and the Family, 66,* 943–958.

Huston, T. L., Niehuis, S., & Smith, S. E. (2001). The early marital roots of conjugal distress and divorce. *Current Directions in Psychological Science, 10,* 116–119.

Hutt, S. J., Tyler, S., Hutt, C., & Foy, H. (1988). *Play exploration and learning: A natural history of the preschool.* New York: Routledge.

Huxley, J. (1941). *The uniqueness of man.* London: Chatto & Windus.

Huxley, J. (1942). *Evolution: The magic synthesis.* New York: Harper.

Hymel, S., Wagner, E., & Butler, L. J. (1990). Reputational bias: View from the peer group. In S. Asher & J. D. Coie (Eds.), *Peer rejection in childhood* (pp. 156–186). New York: Cambridge University Press.

Hymel, S., Bowker, A., & Woody, E. (1993). Aggressive versus withdrawn unpopular children: Variations in peer and self-perceptions of multiple domains. *Child Development, 64,* 879–896.

Iannotti, R. J. (1985). Naturalistic and structured assessments of prosocial behavior in preschool children: The influence of empathy and perspective taking. *Developmental Psychology, 21,* 46–55.

Iannotti, R. J., & Bush, P. J. (1992). Perceived versus actual friends' use of alcohol, cigarettes, marijuana, and cocaine: Which has the most influence? *Journal of Youth and Adolescence, 21,* 375–389.

Idler, E. L. (1987). Religious involvement and the health of the elderly: Some hypotheses and an initial test. *Social Forces, 66,* 226–238.

Ikels, C. (1998). Grandparenthood in cross-cultural perspective. In M. Szinovacz (Ed.), *Handbook on grandparenthood* (pp. 40–52). Westport, CT: Greenwood Press.

Ingersoll-Dayton, B., & Antonucci, T. C. (1988). Reciprocal and nonreciprocal social support: Contrasting sides of intimate relationships. *Journal of Gerontology, 43,* S65–S73.

Inhelder, B., & Piaget, J. (1958). *The growth of logical thinking from childhood to adolescence.* New York: Basic Books.

InteliHealth.com (2002). *Words, not bullets, make the workplace hostile.* Retrieved January 7, 2002, from http://www.intelihealth.com/IH/ihtIH/WSIHW0 00/20813/23598/263562.html?d=dmt-Content

Irwin, C. E., Jr., Burg, S. J., & Cart, C. U. (2002). America's adolescents: Where have we been, where are we going? *Journal of Adolescent Health, 31,* 91–121.

Isaacowitz, D. M., Vaillant, G. E., & Seligman, M. E. P. (2003). Strengths and satisfaction across the lifespan. *International Journal of Aging & Human Development, 57,* 181–201.

Isabella, R. A., & Belsky, J. (1991). Interactional synchrony and the origins of infant–mother attachment: A replication study. *Child Development, 62,* 373–384.

Isabella, R. A., Belsky, J., & vonEye, A. (1989). Origins of infant-mother attachment: An examination of interactional synchrony during the infant's first year. *Developmental Psychology, 25,* 12–21.

Isay, R. (1999). Gender in homosexual boys: Some developmental and clinical considerations. *Psychiatry: Interpersonal and Biological Processes, 62,* 187–194.

Ishii-Kuntz, M. (1997). Japanese American families. In M. K. DeGenova (Ed.), *Families in cultural context: Strengths and challenges in diversity* (pp. 131–153). Mountain View, CA: Mayfield.

IslamOnline. (2003). *Fatwa: What is the sequence of rituals in an Islamic funeral service?* Retrieved March 13, 2005, from http://www.islamonline.net/fatwa/english/FatwaDisplay.asp?hFatwaID=94057

Iverson, J. M., & Thelen, E. (1999). Hand, mouth, and brain: The dynamic emergence of speech and gesture. *Journal of Consciousness Studies, 6,* 11–12.

Izard, C. E. (1977). *Human emotion.* New York: Plenum Press.

Izard, C. E., Haynes, O. M., Chisholm, G., & Baak, K. (1991). Emotional determinants of infant–mother attachment. *Child Development, 62,* 906–917.

Jack, D. C., & Dill, D. (1992). The silencing the self scale: The schemas of intimacy associated with depression in women. *Psychology of Women Quarterly, 16,* 97–106.

Jacklin, C. N., & Maccoby, E. E. (1978). Social behavior at 33 months in same-sex and mixed-sex dyads. *Child Development, 49,* 557–569.

Jackson, P. B. (2004). Role sequencing: Does order matter for mental health? *Journal of Health and Social Behavior, 45,* 132–154.

Jacobson, E. (1964). *The self and the object world.* New York: International Universities Press.

Jacobson, N. S., & Christensen, A. (1996). *Integrative couple therapy: Promoting acceptance and change.* New York: Norton.

Jacobson, S. W., Fein, G. G., Jacobson, J. L., Schwartz, P. M., & Dowler, J. K. (1985). The effect of intrauterine PCB exposure on visual recognition memory. *Child Development, 56,* 853–860.

Jacobson, S. W., & Frye, K. F. (1991). Effect of maternal social support on attachment: Experimental evidence. *Child Development, 62,* 572–582.

Jacobson, S. W., Jacobson, J. L., O'Neill, J. M., Padgett, R. J., Frankowski, J. J., & Bihun,

J. T. (1992). Visual expectation and dimensions of infant information processing. *Child Development, 63,* 711–724.

Jaenisch, R., & Wilmut, I. (2001). Don't clone humans. *Science, 291,* 2552.

Jahoda, M. (1982). *Employment and unemployment.* Cambridge, UK: Cambridge University Press.

James, W. (1892/1961). *Psychology: The briefer course.* New York: Harper & Row.

Jamieson, A., Curry, A., & Martinez, G. (2001). School enrollment in the United States—Social and economic characteristics of students: 1999. *Current Population Reports,* P20-533.

Jarboe, P. J. (1986). *A comparison study of distress and marital adjustment in infertile and expectant couples.* Unpublished doctoral dissertation, Ohio State University.

Jayakody, R., Chatters, L. M., & Taylor, R. J. (1993). Family support to single and married African-American mothers: The provision of financial, emotional, and child care assistance. *Journal of Marriage and the Family, 55,* 261–276.

Jecker, N. S., & Schneiderman, L. J. (1994). Is dying young worse than dying old? *The Gerontologist, 34,* 66–72.

Jeffries, V. (1993). Virtue and attraction: Validation of measure of love. *Journal of Social and Personal Relationships, 10,* 99–118.

Jenkins, J. M., Turrell, S. L., Kogushi, Y., Lollis, S., & Ross, H. S. (2003). A longitudinal investigation of the dynamics of mental state talk in families. *Child Development, 74,* 905–920.

Jenkins, L. E. (1989). The Black family and academic achievement. In G. L. Berry & J. K. Asamen (Eds.), *Black students* (pp. 138–152). Newbury Park, CA: Sage.

Jetten, J., Spears, R., & Manstead, A. S. R. (1996). Intergroup norms and intergroup discrimination: Distinctive self-categorization and social identity effects. *Journal of Personality and Social Psychology, 71,* 1222–1233.

Jockin, V., McGue, M., & Lykken, D. T. (1996). Personality and divorce: A genetic analysis. *Journal of Personality and Social Psychology, 71,* 288–299.

Johnson, H. B. (2005, March–April). My word. Too late to die young. *AARP: The Magazine, 48,* 44–46, 99.

Johnson, K. P. (2004). Adolescent sleep patterns: Biological, social, and psychological influences. *Journal of the American Academy of Child and Adolescent Psychiatry, 43,* 374–375.

Johnson, M. (1999). Ontogenetic constraints on neural and behavioral plasticity: Evidence from imprinting and face processing. *Canadian Journal of Experimental Psychology, 53,* 77–90.

Johnson, M. H. (2001). Functional brain development in humans. *Nature Reviews Neuroscience, 2,* 475–483.

Johnson, M. P. (2002). An exploration of men's experience and role at childbirth. *Journal of Men's Studies, 10,* 165–182.

Johnson, R. E. (2003). Age and the remembering of text. *Developmental Review, 23,* 261–346.

Johnson, S. P. (2000). The development of visual surface perception: Insights into the ontogeny of knowledge. In C. Rovee-Collier, L. P. Lipsitt, & H. Hayne (Eds.), *Progress in infancy research* (Vol. 1, pp. 113–154). Mahwah, NJ: Erlbaum.

Johnson, V. K., Cowan, P. A., & Cowan, C. P. (1991). Children's classroom behavior: The unique contribution of family organization. *Journal of Family Psychology, 13,* 355–371.

Johnston, L. D., O'Malley, P. M., & Bachman, J. D. G. (1996). *National survey results on drug use from Monitoring the Future Study, 1975–1995: Vol. I. Secondary school students.* Rockville, MD: National Institute on Drug Abuse.

Johnston, L. D., O'Malley, P. M., & Bachman, J. G. (1997). *National survey results on drug use from Monitoring the Future Study, 1975–1995: Vol. II. College students and young adults.* Washington, DC: National Institutes of Health.

Johnston, L. D., O'Malley, P. M., & Bachman, J. G. (1999). *National survey results on drug use from Monitoring the Future Study, 1975–1998.* Bethesda, MD: National Institute on Drug Abuse.

Johnston, L. D., O'Malley, P. M., Bachman, J. G., & Schulenberg, J. E. (2004). *Monitoring the Future national results on adolescent drug use: Overview of key findings, 2003* (NIH Publication No. 04-5506). Bethesda, MD: National Institute on Drug Abuse.

Jones, J. B. (1997). Representations of menopause and their health care implications: A qualitative study. *American Journal of Preventive Medicine, 13,* 58–65.

Jones, J. M. (1988). Racism in black and white: A bicultural model of reaction and evolution. In P. A. Katz & D. A. Taylor (Eds.), *Eliminating racism* (pp. 117–136). New York: Plenum Press.

Jones, J. T., & Cunningham, J. D. (1996). Attachment styles and other predictors of relationship satisfaction in dating couples. *Personal Relationships, 3,* 387–399.

Jones, R. M. (1992). Ego identity and adolescent problem behavior. In G. R. Adams, T. P. Gullota, & R. Montemayor (Eds.), *Adolescent identity formation* (pp. 216–233). Newbury Park, CA: Sage.

Jones, S. S., Smith, L. B., & Landau, B. (1991). Object properties and knowledge in early lexical learning. *Child Development 62,* 499–516.

Jones-Webb, R. J., & Snowden, L. R. (1993). Symptoms of depression among Blacks and Whites. *American Journal of Public Health, 83,* 240–244.

Jonker, C., Launer, L. J., Hooijer, C., & Lindeboom, J. (1996). Memory complaints and memory impairment in older individuals. *Journal of the American Geriatrics Society, 44,* 44–49.

Jordan, B. (1983). *Birth in four cultures: A cross-cultural investigation of childbirth in Yucatan, Holland, Sweden and the United States* (3rd ed.). Montreal: Eden Press.

Jordan, C. H., Spencer, S. J., Zanna, M. P., Hoshino-Browne, E., & Correll, J. (2003). Secure and defensive high self-esteem. *Journal of Personality and Social Psychology, 85,* 969–978.

Jordan, J. V. (1997). Relational development through mutual empathy. In A. C. Bohart & L. S. Greenberg (Eds.), *Empathy reconsidered: New directions in psychotherapy* (pp. 343–351). Washington, DC: American Psychological Association.

Jordan, K. F., Lyons, T. S., & McDonough, J. T. (1992). *Funding and financing for programs to serve K–3 at-risk children: A research review.* Washington, DC: National Education Association.

Jordyn, M., & Byrd, M. (2003). The relationship between the living arrangements of university students and their identity development. *Adolescence, 38,* 267–278.

Josephson, W. L. (1987). Television violence and children's aggression: Testing the priming, social script, and disinhibition predictions. *Journal of Personality and Social Psychology, 53,* 882–890.

Josselson, R. (1987). *Finding herself: Pathways to identity development in women.* San Francisco: Jossey-Bass.

Jussim, L. (1990a). Expectancies and social issues: Introduction: *Journal of Social Issues, 46,* 1–8.

Jussim, L. (1990b). Social realities and social problems: The role of expectancies. *Journal of Social Issues, 46,* 9–34.

Justice, L. M., & Ezell, H. K. (2000). Enhancing children's print and word awareness through home-based parent intervention. *American Journal of Speech-Language Pathology, 9,* 257–269.

Kagan, J. (1958). The concept of identification. *Psychological Review, 65,* 296–305.

Kagan, J. (1984). The idea of emotion in human development. In C. E. Izard, J. Kagan, & R. B. Zajonc (Eds.), *Emotions, cognition, and behavior* (pp. 38–72). Cambridge, UK: Cambridge University Press.

Kagan, S. L. (1990). Readiness 2000: Rethinking rhetoric and responsibility. *Phi Delta Kappan, 1,* 21–23.

Kagitcibasi, C. (1990). Family and socialization in cross-cultural perspective: A model of change. In J. J. Berman (Ed.), *Nebraska Symposium on Motivation, 1989: Cross-cultural perspectives* (pp. 135–200). Lincoln: University of Nebraska Press.

Kahana, B. (1982). Social behavior and aging. In B. B. Wolman (Ed.), *Handbook of developmental psychology* (pp. 871–889). Englewood Cliffs, NJ: Prentice Hall.

Kalb, C. (1997, May 5). How old is too old? *Newsweek,* p. 64.

Kalb, C. (2001, August 13). Should you have your baby now? *Newsweek,* pp. 40–48.

Kalichman, S. C. (1998). *Understanding AIDS: Advances in research and treatment* (2nd ed.). Washington, DC: American Psychological Association.

Kalil, K. M., Gruber, J. E., Conley, J., & Sytniac, M. (1993). Social and family pressures on anxiety and stress during pregnancy. *Pre- and Peri-natal Psychology Journal, 8,* 113–118.

Kalish, C. W., & Gelman, S. A. (1992). On wooden pillows: Multiple classification and children's category-based inductions. *Child Development, 63,* 1536–1557.

Kalish, R. A., & Reynolds, D. K. (1976). *Death and ethnicity: A psychocultural study.* Los Angeles: University of Southern California Press.

Kalleberg, A. L., & Rosenfeld, R. A. (1990). Work in the family and in the labor market. *Journal of Marriage and the Family, 52,* 331–346.

Kalman, M. B. (2003). Taking a different path: Menstrual preparation for adolescent girls living apart from their mothers. *Health Care for Women International, 24,* 868–879.

Kalmijn, M. (1991). Shifting boundaries: Trends in religious and educational homogamy. *American Sociological Review, 56,* 786–800.

Kalmijn, M. (1998). Intermarriage and homogamy: Causes, patterns, trends. *Annual Review of Sociology, 24,* 395–421.

Kalmijn, M., & Bernasco, W. (2001). Joint and separated lifestyles in couple relationships. *Journal of Marriage and the Family, 63,* 639–654.

Kalmijn, M., & Flap, H. (2001). Assortative meeting and mating: Unintended consequences of organized settings for partner choices. *Social Forces, 79,* 1289–1312.

Kalverboer, A. F., Hopkins, B., & Geuze, R. (1993). *Motor development in early and later childhood: Longitudinal approaches.* New York: Cambridge University Press.

Kamii, C. K. (1985). *Young children reinvent arithmetic.* New York: Teachers College Press.

Kamii, C. K. (1994). *Young children continue to reinvent arithmetic: 3rd grade.* New York: Teachers College Press.

Kamo, Y. (1993). Determinants of marital satisfaction: A comparison of the United States and Japan. *Journal of Social and Personal Relationships, 10,* 551–568.

Kang, S. M., & Shaver, P. R. (2004). Individual differences in emotional complexity: Their psychological implications. *Journal of Personality, 72,* 687–726.

Kanter, R. M. (2004). *Confidence: How winning and losing streaks begin and end.* New York: Crown.

Kanungo, R. N., & Misra, S. (1992). Managerial resourcefulness: A reconceptualization of management skills. *Human Relations, 45,* 1311–1332.

Kaplan, B. J. (1986). A psychobiological review of depression during pregnancy. *Psychology of Women Quarterly, 10,* 35–48.

Karmel, M. (1983). *Thank you, Dr. Lamaze.* Philadelphia: Lippincott.

Karp, D. A. (1989). The social construction of retirement among professionals 50–60 years old. *The Gerontologist, 29,* 750–760.

Kasper, J. D. (1997). Long-term care moves into the mainstream. *The Gerontologist, 37,* 274–276.

Kastenbaum, R. (1981). *Death, society, and human experience* (2nd ed.). Palo Alto, CA: Mayfield.

Kastenbaum, R. (1985). Dying and death: A life-span approach. In J. Birren and K. W. Schaie (Eds.), *Handbook of the psychology of aging* (pp. 619–643). New York: Van Nostrand Reinhold.

Kastenbaum, R. J. (1992). *The psychology of death* (2nd ed.). New York: Springer Verlag.

Katchadourian, H. (1990). Sexuality. In S. S. Feldman & G. R. Elliott (Eds.), *At the threshold: The developing adolescent* (pp. 330–351). Cambridge, MA: Harvard University Press.

Kaufert, P., Boggs, P. P., Ettinger, B., Woods, M. F., & Utian, W. H. (1998). Women and menopause: Beliefs, attitudes, and behaviors: The North American Menopause Society 1997 Menopause Survey. *Menopause, 5,* 197–202.

Kaufman, G. (1989). *The psychology of shame.* New York: Springer Verlag.

Kavanaugh, R. D., & Engel, S. (1998). The development of pretense and narrative in early childhood. In O. N. Saracho & B. Spodek (Eds.), *Multiple perspectives on play in early childhood education* (pp. 80–99). Albany: University of New York Press.

Kaye, L. W. (1995). *New developments in home care services for the elderly: Innovations in policy, program, and practice.* Binghamton, NY: Haworth Press.

KB Toys. (2004). *Little Tikes Cookin' Fun interactive kitchen.* Retrieved August 29, 2004, from http://www.kbtoys.com/genProduct.html/PID/1992279/ctid/17/1Nstock/Y/D/604

Keating, D. P. (1990). Adolescent thinking. In S. S. Feldman & G. R. Elliott (Eds.), *At the threshold: The developing adolescent* (pp. 54–90). Cambridge, MA: Harvard University Press.

Keating, D. P. (2004). Cognitive and brain development. In R. M. Lerner & L. Steinberg (Eds.), *Handbook of adolescent psychology* (2nd ed., pp. 45–84). New York: Wiley.

Kegan, R. (1982). *The evolving self: Problems and process in human development.* Cambridge, MA: Harvard University Press.

Keith, J. (1994). Old age and age integration: An anthropological perspective. In M. W. Riley, R. L. Kahn, A. Foner, & K. A. Mack (Eds.), *Age and structural lag: Society's failure to provide meaningful opportunities in work, family, and leisure* (pp. 197–216). New York: Wiley.

Keith, V. M., & Finlay, B. (1988). Parental divorce and children's education, marriage, and divorce. *Journal of Marriage and the Family, 50,* 797–810.

Keller, H., Lohaus, A., Kuensemueller, M. A., Yovsi, R., Voelker, S., Jensen, H., et al. (2004). The bio-culture of parenting: Evidence from five cultural communities. *Parenting: Science and Practice, 4,* 25–50.

Kelly, M. L., Power, T. G., & Wimbush, D. D. (1992). Determinants of disciplinary practices in low-income Black mothers. *Child Development, 63,* 573–582.

Kelly, S. J., Ostrowski, N. L., & Wilson, M. A. (1999). Gender differences in brain and behavior: Hormonal and neural bases. *Pharmacology, Biochemistry and Behavior, 64,* 655–664.

Keltenbach, K., Weinraub, M., & Fullard, W. (1980). Infant wariness toward strangers reconsidered: Infants' and mothers' reactions to unfamiliar persons. *Child Development, 51,* 1197–1202.

Kemper, S., Thompson, M., & Marquis, J. (2001). Longitudinal change in language production: Effects of aging and dementia on grammatical complexity and propositional content. *Psychology and Aging, 16,* 600–614.

Kennedy, G. J., & Tanenbaum, S. (2000). Suicide and aging: International perspectives. *Psychiatric Quarterly, 71,* 345–362.

Kermoian, R., & Campos, J. J. (1988). Locomotor experience: A facilitator of spatial cognitive development. *Child Development, 59,* 908–917.

Kernis, M. H. (2003). Toward a conceptualization of optimal self-esteem. *Psychological Inquiry, 14,* 1–26.

Kersting, K. (2004). Improving the end of life for older adults. *Monitor on Psychology, 35,* 53–54.

Kessen, W. (1965). *The child.* New York: Wiley.

Ketterlinus, R. D., Lamb, M. E., Nitz, K., & Elster, A. B. (1992). Adolescent nonsexual and sex-related problem behaviors. *Journal of Adolescent Research, 7,* 431–456.

Khoo, P. N., & Senn, C. Y. (2004). Not wanted in the inbox! Evaluations of unsolicited and harassing e-mail. *Psychology of Women Quarterly, 28,* 204–214.

Kihlstrom, J. L. (1987). The cognitive unconscious. *Science, 237,* 1445–1452.

Kim, H.-J. K. (2002). *Taegyo (fetal education).* Retrieved August 12, 2004, from http://fieldworking.com/historical/kim.html

Kim, O., & Kim, K. (2001). Body weight, self-esteem, and depression in Korean female adolescents. *Adolescence, 36,* 315–322.

Kimura, D. (1992). Sex differences in the brain. *Scientific American, 267,* 119–125.

Kindermann, T. A. (1996). Strategies for the study of individual development within naturally-existing peer groups. *Social Development, 5,* 158–173.

King, L. A. (1993). Emotional expression, ambivalence over expression, and marital satisfaction. *Journal of Social and Personal Relationships, 10,* 601–607.

King, P. M., & Kitchener, K. S. (1994). *Developing reflective judgment: Understanding and promoting intellectual growth and critical thinking in adolescents and adults.* San Francisco: Jossey-Bass.

King, R. A., Schwab-Stone, M., Flisher, A. J., Greenwald, S., Kramer, R. A., Goodman, S. H., et al. (2001). Psychosocial and risk behavior correlates of youth suicide attempts and suicidal ideation. *Journal of the American Academy of Child and Adolescent Psychiatry, 40,* 837–846.

Kinney, J. M., & Stephens, M. A. P. (1989). Hassles and uplifts of giving care to a family member with dementia. *Psychology and Aging, 4,* 402–408.

Kinsella, K., & Velkoff, V. A. (2001). *An aging world: 2001.* U.S. Census Bureau, Series P95/01-1, US Government Printing Office, Washington DC.

Kirby, J. J. (1996). Welfare to work transition. *Human Development Bulletin, 1,* 1–5.

Kirkwood, T. B. L. (2001). Where will it all end? *The Lancet, 357,* 576–577.

Kiselica, M. S., Gorcynski, J., & Capps, S. (1998). Teen mothers and fathers: School counselor perceptions of service needs. *Professional School Counseling, 2,* 146–152.

Kistner, J. A., Ziegert, D. I., Castro, R., & Robertson, B. (2001). Helplessness in early childhood: Prediction of symptoms associated with depression and negative self-worth. *Merrill-Palmer Quarterly, 47,* 336–354.

Kiston, J. M. (1994). Contemporary Eriksonian theory: A psychobiographical illustration. *Gerontology and Geriatrics Education, 14,* 81–91.

Kitayama, S., Karasawa, M., & Mesquita, B. (2004). Collective and personal processes in regulating emotions: Emotion and self in Japan and the United States. In P. Philippot & R. S. Feldman (Eds.), *The regulation of emotion* (pp. 251–276). Mahwah, NJ: Erlbaum.

Kite, M. E. (1996). Age, gender, and occupational label: A test of social role theory. *Psychology of Women Quarterly, 20,* 361–374.

Kite, M. E., Deaux, K., & Miele, M. (1991). Stereotypes of young and old: Does age outweigh gender? *Psychology and Aging, 6,* 19–27.

Kitson, G. C. (1982). Attachment to the spouse in divorce: A scale and its application. *Journal of Marriage and the Family, 44,* 379–393.

Kitzinger, C., & Coyle, A. (1995). Lesbian and gay couples: Speaking of difference. *Psychologist, 8,* 64–69.

Kitzinger, S. (1982). The social context of birth: Some comparisons between childbirth in Jamaica and Britain. In C. P. MacCormack (Ed.), *Ethnography of fertility and birth* (pp. 181–203). London: Academic Press.

Kitzmann, K. M., & Cohen, R. (2003). Parents' versus children's perceptions of interparental conflict as predictors of children's friendship quality. *Journal of Social and Personal Relationships, 20,* 689–700.

Kivnick, H. Q. (1988). Grandparenthood, life review, and psychosocial development. *Journal of Gerontological Social Work, 12,* 63–81.

Klein, H. (1991). Couvade syndrome: Male counterpart to pregnancy. *International Journal of Psychiatry in Medicine, 21,* 57–69.

Klein, M. (1932/1975). *The psychoanalysis of children* (The International Psychoanalytic Library, No. 22). Oxford, UK: Hogarth Press.

Klesges, L. M., Pahor, M., Shorr, R. I., Wan, J. Y., Williamson, J. D., & Guralnik, J. M. (2001). Financial difficulty in acquiring food among elderly disabled women: Results from the Women's Health and Aging Study. *American Journal of Public Health, 91,* 68–75.

Kline, D. W. (1994). Optimizing the visibility of displays for older observers. *Experimental Aging Research, 20,* 11–23.

Kline, D. W., & Scialfa, C. T. (1997). Sensory and perceptual functioning: Basic research and human factors implications. In A. D. Fisk & W. A. Rogers (Eds.), *Handbook of human factors and the older adult* (pp. 27–54). San Diego: Academic Press.

Klinnert, M. D., Emde, R. N., Butterfield, P., & Campos, J. J. (1986). Social referencing: The infant's use of emotional signals from a friendly adult with mother present. *Developmental Psychology, 22,* 427–432.

Klint, K. A., & Weiss, M. R. (1987). Perceived competence and motives for participating in youth sports: A test of Harter's competence motivation theory. *Journal of Sport Psychology, 9,* 55–65.

Kluger, J. (1997, March 10). Will we follow the sheep? *Time,* pp. 67–72.

Knight, C. C., & Fischer, K. W. (1992). Learning to read words: Individual differences in developmental sequences. *Journal of Applied Developmental Psychology, 13,* 377–404.

Knox, D., Zusman, M., & Nieves, W. (1997). College students' homogamous preferences for a date and mate. *College Student Journal, 31,* 445–448.

Kobak, R. (1999). The emotional dynamics of disruptions in attachment relationships. In J. Cassidy & P. Shaver (Eds.), *The handbook of attachment: Theory, research, and clinical applications* (pp. 21–43). New York: Guilford Press.

Koblinsky, S. A., & Anderson, E. A. (1993, Spring–Summer). Studying homeless children and their families: Issues and challenges. *Division 7 Newsletter,* pp. 1–3.

Kochanek, K. D., & Martin, J. A. (2004). *Supplemental analysis of recent trends in infant mortality.* National Center for Health Statistics, U.S. Department of Health and Human Services. Retrieved August 10, 2004, from http://www.cdc.gov/nchs/products/pubs/pubd/hestats/infantmort/infantmort.htm

Kochanska, G. (1997). Multiple pathways to conscience for children with different temperaments: From toddlerhood to age 5. *Developmental Psychology, 33,* 228–240.

Kochanska, G., Aksan, N., & Koenig, A. L. (1995). A longitudinal study of the roots of preschoolers' conscience: Committed compliance and emerging internalization. *Child Development, 66,* 1752–1769.

Kochanska, G., & Knaack, A. (2003). Effortful control as a personality characteristic of young children: Antecedents, correlates, and consequences. *Journal of Personality, 71,* 1087–1112.

Kochanska, G., Murray, K., & Coy, K. C. (1997). Inhibitory control as a contributor to conscience in childhood: From toddler to early school age. *Child Development, 68,* 263–277.

Kochanska, G., Murray, K. T., & Harlan, E. T. (2000). Effortful control in early childhood: Continuity and change, antecedents, and implications for social development. *Developmental Psychology, 36,* 220–232.

Kochanska, G., & Radke-Yarrow, M. (1992). Inhibition in toddlerhood and the dynamics of the child's interactions with an unfa-

miliar peer at age 5. *Child Development, 63,* 325–335.

Kochenderfer-Ladd, B. J., & Wardrop, J. L. (2001). Chronicity and instability of children's peer victimization experiences as predictors of loneliness and social satisfaction trajectories. *Child Development, 72,* 134–151.

Kohlberg, L. (1964). Development of moral character and moral ideology. In M. L. Hoffman & L. W. Hoffman (Eds.), *Review of child development research* (Vol. 1). New York: Sage.

Kohlberg, L. (1966). A cognitive-developmental analysis of children's sex-role concepts and attitudes. In E. E. Maccoby (Ed.), *The development of sex differences.* Stanford, CA: Stanford University Press.

Kohlberg, L. (1969). Stage and sequence: The cognitive-developmental approach to socialization. In D. A. Goslin (Ed.), *Handbook of socialization theory and research.* Chicago: Rand McNally.

Kohlberg, L. (1976). Moral stages and moralization: The cognitive-developmental approach. In T. Lickona (Ed.), *Moral development and behavior.* New York: Holt, Rinehart & Winston.

Kohn, M. L. (1980). Job complexity and adult personality. In N. J. Smelser & E. H. Erikson (Eds.), *Themes of work and love in adulthood* (pp. 193–210). Cambridge, MA: Harvard University Press.

Kohn, M. L. (1999). Social structure and personality under conditions of apparent social stability and radical social change. In A. Jasinska-Kania, M. L. Kohn, & K. Slomczynski (Eds.), *Power and social structure: Essays in honor of Wodzimierz Wesolowski* (pp. 50–69). Warsaw, Poland: University of Warsaw Press.

Kohn, P. M., & Milrose, J. A. (1993). The inventory of high-school students' recent life experiences: A decontaminated measure of adolescents' life hassles. *Journal of Youth and Adolescence, 22,* 43–55.

Kohut, H. (1971). *The analysis of the self.* New York: International Universities Press.

Konopka, G. (1976). *Young girls: A portrait of adolescence.* Englewood Cliffs, NJ: Prentice Hall.

Konrad, P. (1990, August 6). Welcome to the woman-friendly company. *Business Week,* pp. 48–55.

Kopp, C. B. (1982). Antecedents of self-regulation: A developmental perspective. *Developmental Psychology, 18,* 199–214.

Kopp, C. B. (1989). Regulation of distress and negative emotions: A developmental view. *Developmental Psychology, 25,* 343–354.

Kornfield, S. (1990). *Impact of parental marital status, gender, and pubertal development on adolescent.* Unpublished manuscript, University of Georgia.

Kornhaber, A. (2004). *Grandparents' visitation rights.* Retrieved July 27, 2004, from http://www.grandparenting.org/Grandparent%20Visitation.htm

Kosnik, W., Winslow, L., Kline, D., Rasinski, K., & Sekuler, R. (1988). Visual changes in daily life throughout adulthood. *Journal of Gerontology, 43,* P63–P70.

Kotelchuck, M. (1995). Reducing infant mortality and improving birth outcomes for families of poverty. In H. E. Fitzgerald, B. M. Lester, et al. (Eds.), *Children of poverty: Research, health, and policy issues* (pp. 151–166). New York: Garland.

Kotre, J. (1995). Generative outcome. *Journal of Aging Studies, 9*, 33–41.

Kotre, J. N. (1995). *White gloves: How we create ourselves through memory.* New York: Free Press.

Kotre, J., & Kotre, K. B. (1998). Intergenerational buffers: The damage stops here. In D. P. McAdams & E. de St. Aubin (Eds.), *Generativity and adult development: Psychosocial perspectives on caring for and contributing to the next generation* (pp. 367–389). Washington, DC: American Psychological Association.

Kowaz, A. M., & Marcia, J. E. (1991). Development and validation of a measure of Eriksonian industry. *Journal of Personality and Social Psychology, 60*, 390–397.

Kram, K. E. (1985). *Mentoring at work: Developmental relationships in organizational life.* Glenview, IL: Scott, Foresman.

Kramer, A. F., & Willis, S. L. (2002). Enhancing the cognitive vitality of older adults. *Current Directions in Psychological Science, 11*, 173–177.

Krause, N., & Shaw, B. A. (2000). Role-specific feelings of control and mortality. *Psychology and Aging, 15*, 617–626.

Kreider, R. M., & Fields, J. M. (2002). Number, timing, and duration of marriages and divorces: Fall, 1996. *Current Population Reports*, P70-80. Washington, DC: U.S. Census Bureau.

Kremar, M., & Cooke, M. C. (2001). Children's moral reasoning and their perceptions of television violence. *Journal of Communication, 51*, 300–316.

Krestan, J. A., & Bepko, C. S. (1980). The problem of fusion in the lesbian relationship. *Family Process, 19*, 277–289.

Kroger, J. (1993). *Discussions on ego identity.* Hillsdale, NJ: Erlbaum.

Kroger, J. (1997). Gender and identity: The intersection of structure, content, and context. *Sex Roles, 36*, 747–770.

Kroger, J. (2000). *Identity development: Adolescence through adulthood.* Thousand Oaks, CA: Sage.

Kroger, J. (2003). Identity development during adolescence. In G. R. Adams & M. D. Berzonsky (Eds.), *Blackwell handbook of adolescence* (pp. 205–226). Malden, MA: Blackwell.

Kropp, J. P., & Haynes, O. M. (1987). Abusive and nonabusive mothers' ability to identify general and specific emotion signals of infants. *Child Development, 58*, 187–190.

Kruger, J., & Dunning, D. (1999). Unskilled and unaware of it: How difficulties in recognizing one's own incompetence lead to inflated self-assessments. *Journal of Personality and Social Psychology, 77*, 1121–1134.

Kruk, E. (1995). Grandparent–grandchild contact loss: Findings from a study of "grandparents' rights" members. *Canadian Journal on Aging, 14*, 737–754.

Kübler-Ross, E. (1969). *On death and dying.* New York: Macmillan.

Kübler-Ross, E. (1972, February). On death and dying. *Journal of the American Medical Association, 219*, 10–15.

Kübler-Ross, E. (1981). *Living with dying.* New York: Macmillan.

Kübler-Ross, E. (1983). *On children and death.* New York: Macmillan.

Kuczaj, S. A., & Hill, H. M. (2003). The development of language. In A. Slater & G. Bremner (Eds.), *An introduction to developmental psychology* (pp. 211–236). Malden, MA: Blackwell.

Kuczynski, L., Zahn-Waxler, C., & Radke-Yarrow, M. (1987). Development and content of imitation in the second and third years of life: A socialization perspective. *Developmental Psychology, 23*, 276–282.

Kuhl, P. K. (1987). Perception of speech and sound in early infancy. In P. Salapatek & L. Cohen (Eds.), *Handbook of infant perception* (Vol. 1). Orlando, FL: Academic Press.

Kuhn, D., Amsel, E., & O'Loughlin, M. (1988). *The development of scientific thinking skills.* New York: Academic Press.

Kuhn, D., Garcia-Mila, M., Zohar, A., & Andersen, C. (1995). Strategies of knowledge acquisition. *Monographs of the Society for Research in Child Development, 60* (4, Serial No. 245).

Kunjufu. (2004). *Fathers and childbirth.* Retrieved August 11, 2004, from http://www.blackchat.co.uk/theblackforum/forum2/2969.html

Kunz, J., & Kunz, P. R. (1995). Social support during the process of divorce: It does make a difference. *Journal of Divorce and Remarriage, 24*, 111–119.

Kurdek, L. A. (1981). Young adults' moral reasoning about prohibitive and prosocial dilemmas. *Journal of Youth and Adolescence, 10*, 263–272.

Kurdek, L. A. (1993). The allocation of household labor in gay, lesbian, and heterosexual married couples. *Journal of Social Issues, 49*, 127–139.

Kurdek, L. A. (1995). Lesbian and gay couples. In A. R. D'Augelli & C. J. Patterson (Eds.), *Lesbian, gay, and bisexual identities over the lifespan: Psychological perspectives* (pp. 243–261). New York: Oxford University Press.

Kurdek, L. A. (1996). The deterioration of relationship quality of gay and lesbian cohabiting couples: A five-year prospective longitudinal study. *Personal Relationships, 3*, 417–442.

Kurdek, L. A. (2003). Differences between gay and lesbian cohabiting couples. *Journal of Social and Personal Relationships, 20*, 411–436.

Kurdek, L. A. (2004). Are gay and lesbian cohabiting couples *really* different from heterosexual married couples? *Journal of Marriage and the Family, 66*, 880–900.

Kusseling, F. S., Wenger, N. S., & Shapiro, M. F. (1995). Inconsistent contraceptive use among female college students: Implications for intervention. *Journal of American College Health, 43*, 191–195.

Kwon, Y.-J., & Lawson, A. E. (2000). Linking brain growth with the development of scientific reasoning ability and conceptual change during adolescence. *Journal of Research in Science Teaching, 37*, 44–62.

Laberge, L., Petit, D., Simard, C., Vitaro, F., Tremblay, R. E., & Montplaisir, J. (2001). Development of sleep patterns in early adolescence. *Journal of Sleep Research, 10*, 59–67.

Labouvie-Vief, G. (1992). A neo-Piagetian perspective on adult cognitive development. In R. J. Sternberg & C. A. Berg (Eds.), *Intellectual development* (pp. 197–228). New York: Cambridge University Press.

Labouvie-Vief, G., & Diehl, M. (2000). Cognitive complexity and cognitive-affective integration: Related or separate domains of adult development? *Psychology and Aging, 15*, 490–504.

Lacayo, R. (1988, February 15). Baby M. meets Solomon's sword. *Time*, p. 97.

Lachman, M. E., & James, J. B. (1997). *Multiple paths of midlife development.* Chicago: University of Chicago Press.

Lacombe, A. C., & Gay, J. (1998). The role of gender in adolescent identity and intimacy decisions. *Journal of Youth and Adolescence, 27*, 795–802.

Lacroix, V., Pomerleau, A., Malcuit, G., Seguin, R., & Lamarre, G. (2001). Language and cognitive development of the child during the first three years in relation to the duration of maternal vocalizations and the toys present in the environment: Longitudinal study of populations at risk. *Canadian Journal of Behavioural Science, 33*, 65–76.

Ladd, G. W., Price, J. M., & Hart, C. H. (1988). Predicting preschooler's peer status from their playground behaviors. *Child Development, 59*, 986–992.

Ladson-Billings, G. (2002). But that's just good teaching! The case for culturally relevant pedagogy. In S. J. Denbo & L. M. Beaulieu (Eds.), *Improving schools for African American students: A reader for educational leaders* (pp. 95–102). Springfield, IL: Thomas.

Laflamme, D., Pomerleau, A., & Malcuit, G. (2002). A comparison of fathers' and mothers' involvement in childcare and stimulation behaviors during free-play with their infants at 9 and 15 months. *Sex Roles, 47*, 507–518.

LaFreniere, P. J. (2000). *Emotional development: A biosocial perspective.* Belmont, CA: Wadsworth.

Lagattuta, K. H., & Wellman, H. M. (2001). Thinking about the past: Early knowledge about links between prior experience, thinking, and emotion. *Child Development, 72*, 82–102.

Laible, D. J., & Thompson, R. A. (2000). Mother–child discourse, attachment security, shared positive affect, and early conscience development. *Child Development, 71*, 1424–1440.

LaMastro, V. (2001). Childless by choice? Attributions and attitudes concerning family size. *Social Behavior and Personality, 29,* 231–243.

Lamb, M. E. (1976). Twelve-month-olds and their parents: Interaction in a laboratory playroom. *Developmental Psychology, 12,* 237–244.

Lambert, J. D., & Thomasson, G. C. (1997). Mormon American families. In M. K. DeGenova (Ed.), *Families in cultural context: Strengths and challenges in diversity* (pp. 85–108). Mountain View, CA: Mayfield.

Lamborn, S. D., & Steinberg, L. D. (1993). Emotional autonomy redux: Revisiting Ryan and Lynch. *Child Development, 64,* 483–499.

Landale, N. S., & Fennelly, K. S. (1992). Informal unions among mainland Puerto Ricans: Cohabitation or an alternative to legal marriage. *Journal of Marriage and the Family, 54,* 269–280.

Landry, S. H., Miller-Loncar, C. L., Smith, K. E., & Swank, P. R. (2002). The role of early parenting in children's development of executive processes. *Developmental Neuropsychology, 21,* 15–41.

Landry, S. H., Smith, K. E., Swank, P. R., Assel, M. A.. & Vellet, S. (2001). Does early responsive parenting have a special importance for children's development or is consistency across early childhood necessary? *Developmental Psychology, 37,* 387–403.

Landry-Meyer, L. (1999). Research into action: Recommended intervention strategies for grandparent caregivers. *Family Relations: Interdisciplinary Journal of Applied Family Studies, 48,* 381–389.

Lang, F. R., Featherman, D. L., & Nesselroade, J. R. (1997). Social self-efficacy and short-term variability in social relationships: The MacArthur successful aging study. *Psychology and Aging, 12,* 657–666.

Langlois, J. H., Ritter, J. M., Casey, R. J., & Sawin, D. B. (1995). Infant attractiveness predicts maternal behaviors and attitudes. *Developmental Psychology, 31,* 464–472.

Langston, C. A., & Cantor, N. (1989). Social anxiety and social constraint: When making friends is hard. *Journal of Personality and Social Psychology, 56,* 649–661.

Lankford, M. D., & Milone, K. (Illustrator). (1996). *Hopscotch around the world: Nineteen ways to play the game.* New York: Morrow.

Lansford, J. E., & Parker, J. G. (1999). Children's interactions in triads: Behavioral profiles and effects of gender and patterns of friendship among members. *Developmental Psychology, 35,* 80–93.

Larson, M. C., Gunnar, M. R., & Hertsgaard, L. (1991). The effects of morning naps, car trips, and maternal separation on adrenocortical activity in human infants. *Child Development, 62,* 362–372.

Larson, R., & Ham, M. (1993). Stress and "Storm and Stress" in early adolescence: The relationship of negative events with dysphoric affect. *Developmental Psychology, 29,* 130–140.

Larson, R., & Lampman-Petraitis, C. (1989). Daily emotional states as reported by children and adolescents. *Child Development, 60,* 1250–1260.

LaSala, M. C. (2000). Gay male couples: The importance of coming out and being out to parents. *Journal of Homosexuality, 39,* 47–71.

Laszlo, E. (1972). *Introduction to systems philosophy: Toward a new paradigm of contemporary thought.* New York: Harper & Row.

Laumann, E. Q., Ganon, J. H., Michael, R. T., & Michaels, S. (1994). *The social organization of sexuality.* Chicago: University of Chicago Press.

Lavond, D. G., & Steinmetz, J. E. (Eds.). (2003). *Handbook of classical conditioning.* Dordrecht, The Netherlands: Kluwer.

Lawn, R. M., & Vehar, G. A. (1986). The molecular genetics of hemophilia. *Scientific American, 254,* 48–56.

Laws, G., Byrne, A., & Buckley, S. (2000). Language and memory development in children with Down syndrome at mainstream schools and special schools: A comparison. *Educational Psychology, 20,* 447–457.

Lawton, M. P. (2001). Quality of life and the end of life. In J. E. Birren & K. W. Schaie (Eds.), *Handbook of the psychology of aging* (5th ed., pp. 592–616) San Diego: Academic Press.

Lazarus, R. S. (2000). Toward better research on stress and coping. *American Psychologist, 55,* 655–673.

Lazarus, R. S., & Folkman, S. (1984). *Stress, appraisal, and coping.* New York: Springer Verlag.

Le, H.-N., Munoz, R. F., Ippen, C. G., & Stoddard, J. L. (2003). Treatment is not enough: We must prevent major depression in women. *Prevention & Treatment, 6.*

Leadbeater, B. J., Kuperminc, G. P., Blatt, S. J., & Hertzog, C. (1999). A multivariate model of gender differences in adolescents' internalizing and externalizing problems. *Developmental Psychology, 35,* 1268–1282.

Leaper, C. (2000). Gender, affiliation, assertion, and the interactive context of parent–child play. *Developmental Psychology, 36,* 381–393.

Leaper, C., Anderson, K. J., & Sanders, P. (1998). Moderators of gender effects on parents' talk to their children: A meta-analysis. *Developmental Psychology, 34,* 3–27.

Leaper, C., Tenenbaum, H. R., & Shaffer, T. G. (1999). Communication patterns of African American girls and boys from low-income, urban background. *Child Development, 70,* 1489–1503.

Lecanuet, J. P., Graniere-Deferre, C., Jacquet, A. Y., & DeCasper, A. J. (2000). Fetal discrimination of low-pitched musical notes. *Developmental Psychobiology, 36,* 29–39.

Lee, C. (2002). *Cataracts.* Retrieved February 3, 2002, from http://www .allaboutvision.com/conditions/cataracts .htm

Lee, G. R., DeMaris, A., Bavin, S., & Sullivan, R. (2001). Gender differences in the depressive effect of widowhood in later life. *Journal of Gerontology, 56,* S56–S61.

Lee, K., & Allen, N. J. (2002). Organizational citizenship behavior and workplace deviance: The role of affect and cognitions. *Journal of Applied Psychology, 87,* 131–142.

Lee, K., Ashton, M. C., & Shin, K.-H. (2005). Correlates of workplace anti-social behavior. *Applied Psychology, 54,* 81–98.

Lee, K., & Freire, A. (2003). Cognitive development. In A. Slater & G. Bremner (Eds.), *An introduction to developmental psychology* (pp. 359–387). Malden, MA: Blackwell.

Lee, L. C. (1975). Toward a cognitive theory of interpersonal development: Importance of peers. In M. Lewis & L. A. Rosenblum (Eds.), *Friendship and peer relations.* New York: Wiley.

Lee, M. J., Whitehead, J., & Balchin, N. (2000). The measurement of values in youth sport: Development of the Youth Sport Values Questionnaire. *Journal of Sport and Exercise Psychology, 22,* 307–326.

Leerkes, E. M., Crockenberg, S. C., & Burrous, C. E. (2004). Identifying components of maternal sensitivity to infant distress: The role of maternal emotional competencies. *Parenting: Science & Practice, 4,* 1–23.

Lehr, U., Seiler, E., & Thomae, H. (2000). Aging in a cross-cultural perspective. In A. L. Comunian & U. P. Gielen (Eds.), *International perspectives on human development* (pp. 571–589). Lengerich, Germany: Pabst.

Leinbach, M. D., & Fagot, B. I. (1986). Acquisition of gender labels: A test for toddlers. *Sex Roles, 15,* 655–667.

Leis, N. (1982). The not-so-supernatural power of Ijaw children. In S. Ottenberg (Ed.), *African religious groups and beliefs* (pp. 151–169). Meerut, India: Folklore Institute.

Lemaire, P., Arnaud, L., & Lecacheur, M. (2004). Adults' age-related differences in adaptivity of strategy choices: Evidence from computational estimation. *Psychology and Aging, 19,* 467–481.

Lemkau, J. R. (1988). Emotional sequelae of abortion: Implications for clinical practice. *Psychology of Women Quarterly, 12,* 461–472.

Lemonick, M. D. (1997, December 1). The new revolution in making babies. *Time,* pp. 40–46.

Lemonick, M. D. (2000). Teens before their time. *Time, 156,* 66–74.

Leong, F. T. L., Kao, E. M.-C., & Lee, S.-H. (2004). The relationship between family dynamics and career interests among Chinese Americans and European Americans. *Journal of Career Assessment, 12,* 65–84.

Lerman, R. (1993). A national profile of young unwed fathers. In R. Lerman, R. Ooms, & T. Ooms (Eds.), *Young unwed fathers: Changing roles and emerging policies* (pp. 27–51). Philadelphia: Temple University Press.

Lerner, J. V., & Lerner, R. M. (1983). Temperament and adaptation across life: Theoretical and empirical issues. In P. B. Baltes & O. G. Brim (Eds.), *Life span development and behavior, 5* (pp. 197–231). New York: Academic Press.

Lerner, R. M. (2002). *Concepts and theories of human development* (3rd ed.) Mahwah, NJ: Erlbaum.

Lerner, R. M., Dowling, E., & Roth, S. L. (2003). Contributions of lifespan psychology to the future elaboration of developmental systems theory. In U. M. Staudinger & U. Lindenberger (Eds.), *Understanding human development: Dialogues with lifespan psychology* (pp. 413–422). Dordrecht, The Netherlands: Kluwer.

LeVay, S. (1991). A difference in hypothalamic structure between heterosexual and homosexual men. *Science, 253,* 1034–1037.

Levesque, R. P. (1993). The romantic experience of adolescents in satisfying love relationships. *Journal of Youth and Adolescence, 22,* 219–252.

Levin, I. (1986). *Stage and structure: Reopening the debate.* Norwood, NJ: Ablex.

Levine, A., & Nidiffer, J. (1996). *Beating the odds: How the poor get to college.* San Francisco: Jossey-Bass.

LeVine, R. A. (1977). Child rearing as cultural adaptation. In P. H. Leiderman, S. R. Tulkin, & A. Rosenfeld (Eds.), *Culture and infancy: Variations in the human experience* (pp. 15–28). New York: Academic Press.

LeVine, R. A. (1980). Adulthood among the Gusii of Kenya. In N. J. Smelser & E. H. Erikson (Eds.), *Themes of work and love in adulthood* (pp. 77–119). Cambridge, MA: Harvard University Press.

Levine, S. (2003). Erectile dysfunction: Why drug therapy isn't always enough. *Cleveland Clinic Journal of Medicine, 70,* 241–246.

Levinger, G. (1983). Development and change. In H. H. Kelley et al. (Eds.), *Close relationships* (pp. 315–359). New York: Freeman.

Levitt, M. J., Guacci-Franco, N., & Levitt, J. L. (1993). Convoys of social support in childhood and early adolescence: Structure and function. *Developmental Psychology, 29,* 811–818.

Levitt, M. J., Weber, R. A., & Clark, M. C. (1986). Social network relationships as sources of maternal support and well-being. *Developmental Psychology, 22,* 310–316.

Levitt, M. J., Weber, R. A., & Guacci, N. (1993). Convoys of social support: An intergenerational analysis. *Psychology and Aging, 8,* 323–326.

Levy, G. D. (1998). Effects of gender constancy and figure's height and sex on young children's gender-typed attributions. *Journal of General Psychology, 125,* 65–68.

Levy, G. D., Barth, J. M., & Zimmerman, B. J. (1998). *Journal of Genetic Psychology, 159,* 121–126.

Levy, R. I. (1996). Essential contrasts: Differences in parental ideas about learners and teaching in Tahiti and Nepal. In S. Harkness & C. M. Super (Eds.), *Parents' cultural belief systems* (pp. 123–142). New York: Guilford Press.

Levy-Shiff, R., Sharur, H., & Mogilner, M. B. (1989). Mother- and father–preterm infant relationship in the hospital preterm nursery. *Child Development, 60,* 93–102.

Lewinsohn, P. H., Rohde, P., & Crozier, L. C. (1991). Age and depression: Unique and shared effects. *Psychology and Aging, 6,* 247–260.

Lewis, H. B. (1987). Shame and the narcissistic personality. In D. L. Nathanson (Ed.), *The many faces of shame* (pp. 93–132). New York: Guilford Press.

Lewit, E. M., & Baker, L. S. (1995). School readiness. *The Future of Children, 5,* 128–139.

Liang, J., Krause, N. M., & Bennett, J. M. (2001). Social exchange and well-being: Is giving better than receiving? *Psychology and Aging, 16,* 511–523.

Liben, L. S., & Signorella, M. L. (1993). Gender-schematic processing in children: The role of initial interpretations of stimuli. *Developmental Psychology, 29,* 141–149.

Lieberman, A. F., Weston, D. R., & Pawl, J. H. (1991). Preventive intervention and outcome with anxiously attached dyads. *Child Development, 62,* 199–209.

Liebert, R. M., & Sprafkin, J. (1988). *The early window: Effects of television on children and youth* (3rd ed.). New York: Pergamon Press.

Liebow, E. (1966). *Tally's corner.* Boston: Little, Brown.

Lifton, R. J. (1973). The sense of immortality: On death and the continuity of life. *American Journal of Psychoanalysis, 33,* 3–15.

Lin, H.-L., Lawrence, F. R., & Gorrell, J. (2003). Kindergarten teachers' views of children's readiness for school. *Early Childhood Research Quarterly, 18,* 225–237.

Lin, R.-G., II. (2001, February 23). Nation's colleges anticipate end of SATs at UC schools. *Daily Californian,* University of California, Berkeley. Retrieved February 3, 2005, from www.studentadvantage.com article 0,1075,c0-i0-t0-a1333686,00.html

Lindblad, B. S (1987). *Perinatal nutrition.* San Diego: Academic Press.

Lindbohm, M., Hemminki, K., Bonhomme, M. G., Anttila, A., Rantala, K., Heikkilä, P., & Rosenberg, M. J. (1991). Effects of paternal occupational exposure on spontaneous abortions. *American Journal of Public Health, 81,* 1029–1033.

Lindemann, E. (1944). Symptomology and management of acute grief. *American Journal of Psychiatry, 101,* 141–148.

Lindsey, E. W. (1994). Homelessness. In P. C. McKenry & S. J. Price (Eds.), *Families and change: Coping with stressful events* (pp. 281–302). Thousand Oaks, CA: Sage.

Lindsey, E. W., & Colwell, M. J. (2003). Preschoolers' emotional competence: Links to pretend and physical play. *Child Study Journal, 33,* 39–52.

Lindsey, E. W., Mize, J., & Pettit, G. S. (1997). Mutuality in parent–child play: Consequences for children's peer competence. *Journal of Social and Personal Relationships, 14,* 523–538.

Link, B., Phelan, J., Bresnahan, M., & Stueve, A. (1995). Life-time and five-year prevalence of homelessness in the United States: New evidence on an old debate. *American Journal of Orthopsychiatry, 65,* 347–354.

Linn, M. C., Clement, C., Pulos, S., & Sullivan, P. (1989). Scientific reasoning during adolescence: The influence of instruction in science knowledge and reasoning strategies. *Journal of Research in Science Teaching, 26,* 171–187.

Lippert, T., & Prager, K. J. (2001). Daily experiences of intimacy: A study of couples. *Personal Relationships, 8,* 283–298.

Littlefield, D., Robison, C. C., Engelbrecht, L., Gonzalez, B., & Hutcheson, H. (2002). Mobilizing women for minority health and social justice in California. *American Journal of Public Health, 92,* 576–579.

Litwin, H. (1997). Support network type and health service utilization. *Research on Aging, 19,* 274–299.

Litwin, M., Hays, R., Fink, A., Ganz, P., Leake, B., Leach, G., & Brook, R. (1995). Quality of life outcomes in men treated for localized prostate cancer. *Journal of the American Medical Association, 273,* 129–135.

Livesley, W. J., Jackson, D. N., & Schroeder, M. L. (1992). Factorial structure of traits delineating personality disorders in clinical and general population samples, *Journal of Abnormal Psychology, 101,* 432–440.

Lo, R., & Brown, R. (1999). Stress and adaptation: Preparation for successful retirement. *Australian and New Zealand Journal of Mental Health Nursing, 8,* 30–38.

Lobel, T. E., & Menashri, J. (1993). Relations of conceptions of gender-role transgressions and gender constancy to gender-typed toy preferences. *Developmental Psychology, 29,* 150–155.

Lobo, F., & Watkins, G. (1995). Late career unemployment in the 1990s: Its impact on the family. *Journal of Family Studies, 1,* 103–113.

Locker, B. Z. (1997). Job loss and organizational change: Psychological perspectives. In A. J. Pickman (Ed.), *Special challenges in career management: Counselor perspectives* (pp. 13–24). Mahwah, NJ: Erlbaum.

Locker, J., & Cropley, M. (2004). Anxiety, depression, and self-esteem in secondary school children: An investigation into the impact of standard assessment tests (SATs) and other important school examinations. *School Psychology International, 25,* 333–345.

Lockery, S. (1991). Caregiving among racial and ethnic minority elders. *Generations, 15,* 58–62.

Loehlin, J. C. (1992). *Genes and environment in personality development,* Thousand Oaks, CA: Sage.

Loftus, E. F. (1993). The reality of repressed memories. *American Psychologist, 48,* 518–537.

Logan, D. D. (1980). The menarche experience in 23 foreign countries. *Adolescence, 15,* 247–256.

Lohman, B. J. (2000). *School and family contexts: Relationship to coping with conflict during the individuation process.* Unpublished doctoral dissertation, Ohio State University.

Lombardi, D. N., Melchior, E. J., Murphy, J. G., & Brinkerhoff, A. L. (1996). The ubiquity of life-style. *Individual Psychology:*

*Journal of Adlerian Theory, Research and Practice, 52,* 31–41.

Long, E. C. J., Cate, R. M., Fehsenfeld, D. A., & Williams, K. M. (1996). A longitudinal assessment of a measure of premarital sexual conflict. *Family Relations, 45,* 302–308.

Looft, W. R. (1971). Egocentrism and social interaction in adolescence. *Adolescence, 12,* 485–495.

Lopata, H. Z. (1978). Widowhood: Social norms and social integration. In H. Z. Lopata (Ed.), *Family factbook.* Chicago: Marquis Academic Media.

Lopez, A., Gelman, S. A., Gutheil, G., & Smith, E. (1992). The development of category-based inductions. *Child Development, 63,* 1070–1090.

Lopez, S. J., & Snyder, C. R. (2003). *Positive psychological assessment: A handbook of models and measures.* Washington, DC: American Psychological Association.

Lorenz, K. F. (1935). Der Kumpan in der Urwelt des Vogels. *Journal Ornithologie, 83,* 137.

Lorenz, K. F. (1937/1961). Imprinting. In R. C. Birney & R. C. Teevan (Eds.), *Instinct.* Princeton, NJ: Van Nostrand.

Lott, B., & Bullock, H. E. (2001). Who are the poor? *Journal of Social Issues, 57,* 189–206.

Louchheim, T. (1997). *Jewish customs of mourning.* Retrieved March 13, 2005, from http://scheinerman.net/judaism/life-cycle/mourning.html

Lucariello, J. (1987). Spinning fantasy: Themes, structure, and the knowledge base. *Child Development, 58,* 434–442.

Ludemann, P. M. (1991). Generalized discrimination of positive facial expressions by seven- and ten-month-old infants. *Child Development, 62,* 55–67.

Ludemann, P. M., & Nelson, C. A. (1988). Categorical-representation of facial expressions by 7-month-old infants. *Developmental Psychology, 24,* 492–501.

Luhtanen, R., & Crocker, J. (1992). A collective self-esteem scale: Self-evaluation of one's social identity. *Personality and Social Psychology Bulletin, 18,* 302–318.

Lukas, W. D., & Campbell, B. C. (2000). Evolutionary and ecological aspects of early brain malnutrition in humans. *Human Nature, 11,* 1–26.

Lydon, J., Dunkel-Schetter, C., Cohan, C. L., & Pierce, T. (1996). Pregnancy decision making as a significant life event: A commitment approach. *Journal of Personality and Social Psychology, 71,* 141–151.

Lynam, D. R., & Henry, G. (2001). The role of neuropsychological deficits in conduct disorders. In J. Hill & B. Maughan (Eds.), *Conduct disorders in childhood and adolescence* (pp. 235–263). New York: Cambridge University Press.

Lyons-Ruth, K., Connell, D. B., Zoll, D., & Stahl, J. (1987). Infants at social risk: Relations among infant maltreatment, maternal behavior, and infant attachment behavior. *Developmental Psychology, 23,* 223–232.

Lyons-Ruth, K., Lyubchik, A., Wolfe, R., & Bronfman, E. (2002). Parental depression and child attachment: Hostile and helpless profiles of parent and child behavior among families at risk. In S. H. Goodman & I. H. Gotlib (Eds.), *Children of depressed parents: Mechanisms of risk and implications for treatment* (pp. 89–120). Washington, DC: American Psychological Association.

Maccoby, E. E. (1988). Gender as a social category. *Developmental Psychology, 24,* 755–765.

Maccoby, E. E. (1990). Gender and relationships: A developmental account. *American Psychologist, 45,* 513–520.

Maccoby, E. E. (1992). The role of parents in the socialization of children: An historical overview. *Developmental Psychology, 28,* 1006–1017.

Maccoby, E. E. (2002). Perspectives on gender development. In W. W. Hartup & R. K. Silbereisen (Eds.), *Growing points in developmental science* (pp. 202–222). New York: Psychology Press.

Maccoby, E. E., & Jacklin, C. N. (1987). Gender segregation in childhood. In E. H. Reese (Ed.), *Advances in child development and behavior* (Vol. 20, pp. 239–287). New York: Academic Press.

MacDermid, S. M., Huston, T. L., & McHale, S. M. (1990). Changes in marriage associated with transition to parenthood. *Journal of Marriage and the Family, 52,* 475–486.

Mace, D. R. (1982). *Close companions.* New York: Continuum.

MacFarlane, J. A. (1975). Olfaction in the development of social preferences in the human neonate. In Parent–infant interaction. *Ciba Foundation Symposium, 33,* 103–113.

MacKain, S. J. (1997). *"I know he's a boy because my tummy tells me": Social and cognitive contributions to children's understanding of gender.* Unpublished doctoral dissertation, University of North Carolina, Chapel Hill.

Macklin, E. (1987). Non-traditional family forms. In M. B. Sussman & S. K. Steinmetz (Eds.), *Handbook of marriage and the family* (pp. 317–353). New York: Plenum.

MacLean, D. J., & Schuler, M. (1989). Conceptual development in infancy: The understanding of containment. *Child Development, 60,* 1126–1137.

MacTurk, R. H., McCarthy, M. E., Vietze, P. M., & Yarrow, L. J. (1987). Sequential analysis of mastery behavior in 6- and 12-month-old infants. *Developmental Psychology, 23,* 199–203.

Madden, D. J. (2001). Speed and timing of behavioral processes. In J. E. Birren & K. W. Schaie (Eds.), *Handbook of the psychology of aging.* (5th ed., pp. 288–312) San Diego: Academic Press.

Madden, N. A., Slavin, R. E., Karweit, N. L., Doaln, L. J., & Wasik, B. A. (1993). Success for All: Longitudinal effects of a restructuring program for inner-city elementary schools. *American Educational Research Journal, 30,* 123–148.

Madon, S., Jussim, L., & Eccles, J. (1997). In search of the powerful self-fulfilling prophecy. *Journal of Personality and Social Psychology, 72,* 791–809.

Mahler, M. S. (1963). Thoughts about development and individuation. *Psychoanalytic Study of the Child, 18,* 307–324.

Mahler, M., Pine, F., & Bergman, A. (1975). *The psychological birth of the human infant.* New York: Basic Books.

Main, N., Kaplan, N., & Cassidy, J. (1985). Security in infancy, childhood, and adulthood: A move to the level of representation. In I. Bretherton & E. Everett (Eds.), *Growing points of attachment theory and research* (pp. 60–104). *Monographs of the Society for Research in Child Development, 50* (1–2, Serial No. 209).

Malanowski, J. (1997, November 3). Generation www. *Time digital,* pp. 42–49.

Malatesta, C. A., & Izard, C. E. (1984). The ontogenesis of human social signals: From biological imperative to symbol utilization. In N. A. Fox & R. J. Davidson (Eds.), *The psychobiology of affective development* (pp. 161–206). Hillsdale, NJ: Erlbaum.

Malle, B. F., & Horowitz, L. M. (1995). The puzzle of negative self-views: An explanation using the schema concept. *Journal of Personality and Social Psychology, 68,* 470–484.

Maloy, K., & Patterson, M. J. (1992). *Birth or abortion? Private struggles in a political world.* New York: Plenum Press.

Mandel, D. R., Jusczyk, P. W., & Pisoni, D. B. (1995). Infants' recognition of the sound patterns of their own names. *Psychological Science, 6,* 314–317.

Mandel, J. L., Monaco, A. P., Nelson, D. L., Schlessinger, D., & Willard, H. (1992). Genome analysis and the human X chromosome. *Science, 258,* 103–109.

Mangelsdorf, S. C., Plunkett, J. W., Dedrick, C. F., Berlin, M., Meisels, S. J., McHale, J. L., & Dichtellmiller, M. (1996). Attachment security in very low birth weight infants. *Developmental Psychology, 32,* 914–920.

Manning, W. D. (1990). Parenting employed teenagers. *Youth and Society, 22,* 184–200.

Marcia, J. E. (1980). Identity in adolescence. In J. Adelson (Ed.), *Handbook of adolescent psychology* (pp. 159–187). New York: Wiley.

Marcia, J. E. (1993). The relational roots of identity. In J. Kroger (Ed.), *Discussions on ego identity* (pp. 101–120). Hillsdale, NJ: Erlbaum.

Marcia, J. E. (2002). Identity and psychosocial development in adulthood. *Identity, 2,* 7–28.

Marcus, G. F. (1996). Why do children say "breaked"? *Current Directions in Psychological Science, 5,* 81–85.

Marcus, G. R. (2000). *Pabiku* and *Ga Ti Ga*: Two mechanisms infants use to learn about the world. *Current Directions in Psychological Science, 9,* 145–147.

Marjoribanks, K. (1997–1998). Family background, social and academic capital, and adolescents' aspirations: A mediational analysis. *Social Psychology of Education, 2,* 177–197.

Markman, H. I., & Notarius, C. I. (1987). Coding marital and family interaction: Current status. In T. Jacob (Ed.), *Family interaction and psychopathology* (pp. 329–390). New York: Plenum Press.

Markovits, H., Benenson, J., & Dolenszky, E. (2001). Evidence that children and adolescents have internal models of peer interactions that are gender differentiated. *Child Development, 72*, 879–886.

Markovsky, B., & Chaffee, M. (1995). Social identification and solidarity: A reformulation. In B. Markovsky & K. Heimer (Eds.), *Advances in group processes* (Vol. 12, pp. 249–270). Greenwich, CT: Jai Press.

Marks, S. R. (1989). Toward a systems theory of marital quality. *Journal of Marriage and the Family, 51*, 15–26.

Markstrom, C. A., Sabino, V. M., Turner, B. J., & Berman, R. C. (1997). The psychosocial inventory of ego strengths: Development and validation of a new Eriksonian measure. *Journal of Youth and Adolescence, 26*, 705–732.

Markstrom-Adams, C., Hofstra, G., & Dougher, K. (1994). The ego-virtue of fidelity: A case for the study of religion and identity formation in adolescence. *Journal of Youth and Adolescence, 23*, 453–469.

Markus, H. R., Mullally, P., & Kitayama, S. (1997). Selfways: Diversity in modes of cultural participation. In U. Neisser & D. A. Jopling (Eds.), *The conceptual self in context: Culture, experience, self-understanding* (pp. 13–61). Cambridge, UK: Cambridge University Press.

Marsiglio, W. (1988). Adolescent male sexuality and heterosexual masculinity: A conceptual model and review. *Journal of Adolescent Research, 3*, 285–303.

Marsiglio, W. (1989). Adolescent males' pregnancy resolution preferences and family formation intentions: Does family background make a difference for Blacks and Whites? *Journal of Adolescent Research, 4*, 214–237.

Marsiglio, W. (1993). Adolescent males' orientation toward paternity and contraception. *Family Planning Perspectives, 25*, 22–31.

Marsiglio, W. (2004). When stepfathers claim stepchildren: A conceptual analysis. *Journal of Marriage and the Family, 66*, 22–39.

Martikainen, P., & Valkonen, T. (1996). Mortality after the death of a spouse: Rates and causes of death in a large Finnish cohort. *American Journal of Public Health, 86*, 1087–1093.

Martin, C. L. (1989). Children's use of gender-related information in making social judgments. *Developmental Psychology, 25*, 80–88.

Martin, C. L., Eisenbud, L., & Rose, H. (1995). Children's gender-based reasoning about toys. *Child Development, 66*, 1453–1471.

Martin, C. L., & Halverson, C. F. (1987). The roles of cognition in sex roles acquisition. In D. B. Carter (Ed.), *Current conceptions of sex roles and sex typing: Theory and research* (pp. 123–137). New York: Praeger.

Martin, C. L., & Ruble, D. N. (2004). Children's search for gender cues: Cognitive perspectives on gender development. *Current Directions in Psychological Science, 13*, 67–70.

Martin, C. L., Ruble, D. N., & Szkrybalo, J. (2002). Cognitive theories of early gender development. *Psychological Bulletin, 128*, 903–933.

Martin, C. L., Wood, C. H., & Little, J. K. (1990). The development of gender stereotype components. *Child Development, 61*, 1891–1904.

Martin, G. B., & Clark, R. D., III. (1982). Distress crying in neonates: Species and peer specificity. *Developmental Psychology, 18*, 3–9.

Martin, J. A., Hamilton, B. E., Sutton, P. D., Ventura, S. J., Menacker, F., & Munson, M. L. (2003). Births: Final data for 2002. *National Vital Statistics Reports, 52*, No. 10.

Martin, P., Poon, L. W., Kim, E., & Johnson, M. A. (1996). Social and psychological resources in the oldest old. *Experimental Aging Research, 22*, 121–139.

Martin, S., Houseley, K., McCoy, H., Greenhouse, P., Stigger, F., Kenney, M. A., et al. (1988). Self-esteem of adolescent girls as related to weight. *Perceptual and Motor Skills, 67*, 879–884.

Marvin, R. S., & Brittner, P. A. (1999). Normative development: The ontogeny of attachment. In J. Cassidy & P. R. Shaver (Eds.), *Handbook of attachment: Theory, research, and clinical applications* (pp. 44–67). New York: Guilford Press.

Marx, J. (1988). Are aging and death programmed in our genes? *Science, 242*, 33.

Maslow, A. H. (1968). *Toward a psychology of being* (2nd ed.). Princeton, NJ: Van Nostrand.

Mason, M. G., & Gibbs, J. C. (1993). Social perspective taking and moral judgment among college students. *Journal of Adolescent Research, 8*, 109–123.

Masten, A. S., Coatsworth, J. D., Neemann, J., Gest, S. D., Tellegen, A., & Garmezy, N. (1995). The structure and coherence of competence from childhood through adolescence. *Child Development, 66*, 1635–1659.

Masters, W., & Johnson, V. (1966). *Human sexual response*. Boston: Little, Brown.

Masuda, M. (1994). Exclusivity in heterosexual romantic relationships. *Japanese Journal of Experimental Social Psychology, 34*, 164–182.

Masunaga, H., & Horn, J. (2000). Characterizing mature human intelligence: Expertise development. *Learning and Individual Differences, 12*, 5–33.

Masunaga, H., & Horn, J. (2001). Expertise and age-related changes in components of intelligence. *Psychology and Aging, 16*, 293–311.

Masur, E. F., & Turner, M. (2001). Stability and consistency in mothers' and infants' interactive styles. *Merrill-Palmer Quarterly, 47*, 100–120.

Mathiowetz, N. A. (1999). Respondent uncertainty as indicator of response quality. *International Journal of Public Opinion Research, 11*, 289–296.

Mattessich, P., & Hill, R. (1987). Life cycle and family development. In M. B. Sussman & S. K. Steinmetz (Eds.), *Handbook of marriage and the family* (pp. 437–469). New York: Plenum Press.

Mau, R. Y. (1992). The validity and devolution of a concept: Student alienation. *Adolescence, 27*, 731–741.

May, R. B., & Norton, J. M. (1981). Training-task orders and transfer in conservation. *Child Development, 52*, 904–913.

Mayer, R. (1992). *Thinking, problem solving, and cognition* (2nd ed.). New York: Freeman.

McAdams, D. P., & de St. Aubin, E. (1992). A theory of generativity and its assessment through self-report, behavioral acts, and narrative themes in autobiography. *Journal of Personality and Social Psychology, 62*, 1003–1015.

McAdams, D. P., & de St. Aubin, E. (1998). *Generativity and adult development: How and why we care for the next generation.* Washington, DC: American Psychological Association.

McAdams, D. P., de St. Aubin, E., & Logan, R. L. (1993). Generativity among young, midlife, and older adults. *Psychology and Aging, 8*, 221–230.

McAdams, D. P., Diamond, A., de St. Aubin, E., & Mansfield, E. D. (1997). Stories of commitment: The psychosocial construction of generative lives. *Journal of Personality and Social Psychology, 72*, 678–694.

McAdoo, H. P. (1985). Racial attitude and self-concept of young Black children over time. In H. P. McAdoo & J. L. McAdoo (Eds.), *Black children: Social, educational, and parental environments* (pp. 213–242). Newbury Park, CA: Sage.

McAllister, L. E., & Boyle, J. S. (1998). Without money, means, or men: African American women receiving prenatal care in a housing project. *Family and Community Health, 21*, 67–79.

McArdle, J. J., Ferrer-Caja, E., Hamagami, F., & Woodcock, R. W. (2002). Comparative longitudinal structural analyses of the growth and decline of multiple intellectual abilities over the lifespan. *Developmental Psychology, 38*, 115–142.

McAuley, E., Duncan, T. E., & McElroy, M. (1989). Self-efficacy cognitions and causal attributions for children's motor performance: An exploratory investigation. *Journal of Genetic Psychology, 150*, 65–73.

McAuliffe, G. (1997). A constructive developmental perspective on career counseling. In *The Hatherleigh guide to vocational and career counseling* (pp. 1–16). New York: Hatherleigh Press.

McCabe, A. E., Siegel, L. S., Spence, I., & Wilkinson, A. (1982). Class-inclusion reasoning: Patterns of performance from three to eight years. *Child Development, 53*, 780–785.

McCabe, M. P., & Ricciardelli, L. A. (2001). Parent, peer, and media influences on body image and strategies to both increase and decrease body size among adolescent boys and girls. *Adolescence, 36*, 225–240.

McCarthy, J., & Hardy, J. (1993). Age at first birth and birth outcomes. *Journal of Research on Adolescence, 3*, 373–392.

McClearn, G. E., Johansson, B., Berg, S., Pedersen, N. L., Ahern, F., Petrill, S. A., & Plomin, R. (1997). Substantial genetic influence on cognitive abilities in twins 80 or more years old. *Science, 276,* 1560–1563.

McClelland, J. L., & Rumelhart, D. E. (1986). *Parallel distributed processing* (Vol. 2). Cambridge, MA: MIT Press.

McCloskey, L. A., & Stuewig, J. (2001). The quality of peer relationship among children exposed to family violence. *Development and Psychopathology, 13,* 83–96.

McConatha, J. T., McConatha, D., Jackson, J. A., & Bergen, A. (1998). The control factor: Life satisfaction in later adulthood. *Journal of Clinical Geropsychology, 4,* 159–168.

McCool, W. R., Dorn, L. D., & Susman, E. J. (1994). The relation to cortisol reactivity and anxiety to perinatal outcome in primiparous adolescents. *Research in Nursing and Health, 17,* 411–420.

McCord, J. (1990). Problem behaviors. In S. S. Feldman & G. R. Elliott (Eds.), *At the threshold: The developing adolescent* (pp. 414–430). Cambridge, MA: Harvard University Press.

McCreary, L. L., & Dancy, B. L. (2004). Dimensions of family functioning: Perspectives of low-income African American single-parent families. *Journal of Marriage and the Family, 66,* 690–701.

McCubbin, H. I., & Patterson, J. M. (1982). Family adaptation to crisis. In H. I. McCubbin, A. E. Cauble, & J. M. Patterson (Eds.), *Family stress, coping, and social support* (pp. 26–47). Springfield, IL: Thomas.

McDonald, A. D., Armstrong, B. G., & Sloan, M. (1992). Cigarette, alcohol, and coffee consumption and prematurity. *American Journal of Public Health, 82,* 87–90.

McDonough, L. (2002). Basic-level nouns: First learned but misunderstood. *Journal of Child Language, 29,* 357–377.

McGlaughlin, A., & Grayson, A. (2001). Crying in the first year of infancy: Patterns and prevalence. *Journal of Reproductive and Infant Psychology, 19,* 47–59.

McGonagle, K. A., Kessler, R. C., & Gotlib, I. H. (1993). The effects of marital disagreement style, frequency, and outcome on marital disruption. *Journal of Social and Personal Relationships, 10,* 385–404.

McGowen, K. R., & Hart, L. E. (1990). Still different after all these years: Gender differences in professional identity formation. *Professional Psychology: Research and Practice, 21,* 118–123.

McGuffin, P., Riley, B., & Plomin, R. (2001). Toward behavioral genomics. *Science, 291,* 1232–1249.

McIntosh, J. L. (1999). *U.S.A. Suicide: 1999 official final data.* Retrieved October 20, 2001, from http://www.suicidology.org/index.html

McKenry, P. C., & Price, S. J. (2000). Families coping with problems and change. In P. C. McKenry & S. J. Price (Eds.), *Families and change: Coping with stressful events and transitions* (pp. 1–21). Thousand Oaks, CA: Sage.

McKinlay, J. B., McKinlay, S. M., & Brambilla, D. J. (1987). Health status and utilization behavior associated with menopause. *American Journal of Epidemiology, 125,* 110–121.

McLaughlin, D. K., Lichter, D. T., & Johnston, G. M. (1993). Some women marry young: Transitions to first marriage in metropolitan and nonmetropolitan areas. *Journal of Marriage and the Family, 55,* 827–838.

McLeod, J. D., & Shanahan, M. J. (1993). Poverty, parenting, and children's mental health. *American Sociological Review, 58,* 351–366.

McLoyd, V. C. (1990). The impact of economic hardship on Black families and children: Psychological distress, parenting, and socioemotional development. *Child Development, 61,* 311–346.

McLoyd, V. C. (1998). Socioeconomic disadvantage and child development. *American Psychologist, 53,* 185–204.

McLoyd, V. C., & Smith, J. (2002). Physical discipline and behavior problems in African American, European American, and Hispanic children: Emotional support as a moderator. *Journal of Marriage and the Family, 64,* 40–63.

McRae, S. (1997). Cohabitation: A trial run for marriage? *Sexual and Marital Therapy, 12,* 259–273.

Meacham, J. A. (1995). Reminiscing as a process of social construction. In B. K. Haight & J. D. Webster (Eds.), *The art and science of reminiscing: Theory, research, methods, and applications* (pp. 37–48). Philadelphia: Taylor & Francis.

Mead, M. (1928/1950). *Coming of age in Samoa.* New York: New American Library.

Mead, M. (1935). *Sex and temperament in three primitive societies.* New York: Morrow.

Mead, M. (1949/1955). *Male and female: A study of the sexes in a changing world.* New York: Mentor.

Mead, M., & Newton, N. (1967). Cultural patterning of perinatal behavior. In S. A. Richardson & A. F. Guttmacher (Eds.), *Childbearing: Its social and psychological aspects.* Baltimore: Williams & Wilkins.

Means-Christensen, A., Snyder, D., & Negy, C. (2003). Assessing nontraditional couples: Validity of the Marital Satisfaction Inventory–Revised with gay, lesbian, and cohabiting heterosexual couples. *Journal of Marital and Family Therapy, 29,* 69–83.

Meer, J. (1985, July). Loneliness. *Psychology Today, 19,* 28–33.

Meeus, W. (1996). Studies on identity development in adolescence: An overview of research and some new data. *Journal of Youth and Adolescence, 25,* 569–598.

Meeus, W., Iedema, J., Helsen, M., & Vollenbergh, W. (1999). Patterns of adolescent identity development: Review of literature and longitudinal analysis. *Developmental Review, 19,* 419–461.

Meghdari, A., & Aryanpour, M. (2003). Dynamic modeling and analysis of the human jumping process. *Journal of Intelligent and Robotic Systems, 37,* 97–115.

Meins, E. (2003). Emotional development and early attachment relationships. In A. Slater & G. Bremner (Eds.), *An introduction to developmental psychology* (pp. 141–164). Malden, MA: Blackwell.

Melender, H. (2002). Experiences of fears associated with pregnancy and childbirth: A study of 329 pregnant women. *Birth: Issues in Perinatal Care, 29,* 101–111.

Mellor, S. (1989). Gender differences in identity formation as a function of self–other relationships. *Journal of Youth and Adolescence, 18,* 361–375.

Meltzoff, A. N. (2002). Imitation as a mechanism of social cognition: Origins of empathy, theory of mind, and the representation of action. In U. Goswami (Ed.), *Blackwell handbook of childhood cognitive development* (pp. 6–25). Malden, MA: Blackwell.

Meltzoff, A. N., & Borton, R. W. (1979). Intermodal matching by human neonates. *Nature, 282,* 403–404.

Mendel, G. (1866). Experiments with plant hybrids. *Proceedings of the Brunn Natural History Society.*

Merkle, E. R., & Richardson, R. A. (2000). Digital dating and virtual relating: Conceptualizing computer mediated romantic relationships. *Family Relations, 49,* 187–192.

Merton, R. K. (1948). The self-fulfilling prophecy. *Antioch Review, 8,* 193–210.

Meschke, L. L., Bartholomae, S., & Zentall, S. R. (2002). Adolescent sexuality and parent–adolescent processes: Promoting healthy teen choices. *Journal of Adolescent Health, 31,* 264–279.

Meschke, L. L., Zweig, J. M., Barber, B. L., & Eccles, J. S. (2000). Demographic, biological, psychological, and social predictors of the timing of first intercourse. *Journal of Research on Adolescence, 10,* 315–338.

Messer, D. (2000). State of the art: Language acquisition. *Psychologist, 13,* 138–143.

Messer, D. J., Rachford, D., McCarthy, M. E., & Yarrow, L. J. (1987). Assessment of mastery behavior at 30 months: Analysis of task-directed activities. *Developmental Psychology, 23,* 771–781.

Messer, S., & Warren, S. (1995). *Models of brief psychodynamic therapy.* New York: Guilford Press.

Metz, M. E., Rosser, B. R. S., & Strapko, N. (1994). Differences in conflict-resolution styles among heterosexual, gay, and lesbian couples. *Journal of Sex Research, 31,* 293–308.

Meyer, V. (1991). A critique of adolescent pregnancy prevention research: The invisible White male. *Adolescence, 26,* 217–222.

Mikulincer, M. (1998). Attachment working models and a sense of trust: An exploration of interaction goals and affect regulation. *Journal of Personality and Social Psychology, 74,* 1209–1224.

Miller, G. A., & Gildea, P. M. (1987). How children learn words. *Scientific American, 257,* 94–99.

Miller, J., Slomczynski, K. M., & Kohn, M. L. (1988). Continuity of learning-generalization: The effect of job on men's intellective process in the United States and Poland. In J. T. Mortimer & K. M. Borman (Eds.),

*Work experience and psychological development through the lifespan* (pp. 79–107). Boulder, CO: Westview Press.

Miller, N. B., Cowan, P. A., Cowan, C. P., Hetherington, E. M., & Clingempeel, W. G. (1993). Externalizing in preschoolers and early adolescents: A cross-study replication of a family model. *Developmental Psychology, 29,* 3–18.

Miller, N. B., Smerglia, V. L., Gaudet, D. S., & Kitson, G. C. (1998). Stressful life events, social support, and the distress of widowed and divorced women: A counteractive model. *Journal of Family Issues, 19,* 181–203.

Miller, P. H. (1993). *Theories of developmental psychology* (3rd ed.). New York: Freeman.

Miller, P. H. (2002). *Theories of developmental psychology* (4th ed.). New York: Worth.

Miller, P. J., & Sperry, L. L. (1987). The socialization of anger and aggression. *Merrill-Palmer Quarterly, 34,* 217–222.

Miller, W. B. (1992). An empirical study of the psychological antecedents and consequences of induced abortion. *Journal of Social Issues, 48,* 67–93.

Miller-Tiedeman, A. (1999). Development, decision making, and the new (quantum) careering. In A. Miller-Tiedeman (Ed.), *Learning, practicing, and living the new careering* (pp. 96–120). Philadelphia: Accelerated Development.

Millstein, S. G., & Litt, I. F. (1990). Adolescent health. In S. S. Feldman & G. R. Elliott (Eds.), *At the threshold: The developing adolescent* (pp. 431–456). Cambridge, MA: Harvard University Press.

Min, Y. I., Correa-Villasenor, A., & Stewart, P. A. (1996). Parental occupational lead exposure and low birth weight. *American Journal of Industrial Medicine, 30,* 569–578.

Minuchin, S. (1978). Structural family therapy: Activating alternatives within a therapeutic system. In I. Zwerling (Ed.), *The American family.* Philadelphia: Smith, Kline & French.

Mischel, W. (1973). Toward a cognitive social learning reconceptualization of personality. *Psychological Review, 80,* 252–283.

Mischel, W. (1979). On the interface of cognition and personality: Beyond the person-situation debate. *American Psychologist, 34,* 740–754.

Mischel, W., & Ayduk, O. (2002). Self-regulation in a cognitive-affective personality system: Attentional control in the service of the self. *Self & Identity, 1,* 113–120.

Mischel, W., & Ayduk, O. (2004). Willpower in a cognitive-affective processing system: The dynamics of delay of gratification. In R. F. Baumeister & K. D. Vohs (Eds.), *Handbook of self-regulation: Research, theory, and applications* (pp. 99–129). New York: Guilford Press.

Mischel, W., & Shoda Y. (1995). A cognitive-affective system theory of personality: Reconceptualizing situations, dispositions, dynamics, and invariance in personality structure. *Psychological Review, 102,* 246–268.

Mischel, W., Shoda, Y., & Rodriguez, M. L. (1989). Delay of gratification in children. *Science, 244,* 933–938.

Mistretta, C. M., & Bradley, R. M. (1977). Taste in utero: Theoretical considerations. In J. M. Weiffenbach (Ed.), *Taste and development* (pp. 279–291). DHEW Publication no. NIH 77-1068. Bethesda, MD: U.S. Department of Health, Education, and Welfare.

Mitchell, R. W. (2001). Americans' talk to dogs: Similarities and differences with talk to infants. *Research on Language and Social Interaction, 34,* 183–210.

Miyake, K., Campos, J., Kagan, J., & Bradshaw, D. (1986). Issues in socioemotional development in Japan. In H. Azuma, I. Hakuta, & H. Stevenson (Eds.), *Kodomo: Child development and education in Japan* (pp. 239–261). New York: Freeman.

Moen, P., Kim, J., & Hofmeister, H. (2001). Couples' work/retirement transitions, gender, and marital quality. *Social Psychology Quarterly, 64,* 55–71.

Molfese, D. L., Molfese, V. J., & Carrell, P. L. (1982). Early language development. In B. B. Wolman (Ed.), *Handbook of developmental psychology* (pp. 301–322). Englewood Cliffs, NJ: Prentice Hall.

Monroe, S., Rohde, P., Seeley, J., & Lewisohn, P. (1999). Life events and depression in adolescence: Relationship loss as a prospective risk factor for first onset of major depressive disorder *Journal of Abnormal Psychology, 108,* 606–614.

Montemayor, R. (1983). Parents and adolescents in conflict: All families some of the time and some families most of the time. *Journal of Early Adolescence, 3,* 83–103.

Montgomery, D. E. (1993). Young children's understanding of interpretive diversity between different-age listeners. *Developmental Psychology, 29,* 337–345.

Moore, K. A., Myers, D. E., Morrison, D. R., Nord, C. W., Brown, B., & Edmonston, B. (1993). Age at first childbirth and later poverty. *Journal of Research on Adolescence, 3,* 393–422.

Moore, K. L. (1993). *The developing human: Clinically oriented embryology* (5th ed.). Philadelphia: Saunders.

Moore, K. L., & Persaud, T. V. (1998). *The developing human: Clinically oriented embryology* (6th ed.). Philadelphia: Saunders.

Morf, C. C., & Mischel, W. (2002). Epilogue: Self-regulation, vulnerability, and implications for mental health. *Self & Identity, 1,* 191–199.

Morgan, C., Isaac, J. D., & Sansone, C. (2001). The role of interest in understanding the career choices of female and male college students. *Sex Roles, 44,* 295–320.

Morgan, D. M. (1989). Adjusting to widowhood: Do social networks really make it easier? *The Gerontologist, 29,* 101–107.

Morgane, P. J., Austin-LaFrance, R., Bronzino, J. D., Tonkiss, J., et al. (1993). Prenatal malnutrition and development of the brain. *Neuroscience and Biobehavioral Reviews, 17,* 91–128.

Morrison, A. P. (1989). *Shame: The underside of narcissism.* Hillsdale, NJ: Analytic Press.

Morrison, T., Conaway, W. A., & Borden, G. A. (1994). *Kiss, bow, or shake hands: How to do business in sixty countries.* Holbrook, MA: Adams Media Corp.

Morse, C. K. (1993). Does variability increase with age? An archival study of cognitive measures. *Psychology and Aging, 8,* 156–164.

Morse, J. M. (1998). Designing funded qualitative research. In N. K. Denzin & Y. S. Lincoln (Eds.), *Strategies of qualitative inquiry* (pp. 56–85). Thousand Oaks, CA: Sage.

Mortimer, J. T., & Johnson, M. K. (1999). Adolescent part-time work and postsecondary transition pathways in the United States. In W. R. Heinz (Ed.), *From education to work: Cross-national perspectives* (pp. 111–148). New York: Cambridge University Press.

Mortimer, J. T., Finch, M., Shanahan, M., & Ryu, S. (1992). Work experience, mental health, and behavioral adjustment in adolescence. *Journal of Research on Adolescence, 2,* 25–57.

Mosel, S. (1992, Fall). Remembering great teachers at Parker: Chauncey Griffith. *Parker Magazine,* p. 12.

Moshman, D. (2004). From inference to reasoning: The construction of rationality. *Thinking and Reasoning, 10,* 221–239.

Moss, P., & Tilly, C. (1996). "Soft" skills and race: An investigation of Black men's employment problems. *Work and Occupations, 23,* 252–276.

Muir, D., & Lee, K. (2003). The still face effect: Methodological issues and new applications. *Infancy, 4,* 483–491.

Mulder, E. J. H., deMedina, P. G. R., Huizink, A. C., Van den Bergh, B. R. H., Buitelaar, J. K, & Visser, G. H. A. (2002). Prenatal maternal stress: Effects on pregnancy and the (unborn) child. *Early Human Development, 70,* 3–14.

Mulrane, A. (2001). Are boys the weaker sex? *U.S. News and World Report, 131,* 40–47.

Murdock, G. P., & White, D. R. (1969). Standard cross-cultural sample: *Ethnology, 8,* 329–369.

Murphy, L. (1956). *Personality in young children: Vol. 2. Colin, a normal child.* New York: Basic Books.

Murphy, L. B. (1962). *The widening world of childhood: Paths toward mastery.* New York: Basic Books.

Murphy, L. B. (1972). *Infant's play and cognitive development* (pp. 99–126). New York: Norton.

Murray, B. (1997). Why aren't antidrug programs working? *APA Monitor, 28,* p. 30.

Murray, C. I. (2000). Coping with death, dying, and grief in families. In P. C. McKenry & S. J. Price (Eds.), *Families and change: Coping with stressful events and transitions* (2nd ed., pp.120–153) Thousand Oaks, CA: Sage.

Murray, S. L., Homes, J. G., & Griffin, D. W. (1996). The self-fulfilling nature of positive illusions in romantic relationships: Love is not blind, but prescient. *Journal of Personality and Social Psychology, 71,* 1155–1180.

Murrell, S. A., & Norris, F. H. (1991). Differential social support and life change as contributors to the social class–distress relationship in older adults. *Psychology and Aging, 6,* 223–231.

Musch, J., & Grondin, S. (2001). Unequal competition as an impediment to personal development: A review of the relative age effect in sport. *Developmental Review, 21,* 147–167.

Mussen, P. H., & Jones, M. C. (1957). Self-conceptions, motivations, and interpersonal attitudes of late and early maturing boys. *Child Development, 28,* 243–256.

Musser, L. M., & Browne, B. A. (1991). Self-monitoring in middle childhood: Personality and social correlates. *Developmental Psychology, 27,* 994–999.

Myers, S., & Gramick, H. G. (1990). The social rights and responsibilities of pregnant women: An application of Parson's sick role model. *Journal of Applied Behavioral Science, 26,* 157–172.

Namy, L. L., & Waxman, S. R. (2002). Patterns of spontaneous production of novel words and gestures within an experimental setting in children ages 1.6 and 2.2. *Journal of Child Language, 29,* 911–921.

Nangle, D. W., Erdley, C. A., Newman, J. E., Mason, C. A., & Carpenter, E. M. (2003). Popularity, friendship quantity, and friendship quality: Interactive influences on children's loneliness and depression. *Journal of Clinical Child and Adolescent Psychology, 32,* 546–555.

Nash, J. M. (1997, February 3). Fertile minds. *Time,* pp. 48–56.

Nasir, N. S., & Kirshner, B. (2003). The cultural construction of moral and civic identities. *Applied Developmental Science, 7,* 138–147.

Nathanielsz, P. W. (1996). The timing of birth. *American Scientist, 84,* 562–569.

National Academy on an Aging Society. (2000). Depression: A treatable disease. *Challenges for the 21st Century, 9* (Whole).

National Academy on an Aging Society. (2001). What are the attitudes of young retirees and older workers? *Data Profiles: Young Retirees and Older Workers, 5* (Whole).

National Association of School Psychologists. (2002). *Position paper on ability grouping.* Retrieved November 20, 2004, from http://www.nasponline.org/information/pospaper_ag.html

National Center for Education Statistics. (1995). *Digest of education statistics, 1995.* Washington, DC: U.S. Government Printing Office.

National Center for Education Statistics. (2003a). *Digest of educational statistics, 2003.* Retrieved December 19, 2004, from http://nces.ed.gov/programs/digest/

National Center for Education Statistics. (2003b). *The condition of education.* Washington, DC: U.S. Government Printing Office.

National Center for Education Statistics. (2004a). *International comparisons in fourth-grade reading literacy.* Retrieved November 20, 2004, from http://nces.ed.gov/pubs2004/pirlspub/index.asp

National Center for Education Statistics. (2004b). *Highlights from the TIMSS 1999 video study of eight-grade mathematics teaching study.* Retrieved November 20, 2004, from http://nces.ed.gov/pubs2003/timssvideo/3E.asp?nav=3

National Center for Health Statistics. (2004). *NCHS Data on Aging. Factsheet.* Retrieved February 20, 2005, from http://www.cdc.gov/nchs/data/factsheets/agingfactsheet.pdf

National Coalition for the Homeless. (2002). *Why are people homeless?* Retrieved February 12, 2005, from http://www.nationalhomeless.org/causes.html

National Coalition on Television Violence. (1990). Nintendo tainted by extreme violence. *NCTV News, 11*(1–2), 1, 3–4.

National Commission on Children. (1993). *Just the facts: A summary of recent information on America's children and their families.* Washington, DC: Author.

National Hospice and Palliative Care Organization. (2005). *History of hospice care.* Retrieved March 5, 2005, from http://www.nhpco.org/i4a/pages/index.cfm?pageid=3285

National Institutes of Health. (2000). The relation of child care to cognitive and language development. *Child Development, 71,* 960–980.

National Research Council. (1993). *Losing generations: Adolescents in high risk settings.* Washington, DC: National Academy Press.

National Telecommunications and Information Administration. (2002). *Trendline study on electronic access by households: 1984–1998.* Retrieved January 27, 2002, from http://www.ntia.doc.gov/ntiahome/fttn99/appendix.html

National Urban League. (1987). *Adolescent male responsibility, pregnancy prevention, and parenting program: A program development guide.* New York: Author.

Naughton, K., & Thomas, E. (2000, March 13). Did Kayla have to die? *Newsweek,* pp. 24–29.

Naulty, J. S. (1987). Obstetric anesthesia. In G. B. Avery (Ed.), *Neonatology: Pathophysiology and management of the newborn.* Philadelphia: Lippincott.

Nazi, T., & Gopnik, A. (2001). Linguistic cognitive abilities in infancy: When does language become a tool for categorization? *Cognition, 80,* B11–B20.

Neckerman, H. J. (1996). The stability of social groups in childhood and adolescence: The role of the classroom social environment. *Social Development, 5,* 131–145.

Needham, A. (2001). Object recognition and object segregation in 4.5-month-old infants. *Journal of Experimental Child Psychology, 78,* 3–24.

Neeman, J., Hubbard, J., & Masten, A. (1995). The changing importance of romantic relationship involvement to competence from late childhood to late adolescence. *Development and Psychopathology, 7,* 727–750.

Neese, R. M. (2001). Motivation and melancholy: A Darwinian perspective. In R. A. Dienstbier, J. A. French, A. C. Kamil & D. W. Leger (Eds.), *Evolutionary psychology and motivation. Volume 47 of the Nebraska Symposium on Motivation* (pp. 179–204). Lincoln, NE: University of Nebraska Press.

Neff, K. D., & Harter, S. (2003). Relationship styles of self-focused autonomy, other-focused connectedness, and mutuality across multiple relationship contexts. *Journal of Social and Personal Relationships, 20,* 81–99.

Neimark, E. D. (1975). Longitudinal development of formal operations thought. *Genetic Psychology Monographs, 91,* 171–225.

Neimark, E. D. (1982). Adolescent thought: Transition to formal operations. In B. B. Wolman (Ed.), *Handbook of developmental psychology* (pp. 486–499). Englewood Cliffs, NJ: Prentice Hall.

Neisser, U., Boodoo, G., Bouchard, T. J., Jr., Bodkin, A. W., Brody, N., Ceci, S. J., et al. (1996). Intelligence: Knowns and unknowns. *American Psychologist, 51,* 77–101.

Nelson, C. A. (1987). The recognition of facial expressions in the first two years of life: Mechanisms of development. *Child Development, 58,* 889–909.

Nelson, C. A. (2001). The development and neural bases of face recognition. *Infant and Child Development, 10,* 3–18.

Nelson, E. (1987). Learned helplessness and children's achievement. In S. Moore & K. Kolb (Eds.), *Reviews of research for practitioners and parents* (No. 3, pp. 11–22). Minneapolis: Center for Early Education and Development.

Nelson, K. (1973). Structure and strategy in learning to talk. *Monographs of the Society for Research in Child Development, 38*(1–2).

Nelson, K. (1981). Individual differences in language development: Implications for development and language. *Developmental Psychology, 17,* 170–187.

Nelson, K. (1999). Levels and modes of representation: Issues for the theory of conceptual change and development. In E. K. Scholnick & K. Nelson (Eds.), *Conceptual development: Piaget's legacy* (pp. 269–291). Mahwah, NJ: Erlbaum.

Nelson, K. (2000). Narrative, time and the emergence of the encultured self. *Culture and Psychology, 6,* 183–196.

Nemoto, T. (1998). Subjective norms toward social support among Japanese American elderly in New York City: Why help does not always help. *Journal of Community Psychology, 26,* 293–316.

Nesdale, D., & Flesser, D. (2001). Social identity and the development of children's group attitudes. *Child Development, 72,* 506–517.

Neugarten, B. L. (1981). Growing old in 2020: How will it be different? *National Forum, 61*(3), 28–30.

Neugarten, B. L. (1990). The changing meanings of age. In M. Bergener & S. I. Finkel (Eds.), *Clinical and scientific psychogeriatrics: Vol. 1. The holistic approaches* (pp. 1–6). New York: Springer Verlag.

Neugarten, B. L., Moore, J. W., & Lowe, J. C. (1965). Age norms, age constraints, and adult socialization. *American Journal of Sociology, 70,* 710–717.

Neugarten, B., & Weinstein, R. (1964). The changing American grandparent. *Journal of Marriage and the Family, 26,* 199–204.

Neugebauer, R., Hoek, H. W., & Susser, E. (1999). Prenatal exposure to wartime famine and development of antisocial personality disorder in early adulthood. *Journal of the American Medical Association, 282,* 455–462.

Newman, B. M. (1989). The changing nature of the parent–adolescent relationship from early to late adolescence. *Adolescence, 24,* 916–924.

Newman, B. M. (2000). The challenges of parenting infants and children. In P. C. McKenry & S. J. Price (Eds.), *Families and change: Coping with stressful events and transitions* (pp. 45–70). Thousand Oaks, CA: Sage.

Newman, B. M., & Newman, P. R. (2001). Group identity and alienation: Giving the WE its due. *Journal of Youth and Adolescence, 30,* 515–538.

Newman, J. L., Roberts, L. R., & Syre, C. R. (1993). Concepts of family among children and adolescents: Effect of cognitive level, gender, and family structure. *Developmental Psychology, 29,* 951–962.

Newman, P. R. (1982). The peer group. In B. B. Wolman (Ed.), *Handbook of developmental psychology* (pp. 526–535). Englewood Cliffs, NJ: Prentice Hall.

Newman, R. (2001, October 1). The day the world changed, I did too. *Newsweek,* p. 9.

Newman, S., Karip, E., & Faux, R. B. (1995). Everyday memory function of older adults: The impact of intergenerational school volunteer programs. *Educational Gerontology, 21,* 569–580.

NICHD Early Child Care Research Network. (2002). Early child care and children's development prior to school entry: Results from the NICHD Study of Early Child Care. *American Educational Research Journal, 39,* 51–62.

Nichols, M. R. (1993). Paternal perspectives of the childbirth experience. *Maternal-Child Nursing Journal, 21,* 99–108.

Nickols, S. Y. (1994). Work/family stresses. In P. C. McKenry & S. J. Price (Eds.), *Families and change: Coping with stressful events* (pp. 66–87). Thousand Oaks, CA: Sage.

Nicoladis, E. (1998). First clues to the existence of two input languages: Pragmatic and lexical differentiation in a bilingual child. *Bilingualism: Language and Cognition, 1,* 105–116.

Nicoladis, E., & Secco, G. (2000). The role of a child's productive vocabulary in the language choice of a bilingual family. *First Language, 20,* 3–28.

NIH/CEPH Collaborative Mapping Group. (1992). A comprehensive genetic linkage map of the human genome. *Science, 258,* 7–86.

Ninio, A., & Rinott, N. (1988). Fathers' involvement in the care of their infants and their attributions of cognitive competence to infants. *Child Development, 59,* 652–663.

Nisan, M., & Kohlberg, L. (1982). Universality and variation in moral judgment: A longitudinal and cross-sectional study in Turkey. *Child Development, 53,* 865–876.

Noppe, I. C., & Noppe, L. D. (1997). Evolving meanings of death during early, middle, and later adolescence. *Death Studies, 21,* 253–275.

Norem, J. K., & Cantor, N. (1988). Capturing the "flavor" of behavior: Cognition, affect, and integration. In A. Isen & B. Moore (Eds.), *Affect and social behavior.* New York: Academic Press.

Nsamenang, A. B. (1992). *Human development in cultural context: A Third World perspective* (Cross-cultural research and methodology series, Vol. 16). Newbury Park, CA: Sage.

Nucci, L. P., & Turiel, E. (2002). The moral and the personal: Sources of social conflict. In L. P. Nucci & G. B. Saxe (Eds.), *Culture, thought, and development* (pp. 115–137). Mahwah, NJ: Erlbaum.

Nunez, R. (2004). *Beyond the shelter wall: Homeless families speak out.* New York: White Tiger Press.

Nurmi, J.-E. (2004). Socialization and self-development: Channeling, selection, adjustment, and reflection. In R. M. Lerner & L. Steinberg (Eds.), *Handbook of adolescent psychology* (2nd ed., pp. 85–124). New York: Wiley.

O'Brien, S. F., & Bierman, K. L. (1988). Conceptions and perceived influence of peer groups: Interviews with preadolescents and adolescents. *Child Development, 59,* 1360–1365.

O'Bryant, S. (1988). Sibling support and older widows' well-being. *Journal of Marriage and the Family, 50,* 173–183.

O'Bryant, S. L., & Morgan, L. A. (1990). Recent widows' kin support and orientations to self-sufficiency. *The Gerontologist, 30,* 391–398.

O'Campo, P., Gielen, A. C., Faden, R. R., Xue, X., Kass, N., & Wang, M. (1995). Violence by male partners against women during the childbearing years: A contextual analysis. *American Journal of Public Health, 85,* 1092–1097.

O'Leary, P. A., Haley, W. E., & Paul, P. B. (1993). Behavioral assessment in Alzheimer's disease: Use of a 24-hr log. *Psychology and Aging, 8,* 139–143.

O'Leary, S. (1995). Parental discipline mistakes. *Current Directions in Psychological Science, 4,* 11–13.

O'Neil, J. M., Ohlde, C., Barke, C., Prosser-Gelwick, B., & Garfield, N. (1980). Research on a workshop to reduce the effects of sexism and sex-role socialization on women's career planning. *Journal of Counseling Psychology, 27,* 355–363.

O'Neil, J. M., Ohlde, C., Tollefson, N., Barke, C., Piggott, T., & Watts, D. (1980). Factors, correlates, and problem areas affecting career decision making of a cross-sectional sample of students. *Journal of Counseling Psychology, 27,* 571–580.

O'Neill, D. K., & Gopnik, A. (1991). Young children's ability to identify the sources of their beliefs. *Developmental Psychology, 27,* 390–397.

O'Sullivan, L. F., Meyer-Bahlburg, H. F. L., & Watkins, B. X. (2000). Social cognitions associated with pubertal development in a sample of urban, low-income, African-American and Latina girls and mothers. *Journal of Adolescent Health, 27,* 227–235.

Oates, W. E. (1997). Reconciling with unfulfilled dreams at the end of life. In T. D. Hargrave & S. M. Hanna (Eds.), *The aging family: New visions in theory, practice, and reality* (pp. 259–269). New York: Brunner/Mazel.

Obeidallah, D. A., Brennan, R. T., Brooks-Gunn, J., Kindlon, D., & Earls, F. (2000). Socioeconomic status, race, and girls' pubertal maturation: Results from the project on human development in Chicago neighborhoods. *Journal of Research on Adolescence, 10,* 443–464.

Ochberg, R. L. (1986). College dropouts: The developmental logic of psychosocial moratoria. *Journal of Youth and Adolescence, 15,* 287–302.

Offenbacher, D. I., & Poster, C. H. (1985). Aging and the baseline code: An alternative to the "normless elderly." *The Gerontologist, 25,* 526–531.

Ogbu, J. U. (1987). Variability in minority school performance: A problem in search of an explanation. *Anthropology and Education Quarterly, 18,* 312–334.

Ohannessian, C. M., & Crockett, L. J. (1993). A longitudinal investigation of the relationship between educational investment and adolescent sexual activity. *Journal of Adolescent Research, 8,* 167–182.

Okagaki, L., & Sternberg, R. J. (1993). Parental beliefs and children's school performance. *Child Development, 64,* 36–56.

Okimoto, J. T. (2001). The appeal cycle in three cultures: An exploratory comparison of child development. *Journal of the American Psychoanalytic Association, 49,* 187–215.

Okun, M. A., & Keith, V. M. (1998). Effects of positive and negative social exchanges with various sources on depressive symptoms in younger and older adults. *Journal of Gerontology: Psychological Sciences, 53B,* 4–20.

Okundaye, J. N. (2004). Drug trafficking and urban African American youth: Risk factors for PTSD. *Child & Adolescent Social Work Journal, 21,* 285–302.

Olds, D. L., Henderson, C. R., Jr., Tatelbaum, R., & Chamberlin, R. (1988). Improving the life-course development of socially disadvantaged mothers: A randomized trial of nurse home visitation. *American Journal of Public Health, 78,* 1436–1445.

Ollech, D., & McCarthy, J. (1997). Impediments to identity formation in female adolescents. *Psychoanalytic Psychology, 14,* 65–80.

Olshansky, S. J., Carnes, B. A., & Desesquelles, A. (2001). Prospects for human longevity. *Science, 291,* 1492–1492.

Olshansky, S. J., Carnes, B. A., & Grahn, D. (1998). Confronting the boundaries of human longevity. *American Scientist, 86,* 52–61.

Olweus, D. (1993). *Bullying at school: What we know and what we can do.* Cambridge, MA: Blackwell Press.

Olweus, D. (1995). Bullying or peer abuse at school: Facts and intervention. *Current Directions in Psychological Science, 4*, 196–200.

Olweus, D., Limber, S., & Mihalic, S. F. (1999). *Blueprints for violence prevention, Book 9: Bullying prevention program.* Boulder, CO: Center for the Study and Prevention of Violence.

Oosterwegel, A., & Oppenheimer, L. (1993). *The self-system: Developmental changes between and within self-concepts.* Hillsdale, NJ: Erlbaum.

Oppenheim, D., Sagi, A., & Lamb, M. E. (1988). Infant–adult attachments on the kibbutz and their relation to socioemotional development four years later. *Development Psychology, 24*, 427–433.

Orenstein, P. (1994). *Schoolgirls: Young women, self-esteem, and the confidence gap.* New York: Anchor Books.

Orenstein, P. (2000). *Schoolgirls: Young women, self-esteem, and the confidence gap.* New York: Anchor Books.

Osipow, S. H. (1986). Career issues through the life span. In M. S. Pallak & R. Perloff (Eds.), *Psychology and work: Productivity, change, and employment* (pp. 137–168). Washington, DC: American Psychological Association.

Osofsky, J. D. (1995). The effect of exposure to violence on young children. *American Psychologist, 50*, 782–788.

Osofsky, J. D., Hann, D. M., & Peebles, C. (1993). Adolescent parenthood: Risks and opportunities for mothers and infants. In C. H. Zeanah (Ed.), *Handbook of infant mental health* (pp. 106–119). New York: Guilford Press.

Oster, H., Hegley, D., & Nagel, L. (1992). Adult judgments and fine-grained analysis of infant facial expressions: Testing the validity of a priori coding formulas. *Developmental Psychology, 28*, 1115–1131.

Ostrov, E., Offer, D., & Howard, K. I. (1989). Gender differences in adolescent symptomatology: A normative study. *Journal of the American Academy of Child and Adolescent Psychiatry, 28*, 394–398.

Owen, M. T. (1997). *Mother–child interaction and cognitive outcomes associated with early child care: Results of the NICHD study.* Symposium presented at the Biennial Meeting of the Society for Research in Child Development, Symposium No. 2-210.

Pajares, F. (1996). Self-efficacy beliefs in academic settings. *Review of Educational Research, 66*, 543–578.

Palermo, G. B. (1995). Should physician-assisted suicide be legalized? A challenge for the 21st century. *International Journal of Offender Therapy and Comparative Criminology, 39*, 367–376.

Palkovitz, R. (1985). Fathers' attendance, early contact, and extended care with their newborns: A critical review. *Child Development, 56*, 392–406.

Palladino-Schultheiss, D., & Blustein, D. (1994). Contributions of family relationship factors to the identity formation process. *Journal of Counseling Development, 73*, 159–166.

Pallett-Hehn, P., & Lucas, M. (1994). LIFE: Learning informally from elders. *The Gerontologist, 34*, 267–271.

Palm, G. F., & Palkovitz, R. (1988). The challenge of working with new fathers: Implications for support providers. In R. Palkovitz & M. B. Sussman (Eds.), *Transitions to parenthood* (pp. 357–376). New York: Haworth.

Palmer, C. F. (1989). The discriminating nature of infants' exploratory actions. *Developmental Psychology, 25*, 885–893.

Palmore, E. B., Nowlin, J. B., & Wang, H. S. (1985). Predictors of function among the old-old: A 10-year follow-up. *Journal of Gerontology, 40*, 244–250.

Papini, D. R., Datan, N., & McCluskey-Fawcett, K. A. (1988). An observational study of affective and assertive family interactions during adolescence. *Journal of Youth and Adolescence, 17*, 477–492.

Papini, D. R., & Sebby, R. A. (1988). Variations in conflictual family issues by adolescent pubertal status, gender, and family member. *Journal of Early Adolescence, 8*, 1–15.

Parcel, T. L., & Menaghan, E. G. (1994). *Parents' jobs and children's lives.* New York: Aldine de Gruyter.

Parents should talk to college students about alcohol. (1997, October 12). *Columbus Dispatch*, p. 7H.

Park, K. A., & Waters, E. (1989). Security of attachment and preschool friendships. *Child Development, 60*, 1076–1081.

Park, K. A., Lay, K., & Ramsay, L. (1993). Individual differences and developmental changes in preschoolers' friendships. *Developmental Psychology, 29*, 264–270.

Park, S.-Y., Belsky, J., Putnam, S., & Crnic, K. (1997). Infant emotionality, parenting, and 3-year inhibition: Exploring stability and lawful discontinuity in a male sample. *Developmental Psychology, 33*, 218–227.

Parker, J. G., & Asher, S. R. (1993). Friendship and friendship quality in middle childhood: Links with peer group acceptance and feelings of loneliness and social dissatisfaction. *Developmental Psychology, 29*, 611–621.

Parkhurst, J. T., & Asher, S. R. (1992). Peer rejection in middle school: Subgroup differences in behavior, loneliness, and interpersonal concerns. *Developmental Psychology, 28*, 231–241.

Parr, J. M. (1999). Going to school the technological way: Co-constructed classrooms and student perceptions of learning with technology. *Journal of Educational Computing Research, 20*, 365–377.

Parsons, J. E., Adler, T. F., & Kaczala, C. M. (1982). Socialization of achievement attitudes and beliefs: Parental influences. *Child Development, 53*, 310–321.

Parsons, J. E., & Ruble, D. N. (1977). The development of achievement-related expectancies. *Child Development, 48*, 1075–1079.

Parsons, T. (1955). Family structure and the socialization of the child. In T. Parsons & R. F. Bales (Eds.), *Family, socialization, and interaction process.* Glencoe, IL: Free Press.

Parsons, T., & Bales, R. F. (Eds.). (1955). *Family socialization and interaction process.* Glencoe, IL: Free Press.

Pascarella, E. T., & Terenzini, P. T. (1991). *How college affects students: Findings and insights from twenty years of research.* San Francisco: Jossey-Bass.

Passman, R. H., & Longeway, K. P. (1982). The role of vision in maternal attachment: Giving 2-year-olds a photograph of their mother during separation. *Developmental Psychology, 18*, 530–533.

Paterson, G., & Sanson, A. (1999). The association of behavioural adjustment to temperament, parenting and family characteristics among 5 year old children. *Social Development, 8*, 293–309.

Patterson, C. J. (1992). Children of lesbian and gay parents. *Child Development, 63*, 1025–1042.

Patterson, C. J. (1994). Lesbian and gay families. *Current Directions in Psychological Science, 3*, 62–64.

Patterson, C. J. (1995). Families of the lesbian baby boom: Parents' division of labor and children's adjustment. *Developmental Psychology, 31*, 115–123.

Patterson, G. R. (1982). *Coercive family processes.* Eugene, OR: Castalia.

Patterson, G. R. (1992). Developmental changes in antisocial behavior. In R. D. Peters, R. J. McMahon, & V. L. Quignsey (Eds.), *Aggression and violence throughout the lifespan* (pp. 52–82). Newbury Park, CA: Sage.

Patterson, I. (1996). Participation in leisure activities by older adults after a stressful life event: The loss of a spouse. *International Journal of Aging and Human Development, 42*, 123–142.

Patterson, L. E. (1997). Client resistance to career counseling. In *The Hatherleigh guide to vocational and career counseling* (pp. 17–33). New York: Hatherleigh Press.

Patterson, M. L., & Werker, J. F. (1999). Matching phonetic information in lips and voice is robust in 4.5-month-old infants. *Infant Behavior and Development, 22*, 237–247.

Pauli-Pott, U., Mertesacker, B., & Beckman, D. (2004). Predicting the development of infant emotionality from maternal characteristics. *Development and Psychopathology, 16*, 19–42.

Pavetti, L. A. (2000). Creating a new welfare reality: Early implementation of the Temporary Assistance for Needy Families program. *Journal of Social Issues, 56*, 601–615.

Pearn, J. (2003). Children and war. *Journal of Paediatrics & Child Health, 39*, 166–172.

Pearson, D., Rouse, H., Doswell, S., Ainsworth, C., Dawson, O., Simms, K., et al. (2001). Prevalence of imaginary companions in a normal child population. *Child Care, Health, & Development, 27*, 13–22.

Peck, R. C. (1968). Psychological developments in the second half of life. In B. L. Nevgarten (Ed), *Middle age and aging* (p. 88). Chicago: University of Chicago Press.

Peek, M. K., Coward, R. T., & Peek, C. W. (2000). *Research on Aging, 22*, 117–142.

Pelham, B. W. (1991). On the benefits of misery: Self-serving biases in the depressive self concept. *Journal of Personality and Social Psychology, 61*, 670–681.

Pelham, B. W., & Swann, W. B., Jr. (1989). From self-conceptions to self-worth: On the sources and structure of global self-esteem. *Journal of Personality and Social Psychology, 57*, 672–680.

Pell, R. W. (2002). *Hui Malama I Na Kupuna 'O Hawai'i Nei*. Retrieved February 6, 2000, from http://www.pixi.com/huimalam/#beliefs

Pellegrini, A. D., & Bjorklund, D. F. (2004). The ontogeny and phylogeny of children's object and fantasy play. *Human Nature, 15*, 23–43.

Pellegrini, D. S. (1985). Social cognition and competence in middle childhood. *Child Development, 56*, 253–264.

Peltonen, L., & McKusick, V. A. (2001). Dissecting human disease in the postgenomic era. *Science, 291*, 1224–1229.

Pemberton, M. B., Insko, C. A., & Schopler, J. (1996). Memory for and experience of differential competitive behavior of individuals and groups. *Journal of Personality and Social Psychology, 71*, 953–966.

Perfect, T. J. (1994). What can Brinley Plots tell us about cognitive aging? *Journal of Gerontology, 49*, P60–P64.

Pergament, E. (1998). Smoking and pregnancy. *Risk Newsletter, 6*(4). Retrieved January 25, 2002, from http://www.fetal-exposure.org/smoke.html

Peris, A. (2000). *Therapies: Artificial insemination*. Retrieved October 14, 2001, from http://www.fertilitext.org/p2_doctor/ai.html

Perloff, R. M. (2001). *Persuading people to have safer sex: Applications of social science to the AIDS crisis*. Mahwah, NJ: Erlbaum.

Perls, T. T. (2004). The oldest old. *Scientific American, 14*, 6–11.

Perosa, L. M., Perosa, S. L., & Tam, H. P. (1996). The contribution of family structure and differentiation to identity development in females. *Journal of Youth and Adolescence, 25*, 817–837.

Perret-Clermont, A., Perret, J., & Bell, N. (1991). The social construction of meaning and cognitive activity in elementary school children. In L. B. Resnick, J. M. Levine, & S. D. Teasley (Eds.), *Perspectives on socially shared cognition* (pp. 41–62). Washington, DC: American Psychological Association.

Perrucci, C. C., Perrucci, R., & Targ, D. B. (1997). Gender differences in the economic, psychological, and social effects of plant closings in an expanding economy. *Social Science Journal, 34*, 217–233.

Perry, B. D. (1994). Neurobiological sequelae of childhood trauma: PTSD in children. In M. M. Murburg (Ed.), *Catecholamine function in posttraumatic stress disorder: Emerging concepts* (pp. 233–255). Washington, DC: American Psychiatric Press.

Perry, B. D., Pollard, R., Blakley, T., Baker, W., & Vigilante, D. (1995). Childhood trauma, the neurobiology of adaptation and "use-dependent" development of the brain: How states become traits. *Infant Mental Health Journal, 16*, 271–291.

Perusse, D. (1994). Mate choice in modern societies: Testing evolutionary hypotheses with behavioral data. *Human Nature, 5*, 255–278.

Pete, J. M., & DeSantis, L. (1990). Sexual decision making in young Black adolescent females. *Adolescence, 25*, 145–154.

Petersen, A. C., Compas, B. E., Brooks-Gunn, J., Stemmler, M., Ey, S., & Grant, K. E. (1993). Depression in adolescence. *American Psychologist, 48*, 155–168.

Petersen, A. C., Sarigiani, P. A., & Kennedy, R. E. (1991). Adolescent depression: Why more girls? *Journal of Youth and Adolescence, 20*, 247–272.

Peterson, B. D., Newton, C. R., & Rosen, K. H. (2003). Examining congruence between partners' perceived infertility-related stress and its relationship to marital adjustment and depression in infertile couples. *Family Process, 42*, 59–70.

Peterson, B. E., & Stewart, A. J. (1993). Generativity and social motives in young adults. *Journal of Personality and Social Psychology, 65*, 186–198.

Peterson, C., & Seligman, M. E. P. (2003). Character strengths before and after September 11. *Psychological Science, 14*, 381–384.

Peterson, G. (2001). *Infertility is taking its toll*. Retrieved August 9, 2004, from http://www.parentsplace.com/fertility/conception/qas/0,,238711_270929,00.html

Pettit, G. S., Dodge, K. A., & Brown, M. M. (1988). Early family experience, social problem-solving patterns, and children's social competence. *Child Development, 59*, 107–120.

Pfefferbaum, B., Seale, T. W., McDonald, N. B., Brandt, E. N., Jr., Rainwater, S. C., Maynard, B. T., et al. (2000). Posttraumatic stress two years after the Oklahoma City bombing in youth geographically distant from the explosion. *Psychiatry: Interpersonal and Biological Processes, 63*, 358–370.

Phillips, D. A. (1984). The illusion of incompetence among academically competent children. *Child Development, 55*, 2000–2016.

Phillips, D. A. (1987). Socialization of perceived academic competence among highly competent children. *Child Development, 58*, 1308–1320.

Phinney, J. S. (1992). The multigroup ethnic identity measure: A new scale for use with adolescents and young adults from diverse groups. *Journal of Adolescent Research, 7*, 156–176.

Phinney, J. S. (1996a). Understanding ethnic diversity: The role of ethnic identity. *American Behavioral Scientist, 40*, 143–152.

Phinney, J. S. (1996b). When we talk about American ethnic groups, what do we mean? *American Psychologist, 51*, 918–927.

Phinney, J. S. (1997). Variations in bicultural identification among African American and Mexican American adolescents. *Journal of Research on Adolescence, 7*, 3–32.

Piaget, J. (1926). *The language and thought of the child*. New York: Harcourt Brace.

Piaget, J. (1929). *The child's conception of physical causality*. New York: Harcourt Brace. (Originally published in French 1926)

Piaget, J. (1932/1948). *The moral judgment of the child*. Glencoe, IL: Free Press.

Piaget, J. (1936/1952). *The origins of intelligence in children*. New York: International Universities Press.

Piaget, J. (1941/1952). *The child's conception of number*. London: Kegan Paul, Trench & Trubner.

Piaget, J. (1951). *Play, dreams, and imitation in childhood*. New York: Norton.

Piaget, J. (1952). *The language and thought of the child*. London: Routledge & Kegan Paul.

Piaget, J. (1962). *Play, dreams, and imitation in childhood*. New York: Norton.

Piaget, J. (1963). The attainment of invariant and reversible operations in the development of thinking. *Social Research, 30*, 283–299.

Piaget, J. (1970). Piaget's theory. In P. H. Mussen (Ed.), *Carmichael's manual of child psychology* (3rd ed., Vol. 1). New York: Wiley.

Piaget, J. (1972a). Intellectual evolution from adolescence to adulthood. *Human Development, 15*, 1–12.

Piaget, J. (1972b). *The psychology of intelligence*. Totowa, NJ: Littlefield Adams.

Piaget, J. (1978/1985). *The equilibration of cognitive structures*. Chicago: University of Chicago Press.

Piaget, J., & Inhelder, B. (1966/1969). *The psychology of the child*. New York: Basic Books.

Pick, H. L. (1989). Motor development: The control of action. *Developmental Psychology, 25*, 867–870.

Pick, H. L., Jr., & Rosengren, K. S. (1991). Perception and representation in the development of mobility. In R. R. Hoffman & D. S. Palermo (Eds.), *Cognition and the symbolic processes: Applied and ecological perspectives* (pp. 433–454). Hillsdale, NJ: Erlbaum.

Piers, M. W., & Landau, G. M. (1980). *The gift of play*. New York: Walker.

Pillow, B. H. (1991). Children's understanding of biased social cognition. *Developmental Psychology, 27*, 539–551.

Pine, D., Cohen, P., Gurley, D., Brook, J., & Ma, Y. (1998). The risk for early-adulthood anxiety and depressive disorders in adolescents with anxiety and depressive disorders. *Archives of General Psychiatry, 55*, 56–64.

Piotrkowski, C. S., Rapoport, R. N., & Rapoport, R. (1987). Families and work. In M. B. Sussman & S. K. Steinmetz (Eds.), *Handbook of marriage and the family* (pp. 251–283). New York: Plenum Press.

Pirog-Good, M. A. (1995). The family background and attitudes of teen fathers. *Youth and Society, 26*, 351–376.

Planned Parenthood. (2000). *Mifepristone: A brief history*. Retrieved October 23, 2001, from http://www.plannedparenthood.org/library/ABORTION/Mifepristone.html

Pleck, J. H. (1985). *Working wives, working husbands*. New York: Sage.

Pleck, J. H., Sonenstein, F. L., & Ku, L. C. (1991). Adolescent males' condom use: Relationships between perceived cost-benefits and consistency. *Journal of Marriage and the Family, 53*, 733–746.

Plomin R. (1990). *Nature and nurture: An introduction to human behavioral genetics*. Pacific Grove, CA: Brooks/Cole.

Plomin, R. (1994). *Genetics and experience*. Thousand Oaks, CA: Sage.

Plomin, R., DeFries, J. C., Craig, I. W., & McGuffin, P. (Eds.). (2003). *Behavioral genetics in the postgenomic era*. Washington, DC: American Psychological Association.

Plomin, R., & McClearn, G. E. (1993). *Nature, nurture, and psychology*. Hyattsville, MD: American Psychological Association.

Plotnick, R. D. (1992). The effects of attitudes on teenage premarital pregnancy and its resolution. *American Sociological Review, 57*, 800–811.

Plutchik, R. (2001). The nature of emotions. *American Scientist, 89*, 344–350.

Polednak, A. P. (1991). Black–White differences in infant mortality in 38 standard metropolitan statistical areas. *American Journal of Public Health, 81*, 1480–1482.

Pollack, D. (2001, August 17). Seeking secret of longevity in genes of centenarians. *Forward*. Retrieved February 20, 2005, from http://www.forward.com/issues/2001/01.08.17/genetic5.html

Pollack, H. (2000). When pregnant women use crack. *FAS Drug Policy Bulletin, 8*. Retrieved August 11, 2004, from http://www.fas.org/drugs/issue8.htm

Pollard, I. (2000). Substance abuse and parenthood: Biological mechanisms—bioethical challenges. *Women and Health, 30*, 1–24.

Pollitt, E. (1994). Poverty and child development: Relevance of research in developing countries to the United States. *Child Development, 65*, 283–295.

Pomerantz, E. M., & Easton, M. M. (2000). Developmental differences in children's conceptions of parental control: "They love me, but they make me feel incompetent." *Merrill-Palmer Quarterly, 46*, 140–167.

Porter, E. J. (1994). Older widows' experiences of living alone at home. *Image: Journal of Nursing Scholarship, 26*, 19–24.

Porter, R. H., Balogh, R. D., & Makin, J. W. (1988). Olfactory influences on mother–infant interactions. In C. Rovee-Collier & L. Lipsitt (Eds.), *Advances in infancy research* (Vol. 5, pp. 39–68). Norwood, NJ: Ablex.

Posada, G., Gao, Y., Wu, F., Posada, R., Tascon, M., Schoelmerich, A., et al. (1995). The secure-base phenomenon across cultures: Children's behavior, mothers' preferences, and experts' concepts. *Monographs of the Society for Research in Child Development, 60*, 27–48.

Posner, A. (2001). *Skills: Your key to success in the 21st century workplace*. Retrieved December 18, 2001, from http://www.wetfeet.com/asp/article.asp?aid=311&atype=general

Poulin, F. W., & Boivin, M. (2000). The role of proactive and reactive aggression in the formation and development of boys' friendships. *Developmental Psychology, 36*, 233–240.

Poulin, R., Dishion, T. J., & Haas, E. (1999). The peer influence paradox: Friendship quality and deviancy training within male adolescent friendships. *Merrill-Palmer Quarterly, 45*, 42–61.

Power, T. G. (1985). Mother– and father–infant play: A developmental analysis. *Child Development, 56*, 1514–1524.

Powers, S. M. (2002). Merge as a basic mechanism of language: Evidence from language acquisition. In E. Witruk & A. D. Friederici (Eds.), *Basic functions of language, reading and reading disability* (pp. 105–117). Dordrecht, The Netherlands: Kluwer.

Pratt, C. C., Jones, L. L., Shin, H., & Walker, A. J. (1989). Autonomy and decision making between single older women and their caregiving daughters. *The Gerontologist, 29*, 792–797.

Prawat, R. S., Byers, J. L., & Anderson, A. H. (1983). An attributional analysis of teachers' affective reactions to student success and failure. *American Educational Research Journal, 20*, 137–152.

Prentice, D. A., Miller, D. T., & Lightdale, J. R. (1994). Asymmetries in attachments to groups and to their members: Distinguishing between common-identity and common-bond groups. *Personality and Social Psychology Bulletin, 20*, 484–493.

Preski, S., & Shelton, D. (2001). The role of contextual, child and parent factors in predicting criminal outcomes in adolescence. *Issues in Mental Health Nursing, 22*, 197–205.

Presser, H. B. (1989). Some economic complexities of child care provided by grandmothers. *Journal of Marriage and the Family, 51*, 581–591.

Pushkar, D., Arbuckle, T., Conway, M., Chaikelson, J., & Maag, U. (1997). Everyday activity parameters and competence in older adults. *Psychology and Aging, 12*, 600–609.

Putnam, S. P., Sanson, A. V., & Rothbart, M. K. (2002). Child temperament and parenting. In M. H. Bornstein (Ed.), *Handbook of parenting. Vol. 1. Children and parenting* (2nd ed., pp. 255–277). Mahwah, NJ: Erlbaum.

Pye, C. (1986). Quiché Mayan speech to children. *Journal of Child Language, 13*, 85–100.

Pyle, R. P. (2002). Best practices in assessing kindergarten readiness. *California School Psychologist, 7*, 63–73.

Qian, Z., & Preston, S. H. (1993). Changes in American marriage, 1972 to 1987: Availability and forces of attraction by age and education. *American Sociological Review, 58*, 482–495.

Quadrel, M. J., Fischhoff, B., & Davis, W. (1993). Adolescent (in)vulnerability. *American Psychologist, 48*, 102–116.

Quakenbush, S. W., & Barnett, M. A. (1995). Correlates of reminiscence activity among elderly individuals. *International Journal of Aging and Human Development, 41*, 169–181.

Quiggle, N. L., Garber, J., Panak, W. F., & Dodge, K. A. (1992). Social information processing in aggressive and depressed children. *Child Development, 63*, 1305–1320.

Quinn, P. C., Eimas, P. D., & Tarr, M. J. (2001). Perceptual categorization of cat and dog silhouettes by 3- to 4-month-old infants. *Journal of Experimental Child Psychology, 79*, 78–94.

Radin, N. (1982) Primary caregiver and role sharing fathers. In M. E. Lamb (Ed.), *Nontraditional families* (pp. 173–204). Hillsdale, NJ: Erlbaum.

Radin, N. (1988). Primary caregiving fathers of long duration. In P. Bronstein & C. P. Cowan (Eds.), *Fatherhood today* (pp. 127–143). New York: Wiley.

Radin, N. (1993). Primary caregiving fathers in intact families. In A. Gottfried & A. Gottfried (Eds.), *Redefining families* (pp. 11–54). New York: Plenum Press.

Radke-Yarrow, M., Cummings, E. M., Kuczynski, L., & Chipman, M. (1985). Patterns of attachment in two- and three-year-olds in normal families and families with parental depression. *Child Development, 56*, 591–615.

Raina, G., Malhi, P., Malhotra, D., & Jerath, J. M. (2003). Does preference for sons have a differential impact on the intelligence of boys and girls? Evidence from India. *Psychologia: An International Journal of Psychology in the Orient, 46*, 182–189.

Raja, S. N., McGee, R., & Stanton, W. R. (1992). Perceived attachment to parents and peers and psychological well-being in adolescence. *Journal of Youth and Adolescence, 21*, 471–486.

Rakison, D. H., & Poulin-Dubois, D. (2001). Developmental origin of the animate-inanimate distinction. *Psychological Bulletin, 127*, 209–228.

Rakoczy, J., Tomasello, M., & Striano, T. (2004). Young children know that trying is not pretending: A test of the "behaving as if" construal of children's early concept of pretense. *Developmental Psychology, 40*, 388–399.

Raley, R. K. (1996). A shortage of marriageable men? A note on the role of cohabitation in Black–White differences in marriage rates. *American Sociological Review, 61*, 973–983.

Ramey, C. T., Campbell, F. A., & Ramey, S. L. (1999). Early intervention: Successful pathways to improving intellectual development. *Developmental Neuropsychology, 16*, 385–392.

Ramsey, J. L., Langlois, J. H., Hoss, R. A., Rubenstein, A. J., & Griffin, A. M. (2004). Origins of a stereotype: Categorization of facial attractiveness by 6-month-old infants. *Developmental Science, 7*, 201–211.

Rank, M. R. (2000). Poverty and economic hardship in families. In D. H. Demo & K. R. Allen (Eds.), *Handbook of family diversity* (pp. 293–315). New York: Oxford University Press.

Ranzijn, R., Keeves, J., Luszcz, M., & Feather, N. T. (1998). The role of self-perceived usefulness and competence in the self-esteem of elderly adults: Confirmatory factor analyses of the Bachman revision of Rosenberg's self-esteem scale. *Journal of Gerontology, 53*, P96–P104.

Rapkin, B. D., & Fischer, K. (1992a). Framing the construct of life satisfaction in terms of older adults' personal goals. *Psychology and Aging, 7*, 138–149.

Rapkin, B. D., & Fischer, K. (1992b). Personal goals of older adults: Issues in assessment and prediction. *Psychology and Aging, 7*, 127–137.

Raschick, M., & Ingersoll-Dayton, B. (2004). The costs and rewards of caregiving among aging spouses and adult children. *Family Relations, 53*, 317–325.

Raskas, D. F., & Hambrick, D. C. (1992). Multifunctional managerial development: A framework for evaluating the options. *Organizational Dynamics, 21*, 5–17.

Raver, C. C. (1996). Relations between social contingency in mother–child interaction and 2-year-olds' social competence. *Developmental Psychology, 32*, 850–859.

Ray, W. J. (1993). *Methods toward a science of behavior and experience*. Pacific Grove, CA: Brooks/Cole.

Receputo, G., Mazzoleni, G., DiFazio, I., & Alessandria, I. (1996). Study on the sense of taste in a group of Sicilian centenarians. *Archives of Gerontology and Geriatrics, Suppl. 5*, 411–414.

Receputo, G., Mazzoleni, G., Rapisarda, R., & Di Fazio, I. (1996). Sense of smell in centenarians from eastern Sicily. *Archives of Gerontology and Geriatrics, Suppl. 5*, 407–410.

Reddy, V. (2000). Coyness in infancy. *Developmental Science, 3*, 186–192.

Reese, E., & Cox, A. (1999). Quality of adult book reading affects children's emergent literacy. *Developmental Psychology, 35*, 20–28.

Reicher, S., Levine, R. M., & Gordijn, E. (1998). More on deindividuation, power relations between groups, and the expression of social identity: Three studies on the effects of visibility to the in-group. *British Journal of Social Psychology, 37*, 15–40.

Reimer, K. (2003). Committed to caring: Transformation in adolescent moral identity. *Applied Developmental Science, 7*, 129–137.

Reischl, T. M., & Hirsch, B. J. (1989). Identity commitments and coping with a difficult developmental transition. *Journal of Youth and Adolescence, 18*, 55–70.

Remafedi, G. (1987). Adolescent sexuality: Psychosocial and medical implications. *Pediatrics, 79*, 326–330.

Remennick, L. (2000). Childless in the land of imperative motherhood: Stigma and coping among infertile Israeli women. *Sex Roles, 43*, 821–841.

Renshaw, P. D., & Brown, P. J. (1993). Loneliness in middle childhood: Concurrent and longitudinal predictors. *Child Development, 64*, 1271–1284.

Rest, J. R. (1983). Morality. In P. H. Mussen (Gen. Ed.), J. H. Flavell, & E. M. Markman (Vol. Eds.), *Handbook of child psychology: Vol. 3. Cognitive development*. New York: Wiley.

Reynolds, J. R. (1997). The effects of industrial employment conditions on job-related distress. *Journal of Health and Social Behavior, 38*, 105–116.

Rice, M. L. (1989). Children's language acquisition. *American Psychologist, 44*, 149–156.

Rice, P. L. (2000). Baby, souls, name, and health: Traditional customs for a newborn infant among the Hmong in Melbourne. *Early Human Development, 57*, 189–203.

Richards, F., & Commons, M. L. (1990). Postformal cognitive-developmental theory and research: A review of its current status. In C. N. Alexander & E. J. Langer (Eds.), *Higher stages of human development: Perspectives on adult growth* (pp. 229–257). New York: Oxford University Press.

Richards, M. H., & Larson, R. (1993). Pubertal development and the daily subjective states of young adolescents. *Journal of Research on Adolescence, 3*, 145–169.

Richman, J. (2001). Humor and creative life styles. *American Journal of Psychotherapy, 55*, 420–428.

Ricks, M. H. (1985). The social transmission of parental behavior: Attachment across generations. In I. Bretherton & E. Waters (Eds.), *Growing points of attachment: Theory and research* (pp. 211–227). *Monographs of the Society for Research in Child Development, 50* (1–2, Serial No. 209).

Rideout, V. J., Vandewater, E. A., & Wartella, E. A. (2003). *Zero to six: Electronic media in the lives of infants, toddlers and preschoolers. A Kaiser Family Foundation Report*. Retrieved September 19, 2004, from http://www.kff.org/entmedia/loader.cfm?url=/commonspot/security/getfile.cfm&PageID=22754

Ridgeway, C. L., & Correll, S. J. (2004). Motherhood as a status characteristic. *Journal of Social Issues, 60*, 683–700.

Riebe, D., Burbank, P., & Garber, C. E. (2002). Setting the stage for active older adults. In P. M. Burbank & D. Riebe (Eds.), *Promoting exercise and behavior change in older adults: Interventions with the transtheoretical model* (pp. 1–28). New York: Springer Verlag.

Riegel, K. F. (1973). Dialectic operations: The final period of cognitive development. *Human Development, 16*, 346–370.

Riegel, K. F., & Riegel, R. M. (1972). Development, drop, and death. *Developmental Psychology, 6*, 306–319.

Rigsby, L. C., & McDill, E. L. (1975). Value orientations of high school students. In H. R. Stub (Ed.), *The sociology of education: A source book*. Florence, KY: Dorsey Press.

Rindfuss, R. R., & VandenHeuvel, A. (1990). Cohabitation: Precursor to marriage or alternative to being single? *Population and Development Review, 16*, 703–726.

Ringdal, G. I., Jordhoy, M. S., Ringdal, K., & Kaasa, S. (2001). The first year of grief and bereavement in close family members to individuals who have died of cancer. *Palliative Medicine, 15*, 91–105.

Rispoli, M. (2003). Changes in the nature of sentence production during the period of grammatical development. *Journal of Speech, Language, & Hearing Research, 46*, 818–830.

Ritchie, S., & Howes, C. (2003). Program practices, caregiver stability, and child–caregiver relationships. *Journal of Applied Developmental Psychology, 24*, 497–516.

Ritter, C., Hobfoll, S. E., Lavin, J., Cameron, R. P., & Hulsizer, M. R. (2000). Stress, psychosocial resources, and depressive symptomatology during pregnancy in low-income, inner-city women. *Health Psychology, 19*, 576–585.

Robbins, R. N., & Bryan, A. (2004). Relationships between future orientation, impulsive sensation seeking, and risk behavior among adjudicated adolescents. *Journal of Adolescent Research, 19*, 428–445.

Roberts, J. E., Burchinal, M., & Durham, M. (1999). Parents' reports of vocabulary and grammatical development of African American preschoolers: Child and environmental associations. *Child Development, 70*, 92–106.

Roberts, J. S., & Rosenwald, G. C. (2001). Ever upward and not turning back: Social mobility and identity formation among first-generation college students. In D. P. McAdams, R. Josselson, & A. Lieblich (Eds.), *Turns in the road: Narrative studies of lives in transition* (pp. 91–119). Washington, DC: American Psychological Association.

Roberts, L. J., & Krokoff, L. J. (1990). Withdrawal, hostility, and displeasure in marriage. *Journal of Marriage and the Family, 52*, 95–105.

Roberts, R. E., Phinney, J. S., Masse, L. C., Chen, Y. R., Roberts, C. R., & Romero, A. (1999). The structure of ethnic identity of young adolescents from diverse ethnocultural groups. *Journal of Early Adolescence, 19*, 301–322.

Roberts, R. E., & Sobhan, M. (1992). Symptoms of depression in adolescents: A comparison of Anglo, African, and Hispanic Americans. *Journal of Youth and Adolescence, 21*, 639–652.

Robertson, J., & Robertson, J. (1989). *Separation and the very young*. New York: Free Association Books.

Robertson, J. F., & Simons, R. L. (1989). Family factors, self-esteem, and adolescent depression. *Journal of Marriage and the Family, 51*, 125–138.

Robin, D. J., Berthier, N. E., & Clifton, R. K. (1996). Infants' predictive reaching for moving objects in the dark. *Developmental Psychology, 32*, 824–835.

Robinson, B. E. (1988). Teenage pregnancy from the father's perspective. *American Journal of Orthopsychiatry, 58*, 46–51.

Robinson, J. L., & Acevedo, M. C. (2001). Infant reactivity and reliance on mother during emotion challenges: Prediction of cognition and language skills in a low-income sample. *Child Development, 72*, 402–415.

Robinson, J. L., & Emde, R. N. (2004). Mental health moderators of Early Head Start on parenting and child development: Maternal depression and relationship attitudes. *Parenting: Science and Practice, 4*, 73–97.

Rochat, P. (1989). Object manipulation and exploration in 2- to 5-month-old infants. *Developmental Psychology, 25*, 871–884.

Rochat, P., Querido, J. G., & Striano, T. (1999). Emerging sensitivity to the timing and structure of protoconversation in early infancy. *Developmental Psychology, 35*, 950–957.

Rodriguez-Fornells, A., Rotte, M., Heinze, H.-J., Nosselt, T., & Munte, T. F. (2002). Brain potential and functional MRI evidence for how to handle two languages with one brain. *Nature, 415*, 1026–1029.

Rogers, C. R. (1972). *Becoming partners: Marriage and its alternatives.* New York: Delacorte Press.

Rogers, C. R. A. (1959). A theory of therapy, personality, and interpersonal relationships as developed in the client-centered framework. In S. Koch (Ed.), *Psychology: A study of a science* (Vol. 3, pp. 184–156). New York: McGraw-Hill.

Rogers, C. R. A. (1961). *On becoming a person.* Boston: Houghton Mifflin.

Rogers, S. J. (2004). Dollars, dependency, and divorce: Four perspectives on the role of wives' income. *Journal of Marriage and the Family, 66*, 59–74.

Rogoff, B., & Angelillo, C. (2002). Investigating the coordinated functioning of multifaceted cultural practices in human development. *Human Development, 45*, 211–216.

Rogoff, B., Mistry, J., Goncu, A., & Mosier, C. (1993). Guided participation in cultural activity by toddlers and caregivers. *Monograph of the Society for Research in Child Development, 58* (8 Serial No. 236).

Rogoff, B., & Morelli, G. (1989). Perspectives on children's development from cultural psychology. *American Psychologist, 44*, 343–348.

Rogoff, B., Paradise, R., Arauz, R. M., Correa-Chavez, M., & Angelillo, C. (2003). Firsthand learning through intent participation. *Annual Review of Psychology, 54*, 175–203.

Rohner, R. P. (1984). Toward a conception of culture for cross-cultural psychology. *Journal of Cross-Cultural Psychology, 15*, 111–138.

Rokach, A., Bacanli, H., & Ramberan, G., (2000). Coping with loneliness: A cross-cultural comparison. *European Psychologist, 5*, 302–311.

Rokach, A., & Neto, F. (2001). The experience of loneliness in adolescence: A cross-cultural comparison. *International Journal of Adolescence and Youth, 9*, 159–173.

Roosa, M. W. (1984). Maternal age, social class, and the obstetric performance of teenagers. *Journal of Youth and Adolescence, 13*, 365–374.

Rosch, E. (1978). Principles of categorization. In E. Rosch & B. Lloyd (Eds.), *Cognition and categorization* (pp. 27–48). Hillsdale, NJ: Erlbaum.

Roscigno, V., & Ainsworth-Darnell, J. (1999). Race, cultural capital and educational resources: Persistent inequalities and achievement returns. *Sociology of Education, 72*, 158–178.

Rose, S. (2001). Moving on from old dichotomies: Beyond nature–nurture towards a lifeline perspective. *British Journal of Psychiatry, 178*, s3–s7.

Rose, S. A., Feldman, J. F., & Wallace, I. F. (1992). Infant information processing in relation to six-year cognitive outcomes. *Child Development, 63*, 1126–1141.

Rose, S. A., & Ruff, H. A. (1987). Cross-modal abilities in human infants. In J. D. Osofsky (Ed.), *Handbook of infant development* (2nd ed., pp. 318–362). New York: Wiley.

Rosellini, L. (1992, July 6). Sexual desire. *U.S. News and World Report, 113*(1), 60–66.

Rosen, A. B., & Rozin, P. (1993). Now you see it, now you don't: The preschool child's conception of invisible particles in the context of dissolving. *Developmental Psychology, 29*, 300–311.

Rosen, C. S., Schwebel, D. C., & Singer, J. L. (1997). Preschoolers' attributions of mental states in pretense. *Child Development, 68*, 1133–1142.

Rosen, K. S., & Rothbaum, F. (1993). Quality of parental caregiving and security of attachment. *Developmental Psychology, 29*, 358–367.

Rosen, W. D., Adamson, L. B., & Bakeman, R. (1992). An experimental investigation of infant social referencing: Mothers' messages and gender differences. *Developmental Psychology, 28*, 1172–1178.

Rosenberg, M. (1979). *Conceiving the self.* New York: Basic Books.

Rosenberg, M., & McCullough, B. C. (1981). Mattering: Inferred significance and mental health among adolescents. *Research in Community and Mental Health, 2*, 163–182.

Rosenblatt, R. A., Mattis, R., & Hart, L. G. (1995). Abortions in rural Idaho: Physicians' attitudes and practices. *American Journal of Public Health, 85*, 1423–1425.

Rosenfeld, A. H. (1978). *New views on older lives.* Rockville, MD: National Institute of Mental Health.

Rosenfeld, S. (1992). The costs of sharing: Wives' employment and husbands' mental health. *Journal of Health and Social Behavior, 33*, 213–225.

Rosenfield, A., & Figdor, E. (2001). Where is the M in MTCT? The broader issues in mother-to-child transmission of HIV. *American Journal of Public Health, 91*, 703–704.

Rosenkoetter, L. I. (1999). The television situation comedy and children's prosocial behavior. *Journal of Applied Social Psychology, 29*, 979–993.

Rosenkoetter, M. M., & Garris, J. M. (2001). Retirement planning, use of time, and psychosocial adjustment. *Issues in Mental Health Nursing, 22*, 703–722.

Rosenthal, R. (1994). Interpersonal expectancy effects: A 30-year perspective. *Current Directions in Psychological Science, 3*, 176–179.

Rosenthal, R. (1995). Critiquing *Pygmalion:* A 25-year perspective. *Current Directions in Psychological Science, 4*, 171–172.

Rosenthal, R., & Jacobson, L. (1968). *Pygmalion in the classroom: Teacher expectations and student intellectual development.* New York: Holt, Rinehart & Winston.

Rosnick, C. B., Small, B. J., Graves, A. B., & Mortimer, J. A. (2004). The association between health and cognitive performance in a population-based study of older adults: The Charlotte county healthy aging study (CCHAS). *Aging, Neuropsychology, & Cognition, 11*, 89–99.

Ross, G., Kagan, J., Zelazo, P., & Kotelchuck, M. (1975). Separation protest in infants in home and laboratory. *Developmental Psychology, 11*, 256–257.

Ross, M. (1989). Relation of implicit theories to the construction of personal histories. *Psychological Review, 96*, 341–357.

Rostosky, S. S., & Travis, C. B. (1996). Menopause research and the dominance of the biomedical model 1984–1994. *Psychology of Women Quarterly, 20*, 285–312.

Rotenberg, K. J., McDougall, P., Boulton, M. J., Vaillancourt, T., Fox, C., & Hymel, S. (2004). Cross-sectional and longitudinal relations among peer-reported trustworthiness, social relationships, and psychological adjustment in children and early adolescents from the United Kingdom and Canada. *Journal of Experimental Child Psychology, 88*, 46–67.

Roth, D. L., Haley, W. E., Owen, J. E., Clay, O. J., & Goode, K. T. (2001). Latent growth models of the longitudinal effects of dementia caregiving: A comparison of African American and White family caregivers. *Psychology and Aging, 16*, 427–436.

Roth, W. E. (1953). Precautions during pregnancy in New Guinea. In M. Mead & N. Calas (Eds.), *Primitive heritage.* New York: Random House.

Rothbart, M. K. (1991). Temperament: A developmental framework. In J. Strelau & A. Angleitner (Eds.), *Explorations in temperament: International perspectives on theory and measurement* (pp. 235–260). London: Plenum Press.

Rothbart, M. K., Ahadi, S. A., & Evans, D. E. (2000). Temperament and personality: Origins and outcomes. *Journal of Personality and Social Psychology, 78*, 122–135.

Rothbart, M. K., & Derryberry, D. (1981). Development of individual differences in temperament. In M. E. Lamb & A. L. Brown (Eds.), *Advances in developmental psychology* (Vol. 1, pp. 37–86). Hillsdale, NJ: Erlbaum.

Rotheram-Borus, M. J., & Wyche, K. F. (1994). Ethnic differences in identity development in the United States. In S. L. Archer (Ed.), *Interventions for adolescent identity development* (pp. 62–83). Thousand Oaks, CA: Sage.

Rovee-Collier, C. (1987). Learning and memory in infancy. In J. D. Osofsky (Ed.), *Handbook of infant development* (2nd ed., pp. 98–148). New York: Wiley.

Rovee-Collier, C., Schechter, A., Shyi, G. C. W., & Shields, P. (1992). Perceptual identification of contextual attributes and infant memory retrieval. *Developmental Psychology, 28*, 307–318.

Rovet, J., Cole, S., Nulman, I., Scolnik, D., Altmann, D., & Koren, G. (1995). Effects of maternal epilepsy on children's neurodevelopment. *Child Neuropsychology, 1*, 150–157.

Rowe, J. W., & Kahn, R. L. (1997). Successful aging. *The Gerontologist, 37*, 433–440.

Rowe, J. W., & Kahn, R. L. (1998). *Successful aging.* New York: Pantheon Books.

Rowles, G. D., & Ravdal, H. (2002). Aging, place, and meaning in the face of changing circumstances. In R. S. Weiss & S. P. Bass (Eds.), *Challenges of the third age: Meaning and purpose in later life* (pp. 81–114). New York: Oxford University Press.

Rubenstein, R. L. (2002). The third age. In R. S. Weiss & S. A. Bass (Eds.), *Challenges of the third age: Meaning and purpose in later life* (pp. 29–40). London: Oxford University Press.

Rubin, K. H. (1980). Fantasy play: Its role in the development of social skills and social cognition. *New Directions in Child Development, 9*, 69–84.

Rubin, K. H., Hastings, P., Stewart, S. L., Henderson, H. A., & Chen, X. (1997). The consistency and concomitants of inhibition: Some of the children all of the time. *Child Development, 68*, 467–483.

Rubin, K. H., LeMare, L. J., & Lollis, S. (1990). Social withdrawal in children: Developmental pathways to peer rejection. In S. R. Asher & J. D. Coie (Eds.), *Peer rejection in childhood* (pp. 217–252). Cambridge, UK: Cambridge University Press.

Ruff, H. A., Saltarelli, L. M., Capozzoli, M., & Dubiner, K. (1992). The differentiation of activity in infants' exploration of objects. *Developmental Psychology, 28*, 851–861.

Rumelhart, D. E., & McClelland, J. L. (1986). *Parallel distributed processing* (Vol. 1). Cambridge, MA: MIT Press.

Rusbult, C. E., & Arriaga, X. B. (1997). Interdependence theory. In S. Duck (Ed.), *Handbook of personal relationships: Theory, research and interventions* (2nd ed., pp. 221–250). Chichester, UK: Wiley.

Russell, D. W., & Cutrona, C. E. (1991). Social support, stress, and depressive symptoms among the elderly: Test of a process model. *Psychology and Aging, 6*, 190–201.

Russell, S. T., & Joyner, K. (2001). Adolescent sexual orientation and suicide risk: Evidence from a national study. *American Journal of Public Health, 91*, 1276–1281.

Rusting, R. L. (1992). Why do we age? *Scientific American, 267*, 130.

Rutkowska, J. C. (1994). Scaling up sensorimotor systems: Constraints from human infancy. *Adaptive Behavior, 2*, 349–373.

Rutter, M. (1983). School effects on pupil progress: Research findings and policy implications. *Child Development, 54*, 1–29.

Rutter, M. (1990). Commentary: Some focus and process considerations regarding effects of parental depression on children. *Developmental Psychology, 26*, 60–67.

Rutter, M. (1995). Maternal deprivation. In M. H. Bornstein (Ed.), *Handbook of parenting: Vol. 4. Applied and practical parenting* (pp. 3–31). Hillsdale, NJ: Erlbaum.

Ryan, M. K., David, B., & Reynolds, K. J. (2004). Who cares? The effect of gender and context on the self and moral reasoning. *Psychology of Women Quarterly, 28*, 246–255.

Ryan, R. M., & Lynch, J. H. (1989). Emotional autonomy versus detachment: Revisiting the vicissitudes of adolescence and young adulthood. *Child Development, 60*, 340–356.

Ryff, C. D. (1995). Psychological well-being in adult life. *Current Directions in Psychological Science, 4*, 99–104.

Ryff, C. D., & Essex, M. J. (1992). The interpretation of life experiences and well-being: The sample case of relocation. *Psychology and Aging, 7*, 507–517.

Ryff, C. D., & Heincke, S. G. (1983). Subjective organization of personality in adulthood and aging. *Journal of Personality and Social Psychology, 44*, 807–816.

Ryff, C. D., Keyes, C. L., & Hughes, D. L. (2003). Status inequalities, perceived discrimination, and eudaimonic well-being: Do the challenges of minority life hone purpose and growth? *Journal of Health and Social Behavior, 44*, 275–291.

Sabatelli, R. M., Meth, R. L., & Gavazzi, S. M. (1988). Factors mediating the adjustment to involuntary childlessness. *Family Relations, 37*, 338–343.

Sabbagh, M. A., & Baldwin, D. A. (2001). Learning words from knowledgeable versus ignorant speakers: Links between preschoolers' theory of mind and semantic development. *Child Development, 72*, 1054–1070.

Sachs, S. (2001, October 7). The two worlds of Muslim American teenagers. *New York Times*, p. B1.

Saczynski, J. S., Willis, S. L., & Schaie, K. W. (2002). Strategy use in reasoning training with older adults. *Aging, Neuropsychology, & Cognition, 9*, 48–60.

Saffran, J., Aslin, R., & Newport, E. (1996). Statistical learning by 8-month-old infants. *Science, 274*, 1926–1928.

Sagi, A., & Hoffman, M. L. (1976). Empathic distress in the newborn. *Developmental Psychology, 12*, 175–176.

Sagi, A., Koren-Karie, N., Gini, M., Ziv, Y., & Joels, T. (2002). Shedding further light on the effects of various types and quality of early child care on infant–mother attachment relationships: The Haifa study of early child care. *Child Development, 73*, 1166–1186.

Sagi, A., Lamb, M. E., Lewkowicz, K. S., Shoham, R., Dvir, R., & Estes, D. (1985). Security of infant–mother, –father, and –metapelet attachments among kibbutz-reared Israeli children. In I. Bretherton &

E. Everett (Eds.), *Growing points of attachment theory and research* (pp. 257–275). *Monographs of the Society for Research in Child Development, 50* (1–2, Serial No. 209).

Sagi, A., & van IJzendoorn, M. H. (1996). Multiple caregiving environments: The kibbutz experience. In S. Harel & J. P. Shonkoff (Eds.), *Early childhood intervention and family support programs: Accomplishments and challenges* (pp. 143–162). Jerusalem: JDC-Brookdale Institute.

Sagrestano, L. M., Felman, P., Killingsworth Rini, C., Woo, G., & Dunkel-Schetter, C. (1999). Ethnicity and social support during pregnancy. *American Journal of Community Psychology, 27*, 869–898.

Sales, B. C., & Folkman, S. (Eds.). (2000). *Ethics in research with human participants.* Washington, DC: American Psychological Association.

Salisch, M. von (2001). Children's emotional development: Challenges in their relationships to parents, peers, and friends. *International Journal of Behavioral Development, 25*, 310–319.

Salthouse, T. A. (1985). Speed of behavior and its implications for cognition. In J. W. Birren & K. W. Shaie (Eds.), *Handbook of the psychology of aging* (pp. 400–426). New York: Van Nostrand Reinhold.

Salthouse, T. A. (1996). The processing-speed theory of adult age differences in cognition. *Psychological Review, 103*, 403–428.

Saltz, R., & Saltz, E. (1986). Pretend play training and its outcomes. In G. Fein & M. Rivkin (Eds.), *The young child at play: Reviews of research* (Vol. 4, pp. 155–173). Washington, DC: National Association for the Education of Young Children.

Salvatore, N., & Sastre, M. T. M. (2001). Appraisal of life: "Area" versus "dimension" conceptualizations. *Social Indicators Research, 53*, 229–240.

Salzinger, S., Feldman, R. S., Hammer, M., & Rosario, M. (1993). The effects of physical abuse on children's social relationships. *Child Development, 64*, 168–187.

Sameroff, A. J. (1982). Development and the dialectic: The need for a systems approach. In W. A. Collins (Ed.), *The concept of development: The Minnesota Symposia on Child Psychology* (Vol. 15). Hillsdale, NJ: Erlbaum.

Sameroff, A. J. (1987). Psychologic needs of the parent in infant development. In G. B. Avery (Ed.), *Neonatology: Pathophysiology and management of the newborn* (pp. 358–378). Philadelphia: Lippincott.

Sampson, R. J., Raudenbush, S. W., & Earls, F. (1997). Neighborhoods and violent crime: A multilevel study of collective efficacy. *Science, 227*, 918–923.

Sanders, R. E. (1997). Find your partner and do-si-do: The formation of personal relationship between social beings. *Journal of Social and Personal Relationships, 14*, 387–415.

Sandler, J., Holder, A., & Meers, P. M. (1963). The ego ideal and the ideal self. *Psychoanalytic Study of the Child, 18*, 139–158.

Sansavini, A., Bertoncini, J., & Giovanelli, G. (1997). Newborns discriminate the rhythm of multisyllabic stressed words. *Developmental Psychology, 33,* 3–11.

Sanson, A. V., Oberklaid, F., Pedlow, R., & Prior, M. (1991). Risk indicators: Assessment of infancy predictors of preschool behavioural maladjustment. *Journal of Child Psychology and Psychiatry, 32,* 609–626.

Santelli, J. S., Abma, J., Ventura, S., Lindberg, L., Morrow, B., Anderson, J., et al. (2004). Can changes in sexual behaviors among high school students explain the decline in teen pregnancy rates in the 1990s? *Journal of Adolescent Health, 34,* 80–90.

Santillanes, G. F. (1997). Releasing the spirit: A lesson in Native American funeral rituals. *The Director, 69,* 32–34.

Sapp, D. D. (1992). The point of creative frustration and the creative process: A new look at an old model. *Journal of Creative Behavior, 26,* 21–28.

Saracho, O. N., & Shirakawa, Y. (2004). A comparison of the literacy development context of United States and Japanese families. *Early Childhood Education Journal, 31,* 261–266.

Sarkisian, N., & Gerstel, N. (2004). Explaining the gender gap in help to parents: The importance of employment. *Journal of Marriage and the Family, 66,* 431–451.

Savaya, R., & Cohen, O. (2003). Perceptions of the societal image of Muslim Arab divorced men and women in Israel. *Journal of Social and Personal Relationships, 20,* 193–202.

Savin-Williams, R. (1996). Self-labeling and disclosure among gay, lesbian, and bisexual youths. In J. Laird & R-J Green (Eds.), *Lesbians and gays in couples and families: A Handbook for therapists* (pp. 153–182). San Francisco: Jossey-Bass.

Savin-Williams, R. C. & Diamond, L. M. (2004). Sex. In R. M. Lerner & L. Steinberg (Eds.), *Handbook of adolescent psychology* (2nd ed., pp. 189–231). New York: Wiley.

Savitz-Smith, J. (2003). Couples undergoing infertility treatment: Implications for counselors. *Family Journal—Counseling & Therapy for Couples and Families, 11,* 383–387.

Scarbrough, J. W. (2001). Welfare mothers' reflections on personal responsibility. *Journal of Social Issues, 57,* 261–276.

Scarr, S. (1992). Developmental theories for the 1990s: Development and individual differences. *Child Development, 63,* 1–19.

Schaffer, H. R., & Emerson, P. E. (1964). *The development of social attachments in infancy. Monographs of the Society for Research in Child Development, 29* (Whole No. 94).

Schaie, K. E., & Hertzog, C. (1983). Fourteen-year cohort-sequential analyses of adult intellectual development. *Developmental Psychology, 19,* 531–543.

Schaie, K. W. (1965). A general model for the study of developmental problems. *Psychological Bulletin, 64,* 92–107.

Schaie, K. W. (1992). The impact of methodological changes in gerontology. *International Journal of Aging and Human Development, 35,* 19–29.

Schaie, K. W. (1994). The course of adult intellectual development. *American Psychologist, 49,* 304–313.

Schaie, K. W., & Zuo, Y. (2001). Family environments and adult cognitive functioning. In R. Sternberg & E. L. Grigorenko (Eds.), *Environmental effects on cognitive abilities* (pp. 337–361). Mahwah, NJ: Erlbaum.

Schatz, M. (1983). Communication. In J. H. Flavell & E. M. Markman (Eds.), *Handbook of child psychology* (Vol. 3, pp. 841–889). New York: Wiley.

Scheff, T. J. (2003). Shame in self and society. *Symbolic Interaction, 26,* 239–262.

Schickedanz, J. A. (1986). *More than the ABCs: The early stages of reading and writing.* Washington, DC: National Association for the Education of Young People.

Schiedel, D. G., & Marcia, J. E. (1985). Ego identity, intimacy, sex-role orientation, and gender. *Developmental Psychology, 21,* 149–160.

Schieffelin, B. B., & Cochran-Smith, M. (1984). Learning to read culturally: Literacy before schooling. In H. Goelman, A. A. Oberg, & F. Smith (Eds.), *Awakening to literacy* (pp. 3–23). Exeter, NH: Heinemann.

Schlein, S. (1987). *A way of looking at things: Selected papers from 1930 to 1980. Erik H. Erikson.* New York: Norton.

Schmitt-Rodermund, E., & Silbereisen, R. K. (1998). Career maturity determinants: Individual development, social context, and historical time. *Career Development Quarterly, 47,* 16–31.

Schmitz-Scherzer, R. (1995). Reflections on cultural influences on aging and old-age suicide in Germany. *International Psychogeriatrics, 7,* 231–238.

Schnarch, D. (2000). Desire problems: A systematic perspective. In S. Leiblum & R. Rosen (Eds.), *Principles and practice of sex therapy* (pp. 17–56). New York: Guilford Press.

Schneider, B. H., Atkinson, L., & Tardif, C. (2001). Child–parent attachment and children's peer relations: A quantitative review. *Developmental Psychology, 37,* 86–100.

Schneider, D. S., Sledge, P. A., Shuchter, S. R., & Zisook, S. (1996). Dating and remarriage over the first two years of widowhood. *Annals of Clinical Psychiatry, 8,* 51–57.

Schneider, W., & Bjorklund, D. F. (1992). Expertise, aptitude, and strategic remembering. *Child Development, 63,* 461–473.

Schoen, R. (1992). First unions and the stability of first marriages. *Journal of Marriage and the Family, 54,* 281–284.

Schoen, R., & Wooldredge, J. (1989). Marriage choices in North Carolina and Virginia, 1969–71 and 1979–81. *Journal of Marriage and the Family, 51,* 465–482.

Scholnick, E. K. (1995, Fall). Direction I: Knowing and constructing plans. *SRCD Newsletter,* 1–2.

Schooler, C., & Mulatu, M. S. (2001). The reciprocal effects of leisure time activities and intellectual functioning in older people: A longitudinal analysis. *Psychology and Aging, 16,* 466–482.

Schootman, M., Fuortes, L. J., Zwerling, C., Albanese, M. A., & Watson, C. A. (1993). Safety behavior among Iowa junior high and high school students. *American Journal of Public Health, 83,* 1628–1629.

Schrof, J. M. (1994). A lens on maternity. *U.S. News and World Report, 116,* 66–69.

Schulenberg, J., & Maggs, J. L. (2001). Moving targets: Modeling developmental trajectories of adolescent alcohol misuse, individual and peer risk factors, and intervention effects. *Applied Developmental Science, 5,* 237–253.

Schulenberg, J., Vondracek, F. W., & Kim, J. (1993). Career certainty and short-term changes in work values during adolescence. *Career Development Quarterly, 41,* 268–284.

Schultheiss, D. P., & Blustein, D. L. (1994). Contributions of family relationship factors to the identity formation process. *Journal of Counseling and Development, 73,* 159–166.

Schultz, A. (2001, March). 25 women making it big. *Fortune Small Business,* pp. 17–24

Schultz, K. S., Morton, K. R., & Weckerle, J. R. (1998). The influence of push and pull factors on voluntary and involuntary early retirees' retirement decision and adjustment. *Journal of Vocational Behavior, 53,* 45–57.

Schultz, R. I., Grelotti, D. J., & Pober, B. (2001). Genetics of childhood disorders: Vol. 26. Williams syndrome and brain–behavior relationships. *Journal of the American Academy of Child and Adolescent Psychiatry, 40,* 606–609.

Schulz, R., & Willamson, G. M. (1993). Psychosocial and behavioral dimensions of physical frailty. *Journal of Gerontology, 48,* 39–43.

Schuster, C. S. (1986). Intrauterine development. In C. S. Schuster & S. S. Ashburn (Eds.), *The process of human development* (pp. 67–94). Boston: Little, Brown.

Schuster, M. A., Bell, R. M., & Kanouse, D. E. (1996). The sexual practices of adolescent virgins: Genital sexual activities of high school students who have never had vaginal intercourse. *American Journal of Public Health, 86,* 1570–1576.

Schwandt, T. A. (1998). Three epistemological stances for qualitative inquiry: Interpretivism, hermeneutics, and social constructionism. In N. K. Denzin & Y. S. Lincoln (Eds.), *The landscape of qualitative research: Theories and issues* (pp. 221–259). Thousand Oaks, CA: Sage.

Schwartz, A. N., Snyder, C. L., & Peterson, J. A. (1984). *Aging and life: An introduction to gerontology* (2nd ed.). New York: Holt, Rinehart & Winston.

Schwartz, S. J. (2001). The evolution of Eriksonian and neo-Eriksonian identity theory and research: A review and integration. *Identity, 1,* 7–58.

Schweinhart, L. J., & Weikart, D. P. (1988). The High/Scope Perry Preschool Program. In R. H. Price, E. L. Cowen, R. P. Lorion, & J. Ramos-McKay (Eds.), *Fourteen ounces* of prevention (pp. 53–66). Washington, DC: American Psychological Association.

Scogin, F., Storandt, M., & Lott, L. (1985). Memory-skills training, memory complaints, and depression in older adults. *Journal of Gerontology, 40,* 562–568.

Scopesi, A., Zanobini, M., & Carossino, P. (1997). Childbirth in different cultures: Psychophysical reactions of women delivering in U.S., German, French, and Italian hospitals. *Journal of Reproductive and Infant Psychology, 15,* 9–30.

Scott, J. P. (1987). Critical periods in processes of social organization. In M. H. Bornstein (Ed.), *Sensitive periods in development: Interdisciplinary perspectives* (pp. 247–268). Hillsdale, NJ: Erlbaum.

Sears, D. O., Fu, M., Henry. P. J., & Bui, K. (2003). The origins and persistence of ethnic identity among the "new immigrant" groups. *Social Psychology Quarterly, 66,* 419–437.

Sears, P. S., & Barbee, A. H. (1978). Career and life satisfaction among Terman's gifted women. In J. Stanley, W. George, & C. Solano (Eds.), *The gifted and the creative: Fifty year perspective.* Baltimore: Johns Hopkins University Press.

Seccombe, K. (1991). Assessing the costs and benefits of children: Gender comparisons among child-free husbands and wives. *Journal of Marriage and the Family, 53,* 191–202.

Seccombe, K. (2000). Families in poverty in the 1990s: Trends, causes, consequences, and lessons learned. *Journal of Marriage and the Family, 62,* 1094–1113.

Sedikides, C., Gaertner, L., & Toguchi, Y. (2003). Pancultural self-enhancement. *Journal of Personality and Social Psychology, 84,* 60–79.

Seeman, T. E., Berkman, L. F., Blazer, D., & Rowe, J. W. (1994). Social ties and support and neuroendocrine function: The MacArthur studies of successful aging. *Annals of Behavioral Medicine, 16,* 95–106.

Segal, L. B., Oster, H., Cohen, M., Caspi, B., Myers, M., & Brown, D. (1995). Smiling and fussing in seven-month-old preterm and full-term Black infants in the still-face situation. *Child Development, 66,* 1829–1843.

Sehdev, H. M. (2004). *Cesarean delivery.* Retrieved August 9, 2004, from http://www.emedicine.com/med/topic3283.htm

Seligman, M. E. P. (1975). *Helplessness.* San Francisco: Freeman.

Sells, C. W., & Blum, R. W. (1996). Morbidity and mortality among U.S. adolescents: An overview of data and trends. *American Journal of Public Health, 86,* 513–519.

Selman, R. L. (1971). Taking another's perspective: Role-taking development in early childhood. *Child Development, 42,* 1721–1734.

Selman, R. L. (1980). *The growth of interpersonal understanding: Developmental and clinical analysis.* New York: Academic Press.

Selman, R. L. (1994). The relation of role taking to the development of moral judgment in children. In B. Puka (Ed.), *Fundamental research in moral development. Moral devel-*

opment: A compendium, Vol. 2. (pp. 87–99). New York: Garland.

SeniorJournal.com (2004, September 13). *AoA awards $5.1 million to support seniors aging in place.* Retrieved February 22, 2005, from http://www.seniorjournal.com/NEWS/Eldercare/4-09-13AOA.htm

Sera, M. D., Troyer, D., & Smith, L. B. (1988). What do two-year-olds know about the sizes of things? *Child Development, 59,* 1489–1496.

Serbin, L. A., Powlishta, K. K., & Gulko, J. (1993). The development of sex typing in middle childhood. *Monographs of the Society for Research in Child Development, 58* (Whole No. 232).

Seriido, J., Almeida, D. M., & Wetherington, E. (2004). Chronic stressors and daily hassles: Unique and interactive relationship with psychological distress. *Journal of Health and Social Behavior, 45,* 17–33.

Serovich, J. M., & Greene, K. (1997). Predictors of adolescent sexual risk taking behaviors which put them at risk for contracting HIV. *Journal of Youth and Adolescence, 26,* 429–444.

Setterlund, M. B., & Niedenthal, P. M. (1993). "Who am I? Why am I here?": Self-esteem, self-clarity, and prototype matching. *Journal of Personality and Social Psychology, 65,* 769–780.

Sexuality Information and Education Council of the United States. (2001). *Making the connection: Sexuality and reproductive health.* Retrieved November 18, 2001, from http://www.siecus.org/pubs/cnct/cnct0001.html

Shapiro, J. L., Diamond, M. J., & Greenberg, M. (Eds.). (1995). *Becoming a father: Contemporary, social, developmental, and clinical perspectives.* New York: Springer Verlag.

Shapiro, J. P. (2001). Growing old in a good home. *U.S. News and World Report, 130,* 56–61.

Share, D. L., McGee, R., & Silva, P. A. (1989). IQ and reading progress: A test of the capacity notion of IQ. *Journal of the American Academy of Child and Adolescent Psychiatry, 28,* 97–100.

Sharpley, C. F. (1997). Psychometric properties of the Self-Perceived Stress in Retirement Scale. *Psychological Reports, 81,* 319–322.

Sharpley, C. F., & Yardley, P. G. (1999). "What makes me happy now that I'm older": A retrospective report of attitudes and strategies used to adjust to retirement as reported by older persons. *Journal of Applied Health Behavior, 1,* 31–35.

Sharpsteen, D. J., & Kirkpatrick, L. A. (1997). Romantic jealousy and adult romantic attachment. *Journal of Personality and Social Psychology, 72,* 627–640.

Shaver, P. R., Collins, N., & Clark, C. L. (1996). Attachment styles and internal working models of self and relationship partners. In G. J. O. Fletcher & J. Fitness (Eds.), *Knowledge structures in close relationships: A social psychological approach* (pp. 25–61). Hillsdale, NJ: Erlbaum.

Shay, K. A., & Roth, D. L. (1992). Association between aerobic fitness and visuospatial

performance in healthy older adults. *Psychology and Aging, 7,* 15–24.

Sher, T. G., & Weiss, R. L. (1991). Negativity in marital communication? Where's the beef? Special Issue: Negative communication in marital interaction: A misnomer? *Behavioral Assessment, 13,* 1–5.

Sherraden, M. S., & Barrera, R. E. (1996). Maternal support and cultural influences among Mexican immigrant mothers. *Families in Society, 77,* 298–313.

Shibley, P. K. (2000). *The concept of revisitation and the transition to parenthood.* Unpublished doctoral dissertation, Ohio State University.

Shinn, M., & Weitzman, B. (1996). Homeless families are different. In *Homelessness in America.* Washington, DC: National Coalition for the Homeless.

Shostak, A., & McLouth, G. (1985). *Men and abortion.* New York: Praeger.

Shull, R. L., & Grimes, J. A. (2003). Bouts of responding from variable-interval reinforcement of lever pressing by rats. *Journal of Experimental Analysis of Behavior, 80,* 159–171.

Siegel, B. (1996). Is the emperor wearing clothes? Social policy and the empirical support for full inclusion of children with disabilities in the preschool and early elementary grades. *Social Policy Report, 10,* 2–17.

Siegler, I. C., Poon, L. W., Madden, D. J., & Welsh, K. A. (1996). Psychological aspects of normal aging. In E. W. Busse & D. G. Blazer (Eds.), *The American Psychiatric Press textbook of geriatric psychiatry* (pp. 105–127). Washington, DC: American Psychiatric Press.

Siegler, R. S. (2000). Unconscious insights. *Current Directions in Psychological Science, 9,* 79–83.

Siegler, R. S., & Stern, E. (1998). A microgenetic analysis of conscious and unconscious strategy discoveries. *Journal of Experimental Psychology: General, 127,* 377–397.

Sigman, M. (1995). Nutrition and child development: More food for thought. *Current Directions in Psychological Science, 4,* 52–55.

Silver, C. B. (2003). Gendered identities in old age: Toward (de)gendering? *Journal of Aging Studies, 17,* 379–397.

Silver, M. (1995). Sex and violence on TV. *U.S. News and World Report, 119,* 62–68.

Silverman, P. R. (1989). Deconstructing motherhood. *Readings: A Journal of Reviews and Commentary in Mental Health, 4,* 14–18.

Silverstein, A. B., Pearson, L. B., Aguinaldo, N. E., Friedman, S. L., Tokayama, D. L., & Weiss, Z. T. (1982). Identity conservation and equivalence conservation: A question of developmental priority. *Child Development, 53,* 819–821.

Simon, B., & Klandermans, B. (2001). Politicized collective identity. *American Psychologist, 56,* 319–331.

Simon, T. (2002, January 19). Dreaming of the mother who was. *Providence Journal,* p. B7.

Simons, R. L., Beaman, J., Conger, R. D., & Chao, W. (1993). Stress, support and anti-social behavior traits as determinants of emotional well-being and parenting practices among single mothers. *Journal of Marriage and the Family, 55,* 385–398.

Simons, R. L., Lorenz, F. O., Wu, C., & Conger, R. D. (1993). Social network and marital support as mediators and moderators of the impact of stress and depression on parental behaviors. *Developmental Psychology, 29,* 368–381.

Simonton, D. K. (1990). Creativity in the later years: Optimistic prospects for achievement. *The Gerontologist, 30,* 626–631.

Simonton, D. K. (1991). Creative productivity through the adult years. *Generations, 15,* 13–16.

Simonton, D. K. (1997). Creative productivity: A predictive and explanatory model of career trajectories and landmarks. *Psychological Review, 104,* 66–89.

Simons, D. J., Mitroff, S. R., & Franconeri, S. L. (2003). Scene perception: What we can learn from visual integration and change detection. In M.A. Peterson & G. Rhodes (Eds.), *Perception of faces, objects, and scenes: Analytic and holistic processes* (pp. 335–351). London: Oxford University Press.

Sinclair, W., & Pressinger, R. W. (2001). Environmental causes of infertility. *Infertility & Miscarriage Research Summaries.* Retrieved October 31, 2001, from http://www.chem-tox.com/infertility

Singelakis, A. T. (1990). Real estate market trends and the displacement of the aged: Examination of the linkages in Manhattan. *The Gerontologist, 30,* 658–666.

Singer, D. G., & Singer, J. L. (1990). *The house of make-believe: Children's play and developing imagination.* Cambridge, MA: Harvard University Press.

Singer, J. L. (1975). *The inner world of daydreaming.* New York: Colophon Books.

Singer, L. T., Davillier, M., Bruening, P., Hawkins, S., & Yamashita, T. S. (1996). Social support, psychological distress, and parenting strains in mothers of very low birth weight infants. *Family Relations, 45,* 343–350.

Singer, W. (1995). Development and plasticity of cortical processing architectures. *Science, 270,* 758–764.

Singh, L., Morgan, J. L., & Best, C. T. (2002). Infants' listening preferences: Baby talk or happy talk? *Infancy, 3,* 365–394.

Sinnott, J. D., & Cavanaugh, J. C. (1991). *Bridging paradigms: Positive development in adulthood and cognitive aging.* New York: Praeger.

Skaalvik, E. M., & Hagtvet, K. A. (1990). Academic achievement and self-concept: An analysis of causal predominance in a developmental perspective. *Journal of Personality and Social Psychology, 58,* 292–307.

Skaalvik, S., & Skaalvik, E. M. (2004). Frames of reference for self-evaluation of ability in mathematics. *Psychological Reports, 94,* 619–632.

Skerrett, K. (1996). From isolation to mutuality: A feminist collaborative model of

couples therapy. *Women and Therapy, 19,* 93–106.

Skinner, B. F. (1938). *The behavior of organisms.* New York: Appleton-Century-Crofts.

Skinner, B. F. (1983). Intellectual self-management in old age. *American Psychologist, 38,* 239–244.

Skinner, B. F. (1987). Whatever happened to psychology as the science of behavior? *American Psychologist, 42,* 780–786.

Slade, A. (1987). A longitudinal study of maternal involvement and symbolic play during the toddler period. *Child Development, 58,* 367–375.

Slater, A., Carrick, R., Bell, C., & Roberts, E. (1999). Can measures of infant information processing predict later intellectual ability? In A. Slater & D. Muir (Eds.), *The Blackwell reader in developmental psychology* (pp. 55–64). Malden, MA: Blackwell.

Slater, A., & Johnson, S. P. (1998). Visual sensory and perceptual abilities of the newborn: Beyond the blooming, buzzing confusion. In F. Simion & G. Butterworth (Eds.), *The development of sensory, motor and cognitive capacities in early infancy: From perception to cognition* (pp. 121–141). Hove, UK: Psychology Press/Erlbaum.

Slavik, S. (1995). Presenting social interest to different life-styles. Special Issue: Counseling homosexuals and bisexuals. *Individual Psychology: Journal of Adlerian Theory, Research and Practice, 51,* 166–177.

Slavin, R. E. (1987). Grouping for instruction in the elementary school. *Educational Psychologist, 22,* 109–127.

Sliwinski, M. J., Hofer, S.M., Hall, C., Buschke, H., & Lipton, R. B. (2003). Modeling memory decline in older adults: The importance of preclinical dementia, attrition, and chronological age. *Psychology and Aging, 18,* 658–671.

Sliwinski, M., Lipton, R. B., Buschke, H., & Stewart, W. (1996). The effects of preclinical dementia on estimates of normal cognitive functioning in aging. *Journal of Gerontology, 51,* P217–P225.

Slobin, D. I. (1985). *The cross-linguistic study of language acquisition* (Vols. 1, 2). Hillsdale, NJ: Erlbaum.

Sloutsky, V. M., & Fisher, A. V. (2004). Induction and categorization in young children: A similarity-based model. *Journal of Experimental Psychology: General, 133,* 166–188.

Slovak, K., & Singer, M. (2001). Gun violence exposure and trauma among rural youth. *Violence and Victims, 16,* 389–400.

Small, R., Rice, P. L., Yelland, J., & Lumley, J. (1999). Mothers in a new country: The role of culture and communication in Vietnamese, Turkish, and Filipino women's experiences of giving birth in Australia. *Women and Health, 28,* 77–101.

Small, S. A., & Kerns, D. (1993). Unwanted sexual activity among peers during early and middle adolescence: Incidence and risk factors. *Journal of Marriage and the Family, 55,* 941–952.

Small, S. A., & Riley, D. (1990). Assessment of work spillover into family life. *Journal of Marriage and the Family, 52,* 51–62.

Small, S. A., Silverberg, S. B., & Kerns, D. (1993). Adolescents' perceptions of the costs and benefits of engaging in health-compromising behaviors. *Journal of Youth and Adolescence, 22,* 73–88.

Smetana, J. G. (1985). Preschool children's conceptions of transgressions: Effects of varying moral and conventional domain-related attributes. *Developmental Psychology, 21,* 18–29.

Smetana, J. G. (1986). Preschool children's conceptions of sex-role transgressions. *Child Development, 57,* 862–871.

Smetana, J. G., Schlagman, N., & Adams, P. W. (1993). Preschool children's judgments about hypothetical and actual transgressions. *Child Development, 64,* 202–214.

Smetana, J., Yau, J., & Hanson, S. (1991). Conflict resolution in families with adolescents. *Journal of Research on Adolescence, 1,* 189–206.

Smith, A. C., & Smith, D. I. (2001). Emergency and transitional shelter population: 2000. *Census Special Reports,* Series CENSR/01-2. Washington, DC: U.S. Government Printing Office.

Smith, B. A., & Blass, E. M. (1996). Taste-mediated calming in premature, preterm, and full-term human infants. *Developmental Psychology, 32,* 1084–1089.

Smith, D. (2001). Children in the heat of war. *Monitor on Psychology, 32,* 29–31.

Smith, D. C. (1997). *Caregiving: Hospice-proven techniques for healing body and soul.* New York: Macmillan.

Smith, E. M., Ford, J. K., & Kozlowski, S. W. J. (1997). Building adaptive expertise: Implications for training design strategies. In M. S. Quinones & A. Ehrenstein (Eds.), *Training for a rapidly changing workplace: Applications of psychological research* (pp. 89–118). Washington, DC: American Psychological Association.

Smith, J., & Baltes, P. B. (1999). Life-span perspectives on development. In M. H. Bornstein & M. E. Lamb (Eds.), *Developmental psychology: An advanced textbook* (4th ed., pp. 47–72). Mahwah, NJ: Erlbaum.

Smith, L. B., Jones, S. S., & Landau, B. (1992). Count nouns, adjectives, and perceptual properties in children's novel word interpretations. *Developmental Psychology, 28,* 273–286.

Smith, P. K. (Ed.). (1991). *The psychology of grand-parenthood: An international perspective.* London: Routledge.

Smith, P. K., & Drew, L. M. (2002). Grandparenthood. In M. H. Bornstein (Ed.), *Handbook of parenting: Vol. 3, Being and becoming a parent* (pp. 141–147). Mahwah, NJ: Erlbaum.

Smith, P. K., Hunter, T., Carvalho, A. M. A., & Costabile, A. (1992). Children's perceptions of playfighting, playchasing and real fighting: A cross-national interview study. *Social Development, 1,* 211–221.

Smith, T. L. (1986). Self-concepts of youth sport participants and nonparticipants in grades 3 and 6. *Perceptual and Motor Skills, 62,* 863–866.

Smith, Y. L. S., van Goozen, S. H. M., & Cohen-Kettenis, P. T. (2001). Adolescents with gender identity disorder who were accepted or rejected for sex reassignment surgery: A prospective follow-up study. *Journal of the American Academy of Child and Adolescent Psychiatry, 40*, 472–481.

Smock, P. J., & Manning, W. D. (1997). Nonresident parents' characteristics and child support. *Journal of Marriage and the Family, 59*, 789–808.

Smolowe, J. (1997). A battle against biology; a victory in adoption. *Time, 150*, p. 46.

Snarey, J. R., Reimer, J., & Kohlberg, L. (1985). Development of social-moral reasoning among kibbutz adolescents: A longitudinal cross-sectional study. *Developmental Psychology, 21*, 3–17.

Snow, C. E. (1984). Parent–child interaction and the development of communicative ability. In R. L. Schiefelbusch & J. Pickar (Eds.), *Communicative competence: Acquisition and intervention* (pp. 69–108). Baltimore: University Park Press.

Snyder, C. R. (1994). *The psychology of hope: You can get there from here.* New York: Free Press.

Snyder, C. R. (2002). Hope theory: Rainbows in the mind. *Psychological Inquiry, 13*, 249–275.

Snyder, C. R., Cheavens, J., & Sympson, S. C. (1997). Hope: An individual motive for social commerce. *Group Dynamics: Theory, Research, and Practice, 1*, 107–118.

Snyder, C. R., Harris, C., Anderson, J. R., Holleran, S. A., Irving, L. M., Sigmon, S. T., et al. (1991). The will and the ways: Development and validation of an individual-differences measure of hope. *Journal of Personality and Social Psychology, 60*, 570–585.

Sobel, D. M. (2004). Children's developing knowledge of the relationship between mental awareness and pretense. *Child Development, 75*, 704–729.

Social Security Administration. (1998). *Share of income by source, 1998.* Retrieved January 30, 2002, from http://www.ssa.gov/statistics/income_aged/1998/p15.pdf

Soet, J. E., Brack, G. A., & Dilorio, C. (2003). Prevalence and predictors of women's experience of psychological trauma during childbirth. *Birth: Issues in Perinatal Care, 30*, 36–46.

Sokol, R. J., Delaney-Black, V., & Nordstrom, B. (2003). Fetal alcohol spectrum disorder. *Journal of the American Medical Association, 290*, 2996–2999.

Somerfield, M. R., & McCrae, R. R. (2000). Stress and coping research: Methodological challenges, theoretical advances, and clinical applications. *American Psychologist, 55*, 620–625.

Somers, M. D. (1993). A comparison of voluntarily childfree adults and parents. *Journal of Marriage and the Family, 55*, 643–650.

Somerson, M. D. (1997, April 20). Gazing into genetics' crystal ball. *Columbus Dispatch*, pp. 1A–2A.

Sonnentag, S. (1995). Excellent software professionals: Experience, work activities, and perception by peers. *Behavior and Information Technology, 14*, 289–299.

Sophian, C. (1998). A developmental perspective in children's counting. In C. Donlan (Ed.), *The development of mathematical skills* (pp. 27–46). Hove, England: Psychology Press/Taylor & Francis.

Sorkin, D. H., & Rook, K. S. (2004). Interpersonal control strivings and vulnerability to negative social exchanges in later life. *Psychology and Aging, 19*, 555–564.

Sosa, R., Kennell, J., Klaus, M., Robertson, S., & Urrutia, J. (1980). The effect of a supportive companion on perinatal problems, length of labor, and mother–infant interaction. *The New England Journal of Medicine, 303*, 597–600.

South, S. J. (1993). Racial and ethnic differences in the desire to marry. *Journal of Marriage and the Family, 55*, 357–370.

South, S. J., & Lloyd, K. M. (1992). Marriage opportunities and family formation: Further implications of imbalanced sex ratios. *Journal of Marriage and the Family, 54*, 440–451.

Spanier, G. B., Sauer, W., & Larzelere, R. (1979). An empirical evaluation of the family life cycle. *Journal of Marriage and the Family, 41*, 27–38.

Spear, L. P. (2000). The adolescent brain and age-related behavioral manifestations. *Neuroscience and Biobehavioral Reviews, 24*, 417–463.

Spearman, C. (1927). *The abilities of man.* New York: Macmillan.

Speckhard, A. C., & Rue, V. M. (1992). Postabortion syndrome: An emerging public health concern. *Journal of Social Issues, 48*, 95–119.

Spelke, E. S., von Hofsten, C., & Kestenbaum, R. (1989). Object perception in infancy: Interaction of spatial and kinetic information for object boundaries. *Developmental Psychology, 25*, 185–186.

Spence, M. J., & DeCasper, A. J. (1987). Prenatal experience with low-frequency maternal-voice sounds influences neonatal perception of maternal voice samples. *Infant Behavior and Development, 10*, 133–142.

Spencer, M. B. (1982). Personal and group identity of Black children: An alternative synthesis. *Genetic Psychology Monographs, 103*, 59–84.

Spencer, M. B., Cunningham, M., & Swanson, D. P. (1995). Identity as coping: Adolescent African-American males' adaptive responses to high-risk environments. In H. W. Harris, H. C. Blue, & E. E. H. Griffith (Eds.), *Racial and ethnic identity: Psychological development and creative expression* (pp. 31–52). New York: Routledge.

Spencer, M. B., & Markstrom-Adams, C. (1990). Identity processes among racial and ethnic minority children in America. *Child Development, 61*, 290–310.

Sperling, D. (1989, March 10). Success rate for in vitro is only 9%. *USA Today*, p. 1D.

Spitz, R. A. (1945). Hospitalism: An inquiry into the genesis of psychiatric conditions in early childhood. *Psychoanalytic Study of the Child, 1*, 113–117.

Spitz, R. A. (1946). Anaclitic depression. *Psychoanalytic Study of the Child, 2*, 313–342.

Spitze, G., & Logan, J. (1990). Sons, daughters, and intergenerational social support. *Journal of Marriage and the Family, 52*, 420–430.

Sprecher, S., Sullivan, Q., & Hatfield, E. (1994). Mate selection preferences: Gender differences examined in a national sample. *Journal of Personality and Social Psychology, 66*, 1074–1080.

Sprunger, L. W., Boyce, W. T., & Gaines, J. A. (1985). Family–infant congruence: Routines and rhythmicity in family adaptations to a young infant. *Child Development, 56*, 564–572.

Spurlock, J. C., & Magistro, C. A. (1998). *New and improved: The transformation of American women's emotional culture.* New York: New York University Press.

Sroufe, L. A., & Fleeson, J. (1986). Attachment and the construction of relationships. In W. W. Hartup & Z. Rubin (Eds.), *Relationships and development* (pp. 51–72). Hillsdale, NJ: Erlbaum.

Stack, D. M., & Muir, D. W. (1992). Adult tactile stimulation during face-to-face interactions modulates five-month-olds' affect and attention. *Child Development, 63*, 1509–1525.

Stack, S. (1990). The impact of divorce on suicide, 1959–1980. *Journal of Marriage and the Family, 52*, 119–128.

Stahl, S. M. (1990). *The legacy of longevity: Health and health care in later life.* Thousand Oaks, CA: Sage.

Stake, R. E. (1998). Case studies. In N. K. Denzin & Y. S. Lincoln (Eds.), *Strategies of qualitative inquiry* (pp. 86–109). Thousand Oaks, CA: Sage.

Stallings, J. A. (1995). Ensuring teaching and learning in the 21st century. *Educational Researcher, 24*, 4–8.

Standley, K., Soule, B., & Copans, S. A. (1979). Dimensions of prenatal anxiety and their influence on pregnancy outcome. *American Journal of Obstetrics and Gynecology, 135*, 22–26.

Stapley, J. C., & Haviland, J. M. (1989). Beyond depression: Gender differences in normal adolescents' emotional experiences. *Sex Roles, 20*, 295–308.

Stattin, H., & Klackenberg-Larsson, I. (1991). The short- and long-term implications for parent–child relations of parents' prenatal preferences for their child's gender. *Developmental Psychology, 27*, 141–147.

Stechler, G., & Halton, A. (1982). Prenatal influences on human development. In B. B. Wolman (Ed.), *Handbook of developmental psychology* (pp. 175–189). Englewood Cliffs, NJ: Prentice Hall.

Steinberg, L. (1990). Autonomy, conflict, and harmony in the family relationship. In S. S. Feldman & G. R. Elliott (Eds.), *At the threshold: The developing adolescent* (pp. 255–277). Cambridge, MA: Harvard University Press.

Steinberg, L. (2001). We know some things: Parent–adolescent relationships in retrospect and prospect. *Journal of Research on Adolescence, 11*, 1–19.

Steinberg, L. (2005). *Adolescence* (7th ed.). Boston: McGraw-Hill.

Steinberg, L., & Dornbusch, S. M. (1991). Negative correlates of part-time employment during adolescence: Replication and elaboration. *Developmental Psychology, 27,* 304–313.

Steinhauser, K. E., Christakis, N. A., Clipp, E. C., McNeilly, M., Grambow, S., Parker, J., & Tulsky, J. A. (2001). Preparing for the end of life: Preferences of patients, families, physicians, and other care providers. *Journal of Pain and Symptom Management, 22,* 727–737.

Sternberg, R. J. (1985). *Beyond IQ: A triarchic theory of human intelligence.* Cambridge, UK: Cambridge University Press.

Sternberg, R. J. (1988). *The triangle of love.* New York: Basic Books.

Sternberg, R. J. (1990). *Wisdom: Its nature, origins and development.* New York: Cambridge University Press.

Sternberg, R. J., Castejon, J. L., Prieto, M. D., Hautamäki, J., & Grigorenko, E. L. (2001). Confirmatory factor analysis of the Sternberg Triarchic Abilities Test in three international samples: An empirical test of the triarchic theory of intelligence. *European Journal of Psychological Assessment, 17,* 1–16.

Sternberg, R. J., Grigorenko, E. L., & Singer, J. (2004). *Creativity: From potential to realization.* Washington, DC: American Psychological Association.

Sternberg, R. J., Torff, B., & Grigorenko, E. L. (1998). Teaching triarchically improves school achievement. *Journal of Educational Psychology, 90,* 374–384.

Stets, J. E., & Harrod, M. M. (2004). Verification across multiple identities: The role of status. *Social Psychology Quarterly, 67,* 155–171.

Stevens, J. H., Jr. (1988). Social support, locus of control, and parenting in three low-income groups of mothers: Black teenagers, Black adults, and White adults. *Child Development, 59,* 635–642.

Stevens, J. H., Jr., & Bakeman, R. (1985). A factor analytic study of the HOME scale for infants. *Developmental Psychology, 21,* 1196–1203.

Stevens-Long, J., & Commons, M. L. (1992). *Adult life: Developmental processes* (4th ed.). Mountain View, CA: Mayfield.

Stevenson, D. L., & Baker, D. P. (1987). The family–school relation and the child's school performance. *Child Development, 58,* 1348–1357.

Stevenson, H. W. (1992, December). Learning from Asian schools. *Scientific American, 267*(6), 70–77.

Stevenson, H. W., Chen, C., & Lee, S. (1993). Mathematics achievement of Chinese, Japanese, and American children: Ten years later. *Science, 259,* 53–58.

Stewart, A. J., & Vandewater, E. A. (1998). The course of generativity. In D. P. McAdams & E. de St. Aubin (Eds.), *Generativity and adult development* (pp. 75–100). Washington, DC: American Psychological Association.

Stice, E., & Shaw, H. (2002). Role of body dissatisfaction in the onset and maintenance of eating pathology: A synthesis of research findings. *Journal of Psychosomatic Research, 53,* 985–993.

Stice, E., & Shaw, H. (2004). Eating disorder prevention programs: A meta-analytic review. *Psychological Bulletin, 130,* 206–227.

Sticker, E. J. (1991). The importance of grandparenthood during the life cycle in Germany. In P. K. Smith (Ed.), *The psychology of grandparenthood: An international perspective* (pp. 32–49). London: Routledge.

Stipek, D., Recchia, S., & McClintic, S. (1992). Self-evaluation in young children. *Monographs of the Society for Research in Child Development, 57* (1, Serial No. 226).

Stoller, E. P., & Longino, C. F., Jr. (2001). "Going home" or "leaving home"? The impact of person and place ties on anticipated counterstream migration. *The Gerontologist, 41,* 96–102.

Stone, B. K. (1998, Summer). I feel more like 17. *Bryn Mawr Alumnae Bulletin,* p. 4.

Streissguth, A. P., Barr, H. M., Sampson, P. D., Darby, B. L., & Martin, D. C. (1989). IQ at age 4 in relation to maternal alcohol use and smoking during pregnancy. *Developmental Psychology, 25,* 3–11.

Stress and coping research: Methodological challenges, theoretical advances, and clinical applications. *American Psychologist, 55,* 620–625.

Stright, A. D., Neitzel, C., Sears, K. G., & Hoke-Sinex, L. (2001). Instruction begins in the home: Relations between parental instruction and children's self-regulation in the classroom. *Journal of Educational Psychology, 93,* 456–466.

Stringfellow, L. (1978). The Vietnamese. In A. L. Clark (Ed.), *Culture, childbearing, and the health professionals* (pp. 174–182). Philadelphia: Davis.

Strober, M. (1981). A comparative analysis of personality organization in juvenile anorexia nervosa. *Journal of Youth and Adolescence, 10,* 285–295.

Stroebe, M. (1993). Coping with bereavement: A review of the grief work hypothesis. *Omega: Journal of Death and Dying, 26,* 19–42.

Stroh, L. K., & Reilly, A. H. (1997). Rekindling organizational loyalty: The role of career mobility. *Journal of Career Development, 24,* 39–54.

Stromquist, N. P. (1991). *Daring to be different: The choice of nonconventional fields of study by international women.* New York: Institute of International Education.

Strouse, D. L. (1999). Adolescent crowd orientations: A social and temporal analysis. In J. A. McLellan & M. J. V. Pugh (Eds.), *The role of peer groups in adolescent social identity: Exploring the importance of stability and change* (pp. 37–54). San Francisco: Jossey-Bass.

Stuart-Hamilton, I. (1996). Intellectual changes in late life. In R. T. Woods (Ed.), *Handbook of the clinical psychology of ageing* (pp. 23–41). Oxford, England: John Wiley & Sons.

Students, employers disagree on seniors' job readiness, survey shows. (1998, January 23). *Columbus Dispatch,* Employment '98 supplement, p. 9.

Sullivan, H. S. (1949). *The collected works of Harry Stack Sullivan* (Vols. 1, 2). New York: Norton.

Sullivan, H. S. (1953). *The interpersonal theory of psychiatry.* New York: Norton.

Sullivan, K., & Sullivan, A. (1980). Adolescent–parent separation. *Developmental Psychology, 16,* 93–104.

Sullivan, M. D. (2003). Hope and hopelessness at the end of life. *American Journal of Geriatric Psychiatry, 11,* 393–405.

Sullivan, M. W., Lewis, M., & Allesandri, S. M. (1992). Cross-age stability in emotional expressions during learning and extinction. *Developmental Psychology, 28,* 58–63.

Super, C. M., Kagan, J., Morrison, F. J., Haith, M. M., & Weiffenbach, J. (1972). Discrepancy and attention in the five-month infant. *Genetic Psychology Monographs, 85,* 305–331.

Susman, E. J., Dorn, L. D., & Chrousos, G. P. (1991). Negative hormones and affect levels in young adolescents: Concurrent and predictive perspectives. *Journal of Youth and Adolescence, 20,* 167–190.

Sutton-Smith, B. A. (1972). Syntax for play and games. In R. E. Herron & B. Sutton-Smith (Eds.), *Child's play.* New York: Wiley.

Swann, W. B., Jr. (1990). To be known or be adored? The interplay of self-enhancement and self-verification. In E. T. Higgins & R. M. Sorrentino (Eds.), *Handbook of motivation and cognition: Foundations of social behavior* (pp. 404–448). New York: Guilford Press.

Swisher, R., Sweet, S., & Moen, P. L. (2004). The family-friendly community and its life course fit for dual earner couples. *Journal of Marriage and the Family, 66,* 281–292.

Swyer, P. R. (1987). The organization of perinatal care with particular reference to the newborn. In G. B. Avery (Ed.), *Neonatology: Pathophysiology and management of the newborn* (pp. 13–44). Philadelphia: Lippincott.

Tajfel, H. (1981). *Human groups and social categories.* Cambridge, UK: Cambridge University Press.

Takahashi, L. K., Baker, E. W., & Kalin, N. H. (1990). Ontogeny of behavioral and hormonal responses to stress in prenatally stressed male rat pups. *Physiology and Behavior, 47,* 357–364.

Takahashi, L. K., & Kalin, N. H. (1991). Early developmental and temporal characteristics of stress-induced secretion of pituitary-adrenal hormones in prenatally stressed rat pups. *Brain Research, 558,* 75–78.

Tallman, I., & Hsiao, Y.-L. (2004). Resources, cooperation, and problem solving in early marriages. *Social Psychology Quarterly, 67,* 172–188.

Tamis-LeMonda, C. S., Uzgiris, I. C., & Bornstein, M. H. (2002). Play in parent–child interactions. In M. H. Bornstein (Ed.), *Handbook of parenting. Vol. 5: Practical issues in parenting* (pp. 221–242). Mahwah, NJ: Erlbaum.

Tanfer, K. (1987). Premarital cohabitation among never-married women. *Journal of Marriage and the Family, 49,* 483–497.

Tang, C. S. K., Wong, C. S. Y., & Schwarzer, R. (1996). Psychosocial differences between occasional and regular adolescent users of marijuana and heroin. *Journal of Youth and Adolescence, 25,* 219–239.

Tang, C. S., Yeung, D. Y., & Lee, A. M. (2003). Psychosocial correlates of emotional responses to menarche among Chinese adolescent girls. *Journal of Adolescent Health, 33,* 193–201.

Tangney, J. P. (1991). Moral affect: The good, the bad, and the ugly. *Journal of Personality and Social Psychology, 61,* 598–607.

Tangney, J. P. (2001). Constructive and destructive aspects of shame and guilt. In A. C. Bohart & D. J. Stipek (Eds.), *Constructive and destructive behavior: Implications for family, school and society* (pp. 127–145). Washington, DC: American Psychological Association.

Tangney, J. P., & Dearing, R. L. (2002). *Shame and guilt.* New York: Guilford Press.

Tangney, J. P., Wagner, P., Fletcher, C., & Gramzow, R. (1992). Shamed into anger? The relation of shame and guilt to anger and self-reported aggression. *Journal of Personality and Social Psychology, 62,* 669–675.

Tanner, J. M. (1990). *Foetus into man: Physical growth from conception to maturity* (rev. ed.). Cambridge, MA: Harvard University Press.

Tausig, M., & Fenwick, R. (2001). Unbinding time: Alternate work schedules and work-life balance. *Journal of Family and Economic Issues, 22,* 101–119.

Taylor, H. (2002). 2–1 majorities continue to support rights to both euthanasia and doctor-assisted suicide. *The Harris Poll, Harris Interactive.* Retrieved March 5, 2005, from http://www.deathwithdignity.org/fss/opinion/harrispoll.asp

Taylor, H. G., Klein, N., Minich, N. M., & Hack, M. (2000). Middle-school-age outcomes in children with very low birth weight. *Child Development, 71,* 1495–1511.

Taylor, J., & Turner, R. J. (2001). A longitudinal study of the role and significance of mattering to others for depressive symptoms. *Journal of Health and Social Behavior, 42,* 310–325.

Taylor, M., Cartwright, B. S., & Carlson, S. M. (1993). A developmental investigation of children's imaginary companions. *Developmental Psychology, 29,* 276–285.

Taylor, R. D., & Oskay, G. (1995). Identity formation in Turkish and American late adolescents. *Journal of Cross-Cultural Psychology, 26,* 8–22.

Taylor, R. J. (1986). Religious participation among elderly Blacks. *The Gerontologist, 26,* 630–636.

Taylor, R. J., Chatters, L. M., Tucker, M. B., & Lewis, E. (1990). Black families. *Journal of Marriage and the Family, 52,* 993–1014.

Taylor, S. J. (1987) "They're not like you and me": Institutional attendants' perspectives on residents. *Children and Youth Services, 8,* 109–125.

Taylor, S. J., & Bogdan, R. (1998). *Introduction to qualitative research methods* (3rd ed.). New York: Wiley.

Taylor, W. C., Blair, S. N., Cummings, S. S., Wun, C. C., & Malina, R. M. (1999). Childhood and adolescent physical activity patterns and adult physical activity. *Medicine and Science in Sports and Exercise, 31,* 118–123.

Teachman, J. D., Polonko, K. A., & Scanzoni, J. (1987). Demography of the family. In M. B. Sussman & S. K. Steinmetz (Eds.), *Handbook of marriage and the family* (pp. 3–57). New York: Plenum Press.

Teller, D. Y., & Bornstein, J. H. (1987). Infant color vision and color perception. In P. Salapatek & L. Cohen (Eds.), *Handbook of infant perception* (Vol. 1). Orlando, FL: Academic Press.

Tennen, H., Affleck, G., Armeli, S., & Carney, M.A. (2000). A daily process approach to coping: Linking theory, research, and practice. *American Psychologist, 55,* 626–636.

Teong, S. K. (2003). The effect of metacognitive training on mathematical word-problem solving. *Journal of Computer Assisted Learning, 19,* 46–55.

Terman, L. M., & Oden, M. H. (1947). *The gifted child grows up: Twenty-five years' follow-up of a superior group.* Stanford, CA: Stanford University Press.

Terman, L. M., & Oden, M. H. (1959). *The gifted group at mid-life: Thirty-five years' follow-up of a superior group.* Stanford, CA: Stanford University Press.

Teti, D. M., & Lamb, M. E. (1989). Outcomes of adolescent marriage and adolescent childbirth. *Journal of Marriage and the Family, 51,* 203–212.

Teti, D. M., Nakagawa, M., Das, R., & Wirth, O. (1991). Security of attachment between preschoolers and their mothers: Relations among social interaction, parenting stress, and mothers' sorts of the attachment Q-set. *Developmental Psychology, 27,* 440–447.

Thabes, V. (1997). Survey analysis of women's long-term postdivorce adjustment. *Journal of Divorce and Remarriage, 27,* 163–175.

Tharp, R. G. (1989). Psychocultural variables and constants: Effects on teaching and learning in schools. *American Psychologist, 44,* 349–359.

Tharp, R. G., & Gallimore, R. (1988). *Rousing minds to life: Teaching, learning, and schooling in social context.* Cambridge, UK: Cambridge University Press.

Thatcher, R. W., Walker, R. A., & Giudice, S. (1987). Human cerebral hemispheres develop at different rates and ages. *Science, 236,* 1110–1113.

The Names Project Foundation. (2005). *History of the quilt.* Retrieved March 10, 2005, from http://www.aidsquilt.org/history.htm

Thelen, E. (1995). Motor development: A new synthesis. *American Psychologist, 50,* 79–95.

Thoits, P. A. (1999). Self, identity, stress, and mental health. In C. S. Aneshensel & J. C. Phelan (Eds.), *Handbook of sociology of mental health* (pp. 3345–368). New York: Kluwer Academic/Plenum.

Thomas, A., & Chess, S. (1977). *Temperament and development.* New York: Brunner/Mazel.

Thomas, A., & Chess, S. (1980). *The dynamics of psychological development.* New York: Brunner/Mazel.

Thomas, A., & Chess, S. (1986). The New York longitudinal study: From infancy to early adult life. In R. Plomin & J. Dunn (Eds.), *The study of temperament: Changes, continuities, and challenges.* Hillsdale, NJ: Erlbaum.

Thomas, A., Chess, S., & Birch, H. (1970). The origin of personality. *Scientific American, 223,* 102–109.

Thomas, M. H., & Drabman, R. S. (1977). *Effects of television violence on expectations of others' aggression.* Paper presented at the annual convention of the American Psychological Association, San Francisco, CA.

Thomas, R. M. (1999). *Human development theories: Windows on culture.* Thousand Oaks, CA: Sage.

Thomas, V., & Striegel, P. (1994–1995). Stress and grief of a perinatal loss: Integrating qualitative and quantitative methods. *Omega: Journal of Death and Dying, 30,* 299–311.

Thompson, J. J. (1998). Plugging the kegs. *U.S. News and World Report, 124,* 63–67.

Thompson, L. (1993). Conceptualizing gender in marriage: The case of marital care. *Journal of Marriage and the Family, 55,* 557–569.

Thompson, L. W., Gallagher-Thompson, D., Futterman, A., Gilewski, M. J., & Peterson, J. (1991). The effects of late-life spousal bereavement over a 30-month interval. *Psychology and Aging, 6,* 434–441.

Thompson, M. W., McInnes, R. R., & Willard, H. F. (1991). *Genetics in medicine* (5th ed.). Philadelphia: Saunders.

Thompson, R. A. (1990). Emotion and self-regulation. In R. A. Thompson (Ed.), *Nebraska Symposium on Motivation, 1988* (Vol. 36, pp. 367–467). Lincoln: University of Nebraska Press.

Thompson, R. A., Connell, J. P., & Bridges, L. J. (1988). Temperament, emotion, and social interactive behavior in the strange situation: A component process analysis of attachment system functioning. *Child Development, 59,* 1102–1110.

Thompson, S. K. (1975). Gender labels and early sex role development. *Child Development, 46,* 339–347.

Thomson, E., & Colella, U. (1992). Cohabitation and marital stability: Quality or commitment? *Journal of Marriage and the Family, 54,* 259–267.

Thornton, A., Axinn, W. G., & Teachman, J. D. (1995). The influence of school enrollment and accumulation on cohabitation and marriage in early adulthood. *American Sociological Review, 60,* 762–774.

Thornton, A., & Camburn, D. (1989). Religious participation and adolescent sexual behavior. *Journal of Marriage and the Family, 51,* 641–654.

Thornton, A., & Young-DeMarco, L. (2001). Four decades of trends in attitudes toward family issues in the United States: The 1960s through the 1990s. *Journal of Marriage and the Family, 63*, 1009–1037.

Thornton, A., Young-DeMarco, L., & Goldscheider, F. (1993). Leaving the parental nest: The experience of a young wife cohort in the 1980s. *Journal of Marriage and the Family, 55*, 216–229.

Thorpe, I. (2001). *Ian Thorpe's home page.* Retrieved October 21, 2001, from http://www.ianthorpe.telstra.com.au/

Tichauer, R. (1963). The Aymara children of Bolivia. *Journal of Pediatrics, 62*, 399–412.

Thwaites, R., & Dagnan, D. (2004). Moderating variables in the relationship between social comparison and depression: An evolutionary perspective. *Psychology & Psychotherapy: Theory, Research & Practice, 77*, 309–323.

Tiedeman, D. V., & Miller-Tiedeman, A. (1985). The trend of life in the human career. *Journal of Career Development, 11*, 221–250.

Tiedeman, D. V., & O'Hara, R. P. (1963). *Career development: Choice and adjustment.* New York: College Entrance Examination Board.

Tiedje, L. G. (2004). Processes of change in work/home incompatibilities: Employed mothers 1986–1999. *Journal of Social Issues, 60*, 787–800.

Tinsley, H. E. A., Teaff, J. D., Colbs, S. L., & Kaufman, N. (1985). System of classifying leisure activities in terms of the psychological benefits of participation reported by older persons. *Journal of Gerontology, 40*, 172–178.

Tinsley, V. S., & Waters, H. S. (1982). The development of verbal control over motor behavior: A replication and extension of Luria's findings. *Child Development, 53*, 746–753.

Tolman, E. C. (1932/1967). *Purposive behavior in rats and men.* New York: Appleton-Century-Crofts.

Tolman, E. C. (1948). Cognitive maps in rats and men. *Psychological Review, 55*, 189–208.

Tolson, T. F. J., & Wilson, M. N. (1990). The impact of two- and three-generational Black family structure on perceived family climate. *Child Development, 61*, 416–428.

Tomarken, A. J., Dichter, G. S., Garber, J., & Simien, C. (2004). Resting frontal brain activity: Linkages to maternal depression and socio-economic status among adolescents. *Biological Psychology, 67*, 77–102.

Tomer, A., & Eliason, G. (2000). Attitudes about life and death: Toward a comprehensive model of death anxiety. In A. Tomer (Ed.), *Death attitudes and the older adult: Theories, concepts, and applications* (pp. 3–22). New York: Brunner-Routledge.

Tomlin, A. M., & Passman, R. H. (1989). Grandmothers' responsibility in raising 2-year-olds facilitates their grandchildren's adaptive behavior. A preliminary intrafamilial investigation of mothers' and maternal grandmothers' effects. *Psychology and Aging, 4*, 119–121.

Toohey, S. B., Shinn, M., & Weitzman, B. C. (2004). Social networks and homelessness among women heads of household. *American Journal of Community Psychology, 33*, 7–20.

Torbert, W. R. (1994). Cultivating postformal adult development: Higher stages and contrasting interventions. In M. E. Miller & S. R. Cook-Greuter (Eds.), *Transcendence and mature thought in adulthood: The further reaches of adult development* (pp. 181–203). Lanham, MD: Rowman & Littlefield.

Touron, D. R., & Hertzog, C. (2004). Distinguishing age differences in knowledge, strategy use, and confidence during strategic skill acquisition. *Psychology and Aging, 19*, 452–466.

Tracy, J. L., Shaver, P. R., Albino, A. W., & Cooper, M. L. (2003). Attachment styles and adolescent sexuality. In P. Florsheim (Ed.), *Adolescent romantic relationships and sexual behavior: Theory, research, and practical implications* (pp. 137–159). Mahwah, NJ: Erlbaum.

Tracy, R. L., & Ainsworth, M. D. S. (1981). Maternal affectionate behavior and infant–mother attachment patterns. *Child Development, 52*, 1341–1343.

Trawick-Smith, J. (1988). "Let's say you're the baby, OK?": Play leadership and following behavior of young children. *Young Children, 43*, 51–59.

Trends in International Mathematics and Science Study. (2004). *TIMSS results.* Retrieved November 20, 2004, from http://nces.ed.gov/timss/

Trent, K., & South, S. J. (1989). Structural determinants of the divorce rate. *Journal of Marriage and the Family, 51*, 391–404.

Trethowan, W. (1972). The couvade syndrome. In J. Howells (Ed.), *Modern perspectives in psycho-obstetrics.* New York: Brunner/Mazel.

Trevarthen, C., & Aitken, K. J. (2001). Infant intersubjectivity: Research, theory, and clinical applications. *Journal of Child Psychology and Psychiatry and Allied Disciplines, 42*, 3–48.

Triandis, H. C. (1990). Cross-cultural studies of individualism and collectivism. In J. J. Berman (Ed.), *Nebraska Symposium on Motivation, 1989: Cross-cultural perspectives* (pp. 41–133). Lincoln: University of Nebraska Press.

Triandis, H. C. (1994). *Culture and social behavior.* New York: McGraw-Hill.

Triandis, H. C. (Ser. Ed.). (1995). *New directions in social psychology: Individualism and collectivism.* Boulder, CO: Westview Press.

Triandis, H. C. (1998). Vertical and horizontal individualism and collectivism: Theory and research implications for international comparative management. In J. L. C. Cheng & R. B. Peterson (Eds.), *Advances in international comparative management* (Vol. 12, pp. 7–35). Stamford, CT: JAI Press.

Triandis, H., Lambert, W., Berry, J., Lonner, W., Heron, A., Brislin, R., & Draguns, J. (Eds.). (1980). *Handbook of cross-cultural*

*psychology: Vols. 1–6.* Boston: Allyn & Bacon.

Triffon, B. J. (1997). Grandparents: Parenting again. *Columbus Parent, 9*, p. 17.

Troiden, R. R. (1993). The formation of homosexual identities. In L. D. Garnets & D. C. Kimmel (Eds.), *Psychological perspectives on lesbian and gay male experiences. Between men—between women* (pp. 191–217). New York: Columbia University Press.

Tronick, E. Z. (1989). Emotions and emotional communication in infants. *American Psychologist, 44*, 112–119.

Tronick, E. Z. (2003). Emotions and emotional communication with others. In J. Raphael-Leff (Ed.), *Parent–infant psychodynamics: Wild things, mirrors, and ghosts* (pp. 35–53). London: Whurr.

Tronick, E. Z., Als, H., & Brazelton, R. B. (1979). Early development of neonatal and infant behavior. In F. Falkner & J. M. Tanner (Eds.), *Human growth, Vol. 3, Neurobiology and nutrition* (pp. 305–328). New York: Plenum Press.

Tronick, E. Z., & Cohn, J. F. (1989). Infants–mother face-to-face interaction: Age and gender differences in coordination and the occurrence of miscoordination. *Child Development, 60*, 85–92.

Trumbull, E., Rothstein-Fisch, C., & Greenfield, P. M. (2000). *Bridging cultures in our schools: New approaches that work.* Retrieved June 18, 2004, from http://www.wested.org/online_pubs/bridging/ref.shtml

Trzesniewski, K. H., Donnellan, M. B., & Robins, R. W. (2003). Stability of self-esteem across the life span. *Journal of Personality and Social Psychology, 84*, 205–220.

Tsao, F.-M., Liu, H.-M., & Kuhl, P. K. (2004). Speech perception in infancy predicts language development in the second year of life: A longitudinal study. *Child Development, 75*, 1067–1084.

Tschann, J. M., Johnston, J. R, & Wallerstein, J. S. (1989). Factors in adults' adjustment after divorce. *Journal of Marriage and the Family, 51*, 1033–1046.

Tucker, M. B., Taylor, R. J., & Mitchell-Kernan, C. (1993). Marriage and romantic involvement among aged African Americans. *Journal of Gerontology, 48*, S123–S132.

Tudge, J., Putnam, S., & Valsiner, J. (1996). Culture and cognition in developmental perspective. In R. B. Cairns, G. H. Elder Jr., & E. J. Costello (Eds.), *Developmental science* (pp. 190–222). Cambridge, UK: Cambridge University Press.

Tudge, J. R. H. (1992). Processes and consequences of peer collaboration: A Vygotskian analysis. *Child Development, 63*, 1364–1379.

Tudge, J. R. H., & Winterhoff, P. A. (1993). Vygotsky, Piaget, and Bandura: Perspectives on the relations between the social world and cognitive development. *Human Development, 36*, 61–81.

Turiel, E. (1983). *The development of social knowledge: Morality and convention.* Cambridge, UK: Cambridge University Press.

Turiel, E. (2002). *The culture of morality: Social development, context, and conflict*. Cambridge, UK: Cambridge University Press.

Turiel, E. (2003). Resistance and subversion in everyday life. *Journal of Moral Education, 32*, 397–409.

Turner, J. S., & Rubinson, L. (1993). *Contemporary human sexuality*. Englewood Cliffs, NJ: Prentice Hall.

Turner, P. J., & Gervai, J. (1995). A multidimensional study of gender typing in preschool children and their parents: Personality, attitudes, preferences, behavior, and cultural differences. *Developmental Psychology, 31*, 759–772.

Twain, M. (1962). *The adventures of Huckleberry Finn*. New York: Scholastic Book Services.

Tyler, R., Howard, J., Espinosa, M., & Doakes, S. S. (1997). Placement with substance-abusing mothers vs. placement with other relatives: Infant outcomes. *Child Abuse and Neglect, 21*, 337–349.

Tyson, P. (1996). Object relations, affect management, and psychic structure formation: The concept of object constancy. *Psychoanalytic Study of the Child, 51*, 172–189.

U.S. Bureau of the Census. (1976). *Population profile of the United States, 1975*. Current Population Reports (Ser. P-20, No. 292). Washington, DC: U.S. Government Printing Office.

U.S. Bureau of the Census. (1983). *America in transition: An aging society*. Current Population Reports (Ser. P-23, No. 128). Washington, DC: U.S. Government Printing Office.

U.S. Bureau of the Census. (1984). *Demographic and socioeconomic aspects of aging in the United States*. Current Population Reports (Ser. P-23, No. 138), 59. Washington, DC: U.S. Government Printing Office.

U.S. Bureau of the Census. (1986). *Statistical abstract of the United States, 1986*. Washington, DC: U.S. Government Printing Office.

U.S. Bureau of the Census. (1987). *An aging world*. International Population Reports (Ser. P-95, No. 78). Washington, DC: U.S. Government Printing Office.

U.S. Bureau of the Census. (1989a). *Population profile of the United States, 1989*. Current Population Reports (Ser. P-23, No. 159). Washington, DC: U.S. Government Printing Office.

U.S. Bureau of the Census. (1989b). *The Black population in the United States, March, 1988*. Current Population Reports (Ser. P-20, No. 442). Washington, DC: U.S. Government Printing Office.

U.S. Bureau of the Census. (1991). *Statistical abstract of the United States, 1991*. Washington, DC: U.S. Government Printing Office.

U.S. Bureau of the Census. (1992). *Statistical abstract of the United States, 1992*. Washington, DC: U.S. Government Printing Office.

U.S. Bureau of the Census. (1995). *Statistical abstract of the United States, 1995*. Washington, DC: U.S. Government Printing Office.

U.S. Bureau of the Census. (1996). *Statistical abstract of the United States, 1996*. Washington, DC: U.S. Government Printing Office.

U.S. Bureau of the Census. (1997). *Statistical abstract of the United States, 1997*. Washington, DC: U.S. Government Printing Office.

U.S. Bureau of the Census. (1999). *Statistical abstract of the United States, 1999*. Washington, DC: U.S. Government Printing Office.

U.S. Bureau of the Census. (2000). *Statistical abstract of the United States, 2000*. Washington, DC: U.S. Government Printing Office.

U.S. Census Bureau. (2003). *Statistical abstract of the United States, 2003*. Washington, DC: U.S. Government Printing Office.

U.S. Census Bureau. (2004a). *Historical poverty tables*. Retrieved February 13, 2005, from http://www.census.gov/hhes/poverty/histpov/hstpov4.html

U.S. Census Bureau. (2004b). *Statistical Abstract of the United States, 2004*. Washington, DC: U.S. Government Printing Office.

U.S. Conference of Mayors. (1998). *A status report on hunger and homelessness in America's cities*. Washington, DC: Author.

U.S. Department of Commerce. (2003). Student use of computers by level of enrollment and selected characteristics: 1993, 1997, and 2001. Unpublished data. *Bureau of the Census, Current Population Survey*, Table 429. Retrieved November 25, 2004, from http://nces.ed.gov/programs/digest/d03/tables/dt429.asp

U.S. Department of Education. (1995). *Digest of education statistics, 1995*. Washington, DC: U.S. Government Printing Office.

U.S. Department of Education. (2002). *Twenty-fourth annual report to Congress on the implementation of the Individuals with Disabilities Education Act*. Retrieved September 30, 2004, from http://www.ed.gov/about/reports/annual/osep/2002/index.html

U.S. Department of Energy, Office of Science. (2004). *The science behind the Human Genome Project*. Retrieved August 3, 2004, from http://www.ornl.gov/sci/techresources/Human_Genome/project/info.shtml

U.S. Department of Health and Human Services. (1999) *Mental health: A report of the surgeon general—Executive summary*. Rockville, MD: U.S. Department of Health and Human Services, Substance Abuse and Mental Health Services Administration, Center for Mental Health Services, National Institutes of Health, National Institute of Mental Health. Retrieved December 2, 2004, from http://www.surgeongeneral.gov/library/mentalhealth/home.html

U.S. Department of Health and Human Services. (2001a). *Healthy people in healthy communities*. Washington, DC: U.S. Government Printing Office.

U.S. Department of Health and Human Services. (2001b). *Healthy people 2010*. Washington, DC: U.S. Government Printing Office.

U.S. Department of Labor. (1993). *Work and family: Turning thirty—job mobility and labor market attachment*. Report 862. Bureau of Labor Statistics.

U.S. Department of Labor. (2003). *O*NET*. Retrieved February 6, 2005, from http://www.doleta.gov/programs/onet/

U.S. Department of Labor, Employment and Training Administration. (1993). *Selected characteristics of occupations defined in the revised dictionary of occupational titles*. Washington, DC: U.S. Government Printing Office.

U.S. Senate, Special Committee on Aging. (1986). *Aging America: Trends and projections*. Washington, DC: U.S. Government Printing Office.

Udry, J. R., & Billy, J. O. G. (1987). Initiation of coitus in early adolescence. *American Sociological Review, 52*, 841–855.

Udry, J. R., Billy, J. O., Morris, N. M., Groff, T. R, & Raj, M. S. (1985). Serum androgenic hormones motivate sexual behavior in adolescent boys. *Fertility and Sterility, 43*, 90–94.

Umbel, V. M., Pearson, B. Z., Fernandez, M. C., & Oller, D. K. (1992). Measuring bilingual children's receptive vocabularies. *Child Development, 63*, 1012–1020.

Umberson, D., Chen, M. D., House, J. S., Hopkins, K., & Slaten, E. (1996). The effect of social relationships on psychological well-being: Are men and women really so different? *American Sociological Review, 61*, 837–857.

Umberson, D., Wortman, C. B., & Kessler, R. C. (1992). Widowhood and depression: Explaining long-term gender differences in vulnerability. *Journal of Health and Social Behavior, 33*, 10–24.

Uncapher, H., Gallagher-Thompson, D., Osgood, N. J., & Bongar, B. (1998). Hopelessness and suicidal ideation in older adults. *The Gerontologist, 38*, 62–70.

United Nations. (2000). *Child labor, conflict-induced trauma in children, among key topics in Third Committee Survey of children's rights*. Press Release GA/SHC/3590. Retrieved September 8, 2001, from http://srch1.un.org/plwebcgi/fastweb?state_id=999965071&view=unsearch&docrank=3&numhitsfound=12&query=child%20slavery&docid=1804&docdb=pr2000&dbname=web&sorting=BYRELEVANCE&operator=adj&TemplateName=predoc.tmpl&set-Cookie=1

University of California. (2004). *UC and the SAT*. Retrieved November 18, 2004, from http://www.ucop.edu/news/sat/welcome.html

Urban Institute. (2000). *A new look at homelessness in America*. Washington, DC: Author.

Urberg, K. A. (1992). Locus of peer influence: Social crowd and best friend. *Journal of Youth and Adolescence, 21*, 439–450.

Urberg, K. A., Shyu, S. J., & Liang, J. (1990). Peer influence in adolescent cigarette smoking. *Addictive Behavior, 115,* 247–255.

USA Today. (2004). Study: Abstinence pledges not reducing rates of STDs. *The Associated Press.* Retrieved December 4, 2004, from http://www.usatoday .com/news/health/2004-03-09-abstinence-study_x.htm

Utian, W. (2003). What are the key issues women face when ending hormone replacement therapy? *Cleveland Clinic Journal of Medicine, 70,* 93–94.

Vaillant, G. E., & Western, R. J. (2001). Healthy aging among inner-city men. *International Psychogeriatrics, 13,* 425–437.

Valas, H. (2001). Learned helplessness and psychological adjustment II: Effects of learning disabilities and low achievement. *Scandinavian Journal of Educational Research, 45,* 101–114.

Valdez-Menchaca, M. S., & Whitehurst, G. J. (1992). Accelerating language development through picture book reading: A systematic extension to Mexican day care. *Developmental Psychology, 28,* 1106–1114.

Valery, J. H., O'Connor, P., & Jennings, S. (1997). The nature and amount of support college-age adolescents request and receive from parents. *Adolescence, 32,* 323–337.

Valk, A. (2000). Ethnic identity, ethnic attitudes, self-esteem, and esteem toward others among Estonian and Russian adolescents. *Journal of Adolescent Research, 15,* 637–651.

Valsiner, J. (2000). *Culture and human development.* Thousand Oaks, CA: Sage.

Van Boxtel, M. P. J., Paas, F. G. W. C., Houx, P. J., & Adam, J. J. (1997). Aerobic capacity and cognitive performance in a cross-sectional aging study. *Medicine and Science in Sports and Exercise, 29,* 1357–1365.

Van der Mark, I. L., van IJzendoorn, M. H., & Bakermans-Kranenburg, M. J. (2002). Development of empathy in girls during the second year of life: Associations with parenting, attachment, and temperament. *Social Development, 11,* 451–468.

Van der Vegt, G., Emans, B. J. M., & Van De Vliert, E. (2001). Patterns of interdependence in work teams: A two-level investigation of the relations with job and team satisfaction. *Personnel Psychology, 54,* 51–69.

Van IJzendoorn, M. H., Goldberg, S., Kroonenberg, P. M., & Frenkel, O. J. (1992). The relative effects of maternal and child problems on the quality of attachment: A meta-analysis of attachment in clinical samples. *Child Development, 63,* 840–858.

Van IJzendoorn, M. H., & Kroonenberg, P. M. (1988). Cross-cultural patterns of attachment: A meta-analysis of the strange situation. *Child Development, 59,* 147–156.

Van IJzendoorn, M. H., & Sagi, A. (1999). Cross-cultural patterns of attachment: Universal and contextual dimensions. In J. Cassidy & P. R. Shaver (Eds.), *Handbook of attachment: Theory, research, and clinical applications* (pp. 713–734). New York: Guilford Press.

Van Wieringen, J. C. (1978). Secular growth changes. In F. Falkner & J. M. Tanner (Eds.), *Human growth* (Vol. 2, pp. 445–473). New York: Plenum Press.

Van Willigen, M. (2000). Differential benefits of volunteering across the life course. *Journal of Gerontology, 55,* S308–S318.

Vandell, D. L., Henderson, V. K., & Wilson, K. S. (1988). A longitudinal study of children with day-care experiences of varying quality. *Child Development, 59,* 1286–1292.

VanLear, C. A. (1992). Marital communication across the generations: Learning and rebellion, continuity and change. *Journal of Social and Personal Relationships, 9,* 103–123.

Vannoy, D. (1995). A paradigm of roles in the divorce process: Implications for divorce adjustment, future commitments, and personal growth. *Journal of Divorce and Remarriage, 24,* 71–87.

Vanzetti, N., & Duck, S. (1996). *A lifetime of relationships.* Pacific Grove, CA: Brooks/Cole.

Vaughn, B., Egeland, B., Sroufe, L. A., & Waters, E. (1979). Individual differences in infant–mother attachment at 12 and 18 months: Stability and change in families under stress. *Child Development, 50,* 971–975.

Vaughn, B. E., & Bost, K. K. (1999). Attachment and temperament. In J. Cassidy & P. R. Shaver (Eds.), *Handbook of attachment: Theory, research, and clinical applications* (pp. 198–225). New York: Guilford Press.

Vaughn, B. E., Colvin, T. N., Azria, M. R., Caya, L., & Krzysik, L. (2001). Dyadic analyses of friendship in a sample of preschool-age children attending Head Start: Correspondence between measures and implications for social competence. *Child Development, 72,* 862–878.

Vaughn, B. E., Lefever, G. B., Seifer, R., & Barglow, P. (1989). Attachment behavior, attachment security, and temperament during infancy. *Child Development, 60,* 728–737.

Veenhoven, R. (2000). Freedom and happiness: A comparative study in forty-four nations in the early 1990s. In E. Diener & E. M. Suh (Eds.), *Culture and subjective well-being* (pp. 257–288). Cambridge, MA: MIT Press.

Veenman, M. V. J., Wilhelm, P., & Beishuizen, J. J. (2004). The relation between intellectual and metacognitive skills from a developmental perspective. *Learning and Instruction, 14,* 89–109.

Vega, W. A., Zimmerman, R. S., Warheit, G. J., Apospori, E., & Gil, A. G. (1993). Risk factors for adolescent drug use in four ethnic and racial groups. *American Journal of Public Health, 83,* 185–189.

Venter, J. C., et al. (2001). The sequence of the human genome. *Science, 291,* 1304–1351.

Verhaeghen, P., Geraerts, N., & Marcoen, A. (2000). Memory complaints, coping, and well-being in old age: A systemic approach. *The Gerontologist, 40,* 540–548.

Verhoef, H., & Michel, C. (1997). Studying morality within the African context: Model of moral analysis and construction. *Journal of Moral Education, 26,* 389–407.

Verhoeven, L. (2001). Prevention of reading difficulties. In L. Verhoeven & C. Snow (Eds.), *Literacy and motivation: Reading engagement in individuals and groups* (pp. 123–134). Mahwah, NJ: Erlbaum.

Vinokur, A., Caplan, R. D., & Williams, C. C. (1987). Effects of recent and past stress on mental health: Coping with unemployment among Vietnam veterans and nonveterans. *Journal of Applied Social Psychology, 17,* 708–728.

Violato, C., & Holden, W. B. (1988). A confirmatory factor analysis of a four-factor model of adolescent concerns. *Journal of Youth and Adolescence, 17,* 101–113.

Vizziello, G. F., Antonioloi, M. E., Cocci, V., & Invernizzi, R. (1993). From pregnancy to motherhood: The structure of representative and narrative change. *Infant Mental Health Journal, 14,* 4–16.

Vogel, G. (2001). Human cloning plans spark talk of U.S. ban. *Science, 292,* 31.

Vogl-Bauer, S. (2003). Maintaining family relationships. In D. J. Canary & M. Dainton (Eds.), *Maintaining relationships through communication: Relational, contextual, and cultural variations* (pp. 31–49). Mahwah, NJ: Erlbaum.

Volling, B. L., Youngblade, L. M., & Belsky, J. (1997). Young children's social relationships with siblings and friends. *American Journal of Orthopsychiatry, 67,* 102–111.

Vondracek, F. W., Schulenberg, J., Skorikov, V., & Gillespie, L. (1995). The relationship of identity status to career indecision during adolescence. *Journal of Adolescence, 18,* 17–29.

Vorhees, C. V., & Mollnow, E. (1987). Behavioral teratogenesis: Long-term influences on behavior from early exposure to environmental agents. In J. D. Osofsky (Ed.), *Handbook of infant development* (pp. 913–971). New York: Wiley.

Vosler, N. R., & Page-Adams, D. (1996). Predictors of depression among workers at the time of a plant closing. *Journal of Sociology and Social Welfare, 23,* 25–42.

Voydanoff, P. (2004). The effects of work demands and resources on work-to-family conflict and facilitation. *Journal of Marriage and the Family, 66,* 398–412.

Vuchinich, S. (1987). Starting and stopping spontaneous family conflicts. *Journal of Marriage and the Family, 49,* 591–601.

Vygotsky, L. S. (1962). *Thought and language.* Cambridge, MA: MIT Press.

Vygotsky, L. S. (1978). *Mind in society.* Cambridge, MA: Harvard University Press.

Waas, G. A. (1988). Social attributional biases of peer-rejected and aggressive children. *Child Development, 59,* 969–975.

Wager, M. (1998). Women or researchers? The identities of academic women. *Feminism and Psychology, 8,* 236–244.

Wagner, B. M., & Phillips, D. A. (1992). Beyond beliefs: Parent and child behaviors and children's perceived academic competence. *Child Development, 63,* 1380–1391.

Walasky, M., Whitbourne, S. K., & Nehrke, M. F. (1983–1984). Construction and validation of an ego-integrity status interview. *International Journal of Aging and Human Development, 18*, 61–72.

Walden, T. A., & Ogan, T. A. (1988). The development of social referencing: *Child Development, 59*, 1230–1240.

Waldman, I. R. (1996). Aggressive boys' hostile perceptual and response biases: The role of attention and impulsivity. *Child Development, 67*, 1015–1033.

Walker, A. (1991). Beauty: When the other dancer is the self. In H. L. Gates Jr. (Ed.), *Bearing witness: Selections from African-American autobiography in the twentieth century* (pp. 257–258). New York: Pantheon Books.

Walker, L. J. (1989). A longitudinal study of moral reasoning. *Child Development, 60*, 157–166.

Walker, L. J., de Vries, B., & Trevethan, S. D. (1987). Moral stages and moral orientations in real-life and hypothetical dilemmas. *Child Development, 58*, 842–858.

Walker, L. J., Gustafson, P., & Hennig, K. H. (2001). The consolidation/transition model in moral reasoning development. *Developmental Psychology, 37*, 187–197.

Walker, L. J., & Taylor, J. H. (1991). Family interactions and the development of moral reasoning. *Child Development, 62*, 262–283.

Walker, R. (2002). Case study, case records, and multimedia. *Cambridge Journal of Education, 32*, 109–127.

Walker-Andrews, A. S. (1986). Intermodal perception of expressive behaviors: Relation of eye and voice? *Developmental Psychology, 22*, 373–377.

Walker-Andrews, A. S., & Harris, P. L. (1993). Young children's comprehension of pretend causal sequences. *Developmental Psychology, 29*, 915–921.

Wallace, E., Hayes, D., & Jerger, J. (1994). Neurotology of aging: The auditory system. In M. L. Albert & J. E. Knoefel (Eds.), *Clinical neurology of aging* (2nd ed., pp. 448–464). New York: Oxford University Press.

Wallechinsky, D., & Wallace, A. (1993). *The book of lists.* New York: Little, Brown.

Wallechinsky, D., Wallace, I., & Wallace, A. (1977). *The book of lists.* New York: Morrow.

Wallerstein, I., & Smith, J. (1991). Households as an institution of the world-economy. In R. L. Blumberg (Ed.), *Gender, family, and economy: The triple overlap* (pp. 225–242). Newbury Park, CA: Sage.

Wallerstein, J., & Blakeslee, S. (1995). *The good marriage.* New York: Houghton Mifflin.

Wallerstein, J. S., & Corbin, S. B. (1989). Daughters of divorce: Report from a 10-year follow-up. *American Journal of Orthopsychiatry, 59*, 593–604.

Walls, C. T., & Zarit, S. H. (1991). Informal support from Black churches and the well-being of elderly Blacks. *The Gerontologist, 31*, 490–495.

Walther, F. J., den Ouden, A. L., & Verloove-Vanhorick, S. P. (2000). Looking back in time: Outcome of a national cohort of very preterm infants born in The Netherlands in 1983. *Early Human Development, 59*, 175–191.

Wang, G.-Z., & Buffalo, M. D. (2004). Social and cultural determinants of attitudes toward abortion. *Social Science Journal, 41*, 93–105.

Wang, H., & Amato, P. R. (2000). Predictors of divorce adjustment: Stressors, resources, and definition. *Journal of Marriage and the Family, 62*, 655–668.

Wang, Q. (2001). Culture effects on adults' earliest childhood recollection and self-description: Implications for the relation between memory and the self. *Journal of Personality and Social Psychology, 81*, 220–233.

Wang, Q., Leichtman, M. D., & Davies, K. (2000). Sharing memories and telling stories: American and Chinese mothers and their 3-year-olds. *Memory, 8*, 159–177.

Watanabe, N., Hasegawa, K., & Yoshinaga, Y. (1996). Suicide in later life in Japan: Urban and rural differences. In J. L. Pearson & Y. Conwell (Eds.), *Suicide and aging: International perspectives* (pp. 121–129). New York: Springer Verlag.

Waterman, A. (1992). Identity as an aspect of optimal psychological functioning. In G. Adams, T. P. Gullotta, & R. Montemayor (Eds.), *Adolescent identity formation: Advances in adolescent development* (Vol. 4., pp. 50–72). Newbury Park, CA: Sage.

Waterman, A. S. (1982). Identity development from adolescence to adulthood: An extension of theory and a review of research. *Developmental Psychology, 18*, 341–358.

Waterman, A. S., & Whitbourne, S. K. (1981). The inventory of psychosocial development. *Journal Supplement Abstract Service: Catalog of Selected Documents in Psychology, 11* (Ms. No. 2179).

Waters, E., Merick, S., Treboux, D., Crowell, J., & Albersheim, L. (2000). Attachment security in infancy and early adulthood: A twenty-year longitudinal study. *Child Development, 71*, 684–689.

Weatherston, D. J. (2001). Infant mental health: A review of relevant literature. *Psychoanalytic Social Work, 8*, 39–69.

Webb, M. (1997). *The good death: The new American search to reshape the end of life.* New York: Bantam Books.

Weber, C., Hahne, A., Friedrich, M., & Friederici, A. D. (2004). Discrimination of word stress in early infant perception: Electrophysiological evidence. *Cognitive Brain Research, 18*, 149–161.

Weber, E. K. (1999). Children's personal prerogative in home and school contexts. *Early Education and Development, 10*, 499–515.

Webster, D. W., Gainer, P. S., & Champion, H. R. (1993). Weapon carrying among inner-city junior high school students: Defensive behavior vs. aggressive delinquency. *American Journal of Public Health, 83*, 1604–1608.

Webster, R. A., Hunter, M., & Keats, J. A. (1994). Peer and parental influences on adolescents' substance use: A path analysis. *International Journal of Addiction, 29*, 647–657.

Weigel, D. J., Devereux, P., Leigh, G. K., & Ballard-Reisch, D. (1998). A longitudinal study of adolescents' perceptions of support and stress: Stability and change. *Journal of Adolescent Research, 13*, 158–177.

Weinfield, N. S., Sroufe, L. A., Egeland, B., & Carlson, E. A. (1999). The nature of individual differences in infant–caregiver attachment. In J. Cassidy & P. R. Shaver (Eds.), *Handbook of attachment: Theory, research, and clinical applications* (pp. 68–88). New York: Guilford Press.

Weingarten, H. R. (1985). Marital status and well-being: A national study comparing first-married, currently divorced, and re-married adults. *Journal of Marriage and the Family, 47*, 653–662.

Weinraub, M., Clemens, L. P., Sockloff, A., Ethridge, T., Gracely, E., & Meyers, B. (1984). The development of sex role stereotypes in the third year: Relationship to gender labeling, identity, sex-typed toy preference, and family characteristics. *Child Development, 55*, 1493–1503.

Weinreb, L., & Buckner, J. C. (1993). Homeless families: Program responses and public policies. *American Journal of Orthopsychiatry, 63*, 400–409.

Weinstein, R. S., Marshall, H. H., Sharp, L., & Botkin, M. (1987). Pygmalion and the student: Age and classroom differences in children's awareness of teacher expectations. *Child Development, 58*, 1079–1093.

Weinstock, H., Berman, S., & Cates, W., Jr. (2004). Sexually transmitted diseases among American youth: Incidence and prevalence estimates 2000. *Perspectives on Sexual and Reproductive Health, 36*, 6–10.

Weismantle, M. (2001). Reasons people do not work, 1996. *Current Population Reports*, P70-76. Washington, DC: U.S. Department of Commerce.

Weiss, B., Dodge, K. A., Bates, J. E., & Petit. G. S. (1992). Some consequences of early harsh discipline: Child aggression and a maladaptive social information processing style. *Child Development, 63*, 1321–1335.

Weiss, R. S. (1997). Adaptation to retirement. In I. H. Gotlib & B. Wheaton (Eds.), *Stress and adversity over the life course: Trajectories and turning points* (pp. 232–245). New York: Cambridge University Press.

Weissberg, R. P., & O'Brien, M. U. (2004). What works in school-based social and emotional learning programs for positive youth development. *Annals of the American Academy of Political and Social Science, 591*, 86–97.

Weist, M. D., & Cooley-Quille, M. (2001). Advancing efforts to address youth violence involvement. *Journal of Clinical Child Psychology, 30*, 147–151.

Wellman, H. M. (1990). *The child's theory of mind.* Cambridge, MA: MIT Press.

Wellman, H. M., Cross, D., & Bartsch, K. (1986). Infant search and object permanence: A meta-analysis of the A-not-B error. *Monographs of the Society for Research in Child Development, 51* (3, Whole No. 214).

Wellman, H., Cross, D., & Watson, J. (2001). Meta-analysis of theory-of-mind development: The truth about false belief. *Child Development, 71,* 655–684.

Wenar, C. (1982). On negativism. *Human Development, 25,* 1–23.

Wentowski, G. J. (1985). Older women's perceptions of great-grandmotherhood: A research note. *The Gerontologist, 25,* 593–596.

Wentworth, N., & Haith, M. M. (1992). Event-specific expectations of 2- and 3-month-old infants. *Developmental Psychology, 28,* 842–850.

Wentzel, K. R., Barry, C. M., & Caldwell, K. A. (2004). Friendships in middle school: Influences on motivation and school adjustment. *Journal of Educational Psychology, 96,* 195–203.

Werker, J. F., & Tees, R. C. (1999). Influences on infant speech processing: Toward a new synthesis. *Annual Review of Psychology, 50,* 509–535.

Werner, E. E. (1991). Grandparent–grandchild relationships amongst U.S. ethnic groups. In P. K. Smith (Ed.), *The psychology of grandparenthood: An international perspective* (pp. 68–82). London: Routledge.

Wesley, P. W., & Buysse, V. (2003). Making meaning of school readiness in schools and communities. *Early Childhood Research Quarterly, 18,* 351–375.

West, J. R. (1986). *Alcohol and brain development.* London: Oxford University Press.

West, J., Denton, K., & Germino-Hausken, E. (2000). *America's kindergartners: Findings from the Early Childhood Longitudinal Study, Kindergarten Class of 1998–99, Fall 1998.* Washington, DC: U.S. Department of Education, National Center for Education Statistics.

West, K. (1999). Is there a solution to the "Charleston Problem"? Retrieved February 8, 2002, from http://www.crbj.com/articles/1999/04261999/Is%20there%20a%20solution%20to%20the%20Charleston%20problem.htm

West, M., & Newton, P. (1983). *The transition from school to work.* London: Croom Helm.

West, R. L., Crook, T. H., & Barron, K. L. (1992). Everyday memory performance across the life span: Effects of age and noncognitive individual differences. *Psychology and Aging, 7,* 72–82.

Wethington, E., Moen, P., Glasgow, N., & Pillemer, K. (2000). Multiple roles, social integration, and health. In K. Pillemer & P. Moen (Eds.), *Social integration in the second half of life* (pp. 48–71). Baltimore: Johns Hopkins University Press.

Whitaker, M. (1993, November 15). White and black lies. *Newsweek,* pp. 52–54.

Whitall, J., & Getchell, N. (1995). From walking to running: Applying a dynamical systems approach to the development of locomotor skills. *Child Development, 66,* 1541–1553.

Whitbeck, L., Hoyt, D. R., & Huck, S. M. (1994). Early family relationships, intergenerational solidarity, and support provided to parents by their adult children. *Journal of Gerontology, 49,* S85–S94.

Whitbourne, S. K. (1986). *The me I know: A study of adult identity.* New York: Springer Verlag.

Whitbourne, S. K., Zuschlag, M. K., Elliot, L. B., & Waterman, A. S. (1992). Psychosocial development in adulthood: A 22-year sequential study. *Journal of Personality and Social Psychology, 63,* 260–271.

White, B. L., Kaban, B. T., & Attanucci, J. S. (1979). *The origins of human competence.* Lexington, MA: Heath.

White, J. M., Wampler, R. S., & Winn, K. I. (1998). The identity style inventory: A revision with a sixth grade reading level (ISI-6G). *Journal of Adolescent Research, 13,* 223–245.

White, L. K. (1990). Determinants of divorce: A review of research in the eighties. *Journal of Marriage and the Family, 52,* 904–912.

White, L., & Rogers, S. J. (2000). Economic circumstances and family outcomes: A review of the 1990s. *Journal of Marriage and the Family, 62,* 1035–1051.

White, N., & Cunningham, W. R. (1988). Is terminal drop pervasive or specific? *Journal of Gerontology, 43,* P141–P144.

White, R. W. (1959). Motivation reconsidered. The concept of competence. *Psychological Review, 66,* 297–333.

White, R. W. (1960). Competence and the psychosexual stages of development. In M. R. Jones (Ed.), *Nebraska Symposium on Motivation* (Vol. 8). Lincoln: University of Nebraska Press.

White, R. W. (1966). *Lives in progress* (2nd ed.). New York: Holt, Rinehart & Winston.

White, R. W. (1974). Strategies of adaptation: An attempt at systematic description. In G. V. Coelho, D. A. Hamburg, & J. E. Adams (Eds.), *Coping and adaptation* (pp. 47–68). New York: Basic Books.

Wichstrom, L. (2001). The impact of pubertal timing on adolescents' alcohol use. *Journal of Research on Adolescence, 11,* 131–150.

Wierson, M., Long, P. J., & Forehand, R. L. (1993). Toward a new understanding of early menarche: The role of environmental stress in pubertal timing. *Adolescence, 28,* 912–924.

Wilcox, A. J., & Skjoerven, R. (1992). Birth weight and perinatal mortality. The effect of gestational age. *American Journal of Public Health, 82,* 378–382.

Wilcox, T., Schweinle, A., & Chapa, C. (2003). Object individuation in infancy. In H. Hayne & J. Fagen (Eds.), *Progress in infancy research* (Vol. 3, pp. 193–243). Mahwah, NJ: Erlbaum.

Williams, C., & Bybee, J. (1994). What do children feel guilty about? Development and gender differences. *Developmental Psychology, 30,* 617–623.

Williams, D. (2000). Ian Thorpe. *Time, 156,* 76–77.

Williams, H. G., & Abernathy, D. (2000). Assessment of gross motor development. In

B. A. Bracken (Ed.), *The psychoeducational assessment of preschool children* (3rd ed., pp. 204–233). Needham Heights, MA: Allyn & Bacon.

Williams, J. C., & Cooper, H. C. (2004). The public policy of motherhood. *Journal of Social Issues, 60,* 849–865.

Williams, J. M., & Currie, C. (2000). Self-esteem and physical development in early adolescence: Pubertal timing and body image. *Journal of Early Adolescence, 20,* 129–149.

Williams, K. (2003). Has the future of marriage arrived? A contemporary examination of gender, marriage, and psychological well-being. *Journal of Health and Social Behavior, 44,* 470–487.

Williams, T. K., & Thornton, M. C. (1998). Social construction of ethnicity versus personal experience: The case of Afro-Amerasians. *Journal of Comparative Family Studies, 29,* 255–267.

Willinger, M., James, L. S., & Catz, C. (1991). Defining the sudden infant death syndrome (SIDS): Deliberations of an expert panel convened by the National Institute of Child Health and Human Development. *Pediatric Pathology, 11,* 677–684.

Willis, S., Diehl, M., Gruber-Baldini, A., Marsiske, M., & Haessler, S. (1990, March). *Correlates and predictors of intellectual performance and intellectual change in older adults.* Paper presented at the Third Cognitive Aging Conference, Atlanta, GA.

Willwerth, J. (1991, May 13). Should we take away their kids? *Time,* pp. 62–63.

Wilmoth, G. H. (1992). Abortion, public health policy, and informed consent legislation. *Journal of Social Issues, 48,* 1–17.

Wilmoth, J. R. (1998). The future of human longevity: A demographer's perspective. *Science, 280,* 395–397.

Wilson, B. J., Smith, S. L., Potter, W. J., Kunkel, D., Linz, D., Colvin, C. M., & Donnerstein, E. (2002). Violence in children's television programming: Assessing the risks. *Journal of Communication, 52,* 5–35.

Wilson, R. S., & Matheny, A. P., Jr. (1986). Behavior genetics research in infant temperament: The Louisville twin study. In R. Plomin & J. Dunn (Eds.), *The study of temperament: Changes, continuities, and challenges.* Hillsdale, NJ: Erlbaum.

Wilson, S. (1995). Quasi-experimental designs. In G. Breakwell, S. Hammond, & C. Fyfe-Schaw (Eds.), *Research methods in psychology* (pp. 113–132). Thousand Oaks, CA: Sage.

Wilson, S. M., Peterson, G. W., & Wilson, P. (1993). The process of educational and occupational attainment of adolescent females from low-income, rural families. *Journal of Marriage and the Family, 55,* 158–175.

Wilson, T. D., LaFleur, S. J., & Anderson, D. E. (1996). The validity and consequences of verbal reports about attitudes. In N. Schwarz & S. Sudum (Eds.), *Answering questions: Methodology for determining cognitive processes in survey research* (pp. 91–114). San Francisco: Jossey Bass.

Wimmer, H. M., & Perner, J. (1983). Beliefs about beliefs: Representation and constraining function of wrong beliefs in young children's understanding of deception. *Cognition, 13*, 103–128.

Wingfield, A., Poon, L. W., Lombardi, L., & Lowe, D. (1985). Speed of processing in normal aging: Effects of speech rate, linguistic structure, and processing time. *Journal of Gerontology, 40*, 579–585.

Winnicut, D. W. (1948/1958). Paediatrics and psychiatry. In *Collected papers: Through paediatrics to psychoanalysis* (pp. 157–173). London: Tavistock.

Winston, R. M. L., & Handyside, A. H. (1993). New challenges in human in vitro fertilization. *Science, 260*, 932–936.

Wolf, A. M., Gortmaker, S. L., Cheung, L., Gray, H. M., Herzog, D. B., & Colditz, G. A. (1993). Activity, inactivity, and obesity: Racial, ethnic, and age differences among schoolgirls. *American Journal of Public Health, 83*, 1625–1627.

Wolf, S. M. (1996). Gender, feminism, and death: Physician-assisted suicide and euthanasia. In S. M. Wolf (Ed.), *Feminism and bioethics: Beyond reproduction*. New York: Oxford University Press.

Wolff, P. H. (1963). Observations on the early development of smiling. In B. M. Foss (Ed.), *Determinants of infant behavior* (Vol. 2). New York: Wiley.

Wolff, P. H. (1966). Causes, controls, and organization of behavior in the neonate. *Psychological Issues, 5* (1, Whole No. 17).

Wolff, P. H. (1987). *The development of behavioral states and the expression of emotions in early infancy*. Chicago: University of Chicago Press.

Wolfinger, N. H. (2003). Family structure homogamy: The effects of parental divorce on partner selection and marital stability. *Social Science Research, 32*, 80–97.

Wong, P. T. P., & Watt, L. M. (1991). What types of reminiscence are associated with successful aging? *Psychology and Aging, 6*, 272–279.

Wood, W., Rhodes, N., & Biek, M. (1995). Working knowledge and attitude strength: An information-processing analysis. In K. E. Petty & J. A. Krosnick (Eds.), *Attitude strength: Antecedents and consequences* (pp. 283–313). Mahwah, NJ: Erlbaum.

Woodward, K. L. (1997, March 10). Today the sheep. *Newsweek*, p. 60.

Woollett, A., & Dosanjh-Matwala, N. (1990). Asian women's experience of childbirth in East London: The support of fathers and female relatives. *Journal of Reproductive and Infant Psychology, 8*, 11–22.

Woolley, J. D., & Wellman, H. M. (1993). Origin and truth: Young children's understanding of imaginary mental representations. *Child Development, 64*, 1–17.

Worchel, F. F., & Allen, M. (1997). Mothers' ability to discriminate cry types in low birth-weight premature and full-term infants. *Children's Health Care, 26*, 183–195.

Worchel, S. (1998). A developmental view of the search for group identity. In S. Worchel & J. F. Morales (Eds.), *Social identity: International perspectives* (pp. 53–74). Thousand Oaks, CA: Sage.

Woyach, R. B. (1991). *Preparing for leadership: A young adult's guide to leadership skills in a global age*. Columbus: Mershon Center, Ohio State University.

Wright, D. W., Nelson, B. S., & Georgen, K. E. (1994). Marital problems. In P. C. McKenry & S. J. Price (Eds.), *Families and change: Coping with stressful events* (pp. 40–65). Thousand Oaks, CA: Sage.

Wright, J. C., Huston, A. C., Murphy, K. C., St. Peters, M., Pinon, M., Scantlin, R., & Kotler, J. (2001). The relations of early television viewing to school readiness and vocabulary of children from low-income families: The early window project. *Child Development, 72*, 1347–1366.

Wright, J. D., & Devine, J. A. (1993). Family backgrounds and the substance-abusive homeless: The New Orleans experience. *The Community Psychologist, 26*, 35–37.

Wulf, S. (1997). How to teach our children well. (It can be done.) *Time, 150*, 62–69.

Wylleman, P. (2000). Interpersonal relationships in sport: Uncharted territory in sport psychology research. *International Journal of Sport Psychology, 31*, 555–572.

Xu, F. (2003). The development of object individuation in infancy. In H. Hayne & J. Fagen (Eds.), *Progress in infancy research* (Vol. 3, pp. 159–192). Mahwah, NJ: Erlbaum.

Yang, R. K., Zweig, A. R., Douthitt, T. C., & Federman, E. J. (1976). Successive relationships between maternal attitudes during pregnancy, analgesic medication during labor and delivery, and newborn behavior. *Developmental Psychology, 12*, 6–14.

Yarrow, L. J. (1963). Research in dimensions of early maternal care. *Merrill-Palmer Quarterly, 9*, 101–114.

Yarrow, L. J. (1964). Separation from parents in early childhood. In M. L. Hoffman & L. W. Hoffman (Eds.), *Review of child development research* (Vol. 1). New York: Sage.

Yarrow, L. J. (1970). The development of focused relationships during infancy. In J. Hellmuth (Ed.), *Exceptional infant* (Vol. 1). New York: Brunner/Mazel.

Yarrow, L. J., McQuiston, S., MacTurk, R. H., McCarthy, M. E., Klein, R. P., & Vietze, P. M. (1983). The assessment of mastery motivation during the first year of life. *Developmental Psychology, 19*, 159–171.

Yasui, M., Dorham, C. L., & Dishion, T. Y. (2004). Ethnic identity and psychological adjustment: A validity analysis for European American and African American adolescents. *Journal of Adolescent Research, 19*, 807–825.

Yates, A. (1989). Current perspectives on the eating disorders: 1. History, psychological, and biological aspects. *Journal of the American Academy of Child and Adolescent Psychiatry, 28*, 813–828.

Yates, M., & Youniss, J. (1996). Community service and political-moral identity in adolescents. *Journal of Research on Adolescence, 6*, 271–284.

Yau, J., & Smetana, J. G. (2003). Conceptions of moral, social-conventional, and personal events among Chinese preschoolers in Hong Kong. *Child Development, 74*, 647–658.

Yerushalmi, H. (1993). Stagnation in supervision as a result of developmental problems in the middle-aged supervisor. *Clinical Supervisor, 11*, 63–81.

Yeung, W. J., Sandberg, J. F., Davis-Kean, P. E., & Hofferth, S. L. (2001). Children's time with fathers in intact families. *Journal of Marriage and the Family, 63*, 136–154.

Yin, R. K. (1994). *Case study research: Design and methods*. Thousand Oaks, CA: Sage.

Yordanova, J., Kolev, V., Hohnsbein, J., & Falkenstein, M. (2004). Sensory slowing with ageing is mediated by a functional dysregulation of motor-generation processes: Evidence from high-resolution event-related potentials. *Brain, 127*, 351–362.

Youngblade, L. M., & Belsky, J. (1992). Parent–child antecedents of 5-year-olds' close friendships: A longitudinal analysis. *Developmental Psychology, 28*, 700–713.

Youngblade, L. M., & Dunn, J. (1995). Individual differences in young children's pretend play with mother and sibling: Links to relationships and understanding of other people's feelings and beliefs. *Child Development, 66*, 1472–1492.

Younger, B. (1992). Developmental change in infant categorization: The perception of correlations among facial features. *Child Development, 63*, 1526–1535.

Youniss, J. (1980). *Parents and peers in social development: A Sullivan-Piaget perspective*. Chicago: University of Chicago Press.

Youniss, J., McLellan, J. A., & Strouse, D. (1994). "We're popular, but we're not snobs": Adolescents describe their crowds. In R. Montemeyor, G. R., Adams, & T. P. Gwllotta (Eds.), *Personal relationships during adolescence. Advances in adolescent development* (Vol. 6, pp. 101–122). Thousand Oaks, CA: Sage.

Yurdakok, K., Yavuz, T., & Taylor, C. E. (1990). Swaddling and acute respiratory infections. *American Journal of Public Health, 80*, 873–875.

Zahn-Waxler, C., & Kochanska, G. (1990). The origins of guilt. In R. A. Thompson (Ed.), *Nebraska Symposium on Motivation, 1988* (Vol. 36, pp. 183–258). Lincoln: University of Nebraska Press.

Zahn-Waxler, C., Kochanska, G., Krupnick, J., & McKnew, D. (1990). Patterns of guilt in children of depressed and well mothers. *Developmental Psychology, 26*, 51–59.

Zahn-Waxler, C., Radke-Yarrow, M., & King, R. A. (1977). *The impact of the affective environment on young children*. Paper presented at the biennial meeting of the Society for Research in Child Development, New Orleans, LA.

Zahn-Waxler, C., Radke-Yarrow, M., Wagner, E., & Chapman, M. (1992). Development of concern for others. *Developmental Psychology, 28*, 126–136.

Zahn-Waxler, C., Robinson, J. L., & Emde, R. N. (1992). The development of empathy in twins. *Developmental Psychology, 28,* 1038–1047.

Zakriski, A. L., & Coie, J. D. (1996). A comparison of aggressive-rejected and nonaggressive-rejected children's interpretations of self-directed and other-directed rejection. *Child Development, 67,* 1048–1070.

Zarit, S. H., & Eggebeen, D. J. (1995). Parent–child relationships in adulthood and old age. In M. Bornstein (Ed.), *Handbook of parenting: Vol. 1. Children and parenting* (pp. 119–140). Mahwah, NJ: Erlbaum.

Zayas, L. H., & Solari, F. (1994). Early childhood socialization in Hispanic families: Context, culture, and practice implications. *Professional Psychology: Research and Practice, 25,* 200–206.

Zelinski, E. M., & Lewis, K. L. (2003). Adult age differences in multiple cognitive functions: Differentiation, dedifferentiation, or process-specific change. *Psychology and Aging, 18,* 727–745.

Zeskind, P. S. (1983). Cross-cultural differences in maternal perceptions of cries of low- and high-risk infants. *Child Development, 54,* 1119–1128.

Zeskind, P. S., Klein, L., & Marshall, T. R. (1992). Adult's perceptions of experimental modifications of durations of pauses and expiratory sounds in infant crying. *Developmental Psychology, 28,* 1153–1162.

Zettel, L. A., & Rook, K. S. (2004). Substitution and compensation in the social networks of older widowed women. *Psychology and Aging, 19,* 433–443.

Zhao, H., Brooks-Gunn, J., McLanahan, S., & Singer, B. (2000). Studying the real child rather than the ideal child: Bringing the person into developmental studies. In L. R. Bergman, R. B. Cairns, L. Nilsson, & L. Nystedt (Eds.), *Developmental science and the holistic approach* (pp. 393–419). Mahwah, NJ: Erlbaum.

Zick, C. D., & Smith, K. R. (1991). Patterns of economic change surrounding the death of a spouse. *Journal of Gerontology, 46,* S310–S320.

Ziegert, D. I., Kistner, J. A., Castro, R., & Robertson, B. (2001). Longitudinal study of young children's responses to challenging achievement situations. *Child Development, 72,* 609–624.

Zigler, E. F., Kagan, S. L., & Hall, N. W. (1996). *Children, families, and government: Preparing for the twenty-first century.* Cambridge, UK: Cambridge University Press.

Zigler, E., & Styfco, S. (2004). Moving Head Start to the states: One experiment too many. *Applied Developmental Science, 8,* 51–55.

Zilbach, J. J. (1993). Female adolescence: Toward a separate line of female development. In M. Sugar (Ed.), *Female adolescent development* (2nd ed., pp. 45–61). New York: Brunner/Mazel.

Zill, N., & West, J. (2000). *Entering kindergarten: A portrait of American children when they begin school.* Washington, DC: National Center for Educational Statistics. Retrieved August 21, 2001, from http://nces.ed.gov/pubs2000/coe2000/entering_kindergarten.html

Zimmerman, B. J., Bandura, A., & Martinez-Pons, M. (1992). Self-motivation for academic attainment: The role of self-efficacy beliefs and personal goal setting. *American Educational Research Journal, 29,* 663–676.

Zimmerman, M. A., Salem, D. A., & Maton, K. I. (1995). Family structure and psychosocial correlates among urban African-American adolescent males. *Child Development, 66,* 1598–1613.

Ziv, M., & Frye, D. (2003). The relation between desire and false belief in children's theory of mind: No satisfaction? *Developmental Psychology, 39,* 859–876.

Zucker, A. N. (1999, May). The psychological impact of reproductive difficulties in women's lives. *Sex Roles: A Journal of Research,* 767–779.

Zucker, K. J. (1985). The infant's construction of his parents in the first six months of life. In T. M. Field & N. A. Fox (Eds.), *Social perception in infants.* Norwood, NJ: Ablex.

Zuckerman, B., Frank, D. A., & Hingson, R. (1989). Effects of maternal marijuana and cocaine use on fetal growth. *The New England Journal of Medicine, 320,* 762–768.

Zuckerman, C. (1997). Issues concerning end-of-life care. *Journal of Long Term Home Health Care, 16,* 26–34.

Zuo, J. (1992). The reciprocal relationship between marital interaction and marital happiness: A three-wave study. *Journal of Marriage and the Family, 54,* 870–878.

Zur, O., & Gelman, R. (2004). Young children can add and subtract by predicting and checking. *Early Childhood Research Quarterly, 19,* 121–137.

Zuravin, S. J. (1988). Child maltreatment and teenage first births: A relationship mediated by chronic sociodemographic stress? *American Journal of Orthopsychiatry, 58,* 91–103.

# Credits

# Name Index

Abel, E. L., 121
Abell, S. C., 306, 356
Aber, J. L., 203, 297
Abernathy, D., 184, 185
Abrams, L., 358
Acevedo, M. C., 169
Achenbach, T. M., 316
Acitelli, L. K., 402
Acredolo, C., 312
Adam, J. J., 480–81
Adams, A., 312
Adams, B. N., 394
Adams, G. R., 374, 393
Adams, P. W., 234
Adamson, L. B., 166
Adegoke, A. A., 307
Ades, P. A., 508
Adey, P., 314
Adler, A., 289
Adler, J., 322
Adler, N. E., 131
Adler, P., 23
Adler, P. A., 23
Adler, T. F., 283, 387
Adolph, K. E., 144, 146
Affleck, G., 52
Affonso, D. D., 55
Ahadi, S. A., 206
Ainsworth, M. D. S., 149, 151, 152, 153, 154, 156, 169
Ainsworth-Darnell, J., 447
Aitken, K. J., 166
Aksan, N., 204
Alasker, F. D., 308
Albert, M. S., 476
Albert, S., 211
Albino, A. W., 156
Albom, M., 471, 491
Alessandri, S. M., 164, 170
Alessandria, I., 511
Alexander, B. H., 123
Alexander, K. L., 113, 282, 284, 292
Alho, K., 110
Allen, J. P., 323, 349, 352
Allen, K. R., 450
Allen, L., 232
Allen, M., 138, 404
Allen, N. J., 441
Allen, S., 533
Allison, A., 328
Almeida, D. M., 405
Als, H., 161
Alter, R. C., 131
Alvada, J. F., 352
Amato, P. R., 426, 427
Amgott, T., 211
Amlie, C., 229
Amsel, E., 314
Amundson, N. E., 415
Andersen, C., 275
Anderson, A. H., 282
Anderson, C. A., 239
Anderson, D. E., 30
Anderson, D. R., 241
Anderson, E. R., 485
Anderson, R. C., 278
Anderssen, N., 229
Andersson, K., 55
Andrulis, D. P., 533
Aneshensel, C. S., 512, 513, 548
Angelillo, C., 193
Angleitner, A., 96
Anglin, J. M., 191
Annand, M. F., 505
Antonio, A. L., 378
Antonucci, T. C., 529
Aoki, C., 106
Apgar, V., 137
Apospori, E., 343
Appelbaum, M. I., 183
Aquilino, W. S., 450

Arauz, R. M., 193
Arbuckle, T., 530
Archer, J., 62
Archer, S. L., 374, 393
Ardila-Rey, A., 234
Arenberg, D., 476
Arias, E., 12
Aries, E., 224
Armeli, S., 52
Armstrong, B., 332
Armstrong, B. G., 121
Arnaud, L., 508
Arnett, J. J., 351, 352, 372, 392
Arnold, M. L., 234
Aronfreed, J., 231
Arriaga, X. B., 422
Aryanpour, M., 184
Aseltine, R. H., 320
Aseltine, R. H., Jr., 319
Asher, S. R., 267, 268, 270
Ashikaga, T., 508
Ashton, M. C., 441
Aslin, R. N., 139, 140, 189
Assel, M. A., 176
Atchley, R. C., 496, 499
Atkinson, D. R., 378
Atkinson, J. W., 288
Atkinson, L., 156
Atkinson, R., 29, 519
Attie, I., 325
Au, T. K., 272
Avery, C. S., 422
Axinn, W. G., 393
Ayduk, O., 206, 211
Ayers, M., 268
Azar, B., 215
Azria, M. R., 250

Baak, K., 151, 155
Bacanli, H., 420
Bachman, J. G., 341, 342, 343, 381
Bachu, A., 405, 408
Bagwell, C. L., 269
Bailey, J. M., 96, 229
Baillargeon, R., 157, 158, 160
Bakeman, R., 25, 166, 228
Baker, H. A., Jr., 371
Baker, L. S., 258
Bakermans-Kranenburg, M. J., 237
Bakken, L., 272
Balchin, N., 287
Baldacci, H. B., 239
Baldwin, D. A., 195
Bales, R. F., 81
Ballard-Reisch, D., 336
Ballor, D. L., 508
Balogh, R. D., 142
Balter, N., 63
Baltes, M. M., 517
Baltes, P. B., 4, 64, 474, 478, 495, 496, 515, 517
Bandura, A., 75, 76, 203, 207, 232, 240, 254, 280, 281, 293
Bank, B. J., 419
Bank, L., 455
Bankart, B., 114
Barbaranelli, C., 281
Barbee, A. H., 33
Barber, B. L., 327
Barber, J. S., 406
Barbu, S., 250
Bard, K. A., 121
Barinaga, M., 96, 463–64
Barke, C., 362, 363
Barnard, K. E., 118
Barnes, G. M., 342
Barnett, D., 154
Barnett, R. C., 217, 404, 405, 438, 439

Barr, H. M., 121
Barrera, R. E., 114
Barrett, K. C., 165
Barry, C. M., 267
Barth, J. M., 226
Bartholemew, K., 418
Bartholomae, S., 329
Bar-Yam, M., 57
Bar-Yam Hassan, A., 57
Bashore, T. R., 509
Bass, D. M., 485
Bass, S. A., 488
Bassett, M. T., 122
Bates, E., 186, 190
Bates, J. E., 147, 205
Batson, C. D., 237
Bauer, K., 108, 225, 354, 382, 442, 444, 524
Bauer, P. J., 226
Baulieu, E., 128
Baum, S. K., 493
Bauman, K. E., 321
Baumgardner, J., 239
Bavin, S., 486
Beale, R. L., 437
Beall, A. E., 423
Beaman, J., 455
Beard, A. J., 228
Beardsall, L., 197
Beardsley, T., 98
Bearman, P. S., 327
Beaudet, A., 505
Beaulieu, L., 287
Beaumont, R., 486
Beck, J. C., 441
Beck, S., 463–64
Becker, G., 482
Beckman, D., 163, 164
Beere, C. A., 226
Begley, S., 104
Beishuizen, J. J., 275
Beit-Hallahmi, B., 236
Belanger, N. D., 160
Bell, C., 29
Bell, N., 272
Bell, R. M., 381
Bell, S. M., 151, 169
Bellugi, U., 186
Belsky, J., 152, 153, 155, 164, 165, 169, 203, 250, 266, 394, 407, 423, 545
Bem, S. L., 226, 356
Benasich, A. A., 140
Benedict, R., 78, 81
Benenson, J., 250, 251
Benenson, J. F., 251
Bengston, V. L., 481
Bengtsgard, K., 55
Benjet, C., 308
Bennett, J. M., 529
Benson, M. J., 352
Bepko, C. S., 357
Berg, J. H., 420
Berg, K., 533
Bergeman, C. S., 527
Bergen, A., 474
Bergman, A., 182
Berkman, L. F., 528
Berkowitz, L., 203, 240
Berlin, L. J., 266
Berman, R. C., 52
Berman, S., 329
Berman, W. H., 351
Bernard, J., 421
Bernasco, W., 417
Berndt, T., 334
Berndt, T. J., 265
Bernichon, T., 247
Bernier, A., 352
Bertonicini, J., 140
Berzonsky, M. D., 373, 374, 376

Bess, A., 264
Best, C. T., 193
Best, K. M., 349
Betancourt, H., 78
Bettencourt, B. A., 333, 335
Bettinger, M., 358
Bianchi, S. M., 452, 455
Biddle, B. J., 81, 83
Bierman, K. L., 334
Biggar, J. C., 519
Bigler, 226, 287
Bigler, R. S., 226
Bijstra, J., 272
Billy, J. O. G., 326
Bingham, C. R., 327
Birch, D., 288
Birch, H., 147
Birditt, K. S., 453
Biringen, Z., 183
Birren, J. E., 508, 509, 515
Bish, A., 103
Bishop, C. E., 520
Bjorklund, D. F., 200, 287
Blackwell, D. L., 394
Blain, M. D., 352
Blair, C., 259
Blair, S. N., 285
Blair-Loy, M., 409
Blakeslee, S., 443
Blanchard, C., 287
Blanchard, K. H., 453
Blasi, A., 360, 370
Blass, E. M., 142
Blatt, S. J., 316
Blazer, D., 528
Bleeker, M. M., 364
Blehar, M. C., 152, 154
Bliesszner, R., 450
Bloom, L., 189
Bloom, M. V., 351
Blos, P., 39, 182
Bluck, S., 477
Blum, R. W., 318
Blumenfeld, P., 245
Blustein, D., 349
Blustein, D. L., 374
Blyth, D. A., 308, 309
Boardman, S. K., 8, 28
Bobrow, D., 229
Boerner, K., 551
Bogdan, R., 18, 22, 24, 26–27, 28
Boggs, P. P., 445
Bogue, D. J., 338
Bohan, J. S., 224
Bohlin, G., 55
Bohlmeijer, E., 495
Boivin, M., 270
Bolton, F. G., Jr., 307
Bomar, J. A., 349
Bombar, M. L., 398
Bonanno, G. A., 486
Bongar, B., 530
Boom, J., 233
Booth, A., 309, 426
Borden, G. A., 7
Borden, W., 68
Borke, H., 237
Borkenau, P., 96
Borman, K. M., 363
Bornstein, M. H., 178
Bornstein, J. H., 140
Bornstein, M. H., 83, 139, 155, 176, 198, 202
Borrell, K., 524
Borton, R. W., 143
Boss, P., 545, 551, 552
Bosse, R., 499
Bost, K. K., 146
Bosworth, H. B., 529
Botkin, M., 248, 282
Bottge, B. A., 292

Bouchard, T. J., Jr., 96
Boudreau, J. P., 142
Bouldin, P., 201
Boulton, M. J., 267
Bound, J., 485
Bowen, G. L., 413
Bowen, M., 86
Bower, T. G. R., 143
Bowker, A., 269, 270, 334
Bowlby, J., 148–49, 150, 151, 171
Bowman, K., 485
Boyatzis, C. J., 199
Boyce, W. T., 169
Boyer, M. E., 273
Boyes, M., 313
Boykin, A. W., 57
Boyle, F. M., 274
Boyle, J. S., 118
Brack, G. A., 115
Bradbury, R., 541–42
Bradford, J., 401
Bradley, C. B., 306
Bradley, R. H., 213
Bradmetz, J., 274, 315
Bradshaw, D., 165
Bradshaw, Z., 131
Braine, M. D. S., 190
Brainerd, C. J., 272
Braithwaite, V., 173
Brambilla, D. J., 445
Bramlett, M. D., 424, 425
Branch, L. G., 520
Brandenburg, D. L., 320
Brandon, P. E., 485
Brandstadter, J., 471
Branje, S. J. T., 403
Braungart, J. M., 147
Braungart-Rieker, J. M., 154
Braunwold, K., 154
Brazelton, R.B., 161
Brazelton, T. B., 124, 146, 147, 148, 210
Brazy, J. E., 110
Breakwell, G. M., 370
Breault, K. D., 425
Brennan, K. A., 418
Brennan, R. T., 304, 404, 405
Bretherton, I., 152, 153, 245
Brewster, A. L., 163
Bridges, L. J., 152, 204
Brierley, J., 139, 307
Brim, G., 460, 472
Brim, O. G., Jr., 81, 387
Brinkerhoff, A. L., 415
Britner, P. A., 149
Broderick, C. B., 85
Brodersen, L., 151
Bronfenbrenner, U., 84, 453
Bronfman, E., 154
Bronson, G., 123
Bronson, G. W., 149
Bronstein, P., 447
Brook, J., 320, 321, 420
Brookes, H., 142
Brooks-Gunn, J., 9, 303, 304, 306, 307, 325
Brookshire, R. G., 478
Brown, B. B., 321, 322, 323, 324, 336, 337
Brown, D. W., 13
Brown, J., 122, 197, 331
Brown, J. D., 247, 248
Brown, J. L., 124, 213, 297
Brown, J. R., 196, 204
Brown, M. M., 235, 252
Brown, P. J., 268
Brown, R., 81, 498
Brown, S. C., 277
Browne, B. A., 283
Brownell, C. A., 265, 267
Browning, C. R., 533

Brownlee, S., 186, 303
Brubaker, T. H., 449
Brueckner, H., 327
Bruening, P., 138
Brugman, D., 233
Bruner, J., 159
Brustad, R. J., 286
Bryan, A., 342
Bryer, K. B., 547, 548
Buckley, S., 100
Buckwalter, J. G., 114
Buescher, P. A., 118
Buffalo, M. D., 131
Buhler, C., 390
Bui, K., 379
Bui, K.-V. T., 394
Bukowski, W. M., 251, 266
Bulcroft, R., 308, 309
Bullinger, A., 140
Bullock, H. E., 212, 412, 413
Bullock, M., 203
Bullough, V. L., 308
Bumpus, M. F., 439
Bunting, L., 331, 332
Burbank, P., 489
Burchinal, M. R., 195, 215, 379
Burg, S. J., 319
Burgess, E. W., 338
Burke, B., 201
Burleson, B. R., 235, 266, 403,
    404
Burnett, D., 482
Burr, J. A., 518
Burt, R. D., 113
Burtless, G., 413
Burton, S., 285
Bus, A. G., 278
Bush, P. J., 343
Bushnell, E. W., 142
Buss, A. H., 147
Buss, D., 395
Buss, F. L., 224
Butler, R., 248, 280
Butterfield, E. C., 275
Butterfield, N., 201
Butterfield, P., 166
Buunk, B. P., 395, 435
Buzzanca, J., 103
Buzzanca, L., 103
Bybee, J., 253
Byer, A. L., 418
Byers, J. L., 282
Byles, J. E., 486
Byrd, M., 352
Byrd-Craven, J., 277, 395
Byrne, A., 100

Cadigan, D., 282
Cagney, K. A., 533
Cain, K. M., 289
Caldwell, K. A., 267
Calkins, S. D., 147, 164, 174
Calment, J., 504
Calvert, G., 142
Camburn, D., 327
Cameron, R. P., 115
Campbell, B. C., 123
Campbell, F. A., 212
Campbell, S. B., 153
Campos, J. J., 147, 165, 166,
    183
Campos, L., 459, 460
Campos, R. G., 165, 169
Camras, L. A., 163
Canfield, R. L., 140
Canobi, K. H., 274
Cantor, N., 173, 420
Caplan, G., 547
Caplan, R. D., 441
Capozzoli, M., 159
Cappeliez, P., 495
Capps, S., 332
Caprara, G. V., 281
Cardozo, S., 445
Carlson, E. A., 152, 156
Carlson, S. M., 201
Carlson, V., 154
Carmichael, P. J., 4, 6, 7, 8–9,
    11–12
Carnagey, N. I., 239
Carnes, B. A., 13, 505
Carney, M. A., 52
Caro, F. G., 488
Caron, A. J., 141

Caron, R. F., 141
Carossino, P., 124, 128
Carp, F. M., 500
Carpenter, E. M., 268
Carper, J., 13
Carr, D., 485, 524, 542, 548
Carrell, P. L., 187
Carrere, S., 442
Carrick, R., 29
Carroll, J. L., 232
Carskadon, M. A., 310
Cart, C. U., 319
Cartwright, B. S., 201
Carvalho, A. M. A., 250
Casey, R. J., 155
Cashon, C. H., 141
Caspary, G., 217
Casper, L. M., 350, 452, 455
Caspi, A., 288, 309, 389
Cassady, G., 118, 123
Cassia, V. M., 141
Cassidy, J., 152, 171, 266, 268
Castejon, J. L., 276
Castleman, M., 494
Castro, R., 248, 290
Catalan, J., 10
Cate, R. M., 397
Cates, W., Jr., 329
Catherwood, D., 141
Catz, C., 112
Cavanaugh, J. C., 478
Caya, L., 250
Ceballo, R., 212
Cerella, J., 509
Cernkovich, S. A., 340
Cernoch, J. M., 142
Chaffee, M., 335
Chaikelson, J., 530
Chalmers, J. B., 267
Champion, H. R., 318
Chandler, M., 313
Chang, E. C., 474
Chang, K., 521
Chang, J., 236
Chang, M. J., 378
Chao, W., 455
Chapa, C., 160
Chapman, M., 204, 273
Charlesworth, W. R., 63, 64
Chase-Lansdale, P. L., 9
Chatters, L. M., 9, 395
Chaudry, A., 9
Chavez, A., 124
Chavez, V., 297
Chazan, S. E., 160
Cheavens, J., 171
Chen, D. W., 552
Chen, C., 279
Chen, H., 122, 331
Chen, M. D., 419
Chen, X., 148, 310
Cheour-Luhtanen, M., 110
Cherlin, A. J., 330
Chess, S., 146, 147
Chevan, A., 518
Chickering, A. W., 360
Childs, C. P., 146
Chilman, C. S., 355
Chipman, M., 154
Chisholm, G., 151, 155
Choi, N. G., 518
Chopak, J. S., 327
Christensen, A., 443
Christiansen, S. L., 55
Church, G. J., 365
Church, J., 143, 206, 211
Ciaramitaro, V., 142
Cicchetti, D., 154, 165
Cicirelli, V. G., 492
Cinq-Mars, C., 331
Clancy, S. M., 373
Clark, A. L., 127
Clark, B., 336
Clark, C. L., 155
Clark, F. L., 272
Clark, J. E., 183, 184
Clark, K. E., 434
Clark, M. B., 434
Clark, M. L., 268, 292
Clark, R. D., III, 237
Clark, S. D., 490
Clarke, S. C., 524
Clark-Ibanez, M., 397
Clasen, D. R., 337

Clausen, J. A., 308
Clayton, V. P., 515
Clement, C., 314
Clifton, R., 140
Clifton, R. K., 143
Clingempeel, W. G., 182
Clipp, E. C., 389
Clogg, C. C., 451
Cloud, J., 29, 542
Coan, J., 442
Coats, P. B., 286
Cobb, S., 527
Cochran, C. C., 380
Cochran-Smith, M., 279
Cody, H., 100
Cohan, C. L., 405
Cohane, G. H., 307
Cohen, C., 141
Cohen, D., 141
Cohen, L. B., 141
Cohen, M. A., 520
Cohen, O., 425
Cohen, P., 122, 320, 321, 331,
    420
Cohen, R., 266
Cohen, R. S., 446
Cohen-Kettenis, P. T., 354
Cohn, B., 452
Cohn, D. A., 155
Cohn, J. F., 153, 169
Coie, J. D., 269, 270
Colbs, S. L., 488
Colby, A., 359, 361
Coldren, J. T., 140
Cole, M., 292
Coleman, E., 421
Coleman, J. S., 291
Coleman, P. G., 517
Colin, V., 152
Coll, C. G., 136
Collin, A., 412
Collins, K., 521
Collins, N., 155
Collins, W., 324
Colombo, J., 140
Colten, M. E., 320
Colvin, T. N., 250
Colwell, M. J., 201
Comer, J., 259
Commons, M. L., 315, 507
Comstock, G. A., 240
Conaway, W. A., 7
Conger, R. D., 177, 212, 308,
    309, 320, 455
Conley, J., 115
Connell, J. P., 152, 204
Connolly, C., 329
Connolly, J., 270, 325
Connolly, K., 158
Constantinople, A., 55, 56
Contreras, J. M., 482
Conway, M., 530
Cook, K. E., 247
Cook, R., 103
Cooke, M. C., 232
Cool, L. E., 530
Cooley-Quille, M., 296
Coombs, R. H., 343
Cooney, T. M., 350, 407
Cooper, H. C., 409
Cooper, M. L., 156
Copple, C., 197
Corcoran, M. E., 9
Corina, D. P., 186
Cornelius, M. D., 120
Correa-Chavez, M., 193
Correa-Villasenor, A., 123
Correll, S. J., 364, 438, 465
Cosden, M., 122
Cose, E., 464
Cosmides, L., 63
Costa, F. M., 382
Costa, P. T., 473
Costabile, A., 250
Cota-Robles, S., 309
Cotten, S. R., 426
Couzin, J., 13
Cowan, C. P., 23, 83, 155, 182
Cowan, P. A., 23, 83, 155, 182
Coward, R. T., 21
Cox, A., 278
Cox, M., 485
Cox, M. J., 149, 257
Cox, R., 485

Coy, K. C., 206, 336
Coyle, A., 401
Coyne, A., 401
Craig, I. W., 136
Craig, W. M., 270
Craig-Bray, L., 374, 393
Crain, W. C., 55
Crain-Thoreson, C., 195
Cramer, P., 66
Crassini, B., 140
Crawford, J. R., 477
Crawford, T. N., 320, 321
Crick, N. R., 268
Crimmins, E. M., 9
Crnic, K., 164, 203
Crocker, J., 335
Crockett, L. J., 327
Crohan, S. E., 407
Cronbach, L. J., 33
Crooks, R. L., 108, 225, 354,
    382, 442, 444, 524
Cropley, M., 320
Crosby, R. A., 331
Crosnoe, R., 473, 474
Cross, D., 246
Cross, S. I., 296
Cross, W. E., 340, 377
Crouter, A. C., 309, 416, 439
Crowe, J., 409–11
Crowell, J. A., 418
Crozier, L. C., 494
Cuddy, A. J. C., 465
Cuijpers, P., 495
Cukan, A., 465
Culbertson, S. A., 75
Cullen, C., 74
Cummings, E. M., 47, 154, 203
Cummings, J. S., 203
Cummings, S. S., 285
Cunningham, F. G., 97, 110,
    111, 128
Cunningham, J. D., 418
Cunningham, P. B., 318
Cunningham, W. R., 476
Currie, C., 309
Currie, L. A., 275
Cutler, N., 523
Cutrona, C. E., 528
Cutting, A. L., 237
Cyr, M., 331

Dagnan, D., 320
Dahl, R. E., 310
Dale, P. S., 195
Dalgleish, M., 158
Dalgleish, T., 296
Daling, J. R., 113
Dalton, S. S., 293
Damon, W., 233, 243–46, 251,
    359, 361
Dancy, B. L., 455
D'Andrade, R., 292
Danish, S. J., 343
Dann, S., 26
Darby, B. L., 121
Darling, N., 322, 324
Darling-Fisher, C. S., 55
Darwin, C., 38, 62–63, 161
Das, R., 206
Datan, N., 323
Davey, A., 528, 530
Davey, G., 74
David, B., 361
Davidson, K., 524
Davies, K., 246
Davillier, M., 138
Davis, A., 30
Davis, C. C., 210
Davis, K. E., 398
Davis-Floyd, R. E., 127
Davis-Kean, P. E., 176, 248
Davison, M. L., 40
Davydov, V. V., 72
Daw, J., 441
Dawson, T. L., 359
Day, N. L., 120
DeAngelis, T., 156, 317
Dearing, R. L., 210
Deater-Deckard, K., 116, 168
Deaux, K., 82, 522
DeBoer, D. D., 426
DeBord, K. A., 418
DeCasper, A. J., 110, 111, 139
Decety, J., 254
Deeg, D. J. H., 57

Deenen, A. A., 401
Defey, D., 445
DeFrias, C. M., 479
DeFries, J. C., 136, 147
DeGenova, M. K., 393, 482
DeGrazia, D., 540
Dekeyser, M., 23
Delaney-Black, V., 121
De Magalhaes, J. P., 13
DeMaris, A., 340, 486
Demetriou, A., 312
Demetriou, H., 237
Demo, D. H., 426, 427
Deng, S., 306
Denmark, F. L., 438
Denner, J., 355
den Ouden, A. L., 138
Denton, K., 258
Denzin, N. K., 18
Derryberry, D., 147
Desesquelles, A., 13
de Silva, P., 423
Desimone, L. M., 413
DeSoto, M. C., 277
Desrochers, S., 160
de St. Aubin, E., 7, 41, 43, 55,
    131, 458, 459
Devereux, P., 336
DeVos, J., 160
de Vries, B., 361
DeVries, M. R., 209
DeVries, M. W., 209
DeVries, R., 234
Diamond, A., 310
Diamond, L. M., 326, 327
Diamond, M. J., 117
Diaz, J., 444
Diaz, O., 445
Dichter, G. S., 320
Dickinson, D. K., 191
DiClemente, R. J., 331
Diehl, M., 475, 509, 516
Dielman, T., 334
Diener, C. I., 289
Dietz-Uhler, B., 335
DiFazio, I., 511
Dill, D., 420
Dillon, R. F., 120
Dilorio, C., 115
DiMatteo, M. R., 113
Dindia, K., 404
Dion, K. K., 394
Dion, K. L., 394
DiPietro, J. A., 116, 138
DiPietro, L., 489
Dishion, T. J., 266, 336
Dishion, T. Y., 379
DiVitto, B., 138
Dixon, R. A., 476
Doakes, S. S., 122
Dobson, W. R., 374, 393
Dodge, K. A., 205, 235, 252,
    269
Dole, N., 113, 119
Dolenszky, E., 250, 251
Dollahite, D. C., 458
Dollinger, S. J., 373
Domar, A. D., 103
Domino, G., 55
Donald, M., 315, 329
Donnellan, M. B., 248
Donovan, J. E., 382
Dorfman, L., 297
Dorham, C. L., 379
Dornbusch, S. M., 349, 362
Dosanjh-Matwala, N., 117
Dougher, K., 379
Douvan, E., 402
Dowler, J. K., 123
Dowling, E., 85
Doyle, A., 272
Dreman, S., 437
Drew, L. M., 481, 485
Driver, J., 484
Dryfoos, J. G., 260
Dubiner, K., 159
Duff, R. W., 520
Dulberg, C. S., 120
Dun, S. A., 403, 404
Dunbar, E., 335
Dunbar, N., 355
Duncan, G. J., 9, 485
Duncan, T. E., 281

Dunkel-Schetter, C., 114, 128, 405
Dunkley, T. L., 304, 317
Dunn, J. F., 116, 196, 197, 202, 204, 237
Dunn, M., 523
Dunne, M., 329
Dunning, D., 285
Dunphy, D. C., 325
Duran-Aydintug, C., 427
Durbin, D. L., 322, 324
Durham, M., 195, 379
Durik, A. M., 113
Dustman, R., 508
Dutton, K. A., 247
Duvall, E. M., 446
Dweck, C. S., 173, 289
Dwyer, K., 272
Dwyer, P., 466
Dyk, P. H., 393

Earls, F., 297, 304, 533
Early, D. M., 257
East, P. L., 336
Easterbrook, M. A., 139
Easton, M. M., 284
Eccles, J. S., 245, 278, 282, 283, 327, 363
Eckerman, C. O., 202, 210
Edelstein, R. S., 157
Eder, R. A., 247
Edhborg, M., 155
Edin, K., 413, 455
Edwards, C. P., 182, 205, 208, 210, 250
Efklides, A., 312
Egeland, B., 152, 156
Eggebeen, D. J., 451, 528, 530
Eggers, J. H., 437
Egley, A., Jr., 338
Eimas, P. D., 161
Einstein, A., 463
Eisenberg, N., 236, 237, 238, 360, 361
Eisenbud, L., 226
Ekerdt, D. J., 499
Elder, G. H., 388, 389
Elder, G. H., Jr., 8, 308, 309, 389, 432, 473, 474
Eldridge, N. S., 401
Elias, M., 131
Eliason, G., 492
Elkind, D., 313
Ellickson, P., 318
Elliot, L. B., 47, 55, 56
Elliott, D. S., 317
Elliott, K., 122
Ellsworth, C. P., 161
Elmer-Dewitt, P., 103, 105
Elster, A. B., 325
Emans, B. J., 285
Emanuel, E. J., 542
Emanuel, L., 542
Emde, R. N., 166, 183, 204, 205
Emerson, P. E., 149
Emery, A. E. H., 98
Engel, S., 198
Engelbrecht, L., 459
Engles, R. C. M. E., 403
Englis, B. G., 415
Ennett, S. T., 321
Entwisle, D. R., 113, 282, 284, 292
Eppler, M. A., 144, 146
Epstein, S., 243
Erber, J. T., 449, 510
Erdley, C. A., 268
Erikson, E. H., 6, 19, 26, 39, 40, 42, 43, 44, 47, 48, 52, 53–54, 64, 67, 72, 168, 171, 197, 200, 208, 211, 212, 249, 251, 256, 288, 293, 294, 369–70, 373, 374–75, 379, 380, 418, 421, 448, 449, 457, 458, 463, 475, 483, 493, 495, 496, 498, 505, 507, 512, 515–16, 527
Erikson, J. M., 39, 42, 43, 52, 168, 211, 448, 449, 457, 475, 483, 495, 496, 498, 505, 507, 512, 515–16, 527, 530
Eron, L. D., 240, 241
Escalona, S. K., 146
Eshelman, J. R., 397
Eskenazi, B., 121

Espinosa, M., 122
Essau, C. A., 320
Essex, M. J., 520
Ethier, K. A., 82
Ettinger, B., 445
Etzioni, A., 131
Evans, D. E., 206
Evans, D. R., 498
Evans, D. W., 211
Evans, I. M., 201, 202
Evans, W. J., 531
Evers, F. T., 434
Ezell, H. K., 278

Fabes, R. A., 237, 360
Fagot, B. I., 225, 227, 228, 334
Fairbairn, W. R. D., 68
Falkenstein, M., 509
Fanselow, M. S., 74
Farmer, M. C., 361
Farmer, T. W., 269, 334
Farrar, M. J., 273
Farrell, A. D., 343
Faux, R. B., 488
Feagin, J. R., 465, 466
Feather, N. T., 474
Featherman, D. L., 530
Federman, J., 240
Feeney, J. A., 156
Fegley, S., 360
Fehsenfeld, D. A., 397
Feigelman, S., 296
Fein, G. G., 123
Feinman, S., 151
Feldman, J. F., 138
Feldman, P., 128
Feldman, R., 152
Feldman, R. S., 266
Feldman, S., 486
Felinger, M., 282
Felman, P., 114
Felmlee, D., 397
Fenson, L., 188, 189, 190
Fenster, L., 121
Fentress, J. C., 143
Fenwick, R., 415
Fernald, A., 190
Fernandez, M. C., 194
Ferrer-Caja, E., 478, 480
Ferris, M., 437
Ferster, C. B., 75
Fetrow, R. A., 455
Fiatarone, M. A., 531
Ficher, I., 229
Field, D., 272
Field, T., 116, 168
Field, T. M., 116, 141, 151, 170
Fielding, L., 278
Fields, J., 350, 448, 484, 518
Fields, J. M., 402
Fife, B. L., 336
Fifer, W., 139
Figdor, E., 122
Finch, M., 362
Fincham, F., 250
Fine, M. A., 426, 427
Finer, L. B., 129
Fingerman, K. L., 453
Finkenauer, C., 403
Finley, M., 125
Fischer, A. R., 418
Fischer, K. W., 40, 144, 158, 278, 472
Fish, M., 165
Fisher, A. V., 273
Fisher, L. M., 508, 509
Fiske, S. T., 465
Fitch, J., 319, 341
Fitzgerald, B., 229
Fitzgibbon, M., 306
Flaks, D. K., 229
Flannery, D. J., 325
Flap, H., 395
Flavell, E. R., 198
Flavell, J. H., 40, 198, 237, 312
Fleeson, J., 265
Flesser, D., 287
Fletcher, C., 208
Fletcher, W. L., 497, 498
Floyd, F. J., 328, 496, 498
Flynn, C. B., 519
Flynn, K., 306
Folkman, S., 34, 50, 51
Fonagy, P., 154, 155, 236
Fontane, P. E., 490

Foote, D., 103
Ford, C. S., 124
Ford, J. K., 434
Ford, M. E., 293
Fordham, K., 268
Forehand, R. L., 309
Forgatch, M. S., 455
Forman, T. A., 465
Fortenberry, J. D., 382
Fowers, B. J., 426
Fowler, F. L., Jr., 28
Fox, C., 267
Fox, N. A., 147, 152, 174
Foxx, R. M., 75
Fozard, J. L., 57
Fraley, R. C., 418
Franko, D. L., 308
Frazier, P., 418
Frazier, P. A., 380
Frea, W. D., 75
Fredriksen, K., 310
Freedman, V. A., 512
Freeseman, L. J., 140
Freiberg, K., 140, 141
Freire, A., 312
French, D. C., 269, 270
Frese, M., 251
Freud, A., 26, 39, 67
Freud, S., 38, 39, 65, 66, 67, 207, 209, 235, 254, 255, 353, 463
Freund, A. M., 474
Frey, K. S., 248
Fried, P. A., 120
Friederici, A. D., 188
Friedlander, D., 413
Friedman, B. L., 361
Friedman, W. J., 361
Friedrich, M., 188
Froming, W. J., 232, 361
Frone, M. R., 437
Frye, D., 246
Frye, K. F., 155
Fu, M., 379
Fuller, D. W., 147
Fullard, W., 151
Fuller, B., 214, 217
Fuller-Thomson, E., 484
Fullilove, R. E., 332
Fultz, N. H., 522
Funk, J. B., 239
Furman, W., 267, 325
Futterman, A., 550

Gaddis, A., 307
Gaertner, L., 248, 446
Gaina, A., 310
Gainer, P. S., 318
Gaines, J. A., 169
Gall, T. L., 498
Gallagher, D., 530
Gallagher-Thompson, D., 530, 550
Galler, J. R., 123
Galotti, K. M., 361
Galt, A. H., 174
Galyer, K. T., 201, 202
Gandhi, M., 26
Ganea, P. A., 198
Ganon, J. H., 328
Ganong, L. H., 426, 427
Garbarino, J., 296
Garber, C. E., 489
Garber, J., 269, 320
Garcia, R., 141
Garcia-Mila, M., 275
Gardiner, H. W., 354
Gardner, H., 275, 276, 314
Gareis, K. C., 404, 405
Garfield, N., 362, 363
Garguilo, J., 325
Garland, A. F., 319
Garmezy, N., 9, 293
Garris, J. M., 497
Garvey, C., 249
Garwood, M. M., 154
Gati, I., 364
Gattai, F. B., 483
Gaudet, D. S., 428
Gauthier, C. A., 217
Gauze, C., 251
Gavin, L. A., 267
Gay, J., 393
Gazelle, H., 268, 270
Ge, X., 308, 309

Geary, D. C., 277, 395
Gelman, D., 400
Gelman, R., 274
Gelman, S. A., 273
Gentile, D. A., 239
George, C., 155, 157, 352
George, L. K., 432
Georgen, K. E., 439
Geraerts, N., 477
Gerhold, M., 174
Gerlach, S. G., 247
Germino-Hausken, E., 258
Gernsbacher, M. A., 186
Gerstel, N., 450
Gervai, J., 226
Getchell, N., 184
Geuze, R., 184
Geyman, J. P., 97
Gfellner, B. M., 360
Gfroerer, J. C., 381
Ghazanfareeon Karlsson, S., 524
Giambra, L. M., 476
Giarrusso, R., 481
Gibbs, J., 359
Gibbs, J. C., 233, 360
Gibson, E. J., 143, 183
Gibson, F. L., 103
Giele, J. Z., 353
Gielen, U. P., 234
Gifford-Smith, M. E., 265, 267
Gijs, L., 401
Gil, A. G., 343
Gilbert, L. A., 415
Gilbert, L. S., 401
Gilewski, M., 550
Gilewski, M. J., 550
Gillespie, C., 445
Gillespie, L., 363
Gilligan, C., 57, 360–61, 375
Ginsburg, H. P., 274
Ginsburg, S. D., 374
Giordano, P. C., 340
Giovanelli, G., 140
Giudice, S., 315
Givon, M., 364
Glasgow, N., 387
Glass, T. A., 532
Gleason, T. R., 201
Gleckman, H., 466
Glenn, J., 26
Glick, P., 465
Glick, P. C., 425
Gliner, J. A., 20
Glodis, K. A., 370
Gluck, J., 477
Godsil, B. P., 74
Goforth, C. M., 118
Goldbaum, S., 270
Goldberg, S., 138
Goldberg, W. A., 177
Goldfield, E. C., 146
Golding, J., 116
Goldman, H. I., 188
Goldscheider, C., 350
Goldscheider, F. K., 350, 448
Goldshmidt, L., 120
Goldsmith, D. J., 403, 404
Goldsmith, H. H., 147
Golombok, S., 103
Goncu, A., 210
Gonzalez, B., 459
Good, T. L., 282
Goodfellow, J., 485
Goodman, C. C., 484
Goodman, E., 103
Goodman, J. C., 190
Gopnik, A., 157, 161, 275
Gorcynski, J., 332
Gordijn, E., 334, 335
Gordon, K. C., 446
Gore, S., 320
Gorer, G., 125
Gornick, V., 373
Gorrell, J., 259
Gottesman, I. I., 99, 479
Gottman, J. M., 402, 442
Graber, J. A., 318
Grahn, D., 505
Gramick, H. G., 126
Gramzow, R., 208
Grandquist, H., 125
Granger, D. A., 309
Graniere-Deferre, C., 110
Gratch, G., 158
Gray, F. L., 211

Gray, P., 63
Gray, W. M., 312
Grayson, A., 163
Green, L., 401
Green, F. L., 198
Green, R. J., 358, 371
Green, V., 141
Greenberg, E. F., 426
Greenberg, M., 117
Greenberg, R., 141
Greenblatt, J. C., 381
Greene, A. L., 47, 352
Greene, K., 382
Greenfield, P. M., 80, 146
Gregg, T. R., 186
Gregor, T., 250
Gregory, K. M., 195
Gregory, L. W., 292
Grelotti, D. J., 187
Griffin, D. W., 419
Grigorenko, E. L., 276, 462
Grimes, J. A., 75
Groff, T. R., 326
Grolnick, W. S., 204
Grondin, S., 289
Groome, L. J., 110
Grossman, F. K., 117
Gruber, J. E., 115
Gruber-Baldini, A., 509
Grunbaum, J. A., 319
Grunfeld, F. V., 249
Grusec, J. E., 76
Guacci, N., 323
Guacci-Franco, N., 333, 358
Gubrium, J. F., 28
Gulko, J., 225–26, 227, 272
Gulley, B. L., 325
Gunnar, M. R., 151, 166
Gur, R. C., 224
Guralnick, J. M., 13, 531
Gurin, P., 333
Gurley, D., 420
Gustafson, P., 233
Gutheil, G., 273
Guthrie, D., 169
Gutman, L., 447
Guttmann, D. L., 483, 522
Guttmann, B., 125, 474

Haas, E., 336
Habib, M., 396
Hack, M., 21
Hadley, E. C., 531
Haessler, S., 509
Haffner, D. W., 324, 325
Hagtvet, K. A., 280
Hahn, R. A., 114, 124
Hahne, A., 188
Hahn-Smith, A. M., 227
Hains, S. M. J., 161
Haith, M. M., 140, 158
Haley, W. E., 512
Halfon, N., 213
Halford, G. S., 274
Hall, L. J., 270
Hall, N. W., 259
Hall, W. S., 278
Haller, E., 278
Halperin, S., 363
Halton, A., 123
Ham, M., 47, 320
Hamachek, D., 54
Hamagami, F., 478, 480
Hamanishi, S., 310
Hamarat, E., 475
Hamberg, L., 519
Hamblen, J., 296
Hambrick, D. C., 460
Hamilton, B. E., 405
Hamilton, W. D., 63
Hammer, C. S., 195
Hammer, M., 266
Hammill, D. D., 196
Hamon, R. R., 450
Handy, C., 411, 436
Handyside, A. H., 105
Haney, M., 278
Hann, D. M., 120
Hansell, S., 322
Hansford, S. L., 419
Hanson, S., 324
Hansson, R. O., 497, 498
Hao, L., 330
Harding, D. J., 330
Hardy, J., 331

Harel, J., 152
Harkness, S., 208
Harlan, E. T., 23, 206
Harman, D., 13
Harold, R. D., 245, 283
Harrell, J. S., 306
Harrington, C. C., 8, 28
Harrington, M., 121
Harris, M., 189
Harris, M. J., 282
Harris, M. L., 151
Harris, P. B., 352
Harris, P. L., 197, 198, 200
Harris, S. H., 505
Harrod, M. M., 461
Hart, B., 194
Hart, C. H., 201, 235, 266
Hart, D., 243–46, 251, 360
Hart, L. G., 128
Harter, K. S. M., 328
Harter, S., 207, 247, 280, 282, 293, 422
Hartlage, S. A., 320
Hartup, W. W., 201
Harvey, J. H., 495
Harwood, R. L., 155
Hasegawa, K., 527
Haskett, M. E., 266
Haskins, R., 216, 217
Hastings, C. T., 516
Hastings, P., 148
Hatfield, E., 398
Hauser, S. T., 349
Hautamäki, J., 276
Havighurst, R. J., 39, 43
Hawkins, A. J., 437, 458
Hawkins, J. L., 403
Hawkins, S., 138
Hawley, G. A., 55
Hay, E. L., 453
Hayes, D., 511
Hayflick, L., 13
Haynes, J., 102
Haynes, O. M., 151, 155
Hayslip, B., Jr., 478
Hayward, M. D., 9
Hazan, C., 156
Hazell, L. V., 548
Heath, S. B., 194
Heatherington, E. M., 485
Heatherton, T. F., 202
Hedge, B., 10
Heilman, M. E., 358
Heimpel, S. A., 247
Hein, G., 509
Heincke, S. G., 493, 517
Heinicke, C. M., 117, 169, 407
Heinze, H.-J., 194
Heinze, S. D., 116
Heiser, N., 121
Heitlinger, A., 114
Helman, C. G., 125, 126
Helwig, C. C., 233
Henderson, H. A., 148
Henderson, V. K., 149, 216
Hendricks, L. E., 332
Henggeler, S. Q., 318
Henkens, K., 497
Hennig, K. H., 233
Hennighausen, K., 317
Henrich, C. C., 297
Henry, G., 207
Henry, J. D., 477
Henry, P. J., 379
Henshaw, S. K., 129
Herdt, G., 324
Hergovich, A., 282
Herkovits, F., 78
Herman, M. R., 349
Herman-Giddens, M. E., 304
Hernandez, D. J., 8
Hernandez-Guzman, L., 308
Herold, E. S., 357
Herpertz-Dahlmann, B., 317
Herron, M. C., 349
Herting, J. R., 349
Hertsgaard, L., 151
Hertzog, C., 316, 478–79, 509
Hertzog, D., 478–79
Herzog, A. R., 496, 522
Herzog, D. B., 316
Hespos, S. J., 157
Hess, L. E., 336
Hetherington, E. M., 182, 254
Heuveline, P., 399

Heynen, J., 4, 505
Hickson, F. C., 423
Hildebrandt, C., 234
Hill, C. T., 394
Hill, E. J., 437
Hill, H. M., 185
Hill, J. H., 278, 371
Hill, J. P., 309
Hill, N. E., 291
Hill, R., 446
Hillman, J. L., 524
Hilton, J., 505
Hines, M., 533
Hirschfeld, L. A., 334
Hoard, M. K., 277
Hobfoll, S. E., 115
Hochstein, M., 213
Hodges, J., 171
Hodnett, E. D., 115
Hodson, R., 464
Hoeger, W. W. K., 489
Hoek, H. W., 123
Hoeksma, J. B., 315
Hofer, T. P., 417
Hoffman, M. L., 235, 236, 237, 252
Hoffman, S. J., 196
Hoffmann, M. L., 228
Hoffmeyer, L. B., 142
Hofmeister, H., 497
Hofstra, G., 379
Hogan, D. P., 451
Hogan, T. D., 519
Hoge, D. R., 337
Hohnsbein, J., 509
Hoke-Sinex, L., 275
Holahan, C. K., 33
Holden, C., 130
Holder, A., 255
Holland, J. L., 368, 433
Holliday, R., 13
Holloway, S. D., 214, 217
Holmberg, L. I., 132
Holmes, T. H., 115
Holstein, J. A., 28
Holt, C., 141
Holzman, C., 137
Homes, J. G., 419
Hong, L. K., 520
Honig, A. S., 215
Hooijer, C., 477
Hooyman, H., 533
Hooyman, N. R., 451, 512, 540
Hope, T. L., 331
Hopkins, B., 144, 184
Hopkins, D. R., 489
Hopkins, J. R., 54
Hopkins, K., 419
Hopkins, M., 363
Hopper, K., 441, 519
Horn, J., 478, 496
Horn, J. L., 496
Hornblower, M., 259
Hornik, R., 166
Horowitz, A., 551
Horowitz, L. M., 168
Horowitz, M., 98
Horst, E. A., 374
Horwitz, A. V., 393
House, J. S., 419, 485, 496
Houx, P. J., 480–81
Howard, C. W., 343
Howard, D. E., 296
Howard, J., 122, 498
Howell, C., 338
Howell, E. M., 121
Howell-White, S., 393
Howes, C., 198, 202, 217, 251
Howland, R. I., 127
Howse, R. B., 164
Hoyt, D. R., 454
Hoza, B., 251
Hsiao, Y.-L., 403
Hsu, L. K. G., 317
Hubbard, J., 325
Huck, S. M., 454
Huerta, R., 444
Huesmann, L. R., 239, 240, 241
Hughes, D. L., 390
Hughes, F. M., 446
Huizinga, D., 317
Hulsizer, M. R., 115
Hultsch, D. P., 476
Hume, D., 333, 335

Hunt, E. B., 435
Hunter, A. G., 485
Hunter, M., 343
Hunter, T., 250
Hupp, S. D. A., 287
Huston, A. C., 240, 241, 242
Huston, T. L., 402, 403, 407, 442
Hutcheson, H., 459
Huxley, J., 39, 64
Hyde, J. S., 113, 405
Hymel, S., 267, 268, 269, 270, 334

Iannotti, R. J., 238, 343
Idler, E. L., 532
Ikels, C., 482
Indelicato, S., 407
Ingersoll-Dayton, B., 451, 529
Inhelder, B., 158, 270, 310, 311, 312
Inkelas, M., 213
Insko, C. A., 413
Ippen, C. G., 116
Irwin, C. E., Jr., 319
Isaac, J. D., 364–65
Isaacowitz, D. M., 52
Isabella, R. A., 154, 165, 169
Ishii-Kuntz, M., 228
Iversen, J. M., 189
Izard, C. E., 151, 155, 163, 252

Jack, D. C., 420
Jacklin, C. N., 224, 250
Jackson, D. N., 530
Jackson, J. A., 474
Jackson, P. B., 387, 388
Jackson, S., 272
Jacobs, J. E., 283, 364
Jacobson, E., 254
Jacobson, J. L., 123
Jacobson, L., 282
Jacobson, N. S., 443
Jacobson, S. W., 123, 140, 155
Jacquet, A. Y., 110
Jaenisch, R., 99
Jahoda, M., 498
James, J. B., 432
James, L. S., 112
Jaspars, J., 250
Jayakody, R., 9
Jecker, N. S., 493
Jeffries, V., 422
Jenkins, J. M., 197
Jennings, S., 350
Jensen, R., 232
Jerath, J. M., 230
Jerger, J., 511
Jessor, R., 382
Jetten, J., 287
Jockin, V., 426
Johnson, D. R., 309
Johnson, H. B., 540–41
Johnson, J. G., 122, 331
Johnson, K. P., 310
Johnson, M., 139
Johnson, M. A., 57
Johnson, M. H., 310
Johnson, M. K., 362
Johnson, M. P., 117
Johnson, N., 272
Johnson, R. E., 140, 476
Johnson, S. P., 140
Johnson, V., 444
Johnston, G. M., 395
Johnston, J. R., 427
Johnston, L. D., 341, 342, 343, 381
Jones, C., 553
Jones, J. B., 445
Jones, J. M., 464
Jones, J. T., 418
Jones, L. L., 532
Jones, M. C., 308
Jones, R. M., 373
Jones-Webb, R. J., 320
Jonker, C., 477
Jordan, C. H., 247
Jordan, J. V., 419
Jordan, K. F., 274
Jordhov, M. S., 548
Jordyn, M., 352
Joseph, G., 229
Josephson, W. L., 240

Josselson, R., 57
Jouanjean, A., 250
Joyner, K., 319
Juszczyk, P. W., 188
Jussim, L., 282, 283
Justice, L. M., 278

Kaasa, S., 548
Kabbani, N. S., 282, 284, 292
Kaczala, C. M., 283, 387
Kagamimori, S., 310
Kagan, J., 151, 165, 210, 254
Kagan, S. L., 217, 259
Kagitcibasi, C., 78
Kahana, B., 532
Kahn, R. L., 471, 476, 507, 512, 516, 528, 529
Kalb, C., 103, 407
Kalichman, S. C., 10
Kalil, K. M., 115
Kalish, C. W., 273
Kalish, R. A., 492
Kalman, M. B., 306
Kalmijn, M., 395, 397, 417
Kalveboer, A. F., 184
Kamii, C. K., 70
Kamo, Y., 403
Kamphaus, R. W., 100
Kang, S. M., 315, 316
Kann, L., 319
Kanouse, D. E., 381
Kanter, R. M., 434
Kanungo, R. N., 435
Kaplan, B. J., 115
Kaplan, G. A., 13
Kaplan, N., 171, 352
Karasawa, M., 165
Kardaun, J. W. P. F., 57
Karip, E., 488
Karmel, M., 127
Karp, D. A., 500
Karraker, K. H., 47
Karasawa, J. D., 521
Kastenbaum, R., 490
Kastenbaum, R. J., 490
Katchadourian, H., 326
Katz, S. J., 417
Kaufert, P., 445
Kaufman, G., 210
Kaufman, N., 488
Kavanagh, R. D., 197, 198, 200
Kawas, C., 476
Kaye, L. W., 521
Keating, D. P., 309, 314–15
Keats, J. A., 343
Keefe, R., 334
Keeves, J., 474, 521
Kefalas, M. J., 455
Keith, J., 515
Keith, V. M., 529
Keller, H., 155
Kelly, M. L., 9
Kelly, S. J., 224
Keltenbach, K., 151
Kemper, S., 512
Kennedy, G. J., 527
Kennell, J., 115
Kernis, M. H., 247
Kerns, D., 329, 342
Kersting, K., 543
Kessen, W., 23, 140
Kessler, R. C., 485, 486
Ketterlinus, R. D., 325
Keyes, C. L., 390
Khoo, P. N., 380
Kihlstrom, J. L., 65
Killen, M., 234
Killingsworth, C., 128
Killingsworth Rini, C., 114
Kim, A. S., 195
Kim, E., 57
Kim, H.-J. K., 126
Kim, J., 363, 497
Kim, T., 7, 458

Kirkpatrick, L. A., 419
Kirkwood, T. B. L., 13
Kirshner, B., 360
Kiselica, M. S., 332
Kisilevsky, B. S., 139
Kistner, J. A., 248, 266, 290
Kiston, J. M., 54
Kitayama, S., 165, 248
Kitchener, K. S., 40, 475
Kite, M. E., 388, 522
Kitson, G. C., 427, 428
Kitzinger, C., 401
Kitzinger, S., 126
Kitzmann, K. M., 266
Kivnick, H. Q., 43, 52, 168, 211, 448, 449, 457, 475, 483, 495, 496, 498, 505, 507, 512, 515–16, 527
Kiyak, H. A., 451, 512, 533, 540
Klackenberg-Larsson, I., 230
Klandermans, B., 82
Klaus, M., 115
Klebanov, P. K., 9
Klein, H., 125
Klein, L., 163
Klein, M., 68, 235
Klein, N., 21
Klesges, L. M., 507
Kline, D. W., 510
Klinnert, M. D., 166
Klint, K. A., 286
Knaack, A., 206
Knight, C. C., 278
Knox, D., 394
Kobak, R., 352
Kochanek, K. D., 112, 113
Kochanska, G., 23, 204, 205, 206, 238, 252, 253, 336
Kochenderfer-Ladd, B. J., 268
Koenig, A. L., 204
Kogushi, Y., 197
Kohlberg, L., 225, 233, 234, 359, 360
Kohn, M. L., 435
Kohn, P. M., 320
Kohut, H., 68, 235
Kolev, V., 509
Konarski, R., 325
Konrad, P., 466
Koop, E., 130
Kopp, C. B., 164, 202, 203
Kornfield, S., 309
Kornhaber, A., 485
Kornhaber, M. L., 276
Kosmitzki, C., 354
Kosnik, W., 510
Kotelchuck, M., 118, 151
Kotler, J., 242
Kotre, J., 131, 458
Kotre, J. N., 32
Kotre, K. B., 131
Kowalski, P., 293
Kowaz, A. M., 289
Kozberg, S. F., 361
Kozlowski, S. W. J., 434
Kposowa, A. J., 425
Krakow, M., 211
Kram, K. E., 413, 419
Kramer, A. F., 490
Krause, N. M., 529, 534
Kravitz, H. M., 320
Krehbiel, G., 270
Kreider, R. M., 402
Kremar, M., 232
Krestan, J. A., 357
Kroger, J., 55, 370, 372, 373, 374, 375
Kroonenberg, P. M., 168
Kruger, J., 285
Krupnick, J., 253
Krzysik, L., 250
Ku, L. C., 329
Kübler-Ross, E., 490, 540, 541, 543
Kuczaj, S. A., 185
Kuczynski, L., 154, 210
Kuhl, P. K., 139, 188
Kuhn, D., 275, 314
Kuk, L. S., 373
Kunjufu, J., 118
Kunkel, A. W., 403, 404
Kunz, J., 426
Kunz, P. R., 426
Kuperminc, G. P., 316

Kurdek, L. A., 357, 360, 400, 401, 402
Kusseling, F. S., 382
Kwon, Y.-J., 315

Laberge, L., 310
Labouvie-Vief, G., 475, 478
Lacayo, R., 103
Lachman, M. E., 432
Lacombe, A. C., 393
Lacroix, V., 196
Ladd, G. W., 201, 235, 266, 268
Ladson-Billings, G., 293
LaFlamme, D., 176
LaFleur, S. J., 30
LaFreniere, P. J., 63, 324
Lagattuta, K. H., 275
Laible, D. J., 239
Lamarre, G., 196
Lamb, M. E., 152, 325
Lambert, J. D., 409
Lamborn, S. D., 322, 324, 336, 339
Lampman-Petraitis, C., 316
Land, D., 323, 352
Landry, S. H., 176, 195
Landry-Meyer, L., 484
Landsverk, J., 343
Lang, D., 331
Lang, F. R., 530
Langlois, J. H., 155
Langston, C. A., 420
Lankford, M.D., 249
Lansford, J. E., 267
Laplante, D. P., 139
Laren, D. S., 485
Larson, M. C., 151
Larson, R., 47, 308, 316, 320
Larzelere, R., 446
LaSala, M. C., 400, 401
Laszlo, E., 83
Lauer, R., 98
Laumann, E. Q., 328
Launer, L. J., 477
Lavin, J., 115
Lavond, D. G., 73
Lawrence, F. R., 259
Laws, G., 100
Lawson, A. E., 315
Lawson, M., 521
Lawton, M. P., 540
Lay, K., 250
Lazarus, R. S., 50, 51
Le, H.-N., 116
Leadbeater, B. J., 316
Leaper, C., 227, 251
Lecacheur, M., 508
Lecanuet, J. P., 110
Leckman, J. F., 211
Lee, A. M., 307
Lee, C., 510
Lee, G. R., 486
Lee, K., 141, 312, 441
Lee, L. C., 250
Lee, M. J., 287
Lee, S., 279
Leerkes, E. M., 154
Leichtman, M. D., 246
Leidy, N. K., 55
Leigh, G. K., 336
Lein, L., 413
Leinbach, M. D., 225, 227, 334
Leis, N., 202
Lemaire, P., 508
Le Maner-Idrissi, G., 250
LeMare, L. J., 268
Lemkau, J. R., 131
Lemonick, M. D., 103, 104, 306
Lerman, R., 332
Lerner, R. M., 85, 270, 336
Leslie, G. I., 103
Lester, B. M., 147
LeVay, S., 96
Levenson, R. W., 402
Levesque, R. P., 324
Levin, I., 40
Levine, A., 377
Levine, R. A., 175, 406
Levine, R. M., 334, 335
Levine, S., 444
Levitt, J. L., 333, 358
Levitt, M. J., 323, 333, 358
Levkoff, S., 499
Levy, G. D., 226

Levy, R. I., 72
Levy-Shiff, R., 138
Lewinsohn, P., 420
Lewinsohn, P. H., 494
Lewis, E., 395
Lewis, H. B., 210
Lewis, K. L., 477
Lewis, M., 151, 164
Lewit, E. M., 258
Li, P. H. X., 296
Liang, J., 339, 529
Liben, L. S., 226
Lichter, D. T., 394, 395
Lieberman, A. F., 172
Lieberman, M., 359
Liebert, R. M., 240
Liebow, E., 24
Lifton, R. J., 525–26
Lightdale, J. R., 335
Lillard, A. S., 198
Limber, S. P., 269, 318
Lin, H.-L., 259
Lin, R.-G, II, 29
Lincoln, Y. S., 18
Lindblad, B. S., 123
Lindbohm, M., 123
Lindeboom, J., 477
Lindemann, E., 549
Lindenberger, U., 478
Lindsay, E. W., 201, 408
Linebarger, D. L., 241
Linn, M. C., 314
Lippert, T., 403
Litt, I. F., 317
Littig, L. W., 398
Little, J. K., 226, 334
Littlefield, D., 459
Litwin, H., 529
Litwin, M., 444
Liu, H.-M., 188
Liu, W., 182, 205, 208
Livesley, W. J., 530
Lloyd, K. M., 395
Lo, R., 498
Lobel, T. E., 226, 334
Lobo, F., 441
Locker, J., 320
Lockery, S., 482
Loehlin, J. C., 96
Loftus, E. F., 32
Logan, D. D., 306
Logan, J., 451
Logan, R. L., 459
Lohman, B. J., 322
Lollis, S., 197, 268
Lombardi, D. N., 415
Lombardi, L., 476
Long, E. C. J., 397
Long, M. M., 490
Long, P. J., 309
Longeway, K. P., 152
Longino, C. F., Jr., 519
Looft, W. R., 313
Lopata, H. Z., 485
Lopez, A., 273
Lopez, S. J., 52, 55
Lopez, S. R., 78
Lorenz, F. O., 177
Lorenz, K. F., 170
Lott, B., 212, 413
Lott, L., 477
Louchheim, T., 548
Lovett, S., 550
Lowe, D., 476
Lowe, J. C., 388
Lucariello, J., 198
Lucas, D. R., 163
Lucas, M., 533
Lucke, K., 329
Ludemann, P. M., 141
Luhtanen, R., 335
Lukas, W. D., 123
Lumley, J., 128
Lundh, W., 155
Luszcz, M., 474, 521
Lutkenhaus, P., 203
Lydon, J., 405
Lykken, D. T., 426
Lyles, L., 451
Lynam, D. R., 207
Lyubchik, A., 154

Ma, Y., 420
Maag, U., 530
MacCallum, F., 103

Maccoby, E. E., 205, 224, 228, 250, 253
MacDermid, S. M., 407
MacEachron, A. E., 307
MacFarlane, J. A., 142
MacKain, S. J., 228
Macklin, E., 400
MacLean, D. J., 141
MacLeod, M. S., 477
Madden, D. J., 57, 509
Madon, S., 282
Maggs, J. L., 343
Magistro, C. A., 325
Mahler, M. S., 182, 235
Main, M., 352
Main, N., 171
Major, A. K., 338
Makin, J. W., 142
Malacara, J., 444
Malamuth, N. M., 240
Malanowski, J., 295
Malatesta, C., 163
Malcuit, G., 196
Malhi, P., 230
Malhotra, D., 230
Malina, R. M., 285
Malle, B. F., 168
Maloy, K., 132
Mandel, D. R., 188
Mangelsdorf, S. C., 138, 151
Manke, B., 416
Manning, W. D., 9, 362
Manstead, A. S. R., 287
Marcia, J. E., 55, 289, 372, 373, 374
Marcoen, A., 477
Marcus, G. F., 191
Marcus, G. R., 189
Marcus, H., 211
Margand, N. A., 149
Markman, H. I., 402
Markoulis, D. C., 234
Markovits, H., 250, 251
Markovsky, B., 335
Marks, M., 423
Markstrom, C. A., 52
Markstrom-Adams, C., 339, 379
Markus, H. R., 248, 333
Marquis, J., 512
Marshall, H. H., 248, 282
Marshall, M. A., 247
Marshall, N. L., 439
Marshall, S. K., 357
Marshall, T. R., 163
Marsiglio, W., 307, 332, 454
Marsiske, M., 509
Martikainen, P., 486
Martin, C. L., 225, 226, 334
Martin, D. C., 121
Martin, G. B., 237
Martin, J. A., 102, 112, 113, 119
Martin, L. G., 512
Martin, P., 57
Martin, S., 306
Martinez, C., 124
Martinez-Pons, M., 281
Marvin, R. S., 149
Marx, J., 96
Maslow, A. H., 390
Mason, C. A., 268
Mason, M. G., 360
Massarik, F., 390
Masten, A. S., 325
Masten, A. S., 293
Masterpasqua, F., 229
Masters, J. C., 444
Masuda, M., 423
Masunaga, H., 478, 496
Masur, E. F., 169
Matheny, A. P., Jr., 147
Mathieowetz, N. A., 30
Mattis, R., 128
Mau, R. Y., 335
May, R. B., 272
Mazzoleni, G., 511
McAdams, D. P., 7, 32, 41, 43, 55, 131, 458, 459
McAllister, L. E., 118
McArdle, J. J., 478, 480
McAuley, C., 331, 332
McAuley, E., 281
McAuliffe, G., 414
McBride, M. L., 273

McCabe, A. E., 273
McCabe, M. P., 317
McCanne, T. R., 163
McCarthy, J. D., 331, 337, 374
McCarthy, M. E., 206
McClaskey, C. L., 252
McClearn, G. E., 136, 479, 527
McClintic, S., 245
McClintock, M., 324
McCloskey, L. A., 266
McCluskey-Fawcett, K. A., 323
McConatha, D., 474
McConatha, J. T., 474
McCord, J., 317
McCormick, S. E., 237
McCrae, R. R., 50, 473
McCreary, L. L., 455
McCubbin, H. I., 51
McCullough, B. C., 340
McDill, E. L., 336
McDonald, A. D., 121
McDonough, L., 190
McDougall, P., 267
McDuff, P., 331
McElroy, M., 281
McGee, R., 278, 333
McGlaughlin, A., 163
McGregor, J. A., 270
McGue, M., 426
McGuffin, P., 93, 136
McGuigan, K. A., 318
McHale, S. M., 309, 407
McInnes, R. R., 98
McKay, J. K., 413
McKinlay, J. B., 445
McKinlay, S. M., 445
McKinney, K. D., 465, 466
McKnew, D., 253
McKusick, V. A., 98
McLanahan, S., 9
McLaughlin, D. K., 395
McLellan, J. A., 322
McLeod, J. D., 212
McLeod, P. J., 143
McLouth, G., 131
McLoyd, V. C., 8, 9, 212
McMahon, C. A., 103
McManus, J., 361
McMurray, R. G., 306
Meacham, J. A., 494
Mead, M., 78, 79, 124, 125, 127
Means-Christensen, A., 357
Medici Skaggs, N., 336
Meer, J., 420
Meers, P. M., 255
Meeus, W., 374, 403
Meghdari, A., 184
Meins, E., 166
Melchior, E. J., 415
Melender, H., 115
Melton, G. B., 318
Meltzoff, A. N., 143, 157, 161, 210, 237
Melz, H., 442
Mena, A., 444
Menaghan, E. G., 415
Menard, S., 317
Menashri, J., 226, 334
Merkle, E. R., 396
Mertesacker, B., 163, 164
Merton, R. K., 327
Meschke, L. L., 327, 329
Mesquita, B., 165
Messer, D. J., 190, 206
Messer, S., 68
Metter, E. J., 473
Metz, M. E., 401
Meydani, M., 13
Meyer-Bahlburg, H. F. L., 327
Miao, E. S. C. Y., 234
Michael, R. T., 328
Michaels, S., 328
Michealieu, Q., 237
Midgley, C., 447
Midlarsky, E., 320, 321
Miele, M., 522
Mihalic, S. F., 269
Mikach, S., 229
Mikulincer, M., 167
Miles, T. P., 9
Milkie, M. A., 452
Miller, D. T., 335
Miller, J., 102, 435
Miller, N. B., 182, 120

Miller, P. H., 38, 40, 54, 55, 71
Miller, P. J., 203
Miller, W. B., 131
Miller-Loncar, C. L., 195
Miller-Tiedeman, A., 366, 367
Millstein, S. G., 317
Milner, J. S., 163
Milrose, J. A., 320
Min, Y. I., 123
Minich, N. M., 21
Minkler, M., 484
Minuchin, S., 421
Mischel, W., 77, 202–3, 206, 211, 232, 235
Misra, S., 435
Mistry, J., 210
Mitchell, D. W., 140
Mitchell, P., 285
Mitchell, R. W., 193
Miyake, K., 165
Mize, J., 408
Mizrahi, K., 82
Moen, P., 387, 497
Moen, P. L., 415, 461
Moffitt, T. E., 288, 309
Mogilner, M. B., 138
Moise-Titus, J., 241
Molfese, D. L., 187
Molfese, V. J., 187
Mollnow, E., 121
Monroe, S., 420
Montel, K. H., 426
Montemayor, R., 323
Montgomery, D. E., 267
Montplaisir, J., 310
Moore, G., 153
Moore, J. W., 388
Moore, K. A., 330
Moore, K. L., 97, 103, 120
Moradi, A. R., 296
Morales Waugh, I., 412
Morf, C. C., 206
Morgan, C., 364–65
Morgan, D. M., 486
Morgan, G. A., 20
Morgan, J. L., 193
Morgan, J. N., 496
Morgan, L. A., 486
Morgane, P. J., 123
Morimitsu, F., 505
Morisset, C. E., 118
Morris, A. S., 361
Morris, K. A., 418
Morris, N. M., 326
Morrison, T., 7
Morse, C. K., 506
Morse, J. M., 22
Morten, G., 378
Mortimer, J. T., 350, 362
Morton, K. R., 498
Mosel, S., 292
Mosher, W. D., 424, 425
Moshman, D., 270
Mosier, C., 210
Moskowitz, J. T., 51
Moss, P., 434
Mounts, N., 322, 324, 336
Muecke, M. A., 114, 124
Mueller, F. R., 98
Muir, C. P., 161
Muir, D. W., 139, 141
Mulatu, M. S., 517
Mulder, E. J. H., 116
Mullally, P., 248
Mullan, J. T., 512, 513, 548
Mulrane, A., 224
Munholland, K. A., 245
Munoz, R. F., 116
Munte, T. F., 194
Murdock, G. P., 124
Murphy, J. G., 415
Murphy, K. C., 242
Murphy, L., 203–4
Murphy, L. B., 252, 256–57
Murphy, L. M., 265
Murrah, B., 489
Murray, B., 344
Murray, C., 103, 552, 553
Murray, K., 206, 336
Murray, K. T., 23, 206
Murray, S. L., 419
Murrell, A., 335
Murrell, S. A., 528
Musatti, T., 483
Musch, J., 289

Mussen, P. H., 308
Musser, L. M., 283
Mutchler, J. E., 518
Myers, S., 126

Nair, K. S., 508
Nakagawa, M., 206
Namy, L. L., 189
Nangle, D. W., 268
Nasby, W., 361
Nash, J. M., 106, 139
Nasir, N. S., 360
Nathanielsz, P. W., 111
Nation, M. A., 318
Naulty, J. S., 123
Nay, W. R., 426
Nazi, T., 161
Neckerman, H. J., 268
Needham, A., 161
Neeman, J., 325
Neese, R., 485
Neese, R. N., 63
Neff, K. D., 422
Negy, C., 357
Nehrke, M. F., 56, 494
Neimark, E. D., 312, 315
Neiss, M., 309
Neisser, U., 276
Neitzel, C., 275
Nelson, B. S., 439
Nelson, C. A., 140, 160
Nelson, E., 141, 289
Nelson, J. P., 163
Nelson, K., 185, 195, 246
Nelson, T. O., 275
Nemoto, T., 528
Nesdale, D., 287
Neshat-Doost, H. T., 296
Nesse, R. M., 486
Nesselroade, J. R., 527, 530
Neto, F., 419
Neugarten, B., 481
Neugarten, B. L., 388, 506
Neugebauer, R., 123
Newcomb, A. F., 251
Newman, B. M., 83, 333, 407
Newman, J. E., 268
Newman, J. L., 274, 334
Newman, P. R., 321, 333
Newman, R., 377
Newman, S., 488
Newport, E., 189
Newton, C. R., 102
Newton, N., 124, 127
Nichols, M. R., 117
Nichols, S. L., 282
Nickols, S. Y., 437
Nicoladis, E., 194
Nidiffer, J., 377
Niehuis, S., 402, 403
Nieves, W., 394
Nisan, M., 359
Nitz, K., 325
Noppe, l. C., 490
Noppe, L. D., 490
Nordstrom, B., 121
Norem, J. K., 173
Norris, F. H., 528
Norton, J. M., 272
Nosselt, T., 194
Notarius, C. I., 203, 402
Novick, K., 438
Nsamenang, A. B., 80
Nucci, L. P., 234
Nugent, J. K., 147
Nunez, R., 456, 457
Nurmi, J.-E., 372
Nye, C. L., 328
Nyman, M., 237

Oates, W. E., 493
Obeidallah, D. A., 304
Oberklaid, F., 148
O'Brien, M. U., 315
O'Brien, S. F., 334
O'Bryant, S. L., 486
O'Campo, P., 116
O'Connell, M., 405, 408
O'Connor, P., 350
O'Connor, T. G., 168
Oden, M. H., 33
Offenbacher, D. I., 516
Ogan, T. A., 166
Ogbu, J. U., 292
O'Hara, R. P., 366

Ohlde, C., 362, 363
Okagaki, L., 276
Okimoto, J. T., 155
Okun, M. A., 529
Okundaye, J. N., 296
O'Leary, P. A., 512
O'Leary, S., 205
Oleinick, L., 485
Ollech, D., 374
Oller, D. K., 194
O'Loughlin, M., 314
Olshansky, S. J., 13, 505
Olson, A. W., 380
Olson, D. H., 426
Olweus, D., 269
O'Malley, P. M., 341, 342, 343, 381
O'Neil, J. M., 362, 363
O'Neill, D. K., 275
Oosterlaan, J., 315
Oosterwegel, A., 245
Oppenheim, D., 152
Oppenheimer, L., 245
Orenstein, P., 281, 304–5, 317
Orlofsky, J. L., 374
O'Rourke, N., 495
Ory, M. G., 531
Osgood, N. J., 530
Osipow, S. H., 364, 414
Oskay, G., 349
Osofsky, J. D., 120, 296
Ostrowski, N. L., 224
O'Sullivan, L. F., 327
Overman, S. J., 286
Owen, M. T., 149, 215, 216

Paas, F. G. W. C., 480–81
Page-Adams, D., 441
Paik, H., 240
Pajares, F., 281
Palkovitz, R., 55, 407
Palladino-Schultheiss, D., 349
Pallas, A. M., 282
Pallett-Hehn, P., 533
Panak, W. F., 269
Paneth, N., 137
Papini, D. R., 323
Pappas, S., 274
Paquette, J. A., 267, 268
Paradise, R., 193
Parcel, T. L., 415
Park, K. A., 250, 265
Park, S.-Y., 164
Parker, C. A., 40
Parker, J. G., 267, 268
Parkhurst, J. T., 268
Parr, J. M., 293
Parsons, J. E., 282, 283, 387
Parsons, T., 81
Pascarella, E. T., 358
Pasold, T., 239
Passman, R. H., 152, 484
Pastorelli, C., 281
Paterson, G., 148
Patterson, C., 303–4
Patterson, C. J., 229, 401
Patterson, G. R., 266, 455
Patterson, I., 487
Patterson, J. M., 51
Patterson, L. E., 415, 437
Patterson, M. J., 132
Patterson, M. L., 142
Pattison, P. E., 274
Paul, P. B., 512
Pauli-Pott, U., 163, 164
Pavetti, L. A., 8
Pavlov, I., 73
Pawl, J. H., 172
Paxton, S. J., 304, 317
Pearlin, L. I., 512, 513, 548
Pearn, J., 264
Pearson, B. Z., 194
Pearson, D., 201
Pearson, J. L., 155
Peck, R. C., 471
Peck, V., 275
Pedersen, F. A., 407
Pedersen, N. L., 527
Pederson, N., 96
Pedlow, R., 148
Peebles, C., 120
Peek, C. W., 21
Peek, M. K., 21
Peerson, S., 122

Pelham, B. W., 247
Pell, R. W., 526
Pellegrini, A. D., 200, 278
Pellegrini, D. S., 203
Peltonen, L., 98
Pemberton, M. B., 413
Peplau, L. A., 394, 420
Pepler, D., 270
Pergament, E., 120
Peris, A., 148
Perlmutter, M., 247
Perloff, R. M., 10
Perls, T. T., 513
Perner, J., 246
Perosa, L. M., 349
Perosa, S. L., 349
Perreault, S., 287
Perret, J., 272
Perret-Clermont, A., 272
Perris, E., 140
Perrucci, C. C., 441
Perrucci, R., 441
Perry, B. D., 297
Persaud, T. V., 103
Perusse, D., 423
Petersen, A. C., 318, 319, 320
Petersen, R., 184
Peterson, B. D., 102
Peterson, B. E., 55, 458
Peterson, C., 171
Peterson, G., 102
Peterson, G. W., 365
Peterson, J., 550
Peterson, J. A., 521
Petit, D., 310
Petit, G. S., 205
Pettit, G. S., 235, 252, 408
Pfefferbaum, B., 297
Phillips, D. A., 284
Phillips, L. H., 477
Phillips, S. J., 183, 184
Phillipsen, L., 251
Phinney, J. S., 81, 339, 340, 378, 379
Piaget, J., 23, 27, 28, 32, 39, 68–70, 72, 157, 158, 159, 185, 200, 207, 232, 233, 237, 266, 270, 271, 273, 275, 276, 310, 311, 312, 315
Pianta, R. C., 257
Picasso, P., 47, 66, 462, 463, 504
Pick, A. D., 183
Pickering, K., 116
Pierce, T., 405
Pillard, R., 96
Pillemer, K., 387
Pillow, B. H., 267
Pine, D., 420
Pine, F., 182
Pinon, M., 242
Pinto, A., 438
Pinto, J. P., 190
Piotrkowski, C. S., 441
Pirog-Good, M. A., 332
Pisoni, D. B., 188
Pleck, J. H., 329, 439
Plomin, R., 93, 96, 99, 136, 147, 527
Plutchik, R., 161
Pober, B., 187
Podolski, C. L., 241
Pollack, D., 506
Pollack, H., 122
Pollitt, E., 124, 213
Pomerantz, E. M., 284
Pomerleau, A., 196
Poon, L. W., 57, 476
Pope, H. G., Jr., 307
Porges, S. W., 138
Porter, E. J., 518
Porter, R. H., 142
Posada, G., 168
Posner, A., 412
Poster, C. H., 516
Poulin, F., 270, 336
Poulin, R., 336
Poulin-Dubois, D., 161
Power, T. G., 9
Powers, B. P., 154
Powers, S. M., 190
Powlishta, K. K., 225–26, 227, 228
Prager, K. J., 403
Pratt, C., 201

Pratt, C. C., 532
Prawat, R. S., 282
Prentice, D. A., 335
Preski, S., 296
Presser, H. B., 485
Pressinger, R. W., 102
Preston, S. H., 393
Price, J. M., 201
Prieto, M. D., 276
Prior, M., 148
Prosser-Gelwick, B., 362, 363
Pulos, S., 314
Pushkar, D., 530
Putnam, S., 164, 278, 279
Putnam, S. P., 146, 155
Pyle, R. P., 257

Qian, Z., 393
Querido, J. G., 165
Quiggle, N. L., 269
Quinn, J. J., 74
Quinn, P. C., 161

Rachford, D., 206
Radin, N., 228
Radke-Yarrow, M., 154, 204, 205, 210
Rahe, R. H., 115
Raina, G., 230
Raj, M. S., 326
Raja, S. N., 333
Rakison, D. H., 161
Rakoczy, J., 198
Raley, R. K., 395
Ramberan, G., 420
Ramey, C. T., 212
Ramey, S. L., 212
Ramsay, L., 250
Ramsey, J. L., 160
Ranzijn, R., 474
Raphael, D., 329
Rapisarda, R., 511
Rapkin, B. D., 472
Rapoport, R., 441
Rapoport, R. N., 441
Raschick, M., 451
Rasinski, K., 510
Raskas, D. F., 460
Raudenbush, S. W., 297, 533
Ravdal, H., 519
Raver, C. C., 206
Ray, D. W., 403
Ray, W. J., 29, 31
Reagan, R., 130
Recchia, S., 245
Receputo, G., 511
Reddy, M., 310
Reddy, V., 165
Reed, J. M., 455
Reese, R., 278
Reeve, R. A., 274
Reicher, S., 334, 335
Reid, A., 82
Reilly, A. H., 415
Reimer, J., 359
Reimer, K., 360
Reinikainen, K., 110
Reisser, L., 360
Reiter, E. O., 303, 307
Reitman, D., 284
Remafedi, G., 327
Remschmidt, H., 317
Renoir, A., 474
Renshaw, P. D., 268
Rest, J. R., 232, 359
Reynolds, D. K., 492
Reynolds, K. J., 361
Rhodes, J., 310
Rhodes, R. C., 489
Ricciardelli, L. A., 317
Rice, M. L., 190, 193
Rice, P. L., 124, 128
Richards, C., 315
Richards, M. H., 306, 308, 316, 356
Richardson, R. A., 396
Richman, J., 415
Ricks, M. H., 157
Ridderinkhof, K. R., 509
Rideout, V. J., 21, 242
Ridgeway, C. L., 438, 465
Riebe, D., 489
Riegel, K. F., 476, 514
Riegel, R. M., 476

Riemann, R., 96
Rigsby, L. C., 336
Riley, B., 93
Riley, D., 415
Ringdal, G. I., 548
Ringdal, K., 548
Rinne, T., 110
Risley, T. R., 194
Rispoli, M., 191
Ritchie, S., 217
Ritter, C., 115
Ritter, J. M., 155
Robbins, R. N., 342
Roberto, K., 450
Roberts, E., 29
Roberts, J. E., 195, 379
Roberts, J. S., 351
Roberts, L. R., 274, 334
Roberts, R. E., 320
Robertson, B., 248, 290
Robertson, J., 151
Robertson, J. F., 320
Robertson, S., 115
Robin, D. J., 143
Robins, R. W., 248
Robinson, A. B., 361
Robinson, J. L., 169, 204, 205
Robinson, J. P., 452
Robison, C. C., 459
Rochat, P., 143, 165
Rodkin, P. C., 269, 334
Rodriguez, M. L., 202–3, 206, 235
Rodriguez-Fornells, A., 194
Rogers, C. R. A., 390, 398
Rogers, C. S., 352
Rogers, S. J., 425, 426
Rogoff, B., 193, 210
Rohde, P., 420, 494
Rohner, R. P., 78
Rokach, A., 419, 420
Rollins, K. B., 272
Rombach, P., 505
Rook, K. S., 529
Roosa, M. W., 120, 331
Rosario, M., 266
Rosch, E., 160
Roscigno, V., 447
Rose, E., 331
Rose, H., 226
Rose, S., 99
Rose, S. A., 138, 142
Rose, S. P., 144
Rosellini, L., 421
Rosen, A. B., 272
Rosen, C. S., 198
Rosen, K. H., 102
Rosen, K. S., 177
Rosen, W. D., 166
Rosenberg, M., 340
Rosenblatt, R. A., 128
Rosenfeld, A. H., 518, 526
Rosenfeld, S., 404
Rosenfield, A., 122
Rosenkoetter, L. I., 241
Rosenkoetter, M. M., 497
Rosenthal, R., 282
Rosenwald, G. C., 351
Rosnick, C. B., 476
Ross, G., 151
Ross, H. S., 197
Ross, M., 494
Rosser, B. R. S., 401
Rostosky, S. S., 445
Rotenberg, K. J., 267
Roth, D. L., 489, 512
Roth, M. S., 118
Roth, S. L., 85
Roth, W. E., 124
Rothbart, M. K., 146, 147, 155, 206
Rothbaum, F., 177
Rothblum, E. D., 401
Rotheram-Borus, M. J., 378
Rothstein-Fisch, C., 80
Rotte, M., 194
Rovee-Collier, C., 159
Rovet, J., 123
Rovine, M., 407
Rowe, D. C., 309, 325
Rowe, J. W., 471, 476, 507, 512, 516, 528, 529
Rowles, G. D., 519
Rozin, P., 272
Rubenstein, R. L., 470

Rubin, K. H., 148, 268, 448
Ruble, D. N., 225, 226, 248, 282
Rue, V. M., 131
Ruff, H. A., 142, 159
Rusbult, C. E., 422
Rush, J. C., 434
Russell, D. W., 528
Russell, S. T., 319
Rusting, R. L., 13
Rutkowska, J. C., 145
Rutter, M., 170, 171, 292
Ruzany, N., 280
Ryan, C., 401
Ryan, M. K., 361
Ryff, C. D., 390, 493, 517, 520, 530
Ryu, S., 362

Sabatelli, R. M., 349
Sabbagh, M. A., 195
Sabino, V. M., 52
Sachs, J., 340
Saczynski, J. S., 480
Saffran, J., 189
Sagi, A., 152, 168, 237
Sagrestano, L. F., 128
Sagrestano, L. M., 114
Sainio, K., 110
Sales, B. C., 34
Salisch, M. von, 267
Saltarelli, L. M., 159
Salthouse, T. A., 508
Salvatore, N., 475
Salzinger, S., 266
Sameroff, A. J., 82, 83, 127
Sampson, P. D., 121
Sampson, R. J., 297, 533
Samter, W., 403, 404
Sandberg, J. F., 176
Sanders, R. E., 395
Sandler, H. M., 248
Sandler, J., 255
Saner, H., 318
Sanna, L. J., 474
Sansavini, A., 140
Sanson, A., 148
Sanson, A. V., 146, 148, 155
Sansone, C., 364–65
Santelli, J. S., 330
Santillanes, G. F., 546
Saracho, O. N., 278
Sarkisian, N., 450
Sastre, M. T. M., 475
Sauer, W., 446
Saunders, C., 543
Saunders, D. M., 103
Savaya, R., 425
Savin-Williams, R. C., 326, 327, 328
Savitz-Smith, J., 102
Sawin, D. B., 155
Sayer, L. C., 452
Scantlin, R., 242
Scarbrough, J. W., 218
Scarr, S., 96
Schafer, W. D., 152
Schaffer, H. R., 149
Schaie, K. E., 478–79
Schaie, K. W., 33, 478–79, 480, 481, 529
Schatz, J. A., 158
Schechter, A., 159
Scheff, T. J., 208
Scher, A., 152
Schieffelin, B. B., 279
Schiffman, L. G., 490
Schipper, E. M., 315
Schlagman, N., 234
Schlein, S., 58
Schmid, J., 312
Schmitt, K., 241
Schmitt-Rodermund, E., 366
Schmitz-Scherzer, R., 527
Schneider, B. H., 156
Schneider, D. S., 486
Schneider, W., 287
Schneiderman, L. J., 493
Schneider-Rosen, K., 165
Schoen, R., 397
Scholnick, E. K., 256
Schooler, C., 517
Schopler, J., 413

Schouten, R., 441
Schroeder, M. L., 530
Schubert, T., 509
Schulenberg, J., 343, 363
Schulenberg, J. E., 341
Schultheiss, D. P., 374
Schultz, A., 436
Schultz, K. S., 498
Schultz, R. I., 187
Schulz, R., 532, 551
Schunck, D. H., 281
Schuster, C. S., 119
Schuster, M. A., 381
Schwandt, T. A., 20
Schwartz, A. N., 521
Schwartz, M., 490, 491
Schwartz, P. M., 123
Schwartz, S. J., 369
Schwarzer, R., 342
Schwebel, D. C., 198
Schweinhart, L. J., 216, 217
Schweinle, A., 160
Scogin, F., 477
Scopesi, A., 124, 128
Scott, J. P., 170
Scott, P. K., 495
Sears, D. O., 379
Sears, K. G., 275
Sears, P. S., 33
Sears, R. R., 33
Sebanc, A. M., 201
Sebby, R. A., 323
Secco, G., 194
Sedikides, C., 248
Seeley, J., 420
Seeman, T. E., 528
Segal, T., 466
Seguin, R., 196
Sehdev, H. M., 111
Seidner, L. B., 198
Seimyr, L., 155
Sekine, M., 310
Sekuler, R., 510
Seligman, M. E. P., 52, 171, 289
Selman, E., 506
Selman, R. L., 237, 238
Senn, C. Y., 380
Serbin, L. A., 225–26, 227, 272
Seriido, J., 405
Serovich, J. M., 382
Shaffer, T. G., 251
Shakespeare, W., 81
Shanahan, M. J., 212, 362, 389, 432
Shapiro, J. L., 117
Shapiro, J. P., 519, 520
Shapiro, M. F., 382
Share, D. L., 278
Sharp, L., 248, 282
Sharpley, C. F., 497, 498
Sharpsteen, D. J., 419
Sharur, H., 138
Shaver, P. R., 155, 156, 315, 316, 418
Shaw, B. A., 534
Shaw, H., 305, 317
Shay, K. A., 489
Shayer, M., 314
Shelton, D., 296
Sherr, L., 10
Sherraden, M. S., 114
Shibley, P. K., 55
Shields, P., 159
Shin, H., 532
Shin, K.-H., 441
Shinn, M., 457
Shirakawa, Y., 114
Shoda, Y., 77, 202–3, 206, 235
Shostak, A., 131
Shuchter, S. R., 486
Shull, R. L., 75
Shyi, G. C. W., 159
Shyu, S. J., 339
Sidle, A. L., 272
Siegel, B., 260
Siegel, L. S., 273
Siegler, I. C., 57
Siegler, R. S., 66
Siekevitz, P., 106
Sigman, M., 124
Signorella, M. L., 226
Silbereisen, R. K., 366
Silva, P. A., 278, 288

Silver, C. B., 523
Silver, M., 239
Silver, N., 442
Silverberg, S. B., 342
Silverman, P. R., 103
Silvern, L., 40, 158
Silverstein, A. B., 272
Silverstein, M., 481
Simard, C., 310
Simien, C., 320
Simion, F., 141
Simmons, R. G., 308, 309
Simon, B., 82
Simon, T., 513
Simons, R. L., 177, 178, 240, 320, 455
Simonsick, E. M., 531
Simonton, D. K., 480
Sinclair, W., 102
Singelakis, A. T., 519, 520
Singer, B., 9
Singer, D. G., 201, 202
Singer, J. L., 198, 201, 202, 462
Singer, L. T., 138
Singer, M., 318
Singer, W., 139
Singh, L., 193
Sinnott, J. D., 478
Sirsch, U., 282
Skaalvik, E. M., 280
Skaalvik, S., 280
Skerrett, K., 422
Skinner, B. F., 74, 75, 479–80
Skinner, M. L., 266
Skoric, M. M., 239, 240
Skorikov, V., 363
Slade, A., 202, 203
Slade, P., 131
Slater, A., 29, 140
Slavik, S., 415
Slavin, R. E., 278
Sledge, P. A., 486
Sleigh, M. J., 116
Sliwinski, M. J., 476
Sloan, M., 121
Slomczynski, K. M., 435
Sloutsky, V. M., 273
Slovak, K., 318
Smailes, E., 122, 331
Small, R., 128
Small, S. A., 329, 342, 415
Smart, S. A., 247
Smart, T., 466
Smerglia, V. L., 428
Smetana, J. G., 226, 234, 324
Smit, F., 495
Smith, A. C., 456
Smith, B. A., 142
Smith, D., 264
Smith, D. C., 543
Smith, D. I., 456
Smith, E., 273
Smith, E. M., 434
Smith, G., 520
Smith, J., 4, 212, 452, 495, 496
Smith, J. E., 227
Smith, K. E., 176, 195
Smith, K. R., 485
Smith, P. K., 250, 481, 484, 485
Smith, S. E., 402, 403
Smith, T. L., 287
Smith, Y. L. S., 354
Smock, P. J., 9
Snarey, J. R., 359
Snell, P., 103
Snow, C. E., 193
Snowden, L. R., 320
Snyder, C. L., 521
Snyder, C. R., 52, 55, 171, 173
Snyder, D. J., 357
Sobel, D. M., 198
Soberanes, B., 124
Sobhan, M., 320
Soet, J. E., 115
Sokol, R. J., 121
Solari, F., 155
Solomon, J., 155, 157
Solomon, M. R., 415
Somerfield, M. R., 50
Somerson, M. D., 98, 409
Sonenstein, F. L., 329
Sonnentag, S., 434

Sophian, C., 274
Sorkin, D. H., 529
Sosa, R., 115
South, S. J., 393, 395, 425
Spanier, G. B., 446
Spear, L. P., 303
Spearman, C., 276
Spears, R., 287
Speckhard, A. C., 131
Spence, C., 142
Spence, I., 273
Spence, M. J., 111, 139
Spencer, M. B., 336, 339
Sperling, M. B., 351
Sperry, L. L., 203
Spinath, F. M., 96
Spitz, R., 173
Spitze, G., 451
Sprafkin, J., 240
Sprunger, L. W., 169
Spurlock, J. C., 325
Sroufe, L. A., 152, 156, 265
Stack, S., 427
Stahl, S. M., 14
Stake, R. E., 26
Stanley-Hagan, M., 485
Stanton, J. M., 516
Stanton, W. R., 333
Stattin, H., 230
Staudinger, U. M., 495, 496, 515
Stayton, D. J., 151
Stechler, G., 123
Steele, H., 155
Steele, M., 155
Stein, B. E., 142
Stein, S. K., 495
Stein, T. S., 328
Steinberg, L., 322, 323, 324, 336, 349, 362, 447
Steinberg, L. D., 339
Steinhauser, K. E., 542
Steinmetz, J. E., 73
Steinnes, D. N., 519
Stephens, M. A. P., 512
Stern, E., 66, 103
Stern, W., 103
Sternberg, R. J., 276, 422, 423, 444, 462, 523
Stets, J. E., 461
Stevens-Long, J., 507
Stevenson, H. W., 279
Stevenson-Hinde, J., 268
Stewart, A. J., 55, 457, 458
Stewart, P., 202
Stewart, P. A., 123
Stewart, S. L., 148
Stice, E., 305, 317
Stipek, D., 245
Stoddard, J. L., 116
Stoller, E., 519
Stoolmiller, M., 266
Storandt, M., 477
Storch, E., 445
Stovall, J. L., 116
Strange, M., 118, 123
Strapko, N., 401
Strayer, J., 236, 360
Streigel-Moore, R. H., 308
Streissguth, A. P., 121
Striano, T., 165, 198
Stricker, G., 524
Striegel, P., 132
Strober, M., 317
Stroebe, M., 549
Stroebe, W., 164
Stroh, L. K., 415
Stromquist, N. P., 364
Strouse, D., 322
Strouse, D. L., 336
Stuart-Hamilton, I., 475
Stuewig, J., 266
Styfco, S., 217
Sue, D. W., 378
Sullivan, A., 351
Sullivan, C., 376
Sullivan, H. S., 68, 267
Sullivan, K., 351
Sullivan, M. D., 173
Sullivan, M. W., 164
Sullivan, P., 314
Sullivan, R., 486

Sullivan, S. D., 97
Sundin, E., 98
Super, C. H., 208
Susser, E., 123
Sutton-Smith, B. A., 250
Suzman, R., 531
Suzuki, L., 80
Swan, S. H., 121
Swank, P. R., 176, 195
Swann, W. B., Jr., 247
Swanson, C., 442
Sweet, S., 415, 461
Swingly, D., 190
Swisher, R., 415, 461
Swyer, P. R., 118
Sympson, S. C., 171
Syre, C. R., 274, 334
Sytniac, M., 115
Szkrybalo, J., 225

Tabors, P. O., 191
Taghavi, M. R., 296
Tajfel, H., 82
Tallman, I., 403
Tam, H. P., 349
Tamis-LeMonda, C. S., 178, 198, 202
Tanenbaum, S., 527
Tang, C. S., 307
Tang, C. S. K., 342
Tangney, J. P., 208, 210, 252, 253
Tanner, J. M., 124, 303, 308
Tardif, C., 156
Targ, D. B., 441
Tarr, M. J., 161
Tausig, M., 415
Taylor, H., 545
Taylor, H. G., 21
Taylor, J., 340
Taylor, J. H., 239
Taylor, L. C., 257, 291
Taylor, M., 201
Taylor, P. M., 120
Taylor, R. D., 349
Taylor, R. J., 9, 395, 529–30
Taylor, S. J., 18, 22, 24, 26–27, 28
Taylor, W. C., 285
Tazelaar, F., 497
Teachman, J. D., 393
Teaff, J. D., 488
Tees, R. C., 140
Tell, E. J., 520
Teller, D. Y., 140
Tenenbaum, H. R., 251
Tennen, H., 52
Teong, S. K., 275
Terenzini, P. T., 358
Terman, L. M., 33
Teti, D. M., 206
Thabes, V., 9
Tharp, R. G., 292, 293
Thatcher, R. W., 315
Thelen, E., 145, 189
Thoits, P. A., 387
Thomas, A., 146, 147
Thomas, E. J., 81
Thomas, R. M., 43, 50, 57
Thomas, V., 132
Thomasson, G. C., 409
Thompson, J., 272
Thompson, J. J., 381
Thompson, J. M., 352
Thompson, L. W., 224, 550
Thompson, M., 512
Thompson, M. W., 98
Thompson, R. A., 202, 203, 239
Thompson, S. K., 225
Thornton, A., 327, 350, 393, 405, 448
Thornton, M. C., 335
Thwaites, R., 320
Tichauer, R., 125
Tiedeman, D. V., 366
Tiedje, L. G., 433
Tilly, C., 434
Timberlake, J. M., 399
Tinsley, H. E. A., 488
Tinsley, V. S., 191
Tizard, B., 171
Toguchi, Y., 248

Tolman, E., 76–77
Tolson, T. F. J., 485
Tomarken, A. J., 320
Tomasello, M., 198
Tomer, A., 492
Tomlin, A. M., 484
Tonkiss, J., 123
Tooby, J., 63
Toohey, S. B., 457
Torbert, W. R., 315
Torff, B., 276
Touron, D. R., 509
Townsend, M. A. R., 267
Tracy, J. L., 156
Tracy, R. L., 153
Travis, C. B., 445
Trawick-Smith, J., 199–200
Tremblay, R. E., 310
Trent, K., 425
Trethowan, W., 125
Trevarthen, C., 166
Trevethan, S. D., 361
Triandis, H., 78
Triandis, H. C., 78, 79, 287, 333
Triffon, B. J., 484
Troiden, R. R., 357
Tronick, E. Z., 23, 161, 164, 169
Trumbull, E., 80
Trzesniewski, K. H., 248
Tsao, F.-M., 188
Tschann, J. M., 427
Tually, K., 140
Tucker, M. B., 395
Tudge, J., 278, 279
Tudge, J. R. H., 70, 267
Turati, C., 141
Turiel, E., 234, 361
Turkheimer, E., 198
Turner, B. J., 52
Turner, M., 169
Turner, P. J., 226
Turner, R. J., 340
Turrell, S. L., 197
Twain, M., 266
Tyler, R., 122
Tyson, P., 160

Udry, J. R., 326
Uhly, B., 138
Umbel, V. M., 194
Umberson, D., 419, 486
Uncapher, H., 530
Unger, O., 198
Ungerer, J. A., 103
Urberg, K. A., 337, 339
Urrutia, J., 115
Utian, W. H., 445
Utton, J. L., 508
Uzgiris, I. C., 198, 202

Vaid, J., 186
Vaillancourt, T., 267
Vaillant, G. E., 52, 474
Valas, H., 290
Valdez-Menchaca, M. S., 195
Valery, J. H., 350
Valk, A., 335
Valkonen, T., 486
Vallerand, R. J., 287
Valsiner, J., 174, 202, 209, 228, 278, 279, 353, 354
Van Boxtel, M. P. J., 480–81
Vandell, D. L., 216
van der Heijden, P. G. M., 233
van der Mark, I. L., 237
van der Molen, M. W., 509
Van der Vegt, G., 285
Van De Vliert, E., 285

Vandewater, E. A., 21, 242, 457
Van Geert, P., 272
van Goozen, S. H. M., 354
van IJzendoorn, M. H., 152, 154, 168, 237, 278
VanLear, C. A., 446
van Naerssen, A. X., 401
van Nguyen, T., 389
Vannoy, D., 427
Vanrie, J., 23
Van Wieringen, J. C., 308
Van Willigen, M., 488
Vaughan, T. L., 113
Vaughn, B. E., 146, 156, 250
Veenhoven, R., 5
Veenman, M. V. J., 275
Vega, W. A., 343
Vellet, S., 176
Venter, J. C., 93
Verfaillie, K., 23
Verhaeghen, P., 477
Verhoeven, L., 195
Verloove-Vanhorick, S. P., 138
Veroff, J., 402
Vicary, J. R., 327
Vigil, J., 395
Vinokur, A., 441
Vitaro, F., 310
Vittimberga, G. L., 75
Vogl-Bauer, S., 85–86
Volling, B. L., 250
von Bertalanffy, L., 83
Vondracek, F. W., 363
Vorhees, C. V., 121
Vosler, N. R., 441
Voydanoff, P., 438, 439
Vygotsky, L. S., 68, 70–72, 200, 206–7, 257, 272, 273

Wager, M., 409
Wagner, B. M., 284
Wagner, E., 204
Wagner, P., 208
Wahlberg, V., 132
Waihe'e, J., 526
Wake, W. K., 276
Walasky, M., 56, 494
Wald, F., 543
Walden, T. A., 166
Waldman, I. R., 269
Walker, A., 183
Walker, A. J., 532
Walker, A. S., 143
Walker, L. J., 233, 239, 361
Walker, R., 23
Walker, R. A., 315
Walker-Andrews, A. S., 198
Wall, S., 152, 154
Wallace, A., 504
Wallace, E., 511
Wallace, I., 504
Wallace, I. F., 138
Wallack, L., 297
Wallack, S. S., 520
Wallechinsky, D., 504
Wallerstein, I., 452
Wallerstein, J. S., 427, 443
Walls, C. T., 530
Walsh, D. A., 239
Walters, R. H., 75, 76
Walther, E. J., 138
Wampler, R. S., 377
Wander, H., 505
Wang, G. Z., 131
Wang, H., 427
Wang, Q., 246
Wang, X., 154
Wardrop, J. L., 268
Warheit, G. J., 343
Warren, M. P., 306, 325

Warren, S., 68
Wartella, E. A., 21, 242
Watanabe, N., 527
Waterman, A. S., 47, 55, 56, 372, 374, 379
Waterman, M., 278
Waters, E., 152, 154, 156, 265
Waters, H. S., 191
Watkins, B. X., 327
Watkins, G., 441
Watkinson, B., 120
Watson, J., 246
Watson, M. W., 199
Watt, L. M., 495
Watt, T. T., 331
Waxman, S. R., 189
Way, N., 310
Weatherston, D. J., 177
Weber, C., 188
Weber, E. K., 234
Weber, J., 466
Weber, R. A., 323
Webster, D. W., 318
Webster, R. A., 343
Weckerle, J. R., 498
Wehner, E. A., 325
Weigel, D. J., 336
Weikart, D. P., 216, 217
Weindruch, R., 531
Weinfield, N. S., 152, 156
Weingarten, H. R., 427
Weinraub, M., 151, 227
Weinstein, R., 481
Weinstein, R. S., 248, 282
Weinstock, H., 329
Weisberg, C., 403
Weiskopf, S., 140
Weismantle, M., 436
Weiss, B., 205
Weiss, M. R., 286
Weiss, R. S., 497
Weissberg, R. P., 315
Weissman, S. H., 446
Weist, M. D., 296
Weitzman, B. C., 457
Wellman, H. M., 198, 246, 267, 275
Welsh, K. A., 57
Wenar, C., 203
Wendt, G., 68
Wendt, L., 452
Wenger, N. S., 382
Wentowski, G. J., 515
Wentworth, N., 158
Wentzel, K. R., 267
Werker, J. F., 140, 142
Werking, K. J., 403, 404
Wertheim, E. H., 304, 317
West, J., 257, 258, 259, 260
West, K., 519
Western, R. J., 474
Weston, D. R., 172
Wetherington, E., 405
Wethington, E., 387
Wewetzer, C., 317
Wheatley, S. M., 352
Whiffen, V. E., 352
Whiren, A., 195
Whitaker, M., 466
Whitall, J., 184
Whitbeck, L., 454
Whitbourne, S. K., 47, 55, 56, 370, 494
White, D. R., 124, 272
White, H. R., 393
White, J. M., 377
White, L. K., 424, 425
White, N., 476

White, R. W., 39, 51, 207, 209, 293, 390
Whitehead, J., 287
Whitehead, M. B., 103
Whitehurst, G. J., 195
Whitesell, N. R., 293
Whiting, B. B., 250
Whitlatch, C. J., 512, 513, 548
Wichstrom, L., 308
Widstroem, A., 155
Wierson, M., 309
Wigfield, A., 245
Wilcox, T., 160
Wilder, E. I., 331
Wilhelm, P., 275
Wilkinson, A., 273
Willard, H. F., 98
Williams, C., 253
Williams, C. C., 441
Williams, D., 118
Williams, G. A., 268
Williams, H. G., 184, 185
Williams, J. C., 409
Williams, J. M., 309
Williams, K., 393
Williams, K. M., 397
Williams, T. K., 335
Williamson, G. M., 532
Willinger, M., 112
Willis, S. L., 480, 490, 509
Wilmoth, G. H., 130, 504
Wilmut, I., 99
Wilson, B. J., 240
Wilson, K. S., 216
Wilson, M., 233
Wilson, M. A., 224
Wilson, M. N., 485
Wilson, M. S., 237
Wilson, P., 365
Wilson, P. T., 278
Wilson, R. S., 147
Wilson, S., 31
Wilson, S. M., 365
Wilson, T. D., 30
Wimbush, D. D., 9
Wimmer, H. M., 246
Windham, G. C., 121
Wingood, G. M., 331
Winfield, A., 476
Wingood, G. M., 331
Winn, K. I., 377
Winnicut, D., 68
Winnicut, D. W., 235
Winslow, L., 510
Winston, R. M. L., 105
Winterhoff, P. A., 70
Wirth, O., 206
Wiseman, R. F., 519
Wolf, A. M., 306
Wolf, S. M., 544
Wolfe, M., 229
Wolfe, R., 519
Wolff, P. H., 161, 165
Wolfinger, N. H., 394
Wong, C. A., 342
Wong, P. T. P., 495
Woo, G., 114
Wood, C. H., 226, 334
Wood, J. V., 247
Woodcock, R. W., 478, 480
Woodruff, K., 297
Woods, M. F., 445
Woodson, R. W., 141
Woody, E., 269, 270, 334
Wooldredge, J., 397
Woolett, A., 117
Woolley, J. D., 198
Worchel, F. F., 138
Worchel, S., 334
Wortman, C. B., 485, 486
Woyach, R. B., 434, 453

Wright, B. R. E., 288
Wright, D. A., 381
Wright, D. M., 418
Wright, D. W., 439
Wright, E. R., 336
Wright, J., 331
Wright, J. C., 241, 242
Wu, C., 177
Wulf, S., 295
Wun, C. C., 285
Wyche, K. F., 378
Wylie, S. A., 509
Wylleman, P., 287

Xu, F., 159

Yamashita, T. S., 138
Yang, C., 437
Yang, L., 350
Yang, Y., 9
Yardley, P. G., 497
Yarrow, L., 171
Yarrow, L. J., 206
Yasui, M., 379
Yates, M., 360
Yau, J., 234, 324
Yelland, J., 128
Yerushalmi, H., 460
Yeung, D. Y., 307
Yeung, W. J., 176
Yordanova, J., 509
Yoshinaga, Y., 527
Young, R. A., 412
Youngblade, L. M., 202, 250, 266
Young-DeMarco, L., 405, 448
Younger, B., 160
Youniss, J., 267, 322, 360
Ytteroy, E. A., 229
Yule, W., 296

Zacks, E., 358
Zahn-Waxler, C., 204, 205, 210, 252, 253
Zakriski, A. L., 269
Zan, B., 234
Zanko, A., 98
Zanobini, M., 124, 128
Zarit, S. H., 451, 512, 513, 530, 548
Zayas, L. H., 155
Zelazo, P. D., 151, 233
Zelinski, E. M., 477
Zentall, S. R., 329
Zeskind, P. S., 155, 163
Zettel, L. A., 529
Zhao, H., 9
Zick, C. D., 485
Ziegert, D. I., 248, 290
Zigler, E. F., 217, 259, 319
Zilbach, J. J., 356
Zill, N., 257, 259, 260
Zimmerman, B. J., 226, 281
Zimmerman, R. S., 343
Zisook, S., 486
Ziv, M., 246
Zohar, A., 275
Zonderman, A. B., 476
Zucker, A. N., 131
Zucker, K. J., 141
Zuo, J., 442
Zuo, Y., 479
Zur, O., 274
Zuschlag, M. K., 47, 55, 56
Zusman, M., 394
Zweig, J. M., 327

# Subject Index

*Italic* page numbers refer to material in tables or figures.

abdominal reflex, *144*
ability grouping, for reading instruction, 278
abnormal development, genetic determinants of, 97–98
abortions, 128–32
  adolescent mothers, 331, 332
  case study, 130–31
  characteristics of women, 129, *130*
  controversy, 129, 132, 544
  definition, 128
  legalized, 129
  methods, 128
  nonsurgical, 128
  psychosocial impact, 129–32
  spontaneous, 97, 105, 123, 128
abstinence, 328–29
abuse
  consequences, 296
  sexual, 331
academic achievement
  disorders affecting, 290
  effects of child care, 215–16
  obstacles, 290, 292
  parental support, 447
  teachers' expectations and, 282–83
acceptance of life, 471–75, 493
accommodation, 69, *69*
Achilles tendon reflex, *144*
acquired immune deficiency syndrome. *See* AIDS
active euthanasia, 544, 545
activities of daily living (ADLs), 514, 531, *531*
acute brain syndromes, 512–13
adaptation, 69, *69*, 83
adaptive self-organization, 83
adaptive self-regulation, 83
ADHD (attention deficit/hyperactivity disorder), 287
adolescence
  Erikson's stage, 302
  pregnancies, 114, 119–20, 330–33, 485
  stages, 41
  *See also* early adolescence; later adolescence
adulthood
  aggressive behavior, 240–41
  fulfillment theories, 389–92
  life course, 388–89
  social roles, 387–88
  *See also* early adulthood; later adulthood; middle adulthood; very old age
advance directives, 540. *See also* living wills
advocates, parents as, 177
affects, 77, *77*
affiliative values, 522, 523
African Americans
  alcohol use in middle childhood, 343–44
  average ages at menarche, 304
  body images of girls, 305–6, 308
  child care arrangements, 214
  college enrollment, 363
  depression, 115, 320
  ethnic identity, 339
  factors in premature births, 119
  family and peer relations in adolescence, 340
  female-headed families, 455
  funeral rituals, 548
  grandparents as caregivers, 485

income sources in retirement, 499
intergenerational relationships, 482
language used with children, 194
male adolescents' views of parenthood, 332
marriage rates, 395
mothers' perceptions of infant crying, 155
physical activity in adolescence, 306
preschool, 216
religious service attendance, 529–30
role sequencing, 388
social support, 323
teenage pregnancy, 330–31, 485
unemployment, 440, *440*, 464
weapons-related violence, 318
well-being, 391
age-graded expectations, 43
ageism, 493, 524–25
agency
  initiative and, 251–52
  in private self, 370
  in psychosocial theory, 57
  in toddlerhood, 206
  in very old age, 516
aggression
  bullying, 269, 318
  in early adolescence, 316
  exposure to violence and, 240–41, *240*, 296
  neurobiology, 297
  in workplace, 441
aggressive-rejected children (bullies), 269
aggressive-withdrawn children, 270
aging
  behavioral slowing, 508–10
  effects, 13
  genetic influences, 513–14
  physical changes, 507–14, *508*
  sensory changes, 510–12, *510*
  successful, 516, *516*
  usual, 516
  *See also* later adulthood; very old age
AIDS (acquired immune deficiency syndrome)
  in adolescents, 329
  deaths from, 553
  NAMES quilt project, 553
  societal change and, 9–10
  transmission from mothers to children, 122
alcohol
  binge drinking, 342, 343, 381
  effects on prenatal development, 121
  factors associated with use of, 341–43
  physical effects, 341–42
  use in early adolescence, 321, 341–43, *342*
  use in later adolescence, 381, 382
  use in middle childhood, 343–44
alienation, 335–36
alleles, 93–94
Allied Chemical, 123
Alzheimer's disease, 512–13, 540, 543, 551
ambiguous loss, 551, 552
American Academy of Pediatrics, 239–40
American Psychological Association, ethical guidelines, 34
Amish funeral rituals, 547, 548
amniocentesis, 110
amniotic sac, 104
ancestors, honoring, 526, 546
androgens, 356
androgyny, 131, 356, 522
anger, in toddlerhood, 203
anorexia, 316–17. *See also* eating disorders

anxiety
  binding, 212
  death, 492, 525
  in infancy, 163
  retirement, 498
  social, 420.
anxious-avoidant attachment, 153
anxious-resistant attachment, 153
Apgar scoring method, 137, *137*
appraisal, 50
Arab American families, 482
Arab cultures, 424–25
artificial insemination, 104, 229
ARTs. *See* assisted reproductive technologies
Asian Americans
  ethnic identity, 339
  extended families living together, 518
  factors in career choices, 363
  fertility rates, 405
  physical activity in adolescence, 306
  unemployment rates, 440, *440*
assimilation, 69, *69*
assisted living, 521
assisted reproductive technologies (ARTs), 102–3, 104–5, *105*
attachment, 265–66
  anxious-avoidant, 153
  anxious-resistant, 153
  critical period, 170–71
  definition, 148
  development stages, 149–50, *149*
  disorganized, 153–54
  distinction from trust, 167
  to former spouse, 427
  identity formation and, 351, 352
  impact on self-regulation, 206
  in infancy, 148–57
  insecure, 151–52
  in later adolescence, 349, 351
  moral development and, 239
  object permanence and, 160
  patterns, 152–54
  quality, 151–52
  relationship formation and, 418
  relevance to later development, 155–57, 265–66
  secure, 153, 154, 155–57, 349, 352
  separation anxiety and, 151–52
  significant figures, 152
  stranger anxiety and, 150–51
  working models, 153
attachment behavior system, 148–49
attachment formation, challenges for low-birthweight babies, 138
attachment schemes, 150
attention deficit/hyperactivity disorder (ADHD), 287
authority relations, 412, 434
automobiles, car seats, 175
autonomous morality, 232–33
autonomy
  attachment and, 351
  college experience and, 350–51
  conflicts with belonging, 337–39
  definition, 337
  in early adolescence, 337–39
  in later adolescence, 349–53
  leaving home and, 349–50
  from parents, 349–53
  self-sufficiency and, 351–53
  in toddlerhood, 47–48, 208, 251
avoidance conditioning, 231

babbling, 188
babies. *See* infancy
Babinski reflex, 108, *144*

behavioral slowing, 508–10
behaviorism, 76–77, 78, 231
bereavement
  definition, 549
  factors affecting, 551–53
  introjection, 554
  patterns, 550, *550*
  psychosocial growth through, 553–54
  *See also* grief; widowhood
bilingualism, 194
binge drinking, 342, 343, 381
binge eating, 316. *See also* eating disorders
biological system, in psychosocial approach, 6, *6*
birth control, 329–30, 332–33, 382
birth culture, 124–28
birth defects, 97
birth process, 111
  American view, 127
  anesthetics, 123
  cesarean sections, 111–12, 113
  cultural context, 126–28
  doulas, 115
  father's involvement, 117–18
  maternal deaths, 129–30
  stages, 111, *112*
  *See also* newborns; premature infants
Blacks. *See* African Americans
blended families, 446, 454
blindness, 510
body
  care after death, 545–46
  exploration of, 252
  organ inferiority, 289
  physical appearance, 356
  *See also* physical maturation
body image
  of boys, 307
  of girls, 304
  link to depression, 304, 305, 320
  link to eating disorders, 305, *305*, 317
  link to self-esteem, 304
boundaries
  of family, 85
  group, 322–23, 334
boys
  physical changes at puberty, 307, 308–9
  *See also* gender; men
brain
  brainstem, 540
  changes at puberty, 310, *311*
  cortex, 540
  development in infancy, 139, 186
  development throughout childhood, 186
  language processing, 186, *186*
  plasticity, 186
  prenatal development, 106, 108, 111, 121
  sex differences, 224
breastfeeding, 142
Buddhist funeral rituals, 546
bulimia, 317. *See also* eating disorders
bullying, 269, 318
Bush, George H. W., 257

caffeine, 121
capitalist economy, 433
cardiopulmonary death, 539, 540
care, as prime adaptive ego quality, 463
career choice, 361–69
  ages, 366
  decision making, 365–69
  education and, 363–64
  factors in, 362–65, *362*

gender expectations, 358, 363, 364–65
Internet resources, 368
labor market factors, 368–69
phases of decision making, 366–68, 367, 434
career management, 432–42
competence, 433–36
in later adulthood, 480
midlife changes, 436–37
See also employment
career maturity, 366
career phases, 413–15, 414
caregiver-infant interaction
communication repairs, 169
coordination, 169
development of empathy and, 237
differences between mothers and fathers, 152, 176–77
intersubjectivity, 166, 177
matching, 169
mismatch, 169
mutuality, 168–70, 408, 422
sensitivity, 154–55, 154, 170
social referencing, 166–67
synchrony, 149, 169
See also attachment; parent-child relationships; parenting
caregivers
of aging parents, 340–41, 449–51, 532
of Alzheimer's patients, 512–13, 543
cultural context, 154–55
of dying, 543, 551
grandparents as, 484–85
caregiving
attachment and, 149
See also parenting
caring, 360–61
case studies, 25–26, 32
cataracts, 510
categorical identifications, 245–46
categories
classification skills, 273–74
gender labels, 225
people, 334
semantic, 190
categorization
object, 160–61
skill, 273
causality, 157
causal schemes, 157–59, 158
cemeteries, 539, 546
Center for the Prevention of School Violence, 298
Centers for Disease Control and Prevention, 381
central process, 47–48, 48
in early adolescence, 336–40
in early adulthood, 422
in early school age, 254–56
in infancy, 168–70
in later adolescence, 375–79
in later adulthood, 494–95
in middle adulthood, 460–63
in middle childhood, 291–93
in toddlerhood, 210
in very old age, 527–30
cesarean sections, 111–12, 113
childbearing
decisions about, 405–7, 408–9
effects on marriage, 406, 407–8
fertility rates, 405, 407
reproductive technology, 102–3, 104–5, 105, 407
See also birth process; pregnancy
childbirth. See birth process
child care, 214–18
arrangements, 214–15, 214
future of, 217–18
by grandparents, 485
impact on intelligence and academic achievement, 215–16
impact on peer relations, 217
impact on relationship with mother, 216–17
impact on social competence, 216–17
play in, 202
selecting, 177

childhood. See early school age; middle childhood
childrearing. See parenting
children
decision not to have, 408–9
homeless, 457
research with, 34
step-, 454
Chinese Americans
factors in career choice, 363
intergenerational relationships, 482
See also Asian Americans
choice phase, of career decision making, 367, 368
chromosomal disorders, 97–98, 97
chromosomes, 93, 94, 95, 224–25
chronic brain syndrome, 512–13
chronic depression, 460
chronosystems, 84–85
cigarettes. See smoking
clarification phase, of career decision making, 367, 368
classical conditioning, 73–74, 73, 77, 78
classification, 273–74
climacteric, 444
clinical samples, 22–23
cliques, 321, 322, 334. See also peer groups
cloning, 98–99
cocaine, 121–22
codominance, 94–95
coercive escalation, 402
coffee, 121
cognition, 68
meta-, 70, 275
social, 76
cognitive behaviorism, 76–77, 78, 78
cognitive competencies, 77, 77
cognitive developmental theory, 68–72
implications for human development, 70, 72
moral development, 232–34, 243
Piaget's theory, 68–70, 72, 157
psychosocial theory and, 72
stages, 69, 72
view of guilt, 252–53
Vygotsky's theory, 70–72
cognitive functioning
declining mental abilities with age, 478–79, 479
definition, 476
expertise, 495–96
interaction of heredity and environment, 99, 100, 479–81
in later adulthood, 475–81
processing load, 508–9
in very old age, 508–9
workplace productivity and, 480
See also intelligence
cognitive maps, 77
cognitive unconscious, 65, 66
cohabitation, 399–400
cohorts, 389
cohort sequential studies, 33, 33
collective efficacy, 533
collectivism, 79, 80, 80, 361, 393–94, 482
colleges, enrollment, 348, 363
college students
adapting to college, 352
autonomy, 350–51
binge drinking, 381
career decisions, 366
gender role attitudes, 358
goals, 364–65, 365
identities, 370–71
moral reasoning, 359–60
role experimentation, 375–76
See also later adolescence
combinatorial skills, 274
commitment
identity status and, 372–73
love and, 423
common bond, issues of, 336
common identity, issues of, 335–36
communication
gender differences, 403–4
gestures, 188–89

in marriage, 402–4, 426, 442
See also language
communication disorders, 290
communication repairs, 169
communicative competence, 185–87, 189–91
communion, 57
community-based long-term health care, 521
community services, for very old, 533
comparative assessments, 246
competence
illusion of, 284–85
in later adulthood, 474
meanings, 293
in occupation, 433–36
as prime adaptive ego quality, 293–94
relationship to self-esteem, 293–94, 474
social, 216–17, 265–66
competence motivation, 390
competition, 286
compulsions, 211–12
compulsive sexual behavior, 421
computer-mediated relationships, 396
computers
in schools, 295, 295
use by older adults, 488–89
concrete operational thought, 69, 270–75, 276
classification, 273–74
combinatorial skills, 274
comparison to formal operational thought, 310
components, 275
conservation, 271–72, 271
reversibility, 270
confidence, 530
conflicts
among ethnic groups, 81
among friends, 250, 266
in marriage, 266, 402–3, 442–43
role, 437
conformity, 267, 337. See also peer pressure
conscience, 235
consensual unions, 400
conservation, 271–72, 271, 274
constructivist perspective, on gender differences, 224
Consumer Product Safety Commission, 217
contactful interactions, 403
content, of identity, 370–71, 374–75
contextualizing learning, 292–93
continuing care retirement communities, 520
continuity, 78, 81
continuous reinforcement, 75
contraception, 329–30, 332–33, 382
control groups, 30
controlling interactions, 403
conventional morality, 233, 359
conventions. See social conventions
cooperation, 285
coordination, in caregiver-infant interaction, 169
coping behavior, 50–52
core pathologies, 52, 53
in early adolescence, 341
in early adulthood, 423
in early school age, 256–57
in infancy, 173–74
in later adolescence, 379–80
in later adulthood, 496
in middle adulthood, 463
in middle childhood, 294
in toddlerhood, 211–12
in very old age, 530–31
Cornell Retirement and Well-Being Study, 497
correlation, 24–25, 25
couvade, 125
co-workers, friendships with, 412–13, 415, 419
CoZi schools, 259–60
crawling, 144, 146
creativity, 460, 461–63
creeping reflex, 144

crime
gang-related, 338
homicide, 296, 338, 544
victims, 296
See also delinquency; violence
crises, psychosocial. See psychosocial crises
crisis, identity status and, 372–73
critical periods, 257
for attachment, 170–71
in prenatal development, 107
cross-sectional studies, 32–33
crowds, 321–23, 324, 336. See also peer groups
crystallization phase, of career decision making, 367, 368
crystallized intelligence ($G_c$), 478, 509
Cuban Americans
alcohol use in middle childhood, 343–44
mothers' perceptions of infant crying, 155
See also Hispanic Americans
cultural determinism, 78, 79
cultural differences
childrearing, 80, 146, 154–55, 165, 175–76
fantasy play, 202
funeral rituals, 545–46
gender expectations, 224, 226–27
theories of, 78–79
cultural theory, 78–81
implications for human development, 79–81
psychosocial theory and, 81
culture
cognitive development mediated by, 70–71, 72
context of birth and pregnancy, 124–28
definition, 50, 78
influence on development, 7
influences on gender identity, 353–54, 365
physical, 78
social, 78
socialization in, 78–79
taboos, 253
cumulative relation, 94

dating
after death of spouse, 486
in early adolescence, 325
in early adulthood, 392, 394
in later adulthood, 486
online, 395, 396
in very old age, 524
death
ambiguous loss, 551, 552
anxiety about, 492, 525
arrangements, 492, 542
care of body, 545–46
causes, 541
changing views over life span, 490, 538–39
definitions, 539–40
direct experiences of, 539
dying process, 540–42
fear of, 492, 492
good, 542–44
homicide, 296, 338, 544
infant mortality, 112–13, 119
locations, 539, 542
perspectives on in later adulthood, 490–92, 538–39
perspectives on in very old age, 525–27
rituals, 545–48
stigmatized, 552–53
sudden, 550, 551
suffering, 541
survivors, 546–48
terminal illnesses, 540–41, 543, 544
unacknowledged loss, 551–52
See also bereavement; grief; suicides; widowhood
decentering, 312, 313, 334, 370
defense mechanisms, 66
degree of suffering, 541

delayed gratification, 206, 207
delinquency, 317–18
    gangs, 338, 373
    negative identity and, 373
    relationship to physical maturation,
        308–9
dementia, 476, 512–13, 543
dependency, in very old age, 514, 514,
        531, 531, 532–33
dependent variables, 30
depressed mood, 318–19
depression
    anaclitic, 173
    body image and, 304, 305, 320
    chronic, 460
    in early adolescence, 309, 316, 318–
        21, 420
    in early adulthood, 420
    gender differences, 320–21
    grief and, 549, 550
    isolation and, 420
    in later adulthood, 473, 486, 487, 494
    in middle adulthood, 460
    of mothers, 155, 170, 253, 256, 320
    during pregnancy, 115, 116
    risk factors, 320
    in very old age, 530
depressive syndrome, 319
despair, 493–94
development
    abnormal, 97–98
    assumptions, 5
    psychosocial approach, 6–11
    through life span, 5, 11–14
developmental disabilities
    communication disorders, 290
    social relationship problems and, 270
developmental stages, 40–43, 42
    developmental tasks in, 43–44, 45
    ego conflicts, 40
    ego skills, 40
    Erikson's model, 40, 41, 72
    of families, 446–49
    Piaget's theory, 69, 72
    in psychosexual theory, 66
developmental systems theory, 85
developmental tasks, 43–44, 45
    in early adolescence, 303–33
    in early adulthood, 392–417
    in early school age period, 222–51
    in infancy, 137–67
    in later adolescence, 349–69
    in later adulthood, 471–92
    in middle adulthood, 432–57
    in middle childhood, 264–88
    in toddlerhood, 183–207
    in very old age, 507–25
development theories, 38–39, 86–87
    See also cognitive developmental the-
        ory; psychosocial theory
dieting, 305
differentiation, 349
diffidence, 530–31
Digo, toilet training, 209
dilation, 111
disabilities
    children with, 260, 270
    definition, 260
    developmental, 270, 290
    in very old age, 510, 514
discipline
    inductions, 205
    link to social competence, 266
    love withdrawal, 205, 253
    moral development and, 235, 238–39
    power assertion, 205
    in toddlerhood, 204–5
disclosure, of sexual orientation, 327–28,
        357, 400–401
discontinuity, 79, 81
discrimination, employment, 463–66
disdain, 496
disengaged relationships, 421
dismissing avoidant individuals, 418
disorders
    communication, 290
    learning, 290
    motor skills, 290
disorganized attachment, 153–54

displaced homemakers, 437
dissociation, 341
division of labor
    in households, 404, 438, 452, 453
    in teams, 285–86
divorce, 423–28
    attachment to former spouse, 427
    child custody arrangements, 454,
        484–85
    coping with, 426–28
    in early years of marriage, 402
    effects on grandparents, 485
    factors in, 424–26
    family history of, 426
    financial settlements, 452
    rates, 424
dizygotic (fraternal) twins, 99, 102
DNA, 93, 93
dominance relation, 95
doubt, 210
doulas, 115
Down syndrome
    life expectancies of children, 100–101
    risk factors, 120
drugs
    effects on prenatal development, 120–
        23
    fertility, 104
    RU-486, 128
    use in early adolescence, 321, 341–43,
        342
    use in middle childhood, 343–44
dual-earner couples
    adjustment to marriage, 404–5
    adjustment to retirement, 497
    division of household labor, 404, 438,
        452
    effects of children, 406
    lifestyle patterns, 416
    work-family issues, 438–39
    See also women, employment
durable power of attorney, 540, 543
dying process, 540–42. See also death
dying trajectory, 540
DZ twins [dizygotic (fraternal) twins],
        99, 102

early adolescence
    ages, 302
    alcohol and drug use, 321, 341–43,
        342
    central process in, 336–40
    core pathology, 341
    developmental tasks
        emotional development, 315–21
        formal operational thought, 309–
            15
        peer group membership, 321–24,
            333–35, 337
        physical maturation, 303–9
        romantic and sexual relationships,
            313–14, 324–33
    high school experiences, 314–15
    parenthood in, 119–20, 330–33
    prime adaptive ego quality, 340–41
    psychosocial crisis, 333–36
    relationships with parents, 309, 323–
        24, 340, 439, 447–48
    sleep deprivation, 310
    suicides, 319, 321
    work experiences, 362
    See also puberty
early adulthood
    ages, 392
    central process in, 422
    core pathology, 423
    developmental tasks
        childbearing, 405–9
        exploring intimate relationships,
            392–405
        lifestyle, 415–17
        work, 409–15
    prime adaptive ego quality, 422–23
    psychosocial crisis, 417–22
    relationships with parents, 448
early school age
    central process in, 254–56
    concrete operational thought, 274
    core pathology, 256–57

developmental tasks, 222–23
    gender identification, 222, 223–30
    moral development, 222, 230–43
    peer play, 223, 248–51
    self-theory, 222–23, 243–48
egocentrism, 312
gross motor skills, 184
influence of teachers, 267
language development, 191–92
prime adaptive ego quality, 256
psychosocial crisis, 251–54
relationships with parents, 447
school readiness, 257–60
eating disorders, 305, 305, 316–17
ecological niches, 63
education
    as central process of middle child-
        hood, 291–93
    influence on career choice, 363–64
    See also academic achievement; schools
educational attainment
    marriage age and, 393
    relationship to divorce, 425
    relationship to incomes, 363, 363
    unemployment rates and, 440, 440
effacement, 111
efficacy, 76
    collective, 533
effortful control, 205–6
ego, 65, 66, 67
egocentric empathy, 236
egocentric speech, 207
egocentrism
    in adolescence, 312–13
    in early school age, 312
    in infancy, 312
ego ideal, 255
Elder Forums, 533
elderly. See later adulthood; very old age
electronic fetal heart rate monitoring,
        110
embryonic period, 103, 104–6
embryos, 104
emotional development
    age-related changes, 163, 164
    in early adolescence, 315–21
    in infancy, 161–67, 176
    in middle adulthood, 463
    parental influences, 176, 463
    in toddlerhood, 196–97
emotional differentiation, 161–63, 164
emotional regulation, 164–66
emotions
    anger, 203
    as channel for adult-infant communi-
        cation, 166–67
    feedback system, 161, 162
    guilt, 252–54
    sex differences in brain processes, 224
empathy
    for another's feelings, 237
    for another's life conditions, 237
    definition, 236
    development of, 236–37
    distinction from perspective taking,
        237
    in early school age period, 236–37
    gender differences, 361
    guilt based on, 252
    in infancy, 237
    in intimate relationships, 397–98
    levels, 236–37
    in middle childhood, 267
    in toddlerhood, 205, 216
employment
    adaptation to world of work, 409–13
    age and workplace productivity, 480
    authority relations, 412, 434
    career phases, 413–15, 414
    discrimination, 463–66
    in early adolescence, 362
    in early adulthood, 409–15
    of former welfare recipients, 413
    gender discrimination, 358
    hazards, 412
    of high school graduates, 363–64
    interpersonal relationships, 412–13,
        415, 434–35
    job mobility, 366, 411–12, 436

latent functions, 498
retirement, 496–500
role stagnation, 460
sex discrimination, 413, 419, 464–65
sexual harassment, 380, 419
technical skills, 412
training periods, 411, 412
trajectories, 388, 389
typical days, 409–11
work-family issues, 409, 414, 415–17,
        437–40, 438
    See also career choice; career manage-
        ment; dual-earner couples;
        women, employment
enactive attainments, 280, 280
encodings, 77, 77
enculturation, 78
endogamy, 394
enmeshed relationships, 421–22
environment
    influence on behavior, 99–101
    influence on cognitive functioning,
        479–81
    influence on intelligence, 99, 100,
        121, 479–81
    influence on motor development,
        144–46
environmental toxins, 123
epigenetic principle, 42
episodic memory, 476–77
equilibration, 233
equilibrium, 68
estrogen, 356, 444–45
ethical issues
    at end of life, 544–45
    in genetic technology, 98–99
    in reproductive technology, 103
    in research, 34–35
    See also moral development
ethnic group identity
    adjustment and, 379
    in early adolescence, 339–40
    interaction with personal identity,
        378–79
    role experimentation and, 377–79
    social support, 530
    stages, 378
ethnic groups
    bias in standardized tests, 29
    childrearing differences, 155
    conflicts among, 81
    discrimination against, 464, 465
    extended families, 482
    high school crowds, 322
    interethnic intimate relationships, 397
    marriage partner selection, 393–94
    poverty, 9
    subcultures, 50
    unemployment, 464
    unemployment rates, 440, 440
    See also African Americans; Asian
        Americans; cultural differences;
        European Americans; Hispanic
        Americans; minority groups;
        Native Americans
ethology, 63
European Americans
    alcohol use in middle childhood, 343–
        44
    average ages at menarche, 304
    body images of girls, 305, 306, 308
    college enrollment, 363
    depression, 115, 320
    extended families living together, 518
    factors in career choice, 363
    factors in premature births, 119
    female-headed families, 455
    funeral rituals, 545
    income sources in retirement, 499
    intergenerational relationships, 482
    male adolescents' views of parenthood,
        332
    maternal identification of girls, 227
    mothers' perceptions of infant crying,
        155
    physical activity in adolescence, 306
    social support, 323
    teenage pregnancy, 330–31
    unemployment, 440, 440, 464

weapons-related violence, 318
well-being, 391
euthanasia, 543–44, 545
evaluation, of identity, 370–71
evolution, psychosocial, 39–40, 64
evolutionary psychology, 63
evolutionary theory, 62–65
  implications for human development,
    63–64
  psychosocial theory and, 64–65
exclusivity, 423
exercise, 415, 417, 487–88, 489–90,
  508
exosystems, 84
expansion, 195
expectancies, 77, 77
experiential transcendence, 526, 527
experimental groups, 30
experiments, 30–31, 32
expertise, 495–96
exploration phase, of career decision
  making, 367, 368
extended families, 323, 453–54, 481–
  83, 518
external frames of reference, 280
externalizing problems, 316. See also
  aggression; delinquency
external validity, 31
extinction
  fear of, 526–27
  in operant conditioning, 75
extroversion, 473
eye color, genetic determination of, 95, 95

faceness, 140–41, 160
faces
  association with voices, 141–42
  top-heavy configuration, 141, 141
facial expressions
  emotions expressed by, 164
  of infants, 23, 164
  perception by infants, 141, 142, 166
families
  adjustments to new babies, 169
  blended, 446, 454
  developmental stages, 446–49
  disengaged and enmeshed relation-
    ships, 421–22
  divorce in, 426
  extended, 323, 453–54, 481–83, 518
  filial obligation, 340–41, 450
  gendered environment, 227
  gender roles, 354
  Hindu joint, 354
  influence on career choice, 363
  influences on social competence, 265–
    66
  interdependence, 86
  intergenerational solidarity, 481
  rules, 85
  single-parent, 454–56
  as social context, 49–50
  social support, 323, 333
  solidarity, 340–41
  trajectories, 388, 389
  violence in, 266
  work-family issues, 409, 414, 415–17,
    437–40, 438
family households, 452. See also
  households
family systems theories, 85–86
fantasy play, 197–202
fast-mapping, 190
fathers
  adolescent, 331–32
  ages, 120, 406, 407
  attachment of infants, 152
  couvade, 125
  exposure to toxins, 123
  interactions with infants, 176–77
  involvement in childbirth, 117–18
  reactions to abortion, 131–32
  roles during pregnancy, 116–17
  step-, 454
  time spent on household tasks, 438
  See also parents
fear
  of death, 492, 492
  in infancy, 163

fearful avoidant individuals, 418
FedEx, 465
feedback mechanisms, 83
femininity, 356, 358, 374, 522
fertility drugs, 104
fertility rates, 405, 407
fertilization, 101–2
fetal alcohol syndrome, 121
fetal period, 103, 106–8
fetoscopy, 110
fetus, 106
fidelity
  definition, 379
  to others, 340–41
  to values and ideologies, 379
filial obligation, 340–41, 450
fitness
  in early adulthood, 415, 417
  in evolutionary theory, 62
  inclusive, 63
  in later adulthood, 487–88, 489–90
  in very old age, 507–8
flexion reflex, 144
fluid intelligence ($G_f$), 478, 509
foreclosed status. See identity foreclosed
  status
formal operational thought, 69, 276,
  309–15
  conceptual skills, 312, 312
  criticisms of, 315
  egocentrism and decentering, 312–13
  factors promoting, 313–15
  Piaget's theory, 310–12, 315
foundational categories, 161
fragile identity, 421
frail elderly, 531–34
frames of reference, 280
fraternal (dizygotic) twins, 99, 102
friends
  close, 267–68, 325
  conflicts among, 250, 266
  contributions to social development,
    266–68
  co-workers, 412–13, 415, 419
  in early adolescence, 314, 321–23
  in early adulthood, 412–13, 415, 419
  in early school age period, 250–51
  gender differences, 419
  groups and dyads, 251
  imaginary, 201, 202
  loyalty, 340
  in middle childhood, 265–70, 325
  mutuality, 422
  opposite-sex, 251, 267
  same-sex, 228, 250–51
  social support, 419
  in very old age, 524
  See also peers
fulfillment theories, 389–92
funeral rituals, 545–48
  Amish, 547, 548
  planning, 492, 542

$G_c$ (crystallized intelligence), 478, 509
$G_f$ (fluid intelligence), 478, 509
games
  group, 249–50
  hopscotch, 249, 249
  language, 196
  See also play
gamete intrafallopian transfer (GIFT), 105
gangs, 338, 373
gay men
  children of, 229
  emergence of homosexual identity,
    356–57
  gender nonconformity in childhood,
    228
  relationships in very old age, 524
  relationships with partners, 357–58,
    400–402
  stereotypes of, 357
gay rights organizations, 553
gender
  distinction from sex, 224–25
  meaning, 223, 225
  gender constancy, 225–26, 354
gender differences
  best friend relationships, 268

care of aging parents, 450–51
  communication styles, 403–4
  constructivist perspective, 224
  depression, 320–21
  experiences of guilt, 253
  experiences of puberty, 308
  identity formation, 374–75
  incomes, 363, 464
  individual differences perspective, 224
  interaction styles, 419
  interactions with friends, 250–51
  life expectancies, 506
  life objectives, 365, 365
  moral orientations, 360–61
  physical maturation, 304, 305
  play behaviors, 250
  power, 353–54
  prosocial behaviors, 361
gender discrimination, 358
gendered family environment, 227
gender expectations
  for career choice, 358, 363, 364–65
  cultural differences, 224, 226–27
gender identification
  components, 225–30, 225, 230
  in early school age period, 222, 223–
    30
  effects of parent's sexual orientation,
    229
  identification with parents, 227–28,
    355
  understanding gender, 225–26
gender identity
  cultural influences, 353–54, 365
  definition, 353, 356
  in homosexual relationships, 357–58
  integrating, 358
  in later adolescence, 353–58
  sexual dimension, 356
  of transsexuals, 354
gender labels, 225
gender preference, 228–30
gender role convergence, 522–23
gender role preferences, 358
gender roles
  career choice and, 364–65
  cultural influences, 353–54
  factors in socialization, 362–65, 362
  in families, 354
  stereotypes, 363
  in very old age, 522–25
gender role standards, 226–27
  in early school age period, 246
  of older adults, 524
  parental beliefs, 283, 284
  reevaluating in later adolescence, 355
gender schemes, 226, 230
gene pool, 92
generalizability, of research, 21
generativity, 457–59
genes, 92–93
  alleles, 93–94
  chromosomes, 93, 94, 95, 224–25
  DNA, 93, 93
  dominant and recessive relations, 95
  heterozygous, 94, 95
  homozygous, 94
genetic counseling, 98
genetic disorders, 97–98, 97
  hemophilia, 95, 95
  research on, 103
genetics
  aging and, 513–14
  determinants of abnormal develop-
    ment, 97–98
  determinants of development rates, 96
  determinants of individual traits, 96–
    97
  genes and chromosomes, 92–93
  influences on behavior, 99–101
  influences on cognitive functioning,
    479–81
  influences on environment, 96–97
  influences on motor development,
    144–46
  influences on temperaments, 147
  laws of heredity, 93–96
  sex-linked characteristics, 95–96, 95
genetic technology, 98–99

genome, 92, 93
genotypes, 94. See also reaction ranges
gentrification, 519
germinal period, 103, 104
gestures, 188–89
girls
  breast bud development, 304, 306,
    356
  physical changes at puberty, 304–7,
    309, 356
  See also gender; menarche; women
Glick effect, 425
global empathy, 236
goal-corrected partnership, 150
goals
  in cognitive behaviorism, 77, 77
  in later adulthood, 471–73, 473
grammar, 189, 190–91
grand-generativity, 458
grandparenthood, 481–85
  ages, 481
  caregiver role, 484–85
  disrupted relationships with grand-
    children, 485
  effects of divorce, 485
  great-grandchildren, 515
  living with other family members, 482
  meaning of role, 483–84
  in middle adulthood, 448–49
  styles, 481
grasping, by infants, 143–44
grasp reflex, 108, 143, 144
great-grandchildren, 515
grief, 548–50
  duration, 548–49
  expression of, 553
  symptoms, 549–50
  of widows, 486, 487, 550, 550
  See also bereavement
grief work, 549–50
group games, 249–50
group identity, 333–35, 336
  cognitive processes supporting, 333–
    34
  dimensions, 334–35
  ethnic, 339–40, 377–79
  in gangs, 338
group operations, 334
group representations, 333
groups
  boundaries, 322–23, 334
  dominant, 463
  emotional investment in, 335
  histories, 334–35
  ingroup and outgroup attitudes, 287–
    88, 288, 334
  loyalty, 340
  reference, 333, 342–43, 370
  rituals, 334
  shared markers, 334
  See also ethnic groups; peer groups
guilt, 252–54
Gusii people, 406

habituation, 139
hand preference, 146
Hawaiians, Native, 526
Head Start, 215, 217, 218
health
  effects of widowhood, 486
  factors in longevity, 13
  impact of poverty, 213
  impact on cognitive functioning, 476
  in later adulthood, 474, 476, 486
  in very old age, 512–14
health care
  for children, 177
  in very old age, 521
hearing
  in infancy, 139–40
  loss in very old age, 511
  See also sensory/perceptual
    development
helplessness
  learned, 289–90
  See also dependency
hemophilia, 95, 95
heredity, laws of, 93–96. See also
  genetics

heroin, 121
heteronomous morality, 232
heterosexuality. See sexual orientation
heterozygous genes, 94, 95
hierarchy of needs, 390, *391*
high schools
    cliques and crowds, 321–23, 336
    curriculum, 314–15
    See also early adolescence; schools
high self-monitoring children, 283
Hinduism
    funeral rituals, 546
    joint families, 354
Hispanic Americans
    alcohol use in middle childhood, 343–44
    average ages at menarche, 304
    barriers to academic achievement, 292
    child care arrangements, 214
    college enrollment, 363
    depression in adolescence, 320
    ethnic identity, 339
    female-headed families, 455
    fertility rates, 405
    gender role standards, 355
    income sources in retirement, 499
    intergenerational relationships, 482, 484
    maternal identification of girls, 227
    physical activity in adolescence, 306
    social support, 323
    teenage pregnancy, 330–31
    unemployment, 440, *440*
    weapons-related violence, 318
    well-being, 391
HIV (human immunodeficiency virus).
    See AIDS
holophrases, 189
homelessness, 456–57
homemakers, displaced, 437
homicide, 296, 338, 544
homogamy, 394
homosexuality. See gay men; lesbians;
    sexual orientation
homozygous genes, 94
hope, 171–73
hopelessness, 530
hopscotch, 249, *249*
hospice care, 543
households
    definition, 452
    division of labor, 404, 438, 452, *453*
    extended families, 482, 518
    management, 452–57
    one-person, 456, 518
    resource management, 452–53
Human Genome Project, 92
human immunodeficiency virus (HIV).
    See AIDS
humor
    in childhood, 192
    in infancy, 165
hypoactive sexual desire, 421

I, in self-theory, 243–45, *244*, 251
IADLs ( instrumental activities of daily
    living), 531, *531*
IBM, 437–38
id, 65
identical (monozygotic) twins, 99, 102
identification
    categorical, 245–46
    definition, 227
    motives, 254–55, *254*
    with parents, 227–28, 235, 254–56,
        *254*, 355, 366
identity
    in conservation, *271*, 272
    content and evaluation components,
        370–71
    Erikson's concept, 369–70, 373, 374–
        75
    ethnic, 339–40, 377–79, 530
    fragile, 421
    individual, 336, 369–73
    moral, 360
    negative, 373
    private self and public self, 370
    social, 82
    See also gender identity; group identity

identity achieved status, 372, 374
identity confused status, 373
identity confusion, 372, 373–74
identity foreclosed status, 372, 373, 374
identity formation
    attachment and, 351, 352
    gender differences, 374–75
    in later adolescence, 369–75
    turning points, 377
identity statuses, 371–73
    relationship to exploration and com-
        mitment, 376–77, *376*
    relationship to intimacy, 393
illusion of competence, 284–85
illusion of incompetence, 284
imaginary audiences, 313
imaginary companions, 201, 202
imitation
    in infancy, 237
    learning through, 75–76
    in toddlerhood, 47–48, 197, 210
immortality, 525–26
impulse control, 202–6, *205*
inclusive fitness, 63
incomes
    disparities, 464
    relationship to divorce, 425–26
    relationship to educational attainment,
        363, *363*
    in retirement, 499
incompetence, illusion of, 284
independence
    in very old age, 514, 516, 531
    See also autonomy
independent variables, 30
individual differences perspective, 224
individual identity, 336
    versus identity confusion, 369–73
individualism, 79, 80, *80*, 361
Individuals with Disabilities Act, 260
induction, as classification skill, 273
induction phase, of career decision mak-
    ing, 367, 434
inductions, as discipline practice, 205
industry, 288–89
inertia, 294
infancy
    brain development, 139, 186
    central process in, 168–70
    core pathology, 173–74
    crying, 155, 161–63, 169
    developmental tasks, 137–67
        attachment, 148–57
        causal schemes, 157–59, *158*
        emotional development, 161–67,
            *176*
        mortality, 112–13, 119
        motor development, 143–46
        nature and categories of objects,
            159–61
        sensorimotor intelligence, 157–59
        sensory/perceptual development,
            137–43
    egocentrism, 312
    facial expressions, 23, 164
    language development, 187–89
    media exposure, 242
    moral development, 235–36
    mutuality, 168–70, 408, 422
    parents' roles, 174–78, *178*
    prime adaptive ego quality, 171–73
    psychosocial crisis, 167–68
    self-concept, 245
    temperaments, 146–48, *147*, 151,
        155
    See also newborns; premature infants
inferiority, 289–91
infertility, 102–3, 104–5, 407
influence phase, of career decision mak-
    ing, 367–68
ingroup attitudes, 287–88, *288*, 334
inhibited type reactive attachment
    disorder, 156
inhibition
    behavioral, 147
    as core pathology of early school age
        period, 256–57, 294
    definition, 256
    genetic influences, 96
initiative, 251–52

institutional care, in very old age, 520,
    524, 531, 532–33
instrumental activities of daily living
    (IADLs), 531, *531*
instrumental reminiscence, 495
instrumental values, 522, 523
integration phase, of career decision
    making, 368
integrative reminiscence, 495
integrity, 493
intellectual flexibility, 435
intelligence, 509
    crystallized ($G_c$), 478, 509
    effects of child care, 215–16
    fluid ($G_f$), 478, 509
    genetic and environmental influences,
        99, 100, 121, 479–81
    meanings, 276
    multiple, 276, 314
    problems in studying in later life,
        475–76
    sensorimotor, 69, 157–59, 276
    similarities among siblings, 99, *99*
intelligence tests, 29, 276–77
interdependence
    in families, 86
    in teams, 285
intergenerational solidarity, 481
intermittent reinforcement, 75
internal frames of reference, 280
internalization, 231
internalized morality, 358–61
internalizing problems, 316. See also
    depression; eating disorders
internal validity, 31
Internet
    career exploration on, 368
    online dating, 395, 396
    research results on, 34
    use by older adults, 488–89
    use in schools, 295
interobserver reliability, 25
interstate migration, 519
intersubjectivity, 166, 177
interviews, 27, 28, 32
intimacy
    definition, 417
    in early adulthood, 417–19
    enmeshment, 421–22
    expectations, 420
    love and, 422–23, 444
    nurturing in middle adulthood, 442–
        46
    obstacles, 419
    See also friends; marriage; romantic re-
        lationships; sexual activity
intracytoplasmic sperm injection,
    104–5
introjection, 554
introspection, 353, 494–95
*Inventory of Psychosocial Development*, 56,
    *56*
in vitro fertilization, 103, 104
in vivo fertilization, 105
IQs. See intelligence
Islam. See Muslims
isolation, 419–22
Israel
    kibbutz-reared infants, 152
    work-family balance, 463–64

Japanese Americans
    intergenerational relationships, 482
    social support, 528
    See also Asian Americans
Jews, 98, 548
jobs. See career choice; employment
jumping, 184
justice, 360, 361

Kaiser Family Foundation, 21
kibbutz-reared infants, 152
kindergarten
    children with disabilities, 260
    readiness, 257–59
Korea, *taegyo* practices, 126

labor. See birth process
labor market, 368–69, 466. See also
    employment

language
    bilingualism, 194
    communicative competence, 185–87
    as cultural tool, 192–93
    grammar, 189, 190–91
    learning, 69
    native, 140, 188
    receptive, 189
    verbs, 191
    See also words
language development
    in early childhood, 191–92
    environment, 192–97
    in infancy, 187–89
    in middle childhood, 191–92
    milestones, 187, 191, *192*
    sentences, 190
    in toddlerhood, 185–97
    variability, 187
language disorders, 270
language perception, 188
language production, 189
later adolescence
    ages, 302
    central process in, 375–79
    challenges of social life, 380–82
    core pathology, 379–80
    developmental tasks
        autonomy from parents, 349–53
        career choice, 361–69
        gender identity, 353–58
        internalized morality, 358–61
    prime adaptive ego quality, 379
    psychosocial crisis, 369–75
    relationships with parents, 349, 352
    See also college students
later adulthood
    central process in, 494–95
    core pathology, 496
    developmental tasks
        accepting one's life, 471–75
        developing point of view about
            death, 490–92, 538–39
        new roles and activities, 481–90
        promoting intellectual vigor, 475–
            81
    health and illnesses, 474
    life goals, 471–73, *473*
    prime adaptive ego quality, 495–96
    psychosocial crisis, 493–94
    retirement, 496–500
    wisdom, 477, 495–96
Latinos and Latinas. See Hispanic
    Americans
leadership, 434
learned helplessness, 289–90
learning
    contextualizing, 292–93
    zone of proximal development, 71,
        200, 257, 272
learning disorders, 290
learning theories
    classical conditioning, 73–74, *73*, 77,
        78
    cognitive behaviorism, 76–77, 78, *78*
    implications for human development,
        74, 75, 76, 77
    operant conditioning, 74–75, 77, 78
    psychosocial theory and, 78
    social learning theory, 75–76, 77–78,
        *78*, 232
    view of moral development, 231–32,
        241–43
leisure
    activities in later adulthood, 487–90,
        *487*
    activities in very old age, 517
    in early adulthood, 416–17
    of married couples with children, 408,
        *408*
lesbians
    children of, 229
    emergence of homosexual identity,
        356–57
    relationships in very old age, 524
    relationships with partners, 357–58,
        400–402
    stereotypes of, 357
LIFE (Learning Informally From the
    Elderly), 533

life course, 388–89, 389
life expectancies
   changes over time, 12, 12
   definition, 11–12
   effects of technology, 504–5, 545
   gender differences, 506
   influence of social support, 528
   in later adulthood, 471
   projections, 12–13, 13, 504–5
life satisfaction, in later adulthood, 471–73, 488
life-span development, 5, 11–14
lifestyle
   competing role demands, 415–17
   definition, 415
   in early adulthood, 415–17
   pace of life, 415
   in very old age, 516–25
   See also fitness
literacy. See reading
living alone
   in middle adulthood, 456
   in very old age, 518
living arrangements
   cohabitation, 399–400
   in later adolescence, 349–50
   in very old age, 517–21, 517, 532–33
living wills, 540, 543–44, 554
locomotion, 183–85
   See also walking
loneliness, 268–70, 420
longevity. See life expectancies
longitudinal studies, 33
Longitudinal Study of Generations (LSOG), 481
long-term memory, 476–77
love
   definition, 422
   dimensions, 422–23, 444, 523
   in marriage, 393, 442
   as prime adaptive ego quality, 422–23
   in romantic relationships, 398, 422–23
   types, 423, 423
love withdrawal, as discipline practice, 205, 253
low-birthweight babies, 119, 137, 138, 331
loyalty, 340
LSOG. See Longitudinal Study of Generations

MacArthur Foundation Research Network on Successful Aging, 516
macrosystems, 84
major depressive disorder, 319–20
malnutrition, 123–24, 213, 507
managerial resourcefulness, 435–36
marriage
   adjustment in early years, 402–4
   adjustment to retirement, 497
   ages at
      divorce and, 424, 425, 425
      education and, 393
      increase in, 350, 351, 392
   commitment to future, 443–44
   communication in, 402–4, 426, 442
   conflict resolution in, 266, 402–3, 442–43
   divergent spheres of interest, 421
   division of household labor, 404, 438, 452, 453
   effects of childbearing, 406, 407–8
   effects of relationship quality on care of infants, 155, 165, 177
   homogamy, 394
   leisure time without children, 408, 408
   long-lasting, 442–43
   parenting alliance, 446
   partner selection, 393–99, 394
   rates, 392
   readiness, 393
   satisfaction in, 392–93, 403, 407–8, 442
   in very old age, 523
   See also divorce; dual-earner couples; remarriage; widowhood
masculinity, 307, 356, 522

matched groups, 21, 22
matching, in caregiver-infant interaction, 169
mathematics
   competence, 364
   cross-national comparisons of abilities, 279
   skills, 274
maturation. See physical maturation
me, in self-theory, 243–45, 244
media
   educational value, 242
   images of sexual intimacy, 329
   use by infants, toddlers, and preschoolers, 242
   See also television
memory
   changes in late adulthood, 476–77
   earliest, 246
   episodic, 476–77
   long-term, 476–77
   prospective, 477
   reliability, 31–32
   reminiscence, 494–95
   semantic, 476
   sensory register, 476
   short-term, 476
men
   androgens, 356
   changes in sexual responsiveness, 444
   masculinity, 307, 356, 522
   See also fathers
menarche
   average ages, 304, 308
   early, 309
   reactions to, 306–7, 356
menopause, 444–45, 448
menstruation. See menarche
mental retardation. See developmental disabilities; Down syndrome
mercy killing, 544
mesosystems, 84, 453
metacognition, 70, 275
methadone, 121
Mexican Americans
   depression in adolescence, 320
   See also Hispanic Americans
Mexico
   immigrants to United States, 172
   Zinacanteco childrearing, 146
Microsoft, 396, 436
microsystems, 84
middle adulthood
   ages, 432
   central process in, 460–63
   core pathology, 463
   developmental tasks
      expanding caring relationships, 446–52
      household management, 452–57
      managing career, 432–42
      nurturing intimate relationship, 442–46
   prime adaptive ego quality, 463
   psychosocial crisis, 457–60
   relationships with parents, 449–51, 481
middle childhood
   alcohol and drug use, 343–44
   central process in, 291–93
   core pathology, 294
   developmental tasks
      concrete operational thought, 69, 270–75
      friendship, 264–70, 325
      self-evaluation, 280–85
      skill learning, 275–79
      team play, 285–88
   language development, 191–92
   prime adaptive ego quality, 293–94
   psychosocial crisis, 288–91
   relationships with parents, 447
   self-concept, 246
mifepristone, 128
mind, theory of, 246–47
minority groups
   prejudice and discrimination, 390–91, 413
   psychological strength, 391

See also African Americans; Asian Americans; ethnic groups; Hispanic Americans; Native Americans
miscarriages, 128
   See also abortions, spontaneous
mismatch, in caregiver-infant interaction, 169
mistrust, trust versus, 167–68
monozygotic (identical) twins, 99, 102
moral development
   cognitive developmental perspective, 232–34, 243
   in early school age period, 222, 230–43
   experiences promoting, 359–60
   gender differences, 360–61
   in infancy, 235–36
   influence of disciplinary practices, 235, 238–39
   influences, 241–43, 241
   Kohlberg's theory, 233, 359, 360–61
   in later adolescence, 358–61
   learning theory perspective, 231–32, 241–43
   perspective taking, 237–38, 266–67
   psychoanalytic perspective, 235–36, 243
   stages, 233, 233, 359
   television viewing and, 239–41
   See also empathy
moral identity, 360
morality
   autonomous, 232–33
   conventional, 233, 359
   distinction from social convention, 234
moral transgressions, 233–34
moratorium. See psychosocial moratorium
Mormon Church, 393, 408–9
Moro reflex, 144
mortality
   infant, 112–13, 119
   psychosocial development and, 538–39
   See also death
mothers
   adolescent, 119–20, 330–33, 485
   attachment of infants, 152
   breastfeeding, 142
   disrupted relationships with infants, 168, 173–74, 256–57
   distressed, 170, 172
   effects of child care on relationship with child, 216–17
   influences on prenatal development, 118–24
   perceptions of infant crying, 155, 169
   separation anxiety of infants, 151–52
   single, 454–56
   surrogate, 103, 105
   words for, 188
   See also caregiver-infant interaction; parents; pregnancy
motor development
   in early childhood, 184
   in infancy, 143–46
   nature and nurture in, 144–46
   in toddlerhood, 183–85, 184
motor sequence, 144, 145
motor skills disorders, 290
mourning. See bereavement; grief
Muslims
   funeral rituals, 545–46
   identities of adolescents, 340
   selection of marriage partners, 394
mutuality
   among peers, 422
   in infancy, 168–70, 408, 422
MZ twins [monozygotic (identical) twins], 99, 102

NAMES Project AIDS Memorial Quilt, 553
narcissistic people, 460
narcotics
   use in pregnancy, 121–22
   See also drugs
NASA, 14

National Center for Health Statistics, 12
National Coalition for the Homeless, 457
National Hospice Foundation, 543
National Institute of Child Health and Human Development (NICHD), 215–16
National Youth Gang Center, 338
Native Americans
   ethnic identity, 339
   fertility rates, 405
   funeral rituals, 545, 546
Native Hawaiians, 526
naturalistic observation, 24
natural selection, 62–63
negative identity, 373
negative reinforcers, 74, 75
networks, social support, 529–30
neural tube, development of, 106
neuroticism, 96, 473
newborns
   Apgar scores, 137, 137
   arousal states, 161, 162
   birth defects, 97
   low-birthweight, 119, 137, 138, 331
   physical status, 137
   See also birth process; infancy; premature infants
NICHD. See National Institute of Child Health and Human Development
nicotine, 120
nonparental care, 214
   See also child care
norms
   peer group, 323, 336, 343
   reciprocity, 528–29
   social, 267
   in very old age, 516–17, 517
North American Menopause Association, 445
nuclear transplantation, 98–99
numbers, 274
nursing homes, 520, 531, 532–33
nutrition
   impact of poverty, 213
   in pregnancy, 123–24
   for prenatal development, 105, 109, 123–24
   in very old age, 507

obesity
   concerns of adolescent girls, 304–6
   link to self-esteem, 306
obituaries, 548
object categorization, 160–61
objective observations, 19
object names, 189
object permanence, 159–60
object relations theory, 235–36
observation, 23–25, 32
   naturalistic, 24
   objective, 19
   participant, 24
obsessions, 212
obsessive reminiscence, 495
occupational choice. See career choice
older adults. See later adulthood; very old age
old-old, 506
online dating, 395, 396
open systems, 83
operant conditioning, 74–75, 77, 78
operationalization, 18
optimal functioning, 532–33
optimism, 474
Oregon Death with Dignity Act, 544, 545
organic brain syndrome, 512–13
organ inferiority, 289
outgroup attitudes, 287–88, 288, 334
overregularization, 191
ovum, 101

pace of life, 415
parent-child relationships
   conversations, 196–97
   in early adolescence, 309, 323–24, 340, 439, 447–48
   in early adulthood, 448
   in early school age, 447
   impact of poverty, 212
   in infancy, 174–78, 178

parent-child relationships, *continued*
  influence on language development, 193–95, 196–97
  in later adolescence, 349, 352
  in middle adulthood, 449–51, 481
  in middle childhood, 447
  mutuality, 168–70, 408, 422
  *See also* caregiver-infant interaction
parenting
  attachment and, 149
  cultural differences, 80, 146, 154–55, 165, 175–76
  effects of parent's childhood experiences, 156–57, 170
  effects on emotional development, 463
  in middle adulthood, 446–49
  optimizing infant's development, 178, 178
  relationship to adolescent peer group membership, 324, 324, 336
  safety issues, 174–76
  social support, 177–78
  *See also* discipline
parenting alliance, 446
parents
  advocate role, 177
  attitudes toward alcohol and drug use, 343
  care of aging, 340–41, 449–51, 532
  deaths of, 554
  expectations of children, 283–84, 364
  gender role beliefs, 283, 284
  identification with, 227–28, 235, 254–56, 254, 355, 366
  psychological problems, 170
  step-, 454
  *See also* fathers; mothers
participant observation, 24
passion, 423, 444
passive euthanasia, 543–44
pathologies. *See* core pathologies
peer groups
  affiliating with, 337
  attitudes toward alcohol and drug use, 343
  boundaries, 322–23, 334
  cliques, 321, 322, 334
  crowds, 321–23, 324, 336
  in early adolescence, 321–24, 333–35
  gangs, 338, 373
  norms, 323, 336, 343
peer play, 223, 248–51, 252
peer pressure, 267, 336–40, 343
peer review, 34
peers
  in child care, 217
  influence in adolescence, 313, 337
  mutuality, 422
  norms, 267
  rejection, 268–70, 304–5
  *See also* friends
Perry Preschool Project, 216, 217
persistent vegetative state, 540
personal choice, 234
personal fables, 313
personality
  development, 390
  factors in divorce, 426
  genetic influences, 96
  and life satisfaction in later life, 473–74
person-environment interaction, 460–61
perspective taking, 237–38, 266–67
phenotypes, 94
physical activity
  in adolescence, 306
  in early adulthood, 415, 417
  fitness and exercise, 415, 417, 487–88, 489–90, 507–8
  in later adulthood, 487–88, 489–90
  in toddlerhood, 185
  *See also* locomotion; play
physical culture, 78
physical maturation
  in early adolescence, 303–9
  gender differences, 304, 305
  genetic influences, 96
  individual differences, 308–9
  secondary sex characteristics, 303, 304, 305, 307

secular growth trend, 308
  *See also* puberty
physical state, as source of self-efficacy, 280, 281
physician-assisted suicide, 544, 545
placenta, 105–6, 111
plasticity, 5, 139, 186
play
  fantasy, 197–202
  fighting, 250
  gender differences, 250
  gender-typed, 228
  peer, 248–51, 252
  physical, 185
  role of companions, 201–2
  social, 198
  symbolic, 197, 200–201, 462
  toys, 199, 226
  *See also* games
populations, 20–21
positive reinforcers, 74, 75
positivism, 18–20, 19
postconventional morality, 233, 359
postformal thought, 477–78
post-traumatic stress disorder, 296–97, 318
poverty
  conditions leading to, 8–9
  employment opportunities and, 413
  of female-headed families, 455
  impact on infants, 124
  impact on mother-child relationship, 172
  impact on prenatal development, 118, 124
  impact on toddlers' development, 212–13
  infant mortality and, 113
  in later adolescence, 352
  mediating factors, 9
  psychosocial impact, 8–9
  rates, 212
  relationship to teenage pregnancy, 330–31
  violence in neighborhoods, 296
power assertion, as discipline practice, 205
preconventional morality, 233, 359
pregnancy
  in adolescence, 114, 119–20, 330–33, 485
  age of mother, 103, 118–20, 120, 331, 406, 407
  alternative means, 102–3, 407
  contraception, 329–30, 332–33, 382
  cultural context, 124–26
  decisions to have children, 405–7
  drug use during, 120–23
  father's roles, 116–17
  fertilization, 101–2
  impact on mothers, 113–16
  maternal deaths, 129–30
  nutrition, 123–24
  *taegyo* practices, 126
  *See also* birth process; prenatal development
prejudice, 380, 390–91, 413
premature infants
  chances of survival, 110
  disadvantages, 111
  low-birthweight, 137
  psychosocial factors, 119
  risk factors, 119
  of teenage mothers, 119, 331
  *See also* infancy; newborns
prenatal development
  critical periods, 107
  embryonic period, 103, 104–6
  fetal period, 103, 106–8
  first trimester, 103–8, 106
  germinal period, 103, 104
  influence of mother, 118–24
  monitoring, 110
  nutrition, 105, 109, 123–24
  second trimester, 106, 108–10
  sensory development, 109–11, 139
  susceptibility to teratogens, 106, 107, 120–23
  third trimester, 106, 110–11
  *See also* pregnancy

preoccupied individuals, 418
preoperational thought, 69, 185
preschool
  children with disabilities, 260
  *See also* child care; early school age; Head Start
prescription drugs. *See* drugs
President's Commission for the Ethical Study of Problems in Medicine and Biomedical and Behavioral Research, 539
pretend play. *See* fantasy play
prime adaptive ego qualities, 52, 52
  in early adolescence, 340–41
  in early adulthood, 422–23
  in early school age, 256
  in infancy, 171–73
  in later adolescence, 379
  in later adulthood, 495–96
  in middle adulthood, 463
  in middle childhood, 293–94
  in toddlerhood, 211
  in very old age, 530
private self, 370
problem solving, 206–7
  in adolescence, 315
  creative, 435–36, 462
  in marriage, 403
  in middle childhood, 270, 275
processing load, 508–9
productivity, age and, 480
prohibitive moral judgments, 360
prompting, 195
prosocial behaviors
  in early school age period, 238
  gender differences, 361
  promotion in television programs, 241
prosocial judgments, 360
prospective memory, 477
psychoanalytic theory
  moral development, 235–36, 243
  object relations, 235–36
  relational paradigm, 68
  view of guilt, 252
  view of toilet training, 209
psychohistorical perspective, 514–16
psychological system, in psychosocial approach, 6, 7
psychology, evolutionary, 63
psychosexual theory, 65–68
  developmental stages, 66
  implications for human development, 67
  psychosocial theory and, 67–68
psychosocial approach
  biological system in, 6, 6
  overview, 9–11
  psychological system in, 6, 7
  societal system in, 7–8, 7
psychosocial crises, 44–46, 46
  central process for resolving, 47–48, 48
  in early adolescence, 333–36
  in early adulthood, 417–22
  in early school age period, 251–54
  in infancy, 167–68
  in later adolescence, 369–75
  in later adulthood, 493–94
  in middle adulthood, 457–60
  in middle childhood, 288–91
  in toddlerhood, 207–10
  in very old age, 525–27
psychosocial evolution, 39–40, 64
psychosocial moratorium, 373, 374, 375–77
psychosocial theory
  basic concepts, 39–52, 53
  biographical case study, 53–54
  central process, 47–48, 48
  cognitive developmental theory and, 72
  coping behavior, 50–52
  cultural theory and, 81
  developmental stages, 40–43
  developmental tasks, 43–44
  evaluation, 54–58
  evolutionary theory and, 64
  learning theories and, 78
  longitudinal studies, 55, 56
  overview, 58

positive and negative development, 58, 58
  psychosexual theory and, 67–68
  psychosocial crises, 44–46, 46
  radius of significant relationships, 48–50, 49
  rationale for emphasizing, 39
  social role theory and, 82
  strengths, 54–55, 55
  systems theory and, 86
  weaknesses, 55–58, 55
puberty
  in boys, 307, 308–9
  cultural contexts, 308
  emotional development and, 316
  gender identity and, 356
  in girls, 304–7, 309, 356
  hormonal changes, 356
  individual differences, 308–9
  physical changes, 303
  rites of passage, 303
  sleep pattern changes, 310
public self, 370
Puerto Ricans, intergenerational relationships, 482
punishment, 75
pupillary reflex, 144
purpose, 256

qualitative approach to sampling, 22, 23
qualitative inquiry, 18, 20
quasi-experiments, 31
quickening, 108

radius of significant relationships, 48–50, 49, 323
random samples, 21, 22
range of applicability, 38
rapport, 28
Rastafarians, 465
reaching, by infants, 143
reaction ranges, 100, 100, 479, 506
reactive attachment disorder, 156
reactive surveys, 29–30
reactivity, 147
readiness, 257. *See also* school readiness
reading
  to children, 195–96, 278
  learning, 277–79
  parental influences, 278
  social and cultural contexts, 278–79
receptive language, 189
reciprocity
  in conservation, 271, 272
  norm of, 528–29
reference groups, 333, 342–43, 370
reflexes
  of fetuses, 108
  of infants, 143, 144, 158
  sensorimotor adaptation, 157
  startle and Moro, or infancy, 167
reflexive motor responses, 143
reinforcement, 74, 75, 76
rejection, peer, 268–70, 304–5
rejectivity, 463
relational paradigm, 68
reliability
  interobserver, 25
  of tests, 28–29
religious beliefs
  funeral rituals, 545–46
  influence on sexual behavior, 326, 327
  life after death, 525, 545, 546
  selection of marriage partner and, 395
  workplace discrimination and, 465
religious groups, social support from, 529–30
remarriage
  after divorce, 427, 446, 454
  after widowhood, 485, 486, 518, 524
reminiscence, 494–95
repeatability, of research, 19
representational thinking, 185, 276
reproductive systems
  male, 95, 307
  prenatal development, 108
reproductive technology, 102–3, 104–5, 105, 407
repudiation, 379–80

research
  cohort sequential studies, 33, *33*
  cross-sectional studies, 32–33
  design, 20
  ethical issues, 34–35
  evaluating, 33–34
  generalizability, 21
  longitudinal studies, 33
  peer review, 34
  positivist approach, 18–20, *19*
  qualitative inquiry, 18, 20
  repeatability, 19
  retrospective studies, 31–32
  sampling, 20–23
  systematic approach, 19
research methods, 23
  advantages and disadvantages, *32*
  case studies, 25–26, *32*
  experiments, 30–31, *32*
  interviews, 26–28, *32*
  observation, 23–25, *32*
  surveys and tests, 28–30, *32*
resilience, 9, 486
retirement, 496–500
  adjusting to, 497, 499
  definitions, 496
  difficulties, 498
  future of, 499–500
  income loss, 499
retirement anxiety, 498
retirement housing, 519–20
retrospective studies, 31–32
reversibility, *271*, 272
rites of passage, 303
rituals
  death-related, 545–48
  group, 334
  in toddlerhood, 211–12
*Roe v. Wade*, 129
role compatibility, 397–98
role conflict, *387*, 437
role enactment, *387*
role expectations, *387*
role experimentation, in later adolescence, 353, 375–79
role gains, *387*
  in later adulthood, 481
  *See also* grandparenthood
role losses, *387*
  in later adulthood, 481
  in very old age, 516
  *See also* widowhood
role overload, 437
role reversal, 532
roles. *See* social roles
role spillover, 437
role stagnation, 460
role strain, 83, *387*
role transitions
  in later adulthood, 481
  retirement, 496–500
romantic relationships
  attachment and, 156
  cohabitation, 399–400
  in early adolescence, 313–14, 324–33
  in early adulthood, 392–405
  homosexual, 357–58, 400–402, 524
  interracial and interethnic, 397
  in later adulthood, 486
  love, 398, 422–23
  sexual responsiveness, 444–45
  in very old age, 523–24
  *See also* dating; marriage; sexual activity
rooting reflex, *144*
RU-486, 128
rules, in families, 85
running, 184–85

safety
  in child care, 217
  of infants, 174–76
same-sex relationships. *See* gay men; lesbians
sampling, 20–23
SATs (Scholastic Aptitude Tests), 29
scaffolding, 195, 238–39
schedules of reinforcement, 75
Scholastic Aptitude Tests (SATs), 29

school readiness, 257–60
  children with disabilities, 260
  measuring, 257–59
  obstacles, 259
  responsibilities for, 259–60
  skills, *258*
  television viewing and, 242
schools
  ability grouping, 278
  formal education, 291–92
  peer criticism, 248
  peer influences, 267
  risk factors for poor adjustment, 259, *259*
  technology in, 295
  *See also* high schools; preschool
scientific observation, 18–20
scientific process, 18. *See also* research
secondary sex characteristics, 303, 304, *305*, 307
secular growth trend, 308
secure attachment, 153, 154, 155–57, 349, 352
secure individuals, 418
self
  authentic, 390
  private and public, 370
self-acceptance, 390
self-actualization, 390
self-concept, 243, 255
self-control
  development by toddlers, 202–7
  effortful control, 205–6
  impulse control, 202–6, *205*
  self-regulated goal attainment, 206–7
self-efficacy
  competence and, 293
  components, 280–81, *280*
  in middle childhood, 280–81
  in toddlerhood, 207
self-esteem
  body image and, 304
  daily monitoring, 293–94
  in early adolescence, 309
  in early school age period, 247–48
  identification with parents and, 227
  in later adulthood, 473, 474
  in middle childhood, 280, 281–82
  obesity and, 306
  relationship to competence, 293–94, 474
  sources, 247
  stable, 294
self-evaluation
  in middle childhood, 280–85
  social expectations and, 281–85
self-fulfilling prophecy, 282–83
self-labeling, sexual orientation, 327
self-presentation bias, 28
self-regulated goal attainment, 206–7
self-regulation, 147
self-regulatory plans, 77, *77*
self-sufficiency, in later adolescence, 351–53. *See also* autonomy
self-theory, 222–23, 243–48
  developmental changes, 245–46
  function, 243
  me and I, 243–45, *244*, 251
  self-esteem, 247–48
  theory of mind, 246–47
semantic memory, 476
semiotic thinking, 185
senior citizens. *See* later adulthood; very old age
sensitive periods, 43, 257
sensitivity, 154–55, *154*, 170
sensorimotor adaptation, 157
sensorimotor intelligence, 69, 157–59, 276
sensorimotor play, 197
sensory/perceptual development
  changes in very old age, 510–12, *510*
  in infancy, 137–43
  prenatal, 109–11, 139
sensory register, 476
sentences, 189, 190–91
separation anxiety, 151–52
sex
  brain differences, 224
  definition, 224–25

distinction from gender and sexual orientation, 224–25, 356
  preferences of expectant parents, 230
sex discrimination, 380, 413, 419, 464–65
sex education, 328–29
sex hormones, 324, 356
sex-linked characteristics, 95–96, *95*
sex reassignment surgery, 354
*Sex-Role Learning Index*, 226
sexual abuse, 331
sexual activity
  ages of first, 325–26, *326*
  contraception, 329–30, 332–33, 382
  in early adolescence, 324–27
  factors in initiation of, 326–27, *326*
  first intercourse, 325–26
  in later adolescence, 356, 381–82
  taboos, 253
  unwanted attention, 325, 329, 380–81
  virginity pledges, 327
sexual assault, 325, 380
sexual disorders
  compulsive sexual behavior, 421
  hypoactive sexual desire, 421
sexual harassment, 380, 419
sexuality
  problems, 328–30
  in very old age, 523–25
sexually transmitted diseases (STDs), 329, 381–82
sexual orientation
  definition, 225, 356
  disclosure, 327–28, 357, 400–401
  distinction from gender and sex, 224–25, 356
  in early adolescence, 327–28
  effects of parent's sexual orientation, 229
  genetic influences, 96
  in later adolescence, 356–58
  parental acceptance, 328
  self-labeling, 327
  *See also* gay men; lesbians
sexual responsiveness, changes over time, 444–45
SGA (small for their gestational age babies), 137
shame, 208–10, 252
short-term memory, 476
SIDS. *See* sudden infant death syndrome
signs, 185
single-parent families, 454–56
single-person households, 456, 518
skill learning
  in early adulthood, 412
  industry and, 288–89
  in middle adulthood, 435–36
  in middle childhood, 275–79
  process, 277
  reading, 277–79
slave labor and bondage, 264
sleep deprivation, 310
small for their gestational age (SGA) babies, 137
smell, 142, 511. *See also* sensory/perceptual development
smiling, 161, 165
smoking
  in early adolescence, 337
  during pregnancy, 120
social anxiety, 420
social clock, 388
social cognition, 76, 267
social competence
  effects of child care, 216–17
  family influences, 265–66
social conventions
  distinction from moral issues, 358
  transgressions of, 234
social culture, 78
social evolutionary theory, 395
social expectations, self-evaluation and, 281–85
social identity, 82
social integration, 425
socialization
  cultural, 78–79
  drug and alcohol use and, 343
  gender role, 362–65, *362*

social learning theory, 75–76, 77–78, *78*, 232
social networks, 453–54
social norms, 267, 516–17, *517*
social play, 198
social pretend play, 198, 199–200
social referencing, 166–67
social roles, 81
  gender-differentiated, 353
  role strain, 83, *387*
social role theory, 81–82, 353, 387–88
  implications for human development, 82
  major concepts, *387*
  psychosocial theory and, 82
social support
  benefits, 528
  definition, 527
  for divorced women, 427–28
  dynamics, 528–29
  from friends, 419
  networks, 529–30
  for parents, 177–78
  in very old age, 527–30, 533
  in widowhood, 427–28, 486, 524, 529
societal system
  inequality, 361
  multiethnic, 81
  in psychosocial approach, 7–8, *7*
  radius of significant relationships, 48–50, *49*, 323
socioeconomic levels, relationship to divorce, 425–26
SOC model, 474–75, 511–12
solicitude, toward pregnant women, 124–26
solidarity
  family, 340–41
  intergenerational, 481
solitary pretense, 198
speech
  brain areas related to, 186, *186*
  egocentric, 207
  telegraphic, 190
  use in goal attainment, 206–7
  *See also* language
sperm, 101
spontaneous ejaculation, 307
sports
  in later adulthood, 487
  team, 285–88
springing reflex, *144*
stages. *See* developmental stages
stagnation, 457, 460
stalking, 380
startle reflex, *144*
statistical significance, 20
status offenses, 317
STDs. *See* sexually transmitted diseases
stem cell research, 98–99
stepparents, 454
stepping reflex, *144*
stereotypes
  gender role, 363
  of homosexuals, 357
  of older adults, 522–23
  sex, 226–27
stigmatized deaths, 552–53
stranger anxiety, 150–51
strange situation, 152, *153*
stratified samples, 21, 22
substance use. *See* alcohol; drugs
substantive complexity, 435
sucking, 142, 143, *144*
sudden infant death syndrome (SIDS), 112, 120, 121
suffering, in dying process, 541
suicides
  in early adolescence, 319, 321
  physician-assisted, 544, 545
  prevention, 319
  risk factors, 319
  survivors' reactions, 553
  in very old age, 527, 530
superego, 65, 235
Supreme Court, U.S., 129, 131, 544
surrogate mothers, 103, 105
surveys, 28–30, *32*
survival rates, 12, *13*

swaddling, 142, 146
swimming reflex, *144*
symbolic play, 197, 200–201, 462
symbols, 185
synchrony, 23, 149, 169
systematic approach to research, 19
systems theory, 82–86
    implications for human development,
      85–86
    psychosocial theory and, 86
    relationships among systems, *84*

*taegyo*, 126
tasks, developmental. *See* developmental
    tasks
taste, 142, 511. *See also* sensory/
    perceptual development
Tay-Sachs disease, 98
teachable moments, 43
teachers
    expectations of student performance,
      282–83
    influence, 267
team play, 285–88
technical skills, 412, 435–36
technology
    brain imaging, 186
    computers, 295, 488–89
    increased longevity, 504–5, 545
    monitoring fetal development, 110
    risks for infants, 175, 176
    role in study of human development,
      14
    in schools, 295, *295*
    toys, 199
    video recording, 23
    *See also* Internet
teenagers. *See* adolescence
telegraphic speech, 190
television
    educational programming, 241
    impact on moral development, 239–41
    positive effects, 241
    recommendations, 239–40
    school readiness and viewing, 242
    violence on, 239, 240–41, *240*
temperaments, 146–48, *147*, 151, 155,
    238
teratogens, 106, 120–23
Terman Study of Gifted Children, 473
TERRA satellite system, 14
terrorism, 296, 340, 380, 551, 552
testosterone, 356
tests, 28–30, *32*
thalassemia, 98
thalidomide, 122–23
thanatology, 538
theories
    definition, 38
    development, 18
    range of applicability, 38
    *See also* development theories; learning
      theories
theory of mind, 246–47
tobacco. *See* smoking
toddlerhood
    autonomy, 47–48, 208, 251

brain development, 186
central process in, 210
core pathology, 211–12
developmental tasks
    elaboration of locomotion, 183–85
    fantasy play, 197–202
    language development, 185–97
    self-control, 202–7
gross motor skills, *184*
imitation, 47–48, 197, 210
impact of poverty, 212–13
media exposure, 242
prime adaptive ego quality, 211
psychosocial crisis, 207–10
rituals, 211–12
self-concept, 245
toilet training, 208, 209
toilet training, 208, 209
tonic neck reflex, *144*
touch, 142
    *See also* sensory/perceptual
      development
toys, 199, 226
trajectories, 388
transcendence, experiential, 526, 527
transitions
    in life course, 388
    role, 481, 496–500
transsexuals, 354
triangulation, 24
trust
    acceptance of life and, 475
    mistrust versus, 167–68
twins
    fertilization, 101–2
    fraternal (dizygotic), 99, 102
    identical (monozygotic), 99, 102
    intelligence, 99, *99*
    studies of, 96

UDDA (Uniform Determination of Death
    Act), 540
ultrasound, 110
unacknowledged loss, 551–52
unconscious, 65, 66
unemployment, 437, 440–42
    predictors, 288
    rates by ethnicity and educational at-
      tainment, 440, *440*, 464
Uniform Determination of Death Act
    (UDDA), 540
uninhibited type reactive attachment dis-
    order, 156
U.S. Administration on Aging, 531
U.S. Census Bureau, 12
U.S. Department of Commerce, 436
U.S. Department of Education, Early
    Childhood Longitudinal Study,
    257–58
U.S. Department of Energy, Human
    Genome Project, 92
U.S. Department of Labor, Employment
    and Training Administration,
    435
U.S. Senate Special Committee on Aging,
    543
University of California, 29

unwanted sexual attention, 329, 380–81
usefulness/competence, 474

validity
    external, 31
    internal, 31
    of tests, 29
values, 77, *77*, 379, 522
variables
    dependent, 30
    independent, 30
verbal persuasion, as source of self-
    efficacy, *280*, 281
very old age, 505–6
    central process in, 527–30
    core pathology, 530–31
    dependency, 514, *514*, 531, *531*, 532–
      33
    developmental tasks
      coping with physical changes, 507–
        14
      developing psychohistorical per-
        spective, 514–16
      life structures, 516–25
    frailty, 531–34
    individual variations, 506
    living arrangements, 517–21, *517*
    prime adaptive ego quality, 530
    psychosocial crisis, 525–27
    secrets of longevity, 505
    sex composition of population, 506
viability, 129
vicarious experience, *280*, 281
vicarious reinforcement, 76
video games, 239, 242
video recording, 23
violence
    in children's lives, 266, 296–98
    consequences of exposure to, 296–97
    in early adolescence, 317–18
    in families, 266
    reducing exposure to, 297–98
    sexual assault, 325, 380
    on television, 239, 240–41, *240*
    in video games, 239
    weapons-related, 318
    in workplace, 441
    *See also* abuse
vision
    blindness, 510
    changes in very old age, 510–11
    faceness, 140–41, 160
    in infancy, 140–41
    *See also* sensory/perceptual
      development
visual acuity, 140
visual adaptation, 510
vocabulary, 189–90, 195, 476. *See also*
    words
volunteerism, 488, 534
volunteer samples, 21, 22

walking, 144–45, 183
wariness, 167
weapons, 318
welfare recipients, employment of, 413
Whites. *See* European Americans

whole-brain death, 539–40
widowhood
    adaptation to, 485–87, 523, 549
    bereavement patterns, 550, *550*
    identity changes, 554
    living arrangements, 518, 520
    of men, 485, 486
    remarriage, 485, 486, 518, 524
    social support, 427–28, 486, 524, 529
    in very old age, 518, 524
    of women, 427–28, 485–86
will, 211
wills
    living, 540, 543–44, 554
    reading, 548
wisdom, 477, 495–96
withdrawal, 173–74
withdrawn children, 270
women
    changes in sexual responsiveness,
      444–45
    depression in, 420
    employment
      career choices, 358, 366
      childbearing decisions, 406–7
      child care arrangements, 485
      discrimination against, 465
      increased number, 404
      leaving work to raise children, 409
      mothers, 114, 409, 436–37, 443–
        44, 465, 485
      returning to labor force, 436–37,
        443–44
      transition to retirement, 497
      work-family issues, 438–39
      *See also* dual-earner couples
    femininity, 356, 358, 374, 522
    menarche, 304, 306–7, 308, 309, 356
    menopause, 444–45, 448
    *See also* mothers
words
    expanding vocabulary, 189–90, 195
    first, 189
    production, 187, *187*
    as signs, 185
    *See also* language
work
    attitudes toward, 288
    *See also* career choice; employment
work-family facilitation, 439–40
working models, 153
workplace aggression, 441
worldviews, 78

X chromosome, 93, 95

Y chromosome, 93, 95
young-old, 506

Zinacanteco childrearing, 146
zone of proximal development, 71, 200,
    257, 272
zygotes, 97, 101, 104

TO THE OWNER OF THIS BOOK:

I hope that you have found *Development Through Life: A Psychosocial Approach,* Ninth Edition useful. So that this book can be improved in a future edition, would you take the time to complete this sheet and return it? Thank you.

School and address:_____

Department:_____

Instructor's name:_____

1. What I like most about this book is:_____

_____

_____

2. What I like least about this book is:

_____

_____

3. My general reaction to this book is:

_____

_____

4. The name of the course in which I used this book is:

_____

5. Were all of the chapters of the book assigned for you to read?_____

   If not, which ones weren't?_____

6. In the space below, or on a separate sheet of paper, please write specific suggestions for improving this book and anything else you'd care to share about your experience in using this book.

_____

_____

_____

_____

_____

_____

## BUSINESS REPLY MAIL
FIRST-CLASS MAIL      PERMIT NO. 34      BELMONT CA

POSTAGE WILL BE PAID BY ADDRESSEE

Attn:  Psychology: Michele Sordi, Psychology Editor
Wadsworth/Thomson Learning
10 Davis Dr
Belmont CA  94002-9801

OPTIONAL:

Your name:_____ Date: _____

May we quote you, either in promotion for *Development Through Life: A Psychosocial Approach,* Ninth Edition, or in future publishing ventures?

Yes: _____   No: _____

Sincerely yours,

*Barbara M. Newman*

*Philip R. Newman*